1820
Land Lottery
of
Georgia

Compiled By:
The Rev. Silas Emmett Lucas, Jr.

Southern Historical Press, Inc.
Greenville, South Carolina

SOUTHERN HISTORICAL PRESS, INC.
PO BOX 1267
Greenville, SC   29601

ISBN #0-89308-585-5

Printed in the United States of America

THE 1820 LOTTERY

Contrary to an erroneous opinion held by many genealogists, all of Georgia's six Land Lotteries were NOT held for the purpose of granting land to Revolutionary veterans. The 1805, the 1807 and the 1821 Land Lotteries did not even mention military veterans. Only the 1820, 1827 and 1832 Lotteries gave any special consideration to veterans of wars. This Lottery, the 1820, then, is the first of the six which did recognize Revolutionary Soldiers, but only if they were invalid or indigent. Those who had had a fortunate draw, as a citizen of Georgia, in the previous 1805 and 1807 Lotteries, were entitled to one extra draw in this one. If they had not had an extra draw, they were entitled to two extra draws in the 1820 Land Lottery. These extra draws were in addition to those which they might receive as ordinary citizens, and the ordinary citizen was still the main concern in this, as well as all of the Lotteries.

The area which comprised the original counties in this Lottery, was the largest cession of land yet gained by Georgia. The north half of Gwinnett County, and the counties of Hall, Rabun and Habersham were ceded by the Cherokee Nation, but the southern half of Gwinnett, all of Walton, Early, Irwin and Appling Counties were ceded by the Creeks.

One will notice that the letters "R.S." or "Rev. Sol." are listed after the name of the Revolutionary veterans here. That notation IS ALL THAT IS SHOWN IN THE GRANT TO THAT PERSON. Other names show a "sol." and, of course, this means soldier, but the Surveyor General Department does not have any information which can tell you in which war the soldier had fought.

One must also bear in mind, that with the exception of the first, or 1805 Land Lottery, the State of Georgia did NOT keep the list of those persons ENTITLED to draw. Some counties do have such lists and in some county histories these lists have been printed. If you do not see the name you seek in this Lottery, but have seen it elsewhere in lists of those ENTITLED to draw, it simply means that the person drew a blank ticket and received no land.

Please remember also, that those persons who registered to draw in their counties of residence, had to take only an ORAL oath as to their eligibility. Therefore, the Georgia Surveyor General Department has no applications or other written records as to what the registrant may have said about himself, his family, birthplace, age or military service. Copies of grants, and this will be a xerox copy, may be had for one dollar. Write to and make your check payable to the Georgia Surveyor General Department, 330 Capitol Avenue, S. E., Atlanta, Georgia 30334.

Contemporary Map of Georgia
Showing The Land That was
Allocated For Distribution
In The 1820 Land Lottery

GEORGIA

Map Prepared by the
Surveyor General Office
Atlanta, Georgia

THIRD LAND LOTTERY - ALSO KNOWN AS THE 1820 LOTTERY

AUTHORITY

(Act of December 15, 1818
Act of December 21, 1819)

COUNTIES

Appling	13 Districts	(1 thru 13)
Early	26 Districts	(1 thru 23; 26 thru 28)
Gwinnett	3 Districts	(5 thru 7)
Habersham	10 Districts	(1 thru 6; 10 thru 13)
Hall	5 Districts	(8 thru 12)
Irwin	16 Districts	(1 thru 16)
Rabun	5 Districts	(1 thru 5)
Walton	4 Districts	(1 thru 4)

Appling	490 Acres	4620 feet square	
Early	250 "	3300 " "	
Gwinnett	250 "	3300 " "	
Habersham			
(Dist. 1-4; 10-12	250 acres	3300 " "	
(Dist. 5-6)	490 "	4620 " "	
Hall	250 acres	3300 " "	
Irwin	490 "	4620 " "	
Rabun			
(Dists. 1; 3-5	490 acres	4620 " "	
(Dist. 2	250 "	3300 " "	
Walton	250 acres	3300 " "	

GRANT FEE

$18.00 per Land Lot, either size

PERSONS ENTITLED TO DRAW:

Bachelor, 18 years or over, three year residence of Ga., citizen of United States	1 draw
Soldier of Indian War, residence in Georgia during or since military service	1 draw
Invalid or indigent officer or soldier in Revolutionary Army or War of 1812	2 draws
Married man, with wife and/or minor son under 18 and/or unmarried daughter 3 years residence in Ga., citizen of United States	2 draws
Widow, three year residence in Georgia	1 draw
Widow, husband killed in Revolution or War of 1812 or Indian Wars, three year residence in Georgia	2 draws
Family of minor orphans, father dead, mother living three year residence in Georgia	1 draw
Family of three or more minor orphans, father and mother both dead, three year residence in Georgia	2 draws
Family of one or two minor orphans, father and mother both dead, three year residence in Georgia	1 draw
Minor orphan, father killed in Revolution or War of 1812 or Indian Wars, three year residence in Georgia	2 draws
Minor orphans, father dead, three year residence in Georgia	1 draw
Invalid or indigent officer or soldier in Revolutionary Army who had been fortunate drawer in either previous Lottery	1 draw

PERSONS EXCLUDED

Any fortunate drawer in either of two previous Land Lotteries

NOTE:

The oral oath, to be made by an invalid or indigent veteran of the Revolutionary War or by a veteran of the Indian War did not require a detailed statement of his service. The oral oath to be made by a married man, bachelor, widow, spinster or guardian of orphans did not require a detailed statement as to kinship, ancestry or descent. If, by chance, any such oath may have been written or transcribed, it could be found only in the minutes of the Inferior Court of the County where made.

THE 1820

LAND LOTTERY

OF

GEORGIA

NAME	COUNTY	MIL.DIST	LOT/SECT	DREW LAND
Aaron, Jesse	Franklin	Hammonds	233/13	Irwin
Aaron, Wm.	Wilkinson	Lee's	415/5	Appling
Abbet, Bennett	Appling	3	53/3	Early
Abbett, Peter I.	Jasper	Centells	257/10	Irwin
Abbot, William Sr.	Jefferson	Abbots	373/21	Early
Abbot, Wm.W.	Jefferson	Abbots	148/2	Appling
Abbot, Wm.W.	Jefferson	Abbots	265/8	Appling
Abbott, Abner A.	Twiggs	Hodges	223/16	Early
Abbott, Abraham	Putnam	Oslins	70/28	Early
Abbott, Barnett	Tattnall	Tharp's	305/2	Early
Abbott, Elijah	Richmond	Laceys	151/5	Gwinnett
Abbott, George	Glynn		294/6	Appling
Abbott, James O.	Burke	Spiveys	336/1	Early
Abbott, Joel	Wilkes	Gordons	90/2	Rabun
Abbott, Sarah(Wid)	Richmond	Laceys	476/12	Irwin
Abbott, Waddington	Tattnall	Tharp's	92/10	Irwin
Abbott, William Sr.	Jefferson	Abbots	367/17	Early
Abbott, William	Franklin	Morris'	145/13	Irwin
Abercrombie, Anderson	Hancock	Scotts	240/3	Walton
Abercrombie, Charles	Hancock	Danells	288/20	Early
Abercrombie, Nancy(Wid)	Warren	154	30/12	Hall
Abercrombie, Wylie	Putnam	Oslins	284/11	Irwin
Abney, Ezekiel	Jackson	Dicksens Bt.	18/20	Early
Abney, Ezekiel	Jackson	Dicksons Bt.	93/26	Early
Aborn, Joseph R.	McIntosh	Hamilton's	418/15	Early
Abott, Zachariah	Richmond	Lacey's	328/9	Irwin
Abrahams, Isaac	Glynn		400/11	Early
Abrams, Abram D.	Chatham		62/4	Early
Acee, Joshua L.	Hancock			–
Acee, Joshua L.	Hancock	Coopers	272/13	Early
Achols, John	Franklin	Morris'	144/3	Habersham
Achord, Henry	Tattnall	Overstreets	61/3	Rabun
Achord, Lewis D.	Chatham		196/27	Early
Acrage, John	Washington	Cummen's	127/2	Early
Acre, William	Warren	Rodgers	24/26	Early
Acre, William	Warren	Rodgers	55/8	Irwin
Adair, Hiram	Morgan	Talbotts	269/18	Early
Adair, Jones	Morgan	Talbots	53/8	Hall
Adam, Wilaby	Appling	6	280/28	Early
Adams, Absalom	Franklin	Akins	45/6	Appling
Adams, Arthur	Columbia	Watsons	227/8	Appling
Adams, Arthur	Columbia	Watsons	328/1	Appling
Adams, Benj.Jr.	Warren	153	353/7	Irwin
Adams, Chas.H.(Orph)	Richmond	Brantley	13/1	Irwin
Adams, Coalson Jr.	Pulaski	Rays	359/8	Irwin
Adams, Dancy	Columbia	Ob.Morris'	152/4	Walton
Adams, Daniel	Twiggs	Brown's	132/11	Irwin
Adams, David B.(Orph)	Richmond	Brantley	13/1	Irwin
Adams, David E.	Chatham		287/4	Irwin
Adams, David(Little)	Jasper	Blakes	111/8	Appling
Adams, David	Putnam	Bustins	35/12	Irwin
Adams, Dennis	Pulaski	Bryans	312/7	Irwin
Adams, Dennis	Pulaski	Bryans	79/7	Early
Adams, Edward	Jackson	Rogers	67/6	Habersham
Adams, Edward	Jackson	Winters Bt.	405/28	Early
Adams, Eleazer	Jasper	Blakes	13/2	Irwin
Adams, Elizabeth K.(Wid)	Columbia	Watsons	283/9	Early
Adams, Hannah(Wid)	Jackson	Rogers Bt.	376/4	Early
Adams, Hellen(Orph)	Chatham		420/21	Early
Adams, Henry	Putnam	Evans	57/10	Early
Adams, Hester R.(Orph)	Chatham		420/21	Early
Adams, Hezekiah	Clark	Simmons	27/8	Early
Adams, Hopewell	Washington	Mannings	314/21	Early
Adams, Isham	Pulaski	Bryants	197/10	Habersham
Adams, Isham	Pulaski	Bryants	60/3	Rabun
Adams, James B.	Elbert	B.Higginbothams	179/28	Early
Adams, James	Washington	Adams'	391/7	Irwin

NAME	COUNTY	MIL.DIST	LOT/SECT	DREW LAND
Adams, Jefferson	Jasper	Clays	6/15	Early
Adams, Jesse	Jackson	Hamiltons Bt.	171/7	Appling
Adams, John Jr.	Twiggs	Browns	143/4	Walton
Adams, John Sr.	Twiggs	Browns	48/19	Early
Adams, John	Chatham		2/3	Irwin
Adams, John	Chatham		56/4	Appling
Adams, John	Clark	Simms	426/10	Irwin
Adams, John	Clark	Simms	74/23	Early
Adams, John	Hancock			-
Adams, John	Jackson	Henson's Bt.	77/1	Rabun
Adams, John	Jackson	Rogers Bt.	381/2	Appling
Adams, John	Jackson	Rogers Bt.	394/8	Early
Adams, John	Jackson	Winters Bt.	86/2	Irwin
Adams, John	Pulaski	Rays	58/4	Walton
Adams, Kenchin	Columbia	Ob.Morris'	267/18	Early
Adams, Kincheon	Columbia	Ob.Morris	165/8	Irwin
Adams, Levin	Laurens	Jones	156/17	Early
Adams, Lucinda(Orph)	Richmond	Palmers	2/8	Irwin
Adams, Margaret V.(Orph)	Chatham		420/21	Early
Adams, Martha(Orph)	Richmond	Palmers	2/8	Irwin
Adams, Mary B.(Orph)	Chatham		420/21	Early
Adams, Mary	Jasper	Blakes	26/3	Walton
Adams, Nancey	Morgan	Loyds	94/8	Appling
Adams, Patridge	Chatham		221/11	Irwin
Adams, Patsey(Wid)	Greene	Wheelis'	255/18	Early
Adams, Peter	Laurens	Harris	73/4	Habersham
Adams, Reuben	Jones	Mullenses	102/7	Appling
Adams, Richard C.	Elbert	B.Higginbothams	111/7	Irwin
Adams, Richard(Orph)	Chatham		420/21	Early
Adams, Samuel	Chatham		198/6	Early
Adams, Samuel	Elbert	Smiths	411/1	Early
Adams, Sarah(Wid)	Wilkinson	Smiths	39/3	Habersham
Adams, Selwell(Orph)	Richmond	Brantley	13/1	Irwin
Adams, Tarby	Columbia	Watsons	86/5	Appling
Adams, Thomas Sr.	Elbert	B.Higginbothams	15/2	Habersham
Adams, William E.(Orph)	Chatham		420/21	Early
Adams, William	Oglethorpe	Bowls	216/4	Early
Adams, Wm.	Wilkinson	Child's	247/5	Gwinnett
Adamson, Greenberry	Morgan	Knights	337/10	Irwin
Adamson, Wm.C.	Morgan	Knights	77/3	Appling
Adare, Bozeman	Madison	Bones	416/1	Early
Adare, James	Putnam	Morelands	117/3	Appling
Adcock, Edmund	Morgan	Parkers	98/5	Irwin
Adcock, John	Morgan	Jordans	266/2	Appling
Adcock, Stinson	Morgan	Jordans	94/12	Hall
Adderhold, Abraham	Franklin	R.Browns	19/15	Irwin
Adderhold, Abraham	Franklin	R.Browns	23/5	Habersham
Adderhold, Lewis	Franklin	R.Brown's	316/20	Early
Addir, Farmer	Morgan	Hubbards	60/6	Appling
Addir, Robt.T.	Morgan	Campbells	120/3	Appling
Addison, Brazel	Franklin	Kelton's	113/13	Irwin
Addison, Isham(Orphs)	Jasper	Blakes	255/13	Irwin
Addison, Mark	Liberty		88/5	Gwinnett
Aderhold, Frederick.	Franklin	R.Brown's	126/7	Early
Aderhold, John S.	Franklin	R.Brown's	36/14	Early
Adison, John	Franklin	Akins	29/7	Gwinnett
Adkins, Aaron	Warren	150	194/9	Appling
Adkins, Catel J.	Wilkes	Perry's	131/10	Habesham
Adkins, Daniel	Warren	150	108/12	Irwin
Adkins, Daniel	Warren	150	195/17	Early
Adkins, Jesse	Twiggs	W.Belcher	157/3	Appling
Adkins, John	Warren	150	189/6	Early
Adkins, Lewis	Twiggs	Jefferson's	8/11	Habersham
Adkins, Robert	Twiggs	Jeffersons	4/5	Gwinnett
Adkins, Robert	Twiggs	W.Belchers	137/16	Irwin
Adkins, Thomas	Pulaski	Maddoxs	129/4	Irwin
Adkins, William	Twiggs	Jefferson	130/4	Irwin

NAME	COUNTY	MIL.DIST	LOT/SECT	DREW LAND
Adkins, Wm.	Twiggs	Jeffersons	90/12	Irwin
Adkinson, John	Columbia	Burroughs	426/1	Early
Adock, Stenson	Morgan	Jordans	333/9	Early
Ager, Omphra	Wilkes	Ogletrees	299/26	Early
Agerton, Willis(Orph)	Columbia	Shaws	651/2	Appling
Aid, Neil	Pulaski	Senterfeits	84/11	Hall
Aikens, Robert	Wilkes	Josseys	102/9	Irwin
Ajon, Eli	Chatham		206/3	Walton
Aker, William(Orphs)	Greene	Arners	177/5	Early
Akin, Benjamin	Morgan	McClendon	389/1	Early
Akin, Fleming	Chatham		135/15	Early
Akin, James S.	Clark	Applings	207/3	Early
Akin, Peter	Madison	Williford's	345/28	Early
Akin, William	Morgan	McClendon's	266/21	Early
Akins, Alexander	Effingham		70/5	Rabun
Akins, Bartley	Morgan	Hackneys	385/5	Irwin
Akins, Frances	Bulloch	Edwards	190/11	Irwin
Akins, Hillo	Walton	Wagnons	338/16	Early
Akins, James	Greene	Harville	120/3	Habersham
Akins, James	Morgan	Walkers	52/7	Early
Akins, John(Orph)	Warren	Rodgers	375/9	Early
Akins, John(R.S.)	Morgan	Walkers	110/2	Rabun
Akins, Lewis	Bulloch	Edwards	131/4	Irwin
Akins, Robert	Warren	Rodgers	471/8	Irwin
Akins, Robert	Warren	Rogers	90/9	Early
Akins, Thomas	Morgan	Walkers	219/7	Irwin
Akins, Thomas	Morgan	Walkers	5/4	Early
Akins, William	Morgan	Alfords	344/12	Irwin
Akridge, Abel	Montgomery	Alstons	93/3	Rabun
Akridge, Ezekiel	Clark	Oates	172/4	Irwin
Akridge, Levi	Jackson	Hamiltons Bt.	482/6	Appling
Akridge, Simeon	Clark	Jacks	162/15	Irwin
Akridge, William	Baldwin	Stephens'	47/5	Gwinnett
Alberson, Arthur	Laurens	S.Smiths	138/11	Early
Alberson, Joseph	Laurens	S.Smiths	363/1	Early
Alberson, Joseph	Laurens	S.Smiths	68/2	Appling
Albright, Harry	Madison	Willifords	22/1	Walton
Albright, Jacob	Madison	Willifords	400/26	Early
Albright, William	Madison	Willifords	443/5	Irwin
Albrittain, Elizabeth	Hancock	Smiths	309/4	Early
Albritten, William	Laurens	Watsons	322/2	Early
Albritton, Asa	Washington	Avent's	475/8	Appling
Albritton, Henry	Laurens	Watsons	65/9	Appling
Albritton, Jesse	Twiggs	R.Belchers	43/3	Walton
Albritton, Lanier(Orphs)	Hancock	Smiths	92/11	Irwin
Albritton, Matthew	Burke	Spiveys	234/8	Appling
Albritton, Peter	Washington	Avent's	104/7	Appling
Albritton, Peter	Washington	Averitts	345/20	Early
Alday, Isiah	Burke	M.Barde	318/2	Appling
Alday, John P.	Burke	M.Wards	75/2	Irwin
Alderman, James	Bulloch	Tilmans	325/16	Early
Alderman, Samuel	Bulloch	Edwards	103/4	Habersham
Alderman, Thomas	Scriven		265/8	Early
Alderman, William	Bulloch	Tilmans	113/3	Rabun
Alexander, Abdon	Jasper	McMichael's	29/1	Appling
Alexander, Arthur	Habersham	Suttons	237/27	Early
Alexander, Asa C.	Warren	Rodgers	485/7	Appling
Alexander, Asa	Jones	Samuels	224/8	Irwin
Alexander, Benj.	Tattnall	J.Durrences	266/20	Early
Alexander, David	Jefferson	Fountains	318/12	Irwin
Alexander, George	Jasper	Kennedys	417/7	Irwin
Alexander, James	Bryan	19	247/23	Early
Alexander, James	Bryan	19	512/10	Irwin
Alexander, James	Madison	Willifords	107/13	Early
Alexander, Jas.W.	Twiggs	W.Belcher	15/8	Irwin
Alexander, John B.	Bryan	19	245/17	Early
Alexander, John	Elbert	Ruckers	16/11	Early

NAME	COUNTY	MIL.DIST	LOT/SECT	DREW LAND
Alexander, John	Elbert	Ruckers	44/10	Habersham
Alexander, Josiah	Chatham		131/11	Early
Alexander, Nathaniel G.	Greene	144	190/4	Appling
Alexander, Peter	Elbert	Smiths	504/5	Appling
Alexander, Robert	Habersham	Taylors	101/27	Early
Alexander, Susannah(Wid)	Jones	Jeffersons	312/18	Early
Alexander, Travis	Wilkes	Burks	92/9	Appling
Alexander, Wm.(Orps)	Elbert	Ruckers	80/2	Appling
Alexander, Wm.	Elbert	Gaines	91/12	Habersham
Alford, Byas	Jefferson	Lamps	201/11	Early
Alford, Byas	Jefferson	Lamps	21/9	Hall
Alford, Collin	Greene	144	63/7	Appling
Alford, Haywood	Burke	Spiveys	645/2	Appling
Alford, Isham	Jasper	Evans	167/17	Early
Alford, Job	Jones	Kings	155/6	Appling
Alford, Job	Jones	Kings	252/16	Early
Alford, John	Washington	Daniels	80/15	Irwin
Alford, Julious Jr.	Greene	Greers	19/26	Early
Alford, Julious Sr.	Greene	Griers	243/5	Gwinnett
Alford, William	Hancock	Thomas'	34/2	Early
Alford, Wyat	Jefferson	Bothwells	56/22	Early
Alford, Zaddock	Morgan	Leonards	270/28	Early
Alfriend, Abraham	Hancock	Scotts	242/4	Walton
Alfriend, Edward	Greene	Wheelis	337/5	Irwin
Algiers, Williams D.	Laurens	Harry's	110/4	Habersham
Algood, Wm.Sr.	Elbert	Olivers	120/9	Appling
Alinon, Richard	Morgan	Wrights	298/6	Early
Alison, Alexander	Jasper	Northcuts	28/11	Hall
Allcoffee, Mary	Tattnall	Overstreets	284/10	Irwin
Allen, Asa Jr.	Franklin	Turks	78/14	Early
Allen, Asa Sr.	Franklin	Harris	511/4	Appling
Allen, Benjamin	Jones	Permenters	290/5	Gwinnett
Allen, Benjamin	Warren	Rodgers	32/10	Habersham
Allen, Benjamin	Warren	Rodgers	371/9	Irwin
Allen, Beverly	Elbert	Ruckers	256/1	Appling
Allen, Beverly	Putnam	Bustins	360/6	Early
Allen, Boller	Jones	Samuels	131/1	Appling
Allen, Brassel	Camden	Clarkes	449/5	Appling
Allen, Charles	Hancock	Millers	65/12	Habersham
Allen, Clement	Greene	Ragins	109/7	Gwinnett
Allen, Clement	Greene	Ragins	324/14	Early
Allen, David(R.S.)	Morgan	Parkers	73/9	Hall
Allen, Dennis	Jasper	Reids	150/6	Appling
Allen, Drury	Jones	Wallers	255/28	Early
Allen, Drury	Jones	Wallers	308/11	Irwin
Allen, Elijah(Orph)	Burke	Lewis'	472/8	Appling
Allen, Frances T.	Columbia	Olives	489/8	Irwin
Allen, George W.	Clark	Hinton's	360/7	Early
Allen, George(Orphs)	Hancock	Evans'	144/5	Gwinnett
Allen, George(Orphs)	Madison	Orr's	83/2	Habersham
Allen, George(Orphs)	Morgan	Parkers	24/15	Early
Allen, Gideon	Warren	151	121/1	Walton
Allen, Greenberry	Putnam	Oslins	74/3	Appling
Allen, Harris	Baldwin	Marshalls	368/27	Early
Allen, Harris	Baldwin	Marshals	297/8	Appling
Allen, Henry	Oglethorpe	Barnetts	24/6	Early
Allen, Howard	Oglethorpe	Davenports	510/2	Appling
Allen, James Jr.	Putnam	Ectors	283/6	Gwinnett
Allen, James P.	Burke	M.Wards	325/14	Early
Allen, James(Orph)	Richmond	Burtons	300/7	Appling
Allen, John R.	Greene	Garnors	56/2	Irwin
Allen, John Sr.	Franklin	Hammonds	259/8	Appling
Allen, John W.	Elbert	Gaines	233/3	Irwin
Allen, John	Jones	Permenters	308/7	Appling
Allen, John	Pulaski	Lesters	46/2	Appling
Allen, John	Twiggs	Griffins	372/16	Early
Allen, Jordan	Putnam	Oslins	292/7	Irwin

4

NAME	COUNTY	MIL.DIST	LOT/SECT	DREW LAND
Allen, Joseph	Jefferson	Lamps	331/3	Early
Allen, Joseph	Washington	Peabodys	359/2	Early
Allen, Mandy(Orph)	Richmond	Winters	248/5	Early
Allen, Mary(Orph)	Burke	Lewis'	472/8	Appling
Allen, Mary(Wid)	Morgan	Parkers	360/5	Appling
Allen, Nancy(Orph)	Richmond	Winters	248/5	Early
Allen, Rachael(Wid)	Laurens	Kinchens	379/18	Early
Allen, Richard	Richmond	398	102/17	Early
Allen, Richard	Richmond	398	523/8	Irwin
Allen, Robert T.	Columbia	Watsons	327/21	Early
Allen, Robt.(Rev)	Richmond	Palmer	119/7	Irwin
Allen, Scarlet(Orphs)	Warren	151	46/13	Irwin
Allen, Singleton	Elbert	Ruckers	30/21	Early
Allen, Stephen(Orphs)	Scriven	Smiths	72/19	Early
Allen, Stephen	Oglethorpe	Barnetts	106/11	Hall
Allen, Stephen	Oglethorpe	Brittons	359/13	Early
Allen, Theopilus	Greene	141	102/3	Habersham
Allen, Thos.	Morgan	Parkers	264/14	Early
Allen, Waddle	Richmond	Palmers	156/9	Appling
Allen, Welcome	Richmond	122	123/8	Hall
Allen, William B.	Jackson	Rogers Bt.	367/12	Irwin
Allen, William(Orphs)	Jackson	Rodgers Bt.	93/2	Rabun
Allen, William	Clark	Pentecost	235/6	Gwinnett
Allen, William	Morgan	McClendon's	310/8	Appling
Allen, William	Morgan	Parkers	62/5	Rabun
Allen, William	Oglethorpe	Barnetts	448/2	Appling
Allen, William	Oglethorpe	Murrays	116/3	Early
Allen, William	Putnam	Butts	430/11	Irwin
Allen, Wm.(Orph)	Richmond	Burtons	300/7	Appling
Allen, Wm.(R.S.)	Putnam	May's	243/10	Early
Allen, Wm.(R.S.)	Putnam	May's	400/8	Appling
Allen, Wm.F.	Putnam	Coopers	7/7	Early
Allen, Wm.G.	Jones	Wallers	455/5	Irwin
Allen, Young D.	Greene	Ragan's	190/7	Gwinnett
Allerson, Alexr.	Wilkes	Perry's	324/4	Early
Allerson, John	Wilkes	Perry's	336/10	Irwin
Allerson, Robt.	Wilkes	Perry's	12/8	Early
Allgood, Edward	Elbert	Olivers	139/10	Hall
Allgood, John Y.	Elbert	Oliver	486/4	Appling
Allgood, John(R.S.)	Elbert	Olivers	58/16	Irwin
Allgood, Peter	Elbert	Olivers	22/28	Early
Allgood, Samuel	Elbert	Olivers	36/6	Appling
Alligood, Daniel	Laurens	Griffins	17/6	Gwinnett
Alligood, Hillary	Laurens	Griffins	60/21	Early
Allin, Job	Warren	150	74/5	Rabun
Allin, Reuben	Morgan	Selmons	265/27	Early
Allin, Stephen	Morgan	Loyds	158/3	Early
Allison, Jesse	Greene	443	162/17	Early
Allison, John	Morgan	Farrars	240/8	Appling
Allison, Robt.	Oglethorpe	Brittons	220/10	Habersham
Allison, Robt.	Oglethorpe	Brittons	220/5	Gwinnett
Alliston, Elias	Wilkes	Bates	80/9	Irwin
Allman, Ann(Wid)	Elbert	P.Christians	72/10	Hall
Allmond, John	Burke	Bells	205/7	Gwinnett
Alls, Alexander	Glynn		69/1	Habersham
Allums, Edward	Putnam	H.Kindricks	146/4	Walton
Allums, John	Baldwin	Cousins	193/1	Irwin
Allums, Wm.	Putnam	Slaughters	44/10	Early
Almand, Thomas	Elbert	R.Christians	239/1	Early
Almand, Wm.	Gwinnett	Hamilton's B.	108/12	Hall
Almond, John	Burke	Bells	502/3	Appling
Almond,Thomas	Elbert	R.Christians	178/13	Habersham
Alsabrooks, Asa	Jones	Griffiths	290/4	Appling
Alsebrooks, Asa	Jones	Griffiths	59/6	Irwin
Also, Thomas	Twiggs	Browns	108/10	Irwin
Alston, Charity(Wid)	Elbert	Ruckers	469/4	Appling
Alston, Gilly(Wid)	Elbert	Ruckers	94/1	Rabun

5

NAME	COUNTY	MIL.DIST	LOT/SECT	DREW LAN
Alston, James Sr.	Montgomery	Alston's	308/4	Irwin
Alston, John	Telfair	Williams	38/12	Irwin
Alston, John	Telfair	Williams	52/8	Hall
Alston, Philip A.	Elbert	Ruckers	25/5	Habersha
Alston, Wm.H.	Elbert	Ruckers	207/2	Appling
Altman, Thomas	Appling	9	258/4	Walton
Altman, Thomas	Appling	9	319/5	Appling
Alturon, Sampson	Wayne	Johnston	369/7	Appling
Ambrus, Warren	Jasper	Blakes	4/7	Irwin
Ambrus, Warren	Jasper	Blakes	51/2	Irwin
Amerson, Eli	Washington	Cummings'	127/6	Irwin
Amerson, Josiah Sr.	Washington	Cummin's	116/4	Walton
Amerson, Warren	Washington	Cummins	17/7	Early
Amerson, Wm.	Washington	Cummins	182/6	Early
Ames, Eli	Wilkinson	Lees	363/3	Appling
Ammonds, Jacob	Lincoln	Walkers	518/11	Irwin
Ammonds, Jonathan	Lincoln	Jones	148/10	Irwin
Ammonds, William	Effingham		310/26	Early
Ammons, Jesse	Morgan	Campbells	34/2	Appling
Ammons, John	Wayne	Crews	13/2	Habersha
Ammons, John	Wayne	Crews	138/2	Habersha
Ammons, Uriah E.	Morgan	Townsends	200/26	Early
Amos, George	Hancock	Edwards	29/5	Irwin
Amos, James(R.S.)	Hancock	Edwards'	224/13	Early
Amos, James(R.S.)	Hancock	Edwards'	334/9	Early
Amos, James	Jones	Chappels	119/7	Early
Amos, James	Jones	Chappels	254/12	Early
Amos, Milton	Jasper	Kennedys	113/7	Gwinnett
Anders, Frederick	Laurens	(See 1812 Lottery)	—	
Anders, Frederick	Laurens	Carsons	240/7	Early
Anders, Joseph	Baldwin	Cousins	400/15	Early
Anderson, Abijah	Baldwin	Stephens'	126/6	Early
Anderson, Abraham	Columbia	Dodsons	314/15	Early
Anderson, Abraham	Columbia	Dodsons	69/7	Gwinnett
Anderson, Anne(Wid)	Greene	Macon's	336/9	Appling
Anderson, Augustus H.	Burke	Sullivans	178/26	Early
Anderson, Augustus(Orphs)	Jefferson	Abbots	61/4	Appling
Anderson, Braziel(Orphs)	Morgan	Talbots	27/6	Appling
Anderson, Charles W.	Jefferson	Fountains	133/1	Early
Anderson, Elisha Jr.	Richmond	Palmer's	182/15	Early
Anderson, Elisha Jr.	Richmond	Palmers	479/12	Irwin
Anderson, Evan	Washington	Daniels	174/1	Walton
Anderson, George	Elbert	Childer's	410/11	Irwin
Anderson, Henry(Orphs)	Laurens	Griffins	154/6	Appling
Anderson, Henry	Washington	Floyds	220/2	Early
Anderson, Hezekiah	Scriven	36	359/13	Irwin
Anderson, Hezekiah	Scriven	36	409/28	Early
Anderson, Jacob	Madison	Adairs	352/2	Appling
Anderson, James M.	Franklin	Jno.Millers	300/7	Irwin
Anderson, James	Effingham		169/16	Irwin
Anderson, James	Effingham		44/2	Irwin
Anderson, James	Greene	Tally's	138/5	Irwin
Anderson, James	Madison	Adares	34/2	Walton
Anderson, James	Scriven	36	383/9	Appling
Anderson, John M.	Richmond	Burtons	40/6	Appling
Anderson, John Sr.	Madison	Bones	189/2	Appling
Anderson, John Sr.	Madison	Bones	586/2	Appling
Anderson, John Sr.	Twiggs	Evan's	235/15	Early
Anderson, John	Bulloch	Jones	125/2	Appling
Anderson, John	Elbert	Buckners	80/3	Habersha
Anderson, John	Greene	Ragans	95/17	Early
Anderson, John	Greene	Ragins	265/28	Early
Anderson, John	Laurens	Kinchens	293/27	Early
Anderson, John	Twiggs	W.Belchers	27/4	Irwin
Anderson, Jordan	Pulaski	Davis	315/10	Irwin
Anderson, Joseph	Bulloch	Jones	233/1	Walton
Anderson, Joseph	Emanuel	59	59/7	Early

6

NAME	COUNTY	MIL.DIST	LOT/SECT	DREW LAND
Anderson, Mary(Wid)	Laurens	Griffins	458/5	Irwin
Anderson, Moses	Bulloch	Jones	490/10	Irwin
Anderson, Pheriby(Wid)	Twiggs	W.Belchers	96/11	Habersham
Anderson, Phillip	Madison	Milligans	111/28	Early
Anderson, Richard	Wilkes	Mattox's	28/8	Appling
Anderson, Robert	Elbert	R.Christians	142/3	Walton
Anderson, Robt.(Orphs)	Wilkinson	Howards	1/6	Habersham
Anderson, Robt.(Orphs)	Wilkinson	Howards	407/7	Irwin
Anderson, Shadrach	Washington	Peabody's	107/26	Early
Anderson, Shadrach	Washington	Peabodys	391/3	Early
Anderson, Stephen	Morgan	Dennis'	104/14	Early
Anderson, Terel	Madison	Bone's	149/8	Appling
Anderson, Terrell	Madison	Adairs	6/16	Irwin
Anderson, Thomas	Greene	Macon's	166/11	Early
Anderson, Thomas	Wilkes	Bryants	152/9	Appling
Anderson, Thomas	Wilkes	Bryants	443/12	Irwin
Anderson, William	Greene	143	181/4	Walton
Anderson, Wm.	Jefferson	Abbots	86/4	Early
Anderson, Wm.	Morgan	Hubbards	92/13	Irwin
Anderson, Wm.R.	Jackson	Scotts	17/3	Appling
Andersons, Elijah	Jefferson	Mathews	146/2	Habersham
Anderton, Augustus	Jefferson	Jones'	439/6	Irwin
Andress, Evens	Pulaski	Laneais	347/9	Early
Andrew, Benjamin Sr.	Elbert	Penns	113/6	Appling
Andrew, Burley	Elbert	R.Christians	411/6	Irwin
Andrews, Abisha	Twiggs	Thames	161/5	Gwinnett
Andrews, Adam	Greene	142	67/5	Rabun
Andrews, Alexr.(Orphs)	Greene	140	176/4	Irwin
Andrews, Clevfers R.	Twiggs	Hodges	362/3	Appling
Andrews, Daniel	Chatham		109/7	Appling
Andrews, David Jr.	Putnam	Slaughters	473/8	Irwin
Andrews, David R.	Hancock	Mims	105/11	Irwin
Andrews, Edward Q.	Liberty		239/7	Irwin
Andrews, Enoch	Franklin	Vaughns	142/6	Appling
Andrews, Henry W.	Richmond	398	134/6	Irwin
Andrews, John(R.S.)	Oglethorpe	Davenports	107/10	Irwin
Andrews, John	Jones	Permenters	139/6	Early
Andrews, Joseph	Burke	Torrances	114/9	Early
Andrews, Joseph	Burke	Torrances	439/11	Irwin
Andrews, Marcus	Hancock	Canes	79/6	Irwin
Andrews, Mary	Wilkes	Russells	41/11	Early
Andrews, Micajah	Liberty		146/16	Early
Andrews, Moses	Hancock	Daniels	300/4	Walton
Andrews, Richard	Warren	Rodgers	251/11	Early
Andrews, Robert	Hancock	Millers	351/2	Early
Andrews, Thomas R.	Greene	140	377/6	Irwin
Andrews, Warren(Orphs)	Burke	153	171/2	Irwin
Andrews, Wm.(Orphs)	Jasper	Easters	22/1	Rabun
Andrews, Wm.	Oglethorpe	Lees	114/2	Irwin
Andrews, Wm.	Oglethorpe	Lees	307/5	Appling
Andrews, Wm.	Wilkes	Russell's	439/2	Appling
Andrews, Wm.	Wilkes	Russels	270/10	Early
Andrews, Wm.Jr.	Oglethorpe	Lees	33/5	Early
Andrews, Wyatt	Oglethorpe	Lees	181/8	Appling
Andson, Noah(ark)	Twiggs	Thames	140/19	Early
Anees, Jonathan(Orphs)	Bulloch	Knights	411/4	Early
Angelly, Mills A.	Twiggs	R.Belchers	3/13	Habersham
Angilly, Benjamin	Twiggs	Hodge's	287/10	Irwin
Angle, Thomas	Franklin	Tates	299/17	Early
Anglin, Henry(R.S.)	Jackson	Winters Bt.	236/4	Walton
Anglin, Henry(R.S.)	Jackson	Winters Bt.	257/8	Early
Anglin, Henry(R.S.)	Jackson	Winters Bt.	380/6	Appling
Anglin, Henry	Twiggs	Jeffersons	524/7	Irwin
Anglin, Henry	Twiggs	Jeffersons	70/12	Hall
Anglin, James	Jackson	Winters Bt.	31/20	Early
Anglin, John	Oglethorpe	Waters'	152/27	Early
Anglin, John	Putnam	Moreland's	330/8	Appling

NAME	COUNTY	MIL.DIST	LOT/SECT	DREW LAND
Anglin, John	Putnam	Morelands	123/7	Appling
Anglin, Sarah(Wid)	Warren	Parhams	21/28	Early
Anglin, Wm.Jr.	Putnam	Buckners	176/7	Irwin
Ansley, Abel	Warren	152	253/7	Early
Ansley, Gilbert	Jones	Seals	641/2	Appling
Ansley, Jesse	Richmond	120	477/6	Appling
Ansley, Jesse	Warren	152	129/12	Habersham
Ansley, Jesse	Warren	152	188/12	Early
Ansley, Samuel	Greene	Carlton's	413/5	Irwin
Ansley, Samuel	Warren	Parhams'	94/15	Irwin
Anthony, Middleton	Jasper	Reids	431/28	Early
Anthony, Milton(Dr)	Richmond		364/6	Irwin
Anthony, Milton(Dr)	Richmond		78/4	Appling
Anthony, Roling	Wilkes	Smiths	3/10	Habersham
Antony, Isaac	Wilkes	Gordons	109/2	Appling
Aperson, James	Oglethorpe	Waters	240/19	Early
Aperson, John	Morgan	Hubbards	340/16	Early
Appeby, William	Jackson	Winters Bt.	88/15	Early
Applewhite, Robt.	Morgan	Walkers	5/4	Early
Appling, Eleanor D.(Wid)	Columbia	Olives	217/9	Irwin
Appling, Joel	Wilkes	Dents	379/5	Appling
Appling, Walter A.	Columbia	Olives	189/6	Appling
Appling, William	Clark	Stuarts	526/7	Appling
Archer, Alexander	Burke	71	71/4	Rabun
Archer, David	Scriven		35/28	Early
Archer, James	Hancock	Millers	181/6	Appling
Archer, Jonathan(Orp)	Wilkinson	Howards	42/11	Habersham
Archer, Thomas	Burke	71	40/15	Irwin
Ard, Elizabeth	Washington	Barge's	139/2	Walton
Ard, Hector(Orphs)	Wilkinson	Child's	150/8	Appling
Ards, John	Pulaski	Maddox	249/12	Irwin
Arendall, Nathan	Franklin	Harris'	262/9	Irwin
Arendall, Nathan	Franklin	Harris	31/3	Rabun
Arkins, Robert	Wilkes	Josies	308/16	Early
Arline, Henry	Emanuel	56	254/13	Early
Arline, Jesse	Laurens	D.Smiths	272/8	Early
Armer, Robert	Wilkes	Brooks	58/15	Early
Armer, William	Greene	Armers	29/11	Early
Armer, William	Jackson	Hamiltons Bt.	514/12	Irwin
Armor, Andrew	Jackson	Hamiltons	168/3	Habersham
Armor, Andrew	Jackson	Hamiltons	351/20	Early
Armor, Wm.	Jackson	Hamiltons Bt.	36/4	Appling
Armour, Ruth(Wid)	Chatham		274/15	Early
Armsby, William	Camden	Clarks	293/7	Appling
Armsted, John	Greene	Ragins	62/14	Irwin
Armstroff, Gothiel	Effingham		263/11	Irwin
Armstroff, Isreal	Effingham		151/2	Habersham
Armstrong, Alexr.Jr.	Washington	Cummin's	112/13	Early
Armstrong, Alexr.Sr.	Washington	Cummin's	302/9	Early
Armstrong, Edward	Washington	Cummin's	168/10	Early
Armstrong, James W.	Glynn		432/9	Irwin
Armstrong, James W.	Laurens	Harry's	56/27	Early
Armstrong, James	Wilkes	Dents	227/8	Irwin
Armstrong, Jesse	Washington	Avents	96/10	Irwin
Armstrong, John	Greene	Tuggles	188/5	Appling
Armstrong, William	Jasper	Reeds	164/7	Gwinnett
Arnett, Catharine	Wilkes	Holiday's	349/27	Early
Arnett, Perry	Warren	151	171/11	Irwin
Arnett, Peter	Scriven	Lovetts	369/14	Early
Arnett, Timothy	Scriven	Lovetts	226/4	Early
Arnett, Timothy	Scriven	Lovetts	381/6	Irwin
Arnett, Wm.	Wilkes	Holliday's	97/8	Irwin
Arnold, Felix W.	Morgan	Hubbards	111/5	Appling
Arnold, Fielding Sr.	Morgan	Townsends	177/2	Irwin
Arnold, Fielding Sr.	Morgan	Townsends	412/4	Appling
Arnold, Frances	Clark	Simms	318/16	Irwin
Arnold, James B.	Morgan	Townsends	170/10	Early

NAME	COUNTY	MIL.DIST	LOT/SECT	DREW LAND
Arnold, James	Elbert	Ruckers	12/2	Early
Arnold, Jesse H.	Morgan	Townsend	96/5	Early
Arnold, John	Hancock	Edwards'	241/4	Early
Arnold, John	Hancock	Edwards	142/20	Early
Arnold, Jonathan	Richmond	398	118/11	Habersham
Arnold, Joseph	Oglethorpe	Rowlands	103/16	Early
Arnold, Moses	Wilkes	Davis	278/15	Early
Arnold, Stephen	Oglethorpe	Rowlands	24/17	Early
Arnold, Wilie	Hancock	Loyd's	141//2	Walton
Arnold, William Jr.	Hancock	Loyds	503/6	Irwin
Arnold, Wm.	Putnam	Bustins	14/20	Early
Arnold, Wm.	Putnam	Bustins	167/9	Hall
Arnold, Wm.	Washington	Averett's	59/12	Hall
Arnold, Wm.Sr.	Hancock	Loyds	118/3	Irwin
Arnold, Wm.Sr.	Washington	Averets	62/12	Irwin
Arnold, Wyet	Jefferson	Fountains	464/8	Appling
Arnst, Christian	Chatham		328/7	Early
Arnstorff, George Jr.	Effingham		479/9	Irwin
Aron, William	Franklin	Shumates	321/8	Irwin
Arrandal, Wm.	Montgomery	Noble's	308/20	Early
Arrandol, James(Orph)	Montgomery	Noble's	249/17	Early
Arrandol, Wm.	Montgomery	Nobles	101/26	Early
Arrant, Cornelius	Lincoln	Tatoms	526/8	Appling
Arrant, John	Lincoln	Tatoms	145/4	Irwin
Arrant, Wm.Jr.	Lincoln	Tatoms	41/15	Irwin
Arrendell, John	Elbert	Olivers	248/10	Early
Arrington, Isham	Morgan	Parkers	43/12	Habersham
Arrington, James	Jefferson	Bothwells	390/11	Irwin
Arrington, Wm.(R.S.)	Morgan	Townsends	88/9	Early
Arstoff, Christian	Effingham		67/7	Appling
Arther, John	Oglethorpe	Murrays	561/2	Appling
Arthur, Barnabas	Franklin	Holcombs	316/13	Irwin
Arthur, Barnabas	Habersham	Holcombs	11/5	Irwin
Arthur, Caleb	Clark	Applings	53/7	Appling
Arthur, Charles T.	Franklin	Holcombs	335/5	Irwin
Arthur, Lewis	Jackson	Rogers Bt.	5/27	Early
Arthur, Matthew	Franklin	Holcombs	387/17	Early
Asbury, Henry	Greene	Nelms	316/3	Early
Asbury, Jesse	Putnam	Buckners	87/16	Irwin
Asbury, Thomas R.	Greene	Nelms	227/5	Gwinnett
Ash, John H.	Chatham		200/5	Gwinnett
Ash, John H.	Chatham		356/2	Early
Ashley, Cornelias R.	Telfair	Wilsons	370/2	Early
Ashley, Eliz.(wid)	Pulaski	Johnstons	43/7	Irwin
Ashley, James	Burke			—
Ashley, James	Putnam	Mays	221/7	Gwinnett
Ashley, John	Elbert	Dooley's	361/5	Irwin
Ashley, John	Hancock	Canes	255/4	Early
Ashley, Lodewick	Telfair	Wilsons	253/6	Gwinnett
Ashley, Robt.B.	Pulaski	Johnstons'	153/13	Early
Ashley, Stephen	Lincoln	Jeters	288/15	Early
Ashley, Wm.	Lincoln	Jeters	207/26	Early
Ashmore, Anne	Wilkes	Holidays	127/11	Habersham
Ashmore, Joel	Jasper	Barnes	76/27	Early
Ashmore, John	Liberty		398/13	Early
Ashmore, Joseph	Liberty		115/2	Irwin
Ashmore, Joseph	Liberty		196/16	Early
Ashmore, Peter	Lincoln	Tatoms	46/13	Early
Ashnerst, Robt.	Putnam	Buckners	94/10	Irwin
Ashton, Nathaniel	Baldwin	Marshalls	115/2	Habersham
Ashworth, Jonathan	Jackson	Dickerson	90/5	Early
Askew, John(Orphs)	Greene	Macon	406/8	Appling
Askew, Julius A.	Morgan	Hubberts	500/11	Irwin
Askew, Margarett	Chatham		346/17	Early
Askew, Perry	Jasper	Smiths	321/9	Irwin
Askew, Thomas	Jefferson	Cowarts	206/12	Irwin
Askew, William	Jasper	Bentleys	20/5	Early

NAME	COUNTY	MIL.DIST	LOT/SECT	DREW LAND
Aspinwall, Eliza(Wid)	Chatham		260/7	Irwin
Aspinwall, Eliza(Wid)	Chatham		474/6	Appling
Atchison, James A.	Jasper	Hays	118/3	Early
Atchison, John	Warren	Griers	351/13	Irwin
Aters, Peter	Habersham	Grants	41/1	Rabun
Atha's, Elijah(Orphs)	Columbia	Olivers	390/4	Appling
Athey, Zepheniah(Orphs)	Columbia	Burroughs	175/5	Gwinnett
Atkerson, Henry	Jackson	Winters Bt.	242/8	Appling
Atkerson, John Sr.	Baldwin	Haws'	291/3	Early
Atkerson, John Sr.	Baldwin	Haws	3/3	Appling
Atkins, Elizabeth	Scriven	Roberts	147/11	Habersham
Atkins, Ica	Washington	Wimberly's	169/13	Irwin
Atkinson's, John(Orph)	Burke	J.Wards	37/10	Irwin
Atkinson, Arnold	Oglethorpe	Bowls	247/1	Appling
Atkinson, Arnold	Oglethorpe	Bowls	264/27	Early
Atkinson, Arthur C.	Clark	Parrs	150/5	Appling
Atkinson, Cornelius	Jackson	Rogers Bt.	177/13	Early
Atkinson, Cornelius	Jackson	Rogers Bt.	57/8	Hall
Atkinson, Coshiny(Orph)	Camden	32	144/2	Habersham
Atkinson, Edmund(Orph)	Camden	Bailey's	378/20	Early
Atkinson, Elbert	Hancock			-
Atkinson, Henry	Wilkinson	Howards	424/2	Appling
Atkinson, Henry	Wilkinson	Howards	65/4	Rabun
Atkinson, Joseph H.	Clark	Parrs	393/21	Early
Atkinson, Lewis	Hancock	Champions	201/7	Irwin
Atkinson, Nancy(Orph)	Camden	Bailey's	378/20	Early
Atkinson, Robt.Jr.	Jackson	Hamiltons Bt.	145/13	Habersham
Atkinson, Samuel W.	Morgan	Herberts	75/13	Habersham
Atkinson, Thomas P.	Clark	Parrs	126/8	Early
Atkinson, Valentine	Oglethorpe	Barnett's	334/3	Appling
Atkinson, Valentine	Oglethorpe	Barnetts	165/18	Early
Atkinson, Wm.(Orphs)	Burke	J.Wards	177/4	Irwin
Atkison, Littleton	Baldwin	Marshalls	123/12	Hall
Atkison, Nancy	Burke	Bells	344/9	Irwin
Attaway, David	Burke	Sullivans	138/8	Early
Attaway, Elijah	Burke	72	162/6	Appling
Attaway, Elijah	Burke	72	360/1	Appling
Attaway, Elizabeth Jr.	Burke	Sullivans	278/5	Early
Attaway, Harley Jr.	Burke	Sullivans	154/5	Gwinnett
Attaway, James	Elbert	Ruckers	132/8	Hall
Attaway, Jesse Sr.	Burke	Sullivans	47/26	Early
Attaway, Joseph Jr.	Burke	Sullivans	93/5	Irwin
Audulph, Henry	Jones	Permenters	335/28	Early
Austain, Thomas	Gwinnett	Hamilton's B.	56/14	Irwin
Austin, Ann(Orph)	Bryan	20	238/4	Early
Austin, Etheldred	Walton	Williams	262/9	Appling
Austin, Henry(Orph)	Bryan	20	238/4	Early
Austin, Isaac	Walton	Worshains	35/21	Early
Austin, James(Orph)	Bryan	20	238/4	Early
Austin, Jesse	Morgan	Knights	62/19	Early
Austin, John H.	Greene	Armers	63/1	Appling
Austin, John	Baldwin	Taliaferros	457/3	Appling
Austin, John	Bryan	20	238/4	Early
Austin, Joseph(Orph)	Bryan	20	238/4	Early
Austin, Sarah(Orph)	Bryan	20	238/4	Early
Austin, William	Jones	Permenters	8/5	Habersham
Avent, John	Jones	Hansfords	233/12	Early
Avent, John	Jones	Hansfords	94/20	Early
Averea, Samuel	Putnam	Coopers	436/11	Irwin
Averet, David	Putnam	Buckners	122/9	Early
Averet, Drury	Hancock	Smiths	305/8	Appling
Averett, Benjamin	Laurens	Griffins	329/17	Early
Averett, Benjamin	Laurens	Griffins	46/5	Early
Averill, Juda(Wid)	Laurens	Griffins	225/10	Early
Averit, David	Pulaski			-
Averit, David	Putnam	Buckners	180/13	Irwin
Averitt, Abner	Laurens	Ross	61/1	Habersham

NAME	COUNTY	MIL.DIST	LOT/SECT	DREW LAND
Averitt, Jesse	Richmond	Palmer's	22/2	Appling
Averitts, Ralphord(Orphs)	Columbia	Shaws	107/27	Early
Averitts, Ralphord(Orphs)	Columbia	Shaws	513/8	Appling
Avery, Alexander	Warren	150	157/8	Early
Avery, David	Washington	Pools	166/2	Early
Avery, Henry	Franklin	Burroughs	590/2	Appling
Avery, John	Washington	Floyd's	59/11	Early
Avery, Jonathan	Washington	Pool's	43/8	Hall
Avery, Patience(Wid)	Washington	Pools	399/2	Early
Avery, Richard	Putnam	Coopers	404/5	Irwin
Avery, Samuel	Washington	Mannings	36/17	Early
Avery, Thomas	Columbia	Willinghams	47/10	Habersham
Avery, William	Jasper	Kennedys	38/2	Habersham
Avon, Thomas	Franklin	Vaughns	114/8	Early
Avredg, James	Walton	Echols'	111/12	Hall
Awbrey, Thomas	Morgan	Townsends	376/7	Appling
Awbrey, William	Morgan	Townsend's	114/2	Rabun
Awbrey, William	Morgan	Townsends	481/9	Irwin
Awtrey, John	Greene	Ragins	143/15	Irwin
Awtry, Hannah(Wid)	Morgan	Parkers	186/1	Irwin
Awtry, Isaac	Morgan	Raymeys	28/9	Hall
Aycock, James	Lincoln	Thompsons	200/11	Early
Aycock, Joel	Oglethorpe	Waters	379/9	Appling
Aycock, Lorenzo	Lincoln	Thompsons	93/9	Irwin
Aycock, Sebron	Wilkes	Burk's	121/10	Early
Aycock, Zachariah	Oglethorpe	Waters	240/6	Irwin
Ayecock, Reddick	Oglethorpe	Waters	588/2	Appling
Ayecocke, Joel	Oglethorpe	Water's	148/8	Appling
Ayres, Abraham	Lincoln	Graves	274/6	Irwin
Ayres, Daniel	Franklin	R.Browns	264/7	Appling
Ayres, Frances(Wid)	Jackson	Dicksens Bt.	11/1	Appling
Ayres, Jesse	Habersham	Taylors	225/4	Irwin
Ayres, John B.	Lincoln	Parks	238/21	Early
Ayres, John	Columbia	Bealls	56/9	Irwin
Ayres, Nathaniel	Franklin	R.Browns	173/6	Irwin
Ayres, Seaborn	Columbia	Watsons	8/10	Early
Ayres, Thomas	Columbia	Pullins	312/9	Appling
Baas, Daniel A.	Effingham		63/2	Early
Baas, Rebecca(Wid)	Effingham		48/4	Rabun
Baas, Rosannah	Effingham		273/9	Early
Baas, Sarah	Effingham		273/9	Early
Babb, William	Baldwin	Taliaferro	56/4	Walton
Babb, William	Baldwin	Taliaferros	276/3	Early
Babcock, James	Scriven	Moodys	5/1	Walton
Baber, Nathaniel	Morgan	Loyds	203/19	Early
Baber, Thomas	Wilkes	Brook's	59/10	Habersham
Baber, Washington	Morgan	Hackneys	322/13	Early
Baber, William	Oglethorpe	Waters	393/6	Early
Bachelor, Cornelius	Wilkinson	Brooks	153/6	Gwinnett
Bachns, John	Morgan	Parkers	147/13	Habersham
Backlin, John	Chatham		94/3	Rabun
Backus, John	Morgan	Parkers	306/10	Irwin
Bacon, Eugene	Liberty		12/9	Early
Bacon, John	Liberty		307/9	Appling
Bacon, Joseph	Chatham		101/21	Early
Bacon, Lyddall	Jones	Philips'	246/6	Gwinnett
Bacon, Lyddall	Jones	Phillips'	147/12	Hall
Bacon, Thomas W.	Liberty		361/15	Early
Bacon, Wm.Q.	Liberty		404/11	Early
Bagby, John	Walton	Sentells	338/8	Irwin
Baggett, Elias	Columbia	Ob.Morris	81/2	Habersham
Baggett, Jesse	Columbia	Watson	369/9	Irwin
Baggett, Jesse	Columbia	Watsons	329/8	Appling
Baggett, Luke	Twiggs	Ellis	421/10	Irwin
Baggs, David S.	McIntosh	Eigles	196/13	Irwin
Baggs, Esther(Wid)	McIntosh	Eigles	73/3	Walton
Baggs, John	Jefferson	Matthews	134/21	Early

11

NAME	COUNTY	MIL.DIST	LOT/SECT	DREW LAN
Baggs, William	McIntosh	Eigles	453/8	Appling
Baglay, Mary	Franklin	Harris	62/4	Irwin
Bagley, Benj.	Washington	Danells	324/19	Early
Bagley, Harmon	Franklin	Harris	118/18	Early
Bagley, Henry Jr.	Franklin	Harris	313/7	Gwinnett
Bagley, Henry	Greene	Kimbroughs	37/6	Early
Bagley, James	Franklin	Harris'	172/8	Hall
Bagley, James	Franklin	Harris	38/2	Early
Bagley, Joseph	Jackson	Rogers	300/6	Gwinnett
Bagley, Moore	Jasper	Easts	200/8	Appling
Bagley, Wm.	Hancock	Herberts	286/6	Irwin
Bagwell, Fredrk	(R.S.)	Gwinnett	Hamiltons	129/8, A
Bailey, Benjamin H.	Morgan	Walkers	111/3	Walton
Bailey, Charles	Oglethorpe	Brittons	7/12	Early
Bailey, Chas.A.	Hancock	Daniels	117/12	Early
Bailey, Christopher	Effingham		396/26	Early
Bailey, Daniel	Jefferson	Lamps	116/1	Habersha
Bailey, Elizabeth	Morgan	Walkers	259/6	Early
Bailey, Ezekiah	Elbert	Smiths	362/5	Gwinnett
Bailey, George	Laurens	Kinchens'	82/16	Early
Bailey, George	Laurens	Kinchens	91/6	Irwin
Bailey, George	Oglethorpe	Bowls	37/6	Irwin
Bailey, Green	Putnam	Berrys	334/6	Irwin
Bailey, Green	Putnam	Berrys	72/6	Appling
Bailey, Harrison	Telfair	Williams	457/7	Appling
Bailey, Henry J.	Oglethorpe	Brittons	363/5	Irwin
Bailey, Jacob	Oglethorpe	Barnetts	157/3	Habersha
Bailey, Jacob	Oglethorpe	Barnetts	449/2	Appling
Bailey, James	Burke	Royals	483/10	Irwin
Bailey, James	Burke	Royals	73/5	Early
Bailey, James	Jackson	Rogers	458/13	Irwin
Bailey, James	Jones	Kings	312/6	Early
Bailey, James	Jones	Kings	53/27	Early
Bailey, James	Morgan	Campbell's	27/27	Early
Bailey, Jane	Oglethorpe	Brittons	322/8	Appling
Bailey, Jas.(Orph)	Jefferson	Bothwells	25/22	Early
Bailey, John G.	Wilkes	McLendons	114/11	Habersha
Bailey, John S.	Hancock	Danells	40/11	Hall
Bailey, John	Camden	Baileys	208/4	Early
Bailey, John	Morgan	Camels	272/19	Early
Bailey, John	Oglethorpe	Brittons	517/5	Appling
Bailey, John	Warren	Griers	234/8	Irwin
Bailey, John	Washington	Barges	293/6	Early
Bailey, John	Washington	Cummins	137/6	Early
Bailey, John	Washington	Cummins	15/5	Habersha
Bailey, Jonathan	Oglethorpe	Brittons	136/3	Habersha
Bailey, Jos.(Orphs)	Morgan	Walkers	367/6	Early
Bailey, Joseph	Walton	Wagnons	25/21	Early
Bailey, Nathl.(Orphs)	Wilkes	Gordons	169/5	Early
Bailey, Nathl.(Orphs)	Wilkes	Gordons	38/26	Early
Bailey, Nathl.	Wilkes	Gordons	392/1	Early
Bailey, Nathl.	Wilkes	Gordons	65/10	Early
Bailey, Peter	Warren	150	192/9	Irwin
Bailey, Robert	Oglethorpe	Brittons	355/6	Irwin
Bailey, Russell	Wilkes	Baites	176/9	Appling
Bailey, Samuel A.	Hancock	Daniels	70/6	Early
Bailey, Samuel	Jackson	Rogers	332/8	Appling
Bailey, Samuel	Jackson	Scotts	379/11	Irwin
Bailey, Samuel	Twiggs	Evans's	209/8	Appling
Bailey, Thomas Jr.	Warren	150	5/13	Irwin
Bailey, William	Clarke	Harriss	210/14	Early
Bailey, William	Washington	Wimberlys	377/13	Early
Bailey, Wm.	Elbert	Gaines	58/13	Habersha
Bailey, Wm.	Wilkinson	Bowings	183/11	Irwin
Bailey, Wm.Sr.	Oglethorpe	Rowlands	170/3	Habersha
Bailey, Zachariah	Warren	150	99/7	Appling
Baillie, George	Chatham		345/13	Early

NAME	COUNTY	MIL.DIST	LOT/SECT	DREW LAND
Baillie, George	Chatham		473/12	Irwin
Baily, Tellefero	Wilkes	Josseys	294/3	Early
Baily, Wm.	Wilkinson	Bowings	148/6	Appling
Bain, Robert	Morgan	Campbells	43/12	Irwin
Bains, (Altered to Butler)	Scriven	Smiths	166/3	Walton
Baird, Ann(Orph)	Camden	Clarks	43/8	Appling
Baird, Benjamin	Elbert	Whites D./Ns.Bt.	442/5	Irwin
Baird, John P.	Elbert	B.Higginbotham	117/28	Early
Baird, John P.	Elbert	B.Higginbotham	91/18	Irwin
Baird, Martha(Orph)	Camden	Clarks	43/8	Appling
Baird, Robt.M.	Elbert	B.Higginbothams	40/2	Irwin
Baird, Robt.M.	Elbert	G.Higginbothams	17/5	Rabun
Bairdin, Aron	Clarke	Mitchells	231/5	Irwin
Bairdin, Edward	Clarke	Mitchells	351/3	Appling
Bairdin, Elijah	Clarke	Mitchells	285/4	Early
Baisden, Jake	Glynn		34/5	Early
Baisden, Josiah	Liberty		196/8	Appling
Baisdin, Margary(Orph)	McIntosh	Gould's	141/1	Walton
Baisdin, Mary(Orph)	McIntosh	Gould's	141/1	Walton
Baisdin, Thomas(Orph)	McIntosh	Gould's	141/1	Walton
Baismore, Whitmel	Tattnall	Keens	3/2	Early
Baitey, James	Oglethorpe	Barnetts	39/12	Early
Baits, Matthias	Jackson	Hamiltons	159/10	Irwin
Baity, James	Oglethorpe	Barnetts	39/12	Early
Baker, Absalom	Franklin	Hammonds	92/18	Early
Baker, Amos	Elbert	Olivers	104/17	Early
Baker, Artimus	Chatham		88/7	Appling
Baker, Beall	Franklin	Turks	32/10	Hall
Baker, Benj.	Franklin	Haynes	22/9	Appling
Baker, Benjamin	Franklin	Haynes	22/9	Appling
Baker, Benjamin	Gwinnett	Hamiltons	227/1	Appling
Baker, Blake	Washington	Cummins	186/12	Early
Baker, Blake	Washington	Cummins	221/5	Gwinnett
Baker, Chas.Sr.	Franklin	Haynes	330/15	Early
Baker, Chrisphr.Sr.	Gwinnett	Hamiltons	273/10	Irwin
Baker, Christopher	Franklin	Attaways	23/3	Rabun
Baker, Christphr.Sr.	Gwinnett	Hamiltons	399/3	Early
Baker, Demsey(R.S.)	Hancock	Scotts	173/1	Early
Baker, Edward B.	McIntosh	Goulds	448/4	Appling
Baker, Edwin	Warren	Griers	176/8	Early
Baker, Eli	Richmond		308/5	Appling
Baker, Elias Jr.	Franklin	Turk's	153/14	Early
Baker, Elias Jr.	Franklin	Turks	250/12	Irwin
Baker, Elias Sr.	Franklin	Turks	152/10	Habersham
Baker, Elias Sr.	Franklin	Turks	152/10	Habersham
Baker, Elijah	Elbert	Dooleys	55/26	Early
Baker, Elijah	Elbert	Dooleys	67/11	Irwin
Baker, Elijah	Liberty		14/10	Habersham
Baker, Harley	Jasper	Barne's	107/11	Hall
Baker, Harley	Jasper	Barnes	171/9	Irwin
Baker, Hugh	Franklin	Hammonds	211/27	Early
Baker, Hugh	Franklin	Hammonds	224/4	Irwin
Baker, Hugh	Franklin	Hammonds	224/4	Irwin
Baker, James	Bulloch	Edwards	171/5	Appling
Baker, James	Franklin	Attaways	246/5	Irwin
Baker, Jas.(Orphs)	Wilkes	Bryants	43/15	Irwin
Baker, Jeremiah Jr.	Montgomery	Alstons	123/1	Irwin
Baker, Jeremiah	Hancock	Smiths	183/20	Irwin
Baker, Jeremiah	Hancock	Smiths	183/20	Early
Baker, Jeremiah	Hancock	Smiths	370/17	Early
Baker, Jno.(S/O Elias)	Franklin	Turks	251/5	Appling
Baker, John G.	Liberty		521/6	Irwin
Baker, John M.	Franklin	Hammonds	375/13	Early
Baker, John(Son/Elias)	Franklin	Turks	97/5	Appling
Baker, John	Franklin	Vaughns	521/11	Irwin
Baker, John	Greene	Amers	66/11	Hall
Baker, John	Jones	Harrists	355/19	Early

13

NAME	COUNTY	MIL.DIST	LOT/SECT	DREW LAND
Baker, John	Warren	Griers	320/4	Early
Baker, Jonathan	Greene	Talleys	302/27	Early
Baker, Jonathan	Warren	Griers	470/10	Irwin
Baker, Jonathan	Washington	Cummings	48/2	Appling
Baker, Jonathan	Washington	Cummins	134/9	Hall
Baker, Jonathan	Washington	Cummins	25/8	Early
Baker, Jordan	Burke	Spiveys	387/6	Irwin
Baker, Joshua(R.S.)	Franklin	Harris'	160/12	Habersham
Baker, Joshua	Franklin	Ashs	307/11	Irwin
Baker, Joshua	Walton	Green's	139/2	Early
Baker, Margt.R.(Wid)	Liberty		125/2	Early
Baker, Morrell	Laurens	Harris	66/27	Early
Baker, Richard S.	Liberty		226/6	Early
Baker, Richard S.	Liberty		52/1	Rabun
Baker, Samuel	Morgan	Walkers	206/5	Early
Baker, Silas	Greene	Armers	69/5	Irwin
Baker, Solomon	Jackson	Hamiltons	96/11	Early
Baker, Susannah(Wid)	Greene	Tuggles	3/7	Early
Baker, Thomas	Walton	Greens	160/2	Rabun
Baker, Thomas	Walton	Greens	162/3	Walton
Baker, William J.	Liberty		249/8	Early
Baker, William	Jones	Permenters	165/27	Early
Baker, William	Jones	Permenters	42/28	Early
Baker, William	Warren	Griers	290/13	Early
Baker, Willis	Wilkinson	Brooks	94/10	Early
Baker, Wm.	Warren	Griers	391/1	Early
Baker, Wm.I.	Liberty		290/21	Early
Baker, Wm.Jr.	Gwinnett	Hamiltons	176/3	Early
Baker, Wm.L.	Chatham		125/6	Gwinnett
Bakers, John(Orphs)	Burke	Spiveys	23/23	Early
Baldwin, Catherine	Oglethorpe	Barnetts	64/6	Irwin
Baldwin, Charles	Greene	141	233/1	Walton
Baldwin, Elijah	Clarke	Applings	69/5	Irwin
Baldwin, John	Jasper	Smiths	323/12	Irwin
Baldwin, Joseph	Franklin	Davis	375/7	Appling
Baldwin, Lewis	Greene	Greers	405/2	Appling
Baldwin, Wm.Sr.	Jones	Seals	481/6	Irwin
Baldwin, Wm.W.	Oglethorpe	Brittons	281/9	Irwin
Balentine, John	Pulaski	Laniers	84/11	Early
Bales, Emmer	Greene	143	71/11	Habersham
Baley, Eliz.(Wid)	Camden	Longs	3/15	Early
Baley, Eliza.(Orph)	Camden	Long's	48/12	Habersham
Baley, James	Jefferson	Lamps	409/11	Early
Baley, John	Morgan	Alfords	144/19	Early
Baley, Mary(Orph)	Camden	Long's	48/12	Habersham
Baley, Rebecca(Orph)	Camden	Long's	48/12	Habersham
Baley, Sarah(Orph)	Camden	Long's	48/12	Habersham
Baley, Sarah(Wid)	Jefferson	Lamps	30/13	Irwin
Baley, Sarah(Wid)	Morgan	Walkers	231/14	Early
Baley, Thos.Sr.	Columbia	Ob.Morris	180/14	Early
Baley, Wm.(Orphs)	Gwinnett	Hamiltons	48/21	Early
Baley, Wm.(Orphs)	Morgan	Walkers	203/21	Early
Baley, Wm.	Clarke	Harriss	56/13	Irwin
Baleys, Silas(Orphs)	Jefferson	Matthews	99/1	Early
Balir, Janette S.(Orph)	Richmond	398th	332/6	Appling
Ball, Caswell	Pulaski	Bryans	172/9	Early
Ball, Frederick	Chatham		454/5	Irwin
Ball, Hartwell	Warren	Blounts	97/11	Irwin
Ball, Isaac(Orphs)	Warren	Battles	348/5	Irwin
Ball, Isaac	Warren	Blounts	231/12	Early
Ball, Isaac	Warren	Blounts	67/4	Rabun
Ball, John(Orph)	Wilkinson	Lees	32/7	Early
Ball, John	Washington	Brooks	21/27	Early
Ball, Larkin	Telfair	Williams'	247/3	Irwin
Ball, Sarah	Scriven	36th	152/1	Irwin
Ballard, Charles	Pulaski	Maddox'	297/5	Early
Ballard, Edw.	Wilkinson	Smiths	5/1	Habersham

14

NAME	COUNTY	MIL.DIST	LOT/SECT	DREW LAND
Ballard, James(Orph)	Richmond	Burtons	240/18	Early
Ballard, James	Greene	144	79/11	Early
Ballard, Jesse	Morgan	Talbots	177/2	Rabun
Ballard, John P.	Chatham		404/9	Irwin
Ballard, John	Burke	72	135/11	Habersham
Ballard, Lucenia(Orph)	Richmond	Burtons	240/18	Early
Ballard, Micajah(Orph)	Richmond	Burtons	240/18	Early
Ballard, Milly(Orph)	Richmond	Burtons	240/18	Early
Ballard, Ranson	Putnam	Littles	4/9	Hall
Ballard, Thomas(Orph)	Richmond	Burtons	240/18	Early
Ballard, Wharton	Franklin	Attaways	356/8	Appling
Ballard, Wm.	Jones	Shropshiers	107/3	Irwin
Ballinger, John Sr.	Elbert	Whites/Cs.Bt.	263/26	Early
Ballinger, John Sr.	Elbert	Whites/Cs.Bt.	348/8	Irwin
Balls, Joseph(Orphs)	Scriven	36th	72/11	Hall
Baloum, Nancy(Wid)	Twiggs	Ellis	248/1	Walton
Bames, Nathaniel	Madison	Millicans	419/5	Appling
Bandredge, Jesse	Hancock	Herberts	2/26	Early
Bandy, Benjamin	Chatham		507/7	Appling
Bandy, Ephraim	Morgan	Hackney's	106/3	Early
Bandy, James	Morgan	Talbotts	194/12	Irwin
Bandy, John	McIntosh	Goulas	414/21	Early
Bandy, Lovina	McIntosh	Hamiltons	390/5	Irwin
Bandy, Sarah(Wid)	Camden	Baileys	58/4	Habersham
Bane, William	McIntosh	Hamiltons	392/6	Early
Banfield, John	Jones	Harrests	145/26	Early
Banion, John O.	Burke	McNorrills	390/13	Early
Banks, Dunston	Elbert	G.Higginbothams	272/12	Irwin
Banks, Edmund	Jasper	Phillip's	42/2	Irwin
Banks, George	Warren	Parhams	145/2	Rabun
Banks, George	Warren	Parhams	99/8	Irwin
Banks, James J.	Elbert	Childers	66/16	Irwin
Banks, James Jr.	Elbert	Buckners	111/27	Early
Banks, James Sr.	Elbert	Ruckers	431/7	Irwin
Banks, John	Jasper	Phillips	3/11	Irwin
Banks, Joseph	Warren	Parhams	366/13	Irwin
Banks, Josiah C.	Jasper	Phillips	7/7	Gwinnett
Banks, Ralph Jr.	Elbert	B.Higginbothams	187/2	Rabun
Banks, Richard	Oglethorpe	Wises	150/13	Irwin
Banks, Simeon	Emanuel	49	352/7	Gwinnett
Banks, William	Wilkes	Gordons	261/19	Early
Banks, Willis	Elbert	P.Christians	199/8	Appling
Banks, Wm.	Elbert	Dooleys		–
Banks, Wm.	Elbert	Dooleys	52/1	Early
Bankston, Fayette	Morgan	Parkers	76/5	Irwin
Bankston, James E.	Jasper	East's	35/11	Early
Bankston, James S.	Jasper	East's	15/19	Early
Bankston, Sarah(Wid)	Clarke	Moores	517/12	Irwin
Bankston, William	Jackson	Hamiltons	394/12	Irwin
Bankston, Wm.	Jackson	Hamiltons	325/3	Appling
Banlineare, Heloise	Chatham		250/7	Irwin
Banson, Wm.Sr.	Wilkes	McClendons	196/9	Irwin
Barbee, Martha(Wid)	Wilkinson	Lees	332/6	Irwin
Barber, Asa	Washington	Jenkinsons	14/7	Irwin
Barber, Asa	Washington	Jenkinsons	355/28	Early
Barber, Charles(R.S.)	Glynn		203/1	Early
Barber, Chas.(R.S.)	Glynn		109/8	Appling
Barber, Cornelius	Glynn		183/15	Early
Barber, Cornelius	Glynn		29/12	Hall
Barber, Edmund	Clarke	Harpers	114/12	Habersham
Barber, Elisha(Orphs)	Oglethorpe	Murrays	199/12	Irwin
Barber, Frederick	Washington	Wimberleys	435/7	Irwin
Barber, Frederick	Washington	Wimberlys	74/4	Walton
Barber, George W.	Jefferson	Fountains	37/1	Appling
Barber, John	Chatham		401/6	Appling
Barber, John	Franklin	Harris	337/13	Early
Barber, Joseph	Jefferson	Fountains	456/12	Irwin

NAME	COUNTY	MIL.DIST	LOT/SECT	DREW LAN
Barber, Joseph	Twiggs	W.Belchers	195/7	Irwin
Barber, Mary(Wid)	Wilkinson	Childs	232/4	Irwin
Barber, Moses	Washington	Jenkinsons	66/6	Early
Barber, Rebecca(Wid)	Washington	Jenkinsons	298/26	Early
Barber, Samuel	Jefferson	Fountains	399/9	Early
Barber, Samuel	Liberty		450/28	Early
Barber, Stancell(R.S.)	Twiggs	W.Belchers	351/11	Early
Barber, William	Clarke	Harpers	106/1	Habersham
Barber, William	McIntosh	Goulas	464/8	Irwin
Barber, Wm.	Franklin	Harris	95/3	Appling
Barber, Wm.Jr.	Washington	Jenkinsons	345/19	Early
Barbre, John S.	Twiggs	W.Belchers	188/4	Walton
Barbre, Stancell(R.S.)	Twiggs	W.Belcher's	212/8	Appling
Barclay, David	Twiggs	W.Belchers	318/9	Appling
Barclay, John	Twiggs	W.Belchers	4/11	Irwin
Barclay, William	Jasper	Blakes	80/4	Habersham
Barco, Daniel	Camden	33	304/13	Early
Barco, Levice(Orph)	Camden	33	213/27	Early
Barefield, John	Morgan	Hubberts	45/2	Early
Barefield, Lewis F.(Orph)	Richmond		217/11	Irwin
Barefield, Sampson	Jones	Weatherbys	20/4	Irwin
Barefield, William	Morgan	Hubbards	238/15	Early
Barefield, Wm.	Jasper	Trembles	142/4	Early
Barefield, Wm.	Jasper	Trimbles	135/21	Early
Barefield, Wm.W.	Jones	Hurst	234/4	Walton
Barefoot, john	Wilkinson	Bowings	67/14	Irwin
Barfield, James	Warren	151	104/6	Gwinnett
Barfield, James	Warren	151	443/8	Irwin
Barfield, Sampson	Jones	Harrest	140/7	Appling
Bargainer, Wm.	Jefferson	Cowarts	99/21	Early
Bargarner, John(Orphs)	Twiggs	Ellis's	198/16	Irwin
Barge, Abel	Washington	Barges	160/2	Irwin
Barge, Abel	Washington	Barges	427/9	Irwin
Bargemore, Benj.(Orphs)	Burke	Hands	213/3	Appling
Barker, Abraham	Wilkinson	Lee's	19/11	Habersham
Barker, Asaph B.	Jackson	Dickson	86/26	Early
Barker, Benj.(Orphs)	Franklin	Attaways	226/5	Irwin
Barker, Edward	Putnam	Oslins	362/11	Early
Barker, Elijah	Pulaski	Davis	238/11	Irwin
Barker, Hugh	Franklin	Hammonds	211/27	Early
Barker, Isham	Hall		221/6	Irwin
Barker, Isham	Hall		441/5	Irwin
Barker, Jeremiah Sr.	Montgomery	Alston	277/11	Early
Barker, Jesse(R.S.)	Jackson	Hamiltons	272/9	Appling
Barker, Jesse(R.S.)	Jackson	Hamiltons	89/9	Hall
Barker, John B.	Columbia	Shaws	178/3	Habersham
Barker, John	Wilkes	Ogletrees	126/4	Walton
Barker, Lewis Jr.	Jackson	Dicksons	125/8	Early
Barker, Willie	Wilkinson	Brooks	54/11	Irwin
Barker, Wm.	Greene	Tuggles	333/4	Early
Barker, Wm.Jr.	Wilkinson	Lee's	51/5	Gwinnett
Barkley, James	Baldwin	Marshal's	393/12	Early
Barkley, James	Baldwin	Marshalls	20/2	Habersham
Barkley, John	Morgan	Campbell's	11/8	Appling
Barksdale, Hickerson	Lincoln	Thompsons	254/9	Early
Barksdale, Nathanl.	Putnam	Littles	226/6	Gwinnett
Barksdale, Terrell	Baldwin	Doziers	136/8	Irwin
Barksdale, Terrell	Baldwin	Doziers	306/15	Early
Barksdale, Wm.	Hancock	Scotts	230/19	Early
Barksdale, Wm.	Hancock	Scotts	230/19	Early
Barksdall, Nicholas G.	Lincoln	Thompson	486/3	Appling
Barkwell, Julius W.	Oglethorpe	Brittons	35/15	Irwin
Barkwell, Mary	Oglethorpe	Dunnes	271/3	Early
Barler, Jacob(Orphs)	Washington	Jenkinsons	284/7	Irwin
Barlow, James	Laurens	Griffins	411/9	Irwin
Barlow, John	Laurens	Griffins	16/5	Habersham
Barlow, John	Laurens	Griffins	170/8	Hall

NAME	COUNTY	MIL.DIST	LOT/SECT	DREW LAND
Barlow, Thos.(Orph)	Laurens	Griffins	203/13	Early
Barmwell, Alexr.	Greene	Carltons	98/19	Early
Barnard, Ann M.(Orph)	Chatham		490/4	Appling
Barnard, Henry	Chatham		53/11	Early
Barnard, James	Tattnall	Johnsons	260/10	Early
Barnard, James	Tattnall	Johnsons	81/1	Appling
Barnard, Levi(Orphs)	Jones	Green's	299/18	Early
Barnard, William	Chatham		62/3	Habersham
Barnard, William	Jasper	Kennedy	525/7	Irwin
Barnes, Absalom	Morgan	Campbell's	408/12	Irwin
Barnes, Archelus	Twiggs	Hodges	323/1	Appling
Barnes, Burwell L.	Hancock	Danells	319/13	Irwin
Barnes, David	Burke	72	115/15	Irwin
Barnes, Elizabeth	Scriven	36	291/5	Irwin
Barnes, Everlin(Orph)	Pulaski	Johnstons	439/5	Appling
Barnes, George	Hancock	Edwards'	170/21	Early
Barnes, James B.	Lincoln	Parks	20/4	Walton
Barnes, James	Franklin	Morris	38/6	Early
Barnes, James	Jasper	Phillips'	361/27	Early
Barnes, James	Jones	Shropshiers	22/4	Irwin
Barnes, Jethro	Jasper	Bentleys	497/6	Irwin
Barnes, John B.(Orphs)	Columbia	Burroughs	309/17	Early
Barnes, John Jr.	Washington	Renfroes	149/21	Early
Barnes, John Sr.	Washington	Renfroes	138/1	Early
Barnes, John Sr.	Washington	Renfroes	55/8	Early
Barnes, John	Columbia	J.Morris	105/3	Rabun
Barnes, John	Madison	Millicans	267/1	Walton
Barnes, John	Twiggs	W.Belchers	374/8	Irwin
Barnes, Joseph	Hancock	Champions	385/21	Early
Barnes, Lemon	Hancock	Champions	60/3	Irwin
Barnes, Michael	Jasper	Bentleys	198/10	Early
Barnes, Thomas	Hancock	Daniels	11/6	Early
Barnes, Thomas	Wilkes	Josies	40/16	Irwin
Barnes, William F.	Scriven	180	212/6	Gwinnett
Barnes, William	Washington	Renfroes	195/3	Irwin
Barnes, William	Wilkinson	Kettles	208/5	Early
Barnes, William	Wilkinson	Kettles	265/1	Early
Barnes, Wm.(Orps)	Hancock	Danells	114/6	Gwinnett
Barnett, Anne	Oglethorpe	Barnetts	163/1	Appling
Barnett, Avery	Greene	Ragan's	448/8	Irwin
Barnett, Benj.I.	Oglethorpe	Bridges	187/3	Irwin
Barnett, Clabourn	Oglethorpe	Brittons	71/7	Appling
Barnett, Eli	Lincoln	Graves	156/27	Early
Barnett, George	Wilkinson	Howards	185/2	Rabun
Barnett, Isaac	Jones	Samuels	95/4	Appling
Barnett, Isaac	Wilkinson	Smiths	143/8	Appling
Barnett, John	Washington	Pools	147/6	Appling
Barnett, John	Wilkinson	Howards	188/11	Irwin
Barnett, Jos.H.	Greene	Greers	263/7	Gwinnett
Barnett, Leonard	Greene	Ragins	121/16	Irwin
Barnett, Nathan(Orphs)	Greene	Ragans	31/8	Hall
Barnett, Nathl.	Elbert	Olivers	123/2	Rabun
Barnett, Nathl.	Elbert	Olivers	156/1	Irwin
Barnett, Pleasant S.	Greene	Ragins	74/13	Irwin
Barnett, Samuel	Morgan	Wrights	334/28	Early
Barnett, William	Columbia	Bealls	270/3	Appling
Barnett, William	Greene	Griers	104/13	Early
Barnett, William	Greene	Griers	107/21	Early
Barnett, Wm.	Washington	Avents	123/8	Irwin
Barnett, Zadock	Morgan	Townsends	66/9	Irwin
Barnhart, Charles	Greene	144	210/9	Appling
Barnhart, Geo.Jr.	Greene	144	101/1	Early
Barns, Cordin	Scriven	Roberts	316/4	Walton
Barns, Enos	Jasper	Bentley	299/4	Walton
Barns, John	Twiggs	Hodges	186/28	Early
Barnwell, George	Hall		158/20	Early
Barnwell, Henry	Greene	Carltons	417/5	Irwin

NAME	COUNTY	MIL.DIST	LOT/SECT	DREW LAN
Barnwell, Robt.M.	Franklin	J.Millers	324/6	Gwinnett
Barnwell, Wm.	Franklin	J.Millers	47/5	Appling
Barnwell, Wm.	Hall		55/12	Hall
Barnwell, Wm.Sr.	Jackson	Hamiltons	208/4	Irwin
Barr, Bartlett S.	Twiggs	Griffins	55/11	Hall
Barr, David	Elbert			-
Barr, John G.	Jefferson	Bothwells	329/18	Early
Barr, John	Jackson	Winters	280/4	Walton
Barr, John	Twiggs	Thames	266/12	Early
Barr, Joseph	Franklin	Hayne	518/9	Irwin
Barratt, William	Putnam	Coopers	161/4	Appling
Barrentine, Jacob	Baldwin	Doziers	116/1	Irwin
Barrentine, Jacob	Baldwin	Doziers	153/11	Hall
Barret, Lewis	Wilkes	Runnels	195/26	Early
Barrett, Lewis Sr.	Wilkes	Davis	147/8	Hall
Barrett, Richard	Morgan	Farrars	238/9	Irwin
Barrett, Zadock	Morgan	Townsend's	273/7	Appling
Barrie, Lewis	Richmond	Lacey's	312/10	Early
Barrington, Isaac	Jefferson	Waldens	80/13	Irwin
Barrom, James	Jones	Kings	306/13	Irwin
Barron, Barnabas	Jackson	Winters	270/2	Appling
Barron, Edward	Jones	Kings	69/9	Early
Barron, Hiram	Jones	Buckhalters	137/4	Walton
Barron, Jacob	Baldwin	Marshall	50/3	Early
Barron, James	Jasper	Bentleys	206/27	Early
Barron, James	Jones	Kings	87/14	Early
Barron, Jarred(Orphs)	Jones	Buckhalters	289/9	Appling
Barron, John	Jones	Buckhalters	329/7	Irwin
Barron, John	Twiggs	Johnstons	215/14	Early
Barron, Joseph	Telfair	Edwards	79/9	Irwin
Barron, Michael	Warren	Hubbarts	277/1	Walton
Barron, Samuel	Warren	151	58/12	Hall
Barron, Thomas	Elbert	Childers	405/13	Irwin
Barron, Thomas	Jones	Shropshears	314/14	Early
Barron, Thos.	Elbert	Childres	195/3	Appling
Barron, William	Pulaski	Rees	197/3	Walton
Barron, Wm.	Burke	J.Wards	349/3	Early
Barrott, Henry	Warren	Parhams	143/2	Appling
Barrow, Green	Twiggs	Evans	306/20	Early
Barrow, Henry	Baldwin	Irwins	44/6	Appling
Barrow, Henry	Baldwin	Irwins	71/8	Early
Barrow, Hiram	Twiggs	Browns	270/9	Early
Barrow, Warren	Putnam	Slaughters	129/6	Gwinnett
Barrow, William	Putnam	Slaughters	92/12	Hall
Barrow, William	Twiggs	Smiths	405/8	Irwin
Barrow, Wm.	Baldwin	Marshals	81/3	Walton
Barry, John	Richmond	122nd	268/9	Appling
Barry, John	Richmond	122nd	42/13	Habersham
Bartee, James	Wilkinson	Lee's	438/5	Irwin
Barthelmes, Mariah(Wid)	Chatham		119/6	Irwin
Barthelms, John	Chatham		250/3	Irwin
Bartlet, Bussey	Lincoln	Tatums	11/1	Irwin
Bartlett, Bennett	Hancock	Scotts	508/11	Irwin
Bartlett, Celia	Jasper	Bartlett's	93/6	Early
Bartlett, John	Hancock	Scotts	171/7	Gwinnett
Bartlette, Jonathan	Chatham		173/5	Gwinnett
Bartley, James	Emanuel	395	126/8	Irwin
Barton, Eldred	Warren	150	429/6	Irwin
Barton, James	Morgan	Campbells	131/10	Early
Barton, James	Richmond	398th	460/5	Irwin
Barton, John	Twiggs	R.Belchers	137/11	Hall
Barton, Pressley Jr.	Morgan	Campbells	449/9	Irwin
Barton, Richard	Laurens	Griffins	510/11	Irwin
Barton, Robert Sr.	Warren	150	181/2	Early
Barton, Willoughby	Richmond	120th	398/8	Irwin
Barton, Wm.C.	Chatham		18/5	Rabun
Bartow, Henry	Baldwin	Marshalls	62/4	Appling

18

NAME	COUNTY	MIL.DIST	LOT/SECT	DREW LAND
Barwick, Nathan	Emanuel	Chasons	247/5	Irwin
Barwick, Nathan	Emanuel	Chasons	54/8	Appling
Barwick, Wm.	Washington	Renfroes	84/13	Habersham
Bashlott, Joseph	Camden	Clarke's	263/12	Irwin
Baskin, James B.	Wilkinson	Lee's	133/6	Irwin
Baskin, James	Elbert	Whites/Christian 250/3		Appling
Baskin, William	Jackson	Hamiltons	312/3	Appling
Baslain, Jacob	Jackson	Rogers	238/8	Appling
Bass, Benjamin	Hancock	Danells	338/3	Appling
Bass, Buckner	Warren	Blounts	109/10	Early
Bass, Burwell	Hancock	Edwards	347/7	Appling
Bass, Christopher	Oglethorpe	Dunns	20/9	Early
Bass, Christopher	Oglethorpe	Dunns	68/18	Early
Bass, E.S.	Hancock	Edwards	169/19	Early
Bass, Eaton	Putnam	Slaughters	291/7	Irwin
Bass, Edmond S.	Hancock	Edwards	227/2	Early
Bass, Edward	Jones	Buckhalters	307/23	Early
Bass, Elizabeth	Jasper	Bartletts	514/6	Irwin
Bass, Ephraim	Burke	Spiveys	427/7	Irwin
Bass, Ephraim	Burke	Spiveys	76/9	Irwin
Bass, George	Burke	Spiveys	229/27	Early
Bass, Jesse	Burke	Spiveys	30/1	Walton
Bass, John H.	Putnam	Littles	220/1	Walton
Bass, John(Sr)	Burke	Spiveys	355/16	Early
Bass, Louiseana(Orphs)	Burke	Lewis	51/15	Early
Bass, Persons	Warren	Hubberts	160/28	Early
Bassent, Abraham(Orph)	Camden	Clarks	422/1	Early
Bassent, Adaline(Orph)	Camden	Clarks	422/1	Early
Bassent, James(Orph)	Camden	Clarks	422/1	Early
Bassent, Peter(Orph)	Camden	Clarks	422/1	Early
Bassent, Robert(Orph)	Camden	Clarks	422/1	Early
Bassent, Ulysses(Orph)	Camden	Clarks	422/1	Early
Bassett, John	Effingham		1/7	Irwin
Bassett, John	Morgan	Farrars	305/6	Gwinnett
Bassett, Richd.Sr.	Morgan	Farrars	98/13	Habersham
Bassett, Stephen(2)	Jones	Permenters	405/12	Irwin
Bastian, Jacob	Jackson	Rogers	44/4	Early
Baston, Dennis	Twiggs	R.Belchers	382/7	Early
Batchelor, Bearry	Putnam	Jernigans	280/17	Early
Batchelor, Jesse	Putnam	Jurnigans	360/9	Irwin
Batchelor, William	Putnam	Bustins	246/4	Walton
Bateman, Briant	Washington	Pools	143/2	Rabun
Bateman, Bryant	Washington	Pools'	190/5	Gwinnett
Bateman, Elizabeth	Twiggs	Smiths	159/11	Irwin
Bateman, Joseph	Chatham		16/9	Hall
Bateman, Simon	Twiggs	Smiths	311/4	Early
Bateman, Thomas	Richmond	398	203/3	Walton
Bateman, Thomas	Richmond	398	351/4	Early
Bates, Anderson	Wilkes	Bates	184/10	Irwin
Bates, Flemmeng	Putnam	Coopers	147/1	Walton
Bates, Flemming	Warren	153rd	323/8	Irwin
Bates, Jesse	Elbert	Gaines	189/7	Early
Bates, Jesse	Elbert	Gaines	36/3	Rabun
Bates, John W.	Wilkes	Runnels	36/11	Hall
Bates, John(Sr.)	Wilkes	Runnels	400/5	Appling
Bates, John	Elbert	Gaines	147/2	Irwin
Bates, John	Wilkes	Runnels	143/3	Irwin
Bates, Julius	Jackson	Dicksons	148/5	Early
Bates, Julius	Jackson	Dicksons	248/10	Irwin
Bates, Mathew	Greene	142	203/15	Early
Bates, Whram	Jackson	Rogers	101/5	Appling
Bates, Wilson	Warren	153rd	313/6	Gwinnett
Batey, Henry	Jefferson	Matthews	181/13	Irwin
Batey, Henry	Jefferson	Matthews	76/11	Habersham
Batey, James	Jefferson	Rothwells	55/13	Early
Bath, William	Early		109/8	Early
Batie, Hugh	Clarke	Parrs	418/13	Irwin

NAME	COUNTY	MIL.DIST	LOT/SECT	DREW LAN
Batson, David(R.S.)	Pulaski	Maddox's	62/2	Early
Batson, William	Twiggs	R.Belchers	191/1	Early
Battey, Sheldon	Jefferson	Jones'	323/6	Early
Battey, Wm.	Jefferson	Abbots	202/14	Early
Battle, Hartwell	Warren	Rogers	4/20	Early
Battle, John R.	Warren	Rogers	277/15	Early
Battle, Lazarus W.	Warren	Rodgers	373/7	Gwinnett
Battle, Reuben T.	Hancock	Lucas	328/28	Early
Battle, Reuben Y.	Hancock	Lucas'	64/9	Early
Battle, Thomas	Warren	Blounts	231/17	Early
Batty, Sarah(Wid)	Chatham		73/6	Irwin
Baugh, John A.	Greene	143	241/4	Walton
Baugh, John H.	Madison	Willifords	316/2	Early
Baugh, Martin	Franklin	Haynes	121/10	Habersha
Baugh, Mitchell	Franklin			-
Baugh, Mitchell	Franklin	Haynes	203/10	Early
Baugh, Moses	Wilkes	Killgores	238/12	Irwin
Baugh, Nancy(Wid)	Franklin	Haynes	310/13	Early
Baugh, Peter	Putnam	Bustins	198/20	Early
Baugh, Richard	Hancock	Lace's	276/5	Gwinnett
Baugh, Wm.	Franklin	Haynes	134/11	Irwin
Baughan, John	Oglethorpe	Wises	407/8	Appling
Baul, Joel	Morgan	McClendons	32/1	Habersha
Baul, Josiah	Morgan	McClendon's	268/12	Early
Baul, Rebecca(Wid)	Morgan	McClendons	133/11	Irwin
Baxley, Aaron	Tattnall	Overstreets	105/14	Irwin
Baxley, Aron	Jasper	Centills	117/8	Early
Baxley, Caleb	Burke	70	27/8	Appling
Baxley, William	Tattnall	Overstreets	72/28	Early
Baxly, Joshua	Burke	70	361/1	Appling
Baxter, Andrew	Hancock	Danells	4/6	Early
Baxter, Charles	Burke	70	205/6	Early
Baxter, Reuben	Franklin	Harris	220/4	Early
Baxter, Reuben	Greene	Macons	351/8	Appling
Baxter, Thos.M.	Baldwin	Marshalls	448/12	Irwin
Baxter, Thos.W.	Baldwin	Marshalls	159/10	Early
Baylis, Thos.S.	Columbia	Walkers	53/14	Irwin
Bayn, Alexander	Jones	Seals'	169/9	Early
Bayn, William	Jones	Buckhalters	12/10	Irwin
Bayn, William	Jones	Buckhalters	182/28	Early
Baynton, Elijah S.	Morgan	Selmons	308/6	Appling
Bayzer, William	Jones	Wallers	433/28	Early
Bayzor, Edw.(Orphs)	Jones	Wallers	256/6	Appling
Bazer, Wm.(R.S.)	Hancock	Loyds	309/16	Early
Bazer, Wm.(R.S.)	Hancock	Loyds	335/8	Irwin
Bazer, Wm.Jr.	Hancock	Justices	290/2	Appling
Beach, Mary(Wid)	Richmond	122	211/8	Appling
Beach, Miles	Richmond	398	394/26	Early
Beacham, Jane(Wid)	Emanuel	57	91/5	Walton
Beacon, Wm.H.	Jackson	Rogers	158/1	Appling
Beadell, Micajah	Greene	Jones	145/3	Early
Beadles, Joseph(Orph)	Walton	Davis		Appling
Beadles, Joseph(Orph)	Walton	Davis	256/7	Irwin
Beadles, Marh.(Orph)	Walton	Davis		Appling
Beadles, Mary(Orph)	Walton	Davis	256/7	Irwin
Beal, James	Richmond	Winters	128/6	Gwinnett
Beal, Nathaniel	Jefferson	Abbots	282/4	Appling
Beal, Russell G.	Putnam	Littles	155/14	Early
Beal, Tabitha T.(Wid)	Richmond	Winters	179/3	Irwin
Beall, Alexr.E.	Columbia	Ob.Morris	90/7	Irwin
Beall, Alexr.E.	Columbia	Olives	218/8	Irwin
Beall, Alexr.E.	Columbia	Olives	92/5	Gwinnett
Beall, Augustus	Columbia	Burroughs	474/10	Irwin
Beall, Charles T.	Columbia	Walkers	454/9	Irwin
Beall, Charles	Richmond	Palmers	18/6	Gwinnett
Beall, Elias	Oglethorpe	Brittons	27/18	Early
Beall, Elias	Oglethorpe	Brittons	49/18	Early

NAME	COUNTY	MIL.DIST	LOT/SECT	DREW LAND
Beall, Frederick	Franklin	Hammonds	215/3	Appling
Beall, Hezekiah	Columbia	Walkers	106/8	Appling
Beall, Hezekiah	Richmond	Burtons	257/2	Early
Beall, John W.	Richmond	Burtons	432/7	Appling
Beall, Joseph	Hancock	Lucas'	225/14	Early
Beall, Josiah(Orphs)	Warren	153	80/1	Habersham
Beall, Josias B.	Warren	Blounts	145/19	Early
Beall, Nathl.	Burke	Thomas'	167/6	Early
Beall, Noble P.	Franklin	Shumates	14/11	Habersham
Beall, Phebal(Wid)	Franklin	Harris	146/26	Early
Beall, Robert A.	Warren	Griers	93/2	Appling
Beall, Thaddeus	Franklin	Hammonds	445/13	Irwin
Beall, Thadeous	Franklin	Hoopers	17/4	Early
Beall, Thomas	Columbia	Burroughs	135/8	Early
Beall, William	Greene	Jones	221/1	Walton
Beall, Wm.	Franklin	Hammonds	178/9	Early
Beall, Wm.	Franklin	Hammonds	382/18	Early
Bealle, Ann(Wid)	Columbia	Walkers	442/8	Appling
Bealle, Frances(Wid)	Warren	154th	115/26	Early
Bealle, Francis	Warren	154	77/12	Habersham
Bealle, Robert A.	Warren	Greenes	207/1	Appling
Bealle, Robert A.	Warren	Griers	150/28	Early
Bealle, Tandy	Baldwin	Ellis	380/12	Irwin
Bealle, Thomas	Jasper	Clays	223/7	Irwin
Bealle, Wm.P.	Columbia	Walkers	474/11	Irwin
Beals, Joshua	Scriven	36th	260/2	Appling
Bean, John	Jasper	Bentleys	250/5	Early
Bean, John	Jasper	Bentleys	282/55	Appling
Bean, Walter Sr.	Jasper	Posts	324/6	Appling
Bean, Wm.Jr.	Jasper	Posts	22/16	Early
Beard, Archibald	Morgan	Parkers	17/16	Appling
Beard, Benjamin W.	Morgan	Campbells	326/8	Irwin
Beard, Edmond	Jones	Permenters	22/3	Appling
Beard, Hannah(Wid)	Morgan	Walkers	262/19	Early
Beard, Henry	Jones	Permenters	138/11	Irwin
Beard, James	Jones	Permenters	194/2	Rabun
Beard, John L.	Madison	Bone's	170/16	Irwin
Beard, John	Jones	Samuels	317/8	Irwin
Beard, Jos.(Orphs)	Jones	Wallers	194/13	Irwin
Beard, Jos.(Orphs)	Jones	Wallers	93/2	Early
Beard, Mary(Wid)	Jones	Wallers	386/6	Appling
Beard, William	Walton	Greens	83/1	Walton
Bearden, Arull	Hall		308/14	Early
Bearden, Jacob	Hall		200/6	Irwin
Bearden, Richard	Hall		63/3	Walton
Bearden, Rowland	Hall		219/6	Irwin
Beardin, Ambrose	Jasper	Phillips	343/7	Irwin
Beardin, John H.	Putnam	Brooks	37/11	Hall
Beardin, John	Jackson	Dicksons	21/12	Hall
Beardin, Solomon	Jackson	Dicksons	353/27	Early
Beardin, Solomon	Jackson	Dicksons	42/8	Appling
Beardin, Thomas	Putnam	Oslins	29/10	Early
Beardin, Wiley	Jasper	Clays	253/8	Appling
Bearfield, John	Burke	J.Wards	206/19	Early
Beary, Ezekiel(Orphs)	Greene	Jones	228/8	Early
Beary, Frances(Wid)	Greene	Jones'	307/10	Irwin
Beasely, Charles	Putnam	Oslins	167/1	Early
Beasely, John	Oglethorpe	Dunn's	389/3	Appling
Beasely, William	Putnam	Coopers	529/10	Irwin
Beasley, Abram	Jefferson	Connells	64/8	Early
Beasley, Berry W.	Jones	Samuels	364/3	Early
Beasley, David	Jones	Wallers	477/5	Irwin
Beasley, Isaac	Franklin	Flanagans	143/15	Irwin
Beasley, Isaiah	Bulloch	Edwards	237/6	Appling
Beasley, Jacob	Tattnall	J.Durrence	82/3	Rabun
Beasley, James Jr.	Walton	Wests	441/8	Irwin
Beasley, John(R.S.)	Franklin	Flanagans	189/13	Irwin

21

NAME	COUNTY	MIL.DIST	LOT/SECT	DREW LAM
Beasley, John(R.S.)	Franklin	Flanagans	189/13	Irwin
Beasley, John(R.S.)	Franklin	Flannigans	378/6	Early
Beasley, John	Camden	32	153/17	Early
Beasley, John	Franklin	Flanagan's	303/2	Appling
Beasley, John	Oglethorpe	Dunns	189/16	Irwin
Beasley, Richard	Clarke	Mitchell's	217/7	Early
Beasley, Richard	Clarke	Mitchells	353/12	Early
Beasley, Robert	Jones	Wallers	276/27	Early
Beasly, Abram	Jefferson	Connell's	19/12	Early
Beasly, William	Putnam	Coopers	230/8	Appling
Beaty, James Sr.	Burke	72	422/6	Irwin
Beaty, Saml.Sr.(Orphs)	Laurens	Watsons	481/7	Irwin
Beaty, Thomas	Twiggs	Ellis	375/8	Irwin
Beauchamp, Daniel	Jasper	Northents	214/8	Appling
Beauchamp, John	Jasper	Northcuts	5/2	Walton
Beaulard, John A.	Chatham		125/14	Early
Beavers, James	Morgan	Walkers	324/27	Early
Beavers, Joakim	Greene	144	168/9	Appling
Beavers, William	Clarke	Harriss	177/9	Early
Becham, Wm.	Gwinnett	Hamiltons	75/8	Early
Beck, Catharine M.	Glynn		245/6	Appling
Beck, Jesse	Morgan	Dannis'	80/2	Irwin
Beck, John Jr.	Elbert	Wards	198/5	Early
Beck, Reuben C.	Elbert	Ruckers	520/5	Appling
Beck, Wm.	Wilkinson	Smiths	139/3	Appling
Beck, Wm.A.	Elbert	Ruckers	37/1	Habersham
Becker, Daniel	Scriven	180	104/8	Appling
Becker, Daniel	Scriven	180	27/2	Irwin
Beckers, Wm.	Greene	143	201/7	Appling
Beckham, Abel	Washington	Cummins	58/12	Irwin
Beckham, Absalom B.	Baldwin	Marshalls	298/5	Irwin
Beckham, Allen(Orphs)	Baldwin	Irwins	157/1	Walton
Beckham, Laban	Baldwin	Irwins	278/5	Irwin
Beckton, Saml.S.	Jefferson	Cowarts	135/26	Early
Beckwith, Willice	Warren	Rodgers	499/11	Irwin
Beddell, Isaac	Greene	140th	54/2	Rabun
Beddingfield, Jas.(Orphs)	Burke	69	108/26	Early
Bedgood, Eli	Washington	Burneys	300/14	Early
Bedgood, James	Laurens	Griffins	457/13	Irwin
Bedgood, John	Washington	Burneys	239/6	Irwin
Bedgood, John	Washington	Burneys	599/2	Appling
Bedgood, Mathew	Burke	Bells	221/6	Gwinnett
Bee, Wm.	Chatham		121/7	Irwin
Beeks, John	Jackson	Rogers	80/6	Habersham
Beeland, Benjamin	Jones	Seals	28/3	Irwin
Beeman, Nathan S.S.	Hancock	Champions	399/5	Irwin
Beers, Wm.P.	Chatham		40/1	Early
Beesley, Elijah	Telfair	Wilsons	229/3	Walton
Belcher, Abner	Burke	Spivey's	285/20	Early
Belcher, Abram(Orphs)	Burke	Torrance	117/4	Early
Belcher, Ann(Wid)	Chatham		148/10	Habersham
Belcher, Collins H.	Jasper	Bartletts	99/8	Hall
Belcher, Ferrill	Twiggs	W.Belcher	66/13	Irwin
Belcher, John G.	Jasper	Clays	198/18	Early
Belcher, John	Putnam	Coopers	101/1	Irwin
Belcher, McCuin	Twiggs	R.Belchers	273/9	Appling
Belcher, Obediah	Jasper	Posts	433/3	Appling
Belcher, Robert	Twiggs	R.Belchers	105/8	Irwin
Belcher, Wiley	Burke	Spiveys	254/11	Irwin
Bell, (Orphans)	Jackson	Rogers	7/11	Hall
Bell, Arthur	Burke	M.Ward's	47/12	Hall
Bell, Arthur	Wilkes	Bryants	187/5	Appling
Bell, Auther	Wilkes	Bryants	88/9	Appling
Bell, Bailey	Jones	Kings	29/2	Habersham
Bell, Bailey	Wilkes	Kilgores	134/9	Appling
Bell, Bartholomew Jr.	Wilkes	Kilgores	325/8	Appling
Bell, Benjamin	Columbia	J.Morriss	71/3	Habersham

22

NAME	COUNTY	MIL.DIST	LOT/SECT	DREW LAND
Bell, Elias	Burke	M.Wards	124/20	Early
Bell, Elisha	Burke	M.Ward's	484/4	Appling
Bell, Elisha	Burke	M.Wards	18/5	Appling
Bell, Elisha	Burke	M.Wards	38/2	Walton
Bell, Elizabeth(Wid)	Elbert	Olivers	399/26	Early
Bell, George W.	Jackson	Hamiltons	24/12	Irwin
Bell, George	Jasper	Trimbles	111/8	Early
Bell, George	Jasper	Trimbles	146/8	Early
Bell, Hugh	Columbia	Burroughs	397/7	Early
Bell, James	Jackson	Hamiltons	196/12	Irwin
Bell, James	Morgan	Walkers	80/2	Habersham
Bell, James	Richmond	Laceys	280/4	Early
Bell, Jeremiah	Twiggs	Hodges	31/8	Irwin
Bell, Jesse	Oglethorpe	Murray's	26/1	Early
Bell, Jesse	Oglethorpe	Murrays	315/28	Early
Bell, Joe(Orphs)	Warren	153	141/13	Habersham
Bell, John B.	McIntosh	Hamiltons	252/9	Early
Bell, John(Tanner)	Twiggs	Smiths	217/9	Appling
Bell, John	Burke	Bells	189/3	Early
Bell, John	Elbert	Gaines	40/1	Irwin
Bell, Jos.Jr.	Elbert	Olivers	328/13	Irwin
Bell, Joseph S.	Jackson	Hamiltons	77/3	Irwin
Bell, Joseph Sr.	Elbert	P.Christians	374/9	Irwin
Bell, Joshua	Wilkes	Bryants	138/1	Appling
Bell, Joshua	Wilkes	Bryants	400/2	Appling
Bell, Larkin	Hall		362/9	Appling
Bell, Lazarus(Orphs)	Burke	J.Ward's	137/4	Early
Bell, Loyd	Wilkes	Bates	447/3	Appling
Bell, Luister(Wid)	Warren	153rd	14/6	Habersham
Bell, Nathaniel	Tattnall	Tharps'	377/13	Irwin
Bell, Olive(Wid)	Elbert	Olivers	282/3	Early
Bell, Priscilla	Burke	Bells	79/4	Appling
Bell, Richard Sr.	Burke	M.Wards	285/4	Appling
Bell, Sara	Jackson	Hamiltons	97/3	Walton
Bell, Sarah	Morgan	Selmons	69/11	Habersham
Bell, Thos.Jr.	Elbert	Olivers	173/4	Irwin
Bell, William	Burke	J.Ward's	60/27	Early
Bell, William	Burke	J.Wards	253/5	Appling
Bell, William	Richmond	Laceys	276/2	Early
Bell, William	Richmond	Laceys	71/5	Early
Bell, William	Walton	Davis	44/2	Habersham
Bell, Wm.M.	Jackson	Hamiltons	317/4	Early
Bell, Zachariah	Laurens	S.Smiths	132/12	Early
Bell, Zachariah	Laurens	S.Smiths	53/12	Hall
Bellah, James	Morgan	Jordans	177/4	Walton
Bellah, John	Morgan	Talbots	237/5	Early
Bellah, Samuel	Jasper	Bentleys	36/9	Early
Bellah, Samuel	Jasper	Bentleys	76/14	Irwin
Bellard, Elijah	Greene	141st	2/9	Irwin
Bellinger, B.B.	Chatham		374/11	Irwin
Bells, Wm.(Orphs)	Burke	M.Ward's	30/8	Hall
Bells, Wm.(Orphs)	Burke	M.Wards	236/19	Early
Bells, Wm.(Orphs)	Lincoln	Parks	343/6	Irwin
Bender, John(Orphs)	Jasper	Reids	234/9	Appling
Bender, John	Jasper	Reids	34/9	Appling
Bender, Parker	Laurens	Ross	149/4	Early
Benet, Emanuel	Emanuel	49	119/1	Irwin
Bennefield, Hardy	Greene	Ragins	177/7	Early
Bennet, Arnel	Morgan	Knights	8/10	Irwin
Bennet, Randol	Twiggs	Jefferson's	215/7	Gwinnett
Bennet, Reubin	Wilkes	Ogletrees	287/6	Early
Bennet, Thomas	Jackson	Hamiltons	126/11	Habersham
Bennet, Thomas	Madison	Millicans	462/6	Irwin
Bennet, William	Jasper	Easts	95/8	Irwin
Bennet, Winston	Morgan	Knights	21/5	Irwin
Bennett, Anthony	Emanuel	49	349/15	Early
Bennett, Benjamin	Emanuel	49	144/3	Early

NAME	COUNTY	MIL.DIST	LOT/SECT	DREW LAND
Bennett, Dotson	Jackson	Winters	69/4	Walton
Bennett, Edmund	Walton	Sentells	260/7	Early
Bennett, Edmund	Walton	Sentells	506/12	Irwin
Bennett, Edw.B.	McIntosh	Jenkins	245/11	Irwin
Bennett, Eliz.(Wid)	Jones	Chappels	86/8	Irwin
Bennett, Emanuel	Emanuel	49	75/7	Appling
Bennett, James H.	Jones	Samuels	82/14	Early
Bennett, James Sr.	Bulloch	Jones'	325/5	Early
Bennett, James	Franklin	P.Browns	279/6	Early
Bennett, Jane	Burke	71	229/27	Early
Bennett, Jeremiah	Washington	Avients	132/6	Irwin
Bennett, John(Orphs)	Pulaski	Johnstons	144/10	Habersha
Bennett, John	Richmond	Laceys	192/1	Appling
Bennett, John	Richmond	Laceys	48/13	Early
Bennett, John	Walton	Davis'	526/10	Irwin
Bennett, Luke	Wilkinson	Lees	58/7	Early
Bennett, Mary(Wid)	Jones	Samuels	32/5	Early
Bennett, Matthew	Liberty		379/7	Irwin
Bennett, Micajah(R.S.)	Jackson	Rogers	14/5	Rabun
Bennett, Peter	Wilkes	Ogletrees	239/6	Early
Bennett, Peter	Wilkes	Ogletrees	324/2	Early
Bennett, Randol	Twiggs	Jeffersons	372/6	Early
Bennett, Ransom	Gwinnett	Hamiltons	71/16	Irwin
Bennett, Richard	Bryan	19	159/28	Early
Bennett, Richard	Bryan	19	391/12	Early
Bennett, Susan(Wid)	Greene	Tuggles	195/12	Irwin
Bennett, Tapley	Jackson	Hoggards	374/8	Appling
Bennett, Thomas	Columbia	Pullins	114/3	Appling
Bennett, Thos.(Orphs)	Jones	Samuels	23/18	Early
Bennett, Wm.	Bryan	19	140/13	Habersha
Bennett, Wm.	Bryan	19	17/11	Habersha
Bennett, Wm.	Bryan	19	88/2	Appling
Bennett, Wm.	Gwinnett	Hamiltons	156/6	Irwin
Bennett, Wm.	Gwinnett	Hamiltons	314/18	Early
Bennett, Wm.Jr.	Jackson	Winters	158/9	Early
Benning, Joseph	Wilkinson	Howards	32/4	Appling
Benning, Pleasant M.	Columbia	Pullins	446/8	Irwin
Bennock, Peter	Richmond		205/27	Early
Bennyfield, Hardy	Greene	Ragins	75/1	Early
Benson, Esther	Hancock	Coopers	383/27	Early
Benson, George	Twiggs	Bozeman's	73/10	Habersha
Benson, George	Twiggs	Bozemans	59/9	Early
Benson, Jolin Jr.	Putnam	Buckners	43/6	Gwinnett
Benson, Laban	Richmond	122	404/4	Early
Benson, Levi	Morgan	Knights	84/10	Early
Benson, Levi	Putnam	Buckners	217/17	Early
Benson, Robert	Morgan	Townsends	353/6	Early
Benson, Thomas W.	Twiggs	Smiths	132/16	Irwin
Benson, Thomas	Wilkinson	Kettles	266/17	Early
Benson, Willis	Laurens	Watson's	52/13	Early
Bent, Thomas	Madison	Millicans	92/22	Early
Bentley, Abi	Wilkes	Smiths	47/22	Early
Bentley, Benjamin	Lincoln	Graves	335/11	Early
Bentley, Jermiah	Washington	Wimberlys	72/10	Irwin
Bentley, Jesse	Walton	Echols	29/8	Irwin
Bentley, Jesse	Walton	Echols	313/9	Appling
Bentley, Jesse	Walton	Echols	65/9	Early
Bentley, John	Lincoln	Graves	204/14	Early
Bentley, Josiah	Walton	Echols	199/2	Early
Bentley, Saml.Sr.	Elbert	Webb's	265/13	Early
Bentley, Saml.Sr.	Elbert	Webbs	306/8	Early
Bently, Solomon	Oglethorpe	Atkinson	238/3	Irwin
Benton, Abba	Jasper	Evans	321/7	Appling
Benton, Eli	Columbia	Ob.Morris	248/27	Early
Benton, Hardy	Morgan	Farrars	120/3	Irwin
Benton, Hardy	Morgan	Farrars	19/4	Appling
Benton, Isaac	Laurens	Griffins	112/11	Early

NAME	COUNTY	MIL.DIST	LOT/SECT	DREW LAND
Benton, James	Jackson	Winters	93/1	Rabun
Benton, John	Jackson	Winters	166/12	Early
Benton, John	Jones	Samuels	163/9	Early
Benton, John	Lincoln	Stocks	44/4	Appling
Benton, Jonathan	Jasper	Northcuts	63/2	Appling
Benton, Jos.Sr.	Jasper	Northcuts	348/2	Appling
Benton, Lewis	Chatham		393/10	Early
Benton, Mordecai	Jones	Samuel's	173/20	Early
Benton, Nelson M.	Columbia	Olives	360/9	Appling
Benton, Samuel(Orphs)	Jasper	Hays	258/18	Early
Benton, Stephen	Jackson	Rogers	59/5	Early
Benton, William	Jackson	Mays	97/8	Appling
Benton, Wm.(Orph)	Columbia	Walkers	65/17	Early
Benton, Wm.	Wilkinson	Howards	48/4	Irwin
Bergeron, Elijah	Burke	Royals	334/17	Early
Bergeron, Elisha	Burke	Royals	290/11	Early
Bergman, Fredr'k.C.	Effingham		180/7	Appling
Berle, Archibald	Tattnall	Johnsons	85/2	Irwin
Berrien, Williamina(Wid)	Jefferson	Abbots	112/3	Habersham
Berry, Abigal(Orph)	Chatham		53/13	Irwin
Berry, Benajah	Effingham		168/7	Irwin
Berry, Benj.H.	Columbia	Walkers	138/19	Early
Berry, Benj.H.	Columbia	Walkers	53/1	Early
Berry, Bradley	Oglethorpe	Wises	325/6	Gwinnett
Berry, Charles M.	Oglethorpe	Davenports	207/9	Early
Berry, Edmund G.	Morgan	Talbotts	119/9	Early
Berry, Edmund G.	Morgan	Talbotts	526/5	Appling
Berry, Elijah	Elbert	Olivers	234/23	Early
Berry, Eliz.(Wid)	Columbia	Tullins	55/2	Rabun
Berry, George W.	Putnam	Berrys	108/5	Gwinnett
Berry, Hosea	Wilkinson	Child's	290/4	Irwin
Berry, Hosea	Wilkinson	Childs	64/20	Early
Berry, James(Orph)	Chatham		53/13	Irwin
Berry, John	Hancock	Colemans	105/12	Early
Berry, John	Jackson	Hamiltons	413/10	Irwin
Berry, Lewis T.	Morgan	Knights	371/11	Irwin
Berry, Rebecca(Orph)	Chatham		53/13	Irwin
Berry, Talieferro L.	Oglethorpe	Lee's	401/4	Early
Berry, Tealieferro L.	Oglethorpe	Lees	158/2	Appling
Berry, Thomas D.	Putnam	Berrys	275/6	Appling
Berry, Wm.(Orphs)	Pulaski	Bryans	97/16	Early
Berry, Wm.	Wilkes	Kilgores	64/12	Irwin
Berryhill, John	Jasper	Hays	483/8	Appling
Berryhill, Wm.	Jasper	Hays	320/28	Early
Berryhill, Wm.	Oglethorpe	Ellis'	71/13	Irwin
Berryman, John	Elbert	Webbs	138/2	Appling
Berthune, Malcom	Richmond	Palmers	154/9	Hall
Berton, Charles	Burke	M.Ward's	39/6	Irwin
Berton, Martha(Orph)	Burke	McNorrills	39/4	Appling
Berton, Wm.(Orph)	Burke	McNorrills	39/4	Appling
Beshell, John	Wilkes	Bates	105/10	Hall
Beshell, John	Wilkes	Bates	65/8	Appling
Bessom, John	Chatham		372/1	Appling
Best, Absalom	Scriven		105/17	Early
Best, Daniel	Lincoln	Walkers	172/17	Early
Best, George W.	Scriven	36th	272/1	Appling
Best, Jacob	Scriven		86/5	Irwin
Best, Jacob	Scriven		9/3	Habersham
Best, John	Scriven		162/11	Habersham
Bests, Wm.(Orphs)	Wilkes	Holidays	117/11	Irwin
Bethel, Charity(Wid)	Lincoln	Graves	165/2	Early
Bethune, Daniel	Greene	140	359/28	Early
Bethune, John	Greene	143	158/16	Irwin
Bethune, Peter	Richmond	Palmers	384/10	Early
Bett, James	Putnam	Stampers	251/1	Walton
Bettenbock, John	Effingham		421/2	Appling
Bettenbock, John	Effingham		56/18	Early

NAME	COUNTY	MIL.DIST	LOT/SECT	DREW LAND
Bettenbock, Matthew	Effingham		444/28	Early
Betterton, Thomas	Morgan	Parkers	472/9	Irwin
Betterton, Wm.	Franklin	Aikins	502/8	Appling
Betts, Abraham	Jasper	Evans	159/18	Early
Betts, Abraham	Jasper	Evans	278/11	Early
Betts, Elisha	Baldwin	Marshal's	79/8	Irwin
Betts, Elisha	Baldwin	Marshalls	218/5	Appling
Betts, Isaac	Jackson	Hamiltons	188/3	Appling
Betts, Jacob	Jackson	Hamiltons	299/6	Irwin
Betts, James	Jasper	Easts	253/2	Appling
Betts, James	Jasper	Easts	478/12	Irwin
Betts, John	Jackson	Rogers	196/1	Early
Betts, Jonathan	Jackson	Hamiltons	363/28	Early
Betts, Jonathan	Jackson	Hamiltons	61/13	Early
Betts, Joseph	Jasper	Evans	307/15	Early
Betts, William	Columbia	Dodsons	193/13	Irwin
Betty, Henry J.	Morgan	Alfords	45/1	Early
Beverage, James	Oglethorpe	Goolsby	11/1	Habersham
Beverley, William	Tattnall	J.Durrence	130/1	Appling
Beverly, Anthony	Elbert	Smiths	138/16	Irwin
Beverly, Wm.	Tattnall	Jesse Durrences	72/8	Irwin
Bevers, John F.	Jasper	Clays	318/16	Early
Bevil, Eliza W.	Scriven	36th	330/3	Appling
Bevil, Granvill	Scriven		212/3	Walton
Bevil, Paul R.(Orphs)	Scriven	36	451/6	Appling
Beville, Paul Sr.	Scriven	26	21/3	Appling
Bevin, John	Baldwin	Taliaferros	143/21	Early
Bevins, James	Baldwin	Ellis	254/17	Early
Bevins, Stephen	Jones	Harrest	316/6	Appling
Bex, John	Camden	33	43/7	Appling
Bexley, Ann Eliz(Wid)	Richmond	398th	32/11	Habersham
Bibb, Benajah S.	Elbert	Buckners	317/19	Early
Bibb, James	Lincoln	Stokes	179/5	Early
Bibb, Joseph W.	Elbert	Ruckers	424/5	Appling
Bibb, William	Lincoln	Stokes	200/12	Habersham
Bickers, John	Baldwin	Irwin's	349/20	Early
Biggins, Mary	Hancock	Evans	296/3	Early
Biggins, Richd.N.	Hancock	Evans	631/2	Appling
Biggs, Tully(Orphs)	Warren	151	62/12	Habersham
Bilbro, Thomas	Greene	143	119/3	Habersham
Billings, Adam	Pulaski	Maddox	451/8	Irwin
Billingslea, Francis B.	Wilkes	Mattox's	410/26	Early
Billingslea, Francis S.	Wilkes	Mattox	484/6	Irwin
Billingsley, James	Jasper	Smiths	73/7	Gwinnett
Billingsley, Jas.	Jones	Kings	70/15	Early
Billups, Joseph	Clarke	Parrs	90/5	Rabun
Billups, Thomas	Clarke	Parrs	275/14	Early
Billups, William	Clarke	Harriss	511/13	Irwin
Binion, John(Orphs)	Columbia	Bealls	192/19	Early
Binion, Nancy(Wid)	Columbia	Bealls	301/2	Early
Binion, Wm.	Columbia	Bealls	181/1	Early
Binom, Drury(R.S.)	Warren	150	265/12	Early
Binom, Drury(R.S.)	Warren	151st	403/8	Irwin
Binton, Stoddard	Jones	Chappels	300/5	Gwinnett
Bird, Allen	Hancock	Scotts	334/5	Gwinnett
Bird, Andrew	Wayne	Johnstons	84/9	Irwin
Bird, Archibald	Burke	72	148/6	Irwin
Bird, Archibald	Burke	72	379/12	Irwin
Bird, Bluford	Wilkes	Mattoxs	173/21	Early
Bird, Brackston	Greene	Jones	338/8	Appling
Bird, Catharine(Wid)	Warren	154	358/5	Early
Bird, Fitzgerald	Warren	154	386/15	Early
Bird, Harmon	Burke	70	230/2	Irwin
Bird, Henry	Richmond	Winters	17/8	Hall
Bird, Hiram	Putnam	Slaughters	311/1	Appling
Bird, Irwin	Hancock	Lucas	528/7	Irwin
Bird, James	Jefferson	Fountains	69/9	Irwin

NAME	COUNTY	MIL.DIST	LOT/SECT	DREW LAND
Bird, James	Wilkinson	Childs	103/11	Hall
Bird, John	Elbert	Dooleys	191/1	Walton
Bird, John	Emanuel	49	183/19	Early
Bird, John	Pulaski	Johnson's	334/20	Early
Bird, John	Wilkes	Willis	38/8	Early
Bird, Jonas Jr.	Bulloch	Tilmans	102/1	Early
Bird, Judith(Wid)	Putnam	Coopers	404/10	Irwin
Bird, Lee	Lincoln	Tatom	71/3	Rabun
Bird, Mary	Bulloch	Tilmans	354/7	Gwinnett
Bird, Nancy(Wid)	Jones	Hurst	188/27	Early
Bird, Polly	Putnam	Coopers	173/13	Irwin
Bird, Price	Putnam	Coopers	347/8	Irwin
Bird, Robert(Orphs)	Putnam	Coopers	134/10	Habersham
Bird, Robert	Hancock	Scotts	486/5	Appling
Bird, Samuel	Burke	Lewis	172/20	Early
Bird, Sarah(Wid)	Bryan	19	111/5	Early
Bird, Thompson	Baldwin	Marshalls	192/7	Gwinnett
Bird, Thompson	Baldwin	Marshalls	205/19	Early
Bird, Thos.Jr.	Hall		173/10	Early
Bird, William M.	Putnam	Ectors	476/8	Irwin
Bird, William(R.S.)	Twiggs	Ellis's	65/1	Appling
Bird, William(R.S.)	Twiggs	Ellis	335/2	Appling
Bird, William	Effingham		352/16	Early
Bird, William	Putnam	Cooper's	387/11	Irwin
Bird, Wm.	Bulloch	Tilmans	99/1	Rabun
Birds, Philemon(Orph)	Oglethorpe	Myricks	220/12	Irwin
Birds, Robt.(orphs)1st	Putnam	Coopers	505/10	Irwin
Birdsong, Geo.U.	Oglethorpe	Brittains	88/14	Early
Birdsong, James	Putnam	Morelands	120/17	Early
Birdsong, John Jr.	Oglethorpe	Brittons	614/2	Appling
Birdsong, John W.	Oglethorpe	Brittons	177/1	Early
Birdsong, Joseph	Putnam	Morelands	129/9	Irwin
Birdsong, Joseph	Putnam	Morelands	226/12	Early
Biren, Jobe	Gwinnett	Hamiltons	173/3	Early
Bishop, Asa	Greene	Greers	239/2	Early
Bishop, Asa	Greene	Griers	144/7	Early
Bishop, David	Morgan	Loyds	297/2	Appling
Bishop, David	Morgan	Loyds	40/3	Appling
Bishop, Elbert	Pulaski	Senterfeits	547/2	Appling
Bishop, Elijah	Morgan	Loyds	209/4	Early
Bishop, Eliz.(Wid)	Greene	Greers	39/8	Appling
Bishop, Ephraim	Putnam	Slaughters	126/21	Early
Bishop, Ephraim	Warren	Parhams	91/11	Early
Bishop, George	Appling	5	20/3	Irwin
Bishop, George	Appling	5	274/16	Early
Bishop, Golden	Morgan	Leonards	348/14	Early
Bishop, Golden	Morgan	Loyds	236/17	Early
Bishop, Henry	Washington	Jenkinsons	306/7	Appling
Bishop, James(Orphs)	Greene	Greer	379/2	Early
Bishop, John	Emanuel	49	64/2	Habersham
Bishop, John	Warren	Parhams	125/9	Hall
Bishop, Ruthe	Pulaski	Rees	153/16	Early
Bishop, Samuel	Washington	Jenkinsons	9/5	Early
Bishop, Wm.	Emanuel	57	227/27	Early
Biswell, David	Laurens	Griffins	187/10	Early
Biswell, David	Laurens	Griffins	9/16	Irwin
Bitton, William	Chatham		412/15	Early
Bivins, Felix J.	Burke	Bell's	178/7	Early
Bixston, Wm.	Burke	Royal's	4/7	Early
Bixton, Wm.	Burke	Royal's	109/8	Irwin
Black, (Altered to Brack)	Scriven	180th	113/2	Early
Black, Absalom	Putnam	Oslins	426/5	Appling
Black, Coatsworth P.	Jackson	Rogers	316/8	Appling
Black, Gavin	Jackson	Rogers	17/11	Early
Black, James	Jasper	Phillips	123/7	Irwin
Black, John	Hall		36/3	Irwin
Black, John	Hall		377/28	Early

NAME	COUNTY	MIL.DIST	LOT/SECT	DREW LAND
Black, Lemuel	Oglethorpe	Davenports	441/13	Irwin
Black, Mary(Wid)	Twiggs	Jeffersons	14/5	Appling
Black, Richardson	Putnam	J.Kindricks	230/20	Early
Black, Samuel	Jasper	Blacks	249/2	Irwin
Black, Samuel	Morgan	McClendons	162/21	Early
Black, Samuel	Morgan	McClendons	307/8	Irwin
Black, Thomas	Morgan	McClendon's	244/2	Appling
Black, Thomas	Twiggs	Jeffersons	251/10	Irwin
Black, William	Franklin	Harris	292/5	Early
Blackburn, Aron L.	Scriven	36	311/3	Appling
Blackburn, Daniel J.	Bulloch	Jones	44/12	Hall
Blackburn, Elijah	Wilkes	Holidays	154/16	Irwin
Blackburn, John	Oglethorpe	Brittons	91/8	Early
Blackburn, Nathan	Wilkes	Holidays	330/5	Irwin
Blackburn, Thos.	Wilkes	Holidays	48/3	Irwin
Blackburns, John	Lincoln	Walkers	282/7	Early
Blackemore, Thos.	Clarke	Applings	41/9	Early
Blackledge, Jos.G.	Jackson	Rogers	318/3	Early
Blackman, James	Scriven	180th	44/6	Gwinnett
Blackman, John P.	Tattnall	Conyers	388/5	Irwin
Blackmer, Reuben	Richmond	398	192/3	Walton
Blacksel, Sarah(Wid)	Bryan	20	175/1	Early
Blackshar, Jacob	Twiggs	Jeffersons	96/9	Irwin
Blackshar, John	Wilkinson	Brooks'	132/18	Early
Blackshear, David	Laurens	Dean's	315/2	Appling
Blackshear, Randol	Twiggs	Jeffersons	394/1	Early
Blackson, John	Jefferson	Matthews	207/7	Gwinnett
Blackstock, Jas.Sr.	Hall		261/18	Early
Blackstock, Jas.Sr.	Hall		32/3	Walton
Blackstock, Richard	Hall		213/18	Early
Blackstock, Wm.	Hall		292/17	Early
Blackstone, James	Richmond	Palmer's	85/3	Walton
Blackwell, Ambrose	Franklin	Hammonds	196/6	Appling
Blackwell, Banks	Elbert	Smiths	163/17	Early
Blackwell, Hardy	Elbert			—
Blackwell, Isabel(Wid)	Franklin	Haynes	60/17	Early
Blackwell, Ralph	Elbert	Smiths	210/5	Appling
Blackwell, Sally C.	Elbert	Smiths	312/21	Early
Blackwell, Wm.	Franklin	Hammonds	150/4	Walton
Blackwood, Cornelius	Jasper	Sentells	85/1	Habersham
Blackwood, Francis	Jasper	Centells	173/26	Early
Blair, George	Laurens	Harris	165/7	Appling
Blair, James B.	Clarke	Pentecost	147/8	Appling
Blair, James Sr.	Franklin	Powels	41/9	Irwin
Blair, Jemimah(Wid)	Columbia	Gartrells	299/15	Early
Blair, Powell	Franklin	Powells	469/9	Irwin
Blair, Robert	Baldwin	Marshalls	256/7	Gwinnett
Blair, Thomas	Washington	Pools	269/6	Early
Blair, Thomas	Washington	Pools	4/3	Rabun
Blake, Henry	Oglethorpe	Waters	244/23	Early
Blake, John	Jackson	Hamiltons	254/8	Irwin
Blake, Joseph	Jasper	Blake's	215/3	Early
Blake, Thomas	Jackson	Hamiltons	290/17	Early
Blake, William	Jackson	Hamiltons	34/11	Hall
Blakely, Eliz.(Wid)	Washington	Averets	230/14	Early
Blakey, David	Baldwin	Russells	240/5	Appling
Blakey, David	Baldwin	Russels	240/10	Irwin
Blakey, David	Hancock	Herberts	155/8	Hall
Blakey, James	Wilkes	Burks	166/16	Early
Blakey, Jesse	Putnam	Oslins	276/4	Irwin
Blakey, John	Hancock	Herberts	272/18	Early
Blakey, Jos.A.	Wilkes	Smiths	14/3	Irwin
Blakey, Jos.A.	Wilkes	Smiths	214/17	Early
Blakey, Levi	Putnam	J.Kindricks	304/11	Irwin
Blakey, Micajah A.	Wilkes	Burk's	80/1	Rabun
Blakey, Thomas	Jasper	Reids	175/9	Early
Blakey, Thos.Jr.	Wilkes	Burks	228/5	Early

NAME	COUNTY	MIL.DIST	LOT/SECT	DREW LAND
Blakey, William	Jones	Permenters	322/11	Early
Blalock,	Jones	Chappels	292/6	Early
Blalock, Alse(Wid)	Jones	Kings	326/4	Appling
Blalock, Giles	Hall		86/3	Appling
Blalock, Gipson	Lincoln	Jones	16/8	Hall
Blalock, Jas.Jr.	Jones	Chappels	293/3	Early
Blalock, Jas.Sr.	Jones	Chappels	286/6	Early
Blalock, Solomon	Putnam	Slaughters	375/11	Irwin
Blalock, Solomon	Putnam	Slaughters	395/16	Early
Blance, John C.	Chatham		357/18	Early
Blanchard, Benj.(Orph)	Montgomery	Alston	77/7	Irwin
Blanchard, Jeremiah	Columbia	Pullins	364/5	Appling
Blanchard, Jos.(Orph)	Laurens	S.Smiths	115/21	Early
Blanckston, Isaac	Morgan	Farrars	80/9	Appling
Bland, Arthur	Telfair	Loves'	158/3	Appling
Bland, Benjamin	Jackson	Rogers	41/11	Habersham
Bland, Micajah	Washington	Averits	223/3	Irwin
Bland, Wm.	Wilkinson	Howards	522/7	Appling
Blanford, Champ	Warren	153	353/9	Irwin
Blankinship, David(Orphs)	Greene	142	482/7	Appling
Blankinship, Jas.	Jones	Griffiths	372/6	Appling
Blankinship, Solomon	Hancock	Lucas	98/17	Early
Blanks, Littleberry	Jones	Samuels	129/2	Irwin
Blanks, Wm.H.	Greene	Hoggs	97/3	Appling
Blanton, Alexandria	Bulloch	Edwards	304/1	Walton
Blanton, Anna(Orph)	Richmond	Lacey's	341/13	Early
Blanton, Benjamin	Oglethorpe	Dunns	120/7	Gwinnett
Blanton, Chatton(Orph)	Richmond	Winters	323/11	Irwin
Blanton, Eliza(Orph)	Richmond	Lacey's	341/13	Early
Blanton, Joseph(Orph)	Richmond	Lacey's	341/13	Early
Blanton, Sarah(Orph)	Richmond	Lacey's	341/13	Early
Blassingame, Benj.(Orphs)	Morgan	Leonards	29/1	Rabun
Blassingham, Phillip	Greene	Ragans	33/9	Hall
Blassingham, Phillip	Greene	Ragans	82/7	Early
Blaydes, Isarial	Twiggs	Jeffersons	141/18	Early
Blaylock, Elihu W.	Tattnall	Overstreets	398/2	Early
Blaylock, Gipson	Lincoln	Jones	355/4	Early
Bledsoe, Aron(Orphs)	Greene	Carlton	194/27	Early
Bledsoe, Aron(Orps)	Greene	Carltons	149/1	Walton
Bledsoe, James	Greene	Gregorys	157/13	Irwin
Blessit, Stephen	Jasper	Easts	371/1	Early
Bliss, Elias	Chatham		96/2	Irwin
Blitch, Ann(Wid)	Effingham		13/10	Irwin
Blitch, Willis	Effingham		602/2	Appling
Blocker, Jacob	Tattnall	J.Durrence	4/7	Gwinnett
Blocker, Jacob	Tattnall	J.Durrences	75/2	Rabun
Blogg, Mary L.(Orph)	McIntosh	Jinkins	29/28	Early
Blogg, Mary(orph)	Chatham		333/2	Early
Bloodworth, Saml.	Wilkinson	Wiggins	38/34	Habersham
Bloodworth, Wash.I.	Wilkinson	Wiggins	113/3	Early
Blount, Isaac(R.S.)	Hancock	Millers	500/6	Appling
Blount, Isaac(R.S.)	Hancock	Millers	85/8	Irwin
Blount, James G.	Richmond	Burtons	151/27	Early
Blount, James	Burke	72	411/6	Appling
Blount, James	Burke	72	98/11	Habersham
Blount, Marshall	Jones	Shropshiers	202/9	Irwin
Blount, Moab	Hancock	Scotts	342/7	Early
Blount, Penelope(Wid)	Wilkinson	Smiths	103/18	Early
Blount, Reddin(Orphs)	Washington	Burneys	53/23	Early
Blount, Richard	Jones	Shropshiers	2/2	Irwin
Blount, Stephen	Jones	Shropshiers	123/3	Appling
Blow, Benjamin	Hancock	Millers	300/2	Early
Bloxom, Daniel	Richmond	Burtons	431/8	Appling
Blue, Daniel	Glynn		469/5	Irwin
Bluford, Wm.B.	Camden	Tillis	461/5	Irwin
Blunt, Edmund	Wilkes	Gordons	104/10	Hall
Blunt, George M.	Camden	Clarke's	65/4	Appling

NAME	COUNTY	MIL.DIST	LOT/SECT	DREW LAN
Blunt, Henry R.	Columbia	Pullins	28/4	Rabun
Blunt, Isaac	Pulaski	Maddox'	55/7	Appling
Blunt, Isaac	Pulaski	Maddoxs	485/9	Irwin
Blunt, James C.	Chatham		60/28	Early
Blunt, Thomas	Jones	Samuels	191/6	Early
Blunt, Willie	Twiggs	Smiths	228/8	Appling
Boals, Nathaniel	Jackson	Winters	515/6	Irwin
Boals, William	Jackson	Winters	291/10	Irwin
Boals, William	Jackson	Winters	83/2	Early
Boatright, Wm.	Franklin	P.Browns	309/12	Irwin
Boatwright, Betsey(Orph)	Burke		265/11	Irwin
Boatwright, James	Wilkes	McClendons	149/3	Appling
Boatwright, Margt.(Wid)	Emanuel	49	237/11	Irwin
Bobbit, William	Jones	Wallers	243/5	Irwin
Bobitt, Thomas	Twiggs	Evans'	67/10	Irwin
Bobo, Benjamin	Elbert	Dooleys	357/26	Early
Bodine, John	Morgan	Denis	185/8	Appling
Bodine, John	Morgan	Dennis	368/18	Early
Bogan, Albert(Orph)	Richmond	398	103/16	Irwin
Bogan, James(Orph)	Richmond	398	103/16	Irwin
Bogan, John	Jasper	Bailey's	199/9	Irwin
Bogan, John	Jasper	Baleys	413/7	Appling
Bogan, Shadrach	Jackson	Hamiltons	375/13	Irwin
Boggess, Jeremiah	Putnam	Berry's	31/5	Rabun
Boggs, James	Morgan	Leonard's	62/8	Early
Boggus, Jeremiah	Morgan	Farrar's	11/4	Appling
Boggus, Moses	Morgan	Farrars	417/1	Appling
Boggus, Thomas	Franklin	Jas.Millers	144/10	Hall
Bogs, James	Jones	Buckhalters	67/12	Irwin
Bohannon, Henry	Laurens	Watson's	219/11	Early
Bohannon, William	Telfair	Tallies	307/2	Appling
Bointon, James	Jones	Chappels	516/13	Irwin
Boisclair, Michael F.	Richmond	398th	244/15	Early
Bole, Isaac	Warren	151st	150/16	Early
Bolen, Archibald	Franklin	Browns	79/7	Irwin
Boler, Joel(Orph)	Baldwin		62/6	Early
Boler, John(Orph)	Baldwin		62/6	Early
Boler, Nancy(Wid)	Baldwin		65/1	Early
Boler, Zachariah	Lincoln	Parks	413/4	Appling
Boles, Bevvin	Greene	Harvills	18/28	Early
Boles, Henry	Putnam	Littles	32/11	Early
Boles, John A.	Warren	Travis	272/7	Irwin
Boles, John	Jones	Wallers	197/3	Appling
Boles, John	Jones	Wallers	83/12	Early
Boles, Sally(Wid)	Greene	Harvills	158/3	Irwin
Boles, Wm.(Orphs)	Franklin	John Millers	395/2	Early
Boling, Green	Putnam	Bustins	301/4	Appling
Boling, John	Franklin	Jas.Millers	653/2	Appling
Boling, Smith	Morgan	Selmans	116/3	Appling
Bolles, Job T.	Chatham		34/5	Appling
Bolling, Smith	Morgan	Selmons	61/13	Irwin
Bollinger, Eliza(Orph)	Chatham		288/6	Early
Bollinger, John	Twiggs	Bozemans	298/1	Walton
Bolton, Chas.L.(Minor)	Wilkes	Kilgores	81/8	Early
Bolton, Leonard	Oglethorpe	Barnetts	319/12	Irwin
Bolton, Manoah	Oglethorpe	Goolsbys	16/7	Early
Bolton, Mathew	Columbia	Dodsons	6/6	Early
Bolton, Robert	Columbia	Bealls	234/27	Early
Bolton, Thos.C.	Wilkes	Holidays	121/15	Early
Bolton, Thos.C.	Wilkes	Holidays	167/10	Habersham
Boman, Greenberry	Gwinnett	Hamiltons	137/10	Irwin
Boman, Moses(R.S.)	Jackson	Rogers	306/6	Irwin
Boman, Moses(R.S.)	Jackson	Rogers	308/15	Early
Bond, Daniel	Elbert	B.Higginbothams	178/15	Irwin
Bond, Elender(Wid)	Twiggs	Evan's	179/2	Habersham
Bond, Elizabeth	Elbert	Higginbothams	143/9	Early
Bond, George T.	Franklin	Davis	241/3	Walton

30

NAME	COUNTY	MIL.DIST	LOT/SECT	DREW LAND
Bond, James	Richmond	Laceys	94/21	Early
Bond, Joel	Elbert	B.Higginbothams	371/13	Irwin
Bond, Joel	Jones	Hansfords	294/2	Early
Bond, John Jr.	Madison	Willifords	282/14	Early
Bond, John(Dr)	Wilkes	Mattox'	15/12	Early
Bond, Jos.Sr.	Franklin	Hammonds	383/7	Gwinnett
Bond, Leonard	Franklin	Davis	4/17	Early
Bond, Linsey	Franklin	Attaways	135/3	Early
Bond, Mark	Lincoln	Jones	157/3	Irwin
Bond, Robert P.	Franklin	J.Millers	221/2	Irwin
Bond, Samuel M.	Chatham		172/11	Irwin
Bond, Samuel M.	Chatham		78/2	Early
Bond, Samuel	Jones	Shropshiers	145/4	Early
Bond, Sarah	Lincoln	Jones	432/11	Irwin
Bond, Seth	Jones	Shropshiers	8/11	Early
Bond, Solomon	Twiggs	Thames	128/3	Walton
Bond, Wm.S.	Jasper	Kindalls	183/10	Irwin
Bonde, James S.	Chatham		136/28	Early
Bonds, Luke	Jones	Jeffersons	306/5	Early
Bonds, Luke	Jones	Jeffersons	67/5	Irwin
Bonds, Micajah	Columbia	Ob.Morris	4/5	Irwin
Bonds, Seth	Jones	Shropshiers	225/2	Appling
Bone, Wm.Sr.	Madison	Bones	37/3	Appling
Bones, Wm.	Richmond	398th	4/3	Walton
Bonnel, Anthony Jr.	Burke	Hands	284/8	Early
Bonner, Averitt	Warren	Parhams	75/4	Habersham
Bonner, George W.	Jasper	Clay's	338/10	Early
Bonner, Jos.(R.S.)	Jones	Harrest	493/8	Appling
Bonner, Joseph(R.S.)	Jones	Harriss	127/27	Early
Bonner, Robert	Warren	Parham's	51/4	Habersham
Bonner, Robert	Warren	Parhams	107/15	Early
Bonner, Smith	Gwinnett	Hamiltons	362/9	Irwin
Bonner, Thomas M.	Putnam	Littles	190/15	Early
Bonner, Thomas S.	Morgan	Alford's	126/10	Hall
Bonner, Uriah	Jones	Harrest	338/5	Irwin
Bonner, Uriah	Jones	Harrests	135/12	Early
Bonner, William	Jones	Harists	400/21	Early
Bonner, Willis	Clarke	Tredwells	91/12	Hall
Bontwell, Chhapel(?)	Pulaski	Laniers	435/5	Appling
Bontwell, John(Orphs)	Pulaski	Laniers	354/8	Irwin
Booker, John	Wilkes	Mattox's	70/2	Rabun
Booker, John	Wilkes	Mattox	208/3	Irwin
Booker, John	Wilkes	Mattoxs	192/16	Early
Booker, Richison	Wilkes	Holidays	92/21	Early
Booker, William	Columbia	Walkers	17/11	Hall
Booker, William	Richmond	122	186/19	Early
Booker, Wm.	Columbia	Walkers	68/2	Rabun
Booker, Wm.F.(Orphs)	Wilkes	Gordons	170/17	Early
Booker, Wm.M.	Wilkes	Willis	80/3	Appling
Booker, Wm.M.Jr.(Minor)	Wilkes	Holidays	214/3	Walton
Books, William(Orphs)	Scriven	Moody's	245/10	Irwin
Boon, James	Wilkinson	Howards	476/13	Irwin
Boon, John	Baldwin	Marshalls	146/3	Appling
Boon, Lydia	Putnam	Mays	635/2	Appling
Boon, Ratliff	Wilkinson	Howard	107/6	Gwinnett
Boon, Willis	Jones	Wallers	65/8	Irwin
Booren, Joseph	Baldwin	Marshalls	141/3	Early
Booth, Beverly	Greene	Carltons	507/8	Appling
Booth, Edward	Warren	153	320/8	Appling
Booth, Geo.(Orphs)	Elbert	R.Christians	9/7	Early
Booth, John	Clarke	Moores	247/19	Early
Booth, John	Elbert	R.Christians	169/5	Appling
Booth, Richard S.	Richmond	120th	211/5	Gwinnett
Booth, Wiley	Jones	Buckhalters	200/9	Appling
Booth, Wm.Jr.	Jones	Buckhalters	318/5	Early
Booth, Zachariah Sr.	Jones	Griffiths	307/19	Early
Booth, Zachariah Sr.	Jones	Griffiths	338/1	Appling

NAME	COUNTY	MIL.DIST	LOT/SECT	DREW LAND
Boothe, Abraham	Lincoln	Graves	271/8	Appling
Boothe, Melton	Lincoln	Graves	242/4	Early
Booty, Benjamin(Orph)	Warren	Rogers	55/5	Appling
Booty, Nicholas(Orphs)	Warren	Hubberts	229/14	Early
Border, John Sr.	Jackson	Winters	70/23	Early
Borders, John	Putnam	Slaughters	149/8	Early
Borders, John	Putnam	Slaughters	5/3	Early
Boren, William	Baldwin	Marshals	235/16	Early
Boring, Isaac Jr.	Jackson	Rogers	302/17	Early
Boring, John	Jackson	Rogers	380/18	Early
Borins, James(Orphs)	Wilkes	Gordons	70/6	Habersham
Borland, Wm.	Baldwin	Taliaferros	167/16	Irwin
Born, Mary	Oglethorpe	Barnetts	120/8	Hall
Born, Samuel	Oglethorpe	Barnetts	206/1	Appling
Borum, Benjamin	Madison	Willifords	256/4	Irwin
Borum, Flamstead	Oglethorpe	Wises	398/1	Early
Borum, Nathaniel	Oglethorpe	Bridge's	7/2	Walton
Bostick, Amanda(Orph)	Burke	Thomas'	522/6	Irwin
Bostick, Caroline(Orph)	Burke	Thomas'	522/6	Irwin
Bostick, Jacob	Richmond	Winter's	283/4	Walton
Bostick, John G.	Jefferson	Abbots	395/1	Early
Bostick, John G.	Jefferson	Abbots	45/4	Irwin
Bostick, Martha(Orph)	Burke	Thomas'	522/6	Irwin
Bostick, Nathaniel	Jefferson	Langston	8/1	Early
Bostick, Thomas	Burke	Bell's	422/1	Appling
Bostick, Tilman	Hancock	Evans	325/21	Early
Boston, John	Scriven	Burns	28/1	Early
Boston, Pharis	Effingham		13/15	Irwin
Bostwick, Jacob	Richmond	Winters	89/2	Appling
Bostwick, Jane(Wid)	Jefferson	Abbots	364/8	Appling
Bostwick, Joshua D.	Baldwin	McCrarys	277/28	Early
Bostwick, Littleberry Sr.	Jefferson	Abbotts	117/3	Walton
Bostwick, Martha(Wid)	Jefferson	Crowarts	90/1	Early
Bostwick, Nancy(Wid)	Morgan	Townsends	95/22	Early
Boswell, Caroline	Hancock	Justices	35/12	Hall
Boswell, Henly	Richmond	Lacey's	318/1	Early
Boswell, James	Franklin	Davis	97/3	Early
Boswell, John	Putnam	Morelands	12/27	Early
Boswell, John	Wilkes	Runnels	114/10	Irwin
Boswell, John	Wilkes	Runnels	329/9	Irwin
Boswell, Richard	Franklin	Boswells		–
Boswell, Thomas	Jones	Samuels	149/20	Early
Boswell, William S.	Putnam	Stampers	315/14	Early
Boswell, William	Putnam	Berry's	141/10	Early
Boswell, Wm.	Franklin	Ashs	202/5	Irwin
Boswell, Wm.	Franklin	Davis	32/1	Rabun
Bosworth, Britain	Columbia	Shaws	77/6	Habersham
Bosworth, Britton	Columbia	Shaws	119/12	Early
Bosworth, James	Richmond	Lacey's	388/6	Irwin
Bosworth, James	Richmond	Laceys	262/7	Early
Boteman, Calborn	Twiggs	Smith	137/6	Irwin
Bothon, Thos.W.	Wilkes	Kilgores	266/11	Early
Bothwell, Ebenezer	Jefferson	Bothwells	9/14	Irwin
Bothwell, Ebinezer	Jefferson	Bothwell	87/8	Early
Bothwell, John W.	Jefferson	Bothwells	83/19	Early
Bothwell, Saml.Jr.	Jefferson	Bothwells	48/6	Gwinnett
Bothwell, Saml.Sr.	Jefferson	Bothwells	126/11	Early
Bothwell, Saml.Sr.	Jefferson	Bothwells	349/6	Early
Bothwell, Wm.	Jefferson	Bothwells	333/19	Early
Bothwells, James	Jefferson	Bothwells	95/7	Early
Bottoms, Robert	Putnam	Brooks	314/2	Early
Bourguin, Edward	Chatham		454/7	Appling
Bourguin, Henry	Chatham		414/26	Early
Bourke, Robt.(Orph)	Jefferson	Abbots	87/13	Irwin
Bourns, Danniel	Clarke	Parrs	8/4	Early
Bouton, John	Jefferson	Waldens	340/9	Early
Bouyer, Baltazar	Richmond	120	350/13	Early

NAME	COUNTY	MIL.DIST	LOT/SECT	DREW LAND
Bouyer, Baltazar	Richmond	120th	367/3	Appling
Bovet, James	Scriven	180	220/8	Appling
Bowden, James	Jasper	McClendons	14/4	Early
Bowden, William	Oglethorpe	Waters	159/19	Early
Bowdin, Willis	Jasper	McClendons	319/14	Early
Bowdoin, James	Putnam	Tomlinsons	171/3	Early
Bowdon, William	Putnam	Slaughters	304/11	Early
Bowdre, Edmond	Columbia	O.Morris	153/7	Early
Bowdre, Edmund	Columbia	Ob.Morris'	20/26	Early
Bowdre, Geo.W.	Columbia	Cliatts	75/10	Early
Bowdre, Hays	Richmond	120	361/28	Early
Bowdre, Samuel(Orphs)	Columbia	Olives	144/26	Early
Bowdre, Thomas	Columbia	Dodsons	209/9	Appling
Bowen, Elisha	Bulloch	Tilmans	218/5	Early
Bowen, Elisha	Bulloch	Tilmans	97/13	Irwin
Bowen, Gincey	Oglethorpe	Waters	250/27	Early
Bowen, Hezekiah	Bulloch	Edwards	388/2	Appling
Bowen, Hiram	Jackson	Dickson	268/3	Irwin
Bowen, Hiram	Jackson	Rogers	96/4	Appling
Bowen, Horatio	Jones	Samuels	15/3	Walton
Bowen, Mark	Bulloch	Edward's	22/16	Irwin
Bowen, Mereda	Madison	Millicans	6/12	Hall
Bowen, Owen J.	Jackson	Dicksons	61/2	Irwin
Bowen, Raleigh	Jackson	Rogers	41/3	Early
Bowen, Saml.Jr.	Wilkes	Runnels	196/6	Early
Bowen, Thos.J.	Jackson	Dicksons	103/19	Early
Bowen, William	Jackson	Roger's	208/16	Early
Bowen, Wm.	Baldwin	Marshall	374/13	Early
Bowen, Wm.W.	Elbert	Childers	243/26	Early
Bower, Martha	Bulloch	Edwards	164/11	Irwin
Bowers, Jesse	Baldwin	Irwins	57/7	Gwinnett
Bowers, John(Orphs)	Jones	Samuels	316/6	Irwin
Bowers, Wm.	Elbert	White/Christian Bt. 4/1		Habersham
Bowin, Joseph	Baldwin	Marshalls	327/12	Irwin
Bowing, Nathan	Wilkinson	Bowings	226/5	Appling
Bowing, Robert	Jackson	Rogers	257/7	Early
Bowing, Spurtman	Wilkinson	Bowings	167/8	Hall
Bowler, Rhoda(Wid)	Lincoln	Graves	291/7	Gwinnett
Bowlin, Christopher	Effingham		13/1	Walton
Bowlin, Richard	Laurens	Harris	251/20	Early
Bowling, Alexr.B.	Oglethorpe	Waters	243/7	Gwinnett
Bowling, Thomas(Orphs)	Clarke	Deans	162/8	Hall
Bowls, Henry P.	Oglethorpe	Bowles	309/28	Early
Bowls, Henry P.	Oglethorpe	Bowls	68/13	Irwin
Bowls, Jackson	Greene	Tuggles	505/8	Irwin
Bowls, Jackson	Greene	Tugles	47/4	Irwin
Bowls, James Sr.	Jones	Wallers	102/2	Appling
Bowman, Robert	Effingham		489/8	Appling
Bowman, Zachariah	Elbert	Gaines	69/28	Early
Bown, Bennett	Richmond	Palmers	368/8	Early
Box, Phillip	Chatham		385/9	Appling
Boxley, Burwell	Hall	McElhannons	48/10	Hall
Boxton, Silas	Burke	Royals	242/12	Irwin
Boyce, Brinkley	Morgan	Farrars	230/5	Appling
Boyce, Christopher	Twiggs	Evans	341/28	Early
Boyces, John(Orph)	Twiggs	Smiths	141/7	Irwin
Boyd, Aiding	Tattnall	Keens	343/14	Early
Boyd, Andrew	Jackson	Hamiltons	175/21	Early
Boyd, Andrew	Jackson	Hamiltons	246/2	Early
Boyd, David	Tattnall	Keens	58/27	Early
Boyd, James	Chatham		277/6	Irwin
Boyd, John(R.S.)	Warren	150th	284/5	Early
Boyd, John	Jefferson	Fountains	347/11	Early
Boyd, John	Richmond	Palmers	5/2	Irwin
Boyd, John	Richmond	Palmers	74/11	Habersham
Boyd, Samuel	Telfair	Wilsons	182/3	Walton
Boyd, William	Jefferson	Fountains	68/3	Appling

NAME	COUNTY	MIL.DIST	LOT/SECT	DREW LAND
Boyd, William	Richmond	Lacey's	267/9	Appling
Boyd, William	Richmond	Laceys	403/4	Appling
Boyer, John	Richmond		366/7	Irwin
Boyest, Burrel	Tattnall	Keens	272/9	Irwin
Boyet, Phillip	Scriven	180	92/9	Irwin
Boyet, Sabra	Scriven	180th	391/21	Early
Boyet, Stephen Jr.	Scriven	180	4/6	Gwinnett
Boykin, Lodewick	Scriven	26	70/5	Appling
Boykin, Samuel	Baldwin	Marshalls	12/3	Irwin
Boykin, Samuel	Baldwin	Marshalls	70/19	Early
Boyle, Robert	Jackson	Dicksons	332/7	Gwinnett
Boys, James	Jones	Buckhalters	240/28	Early
Boyt, Benjamin	Burke	J.Ward's	37/1	Rabun
Boyt, Benjamin	Burke	J.Wards	118/5	Irwin
Boyt, James	Burke	Bells	315/21	Early
Boytt, Robert	Wilkinson	Bowings	140/28	Early
Bozeman, Elizabeth(Wid)	Twiggs	Bozeman	149/6	Early
Bozeman, Etheldred	Twiggs	Bozeman's	258/4	Appling
Bozeman, Etheldred	Twiggs	Bozemans	451/5	Irwin
Bozeman, James R.	Pulaski	Rees'	236/2	Appling
Bozeman, James	Baldwin	Marshall's	184/12	Irwin
Bozeman, James	Baldwin	Marshalls	380/7	Irwin
Bozeman, John	Baldwin	Marshall's	364/8	Irwin
Bozeman, Ralph	Bulloch	Everitts	102/2	Early
Bozeman, Risdon(Orphs)	Jones	Samuels'	85/13	Habersham
Bozeman, Sarah(Wid)	Wilkinson	Smiths	392/26	Early
Bozeman, Thomas	Wilkinson	Smiths	331/9	Early
Bozewell, Arthur	Washington	Jenkinsons	49/7	Appling
Bracewell, James	Pulaski	Lesters	138/8	Appling
Bracewell, James	Pulaski	Lesters	198/3	Early
Bracewell, Joseph J.	Pulaski	Lesters	250/7	Gwinnett
Bracewell, Richd.Jr.	Laurens	Watson	33/2	Habersham
Bracewell, Samson	Laurens	Deans	167/4	Walton
Bracewell, Samuel	Laurens	Kinchens	43/3	Habersham
Brack, Benjamin	Burke	Lewis	375/5	Appling
Brack, Harden	Burke	Torrances	281/6	Irwin
Brack, Harden	Burke	Torrances	281/6	Irwin
Brack, John	Scriven	180	35/9	Hall
Brack, William	Scriven	180th	113/2	Early
Brack, William	Wilkinson	Bowens	71/4	Early
Brackell, John	Greene	Foster's	43/6	Early
Brackell, John	Greene	Fosters	304/8	Irwin
Brackin, Nancy(Wid)	Twiggs	Ellis'	119/3	Irwin
Brackwood, Francis	Jasper	Centells	380/10	Irwin
Bradberry, James	Columbia	Ob.Morris	68/28	Early
Bradberry, Joseph	Madison	Culbreaths	265/23	Early
Bradberry, Lewis	Walton	Wests	107/11	Early
Bradberry, Lucy(Wid)	Columbia	Burroughs	64/16	Early
Bradberry, Morris	Columbia	Burroughs	359/9	Early
Bradberry, Robert	Madison	Culbreaths	141/12	Irwin
Bradberry, Thos.A.	Richmond	308th	164/16	Irwin
Bradbury, William	Madison	Culbreths	467/13	Irwin
Braddey, Milton	Emanuel	59	403/4	Early
Braddy, John	Jones	Phillips	2/1	Walton
Braddy, Joseph(Orphs)	Twiggs	W.Belchers	142/7	Gwinnett
Braddy, Lewis(R.S.)	Warren	151	268/5	Appling
Braddy, Lienton	Jones	Buckhalters	139/5	Irwin
Braddy, Nathan Jr.	Baldwin	Marshalls	319/21	Early
Braddy, Willie G.	Warren	151	1/8	Appling
Braddy, Willie G.	Warren	151st	383/21	Early
Bradford, Ann	McIntosh	Goulds	112/16	Irwin
Bradford, Archbld.	Jackson	Winters B.	365/3	Appling
Bradford, Archbld.	Jackson	Winters	299/7	Irwin
Bradford, Bartholomew	Clarke	Moores	235/2	Appling
Bradford, David	Jackson	Winters	214/7	Early
Bradford, David	Jackson	Winters	64/2	Appling
Bradford, Eaves	Wilkes	Runnels	374/8	Early

NAME	COUNTY	MIL.DIST	LOT/SECT	DREW LAND
Bradford, Edmund	Jasper	Reids	118/13	Early
Bradford, Fielding	Richmond		314/5	Appling
Bradford, George	Jackson	Winters	53/6	Irwin
Bradford, Joseph	Oglethorpe	Wises	203/4	Walton
Bradford, Joseph	Oglethorpe	Wises	46/4	Appling
Bradford, Richard	Wilkes	Jossey's	244/5	Gwinnett
Bradford, Samuel	Oglethorpe	Goolsbys	83/1	Appling
Bradford, Thomas C.	Richmond	120th	23/16	Early
Bradford, Thomas	Montgomery	Alstons	321/6	Early
Bradford, Thos.M.	Baldwin	Marshalls	361/1	Early
Bradford, Timothy	Putnam	Littles	77/8	Appling
Bradford, William	Montgomery	Alstons	253/8	Irwin
Bradley, Asa	Franklin	Vaughns	337/2	Appling
Bradley, Drury	Morgan	Hackneys	105/19	Early
Bradley, Eli	Liberty		195/5	Gwinnett
Bradley, Ellis	Putnam	Morelands	43/5	Early
Bradley, James	Jackson	Rogers	19/10	Habersham
Bradley, Jesse	Wilkinson	Childs	276/1	Appling
Bradley, Johnson	Jackson	Rogers	25/13	Irwin
Bradley, Joshua	Putnam	Morelands	132/6	Early
Bradley, Josiah	Jackson	Rodgers	17/5	Appling
Bradly, Bryan	Pulaski	Johnston's	98/16	Early
Bradshaw, Brace	Jefferson	Matthews	24/12	Habersham
Bradshaw, Bruce	Jefferson	Matthews	13/20	Early
Bradshaw, Chesley	Twiggs	Ellis	151/10	Irwin
Bradshaw, Chesley	Twiggs	Ellis	295/6	Irwin
Bradshaw, Elijah	Greene	Harvills	112/16	Early
Bradshaw, Jane	Oglethorpe	Waters	79/12	Early
Bradwell, Richard Jr.	Laurens	Watson	33/2	Habersham
Bradwell, Sampson	Laurens	Deans	477/11	Irwin
Brady, John	Jefferson	Lamps	486/12	Irwin
Brady, Saml.Sr.	Wilkinson	Mims'	155/10	Irwin
Brady, Sarah(Wid)	Emanuel	59	366/17	Early
Brady, Thomas	Greene	Kimbroughs	57/11	Habersham
Brag, Benjamin	Hancock	Scotts	60/6	Early
Bragg, George	Elbert	Webbs	6/4	Appling
Bragg, John	Scriven	180	188/8	Irwin
Bragg, Joseph	Elbert	Webbs	424/28	Early
Bragg, Joseph	Oglethorpe	Bowls	117/3	Habersham
Bragg, Mathew	Wilkinson	Brooks'	389/6	Irwin
Bragg, Wm.	Bulloch	Knight	182/10	Habersham
Brake, Matthew	Hancock	Evans	36/11	Early
Bramlet, Enoch Sr.	Franklin	Aikens	476/11	Irwin
Bramlet, Enoch Sr.	Franklin	Aikins	172/13	Early
Bramlet, Enoch	Franklin	Akins	454/8	Irwin
Bramlett, John	Franklin	Attaways	357	-
Bramlett, John	Franklin	Attaways	357/28	Early
Branam, Ishmael	Morgan	Leonards	82/19	Early
Branan, James	Wilkinson	Brooks	167/13	Habersham
Branch, Henry	Appling	5	494/10	Irwin
Branch, William	Tattnall	Overstreets	221/3	Irwin
Brand, Cashwell	Oglethorpe	Barnett's	285/26	Early
Brand, Cashwell	Oglethorpe	Barnetts	44/15	Irwin
Brand, Henry F.	Chatham		357/27	Early
Brand, Jonas	Clarke	Parrs	288/10	Early
Brand, Wm.	Oglethorpe	Barnetts	51/3	Rabun
Brand, Zachariah	Clarke	Parrs	80/2	Walton
Brandon, John	Richmond	Winters	204/4	Early
Brandon, Wm.	Jackson	Hamiltons	51/21	Early
Brandout, Frances L.	Hall	Millers	75/6	Appling
Branham, Elisha(Orph)	Chatham		394/8	Irwin
Branham, Isham	Wilkes	Gordons	193/8	Appling
Branham, Jane(Orph)	Chatham		394/8	Irwin
Branham, Mary	Chatham		43/9	Early
Branham, Thomas	Baldwin	Irwins	77/14	Irwin
Branham, Wm. (Orphs)	Jackson	Hamiltons	183/7	Gwinnett
Branna, John	Morgan	Selmons	200/4	Early

NAME	COUNTY	MIL.DIST	LOT/SECT	DREW LAN
Brannam, Joseph	Putnam	Littles	219/13	Irwin
Brannam, Thomas	Bulloch	Jones	59/11	Hall
Brannan, Russell	Morgan	Jordans'	137/27	Early
Brannan, Wiley	Putnam	Littles	339/12	Irwin
Brannen, Carnes	Pulaski	Davis	103/4	Walton
Brannen, Hope	Scriven	Roberts	249/3	Irwin
Brannen, Huey Sr.	Bulloch	Edwards	149/15	Early
Brannen, Wiley	Pulaski	Davis'	476/10	Irwin
Brannen, Wm.Jr.	Bulloch	Edwards	396/19	Early
Brannin, James	Scriven	Roberts	343/5	Irwin
Brannon, John	Morgan	Selmons	265/18	Early
Brannon, Solomon	Bulloch	Edwards	158/4	Appling
Brannon, Solomon	Bulloch	Edwards	348/12	Early
Brannon, William	Jackson	Winters	54/3	Walton
Brannon, Willy	Putnam	Littles	92/3	Walton
Brannum, Joshua	Washington	Jenkinsons	106/2	Walton
Brannum, Joshua	Washington	Jenkinsons	243/6	Early
Bransby, John	Chatham		382/2	Appling
Branscom, James H.	Telfair	Wilsons	371/10	Irwin
Bransford, James	Clarke	Deans	437/12	Irwin
Bransford, John	Jasper	Centells	430/4	Appling
Branson, Daniel	Twiggs	Smiths	143/12	Irwin
Brantley, Amos(R.S.)	Hancock	Evans	205/7	Early
Brantley, Amos(R.S.)	Hancock	Evans	326/12	Early
Brantley, Amos(R.S.)	Hancock	Evans	453/13	Irwin
Brantley, Benjamin	Laurens	Harris	49/7	Gwinnett
Brantley, Edmund	Baldwin	Ellis'	170/3	Appling
Brantley, Edmund	Baldwin	Ellis's	2155/26	Early
Brantley, Edw.	Washington	Wimberlys	43/11	Early
Brantley, Edward	Washington	Wimberleys	352/27	—
Brantley, Ethelbert	Washington	Brooks	73/13	Irwin
Brantley, Gideon	Washington	Jenkinsons	48/7	Gwinnett
Brantley, Green	Washington	Burneys	105/5	Appling
Brantley, Green	Washington	Burneys	114/3	Habersha
Brantley, James	Hancock	Scotts	336/8	Irwin
Brantley, James	Jones	Jefferson's	124/19	Early
Brantley, James	Laurens	S.Smiths	121/26	Early
Brantley, Jeremiah	Laurens	Kinchens	135/8	Appling
Brantley, Jesse	Morgan	Wrights	88/13	Habersha
Brantley, John	Jones	Green's	67/7	Gwinnett
Brantley, Joseph	Jones	Phillips	13/13	Irwin
Brantley, Joseph	Pulaski	Davis	127/14	Irwin
Brantley, Joseph	Wilkinson	Childs	428/8	Appling
Brantley, Moses	Washington	Wimberlys	114/9	Irwin
Brantley, Moses	Washington	Wimberlys	82/11	Early
Brantley, Solomon(Orphs)	Washington	Brooks	320/19	Early
Brantley, Solomon	Laurens	Harris	375/8	Appling
Brantley, Thomas	Hancock	Danells	137/1	Irwin
Brantley, Thomas	Hancock	Danells	299/3	Early
Brantly, Rebecca(Wid)	Warren	Parhams	1/10	Habersha
Braselton, Amos	Jackson	Hamiltons	79/2	Irwin
Braselton, Amos	Jackson	Rogers	337/7	Early
Braselton, Jacob Sr.	Jackson	Hamiltons	74/14	Early
Braselton, Jacob	Jackson	Hamiltons	341/5	Early
Brasier, Elijah	Lincoln	Jeters	352/20	Early
Brassell, Wm.	Jasper	Blakes	156/3	Walton
Brassell, Wm.	Jasper	Blakes	338/17	Early
Brasswell, William	Twiggs	W.Belchers	45/20	Early
Braswell, Samuel Jr.	Clarke	Oates	154/12	Habersha
Braswell, Turner	Scriven	Moodys	200/7	Appling
Brawner, James	Elbert	P.Christians	416/1	Appling
Brawner, John	Elbert	G.Higginbothams	251/13	Irwin
Brawner, John	Franklin	Turks	96/19	Early
Brawner, Joseph	Elbert	P.Christians	113/6	Gwinnett
Brawner, Joseph	Elbert	P.Christians	162/32	Rabun
Brawner, Talmon	Elbert	P.Christians	114/1	Walton
Brawner, Wenery Sr.	Elbert	P.Christians	140/7	Early

NAME	COUNTY	MIL.DIST	LOT/SECT	DREW LAND
Braxton, John	Twiggs	Evans	167/11	Irwin
Bray, Benjamin	Hancock	Scotts	95/3	Habersham
Bray, Jared	Washington	Daniels	43/9	Irwin
Bray, Jos.	Oglethorpe	Bowls	117/3	Habersham
Bray, Joseph	Oglethorpe	Bowls'	63/3	Early
Brazeal, Catharine(Wid)	McIntosh	Goulds	352/13	Irwin
Brazeel, William	Jones	Permenters	80/4	Walton
Brazel, Britain	Jackson	Rogers	332/18	Early
Brazel, Eliz.(Wid)	Wilkinson	Childs	206/8	Appling
Brazel, James	Jones	Seals	105/15	Early
Brazel, John M.	Jackson	Rogers	236/10	Irwin
Brazel, John M.	Jackson	Rogers	387/8	Irwin
Brazel, Mansfield	Hancock	Smiths	314/17	Early
Brazel, Mathew D.	Appling	5	40/17	Early
Brazell, Britton	Jones	Seals	309/6	Irwin
Brazelton, Jacob Jr.	Jackson	Hamiltons	374/2	Appling
Brazil, Amon	Hancock	Smiths	504/9	Irwin
Brazil, Frederick	Jasper	Posts	105/1	Appling
Brazil, James(Orphs)	Wilkinson	Childs	218/4	Appling
Brazil, Mansfield	Hancock	Smiths	309/2	Early
Breed, Nathan	Columbia	Watsons	156/10	Early
Breedlove, John Jr.	Hancock	Edwards	146/5	Gwinnett
Breedlove, Nathan	Jones	Hansfords'	385/7	Appling
Breedlove, Richard F.	Putnam	J.Kendrick	176/8	Irwin
Breedlove, Samuel	Putnam	Ectors	46/12	Habersham
Breedlove, Sarah(Wid)	Hancock	Edwards	56/2	Early
Breedlove, Wm.(Orphs)	Hancock	Edwards	192/4	Appling
Breedlove, Wm.	Hancock	Edwards	133/13	Habersham
Breedlove, Wm.	Hancock	Edwards	189/2	Early
Brekton, Wm.	Jefferson	Cowarts	124/16	Irwin
Brenson, Josiah	Richmond	Burttons(?)	306/3	Early
Brent, Willoby(Orphs)	Greene	142	370/10	Early
Brewen, Wickliffe	Pulaski	Lesters	47/28	Early
Brewer, Ambrose	Wilkes	Runnels	284/12	Irwin
Brewer, Ambrose	Wilkes	Runnels	400/20	Early
Brewer, Arthur	Telfair	Loves	23/5	Appling
Brewer, Burress	Liberty		250/28	Early
Brewer, Edmund	Morgan	Hubbards	199/20	Early
Brewer, Elijah	Richmond	Lacey's	30/6	Gwinnett
Brewer, Elijah	Richmond	Laceys	444/5	Appling
Brewer, Elisha W.	Jasper	Clays	34/22	Early
Brewer, Henry	Baldwin	Cousins	200/20	Early
Brewer, Henry	Baldwin	Cousins	211/21	Early
Brewer, Horatio G.	Elbert	Childres	34/27	Early
Brewer, Isaac	Jackson	Dicksons	437/7	Appling
Brewer, John	Liberty		135/2	Irwin
Brewer, John	Morgan	Hubbards	84/11	Habersham
Brewer, Joseph	Morgan	Hubbards	223/4	Walton
Brewer, Mary(Wid)	Effingham		435/8	Irwin
Brewer, Mary	Putnam	Bustins	24/1	Rabun
Brewer, Samuel	Wilkinson	Smiths	356/6	Early
Brewerr, David(Orphs)	Jones	Griffiths	8/9	Early
Brewin, Wickliffe	Pulaski	Lesters	339/10	Irwin
Brewton, John	Twiggs	Hodges	204/7	Gwinnett
Briant, James	Camden	Longs	298/12	Irwin
Briant, James	Pulaski	Lesters	137/3	Irwin
Briant, Wm.	Burke	McNorrill's	341/21	Early
Brickley, Benj.	Burke	M.Wards	167/12	Irwin
Briddy, Benj.	Twiggs	Browns	467/7	Appling
Bridger, Wm.F.	Washington	Daniels	254/7	Early
Bridgers, James C.	Baldwin	Marshalls	496/5	Appling
Bridges, Abigal(Wid)	Jackson	Dicksons	59/2	Rabun
Bridges, Barshaba	Warren	151	160/1	Walton
Bridges, Blake	Washington	Jenkins	125/3	Early
Bridges, Blake	Washington	Jenkinsons	112/12	Irwin
Bridges, David	Oglethorpe	McCowen's	196/10	Irwin
Bridges, Jacob	Oglethorpe	Bridges	128/26	Early

NAME	COUNTY	MIL.DIST	LOT/SECT	DREW LAND
Bridges, James Jr.	Oglethorpe	Bridges	224/11	Early
Bridges, James Sr.	Oglethorpe	Bridges	13/7	Appling
Bridges, James	Greene	Jones'	339/8	Appling
Bridges, James	Warren	151	85/1	Rabun
Bridges, John D.	Greene	Jones	161/2	Rabun
Bridges, Jos.	Washington	Robisons	158/14	Irwin
Bridges, Mary	Oglethorpe	Barnetts	152/7	Gwinnett
Bridges, Nancy(Wid)	Jackson	Hamiltons	6/7	Early
Bridges, Solomon	Jackson	Hamiltons	410/3	Appling
Bridges, Solomon	Jackson	Hamiltons	587/2	Appling
Bridges, Wiley J.	Jasper	Bentleys	259/10	Early
Bridges, Wiley	Jackson	Hamiltons	261/2	Early
Bridges, Wilson	Franklin	R.Browns	183/12	Early
Bridges, Wm.	Washington	Jenkinsons	82/2	Irwin
Bridwell, Moses	Wilkes	Willis	364/16	Early
Brigden, William	Scriven		518/9	Irwin
Briggs, John	Richmond		275/18	Early
Briggs, Simeon	Jones	Samuels	193/12	Habersham
Brigham, Emethist	Camden	Tillis	38/20	Early
Bright, Absalom	Burke	Torrance	180/19	Early
Bright, Levi	Washington	Renfroes	121/6	Gwinnett
Bright, Levi	Washington	Renfroes	217/9	Early
Bright, Samuel	Franklin	Flanagans	213/1	Irwin
Bright, Samuel	Franklin	Flanagans	34/4	Walton
Bright, Sarah(Wid)	Franklin	Flanagans	39/13	Early
Bright, William	Franklin	Flanagans	88/3	Rabun
Bright, Wm.	Franklin	Flanagans	88/3	-
Brinkley, Abram	Warren	Blounts	377/1	Appling
Brinkley, Richard	Putnam	Mays	116/11	Early
Brinkley, William	Hancock	Coopers	262/1	Early
Brinkley, Wm.	Hancock	Coopers	132/2	Early
Brinson, Adam Jr.	Scriven		42/12	Habersham
Brinson, David	Jefferson	Matthews	349/2	Early
Brinson, Isaac	Jefferson	Matthews	382/7	Irwin
Brinson, James	Burke	J.Ward's	110/5	Early
Brinson, Mathew	Lincoln	Jeters	91/2	Habersham
Brinson, Noah	Burke	J.Wards	183/28	Early
Brinson, Samuel T.	Tattnall	Conyers	242/6	Appling
Brinson, Shepherd	Burke	Torrence	245/27	Early
Brinson, Wm.	Burke	J.Wards	251/16	Early
Brinsow, Samuel F.	Tattnall	Conyers	69/8	Early
Brisco, John	Oglethorpe	Myricks	33/3	Rabun
Briscoe, John(Orphs)	Clarke	Starnes	220/4	Irwin
Briscoe, John	Columbia	Gartrells	354/4	Early
Briscoe, Patrick(Orph)	Columbia	Olives	5/5	Appling
Briscoe, Waters	Columbia	Gartrells	128/12	Hall
Briton, James	Clarke	Penticost	42/12	Hall
Britt, Amos	Jackson	Rogers	119/16	Irwin
Britt, Hary	Laurens	Watsons	235/12	Early
Britt, Hugh Jr.	Madison	Culbreaths	160/20	Early
Britt, Hugh Sr.	Madison	Culbreths	202/15	Early
Britt, John	Jackson	Rogers	186/8	Appling
Britt, Obed	Baldwin	Stephens	176/10	Early
Britt, Wm.	Washington	Burneys	260/19	Early
Brittenham, Jos.(R.S.)	Warren	150th	391/27	Early
Brittenham, Levi	Warren	150th	520/7	Irwin
Britton, George	Jasper	Phillips'	288/18	Early
Britton, George	Oglethorpe	Brittons	176/7	Appling
Britton, Harriot	Baldwin	Marshalls	326/27	Early
Britton, John(Orphs)	Baldwin	Marshalls	205/6	Appling
Britton, Thos.(Orphs)	Clarke	Starnes	164/15	Irwin
Broach, Wm.H.	Greene	Greene	72/9	Irwin
Broach, Wm.H.	Greene	Griers	13/9	Appling
Broadnax, John H.	Putnam	Bustins	174/6	Irwin
Broadnax, John	Putnam	Bustins	279/13	Irwin
Broadnax, Robert	Putnam	Bustins	80/8	Hall
Broadnax, Robert	Putnam	Bustins	95/7	Irwin

NAME	COUNTY	MIL.DIST	LOT/SECT	DREW LAND
Brock, Benjamin	Effingham		487/12	Irwin
Brock, Daniel	Wilkinson	Brooks	11/11	Early
Brock, Daniel	Wilkinson	Brooks	287/7	Irwin
Brock, William	Franklin	Haynes		-
Brock, Woddy	Walton	Sentills	113/1	Early
Brockinton, Daniel	Camden	Millers	402/4	Appling
Brockman, Elijah	Oglethorpe	Myricks	317/14	Early
Brockman, John	Oglethorpe	Myricks	53/7	Early
Brockman, John	Oglethorpe	Myricks	7/4	Rabun
Brockman, Lewis	Oglethorpe	Myricks	111/2	Rabun
Brockman, Lewis	Oglethorpe	Myricks	164/3	Early
Brocks, Ignatius R.	Putnam	Slaughters	34/4	Early
Brodnax, Henry	Putnam	Bustins	171/14	Early
Brodnax, Robt.B.	Hancock	Champions	207/5	Appling
Brokes, John(Orphs)	Jones	Permenters	252/8	Irwin
Brokes, John	Jones	Permenters	134/16	Early
Brokes, Phillip H.	Jones	Permenters	482/4	Appling
Brook, Ignatius R.	Putnam	Slaughters	87/12	Early
Brooker, John G.(Orph)	Glynn		151/5	Early
Brooker, John	Greene	Jones'	307/4	Irwin
Brooker, Jos.L.(Orph)	Glynn		151/5	Early
Brooker, Lucy(Orph)	Glynn		151/5	Early
Brooker, Wm.E.(Orph)	Glynn		151/5	Early
Brookes, Philip H.	Jones	Permenters	46/2	Walton
Brookes, Sally(Wid)	Jones	Permenters	177/20	Early
Brooking, Francis	Hancock	Millers	144/16	Early
Brooking, Francis	Hancock	Millers	509/4	Appling
Brooking, Robt.N.	Hancock	Scotts	510/4	Appling
Brooking, Wm.	Hancock	Scotts	46/26	Early
Brookins, Benj.	Washington	Brooks'	91/1	Rabun
Brookins, Samuel	Burke	Bells	142/19	Early
Brookins, Wm.	Burke	Sullivans	259/8	Irwin
Brooks, Abijah	Morgan	Loyd's	46/2	Rabun
Brooks, Arthur	Jones	Phillips	79/20	Early
Brooks, Benjamin	Warren	152nd	278/3	Early
Brooks, Burges W.	Warren	153rd	390/21	Early
Brooks, Chas.H.	Jones	Permenters	233/11	Irwin
Brooks, Christopher	Wilkes	Holidays	38/9	Appling
Brooks, Christopher	Wilkes	Holidays	622/2	Appling
Brooks, David(Orphs)	Oglethorpe	Murray's	54/9	Appling
Brooks, Elijah	Jasper	Northcuts	204/2	Early
Brooks, Elisha	Jasper	Northcuts	212/4	Irwin
Brooks, Hannah(Wid)	Jackson	Rogers	382/10	Irwin
Brooks, Isaac	Jackson	Rogers	303/6	Irwin
Brooks, Isaac	Warren	152	37/9	Early
Brooks, Isham	Putnam	Brooks	391/19	Irwin
Brooks, Ivey	Baldwin	Stephens	440/15	Early
Brooks, Jabez	Morgan	Hubbards	277/11	Irwin
Brooks, Jabez	Morgan	Hubbards	81/11	Habersham
Brooks, Jacob R.	Gwinnett	Hamiltons	155/7	Irwin
Brooks, Jacob	Franklin	Jos.Millers	25/20	Early
Brooks, James Jr.	Putnam	Slaughters	291/8	Appling
Brooks, James	Morgan	Jordans	486/7	Appling
Brooks, James	Washington	Burneys	161/14	Irwin
Brooks, Jarvis	Wilkes	Brooks	7/13	Early
Brooks, John T.	Hancock	Herberts	52/6	Gwinnett
Brooks, John(Orphs)	Hancock	Herberts	37/2	Habersham
Brooks, John	Jefferson	Lamps	58/7	Appling
Brooks, John	Jones	Permenters	133/9	Early
Brooks, John	Putnam	Littles	152/2	Appling
Brooks, John	Washington	Averits	302/11	Early
Brooks, John	Washington	Burneys	162/8	-
Brooks, Jordan	Jones	Phillips	251/7	Appling
Brooks, Joseph Jr.	Warren	150	29/1	Walton
Brooks, Joseph	Warren	151	253/3	Walton
Brooks, Lydia(Wid)	Jackson	Rogers	27/14	Irwin
Brooks, Martin	Warren	Pool's	290/5	Irwin

NAME	COUNTY	MIL.DIST	LOT/SECT	DREW LAND
Brooks, Matthew	Jones	Phillips	18/28	Early
Brooks, Maxey	Baldwin	Stephens	438/13	Irwin
Brooks, Micajah	Jasper	Northcuts	94/11	Hall
Brooks, Middleton	Jackson	Dicksons	184/21	Early
Brooks, Paschal	Jasper	McLendons	195/4	Appling
Brooks, Penelope(Wid)	Jackson	Rodgers	239/9	Appling
Brooks, Polly(Wid)	Greene	Tugles	501/8	Appling
Brooks, Posey P.	Morgan	Hubbards	30/5	Irwin
Brooks, Raschal	Jasper	McClendon's	398/21	Early
Brooks, Robert	Greene	Amers	366/9	Appling
Brooks, Robert	Oglethorpe	Myricks	24/4	Irwin
Brooks, Robt.Sr.	Jones	Phillips	116/7	Appling
Brooks, Saml.Sr.	Wilkes	Holidays	49/6	Irwin
Brooks, Saml.W.Jr.(Minor)	Wilkes	Holidays	166/10	Hall
Brooks, Samuel	Baldwin	Doziers	326/7	Gwinnett
Brooks, Samuel	Jones	Phillips'	284/3	Early
Brooks, Samuel	Jones	Phillips	230/7	Gwinnett
Brooks, Sarah	Madison	Millicans	305/8	Irwin
Brooks, Simon	Baldwin	Stephens	79/3	Irwin
Brooks, Stephen(R.S.)	Jackson	Rogers	60/11	Habershar
Brooks, Thomas	Jasper	Bartleys	212/10	Irwin
Brooks, William	Jefferson	Connells	219/8	Early
Brooks, Williee	Twiggs	Hodges	87/1	Irwin
Brooks, Wilson	Oglethorpe	Brittons	35/6	Appling
Brooks, Wilson	Oglethorpe	Brittons	44/21	Early
Brooks, Wm.(Orphs)	Jackson	Rogers	262/8	Appling
Brooks, Wm.	Hancock	Herberts	8/1	Rabun
Brooks, Wm.G.	Washington	Avints	187/6	Gwinnett
Brooks, Wm.H.	Jones	Phillips	139/17	Early
Brooks, Wm.M.	Jones	Phillips	382/5	Irwin
Brooks, Wm.R.	Oglethorpe	Brittons	384/6	Early
Brooks, Wm.Sr.	Greene	Armer's	192/14	Early
Broom, Solomon	Warren	Griers	138/28	Early
Broome, Adam	Warren	Hubberts	278/16	Early
Broughton, Annas	Jasper	Phillips	55/12	Habershar
Broughton, Daniel S.	Liberty		504/2	Appling
Broughton, John C.	Liberty		251/5	Irwin
Broughton, Wm.	Jasper	Phillips'	365/5	Early
Browing, John K.	Morgan	Talbots	73/20	Early
Brown,	Washington	Jenkinsons	106/5	Appling
Brown, Abram	Jones	Phillips	142/11	Hall
Brown, Adam	Elbert	Dooleys	282/6	Irwin
Brown, Alexander	Oglethorpe	Dunns	183/9	Appling
Brown, Alford H.	Jasper	May's	414/10	Irwin
Brown, Alfred	Jasper	Clay's	258/5	Irwin
Brown, Allen W.	Clarke	Stuarts	218/27	Early
Brown, Allen	Bulloch	Knights	153/10	Irwin
Brown, Allexander	Oglethorpe	Dunns	66/26	Early
Brown, Ambrose	Jasper	Ryans	190/10	Irwin
Brown, Andrew	Morgan	Farrar's	455/4	Appling
Brown, Andrew	Wilkinson	Howards	61/16	Early
Brown, Ann(Wid)	Wilkinson	Smiths	65/21	Early
Brown, Armsted(Orphs)	Greene	143	364/4	Early
Brown, Asa	Pulaski	Maddox's	156/28	Early
Brown, Augustus J.	Columbia	J.Morris	54/4	Walton
Brown, Benj.	Hall		4/2	Walton
Brown, Benj.H.	Jones	Phillips	312/4	Appling
Brown, Benj.Jr.	Morgan	Jordans'	459/8	Appling
Brown, Benj.Jr.	Morgan	Jordans	45/3	Walton
Brown, Benj.Sr.	Morgan	Jordans	146/10	Hall
Brown, Benjamin	Burke	Spiveys	25/14	Irwin
Brown, Benjamin	Burke	Spiveys	491/3	Appling
Brown, Benjamin	Hall		135/7	Irwin
Brown, Benjamin	Hall		319/21	Early
Brown, Benjamin	Hall		42/3	Walton
Brown, Benjamin	Morgan	Loyds	170/1	Walton
Brown, Benjamin	Morgan	Loyds	211/6	Early

NAME	COUNTY	MIL.DIST	LOT/SECT	DREW LAND
Brown, Britton	Emanuel	49	154/13	Irwin
Brown, Burrel	Burke	Lewis	102/5	Appling
Brown, Caroline(Orph)	McIntosh	Hamiltons	500/8	Appling
Brown, Caroline(Orph)	McIntosh	Hamiltons	57/7	Irwin
Brown, Charles M.	Oglethorpe	Dunns	72/7	Gwinnett
Brown, Charles	Jones	Buckhalters	382/16	Early
Brown, Charles	Jones	Buckhalters	9/13	Irwin
Brown, Christopher P.	Morgan	Farrars	440/8	Irwin
Brown, Daniel	Laurens	Ross	97/1	Walton
Brown, David	Elbert	Dooley's	260/15	Early
Brown, David	Liberty		294/12	Irwin
Brown, David	Oglethorpe	Brittons	131/8	Hall
Brown, David	Oglethorpe	Brittons	149/7	Early
Brown, David	Warren	Blounts	64/1	Appling
Brown, Edy(Wid)	Camden	32	446/9	Irwin
Brown, Elijah	Jefferson	Langstons	242/17	Early
Brown, Elijah	Jefferson	Langstons	296/7	Gwinnett
Brown, Eliz.(Wid)	Wilkes	Russels	273/1	Walton
Brown, Eliza(Orph)	McIntosh	Hamiltons	500/8	Appling
Brown, Eliza(Orph)	McIntosh	Hamiltons	57/7	Irwin
Brown, Elizabeth	Greene	143	18/6	Appling
Brown, Ephraim	Jackson	Hamiltons	426/7	Appling
Brown, Garrot	Washington	Floyds	204/10	Irwin
Brown, George A.	Twiggs	W.Belchers	342/4	Early
Brown, Gracy(Wid)	Washington	Wimberlys	359/4	Appling
Brown, Green	Pulaski	Ree's	106/5	Early
Brown, Hardy	Elbert	G.Higginbothams	29/1	Habersham
Brown, Henry W.	Burke	Dy's	70/1	Walton
Brown, Henry	Emanuel	49	229/11	Irwin
Brown, Henry	Emanuel	49	353/8	Early
Brown, Henry	Morgan	Jordans'	330/5	Early
Brown, Hezekiah	Washington	Renfroes	41/3	Walton
Brown, Hiram	Elbert	Dobbs	21/5	Early
Brown, Hiram	Elbert	Dobbs	57/7	Early
Brown, Hiram	Hancock	Canes	274/5	Irwin
Brown, Hiram	Lincoln	Jeters	277/12	Irwin
Brown, Hitson	Washington	Pools	235/27	Early
Brown, Irby	Pulaski	Maddox	347/5	Early
Brown, Isaac	Twiggs	Browns	80/10	Habersham
Brown, Jacob	Lincoln	Graves'	260/12	Irwin
Brown, Jacob	Lincoln	Graves	175/17	Early
Brown, James E.	Clarke	Applings	182/4	Early
Brown, James L.	Elbert	Dooleys	45/3	Rabun
Brown, James N.	Elbert	P.Christians	159/1	Early
Brown, James N.	Morgan	Hackney's	310/27	Early
Brown, James	Burke	McNorrils	195/3	Early
Brown, James	Burke	Norl	248/3	Early
Brown, James	Franklin	Flanagans	175/8	Irwin
Brown, James	Franklin	Flanagans	78/7	Irwin
Brown, James	Pulaski	Maddoxs	187/11	Irwin
Brown, James	Putnam	Robinson	68/8	Early
Brown, James	Wilkes	Runnels	515/4	Appling
Brown, James	Wilkinson	Bowings	344/21	Early
Brown, James	Wilkinson	Bowings	475/5	Appling
Brown, Jas.(Orphs)	Jasper	Hays	173/12	Irwin
Brown, Jas.(Orphs)	Jasper	Hays	325/6	Appling
Brown, Jas.(Orphs)	Jasper	Hays	34/11	Irwin
Brown, Jesse	Bulloch	Knights	178/28	Early
Brown, Jesse	Bulloch	Knights	402/9	Early
Brown, Jesse	Elbert	Penn's	144/8	Early
Brown, Jno.Sr.(R.S.)	Franklin	P.Browns	371/2	Early
Brown, John B. (Orphs)	Columbia	Walkers	82/4	Walton
Brown, John D.	Wilkes	Gordons	231/7	Gwinnett
Brown, John F.	Baldwin	Taliaferro's	145/5	Appling
Brown, John F.	Baldwin	Taliaferros	384/4	Appling
Brown, John G.W.	Jasper	Bailey's	15/13	Early
Brown, John H.	Jones	Phillips	289/10	Early

41

NAME	COUNTY	MIL.DIST	LOT/SECT	DREW LAN
Brown, John Jr.	Franklin	P.Browns	376/17	Early
Brown, John L.	Clarke	Stuarts	160/10	Early
Brown, John M.	Baldwin	Marshalls	335/10	Irwin
Brown, John M.	Franklin	Attaways	223/2	Appling
Brown, John S.	Putnam	Coopers	164/9	Irwin
Brown, John Sr.(R.S.)	Franklin	Browns	371/2	Appling
Brown, John Sr.(R.S.)	Franklin	P.Browns	130/11	Irwin
Brown, John Sr.(R.S.)	Franklin	P.Browns	197/13	Early
Brown, John Sr.	Jackson	Hamiltons	399/16	Early
Brown, John Sr.	Jasper	Northcuts	166/10	Habersha
Brown, John Sr.	Jasper	Northcutts	342/8	Early
Brown, John Sr.	Jones	Phillips	24/10	Irwin
Brown, John W.	Jasper	Bartletts	238/27	Early
Brown, John(Orph)	McIntosh	Hamiltons	500/8	Appling
Brown, John(Orph)	McIntosh	Hamiltons	57/7	Irwin
Brown, John	Burke	Lewis	264/20	Early
Brown, John	Chatham		89/13	Habersha
Brown, John	Elbert	Whites of Cs.B.	223/8	Irwin
Brown, John	Greene	Macons	139/9	Early
Brown, John	Greene	Macons	185/3	Irwin
Brown, John	Hancock	Scotts	318/5	Appling
Brown, John	Jones	Buckhalters	157/5	Appling
Brown, John	Liberty		70/2	Early
Brown, John	Morgan	Parkers	160/3	Appling
Brown, John	Pulaski	Maddox's	172/7	Irwin
Brown, Jonathan	Wilkinson	Childs	219/8	Appling
Brown, Joseph(Maj)	Clarke	Mitchells	154/27	Early
Brown, Joseph(Orphs)	Scriven		85/18	Early
Brown, Joseph	Hall		59/1	Rabun
Brown, Julian	Jasper	Clay's	74/4	Early
Brown, Kilby	Twiggs	Smiths	255/9	Appling
Brown, Killis	Franklin	P.Browns	399/18	Early
Brown, Lemuel	Clarke	Mitchells	158/5	Gwinnett
Brown, Leroy	Warren	Blounts	174/9	Appling
Brown, Levin	Twiggs	R.Belchers	73/1	Early
Brown, Lewis	Morgan	Parkers	197/1	Walton
Brown, Lovett	Laurens	S.Smiths	315/16	Early
Brown, Lucy	Chatham		339/16	Early
Brown, Mary Ann(Orph)	McIntosh	Hamiltons	500/8	Appling
Brown, Mary Ann(Orph)	McIntosh	Hamiltons	57/7	Irwin
Brown, Mary S.(Wid)	Elbert	G.Higginbotham	206/16	Early
Brown, Mathew	Jefferson	Mathews	23/10	Habersha
Brown, Mereda	Madison	Millicans	32/10	Irwin
Brown, Michael	Chatham		5/12	Irwin
Brown, Mildred	Baldwin	Taliaferos	494/3	Appling
Brown, Morgan	Washington	Floyds	210/19	Early
Brown, Morgan	Washington	Floyds	368/19	Early
Brown, Nepsa	Pulaski	Johnsons	39/2	Rabun
Brown, Pearson	Pulaski	Maddox	54/5	Rabun
Brown, Phebe	Baldwin	Marshalls	31/12	Hall
Brown, Philip	Morgan	Farrars	216/1	Early
Brown, Richard	Franklin	Morris'	211/13	Early
Brown, Richard	Franklin	Morriss	17/8	Appling
Brown, Richard	Pulaski	Laniers	50/7	Appling
Brown, Richmond	Putnam	Robertson	344/5	Appling
Brown, Robert C.	Camden	270	13/3	Early
Brown, Robert	Jones	Jeffersons	73/1	Rabun
Brown, Robert	Lincoln	Jeters	361/6	Gwinnett
Brown, Robert	Putnam	Coopers	83/1	Early
Brown, Robt.(R.S.)	Franklin	Holcombs	229/5	Irwin
Brown, Robt.(Rev)	Franklin	Holcombs	393/8	Early
Brown, Robt.	Wilkinson	Childs	433/6	Irwin
Brown, Rufus	Warren	153	132/1	Walton
Brown, Sampson	Jones	Buckhalters	21/4	Irwin
Brown, Samuel Sr.	Wilkes	Runnels'	6/11	Hall
Brown, Samuel	Clarke	Applings	180/7	Gwinnett
Brown, Samuel	Jefferson	Matthews	171/11	Early

NAME	COUNTY	MIL.DIST	LOT/SECT	DREW LAND
Brown, Samuel	Putnam	Berry's	214/7	Irwin
Brown, Samuel	Telfair	Williams	98/7	Appling
Brown, Sarah(Wid)	Bulloch	Knights	314/7	Irwin
Brown, Sarah(Wid)	Wilkinson	Childs	179/5	Irwin
Brown, Sarah	Hancock	Scotts	52/1	Irwin
Brown, Silas	Twiggs	Smiths	176/2	Irwin
Brown, Stark(R.S.)	Walton	Wests	18/2	Early
Brown, Stark(R.S.)	Walton	Wests	85/5	Appling
Brown, Thomas	Effingham		68/26	Early
Brown, Thomas	Morgan	Farrars	388/7	Irwin
Brown, Thomas	Morgan	Farrars	399/1	Appling
Brown, Thomas	Morgan	Jordans	317/13	Irwin
Brown, Thos.A.	Oglethorpe	Waters	276/12	Irwin
Brown, Turner	Washington	Cummings	353/4	Early
Brown, Valentine	Wilkes	Ogletrees	112/6	Appling
Brown, Vincent	Jackson	Hamiltons	264/12	Irwin
Brown, Wiatt	Elbert	Whites/At.Cs.	462/7	Appling
Brown, Wiley	Jackson	Hamiltons	6/8	Appling
Brown, William F.	Putnam	Buckners	36/21	Early
Brown, William(Orphs)	Morgan	Jordan's	126/13	Habersham
Brown, William	Bulloch	Knights	204/4	Walton
Brown, William	Chatham		43/14	Irwin
Brown, William	Columbia	Willinghams	268/7	Gwinnett
Brown, William	Columbia	Willinghams	351/12	Early
Brown, William	Hancock	Millers	395/6	Early
Brown, William	Jasper	Bartletts	236/2	Early
Brown, William	Jasper	Hays	378/7	Irwin
Brown, William	Morgan	Lenords	358/12	Early
Brown, William	Oglethorpe	Dunn's	19/22	Early
Brown, William	Twiggs	Smiths	391/8	Early
Brown, Winefred	Jasper	Centells	212/6	Irwin
Brown, Wm.(Orphs)	Wilkinson	Childs	6/3	Rabun
Brown, Wm.(R.S.)	Franklin	Attaways	239/13	Irwin
Brown, Wm.(R.S.)	Franklin	Attaways	25/2	Habersham
Brown, Wm.	Burke	Lewis	295/11	Irwin
Brown, Wm.	Elbert	Smiths	117/13	Irwin
Brown, Wm.	Franklin	Harris	158/8	Irwin
Brown, Wm.	Franklin	Harris	158/8	Irwin
Brown, Wm.	Washington	Cummins	199/26	Early
Brown, Wm.A.	Elbert	Whites Dt/Chs.Bt.	103/6	Gwinnett
Brown, Wm.F.	Putnam	Buckners	285/15	Early
Brown, Wm.H.	Jones	Phillips	307/13	Irwin
Brown, Wm.P.	Baldwin	Irwins	227/14	Early
Brown, Wm.S.	Franklin	Browns	347/7	Early
Brown, Wm.W.	Jones	Philips	56/3	Appling
Brown, Zealous	Jones	Wallers	113/2	Rabun
Brownfield, John	Jasper	Baleys	186/16	Early
Browning, Daniel	Montgomery	McElvins	481/7	Appling
Browning, Edward	Morgan	Talbotts	84/1	Early
Browning, James Sr.	Montgomery	McElvins	57/4	Rabun
Browning, Jas.Jr.	Montgomery	McElvins	447/2	Appling
Browning, Stephen	Wayne	Johnsons	118/10	Early
Browning, Stephen	Wayne	Johnstons	207/4	Early
Brownjohn, Wm.	Chatham		271/6	Early
Brownjohn, Wm.	Chatham		525/12	Irwin
Brownring, John	Greene	Harvills	120/13	Irwin
Brownson, Daniel	Lincoln	Jeters	371/4	Early
Broxton, James	Burke	Royals	396/5	Irwin
Broxton, John	Burke	Royals	267/16	Early
Broxton, John	Burke	Royals	288/5	Appling
Bruce, Aziel	Greene	Wheelis	236/20	Early
Bruce, George	Hancock	Danells	65/23	Early
Bruce, John	Clarke	Stewarts	68/7	Gwinnett
Bruce, John	Greene	Wheelis	384/21	Early
Bruce, Ward	Greene	Jones	299/5	Irwin
Bruckner, Danl.Jr.	Wilkes	Gordons	205/26	Early
Bruen, Cirus	Chatham		34/11	Habersham

43

NAME	COUNTY	MIL.DIST	LOT/SECT	DREW LAND
Bruer, Thos.M.	Clarke	Stuarts	508/5	Appling
Brumbaloe, Wm.	Jackson	Winter's	166/6	Appling
Brumfield, John(R.S.)	Elbert	Webbs	117/7	Irwin
Brumfield, John(R.S.)	Elbert	Webbs	345/3	Early
Brumley, Baptist	Laurens	Griffins	128/9	Appling
Brumley, James	Laurens	Griffins	148/18	Early
Brumley, Stephen	Franklin	Vaughns	358/7	Irwin
Brummit, James	Jasper	Hays	216/6	Appling
Brummitt, James	Jasper	Hays	34/5	Rabun
Brunson, David(R.S.)	Scriven	Lovetts	302/5	Gwinnett
Brunson, Josiah	Richmond	Burtons	180/5	Gwinnett
Brunson, Matthew	Lincoln	Jeters	290/10	Early
Brunson, Nathaniel D.	Scriven	Mills	55/12	Irwin
Bruster, Hugh	Walton	Norshams	136/14	Irwin
Bruster, John Jr.	Morgan	Parkers	109/1	Irwin
Bruster, John	Morgan	Farrars	104/8	Hall
Bruster, John	Morgan	Farrars	167/9	Irwin
Bruster, Sherriff	Morgan	Farrar's	87/13	Early
Bruton, John(Orphs)	Twiggs	Hodges	254/4	Appling
Brux, Albert	Richmond	122	153/2	Walton
Bryan, Alexander	Richmond	398	68/2	Early
Bryan, Alexander	Richmond	398th	478/3	Appling
Bryan, Arthur	Twiggs	W.Belchers	113/10	Habersham
Bryan, Benjamin	Jackson	Dicksons	139/1	Walton
Bryan, Benjamin	Twiggs	W.Belchers	257/15	Early
Bryan, Betey(Wid)	Twiggs	Browns	143/3	Walton
Bryan, David Sr.	Laurens	D.Smiths	4/9	Early
Bryan, David	Franklin	Davis	346/7	Appling
Bryan, Edward	Laurens	Deans	4/12	Habersham
Bryan, Edward	Twiggs	Smiths	27/1	Walton
Bryan, Eli(Orphs)	Franklin	Burroughs	51/18	Early
Bryan, Frederick	Wayne	Johnston's	269/19	Early
Bryan, Jacob	Burke	71	340/2	Early
Bryan, Jacob	Chatham		58/2	Rabun
Bryan, James C.	Twiggs	Smiths	92/15	Early
Bryan, Jesse Jr.	Walton	Echols	84/7	Appling
Bryan, Jesse Sr.	Walton	Echols	125/1	Walton
Bryan, Jesse Sr.	Walton	Echols	270/4	Appling
Bryan, John	Elbert	White/Christian Bt. 165/4		Irwin
Bryan, John	Elbert	Whites	152/9	Early
Bryan, John	Madison	WIllifords	165/9	Hall
Bryan, Joseph B.	Pulaski	Davis	119/16	Early
Bryan, Joseph	Montgomery	Nobles	261/4	Appling
Bryan, Moses Sr.	Burke	Spiveys	179/21	Early
Bryan, Needham	Burke	Spiveys	220/20	Early
Bryan, Peter	Hall		373/8	Irwin
Bryan, Robert	Putnam	Mays	275/10	Irwin
Bryan, Stephen	Hall		339/6	Irwin
Bryan, T.	Wayne	Crews	279/14	Early
Bryan, Thomas	Elbert	Gaines	78/23	Early
Bryan, Thomas	Elbert	Gains	179/4	Appling
Bryan, William	Putnam	Stampers	263/4	Walton
Bryan, William	Twiggs	Smiths	242/8	Irwin
Bryan, Wm.	Franklin		349/17	Early
Bryan, Wm.	Franklin	Burroughs	272/3	Appling
Bryant, Adelia(Orph)	Richmond	Palmers	313/19	Early
Bryant, Austin	Morgan	Talbots	181/3	Early
Bryant, Edward	Pulaski	Maddoxs	241/11	Irwin
Bryant, Edward	Wilkes	Bryants	439/3	Appling
Bryant, Elias	Richmond	Laceys	76/4	Habersham
Bryant, Elias	Wilkes	Mattox	66/3	Habersham
Bryant, Eliz.(Orphs)	Hancock	Millers	14/6	Gwinnett
Bryant, Eliz.(Wid)	Morgan	Wrights	410/13	Irwin
Bryant, Eliza(Orph)	Richmond	Palmers	313/19	Early
Bryant, Hugh	Jackson	Rogers	17/10	Irwin
Bryant, Hugh	Jackson	Rogers	296/5	Gwinnett
Bryant, Isaac(R.S.)	Putnam	Ectors	117/1	Irwin

NAME	COUNTY	MIL.DIST	LOT/SECT	DREW LAND
Bryant, James Sr.	Scriven	Roberts	13/11	Hall
Bryant, James Sr.	Scriven	Roberts	222/3	Appling
Bryant, James	Franklin	Powells	31/1	Appling
Bryant, James	Putnam	Bustins	366/8	Irwin
Bryant, James	Scriven	Lovetts	288/13	Early
Bryant, John Sr.	Franklin	Powels	206/2	Early
Bryant, John(Orphs)	Jefferson	Langstons	48/5	Gwinnett
Bryant, John(Orphs)	Montgomery	McMillans	229/28	Early
Bryant, John	Hancock	Millers	419/26	Early
Bryant, John	Wilkes	Bryants	62/2	Appling
Bryant, Mary	Hancock	Millers	45/1	Habersham
Bryant, Micajah	Franklin	Powels	9/9	Early
Bryant, Moses	Elbert	Whites/Cs.Bt.	429/10	Irwin
Bryant, Moses	Pulaski	Ree's	499/10	Irwin
Bryant, Moses	Pulaski	Rees	68/3	Habersham
Bryant, Rebecca(Wid)	Twiggs	Evan's	437/6	Appling
Bryant, Richmond	Wilkes	Smiths	59/10	Early
Bryant, Robert	Jones	Hurst	212/5	Gwinnett
Bryant, Samuel	Hancock	Millers	237/4	Early
Bryant, Sarah(Wid)	Putnam	Littles	297/1	Walton
Bryant, Solomon	Scriven	Burns	232/2	Appling
Bryant, Stephen	Pulaski	Rees	84/8	Early
Bryant, Susannah(Orph)	Warren	152	289/5	Irwin
Bryant, Thomas(Orphs)	Twiggs	Evans	41/20	Early
Bryant, Thomas	Franklin	Vaughns	395/5	Irwin
Bryant, Thomas	Franklin	Vaughns	395/5	Irwin
Bryant, William	Lincoln	Tatoms	30/3	Rabun
Bryant, William	Lincoln	Tatoms	317/10	Irwin
Bryant, William	Morgan	Talbots	214/3	Irwin
Bryant, William	Morgan	Talbots	32/6	Habersham
Bryant, William	Morgan	Talbots	488/3	Appling
Bryant, William	Oglethorpe	Myricks	231/9	Appling
Bryant, William	Richmond	Palmers	26/3	Early
Bryant, William	Richmond	Palmers	49/10	Hall
Bryant, Willis	Pulaski	Rees'	197/1	Appling
Bryant, Wm.(R.S.)	Jackson	Rogers	338/27	Early
Bryant, Wm.(R.S.)	Jackson	Rogers	473/2	Appling
Bryant, Wm.G.(R.S.)	Putnam	Robertsons	122/10	Habersham
Bryant, Wm.G.(R.S.)	Putnam	Robertsons	141/19	Early
Bryant, Wm.Jr.	Jackson	Rogers	65/8	Hall
Bryens, John(Orphs)	Burke	Sullivans	547/5	Appling
Buchanan, Revinus H.L.	Baldwin	Marshalls	519/2	Appling
Buchannan, Patrick	Madison	Culbreaths	325/5	Irwin
Buchannon, Jas.Sr.(R.S.)	Jasper	Kindalls	90/15	Early
Buchannon, Macelain	Wilkinson	Smiths	269/3	Irwin
Buchannon, Pricella	Jasper	Clays	75/6	Early
Buchanons, John(Orphs)	Jasper	Clays	79/4	Early
Buck, James	Richmond	Palmers	314/8	Appling
Buck, James	Richmond	Palmers	390/27	Early
Buckannon, George	Jasper	Bentleys	351/7	Gwinnett
Buckannon, Jas.T.(R.S.)	Jasper	Kindalls	307/18	Early
Buckannon, Jas.T.(R.S.)	Jasper	Kindalls	363/13	Irwin
Buckannon, Wm.F.	Greene	Nelms	231/5	Early
Buckdew, William	Twiggs	W.Belchers	157/14	Irwin
Buckelew, Fredrk.(R.S.)	Twiggs	Jefferson's	52/11	Irwin
Buckhalter, Catharine	Chatham		65/9	Hall
Buckhalter, Isaac	Pulaski	Senterfeits	403/13	Irwin
Buckhalter, John	Putnam	Slaughters	132/9	Hall
Buckhalter, John	Twiggs	Bozemans	109/11	Early
Buckhalter, Jones	Jones	Buckhalters	128/11	Irwin
Buckhalter, Michael	Jones	Buckhalters	250/16	Early
Buckhalter, Scalier	Warren	Neals'	88/10	Habersham
Buckham, Eliz.(Wid)	Washington	Cummins'	373/26	Early
Buckhannon, Amy(wid)	Richmond	Lacys	91/11	Hall
Buckhannon, James	Jasper	Bentleys	118/10	Hall
Buckhannon, Jane(Orph)	Richmond	Laceys	477/7	Irwin
Buckhannon, Mary(Wid)	Jackson	Hamiltons	518/12	Irwin

NAME	COUNTY	MIL.DIST	LOT/SECT	DREW LAND
Buckle, Caroline I.(Orph)	Richmond	120th	82/2	Habersham
Buckle, Caroline S.(Wid)	Richmond	120th	30/9	Appling
Buckley, Benjamin	Burke	M.Wards	314/27	Early
Buckner, Avria	Putnam	H.Kendricks	55/15	Early
Buckner, Benj.Sr.	Putnam	H.Kendricks	336/11	Early
Buckner, Benj.Sr.	Putnam	H.Kendricks	51/9	Irwin
Buckner, Charles(Orphs)	Putnam	H.Kendricks	366/5	Appling
Buckner, John Sr.	Putnam	Buckners	265/7	Early
Buckner, John(R.S.)	Jones	Jeffersons	184/8	Appling
Buckner, John	Putnam	H.Kendricks	94/2	Rabun
Buckner, Jos.(Orphs)	Hancock	Scotts	113/8	Irwin
Buckner, Parham	Putnam	Slaughters	104/3	Early
Buckner, Polley(Wid)	Putnam	H.Kindricks	228/4	Early
Buckner, Richmond	Putnam	H.Kindricks	60/22	Early
Buddles, William	Oglethorpe	Barnetts	9/8	Irwin
Budles, Bassett A.	Oglethorpe	Barnetts	22/3	Habersham
Buffington, Jas.	Hall	McCutchens	114/9	Appling
Buffington, Samuel	Baldwin	Marshall's	30/23	Early
Buford, John Sr.(R.S.)	Scriven	Moodys	207/5	Irwin
Buford, John(R.S.)	Scriven	Moody's	281/1	Walton
Bugg, Charlott	Richmond	Laceys	355/18	Early
Bugg, Edmund Jr.	Richmond	Laceys	130/7	Appling
Bugg, Edmund	Clarke	Deans	107/9	Irwin
Bugg, John	Chatham		310/12	Early
Bugg, Mary(Wid)	McIntosh	Eigles	132/1	Early
Bugg, Peter T.	Richmond	120th	83/5	Early
Bugg, Samuel(Younger)	Richmond	Winters	342/12	Early
Bugg, William Jr.	Richmond	Laceys	1/5	Appling
Bugg, William Sr.	Richmond	Laceys	210/18	Early
Bugg, William	Oglethorpe	Murrays	310/11	Early
Bugg, Wm.	Richmond	Winters	47/12	Irwin
Buggs, Sarah Ann(Wid)	Columbia	Gartrells	208/7	Irwin
Buie, Hector	Hancock	Justices	212/26	Early
Buie, Neal	Scriven		181/7	Early
Buie, Neil	Scriven		108/14	Early
Buis, John	Jasper	Kennedys	6/4	Early
Buis, Noah	Jones	Seals	152/3	Appling
Buley, William	Jones	Samuels	63/19	Early
Bulger, Daniel	Baldwin	Marshalls	306/14	Early
Bull, Edmond	Warren	Parhams	61/4	Rabun
Bull, Edmund	Warren	Parham's	95/8	Appling
Bull, Jacob	Twiggs	W.Belchers	139/9	Hall
Bull, John	Wilkes	Willis	365/27	Early
Bull, William	Wilkes	Willis	194/12	Early
Bullar, Jarmony G.	Jasper	Kirmedy	453/6	Irwin
Bullard, Elizabeth	Jasper	Bartletts	65/12	Irwin
Bullard, Henry	Burke	Lewis	46/19	Early
Bullard, James	Jasper	Kennedy's	174/28	Early
Bullard, James	Jasper	Kennedys	15/1	Habersham
Bullard, James	Washington	Wimberlys	251/18	Irwin
Bullard, Jesse	Jasper	Kennedys	351/5	Appling
Bullard, John Sr.	Jones	Seal's	22/10	Habersham
Bullard, John U.	Jones	Seals	26/8	Irwin
Bullard, John W.	Jones	Seals	179/4	Irwin
Bullard, John	Morgan	Hubbards	35/3	Irwin
Bullard, Temperance	Jasper	Kennedy's	193/8	Irwin
Buller, Haley	Elbert	Penns	200/2	Appling
Bullis, John	Elbert	Gaines	22/23	Early
Bulloch, Alex.G.	Madison	Adares	474/4	Appling
Bulloch, Alexr.G.	Madison	Adairs	188/3	Walton
Bulloch, James	Columbia	Watsons	202/6	Gwinnett
Bulloch, James	Columbia	Watsons	95/2	Early
Bulloch, John	Gwinnett	Hamiltons	203/3	Appling
Bullock, (Orphs)	Burke	Sullivans	316/9	Early
Bullock, Daniel(R.S.)	Twiggs	Evans'	373/1	Early
Bullock, George	Richmond	Laceys	77/8	Early
Bullock, Hardy	Oglethorpe	Bowles	250/1	Early

NAME	COUNTY	MIL.DIST	LOT/SECT	DREW LAND
Bullock, Hardy	Oglethorpe	Bowls	74/16	Irwin
Bullock, Jesse(Orphs)	Jefferson	Langstons	125/2	Irwin
Bullock, John G.	Oglethorpe	Barnetts	115/12	Early
Bullock, John J.	Chatham		290/6	Gwinnett
Bullock, John	Gwinnett		428/11	Irwin
Bullock, John	Hancock	Lucas	172/3	Habersham
Bullock, John	Twiggs	Jeffersons	245/7	Appling
Bullock, Josiah	Wilkinson	Smiths	186/2	Rabun
Bullock, Lawson	Hancock	Lucas	22/21	Early
Bullock, Mary	Oglethorpe	Barnetts	61/9	Irwin
Bullock, Richard(R.S.)	Twiggs	Jefferson's	151/10	Habersham
Bullock, Willis	Wilkinson	Lees	242/4	Irwin
Bunce, Frederick	Bulloch	Knights	315/12	Early
Bunch, Andrew	Laurens	Harris	46/12	Irwin
Bunkley, James	Warren	Rodgers	187/2	Early
Bunkley, John	Greene	144	55/13	Habersham
Bunyard, James	Jasper	Easts	192/4	Walton
Buran, Jesse(Orphs)	Hancock	Thomas	308/7	Irwin
Buran, Nancy(Wid)	Hancock	Thomas	260/6	Early
Burch, Edward	Richmond	Winters	270/8	Appling
Burch, Edward	Richmond	Winters	277/4	Irwin
Burch, Eliza(Orph)	Richmond	Winter's	490/11	Irwin
Burch, Jerard Sr.	Hancock	Lucas	387/28	Early
Burch, Joseph(Orph)	Richmond	Winters	323/11	Irwin
Burch, Mahal(Orph)	Richmond	Lacey's	341/13	Early
Burch, Mary(Wid)	Laurens	S.Smiths	370/16	Early
Burch, Michael(Orphs)	Laurens	S.Smiths	195/9	Appling
Burckhalter, Peter	Scriven		397/8	Appling
Burckstiner, Matthew	Effingham		231/9	Early
Burdell, Ferdnd.V.(Orph)	Richmond	122nd	238/2	Appling
Burdell, Robt.W.	Greene	Greers	250/4	Appling
Burden, John N.(Orph)	Elbert	B.Higginbothams	395/1	Appling
Burden, Wm.	Elbert	White/Christian Bt.	255/1	Early
Burdett, Margaret	Wilkes	Holidays	423/5	Irwin
Burdine, Jeremiah	Wilkes	Burks	265/13	Irwin
Burdock, Lysander	Richmond		406/21	Early
Burford, Margaret	Greene	Carltons	336/10	Early
Burford, Mitchel	Greene	Tuggles	156/5	Irwin
Burford, Philip H.	Oglethorpe	Barnetts	230/8	Early
Burford, Samuel	Greene	Harvills	231/1	Early
Burford, Thomas	Greene	Harvills	234/6	Gwinnett
Burgamurt, Robt.	Washington	Cummins	262/13	Early
Burgamy, John	Wilkes	Willis'	464/5	Irwin
Burgamy, Nathl.	Wilkes	Dents	104/1	Appling
Burge, John L.	Jones	Shropshiers	207/12	Irwin
Burge, John(Orphs)	Twiggs	Browns	142/9	Irwin
Burge, Mathew	Jones	Griffiths'	141/16	Early
Burge, Rebecca(Wid)	Jones	Shropshiers	314/6	Gwinnett
Burge, Winney(Wid)	Twiggs	Browns	381/2	Early
Burges, William	Jones	Griffiths	99/18	Early
Burgess, Evan	Franklin	Davis	220/13	Irwin
Burgess, Ezekiel	Franklin	Davis'	338/7	Appling
Burgess, Joel	Morgan	Selmans	481/12	Irwin
Burgess, John C.	Morgan	Loyds	285/7	Irwin
Burgess, Josiah	Laurens	Kinchens	372/3	Irwin
Burgess, Samuel	Franklin	Davis	141/3	Walton
Burk, Daniel	Wilkinson	Childs	332/7	Early
Burk, Robt.Jr.	Elbert	Smiths	306/16	Early
Burk, William	Twiggs	Brown's	416/7	Appling
Burke, Carter	Washington	Cummins	423/10	Irwin
Burke, Charles	Greene	140	338/11	Irwin
Burke, David	Scriven	180th	229/4	Walton
Burke, James	Greene	140	365/8	Early
Burke, John	McIntosh	Hamiltons	487/10	Irwin
Burke, Michael	Jefferson	Lamp's	57/12	Hall
Burke, Rebecca(Wid)	Bulloch	Knights	457/8	Irwin
Burke, Robt.Sr.	Elbert	Smiths	308/10	Early

47

NAME	COUNTY	MIL.DIST	LOT/SECT	DREW LAN
Burke, William	Twiggs	Browns	122/4	Irwin
Burke, Wm.	Wilkinson	Childs	287/18	Early
Burkes, James	Madison	Millicans	302/26	Early
Burkhalter, Isaac	Pulaski	Senterfeits	377/18	Early
Burkhalter, Jeremiah	Warren	153	128/3	Habersha
Burks, John Jr.	Clarke	Pentecosts	197/8	Early
Burks, John Sr.	Clarke	Pentecosts	31/9	Early
Burks, Nimrod	Richmond	Palmer's	29/2	Irwin
Burks, Robert	Jackson	Winters	228/28	Early
Burks, Robt.Sr.	Elbert	Smiths	160/9	Early
Burks, William	Madison	Millicans	258/9	Early
Burks, Wm.	Wilkes	Burks	369/13	Irwin
Burley, Samuel	McIntosh	Eigles	312/8	Irwin
Burman, William (Ser)	Pulaski	Davis	127/13	Habersha
Burnam, Joel	Pulaski	Davis	244/4	Early
Burnam, Wm.Sr.	Pulaski	Davis	146/7	Irwin
Burnes, Andrew	Morgan	Farrars	72/2	Irwin
Burnes, David M.	Jackson	Dicksons	36/4	Walton
Burnes, James	Washington	Jenkinsons	107/8	Appling
Burnes, John	Scriven	Roberts	121/28	Early
Burnes, Samuel T.	Wilkes	Runnels	483/6	Irwin
Burnes, Samuel	Jackson	Dicksons	469/6	Appling
Burnet, Ferey	Burke	Spiveys	308/3	Appling
Burnett, Alexander	Jones	Permenters	405/5	Appling
Burnett, Charles	Camden	Clarks	292/11	Irwin
Burnett, Christopher	Laurens	D.Smiths	256/9	Appling
Burnett, Isaac	Jones	Permenters	383/3	Appling
Burnett, James	McIntosh	Hamiltons	32/21	Early
Burnett, James	McIntosh	Hamiltons	412/11	Early
Burnett, Jane(Wid)	Jackson	Dicksons	350/8	Early
Burnett, Jeremiah	Jones	Permenters	82/4	Appling
Burnett, John Jr.	Glynn		327/15	Early
Burnett, John	Jones	Permenters	212/10	Early
Burnett, John	Jones	Permenters	285/13	Early
Burnett, Jos.(Orphs)	Jackson	Dicksons	241/11	Early
Burnett, Mariam(Wid)	Jones	Permenters	320/5	Appling
Burnett, Winston	Morgan	Knights	185/21	Early
Burnett, Zachariah(Orp)	Camden	Clarke's	392/9	Irwin
Burney, David	Glynn		366/10	Early
Burney, Green B.	Wilkinson	Lees	202/8	Early
Burney, Harriss	Washington	Burneys	240/4	Irwin
Burney, John W.	Jasper	Clays	187/13	Early
Burney, John	Bryan	19	478/5	Irwin
Burney, John	Morgan	Hackney's	18/7	Irwin
Burney, William	Glynn		307/12	Early
Burney, Wm.H.	Morgan	Farrars	11/5	Appling
Burnham, Lewis	Twiggs	Hodges	245/13	Irwin
Burnham, Thomas	Pulaski	Bryans	239/4	Walton
Burnham, William	Telfair	Williams'	381/5	Irwin
Burnley, Richmond	Warren	Rogers	289/12	Irwin
Burnley, Stephen W.	Warren	150th	95/6	Irwin
Burns, James	Twiggs	Johnstons	134/8	Early
Burns, William	Scriven	Moodys	380/15	Early
Burns, Wm.	Wilkinson	Moodys	266/8	Early
Burns, Wm.Jr.	Jackson	Dicksons	72/3	Early
Burnside, James	Baldwin	Doziers	113/27	Early
Burnside, John(Orphs)	Morgan	Loyds	21/11	Irwin
Burnside, Matthew	Columbia	Watsons	25/7	Irwin
Burnside, Thos.	Columbia	Shaws	391/18	Early
Burnside, Wm.	Bryan	19	51/11	Hall
Burnsides, Ann(Wid)	Columbia	Shaws	7/1	Appling
Burnsides, Eliz.(Wid)	Walton	Wagnons	341/6	Irwin
Burnsides, James	Bryan	19	319/9	Appling
Burnsides, John	Bryan	20	301/7	Gwinnett
Burnsides, Susanna	Chatham		158/6	Gwinnett
Burnsm, Benjamin	Pulaski	Davis	135/9	Early
Burnsm, Wm.(Sr)	Pulaski	Davis	146/7	Irwin

48

NAME	COUNTY	MIL.DIST	LOT/SECT	DREW LAND
Burrough, Henry	Jasper	Bentleys	180/7	Irwin
Burrough, Phillip	Jasper	Bentleys	66/9	Early
Burroughs, Aquilla(Orphs)	Oglethorpe	Rowlands	217/8	Appling
Burroughs, Benj.	Columbia	Burroughs	249/7	Early
Burroughs, James	Madison	Adare's	28/12	Hall
Burroughs, Raymond	Columbia	Burroughs	38/2	Rabun
Burroughs, Thos.P.	Franklin	Burroughs	232/12	Early
Burson, David	Jones	Shropshears	310/7	Gwinnett
Burson, David	Jones	Shropshiers	42/27	Early
Burson, Isaac Jr.	Jackson	Rogers	354/10	Irwin
Burson, Isaac(Orphs)	Hancock	Coopers	164/12	Early
Burson, John	Warren	152nd	250/5	Gwinnett
Burt, Anderson	Clarke	Mereweathers	158/28	Early
Burt, Anderson	Clarke	Merewether	25/11	Hall
Burt, Cornelius	Tattnall	J.Durrence	156/10	Habersham
Burt, Joseph	Putnam	Robertsons	165/6	Appling
Burt, Spencer	Putnam	H.Kindricks	413/26	Early
Burt, Zacheus	Putnam	Bustins	129/15	Irwin
Burt, Zacheus	Putnam	Bustins	26/7	Irwin
Burton, Alanson	Elbert			-
Burton, Amos	Franklin	Ashs	333/9	Appling
Burton, Benjamin	Chatham		341/7	Appling
Burton, Bins	Elbert	Childers	238/8	Early
Burton, Blackmon	Elbert	Whites/Nunnallys Bt. 187/3		Walton
Burton, Charles	Burke	M.Wards	71/5	Irwin
Burton, Charles	Effingham		14/3	Appling
Burton, Cuthbert H.	Franklin	R.Browns	132/5	Irwin
Burton, Hutchens	Franklin	Turks	72/15	Early
Burton, Jacob	Madison	Mullicans	66/1	Rabun
Burton, James M.	Clarke	Stuarts	518/13	Irwin
Burton, Jarmon(Orphs)	Elbert	Whites/Nunnallys Bt. 99/14		Irwin
Burton, Jesse	Jasper	Northcuts	200/12	Early
Burton, John(J.P.)	Franklin	R.Browns	143/2	Walton
Burton, John(J.P.)	Franklin	R.Browns	161/26	Early
Burton, John	Franklin	R.Browne	161/26	Early
Burton, John	Franklin	Turks	354/9	Irwin
Burton, John	Richmond	398th	321/3	Early
Burton, Lewis	Jones	Kings	262/7	Gwinnett
Burton, Thomas	Jasper	Hays	109/12	Early
Burton, Thos.Jr.	Elbert	Olivers	24/15	Irwin
Burton, Thos.W.	Hancock	Herberts	385/19	Early
Burton, William	Richmond	Burtons	229/2	Early
Burton, William	Richmond	Burtons	256/20	Early
Burton, Willis	Jones	Kings	401/12	Early
Burtt, Prudence	Putnam	Berrys	58/5	Irwin
Busbey, Nathaniel	Jefferson	Matthews	318/4	Early
Busby, Bartholomew A.	Liberty	21	219/6	Early
Busby, Jeremiah	Twiggs	W.Belchers	405/7	Appling
Busby, Nathan	Twiggs	W.Belchers	166/28	Early
Busby, Nimrod	Twiggs	Evans'	224/5	Appling
Bush, Andrew Jr.	Warren	Battles	91/18	Early
Bush, Andrew Sr.	Warren	Blounts	94/3	Irwin
Bush, Charles	Pulaski	Lesters	505/13	Irwin
Bush, David F.	Burke	McNorrells	135/16	Irwin
Bush, David	Franklin	Powells	401/10	Irwin
Bush, Elizabeth(Wid)	Richmond	Lacey's	132/1	Appling
Bush, Gideon	Laurens	Watsons	367/14	Early
Bush, Isaac	Twiggs	Ellis	201/13	Early
Bush, James Sr.	Pulaski	Rees	246/5	Gwinnett
Bush, James	Warren	153rd	463/6	Appling
Bush, Jasper	Oglethorpe	Wises	92/1	Appling
Bush, John(Orph)	Jones	Jeffersons	110/8	Hall
Bush, John	Bulloch	Tilmans	67/20	Early
Bush, Jordan	Pulaski	Rees	461/8	Appling
Bush, Josiah	Pulaski	Ree's	124/9	Appling
Bush, Levi	Burke	Dys	55/1	Appling
Bush, Littleberry	Richmond	122	56/3	Habersham

NAME	COUNTY	MIL.DIST	LOT/SECT	DREW LAND
Bush, Morning	Pulaski	Maddoxs	384/10	Irwin
Bush, Nathan	Burke	McNorrills	72/1	Early
Bush, Nathan	Wilkinson	Brooks'	124/15	Early
Bush, Sanders	Pulaski	Senterfeits	227/8	Early
Bush, Sarah	Burke	Thomas	92/12	Early
Bush, Thomas	Franklin	Turks	268/3	Appling
Bush, Thomas	Franklin	Turks	43/15	Early
Bush, Thomas	Warren	153	375/6	Irwin
Bush, Thomas	Warren	Hutchinsons	245/6	Early
Bush, Thos.(Orphs)	Columbia	Willingham	38/11	Early
Bush, William(Orphs)	Pulaski	Maddox'	339/2	Appling
Bush, William	Franklin	Turks	122/4	Appling
Bush, William	Franklin	Turks	335/12	Irwin
Bush, William	Laurens	Deans	171/4	Irwin
Bush, Zachariah	Laurens	Ross'	166/27	Early
Bush, Zachariah	Laurens	Ross	293/6	Appling
Bussey, Bartlett	Lincoln	Tatoms	556/2	Appling
Bussey, Malachi	Lincoln	Tatoms	137/20	Early
Bussey, Nathan	Lincoln	Graves'	4/3	Early
Bussey, Thomas	Lincoln	Graves	86/13	Habersham
Bussy, David	Putnam	Bustins	320/27	Early
Bustin, Christopher	Putnam	Bustins	54/9	Early
Bustin, Thomas	Warren	Blounts	11/4	Rabun
Butcher, Mary(Wid)	Washington	Cummins	136/14	Irwin
Butler, Barsheba(Wid)	Jones	Permenters	144/4	Appling
Butler, Charles	Jefferson	Fountains	78/15	Early
Butler, Christopher	Hall		381/26	Early
Butler, Christopher	Hall		67/9	Appling
Butler, Currey	Morgan	Parkers	380/16	Early
Butler, Curry	Morgan	Parkers	255/7	Early
Butler, Daniel	Elbert	Olivers	121/4	Early
Butler, David	Wilkes	Gordons	160/3	Irwin
Butler, Demsey	Jones	Greens	139/13	Habersham
Butler, Edward	Morgan	Hubbards	297/11	Irwin
Butler, Fanny	Hancock	Coopers	203/2	Irwin
Butler, James	Morgan	Wrights	361/17	Early
Butler, Jariah(Wid)	Clarke	Oats'	72/4	Early
Butler, Jesse	Bryan	19	206/1	Early
Butler, Joel	Wilkinson	Bowings	285/28	Early
Butler, Joel	Wilkinson	Bowlings	479/6	Irwin
Butler, John M.	Greene	Greers	114/7	Appling
Butler, John W.	Wilkes	Mattox's	304/5	Gwinnett
Butler, John W.	Wilkes	Mattox's	5/5	Habersham
Butler, John	Twiggs	Ellis	294/5	Irwin
Butler, Joseph	Pulaski	Bryans	332/26	Early
Butler, Joseph	Screven	Smiths	157/9	Early
Butler, Joseph	Screven	Smiths	166/3	Walton
Butler, Nathan	Elbert	Olivers	132/4	Irwin
Butler, Nathan	Elbert	Olivers	225/11	Early
Butler, Offerias	Bryan	19	128/2	Rabun
Butler, Patrick Jr.	Elbert	Olivers	76/6	Early
Butler, Patsey(Wid)	Wilkinson	Bowings	55/8	Appling
Butler, Richmond	Madison	Culbreaths	2/10	Early
Butler, Robert	Wilkinson	Lees	166/7	Irwin
Butler, Whitaker(Orph)	Jasper	McClendons	138/10	Early
Butler, Wm.	Wilkinson	Bowings	36/1	Walton
Butrell, Thomas	Warren	Parhams	24/11	Hall
Butridge, Jos.(R.S.)	Hancock	Edwards	49/8	Appling
Butt, Moses	Columbia	Watsons	72/13	Habersham
Butters, Robert(Orphs)	Walton	Davis'	157/2	Appling
Buttock, Benjamin	Warren	150	512/4	Appling
Buttrell, Wm.	Jasper	Clay's	409/13	Irwin
Butts, Anna	Putnam	Ectors	209/6	Appling
Butts, Anthony(Orphs)	Putnam	Ectors	128/17	Early
Butts, Edmond	Hancock	Edward	158/17	Early
Butts, Frederick	Jones	Shropshiers	291/6	Irwin
Butts, Geo.(Orphs)	Hancock	Edwards	82/4	Early

NAME	COUNTY	MIL.DIST	LOT/SECT	DREW LAND
Butts, Henry	Putnam	Little	150/12	Hall
Butts, James	Laurens	Harris	176/19	Early
Butts, James	Laurens	Harris	6/12	Habersham
Butts, John (Orphs)	Putnam	Ectors	354/19	Early
Butts, John	Jefferson	Langston	68/10	Irwin
Butts, Samuel (Orphs)	Hancock	Danells	373/7	Irwin
Butts, Sarah	Putnam	Ectors	90/6	Gwinnett
Butts, Thomas C.	Hancock	Edwards	407/13	Irwin
Butts, Wilson	Laurens	Harriss	129/21	Early
Buxton, Benjamin	Burke	Royals	385/27	Early
Buzbin, Benjamin	Oglethorpe	Barnetts	387/2	Early
Buzbin, John	Oglethorpe	Barnetts	319/5	Gwinnett
Byard, Nicholas J.	Chatham		394/27	Early
Byford, Aquilla	Madison	Adares	16/5	Early
Byford, Aquilla	Madison	Adares	327/8	Early
Byford, John	Clarke	Harriss	207/9	Irwin
Byne, Enoch	Burke	69	347/10	Early
Byne, John S.	Burke	Sullivans	68/1	Appling
Byne, Richard	Burke	Dyes	30/2	Appling
Bynum, James Sr.	Jones	Samuels	251/9	Irwin
Bynum, James	Jones	Samuels	163/6	Appling
Bynum, William	Putnam	Buckners	96/1	Rabun
Byrd, James	Hall	Byrds	15/27	Early
Byrd, Wm.D.	Hall	Byrds	395/5	Early
Byrom, Cynthia (Wid)	Jasper	Whites	191/9	Irwin
Byrom, Isabell (Wid)	Warren	Rodgers	135/1	Appling
Byrom, John S.D.	Jasper	Smiths	318/6	Early
Byron, John	Jasper	McClendons	421/13	Irwin
Byrows, John (Orphs)	Jasper	Whites	238/5	Irwin
Byrum, Wm.	Washington	Renfroes	494/13	Irwin
Cabeniss, Geo. (Orphs)	Jones	Kings	382/20	Early
Cabiness, John	Jones	Kings	44/8	Appling
Cabiness, Wm.	Jones	Shropshiers	284/2	Early
Cabos, John	Chatham		52/2	Rabun
Cade, Robt.Jr.	Wilkes	Russels	288/5	Irwin
Cade, Robt.Sr.	Wilkes	Russells	301/9	Irwin
Cadenhead, Edmund	Jones	Seals	348/8	Appling
Cadenhead, Isham	Jones	Seals	199/4	Appling
Cadenhead, Wm.	Jones	Seals	62/7	Appling
Cagburn, John A.	Putnam	Cooper's	381/8	Irwin
Caggan, William	Morgan	Knights	78/13	Habersham
Caggen, Wm.	Jasper	Baileys	46/20	Early
Caggins, John	Morgan	Wrights	360/8	Early
Cagle, Isham (Orphs)	Clarke	Moores	18/2	Habersham
Cahoun, John	Jones	Hansfords	163/6	Gwinnett
Caigle, George	Franklin	Holcomb's	272/27	Early
Cain, Abel	Richmond	Palmers	22/6	Habersham
Cain, James B.	Morgan	Walkers	30/20	Early
Cain, John	Hancock	Millers	234/2	Irwin
Cain, John	Putnam	J/Kendricks	434/13	Irwin
Cain, Nancy (Wid)	Hall		511/3	Appling
Cain, Thomas	Franklin	Powells	200/9	Irwin
Cain, William	Richmond	LAceys	279/5	Early
Cains, John (Orphs)	Jackson	Dicksons	138/10	Hall
Caits, John	Jackson	Dicksons Bt.	337/15	Early
Calahan, Martha (Wid)	Chatham		104/2	Walton
Calahan, Martha (Wid)	Chatham		188/10	Early
Calaway, Barham	Wilkes	Dents	75/5	Irwin
Calaway, Joel	Wilkes	Dents	70/4	Habersham
Calbreath, Joel	Columbia	Cliatts	95/3	Rabun
Calder, James Jr.	McIntosh	McIntosh	54/11	Habersham
Caldier, James	McIntosh	McIntosh	78/6	Appling
Caldwell, David	Jasper	Blakes	49/3	Irwin
Caldwell, Georgiana (Wid)	Chatham		287/5	Appling
Caldwell, James	Greene	144	259/2	Early
Caldwell, John	Gwinnett	Hamiltons Bt.	143/12	Early
Caldwell, Joshua	Greene	144th	144/1	Early

51

NAME	COUNTY	MIL.DIST	LOT/SECT	DREW LAND
Caldwell, Mathew	Jones	Seals	215/5	Appling
Caldwell, Matthew	Greene	Ragans	218/5	Irwin
Caldwell, Micajah	Laurens	S.Smiths	447/10	Irwin
Caldwell, Robert	Wilkinson	Brook's	280/5	Irwin
Caldwell, Simon	Jefferson	Langstons	169/21	Early
Caldwell, Wm.	Greene	144th	197/9	Early
Caldwell, Wm.	Hancock	Lucas'	310/12	Irwin
Cale, William	Screven	180th	387/20	Early
Calehan, Edward	Clarke	Applings	35/9	Irwin
Caleway, Josiah	Jones	Buckhalters	246/16	Early
Calhoon, Abraham C.	Washington	Robisons	319/13	Early
Calhoon, Anglus	Montgomery	Nobles	84/3	Irwin
Calhoon, Elbert	Baldwin	Doziers	119/28	Early
Calhoon, James	Jones	Jeffersons	89/11	Hall
Calhoon, Lydia(Wid)	Laurens	Jones	66/4	Rabun
Calhoon, Patrick	Jones	Jeffersons	131/8	Irwin
Calhoon, Samuel	Jones	Buckhalters	4/4	Walton
Calhoon, Wm.	Jefferson	Langstons	362/11	Irwin
Calhoon, Wm.	Jefferson	Langstons	493/11	Irwin
Calhoun, John Sr.	Laurens	Deans	127/9	Hall
Calhoun, Axon	Laurens	Jones	162/3	Habersham
Calhoun, James	Jones	Shropshiers	122/1	Walton
Calhoun, James	Washington	Barges	171/3	Irwin
Calhoun, John Sr.	Laurens	Deans	190/6	Irwin
Calhoun, John(Orphs)	Laurens	Jones's	267/14	Early
Caliway, Wm.(Orphs)	Putnam	Morelands	349/7	Gwinnett
Callahan, Jacob	Wilkes	Mattox	73/2	Walton
Callaway, Amasa	Wilkes	Runnels	394/7	Appling
Callaway, Elijah H.	Emanuel	59th	124/3	Appling
Callaway, Frances(Jr)	Franklin	Davis	65/6	Appling
Callaway, Francis	Franklin	Akins	267/7	Irwin
Callaway, Isaac	Madison	Orrs	49/22	Early
Callaway, Jacob	Baldwin	Taliaferro	4/11	Habersham
Callaway, John	Putnam	Brooks	87/2	Appling
Callaway, Levin	Baldwin	Ellis	365/20	Early
Callaway, Parker	Wilkes	Dents	372/7	Gwinnett
Callehan, James	Jackson	Winters Bt.	74/3	Walton
Callehan, Wm.W.	Clarke	Applings	28/8	Irwin
Callehen, John	Jackson	Winters B.	395/8	Early
Callihan, Elizabeth	Oglethorpe	Myricks	142/16	Irwin
Callis, Otto W.	Richmond	398th	109/5	Appling
Calloway, David	Wilkes	Josseys	453/10	Irwin
Calloway, Eli R.	Wilkes	Josseys	40/26	Early
Calloway, Eli R.	Wilkes	Josseys	422/11	Irwin
Calloway, Enoch	Wilkes	Brooks	194/19	Early
Calloway, John	Morgan	Parkers	137/28	Early
Calloway, Jos.H.	Wilkes	Runnels	132/26	Early
Calloway, Jos.M.	Wilkes	Jossey's	20/5	Habersham
Calloway, Luke J.	Wilkes	Brooks	168/7	Appling
Calloway, Noah	Wilkes	Dents	112/14	Early
Calloway, Noah	Wilkes	Dents	112/14	Early
Calloway, Seaborn	Wilkes	Dents	83/23	Early
Calvery, Thomas	Oglethorpe	Goolsbys	195/10	Irwin
Calvery, Thomas	Oglethorpe	Goolsbys	35/15	Early
Cambell, Nicholas	Jackson	Winters	503/8	Irwin
Cambron, Allen	Lincoln	Jones	17/18	Early
Cambron, John M.	Wilkes	Bates's	164/18	Early
Cambron, John M.	Wilkes	Bates	383/5	Appling
Camell, Robert	McIntosh	Hamiltons	155/17	Early
Cameron, Absalom	Jackson	Rogers Bt.	136/2	Early
Cameron, Jas.Sr.	Jasper	Post's	28/21	Early
Cameron, Jas.Sr.	Jasper	Posts	343/20	Early
Cammander, James	Jones	Samuels	168/13	Irwin
Camochan, John	Chatham		83/27	Early
Camp, Abner	Jackson	Hamiltons B.	83/20	Early
Camp, Abner	Jackson	Hamiltons Bt.	283/4	Appling
Camp, Alitha(Wid)	Washington	Danells	61/13	Habersham

NAME	COUNTY	MIL.DIST	LOT/SECT	DREW LAND
Camp, Benjamin	Walton	Williams	202/7	Gwinnett
Camp, Berremon	Jackson	Hamiltons	181/6	Irwin
Camp, Burrell	Walton	Greens	458/7	Irwin
Camp, Clody(Orphs)	Warren	154	160/1	Early
Camp, Henry(orph)	Warren	154th	341/16	Early
Camp, Hosea	Jackson	Rogers Bt.	60/9	Early
Camp, James(R.S.)	Gwinnett	Hamiltons Bt.	185/2	Irwin
Camp, James(R.S.)	Gwinnett	Hamiltons Bt.	200/28	Early
Camp, James(R.S.)	Gwinnett	Hamiltons Bt.	57/5	Gwinnett
Camp, John Sr.	Jackson	Rogers Bt.	120/2	Irwin
Camp, John	Warren	Herberts	315/7	Appling
Camp, Larkin	Jackson	Hamiltons B.	368/5	Irwin
Camp, Samuel	Warren	154th	9/4	Habersham
Camp, Savannah(Wid)	Franklin	J.Millers	412/3	Appling
Camp, Sterling	Jasper	Posts	67/15	Irwin
Camp, Thomas Sr.	Walton	Green's	146/15	Irwin
Camp, Thomas	Jackson	Rogers Bt.	58/5	Gwinnett
Camp, Thomas	Walton	Greens	36/5	Rabun
Camp, Thos.M.	Jackson	Hamiltons Bt.	40/3	Walton
Camp, Thos.M.	Jackson	Hamiltons	40/3	Walton
Camp, Wm.(Orphs)	Washington	Danils	274/9	Early
Camp, Wm.	Jackson	Rodgers Bt.	235/3	Early
Camp, Wm.Jr.	Jackson	Hamiltons Bt.	98/8	Early
Campagnac, Julian	Chatham		166/5	Gwinnett
Campbell, Andrew	Greene	Ragans	311/4	Appling
Campbell, Archibald	Jefferson	Abbotts	524/5	Irwin
Campbell, Archibald	Laurens	B.Smiths	121/8	Hall
Campbell, Archibald	Laurens	D.Smiths	255/5	Gwinnett
Campbell, Burwell	Washington	Broks'	305/4	Early
Campbell, Charles(Orphs)	Morgan	McClendons	329/3	Early
Campbell, Charles	Chatham		278/4	Walton
Campbell, Charter	Morgan	Towmsends	136/15	Habersham
Campbell, Charter	Morgan	Townsends	210/6	Early
Campbell, Daniel	Appling	2	484/5	Appling
Campbell, David	Telfair	Willsons	89/16	Early
Campbell, David	Wilkinson	Bowings	366/4	Early
Campbell, Duncan	Telfair	Loves	424/4	Appling
Campbell, Duncan	Telfair	Loves	79/10	Early
Campbell, Edward F.	Richmond	Laceys	178/19	Early
Campbell, Eli	Tattnall	Overstreets	271/4	Appling
Campbell, Eli	Tattnall	Overstreets	362/12	Early
Campbell, Eliz.	Early		340/27	Early
Campbell, James C.	Richmond	122nd	66/1	Walton
Campbell, James	Camden	Clarks	102/13	Early
Campbell, James	Camden	Clarks	242/3	Early
Campbell, James	Camden	Clarks	88/2	Early
Campbell, Jarrott	Jasper	Smiths	266/13	Irwin
Campbell, Jesse	Liberty		305/15	Early
Campbell, John	Appling	2nd	177/21	Early
Campbell, John	Camden	32nd	488/6	Irwin
Campbell, John	Camden	33rd	88/18	Early
Campbell, John	Jasper	Owen's	143/12	Habersham
Campbell, John	Jasper	Posts	74/4	Appling
Campbell, John	Jones	Wallers	263/21	Early
Campbell, Joseph	Wilkes	Perrys	67/28	Early
Campbell, Juhu	Twiggs	W.Belcher	155/9	Early
Campbell, Juhu	Twiggs	W.Belchers	139/8	Appling
Campbell, Levi	Richmond	Laceys	251/6	Early
Campbell, Levi	Richmond	Laceys	424/6	Appling
Campbell, Mary	Chatham		285/5	Gwinnett
Campbell, Nancy(Wid)	Jefferson	Waldens	157/2	Walton
Campbell, Robert C.	Morgan	Campbells	66/1	Appling
Campbell, Robert R.	Richmond	122	404/8	Irwin
Campbell, Walter L.	Wilkes	Ogletrees	269/27	Early
Campbell, Wm.	Hancock	Thomas'	302/8	Irwin
Campbell, Wm.	Washington	Robinsons	407/8	Early
Campbell, Wm.Sr.	Oglethorpe	Murrays	384/9	Appling

NAME	COUNTY	MIL.DIST	LOT/SECT	DREW LAN
Campbells, Jesse	Liberty		419/21	Early
Camron, Isaac	Bullock	Knights	337/5	Appling
Camron, John	Clarke	Mereweathers	14/5	Gwinnett
Can, Robert	Jackson	Winters	527/5	Irwin
Can, William	Warren	Herberts	78/5	Gwinnett
Cana, Peter	Richmond	122nd	25/9	Early
Canada, Wm.	Emanuel	Dekles	357/19	Early
Canaday, John	Bryan	19th	65/13	Irwin
Canaday, Stephen	Bryan	19th	92/19	Early
Canadell, Elnathan	Franklin	Vaughns	155/12	Early
Canady, James	Washington	Renfro's	101/3	Early
Canady, Milly(Wid)	Lincoln	Graves	76/5	Gwinnett
Candell, Elnathan	Franklin	Vaughn's	398/1	Appling
Candell, John	Franklin	Vaughans	91/5	Irwin
Candle, Joseph	Twiggs	Jamerson's	70/1	Habersha
Candle, Mathew	Twiggs	Jeffersons	50/12	Habersha
Candler, Joseph A.	Columbia	J.Morriss	61/7	Appling
Candler, Mark A.	Columbia	J.Morriss	186/3	Habersha
Candron, Marie Dorothy(Wid)	Richmond	122nd	81/13	Habersha
Cane, Agustis C.	Bullock	Edward	41/8	Appling
Cane, Elijah	Hancock	Canes	384/5	Early
Cane, John Sr.	Hancock	Canes	193/3	Appling
Caneday, David Sr.	Jones	Buckhalters	58/1	Habersha
Caneday, John A.	Jones	Kings	83/1	Habersha
Caneron, Davd.B.	Jasper	Posts	320/15	Early
Canes, William	Washington	Peabodys	245/10	Early
Cannaday, Solomon	Emanuel	59	260/4	Early
Cannady, John	Emanuel	59th	32/17	Early
Cannady, Samuel	Emanuel	59th	182/16	Early
Cannady, Solomon	Emanuel	59th	142/3	Early
Canneday, Caleb	Putnam	Mays	415/5	Irwin
Cannon, Archbd.Sr.	Bullock	Everitts	234/3	Irwin
Cannon, Bailey	Lincoln	Walker's	365/14	Early
Cannon, Eunice(Wid)	Hancock	Edwards	400/3	Appling
Cannon, Henry	Franklin	Vaughns	476/3	Appling
Cannon, Henry	Walton	Sentells	120/4	Habersha
Cannon, James	Laurens	Ross	221/6	Appling
Cannon, Jesse	Pulaski	Johnstons	292/4	Irwin
Cannon, Mathu	Pulaski	Johnston's	251/7	Gwinnett
Cannon, Miles	Wilkinson	Bowing's	104/2	Early
Cannon, Miles	Wilkinson	Bowings	371/1	Appling
Cannon, Nathaniel	Wilkinson	Bowings	165/2	Appling
Cannon, Smith	Camden	Tillis'	245/16	Early
Cannon, Spivey	Hancock	Smiths	107/1	Walton
Cannon, Thomas	Bullock	Jones	195/19	Early
Cansey, Isreal	Jefferson	Langstons	130/10	Habersha
Cantelow, B.W.	Richmond		415/21	Early
Cantelow, L.C.	Richmond	122	166/4	Irwin
Cantelow, Peter L.	Richmond	122nd	50/2	Rabun
Cantelow, Wm.B.	Richmond	122	3/1	Early
Canter, Hester(Wid)	Chatham		134/3	Habersha
Canter, Jacob	Chatham		2/7	Irwin
Canter, Ralph	McIntosh	Hamiltons	189/3	Walton
Canty, Josiah(R.S.)	McIntosh	Hamiltons	179/6	Appling
Canty, Josiah(R.S.)	McIntosh	Hamiltons	26/7	Gwinnett
Canute, Louisa(Wid)	Chatham		116/12	Early
Canyers, Bennett H.	Greene	Harvills	28/7	Appling
Cape, Brinkley	Elbert	Whites Dist.of C's 110/7		Irwin
Capehart, John	Wilkinson	Smiths	202/27	Early
Capeheart, John(R.S.)	Jones	Jeffersons	339/5	Appling
Capeheart, John(R.S.)	Jones	Jeffersons	469/13	Irwin
Capeheart, John	Jones	Jeffersons	442/4	Appling
Capple, Abraham H.	Jones	Chappels	450/12	Irwin
Car, Samuel(Orphs)	Greene	Fosters	483/7	Irwin
Car, Samuel(Orphs)	Greene	Harvills	52/3	Irwin
Caraway, John	Lincoln	Graves	188/7	Irwin
Caraway, Robert	Lincoln	Graves'	122/27	Early

NAME	COUNTY	MIL.DIST	LOT/SECT	DREW LAND
Caraway, Wm.Jr.	Lincoln	Graves'	78/1	Habersham
Carden, Charles	Elbert	Dobbs	292/1	Walton
Carden, James	Jasper	McClendons	46/1	Irwin
Carden, Jefferson(Orphs)	Pulaski	Johnstons	459/6	Appling
Carden, John	Pulaski	Johnston	278/8	Early
Carden, Leonard	Morgan	Selmans	269/3	Early
Carden, Leonard	Morgan	Selmons	229/6	Appling
Cardin, Freeman	Twiggs	Hodges'	89/4	Early
Cardin, James	Jasper	McLendon	133/2	Habersham
Cardin, James	Jasper	Sentills	450/4	Appling
Cardin, Jesse	Jasper	Centtils	338/10	Irwin
Cardin, Jesse	Pulaski	Johnstons	353/11	Irwin
Cardin, John	Jasper	Centells	271/2	Early
Cardin, John	Jasper	Centills	350/7	Gwinnett
Cardin, Wm.	Jasper	McClendons	176/1	Walton
Cardwell, John	Madison	Adares	138/18	Early
Cardwell, John	Madison	Adares	146/15	Early
Careker, Jacob	Laurens	Watsons	394/11	Irwin
Carelish, Tressa	Effingham		6/9	Early
Carew, Mary(Wid)	Hancock	Daniels	114/1	Appling
Carey, Edward	Baldwin	Marshall	377/21	Early
Carey, George	Columbia	Olives	320/12	Early
Carey, James	Franklin	Hammonds	315/11	Irwin
Carey, Vincent	Jefferson	Flemings	309/18	Early
Cargal, John N.	Gwinnett	Hamiltons Bt.	170/15	Irwin
Cargile, James	Jasper	Blakes	122/28	Early
Cargile, John Sr.	Jasper	Reids	186/20	Early
Cargile, Wm.	Jasper	Smiths	414/7	Appling
Cargile, Wm.H.	Jasper	Clays	32/12	Irwin
Carleton, Henry	Warren	154	469/11	Irwin
Carleton, Robt.W.	Morgan	Hubbards	367/6	Irwin
Carlile, John R.	Chatham		152/3	Early
Carlile, John	Jackson	Dicksons Bt.	291/11	Early
Carlisle, Benjamin	Columbia	Willinghams	413/21	Early
Carlisle, James	Jones	Phillips	20/4	Habersham
Carlisle, John B.	Jones	Phillips	52/5	Early
Carlisle, John	Telfair	Williams	341/2	Appling
Carlisle, Robert	Hall		128/1	Early
Carlisle, Robert	Hall		146/8	Hall
Carlisle, Thos.	Jones	Phillips	47/1	Irwin
Carlisle, Wm.(Orphs)	Bullock	Knights	269/17	Early
Carlisle, Wm.	Columbia	Willinghams	77/8	Irwin
Carlisle, Wm.	Wilkinson	Kettles	316/10	Irwin
Carlistle, Jas.	Jackson	Rodgers Bt.	12/21	Early
Carlton, Larkin	Greene	Carltons	311/12	Early
Carlton, Samuel	Screven	Moody's	400/17	Early
Carlton, Wm.(Orphs)	Jones	Phillips	40/23	Early
Carlwell, Samuel	Laurens	Griffins	295/12	Early
Carmean, Celia(Wid)	Hancock	Champions	32/3	Habersham
Carmichael, Duncan	Twiggs	Smiths	134/15	Irwin
Carmichael, Duncan	Twiggs	Smiths	33/3	Appling
Carmichael, John	Wilkinson	Smiths	204/7	Appling
Carmichael, Joseph	Morgan	Walkers	26/27	Early
Carmichael, Joseph	Morgan	Walkers	388/16	Early
Carmichael, Joseph	Morgan	Walkers	486/13	Irwin
Carnes, John(Orphs)	Hall	Millers	76/7	Early
Carnes, John	Wilkes	Ogletrees	13/13	Early
Carnes, Robert W.	Columbia	Walkers	12/2	Appling
Carnes, Wm.W.	Clarke	Applings	81/15	Early
Carney, Cortney(Orph)	Camden	Baileys	375/4	Early
Carnthers, Thomas	Jackson	HAmiltons Bt.	105/4	Appling
Carpenter, Absalom	Elbert	Dooleys	242/27	Early
Carpenter, John	Hancock	Thomas'	145/15	Irwin
Carpenter, John	Hancock	Thomas	33/14	Early
Carpenter, John	Lincoln	Parks'	463/12	Irwin
Carpenter, Wm.	Twiggs	Browns	388/13	Early
Carr, Allan	Pulaski	Bryans	486/6	Appling

NAME	COUNTY	MIL.DIST	LOT/SECT	DREW LAND
Carr, Benjamin	Warren	Hubberts	52/1	Habersham
Carr, Hugh	Pulaski	Rees'	20/9	Appling
Carr, Jesse	Hancock	Herberts	222/7	Irwin
Carr, Nancy	Greene	Ragans	365/9	Early
Carr, Robt.(Orphs)	Jones	Buckhalters	255/5	Early
Carr, Samuel	Elbert	White D./Chs.Bt.	29/12	Habersham
Carr, Susannah(Wid)	Bullock	Williams	145/1	Walton
Carr, Thos.D.Jr.	Columbia	J.Morris	115/2	Early
Carr, William	Twiggs	Evans	231/5	Appling
Carr, Wm.	Hall	Byrds	474/2	Appling
Carra, Peter	Richmond	122nd	365/2	Appling
Carrel, Abner	Madison	Bones	226/7	Early
Carrel, Britton	Columbia	Ob.Morris	274/19	Early
Carrel, Jesse	Wilkes	Runnels	181/13	Habersham
Carrel, Rigdon	Columbia	Ob.Morris	23/11	Hall
Carrel, Sarrah(Wid)	Jackson	Hamiltons Bt.	258/6	Early
Carrel, Wm.	Jasper	Kennedys	297/28	Early
Carrell, George	Franklin	Turk's	458/6	Irwin
Carrell, Jesse W.	Jasper	Hays	249/8	Irwin
Carrell, John(Orphs)	Putnam	Coopers	315/18	Early
Carrell, Rigdon	Columbia	O.Morris	360/6	Appling
Carrie, Joseph	Richmond	122nd	255/4	Walton
Carrington, Timothy	Madison	Orrs	240/11	Early
Carrol, Abner	Madison	Bones	466/5	Appling
Carrol, Clement	Franklin	Aikens	197/2	Early
Carrol, Clement	Franklin	Akins	509/7	Appling
Carrol, John	Jasper	Reids	104/9	Appling
Carroll, Anna	Putnam	Morland's	156/2	Habersham
Carroll, Jas.B.	Jefferson	Lamps	111/18	Early
Carroll, Roan	Jefferson	Lamps	532/2	Appling
Carroll, Thomas B.	Twiggs	Browns	47/6	Gwinnett
Carruth, Adam	Madison	Millicans	308/4	Early
Carruth, Alford	Madison	Millicans	9/1	Rabun
Carruth, Mary	Madison	Adares	63/5	Gwinnett
Cars, Isham(Orphs)	Washington	Burneys	298/20	Early
Carsey, John	Emanuel	59th	96/8	Early
Carson, Adam	Jones	Kings	210/7	Gwinnett
Carson, Adam	Jones	Kings	373/6	Irwin
Carson, David	Franklin	Harris	59/13	Irwin
Carson, David	Jones	Jefferson	479/8	Irwin
Carson, David	Jones	Jeffersons	285/6	Irwin
Carson, James	Franklin	Harris'	159/1	Walton
Carson, James	Pulaski	Maddox's	333/1	Appling
Carson, Samuel	Laurens	Ross	361/6	Appling
Carson, William	Pulaski	Maddoxs	141/26	Early
Carstarphens, Jas.(Orphs)	Putnam	Bustins	379/9	Early
Carstarven, Oran D.	Putnam	Bustins	231/10	Irwin
Carswell, Alexander	Twiggs	Ellis	402/2	Appling
Carswell, Edward	Richmond	Palmers	6/2	Early
Carswell, Samuel M.	Wilkinson	Lee's	114/16	Early
Carswell, William	Tattnall	Overstreets	38/5	Habersham
Carten, Dorothy B.	Jasper	Benleys	258/19	Early
Carten, Thos.	Jasper	Bentleys	162/11	Hall
Carter, Anthony T.	Hancock	Coopers	130/4	Walton
Carter, Candace(Wid)	Jackson	Hamiltons Bt.	189/1	Early
Carter, Charles Jr.	Oglethorpe	Lees	385/8	Early
Carter, Charles Sr.	Oglethorpe	Lees	380/13	Early
Carter, Christopher A.	Clarke	Stuarts	303/4	Walton
Carter, Collam	Jackson	Hamiltons B.	167/2	Appling
Carter, David	Hancock	Coopers	294/3	Appling
Carter, David	Liberty		150/5	Irwin
Carter, David	Tattnall	Overstreets	157/1	Irwin
Carter, David	Washington	Peabodys	26/14	Early
Carter, Elisha	Oglethorpe	Waters	39/4	Habersham
Carter, Eliz.(Orphs)	Appling	4th	493/5	Appling
Carter, Eliz.(Wid)	Wilkes	Willis's	108/3	Irwin
Carter, Eliz.	Elbert	Smiths	108/8	Appling

NAME	COUNTY	MIL.DIST	LOT/SECT	DREW LAND
Carter, Frances	Jasper	Eastes	7/5	Appling
Carter, Francis	Wilkes	Easter's	7/5	Appling
Carter, George Sr.	Tattnall	Overstreets	333/4	Walton
Carter, George Sr.	Tattnall	Overstreets	72/9	Hall
Carter, George	Tattnall	J.Durrnece	281/5	Appling
Carter, Giles Sr.	Laurens	Deans	201/26	Early
Carter, Giles	Washington	Jenkinsons	559/2	Appling
Carter, Hartwell	Hancock	Coopers	286/12	Early
Carter, Henry	Warren	Hutchinsons	46/7	Early
Carter, Isaac	Hancock	Coopers	177/12	Habersham
Carter, Isaac	Jasper	Easts	198/28	Early
Carter, Isaac	Tattnall	Overstreets	139/15	Early
Carter, Isaac	Warren	151	333/3	Appling
Carter, Jacob Sr.	Appling	2nd	246/7	Early
Carter, Jacob	Liberty		294/9	Irwin
Carter, Jacob	Morgan	Afords	85/16	Early
Carter, James F.	Emanuel	59th	32/1	Irwin
Carter, James Jr.	Warren	152	8/9	Appling
Carter, James Jr.	Warren	152nd	2/4	Appling
Carter, James M.	Richmond	120th	356/4	Early
Carter, James	Hancock	Champions	25/12	Early
Carter, James	Warren	Rodgers	194/4	Appling
Carter, Jas.A.	Jasper	Hays	335/13	Early
Carter, Jesse M.	Greene	143rd	16/20	Early
Carter, John D.	Elbert	G.Higginbothams	351/9	Appling
Carter, John T.	Hancock	Millers	416/12	Irwin
Carter, John T.	Wilkes	Holidays	139/3	Habersham
Carter, John	Chatham		96/4	Irwin
Carter, John	Jasper	Bartletts	79/8	Hall
Carter, John	Richmond	Laceys	49/9	Early
Carter, Jonathan	Putnam	Slaughters	175/8	Appling
Carter, Joseph	Appling	4	195/4	Irwin
Carter, Joseph	Jasper	Easts	33/27	Early
Carter, Kindred	Washington	Cummins	190/28	Early
Carter, Letty(Wid)	Liberty		219/2	Early
Carter, Levy H.	Clarke	Starnes	13/18	Early
Carter, Martha(Wid)	Liberty		374/12	Early
Carter, Mary	Baldwin	Irwins	383/5	Early
Carter, Mathew	McIntosh	McIntosh	363/7	Gwinnett
Carter, Mathew	McIntosh	McIntoshs	174/20	Early
Carter, Moore	Warren	152nd	407/5	Appling
Carter, Moore	Warren	152nd	53/10	Habersham
Carter, Moses(Orphs)	Warren	151	430/7	Appling
Carter, Nicholas	Chatham		168/8	Appling
Carter, Obadiah	Oglethorpe	Davenports	208/2	Early
Carter, Paul	Oglethorpe	Bridges	209/4	Walton
Carter, Richard(Orphs)	Appling	3	352/7	Appling
Carter, Richd.	Jasper	Reids	206/8	Irwin
Carter, Richd.	Jasper	Reids	21/13	Early
Carter, Robert G.	Oglethorpe	Lee's	50/4	Rabun
Carter, Robert	Oglethorpe	Brittons	360/7	Gwinnett
Carter, Samuel Sr.	Twiggs	R.Belchers	235/3	Appling
Carter, Samuel(R.S.)	Twiggs	W.Belcher	378/8	Irwin
Carter, Samuel(R.S.)	Twiggs	W.Belchers	102/10	Habersham
Carter, Samuel	Twiggs	Smiths	61/7	Gwinnett
Carter, Sarah(Wid)	Clarke	Otis	82/27	Early
Carter, Sterling	Wilkes	Willis	148/14	Irwin
Carter, Thomas P.	Elbert	G.Higginbotham	60/4	Walton
Carter, Thomas(Orphs)	Putnam	H.Kendricks	320/1	Early
Carter, Thomas	Oglethorpe	Barnett	148/7	Early
Carter, Thos.S.	Elbert	Penn's	296/17	Early
Carter, William	Oglethorpe	Lees	179/3	Early
Carter, Wm.	Oglethorpe	Lees	377/11	Irwin
Carter, Wm.H.	Wilkes	Gordons	73/2	Early
Carter, Wm.R.	Elbert	Dobb's	226/1	Early
Carters, John A.	Jasper	Reids	46/5	Appling
Cartledge, James	Columbia	Willinghams	71/12	Habersham

NAME	COUNTY	MIL.DIST	LOT/SECT	DREW LAN
Cartledge, James	Twiggs	Elis	61/3	Appling
Cartledge, James	Twiggs	Ellis	122/7	Irwin
Cartledge, John	Columbia	Pullins	89/14	Irwin
Cartrigh, Jonas	Greene	143rd	56/6	Habersha
Caruthers, James	Jackson	Hamiltons Bt.	286/6	Gwinnett
Caruthers, Robt.	Jones	Burkhalter's	122/3	Irwin
Caruthers, Saml.L.	Jasper	Baileys	28/2	Rabun
Caruthers, Samuel	Jackson	Hamiltons Bt.	78/12	Hall
Caruthers, Thos.	Jones	Buckhalters	98/1	Walton
Caruthers, Thos.	Jones	Burkhalters	34/7	Early
Carver, James(Orphs)	Telfair	Loves	71/7	Gwinnett
Carver, Samuel	Telfair	Loves	287/8	Early
Carver, William	Montgomery	Noble's	273/5	Appling
Cary, Catharine	Chatham		197/4	Irwin
Cary, George	Columbia	Olives	155/11	Early
Cary, Jesse(orphs)	Laurens	Harris's	90/1	Irwin
Cary, Lucy(Wid)	Clarke	Applings	245/12	Irwin
Cary, Mary(Orph)	Laurens	S.Smiths	31/4	Walton
Cary, Vincent	Jefferson	Flemings	1/3	Early
Casey, Daniel(R.S.)	Elbert	Webb's	209/12	Irwin
Casey, Daniel(R.S.)	Elbert	Webbs	124/7	Irwin
Casey, Daniel(R.S.)	Elbert	Webbs	414/3	Appling
Casey, Elisha	Walton	Williams	395/10	Irwin
Casey, John A.	Chatham		18/7	Early
Cash, Geo.B.	Jackson	Winters Bt.	195/13	Habersha
Cash, Howard	Franklin	Flanagans	67/23	Early
Cash, James	Jackson	Winters	69/3	Walton
Cash, John(Orphs)	Liberty		270/6	Early
Cash, Moses	Elbert	Gaines	342/16	Early
Cash, Moses	Elbert	Gains	292/18	Early
Cash, Nelson	Elbert	Gaines	228/6	Gwinnett
Cash, Patrick	Jackson	Winters Bt.	213/3	Walton
Cason, Canon	Tattnall	Overstreets	98/14	Early
Cason, Dennis	Tattnall	Overstreets	357/21	Early
Cason, Edward	Elbert	Doolys	167/8	Early
Cason, Henry	Screven		402/10	Irwin
Cason, Henry	Washington	Robisons	263/3	Appling
Cason, Hillary	Screven		133/4	Appling
Cason, Jas.Kinnion(Orph)	Bryan	19th	313/4	Walton
Cason, John	Washington	Robinson's	309/19	Early
Cason, Labon(Orph)	Laurens	Dean's	443/11	Irwin
Cason, Mary(Orph)	Bryan	19th	313/4	Walton
Cason, May(Orph)	Bryan	19th	313/4	Walton
Cason, Samuel	Tattnall	Overstreets	178/3	Early
Cason, Willis	Bryan	19th	150/4	Irwin
Cason, Willouby	Bryan	19th	444/6	Appling
Cassy, Joel	Hall	Simmonds	76/2	Rabun
Castalow, James	Washington	Avents	101/3	Irwin
Castalow, Wm.	Washington	Avents	36/1	Rabun
Castellaw, Thomas	Oglethorpe	Goolsby's	411/6	Irwin
Castens, Mary(Wid)	Richmond	122nd	77/4	Walton
Castleberry, Asa	Morgan	Hubbards	384/13	Irwin
Castleberry, David Jr.	Jackson	Hamiltons Bt.	497/8	Irwin
Castleberry, David Sr.	Jackson	Hamiltons B.	362/21	Early
Castleberry, Edw.	Jasper	Posts	144/3	Walton
Castleberry, Elisha	Hancock	Mims	112/12	Habersha
Castleberry, Henry	Telfair	Williams	121/20	Early
Castleberry, Henry	Telfair	Williams	151/10	Early
Castleberry, James	Jackson	Hamiltons Bt.	18/7	Appling
Castleberry, Jeremiah	Putnam	Evans	203/17	Early
Castleberry, Job	Hancock	Mims	311/13	Early
Castleberry, John	Hancock	Mims	24/19	Early
Castleberry, John	Twiggs	Jefferson's	19/4	Irwin
Castleberry, Martha(Wid)	Jackson	Hamiltons Bt.	280/27	Early
Castleberry, Mary(Wid)	Warren	Blounts	136/2	Habersha
Castleberry, R. (Orphs)	Hancock	Mimms	104/6	Early
Castleberry, Thos.	Baldwin	Stephens	7/13	Habersha

58

NAME	COUNTY	MIL.DIST	LOT/SECT	DREW LAND
Castleberry, Thos.	Jackson	Hamiltons B.	82/15	Early
Castleberry, Thos.	Jackson	Hamiltons	393/4	Appling
Castleberry, Timothy	Warren	154th	513/6	Appling
Castleberry, Warren T.	Jasper	Post's	147/5	Irwin
Castlebury, William	Telfair	Williams	339/14	Early
Castles, Absolum	Morgan	Loyd's	161/10	Hall
Caswell, Alexander	Telfair	William's	143/16	Early
Caswell, James	Tattnall	Overstreets	170/20	Early
Caswell, Martin	Bullock	Jones	206/4	Irwin
Caswell, Mathew	Putnam	J.Kindricks	72/21	Early
Cate, Thos.(R.S.)	Jackson	Hamiltons B.	102/13	Habersham
Cates, Charles	Franklin	Harris	301/10	Irwin
Cates, Charles	Jasper	Phillips	3/11	Hall
Cates, Jas.(Orphs)	Jasper	Phillips	131/8	Early
Cates, Richard	Jasper	Posts	177/18	Early
Catlett, William	Montgomery	Alston's	260/9	Appling
Cato, George	Wilkinson	Wiggins	171/18	Early
Cato, William	Laurens	Harriss	1/14	Irwin
Caton, John D.	Jones	Shropshiers	387/4	Appling
Cattelhead, Thos.(Orphs)	Telfair	Loves	31/5	Early
Caulden, Robert(Orph)	Telfair		58/12	Habersham
Caulie, John	Jefferson	Bothwells	306/27	Early
Causey, James	Wayne	Crews	180/15	Early
Causey, John	Jefferson	Fountains	91/9	Early
Caven, Alexander	Hall		340/7	Irwin
Caven, Forgus	Jackson	Dicksons B.	385/12	Irwin
Caven, William	Hall		107/13	Habersham
Caven, William	Hall		300/4	Early
Cavenah, George	Baldwin	Ellis'	53/9	Hall
Cavenah, George	Baldwin	Ellis	71/2	Early
Cavender, Eleaner	Clarke	Appling's	21/4	Rabun
Caver, Jacob	Lincoln	Jeters	422/7	Irwin
Cavin, Alexander	Hall		309/2	Appling
Cawly, Robert	Putnam	Tomlinsons	126/3	Appling
Cawpuld, Charles H.	Chatham		27/4	Early
Cawthon, Chas.	Franklin	Attaways	39/23	Early
Cawthon, Jesse	Wilkes	Kilgores	26/9	Appling
Cawthon, John C.	Franklin	Attaways	236/8	Irwin
Cawthon, John C.	Franklin	Attaways	363/7	Irwin
Cawthon, Larkin	Franklin	P.Browns	240/13	Irwin
Cawthon, William	Laurens	Griffins	360/6	Irwin
Cawthon, Wm.	Franklin	P.Browns	142/3	Irwin
Cawthorn, Chas.	Franklin	Attaways	17/15	Early
Cawthren, John	Morgan	Hackney's	83/7	Irwin
Cawthren, Thomas	Morgan	Hackneys	126/1	Appling
Cerbo, James	Hall		211/12	Habersham
Cessna, Robert B.	Morgan	Campbells	189/13	Early
Cetchens, Stephen	Franklin	Morris	19/13	Habersham
Chadwick, Benj.	Jones	Permenters	133/17	Early
Chaffin, Isam	Wilkes	Ogletrees	192/13	Early
Chaffin, John	Jasper	Posts	18/10	Habersham
Chaffin, Lemuel	Morgan	Wrights	295/16	Early
Chaffin, Leonard	Wilkes	Ogletrees	192/8	Irwin
Chafin, Joshua Sr.	Jasper	Posts	199/8	Early
Chaiffin, Lemuel	Morgan	Wrights	105/16	Irwin
Chain, Isiah(Sr.(Orphs)	Twiggs	R.Belchers	76/16	Early
Chain, Wm.L.	Hancock	Loyds	491/5	Appling
Chaine, Isiah	Twiggs	R.Belchers	248/9	Appling
Chairs, Benjamin	Pulaski	Davis	258/10	Early
Chairs, Benjamin	Pulaski	Davis	84/4	Appling
Chalker, Hodges	Warren	150	303/16	Early
Chalker, Hodges	Warren	150th	33/5	Habersham
Chalker, Nathaniel	Warren	150	412/4	Early
Chalmers, Eliz.(Wid)	Franklin	J.Millers	304/7	Gwinnett
Chalmers, Isaac	Franklin	J.Miller	452/7	Irwin
Chalmers, John	Franklin	John Millers	28/15	Irwin
Chalmers, Wm.	Franklin	John Millers	59/8	Irwin

NAME	COUNTY	MIL.DIST	LOT/SECT	DREW LAN
Chambers, Dicy(Wid)	Warren	151st	434/9	Irwin
Chambers, Edwin	Putnam	Oslin's	171/10	Irwin
Chambers, Joel(Orphs)	Warren	151	33/4	Habersha
Chambers, John	Jefferson	Fountains	434/8	Irwin
Chambers, Jos.	Jones	Chappels	117/7	Appling
Chambers, Joseph	Jones	Chappels	247/27	Early
Chambers, Prudence	Wilkes	Davis'	77/14	Early
Chambless, Edw.(Son/Zach)	Baldwin	Stephens	113/12	Hall
Chambless, Ephraim	Bullock	Knights	508/3	Appling
Chambless, Henry	Bryan	19th	98/5	Gwinnet
Chambless, John	Baldwin	Stephens	66/23	Early
Chambless, John	Jones	Permenters	332/11	Early
Chambless, Littleton	Jones	Permenters	247/13	Irwin
Chambless, Thomas	Wilkinson	Wiggins	242/7	Early
Chambless, Wm.	Jones	Wallers	13/7	Early
Chambless, Wm.	Jones	Wallers	195/5	Early
Chamley, Washington	Jackson	Hamiltons Bt.	23/7	Appling
Champin, Littleberry	Jones	Seal's	177/8	Irwin
Champion, Abner	Putnam	Tomlinsons	363/27	Early
Champion, Abner	Putnam	Tomlinsons	502/11	Irwin
Champion, Alexr.(Orphs)	Putnam	Oslins	204/6	Early
Champion, Eli	Jasper	Hays	152/26	Early
Champion, Elias F.	Laurens	Watson's	525/7	Appling
Champion, Henry Sr.	Greene	142	95/12	Habersha
Champion, Henry Sr.	Greene	142nd	134/7	Irwin
Champion, Henry	Hancock	Champions	33/23	Early
Champion, Jesse	Jasper	Hays	114/4	Appling
Champion, Jesse	Jasper	Hays	34/9	Appling
Champion, John Jr.	Warren	150	117/7	Gwinnett
Champion, John(Orphs)	Hancock	Lucas'	23/10	Early
Champion, John	Jefferson	Mathews	78/14	Irwin
Champion, Mary(Wid)	Laurens	Watsons	211/5	Irwin
Champion, Micajah	Laurens	Harris	293/2	Early
Champion, Micajah	Laurens	Harris	401/2	Appling
Champless, Joseph	Warren	McCrareys	349/4	Appling
Chance, James	Pulaski	Davis	372/2	Early
Chancellor, Levi W.	Chatham		52/8	Early
Chancellor, Levi W.	Chatham		98/3	Rabun
Chancey, Asa	Camden	Tillis'	121/10	Hall
Chancey, John	Jones	Wallers	507/9	Irwin
Chancey, Thos.B.	Morgan	Talbotts	290/7	Appling
Chancey, William	Morgan	Selmons	64/2	Walton
Chancey, Wm.	Morgan	Selmon's	347/5	Appling
Chancy, Aquilla	Morgan	Talbots	148/27	Early
Chancy, John	Morgan	Talbots	519/5	Appling
Chandler, Abraham	Morgan	Townsends	120/3	Early
Chandler, Allan	Franklin	Ash's	272/2	Early
Chandler, Green	Madison	Millicans	176/16	Irwin
Chandler, Henry F.	Franklin	Davis'	64/5	Appling
Chandler, Hezekiah	Franklin	Aikins	30/1	Irwin
Chandler, Isaac	Jackson	Rogers Bt.	398/26	Early
Chandler, Isaac	Jackson	Rogers	162/9	Appling
Chandler, John A.	Franklin	Burroughs	69/7	Early
Chandler, Levi(Alt/1824)	Chatham		52/8	Early
Chandler, Levi(Alt/1824)	Chatham		98/3	Rabun
Chandler, Parkes	Jackson	Rogers' B.	58/19	Early
Chandler, Richardson	Madison	Millicans	185/2	Early
Chandler, Richd.	Franklin	Akin's	140/10	Early
Chandler, Shadrick(Orphs)	Franklin	Ash's	268/11	Irwin
Chandler, Solomon	Jackson	Winters Bt.	94/10	Hall
Chandler, Starling	Franklin	Ash's	360/7	Appling
Chandler, Starling	Franklin	Ashes	344/10	Early
Chandler, Wyatt	Franklin	Ashs	54/2	Appling
Chandler, Zachariah	Franklin	Harriss	162/12	Irwin
Chaney, James	Montgomery	McElvins	241/12	Irwin
Channel, Harmon	Putnam	May's	70/2	Habersha
Channel, John Sr.	Greene	Kimbroughs	283/26	Early

NAME	COUNTY	MIL.DIST	LOT/SECT	DREW LAND
Channing, Mary	Glynn		8/7	Gwinnett
Chapel, John H.	Hancock	Thomas'	15/7	Appling
Chapel, Joseph(Orphs)	Hancock	Danel's	69/4	Appling
Chapman, Abner Jr.	Jasper	Baileys	4/5	Habersham
Chapman, Abner	Putnam	Slaughters	109/3	Early
Chapman, Asa	Warren	Griers	29/9	Early
Chapman, Berry S.	Baldwin	Taliaferro	154/7	Appling
Chapman, Britton W.(Orphs)	Jasper	Clays	150/1	Early
Chapman, Bryant	Wilkes	Bryants	5/20	Early
Chapman, Francis J.	Liberty		366/1	Appling
Chapman, Greenberry(Orphs)	Wilkes	Ogletrees	8/18	Early
Chapman, Hanner	Greene	Armers	56/9	Appling
Chapman, Isaiah	Baldwin	Taliaferros	234/10	Irwin
Chapman, Jane(Wid)	Wilkes	Ogletrees	239/4	Irwin
Chapman, Jesse	Twiggs	Ellis	73/28	Early
Chapman, John	Jasper	Ryans	4/12	Irwin
Chapman, John	Putnam	Slaughters	250/8	Irwin
Chapman, John	Twiggs	Ellis	393/6	Irwin
Chapman, Laborn(Orphs)	Greene	Armers	29/14	Early
Chapman, Robt.C.	Twiggs	R.Belchers	283/8	Irwin
Chapman, Robt.H.	Warren	Greens	57/2	Rabun
Chapman, Samuel	Jones	Perminters	18/18	Early
Chapman, Sanford	Jones	Philips	313/7	Early
Chappel, Allen	Greene	Tuggles	277/7	Appling
Chappel, Benjamin	Putnam	May's	215/11	Early
Chappel, James	Jones	Buckhalters	27/13	Irwin
Chappel, James	Jones	Buckhalters	380/8	Early
Chappel, Robert	Morgan	Hackneys	174/13	Early
Chappel, Wiley	Jones	Chappels	61/6	Early
Chappell, Benjamin	Putnam	Mays	260/10	Irwin
Chappell, George	Walton	Williams	198/12	Early
Chappell, George	Walton	Williams	420/2	Appling
Chappell, Obadiah	Jackson	Rogers Bt.	219/26	Early
Chappell, Thomas S.	Twiggs	Jamisons	467/4	Appling
Charles, Reuben	Chatham		333/8	Early
Charleton, Jno.	Effingham		252/2	Early
Charlton, John K.M.	Wilkes	Gordons	468/6	Appling
Charrier, Joseph	Chatham		147/1	Early
Chasteen, Blassergain	Washington	Burneys	159/13	Habersham
Chasteen, Martin	Washington	Burney's	60/13	Habersham
Chasteen, Peter	Washington	Burneys	148/1	Early
Chasteen, Ramey	Washington	Burneys	153/11	Early
Chasteen, Raney	Washington	Burneys	109/11	Irwin
Chatfield, George	Morgan	Hubbards	345/11	Irwin
Chatfield, John	Jasper	Centells	94/13	Habersham
Chatham, Chaffin	Franklin	Hammonds	246/5	Appling
Chatham, Chaffin	Franklin	Hammonds	322/16	Early
Cheatham, Anthony R.	Jefferson	Flemings	106/3	Irwin
Cheatham, Arthur	Jefferson	Flemmings	346/11	Irwin
Cheatham, Chas.	Jefferson	Abbotts	60/18	Early
Cheatham, John	Jefferson	Walden's	206/4	Early
Cheatham, Thos.	Greene	Harvills	36/10	Habersham
Cheathan, Thomas	Greene	Harville	188/5	Irwin
Cheek, Isaiah	Elbert	White & Christian	270/11	Irwin
Cheeley, Thomas	Hancock	Smiths	41/8	Irwin
Cheely, John	Hancock	Smiths	2/1	Early
Cheely, Thomas	Hancock	Smiths	155/14	Irwin
Cheetam, Amelia	Oglethorpe	Barnetts	108/1	Irwin
Cheetham, Isham	Oglethorpe	Barnetts	74/1	Rabun
Chenault, John	Columbia	Walkers	64/10	Early
Chesher, Turpin	Baldwin	Cousins	257/5	Appling
Cheshers, Wm.(Orphs)	Baldwin	Cousins	146/2	Rabun
Chesser, John T.	Morgan	Alfords	141/6	Irwin
Chesser, Wm.(Orphs)	Morgan	Alfords	264/13	Early
Chester, Abner	Washington	Jenkinsons	464/7	Irwin
Chester, Martin(Br)	Wilkinson	Brooks	199/10	Early
Chevers, James	Wilkes	Mattox	403/1	Appling

NAME	COUNTY	MIL.DIST	LOT/SECT	DREW LAND
Cheves, Thos.(Orphs)	Putnam	Coppers	209/19	Early
Chew, John	Greene	143	26/8	Early
Chewer, Stephen	Jones	Roper	72/7	Early
Chick, Anderson	Madison	Orrs	115/17	Early
Chieves, James	Putnam	Coopers	60/1	Appling
Childers, Isaac	Twiggs	Jefferson	360/10	Early
Childers, John	Twiggs	Browns	202/11	Irwin
Childers, William	Twiggs	Jeffersons	112/12	Irwin
Childers, William	Twiggs	Thames	388/28	Early
Childers, Wm.	Hancock	Champions	439/4	Appling
Childre, Thomas	Twiggs	Evans	104/7	Irwin
Childres, Holman	Elbert	Olivers	196/12	Habersham
Childres, John B.	Hancock	Gilberts	11/5	Gwinnett
Childres, John	Elbert	Childres	27/9	Appling
Childres, Wm.(Orph)	Twiggs	Jefferson's	293/9	Appling
Childress, Edmund	Lincoln	Tatoms	392/18	Early
Childrey, Drury	Wilkinson	Bowings	123/4	Walton
Childrey, Drury	Wilkinson	Bowings	161/8	Early
Childrs, George	Jones	Permenters	171/6	Gwinnett
Childs, Elijah	Elbert	Childres	352/12	Irwin
Childs, Jeremiah	Wilkinson	Lees	122/19	Early
Childs, Mathew	Jones	Buckhalters	238/6	Appling
Childs, Nathan(Orphs)	Wilkes	Josseys	285/2	Appling
Childs, Nimrod(Orphs)	Hancock	Evans	322/5	Appling
Childs, Seaborn	Elbert	Childres	364/9	Irwin
Chiles, Isaac(Orph)	Washington	Barges	82/13	Irwin
Chiles, James	Jones	Seals	106/15	Early
Chiles, John E.	Jones	Seals	225/7	Irwin
Chiles, John Jr.	Jones	Seals	270/20	Early
Chiles, John Sr.	Jones	Seals	271/4	Early
Chiles, John Sr.	Jones	Seals	85/1	Walton
Chiles, Jonathan	Jackson	Hamiltons Bt.	77/11	Habersham
Chiles, Nathan Jr.	Jones	Seals	239/8	Early
Chiles, Nathan	Jones	Seals	531/2	Appling
Chiles, Thos.M.	Jones	Seals	242/23	Early
Chiles, Wm.J.	Jones	Seals	58/14	Irwin
Chilibres, John(Orph)	Wilkinson	Bowings	73/7	Irwin
Chipman, Joseph	Elbert	Smiths	45/17	Early
Chipman, Joseph	Elbert	Smiths	75/1	Rabun
Chisolm, Thos.A.	Morgan	Alfords	422/10	Irwin
Chisolum, Edmond B.	Laurens	Harriss	327/6	Irwin
Chittey, John(Orphs)	Twiggs	R.Belchers	399/21	Early
Chitty, James	Twiggs	Smiths	2/7	Gwinnett
Chitty, Sarah(Wid)	Twiggs	R.Belchers	158/5	Irwin
Chitwood, Daniel	Franklin	Flannigans	158/5	Early
Chivers, Joel(Orphs)	Wilkes	Mattoxs	252/19	Early
Chivers, Joel	Twiggs	R.Belchers	135/13	Early
Chivers, Nancy(Wid)	Washington	Manning	116/3	Irwin
Chivers, Robert	Wilkes	Willis	314/10	Early
Choice, Wm.	Hancock	Edwards'	69/3	Early
Cholston, Leonard B.	Madison	Orrs	78/7	Gwinnett
Chonoway, Chas.	Laurens	Ross'	8/13	Habersham
Chrissup, Fletcher	Hancock	Scotts	116/16	Irwin
Christian, Abda(Orphs)	Columbia	Shaws	346/28	Early
Christian, Chas.	Baldwin	Marshals	7/1	Habersham
Christian, Chas.W.	Elbert	Webbs	76/15	Irwin
Christian, Drury	Franklin	Harris	391/26	Early
Christian, Gabriel	Oglethorpe	Lees	209/5	Irwin
Christian, Isaac	Elbert	R.Christians	205/4	Irwin
Christian, Isaac	Elbert	R.Christians	248/4	Appling
Christian, John	Elbert	Penns	217/14	Early
Christian, John	Elbert	Penns	258/13	Irwin
Christian, Obed M.(Orphs)	Madison	Millicans	198/19	Early
Christian, Presley	Elbert	P.Christian	6/23	Early
Christian, Robt.B.	Elbert	R.Christians	16/3	Appling
Christian, Rufus	Elbert	P.Christians	81/5	Gwinnett
Christian, Rufus	Elbert	R.Christians	97/14	Early

NAME	COUNTY	MIL.DIST	LOT/SECT	DREW LAND
Christian, Simeon	Madison	Willifords	15/20	Early
Christian, Turner H.	Elbert	Webb's	109/13	Early
Christian, Turner(R.S.)	Elbert	Webbs	141/28	Early
Christian, Wm.	Hall		318/4	Appling
Christian, Wm.B.	Elbert	R.Christians	110/3	Walton
Christie, Allen	Hancock	Smiths	360/11	Irwin
Christie, Josiah A.	Hancock	Mims	279/26	Early
Christie, Nathan	Jefferson	Matthews	99/10	Irwin
Christler, Blantern	Elbert	B.Higginbothams	251/4	Irwin
Christler, Jalius	Elbert	B.Higginbothams	406/5	Appling
Christler, Simeon	Elbert	B.Higginbothams	81/4	Early
Christopher, Eliz.(Wid)	Greene	140th	50/17	Early
Christopher, Spencer	Liberty		479/3	Appling
Church, Alanzo	Clarke	Applings	163/4	Irwin
Church, Alanzo	Clarke	Applings	78/5	Appling
Church, Benjamin	Franklin	Morris	191/9	Appling
Church, Benjamin	Franklin	Morris	95/28	Early
Church, Constantine	Wilkes	Gordans	45/28	Early
Church, Constantine	Wilkes	Turners	104/10	Irwin
Church, Silvanus	Camden	Clarks	244/26	Early
Church, Silvanus	Camden	Clarks	296/4	Irwin
Churchwell, Henry	Twiggs	R.Belchers	233/12	Irwin
Cicaty, Augustin D.	Laurens	Harris'	451/20	Early
Cile, Ann & Eliz.(Orphs)	Chatham		518/10	Irwin
Circy, Eliz.(Wid)	Wilkinson	Bowings	66/7	Early
Citchen, Jos.(Orphs)	Greene	Fosters	99/12	Habersham
Claghorn, James	Hall	Millers	71/9	Early
Claiborn, Robt.(Orphs)	Richmond	122	206/6	Irwin
Clanton, Christian(Wid)	Bryan	19th	29/10	Irwin
Clanton, Daniel	Bullock	Knights	58/9	Appling
Clanton, Holt	Columbia	Burroughs	224/13	Irwin
Clanton, Littleberry	Columbia	Walker's	333/1	Early
Clanton, Littleberry	Columbia	Walkers	257/28	Early
Clanton, Samuel	Bryan	19th	382/12	Irwin
Clapp, John	Greene	143	491/8	Irwin
Clark, (Orphans)	McIntosh	Jenkins	226/13	Irwin
Clark, Christphr.Jr.	Elbert	Olivers	208/12	Irwin
Clark, Eli	Jones	Chappels	299/9	Irwin
Clark, Hannah	Wilkes	Russells	57/2	Irwin
Clark, James	McIntosh	Eigles	460/13	Irwin
Clark, James	Morgan	Leonards	163/2	Early
Clark, Jesse	Wilkes	Burks	154/10	Early
Clark, John D.	Gwinnett	Hamiltons Bt.	142/1	Irwin
Clark, John D.	Gwinnett	Hamiltons Bt.	259/2	Appling
Clark, Joshua P.	Jones	Harriss	65/3	Walton
Clark, Joshua(Orphs)	Montgomery	McElvins	72/6	Gwinnett
Clark, Joshua	Elbert	P.Christians	186/12	Irwin
Clark, Nathan	Montgomery	Noble's	164/27	Early
Clark, Nathan	Montgomery	Nobles	286/11	Irwin
Clark, Nathaniel	Richmond	Laceys	110/10	Irwin
Clark, Samuel	Camden	Clarks	339/10	Early
Clark, Solomon W.G.	Laurens	Harris's	378/3	Early
Clark, Thomas	Chatham		125/18	Early
Clark, Thomas	Chatham		186/13	Irwin
Clark, Thomas	Franklin	Akins	59/3	Early
Clark, William	Hancock	Smiths	75/4	Walton
Clark, Williamson	Elbert	Whites D.of Chs.B.	289/1	Early
Clark, Wm.	Franklin	Akins	82/1	Early
Clark, Wm.P.	Chatham		46/18	Early
Clarke, Aaron	Twiggs	Evans'	161/8	Irwin
Clarke, Alfred	Baldwin	Russells	376/8	Irwin
Clarke, Benj.C.	Columbia	Burroughs	108/18	Early
Clarke, David	Elbert	Olivers	52/12	Early
Clarke, Francis	Chatham		418/21	Early
Clarke, James Jr.	Greene	Wheelis	318/20	Early
Clarke, James	Elbert	Ruckers	388/27	Early
Clarke, James	Jefferson	Abbotts	144/13	Irwin

NAME	COUNTY	MIL.DIST	LOT/SECT	DREW LAN
Clarke, James	McIntosh	Eigles	255/3	Irwin
Clarke, James	Twiggs	Smiths	107/5	Appling
Clarke, Jas.Jr.	Greene	Wheelis	80/6	Gwinnett
Clarke, Jas.Sr.	Greene	Wheelis	164/8	Irwin
Clarke, Jesse	Wilkes	Burks	305/2	Appling
Clarke, John A.	Richmond	122nd	81/26	Early
Clarke, John(Orphs)	Jones	Permenters	8/8	Early
Clarke, John	Franklin	Burroughs	240/5	Irwin
Clarke, John	Greene	144th	187/1	Appling
Clarke, John	Greene	144th	37/8	Appling
Clarke, John	Gwinnett	Hamiltons Bt.	226/1	Walton
Clarke, John	Hancock	Scotts	264/4	Irwin
Clarke, John	Jones	Permenters	138/14	Irwin
Clarke, John	Richmond	Palmers	2/13	Irwin
Clarke, John	Warren	Parhams	106/16	Early
Clarke, Lewis	Montgomery	Nobles	138/1	Irwin
Clarke, Mark D.	Richmond	120th	245/26	Early
Clarke, Mary(Wid)	Jefferson	Abbots	110/9	Irwin
Clarke, Michael N.	Richmond	Burtons	40/13	Irwin
Clarke, Samuel	Chatham		177/8	Appling
Clarke, Samuel	Jasper	Northcuts	191/17	Early
Clarke, Samuel	Jefferson	Abbotts	8/4	Appling
Clarke, Samuel	Wilkinson	Lees	187/5	Early
Clarke, Sarah	Lincoln	Jones	308/7	Early
Clarke, Thomas	Laurens	Harris	446/4	Appling
Clarke, Thos.	Jefferson	Lamps	344/7	Early
Clarke, Thos.Jr.	Putnam	Buckners	270/12	Irwin
Clarke, Thos.Sr.	Putnam	Buckners	6/28	Early
Clarke, William	Twiggs	Hodges	69/12	Irwin
Clarke, Williamson	Elbert	White & Christians	196/3	Irwin
Clarke, Wm.(Carpenr.)	Jefferson	Lamps	277/4	Walton
Clarke, Wm.(Orphs)	Warren	Parhams	99/17	Early
Clarke, Wm.	Jasper	Kennedys	103/2	Rabun
Clarke, Wm.	Jefferson	Lamps	387/1	Early
Clarke, Wm.C.W.	Richmond	122	29/16	Early
Clarke, Wm.P.	Chatham		428/5	Irwin
Clarke, Zachariah	Franklin	Burroughs	8/19	Early
Clarkson, John	Franklin	Ashs	445/5	Irwin
Clary, David	Jackson	Rogers Bt.	43/27	Early
Clary, David	Jackson	Rogers Bt.	94/28	Early
Clary, Saml/(Orph)	Effingham		275/4	Walton
Clary, Upton	Laurens	Watsons	181/2	Irwin
Claton, Middleton	Gwinnett	Hamiltons Bt.	144/3	Irwin
Clay, Adam	Wilkinson	Howards	515/2	Appling
Clay, Charles	Columbia	Willinghams	370/4	Appling
Clay, David(Orphs)	Wilkinson	Howards	364/28	Early
Clay, Jesse F.	Jasper	Clay's	341/8	Appling
Clay, Jesse Jr.	Jasper	Clay's	120/20	Early
Clay, Jesse	Columbia	Willinghams	104/12	Irwin
Clay, Jesse	Columbia	Willinghams	342/6	Early
Clay, Pearce	Wilkinson	Howards	7/20	Early
Clay, Robert	Wilkinson	Howards	153/3	Habersha
Clay, Samuel(Orphs)	Greene	Woodhams	352/10	Irwin
Clay, Thomas	Jasper	Hay's	13/6	Early
Clay, Wm.H.	Greene	Woodhams	308/2	Appling
Clayburn, Castleberry	Hall	Millers	218/2	Early
Clayton, Augustus S.	Clarke	Appling's	217/6	Appling
Clayton, Henrietta(Wid)	Jackson	Hamiltons B.	120/1	Habersha
Clayton, Isaac	Morgan	Alfords	35/10	Early
Clayton, James	Hancock	Edwards	77/27	Early
Clayton, Nelson	Pulaski	Dewitts	449/12	Irwin
Clayton, Samuel	Jackson	Hamiltons Bt.	162/3	Irwin
Clayton, Samuel	Jackson	Hamiltons	95/18	Early
Clayton, Simeon	Jackson	Hamiltons B.	369/15	Early
Clayton, Thomas	Hancock	Edwards'	153/1	Early
Clayton, Thomas	Putnam	Berrys	110/4	Early
Clayton, William	Pulaski	Johnstons	143/9	Appling

64

NAME	COUNTY	MIL.DIST	LOT/SECT	DREW LAND
Cleaveland, Larkin	Franklin	P.Browns	276/9	Irwin
Cleaveland, Reuben	Franklin	R.Browns	435/10	Irwin
Cleaveland, Reubin	Franklin	R.Browns	292/9	Appling
Clecker, Jacob	Jasper	Hays	380/21	Early
Cleghorn, Geo.(Dr)	Columbia	Walkers	480/12	Irwin
Cleghorn, George(Dr)	Columbia	Walkers	425/5	Appling
Cleland, Moses	Chatham		48/1	Walton
Clellan, Mc	Camden	32nd	196/8	Early
Clem, David(Orphs)	Washington	Floyd's	56/1	Rabun
Clemants, David	Glynn		124/6	Gwinnett
Clement, Thos.(Orphs)	Lincoln	Stokes	179/5	Early
Clement, Thos.(Orphs)	Putnam	Ectors	69/6	Irwin
Clement, Wm.T.	Greene	Ragan's	235/20	Early
Clements, Allen	Richmond		368/7	Irwin
Clements, Anna	Putnam	Ectors	119/14	Irwin
Clements, Arcibald	Twiggs	R.Belchers	213/2	Early
Clements, Charles	Madison	Culbreths	12/4	Early
Clements, Daniel	Richmond	Laceys	147/20	Early
Clements, David	Putnam	Oslins	101/16	Early
Clements, David	Putnam	Oslins	80/1	Irwin
Clements, Gabriel	Madison	Orrs	46/4	Rabun
Clements, Hosea	Laurens	Dean's	9/11	Habersham
Clements, Hosea	Laurens	Deans	288/8	Early
Clements, Jas.S.	Jefferson	Fountains	261/7	Gwinnett
Clements, Jeptha	Putnam	Ectors	192/17	Early
Clements, John	Jefferson	Fountains	279/16	Early
Clements, Mathew	Baldwin	Stephens	86/6	Early
Clements, Matthews	Baldwin	Stephens'	40/5	Gwinnett
Clements, Ostin	Morgan	Farrar's	120/11	Irwin
Clements, Stephen	Putnam	Ectors	62/3	Appling
Clements, Thos.	Jefferson	Flemmings	171/10	Habersham
Clements, William	Wayne	Crews	73/3	Rabun
Clements, Wm.Jr.	Jackson	Hamiltons Bt.	343/8	Appling
Clemments, James	Jefferson	Fountains	205/1	Early
Clemments, Thos.	Jefferson	Flemmings	248/9	Early
Clemmings, Wm.	Jones	Permenters	215/1	Irwin
Clemmings, Wm.	Jones	Permenters	304/9	Early
Clemmons, Isaac	Wilkes	Perry's	7/11	Habersham
Clemmons, Jacob	Telfair	Love's	22/8	Appling
Clemmons, Jacob	Telfair	Loves	185/10	Early
Clemmons, James J.	Washington	Daniels	190/5	Irwin
Clemons, Wm.A.	Wilkinson	Lees	490/6	Appling
Cleveland, Benj.	Franklin	Akins	322/27	Early
Cliatt, Isham	Richmond	Burtons	156/7	Appling
Cliatt, Isham	Richmond	Burtons	65/2	Early
Cliatt, Samuel M.	Tattnall	Jesse Durrences	198/4	Early
Cliett, Henry	Columbia	Burroughs	31/21	Early
Cliffton, John	Emanuel	49	190/1	Early
Clifton, Daniel	Jones	Phillips	167/10	Irwin
Clifton, Geo.Sr.	Clarke	Pentecosts	19/23	Early
Clifton, John	Emanuel	49th	131/9	Appling
Clifton, Levin	Jackson	Hamiltons B.	143/4	Irwin
Clifton, Levin	Jackson	Hamiltons Bt.	147/12	Irwin
Clifton, Nathan	Tattnall	Johnsons	397/3	Early
Clifton, Richard	Morgan	Pace's	223/6	Gwinnett
Clifton, Thomas	Screven	180th	354/5	Early
Clifton, William	Tattnall	Johnsons	362/14	Early
Clifton, Wm.	Clarke	Pentecosts	232/3	Irwin
Cliles, Elizabeth	Wilkinson	Lees	64/23	Early
Clinch, Edward	Laurens	Griffins	151/12	Habersham
Clinch, Edward	Laurens	Griffins	35/8	Appling
Clisbie, Samuel	Chatham		70/4	Walton
Clopton, Pleasant P.	Jasper	Blakes	83/2	Walton
Clopton, Thomas	Putnam	Bustins	354/17	Early
Clopton, William	Wilkinson	Childs	112/15	Early
Clore, Abel	Jackson	Winters B.	88/4	Habersham
Clore, Abner	Madison	Willifords	22/1	Appling

65

NAME	COUNTY	MIL.DIST	LOT/SECT	DREW LAN
Clore, Abner	Madison	Willifords	91/3	Early
Clore, George	Madison	Mullicans	109/4	Habersha
Cloud, James	Twiggs	W.Belchers	7/4	Irwin
Cloud, William	Twiggs	W.Belchers	115/6	Gwinnett
Clower, David S.	Morgan	Leonards	140/9	Irwin
Clower, Geo.	Jasper	Sentills	27/10	Early
Clower, George	Wilkinson	Bowing's	364/6	Gwinnett
Clower, George	Wilkinson	Bowings	462/2	Appling
Clower, Thomas	Baldwin	Cousins	512/12	Irwin
Clowers, Michael	Morgan	Cheavers	299/11	Irwin
Clubb, Martha(Orph)	Camden	Millers	110/7	Gwinnett
Clubb, Rachell(Orph)	Camden	Millers	110/7	Gwinnett
Clyatt, Samuel M.	Tattnall	Jesse Durrences	254/6	Early
Coal, Rebecca	Jones	Wallers	313/5	Gwinnett
Coal, Reuben	Jones	Wallers	201/5	Gwinnett
Coalding, Samuel B.	Screven	36	363/5	Early
Coales, Wm.(Orphs)	Jones	Permenters	101/11	Hall
Coalson, Mathew	Screven	36th	91/8	Hall
Coates, Josiah(Orphs)	Laurens	Jones'	228/2	Irwin
Coates, Thomas G.	Laurens	Jones'	166/11	Irwin
Coates, Thomas G.	Laurens	Jones	149/28	Early
Coats, Calvin	Wilkes	Runnels	128/28	Early
Coats, Colvin	Wilkes	Runnel's	282/13	Early
Coats, James(Orphs)	Putnam	H.Kendrick's	29/19	Early
Coats, M.E.(Wid)	Chatham		327/4	Early
Coats, Oswell	Twiggs	Smiths	288/11	Early
Cobb, Henry W.	Columbia	J.Morris'	52/9	Appling
Cobb, Horatio	Tattnall	Keans	45/4	Appling
Cobb, Jacob	Hancock	Millers	371/7	Early
Cobb, Jacob	Hancock	Millers	94/11	Habersha
Cobb, James	Wilkinson	Brooks'	230/27	Early
Cobb, Jas.(S/Absalom)	Wilkinson	Brooks	466/10	Irwin
Cobb, Joseph	Hancock	Millers	2/12	Hall
Cobb, Joshua	Wilkinson	Brooks	355/10	Irwin
Cobb, Levi	Baldwin	Russels	249/2	Appling
Cobb, Martha J.(Wid)	Jefferson	Waldens	142/3	Appling
Cobb, Samuel	Pulaski	Bryans	12/10	Early
Cobb, Seth	Wilkinson	Brooks'	175/20	Early
Cobb, Unity	Wilkinson	Brooks	199/3	Irwin
Cobb, Wiley	Pulaski	Maddoxs	293/17	Early
Cobb, William	Hall		218/7	Early
Cobbs, John	Oglethorpe	Wises	248/4	Early
Cochran, Alfred	Wilkes	Runnels	214/12	Habersha
Cochran, Allen	Jasper	Blakes	274/4	Walton
Cochran, Banister	Morgan	McClendons	77/3	Walton
Cochran, Elisha	Morgan	Knights	200/3	Early
Cochran, Elisha	Morgan	Knights	374/6	Early
Cochran, Geo.L.	Effingham		122/11	Irwin
Cochran, Hugh(R.S.)	Effingham		212/1	Appling
Cochran, Hugh(R.S.)	Effingham		301/1	Appling
Cochran, John J.	Columbia	Ob.Morris	157/6	Irwin
Cochran, John(Orphs)	Jasper	Blakes	175/5	Irwin
Cochran, John	Oglethorpe	Bridges	65/27	Early
Cochran, Martin	Jasper	Blakes	459/5	Appling
Cochran, Moses	Morgan	Knights	16/7	Appling
Cochran, Saml.(Orphs)	Greene	Greers	295/1	Appling
Cochran, Thos.	Baldwin	Haws	38/5	Irwin
Cochran, William	Morgan	Knights	193/4	Appling
Cochran, William	Morgan	Knights	447/8	Irwin
Cock, George(Orphs)	Emanuel	58th	110/11	Hall
Cock, Richard(Orphs)	Washington	Daniels	16/22	Early
Cocke, Nathl.(Orphs)	Richmond	Laceys	274/3	Early
Cocker, Jonathan C.	Jackson	Rogers Bt.	159/13	Irwin
Cockerham, Peter	Franklin	Davis'	89/4	Habersha
Cockesham, Richd.	Franklin	Hammonds	91/28	Early
Cockron, Benjamin	Morgan	McClendons	192/6	Irwin
Cocks, Aron	Pulaski	Bryants	72/7	Irwin

NAME	COUNTY	MIL.DIST	LOT/SECT	DREW LAND
Cocks, William	Washington	Barges	111/1	Habersham
Cocran, Abner	Greene	Harvills	56/4	Irwin
Cody, Barnett	Warren	153	214/11	Irwin
Cody, Eliz.(Wid)	Warren	Greenes	303/11	Irwin
Cody, Elizabeth	Jackson	Rogers Bt.	48/2	Walton
Cody, Green	Warren	153	103/5	Irwin
Cody, James Sr.	Warren	153rd	124/27	Early
Cody, James Sr.	Warren	153rd	392/9	Early
Cody, Jesse	Warren	Griers	194/1	Early
Cody, John	Warren	154th	157/12	Hall
Cody, Peter	Warren	153	318/5	Irwin
Cofer, Elizabeth	Wilkes	Runnel's	50/28	Early
Coffee, Rebecca(Wid)	Hall		137/3	Habersham
Coffer, John	Wilkes	Reynolds	366/9	Irwin
Coffer, Joseph b.	Wilkes	Willis	279/7	Gwinnett
Cofield, Grisham(R.S.)	Twiggs	Jeffersons	358/21	Early
Cofield, Grisham	Twiggs	Jeffersons	128/10	Early
Cofman, Amos	Jasper	Hays	284/7	Gwinnett
Coggan, Wm.	Morgan	Knights	97/18	Early
Cohen, Isaac	Chatham		135/7	Gwinnett
Cohoon, Isaac	Jackson	Rogers Bt.	461/7	Appling
Cohorn, Cornelius	Wilkes	Mattox	115/3	Irwin
Cohron, Eliz.(Wid)	Warren	Griers	235/1	Walton
Cohron, James	Twiggs	W.Belchers	158/7	Early
Cohron, James	Twiggs	W.Belchers	274/10	Irwin
Cohron, Wm.M.	Warren	Griers	7/27	Early
Coil, Andrew	Franklin	Ash's	145/7	Irwin
Coker, Cato	Washington	Floyds	390/12	Early
Coker, Elisha	Putnam	Slaughters	216/8	Irwin
Coker, John Sr.	Jackson	Hamiltons	132/11	Early
Coker, John(Orphs)	Walton	Williams	267/3	Appling
Coker, Thomas	Jackson	Rogers B.	137/12	Hall
Coker, Thos.Jr.	Jackson	Hamiltons Bt.	318/13	Irwin
Coker, Thos.Jr.	Jackson	Hamiltons Bt.	324/16	Early
Colawell, John(Orphs)	Morgan	Selmons	301/8	Early
Colbert, John G.	Morgan	Hackneys	375/5	Early
Colbert, Larkin	Oglethorpe	Bridges	95/1	Rabun
Colbert, Lindsey G.	Oglethorpe	Bridges	378/13	Early
Colbert, Richard	Elbert	Ruckers	424/8	Appling
Colbert, Wm.	Elbert	White/Nunelly	204/3	Walton
Colbert, Wm.	Elbert	White/Nunelly	31/4	Appling
Colding, Thomas	Screven	36	197/8	Irwin
Coldwell, Wm.	Clarke	Oates	202/6	Irwin
Cole, Allen(Orph)	Chatham		118/26	Early
Cole, Allen	McIntosh	Hamiltons	387/19	Early
Cole, Brannan	Jefferson	Fountains	289/7	Early
Cole, Bud	Screven	180	317/12	Early
Cole, Duke	Greene	Tuggles	127/3	Early
Cole, Eliza(Orph)	Chatham		118/26	Early
Cole, Elizabeth	McIntosh	Hamiltons	387/19	Early
Cole, George M.	Warren	153rd	277/12	Early
Cole, James D.	Clarke	Deans	159/3	Appling
Cole, Jesse	Jasper	Bentleys	34/2	Rabun
Cole, John D.	Chatham		30/3	Walton
Cole, John D.	Chatham		74/2	Rabun
Cole, John(Orphs)	Greene	Greers	328/5	Appling
Cole, John	Columbia	Willinghams	261/3	Irwin
Cole, John	Habersham	Grants	11/3	Early
Cole, John	Habersham	Grants	239/6	Gwinnett
Cole, John	Habersham	Grants	517/2	Habersham
Cole, Mark	Early		37/16	Irwin
Cole, Robert	Jasper	Bentleys	34/6	Gwinnett
Cole, Robert	Jasper	Northcuts	348/8	Early
Cole, Sarah C.	Wilkes	Smiths	287/21	Early
Cole, Sarah(Wid)	Columbia	Willinghams	90/10	Habersham
Cole, William	Morgan	Campbells	291/6	Appling
Coleby, John	Greene	143	237/6	Irwin

NAME	COUNTY	MIL.DIST	LOT/SECT	DREW LAN
Coleman, Allen W.	Putnam	Littles	110/2	Appling
Coleman, Charles	Jones	Greene's	57/16	Early
Coleman, Daniel	Greene	143rd	589/2	Appling
Coleman, Elisha	Wilkes	Russells	101/7	Early
Coleman, Eliz.(Orphs)	Jackson	Winters Bt.	241/9	Early
Coleman, Harriet(Wid)	Columbia	Willinghams	184/1	Early
Coleman, Isaac	Jasper	Easts	18/5	Irwin
Coleman, Isham	Hancock	Scotts	112/15	Irwin
Coleman, Isham	Hancock	Scotts	44/12	Early
Coleman, Isiah	Washington	Brooks	254/2	Early
Coleman, James	Laurens	Harris'	478/13	Irwin
Coleman, John Sr.	Morgan	Hubbards	229/7	Gwinnett
Coleman, John(Orph)	Chatham		277/8	Irwin
Coleman, John	Bryan	20th	92/12	Habersham
Coleman, John	Wilkes	Bates	270/17	Early
Coleman, John	Wilkinson	Lees	329/8	Early
Coleman, Jonath	Emanuel	57th	324/4	Appling
Coleman, Jonathan	Laurens	Harriss	399/5	Appling
Coleman, Jossey	Laurens	Harriss	112/15	Irwin
Coleman, Margt.S.(Orph)	Chatham		277/8	Irwin
Coleman, Mathew(Sr)	Greene	143rd	13/23	Early
Coleman, Matthew Jr.	Greene	143	225/5	Appling
Coleman, Peter(Orphs)	Columbia	Willinghams	356/12	Early
Coleman, Richard	Franklin	Jno.Millers	56/11	Early
Coleman, Sarah	Baldwin	Ellis'	215/5	Irwin
Coleman, Stephen	Twiggs	Jeffersons	267/4	Irwin
Coleman, Thomas	Hancock	Scotts	154/4	Irwin
Coleman, William	Morgan	Hubbards	84/4	Walton
Coleman, William	Tattnall	Keens	224/6	Early
Coleman, Willis	Baldwin	Ellis	151/15	Irwin
Coleman, Wm.	Jefferson	Cowarts	412/2	Appling
Coleman, Wm.	Jefferson	Cowarts	418/28	Early
Coleson, Sanders	Pulaski	Senterfeits	309/12	Early
Coley, Roland	Jefferson	Lamps	437/5	Irwin
Colhoon, John	Jasper	Evan's	140/6	Early
Colier, Wm.(Dr)	Columbia	Burroughs	346/5	Appling
Collars, Benejah	Lincoln	Jones	42/9	Early
Collars, Isaiah	Lincoln	Jones	319/28	Early
Collars, Richard	Lincoln	Jones	297/4	Walton
Collay, Jonathan	Oglethorpe	Rowlands	156/11	Habersham
Collens, James	Bullock	Tilmans	393/13	Early
Collens, John	Wilkes	McClendons	195/3	Walton
Colley, Edward	Madison	Culbreths	65/3	Rabun
Colley, Frances	Wilkes	Dents	420/6	Irwin
Colley, George	Laurens	Harris's	330/2	Appling
Colley, Joel	Morgan	Wrights	103/12	Early
Colley, Joel	Morgan	Wrights	342/9	Irwin
Colley, John(Orphs)	Wilkes	Dents	430/6	Appling
Colley, John	Madison	Adares	156/5	Early
Colley, Lewis	Jasper	Posts	494/7	Appling
Colley, Nelson	Jasper	Smiths	377/27	Early
Collier, Benjamin	Twiggs	Jefferson's	154/28	Early
Collier, Benjamin	Twiggs	Jefferson's	403/7	Appling
Collier, Charles V.	Oglethorpe	Brittons	374/13	Irwin
Collier, Chas.W.	Hancock	Lucas	50/9	Irwin
Collier, Cuthbert	Oglethorpe	Dunn's	140/10	Habersham
Collier, James	Laurens	Griffins	308/8	Irwin
Collier, James	Laurens	Griffins	369/6	Appling
Collier, Jesse	Twiggs	Jeffersons	61/17	Early
Collier, John	Baldwin	Marshalls	102/7	Early
Collier, John	Baldwin	Marshalls	92/2	Habersham
Collier, John	Franklin	Akins	222/6	Gwinnett
Collier, John	Laurens	Ross	252/10	Irwin
Collier, Martha(Wid)	Columbia	Pullins	6/10	Habersham
Collier, Merril	Jackson	Hamiltons	209/3	Early
Collier, Merrit	Jackson	Hamiltons Bt.	415/2	Appling
Collier, Richard	Baldwin	Marshalls	226/2	Irwin

NAME	COUNTY	MIL.DIST	LOT/SECT	DREW LAND
Collier, Richard	Baldwin	Marshalls	52/14	Early
Collier, Robt.W.	Wilkes	McClendons	202/4	Appling
Collier, Saml.T.	Greene	143	466/4	Appling
Collier, Thomas	Laurens	Ross	117/19	Early
Collier, Thomas	Laurens	Ross	513/4	Appling
Collier, Thomas	Oglethorpe	Dennis	303/13	Irwin
Collier, Thos.	Franklin	Morriss	98/4	Appling
Collier, Thos.W.	Jasper	Baileys	218/3	Early
Collier, Vines	Oglethorpe	Dunn's	170/2	Appling
Collier, Wiatt	Hancock	Danells	67/18	Early
Collier, Wm.(Dr)	Columbia	Burroughs	119/12	Habersham
Collin, Andrew(Orph)	Baldwin	Cousins'	315/6	Early
Collingsworth, Wm.	Morgan	McClendon's	150/27	Early
Collins, Abilm	Wilkinson	Brooks	21/16	Irwin
Collins, Ameila(Orph)	Richmond	Palmers	392/11	Early
Collins, Andrew	Jackson	Winters Bt.	95/5	Walton
Collins, Andrew	Jackson	Winters	133/12	Habersham
Collins, Andrew	Twiggs	Bozemans	148/9	Irwin
Collins, Andrew	Washington	Echols	214/1	Walton
Collins, Catharine(Orph)	Richmond	Palmers	392/11	Early
Collins, Charles	Washington	Cummins	396/9	Early
Collins, Cornelius	Columbia	Walkers	43/4	Rabun
Collins, Creed	Washington	Danels	275/9	Appling
Collins, Creed	Washington	Danels	46/8	Irwin
Collins, Dennis	Baldwin	Cousins	235/7	Appling
Collins, Dennis	Baldwin	Cousins	527/11	Irwin
Collins, Elisha	Twiggs	Browns	242/26	Early
Collins, Eliz.(Orph)	Richmond	Palmers	392/11	Early
Collins, Eliz.(Wid)	Jones	Permenters	363/6	Appling
Collins, George(Orph)	Richmond	Palmers	392/11	Early
Collins, George	Chatham		438/4	Appling
Collins, Gibson	Wilkes	McClendons	155/2	Habersham
Collins, Gibson	Wilkes	McLendons	194/5	Gwinnett
Collins, Henry(Orphs)	Tattnall	Keens	268/3	Early
Collins, James Jr.	Wilkinson	Brooks'	47/4	Early
Collins, James Sr.	Wilkinson	Brooks	201/6	Appling
Collins, James(R.S.)	Richmond	Laceys	87/4	Irwin
Collins, James	Baldwin	Cousins	426/8	Irwin
Collins, James	Baldwin	Cousins	88/13	Early
Collins, James	Bullock	Tilmans	197/18	Early
Collins, James	Hall		380/10	Early
Collins, James	Jackson	Winters Bt.	419/6	Irwin
Collins, Jas.(Big Rd)	Columbia	Ob.Morris	244/10	Irwin
Collins, Jas.(Big Rd)	Columbia	Ob.Morriss	363/6	Early
Collins, Jesse	Tattnall	Keens	132/13	Early
Collins, Joab	Tattnall	Keens	176/7	Gwinnett
Collins, Joab	Tattnall	Keens	217/28	Early
Collins, John B.	Franklin	Morriss	6/12	Irwin
Collins, John	Madison	Orrs	167/1	Walton
Collins, John	Richmond	Palmers	27/17	Early
Collins, John	Warren	152	156/12	Early
Collins, Jos.Sr.	Tattnall	Keens	141/8	Hall
Collins, Joseph Sr.	Tattnall	Keens	433/12	Irwin
Collins, Joseph(R.S.)	Morgan	Leonards	130/15	Irwin
Collins, Joseph(R.S.)	Morgan	Leonards	37/7	Gwinnett
Collins, Joseph	Baldwin	Cousins	67/6	Appling
Collins, Lewis	Washington	Barge's	442/2	Appling
Collins, Lewis	Wilkes	McLendons	382/2	Early
Collins, Mary(Orph)	Richmond	Palmers	392/11	Early
Collins, Merrill	Early		230/7	Appling
Collins, Nathl.F.	Columbia	Willinghams	26/12	Habersham
Collins, Nathnl.	Greene	Ragans	327/7	Early
Collins, Penelope(Wid)	Tattnall	Keens	16/17	Early
Collins, Sarah Jane(Orph)	Richmond	Palmers	392/11	Early
Collins, Seaborn	Columbia	Shaws	63/13	Habersham
Collins, Thomas	Pulaski	Reece	298/7	Irwin
Collins, Thomas	Washington	Cummins	267/2	Irwin

NAME	COUNTY	MIL.DIST	LOT/SECT	DREW LAN
Collins, Thomas	Wilkinson	Brooks	248/5	Irwin
Collins, Thomas	Wilkinson	Brooks	342/8	Appling
Collins, Timothy	Wilkes	Davis'	259/18	Early
Collins, William	Hancock	Coopers	96/6	Irwin
Collins, William	Morgan	Selmons	410/28	Early
Collins, Wiot	Wilkes	Smiths	178/2	Irwin
Collins, Wiot	Wilkes	Smiths	283/11	Early
Collins, Wm.	Jackson	Dicksons Bt.	557/2	Appling
Collins, Wm.	Washington	Danils	31/27	Early
Collum, Eliz.	Jasper	Hay's	278/7	Gwinnett
Colly, Francis	Wilkes	Dents	280/8	Appling
Colly, John	Madison	Adares	4/1	Early
Colly, Lewis	Jasper	Posts	208/8	Irwin
Colly, Spain	Wilkes	Dents	269/13	Early
Colly, Thos.(Orphs)	Oglethorpe	Britton's	13/4	Early
Colly, Zachariah	Oglethorpe	Rowlands	22/11	Early
Collys, George(Orphs)	Wilkinson	Bowings	164/14	Early
Colquette, John T.	Greene	Macon's	450/10	Irwin
Colquitt, John	Oglethorpe	Lees	382/4	Early
Colson, Henry	Bullock	Everitts	136/2	Walton
Colson, Henry	Bullock	Everitts	364/27	Early
Colson, John	Elbert	Dobbs	286/1	Appling
Colter, James	Jefferson	Mathews	48/4	Habersham
Colvard, John G.	Elbert	R.Christians	332/10	Early
Colvin, John	Washington	Peabody's	351/6	Early
Colvin, John	Washington	Peabodys	123/17	Early
Colvin, John	Washington	Peabodys	80/17	Early
Colwell, Alexander	Clarke	Oats	290/12	Early
Colwell, William	Clarke	Oats	224/12	Irwin
Colyer, James	Franklin	Akins	95/18	Early
Combs, Aaron	Jackson	Dicksons B.	269/12	Early
Combs, Aaron	Jackson	Dicksons B.	469/8	Irwin
Combs, Hannah	Jasper	Bentleys	362/2	Appling
Combs, Mark	Wilkes	Harriss	90/14	Early
Combs, Nathaniel	Jasper	Bentleys	79/10	Hall
Combs, Philip Sr.	Wilkes	Bates'	168/2	Early
Combs, Thomas	Wilkes	Runnel's	247/18	Early
Combs, William	Wilkes	Bates	45/7	Early
Commander, Elias	Twiggs	Browns	221/10	Early
Commander, Jas.	Jones	Samuels	256/6	Early
Commander, John	Twiggs	Browns	288/7	Appling
Commer, James	Jones	Burkhalters	99/2	Appling
Compton, John Sr.	Jasper	Evan's	44/5	Early
Compton, John Sr.	Jasper	Evans	345/10	Early
Compton, John W.	Jasper	Clay's	196/7	Early
Compton, Jordon	Jasper	Eastes	35/4	Irwin
Compton, Levi	Pulaski	Lesters	495/7	Irwin
Condon, John	Oglethorpe	Rowlands	11/9	Appling
Condon, John	Oglethorpe	Rowlands	188/10	Irwin
Cone, Archiles	Washington	Cummins	479/4	Appling
Cone, Buzzel	Baldwin	Haws	435/6	Appling
Cone, Ezekiel	Greene	Fosters	520/8	Appling
Cone, Ezekiel	Greene	Fosters	79/15	Irwin
Cone, James	Appling	3rd	125/11	Irwin
Cone, James	Baldwin	Cousins	4/10	Irwin
Cone, James	Washington	Cummins	18/4	Habersham
Cone, James	Washington	Cummins	195/6	Irwin
Cone, John(R.S.)	Baldwin	Haws	337/18	Early
Cone, John	Twiggs	R.Belchers	251/3	Irwin
Cone, Levi	Washington	Peaboddys	30/3	Early
Cone, Lewis	Washington	Wimberleys	254/7	Appling
Cone, Middleton	Jones	Harrest's	37/18	Early
Cone, Robert	Jasper	Northcuts	478/7	Irwin
Cone, Robert	Richmond	Burtons	120/15	Irwin
Cone, Robert	Richmond	Burtons	69/6	Gwinnett
Cone, William	Bullock	Knights	429/3	Appling
Cone, William	Washington	Wimberleys	508/13	Irwin

NAME	COUNTY	MIL.DIST	LOT/SECT	DREW LAND
Conelly, Charles	Clarke	Deans	303/11	Early
Coney, Joseph	Gwinnett	Hamiltons Bt.	148/11	Hall
Conghron, Mathew	Screven		267/4	Early
Conine, Robert	Jackson	Hamiltons Bt.	249/2	Early
Conine, Robert	Jackson	Hamiltons Bt.	43/2	Walton
Conn, John	Franklin	Turks	475/7	Irwin
Conn, Sanders	Franklin	Haynes	90/15	Irwin
Connally, Abner	Franklin	Ash's	181/4	Appling
Connally, Michael	Laurens	Watsons	652/2	Appling
Connaway, Chas.	Bullock	Knights	219/12	Irwin
Connell, Daniel	Jefferson	Mathews	118/1	Early
Connell, Jesse	Jefferson	Matthews	199/8	Irwin
Connell, Thos.Sr.	Greene	Wheelis'	6/22	Early
Connell, Thos.Sr.	Greene	Wheelis	252/4	Irwin
Connell, Wm.	Greene	Wheelis	343/3	Appling
Connelly, Christopher	Madison	Millicans	179/12	Irwin
Connelly, John	Screven	36th	239/19	Early
Connelly, Susannah(Wid)	Jefferson	Abbotts	5/11	Irwin
Connelly, Thomas	Clarke	Pentecosts	24/22	Early
Conner, Benjamin	Putnam	Brooks	144/11	Hall
Conner, Benjamin	Putnam	Brooks	205/4	Appling
Conner, Danl.Sr.(R.S.)	Clarke	Tredwells	235/6	Irwin
Conner, Elijah	Warren	154th	83/2	Appling
Conner, Isaac	Screven	36th	529/2	Appling
Conner, James P.	Putnam	Stampers	116/8	Appling
Conner, James P.	Putnam	Stampers	301/6	Early
Conner, Jesse	Jones	Greenes	21/4	Walton
Conner, Jesse	Jones	Greens	61/1	Early
Conner, John(& Child)	Camden	Longs	60/5	Rabun
Conner, John	Screven		222/16	Early
Conner, Lewis	Screven	Lovetts	4/2	Habersham
Conner, Micajah	Lincoln	Stokes	303/1	Walton
Conner, Tarrence	Jackson	Rogers Bt.	151/2	Rabun
Conner, Thos.	Jackson	Rogers B.	41/9	Hall
Conner, Thos.	Jackson	Rogers Bt.	511/5	Appling
Conner, Thos.B.	Montgomery	Nobles	408/21	Early
Conoway, William	Putnam	Brooks	390/17	Early
Conyers, Daniel	Screven	Burns'	18/4	Early
Conyers, James	Screven	Roberts	256/2	Irwin
Coody, Archibald	Screven	180th	344/4	Appling
Coody, Edward(Orps)	Morgan	Farrars	78/5	Early
Cook, Amos	Bryan	19th	311/7	Early
Cook, Arthur Jr.	Baldwin	Ellis'	440/4	Appling
Cook, Augustin	Jasper	Bartlets	211/12	Early
Cook, Augustin	Jasper	Bartletts	246/28	Early
Cook, Benjamin	Elbert	Ruckers	85/26	Early
Cook, Betty	Elbert	G.Higginbothams	278/13	Irwin
Cook, Buchner	Putnam	May's	83/6	Irwin
Cook, Burrel	Jackson	Hamiltons Bt.	62/11	Irwin
Cook, Caleb	Morgan	Hackneys	227/5	Early
Cook, Elisha(R.S.)	Hancock	Smiths	241/10	Early
Cook, Elisha(R.S.)	Hancock	Smiths	413/9	Irwin
Cook, Elisha(R.S.)	Hancock	Smiths	76/2	Habersham
Cook, Eliz.(Orph)	Laurens	Harris	132/13	Early
Cook, Eliz.(Wid)	Jackson	Winters	280/19	Early
Cook, Fanny	Elbert	Penn's	242/6	Early
Cook, Fortunatus S.	Morgan	Hubbards	393/10	Irwin
Cook, George(Orphs)	Telfair	Wilsons	91/2	Appling
Cook, George	Elbert	Olivers	80/21	Early
Cook, Henry	Baldwin	Ellis'	499/13	Irwin
Cook, Henry	Jefferson	Cowarts	169/6	Appling
Cook, Isachar	Elbert	Olivers	253/27	Early
Cook, Isachar	Elbert	Olivers	370/3	Appling
Cook, Jackson	Elbert	Olivers	92/5	Early
Cook, James C.	Morgan	Hubbards	198/8	Irwin
Cook, James	Jones	Permenters	382/1	Appling
Cook, James	Washington	Pools	268/6	Appling

71

NAME	COUNTY	MIL.DIST	LOT/SECT	DREW LAN
Cook, John Sr.	Washington	Floyds	144/14	Irwin
Cook, John	Elbert	Olivers	329/9	Early
Cook, John	Jackson	Rogers Bt.	249/11	Irwin
Cook, John	Jefferson	Cowarts	160/16	Early
Cook, Joseph(Orphs)	Lincoln	Jeter's	17/14	Irwin
Cook, Joseph	Baldwin	Marshalls	343/28	Early
Cook, Nancy(Wid)	Jackson	Rogers Bt.	348/9	Appling
Cook, Nathan	Washington	Robinsons	275/26	Early
Cook, Philip	Putnam	Mays	193/2	Early
Cook, Pleasant	Putnam	Littles	41/1	Walton
Cook, Ranson	Jackson	Rogers Bt.	83/14	Irwin
Cook, Reuban(R.S.)	Elbert	Olivers	325/12	Early
Cook, Sarah	Effingham		328/17	Early
Cook, Simeon	Twiggs	R.Belchers	235/10	Early
Cook, Sophia(Wid)	Jones	Samuels	335/19	Early
Cook, Theodosius	Elbert	Olivers	324/10	Early
Cook, Thomas	Morgan	Hackneys	170/6	Appling
Cook, Wilie	Jasper	Easts	96/8	Appling
Cook, William	Baldwin	Doziers	53/6	Early
Cook, Wm.(R.S.)	Bullock	Everetts	221/4	Appling
Cook, Wm.	Jefferson	Bothwells	367/9	Appling
Cooker, Abraham	Elbert	Penns	38/21	Early
Cooker, Alsea	Elbert	Webb's	523/6	Appling
Cooker, Alsea	Elbert	Webbs	175/3	Walton
Cooker, Asa	Elbert	Penn's	114/1	Early
Cooker, Isaac	Elbert	Webbs	214/5	Early
Cooker, Newell	Elbert	Webb's	332/27	Early
Cooksey, Caleb	Jefferson	Jones	136/9	Early
Cooksey, John W.	Wilkes	Kilgores	442/3	Appling
Cooksey, John W.	Wilkes	Kilgores	484/6	Appling
Cooksey, John	Laurens	Griffins	224/3	Walton
Cooksley, Hezekiah	Warren	Greens	320/16	Early
Coombs, Nathaniel L.	Richmond	Laceys	120/4	Early
Coon, Henry L.	Twiggs	R.Belchers	184/5	Appling
Coon, Henry L.	Twiggs	R.Belchers	5/6	Gwinnett
Coon, James	Twiggs	R.Belchers	167/16	Early
Cooper, Augustin	Wilkes	Kilgores	324/13	Irwin
Cooper, Benj.	Putnam	Ectors	35/1	Irwin
Cooper, Benjamin	Wilkinson	Brooks'	33/13	Irwin
Cooper, Beverly	Hancock	Edwards	423/12	Irwin
Cooper, Charles M.	McIntosh	Hamiltons	89/1	Habersha
Cooper, David	Columbia	Dodsons	29/2	Irwin
Cooper, Drury	Clarke	Oates	106/3	Walton
Cooper, Edmund(Orphs)	Baldwin	Cousins	525/13	Irwin
Cooper, Elbert	Putnam	Evans	68/13	Habersha
Cooper, Eli	Jasper	Sentills	166/7	Gwinnett
Cooper, Elijah	Twiggs	R.Belchers	68/4	Irwin
Cooper, Eliz.(Wid)	Emanuel	395th	187/7	Irwin
Cooper, Eliza(Orph)	Chatham		120/6	Gwinnett
Cooper, Geo.(Orphs)	Jones	Phillips	400/11	Irwin
Cooper, George(R.S.)	Wayne	Crews	120/10	Early
Cooper, George(R.S.)	Wayne	Crews	174/7	Appling
Cooper, George(R.S.)	Wayne	Crews	176/7	Early
Cooper, George	Montgomery	Nobles	103/15	Irwin
Cooper, Henry	Emanuel	56	378/18	Early
Cooper, Henry	Laurens	Griffins	189/18	Early
Cooper, Herman	Putnam	Evans	204/11	Irwin
Cooper, Howel	Oglethorpe	Golding's	181/12	Irwin
Cooper, Humphrey	Jones	Jeffersons	302/10	Irwin
Cooper, Isaac	Wilkinson	Brooks	124/11	Irwin
Cooper, Isaac	Wilkinson	Brooks	396/13	Irwin
Cooper, James A.	Columbia	Dodsons	174/3	Walton
Cooper, James	Clarke	Starnes	101/3	Walton
Cooper, James	Clarke	Starnes	394/6	Early
Cooper, James	Jones	Hansford	84/12	Hall
Cooper, Jas.(Minor)	Wilkes	Kilgores	224/6	Appling
Cooper, Jesse	Liberty		363/12	Irwin

NAME	COUNTY	MIL.DIST	LOT/SECT	DREW LAND
Cooper, John(Orph)	Chatham		120/6	Gwinnett
Cooper, John	Chatham		195/12	Early
Cooper, John	Twiggs	Smiths	396/10	Early
Cooper, Jos.Sr.(R.S.)	Putnam	Ectors	226/4	Irwin
Cooper, Jos.Sr.(R.S.)	Putnam	Ectors	264/23	Early
Cooper, Jos.Sr.(R.S.)	Putnam	Ectors	468/7	Irwin
Cooper, Joseph	Pulaski	Bryans	322/1	Early
Cooper, Mary(Orph)	Chatham		120/6	Gwinnett
Cooper, Newton	Putnam	Littles	161/8	Appling
Cooper, Samuel Jr.	Putnam	Robertsons	81/12	Irwin
Cooper, Sarah(Orph)	Chatham		120/6	Gwinnett
Cooper, Sarah	Chatham		49/3	Walton
Cooper, Soloma(n)	Chatham		452/6	Appling
Cooper, Thomas	Baldwin	Ellis'	123/3	Early
Cooper, Thomas	Hancock	Lucas'	176/5	Gwinnett
Cooper, Thomas	Hancock	Lucas	321/2	Appling
Cooper, William	Tattnall	Overstreets	358/11	Irwin
Cooper, William	Twiggs	Ellis	274/7	Appling
Cooper, Wm.	Baldwin	Marshalls	25/5	Gwinnett
Cooper, Wm.J.	Warren	151st	133/10	Habersham
Cooper, Wm.J.	Warren	151st	18/9	Irwin
Cootes, John	Jasper	Hays	34/3	Irwin
Cope, George L.	Chatham		421/8	Appling
Copeland, Colston	Greene	Wheelis	76/1	Walton
Copeland, Henry C.	Columbia	Dodson's	334/16	Early
Copeland, Henry C.	Columbia	Dodsons	183/3	Appling
Copeland, Jesse	Tattnall	Overstreets	214/8	Early
Copeland, John(R.S.)	Hancock	Lucas'	36/4	Rabun
Copeland, John	Greene	Kimbroughs	2/13	Irwin
Copeland, John	Jasper	Phillips'	150/26	Early
Copeland, Nancy(Wid)	Greene	Kimbroughs	118/9	Irwin
Copeland, Peter	Morgan	Hubbards	368/3	Early
Copeland, Wm.(Jr)	Greene	Kinnebrough	2/6	Habersham
Copeland, Wm.(Orphs)	Greene	Kimbroughs	388/4	Appling
Copelin, Gilbert	Wilkinson	Smiths	56/8	Hall
Copland, Richard	Morgan	Talbotts	50/5	Rabun
Coplin, Coulson	Wilkinson	Wiggins	162/2	Early
Coplin, Elisha	Wilkinson	Smith's	230/4	Appling
Coplin, Wm.(R.S.)	Gwinnett	Hamiltons Bt.	2/8	Early
Coplin, Wm.(R.S.)	Gwinnett	Hamiltons Bt.	29/2	Rabun
Copp, Betton A.	Camden	Clarks	555/2	Appling
Corbitt, James	Jefferson	Matthews	153/5	Irwin
Corbitt, Richd.	Jefferson	Matthews	199/1	Appling
Cordery, Daniel	Washington	Wimberly	423/9	Irwin
Cordry, Jonathan	Washington	Wimberlys	604/2	Appling
Cordull, Wm.	Washington	Pools	58/6	Early
Corely, Amos	Richmond		3/5	Gwinnett
Corely, Wm.(Orphs)	Morgan	Talbotts	125/5	Gwinnett
Corker, James	Liberty		37/3	Irwin
Corkins, William	Pulaski	Maddox	37/6	Appling
Corley, Isham	Jones	Phillips	41/4	Irwin
Corley, Jeremiah	Jones	Seals	29/6	Gwinnett
Corley, Lewis	Morgan	Talbots	476/7	Irwin
Corley, Tubal	Putnam	Slaughters	53/9	Irwin
Cormick, John	Richmond	120th	169/17	Early
Cornelius, Winnifred(Wid)	Twiggs	R.Belchers	103/4	Irwin
Correy, Jane	Greene	143rd	102/4	Walton
Corry, Robert	Morgan	Alfords	26/5	Irwin
Cortney, Emanuel	Twiggs	Evans	80/1	Early
Corvin, John	Chatham		39/2	Walton
Cosa, Alfred	Washington	Cummins	176/9	Irwin
Cosby, Garland(Orphs)	Wilkes	Kilgores	262/10	Irwin
Cosby, Hickerson D.	Columbia	Dodsons	13/17	Early
Cosby, Wm.T.	Wilkes	Harriss	170/2	Early
Costen, Frances	Jefferson	Langstons	47/3	Habersham
Cothron, James	Morgan	Campbells	219/12	Early
Cotten, Tipton W.(Orphs)	Hall		271/1	Walton

NAME	COUNTY	MIL.DIST	LOT/SECT	DREW LAND
Cotter, David	Jefferson	Fountains	117/15	Irwin
Cotter, James	Jefferson	Matthews	12/6	Irwin
Cotter, James	Jefferson	Matthews	55/6	Early
Cotton, Charles	Chatham		165/12	Early
Cotton, Cyrus	Jones	Kings	261/8	Early
Cotton, Cyrus	Jones	Kings	447/7	Appling
Cotton, Elijah	Jones	King's	268/1	Early
Cotton, Elijah	Jones	Kings	268/1	Early
Cotton, Elijah	Jones	Kings	73/3	Early
Cotton, James	Wilkes	Runnels	180/3	Walton
Cotton, Joseph	Pulaski	Clements	512/11	Irwin
Cotton, Richard	Wilkes	Runnels	107/2	Appling
Cotton, Susan(Wid)	Columbia	Pullens	240/11	Irwin
Cotton, Weaver	Wilkes	Runnels	20/3	Rabun
Cotton, Wm.G.	Putnam	Oslins	322/7	Irwin
Cottongame, Edward	Tattnall	Tharps	204/7	Early
Couch, Mathew	Elbert	Dobbs	303/5	Appling
Couch, Nancy(Wid)	Franklin	Attaways	104/1	Early
Coulter, Moses F.	Morgan	Dennis	265/4	Walton
Coun, Charlotte(Orph)	Richmond	Jefferson	179/10	Irwin
Coun, Eliza(Orph)	Richmond	Jefferson	179/10	Irwin
Coun, Francis(Orph)	Richmond	Jefferson	179/10	Irwin
Coun, George	Richmond	Jefferson	179/10	Irwin
Coursey, Absalom Jr.	Jones	Permenters	402/28	Early
Courson, Absalom Sr.	Jones	Permenters	56/11	Hall
Courson, John	Tattnall	Tharps	103/4	Early
Coursy, Absalom Sr.	Jones	Permenters	240/8	Early
Courter, Edward	Camden	Clarks	135/9	Irwin
Courter, J.K.(I.K.?)	Camden	Clarks	492/8	Irwin
Cousins, Eliz.(Wid)	Columbia	Burroughs	436/7	Irwin
Cousins, Jas.(Orphs)	Columbia	Burroughs	76/13	Early
Cousins, Thomas	Clarke	Starnes	205/16	Gwinnett
Coutier, Peter W.	Jasper	Clays	32/6	Appling
Covey, John	Baldwin	Marshalls	208/9	Appling
Covey, John	Laurens	Griffins	45/5	Irwin
Covington, David	Lincoln	Graves	104/5	Appling
Covington, Edward	Putnam	Coopers	298/9	Early
Covington, Mary(Wid)	Lincoln	Graves'	303/21	Early
Covington, Newbill	Lincoln	Graves	183/9	Irwin
Covington, Silas	Jefferson	Lamps	111/12	Early
Cowan, John	Putnam	Evans	153/2	Appling
Cowan, Joseph	Jackson	Winters B.	63/5	Appling
Cowan, William	Jackson	Winters	236/7	Irwin
Coward, Lewis	Jones	Kings	402/20	Early
Coward, Wm.	Jones	Kings	207/13	Irwin
Coward, Zachariah	Screven	180	58/4	Early
Coward, Zachariah	Screven	180th	5/28	Early
Cowart, David	Emanuel	Lanes	41/3	Appling
Cowart, Edward	Wilkinson	Childs	240/6	Gwinnett
Cowart, Nathanl.	Emanuel	49	248/14	Early
Cowden, Jos.D.	Jackson	Dicksons B.	131/1	Walton
Cowdin, Wm.	Jasper	Trimbles	4/8	Hall
Cowen, David J.	Jones	Seals	311/28	Early
Cowen, Edward	Jackson	Dicksons Bt.	108/5	Early
Cowen, Edward	Jackson	Dicksons Bt.	506/8	Appling
Cowen, James	Jackson	Rogers Bt.	523/12	Irwin
Cowen, Stephen	Oglethorpe	Goolsbys	7/6	Appling
Cowles, Asbury	Putnam	Brooks'	204/13	Irwin
Cowling, Slaughter	Lincoln	Parks'	49/4	Early
Cowling, Slaughter	Lincoln	Parks	397/28	Early
Cox, Adam	Madison	Banes	51/27	Early
Cox, Aries	Hancock	Millers	386/2	Appling
Cox, Benjamin	Bryan	19th	264/3	Early
Cox, Caleb	Wilkinson	Lee's	12/3	Early
Cox, Charles	Wilkinson	Lees	388/15	Early
Cox, Cullin	Washington	Floyd's	190/6	Early
Cox, David	Chatham		188/5	Early

NAME	COUNTY	MIL.DIST	LOT/SECT	DREW LAND
Cox, Devias	Washington	Renfros	361/26	Early
Cox, Edward	Oglethorpe	Brittons	355/13	Early
Cox, Ephraim	Jones	Chappel's	294/4	Early
Cox, Geo.(Orphs)	Jefferson	Bothwells	215/10	Early
Cox, Jacob	Franklin	Davis'	275/13	Irwin
Cox, James	Hall		342/6	Irwin
Cox, James	Jefferson	Langstons	227/4	Walton
Cox, James	Jefferson	Langstons	262/17	Early
Cox, James	Morgan	Parkers	210/13	Irwin
Cox, John I.	Clarke	Deans	35/2	Appling
Cox, John Sr.	Hall	Byrds'	81/2	Rabun
Cox, John(Miller)	Jackson	Dicksons B.	172/2	Early
Cox, John(Orphs)	Baldwin	Irwins	159/4	Appling
Cox, Lemuel	Jones	Weatherbys	60/6	Habersham
Cox, Margarett(Wid)	Hall		454/8	Appling
Cox, Mary(Wid)	Jones	Waltons	391/6	Early
Cox, Presley	Jasper	Dardens	127/9	Irwin
Cox, Richard	Warren	150	11/13	Early
Cox, Samuel(Orphs)	Putnam	Oslins	156/15	Irwin
Cox, Thomas(Orphs)	Liberty		133/19	Early
Cox, William R.	Chatham		393/16	Early
Cox, William	Columbia	Pullins	47/1	Rabun
Cox, William	Putnam	Stampers	355/3	Early
Cox, Willis	Baldwin	Stephens	126/2	Appling
Cox, Willis	Baldwin	Stephens	26/11	Irwin
Cox, Willis	Gwinnett	Pittmans	173/4	Early
Cox, Willis	Putnam	Tomlinsons	5/5	Rabun
Cox, Zachariah	Putnam	Stampers	301/3	Early
Coxwell, Benjamin	Warren	151	131/13	Irwin
Coxwell, Benjan	Warren	151st	300/16	Early
Coxwell, Mitchel	Warren	151	133/10	Irwin
Coxwell, Mitchell	Warren	Travis'	198/12	Habersham
Crabb, Burton	Jones	Chappell's	274/6	Gwinnett
Crabb, Burton	Jones	Chappells	77/2	Rabun
Crabb, Robert	Washington	Danils	160/10	Irwin
Crabb, Samuel	Columbia	J.Morris'	131/17	Early
Crabb, Samuel	Jasper	McClendons	482/3	Appling
Crafford, James	Morgan	Townsends	309/10	Early
Crafford, James	Morgan	Townsends	384/8	Appling
Crafford, John(R.S.)	Twiggs	R.Belchers	66/3	Early
Craft, Charles(Orph)	Wilkinson	Kettles	222/13	Early
Craft, Daniel Sr.	Clarke	Tredwells	273/12	Irwin
Craft, Hugh	Baldwin	Marshals	26/1	Irwin
Craft, Jesse	Pulaski	Lanears	163/13	Early
Craft, John Jr.	Elbert	Gaines	398/10	Early
Craft, Solomon	Elbert	Gaines	6/19	Early
Crafts, Stephen	Chatham		160/4	Early
Crafts, Stephen	Chatham		219/4	Early
Craig, Agnes	Jasper	Posts	202/1	Irwin
Craig, Robert(Orphs)	Twiggs	Smiths	149/10	Habersham
Crain, Spencer	Jasper	Smiths	72/4	Rabun
Crain, Warren	Jasper	Ownes	242/5	Irwin
Crain, Wm.(Orphs)	Franklin	Harris'	19/8	Early
Cramer, Solomon	Effingham		23/4	Habersham
Cramp, Edmond	Clarke	Otis	507/3	Appling
Crane, Joshua R.	Wilkes	Davis	361/8	Early
Crane, Judith	Putnam	Ectors	80/1	Appling
Cranesberry, Aaron	Bullock	Knights	7/6	Irwin
Cranston, Walter(Heirs)	Chatham		8/20	Early
Crary, Benj.G.	Montgomery	McElvins	150/8	Hall
Cravey, Joshua	Bullock	Knights	12/14	Irwin
Cravey, Joshua	Bullock	Knights	48/20	Early
Cravy, David	Telfair	Williams	34/8	Hall
Crawford, (Wid)	Laurens	Harris	344/6	Early
Crawford, Alice S.(Wid)	Columbia	Olives	180/12	Early
Crawford, Anderson(Orp)	Columbia	Olives	38/10	Habersham
Crawford, Ann	Jasper	Baileys	247/2	Early

75

NAME	COUNTY	MIL.DIST	LOT/SECT	DREW LAN
Crawford, Arthur	Jackson	Dicksons Bt.	171/12	Irwin
Crawford, Benj.H.	Greene	Fosters	170/9	Appling
Crawford, Bennet	Jasper	Baileys	281/6	Gwinnett
Crawford, Bennet	Jasper	Baileys	317/12	Irwin
Crawford, Claborn	Morgan	McClendons	246/12	Irwin
Crawford, Claborn	Morgan	McClendons	353/14	Early
Crawford, David	Greene	143rd	305/6	Irwin
Crawford, David	Greene	143rd	516/7	Irwin
Crawford, David	Morgan	Hackneys	536/2	Appling
Crawford, David	Morgan	Hackneys	93/11	Hall
Crawford, Elijah	Franklin	Flanagans	519/6	Appling
Crawford, Ezekiel(Orph)	McIntosh	Eigles	102/5	Early
Crawford, Ezekiel(Orph)	McIntosh	Eigles	367/6	Gwinnett
Crawford, James	Jasper	Bentleys	126/13	Early
Crawford, James	McIntosh	Eigle's	4/2	Irwin
Crawford, Joel	Columbia	Shaw's	369/9	Early
Crawford, John(R.S.)	Twiggs	R.Belchers	119/1	Early
Crawford, John	Effingham		309/8	Early
Crawford, John	Lincoln	Walkers	437/11	Irwin
Crawford, John	Pulaski	Bryans	85/3	Appling
Crawford, Lester(Orphs)	Pulaski	Bryans	368/10	Irwin
Crawford, Mary(Wid)	Franklin	Flannagan's	258/9	Appling
Crawford, Micilla(Wid)	McIntosh	Eigles	312/9	Irwin
Crawford, Philips	Jasper	Posts	127/5	Irwin
Crawford, Reuben(Orph)	McIntosh	Eigles	102/5	Early
Crawford, Reuben(Orph)	McIntosh	Eigles	367/6	Gwinnett
Crawford, Robert	Columbia	Shaws	328/1	Early
Crawford, Russell	Clarke	Deans	110/3	Early
Crawford, Simmons	Columbia	Olives	189/28	Early
Crawford, Strawther	Jefferson	Abbots	328/12	Irwin
Crawford, Thomas(Orph)	McIntosh	Eigles	102/5	Early
Crawford, Thomas(Orph)	McIntosh	Eigles	367/6	Gwinnett
Crawford, Thos.H.	Columbia	Walkers	60/19	Early
Crawford, Thos.Sr.	Greene	Greers	88/6	Early
Crawford, William(Orph)	McIntosh	Eigles	102/5	Early
Crawford, William	Chatham		237/12	Early
Crawford, Williamson	Wilkinson	Kettles	376/9	Early
Crawford, Willis	Warren	150th	241/2	Appling
Crawford, Wm.(Orph)	McIntosh	Eigles	367/6	Gwinnett
Crawford, Wm.	Jasper	Evans	148/3	Habersham
Crawford, Wm.S.P.	Franklin	R.Browns	208/10	Irwin
Crawford, Wm.S.P.	Franklin	R.Browns	500/5	Irwin
Crawl, Mary	Jasper	Phillips	413/11	Irwin
Crayton, John	Jackson	Winters Bt.	18/4	Early
Crayton, John	Jackson	Winters Bt.	347/11	Irwin
Creach, Charles	Laurens	Griffins	155/12	Habersham
Creamer, Henry	Lincoln	Parks	5/8	Early
Creamer, Hugh(Orphs)	Lincoln	Jeters	205/8	Irwin
Creamer, Nancy(Wid)	Lincoln	Jeters	234/5	Appling
Creamer, Samuel	Oglethorpe	Dunns	40/1	Habersham
Creathers, Andrew	Gwinnett	Hamiltons Bt.	180/1	Walton
Credill, Grey	Greene	Wheelis'	82/5	Appling
Credill, Grey	Greene	Wheelis	321/27	Early
Credille, Henry	Greene	Kimbroughs	80/12	Irwin
Creel, Joshua	Morgan	Farrars	358/28	Early
Crensham, Wm.H.	Baldwin	Marshalls	278/12	Irwin
Crenshaw, Benjamin	Warren	Rodgers	331/21	Early
Crenshaw, Benjamin	Warren	Rodgers	41/13	Early
Crenshaw, Fortin	Franklin	Baugh's	255/12	Irwin
Crenshaw, Jarrel W.	Jasper	White	200/5	Appling
Crenshaw, Micajah	Jasper	Reid's	174/10	Habersham
Crenshaw, Paschal	Warren	Rodgers	157/4	Appling
Crenshaw, Paschal	Warren	Rogers	94/3	Walton
Creswell, Ann(Orph)	Richmond	Jefferson	444/9	Irwin
Creswell, Jane(Orph)	Richmond	Jefferson	444/9	Irwin
Creswell, M.Samuel(Orph)	Richmond	Jefferson	444/9	Irwin
Creswell, Mary Ann(Orph)	Richmond	Jefferson	444/9	Irwin

NAME	COUNTY	MIL.DIST	LOT/SECT	DREW LAND
Crews, Alexr.Jr.	Camden	Tillis	279/3	Early
Crews, Asa	Effingham		253/1	Appling
Crews, Isaac	Camden	Clarks	339/11	Irwin
Crews, John	Clarke	Mitchells	218/13	Early
Crews, John	Wilkinson	Brooks'	359/4	Early
Crews, Joseph	Emanuel	59	136/3	Irwin
Crews, Micajah	Camden	32nd	252/4	Walton
Crews, Peter	Morgan	Selmons	111/1	Early
Crews, Sarah(Wid)	Tattnall	Jesse Durrences	150/11	Irwin
Cridale, Jesses	Greene	142	295/27	Early
Cridelle, Moses(Orphs)	Greene	Macons	173/2	Rabun
Crider, Barbara(Wid)	Franklin	Attaways	141/3	Irwin
Crider, David	Franklin	Attaways	460/2	Appling
Crider, John	Franklin	Attaways	369/2	Early
Crim, Clarrissa(Wid)	Wilkes	Kilgores	83/12	Irwin
Crim, Mary(Wid)	Liberty		139/27	Early
Crim, William	Wilkes	Kilgores	284/21	Early
Cristie, Robert	Chatham		240/6	Appling
Cristmas, Saml.(Orphs)	Jackson	Rogers Bt.	417/10	Irwin
Crittendens, Henry(Orph)	Twiggs	R.Belchers	441/6	Appling
Crocker, John	Twiggs	Browns	211/8	Appling
Crocket, Jos.	Gwinnett	Hamiltons Bt.	59/14	Early
Crockett, Martha(Wid)	Morgan	Morrows	253/13	Irwin
Crockett, Martha(Wid)	Morgan	Morrows	363/11	Irwin
Crofford, William	Twiggs	Evan's	281/5	Irwin
Croft, David(R.S.)	Bullock	Everetts	146/7	Appling
Croft, David(R.S.)	Bullock	Everitts	345/9	Early
Croft, Plasant	Lincoln	Stokes	368/11	Early
Croney, Joseph	Gwinnett	Hamiltons Bt.	13/3	Rabun
Crook, Lewis	Oglethorpe	Davenport	9/12	Irwin
Crook, Peter	Oglethorpe	Britton's	319/4	Early
Crook, Robert	Washington	Jinkinsons	373/19	Early
Croose, William	Wilkes	Bryants	179/6	Gwinnett
Crosby, Bailis	Wilkes	Runels	138/6	Appling
Crosby, Henry	Screven	36	67/26	Early
Crosby, John	Columbia	Ob.Morris	127/4	Habersham
Crosby, John	Wilkes	Runnels	53/3	Rabun
Crosby, Robert	Clarke	Tredwells	191/5	Irwin
Crosby, Spencer	Twiggs	Evans	451/10	Irwin
Crosby, Uriah	Wilkes	Runnels	307/3	Appling
Crosier, John	Lincoln	Walkers	172/2	Habersham
Crosier, John	Lincoln	Walkers	71/20	Early
Crosley, Thomas	Effingham		214/10	Habersham
Cross, Harriss	Jasper	Clay's	260/13	Early
Cross, John	Laurens	Watsons	169/16	Early
Cross, John	Laurens	Watsons	402/13	Irwin
Cross, John	Morgan	Hubbards	138/21	Early
Cross, John	Wilkinson	Bowings	7/28	Early
Cross, Richd.	Jasper	Clays	200/10	Irwin
Cross, Richd.	Jasper	Clays	291/7	Early
Crossbey, Edw.(Orphs)	Greene	144th	199/5	Gwinnett
Crossle, Andrew	Jefferson	Abbotts	148/7	Irwin
Crossle, Andrew	Jefferson	Abbotts	256/11	Early
Crossle, John	Jefferson	Fountains	505/6	Irwin
Crosson, John	Lincoln	Tatoms	340/9	Irwin
Crosson, Lewis	Lincoln	Tatoms	12/10	Hall
Crosson, Lewis	Lincoln	Tatoms	158/11	Habersham
Crough, John	Putnam	Mays	83/4	Walton
Crough, Shadrach	Putnam	Mays	8/11	Irwin
Crough, Shadrack	Putnam	Mays	32/22	Early
Crow, Isaac	Clarke	Stewarts	106/10	Habersham
Crow, James	Jackson	Dicksons Bt.	57/16	Irwin
Crow, Thos.S.	Baldwin	Marshalls	104/1	Habersham
Crowder, Frederick Sr.	Putnam	Slaughters	12/16	Early
Crowder, George	Oglethorpe	Barnetts	24/2	Appling
Crowder, John M.	Baldwin	Irwins	243/17	Early
Crowder, Stephen(R.S.)	Richmond	Winters	332/5	Appling

77

NAME	COUNTY	MIL.DIST	LOT/SECT	DREW LAN
Crowdis, Williss	Oglethorpe	Brittons	187/6	Appling
Crowell, Henry	Washington	Floyd's	159/12	Early
Crowell, Henry	Washington	Floyds	3/8	Early
Crowley, Spencer	Oglethorpe	Waters	478/8	Appling
Cruch, Thomas	Jasper	Evans	40/28	Early
Cruise, Arthur	Jones	Permenters	102/5	Rabun
Cruise, Jeremiah	Jefferson	Flemmings	307/6	Appling
Crum, David	Camden	32nd	97/3	Irwin
Crumbly, Alexander	Washington	Avents	17/1	Irwin
Crumbly, George	Washington	Avents	338/20	Early
Crumbly, John	Washington	Avents	276/3	Appling
Crumbly, Wm.	Washington	Avents	128/5	Early
Crump, Charles	Elbert	Gaines	440/10	Irwin
Crump, Phillip	Richmond		12/4	Appling
Crump, Richd.L.	Franklin	Morris'	97/6	Irwin
Crump, Robert	Elbert	Dooleys	72/1	Habersha
Crump, Robt.(Jr)	Franklin	Morriss	148/1	Irwin
Crump, Robt.Sr.	Franklin	Morris	331/28	Early
Crump, Robt.Sr.	Franklin	Morriss	23/3	Appling
Crump, Samuel	Columbia	Pullins	156/3	Appling
Crump, Silas	Franklin	Vaughns	138/9	Irwin
Crumpton, David	Twiggs	R.Belcher's	497/7	Irwin
Crumpton, David	Twiggs	R.Belchers	176/15	Early
Cruse, Catharine	Jasper	Bartletts	389/6	Appling
Cruse, George	Greene	Kimbrows	235/4	Early
Crutchfield, Geo.	Greene	140th	237/11	Early
Cryer, George	Morgan	Hubbard's	219/1	Walton
Cuce, Jas.H.	Jackson	Hamiltons	334/18	Early
Culberhouse, Chas.	Wilkes	Perrys	369/3	Early
Culberson, David	Franklin	Flanagans	124/14	Early
Culberson, Isaac	Morgan	Townsends	123/10	Hall
Culberson, Jas.(Orphs)	Jasper	Hays	205/5	Appling
Culberson, John S.	Laurens	Jones'	229/20	Early
Culbertson, Bird(Orphs)	Gwinnett	Hamiltons Bt.	51/1	Rabun
Culbertson, David B.	Greene	Harvills	232/6	Irwin
Culbertson, Jas.	Greene	Harvills	116/17	Early
Culbertson, Jas.	Greene	Harvills	350/12	Irwin
Culbertson, Jerry F.(Orphs) Greene		Griers	191/3	Habersha
Culbreath, John Sr.	Columbia	Walkers	408/28	Early
Culbreath, Thomas	Columbia	Walkers	241/28	Early
Culbreath, Wm.L.	Columbia	Shaws'	86/2	Habersha
Culbreth, Anguish	Madison	Culbreths	459/9	Irwin
Culbreth, John(Orphs)	Montgomery	Alstons	358/10	Early
Culbreth, Wm.L.	Columbia	Shaws	195/21	Early
Cullifer, Edward	Putnam	Coopers	426/12	Irwin
Cullins, Amos	Jones	Samuels	268/8	Irwin
Culpepper, Allason	Jackson	Dicksons Bt.	131/6	Gwinnett
Culpepper, Benjamin	Warren	Blounts	116/2	Early
Culpepper, Chadwell	Laurens	D.Smiths	240/12	Irwin
Culpepper, Chas.	Wilkinson	Kettles	181/5	Gwinnett
Culpepper, Elijah	Laurens	Deans	181/3	Irwin
Culpepper, Joel	Jones	Buckhalters	85/20	Early
Culpepper, Joel	Laurens	D.Smiths	468/2	Appling
Culpepper, Joseph	Warren	Blounts	122/10	Irwin
Culpepper, Malachiah	Morgan	Talbots	38/14	Appling
Culpepper, Nancy(Wid)	Jackson	Dicksons Bt.	276/4	Appling
Culpepper, Nathan	Warren	154th	179/2	Appling
Culpepper, Sampson	Wilkinson	Kettles	380/17	Early
Culpepper, Thos.K.	Jackson	Dicksons Bt.	198/26	Early
Culpepper, Wm.Sr.	Jones	Wallers	276/28	Early
Culver, George	Hancock	Evans'	201/4	Appling
Culver, Isaac	Hancock	Evan's	36/5	Irwin
Culver, James	Hancock	Evans	360/15	Early
Culver, James	Hancock	Evans	4/5	Rabun
Culver, Joseph	Hancock	Millers	292/8	Irwin
Culver, Levin E.	Hancock	Evans'	303/6	Gwinnett
Culver, Nathan Jr.	Hancock	Champions	220/19	Early

NAME	COUNTY	MIL.DIST	LOT/SECT	DREW LAND
Culver, Salathan(Orphs)	Hancock	Cooper's	18/9	Early
Culverhouse, Jermh.(Orphs)	Hancock	Edwards	62/3	Irwin
Cumbest, John	Baldwin	Marshalls	206/13	Early
Cumings, Joseph	Chatham		201/2	Appling
Cummin, Gideon	Putnam	Brooks	84/5	Early
Cumming, Elizabeth	Chatham		134/8	Appling
Cumming, Jno.Sr.	Jefferson	Bothwells	179/11	Irwin
Cumming, John B.	Richmond	120	201/1	Appling
Cumming, John	Richmond	120th	461/10	Irwin
Cumming, Joseph	Chatham		413/7	Irwin
Cumming, Luther	Richmond		196/9	Early
Cunningham, Jane H.(Wid)	Chatham		395/5	Appling
Cummings, Elijah	Greene	142	527/5	Appling
Cummings, Elijah	Oglethorpe	Murrays	84/3	Rabun
Cummings, James	McIntosh	Hamiltons	275/19	Early
Cummings, Thomas	Oglethorpe	Brittons	8/17	Early
Cummins, Eli	Putnam	Brooks	62/9	Hall
Cummins, Elijah	Greene	142nd	305/20	Early
Cummins, Francis	Greene	141	154/18	Early
Cummins, John	Washington	Cummins	77/2	Irwin
Cummins, Mary	Putnam	Brooks	192/10	Irwin
Cummins, Robt.(Dr)	Twiggs	Hodges	369/6	Irwin
Cummins, Stephen	Putnam	Brooks	130/3	Walton
Cummins, Wm.	Washington	Cummins	97/2	Irwin
Cump, Henry	Gwinnett	Hamiltons Bt.	235/28	Early
Cunnard, John	Jasper	Bentleys	44/11	Hall
Cunningham, Andrew	Jackson	Dicksons Bt.	182/7	Appling
Cunningham, Andrew	Twiggs	Evans	125/4	Appling
Cunningham, Franklin	Elbert	Gaines	321/8	Appling
Cunningham, Franklin	Elbert	Gains	294/6	Irwin
Cunningham, James T.	Richmond	122nd	43/28	Early
Cunningham, James	Washington	Mannings	66/5	Early
Cunningham, Jane H.(Wid)	Chatham		436/9	Irwin
Cunningham, Jas.S.	Wilkinson	Smiths	388/21	Early
Cunningham, John Sr.	Elbert	Ganes	140/2	Appling
Cunningham, John(Orphs)	Elbert	Childers	258/8	Irwin
Cunningham, John	Richmond	122nd	51/8	Early
Cunningham, John	Washington	Mannings	110/4	Appling
Cunningham, Jos.(Orphs)	Wilkes	Ogletrees	209/28	Early
Cunningham, Saml.	Baldwin	Cousins	453/5	Appling
Cunningham, Samuel	Baldwin	Cousins	29/5	Early
Cunningham, Thos.	Greene	143rd	141/3	Habersham
Cunningham, Wm.(R.S.)	Elbert	White & Nunnelly 488/9		Irwin
Cunnongham, Thomas	McIntosh	Hamiltons	378/7	Appling
Cunyers, Henry	Washington	Avents	283/3	Appling
Cunyers, Rachael(Wid)	Washington	Avents	455/8	Irwin
Cunyers, Wm.(Capt)	Tattnall	Cuners	245/28	Early
Cunyers, Wm.(Capt)	Tattnall	Cunyers	313/13	Early
Cunyers, Wm.	Washington	Avents	134/11	Hall
Cunyus, Wm.(Orphs)	Washington	Avents	141/1	Irwin
Cureton, Reason	Hancock	Mims	162/7	Appling
Cureton, Wm.Sr.	Hancock	Smiths	262/6	Early
Curetons, James	Hancock	Mims	284/5	Irwin
Curl, Matthew	Tattnall	Keens	432/4	Appling
Curlee, John(Orphs)	Jackson	Hamiltons Bt.	472/4	Appling
Curlee, Martha(Wid)	Jackson	Hamiltons Bt.	478/6	Irwin
Curlee, Wm.	Jackson	Hamiltons Bt.	201/1	Walton
Currie, Alexr.	Chatham		192/13	Early
Currie, Sarah	Baldwin	Russels	185/13	Irwin
Currier, Eliz.& Hannah(Orp)	Richmond	120th	122/15	Early
Curruthers, Joseph	Chatham		254/3	Early
Curry, Cary(R.S.)	Baldwin	Ellis'	156/6	Early
Curry, Cary(R.S.)	Baldwin	Ellis	353/3	Early
Curry, Charles	Putnam	Evans	335/16	Early
Curry, Charles	Putnam	Evans	57/3	Irwin
Curry, David	Washington	Renfros	415/1	Appling
Curry, Elisha	Baldwin	Ellis	279/12	Irwin

79

NAME	COUNTY	MIL.DIST	LOT/SECT	DREW LAND
Curry, Grace(Wid)	Montgomery	Alstons	265/10	Irwin
Curry, Jacob	Franklin	Morris'	105/26	Early
Curry, Jacob	Franklin	Morris	574/2	Appling
Curry, James	Greene	Harvills	471/2	Appling
Curry, Joel	Tattnall	Jos.Durrences	407/8	Irwin
Curry, John Jr.	Washington	Renfro's	59/12	Irwin
Curry, John Sr.	Washington	Renfro's	498/8	Irwin
Curry, John	Emanuel	55th	137/28	Early
Curry, John	Montgomery	Alstons	116/6	Early
Curry, Joseph	Tattnall	Jos.Durrences	51/1	Habersham
Curry, Josiah	Lincoln	Thompsons	164/7	Irwin
Curry, Thomas	Putnam	Robertsons	174/6	Appling
Curry, Whitmill C.	Wilkinson	Smiths	96/17	Early
Curry, William	Effingham		302/7	Gwinnett
Curtis, David	Screven		371/27	Early
Curtis, Hezekiah	Greene	Fosters	360/27	Early
Curtis, Robert	Greene	141	165/17	Early
Cushman, Allston	Chatham		160/18	Early
Cutchfield, Thos.	Wilkinson	Lees'	115/11	Hall
Cutchfield, Wm.	Wilkinson	Lees'	187/18	Early
Cuthbert, John A.	Putnam	Oslins	49/27	Early
Cutliff, Abraham	Putnam	H.Kendricks	352/9	Appling
Cutliff, Benj.	Elbert	Dobb's	523/9	Irwin
Cutliff, John	Putnam	Oslins	62/9	Appling
Cutts, Elijah	Washington	Daniels	289/8	Irwin
Cutts, Elisha	Washington	Daniels	369/10	Early
Cutts, Paul(Orphs)	Washington	Daniels	274/4	Early
Cuyler, William H.	Chatham		162/10	Early
D'Antignac, A.G.(Orp)	Columbia	Gartrell	127/5	Appling
D'Antignac, Jno.(RS)	Richmond	Lacey	171/3	Habersham
D'Antignac, Jno.(RS)	Richmond	Laceys	187/1	Early
Dadd, Isaac	Baldwin	Irwins	339/27	Early
Dailey, Ann(Wid)	Richmond	Burtons	332/5	Irwin
Dailey, Daniel	Scriven	36th	14/15	Irwin
Dailey, John	Elbert	Childs	270/6	Gwinnett
Dailey, John	Elbert	Childs	512/2	Appling
Dailey, Samuel	Franklin	Harris	49/8	Irwin
Dainill, Wm.	Laurens	S.Smith	32/2	Irwin
Dale, Abraham B.	Jasper	Bailey	330/7	Appling
Dale, Alexr.	Jasper	Bailys	373/8	Appling
Dale, Alexr.	Jasper	Baleys	284/4	Walton
Dale, John	Montgomery	Alstons	94/13	Early
Dalton, Barnabas	Richmond	Burtons	263/5	Irwin
Dalton, Olivia	Putnam	Buckners	277/3	Appling
Dalton, Thos.(RS)	Richmond	Burtons	65/12	Early
Daly, Daniel	Scriven	36th	203/9	Appling
Damper, John	Tattnall	I.Durrence	237/28	Early
Dampler, Stephen	Effingham		393/8	Irwin
Damron, Chas.(RS)	Jackson	Rogers Bt.	29/22	Early
Dancey, Francis	Wilkinson	Kettles	32/16	Early
Danel, Denton	Putnam	Slaughters	333/5	Appling
Danel, Lewis	Putnam	Buckners	1/6	Early
Danell, Jas.L.	Hancock	Herberts	335/7	Appling
Danell, Wm.	Hancock	Danells	95/1	Early
Danells, Amos(Orps)	Putnam	Buckners	316/13	Early
Danells, David	Putnam	H.Kendricks	46/3	Walton
Danels, Stephen(Orps)	Putnam	Buckners	194/11	Early
Daney, Francis	Wilkinson	Kettles	224/18	Early
Danforth, Abraham	Richmond	398	29/16	Irwin
Danforth, Abraham	Richmond	398	331/10	Irwin
Danforth, Ebenz.(Orphs)	Hancock	Lucas	231/7	Appling
Danforth, Jacob	Richmond	398th	73/1	Habersham
Danforth, Jas.K.	Richmond		292/7	Early
Danforth, Joshua	Richmond	398	112/10	Early
Danforth, Oliver	Richmond	398	29/8	Appling
Danforth, Rebecca(Wid)	Hancock	Lucas	71/4	Walton
Daniel, John Jr.	Morgan	Townsend	177/11	Irwin

NAME	COUNTY	MIL.DIST	LOT/SECT	DREW LAND
Daniel, Abraham	Liberty		499/7	Irwin
Daniel, Abraham	Twiggs	Smiths	33/5	Irwin
Daniel, Alexr.	Washington	Renfroes	123/6	Irwin
Daniel, Aron	Columbia	Watson	134/11	Early
Daniel, Aron	Columbia	Watson	158/9	Irwin
Daniel, Bryant	Richmond	Palmer	142/11	Habersham
Daniel, Christopher	Burke	Dye's	35/9	Early
Daniel, David	Bryan	19th	92/11	Habersham
Daniel, David	Burke	Lewis	30/1	Habersham
Daniel, David	Morgan	Farrar	153/10	Early
Daniel, David	Putnam	H.Kendricks	227/6	Appling
Daniel, Denton	Putnam	Slaughters	55/5	Early
Daniel, Edmund	Greene	Nelms	64/9	Irwin
Daniel, Egburt	Jones	Kings	282/4	Walton
Daniel, Elenader(Orp)	Burke	McNorrels	184/7	Gwinnett
Daniel, Ephraim	Twiggs	Smiths	358/9	Early
Daniel, Ezekiel Jr.	Washington	Daniels	187/17	Early
Daniel, Ezekiel Sr.	Washington	Daniels	128/10	Habersham
Daniel, Francis	Washington	Peabodys	181/2	Habersham
Daniel, Geo.W.	Laurens	Deans	168/4	Walton
Daniel, Hering	Greene	Nelms	366/12	Irwin
Daniel, Hopkins	Jasper	Hay's	53/7	Gwinnett
Daniel, Isaac	Tattnall	Jos.Durrence	386/4	Early
Daniel, Isaac	Tattnall	Jos.Durrence	49/9	Appling
Daniel, Jacan(Orp)	Washington	Daniels	348/26	Early
Daniel, James	Greene	Jones	322/6	Early
Daniel, Jas.	Jones	Kings	48/9	Early
Daniel, Jas.	Laurens	Harris	90/1	Rabun
Daniel, Jas.	Laurens	Harriss	51/12	Irwin
Daniel, Jas.J.	Elbert	Gains	225/5	Irwin
Daniel, Jeremiah	Clarke	Stuarts	234/14	Early
Daniel, Jesse	Washington	Avents	323/6	Gwinnett
Daniel, John Sr.	Liberty		57/26	Early
Daniel, John Sr.	Morgan	Townsend	144/7	Appling
Daniel, John Sr.	Morgan	Townsend	372/12	Irwin
Daniel, John	Elbert	Gains	33/19	Early
Daniel, John	Jasper	Reid	57/4	Irwin
Daniel, John	Laurens	Harris	8/7	Appling
Daniel, John	Washington	Wimberly	278/8	Irwin
Daniel, Jos.	Putnam	Oslins	183/3	Appling
Daniel, Jos.	Warren	Ragens	111/11	Early
Daniel, Joseph(Orph)	Burke	McNorrels	184/7	Gwinnett
Daniel, Joseph	Liberty		189/10	Early
Daniel, Josiah	Clarke	Harpers	196/1	Irwin
Daniel, Levy	Jasper	McClendon	239/13	Early
Daniel, Lewis	Putnam	Buckners	16/15	Early
Daniel, Lewis	Twiggs	Smiths	315/6	Irwin
Daniel, Lunsford	Jones	Kings	92/2	Early
Daniel, Mary(Wid)	Washington	Daniel	64/11	Hall
Daniel, Mary	Burke	McNorrills	328/8	Irwin
Daniel, Owen O.	Twiggs	Jamesons	138/8	Gwinnett
Daniel, Peter	Washington	Robisons	134/12	Early
Daniel, Peter	Washington	Wimberlys	95/10	Habersham
Daniel, Pondexter	Walton	Setells	124/2	Appling
Daniel, Reufus	Washington	Renfroes	515/5	Appling
Daniel, Robert C.	Burke	Dye's	354/2	Appling
Daniel, Robert	Chatham		122/8	Early
Daniel, Robert	Chatham		173/8	Appling
Daniel, Roselle(Orph)	Burke	McNorrels	184/7	Gwinnett
Daniel, Ruphus	Washington	Renfros	102/12	Early
Daniel, Russel J.	Madison	Williford	254/9	Irwin
Daniel, Sarah(Orp)	Burke	McNorrels	184/7	Gwinnett
Daniel, Solomon	Burke	J.Wards	105/1	Walton
Daniel, Stephen	Twiggs	Smiths	80/14	Irwin
Daniel, Stephen	Washington	Wimberly	281/7	Appling
Daniel, Thos.(RS)	Richmond	Lacey's	174/5	Appling
Daniel, Thos.(RS)	Richmond	Laceys	354/5	Gwinnett

NAME	COUNTY	MIL.DIST	LOT/SECT	DREW LAN
Daniel, Thos.	Washington	Peabodys	178/3	Appling
Daniel, Wm.	Greene	Jones	17/2	Irwin
Daniel, Wm.	Jones	Walters	319/20	Early
Daniel, Wm.	Laurens	S.Smiths	115/13	Early
Daniel, Wm.	Madison	Williford	92/6	Irwin
Daniel, Wm.	Wilkinson	Brooks	463/13	Irwin
Daniell, John R.	Greene	Carltons	107/3	Early
Daniels, John(Orp)	Washington	Wimberly	384/3	Early
Daniels, Stephen(Orps)	Putnam	Buckners	134/7	Early
Daniels, Wm.(Orps)	Putnam	Oslins	104/10	Habersha
Daniels, Wm.T.(Orphs)	Greene	Carltons	28/3	Habersha
Danman, Richy	Franklin	Davis	323/18	Early
Danney, David	Elbert	Webbs	112/20	Early
Danney, Edward A.	Elbert	Webbs	71/1	Irwin
Danney, Thomas	Elbert	Webbs	286/18	Early
Danset, Augustus	Chatham		412/6	Appling
Dansler, John	Chatham		48/5	Rabun
Darby, James	Baldwin	Haws	173/3	Appling
Darby, Jeremiah	Twiggs	Jameson	60/2	Appling
Darby, John	Laurens	Miltons	150/9	Early
Darby, Micajah	Twiggs	Jefferson	28/6	Early
Darby, Nicholas(RS)	Twiggs	Jefferson	360/8	Irwin
Darby, Nicholas(RS)	Twiggs	Jefferson	375/1	Appling
Darby, Nicholas(RS)	Twiggs	Jefferson	40/16	Early
Darby, Rich.(RS)	Twiggs	Jefferson	375/1	Appling
Darby, Thos.J.	Lincoln	Jeters	286/16	Early
Darcey, Jos.	Laurens	Griffins	255/3	Walton
Darcy, Jas.	Laurens	Griffin	124/17	Early
Darden, Abner	Warren	Griers	81/8	Hall
Darden, Bedford	Jasper	Easts	241/1	Appling
Darden, Elisha Sr.	Wilkinson	Brooks	397/26	Early
Darden, Elisha	Warren	Griers	425/5	Irwin
Darden, Elisha	Warren	Griers	533/2	Appling
Darden, Geo.W.	Jasper	Reids	34/10	Early
Darden, Henry W.	Warren	Hills	33/11	Irwin
Darden, Jas.(Orps)	Jasper	Bartletts	179/12	Habersha
Darden, Jesse	Warren	Griers	164/9	Early
Darden, Jonathan	Warren	Parhams	8/3	Appling
Darden, Micajah	Warren	Griers	359/15	Early
Darden, Micajah	Warren	Griers	480/4	Appling
Darden, Willis	Warren	Rodgers	191/2	Early
Darden, Wilson	Warren	152nd	335/6	Appling
Dardian, Wm.	Jones	Kings	417/28	Early
Dardin, Lemuel	Wilkes	Runnels	337/5	Early
Dardin, Zach.Jr.	Warren	Rodgers	5/14	Irwin
Dark, Agnes	Jones	Samuels	453/2	Appling
Darling, Joseph	Columbia	Burroughs	341/5	Irwin
Darnell, Jeremiah W.	Morgan	Farrar	158/2	Rabun
Darnell, Wm.	Morgan	Townsend	372/17	Early
Darnell, Zachariah	Greene	Carlons	484/8	Irwin
Darnold, Benjamin	Morgan	Loyd	629/2	Appling
Darracott, Wm.	Greene	143rd	308/12	Early
Darrough, Jos.	Jones	Phillip	309/13	Early
Darsey, Benj.Jr.	Laurens	Griffins	419/13	Irwin
Darsey, George	Columbia	Watsons	105/15	Irwin
Darsey, George	Columbia	Watsons	48/2	Irwin
Darsey, James	Liberty		235/21	Early
Darsey, James	Liberty		54/14	Irwin
Darsey, Joel	Columbia	Bealls	203/5	Appling
Darsey, Joel	Jasper	Mathews	220/17	Early
Darsey, Joel	Jasper	Mathews	280/7	Appling
Darsey, John Jr.	Columbia	J.Morris	14/3	Habersham
Darsey, John	Burke	71st	118/28	Early
Darson, Henry C.	Wilkes	Gordans	125/16	Irwin
Dart, Ann(Orph)	Glynn		169/5	Gwinnett
Dart, Ann	Glynn		511/2	Appling
Dart, Edgar(Orph)	Glynn		169/5	Gwinnett

82

NAME	COUNTY	MIL.DIST	LOT/SECT	DREW LAND
Dart, Eliza Ann(Orph)	Glynn		169/5	Gwinnett
Dart, Mariah(Orph)	Glynn		169/5	Gwinnett
Dart, Theodore(Orph)	Glynn		169/5	Gwinnett
Darwell, Jeremiah W.	Morgan	Farrar	371/21	Early
Dasher, Cristian	Effingham		571/2	Appling
Dasher, Eliz.(Wid)	Effingham		82/7	Appling
Dasher, Gottiel	Effingham		63/3	Rabun
Dasher, Herman C.	Effingham		31/2	Appling
Daugharty, Dennis	Appling	2	4733/5	Irwin
Daughtery, Nancy	Tattnall	McKennes	48/2	Rabun
Daughtrey, Mary(Wid)	Wilkinson	Bowings	452/7	Appling
Daughtry, Lemuel	Emanuel	49th	419/8	Appling
Daughtry, Lemuel	Emanuel	59th	130/12	Habersham
Daughtry, Randol(Orps)	Wilkinson	Bowings	419/4	Appling
Daupree, Lewis J.	Jackson	Winters	82/1	Rabun
Dauster, Stephen	Jones	Chappel	101/8	Hall
Dauster, Stephen	Jones	Chappels	321/16	Early
Davenport, Elvey(W)	Jasper	Fountains	518/5	Appling
Davenport, Jack S.	Warren	Rodgers	400/7	Appling
Davenport, Jas.(RS)	Oglethorpe	Davenport	618/2	Appling
Davenport, John M.	Richmond	120	99/8	Early
Davenport, Joiett	Oglethorpe	Davenport	319/26	Early
Davenport, Smith	Jasper	McClendon	170/13	Irwin
Davenport, Smith	Jasper	McClendon	370/4	Early
Davenport, Wm.	Franklin	Harriss	85/3	Rabun
Davico, William	Baldwin	Ellis	98/3	Habersham
David, Henry(Orps)	Madison	Culbreath	70/10	Irwin
David, Henry	Putnam	Stampers	215/7	Early
David, James H.	Franklin	Ash's	465/13	Irwin
David, John F.G.	Chatham		30/15	Early
David, Peter	Elbert	G.Higginbotham	279/8	Early
David, Peter	Madison	Culbreath	162/1	Early
Davidson, Asa	Warren	Travis	131/19	Early
Davidson, Asa	Warren	Travis	75/9	Early
Davidson, Harris	Jackson	Dicksons Bt.	215/9	Irwin
Davidson, Harris	Jackson	Dicksons Bt.	383/4	Early
Davidson, Hugh	Franklin	J.Millers	436/6	Appling
Davidson, John	Twiggs	W.Belchers	124/12	Early
Davidson, John	Wilkinson	Childs	396/7	Irwin
Davidson, John	Wilkinson	Childs	84/16	Early
Davidson, Jos.	Jasper	Blakes	165/4	Irwin
Davidson, Perry P.(Orp)	Warren	153	142/2	Irwin
Davidson, Robt.	Morgan	Alford	448/7	Irwin
Davidson, Talbot	Jones	Samuels	90/1	Appling
Davie, Jos.	Jones	Harris	373/7	Early
Davies, George W.	Chatham		393/13	Irwin
Davies, John	Chatham		391/10	Early
Davies, William	Chatham		15/4	Habersham
Davis, Abrm.(Orps)	Twiggs	Jefferson	401/12	Irwin
Davis, Acenath	Burke	M.Wards	247/15	Early
Davis, Allen J.	Jones	Buckhalter	122/6	Gwinnett
Davis, Allen	Greene	144	222/2	Irwin
Davis, Amos	Bulloch	Knights	186/15	Early
Davis, Ann(Wid)	Bryan	19th	266/7	Appling
Davis, Arthur	Montgomery	Alstons	110/8	Irwin
Davis, Backster R.	Wilkes	Davis	90/11	Hall
Davis, Benj.(Orphs)	Clarke	Pentecosts	76/12	Habersham
Davis, Benj.	Putnam	J.Kendricks	197/28	Early
Davis, Benj.	Putnam	J.Kindricks	50/12	Hall
Davis, Benj.	Wayne	Johnstons	362/3	Early
Davis, Benjamin	Clarke	Parr	324/18	Early
Davis, Benjamin	Effingham		262/4	Irwin
Davis, Britton	Elbert	Webbs	89/18	Early
Davis, Champion	Oglethorpe	Waters	293/20	Early
Davis, Clement	Wilkinson	Howards	255/11	Irwin
Davis, Clement	Wilkinson	Howards	303/9	Irwin
Davis, Clement	Wilkinson	Howards	399/17	Early

NAME	COUNTY	MIL.DIST	LOT/SECT	DREW LAN
Davis, Cornelius	Elbert	Dooleys	148/20	Early
Davis, Daniel Jr.	Montgomery	Alstons	158/9	Hall
Davis, Danl.Jr.	Montgomery	Alston	329/8	Irwin
Davis, Danl.Sr.	Montgomery	Alston	383/1	Early
Davis, David	Jasper	Posts	7/5	Early
Davis, Dennis	Scriven	180	142/2	Early
Davis, Dioclesian	Washington	Brooks	113/20	Early
Davis, Dolfin	Warren	154	328/12	Irwin
Davis, Drury	Morgan	Campbell	359/19	Early
Davis, Eady	Clarke	Pentecosts	52/17	Early
Davis, Edmond(Orps)	Burke	M.Wards	159/20	Early
Davis, Elbert	Twiggs	Smiths	101/9	Irwin
Davis, Eliz.(Wid)	Wilkinson	Howards	384/1	Appling
Davis, Elnatham	Burke	Spiveys	113/1	Walton
Davis, Finch	Jasper	Baleys	101/6	Irwin
Davis, Finch	Jasper	Bayley	227/12	Irwin
Davis, Gardner(Orps)	Jones	Hansford	454/6	Irwin
Davis, Gary	Franklin	P.Browns	1/7	Appling
Davis, Gazaway	Columbia	Ob.Morris	114/3	Irwin
Davis, Geo.C.	Jasper	Trimbles	451/1	Appling
Davis, Geo.Jr.	Oglethorpe	Waters	301/14	Early
Davis, Geo.Sr.	Oglethorpe	Waters	337/17	Early
Davis, George	Columbia	Dodson	203/8	Early
Davis, Goodrum	Washington	Burney	372/1	Early
Davis, Goodrum	Washington	Burneys	439/8	Irwin
Davis, Grant	Morgan	Talbot	128/2	Irwin
Davis, Grant	Morgan	Talbott	84/9	Early
Davis, Hannah	Jasper	Evans	51/13	Habersha
Davis, Henry	Franklin	Vaughn	163/9	Appling
Davis, Henry	Wilkinson	Kettles	266/1	Appling
Davis, Hezekiah	Effingham		99/10	Habersha
Davis, Hieman	Jones	Permenter	143/11	Habersha
Davis, Hosias	Pulaski	Lanears	27/4	Rabun
Davis, Hustus	Bulloch	Jones	44/10	Irwin
Davis, Isaac	Burke	69	78/4	Walton
Davis, Isabel	Morgan	Talbots	85/6	Early
Davis, Isham	Oglethorpe	Wises	58/4	Appling
Davis, James	Elbert	Hannahs	171/11	Habersha
Davis, James	McIntosh	Eigles	500/6	Irwin
Davis, James	McIntosh	McIntosh	210/1	Appling
Davis, Jas.(Orps)	Wilkinson	Howards	42/4	Irwin
Davis, Jas.R.	Jones	Hansford	154/11	Irwin
Davis, Jas.R.	Jones	Hansford	33/6	Irwin
Davis, Jeramiah	Emanuel	55	13/6	Appling
Davis, Jeremiah	Morgan	Jordan	248/3	Walton
Davis, Jeremiah	Morgan	Jordan	35/1	Habersha
Davis, Jesse	Twiggs	Hodges	58/12	Early
Davis, John B.	Laurens	Harris	102/12	Habersha
Davis, John F.	Scriven	180th	157/15	Irwin
Davis, John F.G.	Chatham		27/7	Appling
Davis, John G.	Columbia	Dodsons	193/12	Early
Davis, John J.H.	Pulaski	Rees	129/19	Early
Davis, John T.	Jackson	Rogers Bt.	240/2	Early
Davis, John(Orps)	Wilkinson	Childs	359/26	Early
Davis, John	Baldwin	Stephens	256/3	Early
Davis, John	Elbert	R.Christian	104/5	Rabun
Davis, John	Franklin	Morris	194/7	Irwin
Davis, John	Franklin	Morris	52/15	Irwin
Davis, John	Jasper	Evans	197/17	Early
Davis, John	Jasper	Evans	46/9	Appling
Davis, John	Morgan	Campbell	24/5	Gwinnett
Davis, John	Tattnall	Tharps	139/6	Irwin
Davis, John	Tattnall	Tharps	141/15	Early
Davis, John	Telfair	Williams	129/4	Irwin
Davis, John	Wilkinson	Childs	204/10	Early
Davis, Jonathan	Hancock	Evans	154/3	Habersha
Davis, Jonathan	Jones	Harrist	515/8	Irwin

84

NAME	COUNTY	MIL.DIST	LOT/SECT	DREW LAND
Davis, Jos.	Wilkinson	Howards	175/11	Irwin
Davis, Jos.	Wilkinson	Howards	51/9	Hall
Davis, Joseph	Scriven	180	187/10	Habersham
Davis, Joshua	Jones	Samuels	49/10	Early
Davis, Joshua	Warren	152	2/4	Walton
Davis, Levi Sr.	Effingham		105/13	Early
Davis, Levi Sr.	Effingham		402/5	Irwin
Davis, Lewis(Orps)	Putnam	H.Kendrick	344/2	Appling
Davis, Lewis	Washington	Brooks	286/9	Irwin
Davis, Lewis	Washington	Wimberlys	387/3	Appling
Davis, Littleberry	Warren	152	368/10	Early
Davis, Micajah E.	Pulaski	Davis	400/9	Early
Davis, Moses	Warren	153rd	105/2	Walton
Davis, Mosses	Oglethorpe	Waters	43/2	Appling
Davis, Owen(Orps)	Jasper	McClendon	104/3	Walton
Davis, Palsey(Orph)	Hall	M.Cutchens	465/8	Appling
Davis, Patsey	Jasper	Flemings	30/9	Irwin
Davis, Price	Columbia	J.Morris	392/11	Irwin
Davis, Priscilla(Wid)	Washington	Burney	128/20	Early
Davis, Randolph	Columbia	Willingham	34/21	Early
Davis, Redin	Pulaski	Rees	24/4	Appling
Davis, Reuben	Columbia	Dodsons	97/13	Early
Davis, Reuben	Elbert	Dobbs	198/16	Early
Davis, Richard	Scriven		326/26	Early
Davis, Richd(Orps)	Morgan	Hackney	56/2	Walton
Davis, Richd.	Jasper	Waldens	236/5	Gwinnett
Davis, Robt.H.	Jasper	Evans	37/22	Early
Davis, Samuel	Bulloch	Knights	196/19	Early
Davis, Samuel	Putnam	H.Kendricks	17/9	Early
Davis, Sarah F.(Wid)	Chatham		265/9	Appling
Davis, Sarah(Wid)	Wilkinson	Childs	99/11	Hall
Davis, Stafford	Montgomery	Alstons	285/9	Irwin
Davis, Strawder	Franklin	Greens	361/12	Irwin
Davis, Sylus N.	Greene	Wheelis	415/6	Irwin
Davis, Terry	Elbert	Childs	91/14	Irwin
Davis, Thomas G.	Chatham		234/28	Early
Davis, Thomas W.	Burke	Bells	167/13	Early
Davis, Thomas	Baldwin	Ellis	458/12	Irwin
Davis, Thomas	Elbert	B.Higginbotham	92/27	Early
Davis, Thomas	Franklin	Vaughn	88/5	Rabun
Davis, Thos.	Jones	Harrist	216/7	Gwinnett
Davis, Thos.	Morgan	Hackney	147/17	Early
Davis, Thos.	Morgan	Leonard	488/8	Early
Davis, Thos.	Morgan	Leonards	319/9	Early
Davis, Thos.	Twiggs	Browns	74/6	Appling
Davis, Thos.	Warren	154th	74/3	Habersham
Davis, Thos.	Warren	Parhams	241/16	Early
Davis, Thos.	Warren	Parhams	42/8	Hall
Davis, Thos.Jr.	Franklin	Vaughns	156/15	Early
Davis, Thos.Sr.	Franklin	Vaughns	219/7	Appling
Davis, Thos.W.	Elbert	Childers	43/21	Early
Davis, Thos.W.	Franklin	P.Browns	7/2	Irwin
Davis, Thos.W.	Jones	Wallers	3/27	Early
Davis, Timothy	Baldwin		301/6	Irwin
Davis, Toliver	Baldwin	Stephens	276/5	Early
Davis, Venson	Washington	Cummins	166/1	Appling
Davis, Watkins	Warren	154th	188/6	Irwin
Davis, William Sr.	Columbia	Bealls	150/10	Early
Davis, William	Clarke	Parrs	26/20	Early
Davis, Wm. (Orps)	Hancock	Edwards	45/9	Irwin
Davis, Wm. (R.S.)	Elbert	White & Nunnelly	389/9	Early
Davis, Wm.	Franklin	Vaughans	376/12	Early
Davis, Wm.	Jasper	Clays	271/5	Appling
Davis, Wm.	Jones	Chappels	231/1	Appling
Davis, Wm.	Oglethorpe	Waters	131/27	Early
Davis, Wm.	Tattnall	J.Durrence	94/6	Early
Davis, Wm.	Twiggs	Evan's	308/11	Early

NAME	COUNTY	MIL.DIST	LOT/SECT	DREW LAND
Davis, Wm.	Wilkinson	Kettles	15/4	Irwin
Davis, Wm.H.	Franklin	P.Browns	112/4	Walton
Davis, Wm.N.	Scriven	180	121/19	Early
Davis, Wm.N.	Scriven	180	234/6	Irwin
Davis, Wm.Sr	Columbia	Beall	392/10	Early
Davis, Wright	Twiggs	Bozeman	287/4	Early
Davis, Wright	Twiggs	Bozemans	239/23	Early
Davis, Zachariah	Montgomery	McElvins	64/3	Habersham
Davis, Zadoc	Jones	Seals	392/27	Early
Davison, Allen	Wilkinson	Childs	145/5	Gwinnett
Davison, John	Chatham		314/9	Early
Davisson, Jas.Jr.	Laurens	Jones	140/4	Appling
Dawins, Henry	Jasper	Kennedys	376/1	Early
Dawins, Wm.(Orps)	Putnam	H.Kendricks	247/6	Irwin
Dawkins, Absalum(Orps)	Burke	Dye's	193/1	Early
Dawkins, Daniel	Jasper	Centells	69/2	Irwin
Dawkins, Garland	Jasper	Kennedys	348/13	Irwin
Dawkins, Haney	Jasper	Kennedys	376/1	Early
Dawneng, Mathew B.	Putnam	Jurnigans	313/28	Early
Dawsey, Jarrat	Wilkes	Ogletree	6/2	Irwin
Dawson, Christopher	Chatham		78/6	Irwin
Dawson, Geo.	Greene	143	84/6	Gwinnett
Dawson, Geo.Jr.	Greene	143rd	14/7	Gwinnett
Dawson, Geo.Sr.	Greene	143rd	346/5	Irwin
Dawson, Jno.E.(Orps)	Morgan	Hackney	53/17	Early
Dawson, John	Burke	72nd	48/2	Habersham
Dawson, John	Chatham		152/3	Walton
Dawson, John	Morgan	Campbell	83/10	Early
Dawson, Philemon H.	Putnam	Oslins	60/4	Appling
Dawson, Sabra(Wid)	Richmond	Winters	149/11	Irwin
Dawson, Washington(Orps)	Baldwin	Marshalls	317/9	Appling
Day, Hannah(Wid)	Walton	Worshams	88/17	Early
Day, John	Walton	Sentells	12/11	Irwin
Day, Jos.	Jones	Greens	14/6	Appling
Day, Nimrod	Twiggs	Jefferson	198/7	Early
Day, Richd.R.	Columbia	Shaws	144/6	Irwin
Day, Robt.	Walton	Worshams	434/7	Irwin
Day, Stephen	Columbia	Shaws	61/12	Irwin
Day, William	Columbia	Shaws	184/4	Appling
Day, Wm.(Orps)	Oglethorpe	Bowls	322/1	Appling
DeVillers, Petit F.D.	Chatham		49/12	Irwin
Deafnell, Bush	Pulaski	Johnston	389/11	Early
Deagle, Wm.G.	Emanuel	59th	250/4	Walton
Deake, Robert	Emanuel	57th	145/12	Habersham
Deake, Robert	Emanuel	57th	88/16	Early
Deakle, Thos.	Emanuel	59th	377/17	Early
Deal, Ezekiel	Burke	Lewis	103/7	Irwin
Deal, Ezekiel	Burke	Lewis	331/19	Early
Deal, Lewis	Jasper	Langston	219/18	Early
Deal, Stephen	Jasper	Baileys	191/4	Appling
Deale, John L.B.	Emanuel	59th	250/1	Walton
Deale, Wm.	Franklin	Flanagans	253/10	Early
Deals, John(Orphs)	Emanuel	49th	147/3	Walton
Dean, Agnus(Wid)	Morgan	Jordan	156/20	Early
Dean, Burket	Morgan	Jourdan	197/16	Irwin
Dean, Charles	Clarke	Deans	240/1	Appling
Dean, Charles	Clarke	Deans	51/6	Habersham
Dean, David	Morgan	Jordan	150/17	Early
Dean, Frederich	Elbert	Whites D.Christ Bt. 70/10		Hall
Dean, Fredr.	Morgan	Jordan	15/12	Hall
Dean, Fredr.	Morgan	Jordan	79/12	Hall
Dean, Gideon R.	McIntosh	McIntosh	208/3	Appling
Dean, Henry	Jasper	Blakes	201/10	Irwin
Dean, James(Orps)	Burke	Sullivans	471/5	Appling
Dean, James	Washington	Robisons	169/9	Irwin
Dean, Joel	Washington	Robisons	37/15	Early
Dean, John	Clarke	Deans	285/2	Early

NAME	COUNTY	MIL.DIST	LOT/SECT	DREW LAND
Dean, Mathew	Morgan	Jordan	244/5	Irwin
Dean, Michael	Washington	Robertson	39/5	Irwin
Dean, Richd.Sr.	Laurens	Deans	508/8	Appling
Dean, Richmond(Orp)	McIntosh	Gould	248/13	Early
Dean, Seaborn	Burke	Sullivans	107/1	Appling
Dean, Susannah(Wid)	Laurens	Watson	235/9	Irwin
Dean, Thos.C.	Morgan	Jordan	282/27	Early
Dean, Williamson	Laurens	Deans	519/7	Appling
Dean, Wm.	Franklin	Akins	263/8	Appling
Dean, Wm.	Morgan	Jordan	109/1	Early
Dean, Wm.	Washington	Barges	131/12	Hall
Deans, Henry Jr.	Hancock	Champions	230/3	Irwin
Dearing, Reuben	Wilkes	Dents	395/2	Appling
Dearing, Reuben	Wilkes	Dents	73/8	Appling
Dearing, Wm.	Wilkes	Gordons	64/1	Rabun
Dearring, Joanna	Wilkes	Dents	158/1	Irwin
Deas, Jesse	Wilkinson	Wiggins	157/7	Gwinnett
Deason, Absalom	Washington	Peabodys	254/2	Appling
Deason, Ambrose	Jones	Permenter	235/13	Irwin
Deason, Dempsey	Lincoln	Tatoms	87/3	Early
Deason, Michael	Jasper	Northcut	45/3	Early
Deason, Shepherd	Washington	Peaboddy	191/18	Early
Deaton, Jos.	Hall	Millers	21/5	Habersham
Deaton, Jos.	Hall	Millers	414/15	Early
Deaton, Wm.Jr.	Hall	Millers	89/9	Irwin
Deaton, Wm.Sr.	Hall	Millers	161/1	Walton
Deavenport, Burket	Morgan	Leonard	17/5	Gwinnett
Deavours, Geo.	Franklin	Flanagans	264/21	Early
Deboys, Nancy B.(Wid)	Jones	Buckhalter	103/1	Habersham
Dee, Hulliard(Orps)	Pulaski	Davis	114/12	Irwin
Deen, John	Jackson	Dicksons Bt.	305/7	Appling
Deens, Henry(RS)	Hancock	Champions	186/5	Irwin
Dees, Jacob	Twiggs	Jefferson	233/14	Early
Dees, James(Orps)	Pulaski	Davis	224/2	Appling
Dees, James	Early		277/10	Early
Dees, James	Tattnall	Overstreet	309/15	Early
Dees, James	Tattnall	Overstreet	507/6	Irwin
Dees, Jas.T.	Tattnall	Johnsons	472/7	Appling
Dees, John	Pulaski	Davis	188/7	Appling
Dees, John	Tattnall	Overstreet	486/7	Irwin
Dees, Jordan	Pulaski	Davis	177/19	Early
Dees, Jordan	Pulaski	Davis	187/10	Irwin
Dees, Matthew M.	Tattnall	Overstreet	17/5	Early
Degraffenried, V.	Oglethorpe	Murrays	15/13	Irwin
Delaigle, Nich.	Richmond	Laceys	74/7	Appling
Delbos, John	Tattnall	Overstreet	236/3	Appling
Delegall, Edwd.	McIntosh	Gould	132/10	Early
Delenoy, Ann(Wid)	Chatham		246/4	Irwin
Delenoy, Caraly(Wid)	Chatham		251/4	Walton
Delk, David	Liberty		289/2	Irwin
Delk, Joseph	Wilkinson	Smiths	88/1	Irwin
Dell, Joseph	Scriven	Lovetts	41/5	Rabun
Dellegall, Thos.	McIntosh	Gould	319/2	Appling
Deloach, Hardy	Liberty		130/6	Gwinnett
Deloatch, Abrm.	Tattnall	J.Durrence	325/10	Early
Deloatch, Jesse	Tattnall	J.Durrence	111/11	Hall
Deloatch, Jno.(Orps)	Tattnall	J.Durrence	188/4	Early
Deloatch, Sarah(Wid)	Tattnall	J.Durrence	368/4	Appling
Delport, Wm.(Orps)	Jackson	Rogers	328/2	Early
Denby, Elijah(Orps)	Hancock	Coopers	437/2	Appling
Denes, Reuben	Putnam	Ruckers	78/8	Appling
Denis, Wm.	Hancock	Danells	25/18	Early
Denis, Wm.	Hancock	Danells	41/5	Appling
Denman, Chapleigh	Franklin	Morris	73/5	Irwin
Denmark, James	Bulloch	Knights	64/1	Irwin
Denmark, Malichi	Bulloch	Knights	28/13	Irwin
Dennard, Bird	Twiggs	Browns	348/13	Early

NAME	COUNTY	MIL.DIST	LOT/SECT	DREW LAND
Dennard, Bird	Twiggs	Browns	86/3	Irwin
Dennard, Eliz.(Wid)	Twiggs	Browns	338/12	Early
Dennard, Isaac	Elbert	P.Christians	281/18	Early
Dennard, Jaru	Twiggs	Browns	305/10	Early
Dennard, Jesse	Wilkinson	Lees	77/9	Appling
Dennard, John E.	Twiggs	Browns	166/16	Irwin
Dennard, John Jr.	Elbert	P.Christians	125/8	Appling
Dennard, John Sr.	Twiggs	Browns	188/2	Early
Denneman, James	Franklin	Morriss	59/7	Irwin
Dennis, Abijah	Putnam	Littles	182/5	Early
Dennis, Allen	Lincoln	Tatoms	109/3	Walton
Dennis, Daniel	Hancock	Scotts	27/5	Habershac
Dennis, Jacob	Columbia	Willingham	224/7	Irwin
Dennis, Jesse	Jasper	Bentleys	244/1	Early
Dennis, Jesse	Morgan	Selmon	421/6	Irwin
Dennis, Jesse	Twiggs	Browns	156/4	Walton
Dennis, John	Twiggs	Hodges	196/28	Early
Dennis, Maria	Chatham		204/18	Early
Dennis, Mary	Putnam	Littles	145/3	Walton
Dennis, Richmond	Warren	152	28/2	Early
Dennis, Richmond	Warren	152nd	232/9	Irwin
Dennis, Simeon	Putnam	Evans	160/4	Appling
Dennis, Wm.	Putnam	Bustins	130/2	Habershac
Dennis, Wm.	Putnam	J.Kendicks	157/11	Early
Dennis, Wm.	Putnam	J.Kendrick	157/11	Early
Dennis, Wm.	Putnam	J.Kindrick	5/13	Habershac
Dennis, Wm.Sr.	Lincoln	Parks	52/3	Walton
Dennison, Saml.	McIntosh	Eigles	233/8	Irwin
Dennisson, Wm.(Orp)	Wayne	Johnston	22/17	Early
Denny, John	Effingham		37/7	Irwin
Denny, John	Effingham		383/10	Irwin
Densler, Frederich	Chatham		220/26	Early
Densler, Phillip(Orps)	Effingham		444/7	Appling
Densley, Henry	Baldwin	Cousins	326/8	Appling
Denson, Calley	Putnam	Morelands	62/1	Appling
Denson, Callus	Putnam	Morelands	260/7	Appling
Denson, Eli	Jasper	Trembles	232/27	Early
Denson, Eloanah	Jasper	Trembles	288/27	Early
Denson, Isaac	Twiggs	Hodges	381/9	Early
Denson, John H.	Jasper	Bartlett	474/5	Appling
Denson, Jos.W.	Pulaski	Johnston	356/3	Early
Denson, Richd.	Twiggs	Hodges	126/13	Irwin
Dent, Ann M.(Wid)	Columbia	Burrough	420/4	Appling
Dent, Dennis	Columbia	Burrough	209/13	Early
Dent, Geo.Wash.	Columbia	Burroughs	240/26	Early
Dent, Geo.Washington	Columbia	Burrough	258/4	Irwin
Dent, James T.	Columbia	Buroughs	165/7	Gwinnett
Dent, John	Richmond	120	160/9	Irwin
Dent, Nancy(Wid)	Jones	Jefferson	293/19	Early
Dent, Nathl.	Hancock	Lucas	142/4	Walton
Dent, Nathl.	Hancock	Lucas	90/5	Appling
Dent, Peter(RS)	Hancock	Lucas	259/6	Appling
Dent, Richd.	Oglethorpe	Barnett	18/4	Rabun
Dent, Richd.	Oglethorpe	Barnett	68/20	Early
Dent, Walter C.	Putnam	Littles	107/28	Early
Dent, Wm.(Orps)	Lincoln	Thompson	75/13	Early
Denton, Aaron	Warren	150th	16/13	Early
Denton, Gabriel W.	Chatham		222/8	Early
Denton, John B.	Hancock	Bans	309/9	Appling
Denton, John	Hancock	Evans	128/14	Irwin
Denton, John	Jackson	Dicksons	36/23	Early
Denton, John	Jackson	Dicksons	54/3	Appling
Denton, Joshua(RS)	Jackson	Dicksons	365/10	Irwin
Denton, Joshua(RS)	Jackson	Dicksons	87/5	Appling
Denton, Samuel	Twiggs	R.Belcher	51/4	Appling
Denton, Sarah(Wid)	Twiggs	R.Belchers	208/4	Appling
Denton, Thos.	Twiggs	R.Belchers	506/9	Irwin

NAME	COUNTY	MIL.DIST	LOT/SECT	DREW LAND
Dents, Samuel(Orphs)	Baldwin	Ellis	210/6	Appling
Depreast, Jos.C.	Jackson	Winters Bt.	66/4	Irwin
Deprest, Martin	Morgan	Parker	156/7	Early
Deprest, Martin	Morgan	Parker	199/10	Habersham
Depugh, John	Franklin	J.Miller	54/3	Irwin
Depugh, John	Franklin	J.Millers	325/20	Early
Deracan, Hiram M.	Baldwin	Taliaferros	36/2	Appling
Deracan, Hiram M.	Baldwin	Taliaferros	97/7	Irwin
Derdin, Henry	Emanuel	59	402/7	Irwin
Derifield, John	Hall		479/7	Appling
Derram, Singleton	Jasper	Kennaday	20/16	Early
Desaubleaux, P.L.(Orps)	Laurens	Deans	306/8	Irwin
Deshaze, Wm.	Twiggs	R.Belchers	372/26	Early
Deshazer, Wm.R.	Putnam	Slaughter	298/7	Appling
Deshazer, Wm.R.	Putnam	Slaughters	21/2	Walton
Deshazo, John	Pulaski	Senterfeits	513/7	Irwin
Deshazo, Richd.	Twiggs	R.Belcher	331/18	Early
Deshron, Samuel	Habersham	Flanagans	350/1	Early
Deshroon, Waitman	Habersham	Flannigans	30/12	Habersham
Deublein, Geo.N.	Hancock	Millers	168/13	Early
Devant, James	Chatham		271/26	Early
Devaughn, Wm.	Lincoln	Parks	140/5	Early
Deveaux, Peter(R.S.)	Chatham		264/17	Early
Devenport, Wm.	Franklin	Harriss	481/8	Irwin
Deverages, Jas.	McIntosh	McIntsoh	220/10	Irwin
Devereaux, Chas.(Orps)	Twiggs	Hodges	368/4	Early
Devine, Wm.H.	Putnam	Buckners	102/2	Rabun
Dewart, David	Pulaski	Johnston	153/3	Early
Dewberry, Irby	Warren	Rogers	39/6	Early
Dewberry, John	Warren	Griers	354/6	Irwin
Dewberry, Thos.	Putnam	Cooper	472/5	Appling
Dewit, Robert	Pulaski	Lesters	103/3	Appling
Dews, Robert J.	Chatham		414/1	Early
Dexter, B.W.	McIntosh	Hamilton	221/21	Early
Dexter, B.W.	McIntosh	Hamilton	270/10	Irwin
Dias, Henry	Appling	3	137/7	Irwin
Dick, Thomas	Wilkinson	Brooks	272/2	Appling
Dicken, Isaac	Wilkes	Dents	141/2	Appling
Dicken, James T.	Warren	Hubberts	71/21	Early
Dicken, William	Clarke	Mitchells	97/10	Irwin
Dickens, Ann	Chatham		1/11	Irwin
Dickerson, Alpheus	Hancock	Thomas	265/11	Early
Dickerson, Chas.	Washington	Burney	134/4	Irwin
Dickerson, Clark M.	Hancock	Thomas	61/12	Early
Dickerson, David	Elbert	B.Higginbotham	133/21	Early
Dickerson, Isaac	Hancock	Canes	258/7	Early
Dickerson, Jehu	Laurens	Ross	362/7	Gwinnett
Dickerson, John	Hancock	Lucas	118/20	Early
Dickerson, Jos.	Franklin	Halcombs	126/2	Irwin
Dickerson, Levi	Hancock	Canes	397/9	Irwin
Dickerson, Philipine	Franklin	Holcomb	389/20	Early
Dickerson, Wimbum	Hancock	Canes	452/28	Early
Dickerson, Wm.	Greene	142nd	9/5	Appling
Dickerson, Zachariah	Elbert	Doolys	239/17	Early
Dickerson, Zachr.	Elbert	Higginbotham	401/7	Appling
Dickey, Samuel	Putnam	Slaughter	23/28	Early
Dickin, John	Warren	Travis	249/3	Appling
Dickin, Thomas	Clarke	Stuarts	168/17	Early
Dickin, William	Clarke	Mitchells	54/17	Early
Dickin, Young A.	Elbert	James	101/4	Early
Dickins, John	Washington	Cummins	152/28	Early
Dickinson, Cosby	Richmond	398	252/15	Early
Dickinson, Jezekiah	Richmond	398	506/8	Irwin
Dickinson, John	Hancock	Lucas	303/3	Early
Dickison, James	Clarke	Moores	340/13	Irwin
Dicks, Eliza	Chatham		365/6	Appling
Dicks, James	Oglethorpe	Murray	39/5	Early

NAME	COUNTY	MIL.DIST	LOT/SECT	DREW LAN
Dicks, John(Orp)	Chatham		246/4	Appling
Dicks, John	Oglethorpe	Murrays	203/6	Early
Dicks, John	Oglethorpe	Murrays	55/4	Early
Dickson, Able(Orps)	Pulaski	Rees	56/12	Habersha
Dickson, Benj.	Hancock	Scotts	417/26	Early
Dickson, James	Clarke	Moores	142/5	Appling
Dickson, Jeremiah	Wilkinson	Kettles	181/11	Irwin
Dickson, John B.	Jones	Jefferson	311/11	Early
Dickson, Robt.	Wilkinson	Wiggins	194/15	Early
Dickson, Robt.L.	Scriven		359/12	Irwin
Dickson, Sampson	Wilkinson	Kettles	201/11	Irwin
Dickson, Thomas	Baldwin	Talisferro	174/4	Walton
Dickson, Thos.	Laurens	S.Smiths	45/8	Hall
Dickson, Wm.	Jackson	Dicksons	180/2	Appling
Die, John	Laurens	Harris	349/5	Early
Digbe, Jos.(Orps)	Jasper	Bentley	427/13	Irwin
Digby, William	Baldwin	McCrary	66/9	Irwin
Dill, Jacob	Richmond	120	71/1	Early
Dillard, Allen	Washington	Robinsons	151/13	Habersha
Dillard, David	Emanuel	53rd	505/5	Appling
Dillard, Edmund	Washington	Floyds	16/2	Habersha
Dillard, Elizabeth	Burke	Thomas	55/1	Early
Dillard, Ishmael(Orp)	Burke	Thomas	50/3	Walton
Dillard, Jas.Jr.	Elbert	T.Christian	385/10	Early
Dillard, Jas.Sr.(RS)	Elbert	P.Christian	12/1	Rabun
Dillard, John(Orp)	Burke	Thomas	50/3	Walton
Dillard, John	Jones	Shropsher	336/4	Early
Dillard, John	Jones	Shropshier	145/4	Appling
Dillard, Mary(Orp)	Burke	Thomas	50/3	Walton
Dillard, Phillip	Burke	Dye's	258/6	Appling
Dillard, Reuben	Oglethorpe	Barnett	175/28	Early
Dillard, Tolliver	Burke	69th	220/4	Appling
Dillard, William	Burke	Dye's	293/12	Early
Dillon, John	Chatham		171/8	Early
Dillon, John	Chatham		330/9	Early
Dimsdell, Benj.	Jones	Wallters	91/5	Appling
Dingler, Henry	Jasper	Hay's	425/8	Appling
Dingler, John	Jasper	Hays	403/1	Early
Discombs, Elijah(Orp)	Chatham		470/9	Irwin
Discombs, Margaret(Orp)	Chatham		470/9	Irwin
Disgnath, Christian J.C.	Chatham		340/11	Early
Disheroon, Wm.	Franklin	Flanagan	333/7	Appling
Dismuck, Jeptha V.	Hancock	Herberts	131/2	Irwin
Dismuck, John(Orphs)	Baldwin	Ellis	85/16	Irwin
Dismuck, Jos.T.	Hancock	Herberts	80/20	Early
Dismukes, Edmund	Jones	Chappel	462/13	Irwin
Dismukes, Edmund	Jones	Chappels	81/18	Early
Dismukes, James	Putnam	H.Kendricks	138/2	Walton
Dismukes, Jas.	Putnam	H.Kendricks	12/4	Walton
Dismukes, Jas.	Putnam	J.Kindricks	108/17	Early
Dismukes, Milley(Orp)	Richmond	Burtons	131/16	Early
Dismukes, Reuben	Richmond	Palmer	375/2	Appling
Dix, John	Chatham		66/19	Early
Dixon, Aaron	Early		321/14	Early
Dixon, Aaron	Early		491/7	Irwin
Dixon, Allen	Bulloch	Tilmans	242/4	Appling
Dixon, Benj.	Jones	Seals	395/6	Irwin
Dixon, Curry	Hancock	Scotts	282/13	Irwin
Dixon, Eliz.(Wid)	Emanuel	59	24/4	Early
Dixon, Enoch	Jones	Seals	175/3	Habersha
Dixon, Hickman	Putnam	Brooks	3/21	Early
Dixon, James	Hancock	Danells	180/17	Early
Dixon, James	Twiggs	Browns	300/4	Appling
Dixon, Kirvin	Scriven	180	20/15	Irwin
Dixon, Lemuel(Orps)	Elbert	Whites	300/7	Early
Dixon, Michael	Hall		510/7	Appling
Dixon, Pleasant	Twiggs	Browns	183/4	Walton

NAME	COUNTY	MIL.DIST	LOT/SECT	DREW LAND
Dixon, Robert	Hancock	Smiths	27/12	Irwin
Dixon, Robt.	Wilkinson	Wiggins	179/4	Early
Dixon, Robt.	Wilkinson	Wiggins	82/6	Irwin
Dixon, Robt.H.	Putnam	Majone	484/3	Appling
Dixon, Stephen	Franklin	Harris	192/7	Early
Dixon, Thos.	Jasper	Clays	53/8	Early
Dixon, Thos.	Morgan	Parker	61/10	Early
Dixon, Thos.H.	Wilkes	Gordons	211/8	Irwin
Dixon, Tilman	Washington	Floyd	38/4	Early
Dixon, Tilman	Washington	Floyd	40/12	Hall
Dixon, Wm.	Hancock	Mims	251/4	Appling
Dixon, Wm.	Madison	Williford	155/3	Habersham
Dixon, Wm.	Madison	Williford	21/19	Early
Dixon, Wm.	Twiggs	R.Belchers	329/11	Irwin
Dixon, Wm.	Wilkinson	Childs	356/6	Gwinnett
Dobbage, Wm.	Wilkinson	Howards	300/2	Appling
Dobbage, Wm.	Wilkinson	Howards	4/1	Walton
Dobbins, Jos.	Franklin	Jno.Millers	59/10	Irwin
Dobbs, Asa	Elbert	Dobbs	209/1	Walton
Dobbs, David	Elbert	Dobbs	354/8	Early
Dobbs, James	Franklin	Akins	33/20	Early
Dobbs, Jesse	Elbert	Dobbs	412/13	Irwin
Dobbs, John	Elbert	Dobbs	198/3	Irwin
Dobbs, Silas	Jackson	Hamiltons	110/16	Early
Dobbs, Silas	Jackson	Hamiltons	81/4	Appling
Dobbs, Wm.	Jackson	Hamilton Bt.	128/4	Early
Dobbs, Wm.	Jackson	Hamiltons	435/9	Irwin
Dobins, James	Franklin	Jos.Miller	179/5	Gwinnett
Dobson, John B.	Franklin	Powells	263/7	Irwin
Dobson, Jos.Jr.	Franklin	Powells	134/4	Early
Dobson, Jos.Sr.	Franklin	Powels	87/2	Early
Dobson, Oliver L.	Chatham		314/9	Appling
Dodd, Jas.J.	Franklin	Jos.Miller	283/6	Appling
Dodd, Peter G.	Oglethorpe	Barnett	339/7	Irwin
Dodd, Wm.	Franklin	J.Millers	194/5	Early
Dodd, Wm.Sr.	Franklin	J.Millers	28/18	Early
Dodds, John	Elbert	Higginbotham	75/7	Gwinnett
Dodds, Sarah	Elbert	B.Higginbothams	243/5	Early
Dodds, Thomas	Elbert	Higginbotham	395/20	Early
Dodsen, Presley	Jasper	Baileys	339/6	Early
Dodson, Armsted	Jasper	Trembles	4/1	Rabun
Dodson, Edmund	Morgan	Talbot	274/2	Early
Dodson, Elijah	Jasper	Posts	125/12	Hall
Dodson, Elisha	Clarke	Oats	9/2	Rabun
Dodson, John C.	Wilkes	Dents	187/6	Early
Dodson, John C.	Wilkes	Dents	197/7	Gwinnett
Dodson, Joshua	Morgan	Talbot	221/8	Appling
Dodson, Matthews	Chatham		30/6	Early
Dodson, Wm.	Columbia	Dodsons	67/3	Appling
Dodson, Wm.	Morgan	Walker	3/6	Appling
Dodson, Wm.H.	Morgan	Farrar	402/15	Early
Dogett, William	Clarke	Moores	64/9	Hall
Doggett, Asa(Orps)	Columbia	Pullins	369/7	Gwinnett
Doggett, Garner	Jasper	Kennaday	141/21	Early
Doggett, Garner	Jasper	Kennedy	115/5	Irwin
Doggett, Mark	Walton	Semtells	256/2	Appling
Doggett, Reuben(Orp)	Columbia	Burrough	36/20	Early
Doles, Benjamin	Baldwin	Cousins	35/8	Early
Doles, Benjamin	Baldwin	Cousins	89/16	Irwin
Doles, Jesse(R.S.)	Baldwin	Cousins	159/2	Appling
Doles, Jesse(R.S.)	Baldwin	Cousins	207/5	Early
Dollar, William	Bulloch	Tilmans	127/26	Early
Dollar, William	Bulloch	Tilmans	499/12	Irwin
Doly, Morris	Chatham		105/28	Early
Doly, Morris	Chatham		455/5	Appling
Dominy, John	Emanuel	56th	334/6	Early
Dominy, John	Wilkinson	Bowings	287/9	Appling

NAME	COUNTY	MIL.DIST	LOT/SECT	DREW LAND
Dominy, Jonath.(Orps)	Laurens	Deans	518/8	Irwin
Dominy, Willis	Emanuel	56th	304/4	Early
Donaldson, John	Jasper	Clays	38/7	Gwinnett
Donaldson, Mary	Scriven		16/10	Irwin
Donaldson, Wm.G.	Scriven		188/8	Appling
Donalson, Jesse	Pulaski	Senterfeits	292/12	Irwin
Donalson, Jno.Jr.	Pulaski	Senterfeits	203/4	Early
Donalson, Wm.Sr.	Pulaski	Senterfeits	171/1	Irwin
Donavent, Herbert(Orps)	Washington	Manning	14/9	Irwin
Doney, Louden	Hancock	Lucas	419/15	Early
Donohoo, James	Franklin	Burroughs	109/16	Irwin
Donohoo, James	Franklin	Burroughs	203/5	Irwin
Dooley, Bennett	Elbert	Dooleys	216/11	Irwin
Dooley, James	Habersham	Powels	238/23	Early
Dooley, James	Habersham	Powels	281/8	Irwin
Dooley, John M.	Lincoln	Tatoms	1/1	Rabun
Dooley, John	Franklin	Powels	282/10	Early
Doomas, Moses	Putnam	J.Kendricks	185/18	Early
Doomus, David	Putnam	J.Kendricks	350/11	Irwin
Dorch, Lewis	Franklin	Akins	55/5	Gwinnett
Dorch, Newmans R.	Franklin	Akins	357/17	Early
Dordan, Willie	Twiggs	W.Belchers	276/20	Early
Dorlick, S.C.	Richmond	122	194/9	Early
Dorman, Ephraim	Jones	Buckhalter	68/4	Habersham
Dorman, Lucinda(Orp)	Hancock	Mims	305/21	Early
Dorman, Martha(Wid)	Pulaski	Lesters	28/11	Early
Dorman, Mitchell(Orps)	Pulaski	Lesters	28/7	Irwin
Dormon, Wm.	Twiggs	Hodges	325/4	Appling
Dormons, Willice(Orps)	Twiggs	Hodges	56/21	Early
Dorsett, Elijah	Gwinnett	Hamilton Bt.	84/3	Appling
Dorsett, Elijah	Gwinnett	Hamiltons	11/14	Early
Dorsey, Basdell(Orps)	Franklin	Turks	408/5	Appling
Dorsey, Daniel	Jasper	Phillips	175/10	Irwin
Dorsey, Isaac	Franklin	Turks	36/10	Hall
Dorsey, Isaac	Franklin	Turks	36/12	Hall
Dorsey, Jackey B.	Baldwin	Cousins	45/6	Gwinnett
Dorsey, Thos.	Oglethorpe	Myrick	301/5	Early
Dorsey, Walter B.	Oglethorpe	Myrick	400/28	Early
Dorsey, Walter B.	Oglethorpe	Myrick	455/8	Appling
Dorson, Kinchen	Pulaski	Maddox	71/11	Early
Dorson, Mary	Pulaski	Rees	165/10	Irwin
Dorster, Thos.	Putnam	Slaughter	349/10	Irwin
Dortch, Jas.H.	Franklin	Kettons	387/8	Early
Dortick, S.C.	Richmond	122nd	107/12	Early
Dorton, Eli	Jasper	Clays	215/17	Early
Doss, George	Jackson	Dicksons	339/7	Appling
Doss, Hiram	Jasper	Barnes	281/28	Early
Doss, Isariah	Jasper	Bentleys	398/12	Early
Doss, Izariah	Jasper	Bentley	32/6	Irwin
Doss, Mark	Jackson	Dicksons	14/1	Rabun
Doss, Mark	Jackson	Dicksons	279/21	Early
Doss, Peleg	Greene	142	115/13	Irwin
Doss, Wm.	Jasper	Kennedys	278/9	Appling
Dosset, Augustus	Chatham		382/6	Appling
Dossett, Chas.W.	Columbia	Dodsons	248/8	Irwin
Dossett, Phill.Sr.(RS)	Richmond	Burtons	225/6	Appling
Dossett, Phillip Jr.	Richmond	Burtons	22/27	Walton
Dossett, Rebecca(Wid)	Columbia	Shaws	146/5	Appling
Dossey, Tomas B.	Oglethorpe	Wises	255/16	Early
Doster, Absalom	Jasper	Blakes	34/3	Rabun
Doster, Benj.	Warren	Rogers	309/5	Early
Doster, James J.	Jackson	Rogers	368/20	Early
Doster, Jonathan	Jackson	Rogers	116/1	Early
Doster, Joshua(R.S.)	Baldwin	Marshalls	298/10	Irwin
Doster, Lemuel	Putnam	Slaughters	243/21	Early
Doster, Malachi	Baldwin	Marshalls	234/11	Irwin
Doster, Thos.	Warren	Gains	485/5	Appling

NAME	COUNTY	MIL.DIST	LOT/SECT	DREW LAND
Doster, Wm.	Greene	141	83/6	Gwinnett
Doster, Wm.	Jackson	Rogers Bt.	260/11	Early
Doster, Wm.	Jackson	Rogers Bt.	61/8	Early
Doster, Wm.	Warren	Rodgers	2/3	Habersham
Dotton, Olive	Putnam	Buckner	208.5	Gwinnett
Doud, Amasa	Baldwin	Marshall	151/20	Early
Douehy, Andrew	Jones	Gresham	99/19	Early
Dougharty, Chas.	Jackson	Hamiltons	123/20	Early
Dougharty, Chas.	Jackson	Hamiltons	2/6	Irwin
Dougharty, Demy	Appling	2nd	200/2	Irwin
Dougharty, Latis(Wid)	Laurens	Griffiths	201/5	Appling
Dougherty, Jas.	Jackson	Rogers	432/6	Appling
Doughrty, Rebecca(Wid)	Clarke	Applings	109/15	Irwin
Doughtry, Bryant	Emanuel	53rd	24/7	Appling
Douglas, Hezekiah	Laurens	S.Smith	395/3	Early
Douglas, Lemuel	Emanuel	49th	419/8	Appling
Douglas, Martin	Jasper	Hays	42/3	Appling
Douglas, Peter	Scriven	36th	275/20	Early
Douglass, Alex.Jr.	Scriven		96/15	Irwin
Douglass, Amos	Burke	Sullivans	401/5	Appling
Douglass, Benj.	McIntosh	Hamilton	36/1	Habersham
Douglass, Danl.B.	Jones	Griffith	131/9	Hall
Douglass, David(RS)	Jones	Harrist	49/7	Irwin
Douglass, Eliz.(Wid)	Bryan	19th	318/6	Appling
Douglass, Fredr.	Tattnall	Overstreet	50/6	Early
Douglass, Fredr.	Tattnall	Overstreet	65/5	Rabun
Douglass, James	Emanuel	56th	202/5	Appling
Douglass, Jas.	Putnam	Oslins	209/3	Appling
Douglass, Jas.	Wayne	Jacobs	141/4	Appling
Douglass, Jno.(Orp)	Scriven		120/1	Walton
Douglass, John	Columbia	Gartrell	136/11	Early
Douglass, John	Columbia	Gartrell	167/5	Appling
Douglass, Jones	Baldwin	Stephens	341/1	Appling
Douglass, Lemuel	Emanuel	59th	130/12	Habersham
Douglass, Martin	Jasper	Hays	296/26	Early
Douglass, Michael	Tattnall	Tharps	182/5	Gwinnett
Douglass, Shadrack	Tattnall	Tharps	172/15	Irwin
Douglass, Spencer	Wilkinson	Childs	307/5	Irwin
Douglass, Thomas	Bryan	19th	343/13	Early
Douglass, Willis	Jones	Shropshier	254/5	Early
Douglass, Wm.T.	Wayne	Jacobs	160/4	Irwin
Douglass, Wm.T.	Wayne	Jacobs	380/11	Early
Douglass, Wilson(Orp)	Laurens	S.Smith	176/6	Appling
Doupree, Lewis J.	Oglethorpe	Goolsby	436/12	Irwin
Douring, Wm.	Emanuel	58th	377/5	Appling
Dousier, Bartlett	Chatham		276/7	Irwin
Dow, Amos	Chatham		133/6	Gwinnett
Dowdy, Benj.	Jackson	Dicksons Bt.	390/1	Early
Dowdy, Richd.	Oglethorpe	Davenport	178/1	Appling
Dowdy, Richd.	Oglethorpe	Davenport	48/2	Early
Dowdy, Wily	Scriven	36th	299/16	Early
Dowdy, Wm.	Hall		204/9	Appling
Dowell(Douel), Thos.	Chatham		79/2	Walton
Downer, John	Baldwin	Doziers	103/6	Irwin
Downer, Jos.Jr.	Elbert	T.Christians	49/2	Habersham
Downey, Jas.(Orps)	Jasper	Bartlett	309/6	Appling
Downie, Joseph	Jackson	Rodgers Bt.	66/9	Appling
Downie, Margaret	Chatham		232/11	Irwin
Downies, Jas.(Orps)	Jasper	Bartletts	259/19	Early
Downing, George	Wilkes	Bryants	460/7	Appling
Downs, Ambrose	Franklin	Davis	105/5	Rabun
Downs, David	Morgan	Wright	179/15	Early
Downs, Isaac	Richmond	122	488/13	Irwin
Downs, Jacob	Columbia	Burrough	47/3	Appling
Downs, John	Jasper	Bentleys	49/5	Rabun
Doyle, Dennis	Baldwin	Taliafors	78/13	Irwin
Doyle, William	Chatham		26/3	Irwin

NAME	COUNTY	MIL.DIST	LOT/SECT	DREW LAND
Dozier, Green	Columbia	J.Morris	79/9	Early
Dozier, John	Columbia	Dodson	43/4	Irwin
Dozier, Leonard(Orps)	Warren	152nd	250/6	Gwinnett
Dozier, Thos.	Twiggs	Hodges	44/7	Irwin
Drake, Beverly	Hancock	Lucas	67/1	Irwin
Drake, Eason	Richmond		132/5	Gwinnett
Drake, Eason	Richmond		273/2	Appling
Drake, Elias	Burke	Spiveys	457/10	Irwin
Drake, James	Montgomery	Nobles	74/1	Early
Drake, James	Oglethorpe	Dunns	368/12	Irwin
Drake, Lemuel	Jasper	Abbots	133/4	Walton
Drane, Stephen	Columbia	O.Morris	44/26	Early
Draper, Mary(Wid)	Warren	152nd	105/10	Irwin
Drawdy, Wm.	Tattnall	Overstreet	106/11	Irwin
Drawhorn, Jas.	Jones	Buckhalter	124/26	Early
Drawhorn, Richd.	Jones	Buckhalter	243/5	Appling
Dreding, Samuel	Laurens	Griffin	133/16	Early
Dreding, Samuel	Laurens	Griffin	73/10	Early
Dregors, Jonas	Liberty		154/6	Early
Drigers, Caly(Orp)	McIntosh	Eigles	75/11	Hall
Drigers, Isaac(Orp)	McIntosh	Eigles	75/11	Hall
Drigers, Jacob(Oph)	McIntosh	Eigles	75/11	Hall
Drigers, James	Chatham		284/4	Appling
Drigers, Matthew(Orp)	McIntosh	Eigles	75/11	Hall
Drigers, Reuben(Orp)	McIntosh	Eigles	75/11	Hall
Drigers, Sarah(Orp)	McIntosh	Eigles	75/11	Hall
Driggers, Abrm.	McIntosh	Eigles	233/3	Early
Driggers, Dennis	Bulloch	Tilmans	39/4	Early
Driggers, John	McIntosh	Eigles	195/7	Appling
Driggers, Jonas	Bulloch	Knights	379/7	Gwinnett
Driggers, Jonas	Bulloch	Knights	57/2	Walton
Driscal, Tilman	Jackson	Whites	256/1	Early
Driskell, Wooden	Hancock	Champions	265/1	Walton
Driver, David	Washington	Pool	37/9	Appling
Drummond, Walter	Chatham		158/14	Early
Drury, James	Columbia	Ob.Morris	455/11	Irwin
Drury, Redie	Appling	5th	401/4	Appling
Drury, Samuel	Hancock	Herberts	361/8	Appling
Duberry, Giles	Jasper	Hays	164/10	Hall
Duberry, John	Jasper	Hays	64/26	Early
Duberry, Richd.	Jasper	Phillips	160/2	Walton
Duberry, Thos.	Jasper	Phillips	96/10	Habersham
Dubignnon, Jos.	Glynn		565/2	Appling
Dubose, Elisha	Jones	Hansford	122/5	Gwinnett
Duck, John(RS)	Morgan	Walker	20/5	Appling
Duck, John(RS)	Morgan	Walker	281/27	Early
Duck, John(RS)	Morgan	Walker	295/6	Appling
Duck, Jonathan	Hancock	Millers	389/12	Early
Duck, Mary	Jasper	Baileys	314/1	Appling
Duckworth, Chrst.(Wid)	Jones	Buckhalter	185/11	Irwin
Duckworth, Eleanor(Orp)	Warren	152	200/13	Irwin
Duckworth, Gazaway(Orp)	Warren	152	200/13	Irwin
Duckworth, Jeremiah	Hancock	Smiths	76/9	Appling
Duckworth, John	Hancock	Justices	222/26	Early
Duckworth, Jos.(Orp)	Warren	152nd	200/13	Irwin
Duckworth, Saml.	Warren	153rd	151/2	Walton
Dudley, Anderson	Elbert	Hannahs	120/5	Irwin
Dudley, Ignatius	Elbert	Webbs	111/4	Habersham
Dudley, Jas.Jr.	Elbert	Hannahs	39/11	Hall
Dudley, John(RS)	Hancock	Scotts	167/19	Early
Dudley, Wm.	Hancock	Danells	190/2	Rabun
Dudloy, Thos.	Hancock	Scotts	93/4	Habersham
Duefour, Antony	Chatham		307/4	Early
Duel, Nicholas R.	Chatham		158/2	Irwin
Duffee, Patrick	Chatham		366/20	Early
Duffel, Thos.H.	Twiggs	Bozeman	342/19	Early
Duffie, Thos.	Putnam	Ectors	183/3	Habersham

NAME	COUNTY	MIL.DIST	LOT/SECT	DREW LAND
Dugass, Gustav	Richmond	120	501/10	Irwin
Dugass, M.F.P.(Wid)	Richmond	398	169/1	Appling
Dugger, Chesley	Bulloch	Knights	79/14	Irwin
Dugger, John Jr.	Effingham		124/5	Early
Dugger, Wm.	Bulloch	Knights	115/4	Appling
Duglass, Wm.	Wilkes	McClendon	208/7	Appling
Duhamel, Robt.L.	Chatham		311/2	Appling
Duigler, Nancy(Wid)	Morgan	Leonard	82/20	Early
Duke, Abraham(Orps)	Jackson	Rogers	342/2	Appling
Duke, Bailey	Morgan	Selmon	62/11	Hall
Duke, Charles	Walton	Wagnon's	146/3	Walton
Duke, Chas.	Walton	Bagners	310/8	Early
Duke, Chas.	Wilkes	Gordans	115/10	Hall
Duke, Chas.	Wilkes	Gordons	43/5	Irwin
Duke, David	Jasper	Posts	123/5	Irwin
Duke, David	Morgan	Rainey	80/26	Early
Duke, Edmond	Morgan	Parker	7/9	Irwin
Duke, Eldridge	Morgan	Selmon	22/19	Early
Duke, Eldridge	Morgan	Selmon	383/9	Irwin
Duke, Eliza(Wid)	Laurens	Harris	129/11	Early
Duke, Fredr.	Jasper	McClendons	163/9	Irwin
Duke, Green	Greene	144th	1/13	Early
Duke, Hardiman	Jasper	Eastes	397/10	Irwin
Duke, Henry T.	Clarke	Tredwell	370/7	Early
Duke, Henry(S/Jas)	Morgan	Selmon	332/2	Early
Duke, Isham	Laurens	Harris	98/10	Hall
Duke, James	Burke	70th	3/12	Early
Duke, James	Walton	Wagnons	141/9	Early
Duke, Jane(Wid)	Greene	Jones	188/20	Early
Duke, Jas.(S/Thos)	Morgan	Selmon	43/9	Appling
Duke, Jesse	Jasper	Centells	256/6	Gwinnett
Duke, Jesse	Jasper	Centells	87/1	Appling
Duke, Joseph	Jasper	Bartletts	176/10	Irwin
Duke, Lettice(Wid)	Clarke	Tredwells	146/11	Habersham
Duke, Littleberry	Jasper	Centells	110/13	Early
Duke, Mary	Burke	70th	35/14	Irwin
Duke, Massa(Wid)	Jackson	Rogers Bt.	291/1	Appling
Duke, Reason	Morgan	Selmon	457/7	Irwin
Duke, Richard	Jasper	Trembles	371/10	Early
Duke, Samuel	Burke	70th	160/7	Gwinnett
Duke, Taylor	Morgan	Selmon	52/5	Irwin
Duke, Thos.	Morgan	Dennis	241/27	Early
Duke, Thos.	Morgan	Rainey	515/10	Irwin
Duke, Thos.	Morgan	Selmon	186/2	Appling
Duke, Thos.	Walton	Wagnon's	61/21	Early
Dukes, Doles(Orps)	Burke	70th	176/17	Early
Dukes, John Sr.	Bulloch	Knights	283/3	Early
Dukes, Jos.	Jasper	Posts	313/6	Irwin
Dukes, Robert	Richmond		14/4	Irwin
Dukes, Stephen H.	Jasper	Centells	88/11	Early
Dukes, William	Bryan	19th	57/14	Irwin
Dukes, Wm.P.(Orp)	Laurens	Harris	93/3	Early
Dumas, Jeremiah	Jones	Greens	117/14	Irwin
Dumas, John	Jones	Greens	389/8	Irwin
Dun, Michael	Jackson	Dicksons	165/21	Early
Dunahoo, James	Oglethorpe	Lees	375/2	Early
Dunahoo, Jas.	Oglethorpe	Lees	121/27	Early
Dunaway, Benj.	Warren	153rd	182/7	Early
Dunaway, Edmond	Jackson	Dickson	139/8	Irwin
Dunaway, James	Lincoln	Parks	347/2	Appling
Dunaway, Jeremiah	Wilkes	Burks	61/4	Walton
Dunbar, Thos.S.	Jones	Hansford	47/1	Appling
Duncan, Aaron	Elbert	Smiths	188/2	Appling
Duncan, Benj.	Putnam	H.Kendricks	336/7	Appling
Duncan, Elbert	Laurens	S.Smith	214/6	Irwin
Duncan, Geo.	Jones	Wallers	20/12	Habersham
Duncan, James	Liberty		236/14	Early

NAME	COUNTY	MIL.DIST	LOT/SECT	DREW LAN
Duncan, Jas.A.	Jones	Brooks	108/11	Irwin
Duncan, John Jr.	Elbert	White & Christ.Bt.	354/6	Early
Duncan, Jos.	Putnam	H.Kindricks	14/18	Early
Duncan, Lovina(Orphs)	Greene	Foster	398/19	Early
Duncan, Thos.	Jasper	Northcuts	131/2	Habersha
Duncan, Thos.	Laurens	Harris	168/7	Early
Dunevant, Mann	Warren	152nd	357/16	Early
Dunham, Benj.	Wilkinson	Lees	136/26	Early
Dunham, Charles	Chatham		74/2	Appling
Dunham, Chas.	McIntosh	Goulds	63/10	Irwin
Dunham, Geo.	Jones	Wallers	189/12	Early
Dunham, Jacob H.	Liberty		326/9	Early
Dunkin, Allen	Wilkes	Bryants	105/7	Irwin
Dunkin, John Sr.	Elbert	Whites	9/10	Irwin
Dunkin, Wm.	Wilkes	Ogletrees	195/6	Gwinnett
Dunlap, Joseph	Franklin	Greens	130/12	Irwin
Dunlap, Joseph	Franklin	Greens	175/19	Early
Dunn, Abram	Franklin	Morriss	210/10	Early
Dunn, Alfred(Orp)	Columbia	Gartrell	4/15	Irwin
Dunn, Axum	Jones	Seals	278/27	Early
Dunn, Barney	Jasper	Bentleys	178/13	Early
Dunn, Benj.Sr.(RS)	Twiggs	Browns	248/7	Irwin
Dunn, David Jr.	Twiggs	Browns	11/6	Gwinnett
Dunn, Davis Jr.	Twiggs	Browns	106/8	Early
Dunn, Eliz.(Wid)	Columbia	Olives	206/9	Early
Dunn, Gatewood	Columbia	Gartrells	17/8	Early
Dunn, Geo.W.	Columbia	Gartrell	244/7	Early
Dunn, Harriss	Jasper	Bentleys	137/21	Early
Dunn, Henry L.	Hancock	Evans	323/10	Irwin
Dunn, Henry Sr.	Hancock	Mims	113/5	Gwinnett
Dunn, Henry Sr.	Hancock	Mims	6/6	Gwinnett
Dunn, Hiram	Columbia	Gartrells	2/15	Early
Dunn, Ishmael	Oglethorpe	Dunns	68/7	Irwin
Dunn, James	Franklin	Borroughs	289/5	Gwinnett
Dunn, James	Greene	141	107/10	Early
Dunn, Jas.M.	Putnam	Oslins	59/3	Walton
Dunn, Jeremiah	Jones	Seals	24/3	Rabun
Dunn, Jesse	Jones	Seals	330/4	Appling
Dunn, Joel	Jasper	Posts	382/5	Appling
Dunn, John Sr.	Walton	Sentells	4/12	Early
Dunn, John(Orps)	Hancock	Mims	420/5	Appling
Dunn, John	Hancock	Smiths	9/20	Early
Dunn, John	Jones	Seals	131/11	Hall
Dunn, John	Scriven	Lovetts	161/6	Gwinnett
Dunn, Lewis	Burke	69th	230/4	Walton
Dunn, Mary(Wid)	Columbia	Gartrell	30/2	Irwin
Dunn, Nehamiah	Jones	Shropshier	71/1	Walton
Dunn, Waters	Columbia	Willinghams	263/19	Early
Dunn, Wiley	Early		313/4	Early
Dunn, Wiley	Early		65/1	Habersha
Dunn, William(Orphs)	Columbia	Olive	265/16	Early
Dunn, Wm.	Jasper	Bentleys	330/6	Irwin
Dunn, Wm.	Twiggs	R.Belcher	322/17	Early
Dunn, Wm.Jr.	Twiggs	Browns	115/6	Appling
Dunn, Wm.S.	Columbia	Gartrells	228/4	Walton
Dunn, Wm.S.	Columbia	Willingham	305/9	Early
Dunn, Wm.S.	Columbia	Willinghams	400/10	Early
Dunnagan, Jos.	Hall		401/8	Appling
Dunnavent, Susannah	Greene	Armers	170/4	Irwin
Dunnigan, Joshua	Franklin	Morris	271/27	Early
Dunnmann, John	Hall	Byrds	232/8	Irwin
Dunson, Edmund	Madison	Millican	221/5	Irwin
Dunson, Edmund	Madison	Millican	370/6	Early
Dunson, John	Madison	Millican	133/4	Early
Dunston, Chas.	Jackson	Winters Bt.	46/7	Appling
Dunston, Wm.	Jackson	Winters	64/4	Habersha
Dunwody, John	Liberty		360/3	Appling

NAME	COUNTY	MIL.DIST	LOT/SECT	DREW LAND
Dunwoodie, Mary(Wid)	Twiggs	Smiths	340/8	Early
Dunwoody, Jas.	McIntosh	Hamilton	14/11	Irwin
Dupon, Peter	Chatham		9/2	Irwin
Dupree, Ann(Wid)	Morgan	Campbell	42/9	Appling
Dupree, Bergess	Putnam	Evans	214/4	Appling
Dupree, Cordal	Putnam	Evans	299/2	Early
Dupree, Cordal	Putnam	Evans	330/13	Early
Dupree, Daniel	Wilkinson	Bowings	426/2	Appling
Dupree, Harod	Jasper	Cowarts	34/8	Early
Dupree, James	Jasper	Cowarts	291/10	Early
Dupree, Jeremiah	Twiggs	Smiths	408/6	Appling
Dupree, Jeremiah	Twiggs	Smiths	99/5	Appling
Dupree, John	Greene	143rd	156/18	Early
Dupree, John	Greene	143rd	215/12	Early
Dupree, Simon	Twiggs	Smiths	45/14	Early
Dupree, Wm.H.	Twiggs	Smiths	169/4	Irwin
Dupree, Wm.N.	Twiggs	Smiths	184/14	Early
Duprees, Allen H.	Putnam	Mays	554/2	Appling
Duprees, Burgess	Putnam	Evans	249/5	Irwin
Dupreist, Eliz.(Wid)	Wilkinson	Lees	9/5	Habersham
Durant, Francis	McIntosh	Jinkins	363/26	Early
Durden, Benj.(RS)	Twiggs	W.Bechers	94/4	Habersham
Durden, Benj.(RS)	Twiggs	W.Belcher	261/13	Irwin
Durden, Elisha Sr.	Wilkinson	Brooks	114/2	Walton
Durden, Francis	Washington	Pools	243/11	Early
Durden, John	Columbia	Watson	110/7	Early
Durden, Lewis	Washington	Peaboddys	362/18	Early
Durden, Lewis	Washington	Peabodys	497/7	Appling
Durden, Miles	Columbia	Watsons	12/12	Early
Durden, Washington	Wilkinson	Brooks	335/13	Irwin
Durdin, Wilie	Twiggs	Thames	73/7	Early
Durham, Abner	Jasper	Blakes	212/9	Early
Durham, Abraham	Clarke	Mitchells	295/5	Early
Durham, Hardy	Twiggs	Hodges	262/12	Irwin
Durham, Isbell(Wid)	Greene	Tuggles	381/13	Early
Durham, John	Twiggs	R.Blechers	182/2	Early
Durham, John	Wilkinson	Brooks	444/3	Appling
Durham, John	Wilkinson	Brooks	456/7	Appling
Durham, Matthew	Jones	Buckhalter	268/4	Walton
Durham, Saml.(Orps)	Twiggs	Ellis	185/10	Irwin
Durham, Simeon	Jasper	Kenneday	47/10	Irwin
Durham, Simon	Jasper	Kenadays	245/20	Early
Durham, Thos.	Wilkinson	Smiths	296/14	Early
Durham, Wm.	Twiggs	R.Belchers	239/28	Early
Durkee, Nathl.Sr.	Columbia	Burroughs	413/6	Appling
Durkee, Nathnl.Sr.	Columbia	Burrough	20/3	Habersham
Durkee, Robt.M.	Columbia	Burroughs	15/2	Early
Durker, William H.	Chatham		56/9	Hall
Durr, Michael	Jasper	Baileys	210/11	Irwin
Durrence, Jos.	Tattnall	J.Durrence	257/16	Early
Durrer, Thos.	Morgan	Wright	237/7	Gwinnett
Durrham, Howell J.	Jackson	Winters	300/8	Irwin
Dutton, Henry	Bulloch	Tilmans	107/4	Appling
Dyall, Thos.	McIntosh	Eigles	196/11	Irwin
Dyar, Elisha	Franklin	R.Browns	47/13	Early
Dyar, Elisha	Franklin	R.Browns	58/2	Walton
Dyar, Joel H.	Franklin	P.Browns	45/11	Irwin
Dyar, John	Franklin	R.Browns	180/12	Irwin
Dyche, John(RS)	Jackson	Hamiltons	113/12	Early
Dye, Abel	Warren	150	294/9	Early
Dye, Burwell	Elbert	Christians	427/7	Appling
Dye, David	Elbert	Christians	201/20	Early
Dye, Hopkin	Burke	Dye's	428/8	Irwin
Dye, Hopkins	Richmond	Palmers	475/10	Irwin
Dye, James M.	Richmond	Laceys	58/1	Rabun
Dye, Martin M.	Burke	Dye's	6/2	Walton
Dye, Martin M.	Burke	Dye's	69/20	Early

NAME	COUNTY	MIL.DIST	LOT/SECT	DREW LAND
Dye, William	Elbert	Olivers	202/5	Early
Dye, William	Elbert	Olivers	238/6	Irwin
Dye, Wm.	Twiggs	W.Belchers	399/19	Early
Dyer, Anthony	Jasper	Clay	36/3	Appling
Dyer, Jacob C.	Jones	Jefferson	293/18	Early
Dyer, Obadiah	Greene	Fosters	98/1	Habersham
Dyer, Otis	Jasper	Reids	379/19	Early
Dyer, William	Glynn		126/12	Hall
Dyess, George	Wilkinson	Wiggins	32/2	Walton
Dykes, Allen	Wilkinson	Brooks	232/14	Early
Dykes, Daniel(Orps)	Pulaski	Rees	189/7	Appling
Dykes, David(Orps)	Pulaski	Lanears	185/26	Early
Dykes, George	Wilkinson	Smiths	34/4	Rabun
Dykes, Henry	Pulaski	Rees	36/7	Appling
Dykes, Jacob	Pulaski	Rees	285/3	Early
Dykes, James	Pulaski	Rees	214/3	Appling
Dykes, James	Pulaski	Rees	235/13	Early
Dykes, Jesse	Effingham		306/1	Appling
Dykes, Jesse	Effingham		529/7	Irwin
Dykes, John	Pulaski	Reeces	24/7	Irwin
Dykes, Nathnl.	Pulaski	Lamars	166/8	Hall
Dykes, Samuel	Pulaski	Rees	364/9	Appling
Dyres, Nathan(Orphs)	Greene	Fosters	166/2	Rabun
Dyson, Isaac	Warren	150th	138/27	Early
Dyson, Isaac	Warren	150th	146/19	Early
Eads, Eliz.	Oglethorpe	Goolsby	291/12	Early
Eads, Ruben	Oglethorpe	Davenport	265/6	Early
Eady, Henry	Jasper	Bentleys	17/11	Irwin
Eady, James	Lincoln	Parks	346/19	Early
Eady, John R.	Jasper	Bentleys	258/26	Early
Eady, John R.	Jasper	Bentleys	352/8	Irwin
Eady, Samuel	Jasper	Bentleys	366/26	Early
Eagan, Wm.	Tattnall	Overstreet	220/11	Early
Eagle, Henry	Jones	Buckhalter	149/13	Early
Eakin, James	Jackson	Winters	96/22	Early
Eakin, Thos.	Jackson	Dickson	91/4	Walton
Eakin, Thos.	Jackson	Dicksons	190/16	Early
Eanes, John	Jones	Weatherby	130/21	Early
Eanes, John	Jones	Weatherby	411/12	Irwin
Earby, Tabitha(Wid)	Greene	Jones	112/1	Irwin
Earley, Caleb	Oglethorpe	Dunn's	141/12	Habersham
Early, Ann A.(Wid)	Greene	Greers	207/11	Early
Early, Joel	Greene	Carlton	472/11	Irwin
Early, Sarah	Oglethorpe	Dunn's	247/9	Irwin
Earnest, Nancy(Wid)	Jefferson	Abbots	315/4	Appling
Earnst, Catharine	Chatham		316/6	Early
Earnst, Eliz.	Chatham	8	160/7	Appling
Eason, Abraham Sr.	Morgan	Knight	117/13	Habersham
Eason, John	Wilkes	Davis	150/12	Habersham
Eason, Joseph	Morgan	Knight	381/7	Early
Eason, Parker	Wilkes	Davis	247/11	Early
Eason, Rice	Walton	Worsham	149/10	Early
Eason, Seling D.	Burke	Sullivans	118/13	Habersham
Eason, Seth	Jefferson	Fountains	163/7	Irwin
Eason, Thomas	Morgan	Knight	114/13	Early
Eason, Thomas	Morgan	Knight	333/4	Appling
East, Jos.Sr.	Clarke	Harpers	118/2	Early
East, Martin	Clarke	Harpers	74/6	Gwinnett
East, Stephen	Jackson	Whites	48/27	Early
Easter, John C.	Baldwin	Marshall	3/3	Irwin
Easter, Polly	Jasper	Bartlett	148/11	Habersham
Easterling, Jas.Sr.(RS)	Twiggs	Ellis	94/14	Irwin
Easters, David	Putnam	Littles	159/9	Early
Easterwood, John	Walton	Sentells	585/2	Appling
Eastes, Jas.	Putnam	Brooks	257/27	Early
Eastes, Jas.	Putnam	Brooks	75/7	Irwin
Easton, Elisha	Oglethorpe	Lees	367/7	Irwin

NAME	COUNTY	MIL.DIST	LOT/SECT	DREW LAND
Eastwood, Israel	Burke	Sullivan	150/7	Appling
Eaton, Rebecca(Orp)	Camden	Baileys	17/10	Habersham
Eaves, Rhoday	Elbert	Whites	130/5	Irwin
Eaves, Wm.	Elbert	Whites	58/5	Rabun
Eberhart, Geo.	Madison	Culbreath	21/13	Irwin
Eberhart, Geo.	Madison	Culbreths	226/3	Irwin
Eberhart, James	Madison	Culbreths	181/19	Early
Eberhart, Susanna	Madison	Culbreths	517/8	Appling
Eberheart, Eli	Oglethorpe	Davenport	340/1	Early
Eberheart, Jacob	Oglethorpe	Davenport	348/3	Early
Ebzie, Chas.	Jackson	Hambleton	214/1	Appling
Echels, Wm.	Wilkes	Davis	376/4	Appling*
Echols, Benj.Jr.	Jasper	Bentleys	292/8	Appling
Echols, Benj.Jr.	Jasper	Bentleys	375/1	Early
Echols, Benj.Sr.	Jasper	Bentleys	171/28	Early
Echols, Elijah	Wilkes	Davis	35/11	Irwin
Echols, James	Wilkes	Davis	394/4	Early
Echols, John	Jasper	Northcuts	366/2	Appling
Echols, Jos.(Orps)	Wilkes	Davis	382/8	Irwin
Echols, Levy H.	Wilkes	Gordan	49/11	Habersham
Echols, Milner	Clarke	Harper	341/14	Early
Echols, Milner	Clarke	Harpers	30/6	Appling
Echols, Obadiah(Orps)	Hancock	Thomas	5/16	Irwin
Echols, Obediah	Jasper	Phillips	82/4	Irwin
Echols, Reuben	Wilkes	Davis	20/13	Early
Echols, Richd.(Orps)	Jasper	Bentley	136/7	Early
Echols, Thomas	Wilkes	Davis	56/3	Walton
Ector, Hugh W.	Putnam	Johnston	53/8	Irwin
Ectors, John(Orps)	Jasper	Baileys	384/6	Appling
Eda, Benj.	Columbia	Gartrells	101/16	Irwin
Eddins, Gabriel	Franklin	Powels	471/4	Appling
Eddlemon, Moses	Morgan	Walker	133/28	Early
Eddy, Henry	Wilkinson	Brooks	93/2	Habersham
Eddy, Richd.	Washington	Robison	370/3	Early
Eden, Thomas	Chatham		149/7	Appling
Eden, Thomas	Chatham		274/7	Gwinnett
Edge, Eliz.(Wid)	Emanuel	57	307/9	Irwin
Edge, James	Wilkes	Bryant	122/11	Early
Edge, Joshua	Hancock	Herberts	184/8	Irwin
Edge, Nehemiah	Wilkes	Perrys	52/2	Early
Edge, Nehemiah	Wilkes	Perrys	89/2	Early
Edge, Sarah	Jasper	Bentleys	167/21	Early
Edge, Wm.	Hancock	Herberts	350/9	Irwin
Edges, Jas.(Orps)	Emanuel	57	320/9	Early
Edinfield, Thos.	Emanuel	58th	189/1	Walton
Edins, Job	Wilkinson	Smiths	34/6	Irwin
Edison, Jas.	Oglethorpe	Bowls	69/8	Irwin
Edleman, David	Walton	Echols	319/9	Irwin
Edmonds, Elijah	Oglethorpe	Bowls	52/12	Irwin
Edmonds, James	Jefferson	Abbots	410/10	Irwin
Edmonds, Wm.Sr.	Wilkes	McLendons	403/11	Irwin
Edmondson, Allen	Clarke	Oats	29/5	Rabun
Edmondson, Ambrose	Warren	152	20/8	Early
Edmondson, Ambrose	Warren	152	21/9	Appling
Edmondson, Elijah	Morgan	Wright	162/19	Early
Edmondson, Jas.Jr.	Morgan	Campbell	3/19	Early
Edmondson, Jas.Jr.	Morgan	Campbell	560/2	Appling
Edmondson, Moval(Wid)	Columbia	Pullin	282/9	Irwin
Edmondson, Rebecca	Wilkinson	Howard	282/10	Irwin
Edmondson, Richd.	Jasper	Ryans	43/2	Irwin
Edmondson, Sarah(Wid)	Morgan	Wright	123/2	Habersham
Edmondson, Thos.	Clarke	Oats	161/12	Irwin
Edmondson, Thos.	Clarke	Oats	182/10	Irwin
Edmondson, Wm.	Putnam	Coopers	231/3	Walton
Edmondson, Wm.	Twiggs	Evans	8/21	Early
Edmund, Richd.(Orps)	Wilkes	McLendons	292/6	Irwin
Edmunds, John S.	Lincoln	Jones	252/27	Early

NAME	COUNTY	MIL.DIST	LOT/SECT	DREW LAN
Edmunds, Wm.	Burke	J.Wards	281/15	Early
Edmunds, Wm.	Burke	J.Wards	45/9	Appling
Edmundson, Bryant	Twiggs	Hodges	276/21	Early
Edmundson, Jos.	Wilkinson	Howards	405/8	Appling
Edmundson, Mary A.(Orps)	Columbia	Pullin	398/18	Early
Edmundson, Wm.	Greene	Tuggles	35/7	Gwinnett
Edmundson, Wm.	Putnam	Coopers	205/9	Early
Edward, David	Jasper	Bentleys	130/3	Habersha
Edward, David	Twiggs	Jefferson	270/7	Irwin
Edwards, Andr.N.M.	Columbia	Burrough	363/14	Early
Edwards, Andr.N.M.	Columbia	Burroughs	295/4	Early
Edwards, Ann(Wid)	Emanuel	395	523/2	Appling
Edwards, Augustin	Elbert	Whites	65/20	Early
Edwards, Benj.	Oglethorpe	Britton	153/4	Irwin
Edwards, Britton	Washington	Renfro's	143/12	Hall
Edwards, David	Putnam	Ectors	302/12	Irwin
Edwards, David	Twiggs	Jefferson	346/10	Early
Edwards, Druciller	Hall		108/11	Habersha
Edwards, Elijah	Oglethorpe	Bowls	52/12	Irwin
Edwards, Etheldr.	Greene	Nelms	96/4	Early
Edwards, Isaac A.	Elbert	Olivers	98/8	Appling
Edwards, Isaac	Jackson	Dicksons	293/4	Irwin
Edwards, Isham	Jones	Mullens	89/6	Appling
Edwards, Jas.B.	Hancock	Thomas	139/11	Hall
Edwards, Jas.Jr.	Clarke	Harper	348/17	Early
Edwards, Jesse	Jones	Samuels	252/12	Irwin
Edwards, John Jr.	Jones	Buckhalter	133/11	Early
Edwards, John M.	Oglethorpe	Waters	125/17	Early
Edwards, John Sr.	Jones	Buckhalter	383/28	Early
Edwards, John	Lincoln	Graves	91/10	Early
Edwards, John	Putnam	Moreland	199/6	Early
Edwards, John	Putnam	Moreland	83/15	Early
Edwards, John	Putnam	Moreland	83/2	Rabun
Edwards, John	Washington	Mannings	179/6	Early
Edwards, Ledford	Jasper	Evans	101/5	Rabun
Edwards, Lockey	Jones	Buckhalter	252/6	Gwinnett
Edwards, Mariday	Washington	Cummins	92/10	Early
Edwards, Nathan	Oglethorpe	Waters	499/9	Irwin
Edwards, Obediah	Effingham		288/16	Early
Edwards, Reuben	Oglethorpe	Waters	28/6	Habersha
Edwards, Reubin Sr.	Jasper	Hays	64/16	Irwin
Edwards, Roberts	Warren	Parhams	28/19	Early
Edwards, Robt.	Warren	Parhams	477/	Appling
Edwards, Seaborn	Oglethorpe	Waters	386/9	Irwin
Edwards, Solomon Sr.	Clarke	Harper	205/1	Irwin
Edwards, Solomon Sr.	Clarke	Harper	215/9	Appling
Edwards, Solomon Sr.	Clarke	Harper	324/20	Early
Edwards, Starling	Lincoln	Jeters	149/4	Irwin
Edwards, Thos.G.	Franklin	Davis	51/17	Early
Edwards, Titus	Washington	Mannings	338/14	Early
Edwards, Warren	Jasper	Evans	156/4	Early
Edwards, Wm.(Orps)	Jones	Buckhalter	326/4	Walton
Edwards, Wm.	Baldwin	Ellis's	271/4	Walton
Edwards, Wm.	Clarke	Deans	192/3	Appling
Edwards, Wm.	Effingham		130/27	Early
Edwards, Wm.	Jones	Mullens	133/18	Early
Edwards, Wm.	Madison	Orrs	282/8	Irwin
Edwards, Wm.W.	Oglethorpe	Waters	26/5	Rabun
Edwards, Wm.W.	Oglethorpe	Waters	7/1	Walton
Eidson, Boyes	Oglethorpe	Bowls	280/1	Appling
Eidson, John	Wilkes	Bates	26/6	Habersha
Eidson, Lewis	Oglethorpe	Bowls	164/10	Early
Eidson, Shelton	Oglethorpe	Bowls	244/8	Early
Eidson, Thos.	Oglethorpe	Bowls	77/28	Early
Eiland, Isaiah(Orps)	Baldwin	Taliaferro	15/1	Appling
Eilands, Nancy(Wid)	Jones	Samuels	31/7	Early
Eilands, Stephen	Jones	Samuels	291/12	Irwin

NAME	COUNTY	MIL.DIST	LOT/SECT	DREW LAND
Eisland, David	McIntosh	Jinkins	150/15	Early
Eisland, David	McIntosh	Jinkins	344/8	Irwin
Eisland, Wm.	McIntosh	Jinkins	27/7	Early
Elbert, Hugh W.	Putnam	Ectors	99/1	Walton
Elder, David	Clarke	Merewether	245/12	Early
Elder, Edmond	Elbert	Webbs	158/12	Irwin
Elder, Edmond	Elbert	Webbs	42/1	Walton
Elder, John	Putnam	Mays	369/3	Appling
Elder, Robt.B.	Putnam	Mays	31/1	Irwin
Elder, Sterling	Clarke	Stewart	57/15	Irwin
Elder, Sterling	Clarke	Stuarts	520/6	Appling
Elder, Wm.N.	Putnam	Mays	327/7	Gwinnett
Elders, James	Liberty		103/21	Early
Elders, James	Liberty		90/9	Hall
Eldridge, Jane(Wid)	Twiggs	W.Belcher	8/8	Appling
Eldson, Jas.	Oglethorpe	Bowls	362/8	Appling
Eleby, Isham(Orps)	Bullock	Tilmans	17/15	Early
Eliat, John G.	Morgan	Wright	122/5	Appling
Eliby, Ann(Orph)	Chatham		308/8	Appling
Eliby, Eliza(Orph)	Chatham		308/8	Appling
Eliby, James(Orph)	Chatham		308/8	Appling
Eliby, Lewis(Orph)	Chatham		308/8	Appling
Eliett, Thos.(RS)	Early		85/7	Gwinnett
Elington, Josiah	Jackson	Rogers	356/7	Irwin
Eliott, Abraham	Elbert	Gaines	395/19	Early
Eliott, Andrew	Baldwin	Marshall	323/13	Early
Eliott, Davis	Early		147/13	Irwin
Eliott, Thos.(RS)	Early		52/19	Early
Elis, Nathan	Putnam	Mays	304/3	Early
Elis, Nathan	Putnam	Mays	504/8	Irwin
Elison, Cunningham	Franklin	Davis	214/5	Irwin
Elison, Francis	Jackson	Rogers	324/9	Appling
Elkins, Alexr.	Effingham		70/5	Rabun
Elkins, Erwin	Oglethorpe	Barnett	40/6	Irwin
Elkins, Erwin	Oglethorpe	Barnetts	141/2	Rabun
Elkins, Young	Wilkinson	Kettles	87/13	Habersham
Ellece, Isaac	Jones	Buckhalter	362/7	Early
Ellerson, Moses	Gwinnett	Hamilton	347/14	Early
Elleson, Wm.	Gwinnett	Hamilton	251/28	Early
Ellets, Jas.(Orps)	Elbert	Childers	209/17	Early
Ellett, James	Warren	Griers	336/17	Early
Elliett, Thos.(RS)	Early		240/13	Early
Ellington, David(Orp)	Greene	142nd	28/15	Early
Ellington, E.(Orps)	Wilkes	Bryant	193/16	Early
Ellington, Eliz.	Baldwin	Marshall	254/26	Early
Ellington, Garland	Richmond	120th	23/14	Early
Ellington, Hezekh.	Wilkes	Mattox	9/1	Early
Ellington, J.(Orps)	Wilkes	Ogletree	55/2	Habersham
Ellington, Joshua	Greene	142nd	383/10	Early
Ellington, Josiah	Jackson	Rogers	397/5	Irwin
Ellington, Sarah(Wid)	Wilkes	Perrys	119/2	Rabun
Ellington, Simeon	Laurens	Deans	296/6	Gwinnett
Ellington, Wm.	Jackson	Dicksons	310/20	Early
Elliot, Nelson	Putnam	Leggits	40/27	Early
Elliot, Thomas	Elbert	Olives	140/10	Irwin
Elliot, Wm.	Lincoln	Graves	93/21	Early
Elliott, Alexr.	Camden	Millers	70/3	Irwin
Elliott, Andr.N.	Franklin	Burroughs	537/2	Appling
Elliott, Arthur	Hall		371/8	Early
Elliott, Geo.	Oglethorpe	Davenport	35/5	Rabun
Elliott, Geo.W.	Greene	Greens	240/17	Early
Elliott, Jas.(Orps)	Elbert	G.Higgingbotham	190/4	Walton
Elliott, Jas.	Franklin	Turks	84/4	Habersham
Elliott, Jas.S.	Franklin	Akins	211/4	Irwin
Elliott, John	Burke	M.Wards	20/6	Appling
Elliott, John	Liberty		227/28	Early
Elliott, Larkin M.	Hall	Carnes	62/5	Gwinnett

NAME	COUNTY	MIL.DIST	LOT/SECT	DREW LAN
Elliott, Mary(Wid)	Hancock	Champions	93/7	Gwinnett
Elliott, Randolph	Richmond	Winters	126/10	Habersha
Elliott, Thos.	Lincoln	Graves	275/7	Irwin
Elliott, Thos.	Lincoln	Gray's	396/10	Irwin
Elliott, Thos.	Twiggs	R.Belcher	24/8	Irwin
Elliott, Wm.	Clarke	Mitchell	251/3	Early
Elliott, Wm.	Lincoln	Jeters	148/16	Early
Elliott, Wm.	Lincoln	Jeters	279/15	Early
Elliott, Wm.	Wilkes	Willis	64/5	Irwin
Ellis, Benj.	Greene	141	47/15	Early
Ellis, Benj.	Oglethorpe	Waters	106/3	Appling
Ellis, Davis R.	Oglethorpe	Goldings	18/1	Walton
Ellis, Ephraim	Wilkinson	Brooks	224/17	Early
Ellis, Evans	Twiggs	Ellis	215/3	Irwin
Ellis, Fielding	Baldwin	Ellis	173/1	Irwin
Ellis, Isaac	Jones	Buckhalter	258/3	Early
Ellis, Jas.	Jasper	Bentleys	178/14	Early
Ellis, Jiles	Camden	Baileys	217/2	Early
Ellis, John H.	Oglethorpe	Waters	117/26	Early
Ellis, John	Oglethorpe	Murrays	233/11	Early
Ellis, Jonathan	Jones	Samuels	224/8	Appling
Ellis, Joshua J.	Jones	Buckhalter	136/10	Habersha
Ellis, Mary	Greene	143	57/11	Irwin
Ellis, Nathan	Oglethorpe	Dunn's	63/4	Appling
Ellis, Radford(Orps)	Jasper	Bentleys	259/12	Irwin
Ellis, Rhesa J.	Twiggs	Tisons	390/12	Irwin
Ellis, Saml.	Twiggs	Ellis	11/6	Irwin
Ellis, Thomas	Glynn		193/3	Irwin
Ellis, Thomas	Glynn		41/3	Rabun
Ellis, Thos.	Appling	3rd	166/6	Irwin
Ellis, Thos.	Appling	3rd	7/13	Early
Ellis, Thos.M.	Baldwin	Ellis	135/9	Appling
Ellis, Tricey(Wid)	Jones	Buckhalter	539/2	Appling
Ellis, Walter	Jackson	Rogers	314/13	Early
Ellis, Wiliam	Liberty		28/2	Habersha
Ellis, Wm.	Emanuel	Dekles	311/14	Early
Ellis, Wm.	Greene	141st	197/4	Early
Ellis, Wm.	Twiggs	Ellis	224/16	Early
Ellis, Wm.Sr.	Oglethorpe	Murays	150/2	Irwin
Ellis, Wm.Sr.	Oglethorpe	Murrys	101/3	Appling
Ellison, Charity	Gwinnett	Hamilton	150/10	Habersha
Ellison, Cunningham	Habersham	Suttons	108/4	Habersha
Ellison, David	Franklin	Akins	175/2	Habersha
Ellison, Francis	Jackson	Hamilton	19/16	Early
Ellison, Richd.	Jackson	Hamilton	22/1	Irwin
Ellison, Richd.	Jackson	Hamilton	88/11	Irwin
Ellison, Robt.	Burke	Royals	365/7	Early
Elliss, Wm.(RS)	McIntosh	Jinkins	168/4	Appling
Elliss, Wm.(RS)	McIntosh	Jinkins	93/3	Walton
Elon, Jane	Chatham		172/4	Appling
Elton, Chas.	Washington	Jenkinson	137/1	Walton
Elton, John	Washington	Jenkinson	136/8	Early
Elton, John	Washington	Jenkinson	210/12	Habersha
Elton, Robert	Washington	Floyds	612/2	Appling
Ely, Bennett H.	Greene	Jones	371/19	Early
Ely, Jessee	Greene	Jones	93/4	Appling
Ely, Seaborn	Greene	Mercer	591/2	Appling
Emanuel, John	Scriven	Lovetts	291/17	Early
Emanuel, Lewis(Orps)	Burke	69th	242/2	Irwin
Embre, John	Columbia	J.Morris	22/1	Habersha
Embrey, Hezekiah L.	Warren	Parham	284/16	Early
Embrey, Mirel	Clarke	Parrs	375/28	Early
Embry, Ann	Oglethorpe	Lees	341/27	Early
Emerson, Zacharh.	Jones	Permenter	85/7	Appling
Emmerson, John	Morgan	Knight	46/11	Habersha
Emory, Samuel	Jasper	Bentleys	422/8	Irwin
Emrey, Wm.	Oglethorpe	Bridges	362/8	Early

102

NAME	COUNTY	MIL.DIST	LOT/SECT	DREW LAND
England, Jos.	Franklin	Powels	21/2	Rabun
England, Jos.	Franklin	Powels	6/4	Walton
England, Thos.	Oglethorpe	Lees	359/7	Gwinnett
English, Heary	Oglethorpe	Murrays	97/5	Gwinnett
English, Hiram	Franklin	Turks	36/22	Early
English, Jas.(Orps)	Twiggs	Ellis	155/19	Early
English, John	Jones	Kings	25/10	Hall
English, John	Washington	Pools	355/5	Appling
English, John	Washington	Pools	87/12	Hall
English, Stephen	Oglethorpe	Murry's	93/2	Irwin
Enlow, Phillip	Hall	McCutchen	304/2	Appling
Ennis, Chas.	Hancock	Justices	117/2	Walton
Ennis, Richd.	McIntosh	McIntosh	129/28	Early
Entrecan, Wm.	Columbia	Cockrans	55/10	Irwin
Entricken, Wm.	Warren	152	326/10	Irwin
Enus, (Orphs)	Burke	Royals	515/5	Irwin
Epperson, John	Jackson	Hamilton	172/9	Irwin
Eppinger, John	Chatham		360/9	Early
Epps, Chislon	Columbia	Dodsons	52/1	Walton
Epps, Edward	Twiggs	Jefferson	375/7	Irwin
Epps, Edward	Twiggs	Jefferson	375/7	Irwin
Epps, Jas.T.	Clarke	Stuarts	252/17	Early
Epps, William	Clarke	Deans	167/1	Appling
Epps, Wm.	Clarke	Harpers	162/4	Early
Ervine, Wm.(Orps)	Jones	Parmenter	206/12	Habersham
Erving, John	Hancock	Millers	1/22	Early
Erwin, Alexr.	Jackson	Dicksons	58/10	Early
Erwin, James	Chatham		32/11	Hall
Erwin, James	Jackson	Dicksons	421/1	Appling
Erwin, Leander	Clarke	Appling	155/6	Irwin
Espey, John	Clarke	Applings	356/13	Irwin
Espy, Robt.	Morgan	Loyd	147/26	Early
Espy, Thos.	Putnam	Coopers	280/7	Appling
Etcherson, Jas.	Oglethorpe	Barnett	246/3	Appling
Etherage, Wm.	Jones	Harrist	178/7	Gwinnett
Ethredge, Marmaduke	Baldwin	Stephens	338/8	Early
Ethridge, Abel	Twiggs	R.Belcher	170/3	Irwin
Ethridge, Abel	Twiggs	R.Belcher	367/6	Appling
Ethridge, Caleb	Baldwin	Stephens	295/18	Early
Ethridge, Edmd.	Jones	Permenter	296/5	Appling
Ethridge, Edmund	Jones	Permenters	169/10	Habersham
Ethridge, Edwd.	Wilkinson	Brooks	347/18	Early
Ethridge, Edwd.	Wilkinson	Brooks	411/7	Irwin
Ethridge, John	Twiggs	W.Belcher	2/5	Rabun
Ethridge, John	Twiggs	W.Belcher	206/26	Early
Ethridge, John	Wilkinson	Kettles	248/19	Early
Ethridge, John	Wilkinson	Kettles	29/4	Habersham
Ethridge, Marmaduke	Baldwin	Stephens	145/5	Irwin
Ethridge, Merritt	Wilkinson	Howards	268/6	Irwin
Ethridge, Nathan	Jones	Permenter	133/12	Early
Ethridge, Robt.	Wilkinson	Howards	121/11	Habersham
Ethridge, Robt.	Wilkinson	Howards	132/5	Appling
Ethridge, Wm.	Jones	Hurst	52/7	Gwinnett
Eubank, Caleb	Columbia	Gartrells	18/6	Early
Eubank, Esther(Wid)	Columbia	Pullin	186/6	Irwin
Eubank, John	Columbia	Pullin	285/12	Early
Eubank, Richardson	Wilkes	Bates	273/16	Early
Eubank, Wm.	Lincoln	Graves	362/4	Early
Eubank, Wm.Jr.	Columbia	Pullin	52/26	Early
Eubank, Wm.Sr.	Columbia	Pullin	44/10	Hall
Eubanks, Reuben(Orps)	Columbia	J.Morris	28/5	Rabun
Eubanks, Thos.	Jones	Rossers	69/23	Early
Evan, Zacheus(Orps)	Emanuel	57	323///2	Appling
Evans, Absalom	Jones	Buckhalter	474/5	Irwin
Evans, Adin	Morgan	Lenards	373/17	Early
Evans, Anselm	Jasper	Bartlett	356/5	Irwin
Evans, Anslem	Jasper	Bartlett	49/19	Early

NAME	COUNTY	MIL.DIST	LOT/SECT	DREW LAND
Evans, Benj.	Wilkinson	Lees	128/15	Early
Evans, Benj.	Wilkinson	Lees	88/4	Appling
Evans, Britan W.	Hancock	Evans	280/21	Early
Evans, Brittain W.	Hancock	Evans	320/13	Irwin
Evans, Chas.	Lincoln	Walkers	352/5	Irwin
Evans, Danl.J.	Burke	Thomas	49/12	Irwin
Evans, David Jr.	Laurens	Deans	362/8	Irwin
Evans, David Sr.	Burke	Thomas	16/7	Gwinnett
Evans, David Sr.	Laurens	Deans	210/26	Early
Evans, David	Franklin	Haynes	349/7	Irwin
Evans, Edmund T.	Putnam	Oslins	514/8	Appling
Evans, Edw.H.	Putnam	Evans	210/6	Gwinnett
Evans, Elijah	Putnam	Mays	23/4	Rabun
Evans, Elisha(Orps)	Greene	Jones	156/7	Gwinnett
Evans, Eliz.	Morgan	Talbot	117/27	Early
Evans, Eliza(Orp)	Richmond	Burton	395/10	Early
Evans, Evan	Jasper	Eastes	190/18	Early
Evans, Henry(Orp)	Richmond	Burton	395/10	Early
Evans, Henry(Orps)	Jasper	Bentleys	387/9	Early
Evans, John L.	Wilkinson	Childs	356/18	Early
Evans, John(Orps)	Burke	J.Wards	4/14	Early
Evans, John	Burke	Thomas	181/12	Habersham
Evans, John	Franklin	Haynes	268/7	Appling
Evans, John	Laurens	Deans	271/7	Appling
Evans, Johua	Jasper	Evans	340/12	Irwin
Evans, Josiah	Morgan	Talbot	171/2	Rabun
Evans, Nancy(Orp)	Richmond	Burton	395/10	Early
Evans, Nathan(Orps)	Elbert	Whites	500/9	Irwin
Evans, Polly(Orp)	Richmond	Burton	395/10	Early
Evans, Richd.H.	Burke	Thomas	305/7	Early
Evans, Richd.Sr.	Burke	Dy's	162/6	Gwinnett
Evans, Robt.	Madison	Culbreths	1/11	Hall
Evans, Ruel(Ser)	Scriven		180/5	Early
Evans, Stephen	Putnam	Moreland	99/4	Appling
Evans, Stephen	Wilkinson	Kettles	73/10	Irwin
Evans, Stokeley	Clarke	Pentecost	511/10	Irwin
Evans, Thomas	Baldwin	Hawes	337/7	Irwin
Evans, Thos.	Wilkes	Smiths	21/7	Irwin
Evans, Thos.H.	Putnam	Evans	101/2	Habersham
Evans, Thos.M.	Jones	Shropshier	169/12	Irwin
Evans, Thos.W.	Scriven		34/16	Early
Evans, Thos.W.	Scriven		420/11	Irwin
Evans, Wm.	Elbert	Whites	40/2	Appling
Evans, Wm.Sr.	Greene	Nelms	231/7	Early
Eve, John	Richmond	Laceys	280/3	Early
Eve, Joseph	Richmond	Laceys	108/28	Early
Eveins, Geo.Jr.	Clarke	Pentecost	333/12	Irwin
Even, Peter	Tattnall	Tharps	469/5	Appling
Evenson, Eli	Elbert	G.Higgenbotham	165/10	Early
Evenson, Eli	Elbert	G/Higgenbotham	163/8	Irwin
Everett, Benj.	Hancock	Kindalls	236/1	Early
Everett, John Sr.	Bullock	Jones	26/23	Early
Everett, John(Orps)	Pulaski	Bryans	334/2	Early
Everett, Saml.	Jasper	Evans	411/15	Early
Everett, Saml.H.	Franklin	J.Miller	340/13	Early
Everingham, Thos.	Richmond	Winters	183/5	Early
Everingham, Thos.	Richmond	Winters	355/5	Gwinnett
Everingham, Thos.Jr.	Richmond	Winters	71/9	Early
Everit, Solomon	Jasper	Evans	475/13	Irwin
Everitt, Hardy	Scriven		190/3	Habersham
Everitt, James	Telfair	Williams	73/2	Rabun
Everitt, John C.	Bullock	Tilmans	17/15	Early
Everitt, Wm.	Scriven		265/20	Early
Evers, Gibson	Wilkinson	Childs	301/15	Early
Evers, Gibson	Wilkinson	Childs	337/3	Gwinnett
Evers, John	Effingham		467/6	Appling
Evers, John	Laurens	Harris	229/5	Appling

NAME	COUNTY	MIL.DIST	LOT/SECT	DREW LAND
Everton, John A.	Pulaski	Coles	190/3	Appling
Eves, Wm.	Richmond	120th	200/2	Early
Evins, Banister	Warren	152	70/12	Early
Evins, Charity(Wid)	Hancock	Danells	1/9	Appling
Evins, Howel	Warren	152	331/3	Appling
Evins, John	Gwinnett	Hamilton	84/10	Hall
Evins, Stokely	Clarke	Pentecost	329/5	Gwinnett
Exley, Eliz.(Wid)	Effingham		219/19	Early
Exley, Jacob	Effingham		150/15	Irwin
Exum, Mathew	Twiggs	Smiths	87/2	Rabun
Ezele, Wm.	Laurens	Deans	339/11	Early
Ezell, Jane(Wid)	Twiggs	Browns	428/15	Early
Ezell, Lewis(Orps)	Twiggs	Browns	93/5	Gwinnett
Ezell, Mills	Laurens	Deans	386/6	Irwin
Ezill, Thos.	Jackson	Hamilton	410/8	Irwin
Ezzel, Levy	Twiggs	Barnes	173/4	Appling
Fabian, Jonathan(Orps)	Liberty		310/19	Early
Fagan, Starky	Bulloch	Tilmans	259/9	Early
Fagen, Moses Sr.	Franklin	Flannagan	650/2	Appling
Fagin, Enoch	Bulloch	Tilmans	152/6	Appling
Faglie, John	Warren	150th	113/15	Irwin
Fahm, Jacob	Chatham		501/8	Irwin
Fail, Ely Mc	Liberty		109/3	Rabun
Fails, Arthur(Orps)	Putnam	Robertson	75/10	Habersham
Fails, Sarah(Wid)	Putnam	Robertson	347/8	Early
Fails, Wm.	Putnam	Robertson	240/2	Irwin
Fain, Jesse	Morgan	Hubbard	194/8	Irwin
Fain, John	Morgan	Hackney	342/10	Early
Fair, Jane(Wid)	Jones	Shropshear	50/5	Appling
Fair, William	Franklin	Harris	335/4	Appling
Faircloth, Alexr.	Emanuel	56th	224/5	Gwinnett
Faircloth, Caleb Sr.	Laurens	Griffins	40/1	Rabun
Faircloth, Davis	Laurens	Griffins	16/15	Irwin
Faircloth, Davis	Laurens	Griffins	184/7	Early
Faircloth, Ethelrd.	Emanuel	395th	236/6	Early
Faircloth, Ethelrd.	Emanuel	395th	313/5	Irwin
Faircloth, Ethlrd.	Laurens	Griffins	154/12	Irwin
Faircloth, John	Laurens	Griffins	147/21	Early
Faircloth, John	Scriven	180th	302/5	Irwin
Faircloth, Peter	Laurens	Griffins	85/1	Irwin
Faircloth, Reddin	Scriven	180th	37/5	Rabun
Faircloth, Richd.	Laurens	Griffins	71/14	Early
Faircloth, Robt.	Laurens	Griffins	256/3	Irwin
Faircloth, Wm.	Laurens	Griffins	134/2	Early
Falk, James	Wilkes	Childs	242/5	Early
Falkenbery, Jacob	Richmond	Palmer	298/13	Early
Falkner, Asa(RS)	Twiggs	R.Belchers	76/11	Hall
Falkner, Elisha(Orp)	Twiggs	R.Belchers	297/9	Irwin
Falkner, Henry(Orps)	Twiggs	W.Belchers	72/9	Appling
Falkner, Peter	Morgan	Farrar	77/4	Appling
Falling, John H.	Wilkes	Perrys	278/10	Irwin
Fambrew, Thos.	Greene	Ragins	239/3	Appling
Fambrew, Thos.	Greene	Ragins	487/4	Appling
Fambrough, Gadial	Jasper	Bentley	148/12	Hall
Fambrough, John	Clark	Merriweather	131/9	Irwin
Fambrough, Joshua	Clark	Merriweather	72/10	Habersham
Fambrough, Robertson	Clark	Merriweather	221/3	Appling
Fambrough, Robertson	Clark	Merweather	203/7	Irwin
Fambrough, Wm.	Clark	Merriweather	122/6	Early
Fambrough, Wm.Sr.	Clark	Merewether	42/9	Hall
Fanin, John Jr.	Elbert	Ruckers	251/6	Early
Fanin, Jos.D.(Orps)	Putnam	Littles	351/11	Irwin
Fannen, Hezekiah	Walton	Greens	107/1	Early
Fannen, Jacob W.	Putnam	Buckner	254/3	Appling
Fannen, Jacob.Sr.	Putnam	Buckner	384/9	Irwin
Fannin, Benj.	Elbert	Smiths	87/5	Gwinnett
Fannin, Betsey(Wid)	Putnam	Littles	8/7	Irwin

NAME	COUNTY	MIL.DIST	LOT/SECT	DREW LAND
Fanning, Welcome	Wilkes	Gordon	216/27	Early
Farabee, Jesse	Greene	Alens	377/12	Irwin
Fareleys, Jas.	Jones	Greene	545/2	Appling
Fares, Josiah	Wilkes	Willis	493/10	Irwin
Fargason, Johnston	Morgan	Selmans	77/21	Early
Fargason, Johnston	Morgan	Selmons	90/2	Irwin
Farley, Francis	Morgan	Loyds	427/4	Appling
Farley, Francis	Morgan	Loyds	434/15	Early
Farley, Jas.Sr.	Jasper	Phillips	324/2	Appling
Farley, Jas.Sr.	Jasper	Phillips	334/13	Irwin
Farley, John	Jasper	Owens	208/19	Early
Farley, John	Jasper	Phillips	11/13	Habersham
Farley, Mathew	Putnam	Slaughter	97/3	Rabun
Farman, John S.	Elbert	Dooleys	16/1	Habersham
Farmer, Andrew	Laurens	Griffins	38/9	Irwin
Farmer, Duke	Twiggs	Evans	247/7	Irwin
Farmer, Isaac Jr.	Burke	69th	306/6	Gwinnett
Farmer, James	Wilkes	Mattox	140/4	Walton
Farmer, Jas.Sr.	Jackson	Hamiltons	196/4	Early
Farmer, Jeremiah	Chatham		213/21	Early
Farmer, John(Orps)	Emanuel	55th	308/7	Gwinnett
Farmer, John	Jackson	Hamiltons	167/3	Walton
Farmer, John	Morgan	Campbell	356/8	Irwin
Farmer, John	Washington	Burneys	347/26	Early
Farmer, Luke	Twiggs	Evans	22/12	Early
Farmer, Nancy	Burke	69th	504/5	Irwin
Farmer, Nathan	Morgan	Ramays	127/6	Appling
Farmer, Thos.	Jones	Wallers	42/11	Hall
Farmer, Wm.	Ogelthorpe	Bridges	222/11	Irwin
Farmer, Wm.	Washington	Burneys	97/2	Appling
Farmer, Wm.	Washington	Burneys	97/2	Appling
Farnall, Jas.(Orp)	Burke	Torrance	29/7	Early
Farnando, Moses G.	Chatham		34/13	Early
Farnell, Elisha	Pulaski	Lesters	337/21	Early
Farnell, Elisha	Pulaski	Lesters	493/2	Appling
Farr, John C.	Clark	Parrs	446/11	Irwin
Farra, Geo.Y.	Clark	Starnes	30/8	Irwin
Farrar, John	Columbia	Burroughs	82/28	Early
Farrar, Stephen D.	Morgan	Selmon	8/13	Early
Farrar, Thos.	Clark	Parrs	110/11	Irwin
Farrar, Thos.	Lincoln	Graves	172/16	Early
Farrar, Thos.	Lincoln	Graves	407/9	Early
Farrington, John	Richmond	122	112/4	Habersham
Farris, Samuel	Twiggs	R.Belchers	48/6	Early
Farrow, John S.(Orps)	Morgan	Townsend	70/11	Hall
Farwesworth, Jas.	Wilkes	Kilgores	189/6	Irwin
Faulk, Jesse	Jones	Phillips	343/2	Appling
Faulk, William	Twiggs	Hodges	240/7	Irwin
Faulk, William	Twiggs	Hodges	81/3	Appling
Faulk, Wm.	Elbert	Webbs	23/12	Early
Faulkner, Dozier	Elbert	R.Christian	23/6	Appling
Faulkner, Maston	Elbert	R.Christian	216/4	Walton
Faulkner, Sarah	Madison	Culbreths	220/12	Early
Faulkner, Wm.	Elbert	R.Christian	312/7	Appling
Favor, Isiah	Putnam	Brooks	104/3	Rabun
Favor, Mary	Wilkes	Davis	303/15	Early
Favor, Mathew	Wilkes	Davis	139/3	Early
Favor, Rauben	Wilkes	Davis	9/14	Early
Favour, Vines	Putnam	Brooks	255/6	Gwinnett
Fawnin, John H.	Jones	Samuels	443/6	Appling
Feagan, Saml.	Jones	Permenters	88/12	Hall
Feagin, Benj.	Twiggs	Evans	520/12	Irwin
Feagin, Jas.	Jones	Samuels	309/1	Early
Feagin, Richd.	Jones	Samuels	296/7	Appling
Fean, Isaac	Hancock	Evans	55/4	Habersham
Fears, Richd.	Hancock	Daniels	304/15	Early
Fears, Saml.	Jasper	Bentley	387/12	Early

NAME	COUNTY	MIL.DIST	LOT/SECT	DREW LAND
Fears, Zacheriah	Jasper	Bentley	246/23	Early
Featherston, Richd.	Jasper	Bentley	13/27	Early
Featherston, Richd.	Jasper	Bentley	202/4	Early
Featherston, Wm.	Franklin	J.Miller	89/22	Early
Fell, Eliz.(Wid)	Chatham		404/6	Irwin
Felps, David D.(Orps)	Putnam	Ectors	230/11	Irwin
Felps, Falba(Wid)	Putnam	Ectors	161/4	Irwin
Felps, John	Putnam	Ectors	114/12	Hall
Felps, John	Putnam	Ectors	210/5	Early
Felps, Wm.	Pulaski	Bryans	131/13	Irwin
Felt, Joseph	Chatham		56/20	Early
Felton, John	Ogelthorpe	Barnett	2/14	Irwin
Felts, Cary	Jones	Jefferson	328/12	Irwin
Felts, Jas.(RS)	Jones	Jefferson	321/28	Early
Felts, John	Putnam	Ectors	211/3	Walton
Felts, Simeon	Putnam	Ectors	107/7	Gwinnett
Felts, Wm.	Putnam	Ectors	217/3	Irwin
Fenn, Eli	Washington	Renfro	233/9	Irwin
Fenn, Eli	Washington	Renfroes	450/7	Irwin
Fenn, Elijah	Laurens	Kinchens	290/7	Gwinnett
Fenn, Geo.Sr.	Clark	Pentecost	466/3	Appling
Fenn, George	Clark	Pentecosts	55/2	Early
Fenn, Milmoth(Wid)	Clark	Pentecosts	349/11	Irwin
Fenn, Thos.A.	Clark	Penticosts	389/7	Early
Fenn, Wm.	Clark	Tredwell	339/20	Early
Fenn, Zaches	Wilkes	Childs	2/2	Appling
Fennel, Ephraim	Twiggs	W.Belcher	495/15	Irwin
Fennell, Chas.(Orps)	Columbia	Bealls	119/4	Appling
Fennell, John P.	Washington	Wimberlys	287/5	Irwin
Fennell, Rutha(Wid)	Laurens	S.Smith	152/20	Early
Fereby, Robt.	Franklin	Morris	1/4	Walton
Fergerson, Sally(Orp)	Richmond	Burton	35/17	Early
Fergus, Wm.	Madison	Williford	407/11	Early
Ferguson, Winney(Wid)	Wilkes	Lees	291/11	Irwin
Fernander, Saml.C.	Jasper	Bartlet	38/14	Irwin
Ferrell, Bennett A.	Twiggs	W.Belcher	152/13	Early
Ferrell, Bennett	Wilkes	Kettles	45/1	Rabun
Ferrell, Micajah	Elbert	Gains	398/5	Appling
Ferrell, Mickleberry	Jones	Seals	26/1	Appling
Ferrell, Wm.	Hancock	Loyds	244/7	Irwin
Ferrill, Burton	Pulaski	Davis	305/9	Appling
Ferrill, Cuthbert	Jasper	Kenaday	313/11	Irwin
Ferrill, Cuthbert	Jasper	Kennedys	459/7	Irwin
Ferrill, Ludy	Pulaski	Rees	46/22	Early
Ferris, Joab	Liberty		293/6	Gwinnett
Ferris, Joab	Liberty		6/27	Early
Fetzer, Jonathan	Effingham		61/14	Early
Few, Benj.W.	Columbia	J.Morriss	359/3	Appling
Few, Clement	Morgan	Wrights	7/3	Habersham
Few, Ignacious	Morgan	Wrights	136/15	Irwin
Few, Ignatius(Col)	Columbia	J.Morriss	14/19	Early
Few, James	Morgan	Wright	86/3	Early
Few, Wm.	Columbia	J.Morris	155/11	Hall
Ficklin, Barney W.	Warren	153rd	155/20	Early
Field, Jedidiah	Liberty		107/3	Walton
Fielder, Eliz.(Wid)	Putnam	Littles	175/4	Walton
Fielder, George	Walton	Greens	335/15	Early
Fielder, Isham	Morgan	Walker	225/27	Early
Fielder, John	Walton	Greens	87/10	Habersham
Fielder, Nancy(Wid)	Greene	Griers	38/8	Appling
Fielder, Obed.M.B.	Morgan	Walkers	494/8	Irwin
Fielder, Saml.	Morgan	Knights	38/1	Appling
Fielder, Sarah(Wid)	Morgan	Walker	95/4	Irwin
Fielder, Tyrel	Morgan	Walker	173/13	Early
Fielder, Uriah	Morgan	Selmons	34/1	Appling
Fielder, Wm.L.(Orps)	Greene	Griers	331/12	Irwin
Fields, Horatio	Hancock	Evans	171/17	Early

NAME	COUNTY	MIL.DIST	LOT/SECT	DREW LA
Fields, Jas.	Burke	Spivey	69/7	Irwin
Fields, Jas.	Jefferson	Langston	93/10	Habersh
Fields, Mary	Burke	Spivey	43/1	Appling
Fields, Owen	Laurens	Harris	73/21	Early
Fields, Sarah	Hancock	Evans	165/19	Early
Fields, Sion	Morgan	Selmon	80/10	Irwin
Fields, Thompson	Baldwin	Ellis	254/4	Walton
Figg, John D.R.	Jefferson	Bothwell	29/14	Irwin
Files, Wm.B.	Morgan	Hackney	279/7	Appling
Fillingim, Jarvis Jr.	Twiggs	Evans	226/3	Walton
Filtin, James	Greene	141st	222/9	Appling
Finch, Burdett	Ogelthorpe	Myrick	110/6	Early
Finch, Burdett	Ogelthorpe	Myrick	244/5	Appling
Finch, Gabriel	Franklin	Davis	159/5	Appling
Finch, Gabril	Franklin	Davis	73/15	Early
Finch, Lydia	Madison	Bones	382/9	Early
Finch, Robt.	Putnam	Robertson	142/15	Early
Finch, Thos.	Jones	Seals	413/4	Early
Fincher, Benj.	Jasper	Northcuts	115/1	Appling
Fincher, Jas.(RS)	Jasper	Barnes	184/28	Early
Fincher, Jas.(RS)	Jasper	Barnes	250/8	Appling
Fincher, Jas.(RS)	Jasper	Barnes	29/27	Early
Fincher, Wm.	Jasper	Evans	78/1	Walton
Findalson, Chrst.(Wid)	Telfair	Loves	476/7	Appling
Findalson, Danl.(Orps)	Telfair	Loves	242/11	Irwin
Findley, Jacob	Jasper	Barnes	396/17	Early
Findley, Jas.	Greene	Ragins	154/10	Irwin
Findley, John	Emanuel	58	16/8	Irwin
Findley, John	Emanuel	58th	337/9	Early
Findley, John	Morgan	Ramey	147/1	Irwin
Findley, John	Morgan	Townsend	336/7	Early
Findley, Sarah(Wid)	Glynn		203/8	Appling
Findley, Stephen	Emanuel	58th	165/2	Habersh
Finley, Saml.D.	Ogelthorpe	Murrays	236/9	Early
Finley, Wm.	Clark	Stewart	371/15	Early
Finley, Wm.	Clark	Stewart	391/17	Early
Finn, John(Orps)	Wilkes	Bates	61/10	Irwin
Finnell, Leroy	Columbia	Bealls	67/5	Gwinnet
Finney, Benj.	Jones	Buckhalter	214/6	Early
Finney, Jas.	Jones	Phillips	139/13	Early
Finney, Wm.	Burke	M.Wards	9/18	Early
Finnie, Drury	Jones	Jefferson	400/8	Early
Finnie, John	Jones	Buckhalter	21/3	Early
Finnie, Sarah(Wid)	Jones	Hansford	187/28	Early
Finnie, Ufama	Jones	Harrist	146/11	Early
Finny, Wm.	Burke	M.Wards	119/2	Irwin
Fish, Nathan	Jasper	Baileys	364/18	Early
Fisher, Mikel	Chatham		477/6	Irwin
Fisher, Mikil	Chatham		29/11	Irwin
Fisher, Mittalp	Washington	Barges	178/15	Early
Fisher, Willard	Burke	Hands	313/8	Irwin
Fisher, Wm.	Columbia	Shaws	156/13	Early
Fitchjarrell, Geo.	Franklin	Hammond	369/1	Early
Fitspatrick, Boothe	Jasper	Clays	104/6	Appling
Fittin, John	Greene	141st	111/1	Appling
Fitts, John	Elbert	Ruckers	516/12	Irwin
Fitts, John	Elbert	Ruckers	7/8	Hall
Fitzee, Gottiel	Effingham		249/4	Appling
Fitzgerald, David	Burke	Lewis	348/16	Early
Fitzgerald, John	Burke	Spiveys	200/1	Irwin
Fitzgerald, Nancy(Orp)	Richmond	Palmer	11/15	Early
Fitzgerald, Nancy	Richmond	Palmer	358/3	Appling
Fitzgerald, Reubin	Twiggs	Browns	372/20	Early
Fitzgerald, Sarah(Orp)	Richmond	Palmer	11/15	Early
Fitzpatrick, Alexr.	Morgan	Jordan	243/7	Irwin
Fitzpatrick, Benj.	Morgan	Jordan	53/3	Walton
Fitzpatrick, Booth	Jasper	Clays	202/13	Early

NAME	COUNTY	MIL.DIST	LOT/SECT	DREW LAND
Fitzpatrick, Hamner	Morgan	Jordan	151/1	Appling
Fitzpatrick, Jackson	Jasper	Whites	227/6	Irwin
Fitzpatrick, Jas.	Morgan	Boaseley	412/9	Irwin
Fitzpatrick, Rene	Jasper	Smiths	207/27	Early
Fitzpatrick, Saml.	Effingham		70/17	Early
Fitzpatrick, Wm.	Greene	Tuggles	211/13	Irwin
Flacher, Mary(Wid)	Morgan	Campbell	316/6	Gwinnett
Flake, Thos.	Putnam	Littles	95/5	Rabun
Flake, William Jr.	Warren	154th	546/2	Appling
Flaming, Thos.	Lincoln	Parks	165/4	Appling
Flanagain, Wm.	Franklin	Davis	228/20	Early
Flanders, John	Emanuel	55	210/28	Early
Flanegan, Joel	Walton	Echols	63/11	Early
Flannagan, John	Jackson	Rogers	50/18	Early
Flannigan, Mal.(Wid)	Jones	Buckhalter	280/7	Irwin
Fleaton, Richd.	Jefferson	Flemming	64/12	Early
Fleeton, John	Jefferson	Lamps	502/13	Irwin
Fleming, James	Jefferson	Fleming	131/21	Early
Fleming, James	Warren	Griers	305/7	Irwin
Fleming, James	Warren	Griers	365/7	Gwinnett
Fleming, John Sr.	Columbia	Ob.Morris	275/5	Early
Fleming, John	Jefferson	Fleming	107/15	Irwin
Fleming, John	Jefferson	Fleming	350/3	Early
Fleming, John	Warren	Griers	382/17	Early
Fleming, Royal	Ogelthorpe	Wises	80/23	Early
Fleming, Samuel Jr.	Warren	Griers	273/6	Gwinnett
Flemming, Geo.	Camden	33rd	446/12	Irwin
Flemming, Jas.	Baldwin	Marshall	205/11	Irwin
Flemming, John A.	Columbia	Watson	61/1	Rabun
Flemming, John	Twiggs	R.Belchers	41/6	Habersham
Flemming, Robert A.	Warren	152	142/9	Early
Flemming, Robt.	Franklin	Turks	441/4	Appling
Flemming, Robt.	Morgan	McClendon	370/2	Appling
Flemming, Wm.	Franklin	Turks	172/26	Early
Flemmon, Newton	Franklin	Flemmon	198/1	Appling
Flerl, Isarel(Orps)	Effingham		238/8	Irwin
Fletcher, Ezekiel	Lincoln	Graves	143/8	Hall
Fletcher, Jas.(Orps)	Telfair	Tallies	362/19	Early
Fletcher, John Jr.	Telfair	Tallis	354/11	Irwin
Fletcher, John	Clark	Parrs	344/19	Early
Fletcher, John	Clark	Parrs	416/9	Irwin
Fletcher, Jos.	Telfair	Tallies	321/9	Appling
Fletcher, Jos.	Telfair	Tallies	67/1	Walton
Fletcher, Mary(Wid)	Telfair	Tallies	347/5	Irwin
Fletcher, Richd.	Columbia	Dodson	60/12	Irwin
Fletcher, Thos.	Ogelthorpe	Britton	180/27	Early
Fletcher, Wm.Jr.	Bulloch	Tilmans	157/1	Early
Fletcher, Wm.Jr.	Bulloch	Tilmans	270/11	Early
Fletcher, Ziba	Jones	Samuels	39/13	Irwin
Flewellin, Alexr.	Putnam	Moreland	311/8	Appling
Flewellin, Taylor	Richmond	122	82/1	Appling
Flewellin, Thomas	Warren	Blounts	28/2	Walton
Flewellin, Wm.	Jones	Samuels	227/3	Early
Flinn, James	Warren	152nd	368/8	Irwin
Flinn, John Jr.	Columbia	Watsons	180/13	Early
Flinn, John Sr.	Columbia	Watson	202/10	Habersham
Flint, George W.	Wilkes	Willis	394/18	Early
Flint, John	Clark	Deans	293/28	Early
Flint, Wm.	Morgan	Parker	19/4	Walton
Flippin, Wm.	Clark	Starnes	308/18	Early
Flitcham, Elisa	Chatham		270/15	Early
Flitcham, Jane	Chatham		270/15	Early
Flitcham, Sarah	Chatham		270/15	Early
Flitcham, Senthy	Chatham		270/15	Early
Flitwood, Green(Orp)	Chatham		213/5	Appling
Flitwood, John(Orp)	Chatham		213/5	Appling
Flood, Saml.	Camden	Clarks	140/3	Irwin

NAME	COUNTY	MIL.DIST	LOT/SECT	DREW LAND
Florence, Jane	Lincoln	Jones	15/23	Early
Florence, John	Lincoln	Tatoms	369/6	Irwin
Florence, Thos.Jr.	Lincoln	Jones	221/16	Early
Florence, Wm.(Orp)	Lincoln	Jones	385/11	Early
Flourancy, Marcus	Jefferson	Waldens	90/17	Early
Flourney, Robt.	Putnam	Robertson	499/7	Appling
Flourney, Samuel	Wilkes	Kilgores	196/10	Early
Flourney, Wm.H.	Putnam	Oslins	159/2	Early
Flournoy, Obadiah	Wilkes	Kilgores	264/6	Appling
Flournoy, Simeon	Wilkes	Brooks	201/8	Irwin
Flowers, Abner	Jones	Rosser	264/28	Early
Flowers, Abner	Jones	Rosser	287/7	Early
Flowers, Eliz.(Wid)	Laurens	Kinchens	78/16	Early
Flowers, Harrel	Jones	Waller	286/8	Irwin
Flowers, Harrel	Jones	Wallers	34/14	Irwin
Flowers, John	Liberty		217/12	Habersham
Flowers, Jos.	Emanuel	58th	158/6	Early
Flowers, Joseph	Liberty		219/7	Early
Flowers, Willis	Laurens	Kinchens	219/5	Early
Flowers, Wm.	Camden	33rd	137/9	Hall
Flowers, Wm.	Jasper	Owens	203/13	Irwin
Flowers, Wm.	Jasper	Smiths	159/11	Early
Flowers, Wright	Laurens	Kinchens	493/3	Appling
Floyd, Chas.	Camden	Longs	232/8	Appling
Floyd, Chas.	Camden	Longs	310/10	Early
Floyd, Frederick	Pulaski	Rees	392/21	Early
Floyd, Gallant	Hall		282/17	Early
Floyd, Jabez	Madison	Orrs	392/8	Early
Floyd, James	Burke	Spivey	12/11	Early
Floyd, Jas.	Burke	Spiveys	24/9	Irwin
Floyd, John	Wilkes	Josseys	496/6	Appling
Floyd, Richd.	Ogelthorpe	Davenport	161/6	Appling
Floyd, Richd.	Ogelthorpe	Davenport	398/27	Early
Floyd, Robt.	Madison	Adares	379/10	Early
Floyd, Sarah	Burke	Torrance	185/6	Appling
Floyd, Thomas	Wilkes	Josseys	147/9	Early
Floyd, Thos.	Jones	Samuels	113/26	Early
Floyd, Thos.	Jones	Samuels	56/5	Rabun
Floyd, Wm.Jr.	Ogelthorpe	Bridges	65/2	Habersham
Floyd, Wm.Sr.	Ogelthorpe	Bridges	369/7	Irwin
Floyd, Wm.Sr.	Ogelthorpe	Bridges	428/1	Appling
Floyde, Goodwin	Jones	Samuels	218/3	Walton
Fluker, John	Jasper	Clays	257/13	Irwin
Fluker, Owen	Wilkes	Runnells	152/1	Walton
Fluker, Owen	Wilkes	Runnels	162/9	Irwin
Flury, Handly	Wilkes	Ogletree	147/8	Early
Flynn, Mary Ann	Chatham		494/5	Irwin
Fokes, Amos	Jefferson	Langston	346/7	Gwinnett
Folds,	Morgan	Paces	400/4	Appling
Folds, Amos	Lincoln	Walkers	305/11	Early
Folds, Eli	Morgan	Loyds	70/5	Irwin
Folds, Geo.	Columbia	Shaws	77/7	Early
Folds, Henry	Lincoln	Graves	1/3	Appling
Folds, Jacob	Jasper	Bentley	455/2	Appling
Folds, Richd.	Richmond	Palmer	39/5	Gwinnett
Folly, Asa	Jasper	Eastes	127/14	Early
Folsom, Ebenezer	Laurens	D.Smith	117/9	Appling
Folsom, Geo.	Pulaski	Bryans	77/15	Irwin
Folsom, Randal	Pulaski	Bryans	116/6	Appling
Folsom, Thos.	Pulaski	Lester	171/9	Appling
Folsom, Wm.	Bulloch	Tilmans	257/9	Appling
Folsom, Wm.	Pulaski	Bryans	13/21	Early
Fontain, John	Warren	153rd	217/19	Early
Footman, Richd.H.	Bryan	20th	519/7	Appling
Forbes, Enoch(Orps)	Washington	Burneys	253/11	Irwin
Forbs, Westley	Putnam	Berrys	175/15	Irwin
Ford, Absalom	Jasper	Clays	255/9	Irwin

NAME	COUNTY	MIL.DIST	LOT/SECT	DREW LAND
Ford, Bartholomew	Jasper	Sentals	448/8	Appling
Ford, Elisha	Elbert	Penns	3/2	Hall
Ford, Ephraim	Morgan	Parker	319/10	Early
Ford, Isaac	Elbert	R.Christian	520/5	Irwin
Ford, John	Jefferson	Mathews	190/10	Irwin
Ford, John	Pulaski	Senterfeit	95/10	Hall
Ford, John	Telfair	Williams	120/6	Early
Ford, Joseph(Orps)	Wilkes	Russels	54/3	Early
Ford, Joseph	Warren	153rd	386/10	Irwin
Ford, Mary A.(Wid)	Jefferson	Matthews	206/4	Walton
Ford, Noah	Jasper	Clays	18/5	Gwinnett
Ford, Robt.	Lincoln	Stocks	447/9	Irwin
Ford, Saml.	Jefferson	Bothwell	257/5	Gwinnett
Ford, Samuel	Warren	153	157/5	Early
Fordham, Benj.	Wilkes	Bowlings	138/26	Early
Fore, John	Jefferson	Abbots	283/20	Early
Foredham, Benj.	Wilkes	Bowings	425/15	Early
Forehand, Amos	Twiggs	Ellis	57/1	Irwin
Forehand, Claiborne	Burke	Torrance	106/7	Early
Forehand, Jordan	Washington	Daniels	126/3	Early
Forehand, Jordan	Washington	Daniels	380/4	Early
Foreman, John	Putnam	Mays	406/2	Appling
Forester, Moses	Madison	Millican	226/7	Appling
Forgesson, John(Orps)	Columbia	Shaws	376/7	Irwin
Forgesson, John(Orps)	Columbia	Shaws	384/16	Early
Forguson, David	Emanuel	Olivers	133/9	Hall
Formby, Mathew	Ogelthorpe	Bowls	45/5	Rabun
Formby, Moses	Morgan	Talbotts	258/9	Irwin
Formby, Nathan	Ogelthorpe	Bowls	96/6	Early
Formby, Thomas	Wilkes	Runnels	111/20	Early
Formby, Thomas	Wilkes	Runnels	122/5	Irwin
Formby, Thompson	Morgan	Talbots	360/4	Appling
Formby, William	Wilkes	Runnels	126/7	Gwinnett
Formby, William	Wilkes	Runnels	126/7	Gwinnett
Foroman, Wm.B.	Jefferson	Walton	148/8	Hall
Forrester, Jas.	Madison	Millican	86/8	Early
Forrester, Thos.	Madison	Millican	482/13	Irwin
Forrister, Willis	Greene	Tuggles	176/6	Irwin
Forston, Castin	Elbert	Smiths	459/8	Irwin
Forsyth, Maria B.	Chatham		76/3	Appling
Forsyth, Wm.	Franklin	Turks	167/4	Early
Forsythe, James	Hancock	Loyds	91/3	Rabun
Forsythe, John	Hancock	Loyds	343/12	Early
Forsythe, Robt.M.	Richmond	122	67/4	Irwin
Fort, Elias	Chatham		168/6	Appling
Fort, Elias	Chatham		443/7	Appling
Fort, John	Laurens	Jones	272/5	Early
Fort, Moses	Twiggs	R.Belcher	377/4	Early
Fort, Moses	Twiggs	R.Belchers	157/20	Early
Fort, Owen(Orps)	Jefferson	Cowart	179/17	Early
Fort, Thomas	Twiggs	Brown	130/6	Appling
Fort, Thomas	Twiggs	Browns	380/13	Irwin
Forth, Jool L.	Burke	Sullivan	346/3	Appling
Fortner, James	Washington	Burneys	358/17	Early
Forts, Arthur(Orps)	Hancock	Lucas	347/8	Appling
Fortson, Jesse	Elbert	Higginbotham	146/10	Irwin
Fortson, Wm.	Elbert	Higginbotham	179/7	Early
Foson, Wm.	Hancock	Millers	48/1	Early
Foster, Arthur	Columbia	Burroughs		Gwinnett
Foster, Arthur	Columbia	Burroughs	99/3	Appling
Foster, Arthur	Greene	Fosters	361/12	Irwin
Foster, Charles	Chatham		132/7	Appling
Foster, Collier	Columbia	Walkes	62/11	Early
Foster, Eliz.(Wid)	Hancock	Edwards	54/23	Early
Foster, Fredr.S.	Putnam	Evans	207/8	Early
Foster, Geo.	Richmond	Winters	501/5	Appling
Foster, Geo.W.	Greene	Macons	35/4	Rabun

111

NAME	COUNTY	MIL.DIST	LOT/SECT	DREW LAN
Foster, Harden	Wilkes	Gordons	157/6	Appling
Foster, Hardin	Wilkes	Gordan	472/12	Irwin
Foster, Harrison	Jasper	Bentley	137/2	Rabun
Foster, Jas.M.	Franklin	Flemon	255/12	Early
Foster, Jeremiah	Morgan	Leonard	383/2	Appling
Foster, Jesse	Morgan	Lenards	222/5	Gwinnett
Foster, John H.	Washington	Echols	45/6	Irwin
Foster, John Jr.	Putnam	Oslins	74/27	Early
Foster, John L.	Columbia	Pullins	176/18	Early
Foster, John S.	Elbert	Smiths	230/3	Walton
Foster, John	Clark	Simms	373/13	Irwin
Foster, John	Jasper	Posts	463/2	Appling
Foster, John	Ogelthorpe	Murrays	39/3	Walton
Foster, Joshua	Columbia	Pullins	194/10	Early
Foster, Levi	Hancock	Thomas	274/7	Irwin
Foster, Levi	Hancock	Thomas	340/4	Early
Foster, Richd.	Burke	Thomas	346/18	Early
Foster, Saml.(Orps)	Hancock	Edwards	131/6	Early
Foster, Sterling	Columbia	Burroughs	226/26	Early
Foster, Susannah(Wid)	Greene	Macons	350/2	Appling
Foster, Wm.	Jefferson	Mathews	197/9	Appling
Foster, Wm.	Putnam	Bustins	85/2	Appling
Fosther, Lewis	Wilkes	Mattox	125/7	Appling
Fouch, Daniel	Wilkes	Ogletree	324/8	Appling
Fouch, George	Wilkes	Ogletree	60/3	Walton
Foulley, Joshua	Camden	Clarks	123/5	Gwinnett
Fountain, Benj.R.	Jefferson	Abbots	520/2	Appling
Fountain, Esacas	Laurens	Griffins	268/5	Gwinnett
Fountain, Ethlrd.	Jefferson	Fountain	344/8	Early
Fountain, Henry	Emanuel	53rd	114/5	Appling
Fountain, Israel	Wilkes	Kettles	295/7	Irwin
Fountain, James	Wilkes	Kettles	501/13	Irwin
Fountain, Jas.	Chatham		72/3	Walton
Fountain, Jonath.(Orps)	Jefferson	Langston	130/7	Irwin
Fountain, Owen	Emanuel	59th	375/6	Appling
Fountain, Owen	Emanuel	59th	379/7	Appling
Fountain, Sarah(Wid)	Jefferson	Langston	64/7	Irwin
Fountain, Wm.	Emanuel	59th	22/5	Habersha
Fountain, Wm.	Laurens	Griffins	2/13	Early
Fourchs, Daniel(Orp)	Wilkes	Willis	43/4	Walton
Foutain, Peter	Chatham		266/27	Early
Fowler, Jeremiah	Elbert	Whites	378/4	Early
Fowler, Jeremiah	Washington	Burgis	279/8	Appling
Fowler, John M.	Jasper	Bailey	217/27	Early
Fowler, John	Clark	Appling	178/7	Appling
Fowler, John	Lincoln	Jones	11/2	Irwin
Fowler, Jos.Sr.(RS)	Twiggs	Bozeman	175/13	Habersha
Fowler, Jos.Sr.(RS)	Twiggs	Bozeman	185/1	Appling
Fowler, Jos.Sr.	Twiggs	Bozeman	381/7	Irwin
Fowler, Richd.	Franklin	Flanagans	97/5	Irwin
Fowler, Richd.	Franklin	Flannigan	138/4	Appling
Fowler, Saml.	Elbert	Webbs	205/5	Gwinnett
Fowler, Saml.	Elbert	Webbs	512/13	Irwin
Fowler, Thornton	Wilkes	Childs	120/16	Irwin
Fowler, Thornton	Wilkes	Childs	269/7	Early
Fox, Abel	Chatham		30/4	Appling
Fox, Ann(Wid)	Richmond	398th	489/6	Irwin
Fox, Daniel	McIntosh	Hamilton	358/9	Irwin
Fox, Jas.(Orps)	Scriven		186/27	Early
Fox, Mary(Wid)	Richmond	Laceys	450/9	Irwin
Fox, Mary	Chatham		341/11	Irwin
Fox, Richd.W.	Morgan	Campbell	335/27	Early
Fox, Thomas	Richmond		112/4	Appling
Fox, Thomas	Twiggs	Browns	51/12	Early
Fox, Wm.	Chatham		348/18	Early
Foxey, Wm.	Putnam	Oslins	338/9	Appling
Foy, Darby(Orp)	Columbia	Walker	264/26	Early

NAME	COUNTY	MIL.DIST	LOT/SECT	DREW LAND
Foyil, Eliz.(Wid)	Jefferson	Abbotts	193/7	Irwin
Frambrough, Gadial	Jasper	Bentleys	16/6	Appling
Francis, Sarah(Wid)	Bulloch	Jones	92/1	Walton
Frank, John	Jackson	Winters	113/3	Irwin
Frank, John	Jackson	Winters	202/12	Irwin
Franklin, Bird	Franklin	J.Miller	45/5	Appling
Franklin, Bird	Franklin	Jos.Miller	232/16	Early
Franklin, Eliza	Chatham		169/10	Hall
Franklin, Felix D.	Warren	Parhams	88/3	Appling
Franklin, Henry(Orps)	Elbert	Dobbs	133/2	Walton
Franklin, Job	Elbert	Smiths	4/13	Habersham
Franklin, Job	Elbert	Smiths	89/7	Irwin
Franklin, John(Orps)	Morgan	Townsend	253/17	Early
Franklin, John	Glynn		158/2	Rabun
Franklin, John	Jackson	Rogers	282/5	Early
Franklin, Q.L.C.	Warren	Parhams	199/5	Irwin
Franklin, Singleton	Hancock	Danells	269/7	Irwin
Franklin, Willis R.	Chatham		14/13	Habersham
Fraser, Achbd.	Scriven	180th	199/4	Early
Fraser, Arthur	Lincoln	Jones	110/4	Walton
Fraser, Daniel	Liberty		350/15	Early
Fraser, David	Lincoln	Jones	214/5	Gwinnett
Fraser, John A.	Lincoln	Jones	311/6	Early
Fraser, John E.	Liberty		488/7	Irwin
Fraser, John	Washington	Cummins	249/9	Irwin
Fraser, Joshua D.	Putnam	Oslins	354/21	Early
Fraser, Mary	Lincoln	Jones	80/3	Irwin
Fraser, Simon Sr.	Liberty		62/2	Irwin
Frasier, Barbary(Wid)	Washington	Cummings	283/17	Early
Frasier, Wm.	Washington	Cummings	432/12	Irwin
Frasure, Nancy(Wid)	Hancock	Canes	389/28	Early
Frazer, Archbd.	Scriven	180	63/6	Gwinnett
Frazier, Elijah(Orps)	Putnam	Little	104/12	Early
Frederich, Thos.	Bulloch	Knights	228/9	Irwin
Frederick, Eliz.(Wid)	Wilkes	Lees	91/7	Irwin
Frederick, Louis F.	Hancock	Daniels	20/13	Habersham
Frederick, Wm.	Twiggs	Evans	268/10	Irwin
Fredrick, Delilah(Wid)	Twiggs	Browns	262/6	Appling
Freeman, Ann	Greene	Ragans	106/11	Early
Freeman, Bozzal	Jones	Hansford	66/18	Early
Freeman, Cattrupt(RS)	Clark	Mitchell	301/4	Walton
Freeman, Daniel	Jasper	Smiths	480/3	Appling
Freeman, Drury	Ogelthorpe	Brittons	507/2	Appling
Freeman, Franklin	Wilkes	Burks	53/12	Habersham
Freeman, Garrett	Scriven	Smith	11/7	Appling
Freeman, George W.	Wilkes	Russell	275/15	Early
Freeman, Hawkins	Jasper	Kendalls	467/3	Appling
Freeman, Hugh	Putnam	H.Kendrick	155/6	Early
Freeman, Jacob Jr.	Scriven	Smith	342/17	Early
Freeman, Jacob Jr.	Scriven	Smiths	108/3	Appling
Freeman, Jacob(Orps)	Scriven	Lovett	345/4	Appling
Freeman, James	Wilkes	Kettles	37/28	Early
Freeman, Jas.	Jones	Greene	14/8	Irwin
Freeman, Jesse	Jasper	Posts	297/9	Early
Freeman, John Jr.	Greene	Ragans	223/7	Appling
Freeman, John Sr.(RS)	Scriven	Moody	39/12	Hall
Freeman, John Sr.	Greene	Ragins	130/9	Hall
Freeman, John Sr.	Greene	Ragins	292/4	Walton
Freeman, John W.	Wilkes	Josseys	371/6	Appling
Freeman, John(Orps)	Baldwin	Taliaferro	238/18	Early
Freeman, John	Franklin	Ashs	376/10	Irwin
Freeman, John	Greene	Armers	135/18	Early
Freeman, John	Greene	Tuggles	436/10	Irwin
Freeman, John	Hancock	Lucas	198/9	Irwin
Freeman, John	Jasper	Smiths	294/1	Walton
Freeman, John	Ogelthorpe	Britton	372/8	Appling
Freeman, John	Ogelthorpe	Brittons	98/1	Rabun

NAME	COUNTY	MIL.DIST	LOT/SECT	DREW LAN
Freeman, Josiah Sr.	Jasper	Posts	327/10	Irwin
Freeman, Littleberry	Wilkes	Burks	196/20	Early
Freeman, Lucy	Jasper	McClendon	290/6	Appling
Freeman, Mildred	Jasper	Clays	192/28	Early
Freeman, Penina	Wilkes	Josseys	195/5	Irwin
Freeman, Rhoda	Wilkes	Burks	313/5	Appling
Freeman, Saml.Jr.	Lincoln	Jones	35/19	Early
Freeman, Sarah(Wid)	Jones	Phillips	79/21	Early
Freeman, Theoph.	Jasper	Smith	239/4	Early
Freeman, Thomas	Wilkes	Kettles	13/1	Early
Freeman, Thomas	Wilkes	Kettles	46/23	Early
Freeman, William	Wilkes	Ogletree	34/9	Irwin
Freeman, Wm.(Orps)	Wayne	Johnston	366/7	Gwinnett
Freeman, Wm.	Ogelthorpe	Murrays	132/11	Hall
Freeman, Wm.	Ogelthorpe	Murrays	198/7	Gwinnett
Freeny, Elijah	Baldwin	Russels	285/10	Early
Freeny, Gillah(Orps)	Baldwin	Taliaferro	28/23	Early
Freeny, Wm.B.	Baldwin	Marshall	167/5	Irwin
Freil, Elisa(Orph)	Columbia	Gartrell	72/4	Appling
Freman, Moore	Jefferson	Walden	336/9	Irwin
Freman, Moore	Jefferson	Walden	414/1	Appling
French, Ellis	Wilkes	Brooks	164/2	Irwin
French, James	Warren	Griers	66/7	Gwinnett
French, James	Wilkes	Brooks	246/7	Early
French, John	Jones	Woodson	176/5	Appling
French, Reace	Emanuel	58th	32/12	Early
Freny, Bitsey(Wid)	Jones	Samuels	65/3	Irwin
Frequay, Moses	Liberty		249/7	Irwin
Fretwell, Chas.	Jefferson	Lamps	365/7	Appling
Fretwell, Jas.	Greene	Woodhams	340/3	Appling
Fretwell, John	Putnam	Bustins	26/2	Irwin
Fretwell, Leonard	Putnam	Bustins	103/6	Early
Fretwell, Leonard	Walton	Sentells	263/8	Early
Fretwell, Leonard	Walton	Sentells	75/2	Appling
Fretwell, M.(Orps)	Morgan	Leonards	305/6	Early
Friar, Henderson	Bulloch	Jones	523/5	Appling
Friar, Jarvis T.	Bulloch	Jones	23/9	Early
Frice, Eliz.(Wid)	Jones	Jefferson	32/3	Rabun
Friend, John O.	Warren	154	57/15	Early
Frier, Aaron	Liberty		359/10	Irwin
Frier, Aaron	Liberty		499/6	Appling
Frier, Richd.H.	Jones	Shropshear	72/12	Hall
Frierson, Jas.S.	Jones	Samuels	471/8	Appling
Frith, Sarah	Chatham		10/10	Irwin
Frizevant, Danl.	Bryan	20	37/19	Early
Frost, Edward	Burke	72nd	108/13	Early
Frost, John	Wilkes	Howards	42/6	Appling
Frost, Johnston	Clark	Tredwells	355/2	Early
Frost, William	Wilkes	Howards	403/7	Irwin
Frosts, Jacob(Orps)	Wilkes	Howards	31/22	Early
Fry, Benj.	Jasper	Centills	473/10	Irwin
Fryer, Henderson	Bulloch	Jones	288/6	Appling
Fryor, Feildin	Burke	McNorrill	115/4	Early
Fryor, Fielding	Burke	McNorrill	343/15	Early
Fryor, Robt.	Burke	McNorrill	70/1	Irwin
Fudge, Daniel	Richmond	Laceys	44/19	Early
Fudge, Jacob	Richmond	Palmer	280/26	Early
Fudge, Solomon	Columbia	Shaws	47/3	Early
Fudge, Stephen	Jackson	Rogers	391/12	Irwin
Fulcher, Armsted	Richmond	Winters	33/1	Habersha
Fulcher, Austin	Jackson	Rogers	220/5	Appling
Fulcher, Dillen	Jackson	Rogers	133/2	Appling
Fulcher, Dillen	Jackson	Rogers	26/5	Habersha
Fulcher, Jas.	Jackson	Rogers	302/28	Early
Fulcher, Jesse H.	Jackson	Rogers	158/18	Early
Fulcher, Jessee H.	Jackson	Rogers	158/18	Early
Fulcher, John	Burke	Thomas	135/2	Habersha

114

NAME	COUNTY	MIL.DIST	LOT/SECT	DREW LAND
Fulcher, John	Burke	Thomas	146/13	Early
Fulgham, Jesse	Twiggs	R.Belcher	132/16	Early
Fulgham, John T.	Morgan	Hackney	237/19	Early
Fulgham, Nancy	Hancock	Scotts	506/10	Irwin
Fulgham, Steph.(Orps)	Hancock	Scotts	373/28	Early
Fulgham, Stephen	Morgan	Hackney	318/9	Early
Fulghum, Wm.R.	Franklin	Burroughs	42/17	Early
Fulilove, John	Ogelthorpe	Waters	88/1	Rabun
Fulk, Jacob	Chatham		114/16	Irwin
Fullar, Isral	Gwinnett	Hamiltons	261/26	Early
Fuller, Abraham	Columbia	J.Morris	366/9	Irwin
Fuller, Allen J.	Columbia	Shaws	155/4	Walton
Fuller, Benj.	Columbia	Shaws	25/8	Appling
Fuller, Chas.	Columbia	Watsons	87/7	Appling
Fuller, David J.	Morgan	Selmon	124/1	Irwin
Fuller, Henry	Chatham		241/7	Early
Fuller, Isham	Columbia	Willingham	129/9	Appling
Fuller, Isham	Columbia	Willingham	171/7	Early
Fuller, James	Morgan	Selmons	308/1	Appling
Fuller, Jesse	Greene	Harvills	72/3	Rabun
Fuller, John	Baldwin	Stephens	400/27	Early
Fuller, Jones	Baldwin	Cousins	99/16	Early
Fuller, Joshua Jr.	Columbia	O.Morriss	224/5	Irwin
Fuller, Joshua Sr.	Columbia	Ob.Morris	86/20	Early
Fuller, Joshua Sr.	Columbia	Ob.Morriss	39/5	Appling
Fuller, Saml.	Putnam	Mays	115/16	Irwin
Fuller, Saml.	Putnam	Mays	132/12	Irwin
Fuller, Simion	Putnam	Coopers	316/14	Early
Fuller, Spivey	Warren	Parhams	137/4	Appling
Fuller, Thos.	Columbia	Shaws	164/19	Early
Fuller, William A.	Warren	Parhams	130/16	Irwin
Fuller, Wilson	Chatham		89/8	Irwin
Fuller, Wm.	Camden	Baileys	278/17	Early
Fuller, Wm.	Columbia	Burroughs	302/8	Appling
Fullford, Jesse	Laurens	Deans	36/12	Irwin
Fullford, Valentine	Laurens	Deans	196/14	Early
Fullilove, John	Ogelthorpe	Waters	210/4	Walton
Fullingim, Henry	Morgan	Knights	207/4	Appling
Fullwood, John	Wilkes	Brooks	349/13	Early
Fulson, Elijah	Hancock	Mims	332/3	Early
Fulton, James H.	Twiggs	R.Belcher	35/13	Irwin
Fulton, James	Clark	Parrs	211/10	Irwin
Fulton, Jas.	Clark	Parrs	178/5	Early
Fulton, Thomas Jr.	Twiggs	Griffins	296/5	Irwin
Fulton, Thomas	Twiggs	Jefferson	271/6	Irwin
Fulton, Wm.P.	Liberty		358/1	Early
Fulwood, Robt.Sr.	Clark	Moores	407/6	Irwin
Fulwood, Thomas	Wayne	Johnston	118/3	Habersham
Funderburk, David	Twiggs	Hodges	112/3	Walton
Funderburk, David	Twiggs	Hodges	170/13	Early
Fuqua, Henry C.	Laurens	Harriss	269/1	Appling
Furguson, Ephraim	Greene	144th	485/4	Early
Furlow, Wm.Jr.	Greene	143rd	302/18	Early
Futch, David	Bryan	19	385/8	Appling
Futch, Jacob	Bulloch	Jones	23/12	Habersham
Futch, John	Bulloch	Knights	165/5	Gwinnett
Futch, Wm.	Liberty		140/15	Early
Futch, Wm.	Liberty		24/5	Irwin
Futrall, Micajah	Effingham		79/13	Habersham
Futrel, Micajah	Burke	Thomas	247/4	Irwin
Futrill, Abram	Jasper	Reeds	20/12	Irwin
Futrill, Benj.	Greene	Wheelis	35/2	Irwin
Futrill, Benj.	Greene	Wheelis	84/2	Habersham
Gaborell, Thomas	Burke	Thomas	396/3	Appling
Gaddis, John Jr.	Jackson	Hamiltons	188/18	Early
Gaddis, John	Gwinnett	Hamilton	36/5	Habersham
Gaddy, Mariah(Orp)	Effingham		487/8	Appling

NAME	COUNTY	MIL.DIST	LOT/SECT	DREW LAN[
Gaddy, Sine(Orp)	Effingham		487/8	Appling
Gadwell, Pearce	Irwin	Hamiltons	115/13	Habersha[
Gafford, Hannah	Baldwin	Stephens	172/12	Habersha[
Gafford, John	Baldwin	Stephens	88/5	Early
Gafford, Stephen Jr.	Jones	Harrist	444/10	Irwin
Gafford, Thomas	Baldwin	Stephens	238/19	Early
Gafford, Zachariah	Jones	Hurst	30/7	Irwin
Gahagan, Bridget(Orp)	Richmond	120th	55/5	Irwin
Gahagan, John(Orp)	Richmond	120th	55/5	Irwin
Gahagan, Mariah(Orp)	Richmond	120th	55/5	Irwin
Gailer, James	Baldwin	Marshall	53/7	Irwin
Gailey, James	Hall	Carnes	12/6	Early
Gailey, Mary	Madison	Williford	75/6	Habersha[
Gainer, Lazarus	Washington	Jenkinson	108/4	Early
Gainer, Mary(Wid)	Washington	Jinkinson	25/11	Early
Gainer, Saml.(Orps)	Washington	Burneys	395/13	Early
Gainer, Wm.	Washington	Burneys	269/5	Appling
Gaines, Duncan	Burke	72nd	85/10	Habersha[
Gaines, Henry G.	Twiggs	Bozeman	6/18	Early
Gaines, John	Elbert	Smiths	254/11	Early
Gaines, Phillip	Elbert	Smiths	124/4	Habersha[
Gaines, Richard S.	Elbert	Gaines	452/8	Irwin
Gaines, Richd.S.	Elbert	Gaines	122/12	Hall
Gaines, Salley	Burke	72nd	69/5	Rabun
Gaines, Wm.(Orps)	Washington	Burneys	7/17	Early
Gainey, Bartholomew	Laurens	S.Smiths	478/4	Appling
Gainey, Constant(Wid)	Walton	Greenes	90/3	Rabun
Gainey, McLandon	Tattnall	Johnsons	50/16	Early
Gainey, Micajah	Walton	Greenes	36/15	Irwin
Gainey, Micajah	Walton	Greenes	38/7	Appling
Gains, Robt.T.	Elbert	Gains	383/19	Early
Gairy, John M.	Hancock	Scotts	224/3	Appling
Gairy, Wm.L.	Hancock	Justices	54/11	Early
Gaither, Edward	Lincoln	Parks	353/3	Appling
Gaither, Eli(Orps)	Putnam	Oslins	193/6	Appling
Gaither, Eli(Orps)	Putnam	Oslins	69/13	Habersha[
Gaither, Greenberry	Putnam	J.Kindrick	268/27	Early
Gaither, Meshac	Lincoln	Parks	144/1	Walton
Galding, William	Hancock	Scotts	163/6	Early
Galdwin, Mark	Lincoln	Tatoms	57/14	Early
Gale, Worthington	Chatham		215/18	Early
Galliman, James	Jasper	Hays	238/1	Early
Gallman, Silas	Jasper	Hays	131/13	Early
Galloway, Levy	Oglethorpe	Barnett	21/7	Appling
Galloway, Levy	Oglethorpe	Barnett	317/5	Gwinnett
Galloway, Thomas	Oglethorpe	Goolsby	357/15	Early
Gamage, Wm.(Orps)	Wilkes	Perrys	237/2	Early
Gamble, Hugh T.	Jefferson	Bothwells	383/17	Early
Gamble, James	Scriven	Roberts	160/11	Irwin
Gamel, Israel	Jones	Buckhalter	519/8	Appling
Gamell, John	Lincoln	Graves	142/27	Early
Gamell, John	Lincoln	Graves	28/3	Rabun
Gammage, Alsee	Jones	Griffith	421/5	Appling
Gammage, Saml.(Orps)	Wilkes	Mattox	73/9	Irwin
Gammell, Aires	Jasper	Kenadays	202/20	Early
Gammell, Aires	Jasper	Kenndys	174/4	Early
Gammell, Wm.	Lincoln	Graves	268/7	Early
Gamole, James	Scriven	Roberts	391/11	Irwin
Gana, Richard	Pulaski	Bryans	144/8	Irwin
Gana, Richard	Pulaski	Bryans	2/1	Rabun
Ganaway, Martin	Wilkes	Bates	211/6	Gwinnett
Ganday, Britain(Orps)	Baldwin	Haws	32/2	Habersha[
Gann, James	Clarke	Harpers	79/5	Rabun
Gann, Mary(Wid)	Clarke	Harpers	27/11	Hall
Gann, Micajah	Clarke	Harpers	137/2	Early
Gann, Nathan Jr.	Clarke	Harpers	227/11	Early
Gann, Nathan Sr.(RS)	Clarke	Harpers	26/13	Irwin

NAME	COUNTY	MIL.DIST	LOT/SECT	DREW LAND
Gann, Nathanl.(Orps)	Clarke	Harpers	508/9	Irwin
Gann, Samuel	Clarke	Harpers	135/8	Irwin
Gann, Wm.Sr.	Clarke	Harpers	205/11	Early
Gannt, Joseph	Lincoln	Graves	75/5	Gwinnett
Gant, John	Telfair	Loves	138/1	Walton
Gantt, Charlotte	Lincoln	Tatoms	31/8	Early
Gantt, James	Lincoln	Tatoms	122/21	Early
Ganus, Benj.	Laurens	Dean's	15/2	Walton
Garbett, Wm.	Pulaski	Davis	316/19	Early
Gardian, Rodoric	Washington	Brooks	302/6	Early
Gardner, Christph.	Franklin	Felmons	290/4	Early
Gardner, Elisha(Orps)	Jones	Harrists	93/10	Early
Gardner, Eliz.(Wid)	Morgan	Hubbard	90/2	Appling
Gardner, Ezekiah	Washington	Renfros	143/2	Habersham
Gardner, Isham	Washington	Jenkinson	214/1	Early
Gardner, James	Richmond	120th	149/3	Walton
Gardner, Jas.H.(Orp)	Richmond	120th	211/7	Early
Gardner, Jason	Jones	Harrists	168/3	Irwin
Gardner, John	Jones	Permenter	140/6	Irwin
Gardner, John	Jones	Permenter	50/11	Habersham
Gardner, Mary	Chatham		411/8	Irwin
Gardner, Robert	Clarke	Deans	194/14	Early
Gardner, Robert	Clarke	Deans	257/5	Early
Gardner, Saml.	Twiggs	R.Belcher	274/3	Appling
Gardner, Sarah(Wid)	Wilkinson	Wiggins	354/2	Early
Gardner, Silas	Chatham		74/2	Irwin
Gardner, Thomas	Chatham		208/14	Early
Garland, Henry	Putnam	Brooks	106/4	Appling
Garland, Henry	Putnam	Brooks	233/28	Early
Garland, Patrick	Putnam	Coopers	258/7	Gwinnett
Garland, Patrick	Putnam	Coopers	88/6	Irwin
Garland, Wm.(RS)	Hancock	Justices	127/13	Early
Garlington, Canway	Oglethorpe	Brittons	119/20	Early
Garlington, Christopher	Clarke	Starnes	22/10	Early
Garlington, Doctor	Oglethorpe	Dunnes	123/11	Early
Garner, Asa	Jasper	Bentleys	445/2	Appling
Garner, Bradley	Columbia	Walkers	67/10	Early
Garner, Bradley	Columbia	Walkers	73/6	Gwinnett
Garner, Charles	Morgan	Knights	158/15	Early
Garner, Daniel	Morgan	Knights	293/7	Gwinnett
Garner, Elijah	Clarke	Starnes	194/7	Gwinnett
Garner, Henry	Washington	Cummins	119/18	Early
Garner, James	Jefferson	Waldens	358/7	Appling
Garner, Jesse H.	Clarke	Mitchell	130/13	Early
Garner, John	Richmond	120th	207/18	Early
Garner, Joseph	Clarke	Mitchels	398/7	Appling
Garner, Mark	Putnam	H.Kendrick	114/8	Irwin
Garner, Mark	Putnam	H.Kendrick	84/13	Irwin
Garner, Presley	Morgan	Knights	244/4	Irwin
Garner, Reddick	Baldwin	Taliaferro	428/5	Appling
Garner, Richd.(Orps)	Putnam	H.Kendrick	420/15	Early
Garner, Wm.S.	Greene	Armers	11/9	Irwin
Garnet, Moses	Washington	Cummins	34/28	Early
Garnett, Joseph	Chatham		416/15	Early
Garnett, Joseph	Chatham		91/12	Irwin
Garnett, Rebecca(Wid)	Columbia	Pullins	11/4	Early
Garnett, Thomas	Effingham		82/3	Habersham
Garnett, Wm.	Putnam	Evans	54/7	Appling
Garnett, Zachariah	Jasper	Phillips	40/10	Early
Garnur, David	Franklin	Akins	342/8	Irwin
Garrard, Allen	Wilkes	Bates	555/7	Irwin
Garrard, Anthony(Orps)	Wilkes	Willis	202/13	Irwin
Garrard, Jacob	Jackson	Dicksons	25/4	Irwin
Garrard, John	Wilkes	Willis	102/11	Irwin
Garrard, John	Wilkes	Willis	411/3	Appling
Garrard, Lewis	Jackson	Dicksons	1955/20	Early
Garrason, David	Effingham		285/11	Early

NAME	COUNTY	MIL.DIST	LOT/SECT	DREW LAND
Garrason, Daviss	Effingham		422/4	Appling
Garrell, Thos.B.	Greene	Greers	288/9	Appling
Garret, Asa	Washington	Cummons	132/8	Appling
Garret, Richd.B.(Orps)	Clarke	Deans	24/16	Early
Garrett, Absalom	Jasper	Whites	339/8	Irwin
Garrett, Asa	Washington	Cummins	90/4	Irwin
Garrett, Benj.	Washington	Wimberly	80/12	Hall
Garrett, Cather.(Wid)	Richmond	120th	400/9	Irwin
Garrett, George	Jasper	Whites	109/26	Early
Garrett, Jacob	Putnam	J.Kendrick	399/4	Early
Garrett, Jacob	Warren	152nd	240/12	Early
Garrett, James	Madison	Bones	5/1	Early
Garrett, Jeremiah	Wilkinson	Kettles	118/15	Early
Garrett, Jeremiah	Wilkinson	Kettles	242/9	Irwin
Garrett, John	Greene	Greers	168/2	Walton
Garrett, Miles	Jasper	Blakes	60/11	Hall
Garrett, Miles	Jasper	Blakes	95/14	Early
Garrett, Thomas	Morgan	Townsend	353/4	Appling
Garrett, Thos.C.(Orps)	Jasper	Clays	22/6	Appling
Garrett, William(Orp)	Wilkes	Ogletree	288/4	Early
Garrett, Wm.(Orps)	Hancock	Mims	482/7	Irwin
Garrett, Wm.	Putnam	Evans	268/21	Early
Garrett, Wm.	Putnam	J.Kendrick	44/13	Irwin
Garrett, Wm.	Putnam	J.Kindrick	355/9	Appling
Garrison, James	Franklin	J.Miller	380/11	Irwin
Garrison, Kesiah(Wid)	Franklin	Turks	352/2	Early
Garrison, Michael	Effingham		311/27	Early
Garrison, Thos.	Franklin	Turks	418/6	Irwin
Garrison, Wm.	Franklin	J.Miller	206/3	Appling
Garrisson, Jedediah	Franklin	Turks	79/17	Early
Garritt, Robt.	Greene	Ragins	259/7	Irwin
Garrot, John	Wilkinson	Kettles	348/5	Early
Garrot, Lewis	Wilkes	Mattox	351/19	Early
Garrot, Mary	Burke	McNorrills	74/3	Irwin
Garrot, Samuel	Washington	Wimberley	108/5	Irwin
Garrott, Isom	Twiggs	Barrows	349/7	Appling
Gartman, Daniel	Elbert	B.Higginbotham	462/8	Irwin
Gartrell, Eliz.(Wid)	Columbia	Gartrell	303/26	Early
Gartrell, John	Wilkes	Hollidays	340/7	Appling
Gartrell, Jos.8Orps)	Wilkes	Holidays	9/8	Appling
Gartrell, Margt.(Wid)	Lincoln	Walkers	82/1	Habersham
Gartrell, Wm.	Wilkes	Holidays	419/7	Irwin
Garven, John E.	Pulaski	Lesters	117/17	Early
Garven, John	Elbert	Gaines	87/5	Irwin
Garvin, John	Jefferson	Fountains	178/18	Early
Garvin, Richard	Oglethorpe	Goolsby	467/6	Irwin
Garvin, Robert	Jefferson	Fountains	41/7	Appling
Gary, William	Jasper	Sentells	84/27	Early
Garybill, Henry	Hancock	Edwards	479/8	Appling
Gasaway, Enoch	Hall		161/7	Appling
Gassaway, James	Greene	Macons	292/2	Appling
Gassaway, Jesse	Hall		68/4	Walton
Gassoway, Thos.(RS)	Franklin	Flanagans	261/9	Irwin
Gassoway, Thos.(RS)	Franklin	Flanagans	341/19	Early
Gassoway, Thos.	Franklin	Flannagans	316/3	Appling
Gaster, Matthew	Putnam	Stramper	223/9	Appling
Gaston, Mathew	Putnam	Stampers	173/3	Irwin
Gaston, Rebecca	Putnam	Moreland	153/3	Irwin
Gaston, Thomas	Jasper	Smiths	49/12	Habersham
Gaston, William	Chatham		117/3	Irwin
Gates, Bennett H.H.	Jones	Harrists	226/11	Hall
Gates, Elisha	Jackson	Winters	129/5	Early
Gates, James	Twiggs	Ellis	243/1	Appling
Gates, Joab	Twiggs	Ellis	202/7	Irwin
Gates, Josiah(Orps)	Pulaski	Davis	120/6	Appling
Gates, Saml.K.	Twiggs	Ellis	24/7	Early
Gates, Thomas	Jones	Buckhalter	332/10	Irwin

NAME	COUNTY	MIL.DIST	LOT/SECT	DREW LAND
Gates, Thos.(Orps)	Pulaski	Senterfeit	140/33	Appling
Gatewood, Edmund	Wilkinson	Smiths	248/8	Early
Gatlen, Major	Twiggs	W.Belcher	159/1	Irwin
Gatlin, Edward	Morgan	Leonards	69/1	Early
Gatlin, Hardy(Orps)	Pulaski	Davis	64/3	Irwin
Gatlin, James	Greene	Nelms	36/4	Irwin
Gatlin, Nancy G.	Pulaski	Davis	84/7	Irwin
Gatlin, Patsey	Greene	142nd	162/9	Early
Gatlin, Radford	Greene	Nelms	171/13	Irwin
Gatlin, Shadrach	Greene	142	190/26	Early
Gatlin, Shadrack	Greene	142nd	271/11	Irwin
Gatlin, Shadrack	Greene	142nd	271/11	Irwin
Gatlin, Shadrick	Greene	142nd	50/13	Habersham
Gatlin, Stephen	Pulaski	Johnston	203/12	Irwin
Gatlin, Stephen	Pulaski	Johnston	309/5	Appling
Gattimore, Jas.(Orps)	Twiggs	Ellis	270/5	Irwin
Gattimore, John	Twiggs	Ellis	324/17	Early
Gault, Jno.Henry	Baldwin	Cousins	44/14	Irwin
Gaurtner, Wm.	Franklin	P.Browns	56/4	Rabun
Gay, Benjamin	Jasper	Trimbles	443/2	Appling
Gay, Henry	Laurens	Kinchen	195/21	Early
Gay, James	Pulaski	Maddox	19/2	Rabun
Gay, Joel	Burke	71	184/9	Irwin
Gay, John(Orps)	Jones	Greens	247/6	Appling
Gay, John	Pulaski	Maddox	529/13	Irwin
Gay, John	Wilkinson	Wiggins	356/15	Early
Gay, John	Wilkinson	Wiggins	7/22	Early
Gay, Josiah	Laurens	S.Smiths	68/12	Hall
Gay, Lewis(Orps)	Emanuel	49th	15/3	Early
Gay, Reuben	Laurens	Kinchens	495/11	Irwin
Gay, Sherod H.	Jasper	Bentleys	256/10	Early
Gay, Simon Sr.(RS)	Bulloch	Edwards	488/12	Irwin
Gay, Simon	Emanuel	Lanes	42/2	Walton
Gay, Thomas Sr.	Jefferson	Mathews	49/6	Habersham
Gay, Thomas Sr.	Jefferson	Matthews	379/12	Early
Gay, Thomas	Jasper	Bentleys	248/5	Appling
Gay, William	Jasper	Bentleys	215/19	Early
Gay, William	Jefferson	Bothwells	46/10	Irwin
Gay, William	Jones	Greens	301/7	Irwin
Gayles, Theophilus	Habersham	Powels	232/7	Early
Gazaway, John	Gwinnett	Hamilton	64/28	Early
Gaze, Joseph	Oglethorpe	Myricks	182/1	Irwin
Geddins, Thos.(RS)	Pulaski	Maddox	222/1	Early
Gee, Drury	Madison	Millicans	102/7	Irwin
Gee, Drury	Madison	Millicans	318/10	Early
Geer, Israel	Camden	Clarkes	320/14	Early
Geesham, Marmaduke	Jones	Shropshears	521/2	Appling
Geeslin, Charles	Warren	153rd	65/4	Irwin
Geeslin, Samuel	Warren	153rd	74/16	Early
Geeslin, Wm.	Warren	153	119/5	Gwinnett
Geeslin, Wm.	Warren	153	256/5	Early
Geesling, Samuel	Warren	Torrance	331/8	Early
Gegory, Samuel Jr.	Emanuel	395th	327/13	Early
Geiger, David	Tattnall	J.Durrence	455/7	Appling
Gelnn, Otway	Washington	Robertsons	36/7	Appling
Gent, Peter	Baldwin	Marshall	59/1	Appling
Gente, Peter	Baldwin	Marshall	207/6	Gwinnett
Geoman, Redding	Emanuel	53	255/3	Early
George, Baley(Orps)	Jackson	Rogers	43/10	Irwin
George, Carissa(Orp)	Jefferson	Flemings	359/27	Early
George, Daniel	Laurens	Kinchen	274/4	Walton
George, Daniel	Laurens	Kinchens	229/19	Early
George, Elijah	Jasper	Smiths	394/19	Early
George, Elijah	Jasper	Smiths	524/10	Irwin
George, Elisha	Putnam	Robertson	345/14	Early
George, Gideon	Putnam	Robertson	158/6	Irwin
George, Henry	Jasper	Clays	280/12	Irwin

NAME	COUNTY	MIL.DIST	LOT/SECT	DREW LAN
George, Henry	Jasper	Clays	32/9	Appling
George, James F.	Jones	Shropshier	293/8	Early
George, James R.	Gwinnett	Hamilton	25/2	Appling
George, James	Greene	141	176/3	Habersha
George, Jeptha V.	Jasper	Reids	268/4	Early
George, Jesse	Jasper	Clays	391/2	Appling
George, Jesse	Walton	Worshams	35/5	Irwin
George, Jordan	Columbia	Walkers	396/2	Appling
George, Joseph	Chatham		188/1	Appling
George, Travis	Jackson	Rogers	38/9	Early
Gerald, James	McIntosh	Hamilton	219/4	Irwin
Gerald, James	McIntosh	Hamilton	381/8	Early
Gerardeau, William	Liberty		161/9	Appling
Gerardeau, William	Liberty		24/27	Early
Gerdine, Lewis	Clarke	Deans	272/7	Gwinnett
Geridon, Lewis	Chatham		53/3	Appling
Geridon, Lewis	Chatham		6/2	Rabun
Germaine, Wm.	McIntosh	Hamilton	489/2	Appling
Germany, James(Orps)	Burke	Bells	19/6	Irwin
Germany, Wm.	Morgan	Hubberts	511/8	Irwin
Gerrald, Eliz.(Wid)	Columbia	J.Morris	72/3	Habersha
Gerrald, James	Columbia	J.Morris	307/4	Walton
Geter, Dudley	Elbert	Higginbotham	29/8	Early
Geust, Benj.	Burke	Royals	19/3	Early
Geyne, Hiram	Warren	Rogers	254/19	Early
Gezorme, Adala	Chatham		23/13	Early
Gholdson, John	Putnam	Bustins	265/5	Gwinnett
Gholston, Benj.	Madison	Orrs	22/27	Early
Gibbon, Mary	Chatham		283/16	Early
Gibbons, Harry	Laurens	D.Smiths	211/26	Early
Gibbons, Henry	Laurens	D.Smiths	37/8	Hall
Gibbons, Jos.W.	Chatham		342/1	Early
Gibbons, Mary	Chatham		142/2	Habersha
Gibbons, William	Camden	Tillis	71/13	Habersha
Gibbs, Elhannon	Jasper	Clays	188/13	Early
Gibbs, Elhanon	Jasper	CLays	18/13	Irwin
Gibbs, Fortson	Elbert	B.Higginbotham	43/12	Hall
Gibbs, Herod(RS)	Morgan	Campbells	346/13	Early
Gibbs, Howell	Twiggs	Browns	71/14	Irwin
Gibbs, Jeremiah	Jackson	Dicksons	253/16	Early
Gibbs, John	Greene	Rankins	63/9	Appling
Gibbs, John	Montgomery	Alstons	90/13	Irwin
Gibbs, Jonathan Jr.	Jackson	Dicksons	71/27	Early
Gibbs, Jonathan Sr.	Jackson	Dicksons	302/8	Early
Gibbs, Martha	Morgan	Hubbards	130/3	Early
Gibbs, Thos.F.	Elbert	Ruckers	498/7	Irwin
Gibson, Augustus H.	Wilkes	Gordons	72/13	Irwin
Gibson, Daniel	Franklin	Aikins	110/9	Appling
Gibson, Daniel	Wayne	Johnston	337/11	Irwin
Gibson, Dexter(Ophs)	Columbia	Olives	3/5	Rabun
Gibson, Eliz.(Wid)	Columbia	Olives	315/11	Early
Gibson, Ezekiel	Scriven	Smiths	141/1	Early
Gibson, Felix G.	Richmond	120	339/7	Gwinnett
Gibson, George	Wilkes	Perrys	151/1	Walton
Gibson, Henry	Columbia	Dodsons	171/2	Habersha
Gibson, Henry	Hancock	Smiths	62/10	Habersha
Gibson, James(Orps)	Gwinnett	Hamilton	298/4	Appling
Gibson, James	Twiggs	Jefferson	239/7	Early
Gibson, James	Wilkinson	Bowings	65/4	Early
Gibson, Jas.(Orps)	Warren	150	305/7	Gwinnett
Gibson, John S.	Jasper	Easters	59/5	Rabun
Gibson, John S.	Jasper	Eastes	267/13	Irwin
Gibson, John S.	Jasper	Eastes	308/4	Appling
Gibson, John	Wayne	Crews	221/21	Early
Gibson, Joseph(Orp)	Chatham		164/3	Walton
Gibson, Joseph(Orp)	Chatham		48/28	Early
Gibson, Joshua	Jackson	Winters	330/28	Early

120

NAME	COUNTY	MIL.DIST	LOT/SECT	DREW LAND
Gibson, Louisa(Orp)	Chatham		164/3	Walton
Gibson, Louisa(Orp)	Chatham		48/28	Early
Gibson, Luke	Oglethorpe	Rowland	314/7	Early
Gibson, Luke	Oglethorpe	Rowland	8/3	Irwin
Gibson, Michael	Morgan	Walker	132/3	Early
Gibson, Michael	Morgan	Walkers	211/1	Irwin
Gibson, Michael	Telfair	Tallis	497/3	Appling
Gibson, Richard(Orp)	Chatham		164/3	Walton
Gibson, Richard(Orp)	Chatham		48/28	Early
Gibson, Samuel(Orps)	Burke	71st	313/11	Early
Gibson, Samuel	Franklin	Flanagans	52/4	Habersham
Gibson, Sarah(Wid)	Columbia	Olivers	123/28	Early
Gibson, Shadrack W.	Columbia	Olives	221/9	Early
Gibson, Solomon	Greene	Kimbrough	213/1	Early
Gibson, Sylvanus	Wilkes	Brooks	140/12	Hall
Gibson, Thornton	Warren	152	29/12	Irwin
Gibson, Thornton	Warren	152nd	459/12	Irwin
Gibson, Thos.	Warren	Blounts	122/3	Early
Gibson, Walter	Wilkinson	Bowings	17/7	Appling
Gibson, Wiley J.	Jones	Ropers	397/5	Appling
Gibson, William	Laurens	Harris	130/4	Early
Gibson, Wm.(Orps)	Wilkinson	Howards	82/10	Hall
Gibson, Wm.	Wilkes	Perrys	133/5	Early
Gibson, Wm.C.	Jones	Kings	328/11	Irwin
Gibson, Wm.Jr.	Telfair	Tallis	137/12	Habersham
Gibson, Wm.Sr.	Telfair	Tallis	277/6	Early
Gibson, Wm.Sr.	Telfair	Tallis	81/14	Early
Giddins, Edward	Pulaski	Maddox	358/15	Early
Giddins, Edward	Pulaski	Maddox	93/11	Early
Giger, Phillip	Wayne	Johnston	48/10	Irwin
Gignilliat, James	McIntosh	Goulds	133/3	Early
Gilbert, Bird	Greene	Wheelis	124/5	Irwin
Gilbert, Bird	Greene	Wheelis	129/12	Irwin
Gilbert, Charles L.	Morgan	Jordans	124/1	Walton
Gilbert, Darius	Wilkinson	Lees	106/10	Early
Gilbert, Edward	Madison	Adares	87/28	Early
Gilbert, Edy	Morgan	Farrars	95/9	Irwin
Gilbert, Ezekiel	Morgan	Parker	103/13	Habersham
Gilbert, Ezekiel	Morgan	Parker	93/3	Appling
Gilbert, Felix(Orps)	Wilkes	Gordons	60/2	Rabun
Gilbert, Henry	Chatham		370/28	Early
Gilbert, Hill R.	Walton	Echols	359/6	Appling
Gilbert, Instant H.	Morgan	Jordans	332/12	Early
Gilbert, Isaac	Madison	Millicans	365/11	Irwin
Gilbert, Isaac	Madison	Millicans	91/4	Irwin
Gilbert, John B.	Chatham		22/8	Irwin
Gilbert, John B.	Chatham		300/12	Irwin
Gilbert, John	Oglethorpe	Barnett	235/7	Gwinnett
Gilbert, Morriss(Orps)	Emanuel	49	170/3	Early
Gilbert, Nancy	Greene	143rd	152/16	Early
Gilbert, Richd.(Minor)	Wilkes	Willis	28/5	Appling
Gilbert, Robert(Orps)	Putnam	Bustins	348/6	Appling
Gilbert, Thomas(RS)	Franklin	R.Browns	419/10	Irwin
Gilbert, Thomas	Laurens	Watsons	223/3	Walton
Gilbert, Thos.(RS)	Franklin	R.Browns	170/2	Habersham
Gilbert, Thos.(RS)	Franklin	R.Browns	351/28	Early
Gilbert, William	Wilkinson	Smiths	57/11	Hall
Gilbert, Wm.(RS)	Morgan	Parkers	4/9	Irwin
Gilbert, Wm.	Washington	Barges	42/1	Appling
Gilchrist, Hannah(Wid)	Effingham		140/15	Irwin
Gilchrist, Thos.(Orps)	Effingham		260/12	Early
Gilder, Isaac(RS)	Twiggs	Ellis	392/16	Early
Gilder, James	Twiggs	Ellis	169/20	Early
Gilder, Robert(RS)	Twiggs	Smiths	150/3	Appling
Gildersleeve, Benj.	Hancock	Champions	165/8	Hall
Gildersleeve, Benj.	Hancock	Champions	195/5	Appling
Gilem, John	Oglethorpe	Goolsby	503/2	Appling

NAME	COUNTY	MIL.DIST	LOT/SECT	DREW LAN:
Giles, Alexr.	Washington	Peabodys	202/1	Early
Giles, Alexr.	Washington	Peabodys	56/1	Walton
Giles, Andrew	Putnam	Coopers	183/2	Irwin
Giles, Elizabeth	Putnam	Coopers	324/15	Early
Giles, Jackson B.	Morgan	Farrars	363/4	Early
Giles, Jacob	Washington	Peabodys	65/16	Early
Giles, Jeremiah	Putnam	Stampers	109/28	Early
Giles, John	Hancock	Justices	53/28	Early
Giles, John	Hancock	Justices	58/11	Irwin
Giles, Thomas	Putnam	Coopers	44/4	Irwin
Giles, Wm.	Putnam	Slaughters	40/15	Early
Giles, Wm.	Washington	Peabodys	140/7	Irwin
Gill, Ann	Clarke	Parrs	137/3	Early
Gill, Jesse A.	Jasper	Bentleys	263/1	Early
Gill, Sarah	Scriven	Moodys	115/4	Walton
Gill, Thomas Y.	Jackson	Rogers	47/5	Early
Gill, Thos.Y.	Jackson	Rogers	82/16	Irwin
Gill, William	Baldwin	Cousins	345/7	Appling
Gill, William	Jasper	Smiths	205/9	Irwin
Gill, Wm.	Wilkes	Burks	308/5	Appling
Gill, Young	Morgan	Loyds	125/12	Irwin
Gill, Young	Morgan	Loyds	306/4	Irwin
Gillan, John	Gwinnett	Hamilton	165/7	Early
Gillcoatt, John(Orps)	Jasper	Northcutts	2/9	Early
Gillcoatt, Mary	Jasper	Northcuts	439/3	Appling
Gilleland, Hugh	Hancock	Scotts	405/18	Early
Gilleland, Thomas	Jasper	Dardens	20/14	Irwin
Gilleland, Thos.	Jasper	Dardens	236/7	Gwinnett
Gilleon, John	Wilkinson	Lees	143/1	Appling
Gilley, Charles	Franklin	Vaughns	255/6	Appling
Gilley, Charles	Habersham	Tankersly	217/5	Irwin
Gilley, Leroy	Alstons	Montgomery	267/6	Gwinnett
Gilley, Leroy	Montgomery	Alstons	224/2	Irwin
Gilliam, Peter(Orps)	Lincoln	Tatoms	203/3	Irwin
Gillicoat, Daniel	Jasper	Clays	520/7	Appling
Gilliland, Mary(Orp)	Richmond	122	459/5	Irwin
Gillis, Norman	Montgomery	Alstons	126/16	Irwin
Gillispie, James	Oglethorpe	Brittons	360/26	Early
Gillium, Willis	Washington	Brooks	187/26	Early
Gillson, John	Wilkinson	Lees	322/9	Early
Gillum, Harris	Jasper	McClendons	380/2	Early
Gillum, Moses C.	Oglethorpe	Dunns	53/13	Habershar
Gillum, William	Jones	Samuels	273/4	Appling
Gilly, Charles	Franklin	Vaughns	32/8	Irwin
Gilly, Charles	Franklin	Vaughns	81/2	Appling
Gilly, John	Franklin	Vaughns	189/8	Appling
Gilmer, Eliz.(Wid)	Oglethorpe	McCowns	374/5	Irwin
Gilmer, John	Oglethorpe	Goolsby	259/13	Irwin
Gilmer, Thos.L.	Wilkes	Josseys	5/18	Early
Gilmore, Eliz.(Wid)	Twiggs	Hodges	91/2	Early
Gilmore, George Sr.	Wilkinson	Smiths	174/5	Early
Gilmore, Henry	Wilkinson	Smiths	262/4	Appling
Gilmore, Hugh	Jefferson	Lamps	19/19	Early
Gilmore, Hugh	Jefferson	Lamps	408/8	Irwin
Gilmore, Hugh	Putnam	Oslins	309/9	Early
Gilmore, Humphrey	Morgan	Campbell	14/10	Irwin
Gilmore, Humphrey	Morgan	Campbell	223/9	Early
Gilmore, James Jr.	Jackson	Dicksons	370/6	Appling
Gilmore, James	Putnam	Oslins	370/3	Early
Gilmore, James	Putnam	Oslins	52/4	Irwin
Gilmore, John H.	Jasper	Centells	443/4	Appling
Gilmore, John H.	Twiggs	Hodges	73/10	Hall
Gilmore, John	Hall		238/9	Early
Gilmore, Robert(Orps)	Lincoln	Jones	378/1	Early
Gilmore, Samuel	Wilkinson	Smiths	454/12	Irwin
Gilmore, Stephen H.	Morgan	Loyds	13/7	Gwinnett
Gilmore, Stephen	Wilkinson	Smiths	177/7	Gwinnett

NAME	COUNTY	MIL.DIST	LOT/SECT	DREW LAND
Gilmore, Susan(Wid)	Jones	Seals	46/1	Early
Gilmore, Thos.	Washington	Floyds	302/13	Irwin
Gilpin, Benj.	Putnam	Buckners	415/7	Irwin
Gilpin, Green	Columbia	Shaws	145/2	Irwin
Gilpin, Green	Columbia	Shaws	408/4	Early
Gilpin, Igantius(Orp)	Washington	Mays	199/3	Appling
Gilstrop, Henry	Burke	J.Wards	59/3	Appling
Gilstrop, William	Burke	J.Wards	275/2	Appling
Gilton, James	Chatham		152/3	Irwin
Gindrat, John	Richmond	122	109/15	Early
Ginn, Briant	Elbert	Whites	212/2	Irwin
Ginn, Elisha	Elbert	Whites	204/7	Irwin
Ginn, Isaac	Elbert	B.Higginbotham	232/3	Early
Ginn, Ruffin	Elbert	Christian	425/8	Irwin
Ginnes, William	Oglethorpe	Bowls	144/17	Early
Girardeau, John	Liberty		99/3	Walton
Gitten, John(Orps)	Franklin	Davis	287/15	Early
Gittens, Richard	Franklin	Davis	489/5	Irwin
Glase, John	Putnam	Coopers	8/4	Irwin
Glass, Alexr.(Orps)	Franklin	Hayns	148/10	Early
Glass, James	Oglethorpe	Brittons	213/2	Irwin
Glass, Levi	Laurens	Deans	158/1	Walton
Glass, Mary(Wid)	Emanuel	55th	75/9	Appling
Glass, Richard	Greene	Armour	79/1	Habersham
Glass, Thomas	Oglethorpe	Britton	499/6	Irwin
Glauson, James	Clarke	Harpers	391/11	Early
Glawn, Edmund	Lincoln	Walker	41/19	Early
Glaze, Asa	Lincoln	Jones	336/12	Early
Glaze, Daniel	Hall	M.Cutcheons	439/5	Irwin
Glaze, John	Lincoln	Jones	61/23	Early
Glaze, Milley	Lincoln	Jones	85/15	Irwin
Glaze, Reuben	Oglethorpe	Myricks	427/1	Early
Glaze, Tandy	Lincoln	Stokes	183/5	Gwinnett
Glaze, Thomas	Habersham	Powels	214/19	Early
Glaze, Thomas	Habersham	Powels	50/10	Early
Glaze, Thomas	Putnam	Coopers	73/1	Walton
Glaze, Wm.	Lincoln	Jones	173/27	Irwin
Gleen, James	Baldwin	Marshall	319/6	Appling
Glenn, Andrew	Franklin	Akins	137/15	Early
Glenn, Archbld.S.(Orp)	Chatham		176/5	Early
Glenn, Archibald	Chatham		414/13	Irwin
Glenn, Clement(Orps)	Oglethorpe	Davenport	4/3	Habersham
Glenn, Eliz.	Elbert	Christians	43/2	Early
Glenn, Elizabeth	Oglethorpe	Bowls	21/11	Hall
Glenn, James	Jackson	Dicksons	184/6	Appling
Glenn, James	Jackson	Winters	480/7	Irwin
Glenn, John Sr.	Oglethorpe	Goolsby	121/2	Irwin
Glenn, John Sr.	Oglethorpe	Goolsby	195/28	Early
Glenn, Joseph C.	Oglethorpe	Goolsby	105/6	Gwinnett
Glenn, Margaret	Chatham		414/13	Irwin
Glenn, Margarett S.(Orp)	Chatham		176/5	Early
Glenn, Otway	Washington	Robertsons	186/13	Early
Glenn, Otway	Washington	Robertsons	36/7	Appling
Glenn, Sarah	Chatham		414/13	Irwin
Glenn, Simon(Orp)	Elbert	P.Chrsitian	53/10	Hall
Glenn, Thomas	Hancock	Evans	48/5	Early
Glenn, Wm.	Franklin	Akins	117/6	Appling
Glenn, Wm.	Franklin	Akins	257/8	Irwin
Glenn, Wm.	Putnam	Berrys	241/5	Gwinnett
Glenn, Wm.	Putnam	Berrys	251/1	Appling
Glenn, Wm.Sr.	Oglethorpe	Davenport	63/5	Rabun
Glisson, Barshaba(Orp)	Burke	Royals	343/17	Early
Glisson, John B.	Burke	Royals	31/13	Early
Glisson, Martha(Orp)	Burke	Royals	343/17	Early
Gloss, Churchwell C.	Morgan	Loyds	606/2	Appling
Gloss, Manson	Morgan	Loyds	14/27	Early
Glosson, John	Morgan	Townsend	36/1	Irwin

NAME	COUNTY	MIL.DIST	LOT/SECT	DREW LAN
Glosson, John	Morgan	Townsend	90/6	Irwin
Glouson, Hugh(Orps)	Clarke	Harpers	322/8	Irwin
Glover, Eli	Jasper	Clays	21/1	Irwin
Glover, Elizabeth	Putnam	Oslins	385/5	Early
Glover, Henry	Putnam	Evans	115/16	Early
Glover, Henry	Putnam	Evans	424/5	Irwin
Glover, John Sr.	Putnam	Evans	152/12	Early
Glover, John Sr.	Putnam	Evans	175/16	Irwin
Glover, Joseph	Wilkes	Gordons	195/13	Irwin
Glover, Larkin	Warren	151	245/13	Early
Glover, Mark	Baldwin	Marshall	493/5	Irwin
Glover, Preston	Jackson	Hamiltons	247/5	Early
Glover, Preston	Jackson	Hamiltons	321/7	Gwinnett
Glover, Wiley	Jackson	Hamiltons	136/17	Early
Glover, Wiley	Jackson	Hamiltons	406/7	Appling
Glover, Wm.	Wilkes	Gordons	345/7	Early
Glovers, John(Orps)	Jackson	Hamiltons	204/5	Appling
Gnann, Benj.	Effingham		409/6	Appling
Gnann, Christina(Orps)	Effingham		18/4	Irwin
Gnann, Christopher	Effingham		130/10	Early
Gnann, Jacob Jr.	Effingham		199/7	Irwin
Gnann, Jacob Sr.	Effingham		140/1	Appling
Gnann, Jonathan Jr.	Effingham		299/1	Appling
Gnann, Jonathan Jr.	Effingham		379/6	Irwin
Gnann, Jonathan Sr.	Effingham		104/4	Early
Gnann, Jonathan Sr.	Effingham		320/3	Early
Gnann, Solomon Sr.	Effingham		188/6	Gwinnett
Gnann, Solomon	Effingham		82/2	Walton
Gober, Daniel	Franklin	Ashs	392/7	Early
Gober, Geo.W.	Franklin	Harris	102/1	Irwin
Gober, Geo.W.	Franklin	Harris	186/8	Irwin
Gober, James	Franklin	Harris	350/4	Early
Gober, John Sr.	Franklin	Harris	501/3	Appling
Gober, Thomas	Franklin	Harris	130/7	Early
Gober, Thos.C.	Franklin	Harris	321/10	Irwin
Gober, Wyly	Franklin	Ash's	119/9	Hall
Godard, Frederick	Jones	Greens	108/7	Irwin
Godard, James	Jones	Greens	17/14	Early
Godbee, George(Orp)	Burke	Royals	371/6	Irwin
Godbee, James Jr.	Burke	Royals	251/15	Early
Godbee, Mary	Burke	Royals	348/28	Early
Godbee, Samuel Sr.	Burke	Royals	311/5	Gwinnett
Godbee, Samuel	Burke	Royals	387/4	Early
Godfrey, Caroline(Orp)	Jefferson	Abbotts	165/3	Irwin
Godfrey, Edward	Burke	Royals	108/13	Irwin
Godfrey, Francis H.	Jefferson	Fountains	191/6	Appling
Godfrey, Margaret(Wid)	Jefferson	Abbotts	49/16	Early
Godlee, Samuel Sr.	Burke	Royals	79/9	Hall
Godley, Lipsey(Orp)	Burke	McNorrell	411/26	Early
Godown, Jacob Sr.	Jefferson	Bothwells	81/13	Early
Godphrey, Enoch	Burke	Royals	453/9	Irwin
Godwin, Hardy	Bulloch	Jones	317/6	Irwin
Godwin, James	Baldwin	Russels	90/7	Early
Godwin, Jefferson	Warren	154	353/6	Appling
Godwin, Sion	Twiggs	Ellis	406/9	Early
Godwin, Stephen	Montgomery	Alstons	151/3	Appling
Godwin, Wiley	Montgomery	Alstons	162/20	Early
Goff, Holley	Screven	Moodys	99/7	Early
Goff, Holley	Scriven	Moodys	348/9	Early
Goff, John	Wilkinson	Brooks	413/1	Appling
Goff, Samuel	Montgomery	Alstons	374/14	Early
Goff, Samuel	Richmond	120th	156/2	Appling
Goff, Samuel	Richmond	120th	47/14	Early
Gogant, Francis	Chatham		60/12	Hall
Goin, John	Greene	141st	220/18	Early
Golden, Benj.	Wilkinson	Howards	299/3	Appling
Golden, Caleb	Lincoln	Tatoms	401/11	Early

NAME	COUNTY	MIL.DIST	LOT/SECT	DREW LAND
Golden, Caleb	Lincoln	Tatoms	62/3	Walton
Golden, David(Orps)	Warren	153	290/14	Early
Golden, John	Hancock	Edwards	310/9	Irwin
Golden, John	Lincoln	Tatoms	37/6	Irwin
Golden, Mark Jr.	Lincoln	Parks	178/1	Irwin
Golden, Seaborn	Lincoln	Tatoms	388/5	Appling
Golden, Wm.Sr.	Lincoln	Parks	334/4	Early
Golding, John R.	Clarke	Applings	359/11	Irwin
Goldsmith, Samuel	Chatham		105/14	Early
Goldwire, Caroline(Orp)	Effingham		6/13	Habersham
Goldwire, John	Effingham		204/8	Irwin
Goldwire, Mariah(Orp)	Effingham		6/13	Habersham
Goldwn, Wm.Sr.	Lincoln	Parks	260/18	Early
Golightly, Susannah(W)	Pulaski	Bryans	9/11	Hall
Golightly, Thomas	Columbia	Burroughs	154/9	Irwin
Golitely, Ransom	Pulaski	Senterfeit	6/3	Irwin
Golphin, Milledge	Richmond	120th	153/8	Irwin
Gonder, Mark	Hancock	Evans	274/14	Early
Good, Starling	Jefferson	Flemmings	47/6	Early
Goodall, Samuel	Baldwin	Marshall	298/28	Early
Goodbread, John	Camden	32nd	71/2	Rabun
Goodbread, Phillip	Camden	32nd	362/26	Early
Goodbread, Thomas	Camden	32nd	122/13	Habersham
Goode, ELiz.	Jasper	Smiths	241/3	Early
Goode, Jordan	Jasper	Smiths	121/13	Early
Goode, Samuel W.	Wilkes	Gordons	40/22	Early
Gooden, John S.	Chatham		221/13	Early
Gooden, Thos.	Warren	153	194/1	Appling
Goodger, James	Greene	Nelm's	132/20	Early
Goodman, Isaac	Wilkinson	Bowings	245/3	Walton
Goodman, Jas.Sr.	Wilkes	Runnels	408/1	Early
Goodman, Jesse	Bulloch	Knights	73/4	Walton
Goodman, Jno.Casper	Hancock	Millers	204/3	Early
Goodman, John	Bulloch	Everitt	246/15	Early
Goodman, Timothy	Wilkinson	Bowens	128/12	Habersham
Goodman, Timothy	Wilkinson	Bowings	203/10	Habersham
Goodrow, Thomas	Jones	Chappels	114/3	Walton
Goodson, Abraham	Washington	Barges	44/7	Early
Goodson, Abraham	Washington	Barges	66/8	Appling
Goodson, Arthur(Orps)	Putnam	Slaughter	143/2	Irwin
Goodson, Josiah	Bryan	20	23/5	Gwinnett
Goodson, Martin	Putnam	Slaughters	13/5	Appling
Goodson, Wm.	Warren	153	179/3	Appling
Goodson, Wm.	Warren	153	82/13	Irwin
Goodwin, David	Warren	Rodgers	90/11	Irwin
Goodwin, Hester	Burke	Royals	362/10	Irwin
Goodwin, James C.	Jones	Gresham	280/5	Appling
Goodwin, Jas.Sr.	Wilkes	Runnels	164/13	Early
Goodwin, Jefferson	Warren	154	105/18	Early
Goodwin, John	Gwinnett	Hamilton	235/17	Early
Goodwin, Jonathan	Jones	Permenter	30/17	Early
Goodwin, Lewis	Jones	Permenter	14/1	Habersham
Goodwin, Matthew	Burke	Royals	225/1	Appling
Goodwin, Penalopy(Wid)	Greene	Harvills	428/28	Early
Goodwin, Thos.	Franklin	Morris	521/10	Irwin
Goodwin, Wm.	Franklin	Morris	123/13	Early
Googer, Andr.M.	Lincoln	Thompson	55/6	Irwin
Googer, Stephen	Hancock	Canes	257/10	Early
Googer, Stephen	Hancock	Canes	389/10	Irwin
Goolden, Isaac	Putnam	Slaughter	71/9	Appling
Goolsby, Hezekiah	Oglethorpe	McCowns	44/2	Walton
Goolsby, Isaiah Jr.	Oglethorpe	Goolsby	51/9	Appling
Goolsby, Isiah	Franklin	Attaways	344/28	Early
Goolsby, John A.	Jasper	Owens	88/10	Early
Goolsby, John	Jasper	Smiths	29/1	Irwin
Goolsby, John	Jasper	Smiths	379/28	Early
Goolsby, Reuben	Elbert	P.Christian	131/18	Early

NAME	COUNTY	MIL.DIST	LOT/SECT	DREW LAN
Goolsby, Selah	Oglethorpe	Wises	141/2	Irwin
Goolsby, William	Lincoln	Parks	441/3	Appling
Goolsby, Wm.	Jasper	Smiths	6/2	Habersha
Goolsby, Wm.	Oglethorpe	Devenport	24/1	Early
Goolsby, Wm.	Oglethorpe	Devenport	65/5	Early
Goolsby, Wm.C.	Oglethorpe	Goolsby	377/2	Appling
Goolsy, Curden	Jasper	Whites	86/8	Hall
Goore, Pharis	Hancock	Champions	128/7	Early
Goore, Thomas Jr.	Hancock	Thomas	349/14	Early
Goore, Thos.Jr.	Hancock	Thomas	190/19	Early
Goore, Thos.Sr.(RS)	Hancock	Thomas	218/12	Irwin
Goore, Thos.Sr.(RS)	Hancock	Thomas	433/2	Appling
Gordan, Austin R.	Chatham		346/26	Early
Gordan, Philoman	Oglethorpe	Waters	347/12	Early
Gordan, Rebecca	Jones	Permenters	56/5	Irwin
Gordan, Richard	Washington	Renfroes	262/2	Early
Gordon, (Orphs)	Burke	McNorrills	83/4	Appling
Gordon, Alexr.	Tattnall	Jos.Durrence	430/6	Irwin
Gordon, Asa	Habersham	Flannagans	85/28	Early
Gordon, George	Chatham		200/3	Appling
Gordon, Henry W.	Oglethorpe	Waters	152/14	Irwin
Gordon, James(RS)	Elbert	Maxwells	57/20	Early
Gordon, James(RS)	Elbert	Maxwells	91/7	Appling
Gordon, James	Jefferson	Fountains	75/21	Early
Gordon, James	Jones	Greens	192/11	Early
Gordon, John	Elbert	Dooleys	379/27	Early
Gordon, Sarah(Orp)	Richmond	Laceys	228/17	Early
Gordon, Sarah	Putnam	Slaughter	110/5	Gwinnett
Gordon, William	Burke	71st	17/1	Early
Gordow, John	Elbert	Dooley	94/6	Appling
Gordy, George	Hancock	Justices	276/12	Early
Gordy, Leonard(Orps)	Hancock	Loyds	62/9	Early
Gordy, Leonard(Orps)	Hancock	Loyds	83/13	Early
Gordy, Peter	Morgan	McLendon	26/26	Early
Gordy, Thomas Jr.	Burke	Spiveys	42/23	Early
Gordy, Thomas Sr.	Burke	Spiveys	111/9	Early
Gordy, Thomas	Hancock	Edwards	111/16	Irwin
Gore, Henry	Jones	Chappels	329/13	Irwin
Gore, Pharis	Hancock	Champions	261/16	Early
Gorham, Richard	Chatham		203/11	Early
Gorham, Sandford	Franklin	Hammond	211/14	Early
Gorham, Sanford	Franklin	Hammonds	15/10	Early
Gorham, Willis	Jefferson	Fountains	208/5	Appling
Gorley, Jas.(Orps)	Putnam	J.Kendrick	227/13	Irwin
Gorman, ELiza(Orp)	Camden	Baileys	33/1	Early
Gorman, Eady(Orp)	Camden	Baileys	33/1	Early
Gorman, John(Orp)	Camden	Baileys	33/1	Early
Gorman, Margaret(Orp)	Camden	Baileys	33/1	Early
Gorman, Nathan(Orph)	Camden	Baileys	33/1	Early
Gorman, Richard(Orp)	Camden	Baileys	33/1	Early
Gorman, Sarah(Orp)	Camden	Baileys	33/1	Early
Gortney, Wm.Jr.	Franklin	Davis	226/18	Early
Goryes, Daniel(Orps)	Morgan	Selmons	163/18	Early
Goslin, Barnet	Baldwin	Doziers	30/10	Irwin
Goslin, James	Baldwin	Doziers	90/16	Irwin
Goslin, Simon(Orps)	Jones	Samuels	147/16	Irwin
Goss, Benj.(Orps)	Morgan	Loyals	19/27	Early
Goss, Hezekiah F.	Morgan	Campbell	4/10	Habersha
Goss, Horatio J.	Elbert	P.Christian	53/10	Irwin
Goss, Jesse H.	Morgan	Loyds	116/17	Early
Goss, John	Twiggs	Evans	342/20	Early
Goss, Nathan	Twiggs	Evans	348/5	Gwinnett
Gossett, John	Madison	Adares	300/1	Walton
Gothard, Thomas	Morgan	Parkers	502/10	Irwin
Gough, William	Burke	Dy's	417/5	Appling
Gough, William	Burke	Dy's	61/6	Appling
Gould, Wm.	McIntosh	Goulds	16/6	Irwin

NAME	COUNTY	MIL.DIST	LOT/SECT	DREW LAND
Goulde, Jacob	Chatham		332/9	Appling
Goulden, Jonathan	Liberty		207/28	Early
Goulding, Palmer	Liberty		304/4	Appling
Gouldman, Frances	Lincoln	Walkers	148/3	Early
Gouldman, Francis	Lincoln	Walkers	126/1	Habersham
Gouldsberry, Joshua	Jackson	Winters	150/19	Early
Gowder, Fredrk.	Franklin	Turks	403/15	Early
Gowder, Fredrk.	Franklin	Turks	466/7	Irwin
Gower, Robt.M.	Clarke	Parrs	295/5	Gwinnett
Goza, Martin	Twiggs	Browns	11/12	Early
Gozden, Elizabeth	Oglethorpe	Barnetts	47/23	Early
Gozden, Ezekiel	Oglethorpe	Barnett	112/8	Irwin
Gozden, Waterman	Oglethorpe	Barnetts	147/27	Early
Grabell, Michael	Hancock	Edwards	215/28	Early
Grabill, Henry	Jasper	Kenadays	426/7	Irwin
Grabury, Jonathan	Warren	150th	336/21	Early
Grace, Elizabeth	Burke	71st	231/8	Irwin
Grace, John W.	Jasper	Easts	39/19	Early
Grace, Lantea	Morgan	Selmons	191/10	Early
Grace, Samuel	Jasper	Northcuts	261/28	Early
Grace, Thomas(Orps)	Burke	71	78/7	Appling
Graddy, Arthur	Pulaski	Lesters	250/2	Irwin
Graddy, Winfer	Pulaski	Clements	272/17	Early
Grady, James O.	Franklin	P.Browns	329/10	Early
Gragg, Wm.	Jasper	Kindalls	164/8	Hall
Graham, Alexr.	Laurens	Kinchens	117/13	Irwin
Graham, Daniel	Telfair	Wilsons	472/7	Irwin
Graham, David	Twiggs	Browns	470/6	Irwin
Graham, Duncan	Telfair	Wilsons	409/11	Irwin
Graham, Duncan	Telfair	Wilsons	41/21	Early
Graham, George	Jones	Samuels	485/5	Irwin
Graham, James	Liberty		53/4	Irwin
Graham, Joseph	Telfair	Williams	48/3	Appling
Graham, Josiah	Madison	Orrs	301/9	Irwin
Graham, Nancy(Wid)	Pulaski	Bryans	6/1	Rabun
Graham, Neall	Telfair	Williams	37/15	Irwin
Graham, Robert	Wilkes	Kilgore	90/4	Early
Graham, Robt.	Wilkes	Kilgore	354/20	Early
Graham, Stephen	Oglethorpe	Bowls	311/5	Irwin
Grammar, Peter(RS)	Hancock	Lucas	218/1	Appling
Grammar, Peter(RS)	Hancock	Lucas	470/4	Appling
Granade, James	Warren	152nd	431/8	Irwin
Granade, Joseph	Warren	152nd	326/6	Appling
Granbery, Thomas	Warren	154	124/1	Appling
Granger, Abraham	Oglethorpe	Barnetts	89/4	Appling
Granger, Stephen	Oglethorpe	Barnetts	480/2	Appling
Grant, Chas.(Jr.)	Hancock	Edwards	96/12	Habersham
Grant, Chas.A.Sr.	Hancock	Edwards	374/17	Early
Grant, James	Hancock	Evans	143/5	Appling
Grant, James	Hancock	Evans	74/9	Hall
Grant, John A.	Pulaski	Senterfeit	375/3	Appling
Grant, Jos.Sr.(RS)	Hancock	Lucas	135/3	Irwin
Grant, Jos.Sr.(RS)	Hancock	Lucas	306/3	Appling
Grant, Joseph	Richmond	Burtons	124/6	Irwin
Grant, Robt.Sr.	Glynn		465/11	Irwin
Grant, Thomas	Greene	Jones	362/6	Early
Grant, Thomas	Jasper	Clays	495/2	Appling
Grant, Thomas	Jones	Permenter	238/20	Early
Grantham, Henry	Hancock	Colemans	259/1	Appling
Grantham, Joshua	Hancock	Scotts	190/9	Irwin
Grantham, Thos	(Orps)	Scriven	Lovetts	41/16, Irwin
Granville, Charles	Richmond		126/2	Early
Granville, Chas.	Richmond		257/7	Appling
Gravatt, John	Hall	McElhannon	50/3	Habersham
Graves, Ellis	Lincoln	Graves	54/2	Irwin
Graves, James	Twiggs	Smith	113/4	Walton
Graves, John Sr.	Jasper	Baileys	258/3	Irwin

NAME	COUNTY	MIL.DIST	LOT/SECT	DREW LAN
Graves, John Sr.	Jasper	Baileys	56/10	Hall
Graves, John	Jasper	Baileys	24/4	Rabun
Graves, John	Wilkes	Smiths	192/8	Appling
Graves, Joseph	Lincoln	Graves	126/14	Irwin
Graves, Lucretia(Wid)	Lincoln	Graves	177/1	Appling
Graves, Robert C.	Wilkes	Bates	111/6	Gwinnett
Graves, Stephen	Twiggs	Smiths	39/14	Irwin
Graves, Wm.(Orps)	Jasper	Evans	527/9	Irwin
Gravitt, Randle	Jackson	Dicksons	256/3	Appling
Gray, Absalom	Jackson	Winters	17/9	Appling
Gray, Benj.(Orp)	Jones	Shropshear	163/2	Habersha
Gray, David	Twiggs	R.Belcher	236/18	Early
Gray, Edmond	Burke	70th	66/15	Irwin
Gray, Edmund	Burke	70th	334/5	Appling
Gray, Enoch	Washington	Renfroes	109/19	Early
Gray, George	Clarke	Harris	322/3	Appling
Gray, Gibson	Burke	Bells	171/26	Early
Gray, Green	Putnam	Oslins	396/8	Early
Gray, Hezekiah	Elbert	P.Christian	13/3	Appling
Gray, Hezekiah	Elbert	P.Christian	367/11	Early
Gray, James Sr.	Hancock	Sharps	201/3	Appling
Gray, James	Jones	Samuels	235/6	Early
Gray, James	Putnam	Oslins	225/13	Irwin
Gray, James	Warren	Hubbarts	22/3	Irwin
Gray, John M.	Franklin	Burroughs	81/1	Walton
Gray, John W.	Liberty		253/3	Irwin
Gray, John W.	Liberty		484/7	Appling
Gray, John	Burke	70th	137/13	Habersha
Gray, John	Burke	J.Wards	250/11	Irwin
Gray, John	Lincoln	Walker	150/12	Early
Gray, Minche	Burke	Torrance	37/4	Appling
Gray, Peter	Jones	Greene	221/7	Early
Gray, Priscella(Wid)	Putnam	Roberts	168/16	Irwin
Gray, Priscilla	Baldwin	Marshall	396/1	Early
Gray, Richard	Jasper	Bartletts	54/5	Gwinnett
Gray, Samuel	Lincoln	Tatoms	390/7	Irwin
Gray, Samuel	Lincoln	Walkers	310/13	Irwin
Gray, Sherod H.	Jasper	Bentleys	247/17	Early
Gray, Thomas Sr.	Wilkinson	Smiths	60/9	Irwin
Gray, Thos.Sr.	Walton	Wagnon	154/4	Early
Gray, Thos.Sr.	Walton	Wagnons	263/14	Early
Gray, William	Columbia	Pullins	511/7	Irwin
Gray, William	Jones	Griffith	196/2	Rabun
Gray, William	Richmond	120th	197/2	Appling
Gray, Wm.	Elbert	Ruckers	333/11	Irwin
Gray, Wm.	Putnam	Moreland	246/1	Early
Gray, Wm.	Twiggs	Hodges	49/2	Walton
Graybill, John	Hancock	Edwards	65/6	Irwin
Graybill, Phillip	Glynn		6/5	Habersha
Graye, Jeremiah	Clarke	Harriss	14/2	Walton
Grayham, Archbd.	Effingham		67/5	Appling
Grayham, Isaiah	Hancock	Millers	372/5	Appling
Grayham, John(Orps)	Laurens	Watsons	184/10	Early
Grayham, John	Effingham		423/28	Early
Grayham, Priscilla(W)	Twiggs	Wilie Belcher	48/4	Walton
Grayham, Saml.	Twiggs	Barrows	32/20	Early
Grayson, John R.	Chatham		357/11	Irwin
Greathouse, Archa.	Morgan	Farrars	336/2	Appling
Green, Abraham	Burke	M.Wards	362/20	Early
Green, Abram	Burke	M.Wards	197/4	Walton
Green, Aquilla	Oglethorpe	Myricks	291/26	Early
Green, Augustine	Greene	140th	126/10	Irwin
Green, Berry(Orps)	Putnam	Evans	158/13	Habershar
Green, Boling	Jasper	Blakes	228/19	Early
Green, Burrell(Orps)	Putnam	Coopers	428/6	Appling
Green, Burwell Sr.	Jasper	Reids	492/10	Irwin
Green, Burwell	Jasper	Blakes	344/2	Early

NAME	COUNTY	MIL.DIST	LOT/SECT	DREW LAND
Green, Coleman	Jasper	McLendons	261/12	Early
Green, Daniel	Burke	Lewis	279/17	Early
Green, Daniel	Burke	Spiveys	404/2	Appling
Green, David	Twiggs	Browns	24/5	Habersham
Green, Durant	Richmond	122	493/4	Appling
Green, Forest(RS)	Jackson	Rogers	110/13	Habersham
Green, Gresham	Burke	Thomas	447/6	Irwin
Green, Hardy	Twiggs	W.Belcher	270/1	Early
Green, Hubbard(Orps)	Warren	Rogers	51/3	Irwin
Green, Isaac	Putnam	Slaughter	224/7	Appling
Green, Jesse D.	Richmond	Laceys	246/12	Early
Green, Jesse	Greene	Jones	59/5	Appling
Green, John C.	Clarke	Deans	20/7	Early
Green, John Jr.	Putnam	Slaughter	274/18	Early
Green, John W.	Jackson	Dicksons	212/17	Early
Green, John	Bulloch	Jones	107/12	Irwin
Green, John	Scriven	Roberts	146/1	Walton
Green, John	Wilkinson	Bowings	242/1	Appling
Green, Jos.P.	Walton	Greens	147/2	Habersham
Green, Joseph P.	Walton	Greens	309/20	Early
Green, McKeen	Washington	Floyds	232/20	Early
Green, Nancy	Putnam	Slaughter	168/6	Irwin
Green, Perry(Orp)	Putnam	Evans	191/28	Early
Green, Peter B.	Pulaski	Lester	122/3	Appling
Green, Raleigh	Baldwin	Doziers	281/2	Appling
Green, Rice	Franklin	Vaughns	153/1	Irwin
Green, Richd.(Orps)	Morgan	Hackney	84/14	Irwin
Green, Robert	Greene	144	13/15	Early
Green, Robert	Jackson	Hamiltons	481/5	Irwin
Green, Samuel W.	Morgan	Alfords	491/6	Appling
Green, Sarah(Wid)	Clarke	Pentecosts	14/10	Hall
Green, Shepherd	Jefferson	Fountains	496/3	Appling
Green, Thos.B.	Putnam	Coopers	163/1	Irwin
Green, Thos.B.	Putnam	Coopers	425/10	Irwin
Green, Timothy	Twiggs	Wilie Belcher	142/9	Appling
Green, William B.	Burke	Thomas	66/14	Early
Green, William	Baldwin	Marshall	41/13	Habersham
Green, William	Oglethorpe	Wises	393/4	Early
Green, William	Scriven	Roberts	199/6	Irwin
Green, William	Washington	Brooks	185/20	Early
Greene, Abner	Richmond	122	147/7	Appling
Greene, Allen	Jones	Greens	72/6	Habersham
Greene, Alston H.	Morgan	Hubbard	408/9	Irwin
Greene, Amos	Baldwin	Stephens	6/4	Habersham
Greene, Aquilla	Twiggs	Browns	34/12	Irwin
Greene, Augustine	Greene	140th	330/9	Appling
Greene, Benj.	Baldwin	Stephens	363/19	Early
Greene, Burwell	Jasper	Blakes	378/4	Appling
Greene, Charity(Wid)	Warren	Rogers	317/8	Appling
Greene, Curtice	Jackson	Hamiltons	197/6	Gwinnett
Greene, David	Jackson	Rogers	147/5	Early
Greene, Drury	Jasper	Smiths	39/21	Early
Greene, Edmund	Morgan	Alfords	317/6	Gwinnett
Greene, Ezekiel	Jackson	Rogers	494/11	Irwin
Greene, Forrest(RS)	Jackson	Rogers	15/6	Irwin
Greene, Hartwell B.	Morgan	Cheaves	255/2	Irwin
Greene, Henry	Baldwin	Cousins	516/6	Irwin
Greene, James B.	Clarke	Moors	94/10	Habersham
Greene, James	Hall		380/15	Irwin
Greene, James	Jackson	Rogers	258/27	Early
Greene, John	Burke	Lewis	209/5	Gwinnett
Greene, John	Clarke	Moores	157/2	Early
Greene, John	Putnam	Buckners	488/4	Appling
Greene, John	Scriven	Roberts	80/3	Rabun
Greene, Joseph	Putnam	Slaughter	502/7	Appling
Greene, Larkin	Jackson	Rogers	256/4	Early
Greene, Lewis	Bulloch	Jones	253/13	Early

129

NAME	COUNTY	MIL.DIST	LOT/SECT	DREW LAND
Greene, Moses	Burke	Torrance	208/1	Early
Greene, Myles	Baldwin	Dozier	133/14	Irwin
Greene, Phillip H.	Greene	140th	256/23	Early
Greene, Robert	Jackson	Hamiltons	205/18	Early
Greene, Shadrack	Jackson	Rogers	216/14	Early
Greene, Warren	Burke	Lewis	123/3	Irwin
Greene, William	Greene	Harvills	178/2	Appling
Greene, William	Scriven	Burns	145/12	Irwin
Greene, William	Twiggs	Browns	4/18	Early
Greene, Wm.(Orph)	Burke	Royals	371/6	Irwin
Greene, Wm.(Orps)	Lincoln	Thompson	204/1	Walton
Greene, Wm.	Washington	Brooks	369/12	Irwin
Greene, Wm.Jr.	Greene	140th	1/16	Irwin
Greene, Wm.Sr.	Greene	140th	118/12	Habersha.
Greene, Wm.Sr.	Greene	140th	163/21	Early
Greene, Wm.Sr.	Jasper	Hays	279/7	Early
Greenhog, James G.	Chatham		253/28	Early
Greens, Mathew(Orps)	Burke	72nd	258/28	Early
Greenway, Samuel	Jefferson	Lamps	112/21	Early
Greenwood, Henry	Richmond	Winters	243/20	Early
Greenwood, John	Oglethorpe	Murrays	212/12	Habershar
Greer, Abraham	Greene	Harvills	327/7	Irwin
Greer, Abraham	Greene	Harvills	327/7	Irwin
Greer, Asael	Greene	Ragins	175/6	Early
Greer, Elijah	Morgan	Hackneys	454/28	Early
Greer, Equilla	Greene	Harvills	326/28	Early
Greer, James A.	Jasper	Reids	200/11	Irwin
Greer, James(Orps)	Greene	Ragins	140/2	Rabun
Greer, John G.W.	Wilkinson	Howards	467/5	Appling
Greer, John	Jasper	Reeds	243/13	Irwin
Greer, Richard	Habersham	Flanagans	175/6	Appling
Greer, Robert(RS)	Morgan	Alfords	403/9	Irwin
Greer, Saml.A.	Morgan	Alfords	129/3	Walton
Greer, Thomas Jr.	Morgan	Talbots	423/11	Irwin
Greer, Thomas(Orps)	Morgan	Alfords	340/6	Early
Greer, Thomas	Clarke	Deans	310/17	Early
Greer, Thomas	Jasper	Reeds	168/5	Gwinnett
Greer, Thomas	Jasper	Reeds	282/6	Early
Greer, Thomas	Morgan	Talbots	423/8	Appling
Greer, Thos.Jr.	Greene	143rd	205/2	Appling
Greer, Thos.Sr.	Greene	Carltons	209/11	Early
Greer, Waters W.	Greene	Greers	124/6	Early
Greer, William	Greene	Harvills	229/9	Early
Greer, Wm.Jr.	Greene	Harvills	77/5	Gwinnett
Greer, Wm.Sr.	Greene	Harvills	287/15	Early
Greerer, Robert(RS)	Chatham		220/2	Appling
Greerer, Robert(RS)	Chatham		79/26	Early
Greesham, Wm.	Oglethorpe	Myricks	290/8	Early
Greeson, John	Jackson	Hamiltons	189/4	Appling
Greeson, John	Jackson	Hamiltons	392/12	Irwin
Gregory, Abigail	Richmond	398	194/2	Early
Gregory, Emanuel	Richmond	122nd	393/2	Early
Gregory, Jesse	Scriven	Smiths	449/7	Irwin
Gregory, John(Orps)	Burke	Bells	108/21	Early
Gregory, John(Orps)	Hancock	Mims	167/9	Appling
Gregory, Lewis	Jasper	McLendons	266/5	Appling
Gregory, Mathew	Twiggs	Hodges	375/27	Early
Gregory, Nancy(Wid)	Lincoln	Graves	175/5	Early
Gregory, Thos.H.	Pulaski	Bryans	276/7	Early
Gregory, Thos.J.	Madison	Williford	125/3	Walton
Gregory, Wm.B.	Morgan	Hackneys	137/5	Irwin
Gregory, Wm.G.(Orps)	Lincoln	Craves	98/6	Irwin
Gren, Thos.(S/Gilbert)	Twiggs	141	229/1	Early
Grenad, Johnson	Warren	Hubbards	237/7	Appling
Grenad, Johnson	Warren	Hubberts	144/7	Irwin
Grenad, Solomon	Warren	Hurberts	172/6	Irwin
Grerson, Wm.	Jackson	Hamiltons	45/22	Early

130

NAME	COUNTY	MIL.DIST	LOT/SECT	DREW LAND
Gresham, Archbd.	Greene	140th	248/3	Appling
Gresham, Archbd.	Greene	Carltons	131/20	Early
Gresham, Archbd.	Greene	Carltons	131/20	Early
Gresham, David	Jasper	Bartlett	189/10	Irwin
Gresham, David	Jasper	Bentleys	19/3	Habersham
Gresham, Davis E.	Morgan	Knights	69/10	Hall
Gresham, Eliz.(Wid)	Wilkes	Mattox	33/16	Irwin
Gresham, Isham	Jasper	Bartletts	105/4	Walton
Gresham, Job	Burke	69th	455/9	Irwin
Gresham, John Jr.	Jasper	Bartlets	128/4	Walton
Gresham, John Jr.	Jasper	Bartlets	184/20	Early
Gresham, Lemuel	Morgan	Hackney	424/12	Irwin
Gresham, Lumpkin(Orps)	Oglethorpe	Myricks	166/1	Early
Gresham, Micajah	Morgan	Raimeys	522/8	Appling
Gresham, Micajah	Morgan	Ramseys	245/4	Appling
Gresham, Robert	Oglethorpe	Myricks	153/9	Hall
Gresham, Thos.	Wilkes	Runnels	146/7	Early
Gresham, Thos.	Wilkes	Runnels	230/5	Early
Gresham, Wm.	Wilkes	Bates	419/5	Irwin
Gresham, Young F.	Greene	143rd	318/4	Walton
Greson, Abram Jr.	Warren	Parhams	273/8	Appling
Greson, James	Warren	Palmer	145/11	Hall
Grey, Benjamin	Effingham		71/19	Early
Grey, Joshua	Washington	Mannings	124/10	Habersham
Grey, Stephen	Camden	32	364/12	Early
Grey, Stephen	Camden	32nd	206/5	Appling
Greyer, William E.	Effingham		404/4	Appling
Greyham, John(Orps)	Oglethorpe	Lees	81/3	Habersham
Gribbon, John	Chatham		234/19	Early
Gribbon, Thomas	Chatham		162/10	Irwin
Gribbon, Thomas	Chatham		326/13	Irwin
Grice, Esther	Pulaski	Rees	57/12	Irwin
Grice, John	Burke	M.Wards	345/1	Appling
Grider, Jacob	Montgomery	Nobles	248/28	Early
Grier, Aron W.	Warren	Griers	271/2	Appling
Grier, James(RS)	Clarke	Tredwells	542/2	Appling
Griff, John M.	Pulaski	Rees	328/9	Irwin
Griffeth, John	Oglethorpe	Myricks	34/6	Habersham
Griffin, Abel(Orps)	Washington	Peabodys	356/9	Early
Griffin, Abner	Jefferson	Lamps	72/6	Appling
Griffin, Andrew	Baldwin	Stephens	128/14	Early
Griffin, Andrew	Washington	Floyds	339/28	Early
Griffin, Archbd.	Laurens	Griffins	195/1	Appling
Griffin, Bennet	Laurens	Meltons	134/2	Walton
Griffin, Beverly A.	Jones	Kings	192/2	Rabun
Griffin, Cibel(Wid)	Montgomery	McElvins	245/9	Irwin
Griffin, Clinton	Chatham		127/7	Irwin
Griffin, Demsey	Hancock	Mims	99/16	Irwin
Griffin, Drewry	Wilkes	Smiths	453/5	Irwin
Griffin, Drury	Wilkes	Smiths	54/3	Habersham
Griffin, Enoch	Washington	Peabodys	217/12	Irwin
Griffin, Ezekiel	Oglethorpe	Waters	135/4	Irwin
Griffin, George	Burke	Royals	39/9	Appling
Griffin, Henry	Richmond	Laceys	457/4	Appling
Griffin, James(Orps)	Putnam	Buckner	101/15	Early
Griffin, James(RS)	Jackson	Hamiltons	46/6	Appling
Griffin, James(RS)	Jackson	Hamiltons	60/12	Habersham
Griffin, James	Chatham		235/11	Irwin
Griffin, James	Montgomery	McMillan	98/6	Hall
Griffin, James	Washington	Renfros	333/6	Irwin
Griffin, Jas.(Capt.)	Twiggs	Browns	61/3	Habersham
Griffin, John Sr.(RS)	Hancock	Mims	116/7	Gwinnett
Griffin, John	Baldwin	Marshall	151/14	Early
Griffin, John	Columbia	Bealls	370/9	Early
Griffin, John	Columbia	Willingham	107/4	Walton
Griffin, John	Oglethorpe	Waters	256/1	Walton
Griffin, John	Twiggs	Browns	52/2	Habersham

131

NAME	COUNTY	MIL.DIST	LOT/SECT	DREW LA
Griffin, John	Twiggs	Evans	224/21	Early
Griffin, John	Warren	Parhams	261/15	Early
Griffin, Jonas	Wilkinson	Bowings	149/16	Irwin
Griffin, Jonas	Wilkinson	Bowings	42/1	Irwin
Griffin, Leonard(Orp)	Twiggs	Browns	339/5	Gwinnet
Griffin, Levi	Laurens	Jones	388/1	Appling
Griffin, Levi	Laurens	Jones	497/5	Appling
Griffin, Lewis Jr.	Warren	Parhams	28/27	Early
Griffin, Lucy(Wid)	Bulloch	Knights	65/11	Hall
Griffin, Major	Wilkinson	Bowings	256/5	Gwinnet
Griffin, Major	Wilkinson	Bowings	4/4	Habersh
Griffin, Major	Wilkinson	Bowings	65/12	Early
Griffin, Mary(Wid)	Washington	Avents	376/15	Early
Griffin, Mitchell(Orps)	Telfair	Williams	363/7	Early
Griffin, Mitchell(Wid)	Telfair	Williams	363/7	Early
Griffin, Moses	Twiggs	Evans	21/1	Rabun
Griffin, Nancy	Putnam	Buckner	35/7	Appling
Griffin, Nathan	Morgan	Townsend	183/6	Early
Griffin, Noah	Montgomery	McMillen	107/5	Gwinnet
Griffin, Peter(RS)	Twiggs	Browns	289/5	Appling
Griffin, Peter(RS)	Twiggs	Browns	63/9	Irwin
Griffin, Randph.(Orp)	Wilkinson	Kettles	343/9	Irwin
Griffin, Samuel	Camden	Clark's	217/5	Early
Griffin, Samuel	Camden	Clark's	33/3	Walton
Griffin, Sarah(Wid)	Chatham		19/5	Early
Griffin, Sarah	Washington	Peabodys	19/4	Rabun
Griffin, Shadrach	Montgomery	McMillins	177/27	Early
Griffin, Turner	Jefferson	Lamps	466/11	Irwin
Griffin, William	Jones	Kings	253/12	Early
Griffin, Wm.	Twiggs	W.Belcher	246/26	Early
Griffin, Yancy	Pulaski	Rees	284/1	Appling
Griffin, Yancy	Pulaski	Rees	61/3	Early
Griffis, Charles	Emanuel	Lanes	309/9	Irwin
Griffis, John	Emanuel	53rd	223/5	Gwinnett
Griffis, Matthew	Hancock	Mims	212/7	Appling
Griffith, George	Oglethorpe	Bowls	170/9	Hall
Griffith, Henry	Jones	Griffith	68/8	Irwin
Griffith, John L.	Madison	Orrs	104/27	Early
Griffith, John	Oglethorpe	Bowls	212/9	Appling
Griffith, Peter(RS)	Twiggs	Browns	109/10	Habersha
Griffith, Stephen	Habersham	Flanagans	464/6	Appling
Griffith, Wm.	Oglethorpe	Bowls	367/21	Early
Griffith, Wm.L.	Madison	Culbreths	135/10	Habersha
Griffy, David	Oglethorpe	Bowls	147/11	Hall
Griffy, David	Oglethorpe	Bowls	314/16	Early
Griger, Asa	Bryan	19th	48/16	Irwin
Grigg, Jesse W.	Hancock	Danells	32/14	Irwin
Grigg, William	Baldwin	Irwins	235/11	Early
Grigg, Wm.Sr.	Hancock	Danells	226/11	Irwin
Griggs, Asea	Putnam	Slaughters	426/6	Irwin
Griggs, Geo.(Orps)	Jackson	Hamiltons	358/3	Early
Griggs, Henry	Jones	Greens	199/1	Early
Griggs, Hugh	Jasper	Cantals	67/3	Irwin
Griggs, Lee	Hancock	Daniels	579/13	Irwin
Griggs, Nathnl.	Hancock	Danells	1/4	Rabun
Griggs, Rhodom S.	Baldwin	Marshall	331/26	Early
Griggs, Robert	Hancock	Danells	13/14	Early
Griggs, Robert	Hancock	Danells	61/4	Irwin
Griggs, Robert	Hancock	Herberts	253/6	Irwin
Griggs, Robert	Hancock	Herberts	9/10	Early
Griggs, Rodum	Hancock	Danells	109/4	Walton
Griggs, Thomas	Baldwin	Taliaferro	43/4	Appling
Griggs, Thomas	Hancock	Danells	242/7	Irwin
Griggs, Thomas	Hancock	Danells	357/5	Irwin
Griggs, Wm.M.	Wilkinson	Childs	129/5	Gwinnett
Griggs, Wm.N.	Wilkinson	Childs	120/12	Habersha
Griggs, Wm.Sr.	Hancock	Daniels	181/16	Irwin

NAME	COUNTY	MIL.DIST	LOT/SECT	DREW LAND
Griggs, Wm.Sr.	Hancock	Loyds	343/13	Irwin
Griggs, Wm.Sr.	Hancock	Loyds	81/27	Early
Grigsby, Duncan	Jones	Seals	353/5	Appling
Grimes, Benj.F.	Morgan	Leonard	423/1	Early
Grimes, Cath.J.(Wid)	Chatham		465/5	Irwin
Grimes, H.G.(Orps)	Hancock	Scotts	202/4	Irwin
Grimes, Herbert	Clarke	Merewether	225/4	Appling
Grimes, Jermiah(Orp)	Bulloch	Edwards	109/8	Hall
Grimes, Jesse	Greene	141st	116/11	Habersham
Grimes, Mary	Greene	144th	264/3	Irwin
Grimes, Morriss	Jefferson	Abbotts	292/5	Appling
Grimes, Nathan	Twiggs	R.Belcher	50/7	Early
Grimes, Thos.W.	Greene	143rd	240/6	Early
Grimes, William	Jefferson	Lamps	114/19	Early
Grimon, John	Chatham		226/9	Early
Grimsley, Richards	Early		101/4	Habersham
Grimsley, Zachariah	Lincoln	Thompson	207/13	Early
Griner, Andrew	Effingham		33/10	Early
Griner, Emanuel	Bulloch	Everetts	63/12	Hall
Griner, Emanuel	Bulloch	Everitts	91/9	Irwin
Griner, James	Bulloch	Everitts	275/8	Irwin
Griner, James	Bulloch	Everitts	72/3	Appling
Griner, John	Scriven	9th Bt.	475/11	Irwin
Griner, Jonathan	Bulloch	Edwards	276/6	Appling
Griner, Samuel	Scriven	9th	26/6	Irwin
Griner, William	Scriven	Lovetts	363/6	Irwin
Grineway, Abert(Orp)	Burke	Dy's	88/8	Early
Grineway, James	Burke	Dys	103/9	Appling
Grineway, John(Orp)	Burke	Dy's	88/8	Early
Grineway, William	Burke	Dy's	93/5	Irwin
Grinnage, Joshua	Lincoln	Jeters	129/16	Irwin
Grinnage, Joshua	Lincoln	Jeters	475/8	Irwin
Grinor, Andrew	Effingham		351/10	Irwin
Grinstead, Wm.	Pulaski	Johnston	128/7	Appling
Grisam, George M.	Gwinnett	Hamilton	361/18	Early
Grizzard, Jos.	Warren	154th	89/15	Irwin
Groce, Larkin(Orps)	Lincoln	Stokes	381/9	Irwin
Groce, Shepherd	Lincoln	Thompson	305/14	Early
Grooms, Wiley	Washington	Peabody	2/11	Hall
Grooms, Wright	Jones	Samuels	239/3	Early
Groover, John	Franklin	Attaways	63/5	Irwin
Groover, Joshua	Bulloch	Knights	434/10	Irwin
Gross, Blewford	Jasper	Easts	270/7	Early
Gross, Crecia(Orp)	Bryan	19th	20/3	Walton
Gross, Ellison	Jasper	Easts	103/7	Early
Gross, Lucia(Orp)	Bryan	19th	20/3	Walton
Gross, Mund	Jefferson	Bothwells	128/1	Irwin
Gross, Sarah Ann(Orp)	Bryan	19th	20/3	Walton
Grouver, Elias	Effingham		21/11	Habersham
Grovenstein, Henry J.	Chatham		488/2	Appling
Grover, Charles	Bulloch	Knights	118/15	Early
Grover, Charles	Bulloch	Knights	296/1	Appling
Grover, David	Bulloch	Knights	412/6	Irwin
Grover, Reuben	Clarke	Parrs	22/5	Rabun
Grover, Solomon	Bulloch	Knights	140/3	Walton
Grover, William	Bulloch	Knights	253/20	Early
Grover, William	Bulloch	Knights	293/6	Irwin
Groves, Robert	Madison	Williford	17/9	Irwin
Groves, Samuel	Madison	Orrs	39/3	Irwin
Groves, Stephen	Madison	Williford	179/26	Early
Growett, Joseph	Jasper	Clays	149/7	Gwinnett
Grubbs, Hezekiah	Columbia	Walkers	92/16	Irwin
Grubbs, John	Burke	71st	122/1	Habersham
Grubbs, John	Burke	71st	126/6	Appling
Grumble, William	Jones	Kings	364/11	Irwin
Grumbles, John S.	Richmond	Laceys	111/6	Irwin
Guallat, John	Lincoln	Graves	215/3	Walton

NAME	COUNTY	MIL.DIST	LOT/SECT	DREW LAN?
Guerr, Mercy(Wid)	Twiggs	Browns	321/9	Early
Guerry, John Jr.(Orps)	Twiggs	Browns	214/18	Early
Guerry, John Sr.(RS)	Twiggs	Browns	121/7	Appling
Guerry, John Sr.(RS)	Twiggs	Browns	64/10	Hall
Guerry, Peter V.	Twiggs	Browns	110/12	Early
Guerry, Theodore	Baldwin	Irwins	31/2	Early
Guess, Wm.Sr.	Appling	3rd	405/8	Early
Guest, Adam	Columbia	Watsons	242/12	Early
Guest, Colbert	Franklin	Akins	360/18	Early
Guest, Colbert	Franklin	Akins	96/9	Early
Guest, John	Franklin	Morris	485/4	Appling
Gugel, David	Effingham		519/13	Irwin
Gugel, John C.	Chatham		136/20	Early
Guger, Abraham	Bryan	19th	45/3	Irwin
Gugle, David	Effingham		412/1	Appling
Gugle, John M.	Chatham		53/6	Habersham
Guice, Benajah	Lincoln	Jones	113/19	Early
Guice, Joel	Lincoln	Tatoms	134/6	Appling
Guice, Joel	Lincoln	Tatoms	244/4	Walton
Guice, John	Lincoln	Jones	478/8	Irwin
Guice, Peter	Lincoln	Jones	99/11	Irwin
Guice, Samuel	Lincoln	Parks	388/1	Appling
Guice, William	Lincoln	Jones	259/7	Early
Guilder, John	Montgomery	Nobles	458/11	Irwin
Guimarin, John	Richmond	122	42/7	Early
Guimarne, John	Richmond	122	84/5	Appling
Guinn, Chesley	Jasper	Clays	404/12	Early
Gukey, James	McIntosh	Hamilton	250/9	Appling
Gullat, John	Lincoln	Graves	117/7	Early
Gullatt, Chas.	Lincoln	Jones	167/7	Early
Gullatt, Peter Jr.	Lincoln	Jones	428/2	Appling
Gullatt, Peter Sr.	Lincoln	Jones	115/7	Appling
Gullatt, Peter Sr.	Lincoln	Jones	177/12	Irwin
Gully, John	Elbert	Gains	95/11	Early
Gully, Richd.(RS)	Elbert	Gaines	294/13	Irwin
Gully, Thomas	Elbert	Gains	248/4	Irwin
Gully, Valentine	Elbert	Gaines	210/3	Appling
Gully, William	Elbert	Gains	168/28	Early
Gun, Thomas	Burke	Thomas	98/3	Early
Gunn, Ann(Wid)	Wilkes	Bryants	76/13	Habersham
Gunn, Daniel Jr.	Jones	Griffith	102/10	Irwin
Gunn, James	Jones	Chappels	149/6	Irwin
Gunn, Jesse T.	Morgan	Loyds	28/16	Early
Gunn, John	Hancock	Herberts	182/7	Irwin
Gunn, Moses	Jones	Chapels	28/7	Gwinnett
Gunn, Nelson	Warren	Rodgers	1/20	Early
Gunn, Nelson	Warren	Rodgers	269/7	Appling
Gunn, Nicholas P.	Wilkes	Bryants	445/12	Irwin
Gunn, Radford	Warren	Rodgers	16/21	Early
Gunn, Richard	Warren	Rogers	292/3	Appling
Gunn, Thomas	Jones	Seals	50/1	Early
Gunn, William	Warren	Rogers	205/5	Early
Gunn, William	Wilkinson	Howards	194/12	Habersham
Gunn, Wm.	Warren	Rogers	187/4	Irwin
Gunnel, Daniel(Orps)	Wilkes	Josseys	57/10	Hall
Gunnells, John	Oglethorpe	Bridges	508/2	Appling
Gunnells, Joseph	Jasper	Kennedys	133/11	Habersham
Gunnels, Willis	Jones	Seals	317/3	Early
Gunter, Allen	Jackson	Dicksons	364/6	Early
Gunter, Charles	Jackson	Dicksons	182/5	Irwin
Gunter, Charles	Jackson	Dicksons	38/11	Hall
Gunter, James	Elbert	P.Christian	21/21	Early
Gunter, Jesse	Elbert	Olivers	256/8	Appling
Guthrie, Abner	Warren	152	42/5	Gwinnett
Guthrie, Abner	Warren	152nd	150/8	Irwin
Guthrie, Jane(Wid)	Warren	152	225/18	Early
Guttery, John	Hall		372/2	Appling

NAME	COUNTY	MIL.DIST	LOT/SECT	DREW LAND
Guttery, John	Hall		498/12	Irwin
Guttory, Beverly(Orps)	Oglethorpe	Lees	33/6	Habersham
Guttory, Sarah	Oglethorpe	Lees	59/19	Early
Guy, Hillery	Columbia	Shaws	8/5	Rabun
Guy, James Jr.	Columbia	Ob.Morris	6/3	Habersham
Guy, Joel	Burke	71st	225/7	Appling
Guy, John Jr.	Columbia	Ob.Morris	72/6	Early
Guy, John Sr.	Columbia	Ob.Morris	78/17	Early
Guy, Samuel	Columbia	Ob.Morris	46/1	Rabun
Guyn, Humphrey K.	Jackson	Hamiltons	309/7	Gwinnett
Guyton, John	Laurens	Harris	236/3	Early
Guyton, Joseph	Laurens	Ross	21/1	Walton
Guyton, Joseph	Laurens	Ross	389/7	Gwinnett
Guzzlo, Clement	Warren	Blounts	366/21	Early
Habbord, John	Washington	Daniels	160/12	Early
Habersham, Joseph C.	Chatham		151/6	Early
Habersham, Rich.W.	Chatham		79/18	Early
Habersham, Robert	Chatham		74/17	Early
Hackett, Robert	Franklin	Davis	57/2	Early
Hackey, James T.	Wilkes	Ogletrees	65/5	Appling
Hackle, Christinah(Wid)	Putnam	Robinson	3/3	Habersham
Hackney, Joseph P.	Wilkes	Ogletrees	11/3	Irwin
Hackney, Nathan	Morgan	Jordans	372/9	Irwin
Hackney, Robert	Greene	Jones	177/11	Early
Hackney, Stephen	Morgan	Hackneys	235/4	Irwin
Hadaway, Rebecca(Wid)	Jones	Chappels	181/6	Gwinnett
Haddaway, Amos	Wilkes	Bryants	92/28	Early
Haddaway, Wilson(Orps)	Wilkes	Bryants	5/7	Irwin
Hadden, Thomas	Jefferson	Bothwells	426/9	Irwin
Hadden, Wm.Sr.	Jefferson	Abbotts	49/1	Habersham
Hadduck, William	Pulaski	Johnsons	475/7	Appling
Hadduck, William	Pulaski	Johnstons	208/8	Early
Haden, Daniel B.	Habersham	Byrds	306/17	Early
Haden, George	Jackson	Rogers	261/1	Appling
Hadley, Elizabeth	Burke	McNorrills	85/7	Early
Hadley, John Jr.	Burke	McNorrills	367/15	Early
Hadley, Samuel H.	Montgomery	Alstons	81/7	Appling
Hadley, Simon Sr.	Montgomery	Altons	248/17	Early
Hadley, William(Orps)	Burke	McNorrills	416/5	Appling
Hadway, Lavina(Wid)	Putnam	J.Kindrick	516/5	Gwinnett
Hagan, Charles	Clarke	Tredwells	139/15	Irwin
Hagan, Colsen	Appling	2	209/7	Irwin
Hagan, David	Appling	2nd	374/10	Irwin
Hagan, Edward	Clarke	Tredwells	203/14	Early
Hagan, James(Orps)	Clarke	Mitchells	76/4	Early
Hagan, James	Morgan	Walkers	116/13	Early
Hagan, John	Appling	2nd	252/5	Appling
Hagans, Peter(Orps)	Appling	2nd	117/8	Irwin
Hagin, James	Morgan	Walkers	11/2	Habersham
Hagin, Jesse	Bulloch	Everitts	349/28	Early
Hagin, John	Camden	Balay's	133/3	Appling
Hagin, Joseph	Bulloch	Everits	208/8	Appling
Hagins, John	Emanuel	59th	56/2	Appling
Haigwood, Benj.Jr.	Clarke	Stuarts	405/11	Irwin
Haigwood, Benj.Sr.	Clarke	Stuarts	126/4	Habersham
Hail, Andrew	Morgan	Hackneys	117/15	Early
Hail, John	Clarke	Oates	24/16	Irwin
Hail, Jonas	Madison	Adairs	94/5	Irwin
Hail, Silas	Clarke	Mitchells	281/10	Early
Hail, Stinson	Morgan	Hackneys	121/2	Habersham
Haile, Silas	Morgan	Farrars	434/5	Appling
Haines, John Jr.	Morgan	Rameys	175/3	Appling
Haines, Walter G.	Elbert	Gaines	360/17	Early
Hainey, James	Richmond	Palmers	316/27	Early
Hair, Edmund	Laurens	Griffins	121/4	Irwin
Hairbuck, James	Warren	153	207/7	Early
Hairburk, Eliz.(Orps)	Warren	153rd	349/4	Early

NAME	COUNTY	MIL.DIST	LOT/SECT	DREW LAN
Haistiness, John	Greene	141st	32/12	Habersha
Hale, Hosea	Clarke	Otis	398/4	Early
Hale, James(RS)	Morgan	Campbells	273/2	Early
Hale, James	Clarke	Parrs	101/6	Gwinnett
Hale, Jesse	Greene	Greers	51/3	Early
Hale, John	Morgan	Hackneys	146/14	Early
Hale, John	Putnam	Buckners	433/1	Appling
Hale, Lewis	Jefferson	Matthews	488/10	Irwin
Hale, Nathaniel	Putnam	Stampers	225/1	Walton
Hale, Nathaniel	Putnam	Stampers	291/4	Irwin
Hale, Tharpe	Burke	Lewis	479/2	Appling
Hale, William G.	Columbia	Ob.Morris	160/8	Hall
Hales, Wiley	Clarke	Appling	170/8	Appling
Haley, James	Elbert	Gaines	232/13	Irwin
Haley, John	Elbert	Gaines	237/1	Early
Haley, Ludy	Franklin	Harris	276/26	Early
Haley, Wm.	Elbert	Gaines	64/14	Irwin
Hall, Amy G.	Putnam	H.Kindricks	194/10	Irwin
Hall, Armager	Wilkinson	Lees	38/12	Hall
Hall, Armagor	Wilkinson	Lees	114/4	Habersha
Hall, Asa	Wilkes	Gordons	110/6	Appling
Hall, Benjamin	Richmond	398th	242/14	Early
Hall, Blake	Elbert	Penns	173/2	Habersha
Hall, Daniel Jr.	Wilkinson	Lees	22/3	Early
Hall, Daniel Jr.	Wilkinson	Lees	99/13	Early
Hall, Daniel(s/Danl.)	Wilkinson	Lees	147/7	Irwin
Hall, Daniel	Wilkinson	Lees	141/9	Irwin
Hall, David	Camden	33rd	195/6	Appling
Hall, Demsey	Jefferson	Langston	249/3	Walton
Hall, Edwin	Burke	Torrances	498/9	Irwin
Hall, Epsey(Orp)	Richmond	Laceys	281/6	Gwinnett
Hall, Francis	Greene	143	79/2	Habersha
Hall, Hampton(Orp)	Richmond	Laceys	281/6	Gwinnett
Hall, Henry	Elbert	Childers	74/7	Irwin
Hall, Hewey(Jr)	Greene	Macon	250/15	Early
Hall, Hugh(Orps)	Greene	Macons	180/9	Appling
Hall, Hugh	Putnam	Oslins	174/21	Early
Hall, Hymbrick(Orp)	Richmond	Laceys	281/6	Gwinnett
Hall, Igantius	Montgomery	Nobles	488/5	Appling
Hall, Isaac	Wilkinson	Lees	365/4	Early
Hall, James	Burke	Torrance	20/3	Early
Hall, James	Richmond	Laceys	157/4	Irwin
Hall, James	Washington	Pools	364/13	Irwin
Hall, Jesse	Jefferson	Langston	300/3	Early
Hall, Jesse	Wilkes	Lees	72/2	Habersham
Hall, Jesse	Wilkinson	Lees	199/9	Early
Hall, John A.	Telfair	Tallies	157/5	Gwinnett
Hall, John C.	Greene	Ragins	198/6	Irwin
Hall, John	Clarke	Harriss	63/4	Walton
Hall, John	Hancock	Millers	85/23	Early
Hall, John	Oglethorpe	Murrays	19/7	Appling
Hall, John	Twiggs	Browns	19/8	Irwin
Hall, Joseph	Jefferson	Abbots	12/3	Appling
Hall, Juniper Jr.	Emanuel	57th	270/18	Early
Hall, Juniper Sr.	Emanuel	57th	322/3	Early
Hall, Leonard	Hancock	Danells	589/6	Early
Hall, Louis	Telfair	Tallies	104/1	Irwin
Hall, Mary(Wid)	Chatham		135/12	Habersham
Hall, Mary(Wid)	Chatham		75/5	Appling
Hall, Mathew(Orps)	Jackson	Dicksons	156/3	Habersham
Hall, Morgan(Orp)	Richmond	Laceys	281/6	Gwinnett
Hall, Nancy(Wid)	Wilkinson	Lees	264/10	Early
Hall, Nathaniel	Franklin	Vaughns	316/4	Appling
Hall, Nathnl.(Orps)	Bulloch	Everetts	72/4	Irwin
Hall, Philander	Chatham		204/9	Early
Hall, Philander	Chatham		208/1	Appling
Hall, Red Jr.	Jefferson	Langston	136/13	Habersham

NAME	COUNTY	MIL.DIST	LOT/SECT	DREW LAND
Hall, Robert	Elbert	Smiths	320/18	Early
Hall, Robert	Elbert	Smiths	398/8	Appling
Hall, Robert	Morgan	Loyds	328/5	Early
Hall, Samuel	Greene	Armers	66/2	Walton
Hall, Sarah	Burke	Thomas	317/11	Irwin
Hall, Seaborn	Jasper	Posts	38/1	Early
Hall, Solomon	Laurens	Harris	42/8	Early
Hall, Solomon	Laurens	Harris	5/10	Irwin
Hall, Stephen	Chatham		15/10	Irwin
Hall, Stephen	Chatham		95/16	Early
Hall, Tailiver	Elbert	Smiths	38/1	Rabun
Hall, Thomas H.	Chatham		299/4	Appling
Hall, Thomas L.	Montgomery	Nobles	102/3	Walton
Hall, Thomas(Orps)	Tattnall	Cunyers	310/16	Early
Hall, Thomas	Jefferson	Langston	11/7	Early
Hall, Thomas	Laurens	Harris	69/27	Early
Hall, Thomas	Laurens	Harriss	132/8	Early
Hall, Thomas	Oglethorpe	Murrays	50/15	Irwin
Hall, Thos.(Orp)	Richmond	Laceys	281/6	Gwinnett
Hall, William H.	Morgan	Hubbards	248/10	Irwin
Hall, William	Jefferson	Langston	9/1	Walton
Hall, William	Laurens	Harris	117/5	Early
Hall, William	Telfair	Wilsons	281/14	Early
Hall, William	Washington	Peaboddys	67/8	Appling
Hall, William	Washington	Peabody	44/4	Habersham
Hall, Wm.(Orps)	Elbert	Penns	33/6	Early
Hall, Wm.G.	Columbia	Ob.Morriss	68/3	Early
Hall, Wm.Sr.	Jefferson	Langston	55/14	Early
Hall, Wright Jr.	Hancock	Danells	377/1	Early
Hallansworth, Isaac(RS)	Twiggs	Evans	263/13	Irwin
Hallard, Wilie	Hancock	Evans	252/8	Appling
Halstead, William	Jones	Permenter	6/3	Early
Ham, Gideon	Elbert	Penns	202/16	Early
Ham, James Sr.	Elbert	Olivers	198/6	Irwin
Ham, Jesse	Liberty		84/4	Irwin
Ham, John Jr.	Jasper	Phillips	49/2	Irwin
Ham, John	Bryan	19th	79/1	Appling
Ham, Reubin	Oglethorpe	Lees	281/10	Irwin
Ham, Reubin	Oglethorpe	Lees	66/16	Early
Ham, William(Orps)	Hancock	Lucas	512/9	Irwin
Ham, William	Bryan	20th	385/18	Early
Hamans, Henry	Liberty		113/4	Irwin
Hambleton, Duncan	Washington	Jinkinsons	153/27	Early
Hambleton, William	Pulaski	Lanears	296/3	Appling
Hamblin, John	Jones	Georges	328/4	Early
Hamblin, Richard	Jones	Kings	102/7	Gwinnett
Hambric, Peter	Lincoln	Walkers	66/28	Early
Hambrick, Benjamin	Jasper	Hays	79/14	Early
Hambrick, Peter	Lincoln	Walkers	39/12	Irwin
Hambry, Henry	Jasper	Trembles	120/27	Early
Hamby, Absalom(Orps)	Gwinnett	Hamiltons	107/16	Early
Hamby, Jesse	Jackson	Winters	72/18	Early
Hamby, Jesse	Jasper	Bentleys	107/10	Habersham
Hamby, Mary	Gwinnett	Hamiltons	145/10	Irwin
Hamby, Perry	Jasper	Bentleys	392/8	Irwin
Hamby, Rachel(Wid)	Morgan	Paces	381/7	Gwinnett
Hamby, Thomas	Jasper	Bentleys	294/4	Irwin
Hamby, William(Orps)	Morgan	Paces	355/15	Early
Hames, Joshua	Jasper	McClendons	46/3	Habersham
Hames, Wm.	Hancock	Thomas	42/15	Early
Hamet, John(Orps)	Baldwin	Doziers	373/16	Early
Hamilton, Adin	Twiggs	Browns	384/1	Early
Hamilton, Amy(Wid)	Morgan	Hackneys	167/5	Early
Hamilton, Andrew Jr.	Jackson	Hamilton	285/9	Early
Hamilton, Andrew M.	Jasper	Clays	106/19	Early
Hamilton, Andrew Sr.	Jackson	Hamilton	165/11	Early
Hamilton, Andrew Sr.	Jackson	Hamilton	220/12	Habersham

137

NAME	COUNTY	MIL.DIST	LOT/SECT	DREW LAN
Hamilton, Archbd.Jr.	Jackson	Hamilton	180/11	Irwin
Hamilton, Archbd.Sr.	Jackson	Hamilton	450/7	Appling
Hamilton, Cader	Putnam	Mays	367/26	Early
Hamilton, David	Jasper	Easts	65/1	Walton
Hamilton, Duke	Hancock	Danells	82/3	Irwin
Hamilton, Everand	Hancock	Edwards	251/10	Early
Hamilton, Everard	Hancock	Edwards	93/3	Appling
Hamilton, George W.	Wilkes	Kilgores	186/6	Early
Hamilton, George	Hancock	Danells	180/7	Early
Hamilton, Irwin	Twiggs	Browns	11/13	Irwin
Hamilton, James	Chatham		261/1	Early
Hamilton, James	McIntosh	Hamilton	535/2	Appling
Hamilton, Jas.(Orps)	Elbert	P.Christian	119/13	Irwin
Hamilton, John Jr.	Putnam	Berrys	311/6	g
Hamilton, John L.	Jackson	Hamilton	138/10	Habersha
Hamilton, John(Orps)	Wilkes	Burks	264/7	Early
Hamilton, Martha(Orp)	Washington	Jinkinsons	246/6	Appling
Hamilton, Mathew T.	Jackson	Hamilton	296/12	Early
Hamilton, Moses	Morgan	Hackneys	157/6	Gwinnett
Hamilton, Moses	Morgan	Hackneys	64/13	Early
Hamilton, Peter	Clarke	Treadwells	40/12	Early
Hamilton, Peter	Clarke	Tredwells	200/3	Walton
Hamilton, Robert M.	Jackson	Hamilton	194/6	Irwin
Hamilton, Samuel	McIntosh	Hamilton	163/16	Early
Hamilton, Samuel	McIntosh	Hamilton	415/4	Appling
Hamilton, Turtius A.	Scriven	Smiths	153/10	Hall
Hamilton, Wm.	Habersham	Adairs	460/6	Appling
Hamilton, Wm.	Habersham	Adairs	49/11	Early
Hamilton, Wm.A.	Jackson	Hamilton	54/26	Early
Hamlin, Robert	Jones	Kings	269/11	Early
Hammel, Clarke	Wilkes	Davis	231/18	Early
Hammel, Clarke	Wilkes	Davis	29/10	Hall
Hammel, George	Wilkes	Davis	141/5	Early
Hammel, James Sr.	Wilkes	Davis	125/9	Appling
Hammel, James	Wilkes	Davis	251/3	Appling
Hammel, Susan	Hancock	Scotts	3/1	Appling
Hammel, Wm.S.	Hancock	Scotts	28/1	Walton
Hammer, Samuel	Oglethorpe	Goolsbys	483/6	Appling
Hammet, Wm.	Wilkes	Runnels	92/4	Appling
Hammett, James Sr.	Oglethorpe	Bowls	65/15	Irwin
Hammett, James	Jasper	Eastes	106/3	Rabun
Hammett, James	Jasper	Eastes	35/8	Irwin
Hammett, James	Jefferson	Matthews	380/1	Early
Hammett, James	Jefferson	Matthews	74/11	Hall
Hammett, John Sr.	Jefferson	Bothwells	357/6	Gwinnett
Hammock, Benj.Jr.	Morgan	Campbells	169/2	Early
Hammock, John P.	Jones	Griffiths	140/8	Appling
Hammock, John(Orps)	Jefferson	Abbotts	31/6	Habersha
Hammock, Joshua Jr.	Walton	Sentells	129/6	Early
Hammock, Lewis	Jones	Samuels	39/11	Irwin
Hammock, Simeon	Jones	Samuels	385/2	Early
Hammock, Thomas(Orps)	Wilkes	Runnels	247/8	Early
Hammock, William	Wilkes	Bryants	268/8	Appling
Hammock, William	Wilkes	Bryants	42/4	Habersha
Hammock, Wm.	Jasper	Bentleys	279/2	Early
Hammock, Wm.B.	Jones	Griffiths	281/12	Early
Hammon, John	Jackson	Winters	227/9	Early
Hammon, Mark	Jackson	Dicksons	166/18	Early
Hammon, Thomas	Morgan	Jordans	364/14	Early
Hammond, Abner	Baldwin	Irwins	160/15	Irwin
Hammond, Charles	Oglethorpe	Goolsbys	33/7	Early
Hammond, Daniel	Baldwin	Marshall	124/8	Early
Hammond, Jacob	Wilkes	Kilgores	141/13	Irwin
Hammond, Job Jr.	Franklin	Hammonds	134/2	Rabun
Hammond, Job	Elbert	White/Nully	405/6	Irwin
Hammond, John	Jackson	Winters	277/4	Appling
Hammond, Joshua	Richmond	122	232/4	Appling

NAME	COUNTY	MIL.DIST	LOT/SECT	DREW LAND
Hammond, Joshua	Richmond	122nd	12/6	Habersham
Hammond, Susannah(Wid)	Walton	Greens	39/9	Hall
Hammond, William	Jackson	Dicksons	376/6	Early
Hammonds, Ambrose	Habersham		138/3	Walton
Hammonds, Ambrose	Habersham		96/3	Habersham
Hammonds, Rolley	Oglethorpe	Myricks	440/5	Irwin
Hamock, John Sr.	Lincoln	Walkers	99/12	Early
Hamock, John	Laurens	Harris	39/1	Appling
Hamock, Thomas	Lincoln	Walkers	88/20	Early
Hamonds, James	Burke	McNorrills	231/28	Early
Hamons, Stephen	Burke	McNorrills	42/4	Appling
Hampson(Thompson), Robt.	Washington	Pools	246/8	Appling
Hampton, Andrew	Laurens	Harris	490/5	Appling
Hampton, Barthol.(Orps)	Wilkes	Brooks	275/5	Appling
Hampton, Bartholomew(Op)	Jackson	Rogers	366/8	Early
Hampton, Benj.(Orps)	Jackson	Winters	61/28	Early
Hampton, Benjamin	Walton	Greens	300/20	Early
Hampton, Edward	Putnam	Coopers	429/2	Appling
Hampton, Edward	Putnam	Coopers	458/6	Appling
Hampton, George	Putnam	Slaughters	84/5	Gwinnett
Hampton, Hirum	Madison	Adares	158/10	Habersham
Hampton, James	Jackson	Winters	209/8	Irwin
Hampton, John	Hancock	Daniels	32/9	Hall
Hampton, Joseph	Jackson	Winters	294/7	Gwinnett
Hampton, Reason	Burke	J.Wards	45/8	Early
Hampton, Simeon	Burke	J.Wards	376/1	Appling
Hampton, Thomas	Burke	J.Wards	19/4	Early
Hampton, Wade	Camden	Tillis	211/5	Appling
Hampton, Wade	Camden	Tillis	301/8	Appling
Hamrick, Reuben	Wilkes	Holidays	354/5	Appling
Hanbury, Isrel	Emanuel	57th	246/3	Irwin
Hanbury, Sally(Orp)	Burke	McNorrill	384/11	Early
Hancock, Clement Jr.	Wilkinson	Lees	244/5	Early
Hancock, Durham	Tattnall	J.Durrence	78/2	Appling
Hancock, Enoch	Jones	Harrists	222/12	Early
Hancock, Isac	Jackson	Winters	282/2	Early
Hancock, Isham	Jasper	Smiths	57/4	Walton
Hancock, James	Tattnall	Johnstons	68/1	Walton
Hancock, Joseph(RS)	Oglethorpe	Hoffs	150/9	Irwin
Hancock, Joseph(RS)	Oglethorpe	Hoffs	223/8	Appling
Hancock, Joseph	Wilkes	Brooks	65/10	Habersham
Hancock, Nancy	Wilkes	Davis	348/20	Early
Hancock, Philip	Jasper	Bentleys	392/1	Appling
Hancock, Richardson	Jackson	Winters	119/11	Hall
Hancock, Thomas	Clarke	Pentecost	461/8	Irwin
Hancock, Thomas	Clarke	Pentecosts	256/6	Appling
Hancock, William	Jackson	May's	386/26	Early
Hancock, William	Oglethorpe	Wises	284/27	Early
Hancock, Wm.	Jackson	Mays	74/2	Walton
Hancock, Wm.	Oglethorpe	Wises	331/5	Early
Hancock, Wm.Jr.	Jackson	Winters	95/12	Hall
Hancock, Wm.Sr.	Jackson	Winters	21/4	Appling
Hancock, Wm.Sr.	Jackson	Winters	62/5	Early
Hand, Christopher	Oglethorpe	Murrays	214/14	Early
Hand, Isaac	Jasper	Bentleys	412/7	Irwin
Hand, Joel W.	Scriven	Moodys	113/8	Hall
Hand, John J.	Burke	Royals	38/4	Irwin
Hand, John	Columbia	Watsons	239/3	Early
Hand, John	Columbia	Watsons	422/2	Appling
Hand, John	Jasper	Bentleys	275/3	Early
Hand, Reuben	Jasper	Bentleys	261/4	Irwin
Hand, Sherod H.	Jasper	Barnes	323/11	Early
Hand, Willis	Jasper	Barnes	133/6	Appling
Handberry, Moses	Burke	70th	39/6	Gwinnett
Handcock, Kaidor	Tattnall	Johnsons	15/14	Early
Handley, James	Washington	Brooks	281/21	Early
Handley, Jared(Orps)	Emanuel	57th	148/3	Walton

NAME	COUNTY	MIL.DIST	LOT/SECT	DREW LAND
Handley, Jarratt	Elbert	Penns	7/2	Early
Handley, Jesse(Orps)	Pulaski	Bryans	21/1	Appling
Hanes, Elijah	Morgan	Dennis	135/6	Appling
Hanes, Elijah	Morgan	Selmons	102/26	Early
Haney, William(RS)	Pulaski	Rees	161/5	Appling
Haney, William	Baldwin	Cousins	79/5	Appling
Hanks, Jos.(Orps)	Pulaski	Johnsons	226/4	Walton
Hanks, Thomas	Pulaski	Johnstons	3/1	Habersham
Hanley, Charles W.	Warren	Parhams	301/26	Early
Hannah, Jas.Sr.(RS)	Elbert	Webbs	172/27	Early
Hannah, Nancy(Wid)	Jefferson	Matthews	32/10	Early
Hannah, William	Burke	Hands	228/2	Appling
Hannah, William	Jefferson	Lamps	230/5	Gwinnett
Hanning, Christopher	Effingham		16/26	Early
Hannon, Samuel	Columbia	Olives	203/7	Early
Hanpt, Eliz.(Wid)	Chatham		497/12	Irwin
Hansard, John	Elbert	Smiths	31/2	Rabun
Hansard, Wm.	Elbert	B.Higginbotham	403/21	Early
Hansell, Wm.Y.	Richmond	122nd	25/3	Walton
Hanses, James(Orp)	Oglethorpe	Lees	323/4	Appling
Hansford, Brown	Franklin	Ashs	134/5	Appling
Hansford, George W.	Jones	Hansfords	42/6	Early
Hanshaw, Thomas	Washington	Burneys	179/14	Early
Hanson, Jesse	Morgan	Parkers	475/6	Irwin
Hanson, John W.	Morgan	Talbots	107/18	Early
Hanson, Lazarus	Franklin	Vaughans	131/14	Early
Hanson, Newton	Clarke	Starnes	99/6	Early
Hanson, Reuben	Morgan	Parkers	25/5	Early
Hanson, Samuel	Jackson	Rogers	415/28	Early
Hanson, Samuel	Walton	Echols	163/5	Appling
Hanson, Tapley	Morgan	Townsends	61/8	Appling
Hanson, Thomas(RS)	Jackson	Rogers	173/5	Appling
Hanson, Wm.(Dr)	Columbia	Pullins	234/5	Early
Hany, Shadrach	Twiggs	Tisons	28/2	Appling
Haralson, Jonathan	Greene	Harvills	294/4	Appling
Haralson, Wm.B.	Greene	Harvills	368/5	Irwin
Harason, Joseph	Wilkes	Bryants	195/8	Appling
Harbin, John	Elbert	Whites	90/8	Hall
Harbin, Wm.	Elbert	B.Higginbotham	333/6	Gwinnett
Harbin, Wm.	Elbert	B.Higginbotham	82/17	Early
Harbin, Wm.Sr.(RS)	Elbert	Whites	99/2	Early
Harbock, Michael	Richmond	398th	12/13	Early
Harbon, James	Washington	Barges	621/2	Appling
Harbour, Johny	Franklin	Harriss	242/10	Irwin
Harbour, Thomas	Franklin	Harris	128/6	Irwin
Hardaman, Thomas	Washington	Robinsons	228/13	Irwin
Hardan, James	Washington	Robertson	213/10	Habersham
Hardaway, Stith	Warren	152	154/5	Irwin
Hardee, John R.	Pulaski	Senterfeits	144/13	Habersham
Hardee, Thomas E.	Camden	33rd	177/4	Early
Hardee, Thomas Jr.	Washington	Barges	529/6	Appling
Hardegree, Hiram	Clarke	Jacks	18/1	Appling
Hardeman, John	Oglethorpe	Brittons	483/3	Appling
Hardeman, Robert V.	Jones	Samuels	240/10	Early
Harden, Edward	Chatham		225/5	Gwinnett
Harden, Erasmus	Columbia	Pullins	36/6	Gwinnett
Harden, Henry	Franklin	Powells	200/6	Early
Harden, Henry	Franklin	Powels	341/2	Early
Harden, James	Columbia	Dodsons	90/7	Gwinnett
Harden, James	Greene	142nd	1/9	Irwin
Harden, John(Orps)	Oglethorpe	Waters	327/6	Early
Harden, John	Habersham		89/11	Early
Harden, John	Putnam	Littles	33/5	Gwinnett
Harden, John	Twiggs	Hodges	13/11	Irwin
Harden, Sally	Oglethorpe	Waters	364/1	Appling
Harden, Sarah(Wid)	Franklin	R.Browns	465/6	Appling
Harden, Thomas H.	Bryan	20	2/10	Habersham

140

NAME	COUNTY	MIL.DIST	LOT/SECT	DREW LAND
Harden, Thomas H.	Bryan	20th	140/9	Hall
Harden, Thomas	Columbia	Pullins	123/9	Irwin
Harden, William	Putnam	Littles	159/5	Early
Hardie, Freeman Sr.	Franklin	Akins	133/8	Hall
Hardie, Robert	Wilkinson	Lees	228/5	Irwin
Hardie, William	Wilkinson	Wiggins	84/10	Irwin
Hardigree, Elener	Clarke	Mereweather	119/1	Habersham
Hardigree, Jonathan	Clarke	Mereweather	237/2	Appling
Hardigree, Wm.	Clarke	Mereweather	367/3	Early
Hardigree, Wm.	Clarke	Mereweather	9/11	Irwin
Hardin, Adam	Putnam	Little	272/10	Irwin
Hardin, Benj.C.	Morgan	Walkers	212/7	Irwin
Hardin, Benj.C.	Morgan	Walkers	55/2	Appling
Hardin, Isaac B.	Burke	Sullivans	152/6	Early
Hardin, James	Greene	142	175/6	Gwinnett
Hardin, Martin	Tattnall	Tharps	134/12	Irwin
Hardin, Martin	Tattnall	Tharps	142/4	Appling
Hardin, William	Oglethorpe	Davenports	378/26	Early
Hardin, William	Oglethorpe	Davenports	396/12	Irwin
Hardison, Culin	Jones	Wallers	71/12	Irwin
Hardman, Charles Sr.	Oglethorpe	Goolsbys	422/9	Irwin
Hardman, Elbert	Oglethorpe	Davenport	111/3	Irwin
Hardman, Felix	Oglethorpe	McCowens	291/2	Early
Hardman, Isaiah	Oglethorpe	Lees	136/6	Appling
Hardman, John	Oglethorpe	Burnet	79/8	Early
Hardman, Uel	Oglethorpe	Goolsbys	201/28	Early
Hardway, Answorth	Warren	Neals	251/12	Irwin
Hardway, John	Jones	Chappell	201/12	Habersham
Hardwick, David G.	Morgan	McClendon	74/2	Habersham
Hardwick, Geo.F.	Jackson	Rogers	356/13	Early
Hardwick, James	Morgan	McClendon	182/4	Appling
Hardwick, Jesse	Burke	J.Wards	67/11	Early
Hardwick, John	Jackson	Rogers	4/4	Irwin
Hardy, Aquilla	Jasper	Bentleys	210/11	Early
Hardy, Edward	Lincoln	Tatoms	269/9	Early
Hardy, Freeman Jr.	Franklin	Akins	61/8	Irwin
Hardy, Henry	Franklin	P.Browns	422/5	Appling
Hardy, Henry	Lincoln	Park'S	34/1	Rabun
Hardy, John	Washington	Peabodys	333/7	Gwinnett
Hardy, Lewis	Jackson	Winters	47/7	Gwinnett
Hardy, Preston	Jackson	Winters	129/8	Early
Hardy, R.(Orps)	Bulloch	Everetts	74/3	Early
Hardy, Sutton	Lincoln	Parks	128/12	Early
Hardy, Theophilus	Washington	Mannings	302/20	Early
Hardy, Theophilus	Washington	Mannings	98/2	Rabun
Hardy, Thomas(Orp)	Bulloch	Everetts	45/3	Habersham
Hardy, Thomas	Washington	Peaboddys	163/3	Irwin
Hardy, Thomas	Washington	Peabodys	395/9	Early
Hardy, William W.	Lincoln	Parks	374/28	Early
Hardy, William	Washington	Peabodys	272/5	Irwin
Hardy, Wm.B.	Jasper	Phillips	374/4	Early
Haregroves, William	Washington	Floyds	500/7	Appling
Harell, Isaac	Pulaski	Laners	260/17	Early
Harford, Henry	McIntosh	Hamilton	508/6	Appling
Hargraves, George	Richmond	122	306/18	Early
Hargraves, John S.	Richmond	398th	193/18	Early
Hargreaves, Joseph	Liberty		211/11	Early
Hargrove, Harmon B.	Laurens	Harriss	67/2	Habersham
Hargrove, Jacob	Burke	Hands	165/11	Irwin
Hargrove, James	Franklin	Ashs	103/15	Early
Hargrove, John(Orps)	Jefferson	Fountains	186/10	Habersham
Hargrove, Kinchen W.	Twiggs	Hodges	285/10	Irwin
Hargrove, Pleasant W.	Jefferson	Abbots	155/8	Early
Hargrove, Pleasant W.	Jefferson	Abbotts	41/12	Early
Hargrove, Wm.(Orps)	Hancock	Scotts	302/2	Appling
Hargroves, Hardy	Wilkinson	Childs	201/12	Early
Hargroves, Henry	Emanuel	57th	181/13	Early

141

NAME	COUNTY	MIL.DIST	LOT/SECT	DREW LAND
Hargroves, Loderick	Emanuel	56th	509/2	Appling
Hariston, William	Wilkinson	Howards	300/8	Early
Harkens, Wm.	Walton	Echols	442/13	Irwin
Harkins, Susannah(Orp)	Richmond	Burtons	328/10	Early
Harkins, William	Jones	Griffiths	339/4	Walton
Harkins, Wm.	Jones	Griffith	276/13	Irwin
Harkness, James	Morgan	Hackneys	50/4	Habersham
Harkness, Joseph	Jones	Kings	402/21	Early
Harkness, Mary	Jones	Kings	400/12	Irwin
Harlam, Valentine	Jackson	Dicksons	146/20	Early
Harley, James	Washington	Jinkins	55/11	Habersham
Harlow, Southworth	Burke	Bello	140/20	Early
Harmon, Bartholomew	Jones	Griffiths	68/21	Early
Harmon, John	Franklin	Flannagans	358/4	Appling
Harmon, John	Franklin	Flannagans	4/13	Early
Harnesburger, Step.(Heir)	Lincoln	Jones	25/1	Walton
Harop, Arthur	Putnam	H.Kendricks	240/4	Early
Harop, Arthur	Putnam	H.Kendricks	7/8	Appling
Harper, Allen	Morgan	Campbells	274/27	Early
Harper, Allen	Morgan	Campbells	52/7	Appling
Harper, Benjamin	Jefferson	Flemings	76/18	Early
Harper, Edward	Jasper	Hays	33/12	Irwin
Harper, Edward	Jasper	Hays	5/12	Hall
Harper, Edward	Jasper	Hays	8/7	Early
Harper, Edward	Warren	Griers	273/11	Irwin
Harper, Edward	Warren	Griers	74/4	Habersham
Harper, Eliz.(Wid)	McIntosh	Eigles	388/9	Early
Harper, Frederick	Liberty		465/12	Irwin
Harper, Frederick	Liberty		81/11	Hall
Harper, George(Orps)	Clarke	Harpers	389/3	Early
Harper, George	Habersham		204/8	Appling
Harper, George	Habersham		294/8	Early
Harper, George	Jones	Chappell	521/5	Irwin
Harper, Holcomb G.	Greene	143rd	174/15	Irwin
Harper, James	Wayne	Johnston	63/1	Walton
Harper, James	Wilkes	Davis	155/8	Appling
Harper, John J.	Wilkes	Bryants	292/2	Early
Harper, John W.	Clarke	Stuarts	157/18	Early
Harper, John(Orps)	Jones	Permenters	206/7	Gwinnett
Harper, John	McIntosh	Eigles	185/9	Irwin
Harper, Joseah B.	Morgan	Wrights	99/15	Irwin
Harper, Joseph	Clarke	Stuarts	269/14	Early
Harper, Joseph	Jones	Permenters	40/9	Hall
Harper, Leonard	McIntosh	Eigles	285/21	Early
Harper, Nathaniel	Wilkinson	Kettles	107/6	Irwin
Harper, Prestley	Hancock	Edwards	97/4	Early
Harper, Robert	Habersham		267/12	Irwin
Harper, Sabry	McIntosh	Goulds	199/17	Early
Harper, Sherod	Clarke	Harpers	232/5	Appling
Harper, Sherroll	Clarke	Harpers	178/8	Irwin
Harper, Thos.(Orps)	Jackson	Rogers	120/14	Irwin
Harper, WIlkins	Jasper	McClendons	63/18	Early
Harper, William	Habersham		399/13	Early
Harper, William	Hancock	Herberts	40/9	Appling
Harper, William	Jefferson	Flemmings	222/15	Early
Harper, William	Jones	Griffith	121/2	Appling
Harper, William	Jones	Griffiths	156/1	Early
Harper, William	Lincoln	Thompsons	54/4	Habersham
Harper, William	Wilkes	Davis	146/3	Early
Harper, Wm.A.(Orps)	Franklin	Ashs	79/2	Appling
Harper, Wm.P.	Hancock	Edwards	313/9	Early
Harper, Wm.Sr.(RS)	Hancock	Edwards	212/27	Early
Harper, Wm.T.	Putnam	Bustins	349/3	Appling
Harper, Wyatt	Hancock	Edwards	506/2	Appling
Harper, Wyatt	Putnam	Oslins	113/9	Appling
Harrald, Abner	Camden	32nd	290/7	Early
Harrds, Thomas	Wilkes	Ogletrees	372/8	Irwin

NAME	COUNTY	MIL.DIST	LOT/SECT	DREW LAND
Harrel, David	Warren	Ivys	248/20	Early
Harrel, Elisha	Emanuel	57th	342/5	Appling
Harrel, Jonathan	Putnam	Slaughters	423/8	Irwin
Harrel, Reuben	Wilkinson	Brooks	28/1	Appling
Harrel, Reuben	Wilkinson	Brooks	87/12	Irwin
Harrel, William	Telfair	Talles	7/12	Habersham
Harrell, Alexander	Warren	Iveys	198/27	Early
Harrell, Elijah	Pulaski	Lanears	153/6	Early
Harrell, Esther(Wid)	Pulaski	Lanears	191/3	Walton
Harrell, Jacob	Pulaski	Lanears	165/20	Early
Harrell, Jacob	Pulaski	Laniers	21/12	Irwin
Harrell, Jesse	Pulaski	Laniers	84/12	Irwin
Harrell, John	Bulloch	Jones	208/10	Early
Harrell, John	Liberty		97/12	Hall
Harrell, John	Pulaski	Lanears	160/3	Walton
Harrell, John	Pulaski	Senterfeits	489/5	Appling
Harrell, Joseph(Orps)	Wilkinson	Brooks	113/9	Early
Harrell, Joseph	Jasper	Phillips	48/23	Early
Harrell, Neil	Hancock	Mims	117/9	Irwin
Harrell, Polley	Jasper	Phillips	3/2	Walton
Harrell, Samuel M.	Jasper	Bentleys	122/2	Appling
Harrell, Samuel M.	Jasper	Bentleys	237/6	Gwinnett
Harrell, Wm.	Pulaski	Senterfeits	124/7	Appling
Harrell, Zachariah	Warren	Blounts	566/2	Appling
Harrelson, Reuben	Laurens	S.Smiths	222/3	Early
Harrill, Absalom	Burke	McNorrill	64/11	Habersham
Harrill, Cador	Warren	154th	335/7	Gwinnett
Harrill, Charles	Warren	154th	427/6	Irwin
Harrills, Wm.(Orp)	McIntosh	Hamilton	327/12	Early
Harrington, Thos.(Orps)	Jackson	Hamilton	357/9	Appling
Harrington, Thos.	Liberty		145/3	Appling
Harris, Augustin	Madison	Williford	275/27	Early
Harris, Benj.	Jones	Permenters	440/6	Appling
Harris, Benjamin(RS)	Jones	Permenters	154/21	Early
Harris, Benjamin	Wilkes	McLendons	77/13	Habersham
Harris, Braddock	Franklin	Haynes	85/2	Habersham
Harris, Caleb W.	Washington	Brooks	127/10	Hall
Harris, Charity H.(Wid)	Morgan	Farrars	180/5	Appling
Harris, Charles	Chatham		99/1	Irwin
Harris, David(Orps)	Twiggs	Hughs	294/4	Walton
Harris, Drury	Hancock	Thomas	116/16	Early
Harris, Edward	Jackson	Hamilton	234/13	Early
Harris, Ehud	Jones	Buckhalter	263/5	Early
Harris, Eli	Putnam	H.Kindricks	112/11	Early
Harris, Eliz.(Orp)	McIntosh	Goulds	11/12	Hall
Harris, Ezekiel	Baldwin	Haws	364/20	Early
Harris, Ezekiel	Baldwin	Haws	408/4	Appling
Harris, Ezekiel	Jones	Jeffersons	273/8	Irwin
Harris, Geo.Jr.	Morgan	Parkers	257/4	Irwin
Harris, George	Walton	Wests	168/14	Early
Harris, Hampton	Bryan	19	60/5	Gwinnett
Harris, Hampton	Bryan	19th	249/6	Early
Harris, Harry(Orps)	Putnam	Robertson	103/13	Irwin
Harris, Henry(Orps)	Putnam	Robertson	19/7	Irwin
Harris, Henry	Glynn		75/18	Early
Harris, Henry	Hancock	Danells	193/16	Irwin
Harris, James S.	Chatham		201/18	Early
Harris, James	Jones	Phillips	22/2	Habersham
Harris, James	Lincoln	Tatoms	409/10	Irwin
Harris, James	McIntosh	Gowens	44/12	Early
Harris, James	Washington	Pools	29/13	Habersham
Harris, Jeptha V.	Elbert	G.Higginbotham	156/3	Irwin
Harris, Jeptha V.	Elbert	G.Higginbotham	179/9	Early
Harris, Jesse L.	Wilkinson	Bowings	404/5	Appling
Harris, Jesse	Jackson	Winters	54/1	Habersham
Harris, Jinney	Wilkes	McClendons	259/10	Irwin
Harris, John Sr.	Glynn		153/13	Habersham

143

NAME	COUNTY	MIL.DIST	LOT/SECT	DREW LAI
Harris, John(Orp)	Wilkes	McLendons	284/9	Early
Harris, John	Elbert	Gaines	220/3	Early
Harris, John	Morgan	Hackneys	140/12	Irwin
Harris, John	Morgan	Hackneys	219/2	Appling
Harris, John	Wilkes	Bates	370/10	Irwin
Harris, Leroy G.	Laurens	Harris	295/13	Early
Harris, Lewis	Richmond	Winters	288/11	Irwin
Harris, Littleberry	Hancock	Lucas	287/14	Early
Harris, Mary Ann(Orp)	Elbert	Smiths	177/7	Appling
Harris, Mary Ann	Burke	Spiveys	135/3	Walton
Harris, Mary M.	McIntosh	Goulds	118/2	Irwin
Harris, Micajah	Morgan	Farrars	40/2	Habershä
Harris, Nathan	Oglethorpe	Wises	165/16	Early
Harris, Nathan	Oglethorpe	Wises	31/5	Irwin
Harris, Nelson	Hancock	Thomas	175/26	Early
Harris, Overton	Oglethorpe	Wises	32/12	Hall
Harris, Ozbun	Elbert	Childers	378/11	Irwin
Harris, Payton(Orps)	Lincoln	Tatoms	77/7	Appling
Harris, Robert	Wilkes	Baits	284/4	Early
Harris, Robert	Wilkes	Bates	200/1	Early
Harris, Samuel	Clarke	Applings	522/5	Irwin
Harris, Sarah(Wid)	Franklin	Powells	199/10	Irwin
Harris, Seaborn	Hancock	Thomas	167/26	Early
Harris, Sinsinattis	Columbia	Gartrells	31/1	Early
Harris, Sinsinattus	Columbia	Gartrell	482/8	Irwin
Harris, Spencer	Franklin	Turks	385/6	Early
Harris, Susan(Orp)	McIntosh	Goulds	11/12	Hall
Harris, Thomas W.	Pulaski	Rees	379/17	Early
Harris, Thomas	Jasper	Eastes	130/26	Early
Harris, Thomas	Jasper	Eastes	364/10	Early
Harris, Thomas	Putnam	Oslins	330/6	Early
Harris, Thomas	Putnam	Oslins	42/10	Hall
Harris, Thomas	Warren	Griers	178/6	Appling
Harris, Thomas	Wilkinson	Kettles	514/13	Irwin
Harris, Thompson	Gwinnett	Hamiltons	8/2	Early
Harris, Thos.H.	Chatham		351/7	Early
Harris, William Sr.	Morgan	Townsends	45/2	Walton
Harris, William	Effingham		247/16	Early
Harris, William	Greene	141st	78/15	Irwin
Harris, William	Jones	Hansford	410/2	Appling
Harris, William	Morgan	Leonards	230/3	Early
Harris, William	Morgan	Leonards	237/20	Early
Harris, Wilmut E.	Greene	Ragans	244/6	Early
Harris, Wm.S.	Warren	153	3/22	Early
Harris, Wyllie	Warren	Blounts	229/3	Irwin
Harrison, James	Jasper	Hays	323/1	Early
Harrison, Benj.	Franklin	P.Browns	108/14	Irwin
Harrison, Berrymos S.	Warren	Parhams	219/8	Irwin
Harrison, Caty.B.D.(Wid)	Greene	Harvills	266/3	Appling
Harrison, David(Orps)	Baldwin	Irwins	344/14	Early
Harrison, Duke(Orps)	Greene	143rd	433/8	Irwin
Harrison, James	Columbia	J.Morris	244/3	Irwin
Harrison, Jeremiah	Jasper	Hays	116/11	Irwin
Harrison, Jeremiah	Jasper	Hays	271/5	Irwin
Harrison, John	Franklin	P.Browns	267/3	Irwin
Harrison, John	Putnam	Ectors	288/9	Early
Harrison, John	Scriven		9/3	Walton
Harrison, Joseph	Putnam	Evans	26/6	Appling
Harrison, Joseph	Putnam	Evans	312/13	Early
Harrison, Joseph	Putnam	Stampers	48/11	Early
Harrison, Joseph	Putnam	Stampers	87/3	Early
Harrison, Joseph	Washington	Burneys	119/3	Rabun
Harrison, Joseph	Wilkes	Bryants	176/12	Irwin
Harrison, Moses	Wilkinson	Bowings	149/3	Irwin
Harrison, Nathaniel	Putnam	Bustins	471/6	Irwin
Harrison, Robert	Franklin	P.Browns	333/26	Early
Harrison, Robert	Oglethorpe	Brittons	381/13	Irwin

NAME	COUNTY	MIL.DIST	LOT/SECT	DREW LAND
Harrison, Seaborn	Warren	152	299/28	Early
Harrison, Sterling E.	Jones	Seals	91/16	Irwin
Harrison, Terrill C.	Columbia	J.Morris	202/7	Appling
Harrison, Thos.	Franklin	P.Browns	194/7	Early
Harrison, Vincent Russ	Wilkes	Gordons	285/1	Appling
Harrison, William	McIntosh	Goulds	195/12	Habersham
Harrison, William	Putnam	Oslins	230/17	Early
Harrison, Wm.	Columbia	Ob.Morris	347/3	Early
Harrison, Wm.	Jones	Chappels	201/27	Early
Harrison, Wm.	Jones	Chappels	276/7	Gwinnett
Harrison, Wm.G.	Greene	141	424/7	Irwin
Harriss, (Orps)	Franklin	Powels	109/1	Appling
Harriss, Allen(minor)	Wilkes	Hollidays	345/5	Early
Harriss, Benj.H.Jr.	Richmond	Winters	216/7	Appling
Harriss, Braddock	Franklin	Haines	146/2	Irwin
Harriss, Charles W.	Clarke	Starnes	463/7	Irwin
Harriss, Edmund S.	Putnam	Littles	471/9	Irwin
Harriss, Eliz.	Hancock	Justices	480/9	Irwin
Harriss, Gabriel	Putnam	H.Kindricks	219/4	Appling
Harriss, George Jr.	Morgan	Parker	172/7	Gwinnett
Harriss, George	Jasper	Trimbles	2/21	Early
Harriss, Gillam	Greene	Ragins	27/14	Early
Harriss, Graves	Morgan	Townsend	241/5	Appling
Harriss, Hendley	Clarke	Starnes	296/10	Irwin
Harriss, Hendley	Clarke	Starnes	338/1	Appling
Harriss, Henry	Clarke	Harriss	76/7	Irwin
Harriss, Henry	Wilkes	Runnels	81/8	Irwin
Harriss, Heziah	Jackson	Hamilton	54/12	Habersham
Harriss, Hiram C.	Gwinnett	Hamiltons	389/5	Appling
Harriss, Hiram	Morgan	Farrars	9/3	Rabun
Harriss, James W.	Clarke	Otis	400/4	Early
Harriss, Jesse	Wilkinson	Bowlings	343/7	Early
Harriss, John G.	Putnam	Little	291/5	Appling
Harriss, John Jr.	Morgan	Farrars	76/15	Early
Harriss, John	Camden	33rd	57/20	Early
Harriss, John	Columbia	Shaws	166/9	Early
Harriss, John	Greene	Armers	132/6	Appling
Harriss, Jordan	Greene	Fosters	103/14	Early
Harriss, Joseph	Morgan	Farrars	544/2	Appling
Harriss, Leroy G.	Laurens	Harriss	310/1	Early
Harriss, Moses	Jones	Hansfords	61/3	Irwin
Harriss, Nancy	Lincoln	Tatoms	266/5	Gwinnett
Harriss, Nathaniel	Wilkes	Ogletrees	294/5	Gwinnett
Harriss, Obadiah	Madison	Williford	192/12	Irwin
Harriss, Obediah	Columbia	Gartrills	437/3	Appling
Harriss, Peterson	Hancock	Danells	48/3	Rabun
Harriss, Raymond	Liberty		78/16	Irwin
Harriss, Reddin H.	Jones	Rossers	369/4	Appling
Harriss, Richard	Jones	Wallers	158/15	Irwin
Harriss, Roderick	Greene	Wheels	101/3	Habersham
Harriss, Saml.C.(Orps)	Jones	Chappels	399/15	Early
Harriss, Saml.H.	Hancock	Loyds	30/1	Appling
Harriss, Saml.H.	Hancock	Loyds	93/20	Early
Harriss, Samuel	Clarke	Appling	56/8	Appling
Harriss, Samuel	Morgan	Wrights	163/5	Early
Harriss, Sarah(Wid)	Franklin	Powels	109/1	Appling
Harriss, Sebastian	Jones	Phillips	249/13	Early
Harriss, Stephen W.	Putnam	Oslins	16/10	Early
Harriss, Thomas	Elbert	Olivers	95/3	Early
Harriss, West(Orps)	Liberty		8/6	Appling
Harriss, William M.	Clarke	Garlington	183/11	Early
Harriss, Wm.(Orps)	Clarke	Tredwells	369/7	Early
Harriss, Wm.	Morgan	Beasley	289/18	Early
Harriss, Wylea J.	Clarke	Mitchell	198/2	Appling
Harrist, Archbd.M.	Jones	Harrist	278/9	Early
Harroll, John C.	McIntosh	Hamilton	294/16	Early
Harrolson, Reuben	Laurens	S.Smiths	86/17	Early

NAME	COUNTY	MIL.DIST	LOT/SECT	DREW LAND
Harrup, Wm.	Columbia	Olives	56/19	Early
Harry, Wm.	Jasper	Philips	522/13	Irwin
Harsey, John	Jones	Shropshiers	177/2	Habershan
Harsey, John	Jones	Shropshiers	380/26	Early
Hart, Barney	Washington	Jinkinsons	289/5	Early
Hart, Eli	Hancock	Harts	17/20	Early
Hart, Eliza	Chatham		189/5	Early
Hart, James	Hancock	Canes	354/28	Early
Hart, John(Orps)	Liberty		340/7	Gwinnett
Hart, John	Hancock	Canes	113/10	Early
Hart, John	Jones	Rossers	96/13	Irwin
Hart, Jonathan	Washington	Jenkinson	459/3	Appling
Hart, Marshall	Emanuel	49	461/13	Irwin
Hart, Robert(Orps)	Laurens	Ross	503/7	Appling
Hart, Samuel(Orps)	Hancock	Canes	207/14	Early
Hart, Samuel	Warren	150	307/2	Early
Hart, Silas	Jones	Samuels	30/4	Rabun
Hart, Solomon	Warren	150	163/8	Hall
Hart, Standley	Morgan	Knights	126/15	Early
Hart, Warren	Laurens	Ross	71/6	Habershan
Hart, William H.	Morgan	Knights	110/3	Rabun
Hartfield, Alsy	Wilkes	Brooks	17/4	Appling
Harthorn, Mehaley	McIntosh	Hamilton	97/10	Habershan
Hartley, James	Washington	Jenkinsons	122/11	Hall
Hartley, James	Washington	Wimberlys	226/4	Appling
Hartline, George	Jackson	Rogers	320/5	Irwin
Hartridge, L.A.(Wid)	Chatham		152/10	Early
Hartsfield, Allen	Jasper	Evans	416/13	Irwin
Hartsfield, Eliz.(Wid)	Clarke	Hintons	154/2	Irwin
Hartwell, Nancy(Wid)	Warren	152	172/13	Irwin
Hartwick, Leonard	Franklin	Holcombs	365/8	Irwin
Harvel, Mary(Wid)	Hancock	Danells	73/15	Early
Harvell, Mason(Orps)	Hancock	Danells	497/11	Irwin
Harvey, Benjamin	Putnam	H.Kindricks	190/13	Irwin
Harvey, Blassingame	Burke	J.Wards	150/21	Early
Harvey, Eliz.(Wid)	Bryan	19	140/13	Irwin
Harvey, German	Columbia	Ob.Morriss	393/2	Appling
Harvey, Isaac	Bryan	19th	55/4	Appling
Harvey, Isaac	Jones	Samuels	346/5	Gwinnett
Harvey, Jeremiah	Putnam	Oslins	76/6	Irwin
Harvey, John(Rev)	Clarke	Oates	75/12	Irwin
Harvey, John	Bryan	19th	374/2	Early
Harvey, John	Clarke	Otis	218/26	Early
Harvey, John	Jones	Greenes	23/15	Irwin
Harvey, John	Jones	Greens	83/1	Irwin
Harvey, Michael	Baldwin	Cousins	33/13	Habershan
Harvey, Rebecca	Baldwin	Cousins	28/10	Habershan
Harvey, Richd.Jr.	Bryan	19th	102/5	Gwinnett
Harvey, Richd.Sr.	Bryan	19th	155/11	Irwin
Harvey, Richd.Sr.	Bryan	19th	23/2	Walton
Harvey, Richd.Sr.	Bryan	19th	57/3	Rabun
Harvey, Samuel	Bryan	19th	138/3	Habershan
Harvey, Thomas D.	Jefferson	Cowarts	295/8	Irwin
Harvey, Wm.	Bryan	19	72/11	Irwin
Harvill(?), Hugh	Greene	Harvilles	243/6	Gwinnett
Harvill(?), Wm.	Greene	Harvilles	47/2	Walton
Harvill, Absalom	Burke	McNorrills	346/8	Early
Harvill, Wm.	Warren	154th	371/12	Early
Harwell, Dottson	Jasper	Bentleys	261/20	Early
Harwell, Mason	Jasper	Bentleys	215/21	Early
Harwell, Richard	Morgan	Loyds	40/4	Rabun
Harwell, Samuel	Jasper	Evans	174/5	Gwinnett
Harwell, Sarah	Baldwin	Stephens	5/8	Irwin
Harwell, William	Oglethorpe	Barnetts	312/6	Appling
Hary, Samuel	Washington	Jenkinson	128/8	Irwin
Hary, Samuel	Washington	Jinkinsons	421/4	Appling
Hascall, Elijah N.	Jasper	Clays	266/7	Gwinnett

146

NAME	COUNTY	MIL.DIST	LOT/SECT	DREW LAND
Hasip, Kindall	Burke	Spiveys	491/10	Irwin
Haste, Catharine(Wid)	Chatham		68/16	Irwin
Hastiness, John	Greene	141st	341/9	Irwin
Hataway, Baton	Warren	151	159/9	Irwin
Hataway, Baton	Warren	151st	185/5	Irwin
Hatch, Sarah(Orp)	McIntosh	Goulds	19/2	Irwin
Hatcher, Henry	Wilkinson	Howards	13/10	Hall
Hatcher, Isaac	Wayne	Crews	345/10	Irwin
Hatcher, James	Wilkinson	Howard	157/21	Early
Hatcher, Jesse(Orps)	Jefferson	Waldens	143/11	Hall
Hatcher, Mary(Wid)	Richmond	Lacys	378/6	Irwin
Hatcher, Moses Jr.	Glynn		199/13	Irwin
Hatcher, Moses Jr.	Wayne	Crews	108/7	Gwinnett
Hatcher, Reuben	Wilkinson	Howards	278/1	Walton
Hatcher, Robert	Wayne	Crews	374/9	Early
Hatcher, Robert	Wayne	Crews	492/8	Appling
Hatcher, Robert	Wilkinson	Howard	113/16	Early
Hatcher, Sanders	Wilkinson	Lees	208/13	Early
Hatcher, Wm.Jr.	Wilkinson	Lees	182/19	Early
Hathaway, Nathan	Liberty		73/9	Appling
Hathcock, Hastin	Franklin	Hammonds	160/10	Habersham
Hathorn, Edward(Orps)	Jones	Seals	32/1	Walton
Hathorn, Hugh	Morgan	Hackneys	155/3	Early
Hathorn, James	Morgan	Hackneys	304/4	Irwin
Hathorn, Thos.Jr.	Putnam	Slaughters	213/16	Early
Hathorn, William	Gwinnett	Hamiltons	335/1	Appling
Hathorn, William	Pulaski	Rees	106/13	Early
Hathway, Nathan	Liberty		370/8	Irwin
Hatley, Anderson	Oglethorpe	Bowls	145/9	Appling
Hatley, John(Orps)	Oglethorpe	Bowls	490/7	Appling
Hattaway, John(Orps)	Columbia	Ob.Morris	110/3	Irwin
Hatton, Thomas	Pulaski	Lesters	9/6	Early
Hattoway, Aaron(Orps)	Putnam	Robertson	62/3	Rabun
Hattox, Philip	Jasper	Dosters	224/9	Early
Haughton, Chas.(Orp)	Clarke	Simms	161/2	Habersham
Haupt, Henry	Chatham		384/15	Early
Haven, Andrew	Burke	M.Wards	343/26	Early
Hawes, Payton	Lincoln	Graves	49/1	Early
Hawes, Samuel	Richmond	Laceys	396/7	Appling
Hawes, Spencer	Lincoln	Jeters	86/15	Irwin
Hawes, Walker(Orps)	Lincoln	Graves	64/8	Irwin
Hawk, John	Jasper	Baileys	222/5	Irwin
Hawkins, (Orps)	Franklin	Jos.Millers	133/5	Early
Hawkins, Alexander	Oglethorpe	Waters	94/4	Early
Hawkins, Benj.(Orps)	Jones	Permenter	16/6	Early
Hawkins, Benjamin	Putnam	J.Kindricks	462/7	Irwin
Hawkins, Benjamin	Washington	Barges	348/9	Irwin
Hawkins, Benjamin	Washington	Barges	384/13	Early
Hawkins, Colvin	Twiggs	R.Belcher	144/18	Early
Hawkins, Ezekiel	Jones	Phillips	82/12	Early
Hawkins, Ithamer	Pulaski	Rees	6/1	Early
Hawkins, James	Oglethorpe	Rowlands	83/4	Early
Hawkins, John	Morgan	Hubbards	317/6	Early
Hawkins, John	Oglethorpe	Dunns	418/2	Appling
Hawkins, John	Putnam	Ectors	307/16	Early
Hawkins, Martha	Pulaski	Maddox	282/5	Irwin
Hawkins, Stephen	Jones	Phillips	277/9	Early
Hawkins, Stephen	Washington	Barges	132/4	Walton
Hawkins, Thomas	Morgan	Hubbards	280/2	Early
Hawkins, Thomas	Putnam	Morelands	365/1	Appling
Hawkins, Thomas	Tattnall	Tharps	110/5	Irwin
Hawkins, William	Washington	Barges	195/7	Gwinnett
Hawkins, Wily	Washington	Bargers	228/8	Irwin
Hawks, Frederick	Madison	Culbreaths	164/5	Irwin
Hawks, Frederick	Madison	Culbreaths	256/13	Irwin
Hawks, Wm.(Orps)	Morgan	Parkers	342/26	Early
Haws, Richard	Jones	Greens	471/3	Appling

147

NAME	COUNTY	MIL.DIST	LOT/SECT	DREW LAN
Hawthorn, Benjamin	Morgan	Loyds	31/5	Appling
Hawthorn, John(RS)	Twiggs	Jeffersons	158/7	Gwinnett
Hawthorn, John	Wilkinson	Childs	292/13	Irwin
Hawthorn, Josiah(Orp)	Effingham		200/18	Early
Hawthorn, Kedar	Wilkinson	Childs	174/7	Irwin
Hawthorn, Mahala(Orp)	Effingham		200/18	Early
Hawthorn, Peter	Wilkinson	Childs	306/8	Appling
Hay, Gilbert	Wilkes	Gordons	365/18	Early
Hay, Jesse G.	Franklin	Jas.Miller	154/16	Early
Hay, John G.	Franklin	Jos.Millers	60/1	Irwin
Hay, Samuel	Jackson	Winters	251/1	Early
Hay, William F.	Wilkes	Gordons	90/8	Appling
Haven, Richard	Burke	71st	25/10	Irwin
Hayes, John	Early		162/7	Gwinnett
Hayes, William	Habersham	Powells	377/3	Appling
Hayes, William	Morgan	Townsends	174/2	Rabun
Hayles, Saml.(Orp)	Oglethorpe	Murrys	51/10	Irwin
Hayman, Henry Sr.	Bryan	19th	37/2	Rabun
Hayman, Henry Sr.	Bryan	19th	47/11	Hall
Hayman, John	Laurens	Watsons	28/28	Early
Hayman, Johnson	Jones	Samuels	36/14	Irwin
Haynea, James	Clarke	Mitchells	233/8	Early
Haynes, Elias(Orps)	Jasper	Smiths	190/3	Irwin
Haynes, Green B.	Jackson	Hamilton	1/3	Walton
Haynes, Henry	Morgan	Parkers	386/5	Early
Haynes, Henry	Oglethorpe	Dunns	223/1	Appling
Haynes, James	Clarke	Mitchell	48/13	Irwin
Haynes, Joshua	Morgan	Selmons	167/7	Appling
Haynes, Permemous	Clarke	Tredwells	166/10	Early
Haynes, Permenas Sr.	Morgan	Parkers	144/5	Irwin
Haynes, Permenas Sr.	Morgan	Parkers	79/6	Appling
Haynes, Robert	Oglethorpe	Dunns	432/2	Appling
Haynes, Thomas Jr.	Hancock	Scotts	316/8	Early
Haynes, Thomas	Elbert	Whites	70/3	Walton
Haynes, Wm.	Elbert	Dobbs	174/2	Habersha
Haynes, Wm.	Elbert	Dobbs	301/13	Early
Haynie, Bridgar	Madison	Culbreths	6/14	Early
Haynie, Francis A.S.	Oglethorpe	Lees	283/13	Irwin
Hays, Ambrose	Warren	152nd	284/19	Early
Hays, David	Laurens	Ross	230/1	Appling
Hays, Edward	Franklin	J.Millers	43/13	Habersha
Hays, Geo.(white)	Twiggs	Thames	80/9	Hall
Hays, George	Hancock	Lucas	95/5	Early
Hays, George	Jackson	Rodgers	397/12	Irwin
Hays, Hugh(Orps)	Greene	Ragans	62/8	Hall
Hays, James Sr.(RS)	Putnam	Littles	20/2	Walton
Hays, James	Putnam	Robinson	135/7	Appling
Hays, John(white)	Twiggs	Jefferson	142/11	Early
Hays, John	Jasper	Hays	438/12	Irwin
Hays, John	Warren	152	424/6	Irwin
Hays, Jonathan J.	Franklin	Hammonds	234/6	Early
Hays, Leonard	Madison	Orrs	149/6	Appling
Hays, Richard	Franklin	Baughs	179/13	Irwin
Hays, Thomas S.	Putnam	Littles	332/4	Early
Hays, William	Franklin	Morris	78/2	Irwin
Hays, William	Habersham	Powells	354/8	Irwin
Hays, William	Oglethorpe	Bridges	3/9	Appling
Hays, William	Oglethorpe	Bridges	525/5	Irwin
Haywood, James	Warren	Blounts	325/13	Irwin
Haywood, Lewis	Putnam	Bledsoe	249/15	Early
Hazelett, Andrew	Jackson	Rogers	275/6	Early
Hazlerigg, Benj.	Wilkes	Dents	357/12	Irwin
Hazlerigg, Benj.	Wilkes	Dents	41/16	Early
Heackers, Jas.(Orps)	Clarke	Simms	337/1	Appling
Head, Charles	Jasper	Blakes	103/3	Irwin
Head, James	Jasper	Easts	98/3	Appling
Head, James	Morgan	Campbells	157/8	Irwin

NAME	COUNTY	MIL.DIST	LOT/SECT	DREW LAND
Head, James	Putnam	Berrys	28/5	Appling
Head, James	Putnam	Berrys	42/12	Irwin
Head, John	Elbert	White/Christian	346/9	Early
Head, John	Glynn		288/5	Gwinnett
Head, John	Putnam	Berrys	144/2	Appling
Head, Lewis G.	Morgan	Talbots	304/20	Early
Head, Mattha	Elbert	Gaines	312/16	Early
Head, Richard	Jasper	Kennedys	184/6	Early
Head, Richard	Jones	Seals	287/9	Early
Head, Samuel A.	Jones	Seals	183/7	Early
Head, Thomas	Putnam	Morelands	262/28	Early
Head, William	Jones	Seals	115/1	Early
Head, Wm.R.	Jasper	Eastes	41/5	Irwin
Headen, Tunnel	Wilkinson	Kettles	213/14	Early
Heald, Samuel	Clarke	Applings	328/6	Appling
Healen, Andrew	Wilkes	Turners	508/5	Irwin
Heam, Wm.Sr.	Jasper	Centells	521/7	Appling
Heanah, Adam	Burke	Bells	326/9	Irwin
Heard, Barnard C.	Elbert	Ruckers	117/16	Irwin
Heard, Barnard C.	Elbert	Ruckers	87/6	Early
Heard, Daniel C.	Wilkes	Russels	134/7	Gwinnett
Heard, Eliz.(Wid)	Jackson	Rogers	193/4	Walton
Heard, Geo.W.	Elbert	G.Higginbotham	17/12	Hall
Heard, Jesse F.	Wilkes	Dents	504/12	Irwin
Heard, John A.	Elbert	G.Higginbotham	76/2	Walton
Heard, John S.	Walton	Echols	253/5	Irwin
Heard, Joseph	Morgan	Parkers	195/2	Early
Heard, Joseph	Wilkes	McLendons	141/11	Irwin
Heard, William	Greene	Jones	7/23	Early
Heard, Wm.	Jackson	Winters	356/28	Early
Hearn, Elijah	Putnam	Robertson	284/9	Irwin
Hearn, Francis S.	Morgan	McClendon	52/13	Irwin
Hearn, George	Jasper	Kennedys	194/17	Early
Hearn, Isaac	Jasper	Northcuts	341/18	Early
Hearn, Isaac	Jasper	Northens	140/2	Irwin
Hearn, Jacob	Franklin	Attaways	53/26	Early
Hearn, John	Jasper	Kennedys	111/2	Walton
Hearn, Jonathan	Putnam	Berrys	213/1	Early
Hearn, Jonathan	Putnam	Berrys	64/2	Rabun
Hearn, Joshua	Franklin	Attaways	334/10	Early
Hearn, Joshua	Putnam	Brooks	168/8	Early
Hearn, Stephen	Franklin	Attaways	200/27	Early
Hearn, William	Morgan	Knights	65/9	Irwin
Hearn, Wm.Sr.	Jasper	Centells	162/1	Appling
Hearnden, Wm.	Franklin	Davis	14/5	Habersham
Hearndon, Levi	Clarke	Moores	199/2	Irwin
Hearndon, Silas	Washington	Pools	381/19	Early
Heartfield, Warren	Jasper	Easters	174/4	Appling
Heath, Abraham	Jasper	Barnes	168/12	Irwin
Heath, Benjamin	Jones	Chappels	149/9	Irwin
Heath, Benjamin	Jones	Chappels	150/1	Appling
Heath, Coleson	Putnam	Littles	99/4	Early
Heath, Daniel	Washington	Barges	411/11	Early
Heath, Guilford	Putnam	Oslins	472/8	Irwin
Heath, Hartwell	Warren	Parham	350/7	Early
Heath, Henry	Burke	Royals	311/10	Irwin
Heath, Henry	Warren	Griers	376/11	Irwin
Heath, John B.	Jones	Kings	358/8	Appling
Heath, John H.(Orps)	Washington	Mannings	99/3	Irwin
Heath, Richard	Burke	Royals	401/5	Irwin
Heath, Richard	Habersham		147/10	Habersham
Heath, Samuel	Burke	Royals	331/6	Early
Heath, Tinsley	Wilkinson	Kettles	380/6	Early
Heath, William	Jones	Shropshiers	89/5	Appling
Heath, Winnifred(Wid)	Emanuel	49	483/13	Irwin
Heddy, Nelly(Wid)	Hancock	Canes	179/4	Walton
Heddy, Oliver(Orps)	Hancock	Canes	163/8	Appling

NAME	COUNTY	MIL.DIST	LOT/SECT	DREW LA
Hedrix, William	Bulloch	Edwards	279/4	Irwin
Heeth, Jefferson P.	Warren	Parhams	298/9	Appling
Heeth, Jefferson P.	Warren	Parhams	73/8	Hall
Heeth, Joel	Warren	Hubberts	137/10	Early
Heeth, John	Warren	Hubberts	18/10	Early
Heeth, Rebecca(Wid)	Warren	Griers	226/7	Irwin
Heeth, Richd.	Warren	Hubberts	282/11	Irwin
Heeth, Sarah(Wid)	Warren	Hubberts	237/14	Early
Heeth, William(Orps)	Warren	Hubberts	528/6	Appling
Hefflin, Sarah(Wid)	Warren	Rogers	411/21	Early
Heidt, Christ.J.(R.S.)	Effingham		243/18	Early
Heidt, Christ.J.R.S.	Effingham		132/5	Early
Heit, Abial	Effingham		224/6	Irwin
Heit, George	Effingham		295/3	Early
Heit, Mathew	Effingham		260/14	Early
Helder, Evan	Camden	Baileys	367/16	Early
Helton, Abraham	Washington	Renfros	151/7	Early
Helton, Elijah	Jones	Jefferson	260/1	Walton
Helton, Elisha	Jones	Samuels	179/16	Irwin
Helvenstien, Jos.Sr.	Effingham		46/8	Appling
Helvenstien, Jos.Sr.	Effingham		94/26	Early
Helveston, James	Wayne	Crews	295/6	Early
Helveston, Joshua	Effingham		128/4	Appling
Hemphill, Charles	Jackson	Hemphills	6/7	Irwin
Hemphill, Eliz.(Wid)	Morgan	Jordans	307/7	Gwinnet
Hemphill, Jonathan	Jackson	Dicksons	87/11	Habersh
Hemphill, Marcus	Morgan	Jordans	26/13	Early
Hemphill, Robert	Jackson	Dicksons	203/8	Irwin
Hemphill, Samuel	Clarke	Dickins	363/2	Early
Hemphill, Thomas	Lincoln	Walkers	104/16	Irwin
Hemphill, Tilman	Morgan	Beasleys	140/18	Early
Hemphill, Tilman	Morgan	Beasleys	44/2	Appling
Hemphill, Wade	Morgan	Jordans	315/4	Walton
Henderson, Ciruss	Clarke	Pentecosts	344/1	Appling
Henderson, Daniel	Twiggs	W.Belcher	341/5	Gwinnet
Henderson, Daniel	Twiggs	Wm.Belcher	78/12	Irwin
Henderson, David	Jackson	Rogers	355/8	Irwin
Henderson, David	Jackson	Rogers	372/13	Early
Henderson, Henry	Greene	144th	306/13	Early
Henderson, Henry	Wilkes	Josseys	163/9	Hall
Henderson, Henry	Wilkes	Josseys	398/5	Irwin
Henderson, Isaac P.	Oglethorpe	Goolsbys	293/21	Early
Henderson, James(Orps)	Putnam	Coopers	231/20	Early
Henderson, James	Jasper	Eastes	84/7	Gwinnet
Henderson, James	Jasper	Smiths	24/13	Early
Henderson, Jas.(Orps)	Burke	M.Ward	346/7	Irwin
Henderson, Jas.Sr.	Clarke	Penticost	165/9	Irwin
Henderson, John	Jasper	Hays	109/4	Irwin
Henderson, John	Jones	Chappels	156/19	Early
Henderson, John	Telfair	Tallies	69/12	Hall
Henderson, Jos.	Jackson	Rogers	1/1	Habersha
Henderson, Lawdick	Morgan	Walkers	39/10	Habersha
Henderson, Lodwick	Morgan	Walkers	314/26	Early
Henderson, Mitchel	Wilkes	Runnels	321/12	Irwin
Henderson, Richd.	Wilkes	Runnels	152/5	Appling
Henderson, Samuel	Jackson	Winters	30/3	Early
Henderson, Thomas	Jackson	Winters	510/6	Appling
Henderson, Thomas	Wilkes	Runnels	81/2	Walton
Henderson, William	Putnam	Coopers	66/2	Early
Henderson, William	Wilkes	Brooks	232/13	Early
Henderson, William	Wilkes	Brooks	281/26	Early
Henderson, Wm.	Elbert	G.Higginbotham	97/16	Irwin
Henderson, Wm.	Elbert	Maxwell	367/7	Appling
Henderson, Wm.	Elbert	Smiths	121/6	Early
Henderson, Wm.	Elbert	Smiths	239/6	Appling
Hendley, John C.	Morgan	Alford	401/8	Irwin
Hendley, John(RS)	Morgan	Alfords	7/14	Irwin

NAME	COUNTY	MIL.DIST	LOT/SECT	DREW LAND
Hendley, William	Pulaski	Bryants	81/12	Irwin
Hendley, Wm.	Emanuel	47	435/3	Appling
Hendon, Andrew	Oglethorpe	Bridges	374/1	Appling
Hendon, Israel	Morgan	Townsends	418/4	Appling
Hendon, Roberson	Morgan	Alfords	288/28	Early
Hendon, Wm.	Oglethorpe	Bridges	87/16	Early
Hendrey, Chas.	Elbert	Whites	71/8	Appling
Hendrick, Gustavos	Baldwin	Haws	361/2	Early
Hendrick, Hilrey	Jackson	Dicksons	31/16	Irwin
Hendrick, James	Warren	Griers	456/9	Irwin
Hendrick, Jas.(Orps)	Jackson	Winters	168/8	Hall
Hendrick, Jesse	Elbert	P.Christians	9/6	Habersham
Hendrick, John H.(Orps)	Jasper	Eastes	452/3	Appling
Hendrick, John(Orps)	Baldwin	Haws	433/7	Appling
Hendrick, John	Greene	Gregorys	148/14	Early
Hendrick, John	Madison	Williford	363/9	Early
Hendrick, John	Madison	Williford	389/26	Early
Hendrick, John	Tattnall	J.Durrence	69/6	Appling
Hendrick, Julius C.	Jackson	Scotts	423/5	Appling
Hendrick, Katharine	Putnam	Roberson	341/11	Early
Hendrick, Moses	Franklin	Hayns	226/2	Appling
Hendrick, Sarah(Wid)	Jones	Permenters	206/20	Early
Hendrick, Siah	Jackson	Hamilton	117/2	Early
Hendrick, William	Madison	Williford	194/4	Early
Hendrick, Wm.	Greene	Carltons	260/2	Early
Hendricks, Elias	Elbert	Webbs	12/3	Rabun
Hendricks, Geo.(Orp)	Jones	Permenter	76/11	Early
Hendricks, Hannah(Wid)	Jackson	Winters	122/1	Early
Hendricks, John	Scriven		116/4	Irwin
Hendricks, John	Scriven		36/6	Early
Hendricks, Moses	Franklin	Haynes	159/14	Irwin
Hendricks, Sion	Franklin	R.Browns	312/14	Early
Hendricks, Sion	Franklin	R.Browns	527/2	Appling
Hendricks, Wm.	Montgomery	McMillens	243/3	Appling
Hendrix, Campbell	Elbert	Webbs	101/8	Irwin
Hendrix, James	Bulloch	Edwards	115/5	Gwinnett
Hendrix, Thaxton	Elbert	Webbs	386/28	Early
Hendrix, William	Jackson	Winters	215/10	Habersham
Hendry, Alexr.Jr.	Scriven		86/9	Hall
Hendry, Alexr.Sr.	Scriven		245/1	Appling
Hendry, Alexr.Sr.	Scriven		87/10	Irwin
Hendry, James(Orps)	Scriven		407/28	Early
Hendry, Nancy(Wid)	Morgan	McClendon	95/5	Gwinnett
Hendry, Robert Jr.	Liberty		142/14	Early
Hendry, William	Liberty		74/6	Habersham
Henedy, Josiah	Jones	Buckhalter	374/7	Irwin
Heney, Andrew	Franklin	Vaughns	131/3	Early
Hening, Edmond	Pulaski	Senterfeits	132/10	Habersham
Heninton, Clarissa(Orp)	Camden	53	275/8	Appling
Heninton, J.C.(Orp)	Camden	53	275/8	Appling
Henley, Abner	Wilkes	Kilgores	185/12	Early
Henley, Charles W.	Warren	Parham	389/17	Early
Henley, Fanny(Wid)	Putnam	J.Kindricks	295/9	Irwin
Henley, George(Orp)	Chatham		323/14	Early
Henley, James	Walton	Greens	180/2	Irwin
Henley, Joshua	Putnam	Buckners	312/26	Early
Henman, Alexr.	Madison	Culbreths	142/11	Irwin
Henning, Geo.(Orps)	Franklin	P.Browns	209/7	Appling
Henning, Margt.(Wid)	Franklin	P.Browns	14/7	Early
Henry, Alex.	Elbert	Webbs	248/26	Early
Henry, Alexr.	Elbert	Webbs	300/8	Appling
Henry, Benj.	Elbert	Buckers	58/2	Early
Henry, Benjamin	Elbert	Ruckers	308/17	Early
Henry, David	Warren	Parhams	55/10	Hall
Henry, George	Chatham		179/19	Early
Henry, J.P.	Chatham		278/18	Early
Henry, John	Elbert	Webbs	113/4	Habersham

NAME	COUNTY	MIL.DIST	LOT/SECT	DREW LAN
Henry, John	Twiggs	Ellis	8/5	Appling
Henry, Osborn	Hancock	Canes	172/5	Irwin
Henry, William	Chatham		317/9	Early
Henry, William	Elbert	Webbs	129/27	Early
Henslee, David	Franklin	Yanseys	327/5	Irwin
Henslee, Enoch	Franklin	Yanceys	237/10	Early
Hensley, Davis S.	Franklin	Greene	330/11	Irwin
Henson, James Jr.	Clarke	Simms	158/26	Early
Henson, Lazarus	Franklin	Vaughans	404/6	Appling
Henson, Martha	Pulaski	Senterfeits	57/6	Irwin
Herb, John F.	Chatham		324/3	Early
Herbert, George	Richmond	Burtons	256/7	Appling
Herbert, Isaac	Richmond	120th	256/7	Early
Herbert, J.B.	Chatham		147/16	Early
Herd, Ephraim	Morgan	Walkers	474/7	Appling
Herd, Forkner	Morgan	Alfords	500/8	Irwin
Herd, John G.Sr.	Morgan	Knights	44/22	Early
Herd, Joseph	Morgan	Walkers	70/9	Appling
Herd, Jubil C.	Morgan	Knights	86/10	Early
Herd, Stephen	Morgan	Knights	53/11	Habersha
Herd, Thomas(Orps)	Morgan	Walker	116/18	Early
Herd, William Jr.	Morgan	Knights	275/10	Early
Herendon, Joseph	Washington	Barges	404/8	Appling
Herendon, Lewis(Orps)	Washington	Barges	345/13	Irwin
Herendon, Wyott	Washington	Robinsons	54/12	Irwin
Herington, Isaac	Washington	Wimberlys	136/6	Gwinnett
Herington, Isaac	Washington	Wimberlys	75/4	Irwin
Hernden, Benjamin	Jackson	Dickson	80/12	Habersha
Hernden, Eliz.(Orp)	Elbert	Ruckers	191/12	Habersha
Hernden, James	Wilkinson	Smith	18/11	Irwin
Herndon, Dillard	Elbert	Gaines	52/3	Habersha
Herndon, Edw.Jr.	Elbert	Smiths	70/12	Habersha
Herndon, Elijah	Jackson	Dicksons	152/19	Early
Herndon, George	Habersham		191/7	Gwinnett
Herndon, George	Habersham		81/6	Appling
Herndon, George	Laurens	Kinchens	252/18	Early
Herndon, George	Wilkinson	Smiths	53/9	Early
Herndon, James	Habersham		186/5	Appling
Herndon, John Sr.	Jackson	Dicksons	145/6	Irwin
Herndon, Mereman	Clarke	Moores	77/7	Gwinnett
Herndon, Michael	Elbert	Childres	91/3	Habersha
Herndon, Reuben(Orps)	Jackson	Dicksons	350/10	Irwin
Herndon, Wyott	Washington	Robinsons	423/13	Irwin
Herod, Etheldred	Jefferson	Cowarts	304/19	Early
Herod, Etheldred	Jefferson	Cowarts	385/5	Irwin
Herren, Daniel	Jackson	Hamilton	126/3	Walton
Herrin, Alexander	Jasper	Centells	39/7	Early
Herrin, Daniel	Jackson	Hamilton	241/14	Early
Herrin, Wm.(Orps)	Twiggs	Jefferson	198/10	Habersha
Herring, Arthur	Jasper	Posts	52/3	Rabun
Herring, David	Franklin	Attaways	96/3	Early
Herring, Edmond	Pulaski	Senterfeits	77/10	Habersha
Herring, George	Baldwin	Irwins	190/10	Early
Herring, John	Jefferson	Cowarts	214/10	Irwin
Herring, John	Wayne	Crews	46/1	Appling
Herring, Wm.(Orp)	Clarke	Deans	403/6	Appling
Herrington, Eliz.(Wid)	Wilkinson	Wiggins	13/6	Irwin
Herrington, John	Burke	Thomas	346/4	Walton
Herrington, Stephen	Scriven	Robert's	89/3	Habersha
Herter, Stephen Jr.	Clarke	Simms	262/3	Early
Hervey, James(Orps)	Hancock	Lucas	236/26	Early
Hester, Allen	Montgomery	Alstons	357/5	Gwinnett
Hester, Allen	Montgomery	Altons	229/8	Appling
Hester, David	Burke	Dy's	273/7	Early
Hester, Joseph	Effingham		94/14	Early
Hester, Michael	Putnam	Berry	31/13	Irwin
Hester, Robert	Clarke	Simms	223/10	Irwin

152

NAME	COUNTY	MIL.DIST	LOT/SECT	DREW LAND
Hester, Robert	Jasper	Eastes	187/9	Irwin
Hester, Samuel	Clarke	Sims	183/16	Irwin
Hester, Stephen	Laurens	Kinchens	260/4	Appling
Hester, Wheeler	Hancock	Scotts	370/1	Appling
Hester, Wheeler	Hancock	Scotts	40/4	Appling
Hester, William	Burke	Dy's	236/16	Early
Hester, William	Burke	Royals	147/5	Appling
Hester, Willis	Hancock	Scotts	528/6	Appling
Hester, Wm.B.	Jones	Harrists	56/12	Irwin
Hesters, Jasper	Laurens	Kinchens	67/4	Appling
Heuson, Lazarus	Franklin	Vaughans	169/27	Early
Hewell, Ezekiel	Jackson	Rogers	302/16	Early
Hewell, James D.	Clarke	Tredwells	157/1	Appling
Hewell, Wm.W.	Oglethorpe	Rowlands	32/6	Irwin
Hewet, Washington(Orp)	Chatham		323/17	Early
Hewet, Wm.(Orp)	Chatham		323/17	Early
Hewett, William	Jackson	Rogers	60/2	Habersham
Hewey, John	Morgan	Wrights	15/2	Irwin
Hewey, Joseph	Morgan	Wrights	408/9	Early
Hewey, William	Morgan	Wrights	107/8	Hall
Hewit, James	Jones	Phillips	404/21	Early
Hewye, Andrew	Franklin	Vaughans	14/9	Appling
Hichcock, Joseph	Chatham		230/6	Appling
Hickey, James	Burke	Thomas	303/14	Early
Hicklin, William	Washington	Peabodys	70/10	Habersham
Hickman, Edward	Wilkinson	Brooks	1/16	Early
Hickman, Joshua	Camden	Clarks	344/3	Early
Hickman, Josiah	Habersham		317/7	Gwinnett
Hickman, Stephen	Laurens	Jones	215/6	Gwinnett
Hickman, Stephen	Laurens	Jones	45/2	Irwin
Hickmon, Aron C.	Jasper	Bartletts	66/11	Early
Hicks, Abner	Wilkinson	Howards	126/8	Appling
Hicks, Benjamin	Wilkinson	Howards	78/1	Early
Hicks, Burton	Columbia	Y.E.Bealls	84/13	Early
Hicks, Daniel	Wilkinson	Howards	62/4	Early
Hicks, Isaac R.	Oglethorpe	Barnetts	321/8	Early
Hicks, Isaac R.	Oglethorpe	Burnet	176/28	Early
Hicks, James	Emanuel	56	189/6	Early
Hicks, John B.	Columbia	Walkers	32/1	Early
Hicks, John H.	Baldwin	Taliaferro	73/16	Irwin
Hicks, John Sr.	Warren	154th	106/13	Irwin
Hicks, John	Liberty		77/2	Habersham
Hicks, Johnston	Elbert	Penns	498/8	Appling
Hicks, Joseph	Jasper	Kenadays	449/11	Irwin
Hicks, Nathaniel	Franklin	Harriss	340/3	Early
Hicks, Newsome	Jones	Wallers	191/7	Irwin
Hicks, Reuben	Laurens	D.Smiths	218/11	Early
Hicks, Sarah	Baldwin	Taliaferro	255/9	Irwin
Hicks, Wiatt	Elbert	Penns	62/16	Irwin
Hicks, William	Elbert	R.Christians	55/4	Rabun
Hicks, William	Elbert	R.Christians	71/4	Appling
Hickson, John	Warren	153rd	83/3	Irwin
Hide, George	Franklin	Vaughns	66/3	Appling
Hide, Micajah	Franklin	Jos.Millers	46/6	Irwin
Hide, William	Habersham	Simmonds	20/18	Early
Hifling, Wiley	Jackson	Hamilton	241/19	Early
Higdon, Burrel	Emanuel	57th	145/20	Early
Higdon, Burrell	Emanuel	57th	131/15	Early
Higdon, Terrell	Laurens	Harris	493/12	Irwin
Higgdon, Robert	Pulaski	Rees	118/7	Irwin
Higgerson, Phillemon C.	Jasper	Bentleys	17/2	Appling
Higginbotham, Barley	Elbert	Smiths	271/10	Early
Higginbotham, Bartley	Elbert	Smiths	210/7	Appling
Higginbotham, Benj.G.	Elbert	B.Higginbotham	255/21	Early
Higginbotham, Caleb	Madison	Williford	447/5	Appling
Higginbotham, Jacob Sr.	Elbert	B.Higginbotham	414/12	Irwin
Higginbotham, Jacob	Elbert	B.Higginbotham	259/3	Irwin

NAME	COUNTY	MIL.DIST	LOT/SECT	DREW LAN
Higginbotham, Jacob	Jasper		Hays	21/1
Higginbotham, Jane(Wid)	Elbert	G.Higginbotham	394/1	Appling
Higginbotham, Jno.(Orp)	Morgan	Hubbards	254/6	Gwinnett
Higginbotham, John	Elbert	B.Higginbotham	242/2	Early
Higginbotham, Saml.	Glynn		13/4	Appling
Higginbotham, Saml.	Madison	Williford	16/12	Irwin
Higginbotham, Wm.	Jasper	Hays	466/5	Irwin
Higgins, Burwell	Franklin	Akins	317/3	Appling
Higgins, Henry	Habersham	Grants	295/13	Irwin
Higgins, Henry	Habersham	Grants	299/1	Early
Higgins, James	Greene	143rd	308/26	Early
Higgins, John	Franklin	Holcombs	152/6	Gwinnett
Higgins, Reuben	Franklin	Aikins	300/28	Early
Higgins, Reuben	Habersham	Grants	88/16	Irwin
Higgins, Silas	Franklin	Akins	24/1	Walton
Higgins, Thomas	Franklin	Akins	180/4	Irwin
Higgs, John	Tattnall	Cunyers	271/7	Gwinnett
Higgs, John	Tattnall	Cunyers	74/8	Appling
Higgs, William	Tattnall	Cunyers	116/20	Early
Higgs, William	Tattnall	Cunyers	29/4	Irwin
Highfield, Benjamin	Franklin	Turks	456/5	Appling
Highfield, Lenord	Franklin	Turks	213/13	Irwin
Highnote, Benj.	Jones	Wallers	7/11	Irwin
Highsmith, James	Elbert	Dooley	78/26	Early
Highsmith, James	Elbert	Dooleys	235/10	Irwin
Hight, Henry	Warren	Parhams	214/28	Early
Hight, Julias	Warren	Parhams	368/13	Early
Hightower, Aaron	Clarke	Pentecosts	38/6	Irwin
Hightower, Charnal	Clarke	Starnes	336/5	Appling
Hightower, Charnal	Pulaski	Bryans	44/9	Appling
Hightower, Ephraim	Laurens	Deans	63/2	Rabun
Hightower, Ephram	Laurens	Deans	149/19	Early
Hightower, Jacob D.	Putnam	Oslins	436/2	Appling
Hightower, John T.	Clarke	Mitchells	308/5	Early
Hightower, Joshua Sr.	Clarke	Stewarts	409/15	Early
Hightower, Pleasant	Baldwin	Russels	436/5	Irwin
Hightower, Presley	Putnam	Stampers	303/13	Early
Hightower, Stephen	Greene	Kimbles		—
Hightower, Stephen	Greene	Kimbroughs	126/5	Appling
Hightower, Thos.Jr.	Clarke	Stewarts	54/1	Walton
Hightower, Wm.	Baldwin	Laceys	224/8	Early
Hightower, Wm.	Clarke	Moores	71/17	Early
Hightower, Wm.Sr.	Putnam	Stampers	276/16	Early
Hill, Abraham(Orps)	Oglethorpe	Waters	371/4	Appling
Hill, Abraham	Columbia	Bealls	520/6	Irwin
Hill, Abraham	Wilkes	Brooks	209/26	Early
Hill, Abraham	Wilkes	Brooks	99/8	Appling
Hill, Alexr.F.	Oglethorpe	Waters	60/6	Irwin
Hill, Ambrose	Walton	Wests	253/8	Early
Hill, Ambrose	Walton	Wests	316/4	Early
Hill, Aron	Franklin	Haynes	118/5	Appling
Hill, Benjamin	Warren	Griers	369/27	Early
Hill, Daniel	Laurens	Watsons	2/4	Irwin
Hill, Edmund	Scriven	180th	368/11	Irwin
Hill, Edward	Gwinnett	Hamiltons	37/5	Habersha
Hill, Eli S.	Baldwin	Stephens	226/6	Appling
Hill, Elias	Walton	Williams	5/12	Early
Hill, Elizabeth(Wid)	Richmond	Winters	287/27	Early
Hill, Elizabeth	Putnam	Berrys	68/3	Irwin
Hill, Enoch	Washington	Wimberlys	352/21	Early
Hill, Enoch	Washington	Wimberlys	38/15	Early
Hill, Francis(Wid)	Warren	Blounts	1/8	Early
Hill, Green	Jasper	Bentleys	528/13	Early
Hill, Greene	Warren	Parhams	269/8	Early
Hill, Hardy	Jones	Harrists	98/2	Irwin
Hill, Henry	Oglethorpe	Wises	156/8	Hall
Hill, Isaac(Orps)	Jasper	Kenadays	91/10	Irwin

NAME	COUNTY	MIL.DIST	LOT/SECT	DREW LAND
Hill, Isaac	Clays	Jasper	76/17	Early
Hill, Isaac	Jones	Harriss	89/14	Early
Hill, Isaac	Putnam	H.Kindricks	390/7	Appling
Hill, James A.	Jasper	Reids	75/1	Appling
Hill, James(Orp)	Richmond	Winters	321/11	Early
Hill, James	Gwinnett	Hamiltons	1/28	Early
Hill, James	Warren	Parhams	78/19	Early
Hill, John(Montc.)	Jasper	Clays	19/7	Gwinnett
Hill, John(RS)	Hancock	Lucas	1/2	Irwin
Hill, John(RS)	Hancock	Lucas	202/2	Irwin
Hill, John	Burke	Bells	98/18	Early
Hill, John	Franklin	Haynes	393/9	Irwin
Hill, John	Franklin	Haynes	430/12	Irwin
Hill, John	Jasper	Kennedys	355/13	Irwin
Hill, John	Morgan	Dennis	485/13	Irwin
Hill, John	Richmond	Winters	373/13	Early
Hill, John	Richmond	Winters	70/20	Early
Hill, Joseph	Wilkinson	Kettles	47/3	Rabun
Hill, Joshua	Jackson	Hamilton	183/12	Irwin
Hill, Joshua	Jackson	Hamilton	334/26	Early
Hill, Judith	Baldwin	Russels	16/5	Gwinnett
Hill, Maid	Putnam	Oslins	215/1	Early
Hill, Martha(Wid)	Wayne	Crews	33/3	Habersham
Hill, Martin L.	Hancock	Laccie's	106/10	Irwin
Hill, Martin L.	Hancock	Lacie's	28/14	Early
Hill, Mary(Wid)	Columbia	O.Morriss	111/8	Irwin
Hill, Middleton W.	Clarke	Tredwells	286/2	Early
Hill, Mountain	Warren	Parhams	68/13	Early
Hill, Rebecca(Wid)	Twiggs	R.Belcher	380/5	Appling
Hill, Robert Jr.	Warren	Griers	234/4	Irwin
Hill, Robert Sr.	Warren	Greers	63/7	Gwinnett
Hill, Robert	Emanuel	57	419/9	Irwin
Hill, Robert	Hancock	Herberts	202/10	Irwin
Hill, Robert	Hancock	Herberts	348/27	Early
Hill, Robert	Putnam	H.Kendricks	193/4	Irwin
Hill, Samuel	Laurens	Watsons	372/18	Early
Hill, Senus	Columbia	Shaws	489/6	Appling
Hill, Theophilus(Orps)	Jasper	Centells	57/8	Early
Hill, Waid	Putnam	Oslins	280/11	Early
Hill, William C.	Warren	150th	264/12	Early
Hill, William	Bryan	20th	169/4	Appling
Hill, William	Bryan	20th	173/1	Appling
Hill, William	Lincoln	Stokes	223/4	Irwin
Hill, William	Scriven	180th	214/1	Irwin
Hill, William	Scriven	180th	358/11	Early
Hill, Wm.	Franklin	Attaways	302/9	Irwin
Hill, Wm.	Franklin	Attaways	436/5	Appling
Hill, Wm.	Jackson	Hamilton	338/4	Walton
Hillard, Frances	Laurens	Watsons	40/2	Early
Hillard, Martin	Washington	Danells	121/15	Irwin
Hillard, Silas	Bulloch	Knights	161/11	Irwin
Hilley, Thos.Sr.	Elbert	B.Higginbotham	395/21	Early
Hilley, William	Elbert	Dooleys	312/9	Early
Hillhouse, David P.	Wilkes	Turners	249/5	Appling
Hillhouse, David T.	Wilkes	Turners	332/21	Early
Hilliard, Jane	Burke	Lewis	144/27	Early
Hillis, John	Burke	Royals	380/9	Appling
Hillman, Winder	Warren	152nd	230/4	Early
Hillman, Winder	Warren	152nd	452/4	Appling
Hills, Henry W.	Chatham		187/9	Appling
Hills, Stephen	Richmond	398th	151/14	Irwin
Hillsman, Bennett	Hancock	Cooper	216/17	Early
Hillson, Dicy(Wid)	Warren	151	55/14	Irwin
Hilly, Francis	Oglethorpe	Wises	173/11	Early
Hillyard, Richard	Wilkes	Perrys	63/28	Early
Hillyard, William	Pulaski	Lesters	69/1	Irwin
Hillyard, William	Wilkes	Willis	71/4	Habersham

NAME	COUNTY	MIL.DIST	LOT/SECT	DREW LA
Hillyer, James	Hancock	Herberts	49/3	Early
Hilson, Lewis	Warren	151st	197/6	Appling
Hilton, Sterling	Clarke	Moores	304/9	Appling
Hilton, Sterlingo	Clarke	Moores	290/6	Early
Hilton, Thos.(Orps)	Bulloch	Knights	140/12	Habersh
Hilyard, John(minor)	Wilkes	Willis	25/2	Rabun
Hindrix, Elias	Elbert	Webbs	456/6	Irwin
Hindsman, Israel	Wilkes	Runnels	312/11	Early
Hindsman, Mikel	Wilkes	Runnells	460/3	Appling
Hindsman, Mikel	Wilkes	Runnels	149/2	Early
Hinely, John	Effingham		89/9	Appling
Hinely, Soloman	Effingham		25/12	Habersh
Hiner, Lewis	Jackson	Rogers	54/13	Habersh
Hines, Abner	Baldwin	Doziers	122/2	Habersh
Hines, Abner	Baldwin	Doziers	206/10	Early
Hines, Elizabeth	Laurens	D.Smiths	290/3	Early
Hines, Elizbath L.	Putnam	Mays	338/4	Appling
Hines, John Jr.	Burke	Spiveys	137/1	Appling
Hines, John Sr.	Burke	Spiveys	346/16	Early
Hines, John Sr.	Burke	Spiveys	427/8	Irwin
Hines, Richard K.	Putnam	Mays	369/28	Early
Hines, Rister T.	Jones	Seals	166/10	Irwin
Hines, Stephen	Burke	Spiveys	243/4	Appling
Hinesley, Brittain	Jones	Kings	209/6	Early
Hinesley, John	Clarke	Mitchells	125/12	Early
Hingson, Richard	Wilkes	Davis	86/8	Appling
Hinkston, John	Wilkes	Brooks	40/19	Early
Hinley, David	Bryan	19th	364/5	Irwin
Hinley, David	Effingham		80/13	Early
Hinley, John(Orps)	Effingham		30/4	Habersh
Hinley, Margrt.Ann	Effingham		229/5	Gwinnet
Hinnard, John(RS)	Clarke	Tredwells	145/17	Early
Hinnard, John(RS)	Clarke	Tredwells	523/10	Irwin
Hinsley, Thomas(RS)	Jasper	Trembles	5/26	Early
Hinson, Armstead	Clarke	Simons	184/16	Irwin
Hinson, Samuel	Telfair	Edwards	111/9	Irwin
Hinton, Bradford	Clarke	Moores	210/4	Irwin
Hinton, Christopher	Warren	153	17/19	Early
Hinton, Christopher	Warren	153rd	113/16	Irwin
Hinton, Henry	Warren	153	24/13	Irwin
Hinton, Henry	Warren	153rd	127/20	Early
Hinton, James	Hancock	Danells	425/28	Early
Hinton, John D.	Wilkes	Russels	92/1	Early
Hinton, John	Twiggs	Evans	56/3	Rabun
Hinton, Robert	Warren	153rd	36/13	Irwin
Hinton, Thomas	Warren	153rd	14/11	Hall
Hinton, Wood	Jackson	Roger	256/4	Appling
Hisley, Daniel	Jones	Buckhalter	15/6	Early
Hister, William	Burke	Royals	111/12	Irwin
Histerly, Isham	Elbert	Whites	86/16	Irwin
Hitchcock, David	Hancock	Scotts	589/8	Early
Hitchcock, John	Oglethorpe	Bridges	117/12	Hall
Hitchcock, John	Oglethorpe	Bridges	310/2	Early
Hitchcock, Wm.A.	Morgan	Selmons	49/7	Early
Hitcher, Thomas	Jasper		33/4	Irwin
Hix, Absalom	Franklin	Harris	83/10	Habersha
Hix, Ralph	Appling	2	391/8	Irwin
Hix, Thomas	Jackson	Dicksons	350/17	Early
Hobb, Rebecca(Wid)	Chatham		96/5	Irwin
Hobbs, Abraham(Orps)	Bulloch	Knights	476/6	Appling
Hobbs, David H.	Warren	150th	97/7	Early
Hobbs, James	Warren	150	359/7	Appling
Hobbs, John	Jackson	Hemphills	225/20	Early
Hobbs, John	Putnam	Berrys	112/11	Irwin
Hobbs, Larry	Laurens	Harris	3/9	Irwin
Hobbs, William M.	Jones	Kings	87/22	Early
Hobbs, William	Warren	150th	98/2	Appling

NAME	COUNTY	MIL.DIST	LOT/SECT	DREW LAND
Hobbs, Wm.	Warren	150th	343/6	Appling
Hobby, Alfred	Chatham		293/4	Appling
Hobby, William J.	Richmond	398	92/15	Irwin
Hobby, Wm.J.	Richmond	398th	78/2	Rabun
Hobgood, Asa	Franklin	Akins	316/5	Early
Hobgood, Josiah	Franklin	Davis	521/6	Appling
Hobkerk, John B.	Chatham		128/1	Appling
Hobson, Christopher	Jasper	Clays	101/12	Irwin
Hobson, Christopher	Jasper	Clays	60/1	Habersham
Hobson, Henry(Orps)	Jones	Kings	135/10	Hall
Hobson, John	Jasper	Clays	193/15	Early
Hobson, Mathew	Jackson	Winters	56/26	Early
Hobson, Matthew	Jackson	Winters	62/15	Early
Hodge, Alston	Greene	Mercers	107/4	Irwin
Hodge, Andrew	Jasper	McClendons	352/3	Appling
Hodge, Edmund	Twiggs	Hodges	287/5	Gwinnett
Hodge, James Sr.	Jasper	Posts	19/15	Early
Hodge, John	Franklin	Ashs	3/13	Irwin
Hodge, John	Morgan	Walkers	182/6	Appling
Hodge, P.	Wilkes	Childs	242/5	Early
Hodges, Allen	Jones	Griffiths	92/5	Irwin
Hodges, Benj.	Bulloch	Edwards	366/6	Irwin
Hodges, Drury	Jones	Chappels	358/13	Irwin
Hodges, Elia(Wid)	Liberty		149/17	Early
Hodges, Elias	Jefferson	Cowarts	145/15	Early
Hodges, Elias	Jefferson	Cowarts	28/2	Early
Hodges, James C.	Bulloch	Edwards	90/10	Irwin
Hodges, Jesse	Jones	Greens	342/5	Gwinnett
Hodges, John	Franklin	John Millers	304/6	Appling
Hodges, John	Laurens	Deans	233/19	Early
Hodges, John	Laurens	Deans	399/21	Early
Hodges, John	Twiggs	Smith	337/4	Walton
Hodges, John	Washington	Avents	279/9	Irwin
Hodges, John	Washington	Danells	19/14	Early
Hodges, Joseph(RS)	Bulloch	Edwards	212/5	Early
Hodges, Mathew	Washington	Floyds	279/4	Walton
Hodges, Nancey	Burke	Sullivans	280/4	Appling
Hodges, Robert	Liberty		164/6	Appling
Hodges, Samuel	Scriven	28	128/12	Habersham
Hodges, Seth	Washington	Floyds	145/3	Irwin
Hodges, Sherrod	Clarke	Harpers	238/9	Appling
Hodges, William	Scriven		35/12	Irwin
Hodges, Zachariah	Washington	Avents	177/3	Irwin
Hodnet, Benj.	Jasper	Bentleys	302/14	Early
Hodnett, John	Walton	Sentells	192/1	Walton
Hodnett, John	Walton	Sentills	86/18	Early
Hodo, Nathaniel	Twiggs	R.Belcher	75/8	Appling
Hoff, Peter	Oglethorpe	Goolsbys	384/3	Appling
Hoff, Robert	Oglethorpe	Davenports	54/8	Irwin
Hofman, Elizabeth	Chatham		8/27	Early
Hog, William(Orps)	Wilkinson	Smiths	119/4	Walton
Hogan, Cordy	Laurens	D.Smiths	88/4	Walton
Hogan, Edward	Clarke	Tredwell	514/4	Appling
Hogan, Elijah	Wilkinson	Lees	189/12	Irwin
Hogan, Isham	Baldwin	Haws	284/6	Gwinnett
Hogan, James	Jefferson	Mathews	170/27	Early
Hogan, James	Jefferson	Matthews	137/17	Early
Hogan, John Sr.	Jackson	Dickson	143/7	Appling
Hogan, John	Laurens	Harriss	215/7	Irwin
Hogan, Mary(Wid)	Columbia	Pullins	160/4	Walton
Hogan, Samuel	Emanuel	55th	403/12	Irwin
Hogan, Shadrack	Jackson	Dixons	150/7	Irwin
Hogan, Wm.(Orps)	Lincoln	Graves	142/7	Irwin
Hogans, Thos.(Orps)	Columbia	Pullins	55/19	Early
Hoge, Hosa	Washington	Daniels	27/4	Walton
Hoge, Stephen	Columbia	Ob.Morriss	46/11	Hall
Hoge, William	Columbia	Shaws	30/11	Early

NAME	COUNTY	MIL.DIST	LOT/SECT	DREW LAN
Hoges, James	Washington	Cummins	297/7	Appling
Hoges, Lemuel	Washington	Danells	224/10	Early
Hogg, Jeter A.	Greene	143		-
Hogwood, Griffin	Franklin	Akins	188/2	Irwin
Hogwood, Griffin	Franklin	Akins	425/11	Irwin
Hogwood, Griffin	Franklin	Akins	96/2	Early
Hoket, Henry(Wid)	Jones	Permenters	327/20	Early
Hoket, Richard(Orps)	Jones	Permenters	121/3	Early
Holaway, David	Burke	Dy's	51/3	Walton
Holaway, David	Clarke	Merewether	81/20	Early
Holbrook, Jacob(Orp)	Bryan	19th	296/28	Early
Holbrooks, John	Franklin	Akins	121/9	Appling
Holbrooks, Wm.	Franklin	Hammonds	140/27	Early
Holcomb, (Orphans)	Franklin	Morris	418/10	Irwin
Holcomb, Absalom	Franklin	Holcombs	78/7	Early
Holcomb, Hampton	Franklin	Morris	486/8	Irwin
Holcomb, Jesse	Franklin	Morris	162/26	Early
Holcomb, Jesse	Franklin	Morris	192/11	Irwin
Holcomb, John Sr.	Franklin	Morris	393/19	Early
Holcomb, Sherod	Franklin	Morris	348/2	Early
Holcombe, Henry	Franklin	Morriss	467/2	Appling
Holcombe, Jeremiah	Franklin	Morris	255/8	Early
Holcombe, John C.	Richmond	398	85/12	Habershan
Holcombe, John G.	Chatham		153/13	Irwin
Holcombe, John Jr.	Franklin	Morriss	214/16	Early
Holcombe, John Jr.	Franklin	Morriss	50/4	Irwin
Holcombe, John	Putnam	Stampers	11/3	Walton
Holcombe, Joshua	Jasper	Northcuts	493/9	Irwin
Holcombe, Joshua	Jasper	Northens	360/13	Early
Holcombe, Samuel	Franklin	Holcombs	87/1	Early
Holcome, William	Habersham	Buffington	247/1	Walton
Holden, Jane(Wid)	Warren	Rogers	250/6	Appling
Holden, Jeremiah(Orps)	Warren	Rodgers	364/8	Early
Holder, Jesse	Columbia	Willingham	96/3	Rabun
Holder, John	Clarke	Stuarts	234/3	Early
Holder, Joseph	Camden	Baileys	26/11	Hall
Holder, Wilie	Jefferson	Langston	318/13	Early
Holder, William	Warren	152	111/6	Early
Holderfield, John	Gwinnett	Hamiltons	146/9	Hall
Holdnes, James M.(Orps)	Wilkes	McLendons	2/12	Early
Holebrook, Fleming	Elbert	Whites	436/8	Irwin
Holebrook, Flemming	Elbert	Whites	115/10	Habersham
Holebrooks, (Orps)	Franklin	Akins	210/2	Irwin
Holebrooks, Prisc.(Orp)	Franklin	Aikins	34/9	Irwin
Holebrooks, Prisc.	Franklin	Akins	210/2	Irwin
Holebrooks, Samuel	Franklin	Akins	266/6	Early
Holeman, George	Twiggs	Evans	329/5	Appling
Holeman, Richard	Jones	Shropshiers	94/7	Gwinnett
Holey, Barbary(Wid)	Jefferson	Abbots	264/8	Appling
Holeyfield, Wiley	Jasper	Smiths	69/13	Early
Holiday, Angalina(Orp)	Effingham		121/21	Early
Holiday, Furney	Burke	Torrances	93/10	Irwin
Holiday, Gifford(Orps)	Burke	70th	7/3	Irwin
Holiday, John	Wilkes	Gordons	39/4	Irwin
Holiday, Joseph	Burke	Torrances	80/8	Early
Holiday, Lonezer(Orp)	Effingham		121/21	Early
Holiday, Richd.Ivy	Wilkes	Holidays	114/6	Early
Holiday, Thomas	Lincoln	Walkers	186/9	Early
Holiday, Wm.(RS)	Putnam	J.Kindricks	152/12	Hall
Hollan, Jeremiah	Burke	Royals	169/7	Early
Holland, Andrew	Madison	Millicans	171/8	Appling
Holland, Daniel S.	Twiggs	Browns	386/12	Irwin
Holland, David	Tattnall	Keens	21/2	Early
Holland, Hugh(RS)	Franklin	Davis	320/2	Appling
Holland, Jacob	Wilkinson	Brooks	253/19	Early
Holland, James H.	Madison	Millicans	431/4	Appling
Holland, Jeremiah	Burke	Royals	143/20	Early

158

NAME	COUNTY	MIL.DIST	LOT/SECT	DREW LAND
Holland, Jesse	Franklin	Haynes	89/7	Early
Holland, John(Orps)	Washington	Pools	121/16	Early
Holland, John	Glynn		47/10	Hall
Holland, John	Pulaski	Maddox	27/9	Hall
Holland, John	Putnam	Oslins	124/2	Rabun
Holland, John	Putnam	Oslins	207/17	Early
Holland, John	Tattnall	J.Durrence	328/8	Appling
Holland, Jonas	Jasper	McMichael	182/13	Early
Holland, Joshua	Pulaski	Rees	397/8	Early
Holland, Leucreasa(Wid)	Habersham		117/20	Early
Holland, Lewis C.	Jasper	Phillips	279/5	Irwin
Holland, Lewis	Pulaski	Mattox	7/3	Early
Holland, Moses	Pulaski	Maddox	3/2	Rabun
Holland, William	Jasper	Clays	64/6	Appling
Holland, William	Tattnall	Keens	29/3	Irwin
Holland, Wm.	Glynn		60/16	Early
Hollaway, John(Orps)	Oglethorpe	Lees	7/9	Appling
Hollaway, Samuel	Morgan	Parkers	141/20	Early
Hollbrook, John B.	Franklin	Borroughs	527/7	Appling
Holleman, Abijah	Columbia	Dodsons	33/7	Gwinnett
Holleman, Edmund	Lincoln	Stokes	232/10	Early
Hollen, Moses	Pulaski	Rees	288/19	Early
Hollen, William	Pulaski	Maddox	156/2	Irwin
Holleway, Jeremiah	Bulloch	Tilmans	223/12	Irwin
Holley, Bricey	Pulaski	Rees	71/3	Appling
Holley, Frederich	Franklin	Hammonds	258/5	Gwinnett
Holley, Howel	Morgan	Walkers	476/4	Appling
Holley, James	Burke	Dys	339/4	Appling
Holley, John(Orps)	Jasper	Eastes	529/5	Irwin
Holley, John	Laurens	Watsons	16/5	Appling
Holley, John	Laurens	Watsons	95/15	Early
Holliday, Abner	Burke	Torrance	33/14	Irwin
Holliday, Ashley	Burke	Tarrance	408/10	Irwin
Holliday, Benj.W.	Warren	Rodgers	253/14	Early
Holliday, Joseph	Burke	Torrence	237/5	Irwin
Holliday, Joseph	Burke	Torrences	73/13	Habersham
Holliday, Martin	Jackson	Rogers	119/14	Early
Holliday, Milner	Burke	Torrance	240/9	Early
Holliday, Silas	Putnam	J.Kindricks	295/9	Appling
Holliday, Wm.(RS)	Putnam	J.Kendricks	130/5	Appling
Holliefield, Wm.P.	Jasper	Clays	334/9	Irwin
Holliman, Edmond	Lincoln	Stokes	178/27	Early
Holliman, Edmund P.	Columbia	Pullins	39/2	Irwin
Holliman, James	Columbia	Dodsons	325/9	Early
Holliman, Mary	Jasper	Easts	79/19	Early
Holliman, Richard	Jones	Shropshiers	382/8	Early
Holliman, Wm.	Morgan	Parkers	154/14	Irwin
Hollingshead, Hugh	Lincoln	Parks	511/5	Irwin
Hollingsworth, John	Franklin	Vaughns	66/1	Habersham
Hollingsworth, Matilda(D)	Scriven	Lovets	132/10	Irwin
Hollingsworth, Val.	Emanuel	49	350/3	Appling
Hollinshead, John	Richmond	Laceys	120/11	Hall
Hollis, Elizabeth	Jasper	Posts	65/1	Irwin
Hollis, John	Morgan	Farrars	399/11	Early
Hollis, John	Morgan	Farrars	92/7	Irwin
Hollis, Richard	Putnam	Evans	150/10	Irwin
Hollis, Silas	Chatham		347/26	Early
Hollis, Thomas	Morgan	Farrars	48/3	Walton
Hollis, William	Morgan	Walkers	145/9	Early
Hollis, William	Morgan	Walkers	384/19	Early
Holliway, James	Bulloch	Tilmans	54/20	Early
Holliway, William	Bulloch	Tilmans	144/4	Early
Holloman, David(RS)	Putnam	Littles	162/4	Walton
Holloman, David	Putnam	Littles	441/7	Appling
Holloman, Eaton	Hancock	Danells	12/3	Habersham
Holloman, Hannah	Hancock	Smiths	64/18	Early
Holloway, Asa	Oglethorpe	Wises	8/1	Walton

NAME	COUNTY	MIL.DIST	LOT/SECT	DREW LAN
Holloway, Chesley D.	Jasper	Hays	79/11	Hall
Holloway, Hubbard	Jasper	Hays	212/13	Irwin
Holloway, Hubbard	Jasper	Hays	68/19	Early
Holloway, Martha	Clarke	Parrs	102/16	Irwin
Holloway, Paul	Putnam	Stampers	369/8	Appling
Holloway, Paul	Putnam	Stampers	373/11	Irwin
Holloway, Rebecca(Wid)	Hancock	Edwards	292/9	Early
Holly, Amos	Morgan	Selmons	5/6	Appling
Holly, Editha	Elbert	Dooleys	121/3	Walton
Holly, Henry	Washington	Jinkinsons	330/3	Early
Holly, John(Orps)	Hancock	Millers	347/16	Early
Holly, John(Orps)	Hancock	Millers	396/8	Irwin
Holly, John	Hancock	Herberts	429/4	Appling
Holly, William	Bulloch	Tilmans	168/3	Early
Holly, Wm.Sr.	Franklin	Hammonds	63/1	Rabun
Hollyman, Benjamin	Pulaski	Bryans	118/3	Rabun
Hollyman, Benjamin	Pulaski	Bryans	399/11	Irwin
Holmes, David	Clarke	Deans	380/27	Early
Holmes, Gideon	Habersham	Simmonds	93/11	Irwin
Holmes, Hannah(Wid)	Lincoln	Walkers	174/26	Early
Holmes, Joseph	Wilkes	Willis	452/5	Irwin
Holmes, Josiah B.	Wilkes	Davis	31/4	Habersha
Holmes, Josiah	Twiggs	Hodges	33/4	Appling
Holmes, Rebecca	Chatham		140/5	Appling
Holmes, Richard	Franklin	Akins	319/27	Early
Holmes, Richard	Jasper	Clay	75/1	Habersha
Holmes, Richard	Jasper	Clays	396/18	Early
Holmes, Shadrach	Twiggs	Bosemans	148/10	Early
Holmes, Thomas	Laurens	Kinchens	181/9	Appling
Holmes, Washington	Clarke	Deans	87/9	Appling
Holms, Lewis	Washington	Wimberlys	258/16	Early
Holon, George(Orps)	Washington	Burneys	155/26	Early
Holsclaw, Henry	Wilkes	Dents	283/1	Appling
Holsenbeck, Mathew D.	Richmond	Palmers	159/2	Irwin
Holsombake, Matt.D.	Richmond	Palmers	75/12	Habersha
Holsonbake, Mathew	Richmond	Palmers	66/10	Irwin
Holsondorf, John	Camden	Clarks	18/11	Hall
Holstead, Jonathan(Orps)	Jones	Walles	396/3	Early
Holsteinback, Lewis D.	Franklin	P.Browns	123/2	Early
Holstinback, Lewis D.	Franklin	P.Browns	53/14	Early
Holt, Ann	Putnam	Morlands	289/2	Early
Holt, Asa	Jefferson	Abbots	249/12	Early
Holt, Benj.	Elbert	G.Gogginbotham	136/7	Irwin
Holt, David	Elbert	G.Hogginbotham	83/9	Irwin
Holt, Geo.Eldred	Richmond	398	338/11	Early
Holt, John S.	Richmond	Burtons	327/4	Appling
Holt, Lewis(Orps)	Hancock	Champions	149/5	Gwinnett
Holt, Nathan	Jefferson	Abbots	137/7	Gwinnett
Holt, Newton(Orps)	Putnam	Evans	41/8	Early
Holt, Pulaski S.	Putnam	Oslins	196/13	Early
Holt, Tarpley	Putnam	Bustins	22/7	Gwinnett
Holt, Thomas T.	Richmond	122	76/10	Early
Holt, Thomas	Washington	Burneys	76/12	Irwin
Holt, William	Hancock	Champions	75/23	Early
Holt, William	Jasper	Reids	479/11	Irwin
Holt, Wm. (RS)	Elbert	G.Higginbotham	106/20	Early
Holt, Wm. (RS)	Elbert	G.Higginbotham	380/9	Irwin
Holt, Wm. (RS)	Elbert	Higginbotham	6/1	Habersha
Holt, Wm.B.	Clarke	Merewether	107/13	Irwin
Holt,Thaddeus G.	Baldwin	Marshall	175/7	Appling
Holton, Isaac	Burke	Bells	346/1	Early
Holton, Joseph	Burke	Bells	85/8	Hall
Holton, Metts	Emanuel	53rd	344/27	Early
Holton, Milbra(Wid)	Montgomery	Nobles	71/2	Habersha
Holtzelaw, Hosea(Orps)	Wilkes	Bates	372/27	Early
Holwell, Luther	Scriven	180	122/10	Hall
Holyfield, Alsea	Jasper	Clays	368/2	Early

NAME	COUNTY	MIL.DIST	LOT/SECT	DREW LAND
Holzendorf, John	McIntosh	Hamilton	59/3	Rabun
Homer, Charles	Camden	Clarks	367/10	Early
Homes, Benjamin	Morgan	McClendons	393/27	Early
Homes, Ezekiel	Franklin	Powells	102/4	Appling
Homes, Ezekiel	Franklin	Powells	270/4	Irwin
Homes, James	Pulaski	Bryans	356/7	Early
Hood, Burwell	Wilkes	Davis	297/6	Early
Hood, Joel	Wilkes	Davis	341/20	Early
Hood, John	Columbia	Ob.Morriss	207/16	Early
Hood, John	Columbia	Ob.Morriss	232/1	Appling
Hood, Mary	Jasper	Bentleys	361/11	Early
Hood, Sherrod	Washington	Pools	220/14	Early
Hood, Sion	Washington	Floyds	340/5	Gwinnett
Hood, Wiley	Jasper	Bentleys	225/6	Irwin
Hood, William Sr.	Washington	Pools	393/1	Early
Hood, William	Franklin	Ashs	138/16	Early
Hood, William	Jasper	Smiths	183/16	Early
Hood, Wm.Sr.	Washington	Pools	26/14	Irwin
Hooks, Asa	Wilkinson	Lees	303/8	Early
Hooks, Baldwin H.	Warren	153	52/8	Irwin
Hooks, Barden	Twiggs	Johnston	27/9	Irwin
Hooks, Charles	Putnam	Coopers	129/17	Early
Hooks, Daniel Jr.	Wilkinson	Lees	187/9	Early
Hooks, Daniel	Washington	Mannings	210/17	Early
Hooks, Daniel	Washington	Mannings	582/18	Early
Hooks, Daniel	Wilkinson	Lees	1/10	Early
Hooks, Hillory	Putnam	Stampers	259/3	Early
Hooks, Isaac	Wilkinson	Lees	357/6	Appling
Hooks, Isaac	Wilkinson	Lees	70/8	Early
Hooks, James	Wilkinson	Lees	188/16	Irwin
Hooks, John	Putnam	Coopers	365/13	Early
Hooks, Jonathan	Wilkinson	Lees	163/1	Early
Hooks, Jonathan	Wilkinson	Lees	287/7	Gwinnett
Hooks, Michael	Burke	Torrance	158/13	Irwin
Hooks, William Sr.	Burke	Torrances	404/8	Early
Hooks, William(Orps)	Washington	Mannings	368/9	Appling
Hooks, William	Wilkinson	Lees	158/4	Walton
Hooks, William	Wilkinson	Lees	466/7	Irwin
Hooks, Wm.Jr.	Burke	Lewis	402/1	Early
Hooper, Andrew	Habersham	McCutcheons	356/5	Early
Hooper, James A.	Franklin	Davis	190/9	Appling
Hooper, Joshua	Franklin	Davis	168/1	Appling
Hooper, Joshua	Franklin	Davis	48/11	Habersham
Hooper, Mathew B.	Franklin	Sheumates	72/26	Early
Hooper, Matthew	Franklin	Flanagans	70/27	Early
Hooper, Obadiah	Franklin	Hammonds	114/6	Irwin
Hooper, Richard	Franklin	Davis	525/6	Appling
Hooten, Henry	Jones	Samuels	61/10	Hall
Hooten, Lucy(Wid)	Jones	Samuels	173/6	Early
Hooton, Jeremiah	Elbert	Whites	613/2	Appling
Hooton, Littleton	Jasper	Centals	67/17	Early
Hoover, Jacob	Wilkinson	Kettles	176/15	Irwin
Hoover, John	Wilkinson	Kettles	136/2	Early
Hoover, John	Wilkinson	Kettles	46/3	Early
Hopgood, Henry	Jackson	Rogers	338/7	Irwin
Hopkins, David	Madison	Millicans	196/12	Early
Hopkins, Dennis	Madison	Orrs	165/10	Habersham
Hopkins, Francis Sr.	McIntosh	Jenkins	256/13	Early
Hopkins, Francis Sr.	McIntosh	Jinkins	38/10	Irwin
Hopkins, Isaac	Wilkes	Kilgores	414/5	Irwin
Hopkins, Jesse	Washington	Floyds	278/6	Irwin
Hopkins, John A.	Lincoln	Jones	297/13	Irwin
Hopkins, John A.	Walton	Wests	213/4	Appling
Hopkins, John A.	Walton	Wests	441/7	Irwin
Hopkins, John L.	McIntosh	Jenkins	128/5	Irwin
Hopkins, John	Richmond	Burtons	109/3	Appling
Hopkins, John	Wilkes	Kilgores	157/6	Early

NAME	COUNTY	MIL.DIST	LOT/SECT	DREW LAN
Hopkins, Martha(Wid)	Wilkes	Kilgores	85/1	Appling
Hopkins, Mary	Chatham		449/8	Irwin
Hopkins, Moses(Orps)	Clarke	Harpers	377/8	Appling
Hopkins, Samuel	Clarke	Harpers	1/10	Irwin
Hopkins, William	Richmond	Laceys	251/3	Walton
Hopna, Elizabeth	Chatham		216/6	Irwin
Hopson, William	Washington	Wimberleys	75/3	Walton
Horbach, Henry	Chatham		466/8	Irwin
Horn, Absalom	Elbert	Dooleys	445/10	Irwin
Horn, Beady(Orp)	Laurens	Harris	95/11	Hall
Horn, Brittain	Wilkinson	Kettles	422/3	Appling
Horn, Edward	Morgan	Campbells	110/9	Hall
Horn, Edward	Morgan	Campbells	99/5	Rabun
Horn, Emely W. (Orps)	Burke	Thomas	278/2	Early
Horn, Harris	Jones	Greens	130/6	Early
Horn, Henry(Orp)	Burke	Spiveys	384/2	Appling
Horn, Howel	Jones	Shropshiers	383/13	Irwin
Horn, Howel	Jones	Shropshiers	441/8	Appling
Horn, James	Baldwin	Ellis	138/11	Hall
Horn, James	Baldwin	Ellis	25/2	Walton
Horn, James	Jones	Greens	417/13	Irwin
Horn, Jesse	Jackson	Hamilton	401/15	Early
Horn, John	Greene	Carltons	192/9	Early
Horn, Josiah	Laurens	Harris	73/16	Early
Horn, Julia(Orp)	Burke	Spiveys	384/2	Appling
Horn, Lary	Emanuel	57	119/6	Early
Horn, Margaret(Wid)	Wilkinson	Smiths	246/6	Irwin
Horn, Michael	Pulaski	Bryans	123/3	Habersha
Horn, Needham	Washington	Wimberleys	264/9	Early
Horn, Richard(RS)	McIntosh	Eigles	31/1	Rabun
Horn, Richard(RS)	McIntosh	Eigles	49/2	Early
Horn, Simeon	Jones	Jeffersons	328/16	Early
Horn, William	Baldwin	Ellis	270/9	Irwin
Hornbuckle, Solomon	Jasper	Smiths	102/10	Early
Horne, Eli	Pulaski	Senterfeits	380/7	Gwinnett
Horne, Joab	Pulaski	Senterfeits	122/6	Irwin
Horne, Whitmill D.	Pulaski	Senterfeits	179/2	Rabun
Hornsby, William	McIntosh	McIntosh	3/4	Irwin
Horsford, Isaac	Burke	Royals	118/5	Early
Horton, Daniel	Washington	Peabodys	24/11	Early
Horton, David	Jasper	Sentells	246/11	Early
Horton, Elizabeth	Jasper	Baleys	329/16	Early
Horton, James	Elbert	Whites	496/6	Irwin
Horton, Jeremiah	Jackson	Winters	470/6	Appling
Horton, Jesse	Washington	Peabodys	153/1	Walton
Horton, John	Pulaski	Johnstons	83/3	Rabun
Horton, Kitrill	Washington	Robersons	472/13	Irwin
Horton, Levi	Washington	Barges	108/20	Early
Horton, Levi	Washington	Barges	195/7	Gwinnett
Horton, Robert	Hancock	Millers	27/16	Irwin
Horton, Sally	Putnam	Bustins	499/5	Appling
Horton, Stephen(Orps)	Baldwin	Doziers	268/7	Irwin
Horton, Stephen	Jackson	Hamilton	260/5	Gwinnett
Horton, Thomas Sr.	Elbert	Whites	118/9	Early
Horton, Thos.Jr.	Elbert	Whites	162/14	Early
Horton, William	Baldwin	Doziers	56/2	Habersha
Horton, William	Elbert	Penns	49/14	Early
Horton, William	Putnam	Bustins	247/1	Early
Hoskins, John Sr.	Jones	Samuels	42/3	Irwin
Hoskins, John	Jones	Samuels	371/3	Early
Hotchkiss, Daniel	Chatham		164/11	Hall
Hotchkiss, Daniel	Chatham		359/5	Early
Hoton, John	Jasper	Sentells	357/1	Early
Hotton, Stephen	Washington	Pools	38/12	Early
Hougen, Wm.Sr.	Oglethorpe	Bowls	360/20	Early
Hough, John	Jasper	Bailey	109/2	Irwin
Houghton, Eliz.(Wid)	Wilkes	Holidays	438/10	Irwin

NAME	COUNTY	MIL.DIST	LOT/SECT	DREW LAND
Houghton, George	Hancock	Danells	46/27	Early
Houghton, Jas.M.	Greene	Rankins	25/4	Habersham
Houghton, Joshua	Greene	141st	235/7	Early
Houghton, Sally(Wid)	Hancock	Thomas	271/15	Early
Houghton, Tabitha(Wid)	Greene	Harrills	57/6	Gwinnett
Houghton, Willis	Greene	Harvills	322/4	Appling
House, Binkley(Orps)	Oglethorpe	Lees	140/21	Early
House, Felix	Jackson	Rogers	227/11	Irwin
House, James	Richmond	122nd	255/27	Early
House, John	Jackson	Rogers	256/19	Early
House, Lewis	Lincoln	Thompsons	115/14	Irwin
House, Littleberry	Jackson	Rogers	13/3	Walton
House, Mark	Jasper	Bentleys	106/10	Early
House, Memory	Oglethorpe	Bridges	181/7	Appling
House, Memory	Oglethorpe	Bridges	245/6	Gwinnett
House, Sion	Madison	Orrs	239/8	Appling
Houston, Masmant(Guard.)	McIntosh	Goulds	166/12	Irwin
Houston, Patrick	Chatham		175/10	Habersham
Houston, Sarah	Chatham		330/5	Appling
Houstonn, Harriet E.	Putnam	Oslins	27/2	Appling
How, David	Jones	Wallers	315/2	Early
How, David	Jones	Wallers	40/4	Early
Howard, Absalom	Jasper	Reids	437/9	Irwin
Howard, Acquilla	Columbia	J.Morris	483/7	Appling
Howard, Benjamin	Chatham		113/3	Appling
Howard, Benjamin	Chatham		350/16	Early
Howard, Charles	Chatham		107/4	Early
Howard, Charles	Washington	Jinkinsons	174/1	Irwin
Howard, David	Jones	Phillips	35/9	Appling
Howard, David	Liberty		130/12	Hall
Howard, Edward	Camden	33rd	211/1	Walton
Howard, Elisha	Wilkinson	Lees	49/20	Early
Howard, Frances(Orps)	Putnam	Mays	83/10	Irwin
Howard, George	Liberty		359/8	Early
Howard, George	Liberty		495/6	Irwin
Howard, Harmon	Jones	Phillips	53/1	Rabun
Howard, Henry Sr.	Washington	Jinkinsons	173/7	Irwin
Howard, Henry	Oglethorpe	Dunns	127/4	Irwin
Howard, Hiram Sr.	Clarke	Parrs	375/11	Early
Howard, Isaac(Orps)	Wilkinson	Lees	252/1	Appling
Howard, James	Laurens	Harriss	260/11	Irwin
Howard, James	Washington	Renfroes	26/18	Early
Howard, James	Wilkinson	Howards	5/11	Habersham
Howard, John B.	Jones	Phillips	55/4	Irwin
Howard, John H.	Baldwin	Marshall	107/10	Hall
Howard, John T.	Jasper	Clays	382/21	Early
Howard, John	Laurens	Jones	67/10	Hall
Howard, John	Liberty		504/6	Appling
Howard, John	Oglethorpe	Barnetts	367/2	Early
Howard, John	Oglethorpe	Barnetts	97/15	Irwin
Howard, John	Richmond	120th	188/21	Early
Howard, John	Richmond	120th	207/2	Early
Howard, John	Telfair	Wilsons	207/10	Early
Howard, Joseph(Orps)	Jones	Samuels	57/27	Early
Howard, Joshua	Washington	Jenkinson	5/10	Habersham
Howard, Joshua	Washington	Jinkinsons	385/15	Early
Howard, Josiah	Laurens	Jones	51/6	Early
Howard, Levi(Orps)	Scriven		357/5	Early
Howard, Levi	Scriven		225/9	Appling
Howard, Nauffight	Washington	Renfros	219/10	Irwin
Howard, Ralph	Jones	Phillips	34/12	Hall
Howard, Sally(Wid)	Wilkinson	Lees	120/19	Early
Howard, Samuel	Chatham		221/11	Early
Howard, Samuel	Jasper	Bentleys	195/19	Early
Howard, Samuel	Liberty		328/3	Early
Howard, Sarah(Wid)	Jackson	Rogers	95/27	Early
Howard, Sarah	Scriven		33/28	Early

NAME	COUNTY	MIL.DIST	LOT/SECT	DREW LAN
Howard, Simon	McIntosh	Eigles	178/3	Walton
Howard, Simon	McIntosh	Eigles	36/9	Hall
Howard, Solomon	Washington	Renfroes	145/21	Early
Howard, Solomon	Washington	Renfros	397/18	Early
Howard, Starling	Morgan	Jordans	389/5	Irwin
Howard, Thomas	Oglethorpe	Brittons	116/26	Early
Howard, Thomas	Wilkinson	Lees	283/8	Early
Howard, Vinning	Wilkinson	Howards	99/7	Irwin
Howard, William	Wilkinson	Lees	125/6	Early
Howard, William	Wilkinson	Lees	75/2	Early
Howard, Wm.S.	Wilkes	Russels	295/7	Gwinnett
Howard, Wyllis Jr.	Jefferson	Mathews	367/1	Appling
Howard, Wyllis	Jefferson	Matthews	336/27	Early
Howards, Benj(RS)	Jones	Permenters	440/6	Appling
Howe, James A.	Putnam	Oslin	182/6	Irwin
Howel, Casper	Greene	Wheelis	114/4	Irwin
Howel, Dempsey	Twiggs	Browns	254/7	Irwin
Howel, Gabriel	Wilkinson	Howards	103/20	Early
Howel, Hopkin	Tattnall	Tharps	458/2	Appling
Howel, Josiah(Orp)	Richmond	120th	49/1	Rabun
Howel, Lewis	Warren	152	422/5	Irwin
Howel, Stephen(RS)	Jackson	Hamiltons	184/11	Early
Howel, Theophilus	Wilkinson	Wiggins	80/5	Appling
Howel, William	Jones	Jeffersons	371/6	Early
Howell, Casper	Greene	Wheelis	28/9	Irwin
Howell, Cassandra	Scriven	36	225/3	Appling
Howell, Catharine(Wid)	Camden	Clarks	245/3	Appling
Howell, Daniel Sr.(Orps)	Scriven	Lovetts	118/2	Appling
Howell, Daniel (Orps)	Baldwin	Marshall	133/6	Early
Howell, David	Wilkinson	Howards	123/10	Habersha
Howell, David	Wilkinson	Howards	318/7	Irwin
Howell, Edward Y.	Putnam	Evans	165/3	Habersha
Howell, Etheldred	Pulaski	Senterfeits	179/2	Irwin
Howell, Etheldred	Pulaski	Senterfeits	282/3	Appling
Howell, Gabriel	Wilkinson	Howards	514/10	Irwin
Howell, Hopkins	Tattnall	Tharps	378/10	Early
Howell, James R.	Putnam	Bustins	136/5	Appling
Howell, James(Orps)	Oglethorpe	Brittons	281/2	Early
Howell, Jesse	Jackson	Winters	256/16	Early
Howell, John(Orp)	Chatham		313/6	Early
Howell, John(Orp)	Wilkinson	Howards	92/10	Habersha
Howell, Jos.(Orp.)	Hancock	Mims	412/7	Appling
Howell, Joseph	Hancock	Canes	466/9	Irwin
Howell, Joshua	Jackson	Hamilton	137/8	Hall
Howell, Lewis	Lincoln	Graves	348/4	Appling
Howell, Luannah	Clarke	Treadwell	133/3	Walton
Howell, McKinnie	Hancock	Canes	112/5	Gwinnett
Howell, Saml.D.	Elbert	Olivers	289/1	Appling
Howell, Samuel	Putnam	Evans	181/5	Early
Howell, Solomon(RS)	McIntosh	Eigles	21/5	Appling
Howell, Solomon(RS)	McIntosh	Eigles	64/4	Rabun
Howell, Thomas	Camden	Tillis	157/12	Habersha
Howell, Thomas	Camden	Tillis	254/8	Early
Howell, Thomas	Pulaski	Senterfeits	2/6	Gwinnett
Howell, William	Baldwin	Doziers	83/11	Early
Howell, Wright	Pulaski	Senterfeits	483/9	Irwin
Howenton, Wilson	Madison	Millicans	224/3	Early
Howenton, Wilson	Madison	Millicans	228/4	Appling
Howieell(Howard), Saml.	Washington	Brooks	72/12	Irwin
Howl, Thos.T.	Jones	Seals	44/9	Early
Hoxey, Thomas	Putnam	Oslins	92/1	Rabun
Hoy, Clinton	Baldwin	Taliaferro	294/7	Appling
Hoy, Robert	Chatham		56/9	Early
Hoy, William	Baldwin	Irwins	150/3	Early
Hoze, John	Pulaski	Maddox	46/6	Gwinnett
Hubbard, Benjamin	Wilkes	Josseys	520/8	Appling
Hubbard, Elisha	Morgan	Hubbards	199/16	Early

NAME	COUNTY	MIL.DIST	LOT/SECT	DREW LAND
Hubbard, Eliz.	Greene	143	112/1	Walton
Hubbard, Hannah(Wid)	Richmond	398	183/4	Appling
Hubbard, Jacob	Walton	Echols	123/3	Walton
Hubbard, John(Orp)	Camden	Clarks	132/14	Early
Hubbard, Mannoah(RS)	Baldwin	Russels	319/2	Early
Hubbard, Manoah(RS)	Baldwin	Russels	294/19	Early
Hubbard, Manoah(RS)	Baldwin	Russels	80/11	Habersham
Hubbard, Robert	Oglethorpe	Wises	39/3	Appling
Hubbert, Benjamin	Wilkes	Mattox	50/2	Irwin
Hubbert, Harmon	Warren	Hubberts	272/6	Early
Hubbert, Hiram	Wilkes	Mattox	334/8	Appling
Hubbert, John	Hancock	Herberts	216/9	Irwin
Hubbord, Elijah	Telfair	Loves	275/1	Appling
Hubbord, Elijah	Telfair	Loves	398/8	Irwin
Hubbord, Stephen	Telfair	Loves	329/20	Early
Hubbord, Stephen	Telfair	Loves	387/13	Irwin
Hubert, James(Orps)	Jasper	Baileys	44/12	Irwin
Huchingson, Wm.	Columbia	Willingham	78/9	Early
Huchinson, John	Jasper	Clays	69/2	Rabun
Huckabay, Brittan	Baldwin	Marshall	278/21	Early
Huckaby, Brittain	Baldwin	Marshall	90/11	Early
Huckaby, Charles	Jasper	Reeds	39/8	Hall
Huckaby, Charles	Jasper	Reeds	502/5	Irwin
Huckaby, James B.	Jasper	Centells	166/4	Walton
Huckaby, James	Wilkes	Perrys	223/18	Early
Huckaby, Josiah	Hancock	Mims	432/13	Irwin
Huckaby, William	Jones	Buckhalters	122/4	Walton
Huckaby, William	Jones	Wallers	34/5	Gwinnett
Huckbee, Wm.	Gwinnett	Hamiltons	372/3	Early
Huddleston, George	Wilkes	Davis	29/2	Appling
Huddleston, Jane	Hancock	Evans	25/26	Early
Huddleston, John S.	Oglethorpe	Bowls	223/26	Early
Huddleston, Stephen	Oglethorpe	Bowls	498/13	Irwin
Huddleston, Willis	Oglethorpe	Wises	5/21	Early
Hudgans, Beverly	Jackson	Hamilton	463/3	Appling
Hudggins, Phillip	Pulaski	Davis	425/1	Appling
Hudgins, Beverly	Jackson	Hamilton	172/8	Appling
Hudgins, Josiah	Jones	Griffiths	328/26	Early
Hudgins, Josiah	Jones	Griffiths	511/7	Appling
Hudgins, Wm.W.	Wilkes	Holidays	31/3	Habersham
Hudilisten, Wm.	Elbert	Dooleys	15/1	Early
Hudler, John	Bulloch	Knights	241/23	Early
Hudleston, Allen	Morgan	Campbells	386/4	Appling
Hudman, Ezekiel	Gwinnett	Hamiltons	305/4	Appling
Hudson, Allen	Jones	Seals	218/3	Appling
Hudson, Andrew	Jefferson	Bothwells	93/14	Irwin
Hudson, Ashberry	Jefferson	Bothwells	411/4	Appling
Hudson, Benjamin	Elbert	Olivers	417/1	Early
Hudson, Benjamin	Jefferson	Bothwells	70/10	Early
Hudson, Brooker	Elbert	Whites/Nuly	163/4	Walton
Hudson, Charles	Putnam	Oslins	316/11	Early
Hudson, David Jr.	Elbert	Olivers	361/5	Appling
Hudson, David N.	Jones	Wallers	251/1	Early
Hudson, David Sr.	Elbert	Olivers	56/11	Irwin
Hudson, David	Habersham		289/26	Early
Hudson, David	Jones	Hurst	101/17	Early
Hudson, Elbert	Jefferson	Matthews	339/4	Early
Hudson, Frederick	Greene	Harvills	142/26	Early
Hudson, Hall Sr.	Jefferson	Bothwells	375/12	Early
Hudson, Hall Sr.	Jefferson	Bothwells	387/27	Early
Hudson, Hamilton	Chatham		157/17	Early
Hudson, Hampton(Orps)	Burke	72nd	288/9	Irwin
Hudson, Hillary	Jefferson	Bothwells	438/8	Irwin
Hudson, Irby	Putnam	Oslins	401/7	Irwin
Hudson, James T.	Jefferson	Bothwells	293/12	Irwin
Hudson, James T.	Jefferson	Bothwells	502/12	Irwin
Hudson, John	Laurens	S.Smiths	322/28	Early

NAME	COUNTY	MIL.DIST	LOT/SECT	DREW LAND
Hudson, John	Putnam	Oslins	173/2	Appling
Hudson, Jonathan A.	Jefferson	Abbotts	593/2	Appling
Hudson, Joshua	Franklin	Ashs	20/11	Irwin
Hudson, Joshua	Franklin	Ashs	328/12	Early
Hudson, Mary	Oglethorpe	Lees	135/14	Early
Hudson, Nathaniel	Elbert	Childres	317/18	Early
Hudson, Nathaniel	Elbert	Childres	9/12	Early
Hudson, Phoebe(Wid)	Hancock	Thomas	233/6	Gwinnett
Hudson, Richard	Jefferson	Bothwells	59/4	Appling
Hudson, Roland(Orps)	Oglethorpe	Wises	103/3	Early
Hudson, Thomas	Hancock	Coopers	21/3	Walton
Hudson, William Jr.	Jones	Harrists	285/7	Early
Hudson, William Sr.	Jones	Harrists	129/13	Early
Hudson, William	Franklin	Ashs	204/6	Appling
Hudson, William	Franklin	Ashs	426/8	Appling
Hudson, William	Jackson	Dicksons	255/14	Early
Hudson, Wm.B.	Elbert	Olivers	191/4	Walton
Hudson, Wm.Sr.	Elbert	Whites	281/4	Walton
Hudspeth, Mary	Wilkes	Brooks	207/12	Early
Hue, Joseph	Jackson	Hamilton	448/3	Appling
Huey, Samuel	Jones	Jefferson	36/2	Irwin
Huey, Samuel	Jones	Jeffersons	200/6	Gwinnett
Huff, Andrew	Hancock	Thomas	183/4	Walton
Huff, Clayton	Warren	Parhams	194/3	Appling
Huff, Clayton	Warren	Parhams	244/1	Appling
Huff, Edwin	Putnam	Ectors	54/10	Hall
Huff, George	Greene	Kimbrows	509/13	Irwin
Huff, Green	Hancock	Chamions	38/16	Early
Huff, Harrison	Clarke	Spurlocks	99/4	Habersham
Huff, Henry	Clarke	Mitchells	226/11	Irwin
Huff, Henry	Clarke	Mitchells	26/1	Habersham
Huff, James	Hancock	Thomas	229/1	Appling
Huff, James	Jones	Chappels	20/20	Early
Huff, John	Greene	Wheelis	392/3	Appling
Huff, Mathis	Elbert	P.Christian	74/12	Hall
Huff, Ralph	Jones	Permenters	405/5	Irwin
Huff, Sarah(Wid)	Putnam	Littles	336/11	Early
Huff, Whitfield	Jasper	Reids	109/6	Early
Huff, William	Jones	Chappels	360/2	Early
Huggins, Greene	Franklin	P.Browns	45/5	Early
Huggins, John	Franklin	P.Browns	123/2	Appling
Huggins, Wm.	Franklin	P.Browns	377/7	Early
Hugh, John	Jasper	Clays	47/20	Early
Hughes, Anna	Baldwin	Marshall	85/12	Hall
Hughes, Edward Jr.	Chatham		33/4	Walton
Hughes, Edward	Chatham		249/9	Appling
Hughes, Edward	Chatham		88/28	Early
Hughes, George H.	Wilkes	Dents	173/7	Gwinnett
Hughes, George	Burke	Torrance	232/9	Early
Hughes, James	Wilkes	Josseys	278/4	Appling
Hughes, Jane(Orp)	Wilkes	Bates	247/8	Appling
Hughes, John	Jones	Permenters	76/1	Rabun
Hughes, Micajah	Morgan	Farrars	74/13	Early
Hughes, Thomas	Wilkinson	Lees	322/9	Irwin
Hughes, William	Wilkinson	Lees	33/5	Rabun
Hughes, Wm.(minor)	Wilkes	Bates	141/10	Irwin
Hughey, James	Morgan	Townsends	118/14	Irwin
Hughey, James	Morgan	Townsends	195/11	Early
Hughlin, John	Wilkes	Runnels	134/9	Early
Hughs, David T.	Greene	Jones	220/1	Early
Hughs, George	Burke	Torrance	19/1	Walton
Hughs, John	Jones	Wallers	86/19	Early
Hughs, John	Twiggs	Ellis	74/11	Irwin
Hughs, Mary	Wilkes	Bates	147/6	Gwinnett
Hughs, Matthew	Jefferson	Bothwells	334/10	Irwin
Hughs, Peter M.	Jasper	Bartletts	65/15	Early
Hughs, Sarah(Wid)	Jones	Permenters	473/8	Appling

NAME	COUNTY	MIL.DIST	LOT/SECT	DREW LAND
Hughs, Thomas	Wilkinson	Lees	112/8	Early
Hugnley, Alley(Wid)	Wilkes	Kilgores	186/21	Early
Huguley, Zachariah	Wilkes	Kilgores	291/19	Early
Hulings, James	Wilkes	Gordons	182/11	Early
Hull, Asbury	Clarke	Appling	241/6	Early
Hull, Ezekiel	Burke	71st	186/4	Walton
Hull, Henry	Clarke	Applings	283/2	Early
Hull, Hope(Orps)	Clarke	Applings	265/3	Irwin
Hull, Jane(Wid)	Richmond	398th	47/9	Hall
Hull, Joseph	Camden	33rd	19/11	Irwin
Hull, Richard	Camden	Baileys	83/10	Hall
Hull, Stephen(Orp)	Camden	Baileys	157/14	Early
Hull, Temperance(Orp)	Camden	Baileys	157/14	Early
Hull, William	Camden	Baileys	157/14	Early
Hulsay, Adonyah Jr.	Habersham		5/7	Appling
Hulsey, Adonijah Jr.	Habersham		370/12	Irwin
Hulsey, Armstead	Habersham		379/8	Irwin
Hulsey, Hiram	Habersham		123/12	Irwin
Hulsey, Hopkins	Hancock	Daniels	389/16	Early
Hulsey, Jas.Sr.	Franklin	J.Millers	74/12	Habersham
Hulsey, Jennings	Jackson	Hamilton	107/12	Hall
Hulsey, Jesse Jr.	Jackson	Dicksons	112/7	Irwin
Hulsey, Joel	Franklin	J.Millers	161/1	Irwin
Hulsey, Joel	Franklin	Jos.Millers	2/23	Early
Hulsey, Joel	Habersham		291/5	Gwinnett
Hulsey, Joel	Habersham		329/4	Appling
Hulsey, Micajah	Habersham		207/1	Walton
Hulsey, Pleasant	Franklin	Jos.Millers	235/9	Early
Hulsey, Vinton	Habersham		245/1	Early
Hulson, Charles	Clarke	Penecosts	115/12	Hall
Humber, John	Jackson	Rogers	347/15	Early
Humphrey, Elizabeth	Hancock	Mims	359/9	Irwin
Humphrey, Robert	Hancock	Smiths	232/5	Irwin
Humphrey, Thomas	Hancock	Mims	334/6	Gwinnett
Humphrey, Wm.	Clarke	Deans	128/2	Walton
Humphrey, Wm.	Hancock	Smiths	2/27	Early
Humphrey, Wm.	Hancock	Smiths	56/6	Early
Humphreys, Thos.S.	Jones	Wallers	160/3	Early
Humphries, Thos.(RS)	Baldwin	Cousins	6/7	Gwinnett
Hunk, Christiana W.(Wid)	Chatham		14/2	Rabun
Hunley, Charles W.	Warren	Parhams	184/9	Early
Hunnycut, Henry	Putnam	Buckners	439/9	Irwin
Hunt, Aaron	Jasper	Baileys	263/2	Early
Hunt, Aaron	Jasper	Baileys	525/5	Appling
Hunt, Daniel	Jones	Samuels	163/26	Early
Hunt, Edgfield	Jackson	Hamilton	15/9	Irwin
Hunt, George	Greene	140th	210/16	Early
Hunt, George	Greene	Greens	422/28	Early
Hunt, Henry	Baldwin	Megees	216/1	Walton
Hunt, Henry	Elbert	Gaines	151/9	Irwin
Hunt, James Sr.	Elbert	B.Higginbotham	345/2	Early
Hunt, James	Hancock	Danells	251/5	Early
Hunt, Jerkins	Jasper	McLendons	88/22	Early
Hunt, John	Washington	Wimberlys	193/14	Early
Hunt, Nancy M.(Wid)	Elbert	Penns	181/10	Irwin
Hunt, Nathaniel	Chatham		23/3	Habersham
Hunt, Nathaniel	Chatham		85/27	Early
Hunt, Rachael(Wid)	Greene	Harvilles	512/7	Irwin
Hunt, Sion	Elbert	B.Higginbotham	179/6	Irwin
Hunt, Timothy	Greene	143	290/2	Early
Hunt, Wiley	Jones	Samuels	348/3	Appling
Hunt, William Jr.	Twiggs	Smiths	6/1	Walton
Hunt, William	Columbia	Olives	364/7	Early
Hunt, Wm.	Elbert	B.Higginbotham	184/10	Habersham
Hunter, Archibald S.R.	Hancock	Lucas	113/14	Irwin
Hunter, David	Jasper	Kennedys	61/16	Irwin
Hunter, David	Jasper	Kennedys	62/14	Early

NAME	COUNTY	MIL.DIST	LOT/SECT	DREW LAN
Hunter, David	Telfair	Williams	48/10	Habersha
Hunter, Elizabeth	Oglethorpe	Bowls	188/28	Early
Hunter, Ephraim	Scriven	36th	468/8	Appling
Hunter, James	Appling	5th	27/2	Walton
Hunter, James	Clarke	Pentecost	267/17	Early
Hunter, Jesse	Clarke	Pentecosts	133/15	Early
Hunter, Jesse	Clarke	Pentecosts	278/4	Irwin
Hunter, John	McIntosh	Hamilton	171/4	Early
Hunter, Phillip(Orps)	Greene	140th	79/10	Habersha
Hunter, Redding	Irwin	Lower	227/7	Gwinnet*
Hunter, Thomas	Jackson	Rogers	122/18	Early
Hunter, Wm.(Shetston)	Twiggs	Bozemans	2/16	Irwin
Hunter, Wm.P.	Chatham		417/8	Irwin
Hunter, Wm.R.	Hancock	Millers	241/9	Irwin
Hunters, James	Jasper	McClendons	195/10	Early
Hunton, Hannah(Wid)	Clarke	Mitchells	139/10	Early
Hunton, James	Clarke	Mitchells	388/13	Irwin
Hurrah, Charles	Lincoln	Jeters	331/7	Gwinnet*
Hurson, James	Telfair	Edwards	95/16	Irwin
Hurst, Hardy	Washington	Cummins	334/9	Appling
Hurst, Harmon	Richmond	Palmers	96/3	Walton
Hurst, Jacob(Orp)	Scriven	Smiths	139/4	Irwin
Hurst, James	Effingham		333/2	Appling
Hurst, John	Burke	Royals	56/17	Early
Hurst, John	Burke	Royals	60/9	Appling
Hurst, Major	Burke	Royals	359/6	Irwin
Hurst, Mary(Wid)	Columbia	Willingham	90/21	Early
Hurst, Needman	Scriven	Lovets	499/8	Appling
Hurst, Stephen	Scriven	Moodys	18/3	Irwin
Hurst, Thomas D.	Columbia	Gartrells	285/4	Walton
Hurst, William	Burke	Royals	222/2	Appling
Hurt, Joel	Morgan	Campbells	358/7	Early
Hurt, Spencer	Putnam	H.Kindricks	502/7	Irwin
Hurt, William	Morgan	Leonards	252/6	Appling
Hust, Harmon	Burke	69th	157/8	Hall
Hust, Hester(Orp)	Burke	Thomas	61/7	Irwin
Huston, Oliver	Jasper	Bartlets	16/3	Walton
Hustons, (Orphans)	Burke	Royals	275/11	Irwin
Hutcheons, Redmond	Jackson	Hamilton	157/2	Habersha
Hutcheson, Wm.	Jasper	Easts	284/26	Early
Hutchins, Elijah	Jefferson	Abbots	286/14	Early
Hutchins, Elijah	Jefferson	Abbots	89/3	Appling
Hutchins, Elizabeth	Burke	Lewis	120/9	Irwin
Hutchins, Wm.	Burke	Spiveys	252/5	Irwin
Hutchinson, Ambrose	Greene	Macons	213/13	Early
Hutchinson, Elijah(RS)	Hancock	Smiths	214/7	Gwinnett
Hutchinson, Elijah(RS)	Hancock	Smiths	270/1	Appling
Hutchinson, John	Twiggs	R.Belcher	332/12	Irwin
Hutchinson, Saml.B.	Morgan	Hubbards	84/2	Appling
Hutchinson, Saml.B.	Morgan	Hubbards	94/12	Early
Hutchinson, Shad.(Orp)	Clarke	Merriwether	244/12	Early
Hutchinson, Wm.	Washington	Avents	49/2	Appling
Hutchinson, Wm.	Washington	Avents	77/13	Early
Hutchinton, Moses	Emanuel	395	289/8	Early
Hutckinson, Elijah(R.S.)	Hancock	Smiths	179/3	Habersha
Hutson, Archibald	Clarke	Penticost	416/3	Appling
Hutson, Benjamin	Washington	Brooks	142/1	Early
Hutson, Benjamin	Washington	Brooks	58/22	Early
Hutson, Charles	Jackson	Rogers	127/10	Irwin
Hutson, John	Clarke	Merewether	338/13	Early
Hutson, Leving	Jackson	Rogers	352/4	Appling
Hutson, Thomas	Jasper	Bentleys	182/2	Irwin
Hutto, ELi	Laurens	Watsons	160/11	Early
Hutto, Eli	Laurens	Watsons	291/5	Early
Hutto, Henry	Wilkinson	Kettles	11/16	Early
Hutto, John Sr.	Laurens	Watsons	5/1	Appling
Hutto, Peter	Wilkinson	Kettles	63/9	Early

NAME	COUNTY	MIL.DIST	LOT/SECT	DREW LAND
Hyas, Davis	Laurens	Ross	400/18	Early
Hyde, Samuel	Jasper	Centells	310/28	Early
Hyde, Wm.G.	Richmond	398th	41/4	Habersham
Hylard, Eliz.(Wid)	Wilkes	Perrys	398/7	Irwin
Hynes, Peter	Chatham		12/14	Early
Hysmith, Wm.	Burke	J.Wards	50/1	Rabun
Ihley, John J.	Effingham		207/11	Irwin
Ihly, Samuel	Burke	Bells	278/26	Early
Immanuel, Amos	Montgomery	McMillans	64/11	Early
Imsells, Benj.(Orph)	Emanuel	57th	63/3	Irwin
Inge, Paschal	Warren	Loyless	399/12	Irwin
Inge, William	Warren	150th	173/6	Gwinnett
Inge, William	Warren	150th	257/20	Early
Inger, John(R.S.)	Jackson	Hamilton	470/13	Irwin
Inger, John(R.S.)	Jackson	Hamiltons B.	92/6	Gwinnett
Ingham, David	Laurens	Griffins	515/8	Appling
Ingham, James	Laurens	Jones	141/17	Early
Inglett, Andrew	Richmond	Palmers	174/10	Early
Inglett, Sarah(Wid)	Richmond	Palmers	78/11	Early
Ingraham, David	Twiggs	Tisons	402/12	Irwin
Ingram, Anderson	Wilkinson	Childs	151/3	Irwin
Ingram,.Bartholomew	Hancock	Edwards	69/6	Early
Ingram, Ellen	Jefferson	Langstons	244/6	Appling
Ingram, George	Jefferson	Fountains	179/13	Habersham
Ingram, George	Jefferson	Fountains	374/10	Early
Ingram, George	Putnam	Leggets	238/6	Early
Ingram, Harmon	Jackson	Winters Bt.	250/4	Early
Ingram, John	Madison	Millicans	430/15	Early
Ingram, John	Madison	Millicans	76/20	Early
Ingram, Joseph L.	Twiggs	Smiths	150/4	Appling
Ingram, Joseph T.	Hancock	Lucas	62/27	Early
Ingram, Mary(Wid)	Jefferson	Lamps	33/2	Walton
Ingram, Presley	Putnam	Ectors	347/9	Irwin
Ingram, Thomas	Hancock	Edwards	242/2	Appling
Ingram, Wiley	Hancock	Lucas's	212/4	Appling
Ingrams, Isaac(Orph)	Jefferson	Lamps	317/26	Early
Ingrim, John	Twiggs	Ellis	15/5	Rabun
Ingrim, William	Twiggs	Ellis	297/20	Early
Ingrum, Cely(Wid)	Jefferson	Lamps	55/1	Rabun
Ingrum, John	Franklin	Jos.Millers	242/13	Irwin
Inman, Ezekiel	Burke	Lewis	253/21	Early
Innell, Anthony	Putnam	Morelands	45/16	Irwin
Irby, Abraham	Greene	Jones	219/5	Gwinnett
Irby, Daniel	Columbia	Walkers	138/20	Early
Irby, Henry	Columbia	Ob.Morriss	81/1	Early
Irby, Luke	Lincoln	Thompsons	141/27	Early
Irby, William	Jefferson	Lamps	480/5	Irwin
Irick, Mary(Wid)	Chatham		115/12	Irwin
Irick, Mary(Wid)	Chatham		294/28	Early
Irions, Charlotte(Wid)	Elbert	Olivers	155/7	Gwinnett
Irions, Lewis	Elbert	Olivers	320/7	Irwin
Irions, Lewis	Elbert	Olives	129/7	Gwinnett
Irven, Joseph	Putnam	Jurnigins	221/14	Early
Irvine, Joshua	Putnam	Littles	343/10	Early
Irving, George	Morgan	Townsends	279/4	Early
Irwin, Alexander	Washington	Barges	343/5	Gwinnett
Irwin, Alexander	Washington	Barges	96/13	Habersham
Irwin, Christopher(R.S.)	Morgan	McClendons	288/1	Appling
Irwin, Christopher(R.S.)	Morgan	McClendons	342/13	Irwin
Irwin, Christopher	Jasper	Kennedys	365/21	Early
Irwin, Issabella(Wid)	Washington	Robinsons	286/4	Irwin
Irwin, Jane(Wid)	Chatham		502/6	Irwin
Irwin, Jearrard	Washington	Robersons	49/5	Early
Irwin, John L.	Washington	Robisons	89/1	Early
Irwin, John R.	Effingham		305/18	Early
Irwin, John	Jefferson	Lamps	357/13	Irwin
Irwin, William	Jones	Harrists	398/11	Early

NAME	COUNTY	MIL.DIST	LOT/SECT	DREW LAND
Isaac, Robert	Chatham		223/20	Early
Isel, Priscilla(Wid)	Jones	Jeffersons	371/8	Appling
Isells, Jesse(Orph)	Jones	Jeffersons	138/13	Irwin
Isham, Abraham	Franklin	Jos.Millers	47/1	Early
Isham, Edward	Franklin	Jos.Millers	271/19	Early
Ishley, James	Burke	Torrances	66/3	Walton
Ishly, James	Burke	Torrances	137/11	Habersham
Isles, Nathan	Wilkinson	Bowings	227/6	Gwinnett
Isom, Christian	Morgan	Hubbards	96/1	Appling
Isom, Christian	Morgan	Hubbards	151/11	Irwin
Isom, John	Morgan	Hubbards	346/8	Appling
Isom, John	Morgan	Hubbards	351/17	Early
Iversons, Robert(Orph)	Putnam	Robertsons	426/28	Early
Ivery, Sarah(Wid)	Washington	Pools	217/6	Early
Ivey, Curtice	Jones	Permenters	490/3	Appling
Ivey, John	Appling	9th	59/11	Irwin
Ivey, Jordan	Greene	Wheelis	328/19	Early
Ivey, Joshua	Wilkes	Holidays	243/11	Irwin
Ivey, Peeples	Warren	Hubberts	344/11	Irwin
Ivey, Rives	Hancock	Scotts	81/1	Habersham
Ivey, Sarah	Greene	142nd	233/7	Irwin
Ivy, Benjamin	Warren	Blounts	225/8	Appling
Ivy, Charles	Wilkes	Bates	407/7	Appling
Ivy, Elizabeth(Wid)	Jackson	Rogers Bt.	469/3	Appling
Ivy, Ephraim	Warren	Hubberts	260/1	Early
Ivy, Ephraim	Warren	Hubberts	31/14	Early
Ivy, James S.	Pulaski	Johnstons	192/27	Early
Ivy, Jesse	Warren	Hubberts	281/13	Early
Ivy, Moses	Columbia	Ob.Morris	350/11	Early
Ivy, Moses	Columbia	Ob.Morriss	222/12	Irwin
Ivy, Neemow	Chatham		69/17	Early
Ivy, Sterling	Warren	Huberts	308/27	Early
Ivy, Turner	Wilkinson	Howards	110/13	Irwin
Jack, Elizabeth(Wid)	Jackson	Hamiltons Bt.	455/6	Irwin
Jack, James Jr.	Elbert	Olivers	12/28	Early
Jack, Samuel	Clark	Harris's	342/3	Appling
Jacks, Green B.	Clark	Mereweathers	72/5	Appling
Jacks, Green B.	Clark	Merriweathers	143/4	Appling
Jacks, John	Clark	Mereweathers	103/10	Early
Jackson, Absalom	Wilkinson	Childs	130/3	Irwin
Jackson, Allen W.	Warren	Loyless	227/19	Early
Jackson, Andrew	Richmond	Burtons	386/27	Early
Jackson, Andrew	Wilkinson	Howards	61/6	Irwin
Jackson, Benjamin	Jackson	Hamiltons Bt.	46/2	Habersham
Jackson, Benjamin	Putnam	Buckners	12/1	Early
Jackson, Catherine (Wid)	Bullock	Everitts	8/2	Appling
Jackson, Charles c.	Clark	Pentecosts	205/6	Irwin
Jackson, Claiborn M.	Warren	151	101/2	Walton
Jackson, Daniel M.	Jackson	Rogers Bt.	106/17	Early
Jackson, Daniel(Orph)	Wilkes	Davis	96/21	Early
Jackson, Daniel	Clark	Moores	156/9	Early
Jackson, Daniel	Morgan	Campbells	85/10	Hall
Jackson, Ebenezer Jr.	Chatham		138/4	Walton
Jackson, Ebenezer Sr.	Chatham		64/12	Habersham
Jackson, Edward J.	Laurens	D. Smiths	37/12	Hall
Jackson, Elijah	Franklin	Turks	198/4	Walton
Jackson, Elijah	Franklin	Turks	258/1	Appling
Jackson, Elijah	Franklin	Turks	388/19	Early
Jackson, Elijah	Franklin	Vaugns	303/20	Early
Jackson, Emanuel	Greene	142	523/6	Irwin
Jackson, Ephraim	Greene	Fosters	33/4	Early
Jackson, Ewd.I.	Laurens	D. Smiths	384/9	Early
Jackson, Henry Jr.	Hancock	Lucas	363/9	Appling
Jackson, Henry T.	Franklin	Holcombs	457/8	Appling
Jackson, Henry	Wilkinson	Howards	92/9	Early
Jackson, Isaac	Greene	Macons	167/8	Appling
Jackson, Jacob	Baldwin	Doziers	282/4	Irwin

NAME	COUNTY	MIL.DIST	LOT/SECT	DREW LAND
Jackson, James	Burke	70th	154/6	Irwin
Jackson, James	Burke	70th	24/1	Irwin
Jackson, James	Columbia	Dodsons	123/9	Irwin
Jackson, James	Greene	Armers	262/7	Irwin
Jackson, James	Jefferson	Cowarts	49/5	Irwin
Jackson, James	Jefferson	Waldens	123/1	Habersham
Jackson, James	Putnam	Slaughters	345/21	Early
Jackson, Jesse	Wilkinson	Howards	222/4	Walton
Jackson, Jethro	Putnam	Littles	25/2	Early
Jackson, Jethro	Putnam	Littles	352/28	Early
Jackson, Joel	Franklin	Turks	260/27	Early
Jackson, John B.	Greene	Nelms	56/10	Early
Jackson, John Jr.	Effingham		349/10	Early
Jackson, John Jr.	Effingham		70/4	Early
Jackson, John Sr.	Clark	Stuarts	141/11	Early
Jackson, John Sr.	Clark	Stuarts	178/9	Appling
Jackson, John W.	Warren	151st	367/4	Appling
Jackson, John	Clark	Stuarts	311/12	Irwin
Jackson, John	Jasper	McClendons	23/19	Early
Jackson, John	Jones	Buckhalters	202/16	Irwin
Jackson, John	Jones	Wallers	347/10	Irwin
Jackson, Joseph	Franklin	Davis	157/7	Early
Jackson, Joseph	Jefferson	Cowarts	385/6	Appling
Jackson, Joseph	Putnam	Buckners	2/2	Early
Jackson, Joseph	Putnam	Buckners	72/6	Irwin
Jackson, Joseph	Wilkinson	Smiths	19/9	Irwin
Jackson, Joseph	Wilkinson	Smiths	312/11	Irwin
Jackson, Jourdan	Jasper	Bentleys	331/11	Irwin
Jackson, Kinchan	Washington	Burneys	365/28	Early
Jackson, Kinchen	Washington	Burneys	17/12	Irwin
Jackson, Littleberry	Oglethorpe	Bowls	101/20	Early
Jackson, Littleberry	Oglethorpe	Bowls	394/9	Irwin
Jackson, Mark	Greene	Ragins	168/4	Irwin
Jackson, Mary(Wid)	Greene	Griers	351/18	Early
Jackson, Mary	Jasper	Easters	14/13	Irwin
Jackson, Nelson H.	Greene	Griers	135/19	Early
Jackson, Peter L.	Putnam	Oslins	18/3	Walton
Jackson, Peter	Morgan	Walkers	139/26	Early
Jackson, Phillip	Hancock	Evans	49/4	Rabun
Jackson, Plasant	Clark	Pentecosts	257/6	Gwinnett
Jackson, Robert H.	Hancock	Lucas	101/28	Early
Jackson, Robert(R.S.)	Morgan	Townsends	121/7	Gwinnett
Jackson, Robert(R.S.)	Morgan	Townsends	353/7	Early
Jackson, Robert	Morgan	Selmons	82/15	Irwin
Jackson, Robert	Twiggs	R.Belchers	116/13	Irwin
Jackson, Robert	Twiggs	R.Belchers	125/14	Irwin
Jackson, Sam.B.C.	Twiggs	R.Belchers	213/8	Appling
Jackson, Samuel W.	Jasper	Eastes	64/3	Walton
Jackson, Samuel	Clark	Stuarts	105/6	Early
Jackson, Samuel	Franklin	Vaughans	267/3	Early
Jackson, Samuel	Warren	150	374/12	Irwin
Jackson, Samuel	Warren	150th	301/28	Early
Jackson, Seaborn R.	Warren	150	39/7	Irwin
Jackson, Susannah	Baldwin	Cousins	152/3	Habersham
Jackson, Thomas A.Jr.	Warren	151	138/6	Irwin
Jackson, Thomas	Jasper	Kennedys	101/6	Appling
Jackson, Thompson M.	Morgan	Hubbards	99/2	Rabun
Jackson, Warren	Jasper	McClendons	39/6	Appling
Jackson, Warren	Putnam	Littles	27/15	Habersham
Jackson, Warren	Washington	Jinkinsons	28/3	Walton
Jackson, William S.	Scriven		511/11	Irwin
Jackson, William(Orph)	Jones	Samuels	359/12	Early
Jackson, William	Jones	Griffiths	115/6	Irwin
Jackson, William	Lincoln	Tatoms	57/5	Appling
Jackson, William	Warren	Hubberts	386/3	Appling
Jackson, William	Wilkinson	Childs	95/15	Irwin
Jackson, Williams F.	Columbia	Walkers	33/22	Early

NAME	COUNTY	MIL.DIST	LOT/SECT	DREW LAN
Jackson, Wm.(Orph)	Twiggs	Evans	179/20	Early
Jackson, Wm.	Jackson	Hamiltons Bt.	143/14	Early
Jackson, Wm.P.	Clark	Pentecosts	257/6	Appling
Jackson, Wyche	Wilkes	Kilgores	456/8	Appling
Jacksons, Coleby(Orph)	Jasper	Eastes	296/8	Appling
Jacksons, Jonathan(Orph)	Jones	Wallers	239/26	Early
Jaco, John	Lincoln	Graves	65/28	Early
Jacobs, Benjamin	Chatham		288/14	Early
Jacobs, John B.	Wayne	Jacobs	406/1	Early
Jacobs, Joshua	Jasper	Northcuts	77/4	Early
Jacobs, Shadrack	Washington	Daniels	261/10	Early
Jacobs, Shadrack	Wayne	Jacobs	113/3	Habersham
Jacobs, Susannah(Wid)	Twiggs	R. Belchers	46/2	Irwin
Jamerson, James	Jackson	Hamiltons Bt.	608/2	Appling
Jamerson, Thomas	Jackson	Hamiltons Bt.	310/5	Irwin
Jamerson, William	Jackson	Hamilton	268/18	Early
James, Ardin	Pulaski	Johnstons	238/7	Appling
James, Benjamin	Bryan	19th	199/5	Early
James, Daniel	Jones	Wallers	30/6	Irwin
James, David	Elbert	G. Higginbothams	22/14	Irwin
James, George Sr.	Oglethorpe	Brittons	12/2	Irwin
James, Isaac	Elbert	Smiths	372/3	Appling
James, Jesse	Jasper	Bentleys	236/27	Early
James, John(Orph)	Putnam	Buckners	49/26	Early
James, John	Gwinnett	Hamiltons Bt.	233/10	Irwin
James, John	Richmond	Palmers	37/4	Irwin
James, John	Twiggs	Evans	413/15	Early
James, John	Warren	Hubberts	104/3	Appling
James, Joseph Jr.	Richmond	Palmers	70/1	Rabun
James, Joseph N.	Jackson	Hamilton	5/4	Walton
James, Josiah	Jackson	Hamiltons	124/4	Appling
James, Mary(Wid)	Richmond	Palmers	356/5	Appling
James, Michael	Scriven	Lovetts	118/9	Appling
James, Phillip	Warren	154th	363/11	Early
James, Thomas	Elbert	Doolys	279/6	Irwin
James, William	Oglethorpe	Brittons	6/9	Appling
James, William	Oglethorpe	Brittons	75/11	Early
James, William	Twiggs	R.Belchers	216/7	Early
Jameson, David Jr.	Twiggs	R. Belchers	394/3	Early
Jameson, Henry	Twiggs	Ellis	94/4	Irwin
Jamison, David Sr.(R.S.)	Twiggs	Evans	313/5	Early
Jamison, Henry	Twiggs	Ellis	333/8	Appling
Jamison, Othello	Greene	144th	55/18	Early
Jamson, James	Jackson	Hamiltons Bt.	181/18	Early
Janes, Thomas C.	Wilkes	Bryants	636/2	Appling
Jarmanys, Robert(Orph)	Greene	Harvills	129/12	Hall
Jarrat, Thomas K.	Elbert	P. Christians	25/3	Early
Jarratt, Archelus	Elbert	P. Christians	8/23	Early
Jarratt, Archelus	Jones	Harrists	84/2	Irwin
Jarratt, James D.	Elbert	Ruckers	75/16	Irwin
Jarratt, Nathanl C.	Jackson	Winters B.	88/3	Irwin
Jarratt, William D.	Baldwin	Marshall	339/3	Early
Jarrel, Jacob	Greene	Harvills	51/9	Early
Jarrel, Thomas	Wilkes	Davis	267/7	Appling
Jarrell, Hardy	Greene	141st	259/9	Irwin
Jarrell, Willis	Greene	Kimbroughs	249/7	Appling
Jarret, Buckner	Lincoln	Tatoms	110/28	Early
Jarrett, Nicholas	Wilkes	Runnels	23/17	Early
Jarvis, Benjamin	Morgan	Wrights	233/4	Appling
Jarvis, Floyd(Orph)	Jefferson	Abbotts	162/13	Habersham
Jarvis, Jesse	Oglethorpe	Wises	120/12	Irwin
Jarvis, John W.	Jones	Griffiths	381/9	Appling
Jarvis, John W.	Jones	Griffiths	87/26	Early
Jean, John	Pulaski	Rees	35/4	Walton
Jeane, Green	Baldwin	Russels	226/19	Early
Jefferson, John	Twiggs	Jeffersons	176/1	Irwin
Jefferson, Thomas	Jones	Jeffersons	50/6	Gwinnett

NAME	COUNTY	MIL.DIST	LOT/SECT	DREW LAND
Jeffried, Thomas	Jasper	Phillips	177/9	Irwin
Jeffries, George	Morgan	Alfords	132/9	Irwin
Jelks, William	Pulaski	Johnsons	196/11	Early
Jelks, William	Pulaski	Johnstons	13/8	Appling
Jemison, Christiana S.	Twiggs	Jeffersons	516/5	Irwin
Jenkins, Benjamin	Baldwin	Haws	11/13	Hebersham
Jenkins, Benjamin	Baldwin	Haws	334/6	Appling
Jenkins, Benjn.	Washington	Barges	313/7	Appling
Jenkins, Charles J.	Madison	Millicans	162/6	Early
Jenkins, Charles	Hancock	Loyds	76/26	Early
Jenkins, Chas.	Hancock	Loyd	322/6	Irwin
Jenkins, Edmund	Jasper	Blakes	12/2	Habersham
Jenkins, Evan	Washington	Daniels	59/4	Habersham
Jenkins, George W.	Morgan	Campbells	460/9	Irwin
Jenkins, George	Scriven	Lovetts	252/3	Appling
Jenkins, George	Scriven	Lovetts	70/3	Rabun
Jenkins, James J.	Oglethorpe	Wises	78/10	Irwin
Jenkins, James J.	Oglethorpe	Wises	99/27	Early
Jenkins, John	Jones	Permenters	284/20	Early
Jenkins, Lewis	Washington	Jenkinsons	331/27	Early
Jenkins, Lewis	Washington	Jenkinsons	59/11	Haberhsam
Jenkins, Milley(Wid)	Greene	Carltons	156/2	Early
Jenkins, Mordecai	Warren	154	165/4	Early
Jenkins, Nicholas	Franklin	Jno.Millers	5/6	Early
Jenkins, Oen	Washington	Daniels	221/26	Early
Jenkins, Polley W.	Baldwin	Marshall	139/7	Irwin
Jenkins, Robert	Putnam	H. Kendrick	148/28	Early
Jenkins, Royal	Morgan	Campbells	24/1	Appling
Jenkins, Sampson D.	Columbia	Watsons	239/5	Irwin
Jenkins, Samuel	Burke	J. Wards	294/17	Early
Jenkins, Samuel	Elbert	Gaines	49/15	Early
Jenkins, Uriah	Washington	Jinkinsons	120/7	Appling
Jenkins, Uriah	Washington	Jinkinsons	243/7	Appling
Jenkins, William(Orph)	Morgan	Campbells	207/5	Gwinnett
Jenkins, William	Jones	Permenters	154/4	Appling
Jenkins, William	Scriven	Lovetts	104/5	Gwinnett
Jenney, Edward S.	Chatham		147/9	Hall
Jennings, Coleman	Jackson	Winters B.	96/5	Gwinnett
Jennings, Elijah	Oglethorpe	Barnetts	356/9	Appling
Jennings, James	Lincoln	Parks	285/9	Early
Jennings, Joels	Oglethorpe	Bowls	22/11	Irwin
Jennings, Moody	Lincoln	Parks	124/2	Habersham
Jennings, Nelson	Oglethorpe	Bowls	517/7	Appling
Jennings, Susannah	Oglethorpe	Goolsbys	81/1	Irwin
Jennings, Washington	Columbia	Pullins	96/10	Early
Jenny, Edwards S.	Chatham		256/10	Irwin
Jepson, John	Greene	143	214/2	Irwin
Jerald, David	Tattnall	J.Durrences	220/13	Early
Jerkings, William	Bryan	20th	293/10	Early
Jernagan, William	Putnam	Littles	234/2	Early
Jernigan, Joseph	Telfair	Edward	88/9	Hall
Jernigan, Lewis A.	Warren	153	102/11	Hall
Jernigan, Lewis B.	Laurens	Miltons	142/10	Irwin
Jessop, James	Twiggs	Evans	194/4	Irwin
Jeter, Charles	Morgan	Shaws	46/5	Irwin
Jeter, Dudley	Elbert	G. Higginbothams	74/6	Irwin
Jeter, James	Lincoln	Parks	414/5	Appling
Jeter, Mary(Wid)	Lincoln	Parks	273/12	Early
Jeter, Presly	Lincoln	Parks	231/26	Early
Jeter, Thomas	Lincoln	Parks	214/3	Early
Jeter, William	Lincoln	Tatoms	67/12	Habersham
Jett, Daniel	Greene	143rd	390/18	Early
Jett, Francis	Greene	143	142/10	Early
Jewell, Jane	Oglethorpe	Dunns	76/23	Early
Jewell, Joseph(Orph)	Oglethorpe	Dunns	90/12	Early
Jewell, Kinchin	Emanuel	56th	316/12	Irwin
Jewell, Moses	Emanuel	155th	405/3	Appling

NAME	COUNTY	MIL.DIST	LOT/SECT	DREW LA
Jewell, William	Lincoln	Tatoms	408/11	Irwin
Jewell, William	Oglethorpe	Dunnes	26/10	Hall
Jewells, Jordan(Orph)	Emanuel	55th	328/7	Appling
Jiles, Elijah	Jones	Permenters	387/10	Irwin
Jiles, James H.	Morgan	Farrars	272/8	Appling
Jiles, Joseph	Clark	Pentecost	207/7	Irwin
Jiles, William	Clark	Jacks	44/5	Appling
Jinckings, Francis	Wilkes	McLendons	209/5	Early
Jinckings, Martha	Wilkes	McLendons	393/7	Appling
Jiner, Milly(Wid)	Washington	Burneys	159/7	Appling
Jines, Edmund	Washington	Brooks	219/7	Gwinnet
Jines, Elisha	Washington	Burneys	76/4	Irwin
Jines, Ezekiel	Washington	Brooks	321/6	Irwin
Jinkins, Abisha	Burke	J. Wards	270/4	Early
Jinkins, Elijah	Morgan	Campbells	501/2	Appling
Jinkins, James	Greene	Carltons	238/7	Irwin
Jinkins, Joseph	Gwinnett	Hamiltons Bt.	85/21	Early
Jinks, Abner(Orph)	Madison	Adares	220/3	Irwin
Jinson, Thomas	Chatham		341/7	Gwinnet
John, Saint Lewis	Emanuel	55	49/17	Early
John, William Sr.	Wilkinson	Wiggins	174/8	Irwin
John, William Sr.	Wilkinson	Wiggins	191/21	Early
Johnakin, Aaron	Appling	7th	188/13	Irwin
Johns, Azel	Burke	Sullivans	20/28	Early
Johns, Bartlett C.	Jackson	Dicksons Bt.	205/16	Early
Johns, Booker R.	Jackson	Dicksons Bt.	323/4	Early
Johns, Eli	Burke	72nd	105/9	Appling
Johns, Jeremiah	Wayne	Jacobs	125/15	Irwin
Johns, Jesse	Burke	72	3/1	Irwin
Johns, John D.	Elbert	R.Christians	76/4	Rabun
Johns, John	Madison	Orrs	108/2	Walton
Johns, Lewis	Putnam	Ectors	106/28	Early
Johns, Lewis	Putnam	Ectors	46/10	Habersh
Johns, Mchittable	Camden	Tillis	408/15	Early
Johns, Mehittabel	Camden	Tillis	255/5	Irwin
Johns, Thomas(Orph)	Jasper	Bentleys	93/12	Irwin
Johns, Thomas	Putnam	Oslins	303/5	Irwin
Johns, William	Camden	Tillis	124/8	Irwin
Johns, William	Camden	Tillis	55/3	Rabun
Johns, William	Madison	Orrs	248/15	Early
Johns, William	Madison	Orrs	485/3	Appling
Johns, Zachariah	Putnam	Ectors	46/5	Gwinnet
Johnson, Abner	Greene	Kimbroughs	111/4	Appling
Johnson, Abraham	Wilkes	Dents	141/3	Appling
Johnson, Abraham	Wilkes	Dents	296/7	Early
Johnson, Adam T.	Jackson	Rogers B.	112/11	Hall
Johnson, Allan	Tattnall	Tharps	394/4	Appling
Johnson, Allan	Tattnall	Tharps	77/26	Early
Johnson, Archiabald Sr.	Tattnall	Tharps	335/9	Irwin
Johnson, Archibald Jr.	Elbert	Dooleys	316/26	Early
Johnson, Archibald	Tattnall	Tharps	330/5	Gwinnet
Johnson, Aron	Pulaski	Lesters	108/3	Walton
Johnson, Arthur	Jones	Chappels	27/11	Early
Johnson, Arthur	Jones	Chappels	387/3	Early
Johnson, Asa	Twiggs	Jeffersons	96/20	Early
Johnson, Ashfield	Greene	144th	118/13	Irwin
Johnson, Barnabas B.	Jackson	Rogers	108/6	Irwin
Johnson, Bartholomew	Greene	142nd	163/28	Early
Johnson, Benjamin	Franklin	Keltons	11/12	Irwin
Johnson, Benjamin	Jasper	Centells	136/11	Irwin
Johnson, Calvin	Warren	154	388/18	Early
Johnson, Cary	Warren	Parhams	81/10	Hall
Johnson, Catherine(Wid)	Richmond	Burtons	90/4	Appling
Johnson, Cornelius(Orph)	Putnam	Buckners	169/5	Irwin
Johnson, Crawford	Columbia	O.Morriss	46/4	Walton
Johnson, Daniel	Richmond	Laceys	448/13	Irwin
Johnson, Daniel	Wilkes	Brooks	252/23	Early

NAME	COUNTY	MIL.DIST	LOT/SECT	DREW LAND
Johnson, Darling	Emanuel	55th	284/10	Early
Johnson, David	Clark	Stuarts	326/7	Early
Johnson, David	Columbia	Ob.Morris'	137/14	Early
Johnson, David	Emanuel	58th	107/19	Early
Johnson, David	Wilkinson	Lees	358/5	Irwin
Johnson, David	Wilkinson	Lees	372/21	Early
Johnson, Eleazer(Orph)	Burke	Spiveys	208/27	Early
Johnson, Elizabeth(Wid)	Jones	Phillips	216/19	Early
Johnson, Elizabeth	Burke	Sullivans	26/6	Gwinnett
Johnson, Elizabeth	Oglethorpe	Murrays	183/8	Irwin
Johnson, Ellinder(Orph)	Burke	Spiveys	208/27	Early
Johnson, Frederich	Hancock	Millers	174/4	Irwin
Johnson, George(Orp)	Wilkes	Brooks	417/11	Irwin
Johnson, Grissett	Wilkes	Dents	448/7	Appling
Johnson, Hammet(Orph)	Burke	Spiveys	208/27	Early
Johnson, Hannah	Burke	Torrances	383/3	Early
Johnson, Henry	Oglethorpe	Barnetts	182/14	Early
Johnson, Henry	Oglethorpe	Barnetts	603/2	Appling
Johnson, Henry	Putnam	Stampers	58/7	Gwinnett
Johnson, Hiram	Warren	Hopsons	96/16	Early
Johnson, Howel	Columbia	Watsons	308/9	Appling
Johnson, Isaac W.	Oglethorpe	Bridges	41/23	Early
Johnson, Isaac	Oglethorpe	Waters	488/6	Appling
Johnson, Israel	Hancock	Smiths	446/3	Appling
Johnson, Jack	Oglethorpe	Myricks	213/7	Appling
Johnson, Jack	Oglethorpe	Myricks	227/4	Early
Johnson, Jackson(Orph)	Burke	Spiveys	208/27	Early
Johnson, Jacob(R.S.)	Twiggs	Evans	44/8	Irwin
Johnson, Jacob	Burke	Spiveys	237/8	Early
Johnson, Jacob	Warren	152nd	92/7	Early
Johnson, Jacob	Wilkes	Mattox's	326/7	Early
Johnson, James D.	Morgan	Townsens	518/21	Early
Johnson, James Sr.	Oglethorpe	Barnetts	197/6	Irwin
Johnson, James Sr.	Richmond	398th	481/2	Appling
Johnson, James Sr.	Richmond	398th	607/2	Appling
Johnson, James	Camden	Longs	7/2	Irwin
Johnson, James	Elbert	Childers	87/2	Walton
Johnson, James	Emanuel	55th	189/7	Gwinnett
Johnson, James	Wilkinson	Brooks	237/7	Early
Johnson, Jane(Orph)	Burke	Spiveys	208/27	Early
Johnson, Jeremiah	Oglethorpe	Brittons	320/6	Early
Johnson, Jesse	Greene	Ragins	143/3	Early
Johnson, Jesse	Jackson	Rogers Bt.	249/16	Early
Johnson, Jesse	Richmond	Burtons	237/21	Early
Johnson, John B.(R.S.)	Clark	Treadwell	340/19	Early
Johnson, John C.	Hancock	Scotts	212/8	Early
Johnson, John F.	Jackson	Rodgers (Bt.)	356/5	Gwinnett
Johnson, John G.	Oglethorpe	Bridges	19/9	Hall
Johnson, John	Franklin	John Millers	219/6	Appling
Johnson, John	Hancock	Canes	27/12	Early
Johnson, John	Jones	Hamfords	297/4	Irwin
Johnson, John	Oglethorpe	Murrays	462/5	Irwin
Johnson, John	Tattnall	Cunyers	343/5	Early
Johnson, John	Wilkinson	Wiggins	109/14	Irwin
Johnson, Jonas	Laurens	Deans	27/12	Hall
Johnson, Joseph B.	Wilkes	Hollays	144/6	Gwinnett
Johnson, Joseph C.	Warren	Hubberts	313/13	Irwin
Johnson, Joseph S.	Jasper	Bentleys	431/11	Irwin
Johnson, Joseph	Wilkes	Runnels's	11/10	Hall
Johnson, Josiah	Gwinnett	Hamiltons Bt.	139/12	Irwin
Johnson, Lancelot	Tattnall	J.Durrences	90/26	Early
Johnson, Lear(Wid)	Warren	Herberts	82/5	Irwin
Johnson, Lindsey	Elbert	P.Christians	329/19	Early
Johnson, Lindsey	Elbert	P.Christians	368/2	Appling
Johnson, Littleberry	Emanuel	49th	108/16	Irwin
Johnson, Luke	Hancock	Kindalls	243/8	Early
Johnson, Malcom	Hancock	Carnes	353/10	Early

NAME	COUNTY	MIL.DIST	LOT/SECT	DREW LAND
Johnson, Martin	Jones	Phillips	312/10	Irwin
Johnson, Martin	Warren	151st	177/3	Walton
Johnson, Mary(Wid)	Bullock	Knights	422/15	Early
Johnson, Mary(Wid)	Jackson	Hamiltons Bt.	285/8	Irwin
Johnson, Mary(Wid)	Jones	Shropshiers	357/20	Early
Johnson, Matthew	Emanuel	55th	1/17	Early
Johnson, Mordecai	Warren	Parhams	12/19	Early
Johnson, Moses(Orph)	Burke	M. Wards	385/9	Early
Johnson, Nathan	Oglethorpe	Devenports	294/13	Early
Johnson, Nicholas Jr.	Jasper	Centells	464/11	Irwin
Johnson, Oran(Orph)	Burke	Spiveys	208/27	Early
Johnson, Quinna(Wid)	Washington	Danells	199/27	Early
Johnson, Raborn H.	Oglethorpe	Murrays	221/9	Irwin
Johnson, Rachel(Wid)	Jackson	Dicksons Bt.	494/8	Appling
Johnson, Randall	Tattnall	Johnsons	248/6	Early
Johnson, Rebecca(Wid)	Franklin	Harris	46/3	Irwin
Johnson, Reuben Jr.	Oglethorpe	Barnetts	183/2	Habersham
Johnson, Reuben Sr.	Oglethorpe	Lees	129/16	Early
Johnson, Richmond	Jackson	Dicksons Bt.	374/4	Appling
Johnson, Robert(L.C.)	Warren	Hubberts	60/4	Early
Johnson, Robert	Greene	141	80/1	Walton
Johnson, Robert	Greene	141st	445/8	Irwin
Johnson, Robert	Jones	Permenters	450/5	Appling
Johnson, Robert	Warren	151	24/2	Early
Johnson, Rosannah(Wid)	Morgan	Campbells	181/6	Early
Johnson, Samuel	Lincoln	Parks	326/2	Appling
Johnson, Samuel	Oglethorpe	Murrays	251/7	Irwin
Johnson, Samuel	Oglethorpe	Murrays	331/13	Irwin
Johnson, Sarah(Orph)	Burke	Spiveys	208/27	Early
Johnson, Seborn	Emanuel	49th	315/8	Appling
Johnson, Stephen	Emanuel	49th	310/11	Irwin
Johnson, Stephen	Hancock	Scotts	155/5	Early
Johnson, Susannah	Wilkes	Brooks	36/3	Early
Johnson, Thomas Sr.	Columbia	Dodsons	170/18	Early
Johnson, Thomas Sr.	Pulaski	Senterfeits	88/19	Early
Johnson, Thomas	Elbert	Childres	318/14	Early
Johnson, Thomas	Elbert	Gains	342/21	Early
Johnson, Thomas	Morgan	Loyds	197/11	Early
Johnson, Thomas	Oglethorpe	Bridges	134/15	Early
Johnson, Vincent	Warren	Hubberts	351/14	Early
Johnson, Vinson	Warren	Herberts	510/13	Irwin
Johnson, William B.	Oglethorpe	Lees	213/9	Irwin
Johnson, William B.	Oglethorpe	Lees	368/5	Appling
Johnson, William Jr.	Warren	153	294/6	Early
Johnson, William Jr.	Wilkes	Willis	124/21	Early
Johnson, William Sr.	Franklin	Akins	486/11	Irwin
Johnson, William Sr.	Greene	Wheelis	285/17	Early
Johnson, William Sr.	Warren	153	291/16	Early
Johnson, William Sr.	Warren	153	51/12	Habersham
Johnson, William(Orp)	Morgan	Jordans	357/8	Appling
Johnson, William	Burke	Dys	533/7	Early
Johnson, William	Columbia	Ob.Morris'	14/1	Early
Johnson, William	Emanuel	49th	312/5	Gwinnett
Johnson, William	Emanuel	53	292/11	Early
Johnson, William	Emanuel	55th	396/21	Early
Johnson, William	Hancock	Canes	380/19	Early
Johnson, William	Oglethorpe	Davenports	160/8	Appling
Johnson, William	Tattnall	J.Durrences	56/4	Early
Johnson, William	Warren	153rd	263/2	Appling
Johnson, William	Wilkes	Durrences	56/4	Early
Johnson, Willis A.	Madison	Bones	89/10	Irwin
Johnson, Willis	Wilkinson	Smiths	308/16	Irwin
Johnson, Young	Twiggs	Bozemans	263/5	Gwinnett
Johnston, Aaron	Clark	Parrs	122/7	Gwinnett
Johnston, Abel(Orph)	Bullock	Knights	18/12	Hall
Johnston, Abner	Warren	Herberts	341/1	Early
Johnston, Aman	Jones	Buckhalters	344/7	Irwin

NAME	COUNTY	MIL.DIST	LOT/SECT	DREW LAND
Johnston, Aron	Pulaski	Lester	411/28	Early
Johnston, Bartholomew	Greene	143	52/3	Early
Johnston, Benja.Sr.	Pulaski	Lanears	300/11	Early
Johnston, Benjamin H.	Morgan	Selmons	46/7	Gwinnett
Johnston, Benjamin	Jasper	Centells	249/27	Early
Johnston, Benjamin	Twiggs	Smith	59/3	Irwin
Johnston, Benjamin	Warren	151st	69/2	Habersham
Johnston, Benjm.Sr.	Pulaski	Lanears	290/8	Irwin
Johnston, Cary	Warren	Parhams	265/6	Gwinnett
Johnston, Cyrus	Jones	Phillips	188/9	Appling
Johnston, David	Jasper	Blakes	177/3	Early
Johnston, David	Jasper	Blakes	388/3	Early
Johnston, Edmond	Warren	Rogers	395/6	Appling
Johnston, Edward	Twiggs	Hodges	215/13	Early
Johnston, Elijah	Burke	69th	370/26	Early
Johnston, Elijah	Washington	Daniels	104/2	Rabun
Johnston, Elijah	Washington	Daniels	244/19	Irwin
Johnston, Elizabeth B. (Orph) Elbert		Gaines	55/7	Gwinnett
Johnston, Elizabeth	Hancock	Mimms	52/20	Early
Johnston, Evan	Hancock	Mims	13/8	Early
Johnston, Felix	Pulaski	Lanears	107/14	Early
Johnston, Felix	Pulaski	Lanears	153/5	Appling
Johnston, Frederick	Greene	144	230/6	Gwinnett
Johnston, Harvey	Greene	Wheelis	236/4	Irwin
Johnston, Henry S.	Warren	Griers	115/3	Rabun
Johnston, Hester(Wid)	Chatham		70/7	Irwin
Johnston, Jabez	Jasper	Blacks	454/16	Appling
Johnston, James R.	Pulaski	Johnstons	286/11	Early
Johnston, James	Chatham		498/6	Irwin
Johnston, James	Chatham		74/21	Early
Johnston, James	Jasper	Northcuts	232/4	Early
Johnston, James	Jefferson	Mathews	193/5	Irwin
Johnston, James	McIntosh	Hamiltons	284/18	Early
Johnston, James	Putnam	Coopers	86/1	Early
Johnston, Jeremiah	Twiggs	Evans	227/5	Appling
Johnston, Jesse(Orph)	Oglethorpe	Davenports	425/9	Irwin
Johnston, Jesse	Jones	Wallers	81/19	Early
Johnston, Jesse	Putnam	Coopers	262/10	Early
Johnston, Jesse	Washington	Floyds	306/7	Early
Johnston, Joel	Columbia	Ob.Morriss	155/7	Appling
Johnston, Joel	Walton	Williams	210/4	Appling
Johnston, John B. (R.S.)	Clark	Tredwells	142/6	Irwin
Johnston, John Sr.	Emanuel	49	126/7	Appling
Johnston, John	Elbert	Childres	480/11	Irwin
Johnston, John	Franklin	John Millers	187/3	Early
Johnston, John	Jones	Hansfords	353/5	Gwinnett
Johnston, John	Morgan	Beasleys	18/16	Early
Johnston, John	Tattnall	Cunyers	236/13	Early
Johnston, John	Washington	Daniels	452/6	Irwin
Johnston, Joseph	Clark	Mitchells	456/4	Appling
Johnston, Joseph	Putnam	Bustins	200/17	Early
Johnston, Joshua	Madison	Willifords	158/8	Early
Johnston, Lake	Oglethorpe	Barnetts	8/6	Early
Johnston, Lewis P.	Chatham		68/14	Irwin
Johnston, Lewis	Jones	Seals	388/6	Appling
Johnston, Lewis	Laurens	S.Smiths	165/8	Early
Johnston, Loyd	Baldwin	Doziers	481/6	Appling
Johnston, Malcom	Hancock	Canes	261/3	Early
Johnston, Martin	Warren	151	167/27	Early
Johnston, Michael	Telfair	Wilsons	108/1	Appling
Johnston, Mordica	Warren	Parhams	192/7	Irwin
Johnston, Nehemiah D.	Hancock	Hubberts	371/9	Early
Johnston, Noel	Laurens	Watsons	340/12	Early
Johnston, Phillip	Jefferson	Waldens	14/21	Early
Johnston, Posey	Morgan	Townsends	419/6	Appling
Johnston, Redmond	Jackson	Dicksons Bt.	1/11	Early
Johnston, Robert D.	Jackson	Dicksons Bt.	89/15	Early

NAME	COUNTY	MIL.DIST	LOT/SECT	DREW LAN
Johnston, Robert (R.S.)	Gwinnett	Hamiltons Bt.	61/10	Habersha
Johnston, Robert (R.S.)	Gwinnett	Hamiltons	167/8	Irwin
Johnston, Samuel	Baldwin	Taliaferros	394/2	Early
Johnston, Samuel	Oglethorpe	Rowlands	292/4	Appling
Johnston, Sarah	Baldwin	Talliaferros	50/12	Early
Johnston, Snelling	Jasper	Kennedys	34/5	Irwin
Johnston, Stephen Y.	Wilkes	Dents	85/5	Irwin
Johnston, Stephen	Emanuel	49	319/1	Early
Johnston, Stephen	Pulaski	Lanears	373/6	Appling
Johnston, Thomas C.	Jackson	Hamiltons Bt.	222/12	Habersha
Johnston, Thomas Sr.	Pulaski	Senterfeits	104/11	Early
Johnston, Thomas	Chatham		92/11	Hall
Johnston, Thomas	Greene	141	107/7	Irwin
Johnston, Timothy	Scriven	9 Bt.	288/7	Irwin
Johnston, Vardy	Jackson	Dicksons B.	26/3	Habersha
Johnston, William Sr.	Jasper	Centells	26/7	Early
Johnston, William	Baldwin	Doziers	22/6	Early
Johnston, William	Baldwin	Doziers	72/2	Rabun
Johnston, William	Bullock	Edwards	4/2	Irwin
Johnston, William	Camden	Millers	286/4	Appling
Johnston, William	Franklin	Akins	396/6	Early
Johnston, William	Jasper	Blakes	463/7	Appling
Johnston, William	Jones	Wallers	260/4	Irwin
Johnston, William	Laurens	Harris	38/11	Habersha
Johnston, William	Morgan	Campbells	137/11	Irwin
Johnston, William	Morgan	Selmons	196/5	Gwinnett
Johnston, William	Pulaski	Lanears	222/28	Early
Johnston, William	Pulaski	Lanears	442/21	Early
Johnston, William	Washington	Pools	109/5	Early
Johnston, William	Washington	Pools	428/5	Appling
Johnston, Williams	Clark	Parrs	464/6	Irwin
Johnston, Willis	Washington	Echols	16/12	Hall
Johnston, Wm.	Twiggs	Barrows	451/4	Appling
Johnstons, James (Orph)	Clark	Deans	67/13	Early
Johnstons, John (Orph)	Pulaski	Senterfeits	4/8	Early
Johnstons, William (Orph)	Washington	Daniels	102/14	Irwin
Johnstons, William (Orph)	Wilkes	Josseys	105/12	Hall
Joice, Henry	Tattnall	Tharps	182/17	Early
Joice, John (R.S.)	Tattnall	Tharps	64/8	Hall
Joiner, Benajoe	Morgan	Wright	153/21	Early
Joiner, Bennet	Laurens	Swearingens	46/14	Early
Joiner, Curtis	Laurens	Swearingam	137/8	Irwin
Joiner, Edmund	Washington	Burneys	286/4	Early
Joiner, Edmund	Washington	Burneys	426/3	Appling
Joiner, Hardy	Washington	Danells	336/11	Irwin
Joiner, Jacob	Emanuel	57	71/7	Early
Joiner, Lewis	Laurens	S.Smith	111/1	Walton
Joiner, Nancy	Scriven	Lovetts	24/4	Habersham
Joiner, Samuel	Washington	Cummins	121/8	Irwin
Joiner, Thomas	Burke	J. Wards	184/4	Irwin
Joiner, William H.	Chatham		389/5	Appling
Joiner, William J.	Burke	J. Wards	312/17	Early
Jolley, Bradley	Walton	Worshams	495/3	Appling
Jolley, Joseph	Clark	Applings	108/10	Habersham
Jolliff, Thomas	Jones	Jeffersons	188/6	Early
Jolliff, Thomas	Jones	Jeffersons	292/5	Irwin
Jolly, Benjamin	Gwinnett	Hamiltons Bt.	89/27	Early
Jolly, John	Baldwin	Ellis	224/4	Appling
Jolly, John	Baldwin	Ellis	42/5	Rabun
Jolly, Peter	Jones	Buckhalters	161/3	Habersham
Jones, Aaron O.	Laurens	Ross	392/7	Appling
Jones, Aaron	Lincoln	Jones	151/7	Appling
Jones, Abner	Jasper	Phillips	247/3	Walton
Jones, Abraham	Washington	Floyds	341/17	Early
Jones, Adam Sr.	Warren	154	393/15	Early
Jones, Adam	Columbia	J. Morriss	80/4	Appling
Jones, Adam	Laurens	Jones	233/6	Irwin

NAME	COUNTY	MIL.DIST	LOT/SECT	DREW LAND
Jones, Albritton(Orph)	Putnam	Slaughters	222/2	Early
Jones, Allen H.	Columbia	J. Morris	55/6	Gwinnett
Jones, Allen	Hancock	Lucas	352/19	Early
Jones, Allen	Wilkinson	Kettles	205/13	Irwin
Jones, Amose	Morgan	Selmons	127/3	Walton
Jones, Ann(Wid)	Hancock	Canes	213/6	Appling
Jones, Archwell	Jones	Wallers	290/1	Early
Jones, Arthur	Elbert	Childers	285/13	Irwin
Jones, Augustus S.	Scriven	Moodys	179/27	Early
Jones, Baniee	Jasper	Dasters	17/16	Early
Jones, Barnett	Franklin	Harriss	191/11	Early
Jones, Benjamin B.	Columbia	Ob.Morriss	65/14	Early
Jones, Benjamin R.	Columbia	Ob.Morriss	32/6	Gwinnett
Jones, Benjamin(Orph)	Hall		134/14	Early
Jones, Benjamin	Warren	154	458/8	Irwin
Jones, Brewington	Oglethorpe	Wises	321/15	Early
Jones, Bridger	Bullock	Tilmans	88/7	Irwin
Jones, Bryan	Jones	Rossers	228/3	Early
Jones, Carter	Putnam	Slaughters	110/1	Irwin
Jones, Charity(Wid)	Franklin	Vaughns	93/15	Early
Jones, Charles	Burke	McNorrills	145/10	Hall
Jones, Charles	Franklin	Harris	380/3	Early
Jones, Cornelius	Columbia	Gartrells	513/5	Irwin
Jones, Dabney P.	Madison	Willifords	143/13	Habersham
Jones, Daniel E.	Tattnall	J.Durrences	85/1	Early
Jones, Daniel	Glynn		204/1	Early
Jones, Darling	Pulaski	Johnstons	447/5	Irwin
Jones, David	Wilkinson	Kettles	185/7	Gwinnett
Jones, David	Wilkinson	Kettles	376/26	Early
Jones, Dickerson	Greene	142nd	175/4	Appling
Jones, Drury(Orph)	Emanuel	49th	130/8	Appling
Jones, Drury	Franklin	Flanagans	113/11	Early
Jones, Dudley	Franklin	Hammonds	171/9	Early
Jones, Dudley	Franklin	Hammonds	204/1	Irwin
Jones, Eley	Hancock	Edwards	98/10	Irwin
Jones, Elias	Jasper	Blakes	161/5	Irwin
Jones, Elijah E.	Morgan	Hubbards	335/10	Early
Jones, Elizabeth A.(Wid)	Chatham		354/3	Appling
Jones, Elizabeth(Wid)	Jackson	Dicksons Bt.	158/7	Appling
Jones, Elizabeth	Richmond	398th	39/3	Rabun
Jones, Elizabeth	Scriven	9th Bt.	59/12	Early
Jones, Elizbeth(Wid)	Chatham		234/9	Irwin
Jones, Ephraim	Greene	142nd	156/12	Habersham
Jones, Ephraim	Greene	142nd	308/6	Early
Jones, Evan	Wayne	Jacobs	205/3	Irwin
Jones, Fanney	Morgan	Townsends	327/19	Early
Jones, Frances	Baldwin	Marshalls	47/5	Irwin
Jones, Francis	Bullock	Edwards	16/7	Irwin
Jones, Gabriel	Baldwin	Taliaferros	36/5	Appling
Jones, George W.	Franklin	Akins	322/5	Early
Jones, George W.	Hall		164/2	Rabun
Jones, George	Jefferson	Flemmings	430/3	Appling
Jones, Hardy	Jasper	Kindricks	237/15	Early
Jones, Henly	Warren	154th	134/16	Irwin
Jones, Henry L.	Baldwin	Ellis	404/1	Early
Jones, Henry	Franklin	Halcombs	229/3	Early
Jones, Henry	Habersham	Holcombs	228/26	Early
Jones, Henry	Lincoln	Tatoms	335/17	Early
Jones, Henry	Telfair	William	81/10	Early
Jones, Henry	Warren	Blounts	75/3	Rabun
Jones, Hiram	Wilkinson	Howards	55/28	Early
Jones, Holland(Wid)	Wilkinson	Bowings	365/13	Irwin
Jones, Howell	Jefferson	Cowarts	86/13	Early
Jones, Isaac	Lincoln	Alfords	196/17	Early
Jones, Isaac	Lincoln	Thompsons	34/3	Walton
Jones, Isaac	Wilkinson	Brooks	110/17	Early
Jones, Isaac	Wilkinson	Brooks	277/14	Early

NAME	COUNTY	MIL.DIST	LOT/SECT	DREW LAN
Jones, Isaac	Wilkinson	Brooks	524/6	Irwin
Jones, James D.	Hancock	Coopers	283/28	Early
Jones, James W.	Burke	Betts	360/11	Early
Jones, James(Little)	Twiggs	W. Belcher	21/3	Irwin
Jones, James(Orph)	Twiggs	Hodges	74/19	Early
Jones, James	Bullock	Edwards	285/6	Appling
Jones, James	Bullock	Knight	345/11	Early
Jones, James	Glynn		171/1	Early
Jones, James	Habersham	Taylors	91/2	Rabun
Jones, James	Hancock	Millers	158/10	Early
Jones, James	Putnam	Slaughters	214/6	Gwinnett
Jones, James	Twiggs	W.Belchers	45/9	Hall
Jones, Jane(Wid)	Jones	Childers	43/1	Early
Jones, Jesse L.	Warren	Parhams	407/6	Appling
Jones, Jesse(Orph)	Elbert	Olivers	528/2	Appling
Jones, Jesse	Camden	Baileys	356/9	Irwin
Jones, Jesse	Clark	Applings	395/17	Early
Jones, Jesse	Hancock	Danells	336/8	Early
Jones, Jesse	Jones	Rossers	30/2	Early
Jones, John A.	Baldwin	Haws	67/11	Hall
Jones, John D.	Jones	Weatherbys	218/12	Early
Jones, John H.	Warren	McCrarys	127/10	Habersha
Jones, John J.	Putnam	Berrys	145/10	Early
Jones, John M.	Burke	McNorrills	67/2	Early
Jones, John M.	Hancock	Lucas	23/5	Early
Jones, John P.(Orph)	Wilkes	Mattox	98/12	Irwin
Jones, John Sr.	Washington	Floyds	117/17	Early
Jones, John T.B.	Bullock	Knights	497/13	Irwin
Jones, John W.	Baldwin	Doziers	151/4	Irwin
Jones, John(Son of Rich.)	Columbia	Shaws	22/13	Irwin
Jones, John	Burke	69th	153/16	Irwin
Jones, John	Clark	Simms	241/17	Early
Jones, John	Jasper	Evans	44/5	Hall
Jones, John	Putnam	Buckners	361/6	Early
Jones, John	Richmond	120th	308/13	Irwin
Jones, John	Scriven		355/17	Early
Jones, John	Tattnall	Johnstons	5/6	Irwin
Jones, John	Twiggs	Hodges	81/3	Early
Jones, John	Washington	Floyds	263/1	Appling
Jones, John	Washington	Floyds	294/12	Early
Jones, John	Wilkinson	Howards	255/7	Appling
Jones, Jonathan	Laurens	Ross	299/8	Irwin
Jones, Jonathan	Pulaski	Johnstons	262/8	Irwin
Jones, Jos.B.(Orph)	Baldwin	Marshalls	204/4	Irwin
Jones, Joseph	Clark	Mitchells	5/17	Early
Jones, Joseph	Franklin	P. Brown	89/26	Early
Jones, Joseph	Franklin	P. Browns	183/14	Early
Jones, Joseph	Greene	141	18/11	Early
Jones, Joseph	Greene	141st	158/10	Irwin
Jones, Joseph	Liberty		213/7	Early
Jones, Joseph	Wilkinson	Howard	228/16	Early
Jones, Josiah	Bullock	Tilmans	17/3	Walton
Jones, Josiah	Bullock	Tilmans	329/7	Early
Jones, Josiah	Wilkinson	Kettles	11/23	Early
Jones, Judith(Wid)	Columbia	Olives	330/21	Early
Jones, Julius C.	Columbia	Battles	307/13	Early
Jones, Lemuel(Orph)	Hall		134/14	Early
Jones, Leroy	Oglethorpe	Barnetts	149/5	Early
Jones, Leroy	Oglethorpe	Barnetts	160/7	Irwin
Jones, Lewis	Elbert	Childers	311/9	Early
Jones, Lewis	Franklin	Boswells	406/4	Early
Jones, Lewis	Washington	Peabodys	259/28	Early
Jones, Martha (Wid)	Clark	Applings	212/2	Early
Jones, Martin	Franklin	Flanaganes	28/7	Irwin
Jones, Mary D.	Greene	Ragins	86/2	Rabun
Jones, Mary E.(Wid)	Chatham		293/16	Early
Jones, Mary(Wid)	Columbia	Walkers	384/11	Irwin

NAME	COUNTY	MIL.DIST	LOT/SECT	DREW LAND
Jones, Mary(Wid)	Jones	Buckhalters	358/13	Early
Jones, Mary(Wid)	Twiggs	Bozemans	20/4	Rabun
Jones, Mary(Wid)	Wilkes	Mattox	31/13	Habersham
Jones, Matthew Jr.	Bullock	Edwards	233/5	Gwinnett
Jones, Micajah	Franklin	Turks	157/12	Irwin
Jones, Miles	Chatham		91/13	Early
Jones, Mitchell	Columbia	Olives	230/13	Early
Jones, Moses R.	Lincoln	Walkers	20/8	Appling
Jones, Moses	Lincoln	Jones	261/10	Irwin
Jones, Moses	Montgomery	Alstons	16/4	Habersham
Jones, Nancy(Orp)	Hall		134/14	Early
Jones, Nancy(Wid)	Franklin	Haynes	264/9	Irwin
Jones, Nathaniel	Camden	Tillis	210/9	Early
Jones, Peter	Franklin	Hayns	320/5	Gwinnett
Jones, Polly(Wid.& Or.)	Franklin	Akins	41/13	Irwin
Jones, Rebecca(Orph)	Liberty		213/7	Early
Jones, Rebecca(Wid)	Jones	Chappels	283/4	Early
Jones, Rebecca	Franklin	Flanaganes	519/9	Irwin
Jones, Reuben	Warren	Griers	25/4	Rabun
Jones, Rhisa H.	Columbia	Watsons	147/3	Irwin
Jones, Richard W.	Morgan	Parkers	268/1	Appling
Jones, Richard(R.S.)	Warren	152	229/3	Appling
Jones, Richard	Clark	Starnes	438/15	Early
Jones, Robert	Morgan	Leonards	49/11	Irwin
Jones, Robert	Oglethorpe	Rowlands	407/15	Early
Jones, Russel Sr.	Franklin	Ashs	139/5	Gwinnett
Jones, Samuel Jr.	Pulaski	Johnstons	492/5	Appling
Jones, Samuel Sr.	Pulaski	Lesters	442/9	Irwin
Jones, Samuel Sr.	Putnam	Lesters	139/4	Walton
Jones, Samuel(Orph)	Burke	72d	157/12	Early
Jones, Samuel	Habersham	Tankersleys	486/6	Irwin
Jones, Seaborn	Baldwin	Marshalls	34/8	Irwin
Jones, Seaborn	Baldwin	Marshalls	357/9	Early
Jones, Seaborn	Greene	142	246/18	Early
Jones, Seaborn	Jefferson	Abbots	366/16	Early
Jones, Seaborn	Jefferson	Abbotts	61/5	Rabun
Jones, Seaborn	Morgan	Parker	435/8	Appling
Jones, Seaborn	Morgan	Parkers	256/14	Early
Jones, Simeon	Elbert	Dooleys	83/12	Habersham
Jones, Smith	Richmond	Winters	365/17	Early
Jones, Solomon	Elbert	Childers	47/12	Early
Jones, Standley	Elbert	Ruckers	99/3	Early
Jones, Stephen	Jones	Buckhalters	178/10	Irwin
Jones, Stephen	Jones	Buckhalters	18/14	Irwin
Jones, Stephen	Putnam	Slaughters	82/12	Habersham
Jones, Stephen	Twiggs	Browns	31/9	Hall
Jones, Tandy C.	Jefferson	Abbots	444/4	Appling
Jones, Temperence	Putnam	Slaughters	293/2	Appling
Jones, Thomas B.	Baldwin	Knights	276/11	Early
Jones, Thomas B.	Warren	150th	451/9	Irwin
Jones, Thomas Jr.	Morgan	Jordans	162/13	Early
Jones, Thomas(Orphs)	Greene	Ragins	397/20	Early
Jones, Thomas(R.S.)	Hancock	Edwards	315/5	Gwinnett
Jones, Thomas	Bullock	Knights	133/12	Hall
Jones, Thomas	Burke	Torrances	371/20	Early
Jones, Thomas	Burke	Torrences	361/17	Early
Jones, Thomas	Chatham		102/12	Irwin
Jones, Thomas	Chatham		63/4	Rabun
Jones, Thomas	Columbia	Pullins	45/9	Early
Jones, Thomas	Elbert	Dooleys	134/14	Irwin
Jones, Thomas	Elbert	G. Higginbothams	312/7	Early
Jones, Thomas	Franklin	Harris	44/2	Rabun
Jones, Thomas	Greene	141	521/8	Appling
Jones, Thomas	Hancock	Justices	140/26	Early
Jones, Thomas	Hancock	Justices	195/1	Walton
Jones, Thomas	Putnam	Buckners	63/5	Early
Jones, Thomas	Richmond	120	169/2	Rabun

NAME	COUNTY	MIL.DIST	LOT/SECT	DREW LAND
Jones, Timothy	Morgan	Dennis	152/1	Appling
Jones, Walter	Baldwin	Marshalls	131/15	Irwin
Jones, Warrington	Morgan	Parkers	424/13	Irwin
Jones, Wiley	Jasper	Baileys	56/12	Hall
Jones, Wiley	Morgan	Townsends	226/7	Gwinnett
Jones, Wiley	Wilkinson	Howards	86/4	Habersham
Jones, William H.	Morgan	Knights	17/5	Habersham
Jones, William Jr.	Wilkinson	Kettles	350/7	Appling
Jones, William Rev.	Twiggs	Jeffersons	315/3	Early
Jones, William Sr.	Franklin	Buckhalters	394/17	Early
Jones, William(Orph)	Franklin	Flanagans	130/5	Early
Jones, William(Orph)	Putnam	Robertson	165/5	Early
Jones, William	Chatham		470/7	Appling
Jones, William	Clark	Mitchells	17/3	Rabun
Jones, William	Clark	Mitchells	513/8	Irwin
Jones, William	Columbia	Olives	215/1	Appling
Jones, William	Emanuel	59th	24/9	Appling
Jones, William	Franklin	Ashs	168/11	Irwin
Jones, William	Franklin	Flanagans	251/8	Early
Jones, William	Gwinnett	Hamiltons Bt.	306/6	Early
Jones, William	Hancock	Millers	285/5	Early
Jones, William	Hancock	Thomas	144/7	Gwinnett
Jones, William	Jasper	Kennedys	234/5	Gwinnett
Jones, William	Jasper	Kennedys	80/5	Rabun
Jones, William	Morgan	Loyds	475/4	Appling
Jones, William	Morgan	Parkers	143/11	Irwin
Jones, William	Wilkinson	Kettles	270/5	Appling
Jones, Willie	Warren	152nd	337/26	Early
Jones, Willis	Warren	152nd	329/4	Early
Jones, Wm.(R.S.)	Franklin	Holcombs	269/4	Irwin
Jones, Wm.D.	Lincoln	Parks	24/2	Rabun
Jones, Zera(Orph)	Twiggs	Evans	287/5	Early
Jonson, Henry H.	Jackson	Dicksons Bt.	231/4	Early
Jordan, Abner	Morgan	Jordans	359/7	Early
Jordan, Abraham	Jefferson	Cowarts	143/5	Early
Jordan, Absalom	Wilkinson	Childs	333/15	Irwin
Jordan, Alexr.	Elbert	B.Higginbothams	50/10	Hall
Jordan, Archibald	Habersham	Holcombs	22/7	Appling
Jordan, Asa	Habersham	Flannigans	85/28	Early
Jordan, Benjamin(Orph)	Oglethorpe	Brittons	65/18	Early
Jordan, Briton	Washington	Burneys	145/3	Habersham
Jordan, Cynthia(Wid)	Jones	Shropshiers	37/4	Walton
Jordan, Elijah	Greene	144th	200/7	Irwin
Jordan, Flemming	Oglethorpe	Goolsbys	102/5	Irwin
Jordan, Graham	Richmond	Winters	50/20	Early
Jordan, Greene H.	Laurens	D. Smiths	121/18	Early
Jordan, Henry	Twiggs	Browns	130/17	Early
Jordan, James	Elbert	Whites Dis.of Cs.	224/10	Irwin
Jordan, James	Hall	Simmonds	170/2	Rabun
Jordan, James	Jackson	Hamiltons Bt.	201/2	Early
Jordan, James	Oglethorpe	Bowland	93/4	Irwin
Jordan, James	Washington	Brooks	145/14	Irwin
Jordan, James	Washington	Brooks	176/9	Early
Jordan, John C.	Jasper	Bentleys	273/5	Early
Jordan, John Sr.	Washington	Brooks	217/20	Early
Jordan, John	Lincoln	Parks	224/6	Gwinnett
Jordan, Josiah Sr.	Oglethorpe	Rowlands	364/20	Early
Jordan, Josiah	Jefferson	Lamps	41/1	Irwin
Jordan, Mathew	Oglethorpe	Devenports	70/5	Gwinnett
Jordan, Matthew	Jefferson	Lamps	214/7	Appling
Jordan, Mottimer	Oglethorpe	Goolsbys	23/1	Irwin
Jordan, Nezekiah	Baldwin	Marshalls	351/8	Early
Jordan, Overoff	Baldwin	Marshalls	594/2	Appling
Jordan, Reubin	Oglethorpe	Goolsbys	185/5	Early
Jordan, Richard	Washington	Renfros	262/2	Early
Jordan, Theophilus	Jefferson	Mathews	130/12	Early
Jordan, Thomas D.	Franklin	P.Browns	229/6	Gwinnett

NAME	COUNTY	MIL.DIST	LOT/SECT	DREW LAND
Jordan, Thomas R.	Greene	141st.	20/1	Walton
Jordan, Thomas	Montgomery	McMillans	270/13	Early
Jordan, Warren	Morgan	Jordans	214/20	Early
Jordan, Warren	Morgan	Jordans	453/4	Appling
Jordan, William B.	Baldwin	Irwins	258/10	Irwin
Jordan, William	Emanuel	55th	262/4	Walton
Jordan, William	Wilkes	Brooks	342/3	Early
Jordan, Willouby	Twiggs	Smiths	116/2	Appling
Jordans, Jesse(Orph)	Washington	Brooks	108/6	Appling
Joseph, Samuel	Wilkes	Runnels	290/9	Irwin
Josey, Willis	Burke	Thomas	45/11	Early
Jossey, Henry	Wilkes	Josseys	501/6	Appling
Jouran, Sarah	Chatham		203/16	Irwin
Jourand, J.B.	Chatham		107/2	Rabun
Jourdan, Hezekiah	Baldwin	Marshall	38/3	Walton
Jourdan, Jacob	Lincoln	Parks	558/2	Appling
Jourdan, Levi	Columbia	Watsons	144/28	Early
Jourdan, Sarah	Chatham		288/1	Walton
Jourdan, William	Wilkinson	Bowings	314/7	Appling
Journagan, Alexander	Twiggs	Evins	249/5	Gwinnett
Journagan, Moody	Twiggs	Evans	185/13	Early
Journigan, Mary I.	Bullock	Averits	527/10	Irwin
Jowell, Richard (R.S.)	Baldwin	Marshalls	138/15	Irwin
Jowell, Richard	Baldwin	Marshalls	25/2	Irwin
Joyce, Daniel	Laurens	Deans	278/3	Appling
Joyce, Edward(R.S.)	Putnam	Ectors	72/8	Early
Joyce, Washington	Montgomery	McMillans	351/1	Early
Joyless, John	Putnam	Berrys	263/9	Early
Joyner, Ebenezar	Twiggs	W.Belchers	164/8	Appling
Judgkins, Charles(Orph)	Jefferson	Fountains	94/3	Early
Judkins, Zechariah(R.S.)	Hancock	Millers	317/11	Early
Judkins, Zecheriah(R.S.)	Hancock	Millers	126/3	Irwin
Juirnigains, Isaac(Orph)	Telfair	Williams	19/16	Irwin
Jump, Sarah(Wid)	Pulaski	Johnstons	293/1	Early
Junior, Anthony	Putnam	Morelands	305/1	Appling
Junior, Anthony	Putnam	Morlands	264/6	Early
Junior, Robert	Putnam	Morelands	117/3	Early
Jurdan, Samuel Jr.	Gwinnett	Hamiltons	247/10	Early
Jurnigan, Moses	Tattnall	J. Durences	13/28	Early
Jurnigan, Moses	Tattnall	J.Durrences	114/4	Walton
Justice, Appleton	Jones	Weatherbys	250/10	Early
Justice, Dempsey	Baldwin	Stephens	218/10	Early
Justice, Isaac	Jones	Greens	125/13	Irwin
Justice, Isaac	Jones	Greens	2/19	Early
Justice, Jacob	Wilkinson	Lees	14/13	Early
Justice, James	Hancock	Justices	199/12	Habersham
Justice, James	Wilkinson	Bowings	152/8	Appling
Justice, John	Hancock	Justices	257/1	Appling
Justice, John	Hancock	Justices	370/7	Irwin
Justice, Levi	Baldwin	Stephens	405/6	Appling
Justice, Stephen	Jackson	Winters Bt.	26/4	Appling
Jyner, William	Twiggs	Jeffersons	306/9	Early
Kakler, John	Chatham		56/15	Early
Kallander, Thomas(Orph)	Liberty		223/17	Early
Kallender, Jane(Wid)	Liberty		133/4	Irwin
Kassler, John C.	Twiggs	R.Belchers	12/12	Haberhsam
Kay, Jannet M.	Hall	Byrds	355/27	Early
Kea, Lodowick	Hancock	Mims	342/11	Early
Keal, Abraham	Scriven	Moody	379/1	Appling
Kean, John	Jones	Phillips	222/1	Irwin
Kean, Josiah	Pulaski	Lanears	141/4	Walton
Kean, Robert T.	Wilkes	Willis	13/4	Habersham
Keane, Thomas	Tattnall	Tharps	227/3	Appling
Kearsey, William	Burke	Bells	27/5	Irwin
Keaten, Jesse	Putnam	Oslins	42/3	Habersham
Keath, Ann	Pulaski	Davis	360/12	Irwin
Keaton, Isham	Twiggs	Ellis	304/5	Appling

NAME	COUNTY	MIL.DIST	LOT/SECT	DREW LAND
Keaton, Rader Sr.	Twiggs	Ellis	148/15	Early
Keaton, Rader Sr.	Twiggs	Ellis	327/27	Early
Keaton, Wm.(Orphs)	Washington	Barges	196/9	Appling
Keebler, Geo.(Orp)	Twiggs	Thames	368/14	Early
Keel, John	Wilkinson	Bowings	309/3	Early
Keel, William	Franklin	Greens	261/6	Irwin
Keeling, William H.	Elbert	Dobbs	386/11	Irwin
Keels, (Orphs)	Franklin	Morriss	142/13	Irwin
Keen, Rachel(Wid)	Tattnall	Keens	27/3	Rabun
Keener, Rachel(Wid)	Twiggs	W.Belchers	315/15	Early
Keenum, James	Jackson	Hamiltons Bt.	275/7	Early
Keer, John D.	Greene	Macons	50/2	Walton
Keerbow, Joseph	Jackson	Hamiltons	305/26	Early
Keiffer, Ephraim	Effingham		351/6	Appling
Keith, Jeremiah	Jasper	Posts	282/28	Early
Keith, John	Putnam	Oslins	278/6	Appling
Kell, John	McIntosh	Hamiltons	108/1	Habersham
Kellam, John	Emanuel	53rd	11/20	Early
Kellam, Russell	Washington	Brooks	1/26	Early
Kellar, Willis	Jasper	Phillips	259/4	Irwin
Keller, Godfrey	Jefferson	Lamps	102/6	Irwin
Keller, John A.	Chatham		104/4	Appling
Keller, Justice	Jefferson	Lamps	427/2	Appling
Keller, Paul	Chatham		222/18	Early
Keller, Paul	Chatham		99/5	Early
Kellett, John	Jasper	Clays	199/18	Early
Kelley, Daniel	Hall	McElhannons	481/8	Appling
Kelley, James O.	Oglethorpe	Lees	292/12	Early
Kelley, James	Jones	Griffiths	528/8	Irwin
Kelley, John	Jasper	Kendalls	404/11	Irwin
Kelley, John	Jones	Shropshiers	333/10	Irwin
Kelley, Lewis	Jones	Griffiths	344/5	Irwin
Kelley, Moses	Richmond		251/23	Early
Kelley, William	Jackson	Dicksons	511/6	Appling
Kelley, Wm.	Elbert	Whites Dist.	159/6	Appling
Kelleys, John(Orph)	Hancock	Lucas	331/6	Gwinnett
Kellum, William	Oglethorpe	Barnetts	284/6	Early
Kelly's, Daniel(Orphs)	Jones	Permenters	99/12	Irwin
Kelly, Abraham	Scriven	Lovets	522/8	Irwin
Kelly, Abraham	Scriven	Lovetts	101/5	Gwinnett
Kelly, Daniel	Pulaski	Lesters	215/8	Irwin
Kelly, David	Elbert	Dobbs	365/19	Early
Kelly, David	Morgan	Loyds	7/5	Irwin
Kelly, David	Richmond	Appling	132/4	Appling
Kelly, David	Richmond	Winters	185/7	Irwin
Kelly, Denny	Morgan	Lodys	66/12	Irwin
Kelly, Elijah	Warren	152nd	32/9	Early
Kelly, Elizabeth	Pulaski	Rees	268/19	Early
Kelly, George	Washington	Floyds	127/8	Irwin
Kelly, James A.	Madison	Orrs	86/7	Early
Kelly, James Sr.	Jasper	Kindalls	191/7	Early
Kelly, James	Early		112/17	Early
Kelly, James	Jones	Griffiths	395/4	Early
Kelly, Jiles	Hancock	Smiths	18/8	Appling
Kelly, John	Bryan	19	45/12	Hall
Kelly, John	Chatham		311/19	Early
Kelly, John	Clarke	Moores	162/11	Early
Kelly, John	Hancock	Smiths	242/1	Early
Kelly, John	Hancock	Smiths	34/3	Appling
Kelly, John	Jones	Wallers	220/7	Appling
Kelly, John	Jones	Wallers	91/6	Early
Kelly, John	Pulaski	Rees	55/9	Early
Kelly, Joseph	Jones	Philips	76/13	Irwin
Kelly, Loyd	Jones	Buckhalters	293/4	Early
Kelly, Malakiah	Pulaski	Rees	263/3	Irwin
Kelly, Margaret(Wid)	Wilkinson	Lees	125/3	Irwin
Kelly, Mary(Wid)	Jackson	Hamiltons	169/11	Irwin

NAME	COUNTY	MIL.DIST	LOT/SECT	DREW LAND
Kelly, Moses	Richmond		126/9	Irwin
Kelly, Noah	Morgan	Alfords	113/10	Hall
Kelly, Osborne B.	Hancock	Mims	301/8	Irwin
Kelly, Peggy(Wid)	Hancock	Lucas	72/4	Habersham
Kelly, Randolph	Early		299/10	Early
Kelly, Robert	Bulloch	Tilmans	358/8	Irwin
Kelly, Samuel	Wilkes	Perrys	161/13	Early
Kelly, Tadock	Morgan	Hackneys	132/10	Hall
Kelly, Wm.	Wayne	Jacobs	308/10	Early
Kemp, Alexander	Scriven	Lovetts	64/7	Gwinnett
Kemp, Daniel	Scriven	Lovetts	186/2	Irwin
Kemp, Edward	Franklin	Akins	51/7	Early
Kemp, James	Tattnall	Cunyers	326/4	Early
Kemp, John Sr.(R.S)	Wayne	Johnstons	364/7	Gwinnett
Kemp, John Sr.(R.S.)	Wayne	Johnstons	203/6	Gwinnett
Kemp, John	Scriven	Lovets	55/9	Appling
Kemp, Joseph	Jones	Phillips	487/13	Irwin
Kemp, Joshua(Orphs)	Tattnall	Cunyers	297/7	Irwin
Kemp, Joshua	Montgomery	Nobles	77/9	Irwin
Kemp, Martin	Franklin	Akins	270/8	Early
Kemp, Peter	Tattnall	Cunyers	251/5	Gwinnett
Kemp, Samuel(Orphs)	Scriven	Mills	262/8	Early
Kemp, Simeon	Baldwin	Doziers	155/27	Early
Kemp, Thomas	Jones	Phillips	29/12	Early
Kemph, Folton	Scriven	Smiths	334/14	Early
Kempton, Edward G.	Chatham		123/26	Early
Kenaday, Samuel	Washington	Rogers	69/6	Appling
Kenan, Owen H.	Jasper	Clays	63/17	Early
Kendall, Elisha	Jasper	Posts	351/13	Early
Kendall, Henry	Hancock	Smiths	31/12	Irwin
Kendall, Thomas H.	Hancock	Mims	22/10	Irwin
Kenderson, David	Jasper	Hays	190/8	Early
Kendrick, Alexander	Jasper	Bartletts	183/15	Early
Kendrick, Eli	Columbia	Pullins	351/6	Irwin
Kendrick, James C.	Morgan	Campbells	214/8	Appling
Kendrick, James	Twiggs	Bozemans	393/28	Early
Kendrick, John D.	Lincoln	Tatoms	293/5	Gwinnett
Kendrick, John	Camden	Tillis	222/7	Appling
Kendrick, Joseph	Putnam	H.Kendricks	376/5	Irwin
Kendrick, Merida	Putnam	Slaughters	101/10	Hall
Kendrick, Robert	Hall		407/26	Early
Kendrick, Wm.	Jackson	Dicksons Bt.	301/17	Early
Kendrick, Wm.	Jackson	Dicksons Bt.	319/3	Appling
Kendricks, Sheldrake(Orph)	Jasper	Centells	167/3	Appling
Kenedy, Jonathan	Greene	Harvills	254/7	Gwinnett
Kennard, Barnett	Jasper	Bentleys	241/7	Irwin
Kennard, James(Orphs)	Washington	Averits	363/15	Early
Kennard, John	Jasper	Bentleys	196/5	Appling
Kennard, John	Jasper	Bentleys	300/5	Early
Kennedy, Absalom	Jasper	Centells	76/8	Appling
Kennedy, Benjamin	Effingham		19/6	Habersham
Kennedy, Chestin(Wid)	Jones	Wallers	357/3	Appling
Kennedy, David	Jackson	Hamiltons Bt.	388/10	Irwin
Kennedy, Eli	Bulloch	Everitts	40/14	Irwin
Kennedy, George	Jones	Samuels	290/7	Irwin
Kennedy, Gustavus	Richmond	Laceys	245/3	Irwin
Kennedy, James	Lincoln	Tatoms	102/11	Early
Kennedy, John Jr.	Jackson	Hamiltons	204/3	Irwin
Kennedy, John	Burke	72nd	386/20	Early
Kennedy, John	Jackson	Hamiltons Bt.	67/21	Early
Kennedy, John	Jasper	Kennedys	47/16	Irwin
Kennedy, Jonathan	Greene	Harvills	61/12	Hall
Kennedy, Thomas	Jasper	Centells	293/5	Early
Kennedy, William J.C.	Elbert	B.Higginbothams	167/3	Irwin
Kennedy, William	Jones	Hansford	398/16	Early
Kennedy, Wm.	Jackson	Hamiltons	31/16	Early
Kennedys, John(Orph)	Jones	Wallers	2/9	Hall

NAME	COUNTY	MIL.DIST	LOT/SECT	DREW LAN
Kenney, David	Bulloch	Everitt	297/13	Early
Kenney, John	Jefferson	Lamps	130/28	Early
Kenneyda, Stephen	Tattnall	Keems	118/1	Habersha
Kenneyda, Stephen	Tattnall	Keens	262/4	Early
Kennon, Charef	Morgan	Leonards	38/26	Early
Kennon, Charles L.	Putnam	Slaughters	116/4	Early
Kennon, Charles L.	Putnam	Slaughters	90/6	Appling
Kennon, John	Putnam	J.Kendricks	400/16	Early
Kennon, Lewis(Dr.)	Jefferson	Abbots	97/5	Early
Kennon, William	Baldwin	Irwins	116/3	Walton
Kennon, William	Baldwin	Irwins	22/26	Early
Kennon, William	Jasper	Northcuts	26/16	Irwin
Kennyhorn, Catharine(Wid)	Richmond		408/1	Appling
Kensey, Archibald(Orphs)	Twiggs	R. Belcher	201/7	Early
Kent, Benjamin	Laurens	Watsons	103/17	Early
Kent, Charles	Oglethorpe	Davenports	281/6	Early
Kent, Daniel Sr.	Oglethorpe	Davenports	306/6	Appling
Kent, Daniel Sr.	Oglethorpe	Davenports	77/11	Hall
Kent, Diana	Oglethorpe	Wises	136/2	Appling
Kent, Ezra	Chatham		132/19	Early
Kent, Gilbert	Clarke	Deans	179/1	Appling
Kent, Gilbert	Wilkes	Mattoxs	289/7	Appling
Kent, Hester(Wid)	Pulaski	Johnstons	173/5	Early
Kent, Isaac	Emanuel	49th	87/11	Irwin
Kent, James T.	Wilkes	Josseys	322/10	Early
Kent, James T.	Wilkes	Josseys	529/11	Irwin
Kent, Jesse	Telfair	Talleys	283/13	Early
Kent, John(R.S.)	Warren	150th	230/7	Irwin
Kent, John	Jefferson	Bothwells	31/10	Early
Kent, John	Wilkes	Josseys	296/6	Appling
Kent, Levi	Jefferson	Bothwells	109/5	Irwin
Kent, Lewis	Oglethorpe	Wises	3/28	Early
Kent, Peter	Wilkes	Josseys	267/2	Appling
Kent, Randolph	Clarke	Deans	21/23	Early
Kent, Reuben	Putnam	Bustins	353/5	Early
Kent, Robert F.	Columbia	Watsons	213/5	Gwinnett
Kent, Thomas	Twiggs	Evans's	14/6	Irwin
Kent, Thomas	Warren	Travis	264/11	Early
Ker, Alexander	Chatham		393/5	Appling
Ker, George	Chatham		209/6	Irwin
Ker, Mary	Chatham		72/2	Walton
Ker, Rode	Richmond	120th	431/7	Appling
Kerby, Arthur Jr.	Bulloch	Everitts	187/3	Habersha
Kerby, Arthur Sr.	Bulloch	Everitts	289/6	Irwin
Kerby, Harris	Chatham		256/21	Early
Kerby, John	Twiggs	Browns	168/19	Early
Kerby, Moab	Liberty		146/16	Irwin
Kerby, William	Bulloch	Everitts	238/5	Appling
Kerkland, Richard	Bulloch	Tilmans	120/7	Irwin
Kerklin, William(Orphs)	Putnam	Slaughters	9/15	Irwin
Kerlin, David	Elbert	R. Christians	282/21	Early
Kerling, John	Oglethorpe	Brittons	44/27	Early
Kerlly, Lemma	Jasper	Clays	188/2	Rabun
Kermichael, John Sr.	Jackson	Dicksons Bt.	84/12	Habersha
Kermichal, John Sr.	Jackson	Dicksons Bt.	406/3	Appling
Kerney, John	Washington	Daniels	16/9	Early
Kerr, Andrew	Richmond		31/3	Walton
Kerr, Charles	Jasper	Blake	14/8	Early
Kerr, Charles	Jasper	Blakes	376/6	Irwin
Kerr, David(R.S.)	Oglethorpe	Davenports	164/13	Irwin
Kerr, James M.	Greene	Fosters	214/13	Irwin
Kerrbow, Solomon	Jackson	Hamiltons	417/7	Appling
Kershaw, George	Liberty		378/2	Appling
Kesler, Volantine	Effingham		295/4	Irwin
Ketchum, Ralph	Richmond	398	58/3	Irwin
Ketler, Mildred	Baldwin	Marshalls	195/9	Early
Kettle, Jeremiah	Jackson	Dicksons Bt.	44/3	Irwin

NAME	COUNTY	MIL.DIST	LOT/SECT	DREW LAND
Kettles, Peter(Orphs)	Scriven	Roberts	28/4	Early
Key, Henry H.	Jasper	Northcuts	514/11	Irwin
Key, James	Elbert	Ruckers	111/3	Early
Key, Joseph	Morgan	Alfords	369/1	Appling
Key, Joseph	Morgan	Alfords	393/5	Irwin
Key, Price	Franklin	Ashs	114/18	Early
Key, Samuel	Gwinnett	Hamiltons	357/2	Early
Key, Stephen	Jackson	Hamiltons Bt.	138/3	Appling
Key, Stephen	Jackson	Hamiltons	315/5	Irwin
Key, Talbert	Franklin	Ashs	273/19	Early
Key, Tandey W.	Jasper	Northucts	577/2	Appling
Key, Tandy	Jackson	Hamiltons	326/2	Early
Key, Thomas H.	Burke	J. Wards	162/5	Early
Keys, Moses(Orphs)	Twiggs	Jeffersons	173/28	Early
Keys, Thomas	Early	Ruckers	25/6	Early
Kicklighter, Margt.(Wid)	Bulloch	Jones	78/3	Habersham
Kicklighter, Thomas	Bulloch	Jones	500/13	Irwin
Kidd, Abraham	Oglethorpe	Lees	276/9	Early
Kidd, Absalom	Oglethorpe	Wises	336/7	Gwinnett
Kidd, John W.	Elbert	Smiths	286/13	Early
Kidd, Richard	Oglethorpe	Barnetts	16/4	Irwin
Kidd, Richard	Oglethorpe	Barnetts	3/17	Early
Kidd, Webb	Oglethorpe	Lees	28/7	Early
Kidd, William	Oglethorpe	Lees	78/4	Habersham
Kidd, Zachariah	Oglethorpe	Lees	344/5	Early
Kie, Augustus	Burke	Thomas	315/10	Early
Kie, Henry	Burke	Thomas	195/15	Early
Kie, Henry	Burke	Thomas	3/20	Early
Kieth, James	Jasper	Phillips	79/11	Habersham
Kilcrees, Arthur	Jones	Griffiths	21/22	Early
Kilcrees, Arthur	Jones	Griffiths	3/16	Early
Kilge, Wm.	Walton	Wests	38/10	Early
Kilgo, James	Jackson	Hamiltons	52/12	Hall
Kilgord(e), Allen	Oglethorpe	Wises	157/10	Early
Kilgore, Aaron	Clarke	Mitchells	428/6	Irwin
Kilgore, Absalom(Orphs)	Walton	Wests	315/5	Early
Kilgore, Allen	Oglethorpe	Wises	263/9	Appling
Kilgore, Benjah	Wilkes	Kilgores	363/12	Early
Kilgore, Benjamin	Clarke	Mitchells	296/10	Early
Kilgore, Celia	Lincoln	Tatoms	136/12	Irwin
Kilgore, Charles	Hancock	Evans	416/26	Early
Kilgore, John M.	Putnam	Stampers	218/4	Early
Kilgore, Joseph	Jasper	Hays	14/4	Early
Kilgore, Peter	Clarke	Stuarts	180/12	Habersham
Kilgore, Ralph	Lincoln	Stokes	49/9	Appling
Kilgore, Robert G.	Jasper	Gilmore	30/4	Walton
Kilgore, Robert	Wilkes	Kilgores	146/13	Habersham
Kilgore, Solomon	Clarke	Starnes	76/8	Hall
Kilgore, Theopilus	Clarke	Mitchells	103/11	Irwin
Kilgore, Thomas	Clarke	Mitchells	270/5	Gwinnett
Kilgore, William	Wilkes	Kilgores	197/20	Early
Kilgores, William(Orph)	Jasper	Hays	125/4	Irwin
Killbee, William J.	Montgomery	McMillins	272/26	Early
Killcrease, Robert	Liberty	Tatoms	369/9	Appling
Killibrew, Eliz.(Wid)	Warren	151	261/8	Appling
Killingsworth, Ambrose	Hancock	Mims	646/2	Appling
Killingsworth, Daniel	Columbia	Shaws	69/26	Early
Killingsworth, Freeman	Columbia	Shaws	6/11	Habersham
Killingsworth, Henry	Richmond	Burtons	99/2	Habersham
Killingsworth, Matthew	Columbia	Shaws	289/4	Early
Killingsworth, Matthew	Columbia	Shaws	71/15	Early
Killingsworth, Thomas	Wilkinson	Smiths	64/6	Hall
Killman, John	Emanuel	53rd	44/5	Gwinnett
Killum, John	Oglethorpe	Bridges	187/4	Appling
Kilpatrick, David	Baldwin	Taliaferros	52/2	Irwin
Kilpatrick, John	Burke	J. Wards	388/11	Early
Kimbel, James	Burke	Bells	236/11	Early

NAME	COUNTY	MIL.DIST	LOT/SECT	DREW LAN
Kimbel, Jeremiah	Burke	72nd	311/17	Early
Kimbell, Bartholomew	Richmond		139/14	Early
Kimbell, Thomas	Oglethorpe	Waters	136/1	Early
Kimbell, Thomas	Oglethorpe	Waters	349/9	Early
Kimbrel, Charles	Burke	Hands	185/19	Early
Kimbrel, Mary	Burke	Hands	85/13	Irwin
Kimbrels, (Orph)	Burke	Hands	126/9	Hall
Kimbrough, Adam	Washington	Peabodys	25/4	Appling
Kimbrough, Bradley Sr.	Greene	Kimbroughs	339/1	Appling
Kimbrough, Bradley	Putnam	Evans	18/1	Irwin
Kimbrough, John	Greene	Kimbroughs	374/27	Early
Kimbrough, John	Greene	Kimbroughs	389/27	Early
Kimbrough, Josiah	Greene	Wheelis	136/3	Walton
Kimbrough, Shadrack	Jasper	Evans's	310/1	Walton
Kimbrough, William H.	Jasper	Evans	64/6	Gwinnett
Kimbrough, Wm.H.	Jasper	Evans	38/8	Irwin
Kinblet, Susannah	Morgan	Loyd	232/21	Early
Kindall, Elisha	Jasper	Posts	59/13	Early
Kindall, Henry Sr.	Warren	154	335/5	Appling
Kindall, William	Jasper	Phillips	194/6	Gwinnett
Kinder, David	Lincoln	Parks	4/4	Appling
Kindrick, Isaac	Putnam	Buckners	236/7	Early
Kindrick, John Jr.	Hall		337/28	Early
Kindrick, John Sr.	Hall		156/21	Early
Kindrick, John Sr.	Hall		328/7	Irwin
Kindrick, John	Putnam	J.Kindricks	56/3	Early
Kindrick, Samuel	Putnam	J.Kendricks	152/16	Irwin
Kines, Martin	Clarke	Mitchels	15/14	Irwin
Kineybrew, Littleberry	Oglethorpe	Bowls	99/8	Irwin
King, Barrington	McIntosh	Hamiltons	215/6	Appling
King, Bennett	Wilkinson	Brooks	203/7	Gwinnett
King, Berry	Franklin	Hammonds	321/6	Appling
King, Boswell	McIntosh	Hamiltons	182/3	Appling
King, Daniel	Burke	Spiveys	199/15	Early
King, Dixon P.(Orph)	Columbia	Gartrells	329/7	Appling
King, Edmund	Richmond	122	24/6	Irwin
King, Eliplet	Pulaski	Senterfeits	503/10	Irwin
King, Elisha	Washington	Robinsons	271/7	Irwin
King, Elizabeth(Wid)	Morgan	Morrows	75/9	Irwin
King, Francis	Pulaski	Bryans	392/17	Early
King, George W.	Baldwin	Marshalls	103/5	Appling
King, George W.	Baldwin	Marshalls	105/3	Irwin
King, George	Effingham		93/14	Early
King, George	Putnam	Littles	98/3	Irwin
King, Henry S.	Morgan	Morrows	300/27	Early
King, Henry	Pulaski	Rees	216/2	Early
King, Henry	Pulaski	Rees	93/3	Habershan
King, James	Camden	Clarks	133/7	Early
King, James	Franklin	Browns	242/6	Irwin
King, James	Franklin	Browns	276/5	Appling
King, James	Franklin	Flemmons	355/20	Early
King, James	Jones	Phillips	251/12	Early
King, James	Putnam	Ectors	157/15	Early
King, James	Wilkinson	Lees	174/3	Habersha
King, Jane(Wid)	Franklin	Hammonds	222/21	Early
King, Joel	Washington	Brooks	35/11	Habershan
King, Joel	Wilkinson	Brooks	35/11	Habersha
King, John M.	Jasper	Reids	352/12	Early
King, John M.	Jasper	Reids	66/3	Irwin
King, John P.	Richmond	122	21/5	Rabun
King, John	Columbia	Dodsons	169/3	Early
King, John	Franklin	P. Brown	223/21	Early
King, John	Jefferson	Abbotts	162/16	Irwin
King, John	Twiggs	R.Belchers	93/12	Hall
King, John	Wilkinson	Brooks	2/16	Early
King, John	Wilkinson	Lees	144/20	Early
King, Johnson	Wilkinson	Wiggins	63/2	Habershan

NAME	COUNTY	MIL.DIST	LOT/SECT	DREW LAND
King, Joseph	Chatham		53/11	Irwin
King, Joseph	Greene	141st	201/9	Irwin
King, Kinchen	Wilkes	Perrys	356/1	Early
King, Martha	Putnam	Morelands	18/2	Irwin
King, Martin	Jones	Chappels.	116/2	Walton
King, Martin	Jones	Mulkeys	21/7	Early
King, Mary(Wid)	Jones	Permenters	135/4	Early
King, Mary	Jasper	Blakes	79/6	Early
King, Mikiel	McIntosh	Eigles	338/6	Early
King, Mourning(Wid)	McIntosh	Eigles	344/13	Irwin
King, Nancy(Wid)	Franklin	Attaways	81/28	Early
King, Richard	Jasper	Reids	149/10	Irwin
King, Richard	Wilkes	Bryants	3/12	Irwin
King, Robert	Franklin	Turks	91/2	Early
King, Samuel	Liberty		396/20	Early
King, Stephen	Franklin	Akins	131/3	Habersham
King, Thomas G.	Putnam	Slaughters	102/27	Early
King, Thomas	Camden	Bailuys	233/7	Gwinnett
King, Thomas	Jones	Phillips	29/9	Irwin
King, Thomas	McIntosh	Goulds	3/8	Irwin
King, Thomas	Washington	Peaboddys	338/6	Gwinnett
King, Timothy	Scriven	180	453/3	Appling
King, Wiley	Emanuel	57th	146/3	Habersham
King, William C.	Greene	142	200/9	Early
King, William Jr.	Elbert	Penns	191/3	Early
King, William Sr.	Elbert	Penns	187/1	Walton
King, William	Effingham		351/5	Irwin
King, William	Franklin	P. Browns	521/12	Irwin
King, William	Greene	141st	366/28	Early
King, William	Montgomery	Nobles	244/2	Early
King, William	Montgomery	Nobles	486/5	Irwin
King, William	Warren	Hubberts	227/3	Walton
King, Wm.(Orphs)	Warren	Rodgers	119/9	Appling
King, Yelverton P.	Greene	143rd	38/19	Early
Kinglet, Maryann(Wid)	Baldwin	Marshalls	366/9	Early
Kingrey, Eliz.(Wid)	Wilkinson	Kettles	412/10	Irwin
Kings, Charles(Orph)	Jefferson	Matthews	6/5	Appling
Kings, William(Orph)	Jasper	Blakes	107/3	Rabun
Kingsby, Charles	Pulaski	Lesters	105/2	Habersham
Kingsley, John	Chatham		123/4	Irwin
Kingsly, Genet	Pulaski	Lesters	327/6	Appling
Kinleys, Colvin(Orph)	Burke	Spivey	498/3	Appling
Kinleys, Henry(Orph)	Burke	Spivey	498/3	Appling
Kinleys, Louisa(Orph)	Burke	Spivey	498/3	Appling
Kinleys, Melvana(Orph)	Burke	Spivey	498/3	Appling
Kinleys, Prusiana(Orph)	Burke	Spivey	498/3	Appling
Kinman, Martha(Wid)	Washington	Barges	247/9	Early
Kinmon, Thomas(Orph)	Washington	Barges	333/5	Irwin
Kinnard, Martin	Jasper	Bentleys	619/2	Appling
Kinney, Jesse	Greene	Wheelis	82/26	Early
Kinney, John	Clarke	Appling	161/16	Early
Kinney, John	Richmond	120	13/1	Habersham
Kinney, Jonathan	Clarke	Applings	98/2	Habersham
Kinney, Samuel	Clarke	Appling	274/9	Appling
Kinney, Thomas	Clarke	Moores	201/12	Irwin
Kinney, Thomas	Clarke	Moores	464/7	Appling
Kinneybrew, Littleberry	Oglethorpe	Bowls	119/13	Early
Kinninghams, Howard(Orph)	Jackson	Dicksons Bt.	352/13	Early
Kinnon, Thomas	Morgan	Leonards	114/7	Gwinnett
Kinsey, Cornelius	Twiggs	R.Belchers	361/9	Appling
Kinsey, John	Warren	153rd	42/5	Irwin
Kinsey, Martin	Warren	153	353/8	Irwin
Kinsey, William	Warren	154	152/7	Irwin
Kinsley, Thomas(R.S.)	Jasper	Trembles	264/5	Early
Kirchens, Thomas	Jackson	Rogers Bt.	273/4	Irwin
Kirchens, Wm.	Jackson	Rogers	25/4	Walton
Kirk, George	Jackson	Rogers	117/18	Early

NAME	COUNTY	MIL.DIST	LOT/SECT	DREW LAND
Kirk, George	Jackson	Rogers	198/5	Gwinnett
Kirk, John	Jackson	Rogers Bt.	174/19	Early
Kirk, John	Jackson	Rogers	276/6	Early
Kirk, John	Jones	Kings	380/7	Appling
Kirk, Stephen	Jones	Kings	185/15	Early
Kirk, Wiley	Jasper	Easters	20/2	Irwin
Kirk, Wiley	Jasper	Easts	336/15	Early
Kirkland, Benj.	Jackson	Hamiltons	11/15	Early
Kirkland, Benjamin	Jackson	Hamiltons Bt.	292/9	Irwin
Kirkland, Jesse	Wilkes	Perrys	124/5	Gwinnett
Kirkland, Moses	Pulaski	Maddoxs	360/21	Early
Kirkland, Samuel	Emanuel	49th	336/4	Appling
Kirkland, Samuel	Laurens	Deans	465/6	Irwin
Kirkland, Wm.	Wilkes	Perrys	94/27	Early
Kirklands, John(Orph)	Emanuel	59th	32/23	Early
Kirland, John	Emanuel	49th	200/16	Irwin
Kirlley, Lemma	Jasper	Clays	288/12	Early
Kiser, Muskogee(Wid)	Early		312/28	Early
Kisers, Christopher(Orph)	Early		48/12	Early
Kitchen, Benjamin	Jasper	Bentleys	202/26	Early
Kitchen, Benjamin	Jasper	Bentleys	55/5	Rabun
Kitchen, William	Jasper	Bentleys	52/13	Habersham
Kitchens, Boaz Jr.	Warren	Pools	46/6	Appling
Kitchens, Charles	Jasper	Bentleys	143/28	Early
Kitchens, Garrey	Jones	Philips	35/3	Habersham
Kitchens, James(Orphs)	Telfair	Tallis	362/19	Early
Kitchens, Sarah(Wid)	Washington	Robinsons	136/12	Hall
Kitchens, Thomas	Jackson	Rogers Bt.	130/10	Hall
Kitchens, Willie	Warren	151st	383/8	Early
Kitchens, Wm.	Jackson	Rogers	266/1	Early
Kite, Shadrack	Laurens	Deans	209/7	Gwinnett
Kite, Thomas	Tattnall	Overstreets	67/3	Early
Kites, John(Orphs)	Tattnall	Overstreett	115/2	Walton
Kitle, Jeremiah	Jackson	Dicksons Bt.	158/16	Early
Kitrell, Noah	Washington	Robinsons	248/11	Irwin
Kneely, David	Morgan	Loyds	349/1	Early
Knight, Abel	Twiggs	Smiths	165/12	Early
Knight, Abel	Twiggs	Smiths	75/8	Hall
Knight, Carrington	Jasper	Kennadys	31/3	Early
Knight, Chloe(Wid)	Liberty		27/3	Early
Knight, Elias	Liberty		212/5	Appling
Knight, Elisha	Burke	McNorrills	54/1	Rabun
Knight, Elisha	Walton	Greens	188/10	Habersham
Knight, Frances	Morgan	Knights	375/16	Early
Knight, Isaac	Jackson	Rogers Bt.	131/12	Irwin
Knight, James	Laurens	Watsons	128/6	Early
Knight, James	Twiggs	Smiths	163/15	Irwin
Knight, Jesse	Burke	Thomas	367/8	Early
Knight, John(Orphs)	Twiggs	Smith	188/7	Gwinnett
Knight, John(R.S.)	Wayne	Crews	119/10	Habersham
Knight, John(R.S.)	Wayne	Crews	36/9	Hall
Knight, John	Jasper	Kennedys	114/7	Irwin
Knight, John	Putnam	Oslins	359/11	Early
Knight, Joseph	Bulloch	Knights	139/7	Appling
Knight, Mary(Orph)	Burke	McNorrills	54/1	Rabun
Knight, Mary(Wid)	Twiggs	Smiths	391/9	Irwin
Knight, Robert	Laurens	S.Smith	145/14	Early
Knight, Robert	Twiggs	Bozemans	376/9	Irwin
Knight, Speir	Laurens	S.Smith	60/12	Early
Knight, Thomas	Baldwin	Marshalls	326/12	Irwin
Knight, Thomas	Bulloch	Knights	231/8	Early
Knight, Thomas	Twiggs	Bozemans	110/2	Early
Knight, Thomas	Twiggs	Thames	39/1	Rabun
Knight, Thomas	Wayne	Crews	38/13	Habersham
Knight, Thomas	Wayne	Crews	66/8	Early
Knight, Wm.A.	Wayne	Crews	250/7	Early
Knights, Robert(Orph)	Baldwin	Marshalls	189/4	Walton

NAME	COUNTY	MIL.DIST	LOT/SECT	DREW LAND
Knobles, Elizabeth(Orph)	Camden	Longs	216/11	Early
Knot, Elizabeth	Lincoln	Parks	154/1	Appling
Knots, Reuben(Heirs)	Lincoln	Parks	86/14	Irwin
Knott, Reuben(Heirs)	Lincoln	Parks	440/21	Early
Know, John A.P.	Franklin	Davis	133/13	Early
Knowles, Britten	Greene	Kimbroughs	31/11	Habersham
Knowles, Edmond Jr.	Greene	Kimbroughs	329/15	Early
Knowles, Edmond Jr.	Greene	Kinnbrough	306/1	Walton
Knowles, Edmund Sr.	Greene	Kimbroughs	213/20	Early
Knowles, Ephraim	Burke	Spiveys	413/8	Irwin
Knowles, Isaac	Greene	Kinnbrough	172/1	Irwin
Knowles, James P.	Putnam	Buckners	19/1	Appling
Knowles, Joseph	Greene	Kimbroughs	201/9	Early
Knowles, Rice P.	Jasper	Reids	296/13	Irwin
Knowles, Thomas Jr.	Greene	Kimbroughs	98/6	Gwinnett
Knowles, Thomas Sr.	Greene	Kimbroughs	103/5	Early
Knowles, Thomas Sr.	Greene	Kimbroughs	60/3	Habersham
Knowles, William	Greene	Kimbroughs	243/7	Early
Knowlman, David H.	Oglethorpe	Brittons	217/1	Early
Knox, Andrew	Chatham		119/15	Early
Knox, James(Orphs)	Jackson	Hamiltons Bt.	413/8	Appling
Knox, John	Lincoln	Graves	427/5	Irwin
Knox, Samuel Jr.	Jackson	Dicksons B.	262/9	Early
Knox, Samuel Sr.	Jackson	Dicksons	234/16	Early
Kobbs, Jonathan(Orphs)	Jackson	Winters Bt.	133/9	Irwin
Kolb, Fanny(Wid)	Jones	Phillips	506/7	Appling
Kolb, Hiram	Jackson	Winters	8/2	Habersham
Kollock, Henry(Rev)	Chatham		63/11	Habersham
Koyler, John	Effingham		214/26	Early
Kraatz, John	Baldwin	Taliaferros	85/15	Early
Kramer, David	Baldwin	Marshalls	273/9	Irwin
Kubler, John	Chatham		268/15	Early
Kukman, Josiah	Hall		231/3	Irwin
Kunzee, John M.	Richmond	122nd	95/9	Early
Kurper, Frederick	Chatham		223/6	Irwin
Labamara, Elizabeth	Chatham		399/6	Appling
Labuzan, Bartholomew	Richmond	398	12/11	Hall
Labuzan, Bartholomew	Richmond	398	329/10	Irwin
Lacey, Isaac(Orph)	Richmond	398th	105/21	Early
Lachatier, Plaude	McIntosh	Hamiltons	54/4	Appling
Lacruse, Francis	Baldwin	Marshalls	301/9	Early
Lacy, Eliz.(Wid)	Richmond	398th	54/13	Irwin
Lacy, John	Oglethorpe	Wises	232/5	Gwinnett
Lacy, John	Oglethorpe	Wises	253/11	Early
Lacy, Mary	Pulaski	Morelands	44/5	Irwin
Lacy, Thomas	Morgan	McClendons	368/13	Irwin
Ladson, William F.	Liberty		332/4	Walton
Ladson, Wm.F.	Liberty		490/8	Appling
Lafette, Jane	Chatham		16/2	Walton
Lafiles, Armon	McIntosh	Hamiltons	215/4	Irwin
Lafong, John	McIntosh	Jenkins	169/18	Early
Lagon, Joseph(R.S.)	Clarke	Mitchels	186/9	Appling
Lain, Anderson	Franklin	Flanagans	336/6	Appling
Laird, Lodowich	Tattnall	Cunyers	267/6	Early
Lake, Joseph	Pulaski	Oslins	201/1	Irwin
Lake, Justus	Pulaski	Oslins	524/9	Irwin
Lamar, Benjamin D.	Jones	Kings	420/12	Irwin
Lamar, Benjan S.	Pulaski	Lamars	305/8	Appling
Lamar, Elizabeth	Hancock	Evans	102/6	Gwinnett
Lamar, Harmong	Columbia	Olives	242/10	Early
Lamar, Harmong	Columbia	Olives	344/1	Early
Lamar, James	Jones	Hansfords	519/12	Irwin
Lamar, Jeremiah	Jones	Hansfords	76/3	Habersham
Lamar, John T.	Richmond	122nd	441/2	Appling
Lamar, John	Columbia	J.Morris's	168/7	Gwinnett
Lamar, Lucius Q.C.	Baldwin	Marshalls	142/6	Early
Lamar, Zachariah	Jones	Hansfords	330/18	Early

NAME	COUNTY	MIL.DIST	LOT/SECT	DREW LA
Lamb, Arthur	Twiggs	Ellis	452/12	Irwin
Lamb, Benja.S.	Bryan	20 Dist.	233/6	Appling
Lamb, Benja.S.	Bryan	20 Dist.	84/7	Early
Lamb, Cabel	Chatham		217/11	Early
Lamb, Isaac(R.S.)	Jefferson	Connells	259/13	Early
Lamb, Isaac(R.S.)	Jefferson	Connells	57/13	Early
Lamb, Isham	Twiggs	Ellis	168/13	Habersh
Lamb, Nancy(Wid)	Twiggs	Jefferson	225/3	Appling
Lamb, Reuben	Jefferson	Langstons	116/10	Early
Lamb, Reuben	Jefferson	Langstons	9/2	Early
Lamb, Reubin	Twiggs	Tisons	517/6	Appling
Lamb, Willis	Twiggs	Tisons	215/4	Early
Lambard, Thomas	Clarke	Mereweathers	39/18	Early
Lambard, Thomas	Clarke	Merreweathers	95/10	Irwin
Lambert, Alexander	Jackson	Rogers Bt.	131/5	Gwinnet
Lambert, Betsey(Orph)	Richmond	Laceys	128/6	Appling
Lambert, Irwin	Wilkinson	Brooks	48/14	Irwin
Lambert, Isaac	Wilkes	Brooks	6/26	Early
Lambert, James	Scriven		87/8	Irwin
Lambert, James	Walton	Wagnons	267/4	Appling
Lambert, James	Wilkinson	Brooks	379/7	Early
Lambert, John H.	Richmond	Laceys	322/5	Irwin
Lambert, John	Columbia	Dodsons	287/1	Appling
Lambert, John	Columbia	Dodsons	43/11	Habersh
Lambert, John	Jackson	Hamiltons Bt.	258/14	Early
Lambert, John	Jasper	Bentleys	374/26	Early
Lambert, John	Jones	Phillips	181/14	Early
Lambert, John	Laurens	Ross	248/11	Early
Lambert, John	Laurens	Waltons	113/9	Irwin
Lambert, John	Laurens	Watsons	260/5	Early
Lambert, John	Scriven	Lovetts	21/18	Early
Lambert, Lewis	Pulaski	Berrys	181/8	Irwin
Lambert, Noah	Laurens	Watsons	139/20	Early
Lambert, Patsey(Wid)	Richmond	122	76/5	Early
Lambert, Rebecca(Orph)	Richmond	Laceys	128/6	Appling
Lambert, Ruth	Richmond	Laceys	128/6	Appling
Lambert, Thomas	Burke	Hands	357/7	Irwin
Lambert, William	Morgan	Wrights	103/7	Early
Lambert, William	Scriven	Lovetts	149/1	Appling
Lamberts, Wm.(Orps)	Washington	Cummins	58/11	Early
Lambright, James	Liberty		20/23	Early
Lamkin, Wm.M.	Lincoln	Stokes	85/17	Early
Lamp, Philip	Jefferson	Lamps	197/10	Irwin
Lamp, Phillip	Jefferson	Lamps	216/10	Early
Lampkin, James W.	Richmond	122	368/3	Appling
Lampkin, John	Lincoln	Graves	163/13	Irwin
Lampkins, Jeremiah(Orphs)	Columbia	Pullins	188/16	Early
Lanargam, John	Chatham		137/19	Early
Lanbart, Noah	Laurens	Watsons	444/8	Appling
Lancaster, Benj.	Wilkinson	Howards	172/6	Early
Lancaster, Right	Pulaski	Lesters	18/5	Irwin
Lancaster, Samuel	Greene	141	309/12	Early
Lancaster, Samuel	Greene	141st	228/2	Early
Lancaster, Wash.	Pulaski	Lester	478/6	Appling
Lancaster, William	Hancock	Coopers	113/2	Walton
Lancaster, William	Hancock	Coopers	261/4	Early
Lanchester, Eliz.Ann(Orph)	Liberty		203/27	Early
Land, Frederick	Wilkinson	Childs	62/2	Habersha
Land, Frederick	Wilkinson	Childs	70/1	Early
Land, Thomas	Warren	150	139/1	Appling
Land, Thomas	Warren	150	398/15	Early
Landen, John	Burke	J.Wards	198/2	Irwin
Landers, Humphrey D.	Elbert	B.Higginbothams	177/6	Gwinnett
Landers, Luke	Pulaski	Coopers	136/5	Gwinnett
Landers, Tyre	Elbert	Dooleys	167/4	Irwin
Landers, William	Madison	Willifords	28/1	Irwin
Landers, Wm.	Madison	Willifords	63/8	Early

NAME	COUNTY	MIL.DIST	LOT/SECT	DREW LAND
Landon, Elizabeth	Jefferson	Bothwells	315/8	Irwin
Landrith, Thomas	Warren	151st	112/3	Rabun
Landrum, James B.	Oglethorpe	Brittons	129/8	Hall
Landrum, James B.	Oglethorpe	Brittons	46/9	Early
Landrum, John	Wilkes	Russels	176/6	Early
Landrum, Larkin	Jackson	Rogers Bt.	296/4	Appling
Landrum, William	Oglethorpe	Brittons	249/11	Early
Lane, Abram S.	Emanuel	49th	375/4	Appling
Lane, Alexander	Chatham		267/10	Irwin
Lane, Alexander	Jasper	Phillips	101/15	Irwin
Lane, Alexander	Jasper	Phillips	316/21	Early
Lane, Azariah	Wilkes	Runnels	184/2	Irwin
Lane, Benjamin	Emanuel	49th	36/12	Early
Lane, Benjamin	Pulaski	Evans	469/7	Appling
Lane, Henry	Morgan	Dennis	277/13	Irwin
Lane, James(Orph)	Pulaski	Bryans	236/9	Irwin
Lane, James	Pulaski	Evans	312/3	Early
Lane, John(Orphs)	Bulloch	Knights	40/8	Hall
Lane, John	Burke	Torrences	330/16	Early
Lane, John	Emanuel	49th	303/7	Irwin
Lane, John	Jackson	Dicksons Bt.	147/3	Habersham
Lane, John	Jackson	Dicksons Bt.	181/12	Early
Lane, Jonathan	Clarke	Applings	237/26	Early
Lane, Labon	Madison	Bones	280/4	Irwin
Lane, Labon	Madison	Bones	88/4	Irwin
Lane, Lunsford	Clarke	Applings	305/13	Early
Lane, Richard(Orphs)	Burke	J.Wards	112/19	Early
Lane, Robert	Jackson	Dicksons	77/20	Early
Lane, Sarah	Pulaski	Senterfeits	7/3	Early
Lane, Theldrige	Washington	Daniels	264/5	Irwin
Lane, Theophilus L.	Clarke	Applings	81/5	Irwin
Lane, William T.	Wilkes	Gordons	303/27	Early
Lang, Benjamin	Richmond	398	304/12	Irwin
Lang, David	Scriven		23/1	Appling
Lang, Isaac	Camden	Longs	67/4	Habersham
Lang, Robert	Richmond	398th	228/1	Walton
Lang, Willis	Camden	Longs	58/3	Appling
Langford, Edmund	Hancock	Danells	266/4	Walton
Langford, George	Morgan	Jordans	187/8	Irwin
Langford, James Sr.	Jones	Phillips	386/1	Early
Langford, John	Jones	Hansfords	65/14	Irwin
Langford, Jonathan	Lincoln	Parkers	168/15	Early
Langford, Kurby(Orp)	Morgan	Jordans	312/6	Gwinnett
Langford, Lemuel	Clarke	Deans	89/13	Early
Langford, Robert	Hancock	Thomas	319/8	Appling
Langham, James	Jasper	Blakes	180/13	Habersham
Langham, James	Jasper	Blakes	84/11	Irwin
Langley, Thomas	Jackson	Hamiltons Bt.	233/4	Appling
Langston, Benjamin	Washington	Avents	89/4	Irwin
Langston, David	Oglethorpe	Barnetts	5/23	Early
Langston, David	Oglethorpe	Barnetts	63/14	Irwin
Langston, Dorcas(Wid)	Washington	Floyds	169/6	Irwin
Langston, Isaac	Oglethorpe	Barnetts	570/2	Appling
Langston, Jacob	Jackson	Hamiltons	168/16	Early
Langston, James B.	Jackson	Rogers Bt.	320/7	Gwinnett
Langston, Jason	Washington	Floyds	524/13	Irwin
Langston, Jesse	Elbert	Smiths	215/1	Walton
Langston, Mary(Wid)	Morgan	Alfords	331/2	Appling
Langston, Moses	Morgan	Alfords	144/15	Irwin
Langston, Seth S.	Jefferson	Langstons	207/21	Early
Langston, Seth S.	Jefferson	Langstons	228/6	Irwin
Langston, William	Madison	Millicans	141/11	Irwin
Lanier, Allen	Bulloch	Edwards	17/23	Early
Lanier, Allen	Bulloch	Edwards	69/7	Appling
Lanier, Benjn.	Bulloch	Edwards	343/6	Appling
Lanier, David	Morgan	Cheves	98/21	Early
Lanier, Frederick	Bulloch	Edwards	95/12	Irwin

NAME	COUNTY	MIL.DIST	LOT/SECT	DREW LAND
Lanier, Hannah(Wid)	Bulloch	Edwards	36/2	Habersham
Lanier, James	Bulloch	Edwards	243/3	Early
Lanier, James	Bulloch	Edwards	80/6	Appling
Lanier, James	Morgan	Wrights	11/3	Habersham
Lanier, James	Morgan	Wrights	177/5	Gwinnett
Lanier, John	Jasper	Clays	390/11	Early
Lanier, John	Jefferson	Waldens	121/13	Habersham
Lanier, John	Jefferson	Waldens	245/11	Early
Lanier, Lenniel	Chatham		172/1	Early
Lanier, Lewis	Bulloch	Edwards	26/16	Early
Lanier, Lewis	Bulloch	Edwards	428/10	Irwin
Lanier, Margaret	Bulloch	Edwards	99/5	Gwinnett
Lanier, Nicholas	Hancock	Colemans	256/2	Early
Lanier, Nicholas	Hancock	Colemans	297/19	Early
Lanier, Reuben T.	Greene	143	149/8	Hall
Lanier, Sampson	Morgan	Selmons	13/5	Gwinnett
Lanier, Thomas	Gwinnett	Hamiltons Bt.	382/27	Early
Lanier, William	Washington	Wimberleys	75/11	Habersham
Laniers, Clement(Orph)	Pulaski	Lanairs	25/3	Habersham
Lanis, Wyly(Orph)	Scriven		345/2	Appling
Lankford, Abner	Franklin	Davis	50/11	Hall
Lankford, Bozelul	Clarke	Harpers	233/18	Early
Lankford, Geo.R.	Morgan	Alfords	248/21	Early
Lankford, Henry	Tattnall	Keens	439/7	Irwin
Lankford, James	Clarke	Harpers	114/11	Irwin
Lankford, Moses(R.S.)	Tattnall	Keans	161/3	Walton
Lankford, Moses	Tattnall	Keens	257/1	Walton
Lankford, Wyatt	Franklin	Davis	111/14	Early
Lankford, Wyatt	Franklin	Davis	146/27	Early
Lansford, Henry	Oglethorpe	Brittons	128/16	Early
Laprad, John	Pulaski	J.Kendricks	120/1	Irwin
Lard, James	Clarke	Oates	376/13	Irwin
Lard, John	Morgan	Loyds	345/18	Early
Lard, Lodwick	Morgan	Loyds	69/1	Walton
Lard, Robert Sr.	Clarke	Oates	38/5	Appling
Large, William	Tattnall	Overstreet	303/12	Irwin
Largins, (Orphs)	Jasper	Bentleys	24/8	Early
Lark, Samuel	Richmond	Laceys	356/6	Gwinnett
Larramore, John	Lincoln	Stokes	514/9	Irwin
Larramore, Polly	Lincoln	Stokes	92/14	Early
Larrence, James C.	Morgan	Townsends	335/4	Early
Larrence, Mary(Wid)	Morgan	Townsends	57/12	Habersham
Larry, Thomas	Jones	Buckhalters	51/4	Irwin
Laruce, Joseph	Oglethorpe	Lees	149/15	Irwin
Lary, Andrew	Hancock	Canes	398/11	Irwin
Lary, Betsey	Hancock	Smiths	29/9	Appling
Lary, John B.	Richmond	122nd	33/13	Early
Larys, John(Orphs)	Hancock	Smiths	177/28	Early
Lashee, Lewis	Jones	Permenters	11/8	Irwin
Lashley, Edmond	Pulaski	Johnstons	23/9	Appling
Lashley, Edmund	Pulaski	Johnstons	328/27	Early
Lasiner, John	Chatham		130/2	Rabun
Lasiter, Caswell	Pulaski	Davis	129/3	Irwin
Lassaters, Radford(Orph)	Morgan	Loyals	505/5	Irwin
Lasseter, Jacob	Wilkinson	Smiths	172/8	Irwin
Lasseter, Robert	Columbia	Watsons	83/26	Early
Lasseter, William	Burke	M.Wards	183/2	Early
Lassetter, Mathew	Jasper	Centells	441/6	Irwin
Lassiter, Amos	Twiggs	R.Belchers	225/1	Early
Lassiter, Ann	Jasper	Hays	48/1	Appling
Lassiter, Edward	Burke	M.Wards	265/5	Irwin
Lassiter, Edward	Burke	M.Wards	81/16	Irwin
Lassiter, Emery(Orphs)	Burke	Sullivans	99/1	Habersham
Lassiter, George	Columbia	Watsons	407/9	Irwin
Lassiter, Hansell	Laurens	Watsons	325/7	Irwin
Lassiter, John	Jasper	Blakes	455/11	Irwin
Lassiter, John	Jasper	Blakes	459/7	Appling

NAME	COUNTY	MIL.DIST	LOT/SECT	DREW LAND
Lassiter, Nancy	Jasper	Centells	20/21	Early
Lassiter, Robert	Columbia	Watsons	166/17	Early
Lassiter, Robert	Columbia	Watsons	41/5	Gwinnett
Lassiter, Robert	Jasper	Centells	154/17	Early
Lastinger, Andrew	Bulloch	Knights	185/11	Early
Lastinger, Andrew	Bulloch	Knights	284/13	Early
Lastinger, Janes	Bulloch	Knights	1/4	Habersham
Latan, John	Washington	Jinkinsons	207/7	Appling
Latham, Amos(R.S.)	Glynn		127/11	Irwin
Latham, Amos(R.S.)	Glynn		299/5	Gwinnett
Latham, Amos(R.S.)	Glynn		405/4	Appling
Lathrop, John	Chatham		120/15	Early
Latimer, Charles	Warren	Parhams	86/12	Irwin
Latimer, H.W.	Hancock	Mims	295/17	Early
Latimer, John Sr.	Hancock	Mims	149/9	Appling
Latimer, Robert	Hancock	Mims	105/5	Early
Latimer, Robert	Hancock	Mims	153/20	Early
Latimer, Thomas L.	Hancock	Mimms	335/2	Early
Latimer, William	Warren	Parhams	187/5	Gwinnett
Latimer, William	Warren	Parhams	209/1	Early
Latimere, Benjamin F.	Hancock	Evans	258/4	Early
Latimes, John P.	Oglethorpe	Brittons	60/26	Early
Latimore, George	Oglethorpe	Brittons	282/7	Gwinnett
Latimore, William	Oglethorpe	Brittons	25/6	Habersham
Lattimere, John Sr.	Hancock	Mims	32/2	Early
Laughlin, William	Jackson	Dicksons Bt.	23/1	Walton
Laughlin, Wm.	Jackson	Dicksons Bt.	159/12	Irwin
Laughridge, Benjamin	Franklin	Davis	24/4	Walton
Laughridge, Samuel(Orph)	Franklin	J.Millers	386/7	Appling
Laughter, John T.	Wilkes	Smiths	9/2	Habersham
Laughter, Robt.C.	Wilkes	Kilgores	209/2	Irwin
Launders, John	Lincoln	Graves	157/7	Appling
Launders, Milley(Wid)	Lincoln	Graves	205/10	Irwin
Laurence, Belinder(Orph)	Chatham		429/7	Appling
Laurence, David L.	Pulaski	Buckners	259/12	Early
Laurence, Edward(Orph)	Chatham		429/7	Appling
Laurence, Garrett	Richmond	Burtons	143/17	Early
Laurence, George	Jasper	Sentills	96/7	Appling
Laurence, James	Pulaski	Evans	138/2	Early
Laurence, John Sr.	Greene	Wheeles's	207/19	Early
Laurence, John	Jasper	Kenedays	8/2	Irwin
Laurence, John	Jasper	Kennedys	211/28	Early
Laurence, John	Washington	Wimberleys	237/6	Early
Laurence, Joseph	Chatham		221/28	Early
Laurence, Joseph	Chatham		59/26	Early
Laurence, Josiah	Chatham		7/1	Early
Laurence, Richard	Jasper	Eastes	35/12	Habersham
Laurence, Richard	Jasper	Easts	41/6	Irwin
Laurence, Seaborn	Hancock	Thomas	130/11	Hall
Laurence, Susan(Orph)	Chatham		429/7	Appling
Laurence, Zachariah	Jasper	Easts	52/6	Irwin
Lavander, Benjn.(Orph)	Chatham		7/21	Early
Lavander, Edmond(Orph	Chatham		7/21	Early
Lavander, Martha(Orph)	Chatham		7/21	Early
Lavender, Benjm.(Orph)	Chatham		257/7	Gwinnett
Lavender, Edmund(Orph)	Chatham		257/7	Gwinnett
Lavender, Martha(Orph)	Chatham		275/7	Gwinnett
Lavinder, John	Wilkinson	Kettles	347/12	Irwin
Law, Samuel S.	Liberty		200/15	Early
Law, Wm.	Chatham		216/3	Irwin
Lawder, Hampton	Camden	Tillis	11/16	Irwin
Lawless, John	Oglethorpe	Bridges	15/7	Gwinnett
Lawrence, Isham	Jefferson	Cowarts	77/6	Appling
Lawrence, James	Jasper	Kennedys	17/6	Early
Lawrence, John Sr.	Greene	Wheelis	96/11	Irwin
Lawrence, John	Washington	Brooks	244/11	Early
Lawrence, Silas	Gwinnett	Hamiltons Bt.	85/11	Hall

NAME	COUNTY	MIL.DIST	LOT/SECT	DREW LAN
Lawrence, Thomas	Jasper	Kenedys	81/12	Early
Lawrence, William H.(Orps)	Pulaski	Coopers	172/6	Appling
Lawrence, William	Jasper	Centills	84/20	Early
Laws, Isham	Jasper	Hays	140/3	Early
Laws, Joseph	Morgan	Selmons	113/12	Irwin
Laws, Thomas E.(Orph)	Liberty		73/13	Early
Lawson, Alexander J.	Burke	Bells	252/12	Early
Lawson, Ann(Wid)	Chatham		63/6	Early
Lawson, Arthur	Greene	Armers	68/14	Early
Lawson, Daniel	Laurens	D.Smiths	275/5	Irwin
Lawson, David	Pulaski	J.Kindricks	136/2	Rabun
Lawson, Ivy	Gwinnett	Hamiltons Bt.	29/26	Early
Lawson, James	Wilkinson	Lees	135/11	Hall
Lawson, John H.	Baldwin	Ellis	116/5	Early
Lawson, John	Burke	Bells	384/12	Irwin
Lawson, John	Wilkinson	Lees	213/1	Appling
Lawson, Joy	Gwinnett	Hamiltons Bt.	155/4	Early
Lawson, Margaret	Jefferson	Abbots	73/1	Appling
Lawson, Mary	Elbert	Dooleys	56/6	Irwin
Lawson, Pleasant	Wilkes	Ogletrees	26/22	Early
Lawson, William	Jones	Hansfords	35/20	Early
Lay, Elisha	Jackson	Winters Bt.	267/11	Early
Lay, James	Jackson	Winters Bt.	78/4	Irwin
Layfield, Josiah	Jones	Griffiths	230/2	Appling
Layman, Robert	McIntosh	Hamiltons	51/2	Habersha
Laytham, Eliz.(Wid)	Wilkinson	Childs	15/3	Habersha
Lazenbury, Richard	Warren	152	20/10	Habersha
Lazenby, Elias Jr.	Columbia	Olives	210/1	Walton
Lazenby, John	Jasper	McClendons	305/5	Early
Lazenby, Samuel	Columbia	Dodsons	170/5	Early
Lazenby, Samuel	Columbia	Dodsons	387/15	Appling
LeConte, Louis	Liberty		29/5	Appling
Lea, Burrell	Clarke	Appling	82/6	Gwinnett
Lea, Burrell	Clarke	Applings	272/4	Walton
Lea, Burrell	Clarke	Applings	368/26	Early
Lea, George	Jasper	Baileys	39/16	Irwin
Lea, John	Clarke	Applings	292/5	Gwinnett
Lea, Thomas	Clarke	Sims	329/11	Early
Leach, Burditt	Franklin	Hamiltons Bt.	148/2	Early
Leake, Richard	Chatham		382/13	Irwin
Lealuted, L.	Richmond	Burtons	122/4	Early
Leaptrot, Pritain	Washington	Peabodys	348/15	Early
Leard, William	Morgan	Loyds	65/5	Gwinnett
Learkin, Sertain	Jackson	Dicksons	49/9	Irwin
Leath, Hartwell W.	Camden	Clarks	230/9	Early
Leathers, John	Wilkinson	Smith	83/4	Habersha
Leavens, Jesse	Morgan	Townsends	471/11	Irwin
Leavens, Richard	Wayne	Jacobs	110/7	Irwin
Leavens, Richard	Wayne	Jacobs	36/16	Early
Leavins, Jacob Jr.	Wayne	Jacobs	315/20	Early
Ledbetter, Ann(Wid)	Early		163/2	Rabun
Ledbetter, Elizabeth	Pulaski	Slaughters	64/22	Early
Ledbetter, Isaac	Early		138/5	Appling
Ledbetter, Isaac	Early		163/2	Rabun
Ledbetter, James W.	Hancock	Coopers	285/27	Early
Ledbetter, James	Jasper	Bartletts	342/14	Early
Ledbetter, James	Jasper	Bartletts	365/6	Early
Ledbetter, John	Wilkinson	Kettles	108/2	Rabun
Ledbetter, John	Wilkinson	Kettles	34/26	Early
Ledbetter, John	Wilkinson	Kettles	37/13	Habersha
Ledbetter, Joseph	Jones	Jeffersons	212/6	Appling
Ledbetter, Samuel	Jones	Hansford	124/11	Early
Ledbetter, Samuel	Jones	Hansfords	253/1	Early
Ledbetter, Washington	Greene	Wheelis	121/17	Early
Ledbetter, Washington	Greene	Wheelis	299/12	Irwin
Ledbetter,Silas	Jones	Jeffersons	54/6	Early
Lee, Abel	Bulloch	Knights	298/3	Appling

NAME	COUNTY	MIL.DIST	LOT/SECT	DREW LAND
Lee, Abner	Morgan	Parkers	145/5	Early
Lee, Abram(Orphs)	Bulloch	Jones	162/16	Early
Lee, Anthony	Hancock	Herberts	174/12	Irwin
Lee, Bryant Jr.	Jones	Griffiths	236/5	Early
Lee, Bryant Sr.	Jones	Griffiths	211/1	Early
Lee, Bryant	Jones	Griffiths	86/21	Early
Lee, Cato	Wilkinson	Childs	61/11	Hall
Lee, Daniel	Wilkes	Ogletree	134/27	Early
Lee, Durham	Twiggs	Ellis	413/6	Irwin
Lee, Elias	Washington	Wimberlys	211/16	Early
Lee, Godfrey	Wilkinson	Lees	432/8	Appling
Lee, Isaiah(Orphs)	Bulloch		15/13	Irwin
Lee, Jacob Jr.	Pulaski	J.Kendricks	141/4	Early
Lee, Jacob Sr.	Pulaski	J.Kendricks	160/11	Habersham
Lee, James	Bulloch	Tilmans	108/16	Early
Lee, James	Gwinnett	Hamiltons Bt.	206/6	Gwinnett
Lee, James	Pulaski	Rees	279/3	Appling
Lee, Jesse	Morgan	Knights	367/9	Irwin
Lee, Jesse	Pulaski	Rees	41/27	Early
Lee, John Jr.	Pulaski	Maddox	155/13	Habersham
Lee, John Jr.	Wilkes	Maddoxs	163/16	Irwin
Lee, John Jr.	Wilkes	Mattox	113/2	Habersham
Lee, John S.	Jefferson	Connells	231/3	Appling
Lee, John S.	Twiggs	Ogletrees	379/10	Irwin
Lee, John S.	Wilkes	Ogletrees	306/26	Early
Lee, John Sr.	Pulaski	Maddoxs	125/9	Early
Lee, John Sr.	Pulaski	Rees	318/6	Irwin
Lee, John Sr.	Pulaski	Rees	367/12	Early
Lee, John	Camden	Tillis	220/9	Early
Lee, Joshua	Pulaski	Oslins	191/16	Irwin
Lee, Joshua	Telfair	Williams	11/6	Appling
Lee, Leonard	Jefferson	Bothwells	164/20	Early
Lee, Levi	Jones	Rossers	156/11	Irwin
Lee, Levy	Bulloch	Everritts	73/3	Appling
Lee, Lovard	Jefferson	Bothwells	3/18	Early
Lee, Martin B.	Wilkinson	Childs	143/3	Appling
Lee, Martin B.	Wilkinson	Childs	212/1	Irwin
Lee, Milton	Morgan	Leonards	118/7	Early
Lee, Nathan	Greene	Carltons	11/9	Hall
Lee, Needham	Jefferson	Mathews	203/7	Gwinnett
Lee, Needham	Jones	Griffiths	186/3	Early
Lee, Noah	Wilkes	Runnels	36/15	Early
Lee, Piercy	Bulloch	Everitts	130/13	Irwin
Lee, Polly(Wid)	Franklin	Akins	144/1	Irwin
Lee, Polly(Wid)	Franklin	Akins	350/8	Appling
Lee, Ransom	Morgan	Farrars	81/7	Irwin
Lee, Ranson	Morgan	Farrers	43/13	Irwin
Lee, Saml.M.	Chatham		259/14	Early
Lee, Sampson	Washington	Wimberlys	72/5	Early
Lee, Sarah(Orph)	Scriven	Lovetts	23/14	Irwin
Lee, Seymore	Oglethorpe	Lees	94/5	Early
Lee, Vincent	McIntosh	Eigles	53/8	Appling
Lee, William	Bulloch	Knights	35/6	Irwin
Lee, William	Bulloch	Knights	64/19	Early
Leek, John	Hancock	Smiths	281/12	Irwin
Lees, Godfrey(Orps)	Wilkinson	Lees	254/4	Early
Lefever, James F.	Chatham		103/11	Early
Lefever, James F.	Chatham		150/2	Early
Lefoy, John G.	Richmond	122	52/12	Habersham
Leftvich, James H.	Oglethorpe	Myricks	289/2	Appling
Leftvich, John A.	Greene	Tuggles	514/12	Irwin
Legg, Thomas	Jackson	Rogers Bt.	500/5	Appling
Legg, William	Franklin	Haynes	196/4	Walton
Leggets, Lewis(Orps)	Pulaski	H.Kindricks	254/5	Early
Leggett, Jeremiah	Jasper	Bentleys	514/5	Appling
Leggett, Margarett(Wid)	Franklin	Ashs	39/20	Early
Leggett, Mathew H.	Pulaski	H.Kendricks	183/7	Irwin

NAME	COUNTY	MIL.DIST	LOT/SECT	DREW LAN
Leggetts, Absalom(Orphs)	Franklin	Ash's	144/11	Irwin
Leggit, Benjamin	Burke	Lewis	205/17	Early
Leggit, David	Burke	Lewis's	411/2	Appling
Leggit, Jeremiah	Jasper	Bentleys	305/10	Irwin
Leggitt, Elias	Wilkinson	Wiggins	91/22	Early
Leggitt, Wilson	Burke	Lewis	31/1	Walton
Legon, Alexander	Burke	McNorrills	264/4	Early
Legon, Marshall	Jefferson	Flemmings	143/7	Gwinnett
Legon, Thomas	Greene	143	18/14	Early
Legran, George	Elbert	Whites	377/6	Appling
Leigh, George	Appling	5 Dist	127/5	Early
Leigh, Walter	Richmond	Laceys	261/7	Irwin
Leigh, William Sr.	Greene	Kimbroughs	325/4	Early
Lemester, James	Morgan	Townsends	223/12	Early
Lemley, Mary(Wid)	Effingham		323/12	Early
Lemonds, Joseph Sr.	Morgan	Knights	425/2	Appling
Lemons, Joseph Sr.	Morgan	Hights	185/17	Early
Lennard, Wm.W.P.	Wilkes	Gordons	461/9	Irwin
Lenoir, Robert C.	Burke	Torrences	317/2	Appling
Lenoir, Thomas	Franklin	Yancy	230/7	Early
Lenoir, Thomas	Franklin	Yancys	81/11	Early
Lenore, William	Franklin	Haynes	562/2	Appling
Leo, Abner	Morgan	Parkers	438/8	Appling
Leonard, Benjamin	Baldwin	Taliaferros	19/20	Early
Leonard, Coleman(Orps)	Twiggs	Jefferson	348/12	Irwin
Leonard, James P.	Greene	143rd	431/13	Irwin
Leonard, Michael	Baldwin	Laceys	333/20	Early
Leonard, Thomas	Twiggs	Hodges	51/3	Appling
Leseuer, Drury M.	Baldwin	Stephens	212/16	Early
Leseur, Samuel Jr.	Elbert	P.Christians	180/18	Early
Lesleigh, Mary(Minor)	Burke	70	412/11	Irwin
Lesleys, John(Orps)	Twiggs	R.Belchers	101/8	Appling
Leslie, James	Richmond	122	79/16	Irwin
Leslie, Jane(Wid)	Wilkinson	Howards	430/5	Irwin
Lessel, Aron	Twiggs	R.Belchers	44/12	Habersh
Lessetor, Benjamin	Gwinnett	Hamiltons Bt.	331/2	Early
Lessoms, Patrick	Burke	Sullivans	222/8	Appling
Lester, Alexander	Oglethorpe	Barnetts	103/12	Irwin
Lester, Alexander	Oglethorpe	Barnetts	169/8	Hall
Lester, David	Jones	Jeffersons	20/6	Irwin
Lester, David	Jones	Jeffersons	256/26	Early
Lester, Dolly	Jones	Hansford	63/15	Early
Lester, Eli	Pulaski	Lesters	71/2	Walton
Lester, Ezeajeak	Burke	Dys	114/26	Early
Lester, George D.	Jackson	Winters	30/9	Early
Lester, George	Oglethorpe	Barnetts	271/9	Early
Lester, Hiram	Baldwin	Haws	364/26	Early
Lester, Isaac	Baldwin	Haws	192/10	Irwin
Lester, Issac Jr.	Baldwin	Haws	81/2	Early
Lester, James Sr.	Baldwin	Doziers	9/19	Early
Lester, James(Orphs)	Jones	Hansfords	72/1	Walton
Lester, Jeremiah	McIntosh	Hamiltons	392/13	Early
Lester, Jesse	Pulaski	Dewitts	304/8	Early
Lester, John E.	Jones	Hansfords	142/12	Habersh
Lester, John(Minor)	Burke	69th	249/5	Early
Lester, John	Baldwin	Haws	128/11	Early
Lester, John	Burke	J.Wards	425/12	Irwin
Lester, John	Jones	Hansfords	473/9	Irwin
Lester, John	Oglethorpe	Bridges	367/2	Appling
Lester, Josiah	Pulaski	J.Kendricks	281/4	Appling
Lester, Julius	Baldwin	Haws	353/8	Appling
Lester, Lewis Jr.	Oglethorpe	Barnetts	138/8	Hall
Lester, Nixon(Orps)	Pulaski	Bryans	119/26	Early
Lester, Noel	Burke	Sullivans	83/16	Irwin
Lester, Pleasant	Madison	Bones	166/4	Early
Lester, Samuel	Richmond	120th	31/13	Early
Lester, Wade	Baldwin	Haws	98/6	Appling

NAME	COUNTY	MIL.DIST	LOT/SECT	DREW LAND
Lester, William	Pulaski	Bryans	141/5	Appling
Lesure, Samuel Jr.	Elbert	P.Christian	306/2	Appling
Letbetter, Timothy	Pulaski	Morlands	44/6	Irwin
Letlaw, Lewis	Jones	Buckhalters	52/9	Early
Lett, Hugh	Jasper	Bentleys	187/11	Early
Lett, Robert	Hancock	Thomas	37/2	Appling
Levar, Philip(R.S.)	Hancock	Danells	137/7	Appling
Levar, Phillip(R.S.)	Hancock	Danells	227/10	Irwin
Leveke, Eliza(Wid)	Jones	Phillips	51/5	Early
Levekes, Augustus(Orphs)	Jones	Phillips	312/20	Early
Leverett, Anne	Wilkes	Holidays	42/7	Gwinnett
Leverett, Burrell	Jasper	Hays	240/27	Early
Leverett, Eliz.(Orph)	Burke	Royals	144/5	Early
Leverett, James	Jasper	Eastes	213/9	Appling
Leverett, Jeremiah	Jasper	Eastes	87/1	Rabun
Leverett, John	Gwinnett	Hamiltons Bt.	66/21	Early
Leverett, Mary	Lincoln	Tatoms	569/2	Appling
Leverett, Mathew	Lincoln	Parks	58/2	Irwin
Leverett, Richard H.	Gwinnett	Hamiltons Bt.	144/12	Early
Leverett, Richard H.	Gwinnett	Hamiltons Bt.	83/11	Irwin
Leverett, Susan G. (Orph)	Burke	Royals	144/5	Early
Leverett, William	Gwinnett	Hamiltons Bt.	124/11	Hall
Leveretts, Wm.(Orps)	Tattnall	Tharps	375/3	Early
Leverit, Matthew	Lincoln	Parks	302/6	Gwinnett
Leverit, Sely	Pulaski	Stampers	68/11	Early
Leveritt, Jesse	Jasper	Eastes	5/19	Early
Leveritt, Thomas	Jasper	Easts	264/6	Gwinnett
Leveritt, Thos.Jr.	Pulaski	Coopers	42/5	Appling
Leveritt, William	Gwinnett	Hamiltons Bt.	84/5	Irwin
Levingston, Isaac	Greene	141st	429/28	Early
Levingston, Michael	Clarke	McElvins	150/5	Early
Levingston, William	Jefferson	Waldens	450/6	Irwin
Levington, Thomas	Jones	Buckhalters	396/11	Irwin
Levins, Isaish	Bulloch	Knights	183/4	Early
Leviston, George	Pulaski	Lanears	183/27	Early
Levret, Gideon	Morgan	McClendons	372/13	Irwin
Levritt, Absalom	Lincoln	Jeters	317/5	Early
Lew, James C.	Wayne	Johnstons	173/15	Irwin
Lewelling, William	Jackson	Rogers Bt.	262/5	Irwin
Lewis, Alexnader P.	Burke	Sullivans	15/8	Early
Lewis, Amasa	Twiggs	W.Belchers	85/2	Rabun
Lewis, Archibald(Orphs)	Greene	Harvills	22/4	Habersham
Lewis, Asa	Washington	Peabodys	245/5	Early
Lewis, Augustin	Hancock	Mims	352/1	Appling
Lewis, Benjamin	Walton	Sentills	213/6	Early
Lewis, Charles	Baldwin	Marchalls	271/9	Early
Lewis, Christian	Morgan	Loyds	61/26	Early
Lewis, Daniel(Orphs)	Burke	J.Wards	125/4	Habersham
Lewis, Daniel(Orphs)	Burke	J.Wards	260/5	Appling
Lewis, David	Bulloch	Knights	196/3	Walton
Lewis, Elizabeth	Burke	M.Wards	391/19	Early
Lewis, Fields	Jones	Greenes	54/8	Early
Lewis, Fields	Jones	Greens	258/15	Early
Lewis, Gabriel	Madison	Adairs	36/3	Habersham
Lewis, George	Chatham		155/18	Early
Lewis, George	Jasper	Postss	226/11	Early
Lewis, George	Tattnall	J.Durrence	254/20	Early
Lewis, Harrison	Twiggs	Barrows	192/2	Appling
Lewis, Henry W.	Jones	Buckhalters	373/11	Early
Lewis, Hezekiah	Burke	Sullivans	111/26	Early
Lewis, Hezekiah	Burke	Sullivans	74/4	Rabun
Lewis, Isaac R.	Laurens	D.Smiths	266/3	Early
Lewis, Jacob	Twiggs	W.Belchers	131/10	Irwin
Lewis, James H.	Elbert	Ruckers	225/9	Early
Lewis, James W.	Bulloch	Jones	95/13	Habersham
Lewis, James	Twiggs	R.Belchers	234/15	Early
Lewis, James	Twiggs	R.Belchers	68/6	Appling

NAME	COUNTY	MIL.DIST	LOT/SECT	DREW LAND
Lewis, James	Wilkinson	Lees	146/12	Habersham
Lewis, Jane	Oglethorpe	Bowls	32/8	Hall
Lewis, Jesse(Orphs)	Emanuel	57th	16/11	Hall
Lewis, John(Orphs)	Jones	Buckhalters	161/3	Early
Lewis, John(Orphs)	Jones	Permenters	496/8	Appling
Lewis, John	Chatham		163/4	Early
Lewis, John	Warren	Blounts	212/3	Irwin
Lewis, Joseph	Emanuel	57th	156/10	Hall
Lewis, Joseph	Hancock	Smiths	205/15	Early
Lewis, Josiah	Burke	Sullivans	145/6	Gwinnett
Lewis, Mary(Wid)	Emanuel	57th	322/18	Early
Lewis, Mathew	Chatham		33/9	Appling
Lewis, Matthew	Tattnall	J.Durrences	242/11	Early
Lewis, Nancy(Wid)	Greene	Harvills	283/7	Irwin
Lewis, Nicholas	Greene	143rd	281/16	Early
Lewis, Nimrod	Burke	Lewis	46/1	Habersham
Lewis, Noland R.	Wilkes	Perrys	395/3	Appling
Lewis, Price B.	Jackson	Rogers Bt.	132/15	Irwin
Lewis, Richard	Hancock	Lucas	347/13	Irwin
Lewis, Stephen	Tattnall	Keens	204/19	Early
Lewis, Thomas B.	Scriven	Smiths	311/21	Early
Lewis, Thomas	Richmond	Winters	237/10	Irwin
Lewis, Warner	Pulaski	Mays	2/20	Early
Lewis, William Jr.	Bulloch	Knights	180/11	Early
Lewis, William Jr.	Morgan	Hackneys	159/8	Appling
Lewis, William	Baldwin	Marshalls	505/6	Appling
Lewis, William	Twiggs	Thames	15/10	Habersham
Lewis, William	Twiggs	W.Belchers	23/8	Irwin
Lewis, Wm.Sr.	Morgan	Hackneys	164/1	Appling
Lewis, Wylie	Bulloch	Knights	47/17	Early
Lewis, Zebedee	Morgan	Loyds	65/10	Irwin
Lewis, Zebudee	Morgan	Loyds	468/11	Irwin
Libas, Charles	Wilkes	Ogletrees	26/22	Early
Licet, Delila	Washington	Robinsons	274/13	Early
Liddell, James	Jackson	Dicksons Bt.	7/12	Hall
Liggin, Tabitha	Morgan	Selmons	91/26	Early
Liggin, Willis	Morgan	Knights	101/10	Early
Lighfoot, John A.	Hancock	Canes	371/17	Early
Lighfoot, Thomas	Washington	Wimberlys	136/3	Appling
Lightfoot, Richard	Washington	Floyds	436/15	Early
Lightfoots, (Orphs)	Burke	Sullivans	28/12	Irwin
Lightnor, Phillip(Orps)	Jones	Samuels	414/8	Irwin
Ligin, John	Morgan	Knights	249/4	Early
Lile, Mathew	Walton	Wagnons	30/11	Hall
Lile, William	Jackson	Stricklands	103/13	Early
Liles, Henry	Wayne	Johnsons	113/15	Early
Liles, John	Twiggs	Evans	41/2	Rabun
Liles, Stephen	Columbia	Walkers	483/5	Irwin
Lilibridge, John	Chatham		214/27	Early
Lilis, Benjamin	Glynn		11/19	Early
Limbert, Catharine(Wid)	Chatham		170/1	Appling
Linch, Benjamin	Pulaski	Buckners	309/1	Appling
Linch, Charles	Pulaski	Buckners	97/14	Irwin
Linch, Garett	Pulaski	Littles	352/7	Early
Linch, James H.	Greene	Macons	257/6	Irwin
Linch, Jaqueline	Pulaski	Buckners	259/6	Irwin
Linch, Jaqueline	Pulaski	Buckners	373/2	Early
Linch, Lewis	Pulaski	Buckners	166/2	Habersham
Linder, Lewis	Laurens	Deanss	261/27	Early
Lindsey, Annis	Camden	Clarks	351/21	Early
Lindsey, Clayton	Greene	Tuggles	55/18	Early
Lindsey, David	Greene	Tuggles	327/9	Appling
Lindsey, Henry(Orphs)	Jefferson	Cowarts	303/4	Early
Lindsey, Hester(Wid)	Montgomery	McMillans	25/7	Appling
Lindsey, John(Orph)	Wilkes	Mattox	181/11	Early
Lindsey, John	Hall		46/16	Irwin
Lindsey, John	Wilkinson	Kettles	29/6	Early

NAME	COUNTY	MIL.DIST	LOT/SECT	DREW LAND
Lindsey, John	Wilkinson	Kettles	329/27	Early
Lindsey, Mary	Wilkes	Russells	224/5	Early
Lindsey, Parham	Jasper	Easts	323/5	Appling
Lindsey, William	Jackson	Scotts	334/1	Early
Lindseys, Thomas(Orph)	Montgomery	McMillians	99/15	Early
Lingo, Daniel T.	Washington	Renfores	119/8	Appling
Lingo, Pinkston	Washington	Renfros	46/10	Early
Linier, Sarah(Wid)	Washington	Wimberlys	200/14	Early
Linsey, Benj.F.H.	Wilkes	Bryants	149/2	Rabun
Linsey, Dennis	Warren	151st	319/11	Irwin
Linsey, Isaac	Twiggs	Jeffersons	164/1	Irwin
Linsey, John W.C.	Wilkes	Bryants	151/10	Hall
Linsey, John W.C.	Wilkes	Bryants	494/5	Appling
Linsey, Pegy(Orph)	Wayne	Crews	208/21	Early
Linsey, Stephen	Burke	J.Wards	135/17	Early
Linsey, Thomas	Twiggs	Jefferson	331/5	Irwin
Linsey, William	Warren	151	37/27	Early
Linsey, William	Wilkinson	Bowens	161/3	Habersham
Linton, Alexander B.	Greene	Jones	298/6	Gwinnett
Linton, Hugh	Twiggs	Evans	25/7	Early
Linton, John Sr.(R.S.)	Twiggs	Evans	111/4	Early
Linum, William	Washington	Barges	152/8	Irwin
Linvell, William	Lincoln	Parks	252/7	Irwin
Lipey, James	Jones	Kings	83/14	Early
Lipham, Aaron(Orps)	Wilkes	Ogletrees	276/7	Appling
Lipham, Abraham	Pulaski	Berrys	189/3	Appling
Lipham, Daniel	Pulaski	Stampers	191/14	Early
Lipham, Daniel	Pulaski	Stampers	241/8	Irwin
Lipham, Francis A.	Wilkes	Ogletrees	299/5	Appling
Lipham, John	Pulaski	Berrys	431/5	Irwin
Lipham, Moses	Twiggs	W.Belchers	15/5	Irwin
Lipsey, Barshaba(Wid)	Jones	Samuels	219/3	Early
Lipsey, Hezekiah	Jones	Samuels	226/15	Early
Lipsey, Rasco	Jones	Samuels	230/16	Early
Liptrot, Sarah	Burke	71st	419/5	Appling
Lishners, Geo.(Orps)	Richmond	Laceys	527/7	Irwin
Lister, Nathaniel	Pulaski	Robertson	267/10	Early
Little, Allen	Baldwin	Doziers	122/26	Early
Little, Archibald	Scriven		437/4	Appling
Little, Archibald	Wilkes	Willis	92/4	Early
Little, Forester	Jefferson	Lamps	67/15	Early
Little, Jacob	Richmond	Laceys	112/8	Hall
Little, James H.	Franklin	Harris	407/12	Irwin
Little, John E.	Wilkes	Bryants	191/12	Early
Little, John E.	Wilkes	Bryants	469/12	Irwin
Little, John(Orph)	Baldwin	Cousins	442/11	Early
Little, John(Orphs)	Baldwin	Cousins	323/7	Gwinnett
Little, Josiah	Jackson	Rogers Bt.	374/10	Early
Little, Lewis	Pulaski	Littles	37/20	Early
Little, Little B.	Wilkes	Bryans	165/4	Walton
Little, William	Wilkes	Bryants	178/5	Gwinnett
Littlejohn, Abraham	Greene	Wheelis	156/16	Irwin
Littlejohn, Abraham	Greene	Wheelis	91/1	Early
Littlejohn, Thomas	Jasper	Smiths	148/19	Early
Littles, Abraham(Orphs)	Baldwin	Doziers	90/28	Early
Littles, Joseph(Orps)	Tattnall	Johnsons	139/4	Appling
Littleton, Enoch	Wilkes	Davis	62/26	Early
Littleton, James	Wilkes	Perrys	185/9	Appling
Littleton, John	Warren	153rd	48/5	Irwin
Littleton, Moses	Lincoln	Parks	238/10	Early
Littleton, Susan(Wid)	Chatham		274/17	Early
Littleton, William	Wilkes	Runnels	159/2	Walton
Littleton, William	Wilkes	Runnels	177/12	Early
Littleton, William	Wilkes	Runnels	247/10	Irwin
Luelling, Joseph Jr.	Franklin	Holcombs	111/1	Irwin
Lively, Charles	Morgan	Townsends	85/9	Appling
Lively, Enury	Burke	Royals	467/8	Appling

NAME	COUNTY	MIL.DIST	LOT/SECT	DREW LAN
Lively, Isaac(Orp)	Burke	Royals	467/8	Appling
Lively, Lewis(Orph)	Burke	Royals	467/8	Appling
Lively, Mark	Burke	Royals	160/17	Early
Lively, Polly Ann(Orph)	Burke	Royals	467/8	Appling
Lively, Rhody	Oglethorpe	Lees	239/11	Early
Liverman, Brown	Wilkinson	Brooks	118/21	Early
Liverman, Brown	Wilkinson	Brooks	231/6	Appling
Liverman, John	Richmond	122	213/8	Irwin
Livingston, Jane	Greene	141st	113/10	Irwin
Livingston, Jones	Laurens	D.Smiths	164/5	Gwinnett
Livingston, William R.	Greene	141st	333/6	Early
Livingston, William	Hancock	Scotts	125/19	Early
Livsey, Green H.	Lincoln	Jones	175/2	Appling
Lloyd, Alston	Hancock	Edwards	448/6	Appling
Lloyd, Virginia	Pulaski	Oslins	162/8	Irwin
Loards, William(Orphs)	Hancock	Herberts	94/1	Appling
Lobdell, Jeremiah	Wilkes	Gordons	256/4	Walton
Locay, Rachael(Wid)	Franklin	Haynes	71/23	Early
Lock, David	Greene	141	61/11	Habersha
Locke, Leonard	Laurens	Watsons	296/2	Early
Locke, Winefred(Orph)	Jefferson	Fountains	71/11	Irwin
Locket, David	Wilkes	Bryants	343/2	Early
Locket, James Sr.	Jones	Kings	289/17	Early
Lockett, David	Wilkes	Bryants	343/4	Early
Lockett, Warren	Warren	Hills	309/7	Irwin
Lockey, William	Madison	Willifords	335/11	Irwin
Lockhart, Eli	Lincoln	Graves	108/3	Rabun
Lockhart, Jesse	Hancock	Scotts	25/1	Rabun
Lockhart, Jesse	Hancock	Scotts	346/12	Early
Lockhart, Joel Jr.	Lincoln	Parks	480/5	Appling
Lockhart, Jonathan	Warren	151	237/16	Early
Lockhart, Vincent	Lincoln	Parks	351/9	Irwin
Lockhart, William	Jones	Buckhalters	15/7	Early
Lockheart, David	Lincoln	Graves	147/11	Early
Lockwood, William	Jasper	Hays	197/8	Appling
Lodge, Frances	Burke	Spiveys	52/1	Appling
Lodge, Francis	Burke	Spiveys	212/14	Early
Lodge, Lewis	Burke	Spiveys	295/9	Early
Loe, Bud	Washington	Wimberleys	168/27	Early
Loflin, Elijah	Lincoln	Walkers	108/9	Irwin
Loflin, Elijah	Lincoln	Walkers	319/16	Early
Loftan, Eli	Jefferson	Bothwells	137/12	Irwin
Loftin, Daniel	Pulaski	Coopers	88/8	Hall
Loftin, James	Pulaski	Coopers	119/2	Walton
Lofton, James	Laurens	S.Smith	67/2	Appling
Lofton, Stephen(Orps)	Telfair	Williams	244/12	Irwin
Lofton, Stephen(Orps)	Telfair	Williams	438/9	Irwin
Logan, Hugh(Orphs)	Baldwin	Marshalls	269/7	Gwinnett
Logan, James Jr.	Franklin	Holcombs	204/20	Early
Logan, James Sr.	Franklin	Haynes	114/7	Early
Logan, Phillip	Baldwin	Marshalls	19/2	Appling
Logan, Phillip	Baldwin	Marshalls	350/9	Early
Logue, Charles Jr.	Warren	151st	98/5	Early
Logue, Charls Sr.	Warren	151	95/19	Early
Logue, William	Jefferson	Waldens	275/13	Early
Logue, Wm.Sr.(R.S.)	Hancock	Scotts	163/3	Habersha
Lokey, George	Madison	Willifords	140/11	Irwin
Londay, Macklin	Scriven	36th	129/13	Irwin
London, Jane John G.H.	Effingham		456//8	Irwin
Long, Alfred	Hancock	Danells	233/7	Appling
Long, Aron	Wilkinson	Brooks	193/11	Irwin
Long, Aron	Wilkinson	Brooks	66/2	Appling
Long, Catherine(Wid)	Camden	Longs	116/5	Appling
Long, Charles	Pulaski	Rees	441/12	Irwin
Long, George T	Morgan	Hackneys	103/12	Habersha
Long, George T.	Morgan	Hackneys	129/6	Appling
Long, Henry	Washington	Burneys	206/18	Early

NAME	COUNTY	MIL.DIST	LOT/SECT	DREW LAND
Long, James	Madison	Willifords	287/4	Appling
Long, James	Washington	Cummins	29/11	Habersham
Long, James	Washington	Cummins	360/16	Early
Long, James	Wilkinson	Brooks	42/16	Early
Long, James	Wilkinson	Brooks	87/5	Early
Long, Jesse L.	Jones	Chappels	146/4	Appling
Long, John(Orps)	Washington	Renfroes	53/12	Irwin
Long, John	Hancock	Scotts	56/13	Habersham
Long, John	Jones	Buckhalters	411/7	Appling
Long, John	Morgan	McClendons	483/12	Irwin
Long, John	Morgan	McLendon	21/2	Habersham
Long, Marcus	Morgan	Rameys	296/9	Irwin
Long, Nicholas	Wilkes	Gordons	48/12	Irwin
Long, Nimrod W.	Baldwin	Stephens	192/10	Early
Long, Polly(Wid)	Franklin	Powels	123/11	Habersham
Long, Polly(Wid)	Franklin	Powels	285/12	Irwin
Long, Richard H.	Wilkes	Ogletrees	66/20	Early
Long, Samuel Sr.	Madison	Culbreths	255/19	Early
Long, Samuel	Madison	Culbreaths	63/12	Habersham
Long, Solomon	Jasper	Phillips	15/9	Appling
Long, Solomon	Jasper	Phillips	248/3	Irwin
Long, Thomas	Madison	Culbreaths	138/8	Irwin
Long, Thomas	Madison	Culbreths	167/4	Appling
Long, Thomas	Morgan	Parkers	303/5	Gwinnett
Long, William	Chatham		90/27	Early
Long, William	Washington	Cummins	315/3	Appling
Long, William	Washington	Cummins	54/6	Appling
Longstreet, Gilbert	Richmond	398th	60/4	Irwin
Longstreet, William	Richmond	398th	313/2	Early
Longue, Wm.Sr.(R.S.)	Hancock	Scotts	264/16	Early
Look, Clark	Chatham		299/15	Irwin
Looney, Adam	Franklin	P.Browns	82/18	Early
Lord, Abraham	Tattnall	Keens	299/7	Appling
Lord, Claudius	Bulloch	Knights	409/8	Appling
Lord, Claudius	Bulloch	Knights	515/13	Irwin
Lord, James	Jackson	Mays	216/3	Walton
Lord, John	Wilkinson	Kettles	170/14	Early
Lord, John	Wilkinson	Kettles	19/9	Early
Lord, Matthias	Clarke	Moores	284/8	Appling
Lord, William	Wilkinson	Kettles	154/6	Appling
Lorrecy, William	Scriven	Lovetts	50/13	Early
Lorrecy, Wm.Jr.	Scriven	Lovetts	11/6	Habersham
Lorrez, John B.	Greene	Carltons	448/10	Irwin
Lot, John	Lincoln	Graves	180/3	Habersham
Lots, Ephraim(Orps)	Wilkinson	Brooks	114/15	Early
Lott, Arthur	Jefferson	Mathews	225/7	Gwinnett
Lott, Ellis	Lincoln	Graves	352/26	Early
Lott, Mark	Lincoln	Graves	72/23	Early
Lott, Stephen	Wilkinson	Brooks	256/5	Irwin
Louis, Gale(Orphs)	Hancock	Danells	152/17	Early
Louis, John H.	Hancock	Thomas	7/10	Irwin
Louis, Sarah(Wid)	Hancock	Thomas	147/7	Early
Lounds, Epaphoditus	Greene	142nd	462/9	Irwin
Love, Alexander	Telfair	Loves	18/8	Irwin
Love, Allen	Greene	Carlton	328/20	Early
Love, Amos	Laurens	Harris's	257/19	Early
Love, Amos	Laurens	Harrist	22/8	Hall
Love, Hugh	Greene	143rd	189/15	Early
Love, Ingram	Walton	Sentills	198/14	Early
Love, John	Emanuel	57th	162/3	Early
Love, John	Emanuel	57th	322/18	Early
Love, John	Greene	143	65/2	Walton
Love, John	Greene	143rd	206/13	Irwin
Love, John	Pulaski	Stampers	262/12	Early
Love, Josephus	Greene	142	69/16	Early
Love, Louisa(Wid)	Chatham		515/6	Appling
Love, Nancy(Wid)	Telfair	Loves	20/19	Early

NAME	COUNTY	MIL.DIST	LOT/SECT	DREW LAN
Lovejoy, Edward	Jasper	Posts	73/19	Early
Lovejoy, Samuel	Jasper	Phillips	166/20	Early
Lovejoy, Simeon	Jackson	Rogers Bt.	129/2	Appling
Lovejoy, William	Jasper	Bentleys	251/6	Irwin
Lovejoy, William	Jasper	Bentleys	31/7	Appling
Lovel, William	Columbia	Pullins	73/6	Habersha
Loven, Elijah	Franklin	Harris's	165/5	Irwin
Loven, Gabriel	Oglethorpe	Davenports	200/13	Early
Loves, Edward(Orps)	Telfair	Loves	41/1	Habersha
Loves, Wm.(Orphs)	Jones	Shropshiers	25/27	Early
Lovet, Thomas F.	Scriven	Lovets	30/3	Appling
Lovets, James(Orphs)	Columbia	Willinghams	409/21	Early
Lovett, Aron	Effingham		239/11	Irwin
Lovett, David	Effingham		37/11	Early
Lovett, David	Twiggs	W.Belchers	11/4	Walton
Lovett, David	Twiggs	W.Belchers	416/6	Appling
Lovett, John R.Jr.	Scriven	Lovetts	280/10	Early
Lovett, Moses	Twiggs	R.Belchers	42/1	Habersha
Lovett, N.B.	Chatham		280/8	Irwin
Lovett, Richard	Warren	154	359/17	Early
Lovett, Robert W.	Scriven	Smiths	118/6	Appling
Lovett, Thomas F.	Scriven	Lovetts	397/7	Irwin
Lovin, Lydia	Pulaski	Senterfeits	346/27	Early
Loving, Thomas(R.S.)	Clarke	Moores	24/9	Early
Loving, Thomas(R.S.)	Clarke	Morriss	250/11	Early
Lovins, Arthur	Greene	Carltons	48/6	Irwin
Low, Aquilla(R.S.)	Twiggs	Smiths	206/12	Early
Low, Edmund	Baldwin	Haws	235/18	Early
Low, Elisha	Twiggs	Smiths	105/3	Early
Low, George	Hancock	Thomas	83/7	Gwinnett
Low, Henry Sr.	Jones	Shropshiers	324/6	Irwin
Low, Isaac	Columbia	Dodsons	125/4	Walton
Low, James Sr.	Warren	154	228/7	Appling
Low, John	Gwinnett	Hamiltons Bt.	255/10	Early
Low, Leurana(Wid)	Pulaski	Bustins	46/4	Early
Low, Lunsford	Warren	154	296/19	Early
Low, Mary(Wid)	Twiggs	W.Belchers	249/28	Early
Low, Stephen	Laurens	Jones	74/10	Hall
Low, Thomas	Columbia	Walkers	105/20	Early
Low, William	Hancock	Thomas	173/6	Early
Low, William	Twiggs	Jamesons	108/4	Irwin
Low, Wm.	Hancock	Thomas	366/7	Appling
Lowe, Aaron	Jefferson	Cowarts	617/2	Appling
Lowe, Benjamin	Jones	Shropshiers	42/4	Walton
Lowe, Daniel B.	Jefferson	Cowarts	44/7	Gwinnett
Lowe, David W.	Warren	Parhams	493/7	Appling
Lowe, Dennis	Camden	32nd	303/4	Appling
Lowe, Henry Sr.	Jones	Shopshers	258/8	Appling
Lowe, Isaac	Greene	Tuggles	125/20	Early
Lowe, James	Morgan	Loyds	412/8	Appling
Lowe, James	Wilkinson	Smiths	434/8	Irwin
Lowe, John H.	Clarke	Mereweathers	358/8	Early
Lowe, John	Jones	Wallers	337/20	Early
Lowe, John	Jones	Wallers	37/13	Irwin
Lowe, Ralph R.S.	Pulaski	Bustins	324/13	Early
Lowe, Sarah(Wid)	Pulaski	Ectors	258/5	Appling
Lowery, Charles Sr.	Franklin	Ashs	183/28	Early
Lowery, Henry	McIntosh	Goulds	285/8	Appling
Lowery, John w.	Franklin	Hammonds	178/2	Appling
Lowery, John	Franklin	Ashs	112/26	Early
Lowery, Solomon R.	Franklin	Ash's	528/7	Appling
Lowery, William	Franklin	Turks	79/5	Irwin
Lowre, John	Franklin	Turks	324/7	Early
Lowremore, James	Elbert	Whites D.-C Bt.	140/14	Early
Lowrimore, Andrew	Elbert	P.Christians	44/9	Habersha
Lowry, Andrew	Jefferson	Bothwells	336/13	Early
Lowry, Andrew	Jefferson	Bothwells	76/2	Early

NAME	COUNTY	MIL.DIST	LOT/SECT	DREW LAND
Lowry, Charles	Jackson	Rogers Bt.	330/6	Gwinnett
Lowry, Edmund	Elbert	G.Higginbothams	214/9	Appling
Lowry, James R.	Jackson	Rogers Bt.	13/5	Early
Lowry, John R.	Twiggs	Browns	79/13	Irwin
Lowry, John	Jefferson	Flemmings	286/8	Appling
Lowry, Levi	Jackson	Rogers	27/7	Gwinnett
Lowry, Nathan	Jackson	Hamiltons	298/11	Early
Lowry, Thomas	Jefferson	Flannings	127/16	Early
Lowther, John(Orphs)	Bulloch	Everitts	6/8	Early
Lowther, Samuel	Jones	Samuels	284/17	Early
Loyall, Jesse	Jasper	Clays	338/26	Early
Loyd, Elijah	Morgan	Loyds	172/28	Early
Loyd, Isham	Jones	Griffiths	172/6	Gwinnett
Loyd, James Sr.	Jasper	Evans	103/3	Habersham
Loyd, James Sr.	Jasper	Evans	50/2	Appling
Loyd, John	Jasper	Northcuts	372/7	Appling
Loyd, Joseph	Morgan	Selmons	369/18	Early
Loyd, Mary S.(Wid)	Wilkinson	Childs	344/20	Early
Loyd, Richard J.	Jasper	Northcuts	102/3	Rabun
Loyd, Thomas Jr.	Hancock	Loyds	60/4	Habersham
Loyd, Thomas Sr.(R.S.)	Hancock	Loyds	228/16	Early
Loyd, Thomas	Jasper	Evans	170/5	Gwinnett
Loyds, John(Orphs)	Jones	Permenters	85/14	Irwin
Loyds, Thomas L	Wilkinson	Childs	217/3	Early
Loyless, Henry	Warren	150th	75/6	Irwin
Loyless, James	Warren	153rd	329/5	Early
Loyless, Thomas	Pulaski	Berrys	201/3	Early
Lucas, Abraham B.	Wilkinson	Kettles	192/3	Early
Lucas, Charles	Morgan	Farrars	317/4	Walton
Lucas, Frederick	Jones	Phillips	442/8	Irwin
Lucas, George B.	Jones	Phillips	18/14	Irwin
Lucas, Hampton	Wilkinson	Kettles	308/5	Gwinnett
Lucas, Henry	Hancock	Coopers	113/1	Habersham
Lucas, Hezia	Baldwin	Marshalls	160/8	Early
Lucas, James	Jones	Phillips	56/16	Early
Lucas, John	Baldwin	Marshalls	104/21	Early
Lucas, John	Baldwin	Marshalls	26/17	Early
Lucas, Mary	Hancock	Coopers	157/11	Irwin
Lucas, Thomas(Orph)	Hancock	Coopers	198/11	Irwin
Lucas, William D.	Hancock	Lucas	23/13	Habersham
Lucas, Wm.	Hancock	Coopers	2/22	Early
Luckett, Joseph W.	Warren	Griers	140/16	Early
Luckey, Margaretta(Wid)	Richmond	Palmers	89/12	Early
Luckey, Wm.Sr.R.S.	Pulaski	Evans	218/11	Irwin
Luckeys, John(Orphs)	Jones	Greens	344/6	Appling
Luckie, James	Jackson	Winters Bt.	232/7	Appling
Lucky, William	Columbia	Shaws	112/13	Habersham
Lucky, Wm.	Columbia	Shaws	154/2	Early
Lucky, Wm.Sr. R.S.	Pulaski	Evans	424/1	Appling
Luelling, Joseph Sr.	Franklin	Holcombs	338/6	Irwin
Lufborrows, Matthew	Chatham		84/8	Hall
Luke, Daniel	Jasper	Bartlets	120/2	Habersham
Luke, Ferdinand	Columbia	Pullins	373/10	Irwin
Luke, John	Burke	72nd	353/10	Irwin
Luke, Thomas	Burke	72nd	252/4	Appling
Luke, Wm.B.	Columbia	Pullins	274/5	Early
Luker, Benjamin	Wilkes	Kilgores	429/11	Irwin
Luker, Benjamin	Wilkes	Kilgores	73/18	Early
Lukes, Wm.(Orphs)	Burke	72nd	390/6	Early
Lumkin, Dickson	Madison	Millicans	227/12	Early
Lumkins, John L.	Telfair	Wilsons	172/16	Irwin
Lumkins, John L.	Telfair	Wilsons	231/2	Early
Lumpkin, Henry H.	Oglethorpe	Rowlands	196/5	Irwin
Lumpkin, Jack	Oglethorpe	Murrys	345/12	Irwin
Lumpkin, John	Jasper	Baileys	58/8	Appling
Lumpkin, John	Oglethorpe	Dunns	34/15	Irwin
Lumpkin, Joseph H.	Oglethorpe	Brittains	479/7	Irwin

NAME	COUNTY	MIL.DIST	LOT/SECT	DREW LAND
Lumpkin, Phillip	Burke	Sullivans	135/11	Irwin
Lumpkin, Robert Sr.	Jasper	Baileys	526/11	Irwin
Lumpkin, Walter	Jasper	Baileys	11/14	Irwin
Lumpkin, William	Oglethorpe	Waters	178/2	Habersham
Lumpkin, Wilson	Morgan	Talbots	148/12	Habersham
Lumpkins, Dickerson	Jones	Kings	182/27	Early
Lumpkins, Edwards	Jones	Kings	65/7	Appling
Lumpkins, Robert	Hall		206/2	Appling
Lumsden, Jermiah Jr.	Jasper	Hays	431/12	Irwin
Lumsden, John	Jasper	Posts	186/1	Walton
Lunceford, Leonard	Pulaski	H.Kendricks	313/3	Appling
Lunceford, Moses	Morgan	McClendons	319/6	Irwin
Lunday, Thomas	Hancock	Champions	194/8	Appling
Lunday, William	Scriven		56/13	Early
Lundsden, Jeremiah	Jasper	Hays	67/7	Irwin
Lundy, Peyton	Hancock	Lucas	68/5	Rabun
Lunsford, Bailey	Wilkes	Runnels	75/15	Irwin
Lunsford, George	Elbert	Whites of Chrs.B.	277/3	Early
Lunsford, Hazel	Greene	Jones	336/20	Early
Lunsford, Jacob	Wilkes	Runnels	238/7	Gwinnett
Lunsford, James	Elbert	B.Higginbothams	9/28	Early
Lunsford, Lucinda	Oglethorpe	Brittains	440/12	Irwin
Lunsford, Rolen	Baldwin	Marshalls	176/21	Early
Lyle, Betty(Wid)	Jackson	Hamiltons	159/26	Early
Lyle, James	Jackson	Hamiltons Bt.	275/2	Early
Lyle, John	Jackson	Hamiltons Bt.	423/2	Appling
Lyle, William	Jackson	Rogers Bt.	497/10	Irwin
Lynch, Elizabeth	Burke	Lewis	64/5	Rabun
Lynch, George	Jasper	Centells	479/13	Irwin
Lynch, Henry	Burke	Spiveys	9/6	Appling
Lynch, Mary	Pulaski	Morelands	118/16	Early
Lynch, William	Burke	Spiveys	211/2	Irwin
Lynch, William	Burke	Spiveys	26/12	Early
Lyne, Elizabeth(Wid)	Greene	Nelms	43/1	Rabun
Lyne, James	Greene	Nelms	408/9	Irwin
Lyne, Nancy(Orph)	Greene	Nelms	296/8	Irwin
Lyneburger, Abeloni	Effingham		81/17	Early
Lyneburger, David	Effingham		98/4	Early
Lyneburger, John	Effingham		124/3	Habersham
Lyneburger, Joshua	Effingham		6/5	Irwin
Lynes, James	Richmond	120th	160/8	Irwin
Lynn, Asa	Warren	154	452/8	Appling
Lynn, David	Warren	154	32/13	Habersham
Lynn, David	Warren	154th	23/4	Walton
Lyon, Isaac D.	Chatham		162/2	Irwin
Lyon, James	Richmond	Winters Bt.	346/5	Early
Lyon, Martha	Elbert	B.Higginbothams	436/13	Irwin
Lyon, Nathan	Pulaski	Oslins	9/3	Appling
Lyon, Thomas	Columbia	Pullins	68/11	Hall
Lyon, William T.	Pulaski	Stampers	267/7	Early
Lyons, James	Jones	Permenters	262/3	Irwin
Lyons, John(S/Wm.)	Jefferson	Waldens	69/16	Irwin
Lyons, Jonathan	Richmond	Palmers	284/7	Appling
Lyons, William(Orps)	Oglethorpe	Brittons	204/5	Early
Mabry, Adam(Orps)	Jasper	Posts	122/2	Irwin
Mabry, Adam(Orps)	Jasper	Posts	385/3	Early
Mabry, Allen	Wilkes	Holidays	134/13	Irwin
Mabry, Gray	Greene	140th	339/21	Early
Mabry, Joel	Franklin	Morriss	39/11	Habersham
Mabry, John	Greene	140	140/1	Early
Mabry, Lucy	Jasper	Centells	106/4	Habersham
Mabry, Thomas	Jasper	Posts	372/8	Early
Macarthen, Malcom	Tattnall	Keens	352/6	Appling
Macarthy, Roger	Jones	Samuels	183/13	Irwin
Mace, Mary(Wid)	Bulloch	Knights	183/1	Irwin
Macfairland, John B.	Tattnall	Johnstons	20/4	Appling
Macfarland, Johnson	Tattnall	Johnsons	463/6	Irwin

NAME	COUNTY	MIL.DIST	LOT/SECT	DREW LAND
Mackey, Littleton	Wilkes	Willis	4/11	Early
Mackey, Rebeckah(Wid)	Wilkinson	Howards	87/9	Early
Mackey, Rosanah(W)	Franklin	Harriss	417/6	Irwin
Mackey, Thomas	Jones	Permenters	7/8	Irwin
Mackey, William	Wilkinson	Howards	116/13	Habersham
Mackey, Wm.C.	Franklin	Harris	97/19	Early
Macklin, Lawhin	Washington	Cummins	332/13	Irwin
Maclean, Andrew	Columbia	Olives	359/21	Early
Maclean, Andrew	Columbia	Olives	377/9	Early
Maclin, Edward	Baldwin	Irwins	8/11	Hall
Maclin, John	Baldwin	Irwins	66/6	Irwin
Madcalf, Henry	Jackson	Winters Bt.	273/15	Early
Madcalf, Henry	Jackson	Winters Bt.	73/11	Habersham
Madden, Dennis	Morgan	Selmons	386/1	Appling
Maddin, David(RS)	Morgan	Hubbards	469/7	Irwin
Maddin, Thomas	Morgan	Hubbards	382/11	Irwin
Maddox, Anthoney	Greene	142	466/7	Appling
Maddox, Benjamin	Elbert	Dooleys	341/13	Irwin
Maddox, Clayborn	Greene	142nd	282/8	Early
Maddox, Eliz.	Putnam	Oslins	142/8	Irwin
Maddox, George	Jones	Jeffersons	59/13	Habersham
Maddox, Henley	Elbert	Doolys	346/6	Early
Maddox, Henry	Columbia	Burroughs	463/8	Irwin
Maddox, Henry	Columbia	Burroughs	52/7	Irwin
Maddox, James	Hancock	Herberts	271/18	Early
Maddox, Jesse	Columbia	Burroughs	202/17	Early
Maddox, Jesse	Putnam	Oslins	281/27	Early
Maddox, John	Hancock	Danells	307/6	Early
Maddox, John	Hancock	Danells	406/4	Appling
Maddox, John	Jasper	Evans	360/1	Early
Maddox, Joseph	Jackson	Winters Bt.	328/21	Early
Maddox, Joseph	Putnam	Ectors	136/7	Appling
Maddox, Joseph	Putnam	Oslins	59/15	Irwin
Maddox, Lenta	Oglethorpe	Rowlands	401/21	Early
Maddox, Saml.(R.S.)	Hancock	Lucas	74/9	Early
Maddox, Saml.	Putnam	Morelands	56/19	Early
Maddox, Samuel	Putnam	Morelands	285/15	Early
Maddox, Seaborn	Jackson	Hamiltons Bt.	186/5	Early
Maddox, Thomas	Morgan	Hubbards	223/5	Appling
Maddox, Walter	Columbia	Walkers	90/2	Appling
Maddox, William	Hancock	Danells	81/15	Irwin
Maddox, William	Hancock	Lucas	154/19	Early
Maddox, William	Putnam	Stampers	442/7	Irwin
Maddox, Zachariah	Jackson	Hamiltons Bt.	300/10	Early
Maddox, Zachariah	Jackson	Hamiltons Bt.	305/11	Irwin
Maddux, George	Jones	Jeffersons	18/3	Habersham
Maddux, Patrick N.	Warren	Neals	158/10	Hall
Madry, Benjamin	Burke	70th	261/14	Early
Madry, Joseph	Burke	70th	58/8	Early
Madry, Mary	Burke	70th	318/7	Appling
Maettz, Nathan	Wilkinson	Bowings	69/3	Appling
Magaha, Willis	Columbia	Cochrans	113/4	Early
Magahagan, Wm.	Effingham		77/12	Hall
Magbee, Hiram	Clarke	Mereweather	279/6	Appling
Mageaux, Daniel	Columbia	O.Morris	342/6	Appling
Magee, Daniel	Pulaski	Lester	236/4	Appling
Magee, Lawrence	Twiggs	Thames	417/15	Early
Magee, Mary(Wid)	Richmond	Winters	43/10	Hall
Magee, William	Hancock	Lucas	159/1	Appling
Mages, Ansel	Elbert	Doolys	371/5	Appling
Magill, Baldwin(Orps)	Pulaski	Johnston	213/13	Irwin
Maginta, Alex.	Wilkes	Mattox	351/7	Appling
Magor, Richard	Jackson	Dicksons Bt.	15/5	Gwinnett
Magouirk, James	Jones	Samuels	166/5	Early
Magouirk, John	Walton	Wagnons	12/7	Irwin
Magouirk, Seth	Walton	Williams	292/3	Early
Magruder, George	Richmond	Palmers	291/6	Gwinnett

NAME	COUNTY	MIL.DIST	LOT/SECT	DREW LAN
Magruder, Hezekiah	Columbia	Olives	95/9	Appling
Magruder, John	Columbia	J.Morris	108/5	Rabun
Mahar, John	Greene	Tuggles	468/6	Irwin
Maharry, John	Richmond	122nd	131/4	Appling
Mahon, Nixon	Hancock	Evans	14/4	Appling
Mahon, Wiley A.B.	Lincoln	Jones	14/12	Irwin
Mahon, William	Hancock	Edward	162/5	Irwin
Mahon, William	Hancock	Edwards	219/1	Early
Mahon, Wm.(RS)	Twiggs	R.Belchers	142/12	Irwin
Mahone, Rowland	Putnam	Robertsons	332/8	Early
Mahone, Thomas	Putnam	Robertsons	222/9	Early
Mahoney, James	Lincoln	Thompsons	449/7	Appling
Mahoney, William	Lincoln	Thompsons	32/5	Appling
Mailley, Jeremiah	Jasper	Clays	115/20	Early
Mainer, Hardy	Burke	J.Wards	409/5	Appling
Mainer, Henry G.	Scriven	Roberts	35/5	Early
Mainer, John(R.S.)	Clarke	Oats	527/8	Appling
Mainer, John(R.S.)	Clarke	Otis	92/11	Early
Mainer, Josirus	Burke	J.Wards	173/13	Habersha
Mainer, William	Morgan	Campbells	80/7	Early
Maines, Samuel	Wilkinson	Lees	134/6	Early
Maines, Samuel	Wilkinson	Lees	278/5	Gwinnett
Mainor, John Sr.	Scriven	Roberts	523/13	Irwin
Mainor, John(Orph)	Scriven	Mills	419/12	Irwin
Mains, Samuel	Wilkinson	Lees	6/7	Appling
Majors, Edward	Wilkinson	Brooks	222/1	Walton
Majors, John	Twiggs	Evans	133/12	Irwin
Majors, John	Twiggs	Evans	62/10	Early
Malcom, James Jr.	Morgan	Parkers	262/5	Appling
Malcom, James Jr.	Morgan	Parkers	308/2	Early
Malcom, James Sr.	Morgan	Parks	93/8	Early
Malden, Richard	Franklin	Haynes	381/15	Early
Mallard, Elijah	Columbia	Walkers	103/1	Early
Mallard, Lydia	Liberty		152/11	Hall
Mallet, Joicy(Wid)	Lincoln	Jeters	295/5	Irwin
Mallory, John W.	Wilkes	Burks	126/3	Habersha
Mallory, John W.	Wilkes	Burks	226/3	Early
Mallory, John	Hancock	Canes	106/2	Rabun
Mallory, John	Hancock	Canes	56/5	Appling
Mallory, Stephen	Wilkes	Burks	121/13	Irwin
Mallory, Thomas	Greene	Wheelis	15/6	Habersha
Mallory, Thomas	Greene	Wheelis	187/7	Irwin
Mally, Hendley	Lincoln	Parks	27/1	Appling
Malone, Cherry(Wid)	Washington	Floyds	377/19	Early
Malone, Daniel(Orps)	Walton	Sentells	162/1	Walton
Malone, Edward D.	Morgan	Alfords	146/14	Irwin
Malone, James	Morgan	Leonards	170/4	Appling
Malone, Jemeroon(Orps)	Morgan	Lenords	82/7	Gwinnett
Malone, John	Greene	Carltons	362/16	Early
Malone, John	Putnam	Oslins	103/13	Irwin
Malone, John	Putnam	Oslins	57/6	Appling
Malone, John	Washington	Floyds	400/13	Early
Malone, John	Wilkinson	Wiggins	245/18	Early
Malone, Jones	Greene	Woodhams	456/10	Irwin
Malone, Madison	Washington	Floyds	1/1	Early
Malone, Mary A.(Orph)	Richmond	122	98/12	Early
Malone, Robert	Greene	Carltons	65/11	Early
Malone, Robert	Richmond	122nd	167/6	Appling
Malone, Sherrod	Jasper	Baileys	24/3	Irwin
Malone, Sherrod	Jasper	Baileys	48/12	Hall
Malone, Stephen	Clarke	Tredwells	155/15	Early
Malone, Thomas	Columbia	Pullins	2/2	Walton
Malone, Usla(Wid)	Morgan	Leonards	120/26	Early
Malone, William	Greene	140th	192/13	Irwin
Malpus, Hardy	Washington	Pools	116/10	Irwin
Malpus, Morris	Washington	Mannings	301/18	Early
Malpuss, Hardy	Washington	Pools	340/26	Early

NAME	COUNTY	MIL.DIST	LOT/SECT	DREW LAND
Maltbee, William	Jackson	Hamiltons Bt.	84/8	Irwin
Man, Jane(Wid)	Jefferson	Langstons	60/15	Early
Man, Wm.	Greene	Harvills	39/22	Early
Manary, R.(Orpn)	Madison	Culbreths	254/21	Early
Mancrief, Arthur	Warren	153	98/10	Early
Manders, Samuel	Jackson	Hamiltons Bt.	525/8	Irwin
Manderson, John	Wilkinson	Wiggins	208/3	Early
Mangham, Henry	Hancock	Scotts	364/2	Appling
Mangham, James C.	Glynn		163/7	Appling
Mangham, James	Putnam	Littles	233/4	Early
Mangham, Thomas	Jasper	Reids	201/13	Irwin
Mangnam, Charles	Jones	Wallers	327/8	Appling
Mangram, John C.	Hancock	Danells	9/21	Early
Mangrim, Howell	Franklin	Vaughns	103/27	Early
Mangrum, Sarah	Morgan	Jordans	64/7	Early
Mangum, Howel	Franklin	Vaughns	113/17	Early
Mangum, Howell Sr.	Franklin	Turks	3/15	Irwin
Mangum, Samuel	Franklin	Turks	148/7	Gwinnett
Mankin, Benedicton	Wilkes	Hendersons	73/4	Rabun
Manley, William	Clarke	Stuarts	99/3	Rabun
Manly, John	Putnam	Littles	60/14	Early
Manly, Moses	Franklin	Attaways	331/5	Gwinnett
Manly, Samuel(Orph)	Bryan	20th	104/15	Irwin
Manlys, Dan.(Orps)	Franklin	Attaways	235/17	Early
Mann, Asa	Elbert	Smiths	296/2	Appling
Mann, Baker	Morgan	Farrars	401/26	Early
Mann, David W.	Twiggs	Smiths	269/1	Early
Mann, David W.	Twiggs	Smiths	78/1	Appling
Mann, Henry	Jackson	Hamiltons Bt.	25/5	Irwin
Mann, Joel	Elbert	Penns	246/9	Appling
Mann, Joel	Elbert	Penns	424/10	Irwin
Mann, Joel	Morgan	Farrars	266/26	Early
Mann, John H.	Richmond	122	308/8	Early
Mann, John H.	Richmond	122nd	127/15	Early
Mann, John J.Jr.	Elbert	G.Higginbotham	396/16	Early
Mann, John	Hancock	Millers	358/2	Early
Mann, Judah(Wid)	Richmond	122nd	180/10	Early
Mann, Judeth	Elbert	Penns	34/6	Early
Mann, Kedar(Orps)	Pulaski	Lesters	343/7	Appling
Mann, Shimer	Oglethorpe	Wises	217/26	Early
Mann, Thomas	Bryan	20	80/5	Gwinnett
Mannary, John	Madison	Culbreths	289/9	Irwin
Mannen, Wm.	Madison	Willifords	159/16	Irwin
Mannin, Henry	Madison	Williford	297/26	Early
Manning, Alesey(Wid)	Washington	Avents	262/14	Early
Manning, Kessiah(Orp)	Glynn		155/21	Early
Manning, Laurence	Telfair	Loves	271/8	Irwin
Manning, Littleton	Putnam	Berrys	153/28	Early
Manning, Martin	Glynn		155/21	Early
Manning, Melchisadeck	Glynn		292/4	Early
Manning, Nancy(Orp)	Glynn		155/21	Early
Manning, Shedrick(Orps)	McIntosh	Eigles	83/5	Irwin
Manning, Wright	Pulaski	Maddox	133/5	Gwinnett
Mannings, John(Orph)	Washington	Wimberlys	392/19	Early
Manry, Wm.F.	Greene	144th	66/5	Appling
Mans, John(Orph)	Morgan	McLendons	136/11	Hall
Mansfield, Frederick	Twiggs	Ellis	280/9	Appling
Mansil, George	Pulaski	Rays	445/8	Appling
Manson, William	Jefferson	Flemings	407/4	Appling
Manyard, Thomas	Washington	Peabodys	275/12	Irwin
Manzy, George(RS)	Putnam	Ectors	170/10	Habersham
Mapp, James	Hancock	Lucas	12/7	Appling
Mapp, John F.	Morgan	Townsends	36/1	Appling
Mapp, Littleton	Hancock	Lucas	266/7	Irwin
Mappin, James	Columbia	J.Morriss	217/21	Early
Mappin, Mary(Wid)	Columbia	Bealls	203/6	Appling
Marable, Lucy R.(W)	Clarke	Applings	43/7	Early

NAME	COUNTY	MIL.DIST	LOT/SECT	DREW LAN
Marables, John(Orps)	Clarke	Appling	48/15	Irwin
Marcelin, Richard	Chatham		27/8	Irwin
Marchant, Joseph	Warren	150	420/28	Early
Marchman, John	Baldwin	Russells	381/11	Early
Marchman, Stephen	Putnam	Buckners	240/3	Irwin
Marchman, Stephen	Putnam	Buckners	51/11	Early
Marcrum, James	Jasper	Baileys	148/8	Irwin
Marcrum, James	Jasper	Baileys	90/3	Irwin
Marcus, Thomas	Baldwin	Marshalls	21/8	Hall
Marcus, Thomas	Baldwin	Marshalls	462/3	Appling
Maria, Phillippi	Elbert	Maxwell	197/3	Early
Market, Joseph	Jones	Phillips	283/7	Early
Markey, Patrick	Baldwin	Marshalls	350/21	Early
Marks, Julian	Scriven	36th	151/9	Early
Marks, Stephen	Warren	152	362/15	Early
Marks, William	Madison	Orrs	286/21	Early
Marks, Wm.	Madison	Orrs	145/8	Appling
Marlow, Ann	Scriven		44/4	Rabun
Marlow, Larkin	Jackson	Dicksons Bt.	119/5	Early
Marlow, Stephen	Scriven		206/9	Irwin
Marr, James	Jasper	Smiths	12/23	Early
Marrable, Richard	Clarke	Deans	144/9	Hall
Marrs, Loyd	Clarke	Dickins	131/7	Early
Marrs, Loyd	Clarke	Dickins	213/5	Irwin
Marsh, Hester	Baldwin	Marshalls	284/4	Irwin
Marsh, John	Burke	72nd	224/28	Early
Marsh, John	Burke	Thomas	310/7	Appling
Marsh, Mary(Wid)	Emanuel	59	156/3	Early
Marsh, Reuben	Telfair	Wilsons	522/10	Irwin
Marshall, Allen	Jones	Buckhalters	191/8	Irwin
Marshall, Ann(Wid)	Columbia	Olives	242/1	Walton
Marshall, Asa	Jones	Buckhalters	85/10	Early
Marshall, Chesley	Jones	Buckhalters	146/7	Gwinnett
Marshall, Daniel	Columbia	Walkers	64/5	Gwinnett
Marshall, Elbert	Columbia	Walkers	382/10	Early
Marshall, Henry	Telfair	Williams	130/9	Irwin
Marshall, Henry	Telfair	Williams	218/28	Early
Marshall, James	Chatham		80/9	Early
Marshall, John	Jefferson	Langstons	21/17	Early
Marshall, John	Putnam	Ectors	140/16	Irwin
Marshall, John	Richmond	122nd	481/3	Appling
Marshall, Joseph	Jefferson	Langstons	232/5	Early
Marshall, Jubal	Columbia	Walkers	49/4	Walton
Marshall, Lewis	Jefferson	Fountains	26/9	Early
Marshall, Mathew	Jefferson	Langstons	329/6	Appling
Marshall, Moses(Orps)	Jasper	Bentleys	332/7	Appling
Marshall, Stephen Sr.	Putnam	Robertsons	121/1	Irwin
Marshall, William	Chatham		475/2	Appling
Marshall, Wm.(Orps)	Jones	Shropshier	110/10	Early
Marshall, Wm.B.	Putnam	Robertsons	649/2	Appling
Marshall, Wm.S.	Jefferson	Fountains	270/12	Early
Marshalls, John(Orps)	Burke	72nd	483/8	Irwin
Marshbourn, Daniel	Washington	Jenkinsons	211/12	Irwin
Marshs, James(Orps)	Burke	72nd	101/7	Irwin
Marten, Alexander	Liberty		182/9	Early
Martiangel, Susan(W)	Chatham		83/4	Walton
Martin, Abel	Wilkinson	Kettles	102/2	Habersha
Martin, Abraham Sr.	Gwinnett	Hamiltons Bt.	6/6	Appling
Martin, Absalom	Jackson	Hamiltons Bt.	118/8	Hall
Martin, Absalom	Jackson	Hamiltons Bt.	54/27	Early
Martin, Alex.Sr.	Richmond	122nd	80/4	Early
Martin, Alexander	Clarke	Harris	75/7	Early
Martin, Alexander	Jackson	Dicksons Bt.	85/8	Early
Martin, Alexander	Oglethorpe	Wises	378/12	Early
Martin, Allen	Jasper	Smiths	188/3	Early
Martin, Allen	Jasper	Smiths	244/4	Appling
Martin, Angis	Liberty		183/6	Irwin

NAME	COUNTY	MIL.DIST	LOT/SECT	DREW LAND
Martin, Ann H.(Wid)	Jackson	Hamiltons Bt.	272/6	Gwinnett
Martin, Barnett	Oglethorpe	Brittons	110/2	Habersham
Martin, Benjamin	Baldwin	Haws	105/10	Early
Martin, Benjamin	Columbia	Pullins	25/8	Irwin
Martin, Burton	Jasper	Easts	480/6	Irwin
Martin, Charles	Chatham		251/7	Early
Martin, Charles	Franklin	Ashs	102/8	Hall
Martin, Charles	Franklin	Ashs	309/8	Irwin
Martin, Charles	Jackson	Hamiltons	159/4	Early
Martin, Charles	Richmond		166/2	Irwin
Martin, Charles	Washington	Barges	145/7	Early
Martin, Charles	Washington	Barges	156/4	Appling
Martin, Chas.(Orph)	Richmond	Laceys	88/3	Early
Martin, Cluff	Oglethorpe	Davenports	327/9	Early
Martin, Cluff	Oglethorpe	Davenports	495/5	Appling
Martin, Dabney A.	Wilkes	Brooks	271/1	Appling
Martin, Dabney A.	Wilkes	Brooks	58/1	Early
Martin, Daniel	Jasper	Bentleys	271/4	Irwin
Martin, David	Burke	Thomas	440/13	Irwin
Martin, Dolly	Oglethorpe	Wises	63/4	Habersham
Martin, Edmund	Richmond		222/10	Irwin
Martin, Elijah	Bulloch	Jones	4/1	Appling
Martin, Elijah	Greene	Kimbroughs	89/12	Irwin
Martin, Eliz.(Wid)	Franklin	Holcombs	299/8	Appling
Martin, Eliza(Orph)	Richmond	Laceys	88/3	Early
Martin, Elyah	Jasper	Bentleys	4/23	Early
Martin, Gabriel	Hancock	Danells	310/6	Appling
Martin, Gabriel	Hancock	Danells	345/8	Irwin
Martin, Ganaway	Columbia	Dodsons	88/2	Walton
Martin, George W.	Chatham		61/4	Early
Martin, George W.	Putnam	Coopers	6/8	Irwin
Martin, George(Orph)	Richmond	Laceys	88/3	Early
Martin, Hiram	Twiggs	Jeffersons	433/10	Irwin
Martin, Isaac	Morgan	Talcots	28/4	Walton
Martin, Isabel(Wid)	Liberty		37/6	Gwinnett
Martin, Jacob	Jackson	Hamiltons	326/6	Irwin
Martin, James Sr.	Franklin	Vaughans	226/5	Gwinnett
Martin, James	Greene	Fosters	199/4	Walton
Martin, James	Greene	Fosters	90/9	Appling
Martin, James	Madison	Adares	314/11	Irwin
Martin, Jesse	Oglethorpe	Goolsbys	39/8	Irwin
Martin, John Jr.	Putnam	Bustins	476/5	Appling
Martin, John N.	Laurens	D.Smiths	416/28	Early
Martin, John Sr.	Putnam	Bustins	58/14	Early
Martin, John(Orps)	Jasper	Easts	92/13	Habersham
Martin, John(Orps)	Jones	Wallers	404/7	Irwin
Martin, John	Elbert	Dooleys	335/9	Early
Martin, John	Elbert	Dooleys	412/1	Early
Martin, John	Elbert	Webbs	79/12	Habersham
Martin, John	Jefferson	Lamps	4/11	Hall
Martin, John	Jefferson	Lamps	63/6	Habersham
Martin, John	Telfair	Wilsons	29/3	Rabun
Martin, John	Washington	Barges	343/18	Early
Martin, Jonathan	Jackson	Dicksons Bt.	160/20	Early
Martin, Levi	Jasper	Bentleys	135/1	Early
Martin, Matthew	Clarke	Pentecosts	217/7	Irwin
Martin, Micajah	Franklin	Vaughans	149/26	Early
Martin, Micajah	Jones	Permenters	9/13	Habersham
Martin, Morris	Baldwin	Irwin	118/7	Gwinnett
Martin, Morris	Baldwin	Irwins	321/4	Early
Martin, Naphtah	Madison	Adares	116/14	Irwin
Martin, Oden	Wilkinson	Bowings	171/10	Hall
Martin, Peter	Putnam	Robersons	305/5	Irwin
Martin, Rachel	Burke	J.Wards	250/18	Early
Martin, Robert	Columbia	Olives	112/2	Irwin
Martin, Robert	Columbia	Olives	395/8	Appling
Martin, Robert	Jefferson	Lamps	296/6	Irwin

NAME	COUNTY	MIL.DIST	LOT/SECT	DREW LAN
Martin, Robert	Jones	Jeffersons	526/6	Irwin
Martin, Robert	Twiggs	Browns	71/16	Early
Martin, Sarah(Wid)	Clarke	Oats	71/6	Irwin
Martin, Solomon	Morgan	Loyds	346/14	Early
Martin, Spencer	Clarke	Applings	149/3	Early
Martin, Susan	Jasper	Eastss	71/1	Habersha
Martin, Thomas	Franklin	J.Miller	88/4	Early
Martin, Thomas	Jasper	Clays	155/10	Habersha
Martin, Thompson	Madison	Adares	449/10	Irwin
Martin, Thos.S.	Hancock	Scotts	68/1	Early
Martin, Vincent	Wilkinson	Bowings	501/7	Irwin
Martin, Westley	Franklin	Ashs	252/3	Early
Martin, Wilford	Oglethorpe	Wises	206/15	Early
Martin, William W.	Burke	72	147/13	Early
Martin, William	Emanuel	49th	288/7	Early
Martin, William	Franklin	Vaughns	170/16	Early
Martin, William	Greene	Ragins	385/7	Irwin
Martin, William	Jackson	Hamilton Bt.	187/6	Irwin
Martin, William	Twiggs	Evans	73/8	Irwin
Martin, William	Twiggs	Jeffersons	20/1	Early
Martin, Willis	Warren	150th	244/10	Early
Martin, Wm.	Baldwin	Marshalls	119/3	Early
Martin, Wm.D.	Jackson	Rodgers	105/16	Early
Martin, Wm.Jr.	Madison	Adares	239/7	Gwinnett
Martin, Wm.Jr.	Wilkes	Holidays	231/2	Irwin
Martin, Woody	Warren	Loyless	174/3	Early
Martindale, John	Clarke	Merriweathers	70/3	Early
Martindale, Timothy	Greene	Greers	2/10	Irwin
Martindale, Timothy	Greene	Greers	5/4	Walton
Martius, (Orphs)	Franklin	Harris	151/17	Early
Masburn, Joseph	Jasper	Clays	97/9	Hall
Masey, Daniel	Twiggs	Smiths	505/9	Irwin
Masey, Tabith(Wid)	Effingham		182/1	Early
Mash, John	Warren	150th	25/18	Irwin
Mashburn, Nancy(Wid)	Jones	Chappels	66/11	Irwin
Mason, George	Washington	Daniels	60/11	Irwin
Mason, James	Jones	Jeffersons	39/2	Habersha
Mason, John M.	Hancock	Mims	295/11	Early
Mason, Laban	Jones	Buckhalters	170/3	Walton
Mason, Labon	Jones	Buckwalters	34/20	Early
Mason, Larkin	Jasper	Ryans	52/4	Appling
Mason, Lowell	Chatham		30/11	Habersha
Mason, Lowell	Chatham		139/16	Early
Mason, Peter	Emanuel	57th	61/5	Appling
Mason, Raiford	Washington	Daniels	468/7	Appling
Mason, Redmond B.	Pulaski	Davis	28/7	Gwinnett
Mason, Sarah	Pulaski	Davis	119/11	Irwin
Mason, Timothy B.	Chatham		326/16	Early
Mason, Turner	Laurens	D.Smiths	92/1	Habersha
Mason, William S.	Laurens	D.Smiths	454/3	Appling
Mason, Wm.Sr.	Elbert	Webbs	263/6	Appling
Mason, Wm.Sr.	Elbert	Webbs	445/9	Irwin
Massay, Abraham	Washington	Cummings	275/6	Irwin
Masse, Moore	Effingham		420/13	Irwin
Massey, Abel	Washington	Robisons	150/13	Early
Massey, Abel	Washington	Robisons	467/9	Irwin
Massey, James M.	Greene	144th	350/6	Early
Massey, Jesse	Oglethorpe	Murrays	26/12	Irwin
Massey, Reuben	Morgan	Campbells	285/14	Early
Matherson, Roderick	Richmond	Palmers	70/9	Irwin
Mathess, Cary	Clarke	Parrs	62/12	Early
Mathews, Benjamin	Burke	McNorrills	44/3	Early
Mathews, Benjamin	Wilkinson	Howards	142/1	Appling
Mathews, Charles	Columbia	J.Morris	216/21	Early
Mathews, Chas.B.	Hancock	Danells	141/12	Early
Mathews, Edmond	Glynn		153/5	Irwin
Mathews, Gabriel	Clarke	Harris	106/15	Irwin

NAME	COUNTY	MIL.DIST	LOT/SECT	DREW LAND
Mathews, Galbry	Warren	153	376/7	Gwinnett
Mathews, George G.	Greene	143rd	245/19	Early
Mathews, Green	Putnam	Ectors	75/16	Early
Mathews, James Jr.	Wilkes	Russels	277/2	Early
Mathews, James	Bulloch	Edward	229/12	Irwin
Mathews, James	Clarke	Moores	316/5	Irwin
Mathews, James	Hancock	Lucas	16/16	Irwin
Mathews, James	Jefferson	Bothwells	129/12	Early
Mathews, John G.	Scriven	36th	277/5	Early
Mathews, John(Orps)	Liberty		507/6	Appling
Mathews, John	Appling	5	51/13	Irwin
Mathews, John	Twiggs	Jeffersons	373/27	Early
Mathews, Joseph(R.S.)	Warren	152	402/9	Irwin
Mathews, Littleberry	Oglethorpe	Devinports	151/9	Appling
Mathews, Loderick	Twiggs	W.Belchers	375/20	Early
Mathews, Mathew	Warren	Parhams	174/3	Irwin
Mathews, Matthew	Warren	Parhams	143/3	Habersham
Mathews, Moses	Jackson	Hamiltons Bt.	149/11	Early
Mathews, Noel	Wilkes	Perrys	333/20	Early
Mathews, Phinehas	Franklin	Ashs	187/7	Gwinnett
Mathews, Stephen	Washington	Renfros	35/5	Irwin
Mathews, Temperance(Wid)	Washington	Floyd	31/28	Early
Mathews, Timothy	Twiggs	W.Belchers	114/13	Irwin
Mathews, William	Jackson	Winters Bt.	154/3	Walton
Mathews, William	Jefferson	Bothwells	182/2	Appling
Mathews, William	Oglethorpe	Davenports	238/7	Early
Mathews, Wm.	Putnam	Oslins	287/12	Early
Mathews, Wm.Jr.	Wilkinson	Howards	498/7	Appling
Mathewws, Chas.L.	Oglethorpe	McCowens	313/20	Early
Mathis, Isaac(Orps)	Washington	Mannings	377/6	Early
Mathis, John	Laurens	Watsons	151/2	Appling
Mathis, John	Laurens	Watsons	70/16	Early
Mathis, John	Wilkinson	Smiths	443/5	Appling
Matthew, Chas.(Orps)	Warren	153	94/12	Habersham
Matthews, Aquilla	Jefferson	Bothwell	118/10	Habersham
Matthews, Aquilla	Jefferson	Bothwells	336/7	Irwin
Matthews, Arthur	Warren	Hutcherson	141/10	Habersham
Matthews, Asa	Wilkinson	Howards	273/7	Gwinnett
Matthews, Asa	Wilkinson	Howards	74/5	Early
Matthews, Benj.	Jones	Samuels	94/17	Early
Matthews, Benjamin	Wilkinson	Howards	345/8	Early
Matthews, Brinkley	Putnam	Ectors	11/2	Appling
Matthews, Burwell	Morgan	Loyds	114/19	Early
Matthews, Burwell	Morgan	Loyds	181/20	Irwin
Matthews, Charles	Jefferson	Bothwells	51/6	Irwin
Matthews, Chas.	Richmond	Laceys	33/1	Irwin
Matthews, Elbert	Warren	153	350/6	Appling
Matthews, Elijah	Jones	Harrist	123/12	Habersham
Matthews, Elisha H.	Putnam	Slaughters	425/1	Early
Matthews, Eliz.(Wid)	Elbert	R.Christians	315/26	Early
Matthews, Galbry	Warren	153	383/15	Early
Matthews, Henry	Burke	M.Wards	146/21	Early
Matthews, Henry	Burke	M.Wards	314/12	Irwin
Matthews, Isaac	Warren	Parhams	5/4	Rabun
Matthews, Jacob G.	Oglethorpe	Rowlands	75/10	Irwin
Matthews, James	Bulloch	Edwards	99/6	Appling
Matthews, James	Putnam	Slaughters	88/1	Habersham
Matthews, James	Warren	152	87/15	Early
Matthews, James	Wilkinson	Howards	412/8	Irwin
Matthews, Jane(Wid)	Jefferson	Matthews	397/11	Irwin
Matthews, Jesse	Jackson		8/16	Early
Matthews, John	Jackson	Rogers Bt.	53/11	Irwin
Matthews, John	Lincoln	Stokes	124/15	Irwin
Matthews, John	Lincoln	Stokes	87/9	Early
Matthews, John	Lincoln	Stokes	95/6	Early
Matthews, Joseph F.	Lincoln	Stokes	166/26	Early
Matthews, Lodowick	Washington	Echols	270/7	Irwin

213

NAME	COUNTY	MIL.DIST	LOT/SECT	DREW LAND
Matthews, Mary	Wilkes	Bates	42/3	Rabun
Matthews, Micajah	Jones	Jeffersons	71/10	Early
Matthews, Moses	Jackson	Hamiltons Bt.	190/21	Early
Matthews, Phillip	Elbert	P.Christian	239/9	Early
Matthews, Richard	Jackson	Rogers Bt.	324/4	Walton
Matthews, Robert	Hancock	Justices	463/11	Irwin
Matthews, Seaborn J.	Warren	152	181/5	Appling
Matthews, Stephen	Washington	Renfroes	68/10	Early
Matthews, Thomas	Hancock	Justices	134/5	Irwin
Matthews, Thomas	Richmond	Laceys	33/1	Irwin
Matthews, William Jr.	Jackson	Hamiltons Bt.	9/1	Irwin
Matthews, William	Wilkes	Brooks	95/20	Early
Matthews, Willie	Jefferson	Flemmings	423/6	Irwin
Matthews, Wm.	Jackson	Winters Bt.	371/18	Early
Matthews, Wm.H.	Putnam	H.Kendricks	229/10	Irwin
Matthis, John Sr.	Washington	Avents	175/18	Early
Mattox, Benjamin W.	Jasper	Phillips	478/2	Appling
Mattox, David	Elbert	Olivers	11/11	Hall
Mattox, David	Elbert	Olivers	253/7	Gwinnett
Mattox, Elijah Jr.	Tattnall	Overstreets	181/1	Appling
Mattox, Elijah	Tattnall	J.Durrences	278/4	Appling
Mattox, Hamilton D.	Jackson	Hamiltons Bt.	22/5	Early
Mattox, Hampton	Tattnall	Overstreets	323/9	Irwin
Mattox, John	Jackson	Hamiltons Bt.	472/6	Irwin
Mattox, John	Jones	Griffiths	519/10	Irwin
Mattox, John	Jones	Griffiths	88/8	Irwin
Mattyx, Saml.L.	Jackson	Hamiltons Bt.	110/10	Habersham
Maulden, Andrew	Franklin	Yanseys	104/28	Early
Maulden, Henry	Jasper	Kennedys	33/3	Irwin
Mauldin, James	Liberty		146/9	Irwin
Maulding, Ann	McIntosh	Eiglis	249/26	Early
Maund, Elizabeth	Burke	Torrance	256/6	Gwinnett
Maupin, Jesse(R.S.)	Elbert	Olivers	106/18	Early
Maurin, Paul	Chatham		296/20	Early
Maxell, John J.	Bryan	20th	127/2	Habersham
Maxey, Booz	Jasper	Clays	66/3	Rabun
Maxey, David A.	Baldwin	Stephens	258/5	Early
Maxey, Edward H.	Clarke	Mereweathers	268/2	Early
Maxey, Garland	Jasper	Evans	283/1	Walton
Maxey, Garland	Jasper	Evans	78/11	Hall
Maxey, Lewis	Oglethorpe	Murrays	285/19	Early
Maxey, Moses	Oglethorpe	Myricks	35/5	Habersham
Maxey, Thomas H.	Baldwin	Stephens	200/12	Irwin
Maxey, Yelverton	Oglethorpe	Myricks	74/6	Early
Maxwell, Andley	Liberty		394/7	Early
Maxwell, Benj.	Elbert	B.Higginbotham	228/3	Appling
Maxwell, Eliz.	Wilkes	Brooks	487/6	Irwin
Maxwell, Eliza(Or.)	Bryan	20	233/13	Early
Maxwell, Elizabeth(Wid)	Bryan	20th	41/1	Appling
Maxwell, James(Orp)	Jefferson	Abbotts	209/12	Habersham
Maxwell, James	Franklin	Holcombs	165/2	Irwin
Maxwell, James	Madison	Adares	181/2	Appling
Maxwell, John B.(Or.)	Bryan	20	233/13	Early
Maxwell, John B.	Bryan	20th	318/26	Early
Maxwell, John M.	Chatham		157/7	Irwin
Maxwell, Joseph	Chatham		217/13	Early
Maxwell, Mary(Wid)	Chatham		125/11	Early
Maxwell, Mary(Wid)	Liberty		189/16	Irwin
Maxwell, Robert	Oglethorpe	Brittons	400/6	Irwin
Maxwell, Wm.(Orps)	Putnam	Slaughters	6/16	Early
Maxwells, (Orphs)	Franklin	Morris	248/13	Irwin
May, Allen	Washington	Brooks	220/6	Walton
May, Andrew	Franklin	Turks	69/3	Irwin
May, Bechum	Warren	152	9/4	Walton
May, Drury	Pulaski	Rees	123/4	Habersham
May, George	Chatham		35/7	Early
May, Henry	Putnam	Mays	191/27	Early

NAME	COUNTY	MIL.DIST	LOT/SECT	DREW LAND
May, James A.	Lincoln	Graves	250/13	Early
May, James A.	Lincoln	Graves	62/22	Early
May, James	Jasper	Centills	112/27	Early
May, John Jr.	Warren	153	101/5	Early
May, John Sr.	Pulaski	Rees	266/4	Appling
May, John	Washington	Renfros	356/3	Appling
May, Major W.	Greene	140	525/9	Irwin
May, Martha(Wid)	Lincoln	Graves	6/8	Hall
May, Martha(Wid)	Lincoln	Grays	324/11	Early
May, Peter Sr.	Warren	151st	36/9	Irwin
May, Peter Sr.	Warren	151st	440/7	Irwin
May, Ralph	Chatham		167/6	Irwin
May, Ralph	Chatham		337/10	Early
May, Thomas	Jasper	Kenedys	327/1	Appling
Mayfield, John	Morgan	Campbells	362/5	Irwin
Mayfield, Obediah	Clarke	Simms	50/3	Appling
Mayfield, Philip	Franklin	Attaway	56/7	Appling
Mayn, Matthew	Clarke	Dennis	337/13	Irwin
Maynard, Nathl.(Orps)	Jackson	Hamiltons Bt.	48/7	Early
Maynard, Nicholas	Jackson	Hamiltons	95/4	Habersham
Maynor, John D.	Jefferson	Cowarts	13/4	Walton
Mayo, Benj.	Jackson	Rodgers Bt.	182/11	Irwin
Mayo, Benjamin	Pulaski	Senterfeits	121/14	Early
Mayo, Cyprian	Wilkinson	Wiggins	138/7	Irwin
Mayo, Cyprian	Wilkinson	Wiggins	301/5	Gwinnett
Mayo, Edmund	Washington	Renfros	163/2	Appling
Mayo, Howell	Washington	Wimberleys	321/5	Appling
Mayo, Jesse	Wilkinson	Smiths	156/2	Walton
Mayo, Jethro	Washington	Renfros	206/5	Irwin
Mayo, John	Glynn		196/6	Irwin
Mayo, Jonas	Jefferson	Langstons	143/8	Early
Mayo, Josiah(Orps)	Wilkinson	Wiggins	163/11	Habersham
Mayo, Nathan	Wilkinson	Smiths	46/28	Early
Mays, Andrew G.	Lincoln	Tatoms	354/12	Early
Mays, Edmund	Washington	Renfros	84/17	Early
Mays, Elisha	Wilkinson	Smith	50/15	Early
Mays, James	Lincoln	Tatoms	77/1	Walton
Mays, James	Oglethorpe	Rowlands	14/3	Walton
Mays, John R.	Lincoln	Graves	401/9	Irwin
Mays, John W.	Lincoln	Tatoms	111/21	Early
Mays, John	Jasper	Phillips	399/8	Irwin
Mays, Mattox	Putnam	Coopers	35/4	Habersham
Mays, Priscilla(Wid)	Warren	153	291/18	Early
Mays, Rutherford	Jasper	Sentals	50/6	Appling
Mays, Thos.Sr.	Franklin	Ashs	466/13	Irwin
Mays, William	Franklin	Ashs	259/4	Appling
Mays, William	Franklin	Ashs	341/15	Early
Mayse, Thomas	Morgan	Jordans	26/6	Early
Mazo, John	Glynn		196/6	Irwin
Mazo, William	Richmond	Burtons	382/9	Irwin
McAffee, Robert	Jasper	Reids	362/12	Irwin
McAlhattan, Abram	Morgan	Jordans	226/16	Early
McAlister, Abigail	Elbert	Chiders	293/5	Irwin
McAlley, Thomas	Greene	Ragins	151/7	Irwin
McAllister, Chas.	Warren	154th	111/14	Irwin
McAlpin, Alex.	Greene	Griers	59/1	Irwin
McAlpin, Alexander	Greene	Griers	18/3	Rabun
McAlpin, John	Clarke	Mitchells	120/2	Appling
McAlpin, Wm.	Greene	Greers	141/2	Early
McArdie, Purdis	Chatham		375/8	Early
McArthur, Charles	Telfair	Loves	374/7	Gwinnett
McArthur, John	Hancock	Edwards	112/3	Irwin
McArthur, John	Tattnall	Johnstons	280/18	Early
McArthur, John	Tattnall	Johnstons	492/7	Irwin
McArthur, John	Wilkinson	Kettles	289/12	Early
McAwley, Awley	Montgomery	Nobles	174/9	Hall
McAwley, Awley	Montgomery	Nobles	430/10	Irwin

NAME	COUNTY	MIL.DIST	LOT/SECT	DREW LAN
McAwley, Geo.(Orps)	Montgomery	Alstons	84/1	Walton
McBain, John	Laurens	Harriss	214/3	Irwin
McBean, Daniel	Jasper	Clays	93/13	Habersha
McBee, Isham	Franklin	Ashs	376/5	Appling
McBride, Andrew	Gwinnett	Hamiltons	269/8	Appling
McBride, Jas.Jr.	Jefferson	Fountains	182/2	Rabun
McBride, John	Burke	71	242/28	Early
McBride, John	Jones	Harrists	12/2	Walton
McBride, John	Putnam	Oslins	268/17	Early
McBride, Joseph	Greene	143rd	289/28	Early
McBride, Thomas Sr.	Jefferson	Fountains	178/4	Irwin
McBryde, John	Wilkinson	Wiggins	115/9	Early
McBryde, Nevin	Wilkinson	Kettles	129/5	Appling
McBryde, Nivin	Wilkinson	Kettles	168/9	Early
McBryde, Robert	Jones	Griffiths	407/4	Early
McCain, William D.	Elbert	Whites	96/4	Habersha
McCalee, James(RS)	Jackson	Hamiltons Bt.	143/19	Early
McCalister, John	Jones	Seals	172/8	Early
McCall, Eliz.(Wid)	Bulloch	Edwards	250/8	Early
McCall, John E.(Orps)	Putnam	Morlands	158/11	Early
McCall, John E.	Liberty		433/5	Appling
McCall, John(R.S.)	Effingham		233/2	Early
McCall, John(R.S.)	Effingham		30/19	Early
McCall, Nathaniel	Pulaski	Rees	104/5	Early
McCall, Nathaniel	Pulaski	Rees	14/13	Irwin
McCall, Sherrod	Bulloch	Knights	274/5	Gwinnet
McCall, Thomas	Scriven	180	121/8	Early
McCalla, Margaret(Wid)	Franklin	Ashs	428/13	Irwin
McCallas, Thos.(Orps)	Franklin	Ashs	398/12	Irwin
McCamron, James	Lincoln	Stokes	36/4	Irwin
McCamron, James	Lincoln	Stokes	71/6	Gwinnet
McCan, Charles	Burke	Dys	148/4	Appling
McCar, William	Richmond	120th	296/9	Early
McCardell, Peter	Chatham		188/17	Early
McCaron, Danl.(Orps)	Morgan	Campbells	142/8	Appling
McCaron, Wm.D.	Morgan	Jordans	17/26	Early
McCarrity, Abner	Elbert	Dobbs	85/11	Hall
McCarrity, Gardner	Elbert	B.Higginbotham	2/3	Early
McCarter, Alexr.	Franklin	Harris	212/20	Early
McCarter, John	Franklin	Harriss	91/10	Habersha
McCarter, Mathew	Franklin	Harris	139/10	Irwin
McCarter, Matthew	Franklin	Harriss	1/12	Habersha
McCarther, John B.	Putnam	Bledsoes	390/10	Irwin
McCartie, Benj.(Orps)	Warren	153	124/9	Early
McCartor, Rebecca(Wid)	Jackson	Rogers	237/13	Irwin
McCarty, Anthony	Morgan	Knights	129/3	Early
McCarty, Anthony	Morgan	Nights	406/28	Early
McCarty, Charles	Twiggs	Hodges	62/9	Irwin
McCarty, Cornelius	Baldwin	Marshall	193/10	Irwin
McCarty, John Jr.	Jackson	Winters Bt.	12/1	Habersha
McCarty, John Jr.	Jackson	Winters	220/5	Early
McCarty, John	Walton	Davis	340/6	Appling
McCarty, Sarah	Oglethorpe	Murrays	639/2	Appling
McCarty, Sherod(Orps)	Oglethorpe	Murrays	269/10	Early
McCarty, William	Wilkinson	Kettles	62/11	Habersha
McCarty, Wm.Sr.	Wilkinson	Kettles	174/11	Early
McCarty, Wm.Sr.	Wilkinson	Kettles	262/6	Irwin
McCasell, Mc.	Liberty		357/8	Irwin
McCaughey, Andrew	Washington	Peaboddys	340/7	Early
McCawn, Finlaw	Morgan	Campbells	119/21	Early
McCawn, William	Morgan	Jordans	512/6	Appling
McCeaver, John	Jackson	Hamiltons Bt.	188/3	Irwin
McCeaver, John	Jackson	Hamiltons Bt.	277/5	Irwin
McCeaver, Joseph	Jackson	Hamiltons Bt.	128/13	Early
McCeaver, William	Jackson	Hamiltons Bt.	502/9	Irwin
McChee, Thomas	Jones	Chappels	183/6	Appling
McClain, John	Camden	Baileys	125/7	Irwin

NAME	COUNTY	MIL.DIST	LOT/SECT	DREW LAND
McClain, Silas	Oglethorpe	Dunns	548/2	Appling
McClaine, Mary Ann	Chatham		132/7	Gwinnett
McClammey, Matthew(Orps)	Burke	Lewis	215/4	Walton
McClamry, John	Warren	150	283/5	Irwin
McCleland, Andrew	Tattnall	J.Durrences	279/10	Early
McCleland, Andrew	Tattnall	J.Durrences	53/4	Early
McCleland, John Sr.	Liberty		240/23	Early
McCleland, Mack	Scriven	Moodys	212/5	Irwin
McCleland, William	Scriven	Moodys	421/12	Irwin
McCleland, William	Tattnall	J.Durrences	379/3	Appling
McClellan, Andrew	Camden	32nd	198/8	Early
McClendon, Allen	Jasper	Easts	367/13	Early
McClendon, Amos	Jasper	Blakes	37/1	Walton
McClendon, Amos	Jasper	Blakes	586/2	Appling
McClendon, Eliz.(Wid)	Jones	Phillips	123/16	Early
McClendon, Enoch	Walton	Worshams	16/14	Irwin
McClendon, Haley	Wilkinson	Kittles	50/10	Irwin
McClendon, Holden	Wilkinson	Bowings	269/1	Walton
McClendon, Isham(Orps)	Jefferson	Abbots	126/16	Early
McClendon, Jacob	Jasper	Reids	248/12	Early
McClendon, James	Jasper	Clays	44/14	Early
McClendon, James	Tattnall	J.Durrences	271/16	Early
McClendon, Jeptha	Jasper	Easts	42/15	Irwin
McClendon, Joseph	Jasper	Reeds	234/10	Early
McClendon, Joseph	Jasper	Reids	96/18	Early
McClendon, Nancy(Wid)	Jefferson	Abbots	454/13	Irwin
McClendon, Saml.Jr.	Morgan	McClendons	13/9	Irwin
McClendon, Samuel Jr.	Morgan	McClendons	302/5	Appling
McClendon, Samuel	Morgan	McClendon	329/12	Early
McClendon, Thomas	Gwinnett	Hamiltons Bt.	166/1	Walton
McClendon, Thos.Sr.(RS)	Walton	Worshams	345/1	Early
McClendon, Wiley	Jasper	Easts	448/9	Irwin
McClendon, William	Laurens	Kinchens	47/1	Habersham
McClendon, Wm.	Jones	Phillips	186/5	Gwinnett
McCleng, Geo.(Orps)	Jasper	Reids	423/1	Appling
McClennen, John	Pulaski	Johnsons	346/2	Appling
McCleskey, Thomas	Wilkes	Gordons	116/9	Irwin
McClesky, James R.	Jackson	Rogers Bt.	177/4	Appling
McClesky, James R.	Jackson	Rogers Bt.	79/5	Gwinnett
McClish, James	Chatham		264/5	Appling
McClowen, John	Liberty		329/3	Appling
McClukey, Benj.	Jackson	Dicksons	328/9	Appling
McClung, Drucilla(Orp)	Hall		111/10	Habersham
McClung, Eliz.(Orp)	Hall		111/10	Habersham
McClung, Hiram(Orp)	Hall		111/10	Habersham
McClung, Merida	Jasper	Reids	71/2	Appling
McClung, Robert	Jasper	Reids	45/11	Habersham
McClung, Suel(Orp)	Hall		111/10	Habersham
McClure, John	Jasper	Reids	62/7	Irwin
McCluskey, David G.	Jackson	Dicksons Bt.	341/6	Appling
McCluskley, Benj.	Jackson	Dicksons Bt.	221/5	Early
McCollock, Eliz.(Wid)	McIntosh	Jenkins	79/4	Walton
McCollock, Eliz.(Wid)	McIntosh	Jenkins	79/4	Walton
McCollock, James(Orps)	McIntosh	Jinkins	185/1	Walton
McCollough, Wm.	Gwinnett	Hamiltons	281/3	Early
McColowis, Burwell	Warren	Parhams	278/8	Appling
McConnal, James	Jackson	Hamiltons	437/8	Appling
McConnal, Wm.	Jackson	Hamiltons	435/6	Irwin
McConnel, Burrel(Orps)	Wilkinson	Rooks	329/13	Early
McConnel, William	Putnam	H.Kendricks	287/17	Early
McConnell, Eldredge	Jackson	Rogers Bt.	385/1	Appling
McConnell, Eli	Hall	Millers	177/6	Irwin
McConnell, John Jr.	Hall		350/13	Irwin
McConnell, John Sr.	Hall		364/15	Early
McConnell, John	Hall		18/13	Early
McCook, Alexnader	Wilkinson	Brooks	28/10	Irwin
McCook, Daniel	Wilkinson	Brooks	171/27	Early

NAME	COUNTY	MIL.DIST	LOT/SECT	DREW LAN
McCook, Daniel	Wilkinson	Brooks	83/8	Irwin
McCord, David	Washington	Cummins	221/15	Early
McCord, James(Orph)	Clarke	Moore	38/28	Early
McCord, John	Clarke	Moores	116/9	Early
McCord, John	Lincoln	Graves	12/15	Early
McCord, John	Wilkes	Davis	32/26	Early
McCord, Robert	Oglethorpe	Murrays	390/5	Appling
McCord, William	Jasper	Easts	295/15	Early
McCordell, William	Effingham		96/1	Early
McCork, Robert	Hancock	Smiths	149/18	Early
McCorkle, Archibald	Lincoln	Graves	251/9	Appling
McCormack, James	Elbert	Webbs	23/8	Early
McCormack, John	Pulaski	Johnstons	46/15	Early
McCormack, Thomas	Wilkes	Bryants	354/12	Irwin
McCormick, Abner	Warren	153	263/20	Early
McCormick, James	Pulaski	Johnsons	304/3	Appling
McCormick, John	Jasper	Reids	484/9	Irwin
McCormick, John	Jasper	Reids	93/1	Appling
McCormick, Prucilla(Wid)	Montgomery	Alston	366/6	Gwinnett
McCoullouch, Henry	Richmond	Winters	101/4	Walton
McCoullough, Jacob(RS)	Richmond	Winters	238/2	Early
McCowens, John (Orps)	Warren	Parhams	52/5	Rabun
McCown, Greenberry	Morgan	Jordans	156/6	Gwinnett
McCoy, Benj.R.	Morgan	Hackneys	391/9	Early
McCoy, Daniel	Putnam	Carols	380/2	Appling
McCoy, Esther	Jasper	Eastes	202/2	Appling
McCoy, Ewel	Morgan	Farrars	170/12	Irwin
McCoy, Isaac	Columbia	Watsons	13/5	Habersha
McCoy, John	Morgan	Talberts	71/12	Hall
McCoy, Sarah(Wid)	Morgan	Parkers	42/19	Early
McCracken, David	Franklin	Flanagans	158/21	Early
McCracken, James	Franklin	Flannigans	59/16	Irwin
McCrae, Daniel	Montgomery	Alstons	184/3	Habersha
McCraney, Danl.Jr.	Montgomery	McMillans	64/3	Rabun
McCranie, John	Liberty		23/11	Early
McCrarey, Polley	Wilkinson	Brooks	345/15	Early
McCrary, Bartley Jr.	Baldwin	Irwins	530/2	Appling
McCrary, Bartley Jr.	Baldwin	Irwins	9/1	Habersha
McCrary, Elijah(Minor)	Habersham	Powells	81/23	Early
McCrary, Evans	Warren	154th	123/5	Early
McCrary, Hannah	Baldwin	Irwins	328/11	Early
McCrary, John	Baldwin	Stephens	50/2	Early
McCrary, John	Warren	154	64/10	Habersha
McCrary, Lettice(Wid)	Warren	Parhams	85/4	Irwin
McCrary, Mathew	Baldwin	Irwins	1/2	Early
McCrary, Robert	Baldwin	Ellis	66/4	Walton
McCrary, Robert	Franklin	Powels	35/13	Early
McCrary, Samuel	Warren	154	278/2	Appling
McCrary, Willie	Baldwin	Irwins	80/7	Rabun
McCrary, Wm.	Franklin	Powells	24/10	Habersha
McCray, Eppa	Hancock	Justices	229/9	Irwin
McCrea, Christopher	Pulaski	Davis	299/9	Early
McCrean, John	Wilkinson	Lees	223/11	Irwin
McCrean, Thomas	Wilkinson	Lees	335/26	Early
McCreaver, John Sr.	Jackson	Hamiltons Bt.	73/6	Early
McCree, Rowan	Clarke	Mitchells	71/10	Irwin
McCree, Thomas	Clarke	Mitchells	80/16	Irwin
McCright, James	Jackson	Hamiltons	424/7	Appling
McCright, Mathew	Jackson	Hamiltons Bt.	131/4	Early
McCright, Matthew	Jackson	Hamiltons Bt.	355/10	Early
McCrimon, Archibald	Montgomery	Alstons	148/6	Gwinnett
McCroan, John	Wilkinson	Lees	183/27	Early
McCullan, Benjamin	Wilkinson	Wiggins	154/1	Walton
McCullar, John	Wilkinson	Wiggins	63/10	Hall
McCullers, Britton	Laurens	Harriss	29/3	Walton
McCullers, Chas.	Morgan	Walkers	356/28	Early
McCullers, Mathew	Morgan	Walkers	221/4	Walton

NAME	COUNTY	MIL.DIST	LOT/SECT	DREW LAND
McCullers, Wm.Sr.(RS)	Morgan	Walkers	323/3	Early
McCullough, Jacob(RS)	Richmond	Winters	47/2	Rabun
McCullough, Jacob	Jefferson	Abbots	269/15	Early
McCullough, James	Twiggs	Smiths	112/6	Irwin
McCullough, William	Clarke	Sims	310/7	Early
McCulogh, John	Screven	Roberts	298/4	Walton
McCune, Mary(Wid)	Jackson	Winters Bt.	161/10	Habersham
McCuny, John	Elbert	B.Higginbotham	203/3	Early
McCurdy, James	Madison	Orrs	52/10	Early
McCurdy, Samuel G.	Madison	Orrs	394/15	Early
McCurry, John	Elbert	B. Higginbotham	244/18	Early
McCutchen, Benj.	Hall		110/2	Walton
McCutchen, Joseph R.	Hall		365/6	Irwin
McCutcheon, John	Jackson	Winters Bt.	174/3	Appling
McCutcheon, Mark	Hall		161/21	Early
McCutcheon, William	Hall		191/13	Irwin
McDade, John	Washington	Peabodys	306/7	Irwin
McDade, John	Washington	Peabodys	88/12	Early
McDanels, John(Orps)	Washington	Peabodys	135/20	Early
McDaniel, Albritton	Warren	Parham	55/1	Habersham
McDaniel, Allen	Washington	Peabodys	298/4	Irwin
McDaniel, Annis	Burke	Spiveys	216/18	Early
McDaniel, Bartley	Jones	Wallers	23/3	Walton
McDaniel, Benj.(Orps)	Jones	Chappels	265/6	Irwin
McDaniel, Daniel Sr.	Oglethorpe	Barnetts	512/5	Appling
McDaniel, David	Laurens	Jones	273/10	Early
McDaniel, Elijah	Laurens	Griffins	200/27	Early
McDaniel, Henry(Orps)	Franklin	R.Browns	507/10	Irwin
McDaniel, Isam	Telfair	Wilsons	167/11	Early
McDaniel, Isham	Telfair	Wilsons	175/1	Irwin
McDaniel, Jacob	Jones	Permenters	33/3	Early
McDaniel, James	Jackson	Rogers Bt.	272/11	Early
McDaniel, John	Laurens	Harris	257/3	Early
McDaniel, John	Laurens	Harriss	55/15	Irwin
McDaniel, John	Oglethorpe	Barnetts	11/10	Early
McDaniel, Margaret	Jones	Permenters	60/8	Early
McDaniel, William	Jones	Chappels	189/4	Early
McDaniel, Zadock	Washington	Peabodys	125/6	Irwin
McDirmit, Anguis(Orpn)	Montgomery	Alstons	49/5	Appling
McDonal, Archibald	Franklin	Yanceys	136/12	Early
McDonal, Randal	Burke	Bells	124/7	Gwinnett
McDonal, Randol	Telfair	Wilsons	342/12	Irwin
McDonald, Absalom	Warren	150	355/6	Appling
McDonald, Alexander	McIntosh	McIntosh	149/2	Appling
McDonald, Alexr.	Elbert	Olivers	12/3	Walton
McDonald, Allen	Tattnall	Tharps	332/9	Irwin
McDonald, Allen	Tattnall	Tharps	389/9	Irwin
McDonald, Andrew	Warren	152	392/15	Early
McDonald, Ann(Orph)	McIntosh	Jinkins	406/6	Appling
McDonald, Archibald	Baldwin	Cousins	473/7	Appling
McDonald, Bradley(Orps)	Jackson	Dicksons Bt.	59/27	Early
McDonald, Charles	Oglethorpe	Barnetts	112/12	Irwin
McDonald, Daniel	Washington	Brooks	15/9	Hall
McDonald, Elijah	Jackson	Rogers Bt.	16/3	Irwin
McDonald, Eliz.(Orph)	Chatham		154/17	Gwinnett
McDonald, Ennis	Jefferson	Fountains	302/7	Early
McDonald, Erasmus	Wilkinson	Wiggins	418/8	Appling
McDonald, George(Orps)	Twiggs	Jeffersons	57/10	Early
McDonald, George	Hancock	Scotts	435/28	Early
McDonald, George	McIntosh	Jenkins	125/10	Hall
McDonald, George	McIntosh	Jinkins	406/6	Appling
McDonald, Hiram	Jasper	Reids	194/3	Irwin
McDonald, Hugh	Elbert	Dobbs	154/5	Early
McDonald, Hugh	Franklin	J.Miller	111/13	Early
McDonald, James L.	Warren	152	198/17	Early
McDonald, James	Columbia	Shaws	117/16	Early
McDonald, James	Jasper	Reids	469/10	Irwin

NAME	COUNTY	MIL.DIST	LOT/SECT	DREW LAND
McDonald, Margarett	McIntosh	Jinkins	581/2	Appling
McDonald, Mary(Orph)	Chatham		154/7	Gwinnett
McDonald, Mary	Chatham		294/11	Early
McDonald, Milly	Hancock	Smiths	277/17	Early
McDonald, Moses	Twiggs	Jefferson	109/3	Habersham
McDonald, O.(Orps)	Hancock	Smiths	68/1	Irwin
McDonald, Rich.(Orps)	Hancock	Scotts	193/2	Rabun
McDonald, Robert	Glynn		266/8	Appling
McDonald, Roderick(Orps)	Putnam	Coopers	210/5	Gwinnett
McDonald, Samuel	Baldwin	Marshalls	236/10	Early
McDonald, Tilmon	Jackson	Rogers Bt.	470/2	Appling
McDonald, William	Early		242/13	Early
McDonnal, Auguish	Wayne	Johnstons	350/28	Early
McDonnel, Isaac	Jackson	Rogers Bt.	425/7	Appling
McDormon, Jane(Orph)	Effingham		366/10	Irwin
McDougal, Samuel	Jasper	Baileys	104/18	Early
McDougald, Jonathan	Jasper	Baileys	368/5	Early
McDow, John	Franklin	J.Miller	239/4	Walton
McDowell, Daniel	Jasper	Baileys	160/6	Early
McDowell, Daniel	Jasper	Baileys	402/8	Irwin
McDowell, Isaa	Warren	150th	79/11	Irwin
McDowell, Robert	Warren	150	407/3	Appling
McDowell, Robert	Warren	150th	232/7	Irwin
McDowell, Samuel	Warren	Loyless	231/11	Irwin
McDowell, Thomas	Jones	Samuels	467/12	Irwin
McDowell, Thomas	Warren	150	528/11	Irwin
McDowell, Thos.Sr.	Washington	Renfros	82/11	Habersham
McDowell, William	Jackson	Hamiltons Bt.	154/11	Early
McDowell, Wm.Sr.	Jasper	Bartletts	80/7	Irwin
McDowels, James(Orps)	Jackson	Rogers Bt.	8/4	Walton
McDuffe, Malcom	Washington	Daniels	361/7	Gwinnett
McDuffe, Murdock	Telfair	Williams	23/8	Appling
McDuffee, Duncan	Jones	Griffiths	268/1	Walton
McDuffee, Jane(Wid)	Montgomery	Alstons	4/16	Early
McDuggle, Eliz.(Wid)	Elbert	Webbs	389/4	Appling
McDuggle, Matthew	Elbert	Webbs	18/9	Hall
McDuggles, John(Orps)	Elbert	Webbs	260/26	Early
McElroy, John J.	Jasper	Clays	393/7	Irwin
McElroy, Josiah	Jasper	Eastes	119/12	Irwin
McElroy, Mary	Jasper	Centills	340/20	Early
McElvin, William	Bryan	19th	27/6	Gwinnett
McEver, Andrew	Hall	McCutcheons	107/2	Early
McEwen, Alex.(Orpn)	Washington	Brooks	202/7	Early
McEwen, Isaac A.	Madison	Millicans	383/18	Early
McEwin, Alexander	Oglethorpe	Waters	51/10	Early
McFadden, Henry(Orps)	Jones	Permenters	39/5	Rabun
McFaden, Mary(Wid)	Jones	Permenters	49/13	Early
McFail, James	Liberty		190/7	Appling
McFarland, Ann(Wid)	Richmond	122	493/7	Irwin
McFarland, John	Columbia	Dodsons	142/7	Appling
McFarland, Sherod	Warren	Rogers	104/4	Walton
McFarlin, Harvey	Jones	Hansford	254/27	Early
McFarlin, Sarah(Wid)	Camden	Millers	17/6	Habersham
McFarlin, Thomas	Jasper	Clays	354/5	Irwin
McGalister, Ellender(Wid)	Jasper	Clays	126/1	Walton
McGarrity, Abner	Elbert	Dobbs	34/10	Hall
McGaughey, James	Putnam	Bustins	19/12	Habersham
McGauttrey, Jane(Wid)	Jasper	Sentells	161/9	Early
McGee, David	Jones	Kings	44/6	Early
McGee, Davis	Jones	Kings	248/1	Early
McGee, Geo.W.	Putnam	Jernigans	508/12	Irwin
McGee, Henry	Scriven	36	155/6	Gwinnett
McGee, Henry	Scriven	36th	159/2	Rabun
McGee, James(Orph)	Clarke	Penticost	392/4	Early
McGee, James(orps)	Clarke	Pentecosts	102/21	Early
McGee, John	Burke	Thomas	221/12	Irwin
McGee, John	Columbia	Watsons	312/27	Early

NAME	COUNTY	MIL.DIST	LOT/SECT	DREW LAND
McGee, John	Columbia	Watsons	376/2	Appling
McGee, Josiah(Orps)	Columbia	Watsons	392/12	Early
McGee, Leven	Putnam	Jernigans	96/3	Irwin
McGee, Levin	Twiggs	Browns	135/6	Irwin
McGee, Phillip	Twiggs	Thames	210/1	Early
McGee, Robert	Jones	Griffiths	131/7	Irwin
McGee, Robert	Jones	Griffiths	42/2	Appling
McGeehee, Isaac	Jones	Seals	163/4	Appling
McGeehee, Solomon	Washington	Robersons	260/28	Early
McGehee, Abner	Oglethorpe	Goolsbys	50/3	Irwin
McGehee, Abraham	Oglethorpe	Wises	61/9	Appling
McGehee, James R.	Baldwin	Ellis	432/15	Early
McGehee, Samuel	Baldwin	Marshalls	26/4	Early
McGehee, Solomon	Washington	Robisons	38/1	Habersham
McGennis, James	Laurens	Watsons	112/2	Appling
McGill, John	Jefferson	Fountains	24/7	Gwinnett
McGill, Milly(Wid)	Lincoln	Parks	640/2	Appling
McGill, Morriss	Lincoln	Parks	275/9	Irwin
McGill, Sampson	Pulaski	Dewitts	275/6	Gwinnett
McGinnis, Alexr.	Jackson	Winters Btn.	484/7	Irwin
McGintal, Alexander	Wilkes	Mattox	9/13	Early
McGinty, Abednego	Baldwin	Russells	21/6	Irwin
McGinty, Isaac	Hancock	Herberts	171/5	Early
McGinty, Isaac	Hancock	Herberts	33/26	Early
McGinty, James	Greene	142nd	369/2	Appling
McGinty, John A.	Wilkes	Bates	279/10	Irwin
McGinty, John	Wilkes	Bryants	154/15	Early
McGinty, Robert	Hancock	Danells	399/28	Early
McGlamry, George	Warren	150	90/4	Walton
McGlamry, John (RS)	Warren	150th	327/11	Irwin
McGlamry, John(RS)	Warren	150	15/12	Irwin
McGlawn, Hardy	Putnam	Coopers	7/10	Habersham
McGlawn, Jeremiah	Putnam	Coopers	50/3	Rabun
McGough, John	Jones	Kings	252/7	Appling
McGough, Thomas	Jones	Kings	117/10	Early
McGough, William	Greene	140th	148/12	Irwin
McGouirk, David	Walton	Sentells	221/6	Early
McGowan, Alexander	Scriven	Smiths	151/6	Gwinnett
McGowan, Elijah	Elbert	Gaines	358/9	Early
McGowan, Hamilton	Elbert	Gaines	377/26	Early
McGowan, Jacob	Screven	Smiths	40/7	Appling
McGowan, John	Elbert	Gaines	204/5	Irwin
McGowan, John	Jefferson	Flemmings	9/9	Habersham
McGroans, James(Orps)	Burke	Sullivan	318/1	Appling
McGruder, John Jr.	Burke	Spiveys	361/12	Early
McGuire, Absalom	Morgan	Farrers	94/1	Walton
McGuire, Anderson	Elbert	Gains	175/2	Early
McGuire, David	Greene	Armers	209/10	Irwin
McGuire, Eliz.	Jackson	Hamiltons	304/8	Appling
McGuire, Frances S.	Elbert	Gains	290/9	Early
McGuire, John s.	Elbert	Wards	75/3	Irwin
McGuire, Timma	Jackson	Hamiltons Bt.	239/12	Irwin
McGuire, Timmah	Hall	McCutcheons	31/14	Irwin
McGuire, William	Elbert	Dooleys	34/5	Habersham
McGuires, John	Jackson	Hamiltons Bt.	350/5	Early
McHafey, James	Gwinnett	Hamiltons	205/12	Irwin
McHamilton, Robert	Jackson	Hamiltons Bt.	194/6	Irwin
McHargue, John	Greene	141st	297/12	Irwin
McHenry, Henry	Madison	Culbreath	354/5	Appling
McHenry, James	Chatham		89/3	Irwin
McInnis, Daniel	Irwin	Lower	21/10	Early
McInnis, James	Irwin	Lower	504/11	Irwin
McIntire, James	Franklin	Morriss	18/26	Early
McIntire, Joseph	Franklin	Morris	167/2	Walton
McIntosh, Daniel	Jasper	Smiths	279/5	Gwinnett
McIntosh, Esther(Wid)	McIntosh	McIntosh	275/4	Early
McIntosh, Geo.(Orp)	McIntosh	McIntoshs	286/3	Early

NAME	COUNTY	MIL.DIST	LOT/SECT	DREW LAN
McIntosh, James	Wilkes	Hollidays	43/5	Habersha
McIntosh, Jesse	Morgan	Campbells	275/17	Early
McIntosh, John	McIntosh	McIntoshs	382/5	Irwin
McIntosh, Lachlan H.	Chatham		25/1	Irwin
McIntosh, Lachlan H.	Chatham		75/3	Habersha
McIntosh, Morgan(Orp)	McIntosh	McIntoshs	286/3	Early
McIntosh, Robert	Liberty		303/7	Early
McIntosh, Roderick	Montgomery	Alstons	5/8	Appling
McIntosh, Wm.J.	McIntosh	Hamiltons	308/9	Irwin
McIntosh, Wm.R.W.	McIntosh	McIntoshs	259/26	Early
McInvale, Robert	Jones	Samuels	326/19	Early
McIver, Alexander	McIntosh	Hamiltons	363/16	Early
McIver, Alexander	McIntosh	Hamiltons	78/10	Early
McJohnston, Daniel	Elbert	Higginbotham	200/7	Gwinnett
McKai, Mary(Wid)	Telfair	Tallis	71/4	Irwin
McKamie, John	Twiggs	Smiths	418/12	Irwin
McKary, David S.	Jackson	Rodgers Bt.	16/4	Rabun
McKay, Eliza(Wid)	Chatham		120/8	Early
McKay, George W.	Chatham		89/9	Hall
McKay, James	McIntosh	McIntoshs	267/6	Irwin
McKay, John	McIntosh	McIntoshs	267/6	Irwin
McKay, Thomas	Hall	Byrds	137/9	Irwin
McKay, Wm.R.	McIntosh	McIntosh	267/6	Irwin
McKean, Eliz.(Wid)	Richmond	Burton	105/1	Early
McKean, James	Richmond	Burtons	191/13	Early
McKean, William	Richmond	Burtons	66/4	Appling
McKeans, John(Orps)	Baldwin	Marshalls	263/4	Irwin
McKee, Alexander	Wilkinson	Brooks	148/6	Early
McKee, Elizabeth	Madison	Adares	27/28	Early
McKee, Hezekiah	Franklin	Vaughns	2/1	Appling
McKee, Hezekiah	Franklin	Vaughns	37/3	Rabun
McKee, Jacob	Jasper	Blakes	182/6	Irwin
McKee, Jacob	Jasper	Blakes	437/13	Irwin
McKee, Saml.(Orps)	Madison	Adairs	133/2	Early
McKee, Thomas S.	Wilkes	Gordons	347/20	Early
McKeen, Robert	Greene	143	280/13	Early
McKelroy, Joseph P.	Jackson	Winters Bt.	99/28	Early
McKendley, William	Washington	Avents	62/8	Appling
McKennie, Samuel	Jackson	Winters Bt.	219/9	Irwin
McKennon, Charles	Telfair	Williams	22/7	Irwin
McKensey, George	Jefferson	Langstons	107/8	Early
McKenzie, John H.	Jones	Permenters	20/5	Rabun
McKenzie, John	Richmond	398th	335/14	Early
McKenzie, Samuel	Lincoln	Parks	192/5	Appling
McKey, Daniel	Putnam	Oslins	338/7	Early
McKey, Isaac	Franklin	P.Browns	78/8	Early
McKie, Daniel	Washington	Avents	15/12	Habersha
McKigney, George	Burke	72nd	305/2	Early
McKigney, James	Jefferson	Lamps	374/18	Early
McKingley, Wash.(Orps)	Jasper	Kennedys	67/1	Habersha
McKinney, Caleb(Orps)	Twiggs	W.Belchers	89/7	Gwinnett
McKinney, Chas.Sr.	Jackson	Dicksons Bt.	150/8	Early
McKinney, Chas.Sr.	Jackson	Dicksons	430/5	Appling
McKinney, John Jr.	Lincoln	Walkers	404/12	Irwin
McKinney, John	Scriven	Smiths	299/6	Gwinnett
McKinney, Matthew	Greene	Fosters	367/27	Early
McKinney, Robert	Scriven	Lovett	32/4	Habersha
McKinney, Robert	Scriven	Lovetts	523/11	Irwin
McKinney, Roger	Scriven	Lovetts	279/28	Early
McKinney, Wm.(Orps)	Baldwin	Ellis	438/6	Appling
McKinnie, George	Baldwin	Stephens	271/9	Appling
McKinnie, John Jr.	Lincoln	Walkers	59/22	Early
McKinnie, John	Richmond	398th	311/16	Early
McKinnie, Mary(Wid)	Warren	153	244/3	Early
McKinnie, Saml.	Jackson	Winters Bt.	57/9	Irwin
McKinnie, Travis	Lincoln	Walkers	93/7	Early
McKinnon, Chas.J.	Chatham		63/6	Irwin

NAME	COUNTY	MIL.DIST	LOT/SECT	DREW LAND
McKinnon, John R.	Chatham		457/6	Appling
McKinnon, John	Hancock	Millers	27/1	Early
McKinny, George	Wilkes	Bates	213/7	Irwin
McKinny, John Sr.	Lincoln	Walkers	63/11	Irwin
McKinsack, Wm.	Putnam	Ectors	166/13	Early
McKinsey, Wm.(RS)	Morgan	Campbells	393/6	Appling
McKinzee, Samuel	Greene	143rd	41/7	Gwinnett
McKinzie, Alex.	Richmond	120	292/8	Early
McKinzie, Alexander	Richmond	120th	56/2	Habersham
McKinzie, Dise(Wid)	Jackson	Hamiltons Bt.	83/2	Irwin
McKinzie, James	Morgan	Campbells	13/7	Irwin
McKinzie, John(Orps)	Jackson	Hamiltons Bt.	15/4	Early
McKinzie, Samuel	Lincoln	Parks	85/4	Early
McKinzie, Sanders	Jackson	Hamiltons Bt.	151/11	Early
McKinzie, William	Morgan	Campbells	159/12	Habersham
McKinzie, Wm.	Morgan	Campbells	117/1	Early
McKisack, Archa	Putnam	Slaughters	438/2	Appling
McKisack, John	Putnam	Slaughters	172/7	Early
McKissach, Archbald	Putnam	Slaughters	93/12	Early
McKissick, Thomas	Jones	Griffiths	366/6	Early
McKleroy, Billey	Oglethorpe	Bridges	39/17	Early
McKleroy, Henry(Orps)	Oglethorpe	Lees	77/6	Early
McKleroy, Needham	Clarke	Pentecosts	2/5	Irwin
McKluoy, Henry(Orps)	Oglethorpe	Rogers Bt.	148/13	Irwin
McKnight, Charles	Wilkes	Davis	148/16	Irwin
McKnight, Charles	Wilkes	Davis	371/2	Appling
McKnight, James	Jackson	Winters Bt.	20/1	Appling
McKnight, John	Greene	140th	68/17	Early
McKnight, William	Walton	Echols	39/9	Early
McKnights, Robt.(Orps)	Greene	Tuggles	94/6	Gwinnett
McKonkey, James	Chatham		323/5	Early
McKonkey, M.B.	Chatham		41/4	Early
McKonky, David M.	Jefferson	Abbots	166/7	Early
McKonky, David M.	Jefferson	Abbotts	243/4	Irwin
McKoy, John B.	Putnam	Berrys	295/4	Appling
McLain, Elisha	Greene	Tuggles	310/1	Appling
McLain, James	Jones	Buckhalters	134/3	Irwin
McLain, James	Oglethorpe	Bowls	107/7	Early
McLane, Hugh	Emanuel	395	35/18	Early
McLane, John	Montgomery	Alston	194/16	Irwin
McLanen, Ann(Orph)	Chatham		324/7	Gwinnett
McLanen, Margaret(Orph)	Chatham		324/7	Gwinnett
McLaster, Joseph	Jackson	Winters Bt.	186/10	Early
McLaughlin, John	Warren	Griers	267/2	Appling
McLaughlin, Wm.	Wilkes	Davis	53/9	Early
McLean, Allen	Chatham		164/2	Early
McLean, Allen	Chatham		280/10	Irwin
McLean, Angus	Twiggs	Evans	377/9	Irwin
McLean, Duncan	Washington	Pools	223/15	Early
McLean, John	Columbia	Watsons	344/17	Early
McLellon, Robert	Morgan	Campbells	163/5	Gwinnett
McLemond, John(Orps)	Jasper	Bartletts	176/4	Appling
McLendon, Alsea(Orph)	Jasper	Clays	208/1	Walton
McLendon, Beneniah	Morgan	Selmons	72/6	Appling
McLendon, Burwell	Jones	Phillips	69/3	Habersham
McLendon, Burwell	Laurens	Kinchens	129/4	Appling
McLendon, Francis	Jasper	Reids	206/10	Irwin
McLendon, Francis	Jasper	Reids	240/9	Irwin
McLendon, Hugh	Jones	Phillips	51/19	Early
McLendon, Isaac	Wilkes	Burkes	144/3	Appling
McLendon, Jacob	Wilkinson	Kettles	389/21	Early
McLendon, Jacob	Wilkinson	Kettles	423/7	Appling
McLendon, Joel	Wilkinson	Lees	4/3	Irwin
McLendon, John	Laurens	Kinchens	155/1	Walton
McLendon, Lewis(Orps)	Putnam	Berrys	228/12	Irwin
McLendon, Midad	Wilkes	McLendons	126/12	Irwin
McLendon, Saml.Sr.	Morgan	McLendons	125/10	Early

NAME	COUNTY	MIL.DIST	LOT/SECT	DREW LAN.
McLendon, Simeon	Wilkes	McLendons	525/11	Irwin
McLendon, Simpson	Wilkes	Burks	163/5	Irwin
McLendon, Stephen	Jasper	Blakes	149/12	Habersha
McLendon, Travis	Wilkes	Burks	332/2	Appling
McLendon, William	Wilkes	Burks	50/14	Early
McLeod, Alexander	Telfair	Williams	54/6	Gwinnett
McLeod, Auguis	Montgomery	Alstons	238/5	Appling
McLeod, Catharine(Wid)	Montgomery	Alstons	362/7	Appling
McLeod, James	Montgomery	Alstons	292/6	Gwinnett
McLeod, James	Montgomery	Alstons	361/3	Appling
McLeod, Murdock	Montgomery	Alstons	439/7	Appling
McLeod, Norman Jr.	Telfair	Williams	194/5	Irwin
McLeod, Norman Sr.	Telfair	Williams	43/11	Irwin
McLeod, Norman	Telfair	Williams	55/2	Irwin
McLeod, Wm.	Telfair	Williams	466/6	Irwin
McLeroy, James	Oglethorpe	Lees	39/16	Early
McLeroy, Nathan	Jones	Phillips	297/12	Irwin
McLester, John	Jackson	Winters	366/4	Appling
McLinn, Charles	Columbia	Dodsons	16/14	Early
McLode, Daniel	Lincoln	Thompsons	122/2	Rabun
McLode, Daniel	Lincoln	Thompsons	225/3	Walton
McLord, William	Jasper	Easts	14/14	Irwin
McLoroy, Jesse	Jones	Phillips	92/2	Rabun
McLoy, Andrew	Wilkes	Kilgores	142/16	Early
McLure, George	Jackson	Dicksons Bt.	126/9	Early
McLure, Samuel B.	Jackson	Dicksons Bt.	447/11	Irwin
McLuska, John	Jones	Griffiths	37/14	Irwin
McMahan, Barnett	Walton	Echols	48/22	Early
McMahon, Mosses	Burke	71st	227/3	Irwin
McMahus, Robert	Richmond	Palmers	8/8	Hall
McManns, John(RS)	Richmond	Laceys	217/5	Appling
McManus, John(RS)	Richmond	Laceys	163/8	Early
McMath, William	Jones	Chappels	281/4	Irwin
McMath, Zedekiah	Warren	155	206/2	Irwin
McMichael, Elijah	Jasper	Clays	88/9	Irwin
McMichael, Green S.	Jasper	Centills	440/7	Appling
McMichael, John Jr.	Jasper	Clays	309/26	Early
McMichael, John Jr.	Jasper	Easts	385/1	Early
McMichael, Lemuel	Jones	Jeffersons	9/4	Appling
McMichael, Samuel	Jones	Jeffersons	129/2	Early
McMichael, Shadrack	Jasper	Clays	213/12	Habersha
McMichael, Zachariah	Jasper	Reeds	163/20	Early
McMillan, Alexander	Burke	Royals	287/11	Irwin
McMillan, Archbd.Jr.	Montgomery	Alstons	209/9	Irwin
McMillan, Archibald Jr.	Montgomery	Alstons	358/18	Early
McMillan, Archibald	Montgomery	Alstons	336/14	Early
McMillan, Daniel	Camden	Tillis	410/15	Early
McMillen, James	Jackson	Hamiltons Bt.	161/12	Habersha
McMillin, Anguis	Montgomery	McMillins	24/14	Irwin
McMillion, James Sr.	Jackson	Hamiltons	62/4	Walton
McMillion, Samuel(Orps)	Jackson	Hamiltons Bt.	33/10	Hall
McMullen, James	Baldwin	Cousins	330/12	Early
McMullen, Jeremiah	Elbert	Dooleys	487/8	Irwin
McMullen, Lewis	Elbert	Dooleys	291/13	Early
McMullen, Neil	Elbert	Dooleys	152/2	Habersha
McMullen, Patrick	Elbert	Dooleys	66/15	Early
McMullen, Sarah(Wid)	Telfair	Wilsons	185/9	Early
McMullen, Thomas	Elbert	Doolys	497/2	Appling
McMullen, William	Twiggs	Brown	371/7	Irwin
McMullen, Wm.Sr.	Elbert	Dooleys	177/10	Irwin
McMullen, Wm.Sr.	Elbert	Dooleys	324/3	Appling
McMullin, James	Twiggs	Jamersons	339/2	Early
McMullin, Wm.	Telfair	Wilsons	86/10	Habersha
McMullough, Jacob	Jefferson	Abbots	54/2	Early
McMurphey, Daniel Jr.	Richmond	Laceys	304/6	Gwinnett
McMurphy, Daniel Jr.	Richmond	Laceys	237/4	Walton
McMurphy, Daniel(RS)	Richmond	Laceys	21/7	Gwinnett

NAME	COUNTY	MIL.DIST	LOT/SECT	DREW LAND
McMurphy, Mrs.(Child.)	Clarke	Newtons	362/10	Early
McMurrain, John	Montgomery	Alston	47/10	Early
McMurram, John	Montgomery	Alstons	243/28	Early
McMurran, David Jr.	Jasper	Phillips	32/6	Early
McMurray, James	Greene	141st	62/7	Gwinnett
McMurrin, Frederick	Camden	Clarks	52/27	Early
McMurry, James	Baldwin	Haws	157/10	Hall
McNabb, Daniel	Tattnall	Johnson	122/12	Irwin
McNabb, James	Morgan	Selmons	33/16	Early
McNabb, John	Hancock	Edwards	317/10	Early
McNair, Daniel	Columbia	O.Morriss	115/10	Early
McNair, Daniel	Pulaski	Johnstons	485/10	Irwin
McNair, Duncan	Laurens	Carsons	342/13	Early
McNair, James	Richmond	Palmers	73/3	Irwin
McNair, John	Wilkinson	Childs	90/11	Habersham
McNair, Samuel	Columbia	O.Morriss	74/8	Early
McNair, Turquil	Pulaski	Johnstons	429/8	Irwin
McNat, William	Burke	72nd	427/6	Appling
McNatt, Benjamin	Burke	72nd	146/10	Habersham
McNeal, Daniel	Columbia	O.Morriss	464/5	Appling
McNeal, John C.	Franklin	Burroughs	160/1	Appling
McNeal, John	Columbia	Willinghams	390/3	Early
McNease, William	Warren	153	176/2	Early
McNease, William	Warren	153	390/16	Early
McNeely, John	Jefferson	Fountains	179/7	Irwin
McNees, James	Jackson	Rogers Bt.	80/10	Early
McNees, Ralph	Jackson	Rogers Bt.	1/8	Irwin
McNees, Wm.	Jackson	Rogers Bt.	126/20	Early
McNeil, Neil	Putnam	Oslins	271/6	Appling
McNeil, Riley	Chatham		286/19	Early
McNeill, John	Wilkinson	Smiths	80/3	Walton
McNerril, Feildin	Burke	McNorrills	172/9	Appling
McNiel, Duncan	Columbia	Shaws	55/3	Habersham
McNiel, William	Franklin	Burroughs	236/8	Appling
McNish, William	Camden	Longs	107/2	Habersham
McNorrell, Fielden	Burke	McWarrels	246/19	Early
McPearson, Jas.(Wid)	Franklin	Turks	57/23	Early
McPherson, Duncan	Twiggs	Bozemans	314/10	Irwin
McQuean, Mary(Wid)	Montgomery	Alstons	246/2	Appling
McRae, Phillip	Telfair	Loves	39/2	Appling
McRai, Duncan	Telfair	Tallies	92/5	Rabun
McRea, John Jr.	Telfair	Tallies	232/28	Early
McRees, Saml.	Morgan	Loyds	171/4	Appling
McSparren, Eliz.(Wid)	Clarke	Mitchells	68/15	Irwin
McSwain, Alfred	Morgan	Knights	50/8	Early
McSwain, Elizabeth	Morgan	Campbells	42/5	Early
McSwain, Elizabeth	Morgan	Nights	323/19	Early
McSwain, Elizabeth	Morgan	Nights	323/19	Early
McSwain, Henry	Columbia	O.Morriss	236/6	Gwinnett
McSwain, John Sr.	Columbia	O.Morriss	311/9	Irwin
McTault, John	Liberty		286/1	Early
McTyre, Holland	Richmond	Lacys	352/15	Early
McTyre, John	Richmond		355/11	Irwin
McTyre, Martha(Orph)	Richmond	122	223/5	Irwin
McTyre, William	Putnam	Ectors	344/9	Early
McVay, David	Washington	Wimberlys	311/7	Gwinnett
McVay, John Sr.	Jackson	Rogers Bt.	34/2	Habersham
McVay, William	Twiggs	Jeffersons	477/5	Appling
McWhorter, Hugh	Oglethorpe	Dunnes	276/14	Early
McWhorter, Hugh	Oglethorpe	Dunns	305/8	Early
McWhorter, Jacob G.	Richmond	398	189/9	Irwin
McWhorter, William	Jackson	Hamiltons	425/4	Appling
McWhorters, Wm.	Jackson	Hamiltons Bt.	425/4	Appling
McWilliams, Hodges Sr.	Twiggs	Evans	183/1	Walton
McWilliams, James Sr.	Twiggs	Evans	252/5	Early
McWilliams, Thos.Jr.	Twiggs	Evans	139/18	Early
McWilliams, Thos.M.	Washington	Barges	234/7	Early

NAME	COUNTY	MIL.DIST	LOT/SECT	DREW LAN
Mead, John	Madison	Willifords	90/3	Early
Mead, Joseph H.	Clarke	Deans	35/10	Habersha
Meadow, Wm.	Morgan	Jordans	259/1	Walton
Meadows, Daniel	Greene	Nelms	94/2	Habersha
Meadows, Danniel	Greene	Nelms	346/7	Early
Meadows, Edward	Greene	Nelms	86/11	Habersha
Meadows, Jason	Jones	Permenters	59/9	Appling
Meadows, Micajah	Wilkinson	Lees	199/7	Irwin
Meadows, Micajah	Wilkinson	Lees	263/16	Early
Meadows, William	Clarke	Mereweather	140/8	Irwin
Mealer, George	Oglethorpe	Wises	198/1	Walton
Mealer, Sarah & Orps.	Franklin	Vaughns	16/5	Rabun
Meals, Henry(Orph)	Richmond		174/9	Irwin
Meals, Selestia(Orph)	Richmond		174/9	Irwin
Means, William	Elbert	Gaines	375/10	Early
Means, William	Elbert	Gains	89/6	Irwin
Meariott, Wm.	Greene	140th	147/11	Irwin
Mears, Charity(Wid)	Jefferson	Abbots	58/5	Appling
Meazell, Eliz.(Wid)	Camden	Baileys	202/9	Early
Meazell, Jehu	Camden	Baileys	13/6	Gwinnett
Medcalf, John	Jackson	Winters Bt.	28/12	Early
Medders, Riley	Warren	151	153/15	Irwin
Meddows, Absalom	Oglethorpe	Berdges	169/2	Habersha
Meddows, Absaom	Oglethorpe	Bridges	144/12	Irwin
Meddows, Anna(Wid)	Twiggs	Evan's	29/3	Habersha
Meddows, Benj.	Jones	Griffiths	380/6	Gwinnett
Meddows, Isaac	Oglethorpe	Bridges	396/12	Early
Meddows, Isham	Jones	Griffiths	344/3	Appling
Meddows, Jacob Jr.	Oglethorpe	Bridges	86/12	Hall
Meddows, Jacob	Oglethorpe	Bridges	507/13	Irwin
Meddows, James(Orps)	Putnam	J.Kindricks	253/9	Early
Meddows, Reuben(Orps)	Twiggs	Evans	36/9	Appling
Medlock, Charles	Hancock	Mims	46/7	Irwin
Medlock, Stephen	Tattnall	Overstreet	126/6	Irwin
Medlock, Stephen	Tattnall	Overstreets	335/7	Irwin
Meeds, John	Scriven	Moodys	147/7	Gwinnett
Meeks, Britton	Baldwin	Cousins	60/5	Irwin
Meeks, Littleton	Franklin	Haynes	63/10	Early
Meeks, Seedleton	Franklin	Powels	183/2	Appling
Meeks, William	Franklin	Haynes	112/7	Early
Megahee, David	Columbia	O.Morris	332/20	Early
Megan, Pleasant	Oglethorpe	Brittons	88/8	Appling
Megar, Edward	Richmond	Burton	120/8	Appling
Megarity, John	Elbert	E.Whites	182/3	Irwin
Megee, James	Morgan	Talbots	353/18	Early
Mehaffey, Thomas	Jackson	Hamiltons Bt.	177/16	Early
Meigs, Eliza(Orph)	Richmond	Laceys	78/12	Early
Meigs, Return John	Richmond	398	389/13	Irwin
Meigs, Sarah(Orph)	Richmond	Laceys	78/12	Early
Melan, Barnabas	Emanuel	55th	436/4	Appling
Melanghlin, David	Oglethorpe	Murrys	18/7	Gwinnett
Melaughlin, George	Oglethorpe	Murrays	229/7	Irwin
Meleor, Samuel	Wilkes	Runnels	33/10	Habersha
Melnor, Mary(Wid)	Chatham		351/3	Early
Meloy, Andrew	Wilkes	Kilgores	154/9	Appling
Meloy, Andrew	Wilkes	Kilgores	3/14	Irwin
Melson, Cannon	Jones	Green	269/6	Irwin
Melson, Cannon	Jones	Greens	164/9	Hall
Melton, Henry	Bulloch	Knights	108/27	Early
Melton, John	Columbia	Dodsons	294/21	Early
Melton, John	Columbia	Dodsons	32/13	Irwin
Melton, Joseph	Columbia	Gartrells	124/13	Irwin
Melton, Joseph	Columbia	Gartrells	244/7	Gwinnett
Melton, Mary(Orph)	Camden	Tillis	206/5	Gwinnett
Melton, McKinney	Twiggs	Jeffersons	174/9	Appling
Melton, Robertson	Bulloch	Knights	72/17	Early
Melton, Solomon(Orp)	Camden	Tillis	206/5	Gwinnett

226

NAME	COUNTY	MIL.DIST	LOT/SECT	DREW LAND
Melton, Solomon	Tattnall	Cunyers	312/8	Early
Melton, William	Twiggs	Jeffersons	178/2	Rabun
Meltons, Robt.(Orps)	Franklin	J.Millers	324/7	Appling
Melvin, Martha(Wid)	Chatham		210/9	Irwin
Menabb, David	Tattnall	Johnsons	41/4	Appling
Menard, Peter	Richmond	122nd	290/3	Appling
Mendith, James W.	Richmond		415/1	Early
Mendock, James	Franklin	R.Browns	190/16	Irwin
Meommon, James	Greene	Harvills	53/16	Early
Meran, Bazel(Orph)	Putnam	Buckners	356/12	Irwin
Mercer, Christopher	Tattnall	J.Durrences	110/20	Early
Mercer, Francis	Baldwin	Cousins	86/10	Irwin
Mercer, Hermon	Greene	Jones	22/4	Appling
Mercer, Jacob(R.S.)	Jasper	Baileys	517/13	Irwin
Mercer, Jesse	Hancock	Lucas	45/4	Walton
Mercer, Jesse	Pulaski	Maddox	190/1	Appling
Mercer, Jessee	Pulaski	Maddoxs	38/27	Early
Mercer, John	Elbert	Smiths	66/12	Early
Mercer, John	Scriven	Mills	150/3	Irwin
Mercer, Levi	Jasper	Hays	135/15	Irwin
Mercer, Stephen	Twiggs	Smiths	480/7	Appling
Mercer, William B.	Jones	Chappels	7/12	Irwin
Mercer, William	Burke	J.Wards	390/2	Appling
Mercer, Williby	Burke	Hands	63/15	Irwin
Meredith, Chas.	Wilkinson	Tates	81/6	Irwin
Meredith, James W.	Richmond		158/8	Hall
Meredith, Pleasant	Wilkinson	Howards	218/7	Irwin
Meredith, William	Wilkinson	Howards	188/1	Early
Mereweather, James	Clarke	Harpers	332/11	Irwin
Merewether, George	Clarke	Mereweathers	413/3	Appling
Meridith, Thomas	Wilkinson	Howard	263/28	Early
Meriwether, James S.	Clarke	Meriwethers	410/7	Early
Merodeth, John	Wilkinson	Howard	316/17	Early
Meroney, William	Madison	Adares	93/9	Early
Merrett, Mary	Twiggs	W.Belchers	15/15	Irwin
Merrett, Sherwood	Morgan	Farrars	521/9	Irwin
Merrill, Joshua	Richmond	Laceys	306/4	Early
Merrit, Benj.	Jasper	Kennedys	201/7	Gwinnett
Merrit, Henry C.	Morgan	Jordans	118/8	Irwin
Merrit, Thomas	Greene	Wheelis	433/15	Early
Merrit, Thomas	Greene	Wheelis	97/12	Irwin
Merritt, Benjamin	Jasper	Kennedys	114/10	Hall
Merritt, John B.	Oglethorpe	Lees	72/7	Appling
Merritt, John	Greene	142	187/2	Irwin
Merritt, Lovett	Greene	142nd	57/5	Irwin
Merritt, Madrick	Jasper	Kennedys	218/12	Habersham
Merritt, Madrick	Jasper	Kennedys	24/28	Early
Merritt, Sherwood	Morgan	Farrars	273/8	Early
Merritt, William	Morgan	Jordans	49/23	Early
Merritt, Wm.	Putnam	Brooks	271/12	Early
Merriwether, Geo.W.	Richmond	398	212/12	Early
Merry, Eliz.(Wid)	Washington	Burneys	116/6	Irwin
Mershon, William	Hancock	Scotts	154/4	Walton
Messer, Charles	Jones	Wallers	155/9	Appling
Messer, Charles	Jones	Wallers	27/23	Early
Messer, James	Jasper	Bentleys	38/10	Hall
Messer, John	Richmond	Palmers	146/10	Early
Messer, John	Richmond	Palmers	146/18	Early
Messer, John	Scriven	Lovetts	216/10	Irwin
Messer, Samuel	Jasper	Bentleys	182/21	Early
Messer, William	Jasper	Bentleys	77/3	Early
Messick, George	Washington	Robisons	507/11	Irwin
Messick, Jeremiah	Washington	Robisons	348/10	Irwin
Metcalf, Isaac	Burke	Torrences	6/6	Irwin
Methven, Daniel	Wilkinson	Lees	291/4	Walton
Methvin, Benjamin	Baldwin	Haws	209/7	Early
Methvin, Joseph	Baldwin	Haws	136/5	Irwin

NAME	COUNTY	MIL.DIST	LOT/SECT	DREW LAN
Meton, Tempy(Wid)	Franklin	J.Miller	281/8	Appling
Mettz, Zephaniah(Orps)	Wilkinson	Brooks	47/5	Rabun
Metzgar, Solomon	Effingham		238/2	Appling
Metzger, John J.	Effingham		73/17	Early
Mews, George	Clarke	Parrs	52/2	Walton
Mews, George	Clarke	Parrs	82/4	Habersha
Mezles, Griffin	Telfair	Williams	93/7	Irwin
Michael, John	Oglethorpe	Waters	131/12	Early
Michael, Richard	Jasper	Bentleys	167/7	Gwinnett
Michael, Wm.	Oglethorpe	Goldings	104/11	Hall
Michaell, George	Greene	Ragins	108/10	Hall
Michaell, George	Greene	Ragins	439/6	Appling
Michams, Wm.(Orp)	Jones	Shropshiers	283/12	Early
Micker, Wm.Jr.	Twiggs	Smiths	51/8	Irwin
Mickleberry, James	Oglethorpe	Dunns	119/7	Appling
Micklejohn, Robert	Baldwin	Marshalls	418/3	Appling
Mickler, William	Twiggs	Smiths	147/12	Habersha
Mickler, William	Twiggs	Smiths	213/4	Walton
Micon, William	Richmond	122nd	303/7	Appling
Middlebrook, David	Putnam	Robertsons	146/2	Early
Middlebrooks, Alford	Hancock	Coopers	171/7	Irwin
Middlebrooks, David	Putnam	Robertsons	157/13	Habersha
Middlebrooks, Isaac	Clarke	Starnes	43/11	Hall
Middlebrooks, Micajah	Hancock	Champions	45/4	Rabun
Middlebrooks, Silas T.	Jones	Shropshiers	25/16	Early
Middlebrooks, Wm.S.	Jones	Seals	376/18	Early
Middleton, Emilia(Orp)	McIntosh	Goulds	287/26	Early
Middleton, G.A.	McIntosh	Eiglis	441/5	Appling
Middleton, John	Elbert	Childers	374/16	Early
Middleton, John	Elbert	Childres	262/20	Early
Middleton, Jones	Greene	Harvills	159/3	Early
Middleton, Robert	McIntosh	Eiglis	228/3	Irwin
Middleton, Saml.(R.S.)	Elbert	Whites	506/7	Irwin
Middleton, Saml.(RS)	Elbert	Whites	12/12	Hall
Middleton, Samuel	Emanuel	57th	212/4	Early
Middleton, Samuel	Emanuel	57th	389/11	Irwin
Middleton, Stephen	Emanuel	57th	281/8	Early
Middleton, William	Greene	Harvills	29/15	Irwin
Middleton, William	McIntosh	Goulds	57/1	Walton
Middleton, William	McIntosh	Goulds	57/1	Walton
Middleton, Willma.(Or)	McIntosh	Goulds	287/26	Early
Middleton, Woen	Wilkinson	Lees	18/3	Appling
Middleton, Woen	Wilkinson	Lees	50/27	Early
Midy, Juliett(Orph)	Richmond	Laceys	321/4	Appling
Miers, Absalom	Morgan	Parkerss	87/10	Hall
Mikell, George	Bulloch	Everitts	69/9	Appling
Milamb, Lewis	Jasper	Bentleys	381/10	Irwin
Miles, Abraham Sr.	Twiggs	R.Belchers	316/7	Early
Miles, Abram Jr.	Twiggs	R.Belchers	36/19	Early
Miles, Abram	Washington	Cummins	150/5	Gwinnett
Miles, Gillum	Jones	Permenters	132/2	Habersha
Miles, Joshua	Greene	141st	292/7	Gwinnett
Miles, Lewis	Morgan	Farrars	255/6	Irwin
Miles, Robert P.	Baldwin	Ellis	37/2	Habersha
Miles, Thomas	Baldwin	Ellis	172/5	Gwinnett
Miles, William	Clarke	Pentecost	89/7	Appling
Miles, Zachariah	Franklin	J.Miller	323/4	Walton
Milirons, William	Warren	Parhams	219/13	Early
Mill, Benj.Sr.	Liberty		283/3	Early
Mill, Eliz.S.(Orph)	Liberty		60/3	Early
Mill, John(Orps)	Jones	Buckhalters	198/15	Early
Mill, Wm.Henry	Liberty		184/16	Early
Milland, Anguish	Washington	Daniels	162/7	Irwin
Millear, Master(R.S.)	Jasper	Bentleys	316/10	Early
Milledge, Ann(Wid)	Richmond	Burtons	87/1	Habersha
Milledge, John(Orph)	Richmond	Burtons	290/13	Irwin
Milledge, Wm.(Orph)	Richmond	Burtons	290/13	Irwin

NAME	COUNTY	MIL.DIST	LOT/SECT	DREW LAND
Millen, Eliz.(Wid)	Bulloch	Knights	279/11	Irwin
Millen, Ester(Orph)	Chatham		318/7	Gwinnett
Millen, Frederick(Orph)	Chatham		318/7	Gwinnett
Millen, John	Chatham		396/28	Early
Millen, John	McIntosh	Hamiltons	1/7	Gwinnett
Millener, Dudley	Jasper	Hays	338/12	Irwin
Miller, Alexander	Morgan	Dennis	22/18	Early
Miller, Andrew	Warren	Parhams	432/8	Irwin
Miller, Asa	Franklin	Harris	121/10	Irwin
Miller, Benj.	Wilkes	Mattox	187/15	Early
Miller, Benjamin	Washington	Cummins	283/6	Early
Miller, Charles	Hancock	Herberts	121/5	Appling
Miller, Charles	Jackson	Rogers Bt.	317/1	Appling
Miller, Charles	McIntosh	Jenkins	230/6	Irwin
Miller, Chas.J.	Jones	Hansfords	53/4	Habersham
Miller, Daniel(Orps)	Jasper	Centills	343/1	Appling
Miller, Daniel	Laurens	Kinchens	279/7	Irwin
Miller, David A.(Orph)	Liberty		234/7	Appling
Miller, David	Jasper	Centals	144/2	Irwin
Miller, David	Laurens	Jones	397/2	Early
Miller, Davis	Chatham		104/8	Irwin
Miller, Ebenezer	Richmond	Laceys	370/6	Irwin
Miller, Edy	Hall	Carnes	315/18	Early
Miller, Elias	Jackson	Hamiltons	272/16	Early
Miller, Elias	Jackson	Winters Bt.	30/7	Gwinnett
Miller, Elizabeth	Chatham		298/1	Appling
Miller, Ely	Franklin	J.Miller	431/6	Appling
Miller, Emson	Columbia	J.Morris	263/4	Appling
Miller, Emson	Columbia	J.Morriss	382/8	Appling
Miller, G.J.	Chatham		264/6	Irwin
Miller, Isabella	Glynn		84/6	Appling
Miller, Izabella	Greene	143	23/5	Rabun
Miller, Jacob(Orps)	Camden	Clarkes	180/5	Irwin
Miller, Jacob	Baldwin	Russels	47/8	Irwin
Miller, Jacob	Baldwin	Russels	85/8	Appling
Miller, James Sr.	Franklin	Haynes	118/10	Irwin
Miller, James	Laurens	S.Smith	77/2	Appling
Miller, Jefferson	Jefferson	Lamps	68/3	Rabun
Miller, Jesse	Baldwin	Irwin	189/4	Irwin
Miller, John (RS)	Jackson	Rogers Bt.	2/11	Early
Miller, John Jr.	Hall	Carnes	63/27	Early
Miller, John Jr.	Laurens	Griffins	128/15	Irwin
Miller, John Jr.	Laurens	Griffins	86/2	Appling
Miller, John M.	Putnam	Tomlinsons	208/6	Irwin
Miller, John Sr.	Franklin	J.Millers	327/2	Appling
Miller, John(Orps)	Jackson	Rogers Bt.	416/21	Early
Miller, John	Burke	Lewis	118/6	Early
Miller, John	Franklin	J.Miller	472/5	Irwin
Miller, John	Jones	Shropshiers	266/2	Early
Miller, John	Montgomery	Alstons	238/1	Walton
Miller, John	Pulaski	Rees	27/21	Early
Miller, John	Richmond	122	175/11	Early
Miller, Jonathan Jr.	Laurens	S.Smiths	404/7	Appling
Miller, Jonathan	Hancock	Millers	23/10	Irwin
Miller, Jonathan	Pulaski	Rees	346/6	Appling
Miller, Joshua	Clarke	Merreweather	319/8	Early
Miller, Judith(Wid)	Jackson	Rogers Bt.	72/15	Irwin
Miller, Levi F.	Laurens	S.Smiths	193/5	Appling
Miller, Lewis Jr.	Wilkes	Mattox	399/4	Appling
Miller, Martha(Wid)	Warren	Blounts	262/2	Appling
Miller, Nathaniel	Baldwin	Taliaferro	220/9	Irwin
Miller, Preston	Hall	Simmonds	137/3	Walton
Miller, Preston	Hall	Simmonds	304/7	Irwin
Miller, Richard	Jackson	Hamiltons Bt.	53/6	Gwinnett
Miller, Samuel	Greene	144th	223/10	Irwin
Miller, Solomon	Hancock	Mims	71/26	Early
Miller, Stephen	Burke	Royals	11/22	Early

NAME	COUNTY	MIL.DIST	LOT/SECT	DREW LAND
Miller, Stephen	Burke	Royals	64/3	Appling
Miller, Thomas H.	Camden	Millers	41/17	Early
Miller, William E.	Hancock	Millers	414/6	Appling
Miller, William	Baldwin	Irwins	144/21	Early
Miller, William	Baldwin	Irwins	40/11	Irwin
Miller, William	Bulloch	Jones	292/6	Appling
Miller, William	Hancock	Lucas	317/16	Early
Miller, William	Hancock	Millers	189/3	Habersham
Miller, William	Jackson	Dickson	271/6	Gwinnett
Miller, William	Laurens	S.Smiths	349/9	Appling
Miller, William	McIntosh	Hamiltons	215/2	Irwin
Miller, William	Pulaski	Rees	252/11	Early
Miller, William	Scriven	Lovetts	214/12	Irwin
Miller, Wm.(Orph)	Bulloch	Tilmans	218/9	Early
Millert, Mathew(Wid)	Emanuel	59th	434/8	Appling
Millican, Andrew	Madison	Millicans	236/11	Irwin
Millican, James H.	Elbert	Webbs	149/1	Irwin
Millican, John	Madison	Millicans	245/23	Early
Millican, Josiah	Wilkes	Kilgores	105/27	Early
Millican, Mary Ann	Madison	Culbreths	503/5	Appling
Millican, Robert	Madison	Millicans	112/4	Early
Milligan, Eliz.(Wid)	Chatham		287/7	Appling
Millikan, Stephen	Wilkinson	Howard	81/4	Habersham
Milliner, Martin	Jasper	Baileys	304/26	Early
Milliner, Martin	Jasper	Baileys	376/6	Appling
Millirons, John	Putnam	Ectors	91/19	Early
Millirons, John	Putnam	Ectors	98/4	Irwin
Millirons, John	Putnam	H.Kendricks	27/3	Habersham
Mills, Anthony	Burke	Hands	12/8	Irwin
Mills, Anthony	Burke	Hands	98/7	Irwin
Mills, Archibald(Orps)	Burke	Hands	261/7	Appling
Mills, Charles C.	Morgan	Hubbards	216/5	Early
Mills, Charles E.	Morgan	Hubbards	15/7	Irwin
Mills, Hardy	Pulaski	Dewits	74/4	Irwin
Mills, Harrod	Laurens	Jones	368/16	Early
Mills, Henry	Chatham		137/4	Irwin
Mills, James Jr.	Washington	Mannings	398/10	Irwin
Mills, James	Scriven		153/3	Appling
Mills, Jesse	Washington	Peaboddys	105/2	Rabun
Mills, John	Franklin	Akins	34/4	Habersham
Mills, John	Jones	Seals	46/17	Early
Mills, John	Washington	Cummins	125/11	Habersham
Mills, John	Washington	Mannings	73/20	Early
Mills, Joseph	Camden	33rd	47/4	Appling
Mills, Louisia	Burke	J.Wards	164/12	Irwin
Mills, Peter	Hancock	Thomas	7/3	Appling
Mills, Reuben	Emanuel	57th	61/2	Early
Mills, Richard	Scriven	36th	403/10	Irwin
Mills, Selia(Wid)	Washington	Manning	148/12	Early
Mills, Spire	Pulaski	Senterfeits	241/18	Early
Mills, Stephen	Washington	Cummins	138/5	Early
Mills, Thomas	Franklin	Akins	13/14	Irwin
Mills, Thomas	Pulaski	Lesters	72/12	Early
Mills, Thomas	Scriven	Lovetts	49/13	Habersham
Mills, Thomas	Washington	Pools	7/16	Irwin
Mills, William C.	Chatham		76/8	Early
Mills, William S.	Wilkinson	Wiggins	330/10	Early
Mills, William	Elbert	Childres	191/5	Early
Mills, William	Twiggs	Hodges	381/21	Early
Mills, William	Washington	Cumins	3/11	Irwin
Mills, Wm.(Orps)	Washington	Mannings	98/14	Irwin
Millsaps, Jacob Jr.	Jackson	Rogers Bt.	429/6	Appling
Millsaps, Jacob Sr.	Jackson	Rogers Bt.	359/16	Early
Millsaps, Jacob Sr.	Jackson	Rogers	475/5	Irwin
Millsaps, Locky	Jackson	Rogers Bt.	38/15	Irwin
Millsaps, Marvel	Jackson	Rogers Bt.	25/3	Irwin
Milner, Hopson	Jasper	Bentleys	90/3	Appling

NAME	COUNTY	MIL.DIST	LOT/SECT	DREW LAND
Milner, John B.	Wilkes	Davis	23/6	Gwinnett
Milner, John H.	Jones	Greens	395/7	Appling
Milner, John	Jasper	Bentleys	13/3	Irwin
Milner, John	Jasper	Bentleys	147/2	Rabun
Milner, John	Jasper	Bentleys	20/7	Appling
Milner, John	Jasper	Bentleys	28/11	Habersham
Milner, John	Jasper	Bentleys	340/6	Irwin
Milner, John	Jasper	Bentleys	388/9	Early
Milner, Simeon	Morgan	McClendons	50/9	Appling
Milord, Mary(Wid)	Clarke	Moores	171/5	Irwin
Milton, Eliel	Clarke	Stewarts	103/7	Appling
Milton, Ethen	Clarke	Stuarts	196/26	Early
Milton, Peter	Burke	McNorrills	335/1	Early
Mimms, Britton	Tattnall	Overstreets	174/2	Irwin
Mimms, John(Orps)	Baldwin	Irwin	50/1	Walton
Mimms, Joseph	Tattnall	Cunyers	284/9	Irwin
Mimms, Joseph	Tattnall	Cunyers	347/6	Gwinnett
Mimms, Mary(Wid)	Twiggs	Evans	184/15	Early
Mims, Calvin	Wilkinson	Lees	151/6	Appling
Mims, Henry	Jones	Samuels	280/9	Irwin
Mims, John	Tattnall	Johnstons	296/4	Walton
Mims, Joseph	Wilkinson	Lees	438/7	Appling
Mims, Marshal	Twiggs	Hodges	30/15	Early
Mims, Marshall	Twiggs	Hodges	516/6	Appling
Mims, Needham	Baldwin	Irwins	397/1	Appling
Mims, William	Washington	Barges	331/11	Early
Mims, Williamson	Baldwin	Haws	376/8	Appling
Mims, Wright	Wilkinson	Smiths	175/4	Early
Mincy, Jacob	Bulloch	Tilmans	88/10	Irwin
Mincy, Phillip	Bulloch	Tilmans	349/8	Appling
Mingledorf, John G.	Effingham		375/13	Early
Mingledorf, John G.	Effingham		72/5	Rabun
Minor, Coleman	Putnam	Stampers	145/11	Irwin
Minshaw, Abram	Emanuel	58th	40/4	Habersham
Minshew, Jacob	Twiggs	R.Belchers	124/13	Early
Minter, Anthony	Baldwin	Irwins	23/3	Early
Minter, Richard	Jasper	Evans	182/12	Irwin
Minter, Richard	Jasper	Evans	350/5	Irwin
Minton, Jason	Clarke	Pentecost	3/7	Appling
Minton, Jesse	Hancock	Scotts	92/3	Rabun
Minton, John	Hancock	Lucas	406/8	Early
Minton, John	Wilkes	Dents	220/15	Early
Minton, John	Wilkes	Dents	291/9	Irwin
Minton, John	Wilkes	Dents	334/5	Irwin
Minton, Joseph(Orps)	Hancock	Lucas	217/4	Walton
Minton, Lucretia(Wid)	Hancock	Lucas	45/8	Early
Minton, Moses	Jefferson	Bothwells	204/6	Irwin
Minton, Nancy H.	Burke	Dys	78/6	Habersham
Minton, Stephen(Orps)	Laurens	Kinchens	224/20	Early
Mints, James	Chatham		225/4	Walton
Minyard, John	Gwinnett	Hamiltons Bt.	287/28	Early
Mions, David	Morgan	Parkers	128/13	Irwin
Mires, Abraham	Hall		23/1	Rabun
Mise, James	Jasper	Gilmores	197/27	Early
Misser, Caty(Orph)	Richmond	Palmers	298/15	Early
Misser, Hannah(Orph)	Richmond	Palmers	298/15	Early
Misser, Jesse(Orph)	Richmond	Palmers	298/15	Early
Misser, Peter(Orph)	Richmond	Palmers	298/15	Early
Misser, Wm.(Orph)	Richmond	Palmers	298/15	Early
Mitcalf, William	Burke	Lewis	283/14	Early
Mitcham, Barnett	Jones	Shropshiers	184/6	Irwin
Mitcham, James	Jones	Shropshiers	266/5	Early
Mitcham, Wm.	Jones	Shropshier	238/5	Gwinnett
Mitchel, Thomas G.	Telfair	Williams	301/10	Early
Mitchell, A.G.C.	Washington	Pools	185/4	Early
Mitchell, B.B.	Richmond		16/3	Habersham
Mitchell, B.B.	Richmond		163/10	Early

NAME	COUNTY	MIL.DIST	LOT/SECT	DREW LAN
Mitchell, D.B.Sr.	Baldwin	Russells	153/5	Early
Mitchell, Danvill	Gwinnett	Hamiltons	117/4	Appling
Mitchell, David B.	Chatham		133/20	Early
Mitchell, David	Franklin	Akins	26/4	Irwin
Mitchell, Edward	Morgan	Knights	505/3	Appling
Mitchell, Eldan	Clarke	Cliftons	58/6	Appling
Mitchell, Eliz.(Wid)	Jones	Seals	359/19	Early
Mitchell, Green B.	Putnam	Kendricks	349/13	Irwin
Mitchell, Henry	Jackson	Hamiltons Bt.	11/11	Habersha
Mitchell, Henry	Jones	Wallers	39/28	Early
Mitchell, Henry	Walton	Worshams	111/10	Irwin
Mitchell, Isaac	Hall	McCutcheon	324/8	Early
Mitchell, Isaac	Hall	McCutcheons	418/11	Irwin
Mitchell, Isaac	Wilkinson	Kettles	139/11	Early
Mitchell, Isaac	Wilkinson	Kettles	69/14	Early
Mitchell, James	Jackson	Winters Bt.	202/2	Early
Mitchell, James	Jackson	Winters Bt.	90/19	Early
Mitchell, James	Morgan	Hubbards	73/12	Irwin
Mitchell, Joel	Jasper	Hays	136/9	Irwin
Mitchell, John S.	Wilkes	Gordons	323/10	Early
Mitchell, John	Jones	Samuels	249/3	Early
Mitchell, John	Morgan	Hubbards	145/18	Early
Mitchell, John	Warren	150	289/27	Early
Mitchell, Mary(Wid)	Twiggs	Ellis	152/10	Irwin
Mitchell, Mary(Wid)	Wilkinson	Kettles	88/6	Appling
Mitchell, Nathaniel	McIntosh	McIntosh	272/9	Early
Mitchell, Nathaniel	Montgomery	McMillans	70/4	Appling
Mitchell, Peter	Chatham		102/4	Early
Mitchell, Pleasant R.	Washington	Barges	332/13	Irwin
Mitchell, Reps	Baldwin	Marshalls	108/6	Gwinnett
Mitchell, Reuben	Franklin	Hammonds	193/20	Early
Mitchell, Richard	Pulaski	Lesters	396/8	Appling
Mitchell, Robert	Franklin	Hammonds	117/11	Early
Mitchell, Robert	Jasper	Hays	74/15	Irwin
Mitchell, Robert	Warren	150th	118/8	Appling
Mitchell, Robt.M.	Jones	Seals	178/6	Early
Mitchell, Robt.M.J.	Jones	Seals	376/11	Early
Mitchell, Sterling	(Orps)	Jones	Seals	248/18, 8
Mitchell, Taylor	Montgomery	McMillins	1/6	Gwinnett
Mitchell, Thomas R.	Clarke	Stewarts	33/8	Appling
Mitchell, Thomas R.	Clarke	Stuarts	118/11	Irwin
Mitchell, Thomas	Montgomery	McMillins	234/4	Early
Mitchell, Thomas	Morgan	Knights	269/12	Irwin
Mitchell, William	Madison	Williford	384/17	Early
Mitchell, William	Madison	Williford	79/1	Early
Mitchell, William	Putnam	Morelands	461/12	Irwin
Mitchell, William	Wilkinson	Lees	36/7	Early
Mitchell, Wm.(orps)	Clarke	Applings	193/19	Early
Mitchell, Wm.Jr.	Columbia	Applings	295/5	Appling
Mitchells, John(Orps)	Clarke	Deans	113/11	Hall
Mitchels, Wm.L.	Clarke	Applings	363/17	Early
Mitts, Eleven	Washington	Barges	485/8	Appling
Mitts, Frederick	Washington	Barges	307/5	Gwinnett
Mitts, Meddin	Emanuel	53rd	148/3	Irwin
Mixon, George	Scriven	Moodys	222/5	Early
Mixon, Jesse	Tattnall	Cunyes	109/12	Hall
Mixon, William	Burke	Thomas	387/21	Early
Mize, Anderson	Putnam	Stampers	212/11	Early
Mize, Henry	Jasper	Smiths	163/10	Habersham
Mize, James(Orps)	Jasper	Bartletts	333/7	Early
Mizell, Hardy	Putnam	Ectors	363/8	Appling
Mizzel, Luke	Wilkinson	Brooks	94/18	Early
Mizzle, Luke	Scriven		189/5	Gwinnett
Moat, David	Laurens	Ross's	133/10	Early
Moats, Jethro(Orps)	Laurens	Harriss	276/5	Irwin
Mobley, Abner	Washington	Peabodys	330/19	Early
Mobley, Benjamin	Twiggs	Smiths	119/18	Early

NAME	COUNTY	MIL.DIST	LOT/SECT	DREW LAND
Mobley, Burd	Tattnall	Tharps	413/13	Irwin
Mobley, Eleazar	Jasper	Phillips	52/8	Appling
Mobley, Isaac	Elbert	Olivers	206/11	Early
Mobley, Isaac	Jackson	Rogers Bt.	134/12	Habersham
Mobley, Isaac	Jackson	Rogers Bt.	32/1	Appling
Mobley, James	Scriven	Moodys	311/5	Appling
Mobley, Lydia(Wid)	Effingham		331/9	Irwin
Mobley, Rubin(Orps)	Washington	Mannings	442/5	Appling
Mobley, Sarah Sr.	Burke	Royals	19/5	Rabun
Mobley, Wiley	Washington	Mannings	356/20	Early
Mobley, William	Tattnall	Tharps	141/6	Early
Mobly, John	Baldwin	Irwins	179/10	Early
Mock, Andrew Sr.(Orps)	Scriven	36	576/2	Appling
Mock, Andrew	Scriven	36th	273/1	Appling
Mock, George	Scriven	36	315/5	Appling
Mock, Jacob(Orps)	Wilkinson	Childs	150/14	Early
Mock, John M.	Effingham		201/1	Early
Mock, John M.	Effingham		282/9	Early
Mock, Neall(Orps)	Wilkes	Mattox	1/2	Rabun
Mock, Thomas	Effingham		339/7	Early
Moffatt, Jacob	Jasper	Kennedys	275/20	Early
Moffatt, Thos.	Jasper	Kennedys	67/8	Early
Moffet, Gabriel A.	Clarke	Deans	64/13	Habersham
Moffet, Henry	Clarke	Deans	27/15	Early
Moffett, Henry	Clarke	Deans	498/11	Irwin
Moffott, Gabriel A.	Clarke	Deans	32/15	Irwin
Molborn, John	Effingham		129/8	Irwin
Molder, Lewis	Franklin	R.Browns	379/4	Appling
Moncrief, Caleb	Jones	Hansfords	104/4	Irwin
Moncrief, David	Greene	Kimbroughs	66/1	Irwin
Moncrief, Saml.	Greene	Wheelis	178/5	Irwin
Moncrief, Samuel	Greene	Wheelis	269/3	Appling
Moncrief, Thomas	Wilkes	Hollidays	212/19	Early
Moncrief, Wiley(Orps)	Jones	Hansfords	295/28	Early
Moncrief, William	Columbia	Bealls	241/13	Irwin
Mond, William	Burke	Jones	102/19	Early
Mondon, John B.	Wayne	Johnstons	355/5	Irwin
Monford, John	Greene	143rd	101/12	Habersham
Monford, John	Greene	143rd	123/14	Early
Monford, Lucy R.	Wilkes	Gordons	39/9	Irwin
Monk, George H.	Jasper	Easts	319/17	Early
Monk, George H.	Jasper	Easts	517/7	Irwin
Monk, Hosea	Jones	Phillips	334/7	Appling
Monk, John	Jones	Greens	517/6	Irwin
Monk, Silas	Jones	Greens	300/19	Early
Monk, Silas	Jones	Greens	86/5	Early
Monroe, Neal	Washington	Daniels	335/12	Early
Monrow, John	Burke		73/14	Irwin
Montague, Phillip	Elbert	Higginbottom	2/6	Early
Montcrief, Wm.	Wilkes	Russels	115/5	Appling
Montford, George	Jasper	Bentleys	80/12	Hall
Montford, Henry	Laurens	D.Smiths	155/4	Irwin
Montford, Henry	Laurens	D.Smiths	500/12	Irwin
Montford, John C.	Laurens	D.Smiths	336/18	Early
Montford, John Sr.	Laurens	D.Smiths	9/6	Irwin
Montford, Margry(Wid)	Laurens	Watsons	58/11	Habersham
Montfort, Theodorick	Putnam	Oslins	167/7	Irwin
Montgomery, Ann(Wid)	Jefferson	Fountains	323/2	Early
Montgomery, James Jr.	Jackson	Winters Bt.	284/2	Appling
Montgomery, James	Jackson	Dicksons Bt.	63/3	Appling
Montgomery, James	Wilkes	Dent	97/1	Habersham
Montgomery, John H.	Richmond		122/8	Appling
Montgomery, Margt.(Wid)	Wilkinson	Brook	168/9	Early
Montgomery, Simpson	Wilkes	Smiths	7/2	Rabun
Montgomery, Wm.	Chatham		49/10	Habersham
Montgomery, Wm.W.(Orp)	Jefferson	Fountains	386/9	Irwin
Montgomery, Wright	Jefferson	Fountains	188/7	Gwinnett

NAME	COUNTY	MIL.DIST	LOT/SECT	DREW LAN
Moody, Aerell	Oglethorpe	Bowls	331/8	Appling
Moody, Benj.	Wayne	Johnstons	337/6	Irwin
Moody, Daniel	Greene	143	166/8	Appling
Moody, Daniel	Greene	143	254/16	Early
Moody, Enoch S.	Washington	Barges	408/7	Irwin
Moody, Green	Jasper	Blakes	243/23	Early
Moody, Green	Jasper	Blakes	351/1	Appling
Moody, Jesse	Wayne	Johnstons	268/26	Early
Moody, John	Laurens	Ross	234/26	Early
Moody, John	Oglethorpe	Dunns	165/12	Irwin
Moody, John	Oglethorpe	Dunns	421/5	Irwin
Moody, Perryman	Scriven	Moodys	325/1	Early
Moody, Reuben	Jasper	Smiths	159/8	Irwin
Moody, Robert	Glynn		132/12	Hall
Moody, William	Jasper	Smiths	482/6	Irwin
Moon, Bird	Madison	Orrs	47/9	Appling
Moon, George	Hancock	Loyds	196/2	Early
Moon, Jacob	Madison	Orrs	130/7	Gwinnett
Moon, Jesse Jr.	Columbia	Willinghams	1/14	Early
Moon, Jesse Jr.	Columbia	Willinghams	229/12	Early
Moon, Jesse	Columbia	Willinghams	147/3	Appling
Moon, John W.	Jackson	Rogers Bt.	252/3	Irwin
Moon, John	Jackson	Winters Bt.	81/5	Rabun
Moon, Lewis S.	Columbia	Willinghams	83/3	Habersha
Moon, Pleasant	Twiggs	W.Belchers	139/8	Hall
Moon, Pleasant	Twiggs	W.Belchers	145/8	Early
Moon, Wm.H.	Twiggs	W.Belchers	147/9	Appling
Mooney, Isaac	Morgan	Walkers	516/5	Appling
Mooney, Lewis	Hall		245/8	Early
Moons, Jess(Orps)	Elbert	Olivers	239/7	Appling
Moons, Pleasant(Orps)	Elbert	Webbs	519/8	Irwin
Moor, Benjamin	Richmond		20/6	Appling
Moor, Jacob	Hall		496/7	Appling
Moor, Jason	Wilkinson	Mims	176/1	Appling
Moor, John	Richmond	Lacys	132/7	Early
Moor, John	Richmond	Lacys	323/16	Early
Moor, Moren	Hall		24/23	Early
Moor, Nancy(Wid)	Wilkinson	Mims	331/17	Early
Moor, William	Wayne	Jacobs	328/5	Gwinnett
Moore, Asa	Wilkinson	Bowings	118/6	Irwin
Moore, Abner	Pulaski	Bryans	256/6	Irwin
Moore, Abram	Franklin	Harris	85/6	Irwin
Moore, Alexander	Clarke	Moores	323/21	Early
Moore, Allen	Washington	Wimberly	93/7	Appling
Moore, Alsa	Oglethorpe	Dunns	80/19	Early
Moore, Arthur	Camden	Longs	496/10	Irwin
Moore, Asa	Columbia	Dodsons	110/5	Appling
Moore, Augustus	Burke	Torrances	70/3	Appling
Moore, Bartholomew	Baldwin	Marshalls	182/1	Appling
Moore, Benj.	Greene	Fosters	150/12	Irwin
Moore, Betsey(Wid)	Columbia	Dodsons	211/4	Appling
Moore, Bishop	Wilkes	Perrys	33/2	Rabun
Moore, Charles	Wilkes	Bryants	187/20	Early
Moore, Chas.G.	Oglethorpe	Waters	114/21	Early
Moore, Clement	Haws	Baldwin	212/7	Early
Moore, Daniel	Effingham		80/7	Gwinnett
Moore, David Sr.	Greene	Harvills	113/21	Early
Moore, David	Greene	Marvills	190/2	Early
Moore, David	Hancock	Smiths	306/9	Appling
Moore, David	Hancock	Smiths	462/8	Appling
Moore, David	Madison	Culbreaths	215/20	Early
Moore, Edward	Laurens	Harris	128/21	Early
Moore, Edward	Laurens	Harriss	139/2	Rabun
Moore, Elijah	Baldwin	Haws	239/1	Walton
Moore, Elijah	Elbert	Ruckers	184/15	Early
Moore, Elijah	Greene	Fosters	136/4	Appling
Moore, Elinda(Orph)	Burke	McNorrels	325/17	Early

NAME	COUNTY	MIL.DIST	LOT/SECT	DREW LAND
Moore, Etheldred	Jefferson	Abbots	52/18	Early
Moore, Foeman	Jefferson	Waldens	141/1	Appling
Moore, Frances(R.S.)	Clarke	Mitchells	60/8	Irwin
Moore, Francis(R.S.)	Clarke	Mitchells	340/14	Early
Moore, Francis(R.S.)	Clarke	Mitchells	437/7	Irwin
Moore, Francis(Wid)	Richmond	Laceys	104/12	Habersham
Moore, George	Washington	Wimberlys	500/2	Appling
Moore, Hill	Wilkes	Davis	322/10	Irwin
Moore, Hill	Wilkes	Davis	356/10	Irwin
Moore, Hiram	Baldwin	Milledgeville	33/11	Early
Moore, Hiram	Jasper	Evans	25/12	Irwin
Moore, Hugh	Greene	141	98/13	Irwin
Moore, Isaac Sr.	Jasper	Posts	492/2	Appling
Moore, Isaac	Greene	144th	366/3	Appling
Moore, Isaac	Madison	Bones	8/1	Appling
Moore, Jackson	Greene	144th	93/5	Appling
Moore, James	Camden	Longs	141/5	Gwinnett
Moore, James	Camden	Longs	331/9	Appling
Moore, James	Greene	Gordans	310/8	Irwin
Moore, James	Jasper	Hays	43/9	Hall
Moore, James	Jasper	Smiths	252/20	Early
Moore, James	Jasper	Smiths	32/8	Appling
Moore, James	Laurens	Ross	169/13	Early
Moore, James	Tattnall	Johnsons	418/7	Irwin
Moore, James	Wilkes	Perrys	294/10	Irwin
Moore, Jesse(Orps)	Jones	Permenters	454/2	Appling
Moore, Jesse	Jackson	Rogers B.	315/1	Appling
Moore, Jesse	Jackson	Rogers Bt.	234/18	Early
Moore, Joel	Franklin	Akins	198/8	Early
Moore, John A. (Orps)	Oglethorpe	Barnetts	125/12	Habersham
Moore, John B.	Columbia	Watsons	22/12	Hall
Moore, John Jr.	Baldwin	Russells	25/6	Irwin
Moore, John L.	Greene	Ragins	53/2	Irwin
Moore, John R.	Burke	M.Wards	143/10	Irwin
Moore, John(Orps)	Twiggs	W.Belchers	432/28	Early
Moore, John(R.S.)	Jackson	Winters	384/8	Early
Moore, John	Columbia	Bealls	146/11	Hall
Moore, John	Columbia	Bealls	372/6	Irwin
Moore, John	Columbia	Watsons	16/8	Appling
Moore, John	Emanuel	40th	175/1	Appling
Moore, John	Greene	Greirs	69/19	Early
Moore, John	Greene	Nelms	410/9	Irwin
Moore, John	Hall		3/1	Rabun
Moore, John	Hancock	Millers	72/13	Early
Moore, John	Jackson	Dickson Bt.	215/16	Early
Moore, John	Jackson	Dicksons Bt.	123/27	Early
Moore, John	Jasper	Baileys	151/16	Irwin
Moore, John	Jasper	Clays	320/1	Appling
Moore, John	Washington	Wimberleys	192/26	Early
Moore, John	Wilkes	Davis	15/15	Early
Moore, Joseph (R.S.)	Jasper	Dardens	206/6	Appling
Moore, Joseph J.	Oglethorpe	Barnetts	232/8	Early
Moore, Joseph(RS)	Jasper	Dardins	91/15	Early
Moore, Joseph	Morgan	Hubbards	56/5	Early
Moore, Joshua	Greene	Kimbroughs	82/5	Gwinnett
Moore, Joshua	Jasper	Posts	330/13	Irwin
Moore, Josiah	Washington	Burneys	113/8	Early
Moore, Lemuel Sr.	Greene	142nd	214/9	Irwin
Moore, Lemuel Sr.	Greene	142nd	91/13	Habersham
Moore, Luke	Baldwin	Cousins	341/9	Early
Moore, Margarett	Baldwin	Irwins	343/11	Irwin
Moore, Mark E.	Greene	142nd	82/14	Irwin
Moore, Mary(Wid)	Laurens	Jones	66/1	Early
Moore, Mary(orph)	Burke	Thomas	334/27	Early
Moore, Patience(Wid)	Jackson	Rogers Bt.	184/3	Appling
Moore, Patsey(Wid)	Columbia	Olives	259/7	Gwinnett
Moore, Ransom	Clarke	Pentecosts	219/11	Irwin

NAME	COUNTY	MIL.DIST	LOT/SECT	DREW LAND
Moore, Ransom	Greene	Harvills	89/12	Habershan
Moore, Richard	Madison	Bones	347/3	Appling
Moore, Robert	Wilkes	Bryants	264/1	Appling
Moore, Rowland	Burke	72nd	102/9	Appling
Moore, Sarah	Burke	M.Wards	9/7	Appling
Moore, Seaborn	Wilkes	Davis	122/9	Appling
Moore, Seaborn	Wilkes	Davis	9/4	Early
Moore, Seth	Wilkes	Gordons	233/6	Early
Moore, Susanne(Orp)	Burke	Thomas	334/27	Early
Moore, Syntha(Wid)	Laurens	Harris	34/7	Gwinnett
Moore, Thomas C.	Wilkes	Brooks	440/5	Appling
Moore, Thomas(Orps)	Baldwin	Irwins	400/13	Irwin
Moore, Thomas	Burke	Torrance	62/6	Gwinnett
Moore, Thomas	Elbert	R.Christians	377/5	Early
Moore, Thomas	Madison	Bones	500/7	Irwin
Moore, Thomas	Twiggs	Jeffersons	115/8	Early
Moore, Thomas	Wilkes	Ogletrees	477/12	Irwin
Moore, Thos.J.	Greene	143rd	243/2	Appling
Moore, Turner B.	Burke	M.Wards	638/2	Appling
Moore, Usray	Wilkes	Perrys	58/1	Walton
Moore, Wallace	Jasper	Baileys	277/1	Appling
Moore, Wiley	Jefferson	Jones	382/11	Early
Moore, William A.	Chatham		270/6	Irwin
Moore, William R.	Clarke	Simms	51/8	Appling
Moore, William S.	Columbia	Watsons	378/2	Early
Moore, William	Burke	Royals	304/28	Early
Moore, William	Jasper	Kennedys	89/3	Early
Moore, William	Jasper	Posts	387/5	Irwin
Moore, William	Morgan	Walkers	117/5	Irwin
Moore, William	Oglethorpe	Davenports	266/9	Early
Moore, William	Scriven	9 Bt.	463/8	Appling
Moore, Winfred	Burke	Torrances	279/11	Early
Moore, Wm.	Greene	141st	405/10	Irwin
Moore, Wm.	Jones	Jeffersons	27/7	Irwin
Moore, Wm.A.	Jasper	Baileys	197/26	Early
Moore, Wm.W.	Greene	Fosters	150/3	Habershan
Moore, Wyatt S.	Franklin	Harris	291/8	Early
Moore, Young	Greene	Ragins	91/7	Gwinnett
Mooreland, Robt.Sr.	Pulaski	Lesters	31/6	Irwin
Mooring, James	Wilkinson	Wiggins	350/14	Early
Moorman, Benj.	Laurens	Deans	103/10	Habershan
Moorman, Chas.	Laurens	Deans	129/1	Early
Moran, James	Baldwin	Ellis	243/9	Appling
Moran, Jesse	Jones	Buckhalters	193/6	Irwin
Moran, Jesse	Jones	Buckhalters	281/9	Early
Moran, John	Baldwin	Taliaferro	108/15	Early
Moran, William	Baldwin	Taliaferros	243/8	Appling
Mordecai, Emanuel	Chatham		209/15	Early
Mordecai, Samuel	Chatham		131/5	Irwin
Mordicai, Abraham M.	Pulaski	Johnsons	402/3	Appling
More, Joseph	Morgan	Hubbards	169/7	Gwinnett
More, Susannah S.(Orp)	Jefferson	Abbotts	214/4	Early
Morehead, John	Chatham		67/5	Early
Morel, Ann(Wid)	Chatham		13/2	Walton
Morel, William	Chatham		54/13	Early
Moreland, Colson	Putnam	Morelands	397/10	Early
Moreland, Francis	Pulaski	Lesters	370/21	Early
Moreland, Greene	Jasper	Kennedys	264/8	Irwin
Moreland, John Jr.	Wilkinson	Kettles	336/12	Irwin
Moreland, John	Jasper	McLendons	19/5	Gwinnett
Moreland, John	Putnam	Morelands	163/3	Early
Moreland, Richard	Jasper	Kennedys	198/12	Irwin
Moreland, Turner	Putnam	Morelands	44/1	Appling
Moreland, Wm.	Jones	Phillips	187/16	Early
Morell, Levi	Laurens	Jones	83/3	Walton
Morell, Thomas N.	Chatham		123/7	Gwinnett
Moreman, James	Oglethorpe	Bowls	11/12	Habershan

NAME	COUNTY	MIL.DIST	LOT/SECT	DREW LAND
Moreman, John	Wilkes	Holladays	161/11	Early
Moreman, William	Wilkes	Holidays	172/2	Rabun
Morgan, Blake	Jackson	Mays	120/5	Gwinnett
Morgan, Charlotte(Wid)	Hancock	Edwards	346/17	Early
Morgan, Chas.W.	Laurens	D.Smiths	445/3	Appling
Morgan, Christopher L.	Effingham		357/3	Early
Morgan, David	Jones	Jeffersons	44/1	Irwin
Morgan, Eliz.	Jasper	Smiths	125/20	Early
Morgan, Henrietta	Oglethorpe	Brittons	168/9	Irwin
Morgan, Henry(Orps)	Oglethorpe	Brittons	85/14	Early
Morgan, Isaac	Twiggs	Jeffersons	349/12	Early
Morgan, Isham Jr.	Elbert	Whites	315/6	Gwinnett
Morgan, James B.	Morgan	McClendon	125/10	Habersham
Morgan, James B.	Morgan	McLendons	237/9	Irwin
Morgan, James	Greene	140th	105/3	Habersham
Morgan, James	Jasper	Smiths	12/4	Habersham
Morgan, Jesse	Morgan	Dennis	168/12	Habersham
Morgan, Jesse	Morgan	Dennis	82/6	Appling
Morgan, John E.	Putnam	Oslins	253/6	Early
Morgan, John G.	Twiggs	Jeffersons	299/19	Early
Morgan, John	Glynn		520/8	Irwin
Morgan, John	Jefferson	Waldens	233/3	Irwin
Morgan, John	Jones	Phillips	470/7	Irwin
Morgan, John	Morgan	McClendons	515/9	Irwin
Morgan, John	Putnam	Berrys	249/20	Early
Morgan, Joseph	Jackson	Hamiltons Bt.	171/19	Early
Morgan, Joshua	Clarke	Parrs	126/3	Early
Morgan, Joshua	Clarke	Parrs	458/8	Appling
Morgan, Josiah	Wilkes	Perrys	22/6	Irwin
Morgan, Kiziah	Wilkes	Perrys	409/26	Early
Morgan, Lemuel(Orps)	Morgan	Hackneys	66/10	Early
Morgan, Levi	Liberty		3/26	Early
Morgan, Levi	Liberty		30/15	Early
Morgan, Levi	Liberty		518/7	Appling
Morgan, Lihew	Appling	3rd	346/21	Early
Morgan, Mary D.	Jasper	Clays	162/1	Irwin
Morgan, Peggy W.	Warren	Travis	380/1	Appling
Morgan, Richard M.	Baldwin	Marshalls	48/8	Irwin
Morgan, Rochsalend	Appling	3rd	95/8	Early
Morgan, Solomon	Appling	3rd	425/6	Appling
Morgan, Thomas	Jackson	Dicksons Bt.	94/3	Appling
Morgan, William	Effingham		485/3	Appling
Morgan, William	Jackson	Winters Bt.	370/19	Early
Morgan, William	Liberty		61/6	Gwinnett
Morgan, William	Richmond	Burtons	450/2	Appling
Morgan, Wm.C.	Elbert	R.Christians	319/10	Irwin
Morgan, Wm.F.A.(R.S.)	Hancock	Danells	324/5	Gwinnett
Morgan, Wm.S.	Putnam	Oslins	66/10	Habersham
Morgans, Ellinton(Orps)	Hancock	Edwards	337/11	Early
Morland, Colson	Putnam	Morlands	92/3	Early
Morland, Josiah(Orps)	Clarke	Starnes	98/28	Early
Mornan, Silas	Putnam	Littles	109/1	Habersham
Morrall, John	Chatham		160/13	Early
Morrell, John	Jefferson	Abbots	168/5	Appling
Morrell, John	Jefferson	Abbotts	47/7	Appling
Morris, David L.	Columbia	O.Morris	96/9	Appling
Morris, Abner	Warren	153	79/3	Habersham
Morris, Benj.(Orps)	Putnam	Slaughters	138/6	Early
Morris, Benj.	Hancock	Justices	212/3	Early
Morris, David	Wilkinson	Lees	227/2	Irwin
Morris, David	Wilkinson	Lees	73/2	Appling
Morris, Eliz.(Wid)	Elbert	Olivers	62/13	Early
Morris, George W. .	Clarke	Stewarts	362/13	Early
Morris, George	Warren	Parhams	341/10	Early
Morris, Green	Warren	153	114/4	Early
Morris, Jacob	Washington	Wimberlys	174/1	Early
Morris, Jesse Jr.	Columbia	J.Morris	328/6	Irwin

NAME	COUNTY	MIL.DIST	LOT/SECT	DREW LAND
Morris, John(Orps)	Jasper	McLendons	1733	Walton
Morris, John(Orps)	Jasper	Northcuts	86/14	Early
Morris, John(R.S.)	Clarke	Stewarts	303/28	Early
Morris, John(R.S.)	Clarke	Stewarts	504/7	Appling
Morris, Joseph S.	Columbia	Watsons	377/10	Early
Morris, Joseph	Baldwin	Cousins	498/5	Appling
Morris, Nathan	Hancock	Evans	25/1	Habersham
Morris, Obediah	Baldwin	Taliaferros	13/4	Irwin
Morris, Robert	Richmond	Burtons	141/8	Irwin
Morris, Shadrach	Jackson	Hamiltons Bt.	27/4	Appling
Morris, Spencer	Walton	Sentells	399/6	Irwin
Morris, Thomas Sr.	Jones	Jeffersons	193/5	Early
Morris, Thomas	Columbia	O.Morris	537/9	Appling
Morris, Warren	Jackson	Rogers Bt.	17/21	Early
Morris, Wm.Sr.(R.S.)	Jackson	Hamiltons	192/2	Early
Morris, Wm.Sr.(RS)	Jackson	Hamiltons	266/11	Irwin
Morrison, Daniel	Montgomery	Alstons	311/26	Early
Morrison, Daniel	Montgomery	Alstons	42/14	Irwin
Morrison, Ezra	Elbert	Ruckers	137/5	Gwinnett
Morrison, George	Camden	32nd	378/5	Early
Morrison, James	Chatham		17/5	Irwin
Morrison, James	Wilkinson	Bowings	265/3	Appling
Morrison, John	Burke	Sullivans	287/16	Early
Morrison, Joseph	Walton	Wagnons	25/10	Habersham
Morrison, Mary	Putnam	Tomlinsons	334/3	Early
Morrison, Norman Jr.	Telfair	Williams	43/8	Irwin
Morrison, Norman(Orps)	Telfair	Williams	257/12	Irwin
Morrison, Wm.(Orps)	Telfair	Tallies	68/6	Gwinnett
Morriss, Benjamin	Oglethorpe	Brittons	102/3	Early
Morriss, Eliz.(Wid)	Richmond	Burton	52/9	Irwin
Morriss, Garrett	Clarke	Moore	218/6	Appling
Morriss, George	Jasper	Easts	350/8	Irwin
Morriss, Hannah(Wid)	Clarke	Moores	282/15	Early
Morriss, Isaac	Wilkes	Bates	331/5	Appling
Morriss, James	Jackson	Hamitons Bt.	247/8	Irwin
Morriss, James	Walton	Sentells	167/5	Gwinnett
Morriss, Jesse Sr.	Columbia	J.Morriss	219/5	Irwin
Morriss, Jesse Sr.	Columbia	J.Morriss	6/20	Early
Morriss, John(R.S.)	Clarke	Stewarts	127/4	Early
Morriss, Jonathan	Laurens	S.Smiths	516/7	Appling
Morriss, Joseph	Franklin	Harris	37/11	Irwin
Morriss, Joseph	Franklin	Harriss	43/3	Irwin
Morriss, Simon Jr.	Greene	Nelms	373/20	Early
Morriss, Simon Sr.	Greene	Nelms	43/1	Habersham
Morriss, Thomas	Jasper	Northcuts	297/8	Irwin
Morriss, William	Clarke	Stuarts	103/8	Irwin
Morriss, William	Pulaski	Maddox	239/18	Early
Morrow, Archibald	Montgomery	Alstons	184/5	Early
Morrow, Arthur	Telfair	Tallies	172/13	Habersham
Morrow, Daniel	Montgomery	Alstons	241/6	Appling
Morrow, David	Morgan	Loyds	464/2	Appling
Morrow, Joseph	Morgan	Farrars	303/18	Early
Morrow, Joseph	Morgan	Farrars	42/10	Irwin
Morton, David	Scriven		170/15	Early
Morton, David	Scriven		263/12	Early
Morton, John	Franklin	Flanagans	365/4	Appling
Morton, John	Habersham	Flanigans	322/4	Early
Morton, Judeth	Clarke	Starnes	214/12	Early
Morton, Lewis	Camden	Baileys	354/7	Appling
Morton, Thomas	Morgan	Knights	212/28	Early
Moseley, Silas	Twiggs	Smiths	3/6	Gwinnett
Moseley, Thomas	Jefferson	Bothwells	329/5	Irwin
Moseley, Thomas	Jefferson	Bothwells	82/1	Irwin
Moseley, Wm.H.	Montgomery	Alstons	99/24	Walton
Moseleys, Wm.(Orps)	Tattnall	Cunyers	207/10	Irwin
Mosely, Benj.	Lincoln	Tatoms	30/7	Early
Mosely, Benj.	Morgan	Alfords	238/6	Gwinnett

NAME	COUNTY	MIL.DIST	LOT/SECT	DREW LAND
Mosely, Elisa	Jasper	Hays	246/7	Irwin
Mosely, Jeremiah	Jasper	Smiths	190/5	Early
Mosely, Jeremiah	Jasper	Smiths	317/6	Appling
Mosely, Jesse	Morgan	Talbots	28/5	Irwin
Mosely, Joseph(Orps)	Jones	Permenters	205/3	Appling
Mosely, Mary(Wid)	Twiggs	Jeffersons	27/20	Early
Mosely, Sarah(Wid)	Jones	Permenters	219/5	Appling
Mosely, Silas	Jasper	Hays	197/19	Early
Mosely, William	Twiggs	R.Belchers	144/4	Irwin
Mosely, William	Twiggs	R.Belchers	347/1	Early
Mosely, Wm.	Putnam	Littles	241/4	Irwin
Moses, Delpha(Wid)	Wilkinson	Smiths	198/10	Irwin
Moses, Elisha	Warren	153	451/13	Irwin
Moses, Elisha	Warren	153rd	64/10	Irwin
Mosley, Laban	Morgan	Wrights	18/3	Early
Mosley, Thomas	Greene	Harvills	199/2	Appling
Mosley, Wm.(Orps)	Lincoln	Tatoms	195/10	Habersham
Moss, Abram	Elbert	Smiths	239/5	Appling
Moss, Beverly	Elbert	Smiths	210/5	Irwin
Moss, Danl.D.	Jefferson	Waldens	73/12	Hall
Moss, Duncan I.J.	Lincoln	Thompsons	116/12	Irwin
Moss, Ephraim	Elbert	Smiths	30/3	Habersham
Moss, Ephram	Elbert	Smiths	324/5	Irwin
Moss, Epps	Baldwin	Marshalls	265/6	Appling
Moss, John	Elbert	Smiths	247/11	Irwin
Moss, Michael	Jefferson	Fountains	35/6	Habersham
Moss, William	Franklin	Ashs	198/3	Appling
Moss, Willis	Oglethorpe	Waters	183/9	Early
Moss, Wm.	Clarke	Starns	35/4	Early
Mote, Simeon(R.S)	Jackson	Hamilton	353/6	Irwin
Mote, Vardy	Jackson	Hamiltons	375/12	Irwin
Motes, Ezekel	Warren	150th	330/8	Early
Motes, John	Camden	Longs	222/14	Early
Motley, Abram	Greene	Kimbroughs	62/4	Rabun
Motley, Robt.Sr.	Washington	Floyds	273/14	Early
Motley, Robt.Sr.	Washington	Floyds	285/5	Appling
Motley, William	Washington	Floyds	200/7	Early
Motley, Wilson(Orps)	Washington	Floyds	58/3	Walton
Mott, Ann(Wid)	Wilkinson	Brooks	317/20	Early
Mott, Drusella(Wid)	Jones	Rossers	175/1	Walton
Mott, James	Wilkinson	Brooks	310/2	Appling
Mott, Nathan Sr.	Washington	Cummins	169/8	Early
Moughon, Jesse	Jackson	Haggards	347/21	Early
Moughon, Wiley A.B.	Lincoln	Jones	233/2	Appling
Mouldon, Richard	Emanuel	49th	251/27	Early
Moulton, John	Warren	150th	178/9	Irwin
Moulton, John	Warren	150th	355/1	Early
Mounger, Lucy	Greene	143	240/7	Gwinnett
Mountain, John	Jefferson	Fleming	23/4	Early
Moutree, John(Orp)	Putnam	Buckners	63/26	Early
Moxley, Benjamin	Burke	71st	83/21	Early
Moxley, John	Burke	71st	138/7	Gwinnett
Moxley, Wm.Jr.	Burke	72	310/7	Appling
Moxly, Benj.	Burke	71st	49/8	Early
Moxly, Benjamin	Burke	71st	488/9	Irwin
Moxly, William	Burke	71st	5/5	Gwinnett
Moy, Furney	Scriven		80/6	Early
Moye, Duncan	Washington	Burneys	130/10	Irwin
Moye, George	Washington	Burneys	211/9	Appling
Moye, Wiley	Jones	Permenters	136/21	Early
Moyel, Thomas	Columbia	Burroughs	247/7	Appling
Mozingo, Lewis	Washington	Daniels	194/10	Habersham
Mozingo, Lewis	Washington	Daniels	257/11	Early
Mozo, Ann(Orp)	Glynn		159/15	Irwin
Mozo, James(Orp)	Glynn		159/15	Irwin
Mozo, Margaret(Orp)	Glynn		159/15	Irwin
Mozo, Martha(Orp)	Glynn		159/15	Irwin

NAME	COUNTY	MIL.DIST	LOT/SECT	DREW LAN
Muchum, Marcus	Jones	Chappels	55/3	Irwin
Mulder, Isaac	Oglethorpe	Wises	131/12	Habersha
Mulder, Isaac	Oglethorpe	Wises	70/6	Irwin
Mulkey, Greenberry(Orps)	Wilkes	Mattox	263/8	Irwin
Mulkey, Jane(Wid)	Wilkes	Mattox	271/17	Early
Mulkey, John E.	Franklin	Ahs	8/1	Irwin
Mulkey, John	Jones	Chappels	291/2	Appling
Mulkey, Littleberry	Wilkes	Willis	83/16	Early
Mulkey, Moses	Burke	Royals	159/6	Gwinnett
Mulkey, William	Franklin	Turks	13/12	Irwin
Mulkey, William	Franklin	Turks	152/4	Appling
Mullen, Hardy	Jones	Samuels	102/1	Appling
Mullen, Isaac	Jefferson	Lamps	347/7	Gwinnett
Mullen, Pleasant G.	Jones	Hansfords	240/7	Appling
Mullens, Green	Jefferson	Langstons	11/8	Early
Mullens, Green	Jefferson	Langstons	43/16	Early
Mullens, James	Jones	Seals	42/26	Early
Mullens, John	Jackson	Hamiltons Bt.	176/6	Gwinnett
Mullens, Robt.Sr.	Morgan	Wrights	282/8	Appling
Mullett, Abraham	Effingham		62/5	Irwin
Mullins, Burkley	Hancock	Herberts	204/17	Early
Mullins, Malone(R.S)	Hancock	Herberts	221/27	Early
Mullins, Malone	Hall		177/2	Appling
Mullins, Robt.Sr.	Morgan	Campbells	55/9	Irwin
Muncreif, Labun	Clarke	Otis	130/2	Walton
Muncrief, Thomas	Wilkes	Hollidays	225/3	Early
Muncrief, William	Greene	Carltons	418/5	Irwin
Munkus, Elijah	Jasper	Sentals	3/2	Irwin
Munn, Apollos	Chatham		250/4	Irwin
Munroe, Joseph	Burke	Lewis	332/9	Early
Munroe, Stephen	Burke	Spiveys	76/10	Irwin
Murdock, Joseph	Franklin	Haynes	234/11	Early
Murdock, Milas	Morgan	Dennis	87/2	Habersha
Murkerson, Wm.	Jones	Buckhalters	120/4	Walton
Murph, Jacob Sr.	Lincoln	Parks	82/13	Habersha
Murphey, Alexander	Franklin	J.Miller	178/28	Early
Murphey, Daniel	Hancock	Smiths	365/2	Early
Murphey, Daniel	Hancock	Smiths	472/2	Appling
Murphey, Edward	Richmond	Palmers	74/8	Hall
Murphey, Eliz.(Wid)	Wilkes	Kilgores	172/3	Walton
Murphey, John	Appling	5	24/5	Early
Murphey, John	Wilkinson	Kettles	229/4	Appling
Murphey, Nicholas	Richmond	Palmers	2/5	Appling
Murphey, Wm.(Orps)	Washington	Avents	76/16	Irwin
Murphree, James	Burke	Lewis	196/18	Early
Murphree, Josiah	Burke	Lewis	108/5	Appling
Murphree, Josiah	Burke	Lewis	145/1	Appling
Murphree, Wm.	Burke	Lewis	394/9	Early
Murphree, Wright	Burke	Lewis	367/8	Irwin
Murphy, Benj.	Oglethorpe	Wises	213/11	Irwin
Murphy, Daniel	Warren	151	119/15	Irwin
Murphy, Drury (RS)	Putnam	Bustins	133/5	Appling
Murphy, Drury	Baldwin	Marshalls	63/5	Irwin
Murphy, Hugh	Jefferson	Flemings	431/2	Appling
Murphy, John	Bryan	19	218/13	Irwin
Murphy, John	Franklin	J.Millers	491/3	Irwin
Murphy, John	Hancock	Canes	236/5	Appling
Murphy, John	Jefferson	Lamps	26/4	Walton
Murphy, John	Jefferson	Lamps	312/4	Early
Murphy, John	Wilkinson	Kettles	87/13	Irwin
Murphy, Lucy	Wilkes	Holidays	126/4	Irwin
Murphy, Mallicah	Burke	72	50/9	Hall
Murphy, Mary(Wid)	Twiggs	Ellis	318/7	Early
Murphy, Mastin	Jasper	Centells	393/7	Early
Murphy, Morris	Jefferson	Waldens	326/3	Appling
Murphy, Morris	Jefferson	Waldens	57/8	Appling
Murphy, Murdock	Liberty		8/28	Early

NAME	COUNTY	MIL.DIST	LOT/SECT	DREW LAND
Murphy, Nicholas	Richmond	Palmers	112/2	Early
Murphy, Paschal	Jasper	Clays	288/2	Appling
Murphy, William	Wilkes	Dents	334/1	Appling
Murphy, Wm.Jr.	Burke	72nd	75/28	Early
Murphy, Wright	Jones	Kings	161/7	Gwinnett
Murrah, Moses	Lincoln	Tatoms	151/21	Early
Murray, Alexander	Oglethorpe	Murrys	124/4	Irwin
Murray, David S.	Lincoln	Tatoms	252/13	Early
Murray, Henry	Burke	Hands	53/13	Early
Murray, James	Burke	Hands	51/11	Irwin
Murray, James	Lincoln	Tatoms	44/16	Early
Murray, John Sr.	Burke	Hands	468/8	Appling
Murray, John	Madison	Orrs	68/12	Early
Murray, John	Richmond	Laceys	246/3	Irwin
Murray, Joseph	Warren	151st	3/11	Early
Murray, Stephen	Burke	Hands	60/7	Gwinnett
Murray, Thomas J.	Richmond	122	128/5	Appling
Murray, Thomas W.	Lincoln	Tatoms	300/15	Early
Murray, Thomas W.	Lincoln	Tatoms	49/14	Irwin
Murray, William(Orps)	Twiggs	Evans	75/11	Irwin
Murrell, Thos.W.	Columbia	Gartrells	161/27	Early
Murren, Eliz.(Orph)	Richmond	398	254/13	Irwin
Murren, Margaret(Orph)	Richmond	398	254/13	Irwin
Murren, Reed(Orph)	Richmond	398	254/13	Irwin
Murrow, John	Madison	Millicans	67/1	Early
Murrow, Valentine	Madison	Willifords	169/7	Irwin
Murry, James	Burke	Hands	25/10	Early
Murry, James	Greene	Macons	349/8	Irwin
Murry, John Jr.	Burke	Hands	325/13	Early
Muselwhite, W.	Baldwin	Marshalls	12/1	Appling
Musgrove, John E.	Jefferson	Matathews	388/2	Early
Musgrove, John(Orps)	Wilkes	Holidays	150/9	Appling
Musgrove, Robert H.	Richmond	120th	206/1	Irwin
Musgrove, Willis	Pulaski	Maddox	128/2	Appling
Musgroves, Larkin C.	Warren	150th	404/26	Early
Musick, Major	Jefferson	Bothwells	356/1	Appling
Muze, Daniel	Putnam	Morelands	294/1	Early
Myars, Margaret(Wid)	Morgan	Farrars	362/6	Irwin
Myatt, Walton	Elbert	Ruckers	58/8	Irwin
Myatt, William	Richmond		60/10	Irwin
Myers, George	Greene	141	267/4	Walton
Myers, Mordecai	Chatham		165/1	Early
Myers, Thomas C.	Greene	141st	108/9	Appling
Myhand, Barshaba(Wid)	Morgan	Hubbards	17/10	Early
Myhand, James Sr.(RS)	Morgan	Campbells	80/4	Irwin
Myhand, Thomas	Warren	Guies	40/18	Early
Myhands, John(Orps)	Morgan	Campbells	33/5	Appling
Myres, Burwell	Jones	Wallers	306/12	Irwin
Myres, Eliz.	Greene	141	223/27	Early
Myres, Henry	McIntosh	Goulds	265/9	Irwin
Myres, James	Glynn		23/10	Hall
Myres, Tobias	Chatham		378/27	Early
Myric, John	Chatham		153/10	Habersham
Myrick, Evans	Jones	Samuels	249/9	Early
Myrick, Evans	Jones	Samuels	32/3	Irwin
Myrick, Goodwin	Baldwin	Haws	173/8	Hall
Myrick, Howell	Warren	Blounts	46/1	Walton
Myrick, James	Baldwin	Cousins	370/27	Early
Myrick, John	Baldwin	Cousins	337/27	Early
Myrick, John	Baldwin	Cousins	49/28	Early
Myrick, John	Warren	Blounts	326/20	Early
Myrick, John	Warren	Blounts	33/15	Early
Myrick, Matthew H.	Warren	Blounts	320/26	Early
Myrick, Nathaniel T.	Warren	Blounts	103/26	Early
Myrick, Richard	Warren	154	169/6	Gwinnett
Myrick, Richard	Warren	154th	109/9	Irwin
Myrick, Robert	Oglethorpe	Myricks	146/5	Irwin

NAME	COUNTY	MIL.DIST	LOT/SECT	DREW LAND
Myrick, Robert	Oglethorpe	Myricks	460/8	Irwin
Myrick, Winnefred(Wid)	Wilkinson	Smith	167/18	Early
Nail, John	Putnam	Parkers	299/6	Appling
Nail, Maurice	Tatnall	Cunyers	343/9	Early
Naish, John(RS)	Elbert	Olivers	164/2	Appling
Nally, Cleon	Richmond	Laceys	35/23	Early
Napier, Shelton	Putnam	Ectors	145/16	Early
Napier, Thomas	Putnam	Ectors	99/10	Early
Nappier, John	Wilkinson	Kettles	242/18	Early
Nappier, John	Wilkinson	Kettles	323/28	Early
Nash, Henry E.	Elbert	Tatoms	354/4	Appling
Nash, James	Montgomery	McElvin	49/3	Appling
Nash, John	Columbia	Watsons	122/13	Early
Nash, John	Columbia	Watsons	184/5	Gwinnett
Nash, Pamela(Orph)	Richmond	Laceys	256/8	Irwin
Nash, Wm.	Jones	Buckhalter	230/2	Early
Naull, Nathan	Clark	Pentecost	354/18	Early
Naull, Peggy(Wid)	Clark	Pentecosts	380/20	Early
Navey, Wilson	Burke	McNorrils	81/12	Habersha
Neal, Alexander	Franklin	Davis	80/27	Early
Neal, Harvill	Warren	153	198/6	Appling
Neal, James Sr.	Warren	153	17/8	Irwin
Neal, Joel	Warren	Blounts	367/1	Early
Neal, John Sr.	Warren	153	237/13	Early
Neal, Jonathan	Jones	Wallers	32/4	Early
Neal, Lydia(Wid)	Jones	Griffiths	292/16	Early
Neal, Robert(Orps)	Franklin	Ashs	44/1	Habersha
Neal, Thomas Sr.	Warren	153	80/13	Habersha
Neal, William	Putnam	Oslins	266/28	Early
Nealing, Mary(Wid)	Washington	Renfroes	413/12	Irwin
Neall, Joyce	Putnam	Oslins	25/17	Early
Neally, John (RS)	Morgan	Campbells	150/2	Rabun
Neaves, Wm(RS)	Putnam	Littles	258/20	Early
Neaves, Wm.(RS)	Putnam	Littles	291/6	Early
Needham, Jane(Wid)	Jones	Buckhalter	221/2	Appling
Neel, Elias	Emanuel	53rd	165/6	Gwinnett
Neel, Hezekiah(Orps)	Emanuel	53rd	140/11	Hall
Neel, Jonathan	Emanuel	53rd	57/2	Habersha
Neel, Mary(Wid)	Emanuel	53rd	463/10	Irwin
Neel, Reubin	Emanuel	59th	488/7	Appling
Neel, Thomas	Hancock	Dannels	70/11	Early
Neeland, John(Orps)	Columbia	Dodsons	122/114	Early
Neely, Eliz.(Orph)	Camden	Baileys	345/26	Early
Neely, Geo.(Orph)	Camden	Baileys	345/26	Early
Neely, Mariah(Orph)	Camden	Baileys	345/26	Early
Neely, Samuel W.(Orp)	Camden	Baileys	345/26	Early
Neidlinger, Hannah(Wid)	Effingham		27/15	Irwin
Neighbors, Elizabeth	Burke	Dys	34/17	Early
Neil, Eliz.(Orph)	Richmond	Winters	184/11	Irwin
Neil, Hammon	Montgomery	Alstons	271/13	Irwin
Neil, James T.	Jefferson	Bothwells	313/12	Irwin
Neil, John	Emanuel	53rd	222/20	Early
Neines, Sarah(Wid)	Laurens	Watsons	295/6	Gwinnett
Neise, George Jr.	Effingham		191/1	Appling
Nelmes, David	Franklin	Attaways	92/4	Habersha
Nelmes, Jesse	Franklin	Attaways	190/3	Early
Nelms, Clinous	Greene	Nelms	219/17	Early
Nelms, John	Elbert	B.Higginbotham	337/3	Appling
Nelms, Samuel H.	Greene	Nelms	425/9	Irwin
Nelms, Samuel H.	Greene	Nelms	93/4	Early
Nelms, Thomas	Greene	Fosters	193/28	Early
Nelms, Thomas	Greene	Fosters	74/7	Gwinnett
Nelson, Ambrose	Wilkinson	Howards	30/9	Hall
Nelson, Archibald	Jackson	Hamiltons Bt.	241/3	Appling
Nelson, Archibald	Jackson	Hamiltons	322/12	Irwin
Nelson, Christian	Hancock	Canes	526/8	Irwin
Nelson, David	Chatham		514/7	Irwin

NAME	COUNTY	MIL.DIST	LOT/SECT	DREW LAND
Nelson, David	Chatham		90/10	Early
Nelson, Eliz.(Wid)	Pulaski	Johnstons	82/1	Walton
Nelson, George W.	Hancock	Champions	307/14	Early
Nelson, James	Laurens	Harris	111/15	Irwin
Nelson, Jeremiah(RS)	Hancock	Lucas	323/20	Early
Nelson, Jeremiah(RS)	Hancock	Lucas	504/13	Irwin
Nelson, Jessee	Columbia	Watsons	108/12	Early
Nelson, John	Franklin	P.Browns	106/3	Habersham
Nelson, Levy	Laurens	Kinchens	78/9	Appling
Nelson, Lydia	Franklin	P.Browns	406/1	Appling
Nelson, Mary	Burke	Dys	383/7	Early
Nelson, Moses	Jackson	Dicksons Bt.	294/5	Appling
Nelson, Nicholas	Early		50/6	Irwin
Nelson, Peter	Washington	Barges	473/6	Irwin
Nelson, Thomas	Wilkinson	Howards	352/8	Appling
Nelson, Thomas	Wilkinson	Howards	73/8	Early
Nelson, Thos.(Orps)	Wilkinson	Howards	388/6	Early
Nelson, William	Morgan	Paces	22/8	Early
Nesbett, Patience(Wid)	Greene	Kimbroughs	355/12	Irwin
Nesbitt, Hugh	Richmond	398th	132/28	Early
Nesler, Thomas	Chatham		388/4	Early
Nesmith, James Jr.	Bullock	Jones	415/6	Appling
Nessmith, James Sr.	Bullock	Jones	201/5	Irwin
Nessmith, James Sr.	Bullock	Jones	203/16	Early
Nessmith, John	Bullock	Jones	376/3	Early
Neves, Wm.(RS)	Putnam	Littles	367/5	Early
New, Henry	Madison	Willifords	133/15	Irwin
New, Jesse	Jackson	Winters	2/2	Habersham
New, Joel	Madison	Willifords	114/28	Early
Newberry, James	Jones	Buckhalter	388/8	Early
Newberry, Levi Sr.	Columbia	Dodson	166/9	Hall
Newberry, Thomas	Columbia	Dodsons	323/9	Early
Newberry, Thomas	Columbia	Dodsons	61/5	Gwinnett
Newberry, Wm.(Orps)	Jones	Phillips	208/5	Irwin
Newburn, John	Laurens	Jones	4/9	Appling
Newburn, Mary	Madison	Bones	226/10	Early
Newburn, Thomas	Laurens	Jones	17/4	Irwin
Newby, John	Jasper	Centells	157/9	Irwin
Newell, Catharine	Greene	141st	164/13	Habersham
Newell, James(Orps)	Greene	141st	192/12	Early
Newell, Thomas M.	Chatham		255/4	Irwin
Newly, Jesse Jr.	Jones	Griffiths	66/2	Rabun
Newman, Elwell	Washington	Pools	99/13	Irwin
Newman, Garrett	Wilkes	Brooks	171/5	Gwinnett
Newman, Garrett	Wilkes	Brooks	616/2	Appling
Newman, James A.(Orpn)	Laurens	Kinchens	430/7	Irwin
Newman, James	Richmond	Palmers	455/10	Irwin
Newman, Lemuel	Jasper	Bartlets	279/8	Irwin
Newman, Samuel	Warren	153	175/6	Irwin
Newman, Thomas B.	Columbia	Shaws	469/6	Irwin
Newman, Thomas	Tatnall	Overstreets	157/8	Appling
Newman, Thos.	Tatnall	Overstreets	82/11	Hall
Newman, Willis Sr.	Tatnall	J.Durrences	405/1	Appling
Newman, Willis	Bullock	Everetts	158/27	Early
Newman, Willis	Tatnall	J.Durrences	92/5	Appling
Newmon, Samuel	Warren	153	55/16	Irwin
Newris, Daniel	Camden	Clarks	196/4	Appling
Newsom, Batts	Pulaski	Bryans	62/3	Early
Newsom, Crawford	Warren	150	15/21	Early
Newsom, Crawford	Warren	150	63/9	Hall
Newsom, Henry	Warren	150th	177/5	Irwin
Newsom, James	Greene	Tuggles	151/12	Irwin
Newsom, Joel D.	Hancock	Evans	89/1	Appling
Newsom, Joel Jr.	Hancock	Champions	374/5	Early
Newsom, John	Putnam	Coopers	143/6	Appling
Newsom, Kinchen	Washington	Renfroes	82/11	Irwin
Newsom, Rhoda(Wid)	Warren	150th	214/4	Early

NAME	COUNTY	MIL.DIST	LOT/SECT	DREW LAND
Newsome, Amos	Columbia	Shaws	364/2	Early
Newsome, Asa	Warren	150	218/9	Irwin
Newsome, Green	Warren	150	289/10	Irwin
Newsome, James	Warren	153	232/2	Irwin
Newsome, John	Putnam	Coopers	320/6	Appling
Newsome, John	Warren	153	49/15	Irwin
Newsome, Robert	Greene	140	36/16	Irwin
Newsome, Solomon(Orps)	Warren	150	235/5	Appling
Newsome, Wm.	Columbia	Shaws	28/6	Irwin
Newson, Lucy(Wid)	Wilkinson	Bowings	479/5	Appling
Newton, Ann	Scriven		161/9	Hall
Newton, Aristarchus	Jasper	Haws	30/5	Gwinnett
Newton, Ebenezer	Clark	Applings	94/8	Early
Newton, Elisure L.	Clark	Applings	41/12	Hall
Newton, Geo.& Wm.(Orps)	Richmond	120	420/15	Early
Newton, James	Jasper	Baileys	17/1	Appling
Newton, Samuel	Scriven		254/15	Early
Neyland, Charlotte	Burke	Bells	160/6	Appling
Neyland, Gilbert(Orps)	Burke	Bells	134/5	Gwinnett
Neyle, Sampson	Chatham		285/6	Gwinnett
Nibblett, Edmund	Jones	Greens	293/7	Early
Niblack, Thomas	Jackson	Rogers Bt.	298/8	Early
Niblet, Abel	Jasper	Bentleys	170/1	Irwin
Nicelier, Hugh	Clark	Applings	46/3	Appling
Nichalson, John	Greene	Harvills	280/2	Appling
Nichoeles, Isaac	Pulaski	Rees	296/6	Irwin
Nichol, Joseph(Orps)	Putnam	H.Kendrick	355/17	Early
Nicholas, James	Wilkes	Bryants	113/28	Early
Nichols, Archibald	Jackson	Hamiltons Bt.	370/7	Gwinnett
Nichols, David B.	Chatham		106/11	Habersham
Nichols, David B.	Chatham		160/12	Irwin
Nichols, David D.	Wilkinson	Brooks	119/11	Habersham
Nichols, David	Burke	Bells	235/14	Early
Nichols, George	Warren	153	339/13	Irwin
Nichols, Jarvis	Jasper	Easts	36/5	Early
Nichols, Jefferson	Early		134/1	Appling
Nichols, John	Jackson	Hamiltons Bt.	19/10	Early
Nichols, John	Jasper	Phillips	162/3	Appling
Nichols, Theophilus	Chatham		190/6	Appling
Nichols, Thomas	Burke	72nd	73/4	Appling
Nichols, Timothy(Orph)	Richmond	398	517/5	Irwin
Nichols, William	Washington	Brooks	216/6	Irwin
Nichols, Wm.Sr.	Jones	Wallers	131/16	Irwin
Nicholson, Brittain	Walton	Wests	40/13	Early
Nicholson, George	Oglethorpe	Murrays	49/6	Appling
Nicholson, John	Greene	Harvills	498/5	Irwin
Nicholson, John	Wilkinson	Wiggins	27/2	Early
Nicholson, Margaret	Greene	143	311/10	Early
Nicholson, Nathaniel	Wilkinson	Wiggins	53/12	Early
Nicholson, Saml.(Orps)	Greene	143rd	68/5	Early
Nick, John(Orps)	Washington	Renfroes	23/2	Habersham
Nicks, Darling	Franklin	Sheumates	122/13	Irwin
Nicks, John	Franklin	Akins	236/8	Early
Nicks, William	Franklin	Akins	46/16	Early
Nicks, William	Franklin	Akins	7/6	Early
Nicols, Thomas	Jackson	Hamiltons Bt.	107/5	Irwin
Nicolson, John	Greene	Harvills	50/11	Irwin
Niel, John	Jones	Griffiths	179/1	Walton
Night, Bethany(Wid)	Emanuel	57	196/7	Gwinnett
Night, Westly	Burke	72nd	247/4	Walton
Nipper, Abraham	Pulaski	Lanears	235/26	Early
Nipper, John	Pulaski	Lanears	46/3	Rabun
Nisbitt, John	Wilkes	Perrys	139/7	Early
Nix, Anderson	Madison	Willifords	242/6	Gwinnett
Nix, Benjamin	Burke	70th	137/8	Appling
Nix, Edward	Oglethorpe	Davenports	280/1	Walton
Nix, Elijah	Twiggs	Hodges	133/7	Irwin

NAME	COUNTY	MIL.DIST	LOT/SECT	DREW LAND
Nix, James	Franklin	Harris	121/2	Rabun
Nix, Jeremiah	Elbert	R.Christian	371/16	Early
Nix, Jeremiah	Elbert	R.Christians	299/9	Appling
Nix, John Sr.	Twiggs	Ellis	103/3	Rabun
Nix, Jonas	Franklin	Akins	349/18	Early
Nix, Jonathan	Elbert	R.Christians	87/21	Early
Nix, Thomas	Elbert	R.Christians	158/8	Appling
Nix, William	Twiggs	Ellis	429/5	Irwin
Nix, Williamson	Elbert	R.Christians	121/5	Gwinnett
Nixon, Allen	Oglethorpe	Dunns	175/11	Hall
Nixon, Henry	Franklin	Haynes	204/27	Early
Nixon, Henry	Franklin	Haynes	277/16	Early
Nixon, Honor(Wid)	Wilkinson	Kettles	183/2	Rabun
Nixon, Joseph	Oglethorpe	Murrays	153/2	Early
Noble, Hezekiah(Orps)	Wilkinson	Childs	152/12	Irwin
Noble, Samuel	Pulaski	Johnstons	395/27	Early
Nobles, Eliz.(Wid)	Wilkinson	Childs	92/3	Habersham
Nobles, Lewis S.	McIntosh	Hamiltons	40/11	Habersham
Nobles, Robert	Pulaski	Rees	177/1	Walton
Nobles, Robert	Pulaski	Rees	470/5	Irwin
Nobles, William	Twiggs	R.Belchers	384/6	Irwin
Nobles, William	Twiggs	R.Belchers	64/5	Early
Noell, Beverley	Oglethorpe	Lees	182/13	Irwin
Noell, James	Oglethorpe	Lees	67/3	Rabun
Noell, Thomas	Oglethorpe	Lees	341/6	Early
Nolan, William	Elbert	Olivers	25/13	Early
Nolan, William	Jasper	Bartletts	170/10	Habersham
Noland, Awbry	Morgan	Townsend	63/16	Irwin
Noland, Geo.(Insane)	Morgan	Townsend	63/16	Irwin
Noland, James	Twiggs	Barrows	115/11	Habersham
Noland, John	Twiggs	Evans	132/17	Early
Noland, John	Twiggs	Evans	307/17	Early
Noles, Dencee M.	Jasper	Bentleys	111/17	Early
Nongasen, Daniel	Chatham		139/3	Walton
Nongaser, Georgiana	Chatham		433/9	Irwin
Norman, Argyle	Wilkes	Russels	185/16	Irwin
Norman, Arlaxerxes B.	Tatnall	Keans	420/5	Irwin
Norman, Elijah B.	Wilkes	Russels	277/9	Irwin
Norman, Eliz.(Orph)	Columbia	Burroughs	116/1	Appling
Norman, Elizabeth	Wilkes	Burks	230/4	Irwin
Norman, Esther	Bullock	Jones	56/15	Irwin
Norman, George	Lincoln	Thompsons	274/5	Appling
Norman, Isabella	Wilkes	Burks	29/11	Hall
Norman, John Sr.	Wilkes	Russels	311/20	Early
Norman, Joseph	Liberty		89/20	Early
Norman, Sherwood	Baldwin	Milledgeville	32/5	Rabun
Norman, Talison	Wilkes	Russels	262/15	Early
Norman, William	Lincoln	Stokes	37/5	Gwinnett
Norman, William	Wilkes	Brooks	72/16	Irwin
Normon, James	Twiggs	Evans	299/11	Early
Norris, Abner	Warren	153	36/11	Habersham
Norris, Abner	Warren	153	79/3	Habersham
Norris, Alexander	Wilkes	Mattox	34/12	Habersham
Norris, Benjamin	Lincoln	Parks	134/9	Irwin
Norris, Elisha	Jackson	Dicksons Bt.	294/27	Early
Norris, Eliz.	Chatham		75/2	Walton
Norris, Evans	Jasper	Eastes	17/17	Early
Norris, Green	Twiggs	Barrows	52/4	Rabun
Norris, Green	Warren	153	114/4	Early
Norris, Isaac	Emanuel	55th	5/9	Appling
Norris, James Jr.	Warren	153	253/23	Early
Norris, Jethro	Lincoln	Parks	364/7	Appling
Norris, Joel	Warren	153	151/7	Gwinnett
Norris, John	Putnam	Slaughters	170/11	Early
Norris, Mathew	Wilkinson	Brooks	67/16	Early
Norris, Samuel S.	Jasper	Blakes	159/13	Early
Norris, Samuel S.	Jasper	Blakes	369/16	Early

NAME	COUNTY	MIL.DIST	LOT/SECT	DREW LAN
Norris, Stephen	Putnam	Stampers	210/1	Irwin
Norris, Stephen	Putnam	Stampers	304/7	Early
Norris, William	Jasper	Eastes	286/7	Gwinnet⬛
Norris, Wm.C.	Burke	Royals	482/8	Appling
Norriss, Needham	Jasper	Evans	473/4	Appling
Norriss, Sarah	Morgan	Hubbards	386/8	Appling
Norsworthy, Henry	Twiggs	Evans	491/13	Irwin
North, Anthony	Oglethorpe	Rowlands	199/4	Irwin
North, John	Richmond	398th	184/3	Irwin
North, Robert	Oglethorpe	Rowlands	127/1	Irwin
North, Robert	Oglethorpe	Rowlands	21/9	Early
North, Sarah(Wid)	Jefferson	Abbotts	199/3	Walton
Northcut, Robert	Laurens	S.Smiths	337/6	Gwinnet⬛
Northen, Margaret(Wid)	Jones	Harrist	119/13	Habersh⬛
Northen, William	Jones	Harrist	44/7	Appling
Northern, John	Elbert	Webbs	283/21	Early
Northern, Peter	Jones	Harrist	27/1	Habersh⬛
Northern, Samuel	Putnam	Slaughters	363/4	Appling
Norton, Cylas M.	Clark	Mitchells	397/15	Early
Norton, Elias	Clark	Pentecosts	397/27	Early
Norton, Elisha	Clark	Pentecost	106/1	Walton
Norton, James	Oglethorpe	Brittons	205/28	Early
Norton, John (RS)	Clark	Pentecosts	356/11	Irwin
Norton, John	Clark	Pentecost	77/4	Habersh⬛
Norton, Nathan	Camden	Baileys	261/17	Early
Norton, Nathan	Camden	Baileys	65/16	Irwin
Norton, Thomas	Clark	Pentecosts	59/21	Early
Norton, William	Oglethorpe	Waters	130/18	Early
Norwood, Blakeley	Franklin	Haynes	16/8	Early
Norwood, Blakeley	Franklin	Haynes	42/2	Early
Norwood, Geo.(RS)	Morgan	Farrars	177/3	Habersh⬛
Norwood, George	Pulaski	Maddox	141/9	Appling
Norwood, George	Pulaski	Maddox	257/8	Appling
Norwood, John(Orps)	Wilkinson	Lees	273/18	Early
Norwood, William	Wilkinson	Lees	393/18	Early
Nothen, Wm.(Orps)	Jones	Harrist	336/19	Early
Nottage, Thomas	Chatham		24/3	Habersh⬛
Notts, Nathaniel	Jones	Buckhalater	188/4	Irwin
Nouls, Sarah(Orph)	Franklin	Aikins	376/13	Early
Nowlan, Anthony	Wilkes	McLandons	231/5	Gwinnett
Nowlan, Joseph	Wilkes	McClendons	66/7	Irwin
Nowland, Ann(Wid)	Chatham		298/10	Early
Noyon, Peter	Chatham		92/4	Irwin
Num, Eli	Wilkinson	Lees	298/17	Early
Nunn, Edmond	Twiggs	Barron	429/7	Irwin
Nunn, Joshua(Orps)	Burke	J.Ward	260/16	Early
Nunnele, Simeon	Elbert	Childres	113/6	Early
Nunnelee, Benj.F.	Elbert	Tatoms	280/12	Early
Nunnelee, John	Elbert	Childres	128/10	Hall
Nunnelee, Orsmon F.	Elbert	Childers	184/19	Early
Nunnelee, Willis	Elbert	Childres	37/3	Walton
Nunnelle, James F.	Elbert	Childres	508/8	Irwin
Nunnelly, Horatio	Greene	Nelms	263/7	Appling
Nunnelly, Israel	Greene	Nelms	254/9	Appling
Nunnelly, Israel	Greene	Nelms	61/3	Walton
Nunnelly, Joseah	Oglethorpe	Lees	524/5	Appling
Nunnelly, Willis	Elbert	Childres	318/1	Walton
Nutt, Andrew Sr.	Morgan	Campbells	324/11	Irwin
Nutt, John M.	Clark	Pentecosts	410/7	Appling
Nutt, Matthew	Laurens	Jones	291//4	Early
Nutt, Samuel Jr.	Morgan	Campbells	357/7	Appling
Nutt, William B.	Clark	Pentecost	366/1	Early
Oakes, Jane	Madison	Bones	427/15	Early
Oates, James	Clark	Oates	123/18	Early
Obaions, Elijah(Orps)	Jones	Hurst	303/2	Early
Obannon, John	Wilkinson	Howards	203/6	Gwinnett
Obear, John(Orps)	Washington	Floyds	88/2	Irwin

NAME	COUNTY	MIL.DIST	LOT/SECT	DREW LAND
Oberry, Reuben	McIntosh	Eigles	176/2	Habersham
Oberry, Reuben	McIntosh	Eigles	198/11	Early
Obryant, John	Oglethorpe	Myricks	372/10	Early
Oconner, Arthur	Chatham		419/11	Irwin
Oden, Alexander	Jones	Greens	104/3	Irwin
Odena, Peter	McIntosh	Hamiltons	269/6	Early
Odiam, Archibald	Emanuel	56	120/20	Early
Odian, Archibald	Emanuel	56th	276/15	Early
Odom, Archibald	Pulaski	Maddox's	217/10	Irwin
Odom, Archibald	Pulaski	Maddox's	415/8	Irwin
Odom, Halathia(Orps)	Jones	Wallers	113/11	Irwin
Odom, Honor	Morgan	Selmons	350/6	Irwin
Odom, Jacob Sr.	Washington	Wimberlys	55/6	Appling
Odom, Jesse(Orps)	Bullock	Jones	56/8	Irwin
Odom, John W.	Washington	Wimberlys	420/3	Appling
Odom, John	Washington	Wimberly	260/1	Appling
Odom, John	Washington	Wimberlys	333/5	Early
Odom, Moses	Pulaski	Rees	94/6	Irwin
Odom, Susannah	Burke	71	338/2	Early
Odum, Henry	Burke	McNorrills	109/2	Habersham
Offutt, Jesse	Columbia	Olives	79/16	Early
Ogborn, Jacob	Wilkinson	Lees	135/6	Gwinnett
Ogburn, Littleberry	Wilkinson	Lees	406/6	Irwin
Ogden, Solomon(RS)	Baldwin	Irwins	95/13	Early
Ogilby, Richard	Oglethorpe	Murrays	105/1	Irwin
Ogle, Jessee	Morgan	Paces	444/6	Irwin
Ogle, John	Morgan	Selmans	28/8	Early
Oglesbey, Drury	Elbert	R.Christians	5/1	Rabun
Oglesbey, Drury	Elbert	R.Christians	506/5	Appling
Oglesbey, George	Elbert	R.Christians	431/5	Appling
Oglesby, Daniel	Tatnall	Johnsons	146/1	Appling
Oglesby, Elihu	Liberty		85/19	Early
Oglesby, James	Emanuel	49	108/6	Early
Oglesby, Leroy	Elbert	P.Christians	43/5	Rabun
Oglesby, Robt.C.	Elbert	Penns	439/12	Irwin
Oglesby, Thomas	Elbert	R.Christian	265/5	Appling
Oglesby, Thomas	Madison	Willifords	224/1	Walton
Oglesby, Thomas	Madison	Willifords	38/13	Early
Ogletree, David	Wilkes	Ogletrees	97/20	Early
Ogletree, John B.	Morgan	Leonards	54/5	Appling
Ogletree, Littleton	Greene	Nelms	234/8	Early
Ogletree, Phillamon	Wilkes	Mattox	44/1	Rabun
Ogletree, Richard	Hancock	Thomas	151/8	Habersham
Oguin, Daniel	Washington	Peabodys	275/4	Appling
Okelley, Thomas D.	Madison	Orrs	94/11	Early
Okelly, Charles D.	Oglethorpe	Bridges	73/13	Irwin
Okelly, Francis D.	Oglethorpe	Lees	67/1	Rabun
Okelly, James	Oglethorpe	Bridges	135/10	Early
Okelly, James	Oglethorpe	Bridges	193/7	Early
Okelly, Thomas	Oglethorpe	Lees	317/7	Early
Oliff, John	Bullock	Edwards	550/2	Appling
Oliff, Joseph	Bullock	Edwards	145/12	Hall
Oliphant, Aaron	Hancock	Sharps	98/1	Appling
Olive, Bud	Columbia	O.Morris	42/18	Early
Olive, Bud	Columbia	O.Morriss	12/15	Irwin
Olive, James	Columbia	O.Morriss	127/9	Early
Olive, James	Elbert	B.Higginbotham	474/7	Irwin
Olive, William	Emanuel	58th	38/3	Early
Olive, William	Emanuel	58th	398/7	Early
Oliver, Caleb	Elbert	Ruchers	190/12	Early
Oliver, Dionitious(Orps)	Elbert	Penns	1/13	Habersham
Oliver, Dionysius	Elbert	Olivers	219/21	Early
Oliver, Dionysius	Elbert	Olivers	465/8	Irwin
Oliver, Elijah	Jackson	Rogers Bt.	288/17	Early
Oliver, Elijah	Jackson	Rogers Bt.	348/7	Appling
Oliver, Elijah	Scriven	Smiths	179/6	Irwin
Oliver, Eliz.(Wid)	Jones	Shropshiers	34/1	Irwin

NAME	COUNTY	MIL.DIST	LOT/SECT	DREW LAND
Oliver, James L.	Richmond	398th	47/2	Irwin
Oliver, James V.	Warren	154th	140/9	Early
Oliver, James	McIntosh	Hamiltons	3/10	Early
Oliver, James	McIntosh	Hamiltons	434/7	Appling
Oliver, James	Scriven	Smiths	452/2	Appling
Oliver, John G.	Emanuel	56 Dist.	211/20	Early
Oliver, John(Orps)	Scriven	Smiths	610/2	Appling
Oliver, John	Jones	Buckhalters	394/17	Early
Oliver, John	Jones	Buckhalters	5/3	Early
Oliver, Joseph	Laurens	D.Smiths	58/4	Rabun
Oliver, Moses	Scriven	Moodys	52/14	Irwin
Oliver, Risdon	Laurens	D.Smiths	474/3	Appling
Oliver, Samuel C.	Elbert	Olivers	492/6	Irwin
Oliver, Shelton	Elbert	R.Christian	177/14	Early
Oliver, Simeon	Elbert	Whites	278/10	Early
Oliver, Stephen H.	Richmond	398th	12/6	Gwinnett
Oliver, Terry	Warren	154th	276/19	Early
Oliver, Thomas	Elbert	Gaines	386/5	Appling
Oliver, Thomas	Washington	Jinkinsons	239/10	Irwin
Oliver, Wm.H.	Jones	Buckhalters	285/18	Early
Ollephant, Aaron	Hancock	Sharps	23/7	Early
Olliff, Benjamin	Wilkinson	Brooks	99/20	Early
Onail, Edmund	Putnam	Morlands	278/14	Early
Onail, James	Morgan	Parkers	13/22	Early
Onail, James	Morgan	Parkers	64/27	Early
Oneal, Daniel	Twiggs	R.Belchers	330/20	Early
Oneal, David	Columbia	Willinghams	24/3	Appling
Oneal, Griffin	Warren	154th	59/2	Habersham
Oneal, Harrison	Greene	Nelms	35/9	Irwin
Oneal, James	Morgan	Walkers	515/11	Irwin
Oneal, John	Jackson	Rogers Bt.	322/21	Early
Oneal, Nathan	Bullock	Knights	86/7	Appling
Oneal, Quinny	Greene	Nelms	66/8	Irwin
Oneal, Samuel(Orps)	Washington	Barges	424/8	Irwin
Oneal, Thomas	McIntosh	Hamiltons	381/6	Appling
Oneal, William(Orps)	Columbia	Willinghams	43/26	Early
Onnsel, Daniel	Burke	Betts	241/9	Appling
Ooten, John	Franklin	Akins	260/5	Irwin
Opray, Joseph	Twiggs	Bozemans	57/9	Appling
Oquin, Briant	Washington	Peabodys	148/1	Appling
Oquin, David	Laurens	Kinchens	295/2	Early
Oquin, John Jr.	Washington	Peabodys	28/11	Irwin
Oquin, John Sr.	Washington	Peabodys	72/14	Irwin
Orear, John	Hancock	Danells	280/16	Early
Orear, John	Hancock	Danells	297/17	Early
Orear, Josiah	Hancock	Danells	163/12	Irwin
Orear, Sarah(Wid)	Morgan	Wrights	280/6	Early
Orm, John	McIntosh	Jenkins	123/16	Irwin
Orme, Richard M.	Baldwin	Marshals	483/2	Appling
Orr, Burrell	Madison	Orrs	155/2	Walton
Orr, Jacob	Wilkes	Josseys	157/26	Early
Orr, Jane(Wid)	Washington	Barges	146/13	Irwin
Orr, John	McIntosh	Jinkins	229/18	Early
Orr, John	Washington	Barges	169/1	Irwin
Orr, Mary(Wid)	Richmond	398	247/2	Irwin
Orr, Matthew	Madison	Orrs	25/28	Early
Orr, Phillip	Wilkes	Josseys	193/3	Early
Orr, Phillip	Wilkes	Josseys	202/1	Walton
Orr, Robert	Clark	Applings	313/14	Early
Orr, Watkins	Wilkes	Brooks	473/7	Irwin
Orvis, Susan J.	Jasper	Clays	160/27	Early
Osborn, Aaron	Warren	152nd	180/8	Irwin
Osborn, David	Jackson	Hamiltons Bt.	180/3	Early
Osborn, David	Jackson	Hamiltons Bt.	78/6	Early
Osborn, Jesse	Jackson	Rogers Bt.	144/10	Irwin
Osborn, John Jr.	Jackson	Rogers Bt.	237/1	Appling
Osborn, John	Clark	Mitchells	64/21	Early

NAME	COUNTY	MIL.DIST	LOT/SECT	DREW LAND
Osborne, Ann(Wid)	Chatham		155/9	Irwin
Osborne, James G.H.	Chatham		420/9	Irwin
Osborne, James	Jasper	Posts	90/22	Early
Osborne, John	Hancock	Millers	252/9	Appling
Osborne, Joseph(Orph)	Chatham		15/16	Early
Osborne, Wm.C.	Jones	Jeffersons	273/6	Appling
Osburn, Jessee	Jackson	Rogers Bt.	28/3	Early
Osburn, John Sr.	Jackson	Rogers Bt.	367/28	Early
Osburn, John	Jasper	Kendalls	69/4	Early
Osley, Jesse	Elbert	Childres	164/6	Irwin
Oslin, John	Greene	Amers	433/13	Irwin
Oslin, William W.	Putnam	J.Kendricks	247/20	Early
Oslin, William W.	Putnam	J.Kindricks	160/1	Irwin
Osling, Jesse	Greene	Whelis	12/5	Early
Osling, Jesse	Greene	Whelis	310/18	Early
Osteen, Ezekiel(Orpn)	Camden	32	92/17	Early
Osteen, Jessee	Jefferson	Lamps	20/15	Early
Osteen, John	Appling	8th Dist	507/12	Irwin
Osteen, Leah(Wid)	Camden	32nd	110/21	Early
Osteen, Solomon	Camden	33	164/17	Early
Osteen, Solomon	Camden	33	46/11	Irwin
Osteen, Solomon	Camden	33rd	4/18	Irwin
Osteen, William	Liberty		258/11	Early
Osteen, William	Liberty		277/6	Appling
Otwell, Eliz.(Wid)	Jackson	Hamiltons	503/5	Irwin
Otwells, Benjamin	Jackson	Hamiltons Bt.	331/6	Irwin
Ousley, Jesse C.	Putnam	Buckners	316/12	Early
Ousley, William	Putnam	Buckners	350/9	Appling
Ously, Barbara	Jasper	McClendons	191/4	Early
Oventon, Joel(Orps)	Twiggs	W.Belchers	351/12	Irwin
Overby, Peter(Orps)	Columbia	Dodsons	18/27	Early
Overstreet, Daniel	Emanuel	57th	231/1	Walton
Overstreet, Daniel	Emanuel	57th	526/12	Irwin
Overstreet, John D.	Wilkes	Burks	114/5	Gwinnett
Overstreet, John D.	Wilkes	Burks	65/6	Habersham
Overstreet, Wilas	Tatnall	Overstreets	169/14	Early
Overstreet, Wm.	Burke	Hands	327/3	Appling
Overtim, Henry	Jasper	Bentley	80/10	Hall
Overton, Henry	Jasper	Bentleys	28/5	Gwinnett
Overton, James	Walton	Sentells	188/5	Gwinnett
Overton, John Sr.	Walton	Sentells	114/5	Irwin
Overtree, John B.	Morgan	Leonards	18/13	Habersham
Ovington, Tatom C.	Bullock	Edwards	4/3	Appling
Owen, Benjamin	Oglethorpe	Bowls	449/4	Appling
Owen, Caleb	Burke	Dys	389/2	Early
Owen, Catharine	Morgan	Alfords	396/9	Appling
Owen, Daniel	Greene	Kimbroughs	157/9	Hall
Owen, Jacob	Greene	Kimbroughs	277/21	Early
Owen, John F.	Hancock	Thomas	3/1	Walton
Owen, Nancy	Burke	Dys	314/5	Irwin
Owen, Obediah	Wilkes	Davis	350/5	Gwinnett
Owen, Uriah	Wilkes	Davis	17/9	Hall
Owen, William	Burke	Dys	198/13	Irwin
Owen, William	Greene	Harrils	147/15	Early
Owen, William	Greene	Harvills	255/5	Appling
Owen, William	Greene	Harvills	383/7	Appling
Owen, William	Pulaski	Lanears	116/4	Appling
Owens, Aaron	Baldwin	Ellis	182/2	Habersham
Owens, Aaron	Baldwin	Ellis	63/14	Early
Owens, Andrew	Lincoln	Thompsons	334/5	Early
Owens, Andrew	Lincoln	Thompsons	514/7	Appling
Owens, Anne	Baldwin	Marshalls	250/13	Irwin
Owens, Beachum	Putnam	Evans	319/4	Walton
Owens, Elijah(Orps)	Baldwin	Stephens	5/9	Irwin
Owens, Garland(Orps)	Wilkes	Davis	352/5	Early
Owens, Garland(Orps)	Wilkes	Davis	514/2	Appling
Owens, Geo.W.	Jasper	Smiths	43/17	Early

NAME	COUNTY	MIL.DIST	LOT/SECT	DREW LAN
Owens, George W.	Chatham		391/6	Irwin
Owens, John J.	Baldwin	Stephens	80/15	Early
Owens, John(Orps)	Elbert	Whites	13/3	Habersha
Owens, John	Burke	Sullivans	115/7	Gwinnett
Owens, John	Burke	Sullivans	179/18	Early
Owens, Jonathan	Jones	Phillips	3/5	Irwin
Owens, Joseph	Columbia	Pullins	265/4	Early
Owens, Joseph	Columbia	Pullins	280/5	Gwinnett
Owens, Joseph	Columbia	Pullins	350/10	Early
Owens, Mary(Wid)	Wilkes	Kilgores	266/9	Appling
Owens, Micajah(Orps)	Emanuel	57th	212/9	Irwin
Owens, Parkell	Jones	Phillips	97/8	Hall
Owens, Peter	Jones	Phillips	386/12	Early
Owens, William H.	Twiggs	Evans	108/6	Hall
Owens, William	Jones	Kings	191/20	Early
Owens, Wm.H.	Twiggs	Evans	258/2	Irwin
Owoms, John	Telfair	Wilsons	47/4	Walton
Oxford, Susannah(Wid)	Jones	Greens	118/1	Irwin
Oxford, Tilmond D.	Jones	Greens	339/9	Early
Oxley, William	Burke	70th	61/9	Early
Oxly, George	Burke	J.Wards	436/3	Appling
Ozbourn, George	Jasper	Bentleys	133/2	Rabun
Ozbourn, James	Jasper	Bentleys	187/16	Irwin
Ozbourn, James	Jasper	Bentleys	216/4	Appling
Ozburn, Washington	Wilkes	Maddox	4/8	Appling
Ozburn, Washington	Wilkes	Mattox	248/6	Irwin
Ozburns, Benj.(Orps)	Wilkes	Mattox	131/3	Walton
Pace, Barnabas	Morgan	Longs	263/4	Early
Pace, Barnabas	Morgan	Loyds	246/5	Early
Pace, Bazel	Elbert	Penns	4/6	Appling
Pace, David	Baldwin	Marshalls	7/7	Appling
Pace, Dreasit Sr.	Columbia	Burroughs	113/1	Appling
Pace, Edmund	Warren	152nd	192/4	Early
Pace, Hardy	Twiggs	Smiths	97/8	Early
Pace, James	Oglethorpe	Davenports	177/6	Early
Pace, James	Warren	153rd	340/10	Early
Pace, Jarred	Washington	Robisons	51/10	Hall
Pace, John	Elbert	Hannahs	11/4	Habersha
Pace, Noel	Elbert	Webbs	144/2	Rabun
Pace, Richard	Putnam	Coopers	335/9	Appling
Pace, Solomon	Putnam	Mays	133/3	Irwin
Pace, Thomas	Columbia	J.Morris	30/10	Early
Pace, Thomas	Washington	Barges	147/28	Early
Pace, William Jr.	Putnam	Mays	36/13	Early
Pace, William	Columbia	J.Morriss	215/6	Early
Pace, William	Warren	154	399/2	Appling
Pace, William	Washington	Avents	271/3	Appling
Pack, Lockett	Greene	144th	244/2	Irwin
Padgett, Elijah	Jefferson	Langstons	164/4	Early
Padgett, Elisha	Bulloch	Knights	37/7	Appling
Padgett, Warren J.	Wilkinson	Smiths	132/14	Irwin
Paevy, Anne	Hancock	Loyds	407/10	Irwin
Page, Benjamin	Franklin	Holcombs	88/12	Irwin
Page, Elijah	Jasper	Posts	208/6	Early
Page, Eliz.(Orph)	Pulaski	Johnstons	1/3	Irwin
Page, Eliz.(Wid)	Tattnall	Overstreets	15/5	Appling
Page, James Sr.	Washington	Burneys	276/11	Irwin
Page, John	Chatham		73/23	Early
Page, Levell	Elbert	Hannahs	122/9	Irwin
Page, Solomon	Washington	Wimberlys	106/9	Irwin
Page, Stephen	Twiggs	Browns	17/22	Early
Page, William D.	Elbert	Webbs	37/7	Early
Page, William(Orps)	Jones	Permenters	50/10	Habersha
Page, William	Elbert	Childres	321/4	Walton
Pain, James	Jackson	Winters Bt.	257/6	Early
Paine, Benj.W.	Franklin	Vaughns	42/20	Early
Paine, Hendry D.	Jasper	Phillips	336/6	Early

NAME	COUNTY	MIL.DIST	LOT/SECT	DREW LAND
Paine, William	Jasper	Easter	196/7	Irwin
Painter, Lydia(Wid)	Jefferson	Abbots	142/17	Early
Pair, Elijah	Franklin	Harris	42/7	Appling
Pair, Peggy(Orph)	Franklin	Akins	182/12	Early
Paisley, Thomas	Glynn		101/14	Irwin
Paisley, Thomas	Glynn		211/1	Appling
Palin, James	Chatham		394/8	Irwin
Pall, Moses	Morgan	Farrars	213/6	Irwin
Pall, Moses	Morgan	Farrars	393/11	Irwin
Palman, Watson	Oglethorpe	Goulds	149/13	Irwin
Palmer, Benjamin	Burke	Dys	391/8	Appling
Palmer, Charlotte	Chatham		230/5	Irwin
Palmer, Farmer	Emanuel	58th	376/5	Early
Palmer, Farmer	Greene	58th	376/5	Early
Palmer, Hezekiah	Hancock	Sharps	128/3	Appling
Palmer, Hezekiah	Hancock	Sharps	190/27	Early
Palmer, James S.	Jackson	Winters Bt.	409/4	Appling
Palmer, James	Glynn		331/20	Early
Palmer, Joel	Jones	Permenters	349/9	Irwin
Palmer, John Jr.	Greene	Macons	62/16	Early
Palmer, John	Liberty		283/9	Appling
Palmer, Jonathan	Richmond	Palmers	27/3	Irwin
Palmer, Landon	Greene	Woodhams	179/8	Appling
Palmer, Martin	Glynn		320/20	Early
Palmer, Masa	Greene	Armers	1/5	Rabun
Palmer, Robert	Burke	Dyes	376/12	Irwin
Palmer, Thomas	Hancock	Edwards	510/6	Irwin
Palmer, William	Burke	Drys	178/4	Walton
Palmer, William	Columbia	Shaws	4/4	Rabun
Palmer, William	Richmond	Palmers	99/12	Hall
Palmes, George F.	Chatham		374/5	Appling
Palmes, William	Chatham		159/6	Irwin
Palmore, Elisha	Hancock	Thomas	301/20	Early
Palmore, Russel	Hancock	Thomas	431/5	Appling
Pannell, James	Columbia	Burroughs	305/12	Irwin
Pantlain, Thomas W.	Oglethorpe	Brittons	383/1	Appling
Paradise, Elizabeth	Liberty	Tatoms	185/6	Gwinnett
Paradise, James	Liberty	Tatoms	99/11	Early
Paramore, Redding Sr.	Telfair	Wilsons	70/7	Gwinnett
Pare, Christopher	Telfair	Williams	185/16	Early
Parham, Dixon	Elbert	R.Christians	77/2	Walton
Parham, Edmond	Warren	Parhams	193/13	Early
Parham, Harrison	Elbert	R.Christians	56/7	Early
Parham, Isham	Elbert	R.Christians	132/2	Appling
Parham, John	Putnam	Ectors	31/1	Habersham
Parham, Lewis	Warren	Parhams	372/7	Early
Parham, Lewis	Warren	Parhams	50/13	Irwin
Parham, Robert C.	Warren	Parhams	189/6	Gwinnett
Parham, Rowland	Baldwin	Cousins	390/7	Gwinnett
Parham, Rowland	Baldwin	Cousins	390/7	Gwinnett
Parham, Thomas S.	Baldwin	Haws	192/21	Early
Parham, Williamson	Putnam	Ectors	181/9	Irwin
Paris, Phillip S.	Pulaski	Lesters	354/13	Irwin
Parish, Absalom	Bulloch	Tilmans	173/9	Hall
Parish, Ansel	Bulloch	Tilmans	81/6	Gwinnett
Parish, Charles	Washington	Jenkinsons	155/28	Early
Parish, Hampton	Warren	Hubberts	364/12	Irwin
Parish, John	Telfair	Loves	163/12	Early
Parish, Samuel	Tattnall	Johnsons	175/14	Early
Park, Gabriel	Jasper	Northcuts	246/3	Walton
Park, James S.	Greene	143rd	313/7	Irwin
Park, John	Greene	Greers	147/3	Early
Park, Richard	Greene	Jones	214/4	Walton
Park, Richard	Greene	Jones	480/8	Appling
Park, Robert	Wilkes	Brooks	383/2	Early
Parke, Moses	Putnam	Oslins	192/12	Habersham
Parker, Aaron Sr.	Clark	Harpers	154/8	Irwin

NAME	COUNTY	MIL.DIST	LOT/SECT	DREW LAN
Parker, Acee H.	Hancock	Edwards	35/6	Early
Parker, Benjamin	Emanuel	55th	86/8	Early
Parker, Daniel	Greene	140	125/11	Hall
Parker, Daniel	Habersham	Adairs	290/14	Early
Parker, David	Greene	Macons	505/7	Irwin
Parker, Drury(Orps)	Twiggs	Jeffersons	277/20	Early
Parker, Ebenezer	Chatham		314/4	Walton
Parker, Ebenezer	Chatham		524/7	Appling
Parker, Eli	Effingham		110/6	Irwin
Parker, Gabriel	Twiggs	Evans	114/9	Hall
Parker, Gabriel	Twiggs	Evans	269/10	Irwin
Parker, George P.	Jackson	Hamiltons Bt.	1/4	Appling
Parker, George Sr.	Morgan	Parkers	307/12	Irwin
Parker, George W.	Wilkinson	Kettles	207/8	Appling
Parker, George	Baldwin	Cousins	195/11	Irwin
Parker, Hardy	Emanuel	395	7/4	Walton
Parker, Henry	Baldwin	Irwins	510/5	Irwin
Parker, Hiram	Twiggs	Jeffersons	405/9	Early
Parker, Ica	Washington	Wimberlys	189/10	Habersha
Parker, Isaac A.	Morgan	Talbots	318/2	Early
Parker, Isaiah	Putnam	Oslins	46/4	Irwin
Parker, Jacob(Orps)	Baldwin	Ellis	311/18	Early
Parker, Jacob	Burke	Spiveys	355/7	Irwin
Parker, Jacob	Burke	Spiveys	40/10	Irwin
Parker, James	Walton	Wagnons	124/8	Appling
Parker, Jesse	Emanuel	57th	366/13	Early
Parker, Jesse	Emanuel	57th	91/5	Rabun
Parker, John D.	Franklin	Attaways	41/8	Hall
Parker, John Jr.	Hancock	Mims	144/6	Appling
Parker, John(Orps)	Baldwin	Irwin	325/6	Irwin
Parker, John	Clark	Harpers	342/7	Irwin
Parker, Jonathan Jr.	Laurens	D.Smiths	485/11	Irwin
Parker, Jonathan Sr.	Laurens	D.Smiths	109/18	Early
Parker, Jonathan Sr.	Laurens	D.Smiths	214/21	Early
Parker, Jonathan	Liberty		101/4	Irwin
Parker, Joshua	Morgan	Parkers	71/5	Gwinnett
Parker, Kedar	Washington	Renfros	68/4	Rabun
Parker, Louis Sr.	Hancock	Edwards	285/8	Early
Parker, Maxey	Jones	Kings	50/8	Irwin
Parker, Patience	Greene	144	76/6	Habersha
Parker, Philman	Jones	Griffiths	29/1	Early
Parker, Polly	Baldwin	Ellis	96/1	Habersha
Parker, Robert	Wilkinson	Howards	62/12	Hall
Parker, Samuel S.	Warren	154th	131/2	Appling
Parker, Simon	Burke	Thomas	362/4	Appling
Parker, Simon	Burke	Thomas	89/12	Hall
Parker, Stephen	Gwinnett	Hamiltons Bt.	229/7	Appling
Parker, Stephen	Jefferson	Cowarts	137/7	Early
Parker, Stephen	Jefferson	Cowarts	46/13	Habersha
Parker, Susannah	Burke	Spiveys	300/26	Early
Parker, Teal	Putnam	Stampers	415/8	Appling
Parker, Thomas S.	Jackson	Rogers Bt.	523/8	Appling
Parker, West	Clarke	Moors	243/1	Walton
Parker, William H.	Madison	Millicans	47/11	Early
Parker, William	Chatham		237/9	Early
Parker, William	Clark	Harpers	19/3	Irwin
Parker, William	Hancock	Canes	395/8	Irwin
Parker, William	Jefferson	Bothwells	113/5	Rabun
Parker, William	Liberty		23/6	Habersha
Parker, Wm.C.(R.S.)	Jackson	Rogers	31/6	Appling
Parkerson, Sherwood	Pulaski	Laniers	377/16	Early
Parkins, George S.	Chatham		217/18	Early
Parkinson, Joseph(Min)	Wilkes	Holidays	289/16	Early
Parks, Aron	Columbia	Bealls	1/6	Irwin
Parks, Baptist	Jackson	Winters Bt.	40/10	Habersha
Parks, Benjamin	Franklin	J.Millers	304/1	Appling
Parks, Hannan(Wid)	Jackson	Winters Bt.	14/12	Habersha

252

NAME	COUNTY	MIL.DIST	LOT/SECT	DREW LAND
Parks, Henry Jr.	Franklin	Turks	152/11	Irwin
Parks, Henry Jr.	Franklin	Turks	325/3	Early
Parks, Jeremiah S.	Madison	Bones	165/26	Early
Parks, Jeremiah S.	Madison	Bones	421/15	Early
Parks, Job	Wilkes	Dents	122/7	Appling
Parks, John(Orps)	Jasper	Posts	388/20	Early
Parks, John	Camden	Tillis	95/3	Irwin
Parks, Jonathan(Orps)	Jasper	Centells	120/13	Habersham
Parks, Mathew(Orps)	Jackson	Hamiltons Bt.	492/4	Appling
Parks, Sheerman	Columbia	J.Morriss	166/7	Irwin
Parks, William	Liberty	Parks	91/4	Early
Parks, Wilson	Jackson	Winters Bt.	46/2	Early
Parland, John	Glynn		180/2	Early
Parmer, Charles	Scriven		57/17	Early
Parmer, Jacob	Jones	Wallers	468/8	Irwin
Parmer, Jacob	Jones	Waters	43/3	Rabun
Parmer, Jesse	Jasper	Reeds	35/3	Walton
Parmer, Jesse	Jasper	Reeds	352/6	Gwinnett
Parmer, Joseph	Early		69/10	Irwin
Parmer, Thomas	Hancock	Scotts	129/20	Early
Parr, (Orphs)	Franklin	Akins	319/15	Early
Parr, Bridges	Jasper	Bentleys	157/11	Habersham
Parris, Francis	Burke	Hands	248/4	Walton
Parris, Harris	Putnam	Evans	141/15	Early
Parris, John	Warren	Hubberts	16/13	Irwin
Parrish, Ansel	Bulloch	Tilmans	117/10	Habersham
Parrish, Chas.Jr.	Franklin	Turks	363/1	Appling
Parrish, James	Washington	Peabodys	338/1	Early
Parrish, Joel	Emanuel	59	439/10	Irwin
Parrish, Joel	Greene	Macons	21/8	Irwin
Parrish, John	Warren	Hubberts	22/20	Early
Parrish, Jonathan	Jones	Samuels	213/6	Gwinnett
Parrish, Jonathan	Jones	Samuels	58/18	Early
Parrish, Samuel	Effingham		29/9	Hall
Parrish, Tyran	Camden	Tillis	327/10	Early
Parrish, Wm.	Warren	Hubberts	226/27	Early
Parriss, Phlander O.	Warren	153	37/26	Early
Parrot, John	Glynn		286/7	Irwin
Parrott, Elijah	Glynn		76/5	Irwin
Parrott, James	Twiggs	Hodges	161/20	Early
Parrott, John	Glynn		215/12	Irwin
Parrott, John	Glynn		378/12	Irwin
Parrott, William	Laurens	Harris	421/3	Appling
Parrott, William	Laurens	Harriss	241/2	Irwin
Parsmore, Howsanan	Washington	Cummins	222/6	Appling
Parsons, Francis	Camden	Millers	316/9	Irwin
Partin, Peter	Twiggs	W.Belchers	354/1	Appling
Parting, Britton	Jones	Phillips	264/8	Early
Partrick, Paul	Jackson	Hamiltons Bt.	441/10	Irwin
Partrick, Wm.	Clarke	Tredwills	320/1	Walton
Partridge, Henry	Jefferson	Langstons	279/19	Early
Partridge, Isaac	Washington	Mannings	153/14	Irwin
Partridge, Jesse	Jones	Shopshears	132/2	Rabun
Partridge, John	Oglethorpe	Rowlands	22/9	Irwin
Partridge, Wm.	Washington	Mannings	196/6	Gwinnett
Partridy, Nicholas	Wilkes	Ogletrees	123/2	Irwin
Parymoer, Thos.(Orps)	Emanuel	395th	106/16	Irwin
Paschah, John H.	Oglethorpe	Barnetts	153/8	Early
Pasmore, John	Baldwin	Irwins	341/5	Appling
Pass, John B.	Putnam	Oslins	30/7	Appling
Pass, John	Clarke	Tredwells	492/7	Appling
Pass, Miles	Putnam	Bustins	259/15	Early
Pass, Nathaniel B.	Putnam	Bustins	414/9	Irwin
Pass, Thomas	Elbert	P.Christians	108/15	Irwin
Passmore, Alexander	Wilkinson	Howards	197/12	Early
Passmore, Saml.	Twiggs	Browns	4/5	Early
Patch, William	Glynn		288/3	Early

NAME	COUNTY	MIL.DIST	LOT/SECT	DREW LAND
Pate, Bennet	Emanuel	395th	378/9	Irwin
Pate, Cloe(Wid)	Jefferson	Abbots	19/2	Early
Pate, Corda(Orps)	Oglethorpe	Bowls	144/6	Early
Pate, Dury	Warren	152	104/7	Gwinnett
Pate, James(Orps)	Morgan	Paces	436/6	Irwin
Pate, James	Jasper	Bentleys	341/3	Early
Pate, John	Jasper	Bentleys	355/1	Appling
Pate, Lucretia(Wid)	Richmond	122	25/3	Rabun
Pate, Saml.Sr.(RS)	Twiggs	Jeffersons	312/15	Early
Pate, Samuel Jr.	Twiggs	Jefferson	115/2	Early
Pate, Samuel Jr.	Twiggs	Jeffersons	228/11	Early
Pate, William	Morgan	Selmons	104/2	Habersham
Pate, William	Morgan	Selmons	414/11	Irwin
Pate, Wm.Jr.	Jasper	Bentleys	63/3	Walton
Pate, Wm.Sr.	Jasper	Bentleys	294/10	Early
Patemen, John	Washington	Pools	491/8	Appling
Patey, Elijah	Jasper	Bartletts	145/1	Early
Patey, William	Jasper	Bartlets	454/7	Irwin
Patillo, David(Orps)	Greene	Macons	348/1	Appling
Patillo, George	Greene	Macons	132/3	Habersham
Patillo, John Jr.	Greene	Macons	253/26	Early
Patillo, John Sr.	Greene	Macons	119/8	Early
Patillo, John V.Sr.	Greene	Macons	311/2	Early
Patman, Watson	Oglethorpe	Bowls	209/1	Appling
Patman, Wm.Jr.	Oglethorpe	Wises	218/21	Early
Patnam, Chas.E.	McIntosh	Hamiltons	89/10	Early
Patrann, James B.	Oglethorpe	Barnetts	182/20	Early
Patrick, Alexander	Walton	Williams	259/20	Early
Patrick, Berry	Jackson	Rogers Bt.	289/14	Early
Patrick, Elizabeth	Oglethorpe	Murrys	434/11	Irwin
Patrick, James	Oglethorpe	Murrays	153/9	Early
Patrick, John(Orps)	Jackson	Rogers Bt.	74/26	Early
Patrick, Joshua(Orps)	Morgan	Alford	513/7	Appling
Patrick, Josiah D.	Oglethorpe	Murrays	91/11	Habersham
Patrick, Levy	Bulloch	Edwards	118/5	Gwinnett
Patrick, Luke	Jackson	Rogers Bt.	267.8	Early
Patrick, Robert	Morgan	Walkers	197/4	Appling
Patrick, Robert	Morgan	Walkers	68/9	Irwin
Patrick, William	Franklin	Vaughans	126/14	Early
Patrick, William	Morgan	Alfords	468/9	Irwin
Patten, Catharine	Madison	Culbreths	297/5	Gwinnett
Patten, James H.	Madison	Culbreths	459/11	Irwin
Patten, Silas	Walton	Wagnons	509/8	Appling
Patterson, Andrew B.	Jackson	Dicksons	170/9	Early
Patterson, David C.	Wilkes	172	119/	Hall
Patterson, David	Elbert	Ruckers	438/11	Irwin
Patterson, Ebzy	Elbert	Smiths	72/16	Early
Patterson, Elizabeth(Wid)	Morgan	Campbells	361/20	Early
Patterson, Frances(Orps)	Jasper	Posts	11/17	Early
Patterson, Frederick	Oglethorpe	Barnetts	332/6	Early
Patterson, Geo.D.R.	Scriven	Lovitts	255/2	Early
Patterson, Henry	Elbert	P.Christians	4/19	Early
Patterson, James Jr.	Elbert	Olivers	226/8	Irwin
Patterson, James Sr.	Elbert	Olivers	67/10	Habersham
Patterson, James	Elbert	Wards	282/20	Early
Patterson, James	Jackson	Dicksons Bt.	61/8	Hall
Patterson, James	Jefferson	Matthews	307/1	Appling
Patterson, Jesse	Elbert	Whites	210/21	Early
Patterson, Jessee	Franklin	Haynes	405/9	Irwin
Patterson, John Jr.	Burke	72nd	324/26	Early
Patterson, John T.	Jones	Buckhalters	123/6	Gwinnett
Patterson, John	Elbert	Whites	33/8	Early
Patterson, John	Franklin	Hayns	371/3	Appling
Patterson, John	Morgan	Selmons	249/6	Irwin
Patterson, Joseph	Hancock	Smiths	352/3	Early
Patterson, Margaret	Madison	Orrs	67/1	Appling
Patterson, Margr.(Wid)	Franklin	Harris	320/2	Early

NAME	COUNTY	MIL.DIST	LOT/SECT	DREW LAND
Patterson, Milley	Jones	Griffiths	336/2	Early
Patterson, Robert	Morgan	Parkers	376/3	Appling
Patterson, Samuel L.	Wilkinson	Lees	268/6	Gwinnett
Patterson, Samuel	Burke	72	406/10	Irwin
Patterson, Thomas	Twiggs	R.Belchers	22/15	Early
Patterson, William	Jackson	Rogers	157/18	Early
Patterson, Wm.	Elbert	Smiths	259/21	Early
Patteson, Nimrod	Elbert	Whites	344/11	Early
Patteson, Nimrod	Elbert	Whites	64/1	Early
Pattison, Sarah	Chatham		7/26	Early
Patton, George	Madison	Willifords	1/15	Early
Patton, James	Jasper	Clays	220/28	Early
Patton, Robert	Wilkinson	Brooks	76/14	Early
Patton, Solomon	Oglethorpe	Davenports	3/6	Habersham
Patton, Thomas	Wilkinson	Brooks	218/4	Walton
Patton, William	Jackson	Winters	45/16	Early
Paul, James	Twiggs	R.Belchers	91/27	Early
Paul, Joel	Morgan	McClendons	32/1	Habersham
Paul, Samuel	Richmond	120th	233/20	Early
Paulett, Blassingame	Burke	J.Wards	244/8	Appling
Paulett, Lewis M.	Jackson	Rogers Bt.	143/6	Irwin
Paulin, William	Chatham		306/21	Early
Paulk, James	Laurens	Kinchens	58/6	Gwinnett
Paulk, Samuel	Jefferson	Matthews	164/3	Appling
Paulk, Samuel	Jefferson	Matthews	484/12	Irwin
Paull, Benjamin	Wilkes	Turners	139/5	Early
Paullain, Thomas N.	Oglethorpe	Brittons	193/17	Early
Paullet, Jese	Clark	Simms	389/8	Appling
Pawell, Charles	Laurens	Ross	33/9	Irwin
Payne, Amy	Oglethorpe	Rowlands	236/13	Irwin
Payne, Benedict	Franklin	R.Browns	510/5	Appling
Payne, Bennadick	Franklin	R.Bowens	161/7	Irwin
Payne, Daniel	Twiggs	Hodges	359/7	Irwin
Payne, John Jr.	Franklin	Akins	94/2	Early
Payne, John M.	Franklin	Akins	304/21	Early
Payne, John M.	Franklin	Akins	381/16	Early
Payne, John	Wilkinson	Bowings	16/4	Early
Payne, Landon	Franklin	Akins	130/1	Early
Payne, Leah(Wid)	Wilkinson	Bowings	299/7	Early
Payne, Mary(Wid)	Twiggs	Hodges	260/9	Early
Payne, Middleton	Franklin	Akins	110/27	Early
Payne, Reuben	Franklin	R.Browns	410/7	Irwin
Payne, Thomas Sr.	Franklin	Akins	464/12	Irwin
Payne, Thomas	Franklin	Hammonds	321/1	Appling
Payne, Thomas	Franklin	Hammonds	526/9	Irwin
Payne, Thomas	Franklin	P.Browns	152/18	Early
Payner, John S.	Wilkes	Runnels	316/5	Appling
Payton, Cornelius	Madison	Willifords	105/12	Irwin
Payton, George	Madison	Willifords	96/28	Early
Peace, John	Wilkes	Willis	124/28	Early
Peace, Samuel	Pulaski	Senterfeit	415/15	Early
Peace, William	Burke	McNorrels	481/4	Appling
Peacock, Alfred	Wilkinson	Childs	104/20	Early
Peacock, Archibald	Washington	Jenkinsons	125/10	Irwin
Peacock, Archibald	Washington	Jinkinsons	55/17	Early
Peacock, Isham	Tattnall	J.Durrence	153/6	Appling
Peacock, Isham	Tattnall	J.Durrences	250/12	Early
Peacock, John Sr.	Washington	Jenkinsons	126/9	Appling
Peacock, John(Tinker)	Washington	Jenkinsons	190/4	Irwin
Peacock, John(Tinker)	Washington	Jinkinsons	14/22	Early
Peacock, John	Bulloch	Jones	205/10	Early
Peacock, John	McIntosh	Eigles	106/9	Early
Peacock, John	McIntosh	Eigles	41/7	Irwin
Peacock, Pearsons	Washington	Jinkinsons	87/4	Walton
Peacock, Rebecca(Wid)	Jefferson	Fountains	108/19	Early
Peacock, Saml.(Orps)	Bulloch	Jones	109/10	Irwin
Peacock, Samuel(Orps)	Pulaski	Rees	186/4	Early

NAME	COUNTY	MIL.DIST	LOT/SECT	DREW LAN
Peacock, Seth	Twiggs	Tisons	237/8	Irwin
Peacock, Timothy	Wilkinson	Childs	319/7	Early
Peacock, William	Washington	Jinkinsons	103/8	Irwin
Peak, John	Putnam	Buckners	195/8	Irwin
Peake, John	Putnam	Buckners	74/8	Irwin
Pealer, Anthony	Greene	Armers	33/8	Hall
Pearce, Cador	Burke	Spiveys	63/7	Irwin
Pearce, Ezrous	Twiggs	R.Belchers	30/28	Early
Pearce, Gadwell Sr.(RS)	Jackson	Hamiltons	482/12	Irwin
Pearce, Gadwell	Jones	Hamiltons	115/13	Habersha
Pearce, James B.	Jackson	Hamiltons Bt.	195/9	Irwin
Pearce, James	Franklin	Davis	314/28	Early
Pearce, John	Jackson	Hamiltons Bt.	116/15	Early
Pearce, John	Pulaski	Davis	21/26	Early
Pearce, John	Pulaski	Davis	7/15	Irwin
Pearce, Joseph	Jackson	Hamiltons Bt.	229/26	Early
Pearce, Lazrous	Twiggs	R. Belchers	36/1	Rabun
Pearce, Samuel	Jasper	Centells	345/3	Appling
Pearce, Sion	Jackson	Hamiltons Bt.	74/12	Early
Pearce, Sion	Jackson	Hamiltons	229/11	Early
Pearce, Stafford	Hancock	Justices	215/4	Appling
Pearce, Stephen	Scriven	36th	246/2	Irwin
Pearce, Stephen	Scriven	36th	26/5	Early
Pearce, Theophilus	Twiggs	Evans	94/4	Appling
Pearce, Thomas	Jackson	Hamiltons Bt.	208/7	Early
Pearce, Wiley	Jackson	Hamiltons	223/6	Appling
Pearce, William	Chatham		169/1	Early
Pearce, Wm.(Orps)	Twiggs	Browns	42/10	Habersha
Pearman, Jesse	Clark	Applings	346/11	Early
Pearman, Oran D.	Baldwin	Doziers	1/12	Hall
Pearman, Robert	Morgan	Hubbards	159/17	Early
Pearman, Robert	Morgan	Hubbards	31/14	Irwin
Pearman, Weakly J.	Morgan	Hubbards	221/9	Appling
Pearmon, Izabellah(Wid)	Morgan	McClendons	57/13	Habersha
Pearmon, Whitemell	Putnam	J.Kindricks	222/1	Appling
Pearre, James(Orps)	Columbia	Olives	155/1	Early
Pearre, James	Columbia	Pullins	32/27	Early
Pearre, John	Columbia	Olives	240/3	Early
Pearre, Levi	Columbia	Olives	305/28	Early
Pearre, Nathaniel	Columbia	Olivers	500/10	Irwin
Pearre, William A.	Columbia	Olives	138/7	Appling
Pearson, Benjamin	Bulloch	Edwards	188/11	Early
Pearson, Benjamin	Bulloch	Edwards	347/7	Irwin
Pearson, Benoney	Telfair	Edwards	28/4	Habersha
Pearson, Constant(Orph)	McIntosh	Eigles	529/12	Irwin
Pearson, James	Jasper	Bartletts	109/7	Early
Pearson, James	Jasper	Bartletts	623/2	Appling
Pearson, James	Twiggs	W.Belchers	373/6	Early
Pearson, James	Twiggs	W.Belchers	82/9	Early
Pearson, Jeney(Orph)	McIntosh	Eigles	529/12	Irwin
Pearson, Jeremiah	Jasper	Clays	414/6	Irwin
Pearson, John	Scriven		445/6	Appling
Pearson, Jonathan	Wilkinson	Howards	301/5	Appling
Pearson, Michael	Wilkes	Willis	159/3	Habersha
Pearson, Nancy(Orph)	McIntosh	Eigles	529/12	Irwin
Pearson, Nathan	Wilkinson	Howards	105/7	Gwinnett
Pearson, Nelly(Wid)	McIntosh	Eigles	260/8	Irwin
Pearson, Parland(Orps)	Wilkes	Willis	36/27	Early
Pearson, Peter	Wilkinson	Smiths	384/28	Early
Pearson, Samuel	Twiggs	Browns	30/1	Rabun
Pearson, Stephen	Hancock	Justice	197/12	Irwin
Pearson, William H.	Jasper	Bartletts	47/11	Irwin
Pearsons, William	Jefferson	Abbots	466/2	Appling
Pease, John	Jasper	Clays	154/15	Irwin
Pease, Rodney	Liberty		173/12	Habersha
Peaterson, Chas.	Bulloch	Edwards	297/10	Irwin
Peavey, Joseph(RS)	Clark	Oats	289/20	Early

NAME	COUNTY	MIL.DIST	LOT/SECT	DREW LAND
Peavy, Abram	Warren	Hubberts	245/4	Irwin
Peavy, Ambrose	Warren	Hubberts	32/19	Early
Peavy, Dial	Warren	Hubberts	69/5	Early
Peavy, John	Warren	Hubberts	286/5	Gwinnett
Peavy, Joseph(RS)	Clark	Oates	53/22	Early
Peavy, Joseph(RS)	Clark	Oats	251/18	Early
Peavy, Joseph	Tattnall	J.Durrences	242/8	Early
Peck, Henry	Hancock	Canes	165/7	Early
Peck, Hiram	Greene	144	354/16	Early
Peck, William	Hancock	Canes	262/18	Early
Peck, William	Putnam	Bustins	19/3	Appling
Peddy, Bradford	Jones	Chappels	265/4	Appling
Peddy, Elbert	Washington	Renfroes	191/2	Appling
Peddy, James	Jones	Chappels	101/3	Rabun
Peddy, Jeremiah Jr.	Jones	Chappels	383/7	Irwin
Peddy, Julius	Washington	Renfroes	385/11	Irwin
Peddy, William	Jasper	Kennedys	324/5	Appling
Peddys, Nehemiah	Washington	Renfroes	503/7	Irwin
Peebles, George L.	Elbert	Dobbs	292/1	Appling
Peebles, Henry	Jefferson	Matthews	322/19	Early
Peebles, Henry	Jefferson	Matthews	52/11	Habersham
Peebles, Isaac	Jefferson	Matthews	252/6	Early
Peebles, Isaac	Jefferson	Matthews	315/7	Irwin
Peed, John	Liberty	Graves	150/2	Appling
Peed, John	Liberty	Graves	357/10	Early
Peek, James	Greene	144	257/5	Irwin
Peek, Locket	Greene	144	297/1	Appling
Peel, John	Jefferson	Matthews	25/23	Early
Peeler, Abner	Elbert	Whites	36/3	Walton
Peeples, Archibald	Jefferson	Langstons	367/18	Early
Peeples, Dudley	Morgan	Leonard	77/11	Early
Peeples, Dudley	Morgan	Leonards	62/2	Rabun
Peevy, Eli	Hancock	Loyds	20/3	Appling
Peevy, Eli	Hancock	Loyds	416/4	Appling
Peevy, Ezekiah	Warren	Hubberts	264/11	Irwin
Pelkington, John	Hall		144/2	Walton
Pelly, Edward	Bulloch	Knights	102/28	Early
Pelot, James	McIntosh	Jinkins	358/27	Early
Pelot, James	McIntosh	Jinkins	68/5	Irwin
Pender, Lurany(Wid)	Jones	Wallers	264/4	Appling
Pender, Wright	Jones	Wallers	104/4	Habersham
Pendergrass, Dolly	Greene	143rd	17/8	Irwin
Pendergrass, Hiram	Jasper	Posts	5/15	Early
Pendergrass, John(Orph)	Chatham		53/19	Early
Pendergrass, John(Orph)	Chatham		513//5	Appling
Pendergrass, John	Jackson	Rogers Bt.	329/28	Early
Pendergrass, Margr.(Orp)	Chatham		513/5	Appling
Pendergrass, Margr.(Orph)	Chatham		53/19	Early
Pendergrass, Prince(Orp)	Chatham		513/5	Appling
Pendleton, Coleman	Putnam	Bustins	400/10	Irwin
Pendleton, Jesse	Appling	8th	341/7	Early
Pendrey, John	Jefferson	Flemings	256/17	Early
Pengree, Thomas	Scriven	Roberts	12/8	Hall
Penn, Eliz.(Wid)	Richmond	120th	26/28	Early
Penn, Francis	Madison	Willifords	45/12	Irwin
Penn, John Jr.	Elbert	Webbs	246/13	Early
Penn, John T.	Oglethorpe	Myricks	85/9	Hall
Penn, Thomas H.(Jr)	Elbert	Penns	159/5	Gwinnett
Penn, Thomas Sr.	Elbert	Penns	38/3	Rabun
Penn, William	Jasper	Clays	116/9	Appling
Penn, William	Jasper	Clays	63/4	Irwin
Pennel, Jonathan	Hall		171/9	Hall
Pennell, Jonathan	Hall		161/6	Irwin
Pennell, Richard	Hall		409/6	Irwin
Penney, George	Chatham		243/2	Early
Pennington, Abraham	Jasper	Hays	57/7	Appling
Pennington, Ephriam	Jasper	Posts	125/27	Early

NAME	COUNTY	MIL.DIST	LOT/SECT	DREW LAN
Pennington, Nancey(Wid)	Jefferson	Lamps	311/7	Appling
Pennington, Neddy	Jones	Samuels	206/8	Early
Pennington, Samuel	Jasper	Hays	188/8	Early
Pennington, Sion	Jefferson	Abbots	421/9	Irwin
Pennington, Thomas Jr.	Jasper	Ryans	95/4	Early
Pennington, Thomas	Jefferson	Connells	203/1	Irwin
Pennington, Wm..	Jasper	Hays	6/11	Irwin
Pennington, Wm.P.	Jasper	Hays	126/11	Irwin
Penny, Edward(RS)	Twiggs	Smiths	350/7	Early
Penny, Edward(RS)	Twiggs	Smiths	543/2	Appling
Penny, James	Twiggs	Smiths	257/9	Early
Penny, Thomas M.	Greene	Macons	88/26	Early
Pensel, Michael	Glynn		30/12	Irwin
Pensons, Joseph(Orps)	Oglethorpe	Barnetts	121/4	Appling
Pentecost, George	Jackson	Rogers Bt.	387/1	Appling
Pentecost, John W.	Clark	Pentecosts	139/2	Habersha
Pentecost, John W.	Clark	Pentecosts	212/4	Walton
Penton, David	Glynn		146/12	Early
Peoples, Henry	Jones	Wallers	199/13	Early
Peoples, John	Jackson	Scotts	223/14	Early
Pepper, James G.	Glynn		183/18	Early
Pepper, Parker	Jackson	Hamiltons Bt.	373/3	Early
Perdew, Isaac	Jones	Buckhalters	121/11	Hall
Perdew, James A.	Baldwin	Haws	335/6	Early
Perdue, Daniel	Greene	Macons	29/4	Early
Perdue, James A.	Baldwin	Haws	143/13	Early
Perdue, Leroy	Franklin	Ashs	346/6	Early
Perdue, William	Richmond	Palmers	41/22	Early
Perdue, William	Richmond	Parhams	260/3	Appling
Perfew, Andrew	Twiggs	R.Belchers	56/11	Habersha
Perkin, Joshua(Orps)	Laurens	Jones	29/8	Hall
Perkins, Alexander	Jasper	Baileys	220/6	Irwin
Perkins, Archb.Jr.	Morgan	McClendons	15/6	Gwinnett
Perkins, Ezekiel	Greene	Fosters	172/5	Early
Perkins, Ezekiel	Greene	Fosters	23/15	Early
Perkins, Jesse	Greene	142	154/1	Early
Perkins, Jessee	Greene	142nd	186/3	Walton
Perkins, John	Wilkinson	Smiths	416/5	Irwin
Perkins, Newton	Burke	J.Wards	397/2	Appling
Perkins, Peter	Columbia	Shaws	311/7	Irwin
Perkins, Samuel	Washington	Daniels	60/10	Early
Perkins, Susannah(Wid)	Jefferson	Abbots	273/4	Early
Perkins, Tabitha	Burke	Dyes	297/18	Early
Perkins, William	Burke	Dys	294/11	Irwin
Perkins, William	Jefferson	Abbots	152/14	Early
Perkins, William	Laurens	Griffins	388/2	Early
Perkison, Joel (RS)	Jackson	Hamiltons Bt.	106/13	Early
Perkison, Joel	Jackson	Hamiltons Bt.	140/2	Walton
Permenter, William	Twiggs	R.Belchers	376/21	Early
Perrin, Banister	Elbert	Olivers	223/4	Appling
Perrin, Thomas	Elbert	Olivers	12/4	Irwin
Perritt, John	Jones	Samuels	203/12	Early
Perry, Arthur C.	Twiggs	R.Belchers	329/9	Appling
Perry, Berkley	Putnam	Ectors	123/13	Irwin
Perry, Bird	Warren	Pharraws	196/16	Irwin
Perry, Doctor(RS)	Glynn		355/7	Appling
Perry, Edward	Camden	Clarks	45/10	Habersha
Perry, Elias	Liberty		116/19	Early
Perry, Hardy	Burke	Sullivans	17/2	Rabun
Perry, Henry H.	Twiggs	R.Belchers	297/14	Early
Perry, Hiram	Jackson	Winters Bt.	35/2	Rabun
Perry, Isaac	Twiggs	R.Belchers	363/10	Irwin
Perry, James Jr.	Franklin	John Miller	104/15	Early
Perry, James	Putnam	Berrys	178/5	Appling
Perry, James	Tattnall	Cunyers	97/7	Early
Perry, James	Twiggs	W.Belchers	331/6	Appling
Perry, James	Twiggs	Wm.Belchers	216/9	Appling

NAME	COUNTY	MIL.DIST	LOT/SECT	DREW LAND
Perry, John	Laurens	Watsons	156/6	Appling
Perry, John	Morgan	Rameys	339/5	Early
Perry, John	Twiggs	R.Belchers	126/4	Appling
Perry, John	Warren	Parhams	303/9	Early
Perry, Joseph Sr.	Laurens	D.Smiths	282/12	Irwin
Perry, Joseph	Burke	Sulivans	206/9	Appling
Perry, Josiah	Wilkes	Perry's	184/1	Walton
Perry, Michael W.	Baldwin	Stephens	275/11	Early
Perry, Nicholas	Baldwin	Stephens	213/12	Early
Perry, Obed	Baldwin	Irwins	110/14	Early
Perry, Peter	Baldwin	Marshalls	15/1	Rabun
Perry, Peter	Morgan	Leonards	399/3	Appling
Perry, Peter	Morgan	Leonards	59/4	Irwin
Perry, Richard	Franklin	Turks	12/10	Habersham
Perry, Sion	Franklin	Flanagans	84/9	Appling
Perry, William	Jones	Shropshears	101/12	Early
Perry, Willis	Baldwin	Marshals	158/2	Walton
Perry, Willis	Jackson	Winters Bt.	35/1	Early
Perryman, James	Warren	152nd	337/8	Irwin
Perryman, Matthew	Twiggs	Evans	208/12	Early
Perryman, Robert L.	Pulaski	McPhails	48/13	Habersham
Person, Christopher	Washington	Jinkinsons	193/27	Early
Person, Christopher	Washington	Jinkinsons	236/28	Early
Persons, Jonas	Putnam	Oslins	153/7	Irwin
Pervatt, James D.	Wayne	Crews	15/8	Appling
Pervis, Alfred	Jefferson	Matthews	61/27	Early
Pervis, Nancy(Wid)	Jefferson	Matthews	74/14	Irwin
Petagrew, Robert	Hancock	Hubarts	82/23	Early
Peteet, Chenoth	Wilkes	Ogletrees	379/4	Early
Peter, John(Orps)	Baldwin	Haws	6/12	Early
Peterman, Jacob	Wilkes	Davis	165/5	Appling
Peters, Edmond	Morgan	Talbots	34/12	Early
Peters, Edmond	Morgan	Talbots	378/10	Irwin
Peters, Jesse Jr.	Oglethorpe	Barnetts	19/1	Habersham
Peters, Jesse Jr.	Oglethorpe	Barnetts	326/5	Irwin
Peters, Jesse Sr.	Oglethorpe	Barnetts	187/9	Early
Peters, Matthew	Greene	Ragins	250/5	Appling
Peters, Nathaniel	Jones	Seals	86/6	Appling
Peters, Nathaniel	Jones	Seals	97/26	Early
Peters, Nathaniel	Putnam	Stampers	131/4	Walton
Peters, Robertson	Baldwin	Haws	438/28	Early
Peters, Sarah	Baldwin	Haws	19/17	Early
Peters, William	Baldwin	Haws	294/2	Appling
Peters, Wm.(RS)	Putnam	Littles	229/13	Irwin
Peters, Wm.(RS)	Putnam	Littles	339/15	Early
Peterson, Alimina(Orph)	Burke	Torrances	82/7	Irwin
Peterson, Conrod	Richmond	Laceys	254/10	Irwin
Peterson, John	Appling	6th	79/13	Early
Peterson, Malcum	Montgomery	Nobles	113/7	Early
Peterson, Mary Ann	Pulaski	Rees	353/7	Gwinnett
Peterson, Mary	Burke	Torrances	63/1	Irwin
Peterson, Matilda(Orph)	Burke	Torrances	82/7	Irwin
Peterson, Sarah(Orph)	Burke	Torrances	82/7	Irwin
Peterson, Seaborn(Orph)	Burke	Torrances	82/7	Irwin
Peterson, Thomas B.	Hancock	Millers	463/5	Irwin
Peterson, Thos.B.	Hancock	Millers	310/3	Early
Petigrew, James	Baldwin	Irwins	283/10	Irwin
Petlis, William	Wilkes	Dents	32/3	Early
Pettey, Ambros	Morgan	Townsend	51/10	Habersham
Pettigrew, Ebenezer	Oglethorpe	Barnetts	45/13	Early
Pettis, Moses	Twiggs	Evans	63/12	Early
Pettis, Stephen	Twiggs	Evans	174/16	Irwin
Pettit, John	Columbia	Dodsons	14/17	Early
Pettitt, Constantine	Richmond	122	185/12	Irwin
Petty, Littleton	Jackson	Rogers Bt.	205/9	Appling
Petty, Meredith	Scriven	9th Bt.	354/17	Early
Petty, Zachariah	Jones	Wallers	79/1	Irwin

NAME	COUNTY	MIL.DIST	LOT/SECT	DREW LAND
Pettyjohn, Abraham	Jackson	Dicksons Bt.	163/2	Irwin
Pettyjohn, Abraham	Jackson	Dicksons Bt.	63/8	Irwin
Pettyjohn, Eliz.	Jackson	Dicksons Bt.	102/8	Irwin
Pevey, Allen	Jasper	Reeds	388/12	Early
Pevy, Ambrose	Warren	Hubberts	98/7	Early
Pevy, Henry	Morgan	Talbots	357/5	Appling
Pevy, James	Wilkes	Josseys	35/10	Hall
Pew, Thomas	Laurens	Griffins	351/10	Early
Pewrifoy, Benj.W.	Jasper	Whites	121/9	Irwin
Phan, John H.	Oglethorpe	Waters	225/13	Early
Pharmon, Polly(Orpn)	Morgan	Campbells	170/19	Early
Pharoah, Francis	Richmond	Palmers	392/7	Irwin
Pharoah, Joshuah(RS)	Richmond	Palmers	30/5	Rabun
Pharr, Ephraim	Greene	143	86/16	Early
Pharroah, Frances	Richmond	Palmers	184/18	Early
Phelps, Aquilla	Jasper	Phillips	129/10	Early
Phelps, Francis	Hall	Simmonds	30/3	Irwin
Phelps, Glenn	Clark	Tredwells	34/5	Irwin
Phelps, Overton	Oglethorpe	Dunns	35/1	Appling
Phelps, Thomas	Elbert	R.Christians	113/5	Irwin
Philips, Nathan	Jasper	Evans	129/4	Walton
Philips, Nimrod	Pulaski	Maddox	62/10	Irwin
Philips, Solomon	Jefferson	Fountains	99/26	Early
Phillips, Asa R.	Morgan	Farrars	28/3	Appling
Phillips, Augustus	Morgan	Dennis	92/2	Appling
Phillips, Barthl.(Orps)	Morgan	Wrights	398/3	Early
Phillips, Benjamin	Chatham		438/7	Irwin
Phillips, Benjamin	Scriven	180	306/4	Appling
Phillips, Blewfoot	Putnam	Brooks	151/8	Irwin
Phillips, Burrel	Scriven		410/5	Appling
Phillips, Burwell	Pulaski	Maddox	47/8	Early
Phillips, Caty(Wid)	Morgan	Wrights	34/23	Early
Phillips, Charity(Wid)	Morgan	Parkers	221/8	Irwin
Phillips, Charles	Morgan	Selmons	277/18	Early
Phillips, Daniel A.	Jones	Jeffersons	176/8	Appling
Phillips, Daniel A.	Jones	Jeffersons	18/11	Habersham
Phillips, Daniel E.	Laurens	Griffins	67/6	Early
Phillips, Daniel	Jasper	Evans	64/12	Hall
Phillips, Dawson	Jones	Samuels	315/9	Early
Phillips, Dawson	Jones	Samuels	64/11	Irwin
Phillips, Dempsey	Jasper	Bentleys	103/5	Gwinnett
Phillips, Demsey	Wilkinson	Lees	314/4	Early
Phillips, Demso	Wilkinson	Smith	476/6	Appling
Phillips, Densey	Wilkinson	Lees	156/13	Irwin
Phillips, Early	Wilkes	Davis	183/26	Early
Phillips, Elizabeth	Pulaski	Maddox	59/1	Habersham
Phillips, Ephraim(Orps)	Pulaski	Maddox	255/14	Appling
Phillips, Ephraim	Emanuel	398	60/2	Early
Phillips, Gabriel	Laurens	Ross	285/8	Irwin
Phillips, George	Morgan	Campbells	111/2	Appling
Phillips, George	Morgan	Campbells	65/1	Rabun
Phillips, Hardy	Burke	Spiveys	501/6	Irwin
Phillips, Henry	Greene	Ragins	397/1	Early
Phillips, Henry	Morgan	Campbells	58/1	Appling
Phillips, Henry	Morgan	Raimeys	177/6	Appling
Phillips, Hillery	Jasper	Hays	34/3	Habersham
Phillips, James	Franklin	Ashs	219/3	Appling
Phillips, James	Jasper	McClendon	106/1	Appling
Phillips, James	Jasper	McClendons	168/10	Habersham
Phillips, James	Jasper	Phillips	85/3	Irwin
Phillips, James	Morgan	Loyds	325/2	Appling
Phillips, James	Morgan	Parkers	136/11	Habersham
Phillips, James	Pulaski	Davis	246/9	Early
Phillips, Jeremiah	Jasper	Hays	117/10	Hall
Phillips, Jeremiah	Jasper	Hays	237/5	Gwinnett
Phillips, Jesse	Morgan	Wrights	343/19	Early
Phillips, Joel(Orps)	Morgan	Parkers	137/1	Early

NAME	COUNTY	MIL.DIST	LOT/SECT	DREW LAND
Phillips, John H.	Greene	Fosters	151/11	Hall
Phillips, John J.	Burke	71st	58/17	Early
Phillips, John Sr.	Oglethorpe	Lees	138/13	Habersham
Phillips, John W.	Jasper	Phillips	37/10	Hall
Phillips, John(Orph)	Wilkinson	Childs	352/6	Early
Phillips, John	Burke	72	337/12	Irwin
Phillips, John	Twiggs	Evans	37/3	Early
Phillips, John	Washington	Robisons	311/6	Irwin
Phillips, John	Wilkes	Mattox	300/1	Appling
Phillips, John	Wilkinson	Kettles	49/6	Early
Phillips, Jonathan	Jasper	Centills	324/7	Irwin
Phillips, Joseph J.	Burke	71st	11/4	Irwin
Phillips, Joseph	Warren	151st	77/1	Appling
Phillips, Levi Jr.	Putnam	Coopers	26/2	Early
Phillips, Levi	Jackson	Rogers Bt.	269/2	Appling
Phillips, Levi	Washington	Daniels	414/28	Early
Phillips, Mark(Orps)	Greene	Fosters	144/13	Early
Phillips, Mark	Emanuel	395th	56/10	Irwin
Phillips, Mark	Emanuel	58th	201/4	Irwin
Phillips, Mark	Morgan	Hubbards	22/9	Early
Phillips, Martin	Putnam	Brooks	23/28	Early
Phillips, Martin	Putnam	Brooks	48/7	Irwin
Phillips, Milley(Wid)	Franklin	Attaways	185/1	Irwin
Phillips, Nancy(Wid)	Greene	Fosters	39/27	Early
Phillips, Nathan	Jackson	Evans	129/4	Walton
Phillips, Nathaniel H.	Putnam	Coopers	175/3	Irwin
Phillips, Nimrod	Pulaski	Maddox	343/21	Early
Phillips, Obediah	Richmond	Laceys	20/6	Gwinnett
Phillips, Obediah	Richmond	Laceys	256/12	Early
Phillips, Onesimus	Effingham		438/6	Irwin
Phillips, Richard	Scriven		360/19	Early
Phillips, Robert	Gwinnett	Hamiltons	388/8	Appling
Phillips, Rubin	Wilkes	Josies	163/14	Early
Phillips, Samuel	Laurens	Griffins	185/13	Early
Phillips, Sarah P.(Wid)	Putnam	H.Kendricks	74/28	Early
Phillips, Simeon	Morgan	Wrights	158/4	Irwin
Phillips, Solomon	Jones	Samuel	191/7	Appling
Phillips, Stephen	Franklin	Attaways	60/13	Irwin
Phillips, Thomas C.	Jasper	Phillips	15/16	Irwin
Phillips, Thomas Jr.	Jackson	Rogers Bt.	137/8	Early
Phillips, Thomas Jr.	Jackson	Rogers Bt.	180/20	Early
Phillips, Thomas	Franklin	Attaways	435/5	Irwin
Phillips, Thos.(Orps)	Putnam	H.Kendricks	376/7	Early
Phillips, Wilder Jr.	Columbia	Shaws	57/1	Rabun
Phillips, William C.	Montgomery	Alstons	378/16	Early
Phillips, William	Jasper	Hays	208/20	Early
Phillips, William	Pulaski	Maddox	32/7	Irwin
Phillips, William	Pulaski	Maddox	41/4	Walton
Phillips, William	Twiggs	Hodges	301/4	Early
Phillips, Williamson	Elbert	Pennis	455/7	Irwin
Phillips, Wm.(Orps)	Greene	Horow	227/7	Appling
Phillips, Wm.C.	Montgomery	Alstons	256/8	Early
Phillips, Wm.D.	Jasper	Hays	77/5	Early
Phillips, Zachariah Sr.	Jasper	Clays	62/1	Irwin
Phillips, Zachariah	Morgan	Selmons	20/14	Early
Phinisee, William	Jackson	Dicksons Bt.	212/11	Irwin
Phinizy, Marco(Orps)	Oglethorpe	Dunns	306/5	Irwin
Phinizy, Mary H.	Richmond	122	304/27	Early
Phinzey, John	Richmond	Laceys	173/5	Irwin
Phipps, Lewis	Elbert	Penns	78/7	Gwinnett
Phipps, Lewis	Elbert	Penns	85/6	Appling
Phipps, Richard	Elbert	Ruckers	50/1	Habersham
Phymes, William A.	Greene	Harvills	250/26	Early
Phymes, Wm.Jr.	Greene	Harvills	178/8	Appling
Phymes, Wm.Jr.	Greene	Harvills	217/12	Early
Pichard, Henry	Jones	Buckhalters	17/13	Habersham
Picken, William	Jasper	Northcuts	46/4	Habersham

NAME	COUNTY	MIL.DIST	LOT/SECT	DREW LAN
Pickering, Namon	Laurens	Ross	98/3	Walton
Pickeron, John	Telfair	Loves	356/6	Irwin
Picket, Francis	Jones	Samuels	144/2	Early
Picket, James (RS)	Jones	Jeffersons	163/10	Irwin
Pickett, Daniel	Chatham		282/5	Gwinnett
Pickett, Daniel	Chatham		50/4	Early
Pickett, Francis	Jones	Samuels	156/4	Irwin
Pickett, Martin	Jones	Jeffersons	160/12	Hall
Pickett, Robert	Jones	Greens	170/8	Early
Picquet, Benjamin	Richmond	122	117/2	Rabun
Picquet, Benjamin	Richmond	122	288/14	Early
Pierce, Alexander	Twiggs	Browns	34/1	Habersha
Pierce, Axom	Jackson	Hamiltons Bt.	185/4	Appling
Pierce, Eliz.(Wid)	Wilkinson	Bowins	394/6	Appling
Pierce, Isam	Madison	Willifords	30/14	Irwin
Pierce, Isam	Madison	Willifords	94/2	Appling
Pierce, Jesse(Orps)	Wilkinson	Bowings	303/9	Appling
Pierce, John(Orps)	Burke	71st	363/3	Early
Pierce, Joshua	Scriven	36	135/3	Habersha
Pierce, Levick Sr.(RS)	Baldwin	Marshalls	202/1	Appling
Pierce, Lovick	Greene	143	165/3	Walton
Pierce, Maria(Wid)	Chatham		47/6	Appling
Pierce, Mathew	Hancock	Caines	59/5	Irwin
Pierce, Reuben	Jackson	Dicksons Bt.	45/11	Hall
Pierce, Sherwood(Orps)	Franklin	Attaways	77/19	Early
Pierce, William	Franklin	Morriss	386/9	Early
Pierce, William	Madison	Willifords	17/27	Early
Piercy, Elizabeth	Morgan	Loyds	127/3	Habersha
Piermon, Britton	Jones	Phillips	88/7	Early
Pierson, Elijah	Warren	152	345/27	Early
Pierson, James	Warren	150th	124/4	Walton
Piew, William	Twiggs	Browns	403/11	Early
Piggott, George(Minor)	Wilkes	Willis	154/3	Appling
Pike, John	Richmond	Burtons	123/1	Early
Pikes, Nathaniel(Orps)	Baldwin	Marshalls	128/4	Irwin
Pilcher, Mary(Wid)	Wayne	Johnstons	45/7	Appling
Piles, James	Glynn		391/7	Appling
Piles, John	Glynn		200/4	Walton
Piles, Samuel	Glynn		119/19	Early
Pilgrim, Michael(RS)	Franklin	Flanagans	139/28	Early
Pinchard, Thos.C.	Jasper	Bartletts	1/2	Appling
Pinckington, Uriah	Greene	142nd	83/28	Early
Pinder, James A.	Chatham		291/9	Early
Pines, Daniel	Twiggs	Browns	382/15	Early
Pinkerton, Jas.	Hancock	Scotts	317/13	Early
Pinkston, Shadrack	Wilkes	Ogletrees	123/9	Appling
Pinson, James(Orph)	Jackson	Winters Bt.	153/4	Appling
Pinson, Thomas	Clark	Starnes	165/1	Appling
Pinson, William	Twiggs	Jeffersons	101/4	Appling
Pior, Robert	Jefferson	Bothwells	190/5	Appling
Pipe, Josiah	Oglethorpe	Wises	62/7	Early
Piper, Zadock	Hancock	Scotts	185/3	Habersha
Pipkin, Abram	Pulaski	Maddox	202/3	Walton
Pipkin, Amos	Pulaski	Maddox	230/1	Early
Pipkin, Asa	Pulaski	Maddox	394/13	Irwin
Pipkin, Jesse(Orps)	Pulaski	Maddox	3/7	Gwinnett
Pipkin, Kinchen	Pulaski	Maddox	200/4	Irwin
Pipkin, Moses	Pulaski	Maddox	229/4	Irwin
Pipkin, William	Pulaski	Maddox	443/13	Irwin
Pipkin, William	Pulaski	Maddox	63/20	Early
Piquet, Antoine	Richmond	122	26/5	Gwinnett
Pirkle, Isaac	Jackson	Hamiltons Bt.	315/17	Early
Pirkle, John	Jackson	Hamiltons Bt.	202/3	Irwin
Pitman, Edward	Hall	Buffingtons	193/11	Early
Pitman, Jesse	Twiggs	Hodges	3/10	Irwin
Pitman, Jesse	Wilkes	Russels	200/19	Early
Pitman, John(Orps)	Washington	Posts	106/1	Early

NAME	COUNTY	MIL.DIST	LOT/SECT	DREW LAND
Pitman, John	Jones	Kings	181/4	Early
Pitman, John	Jones	Kings	51/11	Early
Pitman, Martin H.	Jackson	Winters Bt.	364/10	Irwin
Pitman, Robert	Jefferson	Lamps	40/2	Rabun
Pitmon, Jesse	Warren	150th	521/7	Irwin
Pitt, Thomas	Chatham		238/4	Appling
Pittard, William	Oglethorpe	Bridges	221/4	Early
Pittard, William	Oglethorpe	Bridges	35/11	Hall
Pittman, Daniel N.	Columbia	Gartrells	193/4	Early
Pittman, Ichabod	Columbia	Gartrells	104/10	Early
Pittman, Ichabod	Columbia	Gartrells	268/13	Early
Pittman, John G.	Jackson	Winters Bt.	287/12	Irwin
Pittman, Marshall	Columbia	Gartrells	102/14	Early
Pittman, Micajah L.	Wilkes	Bryants	192/2	Irwin
Pittman, Pleasant O.	Jackson	Winters Bt.	86/12	Habersham
Pittman, Timothy	Jones	Samuels	86/3	Rabun
Pitts, Daniel	Effingham		137/5	Appling
Pitts, Hardy G.	Chatham		307/6	Gwinnett
Pitts, Henry	Laurens	Harris	447/7	Irwin
Pitts, John	Baldwin	Russells	163/1	Early
Pitts, Lunsford C.	Laurens	Harris	734/21	Early
Pitts, Martin	Twiggs	Hodges	12/9	Hall
Pitts, Martin	Twiggs	Hodges	431/9	Irwin
Pitts, Nicholas W.	Warren	153	149/8	Irwin
Pitts, Noel (Orps)	Warren	Blounts	99/1	Appling
Pitts, Obediah	Jones	Seals	137/13	Early
Pitts, Obediah	Jones	Seals	254/23	Early
Pitts, Samuel	Warren	Blounts	117/11	Hall
Pitts, Samuel	Warren	Blounts	369/20	Early
Plant, Shadrach	Wilkes	Runnalds	324/6	Early
Plant, William	Wilkes	Ogletrees	489/7	Irwin
Plat, Jane (Wid)	Chatham		507/5	Appling
Platt, David	Bulloch	Jones	147/10	Early
Platt, David	Bulloch	Jones	407/2	Appling
Platt, James (Orps)	Scriven	36th	127/4	Appling
Platts, James (Orps)	Scriven	36th	226/6	Irwin
Pleadger, Thom.Sr.	Elbert	Penns	51/1	Appling
Pleasant, Thomas	Jones	Buckhalters	163/	Appling
Pleddger, James	Elbert	Penns	208/15	Early
Pledge, William M.	Oglethorpe	Goolsbys	347/1	Appling
Pless, Philip	Jasper	Bentleys	67/3	Walton
Plumb, David	Wilkes	Gordons	432/7	Irwin
Plummer, Mary	Burke	Sullivans	142/18	Early
Poake, William	Laurens	Jones	249/19	Early
Poder, Andrew	Wilkes	Killgores	118/4	Walton
Poe, John	Franklin	Vaughns	24/21	Early
Poe, Samuel	Franklin	Vaughns	149/1	Early
Poe, Stephen	Franklin	Vaughns	296/15	Early
Poell, Reuben K.	Jefferson	Cowarts	259/11	Irwin
Pogue, Alfred (Orph)	Richmond	398	289/19	Early
Pogue, Horatio	Jones	Samuels	257/4	Walton
Pogue, John (Orph)	Richmond	398th	289/19	Early
Pogue, Orashie (Orph)	Richmond	398	289/19	Early
Polhill, James	Burke	Dys	568/2	Appling
Polk, Charles	Madison	Millicans	169/15	Irwin
Polk, Eaven	Jackson	Dicksons Bt.	524/21	Early
Polk, Jane (Wid)	Wilkinson	Lees	192/6	Early
Polk, John	Wilkinson	Lees	512/7	Appling
Polk, Uriah	Wilkinson	Lees	392/6	Irwin
Pollard, Irwin	Greene	141st	161/13	Irwin
Pollard, Jane (Wid)	Wilkes	Ogletrees	34/15	Early
Pollard, John	Morgan	Farrars	99/9	Early
Pollard, Richard	Jones	Seals	118/11	Hall
Pollard, Robert	Columbia	Pullins	199/11	Early
Pollard, Seborn	Wilkes	Mattox	66/12	Hall
Pollard, Stephen	Greene	141st	203/10	Irwin
Pollard, William	Wilkes	Ogletrees	167/15	Early

NAME	COUNTY	MIL.DIST	LOT/SECT	DREW LAN
Pollett, Henry	Clark	Harpers	1/5	Early
Pollett, Rich.(RS)	Clark	Harpers	182/3	Early
Pollock, George	Scriven	Smiths	27/5	Early
Pollock, Jesse	Twiggs	Smiths	360/7	Irwin
Pollock, Jesse	Twiggs	Smiths	407/1	Early
Pollock, John	Wilkinson	Kettles	113/7	Appling
Pollock, John	Wilkinson	Kettles	360/3	Early
Pollock, Martin	Twiggs	Smiths	251/2	Early
Pollock, Morris	Twiggs	Smiths	5/16	Early
Polson, Mark	Jasper	Bentleys	259/5	Gwinnett
Ponce, Dimas	Chatham		161/6	Early
Ponce, Dimas	Chatham		390/9	Irwin
Pondar, Hiram	Morgan	Rameys	218/27	Early
Ponder, Amos(Orps)	Oglethorpe	Bridges	35/5	Appling
Ponder, Amos	Jasper	Dardens	142/13	Early
Ponder, Amos	Jasper	Eastes	169/9	Appling
Ponder, Elizabeth	Oglethorpe	Barnetts	370/8	Early
Ponder, Ephraim	Burke	Dys	221/1	Irwin
Ponder, James H.	Jackson	Winters Bt.	526/7	Irwin
Ponder, James	Burke	Easts	15/19	Early
Ponder, John M.	Oglethorpe	Bridges	121/2	Early
Ponder, Margarett	Jasper	Eastes	109/2	Rabun
Ponder, Silas	Jasper	Eastes	170/7	Early
Ponder, Vibate	Oglethorpe	Bridges	401/8	Early
Ponledge, Ephraim	Effingham		462/12	Irwin
Ponney, Anthony	Bulloch	Jones	66/7	Appling
Ponsell, Michael	Glynn		64/8	Appling
Pontil, David(Orph)	Richmond	Laceys	45/1	Irwin
Pontil, Peter(Orph)	Richmond	Laceys	45/1	Irwin
Pool, Aaron	Jefferson	Matthews	189/20	Early
Pool, Hardy	Jefferson	Mathews	491/2	Appling
Pool, James	Wilkinson	Howards	162/2	Appling
Pool, Laban	Baldwin	Ellis	269/4	Walton
Pool, Middleton	Washington	Pools	151/19	Early
Pool, Samuel	Jackson	Dicksons	159/16	Early
Pool, Silas	Gwinnett	Hamiltons Bt.	286/7	Appling
Pool, William	Wilkes	Russels	252/2	Appling
Poole, James S.	Franklin	Turks	583/2	Appling
Poole, James	Warren	153	297/16	Early
Poole, William	Franklin	Turks	245/7	Irwin
Poole, William	Franklin	Turks	45/19	Early
Poole, Wily	Jackson	Dicksons Bt.	223/19	Early
Pope, Abner	Jefferson	Lamps	213/5	Early
Pope, Alexander	Wilkes	Gordons	136/6	Irwin
Pope, Augustine B.	Wilkes	Gordons	109/11	Hall
Pope, Cullen	Jones	Griffiths	210/10	Early
Pope, Henry	Jones	Kings	205/14	Early
Pope, Henry	Wilkes	Dents	410/21	Early
Pope, Jesse(RS)	Hancock	Evans	140/5	Irwin
Pope, Jesse	Jones	Shropshiers	57/5	Early
Pope, Jessee	Twiggs	Hodges	329/2	Early
Pope, John H.	Wilkes	Gordons	322/4	Walton
Pope, John M.	Chatham		282/5	Gwinnett
Pope, John T.	Jones	Shropshiers	372/4	Early
Pope, John	Jasper	Bentleys	54/28	Early
Pope, John	Laurens	Watsons	373/12	Early
Pope, John	Warren	Travis	271/7	Early
Pope, John	Warren	Travis	96/26	Early
Pope, John	Wilkes	Josseys	48/1	Habersha
Pope, Jonathan	Laurens	Deans	144/8	Hall
Pope, Jonathan	Laurens	Deans	36/10	Irwin
Pope, Mary	Oglethorpe	Waters	98/11	Irwin
Pope, Norphlet D.	Hancock	Coopers	452/13	Irwin
Pope, Uriah	Washington	Renfroes	237/5	Appling
Pope, Walter R.	Jones	Mullins	53/5	Appling
Pope, Wiley B.	Jones	Jeffersons	141/6	Appling
Pope, Willis(Dr)	Jackson	Rogers Bt.	289/4	Appling

NAME	COUNTY	MIL.DIST	LOT/SECT	DREW LAND
Pope, Wilson	Greene	Armers	390/2	Early
Popham, John	Franklin	R.Browns	186/7	Appling
Popham, John	Franklin	R.Browns	46/6	Early
Popham, John	Liberty		82/3	Appling
Poppell, John	Appling	4th	462/11	Irwin
Popwell, John (RS)	McIntosh	Eigles	286/7	Early
Porch, Henry	Putnam	Littles	396/2	Early
Porch, Sherod	Clark	Tredwells	158/13	Early
Porter, Archibald	Jasper	Centills	78/20	Early
Porter, Benj.(Orps)	Effingham		519/7	Irwin
Porter, Douglas W.	Morgan	Hackneys	293/8	Irwin
Porter, Edward	Camden	Clarks	135/9	Irwin
Porter, Fayette	Columbia	Dodsons	488/11	Irwin
Porter, Frederick	Early		383/5	Irwin
Porter, George	Jasper	Bentleys	58/21	Early
Porter, Henry	Jones	Phillips	374/1	Early
Porter, John W.	Morgan	Hubbards	380/15	Early
Porter, John	Jasper	Bentleys	278/28	Early
Porter, John	Jasper	McClendons	22/12	Irwin
Porter, Joseph	Wilkinson	Childs	22/2	Rabun
Porter, Joseph	Wilkinson	Childs	47/7	Irwin
Porter, Julius N.	Wilkinson	Lees	255/1	Appling
Porter, Richard	Warren	Blounts	16/10	Habersham
Porter, Richard	Warren	Blounts	69/13	Irwin
Porter, Robert B.	Jasper	McClendons	160/3	Habersham
Porter, Robert	Hancock	Scotts	157/2	Rabun
Porter, Robert	Jasper	Sentells	57/4	Early
Porter, Samuel	Baldwin	Marshalls	118/7	Appling
Porter, Shadrach	Early		128/12	Irwin
Porter, Silvester	Richmond	122	118/12	Irwin
Porter, Silvester	Richmond	122nd	526/2	Appling
Porter, Stinson	Putnam	Littles	81/9	Early
Porter, Thomas D.	Chatham		398/3	Appling
Porter, Uriah	Jones	Phillips	196/3	Early
Porter, Vinson R.	Putnam	Oslins	52/16	Early
Porter, William	Oglethorpe	Bowls	162/10	Habersham
Porterfield, David Sr.	Madison	Willifords	135/11	Early
Porterfield, David Sr.	Madison	Willifords	216/16	Early
Porterfield, David Sr.	Madison	Willifords	386/7	Early
Porterfield, James	Madison	Willifords	87/12	Habersham
Porters, Richard(Orps)	Warren	Battles	30/14	Early
Portwood, Benj.	Jasper	Blakes	156/13	Habersham
Portwood, Dempsey	Wilkes	Bryants	96/7	Early
Portwood, John	Jasper	Blakes	213/3	Early
Posey, Humphrey	Clark	Tredwells	116/5	Irwin
Posey, James	Jasper	Blakes	358/6	Irwin
Posey, John F.	Chatham		59/8	Irwin
Posey, John	Telfair	Williams	201/4	Early
Posey, Nathan	Jones	Jeffersons	36/28	Early
Posey, Nehemiah	Pulaski	Bryans	143/5	Gwinnett
Posey, Thomas	Elbert	R.Christians	38/6	Gwinnett
Poss, Christopher Jr.	Wilkes	Kilgores	250/2	Appling
Poss, George Jr.	Wilkes	Holidays	223/4	Early
Poss, George Sr.	Wilkes	Holidays	327/16	Early
Poss, Henry	Wilkes	Davis	98/5	Appling
Possey, Samuel(Orps)	Warren	153rd	240/16	Early
Posts, Moses H.	Jackson	Winters Bt.	82/8	Irwin
Pots, Moses	Jasper	Posts	239/12	Early
Potter, James	Hancock	Mims	174/13	Irwin
Potter, John S.	Jasper	McClendons	12/1	Irwin
Potts, Alexander	Jackson	Winters Bt.	224/19	Early
Potts, Henry	Jackson	Winters Bt.	361/8	Irwin
Potts, Henry	Jackson	Winters	144/9	Appling
Potts, John	Warren	Loyless	39/15	Irwin
Potts, John	Warren	Loyless	455/13	Irwin
Potts, Moses H.	Jackson	Winters	504/10	Irwin
Potts, Stephen	Jasper	Bentleys	155/2	Irwin

NAME	COUNTY	MIL.DIST	LOT/SECT	DREW LAND
Potts, Wm.	Jasper	Posts	142/5	Early
Potts, Wm.	Jasper	Posts	73/7	Appling
Pounds, Joel	Hancock	Scotts	240/4	Walton
Pounds, Numan	Clark	Moors	187/12	Irwin
Pounds, Wm.	Oglethorpe	Rowlands	509/9	Irwin
Poushier, William	Liberty		26/10	Habersham
Poushier, Wm.	Liberty		26/10	Habersham
Powel, Ambrose	Washington	Barges	270/9	Appling
Powel, Arthumus	Burke	Royals	277/8	Irwin
Powel, Arthumus	Burke	Royals	516/11	Irwin
Powel, Elijah	Burke	McNorrels	57/12	Early
Powel, Killis	Elbert	Doolys	357/4	Appling
Powel, Lewis	Burke	McNorrels	226/28	Early
Powel, Martha(Wid)	Columbia	O.Morris	17/28	Early
Powel, Sion	Jackson	Rogers Bt.	366/7	Early
Powel, Sion	Jackson	Rogers Bt.	377/3	Early
Powell, Abraham F.	Telfair	Wilsons	387/8	Appling
Powell, Asa	Clark	Deans	302/4	Walton
Powell, Benjamin	Burke	McNorrills	111/2	Habersham
Powell, Benjamin	Burke	McNorrills	59/16	Early
Powell, Blair	Habersham	Powells	202/8	Irwin
Powell, Boice	Oglethorpe	Murrays	474/8	Irwin
Powell, Coleman	Jefferson	Langstons	228/12	Early
Powell, Edley	Habersham	Powells	154/2	Walton
Powell, Eliz.(Orph)	Camden	Tillis	77/12	Early
Powell, Elkanah	Twiggs	Jeffersons	112/12	Early
Powell, Francis Jr.	Elbert	Dobbs	257/17	Early
Powell, Francis(RS)	Elbert	Dooleys	120/5	Appling
Powell, Francis(RS)	Elbert	Dooleys	20/10	Irwin
Powell, Francis	Elbert	Dobbs	263/10	Early
Powell, George	Washington	Daniels	33/9	Early
Powell, Hardy	Columbia	O.Morris	350/1	Appling
Powell, Hiram	Twiggs	Evans	30/2	Habersham
Powell, Isaac	Wilkinson	Kettles	250/26	Early
Powell, Isiah	Twiggs	Evans	383/17	Early
Powell, James	Baldwin	Irwins	60/3	Appling
Powell, James	Glynn		327/8	Irwin
Powell, James	Richmond	Burtons	88/1	Appling
Powell, James	Twiggs	R.Belchers	68/11	Hall
Powell, Jason	Jefferson	Cowarts	345/16	Early
Powell, Jeremiah	Twiggs	R.Belchers	50/6	Appling
Powell, Jeremiah	Twiggs	R.Belchers	93/17	Early
Powell, John H.Jr.	Twiggs	Thames	7/10	Early
Powell, John S.	Twiggs	Hodges	54/16	Irwin
Powell, John(Orph)	Camden	Tillis	77/12	Early
Powell, John(Orps)	Twiggs	W.Belchers	104/14	Irwin
Powell, John	Jasper	Centells	353/9	Early
Powell, John	Jefferson	Langstons	234/1	Appling
Powell, Joseph	Scriven	Roberts	510/8	Appling
Powell, Lewis	Columbia	Walkers	108/12	Hall
Powell, Littleberry	Warren	150th	126/4	Early
Powell, Littleberry	Warren	150th	307/4	Appling
Powell, Moses	Clark	Deans	97/10	Early
Powell, Moses	Jasper	Smiths	97/3	Habersham
Powell, Nathan	Morgan	McClendons	231/4	Irwin
Powell, Nelson	Wilkes	Kilgores	146/6	Irwin
Powell, Norborn	Jasper	Clays	302/4	Early
Powell, Perry	Warren	151	444/5	Irwin
Powell, Reuben	Jefferson	Cowarts	17/10	Habersham
Powell, Richard	Warren	151	329/1	Appling
Powell, Richard	Warren	151st	65/11	Irwin
Powell, Robert	Habersham	Powells	107/2	Walton
Powell, Seamore	Clark	Moores	358/1	Appling
Powell, Silas	Emanuel	55th	62/4	Habersham
Powell, Theophilus	Jefferson	Cowarts	264/19	Early
Powell, Thomas J.	Greene	143rd	62/13	Irwin
Powell, Thomas	Clark	Starness	211/4	Walton

NAME	COUNTY	MIL.DIST	LOT/SECT	DREW LAND
Powell, William	Jefferson	Lamps	167/2	Rabun
Powell, William	Jefferson	Lamps	199/19	Early
Powell, Wm.	Washington	Jinkinsons	104/16	Early
Power, James	Madison	Orrs	242/7	Appling
Power, Jesse	Madison	Orrs	16/12	Early
Power, Robert	Jasper	Bartletts	27/5	Appling
Power, Samuel	Franklin	P.Browns	309/6	Appling
Power, Samuel	Franklin	P.Browns	416/7	Appling
Powers, Clem	Effingham		281/3	Appling
Powers, Hardy	Pulaski	Senterfeits	150/2	Habersham
Powers, James	Twiggs	Smiths	41/26	Early
Powers, John	Greene	141st	32/7	Gwinnett
Powers, John	Greene	141st	326/21	Early
Powers, John	McIntosh	Hamiltons	299/20	Early
Powers, Joseph	Camden	Tillis	354/15	Early
Powers, Margaret(Orp)	Chatham		122/1	Appling
Powers, Mary A.(Orph)	Chatham		122/1	Appling
Powers, Senato	Jackson	Hamiltons Bt.	20/6	Early
Powland, Benj.	Richmond	Palmers	420/10	Irwin
Poyner, John W.	Wilkes	Perrys	132/2	Walton
Poyner, Nathan	Wilkes	Perrys	23/16	Irwin
Poythres, Joseph	Warren	Hubberts	98/15	Irwin
Poythress, George	Burke	Bells	194/18	Early
Poythress, Maryann	Scriven	Lovitts	431/10	Irwin
Poytress, Ceaton	Scriven	Roberts	177/10	Early
Prater, Caroline(Orph)	Richmond	Burtons	246/8	Irwin
Prater, Eliz.(orph)	Richmond	Burtons	246/8	Irwin
Prater, Milly(Orph)	Richmond	Burtons	246/8	Irwin
Prater, Polly(Orph)	Richmond	Burtons	246/8	Irwin
Prather, Benajah(minor)	Wilkes	Kilgores	267/9	Early
Pratt, Alexr.T.	Chatham		256/11	Irwin
Pratt, Basdell	Oglethorpe	Bowls	350/12	Early
Pratt, Eliz.(Wid)	Warren	150	512/8	Appling
Pratt, James	Pulaski	Davis	111/11	Habersham
Pratt, John	Oglethorpe	Waters	25/19	Early
Pratt, Leonard	Warren	150th	31/7	Gwinnett
Pratt, Vincent	Warren	150	615/2	Appling
Pratt, Vincent	Warren	150th	33/6	Gwinnett
Pratt, William	Camden	33rd	24/8	Hall
Pratt, Wm.O.	Jones	Buckhalters	359/10	Early
Prescoat, Anthony	Burke	McNorrills	62/10	Hall
Prescoat, Samuel	Burke	McNorrills	244/6	Irwin
Prescoat, William	Burke	McNorrills	158/5	Appling
Prescott, Benj.	Burke	McNorrels	358/16	Early
Prescott, Eliza	Chatham		384/8	Irwin
Prescott, Milledge	Richmond	Winters	89/5	Rabun
Prescott, Thomas	Bulloch	Jones	175/7	Irwin
Prescott, Thomas	Bulloch	Jones	212/13	Early
Prescott, William	Burke	McNorrills	44/5	Rabun
Presley, Elijah	Elbert	P.Christians	105/1	Habersham
Presley, Moses	Putnam	Stampers	98/8	Early
Presley, William	Franklin	Turks	381/4	Early
Presnall, Luke	Walton	Greens	347/4	Early
Presnell, Wm.(RS)	Jackson	Hamiltons Bt.	374/6	Irwin
Prestley, Moses Sr.	Putnam	Stampers	96/11	Hall
Preston, Archibald	Jasper	Phillips	107/4	Habersham
Preston, Thomas Sr.	Jasper	Phillips	86/2	Walton
Preston, Thomas	Jasper	Centells	43/10	Habersham
Prestwood, Terry	Wilkinson	Howards	351/15	Early
Preswood, Robert	Baldwin	Marshalls	161/3	Appling
Prevatt, Morgan	Camden	Tillis	71/12	Early
Prewet, Adam	Jasper	Trimbles	293/9	Early
Prewit, Ancelum	Morgan	Farrars	129/7	Appling
Prewit, James	Morgan	Farrars	96/12	Hall
Price, Benjamin	Putnam	J.Kindricks	168/11	Early
Price, Daniel(Orps)	Putnam	Stampers	141/11	Habersham
Price, Everett	Greene	Woodhams	52/3	Appling

NAME	COUNTY	MIL.DIST	LOT/SECT	DREW LAN
Price, Ezekial	Oglethorpe	Bridges	89/8	Appling
Price, George	Oglethorpe	Brittons	390/8	Irwin
Price, George	Oglethorpe	Murrays	409/7	Irwin
Price, James	Clark	Starnes	143/13	Irwin
Price, John(Orpn)	Wilkinson	Bowings	473/5	Appling
Price, John	Jasper	Northcuts	257/2	Appling
Price, John	Jasper	Northcuts	296/16	Early
Price, John	Jefferson	Langstons	355/4	Appling
Price, John	Laurens	Watsons	98/2	Early
Price, John	Twiggs	Bozemans	364/3	Appling
Price, John	Twiggs	Bozemans	414/7	Irwin
Price, Joseph	Jefferson	Waldens	240/27	Early
Price, Joseph	Jefferson	Waldens	76/1	Irwin
Price, Joshua	Washington	Wimberlys	304/2	Early
Price, Joshua	Washington	Wimberlys	318/11	Irwin
Price, Littleberry	Washington	Burneys	18/5	Habersha
Price, Littleton	Washington	Burneys	311/6	Appling
Price, Moon	Washington	Burneys	364/6	Appling
Price, Parham	Jones	Permenters	390/8	Early
Price, Richard	Washington	Renfroes	106/2	Early
Price, Sarah(Orph)	Laurens	Harris	406/6	Irwin
Price, Thomas B.	Hancock	Lucas	31/10	Hall
Price, William	Clark	Deans	323/8	Early
Price, William	Emanuel	57th	21/6	Early
Price, Willis	Jones	Harrists	401/6	Irwin
Price, Wm.(Orps)	Greene	Jones	145/7	Gwinnett
Price, Wm.(Orps)	Washington	Renfros	204/12	Irwin
Price, Wm.H.	Greene	Harvills	492/9	Irwin
Prichard, Nathl.(Orps)	Baldwin	Stephens	67/6	Gwinnett
Prichard, Presley	Morgan	Beasleys	216/12	Irwin
Pricker, William	Richmond	Laceys	174/6	Gwinnett
Prickett, Geo.	Franklin	Hammonds	25/11	Irwin
Prickett, George	Franklin	Hammonds	86/12	Early
Prickett, John Jr.	Franklin	Turks	141/1	Appling
Prickett, Josiah	Franklin	Turks	112/3	Appling
Prickett, Phillip	Hancock	Daniels	384/18	Early
Prickett, Thomas	Hancock	Daniells	157/10	Habersha
Priddy, Robert	Twiggs	Evans	133/3	Habersha
Pridgen, Amelia(Wid)	Bulloch	Edwards	460/6	Irwin
Pridgen, David	Bulloch	Tilmans	126/5	Irwin
Pridgen, Luke	Bulloch	Tilmans	490/6	Irwin
Pridgen, Susannah(Orph)	Bulloch	Edwards	164/7	Appling
Prier, John H.	Madison	Orrs	225/28	Early
Priest, Gabriel	Camden	Tillis	258/12	Early
Priest, Gabriel	Camden	Tillis	598/2	Appling
Priggin, Edwin(Orps)	Washington	Mannings	273/20	Early
Primrose, Eliz.(Wid)	Richmond	Burtons	63/10	Habersha
Primrose, James	Richmond	Burtons	369/26	Early
Primrose, James	Richmond	Bustins	299/5	Early
Prince, Sarah(Wid)	Jefferson	Abbots	29/2	Walton
Prince, Sylvanus	Washington	Wimberleys	53/6	Appling
Pringle, Banister J.	Clark	Starnes	63/1	Habersha
Prinkley, John	Greene	144th	148/13	Habersha
Prior, John H.	Madison	Orrs	283/19	Early
Prior, John H.	Madison	Orrs	369/12	Early
Prior, John	Burke	Sullivans	129/10	Habersha
Pritchell, Elizabeth	Madison	Willifords	357/6	Early
Pritchett, Benj.	Hancock	Danells	85/2	Early
Procter, Joshua	Wilkinson	Brooks	54/1	Appling
Proctor, Daniel	Chatham		68/2	Walton
Proctor, John Sr.	Wilkinson	Brooks	297/6	Gwinnett
Proctor, John	Jones	Phillips	310/14	Early
Proctor, John	Wilkinson	Brooks	333/9	Irwin
Proctor, Joshua	Wilkinson	Brooks	102/18	Early
Proctor, Melinda(Orps)	Burke	Royals	117/21	Early
Proctor, Stephen	Wilkinson	Brooks	78/21	Early
Proctor, Wm.Jr.	Wilkinson	Brooks	38/17	Early

NAME	COUNTY	MIL.DIST	LOT/SECT	DREW LAND
Procuer, Caroline	Chatham		50/2	Habersham
Prosser, Joab H.	Chatham		268/28	Early
Prosser, John(Orps)	Jones	Wallers	20/4	Appling
Prossy, William	Washington	Peabodys	101/9	Appling
Prothro, Nathaniel	Elbert	Dobbs	2/6	Appling
Prucills, John	Chatham		158/2	Habersham
Pruett, Jacob Sr.	Jones	Seals	226/2	Early
Pruett, William Jr.	Jones	Seals	301/27	Early
Pruett, William Sr.	Jones	Seals	215/5	Gwinnett
Pruit, Hezekiah	Jackson	Dicksons Bt.	62/18	Early
Pruit, Samuel	Putnam	Berrys	389/12	Irwin
Pruit, Tillman	Franklin	Boswells	171/21	Early
Pruitt, Bird	Putnam	J.Kindricks	391/1	Appling
Pruitt, Joseph(Orps)	Franklin	Haynes	89/9	Hall
Pruitt, Joseph	Franklin	Haynes	218/20	Early
Pruitt, Robt.W.	Franklin	Haynes	320/4	Appling
Pruitt, Russel	Hancock	Mimms	497/8	Appling
Pryor, John	Burke	Sullivans	372/19	Early
Pryor, Marlow	Baldwin	Marshals	356/16	Early
Pryor, William	Jasper	Easts	357/10	Irwin
Psalmonds, Thomas	Wilkes	Burks	47/18	Early
Psalter, Zabel	Wilkinson	Smiths	89/2	Habersham
Pucket, Edmund	Putnam	Coopers	49/4	Irwin
Pucket, Joel	Jackson	Hamiltons Bt.	402/4	Early
Pucket, Richard	Jackson	Hamiltons Bt.	35/6	Gwinnett
Puckett, Aaron B.	Pulaski	Lesters	40/7	Gwinnett
Puckett, Richard	Jackson	Hamiltons Bt.	127/12	Hall
Pugh, Dorithy(Wid)	Twiggs	Bozemans	86/28	Early
Pugh, Edwards	Wilkinson	Howards	322/15	Early
Pugh, James	Twiggs	R.Belchers	14/4	Habersham
Pugh, Robert	Burke	Lewis	525/2	Appling
Pugh, Thomas(Orps)	Wilkinson	Lees	17/1	Rabun
Pugh, Thomas	Washington	Barges	172/14	Early
Puham, Nelson	Jones	Permenters	79/1	Rabun
Pulham, Nelson	Jones	Permenters		—
Pullen, Abraham	Wilkes	Burkes	357/2	Appling
Pullen, Athael	Greene	141st	114/6	Appling
Pullen, Elijah Sr.	Wilkes	Russels	390/4	Early
Pullen, Henry	Hancock	Smiths	291/1	Walton
Pullen, John	Wilkes	Russels	103/3	Walton
Pullen, Joseph Sr.	Wilkes	Russells	243/8	Irwin
Pulliam, Benj.	Franklin	P.Browns	327/7	Appling
Pulliam, Joseph Sr.	Franklin	Burroughs	186/4	Appling
Pulliam, Joseph	Elbert	Penns	129/15	Early
Pulliam, Mathew	Elbert	B.Higginbotham	169/7	Appling
Pulliam, Mathew	Elbert	B.Higginbotham	302/5	Early
Pulliam, Robt.Jr.	Franklin	Burroughs	132/3	Walton
Pulliam, Thomas	Franklin	Burroughs	183/5	Appling
Pulliam, Wm.Jr.	Elbert	B.Higginbotham	81/6	Early
Pullims, (Orps)	Franklin	Akins	86/1	Irwin
Pullin, Asher	Columbia	Pullins	387/2	Appling
Pullin, George	Morgan	Hubbards	495/9	Irwin
Pullin, James Jr.	Wilkes	Russells	301/2	Appling
Pullin, John	Columbia	Pullins	142/10	Hall
Pullin, Joseph(Sr)	Wilkes	Russels	180/3	Appling
Pullin, Levan	Hancock	Mims	300/7	Gwinnett
Pullin, Levan	Hancock	Mims	58/16	Early
Pullin, Moses	Laurens	Deans	317/2	Early
Pullin, Samuel	Columbia	Pullins	184/4	Walton
Pullin, Sanford	Wilkes	Russels	124/18	Early
Pulling, Henry	Emanuel	56th	400/6	Early
Pullock, John	Wilkinson	Kettles	113/7	Appling
Pullum, Wm.	Baldwin	Marshalls	112/12	Habersham
Pully, Benjamin	Baldwin	Taliafarro	219/28	Early
Pumphrey, Isham	Jones	Greens	74/9	Appling
Purcy, Benjn.F.	Morgan	Leonards	82/6	Early
Purdee, Larkin	Franklin	Harris	20/8	Hall

NAME	COUNTY	MIL.DIST	LOT/SECT	DREW LAN
Purdue, Larkin	Franklin	Harris	123/6	Early
Purdum, Thomas	Wayne	Crews	317/5	Irwin
Purdum, Thomas	Wayne	Crews	69/6	Habersha
Purify, Archd	Putnam	Slaughters	101/2	Early
Purify, Arrington	Jasper	McClendons	315/4	Early
Purkin, Constantine(Ors)	Jackson	Rogers Bt.	51/2	Appling
Purkins, Joel(RS)	Jackson	Hamiltons	166/3	Early
Purkins, John	Jones	Chappels	206/3	Irwin
Purkins, Lunsford	Wilkes	Bryants	317/5	Appling
Purkins, Robert	Clark	Moors	209/8	Early
Purkins, Wright	Wilkinson	Brooks	219/20	Early
Purkins, Wright	Wilkinson	Brooks	35/3	Appling
Purnel, John	Washington	Wimberlys	8/10	Habersha
Purnell, George	Washington	Wimberleys	339/5	Irwin
Purnell, John(Orps)	Washington	Wimberleys	325/8	Early
Purnell, Samuel	Columbia	O.Morris	303/4	Irwin
Purnington, Neddy	Jones	Samuel	499/5	Irwin
Pursel, James	Franklin	Moores	8/12	Early
Purvis, Bennet	Wilkinson	Bowings	79/5	Early
Putman, Jesse	Franklin	Powels	229/21	Early
Putnam, Ann S.(Wid)	Chatham		47/14	Irwin
Putnam, Henry(Orps)	Putnam	Oslins	193/21	Early
Putnam, Jesse	Franklin	Powels	155/1	Irwin
Putnam, John G.	Chatham		151/13	Early
Pye, Andy(Orps)	Oglethorpe	Davenports	156/16	Early
Pye, James	Scriven	Roberts	251/21	Early
Pye, Jesse	Oglethorpe	Davenports	26/4	Habersha
Pye, Lewis	Jasper	Clays	65/7	Irwin
Pye, William	Oglethorpe	Davenports	97/6	Early
Pyle, Samuel	Walton	Sentells	219/9	Early
Pyron, Drury	Greene	Ragins	489/11	Irwin
Pyron, William	Greene	Ragins	44/11	Early
Qualls, David	Twiggs	W.Belcher	99/5	Irwin
Quals, Peter	Twiggs	Evans	452/9	Irwin
Quarles, Samuel	Twiggs	Evans	292/19	Early
Quarterman, ?	Liberty		180/9	Early
Quarterman, Thomas	Liberty		363/8	Early
Quattleboum, David	Twiggs	Ellis	273/6	Irwin
Quillen, Daniel	Franklin	Aikins	43/14	Early
Quillen, James Jr.	Franklin	Aikins	59/6	Habersha
Quillen, James Sr.	Franklin	Aikins	161/2	Irwin
Quillen, James Sr.	Franklin	Aikins	382/3	Appling
Quin, Allen C.	Washington	Peabodys	227/17	Early
Quiney, Nancy	Jefferson	Flemings	287/10	Early
Quinn, Edward	Richmond	398th	87/6	Irwin
Quinn, John	Lincoln	Walkers	351/1	Early
Quinn, John	Montgomery		5/22	Early
Quinn, William O.	Richmond	Laceys	197/10	Early
Quinn, William Sr.	Lincoln	Walkers	142/2	Rabun
Quinn, William	Baldwin	Russels	455/3	Appling
Quizenberry, David	Richmond	122nd	33/4	Rabun
Quizenberry, Thomas	Richmond	122nd	1/19	Early
Quizenberry, Thomas	Richmond	122nd	261/2	Appling
Rabb, Hezekiah	Laurens	S.Smith	122/11	Habersha
Rabb, Robert	Twiggs	R.Belchers	165/6	Early
Rabourn, Berry	Putnam	Buckners	369/6	Early
Rabun, Bud	Twiggs	Evans	401/13	Irwin
Rabun, Charles	Twiggs	Evans	199/5	Appling
Rabun, Charles	Twiggs	Evans	4/7	Appling
Rabun, Richard	Twiggs	Evans	114/11	Early
Rachael, Ezekiel	Burke	Thomas	147/28	Early
Rachales, Wm.	Washington	Cummings	88/15	Irwin
Rachel, Zadoch	Warren	154th	93/19	Early
Rachel, Zedoch	Warren	154	39/4	Walton
Rackley, Joel	Burke	Hands	563/2	Appling
Radcliff, John	Wilkes	Josseys	233/26	Early
Raddin, James	Greene	Carltons	326/13	Early

NAME	COUNTY	MIL.DIST	LOT/SECT	DREW LAND
Raden, Thomas	Oglethorpe	Myricks	325/27	Early
Radford, Henry(Orps)	Morgan	Farrars	333/27	Early
Radford, John	Morgan	Farrars	314/6	Irwin
Radford, Julina(Wid)	Morgan	Farrars	273/17	Early
Radford, Robert	Twiggs	Hodges	579/2	Appling
Radney, Thomas	Jones	Samuels	325/11	Early
Ragain, Hamilton	Oglethorpe	Barnetts	13/1	Rabun
Ragan, Brice	Wilkinson	Lees	208/9	Irwin
Ragan, Charles	Elbert	Penns	115/8	Appling
Ragan, Charles	Elbert	Penns	236/7	Appling
Ragan, Hamilton	Oglethorpe	Barnett	272/4	Early
Ragan, Jeheu	Oglethorpe	Bowls	440/2	Appling
Ragan, Marcus B.	Oglethorpe	Bowles	211/7	Irwin
Ragan, Mark	Oglethorpe	Barnetts	327/9	Irwin
Ragan, Mark	Oglethorpe	Barnetts	490/8	Irwin
Ragan, Price	Wilkinson	Lees	117/2	Irwin
Ragan, Price	Wilkinson	Lees	380/28	Early
Ragan, Thomas(Orps)	Jackson	Rogers	60/1	Walton
Ragers, Isham(Orps)	Wilkinson	Childs	55/1	Walton
Ragland, Frederick	Jasper	Bailey	198/9	Early
Ragland, William	Jasper	Evans	31/4	Rabun
Ragnes, Josiah(Orp)	Chatham		338/19	Early
Ragnes, Maria(Orp)	Chatham		338/19	Early
Ragsdale, John W.	Gwinnett	Hamiltons Bt.	109/20	Early
Ragsdell, John W.	Gwinnett	Hamiltons Bt.	297/6	Irwin
Rahn, Cletus	Effingham		259/5	Irwin
Rahn, Jonathan S.	Effingham		220/9	Appling
Rahn, Joseph	Effingham		367/10	Irwin
Rahn, Mathew(RS)	Effingham		173/15	Early
Rahn, Mathew(RS)	Effingham		311/8	Irwin
Rahn, Mathew(RS)	Effingham		83/6	Early
Raiford, Alexr.G.	Jefferson	Abbotts	310/5	Gwinnett
Raiford, Morris Jr.	Jefferson	Langston	250/7	Appling
Raiford, Morris Sr.	Jefferson	Langstone	180/26	Early
Railey, Geo.W.	Hancock	Millers	205/5	Irwin
Raily, George W.	Hancock	Millers	7/8	Early
Raily, James	Warren	154th	118/11	Early
Rain, Joseph	Camden	Baileys	101/1	Walton
Rain, Joseph	Camden	Baileys	77/16	Irwin
Raine, Cornelius	Camden	Tillis	27/6	Early
Rainely, John	Putnam	Morelands	460/11	Irwin
Raines, Noah	Jones	Jefferson	243/19	Early
Raines, Sarah(Wid)	Laurens	Watsons	295/6	Gwinnett
Raines, Sarah(Wid)	Twiggs	Browns	204/13	Early
Rainey, Daniel	Oglethorpe	Dunns	112/3	Early
Rainey, Edmond	Oglethorpe	Bowls	207/3	Appling
Rainey, John B.	Oglethorpe	Daniels	137/5	Early
Rainey, John	Putnam	Morelands	348/1	Early
Rainey, Matthew	Oglethorpe	Dunns	76/1	Appling
Raingard, Mary	Chatham		228/27	Early
Rains, Allen	Baldwin	Irwins	410/6	Appling
Rains, Allen	Washington	Robisons	326/7	Appling
Rains, Josiah	Wilkes	Brooks	198/7	Appling
Rains, Noah	Jones	Jefferson	8/13	Irwin
Rains, Washington	Washington	Robinsons	11/28	Early
Rains, William	Morgan	Talbots	24/10	Early
Rakestraw, Robert	Oglethorpe	Brittons	123/1	Appling
Rakestraw, William	Jackson	Hamiltons	316/15	Early
Rakstraw, Margr.(Wid)	Clarke	Harpers	92/4	Walton
Raley, Chas.(RS)	Twiggs	Smiths	23/6	Early
Ralls, Arthur	Laurens	D.Smith	241/6	Gwinnett
Ralls, Caleb	Wilkes	Smiths	231/16	Early
Ralls, Joseph	Jackson	Rogers	186/17	Early
Ralston, Alexander R.	Richmond	120th	64/15	Early
Ralston, Rassta R.	Chatham		231/11	Early
Ramey, Danniel	Clarke	Deans	193/6	Early
Ramey, John Sr.(RS)	Clarke	Moores	79/2	Early

NAME	COUNTY	MIL.DIST	LOT/SECT	DREW LAND
Ramey, Mathew F.	Jackson	Rogers	71/8	Irwin
Rammage, Josiah	Wilkinson	Howards	128/11	Hall
Ramsey, Edmund	Morgan	Parkers	5/1	Irwin
Ramsey, James(Orps)	Franklin	Hammonds	33/18	Early
Ramsey, James	Franklin	Keltons	182/8	Early
Ramsey, James	Greene	143	421/8	Appling
Ramsey, James	Jackson	Winters	112/11	Habersham
Ramsey, James	Jackson	Winters	217/4	Irwin
Ramsey, James	Jones	Kings	181/4	Irwin
Ramsey, James	Jones	Kings	362/5	Appling
Ramsey, Lewis	Laurens	Ross	241/8	Appling
Ramsey, Penelope(Wid)	Laurens	Jones	399/6	Early
Ramsey, Randal	Columbia	Pullins	291/7	Appling
Ramsey, Thomas	Jasper	Northcuts	74/10	Early
Ramsey, Thomas	Wilkes	Brooks	129/1	Irwin
Ramsey, William Sr.	Franklin	Akins	23/12	Hall
Ramsey, Wm.	Franklin	Morris	129/1	Appling
Ramsey, Wm.Sr.	Franklin	Akins	238/3	Early
Randall, William	Greene	140	246/10	Irwin
Randle, James	Greene	141	75/1	Irwin
Randle, Larkington	Hancock	Sharps	133/5	Irwin
Randle, Newton	Jasper	Hays	30/2	Walton
Randle, Peter	Warren	Rodgers	71/1	Rabun
Randle, William	Greene	140th	78/13	Early
Randle, Willis	Morgan	McClendon	220/3	Appling
Randle, Willis	Morgan	McClendons	399/9	Irwin
Randoll, Frederick	Twiggs	Brown	368/6	Appling
Randolph, Ann(Orps)	Burke	M.Wards	103/4	Appling
Randolph, James H.	Richmond	398	20/9	Hall
Randolph, Jeremiah	Jasper	Bentley	82/5	Early
Randolph, John	Jackson	Hamiltons	288/7	Gwinnett
Randolph, John	Jackson	Hamiltons	425/6	Irwin
Randolph, Lee	Jackson	Hamiltons	350/5	Appling
Randolph, Lucy	Wilkes	Gordons	165/14	Early
Randolph, Nimrod F.	Wilkinson	Mims	79/7	Appling
Randolph, Payton	Jackson	Hamiltons	348/7	Gwinnett
Randolph, Richard H.	Morgan	Hubbards	343/6	Early
Randolph, Robert R.	Oglethorpe	Briton	83/8	Early
Randolphm, Augustus W.	Richmond	120th	79/4	Habersham
Ranes, Sarah(Wid)	Jones	Samuels	48/9	Irwin
Raney, Caswell	Telfair	Tallis	92/3	Appling
Raney, George(Orps)	Putnam	Slaughters	382/4	Appling
Raney, Jesse	Oglethorpe	Myricks	264/2	Early
Raney, Matthew	Jasper	Centell	97/10	Hall
Rankin, Adam W.	Greene	141	198/13	Early
Ransom, Davies	Hancock	Evans	54/6	Irwin
Ransom, Dudley	Morgan	Loyds	132/12	Habersham
Ransom, Dudly	Morgan	Loyds	191/26	Early
Ransom, James	Greene	Whoolis	334/7	Gwinnett
Ransom, John	Greene	Kimbroughs	274/8	Appling
Ransom, Reuben Sr.	Greene	Kimbroughs	315/7	Early
Ransom, Samuel	Hancock	Penns	351/4	Appling
Ransworth, Jacob(RS)	Jackson	Rogers	183/17	Early
Rasberry, Joseph	Clarke	Harpers	41/6	Early
Rasberry, William	Jackson	Rogers	55/10	Early
Raseberry, William	Oglethorpe	Davenport	285/5	Irwin
Ratcliff, Wm.(Orps)	Lincoln	Tatoms	177/7	Irwin
Ratherford, David	Jackson	Hamiltons	68/6	Appling
Ratherford, Isaac	Jackson	Hamiltons	90/5	Irwin
Ratherford, James(Orps)	Jackson	Hamiltons	127/17	Early
Ratherford, James	Jackson	Hamiltons	17/2	Early
Ratherford, James	Jackson	Hamiltons	267/5	Appling
Ratherford, Mary	Jackson	Hamiltons	231/8	Appling
Ratliff, James(Orps)	Burke	Sullivans	529/5	Appling
Ratliff, James	Wayne	Crews	88/13	Irwin
Ratliff, John	Hall	Simmonds	331/10	Early
Raulerson, Noel	Appling	9th	27/2	Rabun

NAME	COUNTY	MIL.DIST	LOT/SECT	DREW LAND
Raulerson, William	Appling	9th	53/2	Habersham
Raulerson, William	Appling	9th	66/14	Irwin
Rawles, Arthur	Laurens	D.Smith	390/19	Early
Rawles, Dempsy	Washington	Avents	71/5	Irwin
Rawlison, Jacob	Appling	4th	72/11	Hall
Rawls, Cotton	Columbia	Gartrells	332/17	Early
Rawls, Eliz.(Wid)	Emanuel	57th	233/3	Appling
Rawls, James	Greene	143	24/8	Appling
Rawls, John Sr.	Bulloch	Knights	118/4	Early
Rawls, John	Pulaski	Lesters	304/9	Irwin
Rawls, John	Scriven	Lovetts	11/1	Early
Rawls, Joseph	Scriven	36th	106/27	Early
Rawls, Joseph	Scriven	36th	355/21	Early
Rawls, Seaborn	Tattnall	Overstreets	125/2	Rabun
Rawls, William H.	Jackson	Scotts	6/4	Irwin
Rawls, William	Emanuel	57th	426/13	Irwin
Rawson, Elijah	Franklin	Davis	58/10	Hall
Rawstons, Peter(Orph)	Clarke	Harriss	9/12	Hall
Ray, Ambrose Sr.	Washington	Pools	97/4	Habersham
Ray, Anderson	Morgan	Talbotts	395/15	Early
Ray, Andrew Sr.	Greene	Tuggles	327/1	Early
Ray, Ann	Oglethorpe	Bowls	228/4	Irwin
Ray, Bartlett	Jasper	McClendon	149/12	Hall
Ray, Benjamin	Twiggs	W.Belchers	361/21	Early
Ray, Chesley	Wilkes	Maddox	209/5	Appling
Ray, Chestly	Wilkes	Mattox	67/19	Early
Ray, David	Walton	Davis	301/7	Early
Ray, Duncan	Pulaski	Lesters	148/8	Early
Ray, Elijah	Jasper	Baileys	394/5	Appling
Ray, Elisha	Oglethorpe	Murray	329/2	Appling
Ray, Elisha	Oglethorpe	Murrays	324/8	Irwin
Ray, George A.	Morgan	Selmons	215/27	Early
Ray, Jacob	Wilkes	Perrys	26/4	Rabun
Ray, James(Orph)	Columbia	J.Morris	228/7	Gwinnett
Ray, James	Hancock	Edwards	299/1	Walton
Ray, James	Jasper	Clays	463/5	Appling
Ray, Jeremiah W.	Twiggs	R.Belchers	261/6	Early
Ray, John C.W.	Twiggs	W.Belchers	195/8	Early
Ray, John H.	Greene	Ragins	191/6	Appling
Ray, John Jr.	Morgan	Selmons	176/3	Appling
Ray, John Jr.	Morgan	Selmons	191/10	Habersham
Ray, John(Orps)	Columbia	Bealls	438/5	Appling
Ray, John	Franklin	Morris	281/1	Appling
Ray, Jonathan	Oglethorpe	Murrays	174/17	Early
Ray, Jonathan	Oglethorpe	Murrays	24/6	Appling
Ray, Jos.(Orps)	Columbia	Bealls	111/13	Habersham
Ray, Mark	Jasper	Eastes	273/13	Irwin
Ray, Moses	Franklin	Haynes	21/6	Appling
Ray, Moses	Oglethorpe	Myricks	282/4	Early
Ray, Niell	Putnam	Brooks	353/26	Early
Ray, Solomon	Jasper	Dardens	3/6	Irwin
Ray, Thomas	Franklin	P.Browns	210/27	Early
Ray, Thomas	Walton	Echols	199/6	Gwinnett
Ray, Wiley	Greene	Ragins	59/12	Habersham
Ray, William	Clarke	Mitchells	264/3	Appling
Ray, William	Franklin	Akins	155/3	Irwin
Ray, William	Franklin	Akins	9/15	Early
Ray, William	Hancock	Millers	406/11	Irwin
Ray, William	Hancock	Millers	48/15	Early
Rayford, Patience	Baldwin	Marshalls	149/14	Irwin
Raynes, Joseph	Wilkinson	Bowings	201/9	Appling
Raynes, Robert	Wilkinson	Kittles	159/4	Walton
Rays, Andrew Jr.	Greene	Tuggles	407/5	Irwin
Rea, Bently(RS)	Gwinnett	Hamiltons Bt.	417/4	Appling
Rea, James	Chatham		378/11	Early
Reach, Enoch	Morgan	Parkers	127/7	Gwinnett
Reach, Washington	Emanuel	57th	16/13	Habersham

NAME	COUNTY	MIL.DIST	LOT/SECT	DREW LAN
Reach, Washington	Emanuel	57th	31/4	Early
Read, Frederick	Jasper	Smiths	321/10	Early
Read, Jesse	Morgan	Parkers	346/6	Irwin
Read, John W.	Richmond		82/12	Hall
Read, John	Twiggs	Thames	76/10	Hall
Readick, Peter	Camden	33rd	519/6	Irwin
Reamay, Jacob	Jackson	Hamiltons	152/2	Irwin
Reamay, Thomas	Jackson	Hamiltons	349/12	Irwin
Reason, James	Chatham		78/10	Hall
Reaves, Abner(Orps)	Jasper	Smiths	314/9	Irwin
Reaves, Absalom	Jasper	Clays	394/8	Appling
Reaves, Burges	Jackson	Hamiltons	203/26	Early
Reaves, George	Hancock	Edwards	75/5	Early
Reaves, Sarah(Wid)	Jackson	Hamiltons	229/16	Irwin
Reaves, Tyre	Wilkes	Brooks	174/14	Early
Reaves, Tyre	Wilkes	Brooks	303/6	Early
Reckley, Nathan	Scriven	Lovetts	310/6	Irwin
Reckley, Nathan	Scriven	Lovetts	396/6	Irwin
Recor, William L.	Morgan	Alfords	135/10	Irwin
Red, Andrew(Orp)	Oglethorpe	Myricks	70/9	Early
Red, James	Greene	Macons	234/12	Early
Red, Robert	Greene	Macons	494/6	Appling
Red, Thomas	Burke	McNorrills	495/7	Appling
Reddick, Ann	Chatham		385/3	Appling
Reddick, Eliz.(Wid)	Camden	33rd	370/9	Irwin
Reddick, John(Orp)	Burke	Royals	60/15	Irwin
Reddick, Nicholas(Orp)	Burke	Royals	60/15	Irwin
Reddick, Thomas	Scriven	36th	139/12	Early
Redding, Anderson	Jones	Samuels	365/16	Early
Redding, Edith	Baldwin	Doziers	37/5	Early
Redding, James	Greene	Carltons	363/8	Irwin
Redding, John	Baldwin	Ellis	283/5	Appling
Redding, Rehum(RS)	Twiggs	Ellis	188/1	Walton
Redding, Rehum(RS)	Twiggs	Ellis	340/17	Early
Redding, Rehum(RS)	Twiggs	Ellis	379/5	Early
Redding, Rehum(RS)	Twiggs	Ellis	94/16	Irwin
Redding, Thomas	Baldwin	Doziers	152/2	Rabun
Redding, William C.	Baldwin	Marshalls	78/3	Walton
Reddins, Thos.(Orps)	Wilkinson	Lees	430/8	Irwin
Redford, Elijah	Morgan	Farrars	2/11	Irwin
Redgood, Matthew	Burke	Bells	221/6	Gwinnett
Redick, John	Burke	Hands	178/12	Habersha
Redling, Jacob	Jackson	Mays	248/23	Early
Redmond, Benj.	Richmond	Bentons	202/28	Early
Redon, John	Jackson	Mays	392/3	Early
Redwine, Jacob Jr.	Franklin	Hammonds	40/20	Early
Redwine, Jesse	Franklin	Attaways	4/1	Irwin
Redwine, John	Franklin	Attaways	270/26	Early
Redwine, Lewis	Franklin	Burroughs	84/21	Early
Redwine, Michael	Franklin	Burroughs	427/5	Appling
Redwine, William	Franklin	Attaways	154/10	Habersha
Reece, David A.	Elbert	G.Higginbotham	231/6	Gwinnett
Reece, Richard	Warren	153rd	110/6	Gwinnett
Reed, Elisha	Putnam	Mays	221/20	Early
Reed, Ezekial	Columbia	Pullins	123/1	Walton
Reed, Griffin	Hall		355/12	Early
Reed, Isaac Jr.	Hall		132/3	Irwin
Reed, Isaac Jr.	Hall		293/20	Early
Reed, Jacob	McIntosh	Hamilton	43/12	Early
Reed, James L.	Franklin	Hammonds	129/3	Appling
Reed, James L.	Franklin	Hammonds	288/2	Early
Reed, James Sr.	Franklin	Hammonds	303/5	Early
Reed, James(Orps)	Morgan	Campbells	165/2	Rabun
Reed, James	Lincoln	Walker	337/16	Early
Reed, James	Lincoln	Walkers	283/5	Early
Reed, John C.	Franklin	P.Brown	147/4	Walton
Reed, John S.	Jones	Phillips	191/5	Appling

NAME	COUNTY	MIL.DIST	LOT/SECT	DREW LAND
Reed, John	Franklin	Hoopers	9/2	Appling
Reed, John	Jones	Buckhalter	505/4	Appling
Reed, Joseph	Franklin	Burroughs	18/5	Early
Reed, Joseph	Franklin	Burroughs	200/3	Irwin
Reed, Lydia(Wid)	Columbia	Bealls	64/4	Walton
Reed, Michael	Columbia	Pullins	268/10	Early
Reed, Oliver	Richmond	122nd	244/13	Irwin
Reed, Sampson	McIntosh	McIntoshs	175/7	Early
Reed, Samuel D.	Hancock	Lucas	226/8	Appling
Reed, Zachariah	Putnam	Berrys	229/6	Irwin
Reed, Zephheniah	Baldwin	Ellis	19/6	Habersham
Reeds, Benjamin(Orps)	Hancock	Canes	315/1	Early
Reel, Starling	Warren	152nd	20/17	Early
Rees, Benjamin T.	Columbia	Dodsons	113/9	Appling
Rees, Harris	Warren	153	221/4	Irwin
Rees, Huett	Warren	152	369/10	Irwin
Rees, James	Columbia	J.Morris	454/11	Irwin
Rees, James	Putnam	Butts	18/19	Early
Rees, Joel(Orps)	Putnam	Bustins	26/1	Walton
Rees, John	Putnam	Oslins	292/20	Early
Rees, Nancey(Wid)	Warren	152	282/1	Walton
Rees, Simeon	Columbia	Watsons	261/12	Irwin
Rees, Thaddeus B.	Putnam	Oslins	271/10	Irwin
Reese, Cuthbert	Jasper	Kennedy	15/4	Walton
Reese, Susan	Jasper	Kennedy	33/17	Early
Reese, Williamson C.	Clarke	Oates	123/11	Irwin
Reeves, Drury	Telfair	Williams	451/7	Appling
Reeves, George	Hancock	Edwards	174/15	Early
Reeves, Henry	Jones	Samuels	49/16	Irwin
Reeves, Jesse T.	Putnam	Evans	115/3	Walton
Reeves, Jesse	Tattnall	Jos.Durrences	420/7	Appling
Reeves, Jessee	Camden	Tileses	31/9	Irwin
Reeves, John D.	Wilkes	Burks	327/5	Gwinnett
Reeves, John Sr.	Columbia	O.Morris	335/3	Early
Reeves, John Sr.	Jackson	Hamiltons	333/8	Early
Reeves, John(Orp)	Pulaski	Rees	151/5	Irwin
Reeves, John	Jasper	Evans	204/3	Appling
Reeves, John	Jones	Buckhalter	184/27	Early
Reeves, Jonathan Sr.	Jasper	Smiths	119/4	Irwin
Reeves, Lucius	Putnam	Mays	149/4	Walton
Reeves, Malachi	Jones	Shropshier	326/11	Early
Reeves, Marian(Wid)	Telfair	Loves	237/18	Early
Reeves, Michael	Jones	Shropshier	19/3	Early
Reeves, Spencer	Columbia	Shaws	23/9	Hall
Reeves, Thomas	Wilkes	Burks	140/1	Walton
Reeves, William	Wilkes	Davis	86/2	Early
Reeves, Wyatt	Jasper	Dardens	211/2	Early
Regan, Elias	Pulaski	Rees	513/9	Irwin
Regan, Joseph	Pulaski	Rees	136/4	Early
Regan, Joseph	Pulaski	Rees	180/8	Appling
Regan, Robinson	Twiggs	R.Belchers	330/26	Early
Regan, Wythal	Jones	Buckhalter	572/2	Appling
Regby, William Jr.	Warren	Hopson	16/11	Irwin
Regester, Samuel	Bulloch	Edwards	27/9	Early
Register, Abraham(Orps)	Bulloch	Tilmans	343/16	Early
Register, David	Laurens	Deans	446/5	Appling
Register, Jesse Sr.	Washington	Wimberleys	127/6	Early
Register, John	Laurens	Harriss	45/13	Habersham
Register, John	Washington	Wimberlys	23/4	Irwin
Register, John	Washington	Wimberlys	458/6	Appling
Register, Thomas Jr.	Laurens	Kinchens	85/11	Habersham
Register, Thos.Sr.	Laurens	Kenchins	113/13	Habersham
Register, William C.	Washington	Wimberlys	236/1	Walton
Register, William	Bulloch	Edwards	350/26	Early
Reid, Alfred B.	Twiggs	W.Belchers	128/10	Irwin
Reid, Ama	Madison	Orrs	34/2	Irwin
Reid, Cunningham D.	Putnam	Brooks	331/4	Early

NAME	COUNTY	MIL.DIST	LOT/SECT	DREW LAN
Reid, George(Orps)	Madison	Orrs	120/16	Early
Reid, George	Franklin	Burroughs	443/3	Appling
Reid, Hariet(Orph)	Richmond	120th	53/3	Irwin
Reid, Issac Sr.	Hall		24/29	Early
Reid, James	Putnam	Berrys	397/6	Irwin
Reid, John	Morgan	Cheves	312/1	Appling
Reid, John	Morgan	Loyds	162/8	Appling
Reid, Joseph P.	Early		313/15	Early
Reid, Joseph(Orps)	Telfair	Wilsons	170/6	Gwinnett
Reid, Mary(Wid)	Jones	Wallers	318/18	Early
Reid, Octavia(Orph)	Richmond	120th	53/3	Irwin
Reid, Robert A.	Richmond	398th	140/1	Irwin
Reid, Samuel A.	Putnam	Evans	114/3	Rabun
Reid, Samuel Sr.	Jackson	Hamiltons	55/7	Early
Reid, Samuel	Jasper	Bailey	177/1	Irwin
Reid, Samuel	Putnam	Brooks	51/1	Early
Reid, Stephen	Hall		15/11	Habersha
Reid, Templeton	Baldwin	Marshalls	42/13	Irwin
Reid, Thomas S.	Putnam	Mays	272/8	Irwin
Reid, William	Baldwin	Marshalls	147/18	Early
Reid, William	Baldwin	Marshalls	86/1	Appling
Reighter, Wm.	Chatham		242/9	Early
Reign, Peter	Chatham		55/11	Early
Reins, Mary(Wid)	Emanuel	58th	266/6	Irwin
Reis, David	Putnam	Littles	91/1	Appling
Reisser, Mathew	Effingham		347/6	Irwin
Reisser, Mathew	Effingham		66/10	Hall
Reiver, John(Orps)	Scriven	Roberts	254/10	Early
Rembert, Andrew	Elbert	Whites	202/19	Early
Rembert, Samuel	Elbert	White	155/5	Gwinnett
Remshart, Daniel	Chatham		351/27	Early
Render, Christopher	Wilkes	Dents	108/8	Irwin
Render, Joshua	Wilkes	Dents	153/3	Walton
Render, Susannah	Wilkes	Dents	475/9	Irwin
Renean, William T.	Oglethorpe	Rowlands	137/6	Early
Renean, William T.	Oglethorpe	Rowlands	14/3	Early
Renfro, Enoch	Washington	Mannings	324/10	Irwin
Renfro, Nathan	Washington	Pools	465/7	Irwin
Renfro, Peter	Washington	Renfros	516/4	Appling
Renfroe, Enoch Jr.	Washington	Pools	60/14	Irwin
Renfrow, Edward(Orps)	Twiggs	W.Belchers	184/11	Early
Renis, Thomas	Emanuel	57th	221/18	Early
Renis, Thomas	Emanuel	57th	373/4	Appling
Rennolds, William P.	Putnam	Buckners	78/1	Irwin
Rennols, James	Putnam	Buckners	244/16	Early
Renolds, Charles	Jasper	Bentley	437/27	Early
Renshart, Daniel	Chatham		362/9	Early
Rentfroe, Zachariah	Jasper	Bames	160/14	Early
Rentfrow, Stephen	Morgan	Hubbards	77/2	Early
Respess, Churchwell	Putnam	J.Kendricks	215/9	Early
Respess, Nathan	Putnam	J.Kindricks	94/3	Habersha
Ressent, John	Camden	Clarks	330/27	Early
Retan, John	Chatham		410/4	Appling
Reuton, James H.	Twiggs	W.Belchers	370/13	Irwin
Revel, Hardy	Richmond	122	127/15	Irwin
Revels, Henry	Tattnall	Keens	59/1	Early
Reviere, Holland	Lincoln	Walkers	116/10	Habersha
Revil, Matthew	Twiggs	Bozemans	114/1	Irwin
Reynold, Wm.(Hopping)	Lincoln	Jeters	392/2	Early
Reynolds, Bartemus	Hall		1/5	Habersha
Reynolds, Benj.Jr.	Jones	Greens	187/27	Early
Reynolds, Benjamin	Greene	140th	232/7	Gwinnett
Reynolds, Benjamin	Lincoln	Jeters	249/6	Appling
Reynolds, Berry	Elbert	Dobbs	321/13	Early
Reynolds, Charles	Elbert	B.Higginbotham	460/12	Irwin
Reynolds, Davis	Greene	Tuggles	110/1	Early
Reynolds, Francis	Twiggs	Smiths	11/9	Early

NAME	COUNTY	MIL.DIST	LOT/SECT	DREW LAND
Reynolds, George	Oglethorpe	Waters	145/9	Hall
Reynolds, James Jr.	Greene	Tuggles	426/5	Irwin
Reynolds, James W.	Camden	Baileys	193/3	E(W)alton
Reynolds, James	Hancock	Coopers	440/3	Appling
Reynolds, James	Lincoln	Parks	134/18	Early
Reynolds, James	Putnam	Ectors	151/12	Early
Reynolds, John Sr.	Columbia	Shaws	152/1	Early
Reynolds, John	Greene	Tuggles	508/6	Irwin
Reynolds, John	Richmond	Burtons	250/19	Early
Reynolds, John	Warren	Blounts	321/5	Gwinnett
Reynolds, Johnson	Morgan	Jordan	7/5	Habersham
Reynolds, Joseph	Twiggs	Evans	154/13	Early
Reynolds, Joseph	Twiggs	Evans	363/2	Appling
Reynolds, Meridy	Elbert	Dobbs	72/10	Early
Reynolds, Reuben(Orps)	Columbia	Shaws	58/6	Irwin
Reynolds, Reubin	Jones	Phillips	114/11	Hall
Reynolds, Robert	Lincoln	Jeters	191/11	Irwin
Reynolds, Robert	Twiggs	W.Belchers	391/13	Irwin
Reynolds, Silas	Wilkes	Davis	384/2	Early
Reynolds, Thomas	Richmond	122	176/3	Walton
Reynolds, William(Gov)	Lincoln	Parks	277/26	Early
Reynolds, William(Gov)	Lincoln	Parks	385/20	Early
Reynolds, William	Elbert	Dooleys	396/7	Early
Reynolds, William	Lincoln	Jeters	129/7	Early
Reynolds, Wm.(Wateree)	Lincoln	Parks	120/8	Irwin
Reyns, Thomas	Laurens	S.Smith	114/14	Irwin
Rhan, John	Effingham		254/1	Walton
Rhan, Jonathan S.	Effingham		220/9	Appling
Rheany, Charles	Burke	M.Wards	297/7	Early
Rhendolph, Eliz.(Wid)Jr.	Camden	Clarks	170/11	Habersham
Rhew, William	Jasper	Easts	173/16	Irwin
Rhew, William	Jasper	Easts	99/6	Gwinnett
Rhoades, David	Jones	Samuels	20/13	Irwin
Rhoads, David	Jones	Samuels	119/6	Gwinnett
Rhode, John(Orp)	Pulaski	Davis	211/18	Early
Rhode, Samuel	Pulaski	Davis	201/16	Irwin
Rhodes(?), Christopher	Pulaski	Davis	216/28	Early
Rhodes, Absalom Sr.	Richmond	Palmers	628/2	Appling
Rhodes, Absalom Sr.	Richmond	Palmers	99/3	Habersham
Rhodes, Ann(Wid)	Richmond	Palmers	87/2	Irwin
Rhodes, Benjamin	Oglethorpe	Bowls	81/3	Rabun
Rhodes, Heiflin	Oglethorpe	Bowls	266/19	Early
Rhodes, James	Oglethorpe	Bowels	18/1	Early
Rhodes, John A.	Richmond		86/5	Irwin
Rhodes, John	Greene	Nelms	174/1	Appling
Rhodes, Menimia (Orph)	Richmond	Palmers	53/15	Irwin
Rhodes, Richard Sr.	Oglethorpe	Bowls	174/5	Irwin
Rhodes, Riding Jr.	Wilkes	Bryants	161/4	Early
Rhodes, Sarah	Oglethorpe	Barnetts	25/8	Hall
Rhodes, Thomas	Oglethorpe	Bowls	164/5	Early
Rhodes, William	Scriven	180th	456/13	Irwin
Rholin, Thomas	Scriven	180	115/4	Irwin
Rials, William	Montgomery	Nobles	51/23	Early
Rice, Anderson	Jones	Permenter	272/4	Irwin
Rice, Arthur	Morgan	Loyds	220/21	Early
Rice, Elizabeth(Wid)	Chatham		420/6	Appling
Rice, Elizabeth(Wid)	Jackson	Hamiltons	179/11	Early
Rice, James	Baldwin	Ellis	106/2	Irwin
Rice, James	Baldwin	Ellis	119/4	Early
Rice, James	Greene	Jones	328/7	Gwinnett
Rice, James	Greene	Jones	70/3	Habersham
Rice, Jesse	Elbert	Whites	233/5	Early
Rice, John Jr.	Wilkes	Ogletrees	18/1	Rabun
Rice, John R.	Chatham		8/9	Irwin
Rice, John(Orps)	Baldwin	Ellis	77/9	Early
Rice, John	Franklin	Akins	267/7	Gwinnett
Rice, Juduy	Putnam	Evans	3/14	Early

NAME	COUNTY	MIL.DIST	LOT/SECT	DREW LAND
Rice, Mary(Wid)	Franklin	Hammonds	170/5	Appling
Rice, Mary	Chatham		258/8	Early
Rice, Nancy	Baldwin	Ellis	153/19	Early
Rice, Nathaniel G.	Wilkes	Ogletrees	105/2	Appling
Rice, Richmond	Bryan	19th	295/20	Early
Rice, Robert	Jackson	Winters	344/7	Appling
Rice, Samuel	Columbia	Olives	118/2	Walton
Rice, Samuel	Wilkes	Ogletrees	181/9	Early
Rice, William	Elbert	Webbs	313/1	Appling
Rice, William	Franklin	Akins	80/18	Early
Rice, Wm.	Chatham		173/2	Irwin
Rich, Daniel E.	Emanuel	57th	314/6	Early
Rich, James	Burke	Torrance	234/4	Appling
Rich, James	Burke	Torrance	253/18	Early
Rich, Wm.	Elbert	Whites	33/12	Hall
Richard, John C.	Camden	Clarks	62/20	Early
Richards, Christopher C.	Baldwin	Marshalls	315/13	Irwin
Richards, Ehaphroditus	Greene	Macons	451/12	Irwin
Richards, John	Burke	Spiveys	209/6	Gwinnett
Richards, John	Burke	Spiveys	403/5	Appling
Richards, John	Burke	Spiveys	57/4	Appling
Richards, John	Madison	Williford	279/20	Early
Richards, Johugh	Early		390/6	Appling
Richards, Mathew C.	Morgan	Hubbards	255/6	Early
Richards, Robert	Twiggs	Jeffersons	403/8	Early
Richards, Robert	Twiggs	Jeffersons	404/13	Irwin
Richards, Royal	Madison	Williford	47/1	Walton
Richards, Thomas	Twiggs	Jeffersons	5/2	Appling
Richards, Uriah	Greene	142	74/5	Gwinnett
Richards, Willis	Jasper	Bailey	270/3	Early
Richards, Willis	Jasper	Baileys	152/5	Irwin
Richards, Wm.	Jasper	Bentley	386/21	Early
Richardson, Allen	Oglethorpe	Lees	147/2	Early
Richardson, Allen	Oglethorpe	Lees	68/7	Appling
Richardson, Asa	Wilkinson	Kettles	68/6	Habersham
Richardson, Benj.	Jasper	Blakes	161/2	Appling
Richardson, Benjamin	Hancock	Thomas	18/23	Early
Richardson, Daniel L.	Hancock	Champions	27/4	Habersham
Richardson, David	Gwinnett	Hamiltons Bt.	380/8	Appling
Richardson, David	Twiggs	Jeffersons	156/11	Early
Richardson, Edmund	Camden	Clarks	151/8	Early
Richardson, Edmund	Camden	Clarks	415/11	Irwin
Richardson, Fanny	Putnam	Oslins	148/7	Appling
Richardson, Gabriel	Putnam	Oslins	411/11	Irwin
Richardson, Gatewood	Jasper	Blakes	193/2	Irwin
Richardson, Hugh(Min)	Wilkes	Kilgores	8/14	Early
Richardson, Isaac	Bulloch	Knights	12/12	Irwin
Richardson, James	Columbia	Gatrells	307/7	Appling
Richardson, Jane(Wid)	Hancock	Champions	322/2	Appling
Richardson, John L.	Oglethorpe	Murrays	253/7	Appling
Richardson, John	Clarke	Deans	132/6	Gwinnett
Richardson, John	Wilkinson	Smiths	377/8	Irwin
Richardson, Jonathan	Jones	Chappels	92/6	Early
Richardson, Richard	Chatham		320/13	Early
Richardson, Richard	Chatham		387/18	Early
Richardson, Richard	Elbert	G.Higginbotham	400/2	Early
Richardson, Walker	Elbert	G.Higginbotham	29/5	Habersham
Richardson, William	Chatham		344/13	Early
Richardson, William	Columbia	Gartrells	63/13	Irwin
Richardson, William	Putnam	Brooks	270/7	Gwinnett
Richardson, Winniford(W)	Bulloch	Knights	409/12	Irwin
Richardson, Wm.	Columbia	Gartrells	435/2	Appling
Richardson, Wm.Jr.	Chatham		77/10	Irwin
Richerson, Abram	Hancock	Thomas	183/12	Habersham
Richey, Wm.Sr.	Franklin	Holcombs	320/12	Irwin
Richmond, Samuel	Twiggs	Bozemans	446/7	Appling
Ricketson, Arthur	Warren	Parhams	106/7	Appling

NAME	COUNTY	MIL.DIST	LOT/SECT	DREW LAND
Ricketts, George	Chatham		312/5	Appling
Rickitson, Benjamin	Warren	153rd	17/3	Irwin
Rickitson, Mary(Wid)	Columbia	Burroughs	238/1	Appling
Ricks, Harris	Twiggs	Hodges	86/5	Rabun
Ricks, James	Twiggs	Evans	118/27	Early
Ricks, James	Twiggs	Hodges	160/2	Appling
Ricks, John(Orps)	Emanuel	56th	186/16	Irwin
Ricks, John	Emanuel	395	233/27	Early
Ricks, Larry(Orps)	Jasper	Reeds	216/5	Appling
Riddle, Archibald B.	Wilkes	Smiths	90/7	Appling
Riddle, Cato Sr.	Washington	Brooks	467/7	Irwin
Riddle, Willie	Baldwin	Irwins	108/7	Early
Riddle, Willis	Baldwin	Irwins	300/11	Irwin
Riddleberger, Thomas	Chatham		118/4	Appling
Riddleberger, Thomas	Chatham		137/9	Appling
Riddling, Moses	Jackson	Mays	15/2	Rabun
Rideway, Samuel	Jasper	Clays	238/4	Irwin
Ridge, James(RS)	Gwinnett	Hamiltons Bt.	353/1	Early
Ridgedell, John	Effingham		289/15	Early
Ridgeden, Samuel(RS)	Effingham	Ridgedell	19/6	Appling
Ridgeway, Burrell	Elbert	R.Christians	274/12	Irwin
Ridgeway, Burrell	Elbert	R.Christians	319/3	Early
Ridgeway, Samuel	Elbert	R.Christians	21/5	Rabun
Ridgway, Nelson	Elbert	R.Christians	22/3	Rabun
Ridley, John Jr.	Wilkes	Kilgores	40/9	Early
Ridley, John Sr.	Wilkes	Kilgores	496/5	Irwin
Ridley, Robert(Orps)	Putnam	Littles	133/27	Early
Ridway, Drury	Clarke	Tredwells	88/2	Rabun
Riesser, David	Effingham		386/13	Irwin
Riesser, Sterling N.	Wilkinson	Howards	400/12	Early
Rigby, Jonathan	Laurens	Watsons	32/4	Walton
Rigdon, Anny(Wid)	Bulloch	Everits	209/4	Appling
Rigdon, Daniel	Bulloch	Everitts	12/8	Appling
Rigdon, Daniel	Bulloch	Everitts	232/11	Early
Rigdon, Ephraim(RS)	Scriven	Moodys	188/9	Irwin
Rigdon, Ephraim(RS)	Scriven	Moodys	191/3	Appling
Riggins, James	Jasper	Bentley	458/9	Irwin
Riggs, Stephen(Orps)	Bulloch	Jones	259/3	Appling
Right, Lewis	Jackson	Winters	20/8	Irwin
Right, Thomas(Orps)	Jasper	Northcuts	27/3	Walton
Right, William	Greene	Carltons	155/3	Walton
Rigley, Jonathan	Laurens	Watson	508/4	Appling
Rigsby, Allen	Walton	Wagnons	54/9	Hall
Rigsby, Samuel	Jasper	Bentleys	151/15	Early
Riley, Charles	Wilkinson	Smiths	353/7	Appling
Riley, James	Elbert	Gaines	194/9	Irwin
Riley, James	Elbert	Gains	5/5	Early
Riley, Joseph(Orps)	Wilkinson	Howards	236/15	Early
Riley, Joseph	Greene	141st	144/10	Early
Riley, Lucy(Wid)	Wilkinson	Howards	178/4	Early
Riley, Moses	Richmond	122nd	253/3	Early
Riley, William	Jones	Samuels	14/15	Early
Riley, William	Wilkes	Runnels	3/6	Early
Rilgore, Joseph	Jasper	Hays	14/4	Early
Ringland, George(Orph)	Richmond	120th	249/10	Irwin
Ringland, Jane(Orph)	Richmond	120th	249/10	Irwin
Ripley, Robert	Camden	Clarks	245/4	Walton
Ripley, Robert	Camden	Clarks	330/11	Early
Ripley, Selvenious	Clarke	Pentecosts	357/12	Early
Ritchie, Stewart	Camden	33rd	43/5	Appling
Ritchie, Stewart	Putnam	53	15/3	Appling
Ritler, Catharine	Chatham		130/4	Appling
Ritter, William	Laurens	Griffins	152/7	Early
Ritter, William	Laurens	Griffins	352/8	Early
Rivers, James	Jackson	Reeds	330/2	Early
Rivers, James	Jasper	Reeds	330/2	Early
Rivers, John	Columbia	O.Morris	254/8	Appling

NAME	COUNTY	MIL.DIST	LOT/SECT	DREW LAN
Rivers, John	Jasper	McClendon	37/12	Early
Rivers, Robert T.	Jasper	Smiths	368/12	Early
Rivers, Robert	Jackson	Dicksons	117/10	Irwin
Rivers, Thomas(Jr)	Jasper	McClendon	92/20	Early
Rivers, Thomas	Warren	150th	154/12	Early
Rivers, William	Warren	152nd	451/28	Early
Rives, Harriet E.(Wid)	Washington	Floyds	127/10	Early
Rives, Joel(RS)	Hancock	Millers	310/7	Irwin
Rives, Joel(RS)	Hancock	Millers	87/14	Irwin
Rives, Thomas(Jr)	Jackson	Dicksons	315/19	Early
Rives, Wm.Jr.	Hancock	Millers	79/28	Early
Riviere, Dicy	Wilkes	Bates	219/12	Habersham
Roa, James	Chatham		64/13	Irwin
Roach, James	Franklin	Burroughs	332/1	Appling
Roach, Jesse	Scriven	Roberts	115/15	Early
Roach, Jonathan	Hancock	Danells	242/3	Irwin
Roach, Samuel Jr.	Hancock	Danells	205/7	Irwin
Roads, James(Orps)	Warren	151st	109/9	Appling
Roads, John(Orps)	Laurens	Harris	459/6	Irwin
Roads, Joseph	Warren	Rodgers	180/10	Irwin
Roads, Licam	Warren	151	5/14	Early
Roan, Jesse J.	Morgan	Hackneys	70/7	Early
Roan, Willis J.	Morgan	Hackneys	343/12	Irwin
Roane, Lewis	Jackson	Rogers	40/6	Early
Robbins, Elijah	Scriven		358/9	Appling
Robbins, William	Richmond	Winters	68/1	Habersham
Roben, James	Greene	Macons	32/28	Early
Roberds, Josiah(Orps)	Emanuel	49th	136/4	Irwin
Roberds, Mary(Wid)	Emanuel	395th	16/6	Gwinnett
Roberds, Wm.(Orps)	Emanuel	395th	217/8	Early
Roberson, Elisha	Morgan	Farrars	159/9	Appling
Roberson, Ignatius	Warren	154th	92/8	Hall
Roberson, Isaac(Orps)	Putnam	Coopers	43/8	Early
Roberson, Isaac	Washington	Floyds	366/14	Early
Roberson, James	Oglethorpe	Bowls	324/12	Early
Roberson, John(Orps)	Greene	Macons	12/5	Irwin
Roberson, John	Jackson	Rogerson	2/13	Habersham
Roberson, Sally(Wid)	Jackson	Winters	344/26	Early
Roberson, Samuel H.	Putnam	Coopers	266/12	Irwin
Roberson, William Jr.	Warren	150th	136/19	Early
Roberson, William	Franklin	Haynes	168/6	Early
Roberson, William	Greene	Carltons	349/19	Early
Roberson, Wm.T.	Twiggs	R.Belchers	173/1	Walton
Roberts, Aaron Jr.	Franklin	R.Browns	211/9	Irwin
Roberts, Aaron Sr.	Franklin	R.Browns	71/28	Early
Roberts, Allen	Hancock	Evans	396/4	Appling
Roberts, Arthur	Lincoln	Graves	226/10	Irwin
Roberts, Avery	Jackson	Rogers	332/3	Appling
Roberts, Barnett	Elbert	R.Christians	178/4	Appling
Roberts, Bartley	Morgan	Hackneys	145/8	Irwin
Roberts, Coleman M.	Morgan	Loyds	117/2	Appling
Roberts, David C.	Lincoln	Jeters	118/12	Early
Roberts, David C.	Lincoln	Jeters	159/8	Early
Roberts, David C.	Lincoln	Jeters	45/2	Habersham
Roberts, David(Orps)	Liberty		173/7	Appling
Roberts, David	Jasper	Bentley	161/2	Early
Roberts, Edmond	Columbia	Burroughs	98/26	Early
Roberts, Edward	Warren	Parhams	113/18	Early
Roberts, Elias E.	Chatham		14/5	Early
Roberts, Elias E.	Chatham		423/4	Appling
Roberts, Elijah	Hall		159/6	Early
Roberts, Elijah	Hall		450/6	Appling
Roberts, Eliz.(Wid)	Twiggs	Thames	181/8	Early
Roberts, Elizabeth(Wid)	Liberty		117/13	Early
Roberts, Emlia	Scriven	Roberts	93/11	Habersham
Roberts, George	Jackson	Dicksons	279/18	Early
Roberts, Greystock	Montgomery	McElvins	254/6	Irwin

NAME	COUNTY	MIL.DIST	LOT/SECT	DREW LAND
Roberts, Isom	Emanuel	49th	116/28	Early
Roberts, James H.	Morgan	Walker	227/4	Appling
Roberts, James(Orp)	Liberty		390/7	Early
Roberts, James	Chatham		160/16	Irwin
Roberts, James	Chatham		26/2	Appling
Roberts, Jane(Orph)	Scriven	Lovetts	90/12	Hall
Roberts, Jeremiah	Columbia	Bealls	138/9	Appling
Roberts, Jesse	Columbia	Pullins	249/5	Irwin
Roberts, Jesse	Morgan	Hubbards	357/11	Early
Roberts, Jesse	Morgan	Hubbards	379/9	Irwin
Roberts, John A.	Burke	Thomas	267/9	Irwin
Roberts, John A.	Burke	Thomas	34/7	Appling
Roberts, John A.	Walton	Wests	174/2	Early
Roberts, John B.	Wilkinson	180	444/12	Irwin
Roberts, John G.	Greene	Jones	61/19	Early
Roberts, John H.	Warren	153	371/13	Early
Roberts, John Jr.	Morgan	Farrars	146/4	Early
Roberts, John(Orp)	Liberty		60/7	Irwin
Roberts, John(Orps)	Bulloch	Edwards	397/12	Early
Roberts, John	Jackson	Rogers	7/16	Early
Roberts, John	Jefferson	Cowarts	128/2	Early
Roberts, Joseph	Elbert	Hannahs	255/15	Early
Roberts, Joseph	Morgan	Farrars	283/9	Irwin
Roberts, Joseph	Morgan	Farrars	315/13	Early
Roberts, Josiah(Orps)	Walton	Wests	245/7	Early
Roberts, Josiah	Columbia	Pullins	82/12	Irwin
Roberts, Josiah	Laurens	Swearingen	254/22	Early
Roberts, Josiah	Twiggs	Bozemans	387/16	Early
Roberts, Mary	Burke	70th	197/5	Appling
Roberts, Nancy(Wid)	Laurens	Harris	211/3	Irwin
Roberts, Nathaniel	Scriven	Roberts	116/5	Appling
Roberts, Nathaniel	Scriven	Roberts	248/8	Appling
Roberts, Redden(Orp)	Camden	Baileys	194/5	Appling
Roberts, Reubin Jr.	Jones	Permenter	5/3	Rabun
Roberts, Roland	Scriven	180th	303/3	Appling
Roberts, Shadrack(Orps)	Laurens	S.Smith	211/11	Irwin
Roberts, Sherrod	Warren	Parhams	21/14	Early
Roberts, Simeon	Burke	70th	156/26	Early
Roberts, Simeon	Burke	70th	34/14	Early
Roberts, Tabitha(Wid)	Emanuel	49th	399/19	Early
Roberts, Thomas H.	Chatham		259/9	Appling
Roberts, Thomas(Orps)	Scriven	36th	172/19	Early
Roberts, Thomas(RS)	Clarke	Mitchells	147/19	Early
Roberts, Thomas	Morgan	Parkers	162/28	Early
Roberts, William	Burke	70th	9/17	Early
Roberts, William	Clarke	Harpers	104/12	Hall
Roberts, William	Franklin	Vaughns	301/6	Gwinnett
Roberts, William	Montgomery	Alston	364/5	Early
Roberts, William	Montgomery	Alston	68/12	Irwin
Roberts, Willis	Columbia	Dodsons	33/12	Habersham
Roberts, Wilson	Elbert	Webbs	182/4	Walton
Roberts, Wm.(Orps)	Pulaski	Davis	21/8	Appling
Roberts, Wm.(Orps)	Scriven	Roberts	165/3	Early
Roberts, Wm.	Clarke	Parrs	430/28	Early
Roberts, Zachariah	Camden	Baileys	309/27	Early
Robertson, (Orphans)	Clarke	Dobbins	459/10	Irwin
Robertson, Alexander	Wilkinson	Smiths	395/18	Early
Robertson, Allenr.N.	Greene	Armers	54/8	Hall
Robertson, Aron	Jones	Permenter	166/3	Habersham
Robertson, Benj.(Orps)	Jones	Chappels	70/26	Early
Robertson, Benj.	Putnam	Robertsons	378/28	Early
Robertson, Buckner(Or)	Twiggs	R.Belchers	369/13	Early
Robertson, Edward A.	Jones	Buckhalter	220/7	Irwin
Robertson, Elizabeth(Orp)	Chatham		178/10	Early
Robertson, Frederick	Warren	154	114/27	Early
Robertson, Gilbert	Oglethorpe	Waters	359/8	Appling
Robertson, Henry	Baldwin	Doziers	403/3	Appling

NAME	COUNTY	MIL.DIST	LOT/SECT	DREW LAN
Robertson, Jane(Orp)	Chatham		178/10	Early
Robertson, Jeffry	Warren	Hubberts	75/15	Early
Robertson, Jeffry	Warren	Hubberts	75/2	Habersha
Robertson, John Jr.	Wilkes	Willis	190/5	Early
Robertson, John R.	Baldwin	Taliafiros	1/6	Appling
Robertson, John Sr.	Wilkinson	Willis	8/8	Irwin
Robertson, John(Orph)	Clarke	Meraweathers	506/13	Irwin
Robertson, John(RS)	Jackson	Dicksons	334/15	Early
Robertson, John(RS)	Jones	Wallers	118/1	Walton
Robertson, John(RS)	Jones	Wallers	272/7	Appling
Robertson, John	Jackson	Rogers	85/22	Early
Robertson, John	Jackson	Winters	9/27	Early
Robertson, John	Putnam	Robertsons	111/3	Habersha
Robertson, John	Putnam	Slaughters	417/8	Appling
Robertson, Joseph	Lincoln	Parks	229/4	Early
Robertson, Lewis D.	Hancock	Thomas	274/4	Irwin
Robertson, Matthew	Jefferson	Abbotts	447/13	Irwin
Robertson, Michael	Jones	Shropshier	213/4	Early
Robertson, Michael	Jones	Shropshier	217/7	Gwinnett
Robertson, Nathl.(Orph)	Hancock	Thomas	11/1	Rabun
Robertson, Reddon	Jasper	Posts	88/14	Irwin
Robertson, Robert	Chatham		464/9	Irwin
Robertson, Saml.	Jackson	Dicksons	395/7	Early
Robertson, Sarah(Orp)	Chatham		178/10	Early
Robertson, Seneth(RS)	Clarke	Meraweathers	19/3	Rabun
Robertson, Susannah	Putnam	Slaughters	389/4	Early
Robertson, Thos.(RS)	Jasper	Dosters	257/13	Early
Robertson, Thos.(RS)	Jasper	Dosters	47/27	Early
Robertson, Will	Twiggs	Smith	27/2	Habersha
Robertson, William	Baldwin	Marshalls	77/6	Irwin
Robertson, William	Putnam	Robertsons	120/7	Early
Robertson, William	Walton	Sentells	534/2	Appling
Robertson, Wm.(Orps)	Franklin	Ashs	52/6	Habersha
Robertts, Isaac	Greene	Jones	117/5	Gwinnett
Robeson, James Sr.	Wayne	Crews	402/8	Appling
Robeson, Wiley	Putnam	Tomlinsons	198/8	Appling
Robey, Robert	Jasper	Clays	199/7	Early
Robins, Isaac H.	Chatham		127/1	Walton
Robins, Plinny(Orps)	Oglethorpe	Goolsby	506/4	Appling
Robins, Wm.	Franklin	Jos.Millers	109/7	Irwin
Robinson, Abraham	Burke	Bells	66/11	Irwin
Robinson, Agness(Wid)	Washington	Robinsons	351/5	Early
Robinson, Ann C.(Orp)	McIntosh	McIntosh	429/8	Appling
Robinson, Bird F.	Jasper	Kennedy	95/5	Irwin
Robinson, Darius T.	Burke	69	50/14	Irwin
Robinson, Elizabeth(Orp)	McIntosh	McIntosh	429/8	Appling
Robinson, Ephraim(Orp)	McIntosh	McIntosh	429/8	Appling
Robinson, Henry D.	Morgan	Beaseleys	230/21	Early
Robinson, Isaac	Laurens	S.Smith	414/8	Appling
Robinson, James C.	Twiggs	Browns	1/12	Irwin
Robinson, James T.	Jasper	Phillips	298/1	Early
Robinson, James	Clarke	Deans	95/1	Habersha
Robinson, James	Greene	143	126/26	Early
Robinson, Jesse J.	Richmond	122nd	305/16	Early
Robinson, Jesse	Jefferson	Lamps	326/5	Gwinnett
Robinson, John(Orps)	Jasper	Northcuts	2/8	Appling
Robinson, John	Jasper	Phillips	98/11	Hall
Robinson, John	Morgan	McClendons	106/14	Early
Robinson, John	Morgan	McLendons	371/12	Irwin
Robinson, John	Walton	Echols	200/10	Habersha
Robinson, John	Washington	Renfros	326/15	Early
Robinson, John	Washington	Renfros	76/9	Early
Robinson, Jonathan	Jefferson	Lamps	481/10	Irwin
Robinson, Joseph W.	Wilkes	Gordans	289/1	Walton
Robinson, Joseph W.	Wilkes	Gordons	107/5	Early
Robinson, Joseph	Lincoln	Parks	227/1	Early
Robinson, Lidia	Jasper	Northcuts	235/8	Appling

NAME	COUNTY	MIL.DIST	LOT/SECT	DREW LAND
Robinson, Mary(Orps)	Pulaski	Lesters	111/7	Early
Robinson, Matthew	Franklin	Powels	148/2	Habersham
Robinson, Patrick L.	Columbia	Dodsons	71/6	Appling
Robinson, Patrick	Pulaski	Lesters	454/10	Irwin
Robinson, Richard	Putnam	Stampers	528/5	Irwin
Robinson, Samuel	Washington	Robinsons	186/13	Habersham
Robinson, Serena	Jasper	Easts	283/11	Irwin
Robinson, Solomon	Twiggs	R.Belchers	224/12	Early
Robinson, Solomon	Twiggs	R.Belchers	51/28	Early
Robinson, William	Baldwin	Taliaferros	41/2	Walton
Robinson, William	Wilkes	Ogletrees	341/8	Early
Robinson, Wm.T.L.	Jasper	Hays	490/13	Irwin
Robson, Willie	Wayne	Crews	179/3	Walton
Robson, Willie	Wayne	Crews	339/19	Early
Robuck, Benjamin	McIntosh	Goulds	133/11	Hall
Robuck, Benjamin	McIntosh	Goulds	19/1	Rabun
Roby, Hudley(Orps)	Wilkes	Brooks	111/4	Irwin
Roby, John N.	Putnam	Morelands	432/5	Irwin
Roby, Timothy	Putnam	Brooks	129/2	Walton
Roby, Timothy	Putnam	Brooks	189/12	Habersham
Rockford, George	Clarke	Stuarts	192/6	Appling
Rockford, George	Clarke	Stuarts	91/3	Irwin
Rockmore, John	Putnam	J.Kendricks	206/7	Early
Rodeh, James M.(Orps)	Twiggs	Ellis	13/13	Habersham
Rodgers, Balam	Putnam	Buckners	58/3	Rabun
Rodgers, Cannon R.	Baldwin	Stephens	41/2	Habersham
Rodgers, Daniel	Washington	Peabodys	298/14	Early
Rodgers, Henry	Morgan	Leonards	59/18	Early
Rodgers, James A.	Hancock	Canes	337/3	Early
Rodgers, James	Jackson	Winters	112/2	Habersham
Rodgers, John Sr.	Pulaski	Maddox	216/4	Irwin
Rodgers, John Sr.	Pulaski	Maddox	32/11	Irwin
Rodgers, John	Putnam	Berrys	51/14	Irwin
Rodgers, John	Wilkes	Bryants	105/11	Hall
Rodgers, Reuben	Warren	Griers	388/10	Early
Rodgers, William	Jasper	Bartlett	216/3	Appling
Rodgers, William	Washington	Floyds	95/21	Early
Rodin, James	Jackson	Hamiltons	165/15	Irwin
Rodman, Lucy	Chatham		199/16	Irwin
Rodoh, Victory(Orps)	Effingham		426/6	Appling
Roe, Asia	Putnam	Buckners	203/5	Early
Roe, Judy(Wid)	Jefferson	Lamps	363/28	Early
Roe, Samuel	Chatham		277/3	Appling
Roe, Shadrick	Hancock	Claytons	5/11	Early
Roe, Tryphena(Wid)	Chatham		282/9	Appling
Roebuck, Rolly	Washington	Jenkinsons	112/2	Rabun
Rogers, Acey	Scriven	Lovetts	215/6	Irwin
Rogers, Charles Wm.	Putnam	Oslins	458/3	Appling
Rogers, Charles(Orps)	Wilkinson	Kettles	304/16	Early
Rogers, David	Jackson	Rogers	115/19	Early
Rogers, Dempsey	Jackson	Winters	173/11	Irwin
Rogers, Demsey	Jackson	Winters	335/18	Early
Rogers, Dread	Jasper	McClendon	260/20	Early
Rogers, Edmund	Liberty		163/1	Walton
Rogers, Edward	Washington	Avents	199/6	Appling
Rogers, Elisha	Putnam	Buckners	307/27	Early
Rogers, Enoch	Jackson	Rogers	94/2	Irwin
Rogers, Ephraim	Jasper	Eastes	183/3	Early
Rogers, George A.	Jasper	Kennedy	132/9	Early
Rogers, George	Elbert	Whites	135/2	Walton
Rogers, George	Elbert	Whites	200/4	Appling
Rogers, Henry	Greene	Macons	254/4	Irwin
Rogers, James(Orps)	Jackson	Winters	491/5	Irwin
Rogers, James(RS)	Twiggs	W.Belchers	502/6	Appling
Rogers, James	Jefferson	Bothwells	391/16	Early
Rogers, James	Jefferson	Cowarts	163/10	Hall
Rogers, James	Jefferson	Cowarts	434/12	Irwin

NAME	COUNTY	MIL.DIST	LOT/SECT	DREW LAND
Rogers, James	Washington	Wimberlys	342/10	Irwin
Rogers, Jethro	Burke	71st	55/13	Irwin
Rogers, John (Minor)	Wilkes	Willis	15/28	Early
Rogers, John	Morgan	Hubbards	153/12	Irwin
Rogers, John	Morgan	Hubbards	385/13	Irwin
Rogers, John	Twiggs	Evans	218/7	Gwinnett
Rogers, John	Wilkes	Bryants	94/16	Early
Rogers, John	Wilkinson	Lees	59/28	Early
Rogers, Joseph	Jefferson	Cowarts	351/5	Gwinnett
Rogers, Josiah	Greene	143rd	44/8	Hall
Rogers, Mary Ann	Burke	Sullivans	158/11	Irwin
Rogers, Mashack	Washington	Peabodys	40/2	Walton
Rogers, Mathew	Scriven	Lovetts	321/12	Early
Rogers, Nathan	Washington	Wimberlys	175/2	Irwin
Rogers, Newman	Twiggs	Evans	269/4	Early
Rogers, Peter	Scriven		365/9	Appling
Rogers, Reuben Sr.	Warren	Griers	195/1	Irwin
Rogers, Richard	Scriven	Lovetts	158/19	Early
Rogers, Simeon	Hancock	Daniels	139/8	Early
Rogers, Starkey	Twiggs	Smiths	148/4	Irwin
Rogers, Theophilus	Jackson	Winters	194/7	Appling
Rogers, Thomas	Hancock	Smiths	147/9	Irwin
Rogers, Thomas	Pulaski	Maddox	24/18	Early
Rogers, Unity (Wid)	Jackson	Rogers	192/3	Habersham
Rogers, Wiley	Montgomery		135/27	Early
Rogers, Wiley	Putnam	Kendricks	297/8	Early
Rogers, William	Burke	Thomas	149/3	Habersham
Rogers, William	Putnam	Butts	42/6	Irwin
Rogers, Wm.(Orps)	Elbert	P.Christians	65/4	Walton
Rogers, Wm.(Orps)	Washington	Mannings	80/16	Early
Rogers, Wm.Sr.	Tattnall	Overstreets	82/2	Rabun
Rogers, Wm.Sr.	Tattnall	Overstreets	95/6	Appling
Rogerson, Ames (Orp)	Chatham		69/12	Habersham
Rogerson, Ann	Chatham		79/4	Irwin
Rogerson, James (Orp)	Chatham		69/12	Habersham
Rogerson, Richard (Orp)	Chatham		69/12	Habersham
Roice, Septo	Wilkes	Gordans	30/26	Early
Role, Isaac	Warren	151st	246/9	Irwin
Rolen, Hiram	Greene	Macons	108/2	Habersham
Roler, Michael	Lincoln	Walkers	125/5	Irwin
Roler, Michael	Lincoln	Walkers	31/7	Irwin
Roles, Bevvin	Greene	Harvills	180/28	Early
Roles, John	Camden	Tillis	261/3	Appling
Roles, John	Camden	Tillis	298/7	Early
Roles, Wm.& Geo.(Orps)	Camden	Tillis	403/6	Irwin
Rolin, Hiram	Greene	Macons	238/14	Early
Rollins, Lodewick	Jasper	Bailey	111/5	Gwinnett
Rollins, William	Hall	Buffingtons	98/8	Early
Rollins, William	Washington	Floyds	326/5	Early
Rolls, Wm.& Geo.(Orps)	Chatham		44/4	Walton
Rone, Leonard	Jasper	Evans	345/17	Early
Ronie, James	Richmond	Palmers	170/7	Irwin
Ronie, John	Richmond	Palmers	65/7	Early
Rooks, Frederick	Jefferson	Connells	234/17	Early
Rooks, Hardeman (RS)	Jackson	Rogers	357/9	Irwin
Rooks, James	Jackson	Rogers	248/16	Early
Rooks, John	Putnam	Slaughters	182/13	Habersham
Rooks, John	Putnam	Slaughters	184/2	Rabun
Rooks, John	Wayne	Jacobs	299/2	Appling
Rooks, Joseph	Putnam	Slaughters	184/2	Rabun
Rooks, William	Jefferson	Connells	219/8	Early
Rose, Abner	Chatham		46/10	Hall
Rose, Drury	Franklin	Turks	121/11	Early
Rose, Frederick (RS)	Putnam	J.Kendricks	516/2	Appling
Rose, Grantham	Elbert	P.Christians	416/6	Irwin
Rose, Henry	Wilkes	Kilgores	113/11	Habersham
Rose, Henry	Wilkes	Kilgores	76/2	Irwin

NAME	COUNTY	MIL.DIST	LOT/SECT	DREW LAND
Rose, James	Richmond	122nd	310/9	Appling
Rose, Washington	Putnam	J.Kendrick	206/28	Early
Roseberry, James	Oglethorpe	Davenport	163/13	Habersham
Roseberry, Richard	Oglethorpe	Goolsby	259/5	Early
Rosier, David	Columbia	Shaws	52/15	Early
Rosignol, Paul	Richmond	398th	261/5	Irwin
Ross, Abner	Chatham		202/3	Early
Ross, Catharine(Wid)	Jefferson	Bothwell	340/5	Irwin
Ross, Elizabeth(Wid)	Jackson	Rodgers	352/10	Early
Ross, Frances(Orph)	Columbia	Shaws	75/19	Early
Ross, Godfrey	Twiggs	Smiths	129/5	Irwin
Ross, James	Columbia	Bealls	150/7	Early
Ross, James	Emanuel	57th	49/4	Habersham
Ross, James	Hall		312/13	Irwin
Ross, James	Hall		320/10	Irwin
Ross, James	Putnam	Buckners	175/5	Appling
Ross, James	Putnam	Buckners	244/9	Early
Ross, James	Wilkinson	Lees	23/9	Early
Ross, Jesse	Jones	Griffith	60/23	Early
Ross, John Jr.	Putnam	Buckners	298/27	Early
Ross, John Sr.	Putnam	Buckners	429/12	Irwin
Ross, John Sr.	Putnam	Ruchers	48/3	Early
Ross, John(Sr)	Putnam	Buckners	528/12	Irwin
Ross, Joseph	Wilkinson	Kettles	245/7	Gwinnett
Ross, Mary & John(Orps)	Bryan	20th	201/19	Early
Ross, Riley	Jones	Griffiths	273/28	Early
Ross, Robert	Putnam	Buckners	319/19	Early
Ross, William Sr.	Wilkinson	Lees	485/6	Appling
Ross, William	Chatham		359/2	Appling
Ross, William	Chatham		493/13	Irwin
Ross, William	Emanuel	57	54/9	Irwin
Ross, William	Jasper	Evans	155/10	Early
Ross, William	Jasper	Evans	222/7	Early
Ross, William	Jones	Buckhalter	64/7	Appling
Rossar, Dolly(Orp)	Camden	33	232/6	Early
Rosser(Prosser), J.H.	Chatham		268/28	Early
Rosser, Aaron	Warren	151st	256/9	Early
Rosser, Daniel	Jones	Samuels	105/12	Habersham
Rosser, David	Putnam	Littles	382/6	Irwin
Rosser, Elijah	Franklin	Davis	5/6	Habersham
Rosser, George(Orps)	Putnam	Morelands	90/3	Habersham
Rosser, Jacob H.	Chatham		120/9	Hall
Rosser, James	Putnam	Evans	115/11	Irwin
Rosser, John(Orps)	Jones	Samuels	218/2	Appling
Rosser, Mary(Orp)	Putnam	Butts	242/5	Appling
Rosser, Moses	Jasper	Clays	142/28	Early
Rossetter, White	Clarke	Stuarts	129/6	Irwin
Rossetter, White	Clarke	Stuarts	406/15	Early
Rossignal, Lewis	Chatham		74/13	Habersham
Rottenbury, Wm.	Bulloch	Knights	48/4	Appling
Roughton, Martha	Washington	Brooks	247/4	Early
Roughton, Zachariah	Washington	Brooks	521/13	Irwin
Rountree, Joshua	Emanuel	59th	119/17	Early
Rountree, Joshua	Emanuel	59th	368/4	Irwin
Rountree, Solomon(Orps)	Hancock	Dannells	248/6	Appling
Rous, Martin B.	Emanuel	49th	51/2	Rabun
Rouse, Henry	Twiggs	Hodges	209/18	Early
Rouse, Jesse	Twiggs	Hodges	314/13	Irwin
Rouse, Joseph	Pulaski	Rees	292/10	Early
Rouse, Joseph	Pulaski	Rees	458/7	Appling
Rousseau, George	Putnam	H.Kindricks	13/16	Early
Rousseau, Graves	Putnam	H.Kindricks	227/7	Irwin
Rousseau, James	Baldwin	Marshalls	155/1	Appling
Rousseau, John	Putnam	H.Kendricks	394/12	Early
Rousy, William	Jones	Samuels	217/10	Habersham
Routon, John	Jasper	Smiths	26/10	Early
Routon, Reuben	Jasper	Eastes	158/7	Irwin

NAME	COUNTY	MIL.DIST	LOT/SECT	DREW LAND
Routon, Talbott	Jasper	Easts	417/11	Irwin
Routon, William	Jasper	Easts	349/8	Early
Row, James	Chatham		69/4	Rabun
Row, Samuel	McIntosh	Eigles	216/12	Early
Row, Thomas	Wilkes	Perrys	147/14	Early
Rowe, Chancey	Baldwin	Marshalls	213/3	Irwin
Rowe, Daniel	Warren	Hubberts	393/12	Irwin
Rowe, David	Warren	Hubberts	356/27	Early
Rowe, Joshua Sr.	Warren	Hubberts	181/5	Irwin
Rowe, Joshua Sr.	Warren	Hubberts	285/6	Early
Rowe, Samuel	Wilkes	Bryants	106/6	Gwinnett
Rowe, Samuel	Wilkes	Bryants	155/2	Appling
Rowel, James	Wilkinson	Lees	145/12	Early
Rowell, Edward	Richmond	Winters	468/12	Irwin
Rowell, James	Camden	32nd	218/18	Early
Rowell, James	Twiggs	Evans	7/2	Appling
Rowell, Richard	Chatham		44/9	Irwin
Rowell, William	Franklin	Powells	149/7	Irwin
Rowl, Aldridge	Richmond	398th	63/8	Hall
Rowland, Benj.	Richmond	Palmers	248/2	Irwin
Rowland, Benj.	Richmond	Palmers	420/10	Irwin
Rowland, Charles	Richmond	Palmers	286/5	Appling
Rowland, Daniel	Warren	Parhams	236/12	Irwin
Rowland, David	Wilkinson	Lees	183/21	Early
Rowland, Drury	Franklin	Turks	396/27	Early
Rowland, Eliz.(Wid)	Richmond	Palmers	157/16	Early
Rowland, James	Greene	Carltons	62/2	Walton
Rowland, James	Warren	152nd	204/12	Early
Rowland, John Jr.	Laurens	Jones	97/28	Early
Rowland, John	Oglethorpe	Rowlands	59/20	Early
Rowland, John	Twiggs	W.Belchers	111/16	Early
Rowland, Oliver	Richmond	120th	284/14	Early
Rowland, Robert(Orps)	Franklin	Ashs	307/3	Early
Rowland, Thomas	Warren	152nd	154/13	Habersha
Rowland, William	Emanuel	56th	249/23	Early
Rowlin, James	Burke	Dys	2/4	Early
Rowlin, James	Burke	Dys	471/13	Irwin
Rowlin, John	Pulaski	Rees	227/9	Irwin
Rowlin, William	Pulaski	Rees	250/6	Early
Rowling, William	Lincoln	Walkers	263/6	Irwin
Rowman, James	Richmond	122	274/11	Early
Rowsey, Edward Sr.	Elbert	B.Higginbotham	296/11	Early
Rowson, John B.	Chatham		398/13	Irwin
Rowzee, Winslow	Elbert	Smiths	39/1	Irwin
Roy, Isaac A.(RS)	Morgan	Townsend	346/8	Irwin
Roy, Isaac A.(RS)	Morgan	Townsends	380/12	Early
Royal, Abraham	Elbert	Childers	55/8	Hall
Royal, John	Burke	Royals	77/17	Early
Royal, Mary	Burke	Royals	82/3	Walton
Royal, Samuel	Burke	Royals	227/20	Early
Royal, Sarah	Burke	Royals	420/7	Irwin
Royal, Stephen	Burke	Royals	286/5	Early
Royal, William	Burke	Royals	44/3	Habersha
Royal, Wm.J.J.(Orp)	Burke	Royals	183/5	Irwin
Royals, Abraham	Burke	Hands	135/5	Appling
Royals, Daniel	Burke	Hands	18/12	Habersha
Royals, ELizabeth	Burke	Hands	78/3	Early
Royler, John	Effingham		48/26	Early
Royols, Jonathan(RS)	Richmond	Palmers	6/13	Early
Royston, Robert(Orp)	Clarke	Simms	105/5	Irwin
Royston, William	Chatham		279/27	Early
Rozar, John Jr.	Pulaski	Maddox	416/8	Appling
Rozar, Pinckney	Richmond	Laceys	334/12	Early
Rozar, Shadrack	Richmond	Laceys	362/7	Early
Rozar, Shadrack	Richmond	Laceys	390/26	arly
Rozier, Willey	Camden	Tillis	9/22	Early
Rucher, John Sr.(RS)	Morgan	Leonards	218/16	Early

NAME	COUNTY	MIL.DIST	LOT/SECT	DREW LAND
Rucker, Armon(Orps)	Elbert	P.Christian	13/5	Irwin
Rucker, Barden	Elbert	B.Higginbotham	102/3	Appling
Rucker, Barden	Elbert	B.Higginbotham	61/18	Early
Rucker, Catharine(Wid)	Franklin	J.Millers	78/11	Habersham
Rucker, Fielding	Jasper	Bartlett	73/14	Early
Rucker, George	Franklin	J.Millers	276/10	Irwin
Rucker, James	Elbert	Dooleys	59/1	Walton
Rucker, John	Elbert	Ruckers	295/10	Early
Rucker, John	Elbert	Ruckers	91/2	Irwin
Rucker, Joseph	Elbert	Smiths	509/6	Appling
Rucker, Joseph	Jasper	Kennedy	353/21	Early
Rucker, Mastin	Jasper	Kennedy	407/21	Early
Rucker, Simeon B.	Franklin	J.Millers	16/3	Early
Rucker, Willis	Elbert	Olivers	399/27	Early
Rucker, Wm.Sr.	Elbert	Dooleys	73/5	Gwinnett
Rucknell, Isaac A.	Chatham		138/9	Hall
Ruddell, Mounce	Twiggs	Bosemans	281/13	Irwin
Ruddle, Andrew	Wilkes	Smiths	449/5	Irwin
Ruddle, Celea(Wid)	Twiggs	Bozemans	353/5	Irwin
Ruddle, Hariot(Wid)	Jefferson	Abbotts	84/6	Irwin
Ruff, Shadrack	Elbert	Hammonds	117/5	Appling
Ruffin, Robert R.	Jones	Jefferson	265/1	Appling
Ruford, John	Oglethorpe	Brittons	148/9	Early
Ruford, John	Oglethorpe	Brittons	215/8	Early
Rumsey, Kilbowrn	Elbert	Dooleys	352/11	Irwin
Rumsey, Thomas	Wilkes	Brooks	118/2	Rabun
Runnells, James M.	Wilkes	171	235/2	Early
Runnels, David	Hancock	Coopers	101/6	Early
Runnels, David	Hancock	Daniels	222/10	Early
Runnels, James	Hancock	Canes	399/7	Appling
Runnels, James	Hancock	Canes	58/10	Irwin
Runnels, John	Burke	McNorrils	76/3	Walton
Runnels, John	Hancock	Champions	220/10	Early
Runnels, John	Hancock	Sharps	389/15	Early
Runnels, Levy	Morgan	Knights	5/3	Appling
Runnels, Nancy(Wid)	Hancock	Hubbards	353/15	Early
Runnels, Preston	Jasper	Bentley	366/27	Early
Runnels, Reuben	Columbia	Watsons	138/13	Early
Runnels, Reuben	Columbia	Watsons	320/8	Early
Runnels, Richard	Warren	Gunns	210/12	Irwin
Runnels, Richard	Warren	Gunns	269/4	Appling
Runnels, Sophia	Jasper	Bentley	402/7	Appling
Runnels, Spencer	Wilkes	Runnels	164/3	Habersham
Runnels, Spencer	Wilkes	Runnels	27/5	Gwinnett
Runnels, Spencer	Wilkes	Runnels	278/7	Appling
Runnelson, Andrew	Burke	71	19/6	Early
Runnolds, William	Jones	Buckhalter	103/5	Rabun
Runnolds, Wm.	Jones	Buckhalter	65/19	Early
Rusel, James	Burke	Bells	240/4	Appling
Rush, James	Franklin	Browns	128/8	Early
Rush, James	Hancock	Danells	5/2	Habersham
Rush, Lewis B.	Elbert	Dooleys	420/1	Appling
Rush, Lewis B.	Elbert	Dooleys	509/7	Irwin
Rush, Sarah(Wid)	Franklin	Morris	127/7	Early
Rushin, Joel	Jones	Wallers	12/9	Irwin
Rushin, John Sr.	Jones	Harrist	63/12	Irwin
Rushin, John(Jr)	Jones	Harists	337/4	Appling
Rushin, William	Jones	Harrist	30/6	Habersham
Rushing, William	Tattnall	J.Durrence	41/14	Early
Ruslings, James(Orps)	Washington	Pools	515/7	Irwin
Russau, John	Putnam	J.Kindricks	432/5	Appling
Russel, Benjamin	Wilkes	Russels	330/4	Early
Russel, Burnell	Morgan	Townsends	94/1	Early
Russel, Clary Ann	Lincoln	Thompson	87/6	Gwinnett
Russel, Elijah	Warren	Blounts	365/1	Early
Russel, Ethelbert	Lincoln	Thompson	95/11	Habersham
Russel, Henry & Mary	Glynn		169/9	Hall

NAME	COUNTY	MIL.DIST	LOT/SECT	DREW LAN
Russel, Isaac	Chatham		319/7	Gwinnett
Russel, James	Jackson	Dicksons	81/4	Irwin
Russel, John	Baldwin	Russels	275/7	Gwinnett
Russel, John	Madison	Culbreaths	120/2	Rabun
Russel, Martin	Baldwin	Russels	341/10	Irwin
Russel, Thomas C.	Richmond	122nd	131/5	Early
Russel, William	Jones	Samuels	152/8	Early
Russel, William	Jones	Samuels	440/6	Irwin
Russel, William	Lincoln	Thompson	357/7	Early
Russell, Aaron	Jasper	Smiths	76/3	Early
Russell, David	Jasper	Smiths	90/12	Habersha
Russell, Elijah	Columbia	Walkers	70/6	Gwinnett
Russell, Hiram	Franklin	Flanagans	355/2	Appling
Russell, John R.	Jasper	Bartlett	340/4	Appling
Russell, John W.	Chatham		255/13	Early
Russell, John	Bulloch	Knights	16/1	Walton
Russell, Margarett	Jasper	Bailey	144/1	Appling
Russell, Robert W.	Jackson	Hamiltons	274/20	Early
Russell, Robert	Oglethorpe	Myricks	179/9	Irwin
Russell, Samuel	Chatham		99/2	Irwin
Russell, Stephen	Franklin	Flanagans	421/7	Appling
Russell, Thos.(Orph)	Franklin	Akins	195/2	Appling
Russell, Thos.C.	Richmond	122nd	253/4	Appling
Russell, William R.	Jasper	Smiths	68/4	Appling
Russell, William	Oglethorpe	Myricks	130/2	Early
Ruth, John	Jasper	Reeds	139/1	Early
Rutherford, Franklin	Washington	Floyds	487/2	Appling
Rutherford, John	Twiggs	W.Belchers	323/7	Early
Rutherford, John	Washington	Avents	264/10	Irwin
Rutherford, N.Green	Washington	Floyds	189/27	Early
Rutherford, Robert(Orpn)	Washington	Floyds	77/5	Appling
Rutherford, Robert	Baldwin	Marshalls	8/15	Irwin
Rutherford, Saml.	Warren	Loyless	13/10	Habersha
Ruthing, John	Washington	Pools	276/4	Early
Rutland, Randolph(Orps)	Hancock	Canes	123/8	Appling
Rutledge, Charles	Clarke	Simms	322/8	Early
Rutledge, Christopher(Orp)	Baldwin	Cousins	463/10	Irwin
Rutledge, James	Oglethorpe	Rowlands	103/28	Early
Rutledge, James	Oglethorpe	Rowlands	165/8	Irwin
Rutledge, James	Putnam	Littles	222/3	Walton
Rutledge, James	Putnam	Littles	82/9	Irwin
Rutledge, James	Tattnall	Overstreets	124/5	Appling
Rutledge, John	Burke	J.Ward	279/4	Appling
Rutledge, John	Morgan	Knights	289/6	Appling
Rutledge, Joseph	Oglethorpe	Holtsclaws	358/2	Appling
Rutledge, Joseph	Putnam	Littles	271/13	Early
Rutledge, William	Putnam	Littles	287/6	Appling
Rutledge, Wm.O.	Wilkes	Davis	267/19	Early
Ryal, Samuel(Orps)	Bulloch	Everitts	84/16	Irwin
Ryalls, Henry Sr.(RS)	McIntosh	Eigles	129/27	Early
Ryalls, Henry Sr.(RS)	McIntosh	Eigles	87/7	Early
Ryalls, Herbard	McIntosh	Eigles	438/3	Appling
Ryals, Charles	Effingham		293/11	Early
Ryals, Charles	Effingham		316/7	Irwin
Ryals, Jonathan(RS)	Richmond	Palmers	280/7	Early
Ryals, Jonathan(RS)	Richmond	Palmers	330/8	Irwin
Ryals, Willis	Laurens	Deans	314/8	Irwin
Ryals, Willis	Laurens	Deans	41/18	Early
Ryals, Wright	Laurens	Watsons	47/11	Habersha
Ryam, Peter(Orps)	Jones	Phillips	323/5	Irwin
Ryan, Philip(Sr.)	Jackson	Winters	374/20	Early
Ryan, Rachael(Orp)	Baldwin	Russels	611/2	Appling
Ryan, Richard	Warren	151	50/7	Gwinnett
Ryan, Risdon	Baldwin	Russels	376/28	Early
Ryan, Sally(Wid)	Jones	Phillips	191/6	Irwin
Ryan, William L.	Chatham		193/26	Early
Rye, Dunn	Wilkinson	Lees	261/11	Irwin

NAME	COUNTY	MIL.DIST	LOT/SECT	DREW LAND
Rye, John W.	Wilkinson	Bowings	175/16	Early
Rye, John W.	Wilkinson	Bowings	93/9	Appling
Rye, John	Wilkinson	Bowings	91/8	Appling
Rye, Jonathan	Wilkinson	Bowings	161/15	Irwin
Rye, Joseph	Wilkinson	Bowings	31/2	Walton
Rye, Mary(Wid)	Wilkinson	Bowings	307/7	Early
Rye, William	Laurens	Harris	388/7	Gwinnett
Rye, William	Laurens	Harris	90/13	Early
Ryland, Benjamin	Wilkes	Kilgores	72/4	Walton
Ryland, Benoney	Washington	Cummins	73/3	Habersham
Ryland, Elijah	Washington	Avents	41/2	Appling
Ryle, William Jr.	Putnam	Kindricks	382/28	Early
Ryols, Jonathan(RS)	Richmond	Palmers	442/6	Irwin
Ryon, Benjamin J.	Jefferson	Cowarts	265/9	Early
Saddler, Henry R.	Chatham		66/2	Irwin
Sade, Nathaniel	Scriven	Smiths	21/13	Habersham
Sadler, James	Putnam	Oslins	212/7	Gwinnett
Saffold, Bird	Wilkes	Russels	390/10	Early
Saffold, William	Wilkinson	Lees	268/16	Early
Sage, Mary	Lincoln	Adares	37/3	Rabun
Sailors, David	Jackson	Winters Bt.	496/13	Irwin
Sailors, David	Jackson	Winters Bt.	6/9	Irwin
Sailors, James	Lincoln	Millicans	270/19	Early
Sailors, William	Lincoln	Millicans	250/20	Early
Sale, Gideon	Baldwin	Cousins	172/15	Early
Sale, John	Lincoln	Thompsons	57/3	Early
Sale, Leroy	Wilkes	Dents	188/21	Early
Sale, Richard	Wilkes	Josseys	362/27	Early
Sallins, Caroline(Orph)	McIntosh	Goulds	102/8	Early
Sallins, Caroline(Orph)	McIntosh	Goulds	406/9	Irwin
Sallins, Esther(Orph)	McIntosh	Goulds	406/9	Irwin
Sallins, Martha(Orph)	McIntosh	Goulds	102/8	Early
Sallins, Martha(Orph)	McIntosh	Goulds	406/9	Irwin
Sallins, Robert(Orp)	McIntosh	Goulds	406/9	Irwin
Sallins, Robert(Orph)	McIntosh	Goulds	102/8	Early
Sallins, William(Orph)	McIntosh	Goulds	102/8	Early
Sallins, William(Orph)	McIntosh	Goulds	406/9	Irwin
Salmon, Ephram	Jackson	Rogers Bt.	133/9	Appling
Salmon, Hezekiah	Richmond	Laceys	274/7	Early
Salter, James	Wilkinson	Kettles	389/7	Irwin
Salter, Peter	Warren	154	173/12	Early
Salter, Peter	Warren	154th	186/16	Early
Salter, Richard	Baldwin	Marshalls	390/20	Early
Salter, Simon B.	Washington	Renfros	130/16	Early
Salter, Simon	Clarke	Applings	97/2	Walton
Salter, Simon	Washington	Mannings	122/10	Early
Salter, Simon	Washington	Mannings	525/8	Appling
Salter, West A.J.M.	Laurens	Deans	89/11	Habersham
Salter, Zadock	Washington	Burneys	218/1	Walton
Salters, Jacob	Effingham		468/3	Appling
Saltonstall, Joseph	Laurens	D.Smiths	244/3	Appling
Saltonstall, Joseph	Laurens	D.Smiths	447/6	Appling
Sammons, Charles	Warren	153rd	153/9	Appling
Sammons, Charles	Warren	153rd	68/10	Hall
Sammons, Lewis	Jefferson	Waldens	484/8	Appling
Sample, David	Jefferson	Lamps	172/7	Appling
Sample, John	Jefferson	Lamps	110/12	Habersham
Sampler, Samuel	Columbia	Watsons	56/16	Irwin
Samples, Charles	Walton	Worshams	267/1	Appling
Samples, John	Putnam	Buckners	172/4	Walton
Samples, Uziah C.	Putnam	Buckners	295/7	Early
Sams, James	Oglethorpe	Dunns	221/7	Irwin
Sams, Josiah	Oglethorpe	Brittons	32/15	Early
Samuel, Edward	Lincoln	Walkers	564/2	Appling
Samuel, Thornton	Columbia	Willingham	130/10	Habersham
Sanderford, Benjamin	Warren	Huberts	218/8	Appling
Sanderford, John G.	Warren	154	53/2	Rabun

NAME	COUNTY	MIL.DIST	LOT/SECT	DREW LAND
Sanderlin, Benjamin	Bryan	20	353/12	Early
Sanderlin, Owen	Chatham		302/8	Irwin
Sanderlin, Trebeg	Chatham		361/7	Irwin
Sanders, Ann	Jasper	Centells	296/18	Early
Sanders, Billington M.	Columbia	J.Morriss	112/5	Early
Sanders, Burrell	Warren	151	266/5	Irwin
Sanders, Burrill	Warren	151st	260/13	Irwin
Sanders, Coleman	Laurens	Griffins	77/1	Early
Sanders, Daniel	Washington	Avents	14/2	Habersham
Sanders, David(RS)	Putnam	Robertson	61/15	Irwin
Sanders, David(RS)	Putnam	Robertsons	408/13	Irwin
Sanders, Dennis D.	Twiggs	Bozemans	216/9	Early
Sanders, Elias Sr.	Franklin	R.Brown	96/3	Appling
Sanders, Elias	Elbert	Dobbs	479/10	Irwin
Sanders, Ephraim Sr.	Jones	Chappels	264/9	Appling
Sanders, Isaiah	Jasper	Bentleys	119/3	Walton
Sanders, James H.	Morgan	Wrights	512/6	Irwin
Sanders, James	Putnam	H.Kendricks	160/19	Early
Sanders, James	Warren	152nd	95/9	Hall
Sanders, James	Wilkinson	Kettles	270/3	Irwin
Sanders, Jeremiah(Orp)	Chatham		141/11	Hall
Sanders, Jesse	Wilkinson	Lees	229/16	Early
Sanders, John	Franklin	Pains	86/1	Habersham
Sanders, John	Jasper	Bentleys	396/4	Early
Sanders, John	Jones	Griffiths	178/11	Early
Sanders, John	Lincoln	Thompsons	235/12	Irwin
Sanders, Jonathan	Lincoln	Adares	507/4	Appling
Sanders, Moses(Orps)	Putnam	Buckners	7/1	Irwin
Sanders, Nathaniel	Jones	Seals	381/10	Early
Sanders, Peter	Jones	Harrist	270/8	Irwin
Sanders, Robert	Laurens	Griffins	390/28	Early
Sanders, Samuel	Putnam	Robertsons	188/12	Irwin
Sanders, Thomas W.	Columbia	Bealls	326/7	Irwin
Sanders, Thomas(Orp)	Chatham		141/11	Hall
Sanders, Thomas	Jones	Seals	218/10	Irwin
Sanders, Thomas	Jones	Seals	66/5	Rabun
Sanders, Washington J.	Columbia	Paynes	156/14	Irwin
Sanders, William	Hancock	Edwards	212/6	Early
Sanders, William	Hancock	Edwards	235/7	Irwin
Sanders, Wm.G.	Richmond		327/18	Early
Sanders, Wright	Laurens	Harriss	460/10	Irwin
Sandford, Edward	Emanuel	57	33/12	Early
Sandford, Vincent Jr.	Greene	143rd	138/4	Early
Sandiford, Benjamin	Warren	Hubberts	272/20	Early
Sandiford, Harris	Wilkes	Gordons	223/7	Early
Sandiford, Peter	Warren	Hopsons	129/18	Early
Sandiford, Susannah(Orp)	Burke	Spiveys	330/7	Irwin
Sandredge, Claiborn	Elbert	B.Higginbotham	165/28	Early
Sanford, Britton	Jones	Permenters	333/16	Early
Sanford, Hamilton	Wilkes	Bryans	143/5	Early
Sanford, Henry Sr.	Greene	143	83/17	Early
Sanford, Jesse	Baldwin	Taliaferro	241/3	Irwin
Sanford, John	Wilkes	Bryants	47/3	Walton
Sanford, Presley	Putnam	Littles	45/1	Walton
Sanford, Samuel(Orps)	Laurens	Jones	97/1	Appling
Sanford, William	Greene	143rd	337/4	Early
Sangsters, Peter	Wayne	Crews	325/9	Irwin
Sansom, Archibald(Orps)	Jasper	Evans	356/10	Early
Sansom, Eliz.(Wid)	Wilkes	Kilgores	337/6	Early
Sansom, Elizabeth	Jasper	Bentleys	96/2	Walton
Sansom, Patsey	Jasper	Bentleys	15/8	Hall
Sansom, Thomas	Clarke	Deans	383/11	Irwin
Sap, Aley	Appling	5th	286/10	Irwin
Sapp, Abraham Jr.	Wilkinson	Brooks	336/16	Early
Sapp, Addison	Burke	Hands	27/1	Rabun
Sapp, Adison	Burke	Hands	233/17	Early
Sapp, Benjamin	Tattnall	Johnsons	329/12	Irwin

NAME	COUNTY	MIL.DIST	LOT/SECT	DREW LAND
Sapp, Darling	Liberty		105/11	Habersham
Sapp, Darling	Liberty		359/1	Early
Sapp, Dillson F.	Burke	Hands	23/4	Early
Sapp, Eliz.Ann	Burke	J.Wards	270/5	Early
Sapp, Hardy C.	Burke	Hands	192/3	Irwin
Sapp, Henry(RS)	Twiggs	Ellis	126/27	Early
Sapp, Henry(RS)	Twiggs	Ellis	159/3	Walton
Sapp, Henry	Bulloch	Tilmans	186/9	Irwin
Sapp, Henry	Liberty		250/3	Walton
Sapp, Henry	Tattnall	Tharps	79/1	Walton
Sapp, Henry	Tattnall	Tharps	92/14	Irwin
Sapp, John Jr.	Burke	Hands	386/19	Early
Sapp, John	Burke	M.Wards	18/21	Early
Sapp, John	Jefferson	Langstons	110/1	Habersham
Sapp, John	Tattnall	Johnson	47/16	Early
Sapp, Levi	Emanuel	395	207/4	Walton
Sapp, Margaret(Wid)	Emanuel	57th	1/5	Gwinnett
Sapp, Shadrack Sr.	Liberty		301/12	Irwin
Sapp, William	Burke	M.Wards	29/9	Early
Sapp, William	Tattnall	McKennie	519/5	Irwin
Sappington, Caleb	Wilkes	Davis	185/6	Early
Sappington, Richard	Wilkes	Davis	239/16	Early
Sappington, Richd.	Wilkes	Davis	363/21	Early
Sartin, Elisha	Elbert	Webbs	134/19	Early
Sartin, Elisha	Elbert	Webbs	151/13	Irwin
Sartin, John Jr.	Elbert	Webbs	297/27	Early
Sasser, Bryant	Scriven	180	38/3	Appling
Sasser, Thos.	Scriven	180th	81/8	Appling
Satewhite, Edw.	Jones	Seals	529/8	Irwin
Satterwhite, Charles	Oglethorpe	Goolsbys	86/1	Walton
Satterwhite, Milley(Wid	Columbia	Gartrells	56/7	Irwin
Satterwhite, Thomas	Columbia	Gartrells	388/26	Early
Saucer, John	Putnam	Buckners	362/6	Appling
Saucer, Josiah	Bulloch	Knights	20/4	Early
Saucer, Sarah(Orp)	Burke	McNorrills	408/8	Appling
Sauls, Abraham	Jefferson	Matthews	633/2	Appling
Sauls, Isaac	Liberty		367/20	Early
Sauls, Meredith	Bryan	19th	15/4	Rabun
Sauls, Theophilus	Twiggs	Hodges	153/2	Habersham
Sauls, Thompson	Twiggs	Tisons	528/10	Irwin
Saulter, Nancy(Wid)	Liberty		220/8	Irwin
Sauncey, Thomas	Liberty		59/16	Early
Saunders, Isaiah	Jasper	Bentleys	104/3	Habersham
Saunders, John	Lincoln	Parks	113/2	Irwin
Saunders, John	Lincoln	Parks	516/9	Irwin
Saunders, Lewis	Laurens	D.Smiths	437/10	Irwin
Saunders, Peter	Jones	Harrists	110/14	Irwin
Saunders, Wm.(Orps)	Hancock	Millers	148/15	Irwin
Saundes, Charlotte	Hancock	Scotts	349/5	Appling
Savage, Allen	Franklin	Haynes	105/11	Early
Savage, Mary	Chatham		112/4	Irwin
Savage, Sarah(Wid)	Chatham		245/4	Early
Savage, Sarah(Wid)	Chatham		72/5	Gwinnett
Saveall, William	Franklin	Hanes	286/20	Early
Savill, Lucy(Wid)	Hall		240/2	Appling
Sawyer, Johnson	Putnam	Berrys	183/10	Habersham
Sawyer, Johnson	Putnam	Berrys	60/5	Appling
Sawyers, Margaret	Putnam	Berrys	124/7	Early
Saxon, Benj.A.	Twiggs	Smiths	24/5	Appling
Saxon, Benjamin	Jasper	Bentleys	131/1	Early
Saxon, Eliz. M.(Wid)	Elbert	Whites	510/8	Irwin
Saxon, Henry	Twiggs	Smiths	126/18	Early
Saxon, John M.	Elbert	Whites	366/2	Early
Saxon, John	Burke	Sullivans	112/5	Appling
Saxton, Mary(Wid)	Franklin	Davis	37/1	Early
Sayers, David	Morgan	Parkers	286/13	Irwin
Saylors, Christopher	Jackson	Winters Bt.	403/9	Early

NAME	COUNTY	MIL.DIST	LOT/SECT	DREW LAND
Sayre, Robert S.	Elbert	White/Nun.	213/7	Gwinnett
Sayres, James	Greene	Tuggles	54/4	Early
Scails, Aaron	Elbert	Whites	84/4	Early
Scales, Mary(Wid)	Franklin	Davis	31/15	Irwin
Scales, Simeon	Franklin	Davis	108/11	Early
Scarboro, Samuel	Burke	Spiveys	25/1	Early
Scarborough, Aaron Jr.	Pulaski	Rees	126/6	Gwinnett
Scarborough, Adom	Pulaski	Maddox	23/2	Appling
Scarborough, Allan	Pulaski	Johnstons	7/19	Early
Scarborough, Avan	Pulaski	Maddox	122/8	Irwin
Scarborough, Benj.(Orps)	Jones	Shropshiers	366/3	Early
Scarborough, Frederick	Elbert	Webbs	243/2	Irwin
Scarborough, Frederick	Elbert	Webbs	39/1	Habersham
Scarborough, Irwin	Pulaski	Dewits	101/5	Irwin
Scarborough, Joel	Burke	J.Wards	91/1	Walton
Scarborough, Leml.(Orps)	Burke	J.Wards	325/6	Early
Scarborough, Mary	Burke	Torrance	204/9	Irwin
Scarborough, Mills	Pulaski	Rees	215/8	Appling
Scarborough, Reddie	Bulloch	Everitts	124/4	Early
Scarborough, Reddie	Bulloch	Everitts	174/6	Early
Scarbro, Wm.	Burke	Spiveys	140/2	Habersham
Scarbrough, Elias	Laurens	Watsons	160/13	Habersham
Scarbrough, Elias	Laurens	Watsons	276/13	Early
Scarbrough, James	Laurens	Watsons	17/12	Early
Scarbrough, James	Laurens	Watsons	173/6	Appling
Scarbrough, John	Laurens	Watsons	156/5	Gwinnett
Scarbrough, Lemuel(Orps)	Burke	J.Wards	6/14	Irwin
Scarbrough, Miles	Jones	Greens	136/9	Appling
Scarbrough, Noah	Twiggs	Jeffersons	49/13	Irwin
Scarlett, Francis	Glynn		364/9	Irwin
Scarlett, Francis	Glynn		45/7	Irwin
Schenk, Peter	Chatham		2/1	Habersham
Schley, William	Jefferson	Abbotts	131/9	Early
Schlosser, Matthias	Bryan	20th	78/5	Rabun
Schoder, Letacia(Wid)	Warren	Rogers	440/8	Appling
Schye, Ann	Chatham		24/2	Habersham
Scoder, Roberson	Chatham		582/2	Appling
Scoggens, Fielding	Jasper	Reeds	121/5	Irwin
Scoggin, Chatten D.	Oglethorpe	Bridges	17/12	Habersham
Scoggin, David	Oglethorpe	Barnetts	6/9	Hall
Scoggin, Thomas Sr.	Oglethorpe	Rowlands	56/1	Appling
Scoggin, Wylie	Oglethorpe	Barnetts	12/5	Gwinnett
Scoggins, James	Jones	Griffiths	18/4	Walton
Scoggins, Josiah	Washington	Barges	134/13	Early
Scoggins, Willington	Clarke	Deanes	16/16	Early
Scogin, Mary	Oglethorpe	Barnetts	286/3	Appling
Sconyers, John	Burke	Spiveys	11/26	Early
Scot, Agnatius A.	Warren	Blounts	126/2	Rabun
Scot, Benj. C.	Morgan	Alfords	338/3	Early
Scot, Daniel	Jasper	Posts	79/23	Early
Scot, Daniel	Wilkes	Perrys	266/18	Early
Scot, Gustavus	Wilkes	Perrys	77/13	Irwin
Scot, Henry F.	Greene	Kimbroughs	73/2	Habersham
Scott, Andrew	Burke	69th	209/13	Irwin
Scott, Archibald	Greene	143	157/10	Irwin
Scott, Benjamin	Hancock	Canis	231/6	Irwin
Scott, Charles	Burke	Sullivans	29/15	Early
Scott, Charles	Burke	Sullivans	331/13	Early
Scott, Daniel	Jasper	Posts	234/5	Irwin
Scott, Darins	Twiggs	Jamesons	244/8	Irwin
Scott, Francis	Putnam	Morelands	255/20	Early
Scott, Francis	Putnam	Morlands	222/19	Early
Scott, Francis	Putnam	Morlands	477/13	Irwin
Scott, James C.	Liberty		22/4	Rabun
Scott, James Sr.	Scriven	Lovetts	48/6	Appling
Scott, James	Clarke	Applings	290/5	Early
Scott, James	Lincoln	Willifords	4/12	Hall

292

NAME	COUNTY	MIL.DIST	LOT/SECT	DREW LAND
Scott, James	Montgomery	McMillans	338/2	Appling
Scott, James	Warren	Rogers	349/2	Appling
Scott, John C.	Bryan	19th	415/9	Irwin
Scott, John P.	Greene	Garners	255/10	Irwin
Scott, John P.	Greene	Garners	54/10	Irwin
Scott, John S.	Morgan	Alfords	409/3	Appling
Scott, John (Genl)	Baldwin	Irwins	246/1	Walton
Scott, John	Richmond	122nd	129/14	Early
Scott, John	Wilkes	Perrys	138/10	Irwin
Scott, Joseph A.	Chatham		123/8	Early
Scott, Joseph J.	Franklin	Haynes	46/5	Rabun
Scott, Peter	Hancock	Danells	274/8	Early
Scott, Reuben	Wilkes	Kilgores	495/13	Irwin
Scott, Richard (Orps)	Jones	Greens	145/2	Appling
Scott, Robert	Franklin	Morriss	188/17	Early
Scott, Ross	Baldwin	Russels	457/9	Irwin
Scott, Samuel S.	Jasper	Hays	238/13	Irwin
Scott, Samuel	Warren	Williams	269/16	Early
Scott, Samuel	Warren	Williams	345/4	Early
Scott, Thomas	Jasper	Posts	394/11	Early
Scott, William Sr.	Columbia	Dodson	216/3	Early
Scott, William Sr.	Columbia	Dodsons	3/12	Habersham
Scott, William	Franklin	Davis	249/9	Irwin
Scott, William	Franklin	Davis	436/8	Appling
Scott, William	Jasper	Esly	25/5	Appling
Scott, William	Lincoln	Millicans	172/1	Appling
Scott, William	Scriven	Lovetts	336/7	Gwinnett
Scott, Willis S.	Jones	Wallers	146/17	Early
Scott, Woodliff	Hancock	Danells	410/6	Irwin
Scotts, Orphans	Franklin	Morriss	399/10	Early
Screws, James	Columbia	Ob.Morriss	272/1	Walton
Screws, Nancy (Wid)	Twiggs	Browns	7/15	Early
Scroggin, Barton	Oglethorpe	Wises	197/9	Irwin
Scroggin, Thomas	Oglethorpe	Rowlands	170/9	Irwin
Scroggins, George	Jones	Griffiths	240/9	Appling
Scroggins, Thomas E.	Oglethorpe	Brittons	365/10	Early
Scruggs, Aliotha	Effingham		288/3	Appling
Scruggs, Richard	Scriven	36	352/18	Early
Scurry, E.M.M. (Orp)	Columbia	Ob.Morriss	84/1	Irwin
Seabert, Charles	Pulaski	Dewits	429/13	Irwin
Seabert, Polley (Orph)	Pulaski	Dewits	255/3	Appling
Seabert, Sarah (Orph)	Pulaski	Dewits	255/3	Appling
Seager, John	Burke	Thomas	114/8	Appling
Seagler, Joseph	Walton	Williams	230/6	Early
Seagler, Joseph	Walton	Williams	386/4	Appling
Seagreen, John	Chatham		136/10	Irwin
Seal, Richmond G.	Lincoln	Thompsons	235/5	Early
Seals, Andrew	Twiggs	R.Belchers	147/6	Early
Seals, Andrew	Twiggs	R.Belchers	213/8	Early
Seals, Thomas	Jones	Seals	101/2	Appling
Seals, William W.	Camden	Clarks	278/7	Early
Seals, William W.	Camden	Clarks	393/3	Early
Searkin, L.Sertain	Jackson	Dicksons	49/9	Irwin
Sears, Timothy	Wilkinson	Childs	75/8	Irwin
Searthy, Thomas	Wilkinson	Lees	26/2	Rabun
Searthy, Thomas	Wilkinson	Lees	60/5	Early
Seats, James	Washington	Cummings	71/15	Irwin
Seay, John	Jackson	Rogers Bt.	272/6	Irwin
Seay, John	Jackson	Rogers Bt.	415/3	Appling
Seay, Thomas	Columbia	Bealls	133/8	Appling
Seay, Thomas	Columbia	Bells	434/3	Appling
Seay, William	Greene	Woodhams	253/5	Early
Seckinger, Catharine (Wid)	Effingham		486/2	Appling
Seckinger, John C.	Effingham		108/3	Early
Seckinger, John C.	Effingham		72/11	Early
Seckinger, Joshua	Effingham		265/7	Appling
Seegraves, Burrel	Lincoln	Adares	343/8	Irwin

NAME	COUNTY	MIL.DIST	LOT/SECT	DREW LAN
Selby, Joseph(Orps)	Baldwin	Marshalls	67/14	Early
Self, Baxter	Jasper	Hays	175/4	Irwin
Self, Charnie	Bulloch	Edwards	81/7	Gwinnett
Self, David	Twiggs	W.Belcher	370/11	Irwin
Self, Eliz.(Wid)	Twiggs	W.Belchers	93/12	Habersha
Self, Sincler	Elbert	Dobbs	42/8	Irwin
Selfriege, John	Morgan	Alfords	67/8	Appling
Sell, Jonathan	Warren	Parhams	355/8	Appling
Selleck, Frederick	Chatham		64/4	Irwin
Selleck, Greshom	Richmond	398th	273/26	Early
Sellers, Alfred	Jefferson	Matthews	143/26	Early
Sellers, Alfred	Jefferson	Matthews	247/3	Appling
Sellers, Judith(Wid)	Hall		347/2	Early
Sellers, Solomon	Emanuel	49	212/12	Irwin
Sellers, Solomon	Emanuel	49th	286/27	Early
Sellers, William	Jefferson	Matthews	226/3	Appling
Sellers, William	Jefferson	Matthews	503/8	Appling
Selman, John Sr.	Franklin	Harriss	369/8	Early
Selman, John	Clarke	Oats	418/5	Appling
Selmon, Benjamin	Morgan	Selmons	172/10	Habersha
Selmon, David	Morgan	Loyds	269/28	Early
Selmon, John Sr.	Franklin	Harriss	8/12	Hall
Senderford, Wm.	Burke	Bells	457/6	Irwin
Sentell, Joseph	Jasper	Centells	66/5	Gwinnett
Sentell, Samuel	Walton	Sentells	84/3	Walton
Senterfeit, Henry Jr.	Pulaski	Senterfeit	297/15	Early
Senterfeit, Henry	Pulaski	Senterfeits	381/1	Appling
Senterfeit, Jesse	Pulaski	Senterfeits	229/17	Early
Sermon, John	Pulaski	Dewits	188/4	Appling
Sermon, Jonathan	Emanuel	49	161/8	Hall
Sermons, Joshua	Emanuel	49th	139/11	Irwin
Sessions, Benjamin	Washington	Robsons	134/3	Walton
Sessions, George	Washington	Floyds	5/11	Hall
Sessions, Joseph	Washington	Floyds	491/7	Appling
Sesson, James	Jackson	Dicksons Bt.	133/10	Hall
Sesson, Mary(Wid)	Franklin	Jos.Millers	410/8	Appling
Sesson, Richard M.	Jasper	Baileys	318/8	Early
Sesson, Vardy	Jackson	Dicksons Bt.	251/26	Early
Sevan, Henry	Jackson	Winters Bt.	136/5	Early
Sever, William	Emanuel	49th	335/5	Appling
Seward, William	Laurens	Harris	15/10	Hall
Sewate, William	Wilkes	Russells	33/8	Irwin
Sewell, Greenbury	Franklin	Hammonds	352/9	Early
Sewell, James	Franklin	Harriss	375/5	Irwin
Sewell, John	Franklin	Ashs	109/3	Irwin
Sewell, John	Franklin	Burroughs	265/19	Early
Sewell, Joshua Sr.	Franklin	Burroughs	24/3	Early
Sewell, Moses	Franklin	Ashs	277/27	Early
Sewell, Samuel	Franklin	Ashs	23/1	Habersha
Sewell, Samuel	Franklin	Burroughs	268/4	Irwin
Sexon, Robert	Jackson	Dicksons Bt.	108/4	Appling
Sexton, Archelus	Jasper	Bentleys	328/5	Irwin
Sexton, Henry	Columbia	Watsons	134/3	Early
Seymore, Robert	Jasper	McClendons	172/5	Early
Seymour, John R.	Jasper	Owens	213/4	Irwin
Shackelford, Edmund	Baldwin	Marshalls	392/8	Appling
Shackelford, Edmund	Putnam	Bustins	325/7	Gwinnett
Shackleford, Edmond	Elbert	Smiths	189/16	Early
Shackleford, Edmund	Putnam	Bustins	127/11	Hall
Shackleford, Emd.	Elbert	Smiths	325/7	Early
Shackleford, John	Elbert	R.Christians	219/1	Appling
Shackleford, John	Wilkes	Mattox	44/3	Walton
Shackleford, John	Wilkes	Mattox	89/6	Early
Shackleford, Phillip	Jackson	Rogers Bt.	18/12	Irwin
Shackleford, Richard	Clarke	Mitchells	41/7	Early
Shad, Solomon S.	Chatham		356/17	Early
Shaddock, Anthony	Chatham		54/10	Early

NAME	COUNTY	MIL.DIST	LOT/SECT	DREW LAND
Shaffer, Daniel	Richmond	122	241/7	Appling
Shaffer, Mitchell	Chatham		90/6	Early
Shaftall, Eliza(Orp)	Chatham		238/4	Walton
Shanger, Joseph	Elbert	Dobbs	319/6	Early
Shank, Felix(Minor)	Wilkes	Kilgores	89/17	Early
Shank, Henry	Wilkes	Kilgores	372/4	Appling
Shank, Henry	Wilkes	Kilgores	387/5	Irwin
Shannan, Robert	Jasper	McClendons	176/10	Habersham
Shannon, Thomas C.	Pulaski	Maddox	228/7	Irwin
Shannon, Thomas(RS)	Pulaski	Maddox	198/5	Irwin
Shannon, Thomas(RS)	Pulaski	Madox	354/6	Appling
Shannon, William	Richmond	120th	349/7	Early
Sharger, Wm.Jr.	Franklin	R.Browns	15/3	Rabun
Sharkley, Eleazer	Washington	Wimberleys	223/8	Early
Sharley, Edward Jr.	Jones	Permenters	266/9	Irwin
Sharley, Edward Sr.	Jones	Permenters	94/5	Rabun
Sharley, Edward(RS)	Jones	Permenters	3/3	Early
Sharley, Nathaniel	Jones	Permenters	2/5	Habersham
Sharley, William(Orps)	Jones	Permenters	398/6	Irwin
Sharman, John Jr.(Minor)	Wilkes	Kilgores	397/6	Appling
Sharp, Basdil	Burke	Torrance	8/5	Irwin
Sharp, Cade	Burke	70th	138/3	Early
Sharp, Clemmey	Burke	70th	476/6	Irwin
Sharp, Clemney	Burke	70	311/15	Early
Sharp, Cyrus	Baldwin	Ellis	312/13	Early
Sharp, Daniel	Morgan	Knights	115/9	Appling
Sharp, Daniel	Morgan	Knights	412/12	Irwin
Sharp, Francis J.	Morgan	Dennis	114/20	Early
Sharp, James Jr.	Greene	141st	308/9	Early
Sharp, James	Greene	144th	184/12	Early
Sharp, John(Orps)	Morgan	Jordans	426/11	Irwin
Sharp, John	Baldwin	Stephens	300/6	Early
Sharp, Mathew	Wilkinson	Smiths	367/4	Early
Sharp, Nathan J.	Jackson	Winters Bt.	52/21	Early
Sharpe, Howell	Laurens	D.Smiths	211/13	Irwin
Sharpe, Howell	Laurens	D.Smiths	238/16	Early
Sharpe, James P.	Jasper	Hays	396/1	Appling
Sharuran, John Sr.	Wilkes	Kilgores	140/10	Hall
Sharwood, James	McIntosh	McIntosh	288/17	Early
Shaw, Alexander	Habersham	Powells	173/10	Early
Shaw, Amos	Oglethorpe	Murrays	188/7	Early
Shaw, Daniel	Montgomery	Alstons	222/17	Early
Shaw, Elijah	Jackson	Rogers Bt.	70/4	Irwin
Shaw, Elijah	Jackson	Rogers	102/1	Walton
Shaw, Haley(RS)	Jackson	Hamiltons Bt.	495/12	Irwin
Shaw, Jane(Wid)	Clarke	Harpers	416/7	Irwin
Shaw, Jeremiah Sr.	Liberty		38/22	Early
Shaw, John Jr.	Greene	Ragans	299/4	Irwin
Shaw, John(Orp)	Chatham		398/6	Early
Shaw, John	Greene	Ragans	234/3	Appling
Shaw, John	Greene	Ragins	275/12	Early
Shaw, John	Greene	Ragins	73/6	Appling
Shaw, John	Jasper	Bartletts	132/9	Appling
Shaw, Joseph	Jackson	Hamiltons Bt.	384/7	Early
Shaw, Joseph	Jackson	Rodgers Bt.	101/10	Irwin
Shaw, Lucy(Wid)	Jones	Samuels	209/3	Irwin
Shaw, Margarett	Columbia	Shaws	301/7	Appling
Shaw, Mary(Orp)	Chatham		398/6	Early
Shaw, Neill	Jones	Samuels	397/19	Early
Shaw, Neill	Jones	Samuels	53/20	Early
Shaw, Robert(Orp)	Chatham		398/6	Early
Shaw, Samuel	Jasper	Phillips	95/2	Irwin
Shaw, Thomas	Jasper	Hays	139/6	Appling
Shaw, William Jr.	Clarke	Pentecost	3/23	Early
Shaw, William W.	Greene	Ragans	45/8	Appling
Shay, David(RS)	Clarke	Pentecost	344/4	Early
Shayer, George W.	Franklin	Burtons	214/11	Early

NAME	COUNTY	MIL.DIST	LOT/SECT	DREW LAND
Shearell, Eliz.(Wid)	Greene	140	242/3	Appling
Shearer, Catharine	Chatham		146/28	Early
Shearer, Catharine	Chatham		268/9	Early
Shearer, Elijah	Wilkes	Holidays	93/6	Irwin
Shearer, Francis	Wilkinson	Smiths	487/7	Irwin
Shearer, Gilbert	Richmond	Winters	41/6	Appling
Shearer, Rebecca	Chatham		93/22	Early
Shearer, William	Richmond		119/2	Appling
Shearley, Nathaniel	Jones	Permenters	580/2	Appling
Shearly, William	Jackson	Winters Bt.	421/11	Irwin
Shearman, Edw.Jr.	Camden	Clarkes	180/6	Appling
Shearman, Edward J.	Laurens	Harris	40/3	Appling
Shearman, Edward	Camden	Clarkes	419/2	Appling
Shearman, Usail	Laurens	S.Smiths	305/6	Appling
Sheats, Archibald	Wilkes	Brooks	138/14	Early
Sheats, Taretelon	Wilkes	Smiths	107/8	Irwin
Shebee, A.B.	Washington	Mannings	85/5	Rabun
Sheck, John	Chatham		201/2	Irwin
Shecrouse, Gottel	Effingham		150/18	Early
Shecrouse, Gottiel	Effingham		222/27	Early
Sheets, Linsey	Clarke	Moores	184/3	Walton
Sheffield, John Jr.	Bulloch	Knights	253/7	Irwin
Sheffield, William Jr.	Bulloch	Knights	26/21	Early
Sheffield, Wm.Jr.	Bulloch	Knights	13/1	Appling
Sheffield, Wm.Jr.	Bulloch	Knights	71/5	Rabun
Sheftall, Abram	Chatham		217/10	Early
Sheftall, Emanuel(Orp)	Chatham		238/4	Walton
Sheftall, Moses	Chatham		170/10	Irwin
Sheftall, Rebecca(Orp)	Chatham		238/4	Walton
Sheftall, Solomon(Orp)	Chatham		238/4	Walton
Sheftall, Solomon	Chatham		288/8	Appling
Shehe, John	Washington	Renfros	9/3	Irwin
Shehee, John	Washington	Renfros	164/1	Irwin
Shelby, Evans	Baldwin	Irwins	277/19	Early
Shelby, Rebecca(Wid)	Jones	Harriss	25/12	Hall
Shell, George	Franklin	Attaways	473/3	Appling
Shell, Green	Hancock	Thomas	322/6	Gwinnett
Shell, Green	Hancock	Thomas	74/7	Early
Shelman, Robert B.	Jefferson	Abbots	3/4	Rabun
Shelnut, William	Franklin	Attaways	85/3	Habersham
Shelton, Allen	Greene	141st	377/10	Irwin
Shelton, Charles J.	Telfair	Wilsons	180/4	Appling
Shelton, Joseph	Greene	141	4/13	Irwin
Shepard, Francis	Columbia	Gartrells	241/13	Early
Shepard, Nimrod	Clarke	Tredwell	194/6	Early
Shepard, Thomas(Orps)	Liberty		439/13	Irwin
Shepheard, John	Jefferson	Waldings	496/7	Irwin
Shepheard, Salmon W.	Morgan	Hackneys	85/3	Early
Shepherd, Alford	Morgan	McClendons	325/15	Early
Shepherd, Ann	Jasper	Evans	498/6	Appling
Shepherd, Bazel	Burke	J.Wards	267/5	Early
Shepherd, Bennet	Putnam	Coopers	309/4	Appling
Shepherd, Bennet	Putnam	Coopers	501/12	Irwin
Shepherd, David	Jasper	Baileys	222/7	Gwinnett
Shepherd, Francis	Columbia	Gartrells	269/5	Irwin
Shepherd, Jacob	Wilkinson	Kettles	243/6	Appling
Shepherd, John B.	Scriven	36th	112/14	Irwin
Shepherd, John M.	Putnam	Buckners	69/4	Irwin
Shepherd, John	Scriven	36	74/12	Irwin
Shepherd, Siloma(Wid)	Pulaski	Bryans	230/13	Irwin
Shepherd, Talmon W.	Morgan	McClendons	119/11	Early
Shepherd, Thompson	Wilkes	Willis	446/7	Irwin
Shepherd, William F.	Jefferson	Matthews	167/12	Early
Shepherd, William F.	Jefferson	Matthews	72/20	Early
Shepherd, William(Orps)	Columbia	Burroughs	251/4	Early
Shepherd, William	Scriven	36th	50/9	Early
Shepherd, Wm.	Wilkinson	Smiths	29/4	Rabun

NAME	COUNTY	MIL.DIST	LOT/SECT	DREW LAND
Shepherd, Wm.Sr.	Wilkinson	Kettles	121/12	Habersham
Sheppard, David	Washington	Wimberlys	304/5	Irwin
Sheppard, John	Twiggs	Ellis	70/15	Irwin
Sheppard, Mary(Wid)	Washington	Wimberlys	379/1	Early
Sheppard, Peter	Elbert	Penns	381/27	Early
Sheppard, Peter	Elbert	Penns	40/11	Early
Sheppard, Thomas	Washington	Burneys	150/16	Irwin
Sheppard, Wiles	Wilkinson	Howards	93/13	Irwin
Sheppard, Wiley	Wilkinson	Howards	107/11	Habersham
Sheppard, Willaim(Orps)	Columbia	Burroughs	439/15	Early
Sheppard, William	Baldwin	Haws	105/5	Gwinnett
Sheppars, Charles(Orp)	Baldwin	Cousins	430/2	Appling
Sherer, Isiah	Washington	Robersons	170/8	Irwin
Sheridan, Dennis	Greene	141st	1/1	Appling
Sheridan, Dennis	Greene	141st	109/27	Early
Sherly, James	Burke	Bells	348/19	Early
Sherod, Joel	Pulaski	Johnstons	160/9	Appling
Sherod, Wright	Twiggs	Hodges	328/8	Early
Sherodin, Abner	Franklin	Turks	275/3	Appling
Sherrer, Gilbert	Richmond	Winters	334/4	Walton
Sherrod, Benjamin	Wilkes	Gordons	91/21	Early
Sherrod, Joel	Pulaski	Johnstons	305/13	Irwin
Sherrod, William	Chatham		51/13	Early
Shi, Samuel	Jasper	Posts	117/6	Early
Shick, George	Chatham		154/2	Habersham
Shields, George	Jackson	Rogers Bt.	382/5	Early
Shields, James	Jackson	Rodgers	65/3	Early
Shields, John	Warren	152nd	351/7	Early
Shields, Margaret(Wid)	Jackson	Rogers Bt.	380/6	Irwin
Shields, William	Lincoln	Millicans	110/4	Irwin
Shilley, Samuel D.	Richmond	Burtons	150/14	Irwin
Ship, Daniel	Lincoln	Walkers	281/5	Gwinnett
Shipley, George	Clarke	Moores	216/2	Irwin
Shipp, Thomas	Lincoln	Jeters	265/14	Early
Shippey, John	Hall	McCutcheons	147/10	Irwin
Shirley, Philips	Morgan	Hackneys	305/4	Walton
Shiver, Abraham	Laurens	Jones	402/6	Appling
Shiver, Abraham	Laurens	Jones	6/11	Early
Shiver, Burrell	Laurens	Jones	203/1	Walton
Shiver, Isaiah	Washington	Robisons	390/3	Appling
Shivers, John M.	Hancock	Champions	189/2	Appling
Shivers, Jonas	Hancock	Champions	247/12	Early
Shivers, Thos.W.	Warren	Hubberts	182/26	Early
Shivers, William	Warren	Hurbert	189/11	Irwin
Shockley, James B.	Greene	142nd	60/2	Irwin
Shockley, Thomas	Greene	142	91/11	Irwin
Shockly, Thomas	Jackson	Whites	57/11	Early
Shoemaker, Adam	Lincoln	Willifords	391/15	Early
Shoemaker, Samuel	Lincoln	Millicans	31/2	Irwin
Shoemaker, Samuel	Lincoln	Millicans	434/5	Irwin
Sholar, David	Jasper	Baileys	168/8	Irwin
Sholar, David	Jasper	Baileys	256/17	Irwin
Shop, Joseph	Chatham		102/2	Walton
Shores, John	Laurens	Harriss	478/11	Irwin
Short, Amelia(Wid)	Columbia	Dodsons	312/6	Irwin
Short, Barbary	Wilkes	Brooks	483/5	Appling
Short, Edward	Columbia	J.Morriss	346/3	Early
Short, Jesse	Wilkes	Brooks	81/10	Irwin
Short, Labon	Oglethorpe	Myricks	261/9	Appling
Short, Peter B.	Columbia	J.Morris	113/16	Irwin
Short, Tapley	Clarke	Starnes	125/1	Early
Short, Thomas	Chatham		37/2	Walton
Short, Young W.	Oglethorpe	Barnetts	448/11	Irwin
Shorter, Eli S.	Putnam	Oslins	61/2	Appling
Shorter, Jacob(Orps)	Wilkes	Runnels	420/1	Early
Shropshear, Naman	Jones	Seals	293/11	Irwin
Shuffield, Bartley	Baldwin	Irwins	365/5	Appling

NAME	COUNTY	MIL.DIST	LOT/SECT	DREW LAND
Shuffield, Bartley	Baldwin	Irwins	60/10	Habersham
Shuffield, Eliz.(Wid)	Pulaski	Lanears	350/20	Early
Shuffield, Isham	Pulaski	Lanears	126/1	Irwin
Shuffield, James	Hancock	Herberts	397/9	Early
Shuffield, John(Orps)	Warren	Parhams	112/2	Walton
Shuffield, John(Orps)	Warren	Parhams	197/5	Gwinnett
Shuffield, William	Pulaski	Lanears	503/9	Irwin
Shuftall, Mordecai Sr.	Chatham		13/11	Early
Shults, Christian	Effingham		215/10	Irwin
Shuman, Martin Jr.	Bryan	19th	286/28	Early
Shuman, Samuel	Bryan	19th	38/23	Early
Shumat, Eliz.(Orps)	Liberty		274/11	Irwin
Shumate, Berrymond	Franklin	Shumates	37/10	Habersham
Shumate, Tarlton	Elbert	R.Christians	59/8	Appling
Shurley, Nathan	Warren	154th	134/10	Early
Shurlock, Daniel	Baldwin	Marshalls	391/4	Early
Shute, Giles	Pulaski	Clements	211/5	Early
Siggars, Abel	Franklin	Vaughns	323/13	Irwin
Sikes, Arthur	Appling	4th	175/9	Irwin
Sikes, Arthur	Burke	Dys	314/5	Gwinnett
Sikes, Edward C.	Bryan	19th	368/15	Early
Sikes, Eliza & Mary(Orps)	Burke	Thomas	271/5	Early
Sikes, Jacob(Orph)	Laurens	Harriss	267/1	Early
Sikes, Jacob	Bryan	19th	240/5	Gwinnett
Sikes, Jacob	Bryan	19th	43/16	Irwin
Sikes, James	Telfair	Willsons	124/12	Habersham
Sikes, John B.	Bryan	19th	204/2	Irwin
Sikes, John Sr.	Burke	Sullivans	284/12	Early
Sikes, John	Hancock	Dannells	16/12	Habersham
Sikes, Matthew	Wilkinson	Kettles	502/8	Irwin
Sikes, Sarah	Burke	Thomas	321/2	Early
Sikes, Thomas	Burke	M.Wards	489/7	Appling
Sikes, Willoughby(Orph)	Wilkinson	Kettles	79/2	Rabun
Sikes, Winifred(Wid)	Wilkinson	Kettles	207/15	Early
Sikes, Winney(Wid)	Laurens	Harriss	36/11	Irwin
Silas, Etheldred	Warren	152nd	196/10	Habersham
Silas, Faithy(Wid)	Warren	153	348/6	Irwin
Silbert, Mary(Wid)	Richmond	122nd	148/1	Walton
Sillavant, Christ.(Wid)	Montgomery	Alstons	362/2	Early
Sillavant, William	Montgomery	Alstons	392/6	Appling
Sillivant, Mitch.(Orps)	Montgomery	Alstons	313/26	Early
Sills, Barbara(Orp)	Burke	Dys	116/10	Hall
Sills, Henry(Orp)	Burke	Dys	116/10	Hall
Sills, Macklin	Columbia	Watsons	182/3	Habersham
Sills, Rebecca(Orp)	Burke	Dys	116/10	Hall
Sills, Sarah(Orp)	Burke	Dys	116/10	Hall
Silman, Benjamin	Emanuel	Dekles	171/12	Habersham
Silver, John A.	Chatham		243/12	Early
Silvey, Stephan	Oglethorpe	Bowls	43/19	Early
Silvey, William	Wilkes	Kilgores	487/9	Irwin
Sim, Warren(Orps)	Wilkes	Brooks	42/3	Early
Simeon, Chestnut	Emanuel	53	250/1	Appling
Simimton, Felix	Greene	144	359/11	Early
Siminton, Ezekiel	Greene	141	68/6	Irwin
Siminton, Felix	Greene	144	458/5	Appling
Siminton, Robert	Greene	141st	488/8	Appling
Simmonds, Allen G.	Jasper	Reeds	53/1	Appling
Simmonds, Allen	Jasper	Reids	118/16	Irwin
Simmonds, George	Jasper	Centells	28/5	Early
Simmonds, Green	Jasper	Reeds	257/3	Appling
Simmonds, Wm.B.	Jasper	Easts	136/1	Walton
Simmons, Abijah	Morgan	Leonards	184/26	Early
Simmons, Benjamin	Hancock	Edwards	366/15	Early
Simmons, Brice(Orps)	Bulloch	Everitts	216/13	Early
Simmons, David Jr.	Oglethorpe	Bridges	339/12	Early
Simmons, Henry F.	Jones	Phillips	322/6	Appling
Simmons, Holmon F.	Franklin	J.Millers	368/17	Early

NAME	COUNTY	MIL.DIST	LOT/SECT	DREW LAND
Simmons, James W.L.	Richmond	120th	249/8	Appling
Simmons, James W.L.	Richmond	120th	364/13	Early
Simmons, John B.	Hancock	Edwards	69/1	Appling
Simmons, John Jr.	Lincoln	Thompsons	334/2	Appling
Simmons, John Jr.	Lincoln	Thompsons	5/4	Irwin
Simmons, John K.	Jasper	Clays	435/7	Appling
Simmons, John Sr.	Lincoln	Stocks	62/1	Early
Simmons, John	Jasper	Barnes	63/16	Early
Simmons, John	Oglethorpe	Rowlands	339/8	Early
Simmons, John	Putnam	Mahons	288/12	Irwin
Simmons, John	Putnam	Mahons	526/7	Irwin
Simmons, Jonathan(Orps)	Jones	Permenters	344/5	Gwinnett
Simmons, Margery(Wid)	Bulloch	Everitts	203/1	Appling
Simmons, Martin	Hancock	Cains	170/11	Irwin
Simmons, Martin	Hancock	Canes	13/13	Irwin
Simmons, Rebeckah(Orpn)	Laurens	Deans	320/4	Walton
Simmons, Saml.S.	Morgan	Talbots	75/4	Rabun
Simmons, Samuel	Scriven		87/7	Irwin
Simmons, Samuel	Wilkes	Mattox	129/7	Irwin
Simmons, Thomas T.	Morgan	Leonards	41/14	Irwin
Simmons, Thomas	Lincoln	Stokes	529/9	Irwin
Simmons, William	Columbia	Ob.Morris	407/11	Irwin
Simmons, William	Morgan	Talbots	141/7	Gwinnett
Simmons, William	Twiggs	Evans	237/8	Appling
Simmons, William	Warren	153rd	259/1	Early
Simms, Andrew G.	Chatham		186/1	Early
Simms, Benjamin	Clarke	Mereweather	148/4	Walton
Simms, Britain	Columbia	Walkers	37/21	Early
Simms, Britton	Columbia	Walkers	181/27	Early
Simms, Christian(Wid)	Columbia	Walkers	130/9	Early
Simms, Edmond G.	Jones	Buckhalters	15/18	Early
Simms, Elisha	Franklin	Akins	75/3	Appling
Simms, Herbert	Greene	142	258/12	Irwin
Simms, Horatio	Columbia	Gartrells	266/6	Appling
Simms, Isham	Lincoln	Orrs	231/11	Irwin
Simms, James	Hancock	Coopers	217/1	Appling
Simms, James	McIntosh	Jinkins	151/26	Early
Simms, John	Oglethorpe	Barnetts	107/6	Early
Simms, John	Oglethorpe	Barnetts	124/11	Habersham
Simms, Lewis	Oglethorpe	Lees	61/1	Irwin
Simms, Mark	Oglethorpe	Bridges	161/19	Early
Simms, Mark	Oglethorpe	Bridges	377/4	Appling
Simms, Martin	Franklin	Akins	133/8	Irwin
Simms, Mary P.(Wid)	Columbia	Walkers	149/27	Early
Simms, Murray	Oglethorpe	Bridges	492/12	Irwin
Simms, Richard	Hancock	Canes	35/12	Early
Simms, Robert(Orps)	Hancock	Coopers	235/3	Irwin
Simms, Robert(RS)	Clarke	Pentecost	105/2	Irwin
Simms, Serepta	Franklin	Akins	271/14	Early
Simonet, Augustus	Richmond	122	365/12	Irwin
Simons, Joseph	McIntosh	Jinkins	180/1	Early
Simonton, Robert	Jasper	Reeds	257/14	Early
Simpkins, William M.	Morgan	Knights	108/8	Early
Simpkins, Wm.H.	Morgan	Knights	142/8	Hall
Simpler, William	Warren	153rd	39/7	Gwinnett
Simpson, Alexander	Pulaski	Maddox	144/8	Appling
Simpson, David	Pulaski	Rees	376/10	Early
Simpson, Eliz.(Wid)	Pulaski	Johnstons	12/7	Early
Simpson, Enoch(Orps)	Washington	Peabodys	378/6	Appling
Simpson, Ezekiel	Washington	Peabodys	106/26	Early
Simpson, Ezekiel	Washington	Peabodys	77/11	Irwin
Simpson, Jacob(RS)	Twiggs	Smiths	129/10	Hall
Simpson, James	Hancock	Lucas	396/9	Irwin
Simpson, Jeptha	Washington	Peabodys	127/19	Early
Simpson, John Sr.(RS)	Twiggs	Smiths	194/16	Early
Simpson, Joseph S.	Baldwin	Laceys	74/15	Early
Simpson, Lucy(Wid)	Wilkes	Kilgores	164/4	Walton

NAME	COUNTY	MIL.DIST	LOT/SECT	DREW LAN
Simpson, Mary(Orp)	Camden	Clarkes	11/21	Early
Simpson, Mary(Wid)	Twiggs	Smiths	86/27	Early
Simpson, Solomon	Twiggs	Smiths	337/8	Appling
Simpson, Thomas	Pulaski	Davis	190/7	Early
Simpson, Wm.& Children	Camden	Longs	274/1	Appling
Sims, Benjamin	Jackson	Rogers Bt.	13/6	Habersha
Sims, Benjamin	Jackson	Rogers Bt.	250/9	Early
Sims, Britain	Hancock	Coopers	259/27	Early
Sims, Edmund G.	Jones	Buckhalters	84/22	Early
Sims, Edmund	Wilkinson	Smiths	276/2	Appling
Sims, Edward	Elbert	G.Higginbothams	137/2	Walton
Sims, Elizabeth(Wid)	Clarke	Sims	257/4	Early
Sims, Frederick	Jones	Phillips	181/17	Early
Sims, Hardy	Franklin	Keltons	229/6	Early
Sims, Henry L.	Richmond	120	183/8	Appling
Sims, Horatio	Columbia	Gartrells	303/1	Appling
Sims, Hull	Franklin	Turks	79/6	Gwinnet
Sims, Jacob	Liberty		81/3	Irwin
Sims, James(Orps)	Wilkinson	Brooks	203/5	Gwinnet
Sims, John	Jones	Jeffersons	69/10	Habersha
Sims, John	Twiggs	Ellis	241/2	Early
Sims, John	Warren	151st	131/6	Irwin
Sims, Jonathan F.	Jefferson	Waldens	50/19	Early
Sims, Joseph(Orp)	Baldwin	Marshalls	385/4	Early
Sims, Lemuel	Putnam	Berrys	194/26	Early
Sims, Lucy	Oglethorpe	Rowlands	147/6	Irwin
Sims, Mark Jr.	Oglethorpe	Bridgess	36/1	Early
Sims, Nathan A.	Morgan	Dennis	122/3	Habersha
Sims, Ninam	Columbia	Walkers	155/10	Hall
Sims, Phillip I	Hancock	Danells	462/10	Irwin
Sims, Sarah(Orps)	Burke	Torrance	126/5	Gwinnet
Sims, Sterling	Putnam	Stampers	364/9	Early
Sims, William	Columbia	Walker	295/10	Irwin
Sims, William	Jones	Hansfords	360/8	Appling
Sims, Zachariah	Clarke	Applings	227/5	Irwin
Simson, David	Pulaski	Rees	381/1	Early
Simson, Thomas	Pulaski	Davis	165/6	Irwin
Sinclair, Jesse	Twiggs	Browns	27/6	Habersha
Sinclair, William	Burke	Spiveys	509/5	Appling
Sinclair, Wm.	Burke	Spiveys	187/1	Irwin
Singletary, John	Wilkinson	Smiths	171/6	Irwin
Singletary, Thomas	Telfair	Williams	87/5	Rabun
Singleton, Abner H.	Jones	Griffiths	97/2	Habersha
Singleton, Beggers	Pulaski	Johnstons	74/5	Irwin
Singleton, Lucretia(Wid)	Jones	Griffiths	111/9	Appling
Singleton, William K.	Jones	Griffiths	180/16	Early
Sinkfield, Asa	Jefferson	Fleming	8/12	Irwin
Sinquefield, William	Washington	Brooks	98/12	Habersha
Sisemore, Nazarith	Hancock	Millers	95/1	Appling
Sisk, Elizabeth	Greene	Ragins	496/8	Irwin
Sission, Charles	Franklin	John Millers	524/6	Appling
Sisson, John	Jackson	Dicksons Bt.	14/6	Early
Sisson, John	Jackson	Dicksons Bt.	84/3	Early
Sisson, Noah B.	Chatham		234/20	Early
Sisson, Noah B.	Chatham		259/11	Early
Sistrunk, Jacob	Lincoln	Parks	340/28	Early
Sistrunk, John	Lincoln	Parks	375/19	Early
Sistrunk, Richard	Lincoln	Parks	104/26	Early
Sivear, John	Scriven	Lovetts	235/23	Early
Skaggs, Henry M.	Putnam	Berrys	302/15	Early
Skaggs, John R.	Putnam	Coopers	218/5	Gwinnet
Skaggs, William(Orps)	Putnam	Berrys	398/28	Early
Skelton, Abel	Morgan	Hubbards	283/10	Early
Skelton, Elijah	Elbert	Dooleys	331/7	Appling
Skelton, Hiram R.	Franklin	Holcombs	62/1	Walton
Skelton, John	Elbert	Dooleys	31/6	Gwinnet
Skelton, Robert	Laurens	Griffins	400/6	Appling

300

NAME	COUNTY	MIL.DIST	LOT/SECT	DREW LAND
Skelton, Robt.(RS)	Franklin	Halcombs	191/6	Gwinnett
Skidmore, Samuel	Morgan	Campbells	69/2	Early
Skinner, Ephraim	Putnam	Berrys	67/6	Irwin
Skinner, John	Columbia	Burroughs	110/1	Appling
Skinner, John	Hancock	Lucas	406/12	Irwin
Skinner, John	Hancock	Lucas	92/8	Early
Skinner, John	Putnam	Berrys	194/4	Walton
Skinner, Jonas	Burke	71st	204/8	Early
Skinner, Levingston	Richmond	Burtons	168/26	Early
Skinner, Mary(Wid)	Hancock	Dannells	124/3	Irwin
Skinner, Ollever(Orps)	Hancock	Dannells	230/10	Early
Skinner, Richard	Columbia	Burroughs	175/12	Habersham
Skinner, Robert	Jasper	Bartlets	54/6	Habersham
Skinner, Robert	Jasper	Bartletts	78/2	Habersham
Skinner, Seth	Hancock	Dannells	289/21	Early
Skinner, Thomas	Richmond	Burtons	166/3	Irwin
Skinner, William J.	Richmond	Burtons	76/8	Irwin
Skinner, Wm.Sr.	Richmond	Burtons	168/5	Early
Skipper, Daniel	Wilkinson	Lees	162/5	Appling
Slack, Benjamin	Wilkes	Burks	134/1	Walton
Slack, Benjamin	Wilkes	Burks	184/2	Early
Slack, Jacob	Wilkes	Russels	125/7	Early
Slack, Jesse	Wilkes	McLendons	56/20	Early
Slack, Joseph	Wilkes	Burks	154/11	Hall
Slade, Frederick	Camden	Tillis	142/5	Irwin
Slade, Frederick	Camden	Tillis	300/3	Appling
Slade, Jethro(Orps)	Wilkinson	Howards	288/5	Early
Slade, Joseph P.(Orps)	Baldwin	Taliaferro	333/17	Early
Slappy, Ann(Wid)	Jasper	Clays	76/7	Appling
Slappy, Henry(Orps)	Jasper	Clays	255/2	Appling
Slappy, John G.(Dr)	Twiggs	Johnstons	237/23	Early
Slater, Jesse	Scriven		299/4	Early
Slater, Samuel	Jefferson	Bothwells	70/8	Irwin
Slater, Samuel	Jefferson	Bothwells	99/9	Irwin
Slater, Wm.J.(Orps)	Scriven	36th	141/5	Irwin
Slaton, Barzillai	Tattnall	Johnsons	427/10	Irwin
Slaton, John	Wilkes	Smiths	333/10	Early
Slaton, Thompson N.	Telfair	Williams	42/4	Rabun
Slatorn, Nathaniel	Telfair	Williams	322/19	Early
Slatter, Burwell	Bulloch	Knights	45/13	Irwin
Slatter, James E.	Hancock	Justices	45/15	Irwin
Slatter, Shadrach	Jones	Samuels	225/9	Irwin
Slattings, Malekiah(Orps)	Putnam	Evans	222/4	Irwin
Slaugher, Butler	Jones	Griffiths	342/18	Early
Slaughter, Henry G.	Greene	Wheelis	269/26	Early
Slaughter, Henry	Columbia	Burroughs	262/11	Early
Slaughter, John	Greene	Wheelis	227/16	Early
Slaughter, Martin(Orps)	Putnam	Slaughters	93/1	Walton
Slaughter, Nathl.G.	Putnam	Slaughters	490/2	Appling
Slaughter, Rebecca	Putnam	Slaughters	294/9	Appling
Slaughter, Thos.W.	Greene	142nd	183/3	Walton
Slaughter, William	Putnam	Slaughters	346/2	Early
Slayd, Harriss	Jones	Buckhalters	176/9	Appling
Sledge, Chappell	Hancock	Danells	298/13	Irwin
Sledge, Minsey	Hancock	Thomas	54/4	Rabun
Sledge, Paton(Orps)	Jones	Phillips	394/6	Appling
Sloan, Adam	Elbert	R.Christians	415/12	Irwin
Smalley, James	Columbia	Gartrells	119/3	Appling
Smalley, James	Columbia	Gartrells	143/10	Habersham
Smalley, Levi	Columbia	Gartrells	166/9	Irwin
Smallpeace, Ann	Baldwin	Doziers	394/13	Early
Smallwood, Francis Sr.	Twiggs	R.Belchers	199/14	Early
Smallwood, Mark	Elbert	Webbs	178/11	Irwin
Smallwood, Mark	Elbert	Webbs	35/13	Habersham
Smart, Loanzo(Wid)	Liberty		244/27	Early
Smarts, Alsey(Orps)	Twiggs	Evans	314/3	Appling
Smarts, Francis B.	Jasper	Reeds	219/3	Irwin

NAME	COUNTY	MIL.DIST	LOT/SECT	DREW LAND
Smarts, Littleberry	Jasper	Kenedys	323/6	Appling
Smedley, Thomas M.	Putnam	Berrys	249/1	Appling
Smelt, Mary(Wid)	Richmond	398	169/8	Appling
Smiley, Robert B.	Wilkes	171	69/18	Early
Smiley, Robert B.	Wilkes	171st	176/4	Early
Smith, Aaron	Jackson	Dicksons Bt.	98/9	Early
Smith, Abington F.	Hancock	Mims	510/12	Irwin
Smith, Abram	Warren	Griers	198/4	Appling
Smith, Adam	Franklin	Haynes	354/10	Early
Smith, Alexander	Lincoln	Jeters	45/4	Early
Smith, Alexander	Warren	153rd	342/1	Appling
Smith, Alexnader	Warren	153	384/7	Irwin
Smith, Allen	Washington	Burneys	385/10	Irwin
Smith, Allen	Wilkinson	Childs	46/12	Hall
Smith, Ambrose	Emanuel	53rd	20/11	Habersham
Smith, Ambrose	Telfair	Tallis	126/6	Appling
Smith, Amy & Henry(Orps)	Burke	Royals	8/16	Irwin
Smith, Anderson	Jones	Kings	136/8	Appling
Smith, Ann(Wid)	Jackson	Winters Bt.	123/5	Appling
Smith, Archibald(Orps)	Scriven		98/9	Irwin
Smith, Archibald	Greene	Nelms	254/3	Irwin
Smith, Archibald	Morgan	Loyds	198/4	Irwin
Smith, Archibald	Telfair	Loves	261/7	Early
Smith, Arthur Sr.	Jasper	Smiths	103/8	Hall
Smith, Arthur Sr.	Jasper	Smiths	4/6	Habersham
Smith, Arthur(Orps)	Washington	Renfros	272/15	Early
Smith, Arthur	Walton	Wagnons	7/4	Early
Smith, Asa	Twiggs	Jefferson	51/7	Gwinnett
Smith, Austin	Lincoln	Tatoms	47/9	Early
Smith, Banister	Putnam	Ectors	25/1	Appling
Smith, Benajer	Morgan	Wrights	218/9	Appling
Smith, Benjamin B.	Twiggs	Evans	127/6	Gwinnett
Smith, Benjamin B.	Twiggs	Evans	248/12	Irwin
Smith, Benjamin	Burke	69th	14/16	Irwin
Smith, Benjamin	Elbert	Smiths	144/11	Habersham
Smith, Benjamin	Jackson	Rogers Bt.	22/22	Early
Smith, Benjamin	Jackson	Rogers Bt.	233/9	Appling
Smith, Benjamin	Lincoln	Orrs	367/11	Irwin
Smith, Benjamin	Morgan	Hubbards	265/3	Early
Smith, Benjamin	Oglethorpe	Dunns	103/10	Irwin
Smith, Benjamin	Wilkes	Burks	210/3	Irwin
Smith, Brittain	Franklin	Haynes	155/3	Appling
Smith, Burrell	Lincoln	Parks	452/10	Irwin
Smith, Burton(Orps)	Putnam	Littles	158/6	Appling
Smith, Charles H.	Washington	Barges	221/3	Walton
Smith, Charles H.	Washington	Barges	96/2	Rabun
Smith, Charles Jr.	Oglethorpe	Brittons	477/8	Irwin
Smith, Charles	Appling	5th	262/13	Irwin
Smith, Charles	Baldwin	Stephen	362/5	Early
Smith, Charles	Clarke	Deans	67/9	Irwin
Smith, Charles	Wilkes	Gordons	94/13	Irwin
Smith, Charlton	Putnam	Morelands	446/6	Irwin
Smith, Christiana	Chatham		137/16	Early
Smith, Daniel	Columbia	Ob.Morriss	27/28	Early
Smith, Daniel	Scriven	Lovetts	148/17	Early
Smith, David J.	Montgomery	McElvins	325/10	Irwin
Smith, David Sr.(RS)	Jackson	Rogers Bt.	139/21	Early
Smith, David Sr.(RS)	Jackson	Rogers Bt.	14/3	Rabun
Smith, David Sr.(RS)	Jackson	Rogers Bt.	171/2	Appling
Smith, David Sr.	Jackson	Rogers Bt.	23/22	Early
Smith, David T.	Jefferson	Bothwells	115/27	Early
Smith, David	Burke	Thomas	206/17	Early
Smith, David	Elbert	Olivers	6/1	Appling
Smith, David	Elbert	Smiths	408/11	Early
Smith, David	Greene	Wheelis	427/28	Early
Smith, David	Jasper	Evans	509/12	Irwin
Smith, David	Laurens	D.Smith	172/21	Early

NAME	COUNTY	MIL.DIST	LOT/SECT	DREW LAND
Smith, David	Laurens	D.Smiths	130/5	Gwinnett
Smith, David	Lincoln	Bones	270/1	Walton
Smith, David	Oglethorpe	Lees	16/18	Early
Smith, David	Pulaski	Rees	384/7	Appling
Smith, David	Putnam	Coopers	152/13	Habersham
Smith, David	Putnam	Coopers	314/6	Appling
Smith, David	Richmond	Laceys	41/10	Early
Smith, Delila	Burke	Lewis	221/1	Early
Smith, Ebenezer	Greene	142	166/4	Appling
Smith, Ebenezer	Greene	142	509/11	Irwin
Smith, Edmund	Jackson	Dicksons Bt.	119/6	Appling
Smith, Edmund	Jackson	Dicksons	308/12	Irwin
Smith, Edward	Oglethorpe	Dunns	5/4	Appling
Smith, Elbert	Wilkes	Ogletrees	125/3	Habersham
Smith, Elezander	Lincoln	Jeters	1/12	Early
Smith, Eli	Greene	143rd	219/10	Early
Smith, Elijah	Jackson	Hamiltons Bt.	261/1	Walton
Smith, Elisha	Jefferson	Bothwells	151/1	Early
Smith, Elisha	Wilkinson	Lees	398/6	Appling
Smith, Eliz.(Minor)	Oglethorpe	Myricks	126/12	Early
Smith, Eliz.(Wid)	Greene	Wheelis	9/12	Habersham
Smith, Elizabeth(Wid)	Jones	Jeffersons	321/1	Early
Smith, Ezekial	Emanuel	56	290/19	Early
Smith, Feriby(Wid)	Jones	Kings	118/3	Appling
Smith, France	Lincoln	Tatoms	204/6	Gwinnett
Smith, Frederick	Oglethorpe	Bowls	336/8	Appling
Smith, Gabriel	Franklin	Powells	512/5	Irwin
Smith, George L.	Clarke	Mereweather	24/10	Hall
Smith, George W.	Hancock	Edwards	428/12	Irwin
Smith, George	Bulloch	Knights	298/9	Irwin
Smith, Gideon W.	Morgan	Farrars	267/27	Early
Smith, Gideon	Hancock	Smiths	129/26	Early
Smith, Godhelf	Bryan	19th	18/4	Walton
Smith, Green W.	Franklin	Hammonds	466/8	Appling
Smith, Hampton S.	Putnam	Bledsoes	320/21	Early
Smith, Hardy	Laurens	Kinchens	126/27	Early
Smith, Hardy	Laurens	Kinchens	27/12	Habersham
Smith, Harrison	Jackson	Winters Bt.	24/1	Habersham
Smith, Harrison	Jones	Samuels	117/12	Irwin
Smith, Henderson	Oglethorpe	Hoffs	372/11	Early
Smith, Henry Sr.	Franklin	Powels	125/21	Early
Smith, Henry Sr.	Franklin	Powels	495/8	Appling
Smith, Henry(Orps)	Jasper	Clays	71/10	Hall
Smith, Henry(Orps)	Jasper	Kennedys	166/8	Irwin
Smith, Henry	Burke	Thomas	449/8	Appling
Smith, Henry	Elbert	P.Christians	276/18	Early
Smith, Henry	Franklin	Davis	343/27	Early
Smith, Henry	Franklin	Davis	37/23	Early
Smith, Henry	Jones	Rossers	357/8	Early
Smith, Henry	Lincoln	Bones	248/2	Early
Smith, Henry	Lincoln	Bones	37/12	Irwin
Smith, Henry	Pulaski	Senterfeits	142/2	Appling
Smith, Herbert	Jefferson	Cowarts	189/5	Appling
Smith, Hezekiah	Franklin	Davis	199/11	Irwin
Smith, Hugh	Liberty		189/8	Irwin
Smith, Isaac	Franklin	Vaughns	150/6	Early
Smith, Isaac	Laurens	Ross	142/12	Early
Smith, Isaac	Morgan	McClendons	14/2	Early
Smith, Isaac	Washington	Jenkinsons	49/21	Early
Smith, Isaac	Washington	Jinkinsons	309/14	Early
Smith, Isham	Laurens	Jones	213/10	Irwin
Smith, Isham	Putnam	Morelands	103/8	Appling
Smith, Isham	Putnam	Morlands	141/14	Early
Smith, J.M.(Wid)	Chatham		482/10	Irwin
Smith, Jackson	Clarke	Deans	222/3	Irwin
Smith, Jacob(Orps)	Burke	J.Wards	113/13	Early
Smith, Jacob	Jasper	Bentleys	45/5	Habersham

NAME	COUNTY	MIL.DIST	LOT/SECT	DREW LAN
Smith, Jacob	Laurens	D.Smiths	18/10	Irwin
Smith, James	Wilkes	Bryants	92/7	Appling
Smith, James B.	Jones	Seals	151/4	Early
Smith, James B.	Scriven	180th	362/1	Early
Smith, James D.	Clarke	Moores	80/6	Irwin
Smith, James H.	Oglethorpe	Brittons	281/11	Irwin
Smith, James J.	Burke	69	332/5	Early
Smith, James Jr.	Twiggs	Bozemans	518/7	Irwin
Smith, James L.	Clarke	Mitchells	106/12	Early
Smith, James L.	Clarke	Mitchells	216/1	Appling
Smith, James S.	Jones	Seals	397/17	Early
Smith, James(Orps)	Baldwin	Cousins	161/11	Habersha
Smith, James(Orps)	Burke	Lewis	43/4	Early
Smith, James	Appling	4th	361/13	Early
Smith, James	Baldwin	Taliaferro	23/7	Irwin
Smith, James	Burke	Lewis	223/5	Early
Smith, James	Franklin	Dobsons	165/16	Irwin
Smith, James	Franklin	Powells	9/5	Rabun
Smith, James	Franklin	Vaughns	119/2	Early
Smith, James	Franklin	Vaughns	421/7	Irwin
Smith, James	Jackson	Winters Bt.	201/10	Early
Smith, James	Jackson	Winters Bt.	206/21	Early
Smith, James	Jasper	Bartletts	340/18	Early
Smith, James	Jefferson	Cowarts	136/12	Irwin
Smith, James	Jefferson	Cowarts	265/21	Early
Smith, James	Jones	Jeffersons	177/13	Habersha
Smith, James	Jones	Mullins	422/6	Appling
Smith, James	Jones	Samuels	442/12	Irwin
Smith, James	Richmond	Burtons	287/3	Early
Smith, Jediah	Greene	Wheelis	204/26	Early
Smith, Jeremiah(Orps)	Jasper	Bentleys	573/2	Appling
Smith, Jeremiah	Greene	Harvills	304/6	Early
Smith, Jeremiah	Jones	Griffiths	145/7	Appling
Smith, Jeremiah	Laurens	D.Smiths	186/6	Gwinnett
Smith, Jesse	Franklin	Powels	202/3	Appling
Smith, Jesse	Franklin	Vaughns	102/15	Early
Smith, Jesse	Jackson	Winters Bt.	171/2	Early
Smith, Jessee	Franklin	Vaughns	192/1	Early
Smith, Jewell	Jones	Permenters	479/6	Appling
Smith, Job	Hancock	Scotts	502/2	Appling
Smith, John (Cooper)	Washington	Jenkinsons	39/5	Habersha
Smith, John C.	Jackson	Rogers Bt.	103/2	Appling
Smith, John C.	Jasper	Smiths	101/13	Habersha
Smith, John C.	Jones	Jeffersons	213/1	Walton
Smith, John C.	Jones	Jeffersons	377/20	Early
Smith, John C.	Oglethorpe	Davenports	35/3	Early
Smith, John C.	Warren	Hubberts	158/3	Habersha
Smith, John G.Jr.	Appling	4th	12/18	Early
Smith, John H.	Scriven	Lovetts	381/7	Early
Smith, John H.	Tattnall	J.Durrences	397/16	Early
Smith, John J.	Putnam	Oslins	374/7	Appling
Smith, John Jr.	Jackson	Winters Bt.	108/2	Appling
Smith, John Jr.	Twiggs	Ellis	402/8	Early
Smith, John Jr.	Twiggs	R.Belchers	403/2	Appling
Smith, John M.	Twiggs	Smiths	4/6	Gwinnett
Smith, John N.	Morgan	Selmans	412/25	Early
Smith, John N.	Morgan	Selmons	26/19	Early
Smith, John Sr.(RS)	Morgan	Wrights	218/3	Irwin
Smith, John Sr.(RS)	Morgan	Wrights	366/12	Early
Smith, John Sr.	Chatham		198/5	Appling
Smith, John Sr.	Telfair	Edwards	14/23	Early
Smith, John Sr.	Telfair	Edwards	76/11	Irwin
Smith, John Sr.	Wilkinson	Wiggins	104/5	Irwin
Smith, John(Black)	Twiggs	Bozemans	235/6	Appling
Smith, John(Black)	Twiggs	Bozemans	33/2	Early
Smith, John(Long)	Clarke	Deans	307/20	Early
Smith, John(Orps)	Morgan	McClendons	92/8	Appling

NAME	COUNTY	MIL.DIST	LOT/SECT	DREW LAND
Smith, John(Sandy)	Wilkinson	Lees	139/9	Irwin
Smith, John(Whiskey)	Twiggs	Ellis	326/10	Early
Smith, John	Baldwin	Haws	9/2	Walton
Smith, John	Burke	J.Wards	43/6	Irwin
Smith, John	Burke	Torrence	206/3	Early
Smith, John	Chatham		97/4	Appling
Smith, John	Clarke	Deans	433/8	Appling
Smith, John	Columbia	Ob.Morriss	381/20	Early
Smith, John	Columbia	Olives	19/7	Early
Smith, John	Elbert	Whites	524/8	Appling
Smith, John	Greene	Wheelis	245/5	Gwinnett
Smith, John	Hall		38/18	Early
Smith, John	Laurens	D.Smiths	262/3	Appling
Smith, John	Lincoln	Parks	126/17	Early
Smith, John	Lincoln	Parks	26/12	Hall
Smith, John	Morgan	Loyd	374/11	Early
Smith, John	Oglethorpe	Brittons	29/21	Early
Smith, John	Putnam	Coopers	187/13	Irwin
Smith, John	Putnam	Oslins	29/5	Gwinnett
Smith, John	Warren	152nd	13/16	Irwin
Smith, Jordan Jr.	Jefferson	Langstons	69/2	Walton
Smith, Joseph	Clarke	Simms	382/3	Early
Smith, Joseph	Clarke	Smiths	40/13	Habersham
Smith, Joseph	Elbert	Smiths	134/6	Gwinnett
Smith, Joseph	Elbert	Smiths	19/2	Habersham
Smith, Joseph	Jasper	Evans	267/5	Irwin
Smith, Joseph	Putnam	Robertsons	630/2	Appling
Smith, Joseph	Richmond	Palmers	268/2	Appling
Smith, Joseph	Wilkes	Burks	83/1	Rabun
Smith, Joshua	Bryan	19th	16/9	Irwin
Smith, Josiah	Laurens	Deans	257/9	Irwin
Smith, Josiah	Laurens	Deans	43/6	Appling
Smith, Laddon	Washington	Robinsons	394/28	Early
Smith, Laurence	Morgan	Farrars	134/8	Irwin
Smith, Lemuel	Hancock	Smiths	172/8	Appling
Smith, Lenair E.	Laurens	D.Smiths	8/22	Early
Smith, Leonard B.	Columbia	Shaws	232/19	Early
Smith, Leonard	Elbert	G.Higginbotham	27/6	Irwin
Smith, Levi	Early		313/10	Early
Smith, Levi	Liberty		210/2	Early
Smith, Littleton	Tattnall	J.Durrence	43/2	Rabun
Smith, Lot	Pulaski	J.Kendrick	179/12	Early
Smith, Lott	Putnam	J.Kindricks	179/12	Early
Smith, Luke H.	Scriven	36th	161/13	Irwin
Smith, Luraney	Hancock	Smiths	506/11	Irwin
Smith, Madock	Wilkes	Smiths	470/5	Appling
Smith, Malcomb	Telfair	Edwards	164/16	Early
Smith, Mark	Franklin	Powels	356/19	Early
Smith, Mary(Wid)	Warren	Parhams	152/5	Early
Smith, Mary(Wid)	Washington	Burneys	111/10	Hall
Smith, Mary	Chatham		168/18	Early
Smith, Micajah	Washington	Jenkinson	72/1	Rabun
Smith, Miles	Jackson	Rogers Bt.	62/5	Irwin
Smith, Mittition	Bulloch	Knights	395/9	Irwin
Smith, Morriss	Scriven	Smiths	41/2	Irwin
Smith, Moses	Franklin	Akins	174/16	Early
Smith, Nathan F.	Wilkes	Ogletrees	306/28	Early
Smith, Nathan H.	Oglethorpe	Dunns	245/9	Appling
Smith, Nathan(Orps)	Wilkes	Ogletrees	112/9	Irwin
Smith, Nathan	Camden	Tillis	227/9	Appling
Smith, Nathan	Greene	Macons	279/13	Early
Smith, Nathan	Greene	Macons	316/7	Irwin
Smith, Nathaniel H.	Oglethorpe	Dunns	35/16	Early
Smith, Nathanl.	Richmond		123/10	Early
Smith, Neeham	Washington	Jenkinsons	77/8	Hall
Smith, Paschal	Oglethorpe	Dunns	444/13	Irwin
Smith, Penny(Wid)	Twiggs	Browns	43/5	Gwinnett

NAME	COUNTY	MIL.DIST	LOT/SECT	DREW LAN
Smith, Peter(Orps)	Oglethorpe	Barnetts	50/16	Irwin
Smith, Peter	Morgan	Loyds	298/18	Early
Smith, Peter	Morgan	Loyds	52/10	Habersha
Smith, Peterson	Oglethorpe	Dunns	296/13	Early
Smith, Phillip(Orps)	Telfair	Edwards	136/1	Appling
Smith, Polley(Wid)	Jones	Kings	372/11	Irwin
Smith, Redick	Greene	Kimbroughs	55/3	Early
Smith, Reubin	Greene	Kimbroughs	16/11	Habersha
Smith, Richard	Franklin	Powells	66/5	Irwin
Smith, Richard	Franklin	R.Browns	307/28	Early
Smith, Richard	Hancock	Justices	41/15	Early
Smith, Richard	Morgan	McClendons	125/13	Habersha
Smith, Richard	Morgan	McClendons	306/12	Early
Smith, Richard	Richmond	122nd	417/6	Appling
Smith, Richard	Twiggs	Smiths	50/4	Appling
Smith, Richard	Warren	Blounts	37/5	Irwin
Smith, Richard	Warren	Blounts	90/8	Irwin
Smith, Robens	Morgan	Leonards	186/7	Early
Smith, Robert F.	Clarke	Sims	86/3	Habersha
Smith, Robert R.	Oglethorpe	Davenports	374/3	Appling
Smith, Robert	Washington	Pools	313/17	Early
Smith, Robert	Wayne	Johnsons	102/15	Irwin
Smith, Sally(Wid)	Putnam	Littles	365/8	Appling
Smith, Saml.Jr.(Orps)	Jones	Jeffersons	16/4	Appling
Smith, Samuel R.	Washington	Daniels	527/6	Appling
Smith, Samuel T.	Washington	Daniells	147/8	Irwin
Smith, Samuel(Orps)	Jones	Kings	51/16	Early
Smith, Samuel	Chatham		246/8	Early
Smith, Samuel	Jackson	Winters Bt.	346/20	Early
Smith, Samuel	Lincoln	Bones	344/15	Early
Smith, Samuel	Tattnall	Sunyers	38/5	Rabun
Smith, Samuel	Washington	Barneys	388/7	Appling
Smith, Samuel	Wilkinson	Kettles	343/10	Irwin
Smith, Sarah(Wid)	Tattnall	Overstreet	380/3	Appling
Smith, Sarah	Baldwin	Taleaferro	323/26	Early
Smith, Sarah	Jasper	Evans	360/12	Early
Smith, Silas	Jackson	Winters Bt.	120/18	Early
Smith, Silas	Jackson	Winters Bt.	125/28	Early
Smith, Silas	Twiggs	W.Belchers	109/14	Early
Smith, Silas	Twiggs	W.Belchers	458/4	Appling
Smith, Simeon	Greene	144th	9/7	Irwin
Smith, Simon D.	Jackson	Mays	13/26	Early
Smith, Simon	Laurens	S.Smiths	280/3	Appling
Smith, Solomon	Bryan	19th	172/12	Irwin
Smith, Solomon	Bryan	19th	318/28	Early
Smith, Solomon	Montgomery	McMillans	137/18	Early
Smith, Stephen	Tattnall	J.Durrence	211/3	Appling
Smith, Stephen	Twiggs	Bozemans	195/2	Rabun
Smith, Stephen	Warren	Griers	2/12	Habersha
Smith, Susannah(Wid)	Richmond	Laceys	126/12	Habersha
Smith, Thomas H.	Jasper	Posts	129/11	Irwin
Smith, Thomas K.Jr.	Putnam	Stampers	239/8	Irwin
Smith, Thomas M.	Jasper	Phillips	53/2	Appling
Smith, Thomas Sr.	Jackson	Hamiltons Bt.	68/2	Irwin
Smith, Thomas Sr.	Pulaski	Maddox	162/12	Early
Smith, Thomas	Burke	M.Wards	341/4	Appling
Smith, Thomas	Clarke	Stuarts	217/5	Gwinnett
Smith, Thomas	Franklin	Harriss	64/2	Early
Smith, Thomas	Twiggs	Evans	136/6	Early
Smith, Thomas	Twiggs	Smiths	271/12	Irwin
Smith, Thomas	Twiggs	Smiths	306/9	Irwin
Smith, Thomas	Twiggs	W.Belcher	394/21	Early
Smith, Thomas	Wilkinson	Wiggins	138/4	Irwin
Smith, Thompson	Laurens	Kinchens	487/7	Appling
Smith, Timothy T.	Lincoln	Stokes	346/9	Irwin
Smith, Timothy	Jasper	Dosters	214/2	Early
Smith, Turner	Twiggs	W.Belchers	459/13	Irwin

NAME	COUNTY	MIL.DIST	LOT/SECT	DREW LAND
Smith, Valentine	Elbert	G.Higginbotham	274/12	Early
Smith, Valentine	Elbert	G.Higginbotham	175/15	Early
Smith, Victor	Franklin	Akins	161/4	Walton
Smith, Victor	Franklin	Akins	66/13	Habersham
Smith, Vines	Oglethorpe	Waters	357/4	Early
Smith, Washington	Liberty		286/5	Early
Smith, William C.	Hancock	Mimms	102/10	Hall
Smith, William C.	Jasper	Philips	234/7	Gwinnett
Smith, William E.	Franklin	Powells	109/2	Walton
Smith, William G.	Jasper	Phillips	226/5	Early
Smith, William H.	Wilkinson	Smiths	190/2	Irwin
Smith, William Jr.	Franklin	Vaughns	184/2	Habersham
Smith, William Jr.	Liberty		122/8	Hall
Smith, William(RS)	Jackson	Hamiltons Bt.	227/13	Early
Smith, William(RS)	Morgan	Farrars	62/13	Habersham
Smith, William(RS)	Walton	Wests	361/13	Irwin
Smith, William	Clarke	Pentecosts	2/7	Early
Smith, William	Elbert	P.Christians	121/14	Irwin
Smith, William	Franklin	Harris	206/11	Irwin
Smith, William	Greene	Kimbrows	435/4	Appling
Smith, William	Jackson	Rogers Bt.	98/20	Early
Smith, William	Laurens	D.Smiths	287/11	Early
Smith, William	Laurens	Jones	116/21	Early
Smith, William	Laurens	Jones	73/4	Early
Smith, William	Laurens	Kinchens	41/2	Early
Smith, William	Laurens	Kinchens	69/11	Early
Smith, William	Lincoln	Bones	27/16	Early
Smith, William	Pulaski	Rees	64//3	Early
Smith, William	Putnam	Buckners	7/4	Habersham
Smith, William	Putnam	Ectors	165/10	Hall
Smith, William	Richmond	120th	130/11	Early
Smith, William	Scriven	Lovetts	14/16	Early
Smith, William	Scriven	Lovetts	62/21	Early
Smith, William	Tattnall	Cunyers	244/13	Early
Smith, William	Walton	Wests	430/13	Irwin
Smith, William	Walton	Worthams	276/17	Early
Smith, William	Washington	Avents	867/5	Appling
Smith, Williamson	Telfair	Wilsons	218/10	Habersham
Smith, Willis	Franklin	Jos.Millers	205/12	Early
Smith, Willis	Scriven		3/9	Early
Smith, Wm.(Orps)	Putnam	Berrys	130/6	Irwin
Smith, Wm.(Orps)	Washington	Cummins	28/14	Irwin
Smith, Wm.(RS)	Morgan	Farrars	78/27	Early
Smith, Wm.	Elbert	Ruckers	318/3	Appling
Smith, Wm.	Greene	Kimbroughs	495/6	Appling
Smith, Wm.	Wilkinson	Lees	64/1	Habersham
Smith, Wm.B.	Franklin	Powells	108/4	Walton
Smith, Wm.D.	Jackson	Winters Bt.	101/7	Appling
Smith, Wm.F.	Jefferson	Cowarts	167/3	Habersham
Smith, Wm.R.	Laurens	Griffins	244/11	Irwin
Smith, Wm.W.	Wilkes	Smiths	457/11	Irwin
Smith, Zachariah	Elbert	Ruckers	239/1	Appling
Smiths, Fleming(Orps)	Franklin	Ashs	406/13	Irwin
Smiths, Richard	Washington	Robinsons	179/1	Early
Smiths, Robt.(Orps)	Jackson	Dicksons Bt.	397/6	Early
Smithson, Henry G.	Richmond	Laceys	103/2	Walton
Smithwick, Edmond	Elbert	Webbs	416/10	Irwin
Smithwick, Edmund	Elbert	Webbs	225/12	Irwin
Smuncey, William	Liberty		252/26	Early
Snall, John	Morgan	Walkers	169/3	Irwin
Snall, Saml.	Morgan	Walkers	180/6	Early
Snead, Caroline(Orph)	Richmond		263/11	Early
Sneed, Elijah	Elbert	Smiths	282/16	Early
Sneed, Abijah	Greene	141st	233/21	Early
Sneed, Charlotte(Orph)	Richmond	122nd	21/6	Gwinnett
Sneed, Dudley	Burke	Torrance	199/3	Early
Sneed, Elijah	Hancock	Evans	335/8	Early

NAME	COUNTY	MIL.DIST	LOT/SECT	DREW LAND
Sneed, Hannah	Oglethorpe	Goolsbys	70/21	Early
Sneed, John(Orph)	Richmond	122nd	21/6	Gwinnett
Sneed, Nancy(Wid)	Richmond		135/2	Early
Sneed, Nathaniel(Orph)	Richmond	122nd	21/6	Gwinnett
Sneed, Philip	Burke	Lewis	44/15	Early
Sneed, Samuel	Burke	Torrance	84/14	Early
Snell, David(Orps)	Pulaski	Senterfeits	343/1	Early
Snell, Isaac	Emanuel	56th	3/3	Walton
Snell, Isom	Emanuel	56th	246/27	Early
Snell, Jacob(Orps)	Pulaski	Senterfeits	69/4	Habersham
Snell, John	Emanuel	56th	507/5	Irwin
Snelling, Rebecca(Wid)	Elbert	Olives	333/11	Early
Snellings, Geo.(Orps)	Elbert	Olivers	120/11	Habersham
Snellings, William	Jones	Jeffersons	272/14	Early
Snellings, William	Jones	Jeffersons	496/11	Irwin
Snider, Barnett	Tattnall	Overstreets	164/6	Early
Snider, Barnett	Tattnall	Overstreets	291/13	Irwin
Snider, Barnett	Warren	151st	358/5	Appling
Snider, Christian	Wilkes	Runnels	61/1	Appling
Snider, Samuel	Effingham		165/8	Appling
Snipes, Jonathan	Baldwin	Irwins	116/2	Habersham
Snotling, John	Morgan	Alfords	468/5	Appling
Snow, Ebenezer(Orps)	Baldwin	Irwins	148/26	Early
Snow, Jessee	Pulaski	Rees	327/26	Early
Snow, John P.	Greene	Wheelis	261/3	Walton
Snow, John P.	Greene	Wheelis	80/7	Appling
Snow, Levi	Walton	Greens	23/6	Irwin
Snow, Mark(RS)	Gwinnett	Hamiltons Bt.	444/8	Irwin
Snow, Mark(RS)	Gwinnett	Hamiltons Bt.	524/11	Irwin
Snow, Obediah(Orps)	Gwinnett	Hamiltons Bt.	123/19	Early
Snow, Richard	Wilkinson	Howards	312/19	Hall
Sockwell, James	Jones	Griffiths	34/1	Walton
Solley, Daniel	Putnam	Slaughters	52/2	Appling
Solley, Michael Sr.	Lincoln	Graves	340/10	Irwin
Solly, Michael Sr.	Lincoln	Graves	329/6	Early
Solomon, Henry	Twiggs	R.Belchers	247/28	Early
Solomon, James	Twiggs	Jeffersons	70/11	Irwin
Solomon, Mary(Wid)	Laurens	Harris	282/1	Appling
Solomon, Willis(Orps)	Jackson	Hamiltons Bt.	142/15	Irwin
Solomons, James	Laurens	Harris	159/4	Irwin
Solsberry, James G.	Burke	McNorrills	229/8	Irwin
Somersall, Ann(Wid)	Liberty		496/12	Irwin
Somersall, John	Liberty		481/13	Irwin
Somersall, Stafford A.	Liberty		150/6	Gwinnett
Sorrell, Margarett(Wid)	Tattnall	Keens	111/6	Appling
Sorrels, Thomas	Morgan	Talbots	95/16	Early
Sorrills, William	Lincoln	Adares	35/2	Walton
Sorrow, Etheldred	Oglethorpe	Waters	161/14	Early
Sorrow, John	Oglethorpe	Davenports	168/2	Rabun
Sorrow, Samuel(Orps)	Oglethorpe	Bridges	112/28	Early
Sorrow, William	Oglethorpe	Davenports	154/26	Early
Southall, James	Twiggs	Jeffersons	413/5	Appling
Southerland, John	Greene	Harvills	21/11	Early
Soweks, Henry	Liberty		80/11	Early
Sowel, James	Wilkes	Mattox	302/4	Appling
Sowell, Clayton(Orps)	Jefferson	Lamps	47/2	Appling
Sowell, Nathan	Pulaski	Bryans	412/21	Early
Spain, Marmaduke	Emanuel	58th	69/5	Appling
Spain, Ruffian	Emanuel	58th	246/3	Early
Spalding, Henry	Columbia	Willingham	57/3	Walton
Spalding, Thomas	Twiggs	R.Belchers	180/4	Walton
Span, T.B.	Chatham		59/10	Hall
Spann, Francis(Orps)	Jefferson	Lamps	101/13	Irwin
Spann, Michael	Chatham		154/6	Gwinnett
Spann, Richard C.	Twiggs	Browns	93/3	Irwin
Sparkes, Mathew	Jackson	Hamiltons Bt.	386/10	Early
Sparkman, Stephen	Camden	Tillis	289/4	Irwin

NAME	COUNTY	MIL.DIST	LOT/SECT	DREW LAND
Sparks, Benjamin	Washington	Renfros	31/12	Habersham
Sparks, Benjamin	Washington	Renfros	34/1	Early
Sparks, John Jr.	Putnam	Slaughters	58/28	Early
Sparks, John	Morgan	Wrights	233/8	Appling
Sparks, John	Morgan	Wrights	478/7	Appling
Sparks, Martin P.	Morgan	Townsends	93/1	Habersham
Sparks, Robert	Putnam	Moorlands	55/4	Walton
Sparks, William	Franklin	Morriss	336/3	Early
Sparks, Wm.C.	Franklin	Hammonds	57/5	Rabun
Sparrow, Daniel(Orps)	Pulaski	Johnstons	27/1	Irwin
Sparrow, Daniel	Pulaski	Johnstons	477/9	Irwin
Speake, Kezekiah	Wilkinson	Smiths	16/27	Early
Spean, Nathaniel	Twiggs	Evans	445/5	Appling
Spear, Eliz.(Orph)	Jasper	Clays	11/3	Rabun
Spear, Jane	Jasper	Clays	81/10	Habersham
Spear, John	Jones	Jeffersons	361/19	Early
Spear, William	Jasper	Phillips	201/8	Early
Spears, John	McIntosh	Hamiltons	108/7	Appling
Spears, Joseph S.E.	Warren	Blounts	231/4	Appling
Spears, Lewis	Jasper	Blakes	33/2	Appling
Spears, Sims	Franklin	Harris	79/15	Early
Spears, Thomas	Pulaski	Laniers	29/18	Early
Spears, William	Burke	Sullivans	187/3	Appling
Spears, Wm.	Clarke	Harris	110/1	Walton
Spears, Wm.	Jasper	Posts	70/12	Irwin
Speer, John	Jasper	Phillips	183/6	Gwinnett
Speers, John	Burke	Royals	216/5	Irwin
Speers, John	Burke	Royals	232/3	Walton
Speight, Martha(Wid)	Laurens	Deans	213/12	Irwin
Spell, George	Laurens	D.Smiths	355/9	Irwin
Spence, Ansel	Scriven		263/10	Irwin
Spence, Aron(Orps)	Burke	Lewis	107/16	Irwin
Spence, David	Gwinnett	Hamiltons Bt.	146/5	Early
Spence, David	Gwinnett	Hamiltons Bt.	194/21	Early
Spence, Isaac	Burke	Lewis	119/8	Irwin
Spence, Isaac	Burke	Lewis	126/15	Irwin
Spence, Jane	Burke	Lewis	538/2	Appling
Spence, John	Jasper	Philips	73/27	Early
Spence, John	Morgan	Selmons	412/5	Irwin
Spence, John	Morgan	Selmons	85/13	Early
Spence, Joseph(Orp)	Burke	Spiveys	253/3	Appling
Spence, Joshua	Burke	Lewis	78/10	Habersham
Spence, Jusel	Scriven		314/12	Early
Spence, Leaston(Orp)	Burke	Spiveys	253/3	Appling
Spence, Littleton	Burke	Spiveys	112/6	Early
Spence, Mary	Burke	Lewis	66/17	Early
Spence, Nancy	Burke	Lewis	108/2	Irwin
Spence, Olive & Ann	Burke	Lewis	513/13	Irwin
Spence, Thomas	Wilkinson	Wiggins	5/2	Rabun
Spence, Wm.S.	Elbert	P.Christians	89/3	Rabun
Spencer, Octavo	Elbert	P.Christians	194/6	Appling
Spencer, William	Liberty		36/8	Irwin
Spenholster, John	Liberty		232/18	Early
Spensor, Henry A.	Jones	Buckhalters	23/4	Appling
Spier, David Sr.	Laurens	Deans	22/11	Hall
Spier, David W.	Columbia	Shaws	94/9	Irwin
Spier, James	Laurens	Deans	263/6	Early
Spier, Milley(Wid)	Effingham		59/5	Appling
Spiers, David	Laurens	Harris	136/13	Early
Spiers, Zachariah	Lincoln	Graves	527/13	Irwin
Spights, Asa	Hancock	Evans	319/5	Early
Spights, Asa	Hancock	Evans	383/16	Early
Spikes, Jesse	Hancock	Harts	73/4	Irwin
Spikes, Unity(Wid)	Montgomery	Alstons	37/13	Early
Spillar, Amos	Gwinnett	Hamiltons Bt.	241/1	Early
Spillar, Amos	Gwinnett	Hamiltons Bt.	349/21	Early
Spillars, Warrington	Clarke	Moors	388/12	Irwin

NAME	COUNTY	MIL.DIST	LOT/SECT	DREW LAND
Spinks, Baker S.	Morgan	Dennis	109/21	Early
Spinks, Enoch	Morgan	Selmons	386/7	Irwin
Spinks, Garnett	Clarke	Moores	413/1	Early
Spinks, Presley	Warren	Hubberts	97/15	Early
Spinks, Raleigh	Morgan	Selmons	241/20	Early
Spires, Zachariah	Lincoln	Graves	360/13	Irwin
Spivey, Beverly	Columbia	J.Morris	323/3	Appling
Spivey, James	Warren	152nd	299/10	Irwin
Spivey, Jethro B.	Laurens	Jones	178/2	Early
Spivey, Jethro B.	Laurens	Jones	40/21	Early
Spivey, Mary(Wid)	Columbia	Dodsons	157/2	Irwin
Spivey, Mary	Putnam	Evans	83/4	Irwin
Spivey, Moses	Tattnall	Cunyers	154/8	Early
Spivey, Sherod	Laurens	D.Smiths	167/10	Early
Spivey, Simpson(Orps)	Jefferson	Cowarts	97/11	Habersham
Spivey, Solomon	Laurens	D.Smiths	97/4	Walton
Spiveys, John(Orps)	Hancock	Herberts	206/4	Appling
Spivy, John	Jefferson	Langstons	110/12	Hall
Spivy, John	Putnam	Evans	421/8	Irwin
Splawn, Rosannah	Jasper	Blakes	466/13	Irwin
Splawn, Stephen(Orps)	Jasper	Blakes	128/7	Irwin
Spoon, Jacob	Jackson	Rodgers	252/11	Irwin
Spooner, Loer(Roar?)	Scriven		391/5	Appling
Spradlin, Irwin	Putnam	Littles	8/2	Rabun
Spradlin, Joshua(RS)	Putnam	Littles	254/12	Irwin
Spraggens, William	Jackson	Rogers Bt.	112/9	Early
Spraggins, James	Jackson	Rogers Bt.	296/9	Appling
Spraggins, James	Jackson	Rogers Bt.	48/9	Appling
Sprague, Samuel	Putnam	Evans	294/8	Irwin
Spratling, Henry	Wilkes	Brooks	305/1	Walton
Springer, Jonathan	Warren	Griers	113/6	Irwin
Springer, Jonathan	Warren	Griers	76/4	Appling
Springer, William G.	Hancock	Danells	57/6	Gwinnett
Springer, Wm.G.	Hancock	Dannells	335/8	Appling
Springfield, Aaron(RS)	Jackson	Winters Bt.	45/21	Early
Springfield, Aron(RS)	Jackson	Winters Bt.	340/8	Irwin
Springfield, Moses	Jackson	Rogers Bt.	398/4	Appling
Springs, Bartholomew	Burke	Dys	222/9	Irwin
Springs, Jacob(Orps)	Emanuel	53rd	123/21	Early
Spurgen, Thomas R.	Gwinnett	Hamiltons Bt.	167/2	Early
Spurgin, Thomas R.	Gwinnett	Hamiltons Bt.	125/9	Irwin
Spurlin, Levi	Warren	151st	340/7	Irwin
Spurlin, Silas	Warren	151st	210/8	Early
Spurling, John	Jones	Permenters	472/3	Appling
Spurlock, Britton	Laurens	Ross	21/4	Habersham
Spurlock, John	Jackson	Winters Bt.	388/8	Irwin
Spurlock, John	Twiggs	Evans	294/5	Early
Spurlock, Mary(Wid)	Twiggs	Browns	411/5	Appling
Spurlock, Solomon	Washington	Peabodys	60/20	Early
Spurlock, William	Washington	Peabodys	185/2	Habersham
St.John, John	Jasper	Hays	252/7	Gwinnett
St.John, John	Jasper	Hays	290/26	Early
St.Johns, William	Washington	Burneys	58/1	Irwin
Stacy, John W.	Liberty		307/11	Early
Stafford, George	Camden	Longs	288/26	Early
Stafford, Joseph(Orps)	Appling	9th	122/20	Early
Stafford, Joshua	Twiggs	R.Belchers	110/12	Irwin
Stafford, Robert(RS)	Wayne	Crews	11/11	Irwin
Stafford, William	McIntosh	Hamiltons	355/9	Early
Stallings, James(Orps)	Greene	Armers	303/3	Appling
Stallings, Jesse	Jones	Buckhalters	434/6	Appling
Stallings, John	Jones	Rossers	65/3	Appling
Stallings, Lovet	Columbia	Bealls	243/27	Early
Stallings, Lydia(Wid)	Greene	Armers	503/7	Appling
Stallings, Palisiah	Morgan	Campbells	181/10	Early
Stallings, Sanders	Jasper	Baileys	18/8	Early
Stallings, William	Columbia	Bealls	23/21	Early

NAME	COUNTY	MIL.DIST	LOT/SECT	DREW LAND
Stallings, William	Morgan	Knights	212/21	Early
Stamper, Martin W.	Putnam	Stampers	87/8	Hall
Stamper, Spencer	Putnam	Stampers	44/3	Rabun
Stamper, Susannah(Wid)	Morgan	McClendons	51/11	Habersham
Stamps, Brittian	Oglethorpe	Bridges	70/2	Irwin
Stamps, Britton	Oglethorpe	Bridges	272/29	Early
Stamps, James	Jackson	Rogers Bt.	97/9	Appling
Stamps, Thomas J.	Oglethorpe	Barnetts	135/2	Rabun
Stamps, Thomas Sr.(RS)	Clarke	Oates	136/7	Gwinnett
Stamps, Thos.Jr.	Jasper	Bentleys	306/19	Early
Stamps, Timothy	Putnam	Morelands	116/8	Early
Stanaland, Joseph	Tattnall	Overstreets	15/27	Early
Stanaland, Samuel	Tattnall	Overstreets	181/3	Habersham
Stanaton, Jonathan	Jackson	Winters Bt.	237/3	Irwin
Standard, John	Lincoln	Tatoms	272/6	Appling
Standard, Kimbro	Lincoln	Tatoms	266/8	Irwin
Standard, William	Lincoln	Stokes	91/8	Irwin
Standback, Nancy(Wid)	Warren	Herberts	234/2	Habersham
Standifer, Archd.	Jasper	Centells	288/4	Irwin
Standland, Richard T.	Bulloch	Knights	149/12	Early
Standley, Robert	Tattnall	Johnstons	142/21	Early
Standley, Robert	Tattnall	Johnstons	153/12	Early
Standley, William	Camden	Tillis	354/3	Early
Standly, John	McIntosh	Eigles	67/12	Hall
Stanfield, John	Montgomery	Nobles	379/6	Appling
Stanfield, Littleton	Scriven		83/7	Early
Stanfield, Richard	Walton	Wagnons	209/21	Early
Stanfield, Wm.B.(Orps)	Oglethorpe	Barnetts	225/16	Early
Stanford, Betsey(Wid)	Jefferson	Waldens	38/7	Irwin
Stanford, David	Richmond	Augusta	313/9	Irwin
Stanford, J.W.	Warren	152nd	85/4	Walton
Stanford, James	Baldwin	Marshalls	42/4	Early
Stanford, Johnathan	Columbia	Ob.Morris	64/14	Early
Stanford, Jonathan Sr.	Warren	152	318/27	Early
Stanford, Joseph(Orps)	Warren	Blounts	118/4	Habersham
Stanford, Joshua	Columbia	Watsons	338/9	Irwin
Stanford, Josiah	Warren	152nd	36/10	Early
Stanford, Levi	Warren	152nd	152/4	Irwin
Stanford, Robert(RS)	Twiggs	W.Belchers	86/6	Gwinnett
Stanford, William D.	Columbia	Watsons	80/12	Early
Stanford, Wm.W.	Twiggs	W.Belchers	174/7	Early
Stanley, Ezekiel	Clarke	Sims	424/3	Appling
Stanley, Felix	Jasper	Baileys	115/4	Habersham
Stanley, James	Laurens	Watsons	197/14	Early
Stanley, Lewis	Greene	Fosterse	391/2	Early
Stanley, Martin	Jasper	Hays	492/13	Irwin
Stanly, Benjamin	Effingham		107/9	Appling
Stansel, Joel	Wilkinson	Bowings	37/4	Habersham
Stansel, Levi	Wilkinson	Bowens	248/7	Appling
Stansill, Richard O.	Tattnall	Cunyers	230/18	Early
Stanton, Batt	Putnam	Robertsons	128/1	Walton
Stanton, Batt	Putnam	Robertsons	55/20	Early
Stanton, Henry	Columbia	Burroughs	311/1	Walton
Stanton, Jonathan	Jackson	Winters Bt.	3/12	Habersham
Stanton, Patrick	Chatham		1/15	Irwin
Stanton, William	Hancock	Justice	460/8	Appling
Stanton, Wm.	Elbert	Whites	451/2	Appling
Staples, Elizabeth	Wilkes	Harris	476/5	Irwin
Staples, Thomas	Elbert	Webbs	30/8	Appling
Stapleton, George Sr.	Jefferson	Matthews	385/5	Appling
Stapleton, Thomas	Jefferson	Matthews	380/5	Early
Stapleton, Wm.	Jefferson	Mathews	148/9	Appling
Stapp, John	Jefferson	Langstons	222/13	Irwin
Stare, Henry	Wilkes	Reynolds	18/1	Habersham
Stark, Fielding	Lincoln	Thompsons	282/19	Early
Stark, Mary(Wid)	Wilkes	Runnels	283/8	Appling
Stark, Philip J.(Orps)	Wilkes	Reynolds	22/3	Walton

NAME	COUNTY	MIL.DIST	LOT/SECT	DREW LAN
Starkes, Thomas	Morgan	McClendons	52/16	Irwin
Starks, Fielding	Lincoln	Thompson	255/7	Irwin
Starks, William J.	Columbia	Dodsons	25/14	Early
Starky, Semore	Wilkinson	Lees	46/15	Irwin
Starley, John	Wilkinson	Wiggins	365/15	Early
Starling, Abram	Appling	4th	68/5	Appling
Starling, Francis	Camden	Longs	299/13	Early
Starling, John	Washington	Renfroes	274/10	Early
Starling, Starky	Wilkinson	Lees	28/22	Early
Starnes, Saml.S.	Richmond	122nd	212/3	Appling
Starnes, Samuel G.	Richmond	122	133/26	Early
Starnes, Titus	Jones	Shropshiers	19/14	Irwin
Starnes, Titus	Jones	Shropshiers	348/11	Irwin
Starr, Asa(Orps)	Wilkes	Ogletrees	2/3	Rabun
Starr, Benjamin	Wilkes	Ogletrees	249/1	Walton
Starr, Joshua	Wilkes	Runnels	316/1	Appling
Starr, Samuel	Wilkes	Ogletrees	264/7	Irwin
Starr, William Jr.	Chatham		491/11	Irwin
Starrett, Benj.	Franklin	Vaughans	370/5	Appling
Starritt, James	Franklin	Powells	269/9	Appling
Startin, Eliz.(Wid)	Chatham		5/4	Habersha
Statam, Pleasant	Morgan	Townsends	114/3	Early
Statam, Plesant(Orps)	Gwinnett	Hamiltons Bt.	119/2	Habersha
Stateham, Anderson	Clarke	Oates	16/1	Appling
Stateham, John	Wilkinson	Lees	20/12	Hall
Statham, James	Elbert	Penns	310/5	Appling
Statham, William	Lincoln	Stokes	181/3	Appling
Statham, William	Lincoln	Stokes	191/2	Rabun
Statnaker, James	Warren	151	132/4	Early
Statnaker, James	Warren	151st	329/7	Appling
Staton, Danl.(Orps)	Wilkes	Ogletree	161/10	Irwin
Statum, James	Telfair	Williams	163/3	Walton
Stay, John	Camden	Clarks	351/26	Early
Stayle, John	Chatham		358/4	Early
Steed, Green	Jackson	Rogers	102/4	Irwin
Steed, Leonard	Columbia	J.Morris	279/2	Appling
Steed, Phillip Jr.	Columbia	J.Morris	143/7	Irwin
Steed, William P.	Columbia	J.Morriss	457/12	Irwin
Steedley, William	Franklin	Powels	20/1	Habersha
Steel, Henry	Jasper	Northcuts	2/11	Habersha
Steel, Henry	Jasper	Northcuts	40/8	Appling
Steel, John	Walton	Wagnons	349/26	Early
Steele, Joseph	Morgan	Farrars	59/23	Early
Steeles, Joseph(Orp)	Baldwin	Marshalls	322/7	Gwinnett
Steely, James	Baldwin	Taliaferro	93/5	Early
Stell, Eliz.(Wid)	Morgan	Hackneys	3/4	Appling
Stelson, David	Liberty		519/11	Irwin
Stembridge, Henry R.	Putnam	Littles	103/9	Irwin
Stembridge, John	Putnam	Stampers	43/3	Early
Stembridge, Wm.Jr.	Hancock	Edwards	119/9	Irwin
Stephen, Andrew B.	Wilkes	Bryants	29/17	Early
Stephens, Abraham	Washington	Peabodys	84/15	Irwin
Stephens, Absalom	Franklin	Vaughns	340/5	Appling
Stephens, Allen	Putnam	J.Kendricks	450/13	Irwin
Stephens, Aquilla	Warren	Rodgers	68/1	Rabun
Stephens, Barnett	Oglethorpe	Bridges	125/1	Irwin
Stephens, Caleb	Lincoln	Willifords	62/6	Habersha
Stephens, Charles	Chatham		233/7	Early
Stephens, Charles	Jefferson	Jones	309/1	Walton
Stephens, David	Laurens	Watsons	40/5	Habersha
Stephens, Eady(Wid)	Jefferson	Lamps	14/11	Early
Stephens, Ebenezer	Laurens	Haleys	338/18	Early
Stephens, Ebenezer	Laurens	Watsons	298/6	Appling
Stephens, Eveline	Chatham		484/13	Irwin
Stephens, Hailey	Lincoln	Willifords	7/18	Early
Stephens, Henry	Jasper	Clays	221/19	Early
Stephens, Herbert	Jones	Permenters	101/11	Irwin

NAME	COUNTY	MIL.DIST	LOT/SECT	DREW LAND
Stephens, Herbert	Jones	Permenters	6/5	Early
Stephens, Holman	Twiggs	Bozemans	16/3	Irwin
Stephens, Holman	Twiggs	Bozemans	302/3	Early
Stephens, Hubert(RS)	Baldwin	Marshalls	74/3	Rabun
Stephens, Hugh	Tattnall	Overstreets	518/8	Appling
Stephens, Isaac	Burke	McNorrell	513/11	Irwin
Stephens, Isaac	Burke	McNorrill	373/3	Appling
Stephens, Jacob Sr.	Washington	Peabodys	196/15	Early
Stephens, James Sr.	Burke	Spiveys	65/3	Habersham
Stephens, James(Orps)	Jasper	McClendons	178/16	Early
Stephens, James	Clarke	Deans	26/2	Walton
Stephens, James	Clarke	Deans	85/4	Habersham
Stephens, James	Morgan	Campbells	42/5	Early
Stephens, James	Tattnall	J.Durrences	5/8	Hall
Stephens, James	Twiggs	Bozemans	230/10	Irwin
Stephens, Jared	Washington	Robinsons	111/3	Rabun
Stephens, John Sr.	Washington	Peabodys	253/4	Walton
Stephens, John W.	Wilkes	Bryants	437/5	Appling
Stephens, John W.	Wilkinson	Lees	239/4	Appling
Stephens, John	Jones	Shropshiers	195/18	Early
Stephens, John	Wilkinson	Smiths	340/11	Irwin
Stephens, Joseph Jr.	Wilkinson	Brooks	358/12	Irwin
Stephens, Joseph	Oglethorpe	Davenports	135/1	Walton
Stephens, Joshua(Orph)	Oglethorpe	Barnetts	105/2	Early
Stephens, Joshua(Orps)	Putnam	J.Kendricks	215/11	Irwin
Stephens, Josiah T.	Wilkinson	Lees	309/5	Gwinnett
Stephens, Josiah	Twiggs	Hodges	202/6	Appling
Stephens, Maria A.(Orp)	Chatham		89/5	Early
Stephens, Mary(Wid)	Montgomery	Alstons	330/10	Irwin
Stephens, Mary	Jasper	McClendons	225/17	Early
Stephens, Matthew	Burke	Spiveys	240/20	Early
Stephens, Micajah	Richmond	Palmers	378/9	Early
Stephens, Minor M.	Oglethorpe	Brittons	45/5	Gwinnett
Stephens, Nathaniel	Camden	32nd	112/10	Hall
Stephens, Needham	Pulaski	86th Bt.	54/7	Irwin
Stephens, Oliver	Liberty		402/5	Appling
Stephens, Oliver	Liberty		69/2	Appling
Stephens, Orran	Pulaski	Rees	313/27	Early
Stephens, Orren	Pulaski	Rees	382/6	Early
Stephens, Peggy(Orp)	Chatham		89/5	Early
Stephens, Reuben(RS)	Clarke	Moores	49/2	Rabun
Stephens, Richard Sr.(RS)	Twiggs	Belchers	77/18	Early
Stephens, Robert	Bulloch	Knights	389/13	Early
Stephens, Robert	Bulloch	Knights	45/1	Appling
Stephens, Robert	Jefferson	Waldens	4/22	Early
Stephens, Rossell	Warren	Rogers	311/11	Irwin
Stephens, Samuel(Orps)	Jefferson	Lamps	107/2	Irwin
Stephens, Silas	Jones	Griffiths	110/26	Early
Stephens, Simeon L.	Baldwin	Marshalls	238/12	Early
Stephens, Thomas	Jones	Seals	32/5	Irwin
Stephens, William	Baldwin	Cousins	164/1	Walton
Stephens, William	Clarke	Deans	64/1	Walton
Stephens, William	Emanuel	57th	171/8	Hall
Stephens, William	Jasper	Reids	386/16	Early
Stephens, William	Oglethorpe	Goolsby	146/12	Irwin
Stephens, William	Oglethorpe	Goolsbys	326/5	Appling
Stephens, William	Twiggs	Bozemans	217/3	Appling
Stephens, Willie	Tattnall	Overstreets	361/4	Appling
Stephens, Wm.	Putnam	Slaughters	139/1	Irwin
Stephenson, Silas	Laurens	Harriss	149/5	Appling
Stephenson, Thos.	Clarke	Applings	45/7	Gwinnett
Stephenson, Thos.	Clarke	Applings	53/11	Hall
Stephenson, Wm.M.	Clarke	Penticost	334/11	Irwin
Stepleton, George Jr.	Warren	153rd	90/18	Early
Steptoe, John	Burke	Sullivans	249/13	Irwin
Steptoe, John	Burke	Sullivans	265/8	Irwin
Steptoe, Thomas(Orps)	Wilkinson	Brooks	327/5	Early

NAME	COUNTY	MIL.DIST	LOT/SECT	DREW LAND
Sterling, Burwell	Oglethorpe	Bridges	177/16	Irwin
Sterling, James	Lincoln	Adares	168/1	Early
Sterling, Josiah	Oglethorpe	Bridges	162/13	Irwin
Stevens, Benjamin	Camden	Longs	216/26	Early
Stevens, Beverly	Laurens	Watsons	52/6	Early
Stevens, Edmund	Greene	144	5/13	Early
Stevens, Edmund	Greene	144th	243/4	Early
Stevens, John	Baldwin	Stevens	505/8	Appling
Stevens, William	Putnam	Slaughters	154/20	Early
Stevens, Wm.J.	Putnam	Buckners	38/11	Irwin
Stevenson, John	Greene	141st	163/11	Early
Stevenson, John	Greene	141st	303/7	Gwinnett
Stevenson, John	Jefferson	Flemmings	327/28	Early
Steward, Daniel	Chatham		106/4	Irwin
Steward, David	Burke	Thomas	394/16	Early
Steward, Isaac	Burke	Thomas	221/3	Early
Steward, James	Jasper	Hays	129/11	Hall
Steward, John P.	Pulaski	Maddoxs	132/15	Early
Steward, John	Emanuel	59th	376/16	Early
Steward, Mary	Burke	Royals	231/19	Early
Steward, Thomas	Clarke	Deans	142/5	Gwinnett
Stewart, Alexander	Morgan	Leonards	373/9	Irwin
Stewart, Amous	Wilkes	Bryants	266/4	Early
Stewart, Benjamin	Jones	Mulkeys	315/6	Appling
Stewart, Charles(Orps)	Oglethorpe	Wises	24/12	Early
Stewart, Charles	Clarke	Mereweather	161/28	Early
Stewart, Charles	Clarke	Mereweather	304/13	Irwin
Stewart, Charles	Effingham		502/5	Appling
Stewart, Charles	Effingham		53/10	Early
Stewart, Charles	Jones	Greens	276/8	Irwin
Stewart, Charles	Jones	Greens	522/5	Appling
Stewart, Charles	Pulaski	Maddox	465/2	Appling
Stewart, Chas.J.W.	McIntosh	Hamiltons	304/6	Irwin
Stewart, Chas.Jr.	Wilkinson	Brooks	134/5	Early
Stewart, Daniel M.	Liberty		72/9	Early
Stewart, Daniel	Liberty		110/115	Early
Stewart, David	Bulloch	Everitts	48/18	Early
Stewart, David	Warren	150th	363/13	Early
Stewart, Eli	Jones	Wallers	88/2	Habersham
Stewart, Floyd	Oglethorpe	Myricks	167/14	Early
Stewart, Fredr. S.	Oglethorpe	Brittons	50/6	Habersham
Stewart, Henry(Orps)	Jasper	Baileys	303/10	Early
Stewart, Henry	Bulloch	Knights	444/7	Irwin
Stewart, Hugh B.	Jasper	Northcut	274/7	Appling
Stewart, Hugh B.	Jasper	Northcuts	39/11	Early
Stewart, James P.	Camden	32nd	56/7	Gwinnett
Stewart, James(Orph)	Pulaski	Maddox	254/18	Early
Stewart, James	Camden	32nd	228/27	Early
Stewart, James	Greene	141st	341/26	Early
Stewart, James	Greene	144th	261/13	Early
Stewart, James	Jasper	Barnes	84/1	Rabun
Stewart, James	Jasper	Hays	186/14	Early
Stewart, James	Jefferson	Bothwells	65/4	Habersham
Stewart, James	Oglethorpe	Myricks	176/16	Early
Stewart, James	Richmond	Laceys	9/11	Early
Stewart, John Jr.	Bulloch	Everitts	284/6	Irwin
Stewart, John(Orps)	Burke	Sullivans	103/2	Early
Stewart, John	Bulloch	Everitts	322/12	Early
Stewart, John	Jasper	Centells	378/1	Appling
Stewart, John	Jasper	Easters	215/2	Early
Stewart, John	Jones	Hansfords	233/10	Early
Stewart, John	Lincoln	Tatoms	420/8	Appling
Stewart, John	Oglethorpe	Wises	79/9	Appling
Stewart, John	Tattnall	Conyers	376/13	Irwin
Stewart, John	Warren	151st	306/4	Walton
Stewart, Josiah	Twiggs	Browns	226/12	Irwin
Stewart, Lewis	Jefferson	Bothwells	338/5	Appling

NAME	COUNTY	MIL.DIST	LOT/SECT	DREW LAND
Stewart, Mathew	Greene	144th	180/6	Gwinnett
Stewart, Nathaniel W.	Washington	Avents	162/18	Early
Stewart, Nathanl.W.	Washington	Avents	391/5	Irwin
Stewart, Reuben	Clarke	Oates	138/2	Rabun
Stewart, Reuben	Clarke	Otis	281/20	Early
Stewart, Richard(Orps)	Clarke	Simms	280/6	Irwin
Stewart, Saml.(Orps)	Jackson	Winters Bt.	3/5	Habersham
Stewart, Samuel D.	Jones	Chappels	240/8	Irwin
Stewart, Susannah(Orps)	Scriven	Lovetts	76/4	Walton
Stewart, Sylvanus	Jasper	Hayes	159/15	Early
Stewart, Thomas	Oglethorpe	Myricks	1/3	Rabun
Stewart, Thomas	Richmond	Laceys	224/11	Irwin
Stewart, Walter	Effingham		298/2	Early
Stewart, William M.	Tattnall	Johnstons	297/4	Early
Stewart, William	Burke	Bells	188/3	Habersham
Stewart, William	Burke	Bells	356/21	Early
Stewart, William	Jones	Jeffersons	194/1	Irwin
Stewart, William	Lincoln	Tatoms	347/6	Appling
Stewart, William	Oglethorpe	Myricks	148/5	Appling
Stewart, William	Pulaski	Maddox	372/12	Early
Stewart, Wm.	Hall		255/17	Early
Stewart, Wm.	Morgan	Farrars	484/2	Appling
Stewart, Wm.	Tattnall	Cunyers	9/3	Early
Stewarts, John	Jones	Hansford	96/8	Irwin
Stibbins, Edward	Chatham		441/11	Irwin
Stibbs, Ann	Chatham		195/7	Early
Stibbs, Ann	Chatham		412/5	Appling
Stidivant, John	Putnam	Morelands	214/10	Early
Stigall, Samuel	Jasper	Centills	139/2	Appling
Stile, Joseph	Morgan	Farrars	146/6	Gwinnett
Stiles, Benj(Orp)	Chatham		518/5	Irwin
Stiles, Edmond(Orp)	Chatham		518/5	Irwin
Stiles, Jane(Orp)	Chatham		518/5	Irwin
Stiles, John(RS)	Twiggs	Evans	118/19	Early
Stiles, Joseph G.	Jones	Permenters	169/3	Walton
Stiles, Nicholas	Jackson	Dicksons Bt.	96/2	Habersham
Stiles, S.A.(Orp)	Chatham		139/16	Irwin
Stiles, Sarah(Orp)	Chatham		518/5	Irwin
Stiles, W.E.C.(Orp)	Chatham		139/16	Irwin
Stills, Robert(Orps)	Morgan	Hackneys	216/6	Gwinnett
Stillwell, Jane(Wid)	Chatham		75/27	Early
Stilwell, Abigail(Orp)	Chatham		379/11	Early
Stilwell, Eliza(Orp)	Chatham		379/11	Early
Stilwell, Green S.	Jones	Kings	375/6	Early
Stilwell, Jane(Orp)	Chatham		379/11	Early
Stilwell, John	Chatham		379/11	Early
Stilwell, John	Jones	Buckhalters	143/2	Early
Stilwell, Rebecca(Orp)	Chatham		379/11	Early
Stilwell, Sarah(Orp)	Chatham		379/11	Early
Stinchomb, Phillip	Elbert	Penns	290/1	Appling
Stinger, John Jr.	Hall	McCutcheons	194/3	Early
Stinson, George	Jones	Phillips	83/3	Appling
Stinson, James W.	Putnam	Littles	506/6	Irwin
Stinson, John	Putnam	Jurnigans	38/16	Irwin
Stinson, Joseph	Jones	Permenters	448/6	Irwin
Stinson, Michael Sr.	Putnam	Littles	386/13	Early
Stinson, Michael Sr.	Putnam	Littles	400/1	Early
Stinson, Porter	Putnam	Littles	81/19	Early
Stinson, Robert H.	Putnam	Jurnigans	97/12	Habersham
Stirk, John W.	Chatham		185/3	Walton
Stirk, William	Chatham		373/10	Early
Stockdale, John	Burke	Dys	160/5	Appling
Stockley, Silas	Greene	144st	261/5	Early
Stocks, John	Walton	Davis	144/9	Early
Stocks, William	Morgan	Alfords	120/1	Appling
Stoker, Mathew	Clarke	Moores	171/15	Irwin
Stoker, Mathew	Clarke	Moores	212/8	Irwin

NAME	COUNTY	MIL.DIST	LOT/SECT	DREW LAN
Stokes, Allen	Jasper	Sentals	242/16	Early
Stokes, Archibald	Elbert	Whites	165/12	Habersha
Stokes, Drury	Washington	Floyds	459/2	Appling
Stokes, Henry	Oglethorpe	Davenports	172/3	Irwin
Stokes, Ignatius	Jasper	Barnes	360/10	Irwin
Stokes, John	Walton	Wests	190/10	Habersha
Stokes, John	Walton	Wests	294/26	Early
Stokes, Martha	Burke	Torrance	272/11	Irwin
Stokes, Mathew	Lincoln	Tatoms	141/7	Appling
Stokes, Matthew	Lincoln	Tatoms	147/13	Early
Stokes, Selvanas(Orps)	Washington	Burneys	20/1	Rabun
Stokes, Susannah(Wid)	Clarke	Simms	24/2	Walton
Stokes, William A.	Wilkes	Russells	124/13	Habersha
Stokes, William M.	Oglethorpe	Barnetts	41/1	Early
Stokes, William W.	Lincoln	Stokes	50/7	Irwin
Stokes, William	Washington	Floyds	24/12	Hall
Stokes, Young	Wilkinson	Bowings	228/10	Early
Stone, Benj.(Orps)	Lincoln	Thompsons	118/4	Irwin
Stone, Betsey(Orp)	Jasper	Eastes	149/4	Appling
Stone, Edmund	Wilkes	Josseys	187/7	Appling
Stone, Francis M.	Chatham		325/5	Appling
Stone, James B.	Liberty		282/7	Irwin
Stone, James	Jefferson	Abbots	24/5	Rabun
Stone, Jane(Wid)	Jefferson	Flemings	13/8	Irwin
Stone, John B.	Liberty		120/11	Early
Stone, John B.	Liberty		199/1	Walton
Stone, John R.	Washington	Barges	216/8	Early
Stone, Joshua	Columbia	Gartrells	26/10	Irwin
Stone, Margaret(Orph)	Jefferson	Flemmings	110/18	Early
Stone, Marvil	Tattnall	Tharps	74/18	Early
Stone, Michael	Baldwin	Marshalls	498/10	Irwin
Stone, Nancy(Wid)	Jones	Buckhalters	31/26	Early
Stone, Nancy	Lincoln	Thompsons	125/15	Early
Stone, Neil	Jasper	Ryans	15/5	Early
Stone, Neil	Jasper	Ryans	279/9	Early
Stone, Rene	Columbia	Gartrells	52/9	Hall
Stone, Samuel	Bulloch	Knights	217/7	Appling
Stone, Samuel	Bulloch	Knights	326/18	Early
Stone, Sarah(Wid)	Chatham		295/4	Walton
Stone, Thomas M.L.	Liberty		433/4	Appling
Stone, Thomas	Putnam	Buckners	221/12	Early
Stone, Thomas	Putnam	Buckners	254/6	Appling
Stone, William	Jones	Buckhalters	288/21	Early
Stone, William	Twiggs	Browns	218/19	Early
Stone, William	Warren	Griers	499/8	Irwin
Stoneham, Henry(Orps)	Jackson	Winters Bt.	68/8	Appling
Stones, James(Orps)	Wilkes	Josseys	33/6	Appling
Stones, Micajah(Orps)	Warren	Griers	169/15	Early
Stonestreet, Rich.	Warren	Hubberts	112/10	Habersha
Stonestreet, Rich.	Warren	Hubberts	140/2	Early
Stonesypher, Benj.	Franklin	Powells	50/26	Early
Stonesypher, Jas.	Franklin	Morris	38/8	Hall
Storey, Edward	Jackson	Dicksons Bt.	197/5	Irwin
Storey, James	Jasper	Barnes	121/3	Appling
Storey, Wm.F.	Jackson	Dicksons Bt.	265/10	Early
Storie, Margt.(Wid)	Camden	Clarks	89/6	Gwinnett
Story, Edey	Pulaski	Davis	45/26	Early
Story, James	Warren	150th	386/6	Early
Story, John T.	Jackson	Dicksons Bt.	179/7	Appling
Story, John T.	Jackson	Dicksons Bt.	97/11	Hall
Story, Prudence(Wid)	Jackson	Winters	91/6	Gwinnett
Story, Richard	Laurens	Harris	509/6	Irwin
Story, Richard	Laurens	Harriss	410/12	Irwin
Story, Samuel	Pulaski	Lanears	29/4	Walton
Story, Samuel	Pulaski	Lanears	440/11	Irwin
Story, Samuel	Warren	150	227/10	Early
Story, Solomon	Warren	150	4/16	Irwin

NAME	COUNTY	MIL.DIST	LOT/SECT	DREW LAND
Stovall, Benj.Jr.	Lincoln	Jones	29/4	Appling
Stovall, Benj.Jr.	Lincoln	Jones	424/15	Early
Stovall, Geo.(Orps)	Greene	Greers	94/7	Irwin
Stovall, Geo.Sr.	Franklin	P.Browns	377/7	Appling
Stovall, George	Franklin	Davis	392/5	Appling
Stovall, George	Franklin	Davis	417/12	Irwin
Stovall, John	Clarke	Stuarts	228/10	Irwin
Stovall, John	Jackson	Winters Bt.	123/6	Appling
Stovall, Josiah	Franklin	Davis	211/17	Early
Stovall, Littleberry	Greene	Ragins	113/12	Habersham
Stovall, Pleasant	Richmond	120	3/16	Irwin
Stovall, Pleasant	Richmond	120th	366/3	Early
Stovall, Powhattan	Greene	Greers	592/2	Appling
Stovall, Samuel	Morgan	Parkers	360/5	Irwin
Stoveall, Mary(Wid)	Greene	Griers	59/9	Irwin
Stower, Hugh(Orps)	Franklin	Harris	130/1	Irwin
Stowers, Benjamin	Elbert	Dooleys	274/8	Irwin
Stowers, Benjamin	Elbert	Dooleys	331/7	Irwin
Stowers, Unity(Wid)	Franklin	Harris	45/10	Irwin
Stoy, Frederick	Richmond	122nd	139/19	Early
Stoy, Frederick	Richmond	122nd	57/6	Irwin
Stoy, William	Richmond		109/5	Gwinnett
Strahan, Rachel(Wid)	Screven		125/4	Early
Strain, Sarah(Wid)	Hancock	Champions	80/8	Appling
Strange, Edmond	Gwinnett	Hamiltons Bt.	40/7	Early
Strange, Samuel	Emanuel	58th	317/21	Early
Strange, William	Franklin	Turks	187/8	Early
Stranger, Abner	Burke	J.Wards	313/4	Appling
Straw, James	Jasper	Northcuts	237/17	Early
Strawn, Amos	Elbert	Ruckers	114/15	Irwin
Streckling, Stephen D.	Appling	4	22/4	Walton
Street, Samuel	Jackson	Winters Bt.	304/11	Early
Street, Thomas	Clarke	Moores	418/1	Early
Street, Thomas	Jackson	Winters Bt.	91/16	Early
Streetman, Martin	Lincoln	Bones	53/4	Rabun
Streetman, William	Jefferson	Mathews	113/1	Irwin
Stregel, Nicholas(RS)	Scriven	Moodys	107/17	Early
Strickey, Mary(Wid)	Laurens	Harriss	214/9	Early
Strickland, Aaron	Tattnall	Overstreets	198/9	Appling
Strickland, Aaron	Tattnall	Overstreets	41/10	Habersham
Strickland, Burgess	Lincoln	Bones	118/12	Hall
Strickland, Burgess	Lincoln	Bones	128/2	Habersham
Strickland, Carless	Jackson	Winters Bt.	390/8	Appling
Strickland, Carlis	Jackson	Rogers Bt.	125/8	Irwin
Strickland, David	Tattnall	Overstreets	401/20	Early
Strickland, Hardy	Lincoln	Millicans	34/10	Habersham
Strickland, Hardy	Lincoln	Willifords	127/2	Rabun
Strickland, Henry	Hancock	Loyds	306/19	Early
Strickland, Henry	Tattnall	Overstreets	8/26	Early
Strickland, Isaac	Jasper	Bentleys	209/20	Early
Strickland, Isaac	Lincoln	Millicans	35/1	Walton
Strickland, James	Wilkinson	Kettles	312/19	Early
Strickland, James	Wilkinson	Kettles	520/11	Irwin
Strickland, Joel	Tattnall	Overstreets	96/1	Walton
Strickland, Joel	Tattnall	Overstreets	96/1	Walton
Strickland, John	Tattnall	Overstreets	317/8	Early
Strickland, Julius(Ors)	Jackson	Hamiltons Bt.	522/9	Irwin
Strickland, Kintchen	Lincoln	Adares	487/3	Appling
Strickland, Martha(Wid)	Tattnall	Overstreets	1/5	Irwin
Strickland, Martha(Wid)	Tattnall	Overstreets	111/11	Irwin
Strickland, Matthew	Lincoln	Millicans	46/12	Early
Strickland, Pheriba(Wid)	Twiggs	Evans	121/7	Early
Strickland, Richard	Jackson	Winters Bt.	294/7	Early
Strickland, Simeon	Gwinnett	Hamiltons Bt.	39/1	Early
Strickland, Simeon	Gwinnett	Hamiltons	195/16	Irwin
Strickland, Solomon	Jasper	Northcuts	370/7	Appling
Strickland, Wilson	Gwinnett	Hamiltons Bt.	262/1	Walton

NAME	COUNTY	MIL.DIST	LOT/SECT	DREW LAND
Strickland, Wilson	Gwinnett	Hamiltons Bt.	93/6	Appling
Strickland, Wm.Jr.	Liberty		51/14	Early
Strickland, Wm.Sr.	Liberty		12/20	Early
Strickling, Allen	Jones	Shropshiers	135/16	Early
Strickling, Allen	Jones	Shropshiers	344/6	Irwin
Strine, David	Hall		320/10	Early
Stringer, Daniel	Emanuel	57	217/4	Early
Stringer, John Sr.	Hall	Byrds	387/13	Early
Stringer, John(Sr)	Hall	Byrds	43/23	Early
Stringer, Willis	Putnam	H.Kindricks	150/11	Early
Stripling, Aaron	Jones	Wallers	265/2	Early
Stripling, Arthur	Jones	Wallers	127/28	Early
Stripling, Benj.Sr.	Jones	Walkers	8/21	Early
Stripling, Benjamin	Tattnall	Johnson	382/7	Appling
Stripling, Caleb	Jones	Wallers	29/13	Early
Stripling, James B.	Tattnall	Johnsons	43/7	Gwinnett
Stripling, Piercy(Wid)	Jones	Wallers	286/2	Appling
Stripling, Wiley	Jones	Wallers	71/10	Habersha
Stripling, Wm.	Jones	Wallers	359/18	Early
Strodghill, Durrott	Elbert	G.Higginbotham	137/11	Early
Stron, David	Hall		252/9	Irwin
Strong, Charles	Oglethorpe	Barnetts	423/6	Appling
Strong, Elijah Sr.	Clarke	Parrs	183/13	Early
Strong, Elisha	Oglethorpe	Brittons	44/18	Early
Strong, Fanney	Clarke	Deans	340/21	Early
Strong, John B.	Oglethorpe	Brittons	297/2	Early
Strong, Major	Washington	Jinkinsons	381/3	Early
Strong, Peggy	Clarke	Starns	85/10	Irwin
Strong, Robert	Clarke	Starnes	446/13	Irwin
Strong, Wm.J.	Clarke	Starnes	313/3	Early
Strother, David	Hancock	Evans	120/9	Early
Strother, George	Jones	Buckhalters	284/13	Irwin
Stroud, James	Jones	Phillips	217/3	Walton
Stroud, John D.	Wilkes	Russells	161/9	Irwin
Stroud, John D.	Wilkes	Russels	37/8	Irwin
Stroud, John	Wilkes	Burks	56/1	Irwin
Stroud, Leevei	Clarke	Stuarts	73/11	Irwin
Stroud, Mathew	Franklin	Ashs	337/2	Early
Stroud, Matthew	Franklin	Ashs	475/12	Irwin
Strowd, Wm.	Jasper	Northcuts	445/11	Irwin
Strowd, Yerby	Jasper	Bentleys	149/6	Gwinnett
Strums, Henry(Orps)	Liberty		290/5	Appling
Struttren, Solomon	Jackson	Rogers Bt.	146/1	Irwin
Stuart, George	Jones	Chappels	124/2	Irwin
Stuart, John	Jones	Chappels	115/9	Irwin
Stuart, John	Jones	Chappels	337/14	Early
Stuart, Josiah	Hall	Tanners	79/3	Early
Stuart, Matthew	Twiggs	R.Belchers	226/8	Early
Stubblefield, Colvin	Oglethorpe	Rowlands	50/5	Irwin
Stubblefield, Peter	Wilkes	171st	323/9	Appling
Stubblefield, Peter	Wilkes	Runnalds	207/1	Early
Stubblefield, Peter	Wilkes	Runnalds	8/3	Walton
Stubblefold, Wm.G.	Richmond	Palmers	125/13	Early
Stubbs, Abner	Bulloch	Tilmans	30/5	Appling
Stubbs, Francis Jr.	Putnam	Buckners	250/6	Irwin
Stubbs, James(Orps)	Wilkinson	Brooks	197/5	Early
Stubbs, James	Putnam	J.Kendricks	74/1	Habersha
Stubbs, John	Jones	Harrists	181/28	Early
Stubbs, Peter	Baldwin	Marshalls	495/6	Appling
Stubbs, Thomas B.	Baldwin	Marshalls	507/8	Irwin
Stubbs, Thomas	Jones	Samuels	367/8	Appling
Stubbs, William B.	Jones	Harrist	16/2	Rabun
Stubbs, William B.	Jones	Harrist	29/6	Irwin
Stubbs, William	Wilkinson	Smiths	262/3	Walton
Stubs, John	Washington	Renfroes	374/7	Early
Stuckland, Joel	Twiggs	Evans	59/7	Irwin
Studivan, William	Morgan	Jordans	34/9	Hall

NAME	COUNTY	MIL.DIST	LOT/SECT	DREW LAND
Studman, Mary	Jasper	Baileys	464/3	Appling
Studman, Thomas	Jasper	Clays	106/8	Irwin
Studsell, John	Emanuel	49th	255/11	Early
Stugel, Nicholas(RS)	Scriven	Moodys	270/16	Early
Stuns, John O.	Wilkinson	Childs	45/12	Early
Sturdevant, Allen	Putnam	Stampers	259/4	Early
Sturdivant, Edwin	Jasper	Hays	395/28	Early
Sturdivant, Joel	Jasper	Blakes	296/7	Irwin
Sturdivant, Robert	Jasper	Smiths	295/26	Early
Sturges, Ama U.(Wid)	Richmond	122	201/3	Irwin
Sturges, Andrew B.	Richmond	122nd	119/10	Irwin
Sturges, Benj.H.	Baldwin	Marshalls	105/6	Irwin
Sturges, Nathanl. L.	Richmond	122nd	313/6	Appling
Sturges, Robert(Orps)	Pulaski	Johnstons	70/2	Walton
Sturges, Samuel Jr.	Richmond	122	181/1	Irwin
Sturgess, John	Columbia	Olives	81/11	Irwin
Sturgess, Robert	Columbia	Olives	444/11	Irwin
Sturgess, Samuel	Burke	Bells	385/13	Early
Sturgis, Joseph	Wilkes	Holidays	351/2	Appling
Sturkey, Benjamin	Richmond	Burtons	510/7	Irwin
Stutam, Mary	Gwinnett	Hamiltons Bt.	373/7	Appling
Styron, William	Hancock	Thomas	210/6	Irwin
Suals, Daniel	Washington	Floyds	177/3	Appling
Suddeth, Lewis(Orps)	Oglethorpe	Brittons	390/15	Early
Suddoth, John	Lincoln	Stocks	391/6	Appling
Sudduth, Henry	Lincoln	Walkers	75/14	Irwin
Sudduth, John	Lincoln	Walkers	87/7	Gwinnett
Sudduth, Laurence	Lincoln	Stokes	383/4	Appling
Sudduth, Nancy(Wid)	Lincoln	Walkers	337/6	Appling
Sudduth, Willis	Lincoln	Stokes	196/2	Appling
Sulds, John	Wilkes	Perrys	305/5	Irwin
Sulds, Robert	Wilkes	Perry	109/16	Early
Sullavan, John	Pulaski	Davis	359/9	Appling
Sullin, Hasay W.	Burke	Sullivans	5/3	Habersham
Sullivan, Daniel F.	Liberty		77/10	Early
Sullivan, Dennis	Burke	J.Wards	48/10	Early
Sullivan, Eliz.(Wid)	Columbia	Shaws	130/9	Appling
Sullivan, Jones	Scriven		315/9	Appling
Sullivan, Mark	Columbia	Willingham	250/9	Irwin
Sullivan, Samuel(Orps)	Columbia	Willinghams	3/8	Hall
Sullivan, William	Burke	Sullivans	98/1	Irwin
Sullivans, Daniel(Orps)	Liberty		394/5	Irwin
Sumerset, Rebeccah(Orp)	Burke	Royals	239/10	Early
Summer, James	Jones	Wallers	40/4	Irwin
Summerall, N.W.	Scriven	Smiths	296/12	Irwin
Summerford, Abrm.(Orps)	Wilkinson	Lees	382/19	Early
Summerford, Wm.D.	Wilkinson	Childs	396/6	Appling
Summerland, Lasarus	Clarke	Oates	404/9	Early
Summerland, Luke	Glynn		218/7	Appling
Summerland, Thomas	Glynn		11/2	Walton
Summerland, Thomas	Tattnall	Tharps	127/12	Habersham
Summerlin, Hardy	Bulloch	Tilmans	193/10	Habersham
Summerlin, Henry	Clarke	Spurlocks	124/1	Early
Summerlin, Jonas	Tattnall	Keens	28/5	Habersham
Summerlin, Lazeunus	Clarke	Oats	302/7	Appling
Summerlin, Thomas	Morgan	Farrars	208/18	Early
Summerlon, Thomas	Baldwin	Taliaferro	49/12	Hall
Summerlon, Thomas	Baldwin	Taliaferro	492/3	Appling
Summers, Daniel	Clarke	Stuarts	18/15	Irwin
Summers, Duell	Clarke	Harpers	393/26	Early
Summers, Edward	Clarke	Stewarts	109/4	Early
Summers, James(RS)	Jones	Permenters	345/9	Irwin
Summers, Nicholas	Jones	Permenters	450/5	Irwin
Summersall, Stafford	Liberty		174/7	Gwinnett
Sumner, Alexander	Emanuel	55	312/2	Early
Sumner, Alexander	Emanuel	55th	372/7	Irwin
Sumner, Jesse	Emanuel	55th	143/10	Hall

NAME	COUNTY	MIL.DIST	LOT/SECT	DREW LAND
Sunday, John	Wilkinson	Brooks	146/3	Appling
Sunency, James Sr.	Liberty		124/10	Irwin
Sunincy, Jacob	Liberty		433/7	Irwin
Sunnency, Thomas	Liberty		3/4	Early
Surmer, Richard	Emanuel	55th	322/7	Early
Sutherland, Edmond	Oglethorpe	Waters	137/9	Early
Sutley, Michael	Franklin	Hammonds	47/12	Habersham
Suton, Martha(Wid)	Jefferson	Waldens	260/6	Appling
Suttan, Joseph	Jasper	Northcuts	42/21	Early
Sutten, Abimaledge	Emanuel	59	141/8	Appling
Sutten, John	Wilkes	Burks	2/28	Early
Sutten, John	Wilkes	Burks	90/4	Habersham
Suttingfield, Wm.	Washington	Robinsons	123/11	Hall
Suttles, Micajah	Franklin	Vaughns	302/1	Appling
Suttles, Micajah	Franklin	Vaughns	36/2	Walton
Suttles, Millian	Franklin	Akins	87/11	Hall
Suttles, William	Franklin	Akins	46/9	Irwin
Suttles, Wm.	Clarke	Pentecost	388/7	Early
Sutton, Abner	Emanuel	59th	188/6	Appling
Sutton, Anthony	Warren	151st	133/2	Irwin
Sutton, Anthony	Warren	151st	389/7	Appling
Sutton, Benj.(Orps)	Jefferson	Waldens	216/1	Irwin
Sutton, Booker	Columbia	J.Morris	176/13	Habersham
Sutton, Charles	Twiggs	Johnstons	317/1	Early
Sutton, Cullin	Jefferson	Langstons	69/11	Irwin
Sutton, Erwin	Wilkinson	Kettles	230/3	Appling
Sutton, Hardee	Jefferson	Abbots	66/4	Habersham
Sutton, Jesse	Pulaski	Rees	21/3	Habersham
Sutton, Jesse	Pulaski	Rees	503/13	Irwin
Sutton, John C.	Jefferson	Langstons	343/3	Early
Sutton, John	Franklin	Morris	169/28	Early
Sutton, John	Franklin	Morris	49/1	Appling
Sutton, John	Laurens	Ross	85/4	Appling
Sutton, Jordan	Emanuel	59th	32/18	Early
Sutton, Moses	Wilkes	Smiths	160/5	Gwinnett
Sutton, Moses	Wilkes	Smiths	197/16	Early
Sutton, Sarah(Wid)	Pulaski	Johnstons	186/11	Early
Sutton, Stephen	Wilkinson	Kettles	395/10	Irwin
Sutton, Theophilus	Jefferson	Cowarts	65/2	Rabun
Sutton, Wiley	Jefferson	Langstons	11/2	Rabun
Sutton, Wiley	Jefferson	Langstons	268/8	Early
Sutton, Zachariah	Wilkinson	Lees	156/1	Appling
Sutton, Zachariah	Wilkinson	Lees	68/10	Habersham
Swain, Conneth	Emanuel	55th	233/1	Early
Swain, Dred	Emanuel	55	279/1	Walton
Swain, Jeremiah R.	Columbia	Watsons	391/4	Appling
Swain, Nelly	Scriven	Moodys	53/5	Rabun
Swain, Richard	Warren	Rogers	13/12	Appling
Swain, Thomas S.	Telfair	Willsons	98/15	Early
Swan, Archibald	Greene	141	86/22	Early
Swan, Edward Sr.	Franklin	Burtons	365/26	Early
Swan, Henry	Jackson	Winters Bt.	223/10	Early
Swan, Jonathan	Columbia	Pullins	516/10	Irwin
Swan, Mary	Greene	141	82/5	Rabun
Swan, William	Jones	Samuels	88/11	Habersham
Swann, John	Greene	Jones	201/6	Early
Swann, Joseph	Greene	142nd	387/7	Irwin
Swann, Lany(Wid)	Jefferson	Lamps	316/8	Irwin
Swann, Thomas	Greene	Jones	74/20	Early
Swanson, John	Oglethorpe	Myricks	173/9	Irwin
Swanson, Nathan	Morgan	Alfords	119/5	Appling
Swarringin, Samuel	Camden	Baileys	47/9	Irwin
Sway, George W.	Franklin	Vaughns	511/9	Irwin
Sway, George(RS)	Jackson	Hamiltons Bt.	217/4	Appling
Sway, George(RS)	Jackson	Hamiltons Bt.	228/13	Early
Swearingam, Bowlin	Pulaski	Davis	361/4	Early
Swearingin, Martin	Laurens	S.Smith	230/8	Irwin

NAME	COUNTY	MIL.DIST	LOT/SECT	DREW LAND
Sweet, James	Bulloch	Tilmans	153/7	Appling
Sweet, John	Bulloch	Tilmans	115/28	Early
Sweet, Nathan Jr.	Bulloch	Tilmans	137/14	Irwin
Sweet, Rachael (Wid)	Chatham		111/8	Hall
Swendall, Henry	Greene	Macons	110/11	Early
Swendall, Henry	Greene	Macons	26/9	Irwin
Swift, John	Morgan	Hubbards	310/9	Early
Swilley, Nicholas	Laurens	Jones	242/20	Early
Swilley, Nicholas	Laurens	Jones	26/15	Irwin
Swilley, Satclif (Orph)	Liberty		168/3	Appling
Swillivan, Darcus	Burke	J.Wards	151/2	Irwin
Swillivant, Elijah	Baldwin	Stephens	195/16	Early
Swilly, Samuel	Twiggs	W.Belchers	477/8	Appling
Swilly, Sarah (Wid)	Liberty		352/5	Gwinnett
Swinney, Ellis	Jackson	Hamiltons Bt.	71/18	Early
Swinney, Henry	Lincoln	Millicans	128/5	Gwinnett
Swinney, James	Jackson	Hamiltons Bt.	68/11	Irwin
Swinney, John	Putnam	Mays	285/7	Gwinnett
Swinney, Timothy	Greene	Griers	308/28	Early
Swinney, Wiley	Greene	Greers	428/3	Appling
Swinney, William H.	Clarke	Simmons	203/9	Early
Swinson, Stark	Laurens	Harris	322/20	Early
Swinson, Thomas	Laurens	Watsons	276/10	Early
Swint, John	Columbia	Willingham	461/7	Irwin
Swint, Samuel	Washington	Pools	246/11	Irwin
Swords, James Jr.	Lincoln	Parks	58/9	Irwin
Swords, John	Lincoln	Parks	480/8	Irwin
Sykes, Wm.B.	Putnam	Ectors	69/3	Rabun
Sylvester, Augustin Sr.	Liberty		286/10	Early
Taber, John	Franklin	Akins	257/23	Early
Taber, William	Franklin	Aikens	209/4	Irwin
Taber, William	Franklin	Akins	3/12	Hall
Taber, Zachariah	Twiggs	Browns	334/11	Early
Taber, Zachariah	Twiggs	Browns	348/7	Irwin
Tabor, Charles B.	Laurens	Smiths	237/12	Irwin
Tackwell, Benjamin	Oglethorpe	Brittons	224/9	Appling
Tackwell, Benjamin	Oglethorpe	Galdings	418/9	Irwin
Taff, Elizabeth (Wid)	Wilkinson	Bowings	156/10	Irwin
Taff, James	Wilkinson	Bowings	144/4	Walton
Taff, Richard	Wilkinson	Bowings	183/3	Irwin
Taff, Wm.	Putnam	Slaughters	251/17	Early
Tagart, Joseph	Columbia	Dodsons	445/4	Appling
Tailor, David	Telfair	Wilsons	326/6	Early
Tailor, John	Telfair	Wilsons	26/15	Early
Tailor, Johnathan (Orps)	Telfair	Wilsons	349/5	Gwinnett
Tailor, Joseph	Wilkes	Runnels	111/7	Gwinnett
Tait, James M.	Elbert	Whites	399/7	Irwin
Tait, Sarah	Hancock	Smiths	55/9	Hall
Talbot, Benjamin (RS)	Baldwin	Cousins	56/8	Early
Talbot, Greene	Morgan	Talbots	352/1	Early
Talbot, James	Clarke	Harriss	155/7	Early
Talbot, Mathew Sr.	Wilkes	Bates	52/10	Hall
Talbot, Matthew	Morgan	Farrars	51/7	Irwin
Talbot, Thomas	Wilkes	Bates	332/28	Early
Talbott, Benj. (RS)	Baldwin	Cousins	179/16	Early
Talbott, Mathew Jr.	Wilkes	Bates	299/8	Early
Taliaferro, Benj.	Wilkes	Russels	289/11	Irwin
Tallant, Mary	Bulloch	Edwards	153/6	Irwin
Talley, Littleton	Morgan	Talbots	161/1	Early
Talley, Littleton	Morgan	Talbots	297/4	Appling
Talley, Nathan	Greene	Macons	87/3	Habersham
Talliaferro, John	Wilkinson	Howards	144/12	Habersham
Tally, Larkin	Richmond	Laceys	161/10	Early
Tally, Peyton	Hancock	Scotts	127/3	Appling
Tally, Thomas	Morgan	Talbotts	469/2	Appling
Tamplin, Edward (Orps)	Jones	Samuels	299/27	Early
Tamplin, Fanny (Wid)	Jones	Griffiths	14/10	Early

NAME	COUNTY	MIL.DIST	LOT/SECT	DREW LAN
Tamplin, John	Jones	Griffiths	457/5	Irwin
Tankerslay, Andr.(Orps)	Lincoln	Jones	383/12	Early
Tankersley, Bennett	Hall		252/8	Early
Tankersley, Cassa	Lincoln	Jones	470/8	Irwin
Tankersley, Eliz.(Orps)	Habersham	Garretts	34/15	Irwin
Tankersley, Jos.Jr.	Columbia	Gartrells	407/1	Appling
Tankersley, Joseph Jr.	Columbia	Gartrells	407/1	Appling
Tankersley, Wm.	Clarke	Tredwells	306/7	Gwinnett
Tankersly, Absalom	Lincoln	Jones	67/17	Early
Tanner, Bruwell	Jones	Jefferson	39/10	Early
Tanner, Burwell	Jones	Jefferson	513/12	Irwin
Tanner, Eli	Hall	Tanners	243/10	Irwin
Tanner, Grey	Emanuel	56th	12/7	Gwinnett
Tanner, Joseph	Washington	Wimberlys	385/4	Appling
Tanner, Lewis	Jones	Jefferson	22/5	Gwinnett
Tanner, Mathew	Jackson	Hamiltons	291/8	Irwin
Tanner, Rebecca(Wid)	Washington	Wimberleys	485/8	Irwin
Tanner, William	Liberty		199/28	Early
Tanner, William	Liberty		54/1	Early
Tanner, Wilson	Emanuel	56th	162/12	Habersha
Tanner, Wilson	Emanuel	56th	173/9	Early
Tannton, Nathan	Wilkinson	Smiths	174/10	Irwin
Tansy, William A.	Habersham	Holcombs	37/1	Irwin
Tarabee, Jesse	Greene	Allens	377/12	Irwin
Tarbutton, Wm.	Washington	Jenkinsons	36/4	Habersha
Tarbutton, Wm.	Washington	Jinkinsons	161/18	Early
Tardy, Alexis Jr.	Richmond	122nd	69/14	Irwin
Tarentine, Samuel	Baldwin	Cousins	487/6	Appling
Tarple, Ann	Oglethorpe	Murrays	127/3	Irwin
Tarpley, Archibald	Greene	Macons	293/4	Walton
Tarpley, Elizabeth(Wid)	Emanuel	55	156/9	Hall
Tarpley, John	Oglethorpe	Waters	434/4	Appling
Tarpley, Joseph	Clarke	Simms	445/5	Irwin
Tarpley, Joseph	Clarke	Sims	138/3	Gwinnett
Tarven, Churchwell	Columbia	Shaws	213/19	Early
Tarven, Samuel	Richmond	Palmers	471/5	Irwin
Tarver, Absalom	Hancock	Justices	231/21	Early
Tarver, Absalom	Hancock	Justices	255/8	Appling
Tarver, Andrew	Wilkes	Perrys	504/8	Appling
Tarver, Benjamin	Putnam	H.Kendrick	245/2	Appling
Tarver, Benjamin	Washington	Robison	243/13	Early
Tarver, Elijah	Jones	Phillips	293/8	Appling
Tarver, Jacob	Burke	Torrances	234/7	Irwin
Tarver, Mariah	Burke	Dys	114/2	Appling
Tarver, Martin	Hancock	Mims	336/26	Early
Tarver, Richard	Wilkes	Perrys	124/12	Hall
Tarver, Robert	Washington	Robinson	63/2	Walton
Tarver, Robert	Washington	Robinsons	238/28	Early
Tarver, Sterling	Washington	Floyds	267/8	Appling
Tarvin, Harswell H.	Wilkes	Perrys	70/6	Appling
Tarvin, Ignatius(Orp)	Richmond	Laceys	35/14	Early
Tate, Andrew A.(RS)	Franklin	P.Browns	191/2	Irwin
Tate, Andrew A.(RS)	Franklin	T.Browns	346/10	Irwin
Tate, Andrew(RS)	Franklin	P.Browns	1/9	Early
Tate, Elishaba(Wid)	Elbert	Whites	58/2	Appling
Tate, Enos Sr.	Elbert	Childers	232/9	Appling
Tate, James	Jackson	Rogers	44/17	Early
Tate, John O.	Franklin	Morriss	60/7	Appling
Tate, Permelia(Wid)	Elbert	Whites	114/12	Early
Tate, Samuel	Franklin	P.Browns	184/17	Early
Tate, William	Franklin	T.Browns	137/2	Appling
Tatom, Abel	Lincoln	Tatoms	427/3	Appling
Tatom, James	Putnam	Morlands	24/15	Early
Tatom, Jane(Orps)	Lincoln	Tatoms	106/5	Gwinnett
Tatom, Jesse	Elbert	Tatoms	247/6	Early
Tatom, Nathaniel	Twiggs	W.Belchers	317/4	Appling
Tatom, Nathl.	Twiggs	W.Belchers	66/12	Habersha

NAME	COUNTY	MIL.DIST	LOT/SECT	DREW LAND
Tatom, Silas	Lincoln	Tatoms	273/6	Irwin
Tatom, Thomas	Elbert	Childers	288/10	Irwin
Tatom, Wiley G.	Lincoln	Jones	393/11	Early
Tatterton, Thomas	Chatham		115/11	Early
Tatum, Jesse Sr.	Elbert	Childers	22/14	Early
Tatum, Peter	Early		393/8	Appling
Taunton, Henry	Wilkinson	Smiths	28/6	Irwin
Tayler, Demsey	Emanuel	58th	195/4	Walton
Taylor, Absalom	Greene	Armours	56/1	Early
Taylor, Alexander B.	Greene	141	443/7	Irwin
Taylor, Alexander B.	Greene	141st	78/28	Early
Taylor, Ann (Wid)	Richmond	122nd	103/2	Habersham
Taylor, Avorit	Wilkinson	Brooks	277/7	Gwinnett
Taylor, Burrel	Wilkinson	Kettles	58/6	Habersham
Taylor, Clarke	Oglethorpe	Wises	111/15	Early
Taylor, Daniel	Madison	Bones	371/7	Appling
Taylor, Davenport	Lincoln	Stokes	239/21	Early
Taylor, David	Laurens	Watsons	216/8	Appling
Taylor, Dory	Jasper	Northcuts	388/11	Irwin
Taylor, Edmund	Jackson	Winters	305/27	Early
Taylor, Edmund	Twiggs	Browns	89/8	Early
Taylor, Edmund	Twiggs	Jeffersons	74/10	Habersham
Taylor, Elizabeth A.	Pulaski	Maddox	40/4	Walton
Taylor, Ezekiel	Pulaski	Davis	323/15	Early
Taylor, Frederick (Orps)	Morgan	Leonards	191/8	Early
Taylor, George C.	Franklin	Davis	6/5	Rabun
Taylor, George L.	Jones	Shropshiers	21/15	Irwin
Taylor, George	Habersham	Suttons	1/1	Habersham
Taylor, George	Jones	Hansfords	21/8	Early
Taylor, Grant R.	Madison	Milligans	164/5	Appling
Taylor, Grant R.	Madison	Milligans	356/26	Early
Taylor, Harbort	Pulaski	Rees	17/3	Habersham
Taylor, Henry	Emanuel	55th	93/26	Early
Taylor, Henry	Hancock	Danells	73/8	Irwin
Taylor, Hezeiah	Appling	4th	158/12	Early
Taylor, Hubard	Jones	Wallers	87/19	Early
Taylor, Hugh	Pulaski	Bryans	216/13	Irwin
Taylor, Hugh	Pulaski	Bryans	293/1	Walton
Taylor, Hyram	Franklin	Dodsons	184/13	Early
Taylor, James M.	Pulaski	Johnstons	78/1	Rabun
Taylor, James	Washington	Barges	155/11	Habersham
Taylor, Jeremiah	Franklin	Morris	257/18	Early
Taylor, Jesse B.	Twiggs	Browns	101/2	Rabun
Taylor, Jesse	Putnam	Robertsons	21/9	Irwin
Taylor, Job	Jones	Hansfords	127/16	Irwin
Taylor, John C.	Elbert	Olivers	278/7	Irwin
Taylor, John	Elbert	Gaines	219/3	Walton
Taylor, John	Greene	Fosters	277/9	Appling
Taylor, John	Laurens	Watson	51/6	Appling
Taylor, John	Wilkinson	Brooks	125/3	Appling
Taylor, Joseph	Jones	Harrists	112/7	Appling
Taylor, Joseph	Jones	Harrists	198/1	Irwin
Taylor, Joseph	McIntosh	Hamiltons	53/4	Appling
Taylor, Joshua	Jasper	Northcuts	8/3	Early
Taylor, Lemuel	Jefferson	Abbots	127/2	Irwin
Taylor, Lemuel	Jefferson	Abbots	80/14	Early
Taylor, Moses	Jones	Harrist	25/15	Early
Taylor, Nothias (Orps)	Elbert	Olivers	90/5	Gwinnett
Taylor, Peter	Walton	Greenes	57/3	Habersham
Taylor, Randolph D.	Lincoln	Tatoms	314/3	Early
Taylor, Robert Sr.	Jackson	Dicksons	106/1	Irwin
Taylor, Robert	Burke	M.Wards	272/13	Irwin
Taylor, Robert	Chatham		20/16	Irwin
Taylor, Robert	Chatham		273/27	Early
Taylor, Robert	Franklin	Ashs	147/2	Appling
Taylor, Robert	Franklin	Ashs	57/6	Early
Taylor, Robert	Jones	Kings	461/3	Appling

NAME	COUNTY	MIL.DIST	LOT/SECT	DREW LAND
Taylor, Robert	Jones	Kings	98/4	Habershan
Taylor, Roland	Clarke	Oates	204/16	Early
Taylor, Samuel	Twiggs	Browns	195/14	Early
Taylor, Sarah(Wid)	Jones	Shropshears	131/10	Hall
Taylor, Sarah(Wid)	Pulaski	Johnstons	226/1	Appling
Taylor, Stephen	Greene	143rd	157/27	Early
Taylor, Swepston	Oglethorpe	Wises	152/6	Irwin
Taylor, Theophilus	Franklin	Powells	473/6	Appling
Taylor, Thomas	Greene	143	446/6	Appling
Taylor, Thomas	Twiggs	Evans	61/2	Walton
Taylor, William(Orps)	Baldwin	Taliaferro	185/14	Early
Taylor, William	Franklin	Morris	211/6	Irwin
Taylor, William	Hancock	Scotts	252/1	Early
Taylor, William	Lincoln	Stokes	126/10	Early
Taylor, William	Scriven	Lovetts	142/2	Walton
Taylor, William	Wilkinson	Smiths	25/9	Appling
Taylor, Willis	Elbert	Gaines	363/20	Early
Taylor, Willis	Scriven	Lovetts	176/27	Early
Taylor, Willis	Scriven	Lovetts	420/8	Irwin
Taylor, Wm.	Jones	Samuels	228/1	Early
Taylor, Wm.D.	Baldwin	Stephens	278/4	Early
Taylor, Wm.Jr.	Scriven	Lovetts	16/1	Early
Taylor, Wm.Therby	Jasper	Northcuts	128/7	Gwinnett
Teabeau, Frederick E.	Chatham		74/1	Appling
Teal, John	Pulaski	Johnstons	295/7	Appling
Tealieferro, L.Berry	Oglethorpe	Lees	401/4	Irwin
Teasley, Joshua	Elbert	B.Higginbotham	185/3	Early
Teasley, Levi	Elbert	B.Higginbotham	32/7	Appling
Teasley, Levi	Elbert	B.Higginbotham	464/10	Irwin
Teasley, Silas Sr.	Elbert	B.Higginbotham	184/12	Habershal
Teasley, Silas Sr.	Elbert	B.Higginbotham	196/7	Appling
Teasley, Thomas	Elbert	Dooleys	449/6	Appling
Teasley, Wm.	Elbert	B.Higginbotham	261/5	Appling
Teat, Edwin	Putnam	Morelands	166/6	Gwinnett
Teat, Henry D.	Walton	Echols	382/26	Early
Teatt, John	Putnam	Morelands	170/28	Early
Teatt, Thomas B.	Putnam	Morelands	443/9	Irwin
Teatt, Thomas B.	Putnam	Morelands	58/15	Irwin
Tedder, Solomon	Clarke	Stuarts	88/11	Hall
Tedders, Samuel	Jasper	Northcuts	198/6	Gwinnett
Teel, Jerry	Jasper	Northcuts	134/26	Early
Teel, Lodrick	Jasper	Northcuts	63/23	Early
Teele, Jordan	Jasper	Northcuts	178/1	Walton
Teirce, Mary Green	Chatham		70/14	Irwin
Telfair, Margarett	Wilkes	Gordons	35/22	Early
Telfair, Sarah(Wid)	Chatham		503/11	Irwin
Telghmon, Nancy(Wid)	Clarke	Pentecosts	316/18	Early
Temple, Ann(Wid)	Hancock	Danells	185/7	Early
Temples, James	Chatham		486/9	Irwin
Temples, John	Franklin	T.Browns	108/1	Walton
Templeton, Annis(Wid)	Wilkinson	Lees	415/10	Irwin
Templeton, Greenberry	Morgan	McLendons	154/5	Appling
Templeton, Mathew	Richmond	Palmers	287/8	Appling
Templeton, Milton	Morgan	McClendon	254/5	Appling
Templeton, Zephemiah	Morgan	Hackneys	264/6	Appling
Templin, Charles	Hancock	Evans	75/4	Early
Templin, Reuben	Hancock	Evans	97/27	Early
Tenison, Lemuel	Elbert	Whites	181/16	Early
Tennel, Mary B.(Wid)	Washington	Mannings	27/10	Habershal
Tennell, Francis(Orps)	Washington	Mannings	353/2	Appling
Tennell, John P.	Washington	Wimberlys	205/4	Early
Tennell, Wm.A.	Washington	Mannings	203/28	Early
Tenney, Edward R.(RS)	Chatham		116/11	Hall
Tenney, Edward R.(RS)	Chatham		55/1	Irwin
Tennison, Jesse	Burke	Bells	31/5	Gwinnett
Teppins, Lemuel	Tatnall	Jos.Durrence	364/7	Irwin
Terentine, Wm.	Jones	Griffiths	18/17	Early

NAME	COUNTY	MIL.DIST	LOT/SECT	DREW LAND
Terrell, Bennett	Wilkinson	Kettles	45/1	Rabun
Terrell, Carland B.	Jasper	Baileys	147/15	Irwin
Terrell, Henry M.	Twiggs	R.Belchers	72/2	Appling
Terrell, Henry	Wilkes	Gordans	370/12	Early
Terrell, Hezekiah	Franklin	Hammonds	109/1	Walton
Terrell, James	Franklin	Hammonds	149/5	Irwin
Terrell, Joel H.	Wilkes	Mattox	131/6	Appling
Terrell, John B.	Jefferson	Lamps	47/19	Early
Terrell, John	Wilkes	Willis	35/4	Appling
Terrell, John	Wilkes	Willis	63/22	Early
Terrell, Joseph	Elbert	White	142/13	Habersham
Terrell, Peter B.	Wilkes	Gordons	470/11	Irwin
Terrell, Richmond	Jefferson	Lamps	131/5	Appling
Terrell, Richmond	Liberty		210/3	Walton
Terrell, Richmond	Liberty		334/7	Early
Terrell, Solomon	Putnam	Ectors	65/6	Early
Terrell, Thomas D.	Jefferson	Lamps	196/1	Walton
Terrell, Thomas F.	Hall	Simmonds	156/14	Early
Terrell, Thomas W.	Twiggs	R.Belchers	454/4	Appling
Terrell, Thomas	Wilkes	Gordons	43/4	Habersham
Terrell, Thompson	Franklin	Hammonds	213/28	Early
Terrell, Timothy	Elbert	Childers	480/10	Irwin
Terrell, William	Franklin	Hammonds	80/9	Appling
Terrell, William	Jasper	Lamps	114/17	Early
Terrell, Wm.C.	Elbert	Childers	25/6	Appling
Terry, Champion	Jasper	Centells	411/5	Irwin
Terry, James	Lincoln	Thompsons	328/15	Early
Terry, John	Morgan	Wrights	341/3	Appling
Terry, Joseph	Elbert	Gaines	301/6	Appling
Terry, Nathaniel	Baldwin	Stephens	104/6	Irwin
Terry, Nathaniel	Baldwin	Stephens	393/9	Early
Terry, Thomas	Elbert	R.Christian	269/5	Gwinnett
Terry, Thomas	Putnam	Oslins	366/11	Early
Terry, Thoms	Warren	152	238/13	Early
Terry, William	Warren	Hubbards	524/2	Appling
Thacker, James(Orps)	Clarke	Simms	337/1	Appling
Thacker, Lucretia	Clarke	Simms	309/11	Irwin
Thackston, Nathaniel	Greene	Tuggles	356/6	Appling
Thames, Amos	Twiggs	W.Belchers	224/7	Early
Thames, Wm.	Putnam	Slaughters	235/5	Irwin
Thames, Wm.	Putnam	Slaughters	45/2	Rabun
Tharp, John A.Sr.	Twiggs	Evans	391/7	Early
Tharp, Presley A.Sr.	Pulaski	Rees	2/5	Gwinnett
Tharp, Ralph	Hall	Byrds	88/27	Early
Tharpe, John A.Sr.(RS)	Twiggs	Evans	30/27	Early
Tharpe, John A.Sr.(RS)	Twiggs	Evans	379/8	Appling
Tharpe, Mary(Wid)	Twiggs	Bozemans	493/8	Irwin
Tharpm, Charles	McIntosh	Goulds	127/13	Irwin
Thate, John	Chatham		6/10	Early
Thaxton, Charles	Oglethorpe	Murrays	305/4	Irwin
Thaxton, James	Oglethorpe	Bowls	277/2	Appling
Thaxton, Peter	Oglethorpe	Bowls	235/2	Irwin
Thaxton, Yelverton	Oglethorpe	Murrays	501/9	Irwin
Thaxton, Yelverton	Oglethorpe	Murrays	83/9	Appling
Thearman, John G.	Chatham		177/9	Appling
Therrell, John(Orps)	Bulloch	Knights	11/2	Early
Theweatt, Peterson	Hancock	Danells	268/4	Appling
Thigpen, Cullen	Warren	Travis	175/3	Early
Thigpen, Job	Warren	Travis	111/7	Appling
Thigpen, Melus	Warren	Hutchinsons	515/12	Irwin
Thigpen, William	Emanuel	395th	258/2	Early
Thomas, Absalom	Appling	4th	86/11	Hall
Thomas, Absalom	Burke	McNorrels	32/13	Early
Thomas, Barnabas	Hall		11/7	Gwinnett
Thomas, Benjamin	Jefferson	Flemings	108/5	Irwin
Thomas, Benjamin	Jefferson	Flemmings	184/13	Irwin
Thomas, Bud C.	Chatham		304/14	Early

NAME	COUNTY	MIL.DIST	LOT/SECT	DREW LAND
Thomas, Caleb L.S.R.	Tatnall	J.Durrence	497/5	Irwin
Thomas, Clary(Wid)	McIntosh	Eigles	36/8	Appling
Thomas, Clayborn	Emanuel	53rd	137/15	Irwin
Thomas, Clayton	Emanuel	53	164/2	Habersham
Thomas, Daniel	Laurens	Jones	20/11	Hall
Thomas, David	Baldwin	Taliaferro	385/28	Early
Thomas, David	Jackson	Rogers	98/4	Walton
Thomas, Doctor W.	Hancock	Champions	308/5	Irwin
Thomas, Edward B.	Wilkes	Dents	63/21	Early
Thomas, Edwin	Twiggs	Jeffersons	257/4	Appling
Thomas, Elijah M.	Putnam	Littles	19/3	Walton
Thomas, Eliz.(Wid)	Clarke	Moores	151/3	Irwin
Thomas, Eliz.Mary L.(Orp)	Hall		446/5	Irwin
Thomas, Elliott	Wilkinson	Childs	12/13	Irwin
Thomas, Etheldred	Burke	72	197/11	Irwin
Thomas, Evan(Orps)	Pulaski	Bryans	246/4	Early
Thomas, Ezekiel	Franklin	Ashs	496/2	Appling
Thomas, Gracy	Baldwin	Haws	75/5	Rabun
Thomas, Granville(Orp)	Jackson	Dicksons	258/13	Early
Thomas, Greenberry	Tatnall	Keens	149/14	Early
Thomas, Grigsby E.	Hancock	Thomas	42/16	Irwin
Thomas, Hannah(Wid)	Emanuel	53rd	93/6	Gwinnett
Thomas, Hinchee	Lincoln	Graves	146/8	Irwin
Thomas, Hugh	Laurens	Watsons	204/5	Gwinnett
Thomas, James Sr.	Twiggs	Ellis	136/16	Irwin
Thomas, James	Baldwin	Russels	59/6	Early
Thomas, James	Hancock	Evans	350/19	Early
Thomas, James	Liberty		134/	Irwin
Thomas, James	Liberty		57/8	Irwin
Thomas, James	Oglethorpe	Bridges	120/10	Irwin
Thomas, James	Oglethorpe	Waters	414/4	Appling
Thomas, James	Putnam	Evans	331/1	Appling
Thomas, James	Putnam	Evans	332/5	Gwinnett
Thomas, James	Twiggs	Jeffersons	33/1	Walton
Thomas, John E.	Chatham		395/13	Irwin
Thomas, John G.	Morgan	Farrars	206/11	Early
Thomas, John L.	Laurens	Watsons	96/6	Appling
Thomas, John L.	Richmond	122nd	310/4	Early
Thomas, John Sr.	Putnam	Coopers	80/11	Irwin
Thomas, John(Orps)	Greene	Nelms	43/20	Early
Thomas, John(Orps)	Hancock	Champions	258/11	Irwin
Thomas, John	Bulloch	Knights	160/26	Early
Thomas, John	Bulloch	Knights	245/15	Early
Thomas, John	Jackson	Dicksons	159/2	Habersham
Thomas, John	Jackson	Dicksons	319/5	Irwin
Thomas, John	Jones	Shropshears	293/13	Irwin
Thomas, John	Pulaski	Rees	464/13	Irwin
Thomas, John	Washington	Renfros	164/3	Irwin
Thomas, Jonathan	Putnam	Coopers	50/23	Early
Thomas, Joshua	Pulaski	Rees	184/9	Appling
Thomas, Lewis	Franklin	J.Millers	190/6	Gwinnett
Thomas, Lewis	McIntosh	Eigles	341/12	Early
Thomas, Lewis	Pulaski	Rees	146/6	Early
Thomas, Louis(Orps)	Hancock	Thomas	309/7	Early
Thomas, Madderson	Emanuel	55th	221/5	Irwin
Thomas, Mark S.	Hancock	Thomas	270/14	Early
Thomas, Mary(Orp)	Jackson	Dicksons	258/13	Early
Thomas, Mary(Wid)	Hancock	Thomas	202/10	Early
Thomas, Micajah	Hancock	Lucas	199/9	Appling
Thomas, Michael L.	Warren	Hobsons	57/28	Early
Thomas, Nancy(Wid)	Franklin	Turks	262/5	Early
Thomas, Patrick	McIntosh	Eigles	2/9	Appling
Thomas, Peter	Laurens	Ross	9/1	Appling
Thomas, Phebs(Wid)	Jones	Samuels	300/13	Early
Thomas, Phillip(Orps)	Wilkes	Gordons	146/6	Appling
Thomas, Phillip	Wilkes	Dents	260/8	Appling
Thomas, Polley(Wid)	Clarke	Oates	134/28	Early

NAME	COUNTY	MIL.DIST	LOT/SECT	DREW LAND
Thomas, Rebecca(Wid)	Morgan	Farrars	34/18	Early
Thomas, Richard H.	Pulaski	Johnstons	89/5	Gwinnett
Thomas, Richard	Burke	72nd	102/20	Early
Thomas, Richard	Jones	Griffiths	205/20	Early
Thomas, Richard	Oglethorpe	Holtsclaws	143/11	Early
Thomas, Robert	Burke	Thomas	333/18	Early
Thomas, Robert	Wilkes	Gordons	491/4	Appling
Thomas, Samuel	Bulloch	Jones	31/8	Appling
Thomas, Spencer Jr.	Baldwin	Haws	223/9	Irwin
Thomas, Spencer Sr.	Baldwin	Haws	36/1	Appling
Thomas, Thomas	Lincoln	Tatoms	178/6	Irwin
Thomas, Turner	Franklin	Davis	99/14	Early
Thomas, Ulsby(Orp)	Hall		446/5	Irwin
Thomas, William L.	Wilkinson	Bowings	302/19	Early
Thomas, William W.	Putnam	Littles	3/11	Habersham
Thomas, William	Bulloch	Jones	305/9	Irwin
Thomas, William	Franklin	Ashs	152/15	Irwin
Thomas, William	Oglethorpe	Bridges	197/12	Habersham
Thomas, Wm.	Oglethorpe	Holtsclaws	140/8	Hall
Thomason, John Jr.	Elbert	Smiths	358/19	Early
Thomason, Paul P.	Chatham		171/6	Appling
Thomason, Vincent	Hall	McElhannons	257/26	Early
Thomason, William R.	Walton	Davis	57/7	Appling
Thomason, William(Orps)	Putnam	Robertsons	2/4	Habersham
Thomaston, Wm.R.	Walton	Davis	327/3	Early
Thomerson, Thomas	Jasper	Evans	153/5	Gwinnett
Thomerson, Thomas	Jasper	Evans	91/5	Gwinnett
Thomison, William	Jasper	Evans	376/20	Early
Thomison, William	Jasper	Evans	392/2	Appling
Thomley, Thomas(RS)	Pulaski	Maddox	101/12	Hall
Thomley, Thomas(RS)	Pulaski	Maddox	224/1	Early
Thomley, Thomas(RS)	Pulaski	Maddox	369/5	Irwin
Thompkins, Nicholas	Putnam	Stampers	23/20	Early
Thompson, A.(Orps)	Jasper	Blakes	65/13	Habersham
Thompson, Alexander	Jackson	Meigs	475/3	Appling
Thompson, Alexander	Jackson	Rogers	70/8	Appling
Thompson, Alexander	Twiggs	Ellis	117/2	Habersham
Thompson, Alfred	Laurens	Harris	231/13	Early
Thompson, Andrew	Jackson	Dicksons	84/3	Habersham
Thompson, Ann	Morgan	Talbots	316/2	Appling
Thompson, Anne(Wid)	Jefferson	Bothwell	276/6	Appling
Thompson, Archibald	Bryan	19	213/9	Early
Thompson, Asa	Elbert	Whites	51/15	Irwin
Thompson, Barbary(Wid)	Warren	150th	495/8	Irwin
Thompson, Benjamin	Columbia	Watsons	58/11	Hall
Thompson, Benjamin	Columbia	Watsons	58/11	Hall
Thompson, Benjamin	Hancock	Scotts	143/7	Early
Thompson, Benjamin	Hancock	Scotts	352/7	Irwin
Thompson, Benjamin	Twiggs	Hodges	154/9	Early
Thompson, Buckner(Orps)	Morgan	Wrights	86/9	Early
Thompson, Charity(Wid)	Franklin	Jos.Miller	162/9	Hall
Thompson, Charity	Burke	Hands	383/6	Appling
Thompson, Charles	Twiggs	Ellis	19/12	Hall
Thompson, Christian(Wid)	Elbert	Webbs	240/1	Early
Thompson, Clayton	Lincoln	Thompsons	347/4	Appling
Thompson, Daniel	Twiggs	Browns	12/5	Appling
Thompson, Elijah	Jackson	Rogers	390/1	Appling
Thompson, Elipnes	Burke	M.Wards	297/6	Appling
Thompson, Eliz.(Wid)	Jackson	Hamiltons	50/21	Early
Thompson, Elizabeth A.	Chatham		152/4	Early
Thompson, Ezekiel	Greene	140th	126/7	Irwin
Thompson, George	Twiggs	Ellis	152/2	Early
Thompson, George	Twiggs	Ellis	23/9	Irwin
Thompson, Gideon(Orp)	Jefferson	Bothwells	110/3	Habersham
Thompson, Hannah	Jasper	Blakes	522/2	Appling
Thompson, Henry B.	Twiggs	Ellis	354/13	Early
Thompson, Henry T.	Twiggs	Browns	187/5	Irwin

NAME	COUNTY	MIL.DIST	LOT/SECT	DREW LAND
Thompson, Henry	Baldwin	Doziers	431/6	Irwin
Thompson, Henry	Jackson	Hamiltons	228/9	Appling
Thompson, Isaac	Burke	Hands	419/8	Irwin
Thompson, Isaiah E.	Jones	Phillips	74/10	Irwin
Thompson, Isham	Hancock	Millers	115/3	Habersham
Thompson, Isham	Hancock	Millers	70/16	Irwin
Thompson, Isham	Richmond	120	287/6	Gwinnett
Thompson, James G.	Greene	Garners	32/5	Habersham
Thompson, James	Baldwin	Irwins	127/12	Early
Thompson, James	Baldwin	Irwins	199/7	Appling
Thompson, James	Jackson	Rogers	203/9	Irwin
Thompson, James	Jones	Permenters	84/15	Early
Thompson, James	Madison	Adares	180/9	Irwin
Thompson, James	Madison	Adares	271/21	Early
Thompson, James	Warren	152	72/2	Early
Thompson, Jane(Wid)	Jones	Seals	53/1	Walton
Thompson, Jeremiah	Jasper	Kennedys	278/11	Irwin
Thompson, Jeremiah	Jasper	Kennedys	372/15	Early
Thompson, Jeremiah	Lincoln	Tatoms	220/5	Irwin
Thompson, Jesse(Orp)	Bryan	19th	83/5	Appling
Thompson, Jesse	Richmond	120th	384/4	Early
Thompson, Joel	Elbert	Webbs	149/12	Irwin
Thompson, John D.	Wilkes	Gordons	85/11	Irwin
Thompson, John H.	Twiggs	Ellis	170/7	Appling
Thompson, John Jr.	Twiggs	Ellis	63/6	Appling
Thompson, John McD.(Orp)	Jefferson	Bothwells	110/3	Habersham
Thompson, John N.	Twiggs	Ellis	309/3	Appling
Thompson, John N.	Twiggs	Ellis	370/11	Irwin
Thompson, John(Orp)	Oglethorpe	Barnetts	59/4	Early
Thompson, John(Orps)	Elbert	Webbs	102/3	Irwin
Thompson, John(Orps)	Jackson	Hamiltons	333/14	Early
Thompson, John(Orps)	Lincoln	Parks	76/12	Hall
Thompson, John	Elbert	Webbs	82/11	Irwin
Thompson, John	Jackson	Hamiltons	312/7	Gwinnett
Thompson, John	Jasper	Reids	140/8	Appling
Thompson, John	Morgan	Loyds	336/4	Walton
Thompson, John	Oglethorpe	Myricks	458/6	Appling
Thompson, John	Scriven	36th	193/9	Appling
Thompson, John	Twiggs	Hodges	269/9	Irwin
Thompson, John	Wilkinson	Lees	29/3	Appling
Thompson, Joseph	Hall	Buffington	98/2	Walton
Thompson, Joseph	Jackson	Hamiltons	278/9	Irwin
Thompson, Joseph	Jasper	Hays	91/1	Irwin
Thompson, Laben	Burke	M.Wards	251/11	Irwin
Thompson, Labon(Orps)	Laurens	Kinchens	208/26	Early
Thompson, Lesley	Chatham		363/18	Early
Thompson, Louisa(Orp)	Bryan	19th	83/5	Appling
Thompson, Moses	Burke	Hands	259/17	Early
Thompson, Nathaniel Jr.	Warren	152nd	48/14	Irwin
Thompson, Nelson	Twiggs	R.Belchers	223/6	Early
Thompson, Rebecca(Wid)	Jefferson	Bothwells	303/8	Irwin
Thompson, Reef(Orps)	Jones	Seals	131/2	Rabun
Thompson, Richard	Clarke	Starnes	236/5	Irwin
Thompson, Richard	Hancock	Millers	141/2	Habersham
Thompson, Richard	Jackson	Burns	359/3	Early
Thompson, Richard	Jackson	Dicksons	260/9	Irwin
Thompson, Robert	Washington	Pools	246/8	Appling
Thompson, Robert	Washington	Pools	283/4	Irwin
Thompson, Salvadors	Jackson	Hamiltons	167/13	Irwin
Thompson, Samuel	Greene	Armers	521/5	Appling
Thompson, Samuel	Jackson	Winters	281/4	Early
Thompson, Samuel	Oglethorpe	Murrays	289/13	Early
Thompson, Samuel	Oglethorpe	Waters	510/10	Irwin
Thompson, Sarah(Orp)	Warren	150	23/3	Irwin
Thompson, Shadrack	Jefferson	Waldens	312/5	Early
Thompson, Sherod	Jackson	Winters	298/19	Early
Thompson, Silas	Franklin	Jos.Millers	193/9	Early

NAME	COUNTY	MIL.DIST	LOT/SECT	DREW LAND
Thompson, Solomon(Orps)	Wilkinson	Kettles	437/6	Irwin
Thompson, Solomon	Wilkinson	Smiths	335/4	Walton
Thompson, Stephen	Warren	153rd	83/5	Gwinnett
Thompson, Thomas B.	Bryan	19th	404/28	Early
Thompson, Thomas P.	Columbia	J.Morriss	269/8	Irwin
Thompson, Thomas P.	Greene	Armers	380/7	Early
Thompson, Wiley	Elbert	G.Higginbotham	50/4	Walton
Thompson, William C.	Clarke	Pentecosts	142/7	Early
Thompson, William H.	Chatham		42/11	Early
Thompson, William(RS)	Jackson	Hamiltons	352/9	Irwin
Thompson, William	Baldwin	Irwins	245/8	Appling
Thompson, William	Baldwin	Irwins	51/7	Appling
Thompson, William	Burke	M.Wards	61/6	Habersham
Thompson, William	Columbia	Willingham	75/14	Early
Thompson, William	Jackson	Winters	155/7	Early
Thompson, William	Jefferson	Waldens	264/4	Appling
Thompson, William	Oglethorpe	Myricks	242/3	Walton
Thompson, William	Washington	Danells	142/8	Early
Thompson, Wm.	Elbert	Webbs	528/8	Appling
Thompson, Wm.	Lincoln	Graves	60/1	Rabun
Thompson, Wm.C.	Clarke	Pentecosts	18/21	Early
Thompson, Zachariah	Jackson	Hamiltons	97/7	Appling
Thompson, Zechariah	Jackson	Hamiltons	474/13	Irwin
Thomson, Daniel	Burke	Hands	358/6	Early
Thomson, Daniel	Burke	Hands	359/5	Appling
Thomson, Marender	Warren	150	368/7	Early
Thomson, Richard	Jackson	Barnes	219/10	Habersham
Thomson, Samuel	Greene	Nelms	448/5	Appling
Thomson, William	Emanuel	59th	31/23	Early
Thorn, Mary Ann	Laurens	Ross	65/7	Gwinnett
Thorn, Sophia	Scriven	36	266/3	Irwin
Thorn, William	Scriven		118/14	Early
Thornton, Benjamin	Elbert	Higginbotham	85/5	Early
Thornton, David	Oglethorpe	Wises	316/9	Appling
Thornton, Dozier	Elbert	Maxwells	277/5	Appling
Thornton, Dozier	Elbert	Smiths	122/15	Irwin
Thornton, Dozier	Elbert	Smiths	33/11	Habersham
Thornton, Elijah	Franklin	Haynes	59/2	Irwin
Thornton, Evans	Elbert	Smiths	1/13	Irwin
Thornton, Evans	Elbert	Smiths	131/2	Walton
Thornton, Ezekiel	Bulloch	Knight	472/6	Appling
Thornton, Ezekiel	Bulloch	Knights	133/14	Early
Thornton, Harrison L.	Oglethorpe	M.Cowns	133/8	Early
Thornton, Henry	Baldwin	Marshalls	373/1	Appling
Thornton, Herod Jr.	Oglethorpe	Goolsby	36/5	Gwinnett
Thornton, Hudson A.	Elbert	Smiths	132/13	Habersham
Thornton, Isham	Hancock	Herberts	347/4	Walton
Thornton, James	Hancock	Loyds	29/23	Early
Thornton, James	Jones	Mullens	33/2	Irwin
Thornton, Jeremiah	Elbert	Smiths	44/11	Habersham
Thornton, John	Chatham		404/3	Appling
Thornton, John	Elbert	Ruchers	184/2	Appling
Thornton, John	Hancock	Herberts	109/6	Irwin
Thornton, John	Hancock	Herberts	301/3	Appling
Thornton, John	Wilkes	Hollidays	515/7	Appling
Thornton, Jourdan	Jasper	Posts	74/2	Early
Thornton, Lindsey	Jones	Mullins	146/11	Irwin
Thornton, Lucy(Wid)	Jefferson	Walden	578/2	Appling
Thornton, Middleton	Elbert	Smiths	32/2	Appling
Thornton, Moses	Burke	Torrances	88/12	Habersham
Thornton, Patience(Wid)	Tatnall	Overstreets	124/9	Irwin
Thornton, Penelope	Jackson	Winters	141/16	Irwin
Thornton, Rachel	Wilkes	Kilgores	231/10	Early
Thornton, Rebecca(Wid)	Jones	Griffiths	57/1	Habersham
Thornton, Reddick	Bulloch	Knights	147/5	Gwinnett
Thornton, Reddick	Bulloch	Knights	31/5	Habersham
Thornton, Redmon	Greene	140th	474/6	Irwin

NAME	COUNTY	MIL.DIST	LOT/SECT	DREW LAN
Thornton, Reuben	Elbert	B.Higginbotham	192/5	Gwinnett
Thornton, Reuben	Greene	Allens	224/2	Early
Thornton, Richard(Orps)	Oglethorpe	Goolsbys	103/1	Appling
Thornton, Samuel	Tatnall	Overstreets	223/11	Early
Thornton, Sherod Jr.	Oglethorpe	Goolsbys	423/3	Appling
Thornton, Solomon(Orps)	Jones	Griffith	159/11	Habersha
Thornton, Solomon(Orps)	Putnam	Mays	5/9	Hall
Thornton, Solomon	Jasper	Bartletts	140/11	Early
Thornton, Thomas Sr.	Walton	Sentells	383/9	Early
Thornton, Thomas Sr.	Walton	Sentells	44/11	Irwin
Thornton, Thomas(S/Benj.)	Elbert	B.Higginbotham	313/12	Early
Thornton, Tilphy	Burke	Bells	88/6	Gwinnett
Thornton, William	Elbert	B.Higginbotham	200/8	Irwin
Thornton, William	Jasper	Kennedys	129/10	Irwin
Thornton, Wm.Jr.	Jasper	Bartletts	242/5	Gwinnett
Thornton, Young	Jasper	Kennedys	47/3	Irwin
Thorp, Henry C.	Chatham		4/2	Appling
Thorpes, Joseph(Orps)	Hancock	Edwards	271/28	Early
Thower, Thomas	Gwinnett	Hamiltons	301/16	Early
Thrash, Jacob Jr.	Putnam	Buckners	176/2	Rabun
Thrash, John	Putnam	Oslins	110/5	Rabun
Thrash, Joseph	Putnam	Oslins	132/7	Irwin
Thrash, Martin	Jasper	Blakes	286/26	Early
Thrasher, David	Morgan	Wrights	21/15	Early
Thrasher, George Jr.	Franklin	Hammonds	306/10	Early
Thrasher, George Sr.	Franklin	Hammonds	143/10	Early
Thrasher, Isaac(Orps)	Clarke	Merriwethers	57/4	Habersha
Thrasher, Isaac	Clarke	Simms	42/10	Early
Thrasher, John Jr.	Clarke	Simms	287/19	Early
Thrasher, Pinkney	Clarke	Jacks	158/2	Early
Thrasher, Tillitha(Wid)	Clarke	Merewethers	385/7	Early
Thrasher, William	Franklin	Hammonds	235/4	Walton
Thrasher, Wm.	Franklin	Hammonds	375/15	Early
Threadcraft, Seth G.	Effingham		200/8	Early
Threasher, Thomas	Franklin	Vaughns	297/7	Gwinnett
Threewits, James(Orps)	Jefferson	Lamps	43/2	Habersha
Thrifit, Robert T.	Washington	Cummins	166/21	Early
Thrower, Clement	McIntosh	Hamiltons	322/13	Irwin
Thrower, Clement	McIntosh	Hamiltons	77/4	Irwin
Thrower, Margaret	Putnam	Buckners	232/12	Irwin
Thrush, Isaac	Putnam	Oslins	345/8	Appling
Thud, George	Wilkes	Gordans	529/6	Irwin
Thurman, John(Little)	Wilkes	Russels	44/3	Appling
Thurman, Micajah	Walton	Echols	58/13	Irwin
Thurman, Robert	Jackson	Rogers	246/17	Early
Thurman, Thos.R.(Orp)	Wilkes	Burks	418/26	Early
Thurmand, Phillip	Jasper	Smiths	45/12	Habersha
Thurmon, William(Orps)	Jasper	Northcuts	33/10	Irwin
Thurmon, William	Jackson	Winters	316/7	Gwinnett
Thurmond, Benj.(Orps)	Oglethorpe	Barnetts	193/12	Irwin
Thurmond, Harris F.	Morgan	Farrars	164/4	Irwin
Thurmond, Harrson	Jackson	Hamiltons	313/16	Early
Thurmond, John	Morgan	Farrars	110/8	Appling
Thurmond, John	Morgan	Selmons	273/5	Early
Thurmond, William	Jackson	Hamiltons	243/12	Irwin
Thurmond, William	Wilkes	Russels	172/3	Early
Thurmond, Willis	Jackson	Hamilton	136/21	Early
Thurmond, Wm.	Jackson	Hamiltons	453/11	Irwin
Thweatt, John	Hancock	Thomas	301/11	Early
Thweatt, Kinchen P.	Jones	Kings	13/12	Hall
Thweatt, Susannah(Wid)	Jones	Samuels	388/6	Appling
Thweatt, Wm.	Hancock	Edwards	201/3	Walton
Tice, James	Warren	152	358/26	Early
Tickle, John	Clarke	Treadwells	84/10	Habersha
Tickle, John	Clarke	Tredwells	53/1	Irwin
Tidd, Joseph	Jones	Buckhalters	185/4	Irwin
Tidol, Bailey	Washington	Barges	106/12	Irwin

NAME	COUNTY	MIL.DIST	LOT/SECT	DREW LAND
Tidwell, Isaiah	Putnam	J.Kendricks	181/2	Rabun
Tidwell, John	Putnam	Ectors	87/4	Habersham
Tidwell, Mary(Wid)	Wilkinson	Brooks	33/7	Irwin
Tidwell, Miner	Jones	Seals	145/4	Walton
Tidwell, Miner	Jones	Seals	209/12	Early
Tidwell, Wiley	Jones	Seals	454/5	Appling
Tiller, John	Oglethorpe	Davenports	38/28	Early
Tiller, Maitin	Oglethorpe	Davenports	1/1	Walton
Tiller, Randol	Oglethorpe	Davenports	397/3	Appling
Tillery, Alford	Putnam	Robertsons	130/8	Hall
Tillery, Alford	Putnam	Robinsons	273/5	Gwinnett
Tillery, Henry(Orps)	Putnam	Robertsons	223/2	Early
Tillery, Hudson	Montgomery		245/5	Appling
Tillery, John	Jasper	Bentleys	395/12	Irwin
Tillery, John	Jasper	Bentleys	84/4	Appling
Tillery, Ruth(Wid)	Putnam	Robinson	336/5	Early
Tilley, William Sr.	Richmond	Palmers	19/6	Gwinnett
Tilley, William Sr.	Richmond	Palmers	31/3	Appling
Tillman, Dixon	Jackson	Winters	522/6	Appling
Tillman, Green B.	McIntosh	Jinkins	135/5	Appling
Tillman, Littleberry(Op)	Hancock	Thomas	410/1	Early
Tilly, Isaac	Burke	Bells	290/11	Irwin
Tilly, James Jr.	Burke	Bells	145/16	Irwin
Tilly, John	Richmond	Palmers	109/11	Habersham
Tilly, William	Burke	Bells	333/6	Appling
Tilman, Aaron	Clarke	Applings	234/13	Irwin
Tilman, James	Tatnall	Thorps	274/6	Early
Tilman, John	Bulloch	Tilmans	223/2	Irwin
Tilman, John	Bulloch	Tilmans	233/1	Appling
Tilman, Joseph	Bulloch	Tilmans	12/9	Appling
Tilman, Mary(Wid)	Tatnall	Josh.Durrence	129/3	Habersham
Tilman, Penelope	Jasper	Kennedys	275/16	Early
Tilman, Richard(Orps)	Jasper	Kennedys	277/4	Early
Tilmon, Asa	Putnam	Kindrick	35/2	Early
Timmon, Elizabeth(Wid)	Appling	2nd	35/16	Irwin
Timmons, John	Pulaski	Johnstons	154/2	Appling
Timmons, Noble	Franklin	P.Browns	184/5	Irwin
Timmons, Stephen H.	Chatham		361/9	Early
Timmons, William	Appling	2nd	168/10	Irwin
Timmons, William	Jasper	Blakes	345/6	Early
Timmons, William	McIntosh	Goulds	29/7	Appling
Tindal, Alexander	Washington	Daniells	57/1	Appling
Tindal, Joshua(RS)	Washington	Wimberlys	110/9	Early
Tindal, Samuel	Morgan	Farrars	246/7	Appling
Tindale, James Sr.	Burke	J.Wards	175/13	Early
Tindale, Wiley	Burke	Bells	239/20	Early
Tindall, Joshua(RS)	Washington	Wimberlys	445/6	Irwin
Tindall, Richard	Scriven	Roberts	162/10	Hall
Tindall, Samuel	Morgan	Farrars	182/4	Irwin
Tindall, Thomas B.(Orps)	Wilkes		17/6	Irwin
Tindley, Sarah	Glynn		203/8	Appling
Tiner, Gideon	Effingham		134/3	Appling
Tiner, Gideon	Effingham		19/8	Appling
Tiner, Jackson	Jones	Greens	504/3	Appling
Tingle, Solomon(Orps)	Jasper	McLendon	255/9	Early
Tinley, David	Richmond	Winters	126/19	Early
Tinley, David	Richmond	Winters	320/11	Early
Tinley, John Jr.	Richmond	Winters	109/6	Gwinnett
Tinley, Phillip	Richmond	Winters	153/2	Irwin
Tinley, Thomas	Wilkinson	Smiths	130/19	Early
Tinney, William	Wilkinson	Howards	127/12	Irwin
Tinny, Isaac	Wilkinson	Howards	305/19	Early
Tinny, William(Orps)	Wilkinson	Howards	38/3	Irwin
Tinny, William	Wilkinson	Howards	5/2	Early
Tinor, Ephraim	Effingham		134/2	Appling
Tinsley, Abram	Columbia	Shaws	72/3	Irwin
Tinsley, Abram	Columbia	Shaws	72/3	Irwin

NAME	COUNTY	MIL.DIST	LOT/SECT	DREW LAND
Tinsley, John	Columbia	J.Morris	309/10	Irwin
Tinsley, John	Columbia	Ob.Morris	390/6	Irwin
Tinsley, John	Pulaski	Senterfeits	77/15	Early
Tiot, Charles	Chatham		374/3	Early
Tipper, James	Oglethorpe	Davenports	288/8	Irwin
Tipper, Wilie	Oglethorpe	Barnetts	514/5	Irwin
Tippets, William	Greene	Harvills	268/6	Early
Tippett, Frederick	Twiggs	Hodges	11/7	Irwin
Tippins, Dennis	Gwinnett	Hamiltons	145/11	Early
Tippins, John W.	Tatnall	J.Durrences	176/11	Early
Tippins, Lemuel	Tatnall	J.Durrences	471/7	Appling
Tippins, Phillip	Tatnall	J.Durrences	115/6	Early
Tippins, William	Tatnall	Jos.Durrence	8/6	Irwin
Tippitt, Susan	Greene	142nd	80/5	Irwin
Tippron, Emanuel	Effingham		108/11	Hall
Tipton, Jacob	Burke	Bells	234/6	Appling
Tipton, Reuben	Burke	J.Wards	387/12	Irwin
Tipton, Reuben	Burke	J.Wards	41/12	Irwin
Tisdal, Haley	Washington	Daniels	344/8	Appling
Tisdol, Hailey	Washington	Barges	409/1	Early
Tison, Aaron	Putnam	Slaughters	313/21	Early
Tison, Aron	Putnam	Slaughters	6/4	Rabun
Tison, Cornelius	Laurens	Kinchens	108/2	Early
Tison, Cornelius	Laurens	Kinchens	113/2	Appling
Tison, Eliz.(Wid)	Laurens	Kinchens	42/14	Early
Tison, Jacob	Twiggs	Ellis	104/7	Early
Tison, James S.	Jones	Seals	326/17	Early
Tison, James(RS)	Effingham		113/7	Irwin
Tison, Luther	Effingham		290/6	Irwin
Tison, Moses Jr.	Laurens	Ross	446/8	Appling
Tison, Moses Sr.	Laurens	Ross	252/13	Irwin
Tittle, John	Elbert	Olivers	48/7	Appling
Toadvines, Wm.(Orps)	Jones	Phillips	429/15	Early
Tod, Eliz.(Wid)	Warren	154th	144/11	Early
Tod, Job	Warren	151	310/5	Early
Tod, Job	Warren	151	94/8	Irwin
Todd, Ann W.	Greene	143rd	277/5	Gwinnett
Todd, Archibald	Jackson	Hamiltons	209/10	Early
Todd, James	Burke	Thomas	32/8	Early
Todd, James	Chatham		129/2	Rabun
Todd, James	Jackson	Dicksons	123/4	Appling
Todd, James	Wilkinson	Lees	38/6	Appling
Todd, John	Putnam	Coopers	219/14	Early
Todd, Joseph	Wilkes	Gordons	253/9	Appling
Todd, William	Jackson	Hamiltons	239/27	Early
Todd, William	Jackson	Hamiltons	52/11	Early
Tolason, Eli	Hall	Byrds	171/16	Irwin
Tolason, Eli	Hall	Byrds	261/5	Gwinnett
Tolbert, John	Jones	Greens	20/9	Irwin
Tolbert, Westley	Jackson	Rogers	93/13	Early
Tolbert, William	Clarke	Harris	31/9	Appling
Tolbert, William	Clarke	Harris	354/7	Early
Tole, James	Wilkes	Burks	257/11	Irwin
Tole, Prissilla	Wilkes	Burks	282/7	Appling
Tole, Rebekah(Orp)	Wilkes	Burkes	236/1	Appling
Toler, Robert(Orps)	Twiggs	W.Belchers	101/9	Early
Toller, Daniel	Burke	M.Wards	335/7	Early
Tomkins, John Jr.	Jefferson	Fountains	96/13	Early
Tomkins, John Sr.	Jefferson	Fountains	220/7	Early
Tomkins, Rukins	Washington	Floyds	186/11	Irwin
Tomkins, Rukins	Washington	Floyds	363/9	Irwin
Tomkins, Samuel	Washington	Floyds	11/18	Early
Tomley, Mitchell	Pulaski	Maddox	310/4	Appling
Tomlin, Owen	Burke	McNorrills	13/8	Hall
Tomlinson, Aaron	Jefferson	Cowarts	307/10	Early
Tomlinson, Daniel	Morgan	McClendons	148/11	Habersham
Tomlinson, John	Appling	4th	217/13	Irwin

NAME	COUNTY	MIL.DIST	LOT/SECT	DREW LAND
Tomlinson, John	Putnam	Slaughters	111/19	Early
Tomlinson, Wm.	Appling	4th	366/19	Early
Tommey, John W.	Putnam	Stampers	264/5	Gwinnett
Tompkins, Donald	Camden	Longs	255/23	Early
Tompkins, Giles	Putnam	Stampers	257/3	Irwin
Tompkins, John	Baldwin	Irwins	53/5	Irwin
Tompkins, John	Baldwin	Irwins	83/11	Habersham
Toney, Headrick	Franklin	Boswells	321/7	Early
Toney, John Sr.	Franklin	Ashs	271/11	Early
Tooke, Arthur	Pulaski	Johnstons	387/7	Appling
Tooke, Starling	Pulaski	Davis	444/2	Appling
Tookes, William(Orps)	Pulaski	Johnsons	34/10	Irwin
Tookes, William(Orps)	Pulaski	Johnsons	342/9	Early
Tool, Boland	Jones	Samuels	134/10	Irwin
Tool, James	Jones	Phillips	55/27	Early
Tool, James	Richmond	Burtons	42/7	Irwin
Tool, John(Orps)	Washington	Jinkinsons	432/6	Irwin
Toole, James Jr.	Columbia	Pullins	298/11	Irwin
Toole, Jane(Wid)	Jones	Samuels	141/15	Irwin
Toombs, Catharine(Wid)	Wilkes	Runnels	289/7	Early
Toombs, Robert(Orps)	Wilkes	Runnels	127/8	Appling
Tootle, Wiley	Appling	5th	12/5	Habersham
Torbert, James	Oglethorpe	Wises	103/6	Appling
Torrance, John	Warren	Griers	177/2	Early
Torrence, Benj.	Warren	Griers	30/22	Early
Torrence, Setpemus	Warren	Griers	327/5	Appling
Torrens, John	Jackson	Hamiltons	7/9	Hall
Tosia, Mary	Chatham		97/1	Rabun
Totly, Abner(Orps)	Greene	142	8/5	Gwinnett
Touchstone, Experience	Appling	5	333/13	Early
Towers, Benjamin	Greene	Garners	249/14	Early
Towers, Benjamin	Greene	Garners	89/2	Rabun
Towls, James	Bryan	19th	162/7	Early
Towls, James	Bryan	19th	97/11	Early
Town, Bartlett(Orps)	Jasper	Bartletts	236/3	Irwin
Towns, Drury	Greene	Jones	14/8	Hall
Towns, Drury	Greene	Jones	251/13	Early
Towns, Hawkey	Wilkes	Mattox	54/18	Early
Towns, James	Madison	Willifords	191/10	Irwin
Towns, John G.	Jasper	Bartlets	244/9	Appling
Towns, John G.	Jasper	Bartletts	483/11	Irwin
Towns, Rebecca(Wid)	Wilkes	Mattox	397/21	Early
Towns, Williams	Jasper	Blakes	86/11	Early
Townsend, Jesse	Jackson	Hamiltons	225/5	Early
Townsend, John	Greene	Whelis	185/27	Early
Townsend, John	Jackson	Hamiltons	205/7	Appling
Townsend, John	Jones	Samuels	364/4	Appling
Townsend, Solomon	Jackson	Hamiltons	177/15	Irwin
Townsend, Thomas Jr.	Franklin	Morris	84/12	Early
Townsend, Thomas Sr.	Franklin	Morris	462/5	Appling
Townsley, Job	Jefferson	Abbots	295/14	Early
Townsley, Lott S.	Washington	Floyds	292/13	Early
Towson, Asa	McIntosh	Eigles	174/2	Appling
Tradwell, Adoniah	Richmond	Laceys	231/7	Irwin
Tramble, William	Burke	71st	166/21	Early
Tramel, Daniel(Orps)	Jasper	Posts	117/9	Early
Tramel, Frances M.	Clarke	Mitchels	24/6	Habersham
Trammel, David	Lincoln	Jones	16/28	Early
Trammel, Fanny	Jasper	Posts	284/5	Gwinnett
Trammel, Peter	Lincoln	Walkers	250/17	Early
Trammel, Thomas Sr.	Lincoln	Tatoms	144/16	Irwin
Trammel, Thomas Sr.	Lincoln	Tatoms	93/15	Irwin
Trammel, Thomas W.	Lincoln	Tatoms	102/6	Appling
Trammel, William(RS)	Elbert	Webbs	227/4	Irwin
Trammel, Woodward	Wilkes	Runnels	280/9	Early
Trammell, David	Laurens	Griffith	8/15	Early
Trammell, Drakford	Clarke	Moores	54/21	Early

NAME	COUNTY	MIL.DIST	LOT/SECT	DREW LAND
Trammell, Jared(Orps)	Laurens	Griffins	257/1	Early
Trammell, John	Walton	Davis	83/3	Early
Trammell, Thomas Sr.	Lincoln	Tatoms	113/5	Early
Trammell, Wm.(RS)	Elbert	Webbs	282/1	Early
Trapnell, Elijah	Burke	Spiveys	6/13	Irwin
Trapp, Benjamin	Jones	Rossers	171/6	Early
Trapp, John L.	Jackson	Haggards	139/12	Hall
Trapp, Timothy	Baldwin	Irwins	112/18	Early
Trapp, Timothy	Baldwin	Irwins	7/4	Appling
Trapp, William	Jones	Samuels	273/3	Appling
Trappnett, Archibald(Orps)	Burke	J.Wards	123/13	Habersham
Travice, Asa(Orps)	Washington	Mannings	31/18	Early
Travis, Amos	Warren	151st	13/10	Early
Travis, Simeon	Warren	151	9/8	Early
Travis, Whitmill	Warren	151	107/3	Appling
Travis, Whitmill	Warren	151	117/11	Habersham
Travis, William	Morgan	Hackneys	77/10	Hall
Trawick, Henry	Hancock	Millers	132/2	Irwin
Trawick, Henry	Hancock	Millers	318/8	Appling
Trawick, James	Washington	Peabodys	30/5	Habersham
Trawick, Jesse(Orps)	Washington	Peabodys	235/5	Gwinnett
Trayler, Edward	Oglethorpe	Wise	224/4	Early
Traylor, John	Jasper	Bentleys	265/7	Irwin
Traylor, Richard	Greene	Whelises	387/5	Appling
Traylor, Thomas H.	Jasper	Smiths	129/9	Hall
Traylor, Wiley	Jasper	Blakes	224/9	Irwin
Traywick, Anne	Hancock	Millers	345/6	Irwin
Traywick, Frances M.	Hancock	Justice	335/5	Early
Traywick, Francis M.	Hancock	Justices	409/8	Irwin
Treadaway, Elias	Jackson	Dicksons	34/16	Irwin
Treadway, Thomas	Hall		203/4	Irwin
Treadway, Thomas	Hall		244/14	Early
Treadwell, David	Jasper	Centells	176/28	Early
Treble, Benjamin	Oglethorpe	Barnetts	119/1	Appling
Treble, Benjamin	Oglethorpe	Barnetts	137/3	Appling
Tredaway, Elias	Jackson	Dickson	136/10	Early
Tredwell, Greene(Orp)	Jasper	Centells	237/7	Irwin
Tredwell, Hardy	Clarke	Tredwells	477/4	Appling
Tredwell, Jacob	Clarke	Tredwells	325/9	Appling
Tredwell, Mary(Orp)	Richmond	Laceys	23/2	Rabun
Tredwell, Sarah(Orp)	Jasper	Centells	237/7	Irwin
Treemle, William	Morgan	Loyds	185/5	Early
Tremble, James Sr.	Jefferson	Mathews	43/13	Early
Tremble, John H.	Jasper	Bentleys	176/13	Irwin
Tremble, Moses	Morgan	Loyds	21/20	Early
Trent, James	Jones	Permenters	144/14	Early
Trenthams, Levy(Orp)	Madison	Milligans	442/7	Appling
Tretwell, James	Jasper	Bentleys	320/9	Appling
Tribble, Martha(Wid)	Wilkinson	Howards	3/9	Hall
Trice, Elisha	Jones	Samuels	273/3	Appling
Trice, William	Jones	Griffith	287/2	Early
Tricker, William	Richmond	Laceys	3/13	Early
Tridwell, William	Franklin	Harriss	5/7	Gwinnett
Trigg, John	Franklin	Hammonds	513/2	Appling
Trimble, John H.	Jasper	Bentleys	387/9	Irwin
Trimble, Martha(Wid)	Morgan	Townsends	109/12	Habersham
Trimble, Moses	Franklin	Harris	153/26	Early
Trimble, Moses	Morgan	Loyds	2/18	Early
Trimble, William	Morgan	Loyds	269/5	Early
Triplett, William	Tatnall	Tharps	486/10	Irwin
Tripp, Henry Jr.	Hancock	Danells	379/13	Early
Tripplett, Daniel(Orps)	Baldwin	Irwins	346/13	Irwin
Tripps, Henry	Hancock	Edwards	195/6	Early
Trot, Charles	Chatham		393/3	Appling
Trotman, Blount	Washington	Robinson	283/2	Appling
Trotman, Cullin	Washington	Robinsons	14/4	Walton
Trouchelutt, Joseph	Chatham		225/3	Irwin

NAME	COUNTY	MIL.DIST	LOT/SECT	DREW LAND
Troup, Robert L.	Montgomery	Alstons	187/8	Appling
Trout, George	Jackson	Hamiltons	38/3	Habersham
Trout, Tilman	Jackson	Rodgers	467/11	Irwin
Troutman, Henry	Camden	Baileys	482/5	Irwin
Troutman, John	Baldwin	Irwins	514/6	Appling
Troutman, John	Baldwin	Irwins	605/2	Appling
Trueluck, Sutton	Pulaski	Bryants	135/13	Irwin
Truesdell, Nathaniel	Richmond	398th	365/9	Irwin
Truet, Thomas	Wilkes	Ogletrees	339/13	Early
Truit, Nathan	Wilkes	Runnels	379/26	Early
Trull, James	Pulaski	Maddox	509/5	Irwin
Truman, Ann	Greene	Ragans	106/11	Early
Trussel, John	Scriven	180th	340/5	Early
Tuchstone, Daniel(Orps)	Washington	Barges	309/13	Irwin
Tuck, Josiah	Oglethorpe	Rowlands	55/3	Walton
Tucker, Andrew	Camden	33rd	153/4	Early
Tucker, Andrew	Camden	33rd	506/3	Appling
Tucker, Benjamin	Franklin	Hammonds	121/8	Appling
Tucker, Benjamin	Franklin	Hammonds	63/11	Hall
Tucker, Dean	Oglethorpe	Lees	379/2	Appling
Tucker, Elijah	Camden	33rd	104/9	Early
Tucker, Frederick(Orp)	Hancock	Lucas	295/10	Irwin
Tucker, Henry(Orp)	Chatham		350/27	Early
Tucker, Jacob	Hancock	Danells	324/9	Irwin
Tucker, Jeremiah	Jasper	Hays	36/6	Habersham
Tucker, John & Sarah(Orps)	Chatham		350/27	Early
Tucker, John	Jasper	Hays	353/16	Early
Tucker, John	Laurens	Kinchens	133/7	Appling
Tucker, John	Laurens	Kinchens	303/10	Irwin
Tucker, John	Oglethorpe	Brittons	53/18	Early
Tucker, Joseph	Baldwin	Taliaferro	312/12	Early
Tucker, Oran	Twiggs	Bozemans	76/5	Appling
Tucker, Pointun	Jasper	Hays	75/9	Hall
Tucker, Reuben	Elbert	Ruchers	116/8	Irwin
Tucker, Robert	Columbia	Watsons	288/6	Gwinnett
Tucker, Robert	Columbia	Watsons	333/28	Early
Tucker, Robert	Columbia	Watsons	333/28	Early
Tucker, Robert	Jasper	Evans	150/7	Gwinnett
Tucker, Robert	Jasper	Evans	385/17	Early
Tucker, Tarpley	Oglethorpe	Lees	230/12	Early
Tucker, Tarpley	Oglethorpe	Lees	80/28	Early
Tucker, Thomas	Camden	33	325/4	Walton
Tucker, Thomas	Jasper	Evans	53/5	Early
Tucker, Thomas	Jasper	Kennedys	381/5	Early
Tucker, Timothy	Hancock	Coopers	503/6	Appling
Tucker, William	Franklin	R.Browns	83/6	Appling
Tucker, William	Greene	Fosters	144/15	Early
Tucker, William	Greene	Fosters	325/28	Early
Tucker, Woodward	Emanuel	53	260/6	Irwin
Tuder, John	Morgan	Farrars	232/5	Early
Tuder, Sarah(Orp)	Columbia	Walkers	221/5	Appling
Tuggle, Leonard	Morgan	Hubbards	298/5	Appling
Tuggle, Leonard	Morgan	Hubbards	59/14	Irwin
Tuggle, Lodowick	Jasper	Hays	166/15	Irwin
Tuggle, Lodowick	Jasper	Hays	525/10	Irwin
Tuggle, Robert	Jasper	Baileys	78/3	Irwin
Tulless, John R.	Columbia	Pullins	104/9	Irwin
Tullis, Patience(Wid)	Effingham		295/2	Appling
Tullis, Stephen	Chatham		175/7	Gwinnett
Tullis, Stephen	Chatham		305/5	Appling
Tullos, Richard	Tatnall	Overstreets	20/5	Gwinnett
Tully, Charles	Jefferson	Fountains	91/7	Early
Tully, John A.	Baldwin	Marshals	15/6	Appling
Tumbling, Rebecca	Effingham		400/1	Appling
Tumlin, William	Jackson	Hamiltons	231/2	Appling
Tumlin, William	Jackson	Hamiltons	367/9	Early
Turk, John(Orps)	Franklin	Turks	154/7	Early

NAME	COUNTY	MIL.DIST	LOT/SECT	DREW LAND
Turk, Thomas	Baldwin	Stephens	51/16	Irwin
Turlington, Thomas	Washington	Burneys	223/28	Early
Turman, Edward	Jones	Permenters	518/6	Appling
Turman, George	Elbert	Childers	316/11	Irwin
Turman, Martin B.	Oglethorpe	Goolsbys	94/11	Irwin
Turman, Mary (Wid)	Elbert	Olivers	106/13	Habersham
Turman, Robert (Orps)	Elbert	Olivers	325/8	Irwin
Turman, Yancey	Elbert	Olivers	311/8	Early
Turmon, James Sr.	Franklin	Burroughs	184/3	Early
Turmon, Martin	Franklin	Davis	127/4	Walton
Turmon, Martin	Franklin	Davis	221/7	Appling
Turnbull, John	McIntosh	Hamiltons	328/3	Appling
Turnbull, Nicholas	Chatham		300/4	Irwin
Turnbull, Nicholas	Chatham		362/13	Irwin
Turner, Abednago	Lincoln	Tatoms	200/5	Irwin
Turner, Aisha	Bulloch	Tilmans	6/1	Irwin
Turner, Alfred	Jefferson	Fountains	172/2	Appling
Turner, Allen	Morgan	Talbots	491/12	Irwin
Turner, Andrew	Oglethorpe	Lees	145/2	Early
Turner, Benjamin	Bulloch	Tilmans	268/11	Early
Turner, Betsey	Hancock	Mims	368/9	Early
Turner, Butler (Orps)	Morgan	Talbots	446/2	Appling
Turner, David	Tatnall	Jos. Durrence	172/3	Appling
Turner, Dempsey	Laurens	Swearingans	247/7	Early
Turner, Eason	Jasper	Posts	272/7	Early
Turner, Eliz.M. (Orps)	Elbert	Gains	135/25	Gwinnett
Turner, George (Orps)	Jefferson	Bothwells	208/6	Appling
Turner, George	Putnam	Berrys	51/8	Hall
Turner, George	Warren	Hubberts	131/11	Irwin
Turner, Henry Jr.	Hancock	Danells	333/5	Gwinnett
Turner, Henry (s/Zadock)	Putnam	Littles	230/12	Irwin
Turner, Henry	Baldwin	Stephens	28/10	Early
Turner, Henry	Wilkes	Russels	124/16	Early
Turner, James B.	Lincoln	Parks	36/8	Hall
Turner, James F.	Jasper	Centells	66/6	Gwinnett
Turner, James	Jasper	Bentleys	194/14	Early
Turner, James	Jasper	Kendalls	375/9	Irwin
Turner, James	Jones	Samuels	397/7	Appling
Turner, Jehu	Hancock	Danells	57/21	Early
Turner, Jesse	Bulloch	Tilmans	20/11	Early
Turner, John D.	Elbert	Hannahs	232/2	Early
Turner, John G.	Jasper	McClendons	157/3	Walton
Turner, John R.	Wilkinson	Bowings	153/18	Early
Turner, John	Burke	70th	49/6	Gwinnett
Turner, John	Burke	70th	82/7	Appling
Turner, John	Greene	Kimbrough	83/18	Early
Turner, John	Greene	Kimbrows	106/10	Hall
Turner, John	Hancock	Danells	342/4	Appling
Turner, John	Laurens	Swearingans	176/5	Irwin
Turner, John	Laurens	Swearingans	37/11	Habersham
Turner, John	Pulaski	Maddox	90/8	Early
Turner, John	Putnam	Oslins	104/2	Appling
Turner, John	Tatnall	Johnstons	209/11	Irwin
Turner, John	Wayne	Crews	73/11	Early
Turner, Jonathan	Hancock	Scotts	109/5	Rabun
Turner, Joseph	Laurens	S. Smiths	71/3	Walton
Turner, Joseph	Putnam	Berrys	172/1	Walton
Turner, Joshua	Baldwin	Taliaferro	432/3	Appling
Turner, Joshua	Baldwin	Taliaferro	69/10	Early
Turner, Julius	Jones	Harrists	157/13	Early
Turner, Larkin	Jasper	Hays	352/4	Early
Turner, Levin	Hancock	Danells	189/19	Early
Turner, Lewis	Lincoln	Tatoms	115/18	Early
Turner, Lewis	Lincoln	Tatoms	383/6	Early
Turner, Luke	Wilkes	Gordons	66/2	Habersham
Turner, Manson	Jasper	Centells	353/9	Appling
Turner, Milburn	Baldwin	Taliaferro	130/15	Early

NAME	COUNTY	MIL.DIST	LOT/SECT	DREW LAND
Turner, Robert	Wilkinson	Bowings	194/2	Appling
Turner, Robert	Wilkinson	Bowings	397/13	Early
Turner, Samuel Jr.	Hancock	Daniels	96/7	Irwin
Turner, Samuel P.	Putnam	Buckners	272/5	Appling
Turner, Solomon(Orps)	Wilkinson	Kettles	138/3	Irwin
Turner, Stephen	Laurens	Swearingans	107/1	Irwin
Turner, Thomas B.	Gwinnett	Hamiltons	284/8	Irwin
Turner, Thomas	Elbert	Hannahs	12/22	Early
Turner, Thomas	Hancock	Thomas	245/2	Early
Turner, Thomas	Jones	Harrists	51/3	Habersham
Turner, Wade H.	Jasper	Hays	371/8	Irwin
Turner, William T.	Hancock	Feuns	252/7	Early
Turner, William	Glynn		83/15	Irwin
Turner, William	Lincoln	Stokes	168/10	Hall
Turner, William	Putnam	Brooks	226/9	Appling
Turner, William	Putnam	Evans	253/6	Appling
Turpin, Allen	Franklin	Powels	115/10	Irwin
Turpin, John	Richmond	Laceys	279/12	Early
Turpin, William H.	Richmond	120th	386/17	Early
Tuterall, Micager	Effingham		79/13	Habersham
Tutrall, Micajah	Effingham		79/13	Habersham
Tuttle, Catharine(Wid)	Jackson	Hamiltons	222/4	Appling
Twidwell, Wm.(R.S.)	Franklin	Harris	369/19	Early
Twiggs, Asa	Richmond	Winters	458/10	Irwin
Twiggs, David	Richmond	Winters	154/2	Rabun
Twiggs, Ruth(Wid)	Richmond	Winters	433/6	Appling
Twik, Abbington	Jasper	Baileys	303/6	Appling
Twilley, Joseph	Hancock	Edwards	69/15	Early
Twilley, Nathan	Jasper	Evans	119/7	Gwinnett
Twilly, ELijah	Jasper	Evans	111/2	Early
Twiner, Ezekiah	Putnam	Oslins	121/6	Appling
Twinning, Nathaniel(Orps)	Clarke	Mitchells	481/5	Appling
Twitty, Thomas	Jackson	Rogers	2/14	Early
Tyas, Louis	Hancock	Champions	166/13	Irwin
Tyas, Mary(Wid)	Hancock	Thomas	26/1	Rabun
Tye, Henry	Oglethorpe	Waters	22/5	Appling
Tyler, Anna	Jasper	Centells	180/8	Early
Tyler, Needham(RS)	Twiggs	Smiths	494/4	Appling
Tyler, Needham(RS)	Twiggs	Smiths	67/3	Habersham
Tynar, James	Lincoln	Parks	205/4	Walton
Tyner, Benjamin	Pulaski	Lanears	173/17	Early
Tyner, Harris	Elbert	Dooley	135/28	Early
Tyner, James	Lincoln	Parks	41/9	Appling
Tyner, Kneeland	Chatham		41/3	Habersham
Tyner, Samuel	Elbert	Dooleys	9/5	Early
Tyner, William	Pulaski	Bryans	31/11	Hall
Tyner, Wm.	Tatnall	Overstreets	461/6	Appling
Tyre, Cannon	Tatnall	Johnsons	16/19	Early
Tyson, Eugany H.	Clarke	Deans	210/20	Early
Tyson, Job	Glynn		155/5	Appling
Tyson, Job	Glynn		218/4	Irwin
Tyson, Kinchen P.	Jones	Wallers	497/9	Irwin
Uha, Henry	Columbia	Walkers	146/12	Hall
Ulsery, John Jr.	Jones	Griffiths	38/7	Early
Umpres, Wm.	Burke	McNorrills	359/1	Appling
Underhill, Joseph	Bulloch	Jones	225/7	Early
Underwood, Benjamin	Wilkinson	Brooks	44/23	Early
Underwood, Daniel	Greene	141st	163/19	Early
Underwood, Daniel	Greene	141st	44/20	Early
Underwood, Enoch	Baldwin	Irwins	166/8	Early
Underwood, Enoch	Baldwin	Irwins	88/21	Early
Underwood, Isham	Wilkinson	Kettles	261/9	Early
Underwood, Jared	Elbert	B.Higginbothams	209/2	Early
Underwood, John	Laurens	Jones	5/9	Early
Underwood, Joseph	Elbert	Gaines	178/16	Irwin
Underwood, Josiah	Columbia	Shaws	290/1	Walton
Underwood, Lemuel	Elbert	B.Higginbothams	389/2	Appling

337

NAME	COUNTY	MIL.DIST	LOT/SECT	DREW LAND
Underwood, Thomas	Tattnall	Overstreet	34/4	Appling
Underwood, Thomas	Wilkinson	Howards	356/2	Appling
Underwood, William A.	Laurens	S.Smiths	112/1	Habersham
Underwood, William	Morgan	Townsends	105/4	Irwin
Underwood, William	Wilkinson	Wiggins	55/22	Early
Underwood, Wm.Sr.	Tattnall	Overstreet	13/19	Early
Upshaw, Atkins	Madison	Culbreths	156/5	Appling
Upshaw, Haston	Elbert	R.Christians	430/8	Appling
Upshaw, John Jr.	Elbert	B.Higginbothams	222/5	Appling
Upshaw, Rebecca(Wid)	Elbert	Penns	479/5	Irwin
Upshaw, Richard	Elbert	R.Christians	449/13	Irwin
Upson, Stephen	Oglethorpe	Brittons	360/4	Early
Upton, Benjamin	Warren	151st	237/3	Appling
Upton, Jane	Warren	151st	205/3	Walton
Upton, Tobias	Warren	151st	66/6	Habersham
Urquhart, David	Richmond	Laceys	371/28	Early
Ursury, Levi	Wilkinson	Kettles	96/10	Hall
Usery, Abner	Burke	Bells	170/8	Early
Usery, John Sr.	Jones	Griffiths	317/28	Early
Usher, Daniel(RS)	Richmond	Palmers	50/5	Early
Usry, Carroll	Warren	150th	18/16	Irwin
Usry, William	Warren	150th	219/27	Early
Ussery, David(Orps)	Twiggs	R.Belchers	335/6	Irwin
Ussery, John	Hall	Millers	293/3	Appling
Ussery, Meredith	Laurens	Watsons	287/8	Irwin
Ussery, Meredith	Laurens	Watsons	6/2	Appling
Utley, Henry	Burke	McNorrills	340/15	Early
Vadeviere, Lampkin	Jackson	Rodgers	169/11	Habersham
Valentine, Levi	Wilkinson	Brooks	14/28	Early
Valentine, Levi	Wilkinson	Brooks	209/14	Early
Valentine, Thomas	Wilkinson	Brooks	323/7	Appling
Van, Samuel	Washington	Daniels	278/12	Early
Vanalen, Caroline M.C.S.(Orp)	Wilkes	Kilgores	381/8	Appling
Vanbrackle, John	Bryan	19th	447/8	Appling
Vancant, Joseph	Richmond	122nd	322/11	Irwin
Vance, John	Jones	Chappels	153/2	Rabun
Vandefar, Richard	Clarke	Tredwells	354/8	Appling
Vandeviere, Lampkin	Jackson	Rogers	24/7	Appling
Vanlandingham, Benj.	Wilkinson	Kettles	380/4	Appling
Vanlandingham, John	Morgan	Talbots	231/12	Irwin
Vanlandingham, Peter	Wilkinson	Bowings	54/2	Habersham
Vanlandingham, Thos.	Morgan	Leonards	162/4	Appling
Vann, James	Burke	Thomas	238/3	Appling
Vann, William	Burke	Thomas	28/10	Hall
Vardamon, Joseph	Morgan	Leonard	152/2	Walton
Vardel, Peter	Chatham		424/26	Early
Vardery, Mathurin	Richmond	Laceys	123/10	Irwin
Varn, Isaac	Camden	Tillis	143/18	Early
Varnado, John	Laurens	Ross	143/6	Gwinnett
Varnadoe, Nathaniel	Liberty		361/10	Irwin
Varnedore, Joseph	Washington	Cummins	87/4	Early
Varner, Alexander	Baldwin	Ellis	40/8	Irwin
Varner, George	Putnam	Oslins	433/3	Irwin
Varner, Henly	Putnam	Oslins	107/7	Appling
Varner, John	Oglethorpe	Bowls	108/13	Irwin
Varner, Mathew	Oglethorpe	Murrays	368/6	Early
Varner, Matthew	Oglethorpe	Murrays	211/7	Appling
Varner, William	Putnam	Oslins	364/19	Early
Vason, Joseph	Morgan	Talbots	18/2	Rabun
Vass, Alexander	Putnam	Brooks	327/13	Irwin
Vass, John M.	Baldwin	Marshalls	227/6	Early
Vassal, John	Hancock	Herberts	2/10	Irwin
Vasser, Elizabeth	Scriven	Moodys	370/8	Appling
Vasser, John	Lincoln	Graves	17/13	Early
Vaughan, Alexander	Warren	Greers	202/18	Early
Vaughan, Edward	Clarke	Stuarts	287/13	Irwin
Vaughan, Francis	Twiggs	R.Belchers	522/11	Irwin

NAME	COUNTY	MIL.DIST	LOT/SECT	DREW LAND
Vaughan, Isaac	Columbia	Walkers	61/22	Early
Vaughan, Jane (Wid)	Warren	Greens	335/28	Early
Vaughan, John Sr.	Morgan	Walkers	315/12	Irwin
Vaughan, John	Morgan	Hackneys	30/13	Early
Vaughan, John	Wilkinson	Howards	396/5	Appling
Vaughan, Joshua	Columbia	Olives	19/4	Habersham
Vaughan, Joshua	Franklin	Burroughs	452/5	Appling
Vaughan, Peter	Franklin	Burroughs	151/6	Irwin
Vaughn, Alexander	Elbert	R.Christians	490/5	Irwin
Vaughn, Benj.	Franklin	Vaughns	458/7	Irwin
Vaughn, Felix	Franklin	Turks	18/4	Appling
Vaughn, Michael Jr.	Laurens	S.Smiths	294/8	Appling
Vaughn, Sterling	Franklin	Turks	294/20	Early
Vaughn, Thomas	Richmond		189/11	Early
Vaughn, William	Jasper	Centells	51/2	Walton
Vauters, Cornelius H.	Jones	Buckhalters	88/1	Early
Vawter, Anna	Elbert	Dobbs	412/28	Early
Vawter, Richard	Elbert	Smiths	332/7	Irwin
Vawter, Wm.	Elbert	Dobbs	290/20	Early
Veal, Carnaby	Putnam	Stampers	522/12	Irwin
Veal, Edward	Washington	Peabodys	142/3	Habersham
Veal, Edward	Washington	Peabodys	518/2	Appling
Veal, Francis	Washington	Peabodys	189/3	Irwin
Veal, George	Washington	Peabodys	173/10	Irwin
Veal, James	Madison	Willifords	289/14	Early
Veal, John	Putnam	Stampers	125/2	Habersham
Veal, Lewis D.	Putnam	Oslins	34/11	Early
Veal, Nathan Sr.	Washington	Peabodys	442/6	Appling
Veal, William Sr.	Putnam	Stampers	19/5	Habersham
Veal, Wm.Jr.	Putnam	Stampers	309/7	Early
Veasey, Abner	Putnam	Oslins	30/5	Gwinnett
Veasey, Andrew B.	Hancock	Scotts	111/2	Irwin
Veasey, Ezekiel	Morgan	Jordans	155/2	Early
Veasey, Ezekiel	Morgan	Jordans	243/9	Irwin
Veasey, Jesse H.	Jones	Kings	32/16	Irwin
Veasey, Jesse H.	Jones	Kings	85/6	Gwinnett
Veasey, Jesse Sr.	Hancock	Canes	331/1	Early
Veasey, Stephen	Hancock	Canes	197/15	Early
Veasey, Stephen	Hancock	Canes	254/5	Gwinnett
Veasey, Zebulon	Hancock	Canes	304/5	Early
Veasley, James	Hancock	Canes	8/4	Rabun
Veazey, Timothy	Greene	141	36/6	Irwin
Veazy, John	Greene	Carletons	408/5	Irwin
Veazy, Timothy	Greene	141	475/6	Appling
Venable, Abraham	Oglethorpe	Waters	271/5	Gwinnett
Venable, Abram	Oglethorpe	Waters	175/13	Irwin
Venible, Robert	Jackson	Hamiltons	259/6	Gwinnett
Venible, Thomas U.	Jackson	Hamiltons	368/1	Early
Venters, Cornelius	Jones	Buckhalters	273/11	Early
Venters, Stephen	Telfair	Wilsons	231/27	Early
Verdery, Benj.F.	Richmond	120th	146/1	Early
Vessels, James	Franklin	Akins	129/2	Habersham
Vessels, James	Franklin	Akins	205/6	Appling
Vessels, James	Franklin	Akins	50/22	Early
Vessels, James	Franklin	Akins	65/26	Early
Vicars, Silas	Walton	Wests	77/23	Early
Viccars, Joel	Montgomery	Alstons	124/6	Appling
Vick, Elisha	Elbert	Dooleys	372/10	Irwin
Vick, Moses	Appling	4th	110/3	Appling
Vick, Moses	Appling	4th	145/6	Appling
Vicker, Thomas	Wilkinson	Childs	129/14	Irwin
Vickers, Drury	Montgomery	McMillans	397/13	Irwin
Vickers, Elijah	Jasper	Kendalls	103/7	Gwinnett
Vickers, Frederick	Jefferson	Fountains	405/15	Early
Vickers, Graham	Oglethorpe	Waters	497/6	Appling
Vickers, Hatcher	Baldwin	Marshalls	47/15	Irwin
Vickers, Jacob	Twiggs	Ellis	155/4	Appling

NAME	COUNTY	MIL.DIST	LOT/SECT	DREW LAND
Vickers, Jacob	Twiggs	Ellis	47/8	Appling
Vickers, James	Greene	Greers	112/8	Appling
Vickers, James	Greene	Greers	31/6	Early
Vickers, Joel	Jasper	Phillips	317/7	Irwin
Vickers, Joshua	Twiggs	Ellis	147/14	Irwin
Vickers, Joshua	Twiggs	Ellis	19/28	Early
Vickers, Mirium	Hancock	Millers	117/8	Hall
Vickers, Penelope	Burke	Torrances	104/19	Early
Vickers, Solomon R.	Washington	Floyds	225/8	Irwin
Vickers, Stephen	Laurens	Jones	29/6	Appling
Vickers, Thomas	Hancock	Millers	24/3	Walton
Vickers, Young	Twiggs	Ellis	23/27	Early
Vickery, Ely	Scriven	180th	153/8	Appling
Vickery, Hezekiah	Scriven	Lovetts	325/18	Early
Vickery, John	Elbert	Dobbs	324/1	Appling
Vickery, Joseph	Elbert	Gaines	311/9	Appling
Vickery, William	Scriven	180th	96/15	Early
Vigal, George	Lincoln	Thompsons	320/8	Irwin
Vincent, Benjamin	Baldwin	Ellis	186/3	Irwin
Vincent, James	Washington	Peabodys	174/9	Early
Vincent, Levin Sr.	Washington	Peabodys	115/1	Habersham
Vincent, Margarett(Wid)	Richmond	122nd	171/1	Appling
Vincent, Richard	Burke	72nd	63/3	Habersham
Vineyard, Joseph	Madison	Orrs	285/16	Early
Vining, Abraham	Jefferson	Lamps	63/13	Early
Vining, Cader	Effingham		77/5	Rabun
Vining, Nancey(Wid)	Jefferson	Waldens	96/5	Appling
Vinsen, Levin	Hancock	Justices	225/26	Early
Vinson, Elijah	Wilkinson	Brooks	190/8	Appling
Vinson, Henry	Jones	Wallers	284/28	Early
Vinson, James	Twiggs	Jefferson	466/12	Irwin
Vinson, John	Hancock	Champions	152/15	Early
Vinson, John	Jones	Wallers	106/14	Irwin
Vinson, Nimrod	Putnam	Morelands	56/23	Early
Vinson, Obediah	Clarke	Harpers	180/2	Rabun
Vintress, Stephen	Jones	Greens	119/1	Walton
Vinzant, William	Tatnall	Durrence	131/2	Early
Vivion, Virgil H.	McIntosh	Hamiltons	186/7	Irwin
Voleton, Francis	Burke	Dye's	121/11	Irwin
Voleton, Francis	Burke	Dye's	31/19	Early
Volloton, Paul J.	Chatham		424/1	Early
W-lkinson, A.McL.	Laurens	Deans	105/4	Habersham
Waddle, Thomas	Morgan	Farrars	42/20	Early
Wade, Archibald	Morgan	Knights	207/6	Irwin
Wade, Edward	Columbia	Bealls	305/17	Early
Wade, Elijah	Scriven	Moodys	56/5	Gwinnett
Wade, Hudson	Morgan	McLendons	404/1	Appling
Wade, James H.	Scriven	Lovetts	288/4	Appling
Wade, James Jr.	Morgan	McClendons	62/1	Rabun
Wade, James	Jackson	Hambletons	96/5	Early
Wade, Jeremiah	Burke	Royals	224/1	Appling
Wade, Jesse	Morgan	Knights	19/1	Early
Wade, Jesse	Morgan	Knights	190/11	Early
Wade, Jesse	Twiggs	Hodges	97/2	Early
Wade, John M.	Scriven	Smiths	164/28	Early
Wade, John	Franklin	R.Browns	382/9	Appling
Wade, John	Franklin	R.Browns	54/7	Gwinnett
Wade, John	Jackson	Hamiltons	186/26	Early
Wade, Moses	Wilkes	Hollidays	97/9	Irwin
Wade, Nathaniel	Scriven	Smiths	21/13	Habersham
Wade, Nathaniel	Scriven	Smiths	89/1	Irwin
Wade, Richard	Franklin	Turks	383/13	Early
Wade, Richard	Franklin	Turks	388/3	Appling
Wade, Sarah	Wilkes	Russells	132/8	Irwin
Wade, Thomas	Clarke	Mitchells	16/3	Rabun
Wade, Thomas	Clarke	Mitchells	259/16	Early
Wade, William	Jackson	Hamiltons	148/2	Rabun

NAME	COUNTY	MIL.DIST	LOT/SECT	DREW LAND
Wadkins, David	Jackson	Dicksons	511/12	Irwin
Wadkins, Henry	Jackson	Dicksons	113/3	Walton
Wadkins, Henry	Jackson	Dicksons	73/11	Hall
Wadkins, John C.	Jackson	Dicksons	41/28	Early
Wadkins, Phillip Jr.	Oglethorpe	Wises	73/5	Rabun
Wadkins, Reding	Washington	Renfros	87/4	Appling
Wadkins, William	Franklin	Haynes	121/3	Irwin
Wadkins, William	Franklin	Haynes	321/3	Appling
Wadkins, William	Jackson	Dicksons	83/11	Early
Wads, John B.	Franklin	P.Browns	366/5	Early
Wads, Robert	Columbia	Bealls	82/10	Irwin
Wadsworth, Elbert	Jones	Wallers	70/18	Early
Wadsworth, James	Jones	Wallers	394/3	Appling
Wadsworth, John	Hancock	Justices	19/11	Early
Wadsworth, John	Jones	Wallers	171/3	Walton
Wadsworth, John	Jones	Wallers	78/12	Habersham
Wadsworth, Thomas	Hancock	Justices	342/11	Irwin
Wadsworth, William	Jackson	Hamiltons	67/8	Hall
Wadsworth, William	Jones	Harrists	55/3	Appling
Wadsworth, William	Lincoln	Parks	95/7	Appling
Wadsworth, Wm.(Orps)	Lincoln	Parks	338/15	Early
Wadsworth, Wm.Jr.	Lincoln	Parks	342/15	Early
Wadsworth, Wm.Jr.	Lincoln	Parks	368/8	Appling
Wafford, Absalom	Jackson	Hamiltons	40/5	Rabun
Wafford, Benjamin	Franklin	Flannagan	1/21	Early
Wafford, Daniel	Jackson	Rogers	350/16	Early
Wafford, Joseph	Franklin	Holcombs	275/7	Appling
Wafford, Solomon	Jackson	Rogers	192/5	Early
Wages, William	Richmond	Burtons	632/2	Appling
Waggoner, Amos	Putnam	Buckners	192/8	Early
Waggoner, David W.	Warren	Parhams	352/6	Gwinnett
Waggoner, Henry H.	Warren	Parhams	238/6	Irwin
Waggoner, Hiram	Warren	150th	211/8	Early
Waggoner, James(Orps)	Warren	Parhams	164/8	Early
Waggoner, Joseph S.	Warren	Parhams	159/10	Habersham
Waggoner, Nicholas	Jones	Jeffersons	238/17	Early
Waggoner, Nicholas	Jones	Jeffersons	9/4	Rabun
Waggoner, Wm.Jr.	Greene	Ragins	12/2	Rabun
Waggoner, Zacheus	Warren	Parhams	415/7	Appling
Wagnon, Richard	Greene	Kimbrough	298/8	Appling
Wagnon, Richard	Greene	Kimbroughs	307/9	Early
Wagnon, William O.	Walton	Wagnons	153/7	Gwinnett
Wagoner, Simeon	Putnam	Ectors	333/3	Early
Wainwright, Daniel	Jones	Permenters	298/16	Early
Waits, Jeremiah	Hall		300/13	Irwin
Waits, Jeremiah	Hall		98/10	Habersham
Waits, John	Jackson	Dicksons	20/10	Early
Waits, Joseph	Jasper	Smiths	109/6	Appling
Waits, Samuel	Hall	Byrds	119/8	Hall
Wakefield, George	Morgan	Rameys	71/13	Early
Wakefield, John	Morgan	Parkers	353/12	Irwin
Wakefield, John	Morgan	Parkers	51/1	Walton
Walden, Edward	Jefferson	Waldens	473/13	Irwin
Walden, Henry	Jasper	Hays	19/5	Appling
Walden, Henry	Jefferson	Waldens	120/2	Walton
Walden, Henry	Jefferson	Waldens	209/16	Early
Walden, James	Warren	151st	344/10	Irwin
Walden, Osborn	Jefferson	Waldens	168/5	Irwin
Walden, Reuben	Pulaski	Rees	75/12	Hall
Walden, Richard(RS)	Jones	Permenters	365/11	Early
Walden, Samuel	Twiggs	Bozemans	171/8	Irwin
Walder, Alexander	Clarke	Pentecost	134/20	Early
Walder, Alexander	Clarke	Pentecost	147/4	Irwin
Walder, John	Effingham		322/5	Gwinnett
Waldhaner, John Sr.	Effingham		501/5	Irwin
Waldhaner, William	Effingham		130/8	Early
Waldon, Green	Twiggs	Bozemans	7/5	Gwinnett

341

NAME	COUNTY	MIL.DIST	LOT/SECT	DREW LAN'
Waldrip, Josiah	Jones	Seals	83/7	Appling
Waldrobe, Abraham	Jasper	Centells	192/18	Early
Waldrobe, Elihu	Jasper	Centells	70/11	Habersha
Waldrobe, James	Jasper	Centells	244/6	Gwinnett
Waldrobe, James	Jasper	Centills	1/7	Early
Waldrop, Benjamin	Jones	Griffiths	180/1	Appling
Waldrope, James	Putnam	Morelands	377/15	Early
Waldrope, William	Putnam	Morelands	184/9	Appling
Wales, Sarah B.	Madison	Culbreaths	274/9	Irwin
Wales, Wm.	Emanuel	57th	106/2	Habersha
Waley, Gabriel	Emanuel	53rd	22/9	Hall
Walker, Abraham	Burke	Sullivans	278/19	Early
Walker, Amos	Burke	Sullivans	142/4	Irwin
Walker, Benj.G.	Richmond		207/20	Early
Walker, Benjamin	Putnam	Butts	200/6	Appling
Walker, Benjamin	Putnam	Butts	332/4	Appling
Walker, Charlotte(Wid)	Twiggs	Smiths	131/28	Early
Walker, Churchwell	Putnam	Slaughters	60/16	Irwin
Walker, Cornelia(Orp)	Richmond	122nd	379/20	Early
Walker, Daniel R.	Putnam	Ectors	52/5	Gwinnett
Walker, David	Wilkes	Kilgores	476/8	Appling
Walker, Dosey	Washington	Mannings	306/11	Early
Walker, Edmund	Morgan	Walkers	110/19	Early
Walker, Edwin	Columbia	Olives	78/19	Early
Walker, Elisha S.	Columbia	Shaws	298/5	Early
Walker, Elisha Sr.	Columbia	Walkers	526/5	Irwin
Walker, Elisha(Orps)	Laurens	D.Smiths	51/26	Early
Walker, Elisha(Orps)	Washington	Cummins	379/15	Early
Walker, Eliz.Jr.(Wid)	Hancock	Champions	393/2	Early
Walker, Elizabeth(Wid)	Jefferson	Cowarts	35/2	Habersha
Walker, George H.	Jackson	Winters	28/16	Irwin
Walker, George Jr.	Pulaski	Davis	164/26	Early
Walker, George M.	Wilkes	Gordons	143/16	Irwin
Walker, Henry(of Joel)	Jefferson	Cowarts	78/5	Irwin
Walker, Henry	Warren	Jackson	56/1	Habersha
Walker, Isaac	Morgan	Walkers	154/3	Irwin
Walker, Isaiah C.	Lincoln	Graves	206/7	Appling
Walker, Isaiah	Lincoln	Graves	17/13	Irwin
Walker, James(Orph)	Richmond	122nd	379/20	Early
Walker, James	Camden	32nd	185/5	Gwinnett
Walker, James	Franklin	Harriss	271/9	Irwin
Walker, Jeremiah	Lincoln	Thompsons	405/7	Irwin
Walker, Jesse	Lincoln	Graves	634/2	Appling
Walker, Joel(Orps)	Warren	Blounts	38/13	Irwin
Walker, Joel	Pulaski	Davis	160/7	Early
Walker, John C.	Columbia	Shaws	336/13	Irwin
Walker, John H.Jr.	Putnam	J.Kendricks	521/8	Irwin
Walker, John S.	Columbia	Dodsons	274/4	Appling
Walker, John S.	Warren	150th	244/9	Irwin
Walker, John S.	Warren	150th	33/27	Early
Walker, John S.	Wilkes	Smiths	140/4	Irwin
Walker, John Sr.	Morgan	Walkers	155/9	Hall
Walker, John	Chatham		20/12	Early
Walker, John	Greene	Macons	151/3	Habersha
Walker, John	Hancock	Thomas	9/9	Irwin
Walker, John	Morgan	Hubbards	236/23	Early
Walker, Joseph	Columbia	Bealls	508/7	Appling
Walker, Joseph	Putnam	Eavens	171/15	Early
Walker, Joseph	Putnam	Stampers	155/12	Irwin
Walker, Joseph	Wilkes	Kilgores	40/5	Appling
Walker, Joshua(Orp)	Richmond	122nd	379/20	Early
Walker, Levi L.	Putnam	Evans	86/13	Irwin
Walker, Littleberry Sr.	Appling	4th	89/11	Irwin
Walker, Londy	Gwinnett	Hamiltons	384/5	Appling
Walker, Margarett(Orp)	Richmond	122nd	379/20	Early
Walker, Mary(Wid)	Richmond		307/5	Early
Walker, Mary(Wid)	Wayne	Johnstons	306/11	Irwin

NAME	COUNTY	MIL.DIST	LOT/SECT	DREW LAND
Walker, Meredith	Twiggs	Jeffersons	85/5	Gwinnett
Walker, Moses P.	Putnam	Stampers	19/9	Appling
Walker, Moses	Jones	Seals	5/3	Walton
Walker, Nathaniel	Putnam	J.Kendricks	105/3	Walton
Walker, Noah	Laurens	D.Smiths	67/27	Early
Walker, Polly A.	Lincoln	Tatoms	234/9	Early
Walker, Richard	Appling	4th	409/5	Irwin
Walker, Robert	Hancock	Thomas	28/20	Early
Walker, Shadrack	Richmond	Palmers	391/13	Early
Walker, Solomon	Camden	32nd	370/1	Early
Walker, Thomas T.	Jasper	Centells	190/9	Irwin
Walker, Thomas T.	Jasper	Centells	291/9	Appling
Walker, Thomas(Orps)	Lincoln	Graves	300/9	Early
Walker, Wells	Warren	Parhams	202/12	Early
Walker, William(Orp)	Richmond	122nd	379/20	Early
Walker, William(Orps)	Franklin	Flanagans	489/10	Irwin
Walker, William(Orps)	Putnam	Coopers	244/17	Early
Walker, William	Greene	Macons	71/2	Irwin
Walker, William	Hancock	Thomas	8/5	Early
Walker, William	Lincoln	Walkers	130/20	Early
Walker, William	Lincoln	Walkers	410/5	Irwin
Walker, William	Montgomery	McElvins	226/14	Early
Walker, William	Richmond	Palmers	503/3	Appling
Walker, William	Wayne	Johnstons	490/12	Irwin
Walker, Wm.B.C.	Richmond	Palmers	295/8	Early
Walker, Wm.Jr.	Washington	Floyds	9/23	Early
Walker, Wm.L.	Putnam	Coopers	127/2	Appling
Walker, Wm.L.	Putnam	Coopers	335/3	Appling
Walker, Wm.Sr.	Greene	Macons	84/2	Walton
Wall, Arthur	Jackson	Rogers	32/4	Rabun
Wall, Benajmin	Chatham		143/8	Irwin
Wall, Elizabeth(Wid)	Chatham		113/8	Appling
Wall, Ezekiel	Washington	Wimberleys	2/7	Appling
Wall, Ezekiel	Washington	Wimberlys	314/2	Appling
Wall, Isaac	Burke	Dys	131/7	Appling
Wall, James G.	Twiggs	Evans	12/6	Appling
Wall, James Jr.	Twiggs	Jeffersons	176/11	Irwin
Wall, Jesse Jr.	Twiggs	Jeffersons	305/3	Early
Wall, Jesse R.	Twiggs	Evans	40/3	Rabun
Wall, John Jr.	Wilkes	Holidays	217/16	Early
Wall, John	Chatham		228/13	Early
Wall, John	Twiggs	Jeffersons	76/1	Early
Wall, King D.	Twiggs	Evans	28/9	Appling
Wall, Mary(Wid)	Chatham		61/14	Irwin
Wall, Mayor	Twiggs	W.Belcher	178/6	Gwinnett
Wall, Shadrack	Twiggs	Jeffersons	73/26	Early
Wall, Solomon	Washington	Robersons	79/6	Habersham
Wallace, Abram	Putnam	Robertsons	401/1	Appling
Wallace, Benjamin	Wilkes	Ogletrees	163/11	Hall
Wallace, Enoch	Baldwin	Stephens	346/7	Early
Wallace, George	Richmond	122nd	522/7	Irwin
Wallace, John H.	Oglethorpe	Atchisons	208/2	Irwin
Wallace, John	Jackson	Hamiltons	18/9	Appling
Wallace, John	Putnam	Bustins	238/6	Irwin
Wallace, Joseph	Jasper	Ryans	161/7	Early
Wallace, Mary(Wid)	Chatham		279/9	Appling
Wallace, Robert	Lincoln	Jeters	94/7	Appling
Wallace, Thomas(Orps)	Lincoln	Jeters	173/16	Early
Wallace, William(Orps)	Hancock	Edwards	62/23	Early
Wallace, William	Laurens	Deans	81/9	Appling
Wallace, William	Lincoln	Parks	266/16	Early
Wallace, William	Lincoln	Parks	50/11	Early
Wallace, William	Morgan	Selmons	150/1	Walton
Wallace, William	Richmond		122/1	Irwin
Wallace, William	Twiggs	Barrows	371/11	Irwin
Wallace, Wm.(Orps)	Wilkes	Josseys	188/26	Early
Wallas, Charles	Jackson	Dicksons	227/18	Early

NAME	COUNTY	MIL.DIST	LOT/SECT	DREW LAND
Wallas, Charles	Jackson	Dicksons	575/2	Appling
Wallas, Daniel	Jackson	Dicksons	194/13	Early
Wallas, Levi	Jackson	Dicksons	1/18	Early
Wallen, Elias	Chatham		16/9	Appling
Wallen, William	Jackson	Rogers	300/10	Irwin
Waller(Walker), Elias M.	Hancock	Champions	27/5	Rabun
Waller, Archelaus	Jasper	Smith	211/7	Gwinnett
Waller, Benjamin(Orps)	Hancock	Champions	236/12	Early
Waller, Burwell	Twiggs	Smiths	187/19	Early
Waller, Burwell	Twiggs	Smiths	94/5	Gwinnett
Waller, Elijah	Greene	Armers	321/11	Irwin
Waller, Hiram	Bryan	19th	266/4	Irwin
Waller, James(Orps)	Hancock	Champions	361/10	Early
Waller, Jeremiah	Jasper	Clays	65/2	Appling
Waller, Job	Hancock	Loyds	472/10	Irwin
Waller, John Key	Jackson	Winters	88/6	Early
Waller, John	Hancock	Loyds	35/8	Hall
Waller, John	Wilkes	Russels	511/6	Irwin
Waller, Joseph	Jasper	Owens	254/1	Appling
Waller, Joseph	Jasper	Owens	280/13	Irwin
Waller, Loxla	Jones	Buckhalters	113/4	Appling
Waller, Martha(Wid)	Laurens	Harris	17/7	Irwin
Waller, Pheba	Hancock	Justices	6/10	Irwin
Waller, William G.	Hancock	Champions	11/5	Habersham
Waller, William Sr.	Washington	Floyds	392/13	Irwin
Waller, Wm.Sr.	Putnam	Mays	12/7	Early
Waller, Zephaniah	Hancock	Loyds	246/1	Appling
Walley, Abner	Putnam	Mays	139/7	Early
Walley, Abner	Putnam	Mays	35/5	Gwinnett
Walling, Michael	Jackson	Dicksons	176/12	Habersham
Wallis, Burrel	Elbert	Dooleys	471/12	Irwin
Wallis, James	Jackson	Rogers	279/6	Early
Wallis, Jesse	Elbert	Dooley	480/6	Appling
Wallis, John	Laurens	Deans	28/26	Early
Wallis, Thomas	Jackson	Rogers	122/7	Early
Wallis, William	Putnam	Morlands	113/3	Appling
Wallpole, John	Wilkinson	Kettles	375/26	Early
Wallraven, Isaac	Jasper	Post	43/10	Early
Walls, John Sr.	Jackson	Hamiltons	244/28	Early
Walls, John	Putnam	J.Kendricks	54/14	Early
Walpole, Thomas	Wilkinson	Kettles	99/13	Habersham
Walraven, Archibald	Jackson	Dicksons	83/13	Habersham
Walraven, Isaac	Jasper	Posts	320/6	Irwin
Walser, David	Wilkes	Runnels	97/6	Appling
Walsh, Isaac	Jones	Samuels	373/18	Early
Walsingham, Catharine	Effingham		21/2	Habersham
Walsingham, Elisha	Richmond		414/2	Appling
Walsingham, John(Orps)	Effingham		42/2	Habersham
Walston, Benj.B.	Franklin	Yanseys	339/9	Irwin
Walston, Ridson F.	Greene	140th	165/9	Early
Waltcur, Averett	Burke	72	330/17	Early
Walter, Ann(Wid)	Walton	Wagnons	244/3	Walton
Walter, J.H.	Chatham		260/3	Early
Walters, Elijah Jr.	Franklin	P.Browns	157/16	Irwin
Walters, John C.	Franklin	P.Browns	8/2	Walton
Walters, John C.	Franklin	P.Browns	87/1	Walton
Walters, Michael	Scriven	Lovetts	103/8	Early
Walters, Nancy(Wid)	Habersham	Taylors	404/15	Early
Walters, Peter	Franklin	P.Browns	243/9	Early
Walters, Robert Jr.	Franklin	P.Browns	162/5	Gwinnett
Walters, Thomas	Franklin	Morris	168/3	Walton
Walters, Thomas	Franklin	Morris	192/20	Early
Walters, William	Franklin	Morriss	159/14	Early
Walthall, John H.	Jasper	Northcuts	164/7	Early
Walthall, Turmon	Jasper	Northcuts	96/12	Irwin
Walthour, Andrew	Liberty		7/13	Irwin
Walton, Daniel	Burke	72	241/4	Appling

NAME	COUNTY	MIL.DIST	LOT/SECT	DREW LAND
Walton, Daniel	Burke	72nd	176/14	Early
Walton, Dorothy(Wid)	Richmond	Palmers	230/16	Irwin
Walton, Edmond	Jones	Samuels	390/9	Early
Walton, George(Col)	Richmond	Palmers	14/12	Hall
Walton, George(Orps)	Wilkes	Kilgores	444/7	Appling
Walton, Gibson	Wilkes	Russels	362/1	Appling
Walton, Jesse	Burke	72nd	45/3	Appling
Walton, John	Lincoln	Graves	229/9	Appling
Walton, John	Oglethorpe	Brittons	190/12	Habersham
Walton, John	Putnam	Mahones	116/12	Hall
Walton, Mathew	Columbia	Olives	225/12	Early
Walton, Newell Jr.	Lincoln	Tatoms	210/7	Early
Walton, Newell Sr.	Lincoln	Stokes	281/7	Irwin
Walton, Newell Sr.	Lincoln	Stokes	312/5	Irwin
Walton, Robert	Lincoln	Graves	181/2	Early
Walton, Robert	Lincoln	Graves	302/11	Irwin
Walton, Robert	Richmond	398th	60/13	Early
Walton, Simeon	Warren	Parhams	71/11	Hall
Walton, Thomas J.	Lincoln	Stokes	355/6	Early
Walton, Thomas J.	Richmond	120th	187/2	Appling
Walton, Thomas J.	Richmond	120th	274/26	Early
Walton, William T.	Columbia	J.Morris	400/7	Early
Walton, William	Wilkes	Russells	91/14	Early
Waltons, (Orphans)	Burke	McNorrills	207/3	Irwin
Wamble, John	Twiggs	Bozemans	204/1	Appling
Wamble, Lucy(Wid)	Richmond	Winters	361/6	Irwin
Wamble, Wm.(Orp)	Richmond	Winters	229/10	Early
Wammack, Bird	Greene	Juggles	311/5	Early
Wanton, Eliz.T.(Wid)	Richmond		56/4	Habersham
Ward, Abner	Oglethorpe	Dunns	106/21	Early
Ward, Anderson	Putnam	Bustins	409/4	Early
Ward, Benjamin	Bryan	20th	148/5	Irwin
Ward, Benjamin	Clarke	Treadwell	67/7	Early
Ward, Benjamin	Clarke	Treadwells	97/1	Irwin
Ward, David & Jane(Orps)	Richmond		129/4	Early
Ward, Elam	Clarke	Simms	47/21	Early
Ward, Eli	Wilkinson	Lees	109/12	Irwin
Ward, Elijah Jr.	Twiggs	Smiths	13/2	Rabun
Ward, Elisha	Twiggs	Smiths	386/5	Early
Ward, Elisha	Twiggs	Smiths	447/7	Irwin
Ward, Eliz.& Ethuel(Orps)	Richmond		124/4	Early
Ward, Enoch	Twiggs	Browns	410/9	Early
Ward, Enoch	Twiggs	Browns	430/11	Irwin
Ward, James L.	Appling	6	91/4	Habersham
Ward, James S.	Appling	6th	170/4	Early
Ward, James(Orp)	Richmond		129/4	Early
Ward, James	Putnam	Brooks	324/5	Early
Ward, James	Wilkinson	Smiths	406/7	Irwin
Ward, John(Orps)	Putnam	Brooks	249/10	Early
Ward, John	Burke	J.Wards	118/8	Early
Ward, John	Oglethorpe	Murrays	387/6	Early
Ward, John	Warren	150th	159/21	Early
Ward, John	Wilkinson	Childs	79/3	Rabun
Ward, Mary(Wid)	Wilkinson	Bowings	318/8	Irwin
Ward, Maryann(Orp)	Richmond		124/4	Early
Ward, Micajah B.	Burke	M.Wards	297/10	Early
Ward, Michael(Orp)	Richmond		129/4	Early
Ward, Nancey(Wid)	Morgan	Hackneys	168/15	Irwin
Ward, Nancy(Wid)	Richmond		301/4	Irwin
Ward, Nathaniel	Twiggs	Jeffersons	36/4	Early
Ward, Obediah	Jasper	Bentleys	289/3	Appling
Ward, Obediah	Jasper	Bentleys	77/12	Irwin
Ward, Pulinia	Oglethorpe	Murrays	145/1	Irwin
Ward, Richard G.	Putnam	Berrys	316/16	Early
Ward, Richard G.	Putnam	Berrys	51/1	Irwin
Ward, Richard M.	Greene	Kimbroughs	57/18	Early
Ward, Richard(Orps)	Greene	Kimbroughs	99/9	Appling

NAME	COUNTY	MIL.DIST	LOT/SECT	DREW LAND
Ward, Robert	Camden	32nd	269/20	Early
Ward, Robert	Wilkinson	Lees	217/8	Irwin
Ward, Samuel Jr.	Jackson	Hamiltons	60/2	Walton
Ward, Samuel P.	Twiggs	Hodges	115/7	Irwin
Ward, Samuel	Habersham	Taylors	232/26	Early
Ward, Samuel	Oglethorpe	Murrays	166/5	Irwin
Ward, Sarah(Orp)	Richmond		129/4	Early
Ward, Seaborn	Burke	McNords	349/6	Irwin
Ward, Seth	Oglethorpe	Dunns	222/8	Irwin
Ward, Simon & Danl.(Orps)	Richmond		124/4	Early
Ward, Stephen	Greene	Wheelis	490/7	Irwin
Ward, Thomas E.	Emanuel	56th	103/14	Irwin
Ward, Thomas(Orp)	Jackson	Rogers	139/5	Appling
Ward, Thomas	Burke	Bells	60/8	Appling
Ward, West	Twiggs	Ellis	17/7	Gwinnett
Ward, William	Jones	Phillips	482/9	Early
Ward, William	Morgan	Farrars	178/7	Irwin
Ward, William	Putnam	Berrys	470/12	Irwin
Ward, Willis	Twiggs	Smiths	95/2	Appling
Ward, Winney(Wid)	Greene	Kimbroughs	173/10	Habersham
Ward, Zachariah	Wilkinson	Childs	74/5	Appling
Warden, John	Franklin	Jas.Miller	52/5	Appling
Warden, Lovel	Chatham		262/26	Early
Warden, Samuel(RS)	Franklin	Jno.Miller	190/20	Early
Warderobs, Harriott	Chatham		526/6	Appling
Wardlaw, James	Jackson	Hamiltons	289/3	Early
Wardlow, William	Jackson	Hamiltons	178/13	Irwin
Wardlow, Wm.	Jackson	Hamiltons	13/11	Habersham
Ware, Alexander	Madison	Willifords	348/10	Early
Ware, David	Jones	Shropshiers	443/10	Irwin
Ware, Edward Sr.	Madison	Willifords	49/5	Gwinnett
Ware, Elisha	Madison	Willifords	45/6	Early
Ware, Elisha	Madison	Willifords	95/2	Rabun
Ware, Henry	Madison	Willifords	280/14	Early
Ware, James Sr.	Madison	Willifords	62/5	Appling
Ware, John M.	Lincoln	Parks	284/3	Appling
Ware, Phillip	Madison	Willifords	93/27	Early
Ware, Robert	Lincoln	Thompsons	189/2	Rabun
Ware, Robert	Lincoln	Thompsons	250/5	Irwin
Ware, Robert	Wilkinson	Lees	92/1	Irwin
Ware, Susannah	Jasper	Northcuts	37/10	Early
Ware, William C.	Richmond	122nd	23/8	Hall
Ware, William C.	Richmond	122nd	387/7	Early
Waring, Wm.	Chatham		117/1	Appling
Warnall, Asa	Liberty		441/9	Irwin
Warnall, Phillip	Liberty		101/8	Early
Warner, Benjamin	Jefferson	Waldens	136/15	Early
Warner, Elijah	Jefferson	Flemmings	337/12	Early
Warner, Jeremiah(Orps)	Jefferson	Waldens	409/7	Appling
Warnock, Benjamin	Burke	J.Wards	235/19	Early
Warnock, James	Burke	M.Wards	273/5	Irwin
Warren, Allen(Orps)	Columbia	Dodsons	3/2	Appling
Warren, Archibald(Orps)	Greene	Armers	143/27	Early
Warren, Benjamin	Emanuel	58th	280/20	Early
Warren, Carlor	Burke	70th	263/5	Appling
Warren, Edmund	Jasper	Philips	284/7	Early
Warren, Harrison	Elbert	Grimes	155/13	Early
Warren, Hinchi	Jefferson	Fountains	170/6	Irwin
Warren, Isaiah	Emanuel	58th	358/10	Irwin
Warren, James M.	Franklin	Jos.Miller	88/5	Appling
Warren, James	Hall		336/5	Irwin
Warren, James	Jefferson	Lamps	151/18	Early
Warren, Jeremiah S.	Elbert	Gaines	27/26	Early
Warren, Jeremiah	Hancock	Edwards	289/11	Early
Warren, Jeremiah	Jones	Seals	329/26	Early
Warren, Jesse	Hancock	Edwards	290/28	Early
Warren, John(Orps)	Tattnall	Overstreets	487/8	Irwin

NAME	COUNTY	MIL.DIST	LOT/SECT	DREW LAND
Warren, Josiah(Orps)	Wilkinson	Kettles	501/11	Irwin
Warren, Josiah	Emanuel	58th	330/6	Appling
Warren, Josiah	Wilkinson	Kettles	37/8	Early
Warren, Mary(Wid)	Liberty		411/13	Irwin
Warren, Mary(Wid)	Tattnall	Overstreets	491/9	Irwin
Warren, Moses	Emanuel	58th	312/12	Irwin
Warren, Peter	Jackson	Rogers	384/27	Early
Warren, Reuben(Orps)	Franklin	Flanagans	21/6	Appling
Warren, Reuben	Laurens	Harris	28/1	Habersham
Warren, Robert	Baldwin	Doziers	447/4	Appling
Warren, Robert	Hall		42/2	Rabun
Warren, Sladey	Greene	Hoggs	67/2	Irwin
Warren, Stephen	Morgan	McClendons	122/12	Habersham
Warren, Wm.	Putnam	Berrys	220/16	Early
Warron, Dennis	Wilkinson	Brooks	57/3	Appling
Wars, Morse	Jackson	Rogers	127/18	Early
Warters, Littleberry	Pulaski	Davis	105/6	Appling
Wasden, Phillip M.	Jefferson	Waldens	194/11	Irwin
Washam, Edmond	Hancock	Thomas	403/5	Irwin
Washam, Robert	Putnam	Littles	2/4	Rabun
Washam, Thomas	Hancock	Thomas	34/13	Habersham
Washburn, Nancy(Wid)	Jones	Chappels	86/11	Irwin
Washington, James	Columbia	Shaws	307/8	Early
Washington, James	Putnam	Slaughters	333/21	Early
Washington, Robert B.	Baldwin	Marshals	516/8	Appling
Washington, Robt.B.Jr.	Baldwin	Marshalls	75/10	Hall
Waterfield, John H.	Chatham		126/1	Early
Waterfield, John H.	Chatham		337/7	Appling
Waters, Calison	Jackson	Hambletons	35/3	Rabun
Waters, Callinson	Jackson	Hamiltons	453/8	Irwin
Waters, Collins	Clarke	Starns	140/17	Early
Waters, David	Jackson	Hamiltons	473/11	Irwin
Waters, James	Wilkinson	Kettles	78/4	Rabun
Waters, Jane	Wilkes	Bates	164/21	Early
Waters, John	Wilkinson	Kittles	287/11	Irwin
Waters, Joseph	Franklin	P.Browns	91/3	Appling
Waters, Joseph	Oglethorpe		19/1	Irwin
Waters, Mary(Orp)	Jefferson	Langstons	237/4	Irwin
Waters, Morris	Oglethorpe	Murrays	36/13	Habersham
Waters, Philamon	Washington	Jenkins	173/18	Early
Waters, Richard	Washington	Daniels	76/28	Early
Wates, Sally	Jasper	Smiths	92/8	Irwin
Watins, Martin S.	Columbia	Shaws	46/1	Early
Watkins, Andrew G.	Franklin	J.Millers	311/3	Early
Watkins, Ansel L.	Columbia	Shaws	162/4	Irwin
Watkins, Daniel M.	Columbia	Shaws	27/1	Walton
Watkins, Gillim	Columbia	Gartrells	84/18	Early
Watkins, Henry B.	Jackson	Rodgers	293/9	Irwin
Watkins, James Jr.	Elbert	Whites	455/12	Irwin
Watkins, James M. (Orp)	Pulaski	Johnsons	83/12	Hall
Watkins, James(Orps)	Jones	Phillips	124/2	Early
Watkins, James	Franklin	J.Millers	32/2	Rabun
Watkins, James	Franklin	Jno.Millers	81/2	Irwin
Watkins, Jason	Richmond		251/6	Gwinnett
Watkins, Jobe	Franklin	Flanagans	198/7	Irwin
Watkins, John	Franklin	J.Millers	383/8	Appling
Watkins, John	Jefferson	Cowarts	264/4	Walton
Watkins, Josiah	Greene	Wheelis	185/1	Early
Watkins, Josiah	Greene	Wheelis	492/5	Irwin
Watkins, Labun	Oglethorpe	Thorntons	336/3	Appling
Watkins, Lydia(Wid)	Washington	Pools	268/14	Early
Watkins, Mathew	Franklin	Jos.Miller	118/3	Walton
Watkins, Moses	Madison	Adares	193/10	Early
Watkins, Mosses	Madison	Adares	15/3	Irwin
Watkins, Robert H.	Elbert	Whites	164/10	Irwin
Watkins, Robert	Jackson	Rodgers	366/11	Irwin
Watkins, Robert	Richmond	Laceys	92/3	Irwin

347

NAME	COUNTY	MIL.DIST	LOT/SECT	DREW LAN
Watkins, Samuel	Elbert	Childers	145/9	Irwin
Watkins, Thomas(Orps)	Laurens	Harris	256/18	Early
Watkins, Thompson	Wilkes	Josseys	166/2	Early
Watkins, Vinson	Clarke	Pentecost	370/5	Irwin
Watkins, Vinson	Clarke	Pentecost	382/13	Early
Watkins, Wm.(Orp)	Richmond	122nd	161/17	Early
Watkins, Wm.(Orps)	Putnam	Coopers	98/16	Irwin
Watley, Arnold	Morgan	Farrars	451/7	Irwin
Watley, James Sr.(RS)	Jackson	Hamiltons	184/1	Appling
Watley, James Sr.	Jackson	Hamiltons	265/12	Irwin
Watson, Arthur T.	Walton	Wagnons	84/19	Early
Watson, Asa	Laurens	Watsons	290/4	Walton
Watson, David	Columbia	Ob.Morriss	173/7	Early
Watson, David	Jasper	Bentleys	242/19	Early
Watson, David	Laurens	Watsons	18/2	Appling
Watson, Edward	Richmond	Palmers	504/6	Irwin
Watson, George	Columbia	Bealls	291/28	Early
Watson, George	Columbia	Bealls	3/5	Early
Watson, Guilford D.	Madison	Adares	317/7	Appling
Watson, Isaiah(Orps)	Laurens	Watsons	310/10	Irwin
Watson, Jacob	Pulaski	Lesters	477/7	Appling
Watson, James C.	Baldwin	Cousins	115/5	Early
Watson, James H.	Chatham		182/5	Appling
Watson, James(S/Jos)	Columbia	Ob.Morriss	49/1	Walton
Watson, James	Columbia	Watsons	154/13	Irwin
Watson, James	Tattnall	Johnsons	4/5	Appling
Watson, John	Elbert	Dooleys	55/6	Habersha
Watson, John	Elbert	Whites	389/1	Appling
Watson, John	Madison	Bones	192/16	Irwin
Watson, John	Wilkinson	Wiggins	182/18	Early
Watson, John	Wilkinson	Wiggins	182/9	Appling
Watson, Joshua	Jefferson	Langstons	7/5	Rabun
Watson, Margaret(Wid)	Wilkinson	Wiggins	28/4	Irwin
Watson, Mary(Wid)	Greene	Wheelis	56/12	Early
Watson, Michael	Jefferson	Langstons	351/6	Gwinnett
Watson, Nehemiah	Greene	142nd	195/4	Early
Watson, Reason	Laurens	Watsons	8/4	Habersha
Watson, Rebecca(Wid)	Columbia	Watsons	39/26	Early
Watson, Reuben	Putnam	Brooks	208/17	Early
Watson, Reuben	Putnam	Brooks	78/4	Early
Watson, Richard L.	Wilkinson	Smiths	431/3	Appling
Watson, Richard	Laurens	Watsons	49/3	Habersha
Watson, Robert	Elbert	Dooleys	328/2	Appling
Watson, Robert	Morgan	Hackneys	54/22	Early
Watson, Robert	Tattnall	Overstreets	61/7	Early
Watson, Samuel	Baldwin	Cousins	82/9	Appling
Watson, Sarah	Twiggs	Browns	366/6	Appling
Watson, Silas	Laurens	Watsons	129/8	Early
Watson, Silas	Laurens	Watsons	409/9	Early
Watson, Solomon	Wilkes	Runnels	246/20	Early
Watson, Terry B.	Morgan	Hackneys	447/12	Irwin
Watson, William C.	Baldwin	Cousins	15/2	Appling
Watson, William W.	Pulaski	Johnsons	43/22	Early
Watson, William	Columbia	Bealls	57/2	Appling
Watson, William	Jasper	Bartletts	297/3	Early
Watson, Wm.	Columbia	Bealls	110/16	Irwin
Watson, Zadock	Laurens	Watsons	361/11	Irwin
Watt, Alexander	Chatham		18/9	Appling
Watt, Ann(Wid)	Chatham		342/5	Irwin
Watt, Ann(Wid)	Chatham		385/6	Irwin
Watters, Charles	Franklin	R.Browns	485/6	Irwin
Watters, William	Tattnall	J.Durrences	31/17	Early
Watts, Ann	Chatham		183/10	Early
Watts, Archibald(Orps)	Morgan	Hubbards	332/16	Early
Watts, Edmund	Putnam	Mays	381/7	Appling
Watts, Francis	Chatham		204/11	Early
Watts, Hope H.	Jackson	Hamiltons	52/23	Early

NAME	COUNTY	MIL.DIST	LOT/SECT	DREW LAND
Watts, Jacob(Orps)	Laurens	D.Smiths	56/2	Rabun
Watts, John Y.E.	Morgan	Walkers	35/26	Early
Watts, John(Orps)	Montgomery	McElvins	263/27	Early
Watts, John	Morgan	Knights	155/16	Irwin
Watts, John	Morgan	Knights	186/18	Early
Watts, Joseph	Wilkinson	Kettles	477/3	Appling
Watts, Josiah	Greene	Carltons	397/4	Early
Watts, Jubal E.	Morgan	Hubbards	171/20	Early
Watts, Littleberry	Morgan	Hubbards	136/8	Appling
Watts, Presley(Orps)	Greene	Carltons	328/13	Early
Watts, Redmon	Morgan	Alfords	207/9	Appling
Watts, Richard J.	Jackson	Hamiltons	112/10	Irwin
Watts, Richard J.	Jackson	Hamiltons	229/2	Appling
Watts, Richard(Orps)	Greene	Jones	120/6	Irwin
Watts, Robert	Chatham		108/7	Irwin
Watts, Samuel	Jones	Kings	290/9	Appling
Watts, Samuel	Morgan	Walkers	228/3	Walton
Watts, Sarah	Chatham		425/3	Appling
Watts, Spencer	Hancock	Evans	326/8	Early
Watts, Thomas	Laurens	Smiths	302/6	Appling
Watts, Thomas	Morgan	Alfords	61/2	Habersham
Watts, William	Hancock	Edwards	54/10	Early
Watts, William	Laurens	D.Smiths	66/3	Appling
Wattson, James T.	Jasper	Kennedys	261/11	Early
Wattson, John	Jackson	Haggards	383/8	Irwin
Way, Thomas G.	Liberty		527/8	Irwin
Way, William	Chatham		363/7	Appling
Wayne, George	Wilkinson	Brooks	321/6	Gwinnett
Wayne, Greene	Hancock	Claytons	42/12	Early
Wayne, John	Hancock	Edwards	152/8	Hall
Wayne, Wm.C.	Chatham		179/9	Appling
Ways, Wm.Sr.(Orps)	Liberty		324/12	Irwin
Weatherby, George M.	Jones	Harrists	268/20	Early
Weatherby, John	Wilkes	Davis	523/7	Irwin
Weatherby, Septamus	Putnam	Buckners	30/13	Habersham
Weatherby, Septimus Sr.	Jones	Harrists	82/3	Early
Weatherby, Septimus	Jones	Weatherbys	274/6	Appling
Weatherington, John	Montgomery	McElvins	124/3	Early
Weatherington, Thos.	Jasper	Easts	66/13	Early
Weatherington, Wm.	Montgomery	McElvins	395/7	Irwin
Weathers, Elisha	Lincoln	Jeters	247/12	Irwin
Weathers, George(Orps)	Burke	J.Wards	478/9	Irwin
Weathers, Jenkins	Jones	Samuels	34/19	Early
Weathers, Jenkins	Jones	Samuels	481/11	Irwin
Weathers, Samuel	Twiggs	Hodges	205/13	Early
Weathers, Samuel	Twiggs	Hodges	300/5	Irwin
Weathers, Stephen(Orps)	Twiggs	Smiths	277/13	Early
Weathers, Valentine	Lincoln	Jeters	266/10	Irwin
Weathersby, Levin	Twiggs	Jeffersons	124/12	Irwin
Weathersby, Stephen	Twiggs	W.Belchers	91/20	Early
Weathington, Richard(RS)	Elbert	Webbs	217/6	Gwinnett
Weathington, Richard(RS)	Elbert	Webbs	39/10	Irwin
Weaver, Andrew	Oglethorpe	Davenports	56/6	Appling
Weaver, Christian	Warren	132nd	203/20	Early
Weaver, David	Putnam	Coopers	173/3	Habersham
Weaver, Drury A.	Warren	Blounts	101/11	Early
Weaver, Ira	Warren	152nd	185/6	Irwin
Weaver, Isham	Oglethorpe	Davenports	329/1	Early
Weaver, Jacob	Hancock	Justices	125/5	Appling
Weaver, Jane	Wilkes	Gordons	39/8	Early
Weaver, Jetha & Lucy(Orp)	Richmond	Burtins	344/16	Early
Weaver, John C.	Pulaski		14/1	Appling
Weaver, John C.	Pulaski	Davis	220/27	Early
Weaver, John	Jones	Samuels	114/10	Habersham
Weaver, John	Twiggs	Tisons	235/1	Appling
Weaver, Julius	Twiggs	R.Belchers	331/12	Early
Weaver, Rebecca(Wid)	Early		200/None	Early

NAME	COUNTY	MIL.DIST	LOT/SECT	DREW LAND
Weaver, Reubin	Putnam	Mays	513/6	Irwin
Weaver, Stephen	Emanuel	53rd	314/20	Early
Weaver, Stephen	Emanuel	53rd	68/8	Hall
Weaver, Susannah(Wid)	Morgan	Wrights	200/1	Appling
Weaver, William R.	Morgan	Wrights	20/2	Early
Weaver, William	Morgan	Wrights	150/4	Early
Weaver, William	Wilkes	Davis	72/1	Appling
Webb, Austin Jr.	Elbert	R.Christians	466/14	Early
Webb, Axiom	Wilkinson	Smiths	339/17	Early
Webb, Benjamin	Emanuel	55th	95/10	Early
Webb, Bridger	Elbert	Webb	134/17	Early
Webb, Burrell	Elbert	R.Christians	110/8	Early
Webb, Charles	Jasper	Baileys	295/8	Appling
Webb, Clabourn(RS)	Jackson	Winters	169/8	Irwin
Webb, Dawson	Wilkinson	Kettles	164/4	Appling
Webb, Eli	Emanuel	53rd	173/9	Appling
Webb, Eli	Emanuel	53rd	190/12	Irwin
Webb, Etheldred	Wilkinson	Kettles	9/16	Early
Webb, Etheldred	Wilkinson	Kettles	92/12	Irwin
Webb, James H.	Twiggs	Ellis	310/3	Appling
Webb, James	Elbert	R.Christian	154/7	Irwin
Webb, James	Elbert	R.Christians	219/4	Walton
Webb, John	Elbert	Penns	270/4	Walton
Webb, John	Putnam	Oslins	158/12	Habersham
Webb, John	Washington	Floyds	38/1	Walton
Webb, John	Wilkes	Smiths	340/4	Walton
Webb, Josiah(Orps)	Washington	Floyds	92/16	Early
Webb, Mary(Wid)	Greene	Armers	92/7	Gwinnett
Webb, Oren(Orps)	Jones	Kings	468/5	Irwin
Webb, Pleasant	Oglethorpe	Bridges	359/5	Irwin
Webb, Rockett	Walton	Sentells	23/7	Gwinnett
Webb, Samuel	Washington	Danells	272/5	Gwinnett
Webb, Stephen	Walton	Sentells	64/15	Irwin
Webb, Thomas T.	Liberty		216/7	Irwin
Webb, Wiley	Elbert	R.Christians	143/6	Early
Webb, Wiley	Elbert	R.Christians	190/13	Early
Webb, Wilie	Jefferson	Cowarts	288/6	Irwin
Webb, Willis	Jackson	Winters	269/6	Gwinnett
Webbs, Machariah	Bryan	20th	45/8	Irwin
Webbs, Micajah(Orps)	Greene	Armers	89/21	Early
Webbs, Milton P.	Elbert	R.Christians	86/6	Irwin
Webbs, William	Bryan	20th	121/3	Habersham
Webster, George B.	Richmond		307/8	Appling
Webster, George B.	Richmond	120th	453/28	Early
Webster, Hosea	Richmond	120th	176/13	Early
Webster, John	Columbia	Willingham	106/2	Appling
Webster, Labon	Wilkes	Bates	153/15	Early
Webster, Martin	Wilkes	Bates	512/8	Irwin
Webster, Reuben	Wilkes	Bates	467/5	Irwin
Webster, Samuel	Columbia	Willingham	453/7	Irwin
Webster, Seaborn	Elbert	Olivers	309/11	Early
Webster, William	Hall	Byrds	476/9	Irwin
Weeaden, Rowland	Franklin	Ashs	302/4	Irwin
Weeds, Bartholomew	Jasper	Evans	23/16	Irwin
Weekes, John	Jasper	Bartletts	34/6	Appling
Weeks, Ezekiel	Camden	32nd	224/27	Early
Weeks, James S.	Jasper	Clays	106/6	Early
Weeks, James S.	Jasper	Clays	481/3	Appling
Weeks, James	Putnam	Slaughters	102/4	Habersham
Weeks, John	Jasper	Bartletts	279/1	Appling
Weeks, Joshua	Jones	Wallers	375/21	Early
Weeks, Mary(Wid)	Washington	Avents	93/1	Early
Weeks, Poleman	Jasper	McClendons	139/13	Irwin
Weeks, Seabron	Hancock	Lucas	170/1	Early
Weeks, Theophilus	Camden	32nd	395/26	Early
Weeks, Thomas	Burke	72	258/1	Early
Weeks, William	Baldwin	Marshals	233/16	Early

NAME	COUNTY	MIL.DIST	LOT/SECT	DREW LAND
Weems, George	Jackson	Hamiltons	9/10	Hall
Weems, John S.	Jasper	Clays	67/12	Early
Weems, Walter H.	Wilkes	164th	514/8	Irwin
Weitman, Hannah(Wid)	Effingham		152/13	Irwin
Weitman, Jediah(Orps)	Effingham		297/1	Early
Weitman, Lewis	Effingham		28/1	Rabun
Weitman, Mathew	Effingham		88/5	Irwin
Weitman, Solomon(Orps)	Effingham		81/1	Rabun
Wekelly, George	Franklin	Turks	174/18	Early
Welborn, Abner	Wilkes	Holidays	257/2	Irwin
Welborn, David	Morgan	Paces	299/6	Early
Welborn, Ezekiel(Orps)	Wilkes	McLendons	53/2	Early
Welborn, John R.	Morgan	Hubbard	42/13	Early
Welborn, Josiah	Morgan	Campbells	47/4	Rabun
Welborn, Kurtus	Morgan	Campbells	145/10	Habersham
Welborn, Levi T.	Morgan	Hubbards	127/5	Gwinnett
Welborn, William R.	Morgan	Hubbards	68/15	Early
Welch, Asa	Washington	Brooks	349/5	Irwin
Welch, Benjamin(RS)	Jackson	Hamiltons	213/17	Early
Welch, David	Wilkinson	Kettles	148/11	Irwin
Welch, David	Wilkinson	Kettles	389/10	Early
Welch, Edmond	Morgan	Knights	54/1	Irwin
Welch, Elizabeth	Morgan	Knights	105/3	Appling
Welch, George	Columbia	Walkers	42/9	Irwin
Welch, Isaac	Burke	69th	216/20	Early
Welch, James	Burke	69th	30/10	Hall
Welch, James	Burke	69th	428/4	Appling
Welch, James	Jasper	Baileys	157/5	Irwin
Welch, Jesse	Columbia	Shaws	294/14	Early
Welch, John James(Min)	Burke	69th	167/15	Irwin
Welch, John(Orps)	Morgan	Knights	75/6	Gwinnett
Welch, John	Jasper	Centells	48/14	Early
Welch, Luke	Morgan	Knights	77/16	Early
Welch, Michael	Warren	153rd	264/11	Early
Welch, Michael	Warren	153rd	32/14	Early
Welch, Stephen	Chatham		13/9	Early
Welch, William	Baldwin	Taliaferro	243/4	Walton
Welch, William	Baldwin	Taliaferro	68/7	Early
Welch, William	Washington	Brooks	19/21	Early
Welden, John	Jones	Seals	263/17	Early
Weldon, Isaac	Jasper	Easts	199/7	Gwinnett
Weldon, James	Jasper	Reids	297/9	Appling
Weldon, James	Twiggs	R.Belchers	71/1	Appling
Weldon, Jesse	Jasper	Blakes	251/19	Early
Weldon, John	Jasper	Blakes	135/2	Appling
Weldon, Robert	Twiggs	R.Belchers	181/7	Irwin
Wellborn, Alfred	Wilkes	Dents	152/5	Gwinnett
Wellborn, Elias	Columbia	Gartrells	225/11	Irwin
Wellborn, Johnson	Wilkes	Dents	191/3	Irwin
Wellborn, Shubel S.	Wilkes	Hollidays	65/13	Early
Wellon, Thomas	Pulaski	Lesters	47/2	Early
Wells, Abner(Orps)	Greene	143rd	144/5	Appling
Wells, Andrew	Morgan	Farrars	45/14	Irwin
Wells, Benj.Jr.	Putnam	Buckners	62/6	Appling
Wells, George	Putnam	Littles	79/12	Irwin
Wells, John	Elbert	Olivers	176/1	Early
Wells, Joshua S.	Putnam	Stampers	30/18	Early
Wells, Julius(RS)	Twiggs	Ellis	131/1	Irwin
Wells, Marten Jr.	Jefferson	Langstons	267/28	Early
Wells, Martin Sr.	Jefferson	Langstons	44/13	Habersham
Wells, Matthew	Greene	143	99/10	Hall
Wells, Nicholas M.	Jones	Permenters	220/1	Appling
Wells, Salley	Oglethorpe	Brittons	379/6	Early
Wells, Samuel	Twiggs	Jeffersons	120/10	Habersham
Wells, Samuel	Wilkinson	Smiths	103/1	Irwin
Wells, Thomas B.	Jefferson	Bothwells	461/11	Irwin
Wells, Thomas	Putnam	Stampers	2/3	Walton

NAME	COUNTY	MIL.DIST	LOT/SECT	DREW LAND
Wells, Thomas	Putnam	Stampers	436/5	Irwin
Wells, William H.	Jasper	Clays	272/12	Early
Wells, William	Jones	Walters	426/1	Appling
Wells, Williams	Clarke	Starnes	77/1	Irwin
Wells, Wm.	Putnam	Buckners	121/1	Habersham
Welsh, Jane & Ann(Orps)	Chatham		388/9	Early
Welsh, Stephen(Orp)	Chatham		388/9	Early
Welsh, Thomas(Orp)	Chatham		388/9	Early
Wence, John	Chatham		166/14	Early
Wence, John	Chatham		78/9	Irwin
Werrell, Axum	Burke	Thomas	52/22	Early
Wesley, John(Orps)	Jasper	Posts	186/10	Irwin
West, Andrew Sr.	Elbert	P.Christian	243/1	Early
West, Cranford	Putnam	Robertsons	71/6	Early
West, Crawford	Putnam	Robertsons	182/9	Irwin
West, Edward	Wilkinson	Howards	276/8	Early
West, Francis	Greene	Jones	139/4	Early
West, Francis	Greene	Jones	234/12	Irwin
West, James(1st Orps)	Morgan	Selmons	15/11	Hall
West, James(Last Orps)	Morgan	Selmons	260/21	Early
West, James	Jones	Seals	353/2	Early
West, James	Oglethorpe	Bowls	368/21	Early
West, James	Walton	Wests	354/9	Appling
West, Jeremiah	Washington	Renfros	428/1	Early
West, John Jr.	Greene	143rd	28/6	Gwinnett
West, John	Jackson	Haggards	75/17	Early
West, John	Jasper	Evans	200/10	Early
West, Jonathan	Twiggs	Evans	373/4	Early
West, Levin	Washington	Wimberlys	179/5	Appling
West, Matthew K.	Burke	72nd	149/2	Habersham
West, Nathan(Orps)	Twiggs	Evans	595/2	Appling
West, Robert	Jasper	Evans	275/8	Early
West, Tabitha	Morgan	Selmons	97/17	Early
West, Wiley	Washington	Wimberlys	20/22	Early
West, William(RS)	Morgan	Hackneys	216/10	Habersham
West, William(RS)	Morgan	Hackneys	476/2	Appling
West, William	Columbia	Dodsons	435/13	Irwin
West, William	Wilkinson	Howards	339/1	Early
West, William	Wilkinson	Howards	91/6	Appling
Westbrook, Allen	Greene	Wheeler	203/4	Appling
Westbrook, James	Franklin	Harriss	6/3	Walton
Westbrook, John Jr.	Franklin	Harris	337/19	Early
Westbrook, John Jr.	Franklin	Harris	416/8	Irwin
Westbrook, Thos.B.	Franklin	Harris	77/1	Habersham
Westbrook, Thos.Sr.	Franklin	Harris	87/6	Appling
Wester, Benjamin	Morgan	Cammels	244/1	Walton
Wester, Daniel	Gwinnett	Hamiltons	49/4	Appling
Wester, Daniel	Gwinnett	Hamiltons	6/15	Irwin
Wester, Elias(Orps)	Tattnall	Cunyers	252/5	Gwinnett
Wester, Richard	Tattnall	Cunyers	451/3	Appling
Westermyres, Eliz.(Wid)	Chatham		125/6	Appling
Westermyres, Eliz.(Wid)	Chatham		33/1	Rabun
Western, Stephen	Hancock	Lucas	62/28	Early
Western, Thomas	Wilkes	McCendons	56/14	Early
Westly, Evans	Emanuel	55th	53/1	Habersham
Westmoreland, James	Jasper	Centells	106/6	Appling
Westmoreland, Reuben	Jasper	Centells	121/6	Irwin
Westmoreland, Robt.	Jasper	Reids	298/5	Gwinnett
Westmoreland, Wilborne	Jasper	Reids	411/8	Appling
Weston, Ezekiel	Burke	Hands	23/13	Irwin
Weston, William	Tattnall	Johnstons	567/2	Appling
Wethers, Samuel Sr.	Lincoln	Jeters	19/11	Hall
Whaley, Ebnezer	Jasper	Bentleys	415/26	Early
Whaley, Eli	Jackson	Rogers	56/6	Gwinnett
Whaley, Elijah	Jasper	Posts	231/9	Irwin
Whaley, Isaac	Morgan	Walkers	214/13	Early
Whaley, John	Putnam	Coopers	372/9	Early

NAME	COUNTY	MIL.DIST	LOT/SECT	DREW LAND
Whaley, Nathaniel	Jasper	Potts	277/10	Irwin
Whallis, Francis	Baldwin	Marshals	174/11	Irwin
Whallis, Francis	Baldwin	Marshals	257/7	Irwin
Whatley, Allen J.	Jones	Wallers	128/8	Hall
Whatley, Allen J.	Jones	Wallers	98/13	Early
Whatley, Elisha	Jones	Buckhalters	47/13	Habersham
Whatley, Fanny	Jasper	Centells	33/7	Appling
Whatley, Floyd	Greene	Tuggles	170/12	Habersham
Whatley, Green	Jones	Griffiths	197/1	Irwin
Whatley, Green	Wilkinson	Brooks	27/11	Irwin
Whatley, James	Jasper	Bentley	13/2	Early
Whatley, James	Jones	Buckhalters	213/26	Early
Whatley, John Sr.(RS)	Jones	Wallers	166/19	Early
Whatley, John(Orps)	Greene	Jones	68/2	Habersham
Whatley, Oran(Orps)	Morgan	Selmons	163/11	Irwin
Whatley, Solomon	Jones	Buckhalters	156/9	Irwin
Whatley, William	Jones	Kings	369/11	Irwin
Whatley, William	Jones	Kings	455/6	Appling
Whatley, Willis	Jones	Griffiths	203/7	Appling
Whatley, Wilmot	Jones	Samuels	19/5	Irwin
Whatley, Wm.R.(Orps)	Morgan	Alfords	283/7	Appling
Whatley, Wyat	Putnam	Berrys	347/19	Early
Whatley, Wyatt	Putnam	Berrys	342/5	Early
Wheat, Harvey	Lincoln	Walkers	394/10	Early
Wheat, Ila	Columbia	Bealls	228/5	Appling
Wheat, Wesley	Hall		201/16	Early
Wheatley, Curtis	Wilkes	Davis	220/6	Appling
Wheatly, Joseph	Wilkes	McLendons	148/1	Irwin
Wheddon, William	Tattnall	Overtsreets	70/5	Early
Wheeler, (Orps)	Franklin	Akins	141/9	Hall
Wheeler, Benjamin	Elbert	Gaines	174/12	Habersham
Wheeler, David	Baldwin	Taliaferro	153/11	Irwin
Wheeler, George W.	Jefferson	Abbots	267/5	Gwinnett
Wheeler, Hardy	Jones	Chappells	103/10	Habersham
Wheeler, James Sr.(RS)	Jackson	Rogers	114/1	Habersham
Wheeler, James Sr.(RS)	Jackson	Rogers	23/5	Irwin
Wheeler, James	Twiggs	R.Belchers	297/3	Appling
Wheeler, James	Warren	Hubberts	38/2	Appling
Wheeler, Jessee	Baldwin	Cousins	161/1	Appling
Wheeler, John Sr.	Jackson	Winters	293/7	Irwin
Wheeler, Leroy	Elbert	Doolys	318/12	Early
Wheeler, Noah	Twiggs	R.Belchers	36/14	Irwin
Wheeler, Noah	Twiggs	R.Belchers	89/19	Early
Wheeler, Reuben	Wilkinson	Lees	81/7	Early
Wheeler, Robert J.	Liberty		505/12	Irwin
Wheeler, Thomas	Elbert	Smiths	153/9	Irwin
Wheeler, Tierey(Minor)	Burke	70th	69/15	Irwin
Wheeler, William	Emanuel	53rd	201/15	Early
Wheeler, Wm.(RS)	Twiggs	R.Belchers	386/18	Early
Wheelis, Hardy	Jones	Kings	250/2	Early
Wheelis, Mark	Morgan	Wrights	78/9	Hall
Wheelis, Matthew	Jones	Shropshiers	167/3	Early
Wheelis, Wilborn	Greene	Wheelis	392/28	Early
Wheeller, Benjamin	Jackson	Hamiltons	461/5	Appling
Wheelous, Lewis Jr.	Morgan	Wrights	196/5	Early
Wheelus, Hardy	Jones	Chappels	194/28	Early
Wheelus, Lewis Sr.(RS)	Morgan	Wrights	361/3	Early
Wheler, William A.	Wilkes	Ogletrees	19/2	Walton
Whelis, Burton	Greene	Wheelis	222/11	Early
Whesenant, Jacob	Franklin	Powels	132/21	Early
Whiddon, John	Bulloch	Jones	319/12	Early
Whiddon, Lott	Laurens	Deans	41/3	Irwin
Whigham, Alexander	Jefferson	Lamps	488/5	Irwin
Whigham, Alexander	Jefferson	Lamps	97/13	Habersham
Whigham, Andrew	Jefferson	Flemmings	48/11	Hall
Whigham, John Jr.	Jefferson	Lamps	176/20	Early
Whigham, Joseph	Jefferson	Lamps	162/11	Irwin

353

NAME	COUNTY	MIL.DIST	LOT/SECT	DREW LAND
Whigham, Thomas	Jefferson	Lamps	12/17	Early
Whigham, William	Jefferson	Lamps	160/5	Irwin
Whigham, William	Pulaski	Senterfeits	26/9	Irwin
Whilley, Michael(Orps)	Jefferson	Abbots	267/12	Early
Whilley, Wiley	Morgan	Rameys	106/5	Rabun
Whipple, Jesse	Elbert	G.Higginbotham	225/8	Early
Whisenant, Adam	Franklin	Powels	151/8	Appling
Whitaker, Abel	Warren	Loyless	259/4	Walton
Whitaker, Arnold	Wilkes	Runnels	237/9	Appling
Whitaker, Benjamin	Franklin	Hammonds	158/9	Appling
Whitaker, David E.	Jefferson	Flemmings	145/26	Early
Whitaker, Edwin	Washington	Floyds	296/4	Early
Whitaker, Joel	Columbia	Shaws	225/2	Irwin
Whitaker, John Jr.	Morgan	Talbotts	308/3	Early
Whitaker, John Sr.	Morgan	Knights	323/7	Irwin
Whitaker, John	Wilkinson	Kettles	297/5	Irwin
Whitaker, Joshua Jr.	Columbia	Shaws	350/4	Early
Whitaker, Joshua	Richmond	Palmers	313/8	Early
Whitaker, Mark	Baldwin	Stephens	485/7	Irwin
Whitaker, Mary	Putnam	Slaughters	16/6	Habersham
Whitaker, Richard	Wilkinson	Smiths	286/13	Irwin
Whitaker, Samuel H.	Washington	Floyds	73/12	Early
Whitaker, Simon	Baldwin	Marshalls	248/2	Appling
Whitaker, Simon	Baldwin	Marshalls	72/27	Early
Whitaker, Thos.	Putnam	Slaughters	115/12	Habersha.
Whitaker, William	Madison	Adares	232/1	Early
Whitaker, William	Washington	Avents	30/1	Early
Whitaker, Wm.	Washington	Avents	207/6	Appling
Whitcombe, William	Columbia	Burroughs	435/15	Early
White, Alford	Madison	Hamiltons	384/5	Irwin
White, Allen	Emanuel	55th	268/12	Irwin
White, Allen	Emanuel	55th	311/13	Irwin
White, Arthur	Burke	Hands	246/10	Early
White, Asa	Elbert	Childers	469/8	Appling
White, Benedick	Baldwin	Cousins	16/2	Early
White, Benedict	Baldwin	Cousins	256/9	Irwin
White, Benjamin	Washington	Floyds	127/11	Early
White, Carter	Franklin	Heltons	198/1	Early
White, Constant	Burke	Spiveys	127/1	Appling
White, Cyrus	Jasper	Clays	136/1	Irwin
White, Daniel	Burke	70	484/10	Irwin
White, Daniel	Putnam	Bustins	374/6	Irwin
White, David	Elbert	Ruckers	189/1	Appling
White, Elbert	Morgan	Wrights	70/2	Appling
White, Elisha	Warren	150th	143/1	Early
White, Ezekiel	Burke	Hands	194/3	Walton
White, George	Chatham		143/9	Irwin
White, George	Madison	Jinkins	210/8	Irwin
White, George	Wilkinson	Smiths	329/6	Irwin
White, Henry	Burke	Spiveys	373/8	Early
White, Henry	Clarke	Harris	205/3	Early
White, Henry	Effingham		17/3	Early
White, Henry	Elbert	Smiths	210/13	Early
White, Isham	Elbert	Penns	224/26	Early
White, Jacob	Franklin	Vaughns	213/10	Early
White, Jacob	Franklin	Vaughns	35/10	Irwin
White, James(Orps)	Laurens	Jones	410/1	Appling
White, Jepthah Jr.	Franklin	Morris	316/28	Early
White, Jepthah Sr.	Franklin	Morris	54/15	Early
White, Jesse	Burke	Bells	137/10	Habersham
White, Jesse	Franklin	Burroughs	243/14	Early
White, John M.	Elbert	Whites	446/10	Irwin
White, John Sr.	Elbert	P.Christians	190/8	Irwin
White, John Sr.	Elbert	P.Christians	506/6	Appling
White, John Y.	Chatham		60/1	Early
White, John	Elbert	White/Chrsts.	15/17	Early
White, John	Greene	143rd	302/13	Early

NAME	COUNTY	MIL.DIST	LOT/SECT	DREW LAND
White, John	Greene	143rd	81/5	Appling
White, John	Greene	144th	263/6	Gwinnett
White, John	Jones	Buckhalters	291/20	Early
White, Joseph(Orps)	Jasper	Kennedys	317/27	Early
White, Joseph	Jasper	Smiths	21/5	Gwinnett
White, Joseph	Jones	Samuels	422/13	Irwin
White, Joshua	Jasper	Whites	67/2	Rabun
White, Judy(Wid)	Washington	Floyds	375/7	Gwinnett
White, Levi	Greene	142nd	403/12	Early
White, Levi	Putnam	H.Kendricks	125/5	Early
White, M.L.	Chatham		325/5	Gwinnett
White, Marten	Franklin	Morris	77/3	Habersham
White, Mary(Wid)	Bryan	20th	21/1	Early
White, Mary(Wid)	Franklin	Akins	262/16	Early
White, Nathaniel H.	Franklin	Hammonds	4/28	Early
White, Nicholas	Putnam	Slaughters	353/19	Early
White, Pleasant	Jasper	McClendons	68/16	Early
White, Pressley(Orps)	Columbia	Olives	302/7	Irwin
White, Resolved	Madison	Hamiltons	110/15	Irwin
White, Reuben	Elbert	Buckners	413/28	Early
White, Richard	Franklin	Akins	64/17	Early
White, Robert	Warren	152nd	449/6	Irwin
White, Robert	Wilkinson	Childs	140/12	Early
White, Robert	Wilkinson	Childs	241/5	Irwin
White, Samuel(Orps)	Jasper	Kennedys	225/2	Early
White, Samuel	Wilkinson	Childs	363/5	Appling
White, Samuel	Wilkinson	Childs	57/1	Early
White, Shelton		Elbert	P.Christians8/10, Hall	
White, Shelton	Elbert	P.Christians	355/7	Early
White, Stephen	Elbert	B.Higginbotham	228/21	Early
White, Stephen	Morgan	Knights	136/18	Early
White, Stephen	Morgan	Nights	223/3	Appling
White, Stephen	Wilkes	Holidays	153/4	Walton
White, Stut	Chatham		341/8	Irwin
White, Timothy	Morgan	Wrights	471/6	Appling
White, Venson	Hall	McCutcheons	258/3	Appling
White, Ward	Clarke	Moores	32/9	Irwin
White, William H.	Putnam	Coopers	48/17	Early
White, William Sr.	Elbert	Dobbs	189/9	Early
White, William(Orps)	Jones	Samuels	41/5	Habersham
White, William(Orps)	Twiggs	Evans	51/22	Early
White, William	Elbert	Ruckers	111/10	Early
White, William	Montgomery	Allstons	263/18	Early
White, Willie	Morgan	Wrights	146/2	Appling
White, Wilson	Franklin	Davis	85/2	Walton
White, Wm.(Bro/Levi)	Greene	142nd	192/7	Appling
White, Zachariah	Effingham		436/7	Appling
Whiteaker, William	Madison	Adares	79/10	Irwin
Whitefield, John	Chatham		108/1	Early
Whitehead, Austin	Wilkinson	Lees	392/10	Irwin
Whitehead, Henry	Jefferson	Mathews	431/15	Early
Whitehead, Henry	Jefferson	Matthews	377/12	Early
Whitehead, Jacky	Wilkinson	Lees	99/2	Walton
Whitehead, Jeminah	Putnam	J.Kindricks	51/2	Early
Whitehead, Joel	Oglethorpe	Bridges	139/9	Appling
Whitehead, John	Burke	Sullivans	307/17	Early
Whitehead, Martha(Wid)	Twiggs	Hodges	104/8	Early
Whitehead, Peter	Clarke	Pentecost	281/9	Appling
Whitehead, Rachel(Wid)	Clarke	Moores	366/7	Appling
Whitehead, Richard	Twiggs	R.Belchers	29/6	Habersham
Whitehead, Samuel Sr.	Oglethorpe	Bridges	103/9	Early
Whitehead, Thos.Jr.(Orps)	Putnam	J.Kendricks	140/9	Appling
Whitehead, Wm.	Jackson	Rogers	88/10	Hall
Whitehead, Zemula(Wid)	Richmond	122nd	256/28	Early
Whitehurst, Hilly	Appling	2nd	217/6	Irwin
Whitehurst, Levi	Montgomery	McElvins	241/12	Early
Whitehurst, Levi	Montgomery	McElvins	381/5	Appling

NAME	COUNTY	MIL.DIST	LOT/SECT	DREW LAND
Whitesides, Samuel	Putnam	Evans	241/26	Early
Whitfield, Alexander	Clarke	Pentecost	263/13	Early
Whitfield, Arthur	Washington	Burneys	117/14	Early
Whitfield, Arthur	Washington	Burneys	314/19	Early
Whitfield, Horatio S.	Putnam	Oslins	417/2	Appling
Whitfield, James	Jefferson	Flemmings	321/13	Irwin
Whitfield, James	Jefferson	Flemmings	87/3	Irwin
Whitfield, James	Putnam	Oslins	152/12	Habersham
Whitfield, Lewis	Burke	McNorrells	269/2	Early
Whitfield, Mathew	Putnam	Oslins	302/3	Appling
Whitfield, Matilda(Wid)	Jasper	Dardins	17/4	Habersham
Whitfield, Matthew	Putnam	Bledsoes	63/21	Early
Whitfield, Miles	Washington	Burneys	147/4	Appling
Whitfield, William H.	Laurens	D.Smiths	317/9	Irwin
Whitlock, Beasley	Morgan	Farrars	517/10	Irwin
Whitlock, Catharine(Wid)	Jasper	Hays	53/15	Early
Whitlock, Charles	Franklin	Jos.Millers	230/28	Early
Whitlock, George W.	Greene	Jones	349/16	Early
Whitlock, James	Jackson	Dicksons	27/10	Irwin
Whitlock, Josiah	Morgan	Farrars	153/1	Appling
Whitlock, Thomas	Franklin	J.Millers	21/16	Early
Whitlock, Wm.(Orps)	Jasper	Hays	271/20	Early
Whitman, Parley	Camden	Baileys	283/13	Early
Whiton, Robert(RS)	Jasper	Dosters	176/4	Walton
Whitsell, James	Oglethorpe	Barnetts	60/11	Early
Whittaker, Abel	Warren	Loyless	518/6	Irwin
Whitteaker, John Jr.	Morgan	Talbotts	637/2	Appling
Whitteaker, Joshua Jr.	Columbia	Shaws	419/7	Appling
Whitteaker, Wm.	Columbia	Shaws	172/5	Appling
Whittemore, Parley	Camden	Baileys	374/6	Appling
Whitten, Dempsey	Washington	Wimberlys	181/4	Walton
Whitten, Inman	Clarke	Mitchells	486/8	Appling
Whitten, Inman	Clarke	Mitchels	182/8	Appling
Whitten, James	Appling	4th	102/8	Appling
Whitten, James	Appling	4th	23/12	Irwin
Whitten, John	Clarke	Mitchells	471/10	Irwin
Whittington, Ephraim	Columbia	Whittington	405/21	Early
Whittington, Faddy	Jasper	Bentleys	188/19	Early
Whittington, Irwin	Warren	150th	53/16	Irwin
Whittington, Jack	Hancock	Millers	144/12	Hall
Whittington, John Sr.	Hancock	Millers	338/5	Gwinnett
Whittington, Mary(Wid)	Columbia	Ob.Morris	14/9	Hall
Whittingtong, Wm.	Bryan	19th	182/12	Habersham
Whittish, Dorothy	Morgan	Hubbards	321/21	Early
Whittle, Burwell	Washington	Renfroes	78/8	Hall
Whittle, Burwell	Washington	Renfros	267/20	Early
Whitton, Bowling	Clarke	Parrs	357/1	Appling
Whitton, Wileby	Camden	Tileses	173/2	Early
Whittons, Allen	Morgan	Wrights	131/8	Appling
Whitworth, Jospeh S.	Franklin	Davis	45/4	Habersham
Whitworth, Richard W.	Madison	Millicans	253/5	Gwinnett
Whitworth, Samuel Jr.	Madison	Milicans	2/12	Irwin
Whitworth, Thomas	Franklin	Davis	101/19	Early
Whitworth, Thomas	Franklin	Davis	156/7	Irwin
Whitworth, Winston	Madison	Millicans	261/6	Appling
Whorton, Benjamin	Hall		121/4	Walton
Whorton, Isaac	Hall	McCutchens	99/4	Irwin
Whorton, Joseph	Jackson	Dicksons	195/13	Early
Whorton, Joseph	Jackson	Dicksons	97/1	Early
Whorton, Rachael(Wid)	Jackson	Dicksons	33/15	Irwin
Whorton, William	Walton	Sentells	283/5	Gwinnett
Wiat, Benj.	Twiggs	Smiths	286/6	Appling
Wiatt, Elijah	Twiggs	Smiths	122/6	Appling
Wicker, James	Washington	Pools	418/6	Appling
Wicker, William	Wilkinson	Smiths	1/2	Walton
Wicker, William	Wilkinson	Smiths	191/19	Early
Wickers, Allen(RS)	Twiggs	R.Belchers	289/13	Irwin

NAME	COUNTY	MIL.DIST	LOT/SECT	DREW LAND
Widden, Eli	Emanuel	53rd	111/13	Irwin
Widden, Eli	Emanuel	53rd	229/2	Irwin
Widdington, Neno	Putnam	Mays	361/9	Irwin
Widemon, Henry	Jasper	Northcuts	20/2	Appling
Wienfry, Barbary	Burke	Thomas	232/3	Appling
Wier, Isaac	Jackson	Rogers	151/4	Appling
Wier, William(RS)	Clarke	Simms	492/11	Irwin
Wiggins, Allen	Wilkinson	Brooks	336/6	Irwin
Wiggins, Amos	Burke	Dys	116/27	Early
Wiggins, Dorothy B.(Wid)	Washington	Avents	48/5	Appling
Wiggins, James	Burke	Dys	273/4	Walton
Wiggins, James	Burke	Dys	44/16	Irwin
Wiggins, Jesse	Emanuel	57th	228/9	Early
Wiggins, Lemuel(Orps)	Washington	Avents	278/13	Early
Wiggins, Orren	Greene	Nelms	324/1	Early
Wiggins, Peter	Liberty		294/1	Appling
Wiggins, Peter	Liberty		98/12	Hall
Wiggins, Richard	Warren	151st	235/1	Walton
Wiggins, William	Burke	Dys	170/7	Gwinnett
Wiggins, William	Burke	Dys	212/18	Early
Wiggins, William	Burke	Dys	320/7	Early
Wiggins, William	Burke	Dys	378/15	Early
Wiggins, William	Warren	152nd	18/22	Early
Wiggins, William	Washington	Brooks	114/13	Habersham
Wigins, Richard	Warren	151st	292/28	Early
Wigley, Allen	Jackson	Hamiltons	133/1	Walton
Wigley, Joseph Jr.	Jackson	Hamiltons	449/9	Irwin
Wigley, Joseph Sr.	Jackson	Hamiltons	102/16	Early
Wigley, Joseph Sr.	Jackson	Hamiltons	126/28	Early
Wikham, Richard	Madison	Goulds	139/11	Habersham
Wilborn, Cordral T.	Greene	Nelms	346/4	Appling
Wilcher, Larkin	Warren	151st	89/4	Walton
Wilcocks, Elijah	Madison	Eigles	4/2	Early
Wilcox, Cyprian	Hancock	Colemans	156/10	Early
Wilcox, Gincey(Wid)	Richmond	Burtons	231/13	Irwin
Wilcox, John Jr.	Richmond	Burtons	302/2	Early
Wilcox, Samson(Orp)	Richmond	Burtons	185/10	Habersham
Wilde, Ann(Orp)	Richmond	122nd	128/8	Appling
Wilde, Richard H.	Richmond		323/6	Irwin
Wilde, Richard H.	Richmond	122	243/9	Early
Wilder, Edward	Jones	Permenters	347/5	Gwinnett
Wilder, Etheldred	Warren	153rd	150/1	Irwin
Wilder, Graves	Jones	Permenters	119/10	Early
Wilder, Henson	Chatham		349/1	Appling
Wilder, Joseph	Hancock	Canes	146/9	Appling
Wilder, Mary(Wid)	Jones	Permenters	339/5	Gwinnett
Wilder, Rachel(Wid)	Hancock	Canes	237/3	Early
Wilder, Selomon	Warren	Parhams	435/12	Irwin
Wilder, Ward	Jones	Permenters	151/2	Early
Wilder, Willis(RS)	Jones	Permenters	379/16	Early
Wilder, Winfred	Jasper	Baileys	283/12	Irwin
Wiley, Alexander C.	Glynn		38/2	Irwin
Wiley, Alphus(Orps)	Scriven	Moodys	54/7	Early
Wiley, Ann M.(Wid)	Hancock	Lucas	134/2	Habersham
Wiley, Burrel	Madison	Bones	287/3	Appling
Wiley, Edward	Richmond	120th	199/8	Early
Wiley, Enoch	Madison	Eigles	27/10	Hall
Wiley, Fanny(Wid)	Greene	Armis	7/11	Early
Wiley, John Jr.	Madison	Bones	29/20	Early
Wiley, John	Madison	Eigles	15/11	Irwin
Wiley, Moses	Hancock	Daniels	366/18	Early
Wiley, Taylor	Columbia	Bealls	290/8	Appling
Wiley, William	Gwinnett	Hamiltons	82/2	Appling
Wilford, John	Montgomery	Nobles	15/4	Appling
Wilhite, Philemon	Elbert	R.Christians	137/6	Appling
Wilkerson, Nancy	Baldwin	Irwins	172/10	Early
Wilkerson, Thos.(Orps)	Greene	Greens	48/16	Early

NAME	COUNTY	MIL.DIST	LOT/SECT	DREW LAND
Wilkes, Elisha	Emanuel	58th	338/21	Early
Wilkes, John C.	Jasper	Bartletts	71/5	Appling
Wilkes, John Jr.	Oglethorpe	Brittons	76/6	Gwinnett
Wilkes, Silas	Laurens	Deans	318/17	Early
Wilkey, Eliz.(Wid)	Washington	Pools	277/7	Early
Wilkey, Thomas(Orps)	Morgan	Farrars	169/12	Habersham
Wilkins, Alladon	Jasper	McClendons	236/21	Early
Wilkins, Alladon	Jasper	McClendons	31/2	Habersham
Wilkins, Archibald O.	Chatham		95/1	Walton
Wilkins, Clement	Elbert	P.Christian	319/7	Irwin
Wilkins, Henry	Columbia	Walkers	474/8	Appling
Wilkins, James	Clarke	Harpers	338/5	Early
Wilkins, James	Gwinnett	Hamiltons	22/7	Early
Wilkins, Job	Clarke	Stewarts	169/11	Early
Wilkins, Job	Clarke	Stuarts	65/6	Gwinnett
Wilkins, John	Columbia	Willingham	285/1	Early
Wilkins, John	Elbert	P.Christians	95/5	Appling
Wilkins, Leroy	Wilkes	Jossey	138/15	Early
Wilkins, Leroy	Wilkes	Josseys	23/2	Early
Wilkins, Mary A.	Chatham		148/2	Irwin
Wilkins, Robert	Clarke	Hentons	211/9	Early
Wilkins, Samuel	Liberty		467/10	Irwin
Wilkins, Thomas Jr.	Franklin	Davis	269/5	Early
Wilkins, Thomas	Columbia	Shaws	260/3	Irwin
Wilkins, William	Columbia	Willingham	313/8	Appling
Wilkins, William	Jackson	Dicksons	362/12	Early
Wilkins, William	Putnam	Oslins	146/3	Irwin
Wilkins, Wm.A.	Columbia	J.Morris	239/9	Irwin
Wilkinson, Abner	Greene	142nd	55/2	Walton
Wilkinson, Caleb	Jasper	Hays	66/23	Early
Wilkinson, Daniel	Greene	Greers	391/28	Early
Wilkinson, Eldred	Jasper	Hays	322/7	Appling
Wilkinson, Elisha	Franklin	Davis	12/1	Walton
Wilkinson, Francis	Wilkes	Ogletrees	310/15	Early
Wilkinson, James M.	Bulloch	Knights	314/4	Appling
Wilkinson, James	Jasper	Kennedys	362/28	Early
Wilkinson, John B.	Columbia	Burroughs	347/13	Early
Wilkinson, John	Bulloch	Jones	58/3	Habersham
Wilkinson, John	Columbia	Dodsons	487/5	Irwin
Wilkinson, John	Jasper	Bartlets	84/23	Early
Wilkinson, John	Twiggs	Bozemans	312/4	Walton
Wilkinson, John	Wilkes	Josseys	20/2	Rabun
Wilkinson, John	Wilkes	Josseys	235/9	Appling
Wilkinson, Lemuel	Putnam	Coopers	247/9	Appling
Wilkinson, Malcomb G.	Baldwin	Stephens	110/7	Appling
Wilkinson, Micajah	Twiggs	Bozemans	248/4	Appling
Wilkinson, Pleasant(Orps)	Wilkes	Mattox	45/23	Early
Wilkinson, Sherod(Orps)	Baldwin	Irwins	30/12	Irwin
Wilkinson, Simon	Jasper	Hays	191/5	Gwinnett
Wilkinson, Thomas(Orps)	Hancock	Lucas	354/7	Irwin
Wilkinson, Thomas(Orps)	Morgan	McClendons	273/13	Early
Wilkinson, Thomas	Morgan	McClendons	194/20	Early
Wilkinson, Thomas	Morgan	McClendons	325/2	Early
Wilkinson, Thomas	Wilkes	Ogletrees	251/2	Appling
Wilkinson, William	Franklin	P.Browns	304/18	Early
Wilkinson, William	Putnam	Coopers	323/19	Early
Wilkinson, Willis	Liberty		47/6	Irwin
Wilkinson, Wm.	Putnam	Coopers	292/20	Early
Wilkinson, Zarah	Putnam	Coopers	342/2	Early
Wilkite, Philip(Orps)	Elbert	R.Christians	40/3	Irwin
Wilkite, Phillip(Orps)	Elbert	Christians	110/11	Habersham
Willard, Sarah(Wid)	Morgan	Parkers	371/26	Early
Willborn, James	Jackson	Rogers	11/3	Appling
Willcox, Martin	Richmond	Burtons	101/7	Gwinnett
Willcox, Martin	Richmond	Burtons	138/11	Habersham
Willden, Wm.H.(Orps)	Scriven	36th	85/7	Irwin
Willder, Elizabeth	Scriven	36th	135/12	Irwin

NAME	COUNTY	MIL.DIST	LOT/SECT	DREW LAND
Willeby, John(RS)	Twiggs	W.Belchers	31/3	Irwin
Willes, Elisha	Emanuel	58th	57/22	Early
Willet, Henry(RS)	Effingham		88/3	Habersham
Willet, Sarah	Warren	150th	76/5	Rabun
Willets, Samuel	Jefferson	Cowarts	229/13	Early
Willey, Osburn	Madison	Adares	187/7	Early
Willey, Solomon	Jefferson	Waldens	262/5	Gwinnett
Willey, William	Hancock	Danells	191/12	Irwin
Willhite, Meshack T.	Madison	Adares	350/2	Early
Willhite, Morning(Wid)	Oglethorpe	Brittons	175/27	Early
Willhite, Philemon R.	Elbert	R.Christians	156/12	Irwin
William, John(Orps)	Elbert	Olivers	187/12	Early
William, John	Franklin	Akins	330/12	Irwin
William, John	Franklin	Akins	44/8	Early
William, Robert	Franklin	Akins	301/13	Irwin
Williams, Abigail	Greene	Hoggs	274/13	Irwin
Williams, Abraham M.	Hancock	Champions	101/1	Appling
Williams, Abraham M.	Hancock	Champions	197/7	Appling
Williams, Abraham	Twiggs	Evans	186/4	Irwin
Williams, Absalom	Wilkes	Mattox	271/1	Appling
Williams, Allen	Washington	Barges	165/2	Appling
Williams, Amos	Franklin	Hynes	127/2	Walton
Williams, Avington B.	Jasper	Eastes	95/14	Irwin
Williams, Benj.	Twiggs	Barrows	81/12	Hall
Williams, Benjamin	Morgan	Knights	487/5	Appling
Williams, Benjamin	Twiggs	Barrows	82/10	Early
Williams, Benjamin	Walton	Worshams	328/9	Early
Williams, Berry C.	Walton	Williams	134/1	Early
Williams, Blake	Liberty		227/2	Appling
Williams, Briant	Clarke	Tredwells	214/5	Appling
Williams, Burdy	Madison	Bones	353/13	Early
Williams, Caroline E.	Chatham		126/2	Habersham
Williams, Charles Jr.	Jasper	Bentleys	378/17	Early
Williams, Charles	Pulaski	Bryans	135/4	Appling
Williams, Cornelius M.	Liberty		232/6	Appling
Williams, Cornelius M.	Liberty		399/13	Irwin
Williams, Daniel	Washington	Avents	346/12	Irwin
Williams, Daniel	Washington	Floyds	110/2	Irwin
Williams, Daniel	Wilkes	Willis	247/2	Appling
Williams, Danl.McDonald	Putnam	Kendrick	232/1	Walton
Williams, Danl.McDonald	Putnam	Kendricks	4/26	Early
Williams, David(RS)	Twiggs	Evans	25/5	Rabun
Williams, David	Wilkinson	Kettles	419/1	Early
Williams, David	Wilkinson	Kettles	61/5	Irwin
Williams, Dicy(Wid)	Twiggs	Evans	411/10	Irwin
Williams, Dorson	Madison	Bones	380/8	Early
Williams, Drury	Twiggs	Willice & Chris.	106/6	Irwin
Williams, Drury	Wilkinson	Brooks	88/7	Gwinnett
Williams, Edward	Camden	33rd	218/14	Early
Williams, Edward	Camden	33rd	34/5	Early
Williams, Edward	Wilkinson	Kettles	87/10	Early
Williams, Elben(Orp)	Chatham		7/9	Early
Williams, Elijah	Madison	Bones	272/4	Appling
Williams, Elilm	Franklin	Yanseys	348/4	Early
Williams, Elisha	Hall		81/9	Irwin
Williams, Elisha	Putnam	Stampers	39/1	Walton
Williams, Elisha	Putnam	Stampers	51/12	Hall
Williams, Eliza(Orp)	Chatham		304/4	Walton
Williams, Eliza	Chatham		212/1	Walton
Williams, Elizabeth	Pulaski	Davis	390/13	Irwin
Williams, Emanuel	Wilkinson	Smiths	220/4	Irwin
Williams, Frances	Putnam	Robertsons	351/9	Early
Williams, Garrett Sr.	Bulloch	Edwards	206/14	Early
Williams, Garrett	Bulloch	Tilmans	490/9	Irwin
Williams, Garrot Sr.	Bulloch	Edwards	85/9	Early
Williams, George	Washington	Jinkinsons	29/3	Early
Williams, Green	Jackson	Rogers	148/13	Irwin

NAME	COUNTY	MIL.DIST	LOT/SECT	DREW LAND
Williams, Hannah(Orp)	Chatham		7/9	Early
Williams, Hardy S.	Morgan	Jordans	269/13	Irwin
Williams, Hardy	Washington	Barges	30/16	Early
Williams, Henry J.	Morgan	Walkers	41/10	Irwin
Williams, Henry	Twiggs	W.Belchers	304/7	Appling
Williams, Hezekiah	Jackson	Hamiltons	294/18	Early
Williams, Hiram	Oglethorpe	Myricks	26/8	Appling
Williams, Hodges M.Sr.	Twiggs	Evans	480/13	Irwin
Williams, Hope H.	Twiggs	Smiths	180/21	Early
Williams, Hope H.	Twiggs	Smiths	361/4	Appling
Williams, Hugh	Jasper	Kennedys	381/12	Early
Williams, Isaac	Jefferson	Lamps	325/11	Irwin
Williams, Isaac	Morgan	Farrars	34/8	Appling
Williams, Isham	Jackson	Hamiltons	112/7	Gwinnett
Williams, James H.	Jasper	Eastes	116/3	Habershaⅿ
Williams, James(Orps)	Pulaski	Davis	209/27	Early
Williams, James	Bryan	20th	38/5	Gwinnett
Williams, James	Bulloch	Edwards	73/5	Appling
Williams, James	Camden	32nd	30/11	Irwin
Williams, James	Camden	32nd	484/5	Irwin
Williams, James	Clarke	Mitchells	97/12	Early
Williams, James	Franklin	Jos.Millers	45/10	Hall
Williams, James	Jefferson	Lamps	399/7	Early
Williams, James	Madison	Bones	365/7	Irwin
Williams, James	Telfair	Williams	86/7	Gwinnett
Williams, Jas.M.Sr.	Twiggs	Evans	328/11	Irwin
Williams, Jeremiah W.	Putnam	Evans	451/8	Appling
Williams, Jesse	Twiggs	Evans	340/2	Appling
Williams, Jesse	Twiggs	Evans	80/3	Early
Williams, Joel	Laurens	D.Smiths	67/4	Walton
Williams, Joel	Washington	Refros	401/11	Irwin
Williams, John G.	Morgan	Knights	166/9	Appling
Williams, John Jr.	Madison	Bones	120/13	Early
Williams, John Jr.	Madison	Bones	225/6	Early
Williams, John Jr.	Washington	Floyds	298/4	Early
Williams, John L.	Putnam	Evans	151/28	Early
Williams, John Sr.	Washington	Floyds	135/12	Hall
Williams, John Sr.	Washington	Floyds	14/7	Gwinnett
Williams, John	Baldwin	Milledgeville	136/14	Early
Williams, John	Clarke	Oates	140/6	Appling
Williams, John	Franklin	Davis	58/5	Early
Williams, John	Hancock	Edwards	331/8	Irwin
Williams, John	Madison	Hamiltons	310/6	Early
Williams, John	Oglethorpe	Myricks	78/2	Walton
Williams, John	Warren	150th	98/11	Early
Williams, John	Wilkes	Holidays	79/27	Early
Williams, John	Wilkes	Kilgores	184/6	Gwinnett
Williams, John	Wilkes	Kilgores	337/1	Early
Williams, John	Wilkinson	Kettles	262/7	Appling
Williams, Jones	Morgan	Townsends	40/12	Irwin
Williams, Jos.Sr.(RS)	Warren	150th	17/4	Rabun
Williams, Joseph	Greene	Tuggles	69/1	Rabun
Williams, Joseph	Warren	150th	75/26	Early
Williams, Joshua(Orps)	Twiggs	Evans	40/1	Walton
Williams, Julian(Orp)	Chatham		304/4	Walton
Williams, Lavina(Wid)	Putnam	J.Kendricks	182/8	Irwin
Williams, Lewis Sr.	Franklin	Haynes	17/2	Habershaⅿ
Williams, Lewis	Tattnall	J.Durrences	116/3	Rabun
Williams, Lewis	Tattnall	J.Durrences	461/2	Appling
Williams, Lightfoot B.	Warren	150th	2/5	Early
Williams, Lightfoot B.	Warren	150th	400/3	Early
Williams, Louis Jr.	Franklin	Hains	22/6	Gwinnett
Williams, Luke	Jasper	Evans	104/13	Early
Williams, Mark	Twiggs	Ellis	60/10	Hall
Williams, Mary	Baldwin	Stephens	115/2	Rabun
Williams, Matthew J.	Elbert	Olivers	123/15	Early
Williams, Matthew	Morgan	Hackneys	37/5	Appling

NAME	COUNTY	MIL.DIST	LOT/SECT	DREW LAND
Williams, Micajah	Wilkinson	Lees	453/7	Appling
Williams, Micajah	Wilkinson	Lees	76/21	Early
Williams, Nathaniel	Franklin	Vaughns	308/13	Early
Williams, Nathaniel	Franklin	Vaughns	89/9	Early
Williams, Nathaniel	Twiggs	W.Belchers	2/2	Rabun
Williams, Nathanl.L.	Morgan	Farrars	456/3	Appling
Williams, Nicholas	Warren	Blounts	434/2	Appling
Williams, Patsey	Oglethorpe	Barnetts	115/8	Irwin
Williams, Peter J.	Greene	Harvills	262/6	Gwinnett
Williams, Polly	Jones	Greens	417/21	Early
Williams, Rebecca	Chatham		399/1	Early
Williams, Richard	Jones	Phillips	524/8	Irwin
Williams, Richard	Wilkinson	Lees	103/8	Appling
Williams, Robert Jr.	Madison	Bons	245/3	Early
Williams, Robert Sr.	Scriven		61/15	Early
Williams, Robert(Orps)	Jackson	Dicksons	87/18	Early
Williams, Robert	Franklin	Akins	345/5	Gwinnett
Williams, Robert	Wilkes	Kilgores	270/27	Early
Williams, Robert	Wilkes	Runnels	377/2	Early
Williams, Rowland(Orps)	Emanuel	59th	432/10	Irwin
Williams, Rowland	Wilkinson	Childs	156/11	Hall
Williams, Saml.Jr.	Bulloch	Edwards	149/2	Irwin
Williams, Saml.Sr.(Orps)	Bulloch	Edwards	80/2	Habersham
Williams, Samuel Jr.	Bulloch	Edwards	7/7	Irwin
Williams, Samuel Sr.	Twiggs	Hodges	327/2	Early
Williams, Samuel T.	Twiggs	Thames	267/6	Appling
Williams, Samuel	Twiggs	R.Belchers	406/5	Irwin
Williams, Samuel	Wilkinson	Smiths	114/2	Early
Williams, Sarah(Wid)	Laurens	Harris	408/6	Irwin
Williams, Sarah(Wid)	Twiggs	Hodges	45/27	Early
Williams, Silas	Pulaski	Johnson	52/28	Early
Williams, Silas	Pulaski	Johnstons	230/9	Appling
Williams, Smith	Chatham		267/26	Early
Williams, Solomon	Laurens	Kinchens	54/3	Rabun
Williams, Stafford	Jones	Griffiths	75/4	Appling
Williams, Stephen S.	Chatham		249/18	Early
Williams, Stephen W.	Wilkinson	Smiths	71/3	Early
Williams, Stephen	Laurens	Watsons	402/26	Early
Williams, Stephen	Putnam	Buckners	138/17	Early
Williams, Stephen	Putnam	Buckners	4/4	Early
Williams, Stephen	Putnam	Mahons	116/2	Rabun
Williams, Stephen	Tattnall	J.Durrences	282/6	Gwinnett
Williams, Stephen	Washington	Brooks	499/2	Appling
Williams, Stephen	Washington	Floyds	493/6	Irwin
Williams, Susannah(Wid)	Warren	Blounts	221/17	Early
Williams, Syllatus	Washington	Floyds	371/5	Irwin
Williams, Theophilus	Twiggs	Hodges	48/3	Habersham
Williams, Thomas H.	Chatham		147/1	Appling
Williams, Thomas Sr.(RS)	Jackson	Rogers	154/3	Early
Williams, Thomas Sr.(RS)	Jackson	Rogers	96/14	Early
Williams, Thomas Sr.	Washington	Floyds	196/3	Appling
Williams, Thomas Sr.	Washington	Floyds	430/9	Irwin
Williams, Thomas(RS)	Jackson	Rodgers	264/18	Early
Williams, Thomas	Baldwin	Stephens	307/7	Irwin
Williams, Thomas	Chatham		127/21	Early
Williams, William(Orps)	Clarke	Mitchells	233/8	Early
Williams, William	Bryan	19th	134/2	Irwin
Williams, William	Bulloch	Edwards	127/9	Appling
Williams, William	Bulloch	Edwards	96/16	Irwin
Williams, William	Effingham		165/9	Appling
Williams, William	Jackson	Rogers	47/13	Irwin
Williams, William	Putnam	Buckners	30/16	Irwin
Williams, William	Scriven		518/15	Early
Williams, William	Warren	McCrarys	39/3	Early
Williams, William	Washington	Cummins	193/9	Irwin
Williams, Wilson	Greene	Kimbroughs	148/9	Hall
Williams, Wilson	Jones	Seals	152/10	Hall

NAME	COUNTY	MIL.DIST	LOT/SECT	DREW LAND
Williams, Wilson	Jones	Seals	298/2	Appling
Williams, Wilson	Putnam	Oslins	484/11	Irwin
Williams, Winfrey	Baldwin	Haws	153/12	Hall
Williams, Wiott	Oglethorpe	Dunns	29/2	Early
Williams, Wm.(Bare C)	Jackson	Rogers	382/1	Early
Williams, Wm.	Elbert	Dobbs	79/1	Appling
Williams, Wm.	Telfair	Wilsons	237/1	Walton
Williams, Wm.M.	Wilkes	McClendons	393/5	Early
Williams, Wm.M.	Wilkes	McLendons	51/5	Rabun
Williams, Wm.Sr.	Wilkes	Russels	297/11	Early
Williams, Zachariah(RS)	Wayne	Crews	207/4	Irwin
Williams, Zachariah(RS)	Wayne	Crews	395/12	Early
Williams, Zachariah(RS)	Wayne	Crews	504/7	Irwin
Williamson, Adam(RS)	Jackson	Rogers	140/3	Habersham
Williamson, Adam(RS)	Jackson	Rogers	281/7	Early
Williamson, Benj.	Jasper	Evans	239/5	Appling
Williamson, Benj.	Putnam	Oslins	168/2	Appling
Williamson, Calbrook	Wilkes	Brooks	128/9	Early
Williamson, Charles	Baldwin	Marshals	171/16	Early
Williamson, Charles	Hancock	Lucas	456/11	Irwin
Williamson, Eliz.(Wid)	Wilkinson	Lees	347/17	Early
Williamson, Eugene J.	Baldwin	Marshalls	145/6	Early
Williamson, George	Jackson	Winters	387/6	Appling
Williamson, George	Jackson	Winters	78/18	Early
Williamson, Isaac	Wilkes	Rennolds	230/9	Irwin
Williamson, James(Orp)	Wilkinson	Lees	115/3	Early
Williamson, James	Camden	Clarkes	474/12	Irwin
Williamson, James	Camden	Clarks	39/15	Early
Williamson, James	Franklin	Hammonds	211/3	Early
Williamson, James	Jasper	Reids	399/12	Early
Williamson, John T.	Chatham		97/4	Irwin
Williamson, John	Montgomery	Alstons	200/1	Walton
Williamson, John	Montgomery	Alstons	69/12	Early
Williamson, John	Scriven	Roberts	193/7	Gwinnett
Williamson, Lilborn	Jones	Buckhalters	527/6	Irwin
Williamson, M.R.Jr.	Scriven	Roberts	18/12	Early
Williamson, M.R.Jr.	Scriven	Roberts	38/4	Walton
Williamson, Malachi	Washington	Wemberly	91/4	Appling
Williamson, Margaret(Wid)	Laurens	Harris	155/16	Early
Williamson, Mary(Wid)	Jones	Buckhalters	189/2	Irwin
Williamson, Nathan	Liberty		221/1	Appling
Williamson, Nathan	Liberty		5/10	Early
Williamson, Penellopy	Montgomery	Alstons	321/7	Irwin
Williamson, Reuben	Putnam	J.Kendricks	202/6	Early
Williamson, Reuben	Putnam	J.Kindricks	252/3	Walton
Williamson, Richard	Scriven	Roberts	225/19	Early
Williamson, Robert	Burke	Dys	94/5	Appling
Williamson, Robert	Jasper	Clays	232/17	Early
Williamson, Samuel	Jasper	Evans	375/7	Early
Williamson, Samuel	Jasper	Evans	67/13	Irwin
Williamson, Seth	Jones	Seals	61/1	Walton
Williamson, Silas	Putnam	Bustins	205/1	Appling
Williamson, Stephen	Burke	Royals	209/9	Early
Williamson, Thomas W.	Jackson	Rogers	379/3	Irwin
Williamson, Thomas	Oglethorpe	Murrays	28/13	Habersham
Williamson, Thos.C.	Hancock	Mims	400/5	Irwin
Williamson, Wiatt C.	Jones	Jeffersons	352/17	Early
Williamson, William	Camden	32nd	376/2	Early
Williamson, William	Camden	32nd	40/19	Irwin
Williamson, William	Jasper	Phillips	228/11	Irwin
Williamson, Wm.(Orps)	Franklin	Hammonds	39/10	Hall
Williamson, Wm.	Jackson	Winters	183/7	Appling
Williamson, Wm.	Oglethorpe	Murrays	196/4	Irwin
Willibah, James	Morgan	Wrights	48/4	Early
Williby, John(RS)	Twiggs	W.Belchers	66/8	Hall
Williby, John(RS)	Twiggs	W.Belchers	68/5	Gwinnett
Willice, Aldridge	Laurens	D.Smiths	321/5	Irwin

NAME	COUNTY	MIL.DIST	LOT/SECT	DREW LAND
Willie, Flora(Orp)	Richmond	Palmers	363/6	Irwin
Willie, John(Orp)	Richmond	Palmers	363/6	Irwin
Willie, Sarah(Orp)	Richmond	Palmers	363/6	Irwin
Willie, Wesley(Orp)	Richmond	Palmers	363/6	Irwin
Williford, Benjamin	Warren	Blounts	503/11	Irwin
Williford, Britain	Madison	Willifords	182/10	Early
Williford, Brittain	Madison	Willifords	354/9	Early
Williford, David	Chatham		113/5	Appling
Williford, Hansel	Warren	151st	245/2	Irwin
Williford, Hezekiah	Warren	154th	87/8	Appling
Williford, Jeptha V.	Madison	Willifords	468/10	Irwin
Williford, Nathan	Madison	Willifords	243/3	Irwin
Williford, Samuel	Madison	Willifords	304/10	Irwin
Willin, Benjamin	Telfair	Williams	223/3	Early
Willingham, Alban	Oglethorpe	Davenports	123/15	Irwin
Willingham, Archer	Jasper	Clays	229/5	Early
Willingham, Caleb	Jones	Permenters	422/7	Appling
Willingham, Charles	Baldwin	Cousins	348/5	Appling
Willingham, George	Columbia	Willingham	210/15	Early
Willingham, Hardman	Jasper	Posts	189/26	Early
Willingham, Isaac(Orps)	Lincoln	Graves	192/5	Irwin
Willingham, James	Baldwin	Cousins	204/28	Early
Willingham, John C.	Columbia	Willingham	39/13	Habersham
Willingham, John G.	Columbia	Willinghams	304/17	Early
Willingham, John(RS)	Columbia	Gartrells	253/7	Appling
Willingham, John(RS)	Columbia	Gartrells	376/8	Early
Willingham, Rolla	Columbia	Willingham	243/8	Irwin
Willingham, Samuel	Jackson	Winters	294/6	Gwinnett
Willingham, Thomas	Columbia	Willingham	169/7	Gwinnett
Willingham, Thomas	Jasper	Hays	441/21	Early
Willingham, Thomas	Morgan	Wrights	8/14	Irwin
Willingham, Troy	Oglethorpe	Davenports	26/2	Habersham
Willingham, William	Jasper	Reids	422/8	Appling
Willingham, Wm.B.	Columbia	Willingham	381/6	Early
Willis, Aron	Burke	J.Wards	207/12	Habersham
Willis, Arthur	Jasper	Hays	109/17	Early
Willis, Arthur	Jasper	Hays	8/12	Habersham
Willis, Benj.(RS)	Telfair	Williams	424/11	Irwin
Willis, Benjamin	Laurens	Harris	23/11	Irwin
Willis, Daniel H.	Jasper	McClendons	340/8	Appling
Willis, Daniel H.	Jasper	McClendons	90/13	Habersham
Willis, David	Laurens	Watsons	451/6	Irwin
Willis, Dempsey Sr.	Jones	Shropshiers	222/6	Irwin
Willis, Dempsey Sr.	Jones	Shropshiers	394/10	Irwin
Willis, Edney(Wid)	Wilkes	Willis	203/2	Early
Willis, Eliz.	Wilkes	Gordons	443/8	Appling
Willis, Ennis	Lincoln	Thompsons	171/3	Appling
Willis, George	Laurens	Ross	44/1	Early
Willis, Henry	Greene	Ragins	352/6	Irwin
Willis, Hosea	Jones	Shropshiers	111/3	Appling
Willis, Jacob	Scriven	Lovetts	51/5	Irwin
Willis, James(Orps)	Jones	Buckhalters	22/13	Early
Willis, Jesse	Lincoln	Thompson	252/10	Early
Willis, John C.	Jasper	Bartletts	291/4	Appling
Willis, John W.	Wilkes	Willis	258/7	Irwin
Willis, John W.	Wilkes	Willis	395/11	Irwin
Willis, John	Elbert	G.Higginbotham	324/28	Early
Willis, John	Twiggs	Evans	203/6	Irwin
Willis, John	Twiggs	Evans	370/13	Early
Willis, Jonathan	Liberty		156/8	Irwin
Willis, Jonathan	Liberty		387/11	Early
Willis, Joseph Sr. (RS)	Effingham		291/21	Early
Willis, Joseph Sr. (RS)	Effingham		98/1	Early
Willis, Joshua	Wilkes	Perrys	380/9	Early
Willis, Lewis(Orps)	Wilkes	Willis	79/3	Walton
Willis, Lowden	Hancock	Daniels	21/14	Irwin
Willis, Martha(Wid)	Jones	Buckhalters	517/9	Irwin

NAME	COUNTY	MIL.DIST	LOT/SECT	DREW LAND
Willis, Nicholas	Jackson	Rogers	6/5	Gwinnett
Willis, Paul T.	Wilkes	Willis	89/10	Habersham
Willis, Perry	Effingham		35/1	Rabun
Willis, Price	Baldwin	Irwins	298/3	Early
Willis, Rachel(Wid)	Jackson	Rogers	184/4	Early
Willis, Redden	Wilkinson	Lees	90/3	Walton
Willis, Reddin	Wilkinson	Lees	2/17	Early
Willis, Richard J.	Wilkes	Brooks	148/11	Early
Willis, Richard J.	Wilkes	Brooks	276/6	Irwin
Willis, Robert	Jefferson	Waldens	428/7	Irwin
Willis, Thomas(Orps)	Wilkes	Gordons	152/9	Irwin
Willis, Thomas	Elbert	G.Higginbotham	275/4	Irwin
Willis, Thomas	Jones	Phillips	289/8	Appling
Willis, Thomas	Jones	Phillips	319/10	Early
Willis, Thomas	Lincoln	Graves	84/6	Early
Willis, Thomas	Twiggs	Evans	434/28	Early
Willis, William Sr.	Jones	Chappels	292/21	Early
Willis, William	Baldwin	Marshalls	178/12	Irwin
Willis, William	Greene	Carltons	120/4	Appling
Willis, William	Jasper	Bentleys	328/6	Early
Willis, William	Putnam	Morelands	106/9	Appling
Willis, Williamson	Baldwin	Irwins	427/1	Appling
Willmaker, John Jr.	Wilkes	Killgores	255/8	Irwin
Willmaker, John	Wilkes	Kilgores	274/28	Early
Willobers, Elijah	Clarke	Mereweather	153/12	Habersham
Willobers, Robert	Clarke	Merreweather	118/1	Appling
Willobers, Thomas	Clarke	Merreweather	88/15	Early
Willobers, Wm.B.	Clarke	Merreweather	98/27	Early
Willoughby, Aaron	Wilkinson	Kettles	196/8	Irwin
Willoughby, Lemuel D.W.	Twiggs	Thames	175/2	Rabun
Wills, William H.	Jasper	Clays	91/15	Irwin
Willshire, Charles	Jasper	Bentleys	293/13	Early
Willson, James Sr.	Jasper	Posts	373/5	Appling
Willson, James	Jasper	Evans	287/9	Irwin
Willson, Jesse A.	Chatham		136/3	Early
Willson, John	Chatham		140/4	Early
Willson, John	Jasper	Clays	247/4	Appling
Willson, John	Richmond	398	199/12	Early
Willson, Joseph	Jasper	Barnes	115/7	Early
Willson, Julia	Chatham		107/1	Habersham
Willson, Samuel	Scriven	Lovetts	238/11	Early
Willson, Thomas	Jasper	Centells	364/17	Early
Willson, William	Chatham		130/4	Early
Wilmouth, William	Franklin	Akins	121/9	Early
Wilson, Alexander	Morgan	Townsends	191/4	Irwin
Wilson, Barbary(Wid)	Washington	Jinkinsons	122/3	Walton
Wilson, Benjamin	Hancock	Smiths	127/7	Appling
Wilson, Charles	Richmond	398	321/17	Early
Wilson, Charles	Richmond	398th	67/4	Early
Wilson, Craven	Hall		72/14	Early
Wilson, Daniel	Greene	Jordans	208/11	Irwin
Wilson, David	Chatham		173/8	Irwin
Wilson, David	Chatham		225/6	Gwinnett
Wilson, David	Warren	152nd	114/2	Habersham
Wilson, Drury	Jefferson	Cowarts	77/5	Irwin
Wilson, Elias	Warren	132nd	74/11	Early
Wilson, Elias	Warren	152nd	155/15	Irwin
Wilson, Elijah	Jasper	Bentleys	149/16	Early
Wilson, Elijah	Jasper	Centells	130/14	Irwin
Wilson, Gabriel(Orps)	Effingham		400/8	Irwin
Wilson, George	Twiggs	W.Belchers	130/14	Early
Wilson, Henry	Jackson	Dicksons	192/10	Habersham
Wilson, Henry	Telfair	Wilsons	97/21	Early
Wilson, Hudson B.	Greene	143rd	450/8	Appling
Wilson, Hugh	Jasper	Northcuts	173/14	Early
Wilson, Hugh	Jefferson	Abbotts	70/13	Irwin
Wilson, Isaac	Putnam	Evans	418/7	Appling

NAME	COUNTY	MIL.DIST	LOT/SECT	DREW LAND
Wilson, James G.	Chatham		285/4	Irwin
Wilson, James G.	Jackson	Haggards	46/21	Early
Wilson, James J.	Jackson	Winters	145/13	Early
Wilson, James Jr.	Jackson	Winters	120/14	Early
Wilson, James Sr.	Elbert	Doolys	549/2	Appling
Wilson, James Sr.	Jasper	Posts	326/3	Early
Wilson, James Sr.	Jasper	Posts	403/26	Early
Wilson, James(RS)	Franklin	Attaways	133/1	Appling
Wilson, James	Baldwin	Marshalls	343/8	Early
Wilson, James	Burke	Bells	402/12	Early
Wilson, James	Camden	Baileys	245/6	Irwin
Wilson, James	Columbia	Burroughs	300/6	Appling
Wilson, James	Columbia	Burroughs	59/5	Gwinnett
Wilson, James	Effingham		19/3	Walton
Wilson, James	Effingham		207/6	Early
Wilson, James	Hall	Byards	126/5	Early
Wilson, James	Hancock	Millers	103/10	Hall
Wilson, James	Jasper	Evans	133/7	Gwinnett
Wilson, James	Liberty		238/26	Early
Wilson, Jeremiah	Effingham		388/8	Irwin
Wilson, Jessey A.	Chatham		178/10	Irwin
Wilson, John S.	Jasper	Hays	145/11	Habersham
Wilson, John(Minor)	Burke	70th	354/7	Early
Wilson, John	Clarke	Tredwells	178/20	Early
Wilson, John	Franklin	Attaways	303/19	Early
Wilson, John	Greene	Ragans	141/10	Hall
Wilson, John	Greene	Ragans	377/15	Irwin
Wilson, John	Jasper	Bentleys	206/7	Irwin
Wilson, John	Jasper	Bentleys	340/2	Appling
Wilson, John	Twiggs	Evans	403/26	Early
Wilson, Joseph	Putnam	J.Kendricks	207/8	Irwin
Wilson, Joseph	Richmond	Palmers	101/14	Early
Wilson, Josiah	Liberty		25/9	Irwin
Wilson, Lemuel (Orps)	Baldwin	Irwins	105/9	Irwin
Wilson, Leonard	Jasper	Hays	107/3	Habersham
Wilson, Margaret(Wid)	Columbia	Willingham	48/11	Irwin
Wilson, Moses	Jackson	Winters	167/20	Early
Wilson, Moses	Pulaski	Senterfeits	402/11	Early
Wilson, Peter	Franklin	Attaways	362/17	Early
Wilson, Redding	Jones	Samuels	489/3	Appling
Wilson, Richard	Greene	143rd	396/13	Early
Wilson, Richard	Jasper	Northcuts	245/1	Walton
Wilson, Richard	Jasper	Northcuts	477/10	Irwin
Wilson, Robert(Orps)	Washington	Jinkinsons	22/1	Early
Wilson, Robert	Hancock	Millers	127/1	Early
Wilson, Saml.	Twiggs	W.Belchers	173/19	Early
Wilson, Samuel L.	Franklin	Hoopers	203/2	Appling
Wilson, Samuel	Burke	Bells	94/19	Early
Wilson, Sinson(Orp)	Washington	Barges	178/1	Early
Wilson, Solomon	Jones	Permenters	190/3	Walton
Wilson, Solomon	Jones	Permenters	451/11	Irwin
Wilson, Stainback	Richmond	398th	427/12	Irwin
Wilson, Stephen	Jackson	Winters	159/3	Irwin
Wilson, Thomas M.	Hall		369/17	Early
Wilson, Thomas R.	Hancock	Harts	232/6	Gwinnett
Wilson, Thomas	Elbert	Dooleys	356/7	Gwinnett
Wilson, Thomas	Elbert	Doolys	169/26	Early
Wilson, Thomas	Greene	143rd	124/10	Early
Wilson, Thomas	Greene	143rd	344/18	Early
Wilson, Thomas	Hall		19/13	Irwin
Wilson, Thomas	Hall		376/19	Early
Wilson, Thomas	Jackson	Winters	86/7	Irwin
Wilson, Thomas	Jasper	Bentleys	84/2	Rabun
Wilson, William(Orps)	Jones	Samuels	208/28	Early
Wilson, William	Effingham		351/16	Early
Wilson, William	Greene	Tuggles	427/11	Irwin
Wilson, William	Jasper	Bentleys	326/1	Early

NAME	COUNTY	MIL.DIST	LOT/SECT	DREW LAND
Wilson, William	Jones	Kings	339/6	Appling
Wilson, William	Madison	Orrs	339/18	Early
Wilson, William	Twiggs	R.Belchers	400/19	Early
Wily, Wm.	Jackson	Dicksons	107/20	Early
Wimbash, Edwd.	Putnam	Buckners	124/14	Irwin
Wimberley, Lewis(Sr)	Jones	Samuels	331/16	Early
Wimberley, Titus	Jones	Samuels	317/15	Early
Wimberly, Abner	Jones	Permenters	204/2	Appling
Wimberly, Ezekiel Jr.	Twiggs	Browns	318/5	Gwinnett
Wimberly, Henry	Jones	Permenters	136/13	Irwin
Wimberly, James	Twiggs	Browns	206/9	Early
Wimberly, John	Burke	Royals	115/1	Walton
Wimberly, John	Burke	Royals	409/1	Appling
Wimberly, John	Jones	Permenters	270/13	Irwin
Wimberly, Joshua	Twiggs	Bozemans	263/9	Irwin
Wimberly, Lewis D.	Jones	Samuels	123/14	Irwin
Wimberly, Mary(Wid)	Washington	Wimberlys	122/2	Early
Wimberly, William	Burke	71st	225/4	Early
Wimberly, William	Twiggs	Hodges	383/12	Irwin
Winchester, Jesse	Jasper	Smiths	184/7	Irwin
Windham, Edward	Warren	154th	377/11	Early
Windham, John	Baldwin	Ellis	171/10	Early
Windham, John	Baldwin	Ellis	294/7	Irwin
Windom, Francis	Jasper	Bartletts	204/21	Early
Winefred, Joakin	Greene	143rd	368/8	Appling
Winfield, Joel	Jackson	Stricklings	193/2	Appling
Winfield, John	Greene	Fosters	330/1	Appling
Winfield, William	Greene	Fosters	24/11	Irwin
Winfrey, George	Jackson	Rogers	80/8	Irwin
Winfrey, Isaac(Orps)	Columbia	Bealls	509/10	Irwin
Winfrey, John	Columbia	Bealls	302/10	Early
Winfrey, John	Oglethorpe	Lees	33/11	Hall
Winfrey, John	Putnam	Morelands	160/2	Early
Winfrey, Reuben	Clarke	Simms	286/12	Irwin
Winfrey, Reuben	Columbia	Bealls	83/8	Appling
Wing, George(Heirs)	Madison	Hamiltons	101/1	Habersham
Wingate, Michael	Baldwin	Taliaferro	17/16	Irwin
Wingate, Michael	Baldwin	Taliaferro	94/22	Early
Wingates, Wm.(Orp)	Twiggs	R.Belchers	20/27	Early
Winget, Mary(Wid)	Richmond	120th	261/8	Irwin
Winget, Permelia(Orp)	Richmond	120th	207/2	Irwin
Wingfield, Edward B.	Wilkes	Mattox	249/4	Irwin
Wingfield, Garland Jr.	Wilkes	Mattox	98/9	Appling
Wingfield, James	Wilkes	Gordons	58/13	Early
Wingfield, John L.	Wilkes	Freemans	79/7	Gwinnett
Wingfield, John(RS)	Elbert	G.Higginbotham	177/26	Early
Wingfield, John(RS)	Elbert	G.Higginbotham	348/11	Early
Wingfield, John(RS)	Elbert	G.Higginbotham	46/8	Early
Wingfield, John	Morgan	Hubbards	32/5	Gwinnett
Wingfield, John	Morgan	Hubbards	367/7	Early
Wingfield, John	Wilkes	Mattox	138/9	Early
Wingfield, Mathew	Greene	Fosters	15/11	Early
Wingfield, Thomas	Wilkes	Gordons	378/8	Appling
Wingham, John	Jones	Permenters	45/2	Appling
Winkfield, Nathan	Greene	Macons	300/17	Early
Winkler, Elizabeth(Wid)	Chatham		91/17	Early
Winn, Elisha	Jackson	Hamiltons	250/23	Early
Winn, Francis Sr.	Gwinnett	Hamiltons	91/9	Appling
Winn, John	Columbia	Olives	208/13	Irwin
Winn, John	Lincoln	Graves	3/8	Appling
Winn, John	Oglethorpe	Rowlands	259/7	Appling
Winn, Mariah(Orps)	Madison	Eigles	334/8	Early
Winn, Minor	Chatham		63/7	Early
Winn, Peter Farley	Liberty		422/12	Irwin
Winn, Richard(Orps)	Lincoln	Jeters	16/10	Hall
Winn, Richard(Orps)	Pulaski	Dais	260/6	Gwinnett
Winn, Washington	Liberty		170/5	Irwin

NAME	COUNTY	MIL.DIST	LOT/SECT	DREW LAND
Winne, Robert	Columbia	J.Morris	62/17	Early
Winne, Robert	Columbia	J.Morris	81/26	Early
Winningham, Caleb	Jones	Seals	241/10	Irwin
Winslett, Richard	Greene	Kimbroughs	283/6	Irwin
Winslett, Sally(Wid)	Greene	Kimbrough	419/26	Early
Winter, Morgan(Orps)	Jones	Jefferson	272/3	Early
Winters, Albert	Jackson	Winters	418/8	Irwin
Winters, Frederick	Richmond	Winters	253/2	Early
Winters, George W.	Jackson	Haggards	52/6	Appling
Winters, John Sr.	Jackson	Winters	453/12	Irwin
Winters, John	Jackson	Winters	87/15	Irwin
Wise, Abner	Oglethorpe	Thornton	160/13	Irwin
Wise, Daniel	Wilkinson	Bowings	352/5	Appling
Wise, Henry	Wilkes	Brooks	345/5	Irwin
Wise, Herren	Wilkinson	Bowings	34/4	Irwin
Wise, Isaac	Jackson	Rodgers	298/8	Irwin
Wise, John	Oglethorpe	Wises	261/17	Early
Wise, John	Oglethorpe	Wises	73/2	Irwin
Wise, John	Wilkes	Brooks	370/20	Early
Wise, Josiah	Wilkes	Brooks	3/4	Habersham
Wiseman, John	Lincoln	Thompsons	186/1	Appling
Wiseman, Robert Sr.	Columbia	Dodsons	364/21	Early
Wiseman, Robert Sr.	Columbia	Dodsons	8/9	Hall
Wiseman, Samuel	Jasper	Clays	317/17	Early
Wiseman, Samuel	Jasper	Clays	482/2	Appling
Wiseman, Wm.	Chatham		327/17	Early
Wisenbaker, Christian	Effingham		157/3	Early
Wisenor, William	Morgan	Dennis	106/4	Walton
Witcher, Benjamin	Madison	Culbreaths	285/3	Appling
Withington, Nathan	Jones	Seals	4/14	Irwin
Witlich, Charles	Elbert	Whites	20/5	Irwin
Witmire, Henry	Jackson	Dicksons	11/10	Irwin
Witmire, Henry	Jackson	Dicksons	221/10	Irwin
Witt, Adam	Franklin	Harris	128/3	Irwin
Wittich, Frederick	Wilkes	Burks	399/8	Appling
Witton, William	Chatham		412/15	Early
Woddale, Noel	Morgan	Farrars	334/7	Irwin
Wofford, Solomon	Jackson	Rogers	169/3	Habersham
Wofford, William H.	Franklin	Flannagans	150/2	Irwin
Wofford, William	Habersham	Powells	424/9	Irwin
Wofford, William	Habersham	Powells	81/16	Early
Wollis, William	Jackson	Rogers	253/4	Irwin
Wolten, Hannah(Wid)	Elbert	R.Christians	38/5	Early
Womack, Benjamin	Twiggs	Bozemans	164/10	Habersham
Womack, Jacob	Wilkinson	Kettles	165/3	Appling
Womack, James	Effingham		49/12	Early
Womack, Josiah	Putnam	Littles	156/3	Walton
Womack, Mark	Baldwin	Doziers	169/10	Irwin
Womack, Nancy(Wid)	Hancock	Canes	148/5	Gwinnett
Womack, Sherard(Orps)	Hancock	Canes	1/4	Early
Womack, Thomas	Putnam	Littles	507/7	Irwin
Womack, Wiley	Hancock	Canes	492/6	Appling
Womack, William Sr.	Effingham		242/9	Appling
Womack, William(Orps)	Jones	Buckhalters	282/12	Early
Womack, William	Hancock	Canes	220/11	Irwin
Womble, Allen	Warren	151st	155/2	Rabun
Womble, Allen	Warren	151st	218/6	Irwin
Womble, Daniel	Pulaski	Davis	423/15	Early
Womble, Daniel	Pulaski	Davis	452/11	Irwin
Womble, Redden	Warren	Travis	155/13	Irwin
Wommack, Edmund	Jackson	Rogers	190/17	Early
Wommack, Green	Baldwin	Cousins	397/4	Appling
Wommock, Edmund	Jackson	Rogers	212/1	Early
Wommock, Nancy(Wid)	Hancock	Canes	148/5	Gwinnett
Womock, Charles	Jones	Kings	234/21	Early
Womock, Frederick	Effingham		413/2	Appling
Wood, Allen	Warren	150th	116/55	Gwinnett

367

NAME	COUNTY	MIL.DIST	LOT/SECT	DREW LAND
Wood, Archibald	Morgan	Farrers	219/15	Early
Wood, Augustus	Columbia	Ob.Morris	152/11	Early
Wood, Ballenger	Jefferson	Lamps	54/11	Hall
Wood, David	Jefferson	Lamps	120/28	Early
Wood, David	Jefferson	Lamps	202/5	Gwinnett
Wood, David	Twiggs	Hodges	56/3	Irwin
Wood, Edridge	Putnam	Oslins	109/4	Appling
Wood, Elisha	Baldwin	Marshalls	281/6	Appling
Wood, Elizabeth(Wid)	Jefferson	Langstons	178/3	Irwin
Wood, George R.	Washington	Robinsons	297/5	Appling
Wood, Henry Sr.	Morgan	Knights	174/27	Early
Wood, Henry(Orps)	Elbert	P.Christian	437/8	Irwin
Wood, Jacob	Madison	Hamiltons	300/5	Appling
Wood, Jacob	Madison	Hamiltons	96/27	Early
Wood, James(Orps)	Washington	Robinsons	324/9	Early
Wood, James	Columbia	Burroughs	65/12	Hall
Wood, James	Jackson	Winters	160/6	Gwinnett
Wood, Jared	Washington	Robinsons	331/7	Early
Wood, John	Putnam	Evans	58/3	Hall
Wood, John Jr.	Wilkes	Runnels	197/6	Early
Wood, John W.	Clarke	Appling	90/14	Irwin
Wood, John W.	Morgan	Farrars	290/12	Irwin
Wood, John(Orps)	Madison	Orrs	119/4	Habersham
Wood, John	Morgan	Talbots	378/19	Early
Wood, Joseph	Pulaski	Lesters	338/6	Appling
Wood, Joseph	Twiggs	Jeffersons	319/18	Irwin
Wood, Joseph	Twiggs	Jeffersons	32/3	Appling
Wood, Joseph	Warren	Hutchinsons	347/6	Early
Wood, Martin	Pulaski	Bryans	198/2	Early
Wood, Mathew M.	Burke	71st	523/7	Appling
Wood, Miset	Washington	Robinsons	372/28	Early
Wood, Nancy(Wid)	Elbert	P.Christians	40/3	Habersham
Wood, Peter	Washington	Peabody	341/4	Early
Wood, Rhoda(Wid)	Jefferson	Cowarts	340/1	Appling
Wood, Robert T.	Washington	Averits	252/28	Early
Wood, Stephen	Glynn		359/6	Early
Wood, Tabitha(Wid)	Walton	Echols	84/26	Early
Wood, Terrell	Jackson	Rogers	421/1	Early
Wood, Thomas L.	Richmond	398	15/26	Early
Wood, Thomas	Morgan	Farrars	124/3	Walton
Wood, Thomas	Morgan	Knights	86/4	Appling
Wood, Thomas	Oglethorpe	Warters	243/3	Walton
Wood, Whitmill	Wilkinson	Smiths	21/10	Habersham
Wood, Whitmill	Wilkinson	Smiths	34/3	Early
Wood, William Jr.	Jackson	Winters	45/18	Early
Wood, William	Morgan	Farrars	134/12	Hall
Wood, Willis	Laurens	Jones	266/1	Walton
Wood, Willis	Laurens	Jones	59/2	Early
Woodal, Williamson	Wilkes	Bates	180/4	Early
Woodall, Archibald	Baldwin	Marshalls	202/9	Appling
Woodall, John	Jasper	Centells	18/15	Early
Woodall, Robert	Jones	Shropshiers	89/28	Early
Woodard, John	Putnam	Brooks	288/13	Irwin
Woodard, Joshua	Lincoln	Tatoms	511/8	Appling
Woodard, Paschal	Morgan	Loyds	108/3	Habersham
Woodard, Thomas	Laurens	Harris	114/5	Early
Wooden, Samuel	Burke	71	34/13	Early
Woodford, Mary(Wid)	Wilkes	Willis	334/12	Irwin
Woodham, Everett	Greene	143rd	112/1	Appling
Woodham, James	Greene	Armers	134/13	Habersham
Woodley, Caleb	Jasper	Reids	41/11	Hall
Woodley, Garrett	Jones	Jefferson	190/2	Appling
Woodley, Garrett	Jones	Jeffersons	38/1	Irwin
Woodley, John	Elbert	P.Christians	269/11	Irwin
Woodliff, Wm.	Clarke	Harriss	255/26	Early
Woodmason, Calder	Jones	Permenters	423/7	Irwin
Woodmason, Calder	Jones	Permenters	9/28	Early

NAME	COUNTY	MIL.DIST	LOT/SECT	DREW LAND
Woodram, J.	Bulloch	Williams	128/19	Early
Woodruff, Benj.	Oglethorpe	Lees	400/7	Irwin
Woodruff, Clifford	Jasper	Evans	135/5	Irwin
Woodruff, Clifford	Oglethorpe	Lees	123/4	Early
Woodruff, Ephram Sr.	Chatham		292/7	Appling
Woodruff, James	Jasper	Eastes	106/7	Irwin
Woodruff, Reuben	Oglethorpe	Lees	494/2	Appling
Woods, Charles	Jasper	Baileys	117/12	Habersham
Woods, Isaac	Jefferson	Langstons	349/21	Early
Woods, John	Madison	Culbreaths	84/1	Habersham
Woods, Matthew M.	Jefferson	Langstons	1/23	Early
Woods, Robert	Effingham		61/5	Early
Woods, Samuel	Madison	Culbreaths	338/4	Early
Woods, Thomas(Orps)	Washington	Jinkinsons	375/18	Early
Woodson, Wm.P.W.	Franklin	Burtons	254/14	Early
Woodward, Barnes	Burke	Abbotts	325/1	Appling
Woodward, Eliz.(Wid)	Warren	Hubberts	303/12	Irwin
Woodward, F.(Orps)	Warren	Hubberts	91/12	Early
Woodward, Jemimah	Burke	Thomas	229/27	Early
Woodward, Lemuel	Burke	71st	228/6	Early
Woodward, Leroy(Orp)	Wilkes	Burks	494/6	Irwin
Woodward, Paschal	Morgan	Loyds	171/13	Early
Woodworth, Darius	Camden	Clarkes	134/7	Appling
Woodworth, Darius	Camden	Clarks	55/21	Early
Woody, Henry T.(Orps)	Oglethorpe	Goolsbys	200/16	Early
Woodyard, Jessee	Morgan	Jordans	308/5	Gwinnett
Woolbridgt, Jacob Sr.	Wilkes	Davis	242/7	Gwinnett
Woolbright, Barnaba	Greene	Fosters	322/9	Appling
Woolbright, Barnaba	Greene	Fosters	415/13	Irwin
Woolbright, Jacob Sr.	Wilkes	Davis	218/6	Early
Wooldridge, Absalom	Putnam	Ectors	154/10	Hall
Woolf, Frederick	Pulaski	Senterfeits	194/7	Irwin
Woolf, Stephen	Effingham		437/15	Early
Woolfork, Rustin	Richmond	222nd	183/8	Early
Woolfork, Sowel	Richmond		301/11	Irwin
Woolfork, Thomas	Jones	Wallers	334/4	Appling
Woolfork, Thomas	Jones	Wallers	72/5	Irwin
Woolhopter, Mrs.(Wid)	Chatham		54/16	Early
Woolhopter, Mrs.(Wid)	Chatham		93/1	Irwin
Woolsey, Benjamin	Baldwin	Irwins	54/4	Irwin
Woolsey, John M.	Putnam	Evans	140/13	Early
Woolsey, John M.	Putnam	Evans	197/7	Early
Woolsey, Seth	Putnam	Ectors	195/27	Early
Wooten, Allen R.	Wilkes	Burks	262/1	Appling
Wooten, Benjamin	Wilkes	Dents	293/5	Appling
Wooten, Betsey(Orp)	Burke	Lewis	51/4	Early
Wooten, Betty(Wid)	Telfair	Loves	41/4	Rabun
Wooten, Branson D.	Greene	Wheelis	107/11	Irwin
Wooten, Bryant	Telfair	Loves	234/1	Walton
Wooten, David	Burke	72nd	122/16	Irwin
Wooten, Eli(Orp)	Burke	Lewis	51/4	Early
Wooten, Eliz.(Wid)	Wilkinson	Kettles	109/2	Early
Wooten, Hardy(Orp)	Burke	Lewis	51/4	Early
Wooten, James	Jackson	Rogers	388/1	Early
Wooten, Jesse	Walton	Wagnons	151/16	Early
Wooten, Joel(Orps)	Telfair	Loves	394/2	Appling
Wooten, John	Jefferson	Waldens	74/9	Irwin
Wooten, Martha(Orp)	Burke	Lewis	51/4	Early
Wooten, Richard B.	Wilkes	Burks	26/11	Early
Wooten, Thomas(Orps)	Jefferson	Lamps	134/4	Appling
Wooten, Thomas	Richmond	Laceys	16/1	Irwin
Wooten, Wm.B.	Putnam	Bustins	117/6	Irwin
Wootson, Jonathan C.Jr.	Jones	Wallers	296/27	Early
Wootson, Jonathan C.Sr.	Jones	Wallers	202/8	Appling
Word, Charles	Franklin	Davis	378/3	Appling
Word, James	Burke	McNorrills	300/9	Irwin
Word, Thomas	Franklin	Holcombs	352/14	Early

NAME	COUNTY	MIL.DIST	LOT/SECT	DREW LAND
Worhtam(?), William B.	Washington	Cummins	180/6	Irwin
Works, Eli	Baldwin	Ellis	91/5	Early
Worlley, Jacob	Camden	Baleys	28/13	Early
Wormock, Sarah(Wid)	Washington	Daniels	428/7	Appling
Worrell, Alexander	Jefferson	Lamps	57/2	Irwin
Worrell, Stephen	Jefferson	Lamps	152/7	Appling
Worrill, Solomon	Wilkinson	Smiths	134/10	Hall
Worsham, Archer Jr.	Baldwin	Stephens	12/13	Habersham
Worsham, Archer Sr.	Baldwin	Stephens	122/4	Habersham
Worsham, Daniel B.	Baldwin	Stephens	52/4	Early
Worsham, John	Jasper	Clays	163/7	Gwinnett
Worsley, Sampson	Warren	Travis	373/2	Appling
Worsley, Thomas	Pulaski	Madison	189/5	Irwin
Wortham, Elijah Sr.	Washington	Cummins	275/5	Gwinnett
Wortham, Elijah	Washington	Cummins	233/5	Appling
Wortham, John	Wilkes	Josseys	282/18	Early
Wortham, John	Wilkes	Josseys	364/1	Early
Wortham, Theophilus	Wilkes	Brooks	172/2	Irwin
Wortham, William	Morgan	Parkers	56/26	Early
Wortham, William	Washington	Cummins	485/12	Irwin
Wortham, Zachariah	Clarke	Deans	122/5	Early
Worthy, Anderson	Jasper	Bartlets	342/7	Appling
Worthy, Arnul	Franklin	Vaughns	117/8	Appling
Worthy, George	Franklin	Vaughns	61/12	Habersham
Worthy, Leonard	Jasper	Bartletts	373/5	Early
Worthy, Margaret(Wid)	Washington	Mannings	50/1	Appling
Worthy, Robert	Washington	Avents	22/12	Habersham
Worthy, Thomas(Orps)	Washington	Mannings	280/6	Gwinnett
Worthy, William	Putnam	J.Kindricks	89/1	Rabun
Worthy, Williamson	Putnam	J.Kendricks	121/1	Appling
Wortley, George	Franklin	Vaughns	157/4	Early
Wothall, Charles T.	Jasper	Northcuts	130/3	Irwin
Wratehford, Robert	Jackson	Rodgers	489/13	Irwin
Wright, Abel	Laurens	S.Smiths	177/5	Appling
Wright, Asa	Oglethorpe	Lees	342/27	Early
Wright, Bazel(Orps)	Warren	Parhams	173/8	Early
Wright, Benj.(Orps)	Putnam	Ectors	394/7	Irwin
Wright, Benjamin	Lincoln	Jones	241/8	Early
Wright, David	Elbert	P.Christians	43/18	Early
Wright, David	Jasper	Blakes	59/3	Habersham
Wright, David	Morgan	Townsends	450/8	Irwin
Wright, Elias S.	Jones	Mulkeys	286/8	Early
Wright, Elliot	Jones	Chappels	313/12	Irwin
Wright, Elliott	Jones	Chappels	175/12	Irwin
Wright, Eve(Wid)	Camden	Clarks	541/2	Appling
Wright, George W.	Jasper	Eastes	597/2	Appling
Wright, George(Orps)	Oglethorpe	Bridges	265/5	Early
Wright, George	Wilkinson	Bowings	69/27	Early
Wright, Henry	Oglethorpe	Lees	353/28	Early
Wright, Henry	Wilkinson	Bowlings	48/1	Rabun
Wright, James B.	Glynn		53/9	Appling
Wright, James(RS)	Elbert	Olivers	160/21	Early
Wright, James	Columbia	Dodsons	87/27	Early
Wright, James	Putnam	Robertsons	83/13	Irwin
Wright, James	Warren	Parhams	12/16	Irwin
Wright, Jared	Laurens	Deans	204/16	Irwin
Wright, John H.	Baldwin	Marshalls	393/1	Appling
Wright, John L.	Clarke	Starnes	95/2	Habersham
Wright, John L.	Clarke	Starns	357/6	Irwin
Wright, John M.	Washington	Daniels	71/7	Irwin
Wright, John S.	Putnam	Ectors	170/26	Early
Wright, John(RS)	Walton	Wagnons	232/11	Early
Wright, John(RS)	Walton	Wagnons	428/9	Irwin
Wright, John	Columbia	Willingham	107/6	Appling
Wright, John	Jackson	Dicksons	235/8	Irwin
Wright, John	Lincoln	Stokes	70/14	Early
Wright, John	Putnam	Robertsons	67/13	Habersham

NAME	COUNTY	MIL.DIST	LOT/SECT	DREW LAND
Wright, John	Wilkes	Rennolds	421/28	Early
Wright, John	Wilkinson	Bowings	222/4	Early
Wright, Johnson	Oglethorpe	Bridges	337/9	Irwin
Wright, Joseph	Jasper	Eastes	337/5	Gwinnett
Wright, Joseph	Warren	Parhams	341/7	Irwin
Wright, Joseph	Warren	Parhams	49/11	Hall
Wright, Kennon	Laurens	S.Smiths	26/7	Appling
Wright, Kennon	Laurens	S.Smiths	272/10	Early
Wright, Lewis	Putnam	H.Kendricks	307/6	Irwin
Wright, Lewis	Putnam	H.Kendricks	47/7	Early
Wright, Mary	Elbert	Doolys	119/10	Hall
Wright, Melton	Warren	Blounts	1/27	Early
Wright, Nancey(Wid)	Warren	Blounts	128/18	Early
Wright, Nancy(Wid)	Oglethorpe	Lees	33/21	Early
Wright, Nathan Jr.	Lincoln	Tatoms	172/9	Hall
Wright, Polly	Wilkes	Russells	250/10	Irwin
Wright, Rachell(Orps)	Warren	Parhams	159/5	Irwin
Wright, Randal	Putnam	Stampers	335/5	Early
Wright, Richard	Putnam	Robertsons	494/12	Irwin
Wright, Robert	Putnam	Berrys	328/4	Appling
Wright, Robert	Putnam	Berrys	528/5	Appling
Wright, Sally	Greene	Ragins	210/12	Early
Wright, Sampson	Hancock	Edwards	284/9	Appling
Wright, Stephen	Greene	Harris	465/5	Appling
Wright, Thomas Jr.	Chatham		161/3	Irwin
Wright, Thomas	Putnam	Berrys	462/6	Appling
Wright, Thomas	Putnam	Ectors	146/4	Irwin
Wright, Wiley	Chatham		406/26	Early
Wright, William S.	Warren	Parhams	3/4	Walton
Wright, William Sr.	Lincoln	Jones	61/4	Habersham
Wright, William(Orps)	Warren	Blounts	36/26	Early
Wright, William	Greene	142nd	275/9	Early
Wright, William	Laurens	S.Smiths	427/8	Appling
Wright, William	Oglethorpe	Bridges	244/20	Early
Wright, William	Wilkinson	Howards	411/1	Appling
Wright, Willis	Wilkinson	Bowings	79/8	Appling
Wright, Winfield J.	Clarke	Starnes	211/10	Early
Wright, Winfield J.	Clarke	Starnes	387/10	Early
Wright, Wm.G.	Clarke	Starns	138/12	Hall
Wright, Wm.H.B.	Columbia	Watsons	4/10	Early
Wright, Wm.Sr.	Lincoln	Jones	248/5	Gwinnett
Wright, Zacheus	Greene	Kinbrough	169/10	Early
Wyat, William	Jones	Buckhalters	470/3	Appling
Wyche, Batt	Montgomery	McElvins	30/5	Early
Wyche, Clarke	Jones	Shropshiers	3/3	Rabun
Wyche, George	Elbert	P.Christians	483/4	Appling
Wyche, George	Elbert	P.Christians	60/7	Early
Wyche, Henry	Jones	Samuels	146/8	Appling
Wyche, Littleton	Montgomery	Nobles	226/17	Early
Wyche, Samuel C.	Elbert	P.Christians	277/16	Gwinnett
Wyett, John	Morgan	Selmons	210/10	Habersham
Wylie, Nicholas	Wilkes	Dents	180/2	Habersham
Wylly, Thomas	Effingham		3/7	Irwin
Wyly, David	Scriven		22/2	Early
Wynn, Bartley	Emanuel	57th	64/4	Appling
Wynn, Burwell J.	Hancock	Edwards	228/1	Appling
Wynn, Green	Jones	Seals	256/27	Early
Wynn, John	Emanuel	59th	376/27	Early
Wynn, Jones	Putnam	Coopers	321/19	Early
Wynn, Lewis	Jones	Seals	325/26	Early
Wynn, Richmond W.	Jasper	Blakes	346/4	Early
Wynn, William	Wilkinson	Kettles	345/6	Appling
Wynn, Wm.	Jones	Seals	501/7	Appling
Wynne, Clament	Warren	Rodgers	283/7	Appling
Wynne, Cynthia(Orp)	Warren	Rodgers	205/8	Early
Wynne, John W.	Twiggs	W.Belchers	334/19	Early
Wynne, John	Putnam	Bustins	208/4	Walton

NAME	COUNTY	MIL.DIST	LOT/SECT	DREW LAND
Wynne, John	Putnam	Robersons	333/12	Early
Wynne, Jones	Putnam	Coopers	367/13	Irwin
Wynne, Lemuel	Jasper	Bentleys	286/9	Appling
Wynne, Lemuel	Jasper	Bentleys	498/2	Appling
Wynne, Thomas	Warren	Rodgers	90/20	Early
Wynne, Wm.	Warren	Hubberts	67/16	Irwin
Wynns, Henry(Orps)	Burke	Bells	224/14	Early
Wyot, Thomas	Morgan	Walkers	227/1	Walton
Wyot, William	Morgan	Walkers	249/4	Walton
Wyot, Wm.	Morgan	Walkers	320/9	Irwin
Yancey, James	Jasper	Bentleys	416/11	Irwin
Yancey, Lewis D.	Jasper	Bentleys	53/5	Gwinnett
Yancey, Thomas	Oglethorpe	Barnetts	147/12	Early
Yancy, Ezekiel	Jackson	Hamiltons	222/6	Early
Yancy, James Banis	Jasper	Hays	148/13	Early
Yancy, James Jr.	Jackson	Hamiltons	385/2	Appling
Yancy, Lewis D.	Jasper	Bentley	131/7	Gwinnett
Yancy, Richard	Jackson	Hamiltons	240/14	Early
Yancy, Wesley	Jackson	Hamiltons	301/19	Early
Yansey, Absalom	Franklin	Yanseys	202/11	Early
Yarborough, Benjamin	Baldwin	Marshalls	520/13	Irwin
Yarborough, Thos.	Columbia	Dodsons	375/10	Irwin
Yarbrough, Ambrose	Jackson	Dicksons	11/15	Irwin
Yarbrough, Ambrose	Jackson	Dicksons	78/11	Irwin
Yarbrough, Jas.G.(Orp)	Warren	154	398/2	Appling
Yarbrough, Jeptha	Jasper	Evans	2/3	Appling
Yarbrough, Jeremiah	Morgan	Townsends	45/10	Early
Yarbrough, Joseph	Jefferson	Lamps	282/6	Appling
Yarbrough, Joshua	Oglethorpe	Myricks	525/6	Irwin
Yarbrough, Josiah	Jasper	Kennedys	203/11	Irwin
Yarbrough, Lewis(Orps)	Pulaksi	Johnstons	178/17	Early
Yarbrough, Lewis	Morgan	Parkers	111/4	Walton
Yarbrough, Lewis	Pulaksi	Johnstons	267/13	Early
Yarbrough, Mary(Wid)	Warren	154	233/2	Irwin
Yarbrough, Nimrod	Warren	154	293/1	Appling
Yarbrough, Nimrod	Warren	154	64/6	Early
Yarbrough, Samuel Sr.	Warren	Hubberts	402/6	Irwin
Yarbrough, William	Pulaksi	Johnsons	283/15	Early
Yarbrough, William	Walton	Wagnons	148/4	Early
Yarbry, Joseph	Morgan	Paces	5/5	Irwin
Yates, Burrel	Emanuel	55th	460/5	Appling
Yates, James Jr.	Laurens	Deans	152/21	Early
Yates, James Jr.	Laurens	Deans	309/6	Early
Yates, John	Clark	Harpers	264/13	Irwin
Yates, John	Laurens	Jones	210/3	Early
Yates, John	Laurens	Jones	95/13	Irwin
Yates, Joseph	Franklin	Akins	58/3	Early
Yates, Peter(RS)	Clark	Applings	42/1	Early
Yates, Peter	Clark	Applings	339/26	Early
Yates, William	Clark	Applings	361/7	Appling
Yates, Willis	Baldwin	Russels	307/21	Early
Yawn, Joseph	Burke	McNorrills	343/4	Appling
Yawn, Lewis	Jefferson	Mathews	494/9	Irwin
Yeamans, Frederick	Glynn		520/10	Irwin
Yeargin, Andrew	Franklin	Weltons	395/4	Appling
Yeargin, John B.	Franklin	Weltons	236/6	Appling
Yeargin, Samuel	Franklin	Weltons	378/5	Appling
Yeargin, Samuel	Franklin	Weltons	40/8	Early
Yearta, Jacob	Twiggs	Bozeman	251/6	Appling
Yearwood, Andrew	Franklin	Powells	250/3	Early
Yelvengton, Bryant	Twiggs	Bozemans	417/3	Appling
Yon, Nicholas(RS)	Columbia	Watsons	24/9	Hall
Yon, Nicholas(RS)	Columbia	Willinghams	224/4	Walton
York, Absalom	Lincoln	Jones	116/2	Irwin
York, Burwell M.	Wilkes	McLendons	157/9	Appling
York, David S.	Lincoln	Jones	290/16	Early
York, David	Columbia	Pullins	402/11	Irwin

NAME	COUNTY	MIL.DIST	LOT/SECT	DREW LAND
York, David	Columbia	Pullins	41/11	Irwin
York, James	Lincoln	Jones	223/1	Early
York, John	Lincoln	Jeters	58/23	Early
York, William	Franklin	Ashs	105/7	Appling
Yotty, Abner(Orps)	Greene	142	8/5	Gwinnett
Youman, Redding	Emanuel	53rd	255/3	Early
Youn, Jesse	Laurens	Harriss	312/8	Appling
Youn, Jesse	Laurens	Harriss	318/6	Gwinnett
Youn, John	Pulaksi	Rees	224/3	Irwin
Youn, John	Pulaksi	Rees	508/10	Irwin
Young, Alexander	Jones	Permenters	320/3	Appling
Young, Amos(Orps)	Jones	Phillips	47/4	Habersham
Young, Amos	Baldwin	Irwins	102/13	Irwin
Young, Benjamin	Jefferson	Bothwells	358/7	Appling
Young, Benjamin	Laurens	S.Smiths	75/3	Early
Young, Charles	Wilkinson	Brooks	30/4	Early
Young, Dinah(Wid)	Jackson	Hamiltons	215/5	Early
Young, E.R.	Jackson	Dicksons	43/1	Irwin
Young, Elam	Burke	72nd	215/7	Appling
Young, Elizabeth(Wid)	Jefferson	Bothwells	228/5	Gwinnett
Young, Frederick	Oglethorpe	Dunns	197/3	Irwin
Young, George H.	Oglethorpe	Brittons	330/9	Irwin
Young, Giles	Oglethorpe	Dunns	381/11	Irwin
Young, Henry F.	Morgan	Loyds	18/6	Irwin
Young, Henry	Jefferson	Mathews	190/1	Walton
Young, Hezekiah	Columbia	Olives	325/7	Appling
Young, James A.	Morgan	Loyds	16/23	Early
Young, James C.	Lincoln	Walkers	116/15	Irwin
Young, James T.	Columbia	Burroughs	378/7	Early
Young, James	Bulloch	Edwards	112/6	Gwinnett
Young, James	Bulloch	Edwards	180/3	Irwin
Young, James	Jefferson	Bothwells	97/2	Rabun
Young, James	Oglethorpe	Dunns	385/16	Early
Young, Jennett	Chatham		62/8	Irwin
Young, Jesse(Orps)	Wilkinson	Smiths	66/1	Rabun
Young, John W.	Hancock	Smiths	6/3	Appling
Young, John	Camden	32nd	17/1	Walton
Young, John	Jackson	Dicksons	93/16	Irwin
Young, Joseph	Wilkinson	Lees	159/27	Early
Young, Margaret(Orp)	Laurens	Griffins	489/4	Appling
Young, Michael	Bulloch	Edwards	239/2	Appling
Young, Moses	McIntosh	Jenkins	8/1	Habersham
Young, Pearson	Laurens	Griffin	169/3	Appling
Young, Pearson	Laurens	Griffins	14/8	Appling
Young, Phillip	Chatham		433/11	Irwin
Young, Phillip	Chatham		69/5	Gwinnett
Young, Robert	Jackson	Hamiltons	57/13	Irwin
Young, Samuel	Wilkes	Russels	195/1	Appling
Young, Sarah(Wid)	Columbia	Olives	381/18	Early
Young, Sarah(Wid)	Twiggs	Evans	14/26	Early
Young, Thomas H.	Oglethorpe	Waters	314/11	Early
Young, Thomas(Orps)	Wilkes	Burks	270/2	Early
Young, Thomas	Baldwin	Harris	182/16	Irwin
Young, Turner(Orps)	Baldwin	Haws	465/7	Appling
Young, William	Columbia	Olives	351/8	Irwin
Young, Wm.Sr.(Orps)	Bulloch	Edwards	398/17	Early
Youngblood, Abraham	Burke	72nd	196/1	Appling
Youngblood, Abraham	Columbia	Ob.Morris	21/2	Appling
Youngblood, Arthur	Hancock	Justices	373/5	Irwin
Youngblood, Henry	Morgan	Alfords	94/12	Irwin
Youngblood, James Jr.	Hancock	Justices	36/7	Irwin
Youngblood, James(RS)	Hancock	Justices	318/19	Early
Youngblood, Joel	Twiggs	Browns	95/26	Early
Youngblood, John	Jones	Wallers	425/13	Irwin
Youngblood, Peter	Twiggs	Browns	268/9	Irwin
Youngblood, Wm.L.	Hancock	Justices	237/4	Appling
Yowman, John	Emanuel	55th	369/4	Early

NAME	COUNTY	MIL.DIST	LOT/SECT	DREW LAND
Zachary, Asa C.	Morgan	Leonards	29/13	Irwin
Zachary, Clementey R.	Morgan	Leonards	133/13	Irwin
Zachery, Archimides G.S.L.	Columbia	Shaws	179/7	Gwinnett
Zachery, John L.	Columbia	Olives	63/8	Appling
Zachry, Daniel M.(Orps)	Jasper	Hays	125/16	Early
Zachry, James B.	Putnam	Brooks	336/9	Early
Zant, Joshua(Orps)	Effingham		87/11	Early
Zant, Joshua	Effingham		213/11	Early
Zeigler, David Jr.	Effingham		104/13	Irwin
Zeigler, Emanuel	Effingham		360/28	Early
Zeigler, John	Scriven	Roberts	42/1	Rabun
Zeigler, Solomon	Scriven	Roberts	188/1	Irwin
Zettarauer, Nathaniel	Twiggs	R.Belchers	370/18	Early
Zimmerman, Simon	Wilkes	Kilgores	59/2	Appling
Zipperer, Guardian	Chatham		43/3	Appling
Zipperer, John M.	Chatham		118/2	Habersham
Zipporah, Geo.W.(Orp)	Chatham		333/13	Early
Zipporah, Lucretia(Orp)	Chatham		333/13	Early
Zipporah, Paul W.(Orp)	Chatham		333/13	Early
Zipporah, Richard(Orp)	Chatham		333/13	Early
Zipporah, Susannah(Orp)	Chatham		333/13	Early
Zipprow, Emanuel	Effingham		108/11	Hall
Zitrouer, David	Effingham		104/11	Irwin
Zitrouer, Godhelf J.	Effingham		189/7	Irwin
Zitrouer, Godhelf J.	Effingham		9/9	Appling
Zitrouer, William	Effingham		466/6	Appling
Zorner, Henry	Twiggs	R.Belchers	308/21	Early
Zoullner, George	Lincoln	Walkers	258/1	Walton
Zoullner, George	Lincoln	Walkers	4/27	Early
Zuber, Abraham	Twiggs	R.Belchers	408/3	Appling
Zuber, Caleb B.	Twiggs	R.Belchers	151/5	Appling
Zuber, Emanuel	Oglethorpe	Murrays	76/10	Habersham
Zuber, Joshua	Twiggs	R.Belchers	345/7	Irwin